D1465876

THIRTEENTH EDITION

AN INTRODUCTION TO
MANAGEMENT SCIENCE
QUANTITATIVE APPROACHES
TO DECISION MAKING

David R. Anderson
University of Cincinnati

Dennis J. Sweeney
University of Cincinnati

Thomas A. Williams
Rochester Institute of Technology

Jeffrey D. Camm
University of Cincinnati

Kipp Martin
University of Chicago

SOUTH-WESTERN
CENGAGE Learning

Australia • Brazil • Japan • Korea • Mexico • Singapore • Spain • United Kingdom • United States

SOUTH-WESTERN
CENGAGE Learning

An Introduction to Management Science: Quantitative Approaches to Decision Making, Thirteenth Edition
David R. Anderson, Dennis J. Sweeney, Thomas A. Williams, Jeffrey D. Camm, & Kipp Martin

VP/Editorial Director:
Jack W. Calhoun

Publisher:
Joe Sabatino

Senior Acquisitions Editor:
Charles McCormick, Jr.

Developmental Editor:
Maggie Kubale

Editorial Assistant:
Nora Heink

Marketing Communications Manager:
Libby Shipp

Content Project Manager:
Jacquelyn K Featherly

Media Editor:
Chris Valentine

Manufacturing Coordinator:
Miranda Klapper

Production House/Compositor:
MPS Limited, A Macmillan Company

Senior Art Director:
Stacy Jenkins Shirley

Internal Designer:
Michael Stratton/Chris Miller Design

Cover Designer:
Craig Ramsdell

Cover Images:
© Getty Images/GlowImages

For product information and technology assistance, contact us at
Cengage Learning Customer & Sales Support, 1-800-354-9706

For permission to use material from this text or product,
submit all requests online at **www.cengage.com/permissions**
Further permissions questions can be emailed to
permissionrequest@cengage.com

ExamView® and ExamView Pro® are registered trademarks of FSCreations, Inc. Windows is a registered trademark of the Microsoft Corporation used herein under license. Macintosh and Power Macintosh are registered trademarks of Apple Computer, Inc. used herein under license.

Library of Congress Control Number: 2009935881

Student Edition ISBN 13: 978-1-4390-4323-3
Student Edition ISBN 10: 1-4390-4323-X
Package Student Edition ISBN 13: 978-1-4390-4327-1
Package Student Edition ISBN 10: 1-4390-4327-2

South-Western Cengage Learning
5191 Natorp Boulevard
Mason, OH 45040
USA

Cengage Learning products are represented in Canada by Nelson Education, Ltd.

For your course and learning solutions, visit **www.cengage.com**

Purchase any of our products at your local college store or at our preferred online store **www.CengageBrain.com**

Printed in the United States of America
1 2 3 4 5 6 7 14 13 12 11 10

Dedication

To My Parents
Ray and Ilene Anderson
DRA

To My Parents
James and Gladys Sweeney
DJS

To My Parents
Phil and Ann Williams
TAW

To My Wife
Karen Camm
JDC

To My Wife
Gail Honda
KM

Brief Contents

Preface xxv

About the Authors xxix

Chapter 1   **Introduction** 1

Chapter 2   **An Introduction to Linear Programming** 28

Chapter 3   **Linear Programming: Sensitivity Analysis and Interpretation of Solution** 92

Chapter 4   **Linear Programming Applications in Marketing, Finance, and Operations Management** 153

Chapter 5   **Advanced Linear Programming Applications** 214

Chapter 6   **Distribution and Network Models** 255

Chapter 7   **Integer Linear Programming** 315

Chapter 8   **Nonlinear Optimization Models** 363

Chapter 9   **Project Scheduling: PERT/CPM** 410

Chapter 10   **Inventory Models** 451

Chapter 11   **Waiting Line Models** 500

Chapter 12   **Simulation** 540

Chapter 13   **Decision Analysis** 600

Chapter 14   **Multicriteria Decisions** 657

Chapter 15   **Time Series Analysis and Forecasting** 701

Chapter 16   **Markov Processes** 759

Chapter 17   **Linear Programming: Simplex Method** On Website

Chapter 18   **Simplex-Based Sensitivity Analysis and Duality** On Website

Chapter 19   **Solution Procedures for Transportation and Assignment Problems** On Website

Chapter 20   **Minimal Spanning Tree** On Website

Chapter 21   **Dynamic Programming** On Website

Appendixes 785

Appendix A   **Building Spreadsheet Models** 786

Appendix B   **Areas for the Standard Normal Distribution** 813

Appendix C   **Values of $e^{-\lambda}$** 815

Appendix D   **References and Bibliography** 816

Appendix E   **Self-Test Solutions and Answers to Even-Numbered Problems** 818

Index 851

Contents

Preface xxv
About the Authors xxix

Chapter 1 Introduction 1

1.1 Problem Solving and Decision Making 3
1.2 Quantitative Analysis and Decision Making 4
1.3 Quantitative Analysis 6
Model Development 7
Data Preparation 10
Model Solution 11
Report Generation 12
A Note Regarding Implementation 12
1.4 Models of Cost, Revenue, and Profit 14
Cost and Volume Models 14
Revenue and Volume Models 15
Profit and Volume Models 15
Breakeven Analysis 16
1.5 Management Science Techniques 16
Methods Used Most Frequently 18
Summary 19
Glossary 19
Problems 20
Case Problem **Scheduling a Golf League 23**
Appendix 1.1 Using Excel for Breakeven Analysis 24

Chapter 2 An Introduction to Linear Programming 28

2.1 A Simple Maximization Problem 30
Problem Formulation 31
Mathematical Statement of the Par, Inc., Problem 33
2.2 Graphical Solution Procedure 35
A Note on Graphing Lines 44
Summary of the Graphical Solution Procedure
  for Maximization Problems 46
Slack Variables 47
2.3 Extreme Points and the Optimal Solution 48
2.4 Computer Solution of the Par, Inc., Problem 50
Interpretation of Computer Output 51

2.5   A Simple Minimization Problem 52
Summary of the Graphical Solution Procedure
for Minimization Problems 54
Surplus Variables 55
Computer Solution of the M&D Chemicals Problem 56

2.6   Special Cases 57
Alternative Optimal Solutions 57
Infeasibility 58
Unbounded 60

2.7   General Linear Programming Notation 62
Summary 64
Glossary 65
Problems 66
Case Problem 1 **Workload Balancing 82**
Case Problem 2 **Production Strategy 83**
Case Problem 3 **Hart Venture Capital 84**
Appendix 2.1 Solving Linear Programs with LINGO 85
Appendix 2.2 Solving Linear Programs with Excel 87

**Chapter 3   Linear Programming: Sensitivity Analysis
and Interpretation of Solution 92**

3.1   Introduction to Sensitivity Analysis 94
3.2   Graphical Sensitivity Analysis 95
Objective Function Coefficients 95
Right-Hand Sides 100

3.3   Sensitivity Analysis: Computer Solution 103
Interpretation of Computer Output 103
Cautionary Note on the Interpretation of Dual Values 106
The Modified Par, Inc., Problem 106

3.4   Limitations of Classical Sensitivity Analysis 110
Simultaneous Changes 111
Changes in Constraint Coefficients 112
Nonintuitive Dual Values 112

3.5   The Electronic Communications Problem 116
Problem Formulation 117
Computer Solution and Interpretation 118
Summary 122
Glossary 123
Problems 123
Case Problem 1 **Product Mix 145**
Case Problem 2 **Investment Strategy 146**
Case Problem 3 **Truck Leasing Strategy 147**
Appendix 3.1 Sensitivity Analysis with Excel 148
Appendix 3.2 Sensitivity Analysis with LINGO 150

Chapter 4 Linear Programming Applications in Marketing, Finance, and Operations Management 153

4.1 Marketing Applications 154
Media Selection 155
Marketing Research 158

4.2 Financial Applications 161
Portfolio Selection 161
Financial Planning 164

4.3 Operations Management Applications 168
A Make-or-Buy Decision 168
Production Scheduling 172
Workforce Assignment 179
Blending Problems 183
Summary 188
Problems 189
Case Problem 1 **Planning an Advertising Campaign 202**
Case Problem 2 **Phoenix Computer 203**
Case Problem 3 **Textile Mill Scheduling 204**
Case Problem 4 **Workforce Scheduling 205**
Case Problem 5 **Duke Energy Coal Allocation 207**
Appendix 4.1 Excel Solution of Hewlitt Corporation Financial Planning Problem 210

Chapter 5 Advanced Linear Programming Applications 214

5.1 Data Envelopment Analysis 215
Evaluating the Performance of Hospitals 216
Overview of the DEA Approach 216
DEA Linear Programming Model 217
Summary of the DEA Approach 222

5.2 Revenue Management 223

5.3 Portfolio Models and Asset Allocation 229
A Portfolio of Mutual Funds 229
Conservative Portfolio 230
Moderate Risk Portfolio 232

5.4 Game Theory 236
Competing for Market Share 236
Identifying a Pure Strategy Solution 238
Identifying a Mixed Strategy Solution 239
Summary 247
Glossary 247
Problems 248

Chapter 6 Distribution and Network Models 255

6.1 Transportation Problem 256
Problem Variations 260
A General Linear Programming Model 262

6.2 Assignment Problem 263
Problem Variations 266
A General Linear Programming Model 267

6.3 Transshipment Problem 268
Problem Variations 274
A General Linear Programming Model 274

6.4 Shortest-Route Problem 276
A General Linear Programming Model 279

6.5 Maximal Flow Problem 279

6.6 A Production and Inventory Application 283

Summary 286

Glossary 287

Problems 288

Case Problem 1 **Solutions Plus 305**

Case Problem 2 **Distribution System Design 306**

Appendix 6.1 Excel Solution of Transportation, Assignment, and Transshipment Problems 308

Chapter 7 Integer Linear Programming 315

7.1 Types of Integer Linear Programming Models 317

7.2 Graphical and Computer Solutions for an All-Integer Linear Program 319
Graphical Solution of the LP Relaxation 320
Rounding to Obtain an Integer Solution 320
Graphical Solution of the All-Integer Problem 321
Using the LP Relaxation to Establish Bounds 321
Computer Solution 322

7.3 Applications Involving 0-1 Variables 323
Capital Budgeting 323
Fixed Cost 324
Distribution System Design 327
Bank Location 332
Product Design and Market Share Optimization 335

7.4 Modeling Flexibility Provided by 0-1 Integer Variables 339
Multiple-Choice and Mutually Exclusive Constraints 339
k out of n Alternatives Constraint 340
Conditional and Corequisite Constraints 340
A Cautionary Note About Sensitivity Analysis 342

Summary 342
Glossary 343
Problems 344
Case Problem 1 Textbook Publishing 355
Case Problem 2 Yeager National Bank 356
Case Problem 3 Production Scheduling with Changeover Costs 357
Appendix 7.1 Excel Solution of Integer Linear Programs 358
Appendix 7.2 LINGO Solution of Integer Linear Programs 360

Chapter 8   Nonlinear Optimization Models 363

8.1 A Production Application—Par, Inc., Revisited 365
An Unconstrained Problem 365
A Constrained Problem 366
Local and Global Optima 369
Dual Values 372
8.2 Constructing an Index Fund 372
8.3 Markowitz Portfolio Model 377
8.4 Blending: The Pooling Problem 380
8.5 Forecasting Adoption of a New Product 385
Summary 390
Glossary 390
Problems 391
Case Problem 1 Portfolio Optimization with Transaction
Costs 400
Case Problem 2 CAFE Compliance in the Auto Industry 403
Appendix 8.1 Solving Nonlinear Problems with LINGO 406
Appendix 8.2 Solving Nonlinear Problems with Excel Solver 407

Chapter 9   Project Scheduling: PERT/CPM 410

9.1 Project Scheduling with Known Activity Times 411
The Concept of a Critical Path 412
Determining the Critical Path 414
Contributions of PERT/CPM 418
Summary of the PERT/CPM Critical Path Procedure 419
9.2 Project Scheduling with Uncertain Activity Times 420
The Daugherty Porta-Vac Project 421
Uncertain Activity Times 421
The Critical Path 423
Variability in Project Completion Time 426
9.3 Considering Time-Cost Trade-Offs 429
Crashing Activity Times 430
Linear Programming Model for Crashing 432

Summary 434
Glossary 435
Problems 436
Case Problem **R. C. Coleman 446**
Appendix 9.1 Using Microsoft Office Project 448

Chapter 10   Inventory Models 451

10.1 Economic Order Quantity (EOQ) Model 452
The How-Much-to-Order Decision 457
The When-to-Order Decision 458
Sensitivity Analysis for the EOQ Model 459
Excel Solution of the EOQ Model 460
Summary of the EOQ Model Assumptions 461

10.2 Economic Production Lot Size Model 462
Total Cost Model 463
Economic Production Lot Size 465

10.3 Inventory Model with Planned Shortages 465

10.4 Quantity Discounts for the EOQ Model 470

10.5 Single-Period Inventory Model with Probabilistic Demand 472
Johnson Shoe Company 473
Nationwide Car Rental 477

10.6 Order-Quantity, Reorder Point Model with Probabilistic Demand 478
The How-Much-to-Order Decision 479
The When-to-Order Decision 480

10.7 Periodic Review Model with Probabilistic Demand 482
More Complex Periodic Review Models 485
Summary 486
Glossary 487
Problems 489
Case Problem 1 **Wagner Fabricating Company 496**
Case Problem 2 **River City Fire Department 497**
Appendix 10.1 Development of the Optimal Order Quantity (Q^*) Formula for the EOQ Model 498
Appendix 10.2 Development of the Optimal Lot Size (Q^*) Formula for the Production Lot Size Model 499

Chapter 11   Waiting Line Models 500

11.1 Structure of a Waiting Line System 502
Single-Channel Waiting Line 502
Distribution of Arrivals 502
Distribution of Service Times 504

Queue Discipline 505
Steady-State Operation 505

11.2 Single-Channel Waiting Line Model with Poisson Arrivals and Exponential Service Times 506
Operating Characteristics 506
Operating Characteristics for the Burger Dome Problem 507
Managers' Use of Waiting Line Models 508
Improving the Waiting Line Operation 508
Excel Solution of Waiting Line Model 509

11.3 Multiple-Channel Waiting Line Model with Poisson Arrivals and Exponential Service Times 510
Operating Characteristics 511
Operating Characteristics for the Burger Dome Problem 513

11.4 Some General Relationships for Waiting Line Models 515

11.5 Economic Analysis of Waiting Lines 517

11.6 Other Waiting Line Models 518

11.7 Single-Channel Waiting Line Model with Poisson Arrivals and Arbitrary Service Times 519
Operating Characteristics for the $M/G/1$ Model 519
Constant Service Times 521

11.8 Multiple-Channel Model with Poisson Arrivals, Arbitrary Service Times, and No Waiting Line 522
Operating Characteristics for the $M/G/k$ Model with Blocked Customers Cleared 522

11.9 Waiting Line Models with Finite Calling Populations 524
Operating Characteristics for the $M/M/1$ Model with a Finite Calling Population 525
Summary 527
Glossary 529
Problems 529
Case Problem 1 **Regional Airlines 537**
Case Problem 2 **Office Equipment, Inc. 538**

Chapter 12 Simulation 540

12.1 Risk Analysis 543
PortaCom Project 543
What-If Analysis 543
Simulation 545
Simulation of the PortaCom Project 552

12.2 Inventory Simulation 556
Butler Inventory Simulation 559

12.3 Waiting Line Simulation 561
Hammondsport Savings Bank ATM Waiting Line 561
Customer Arrival Times 562

Customer Service Times 563
Simulation Model 563
Hammondsport Savings Bank ATM Simulation 567
Simulation with Two ATMs 568
Simulation Results with Two ATMs 570

12.4 Other Simulation Issues 572
Computer Implementation 572
Verification and Validation 573
Advantages and Disadvantages of Using Simulation 573
Summary 574
Glossary 575
Problems 576
Case Problem 1 **Tri-State Corporation 583**
Case Problem 2 **Harbor Dunes Golf Course 585**
Case Problem 3 **County Beverage Drive-Thru 587**
Appendix 12.1 Simulation with Excel 588
Appendix 12.2 Simulation Using Crystal Ball 595

Chapter 13 **Decision Analysis 600**

13.1 Problem Formulation 602
Influence Diagrams 603
Payoff Tables 603
Decision Trees 604
13.2 Decision Making Without Probabilities 605
Optimistic Approach 605
Conservative Approach 605
Minimax Regret Approach   606
13.3 Decision Making with Probabilities 608
Expected Value of Perfect Information 611
13.4 Risk Analysis and Sensitivity Analysis 613
Risk Analysis 613
Sensitivity Analysis 614
13.5 Decision Analysis with Sample Information 618
Influence Diagram 618
Decision Tree 619
Decision Strategy 621
Risk Profile 625
Expected Value of Sample Information 627
Efficiency of Sample Information 628
13.6 Computing Branch Probabilities 628
Summary 632
Glossary 633
Problems 635
Case Problem 1 **Property Purchase Strategy 649**

Case Problem 2 **Lawsuit Defense Strategy 650**
Appendix 13.1 Decision Analysis with Treeplan 651

Chapter 14 Multicriteria Decisions 657

14.1 Goal Programming: Formulation and Graphical Solution 658
Developing the Constraints and the Goal Equations 659
Developing an Objective Function with Preemptive Priorities 661
Graphical Solution Procedure 662
Goal Programming Model 665
14.2 Goal Programming: Solving More Complex Problems 666
Suncoast Office Supplies Problem 666
Formulating the Goal Equations 667
Formulating the Objective Function 668
Computer Solution 669
14.3 Scoring Models 672
14.4 Analytic Hierarchy Process 677
Developing the Hierarchy 678
14.5 Establishing Priorities Using AHP 678
Pairwise Comparisons 679
Pairwise Comparison Matrix 680
Synthesization 682
Consistency 683
Other Pairwise Comparisons for the Car Selection Problem 685
14.6 Using AHP to Develop an Overall Priority Ranking 686
Summary 688
Glossary 688
Problems 689
Case Problem **EZ Trailers, Inc. 698**
Appendix 14.1 Scoring Models with Excel 699

Chapter 15 Time Series Analysis and Forecasting 701

15.1 Time Series Patterns 703
Horizontal Pattern 703
Trend Pattern 705
Seasonal Pattern 707
Trend and Seasonal Pattern 708
Cyclical Pattern 711
Selecting a Forecasting Method 711
15.2 Forecast Accuracy 711
15.3 Moving Averages and Exponential Smoothing 715
Moving Averages 715
Weighted Moving Averages 718
Exponential Smoothing 719

15.4 Trend Projection 724
    Linear Trend 724
    Nonlinear Trend 728
15.5 Seasonality 731
    Seasonality Without Trend 732
    Seasonality and Trend 735
    Models Based on Monthly Data 737
    Summary 738
    Glossary 739
    Problems 739
    Case Problem 1 **Forecasting Food and Beverage Sales 749**
    Case Problem 2 **Forecasting Lost Sales 749**
    Appendix 15.1 Forecasting with Excel Data Analysis Tools 751
    Appendix 15.2 Forecasting with Excel Solver 752
    Appendix 15.3 Forecasting with LINGO 756

Chapter 16   Markov Processes 759

16.1 Market Share Analysis 761
16.2 Accounts Receivable Analysis 769
    Fundamental Matrix and Associated Calculations 770
    Establishing the Allowance for Doubtful Accounts 772
    Summary 774
    Glossary 774
    Problems 775
    Case Problem **Dealer's Absorbing State Probabilities in Blackjack 779**
    Appendix 16.1 Matrix Notation and Operations 780
    Appendix 16.2 Matrix Inversion with Excel 783

Chapter 17   Linear Programming: Simplex Method On Website

17.1 An Algebraic Overview of the Simplex Method 17-2
    Algebraic Properties of the Simplex Method 17-3
    Determining a Basic Solution 17-3
    Basic Feasible Solution 17-4
17.2 Tableau Form 17-5
17.3 Setting up the Initial Simplex Tableau 17-7
17.4 Improving the Solution 17-10
17.5 Calculating the Next Tableau 17-12
    Interpreting the Results of an Iteration 17-15
    Moving Toward a Better Solution 17-15
    Interpreting the Optimal Solution 17-18
    Summary of the Simplex Method 17-19

17.6 Tableau Form: The General Case 17-20
Greater-Than-or-Equal-to Constraints 17-20
Equality Constraints 17-24
Eliminating Negative Right-Hand-Side Values 17-25
Summary of the Steps to Create Tableau Form 17-26
17.7 Solving a Minimization Problem 17-27
17.8 Special Cases 17-29
Infeasibility 17-29
Unboundedness 17-31
Alternative Optimal Solutions 17-32
Degeneracy 17-33
Summary 17-35
Glossary 17-36
Problems 17-37

**Chapter 18   Simplex-Based Sensitivity Analysis and Duality
                         On Website**

18.1 Sensitivity Analysis with the Simplex Tableau 18-2
Objective Function Coefficients 18-2
Right-Hand-Side Values 18-6
Simultaneous Changes 18-13
18.2 Duality 18-14
Economic Interpretation of the Dual Variables 18-16
Using the Dual to Identify the Primal Solution 18-18
Finding the Dual of Any Primal Problem 18-18
Summary 18-20
Glossary 18-21
Problems 18-21

**Chapter 19   Solution Procedures for Transportation
                         and Assignment Problems On Website**

**19.1 Transportation Simplex Method: A Special-Purpose Solution
           Procedure 19-2**
Phase I: Finding an Initial Feasible Solution 19-2
Phase II: Iterating to the Optimal Solution 19-7
Summary of the Transportation Simplex Method 19-17
Problem Variations 19-17
19.2 Assignment Problem: A Special-Purpose Solution Procedure 19-18
Finding the Minimum Number of Lines 19-21
Problem Variations 19-21
Glossary 19-25
Problems 19-26

Chapter 20   Minimal Spanning Tree On Website

A Minimal Spanning Tree Algorithm 20-2
Glossary 20-5
Problems 20-5

Chapter 21   Dynamic Programming On Website

21.1 A Shortest-Route Problem 21-2
21.2 Dynamic Programming Notation 21-6
21.3 The Knapsack Problem 21-10
21.4 A Production and Inventory Control Problem 21-16
Summary 21-20
Glossary 21-21
Problems 21-22
Case Problem Process Design 21-26

Appendixes 785

Appendix A   Building Spreadsheet Models 786

Appendix B   Areas for the Standard Normal Distribution 813

Appendix C   Values of $e^{-\lambda}$ 815

Appendix D   References and Bibliography 816

Appendix E   Self-Test Solutions and Answers to Even-Numbered Problems 818

Index 851

Preface

We are very excited to publish the thirteenth edition of a text that has been a leader in the field for over 20 years. The purpose of this thirteenth edition, as with previous editions, is to provide undergraduate and graduate students with a sound conceptual understanding of the role that management science plays in the decision-making process. The text describes many of the applications where management science is used successfully. Former users of this text have told us that the applications we describe have led them to find new ways to use management science in their organizations.

An Introduction to Management Science is applications oriented and continues to use the problem-scenario approach that is a hallmark of every edition of the text. Using the problem-scenario approach, we describe a problem in conjunction with the management science model being introduced. The model is then solved to generate a solution and recommendation to management. We have found that this approach helps to motivate the student by not only demonstrating how the procedure works, but also how it contributes to the decision-making process.

From the very first edition we have been committed to the challenge of writing a textbook that would help make the mathematical and technical concepts of management science understandable and useful to students of business and economics. Judging from the responses from our teaching colleagues and thousands of students, we have successfully met the challenge. Indeed, it is the helpful comments and suggestions of many loyal users that have been a major reason why the text is so successful.

Throughout the text we have utilized generally accepted notation for the topic being covered so those students who pursue study beyond the level of this text should be comfortable reading more advanced material. To assist in further study, a references and bibliography section is included at the back of the book.

CHANGES IN THE THIRTEENTH EDITION

The thirteenth edition of *Management Science* is a major revision. We are very excited about it and want to tell you about some of the changes we have made and why.

New Member of the ASWM Team

Prior to getting into the content changes, we want to announce that we are adding a new member to the ASWM author team. His name is Jeffrey Camm. Jeff received his Ph.D. from Clemson University. He has been at the University of Cincinnati since 1984, and has been a visiting scholar at Stanford University and a visiting professor of business administration at the Tuck School of Business at Dartmouth College. Jeff has published over 30 papers in the general area of optimization applied to problems in operations management. At the University of Cincinnati, he was named the Dornoff Fellow of Teaching Excellence and he was the 2006 recipient of the INFORMS Prize for the Teaching of Operations Research Practice. He currently serves as editor-in-chief of *Interfaces,* and is on the editorial board of *INFORMS Transactions on Education.* We welcome Jeff to the new ASWCM team and expect the new ideas from Jeff will make the text even better in the years to come.

In preparing this thirteenth edition, we have been careful to maintain the overall format and approach of the previous edition. However, based on our classroom experiences and suggestions from users of previous editions, a number of changes have been made to enhance the text.

Made the Book Less Reliant on Specific Software

The first eight chapters on optimization no longer use output from The Management Scientist software. All figures illustrating computer output are generic and are totally independent of software selection. This provides flexibility for the instructor. In addition, we provide appendices that describe how to use Excel Solver and LINGO. For every model illustrated in the text we have both Excel and LINGO files available at the website. Prior users of The Management Scientist wishing to upgrade to similar software should consider using LINGO. This will be an easy transition and LINGO is far more flexible than The Management Scientist. The documented LINGO models (not available in MS 12e), available at the website, will aide in the transition. Excel Solver and LINGO have an advantage over The Management Scientist in that they do not require the user to move all variables to the left-hand side of the constraint. This eliminates the need to algebraically manipulate the model and allows the student to enter the model in the computer in its more natural form. For users wishing to use The Management Scientist, it will continue to be available on the website for the text.

New Appendix A: Building Spreadsheet Models

This appendix will prove useful to professors and students wishing to solve optimization models with Excel Solver. The appendix also contains a section on the principles of good spreadsheet modeling and a section on auditing tips. Exercises are also provided.

Chapter 15 Thoroughly Revised

Chapter 15, Times Series Analysis and Forecasting, has been thoroughly revised. The revised chapter is more focused on time series data and methods. A new section on forecast accuracy has been added and there is more emphasis on curve fitting. A new section on nonlinear trend has been added. In order to better integrate this chapter with the text, we show how finding the best parameter values in forecasting models is an application of optimization, and illustrate with Excel Solver and LINGO.

New Project Management Software

In Chapter 9, Project Scheduling: PERT/CPM, we added an appendix on Microsoft Office Project. This popular software is a valuable aid for project management and is software that the student may well encounter on the job. This software is available on the CD that is packaged with every new copy of the text.

Chapter 3 Significantly Revised

We significantly revised Chapter 3, Linear Programming: Sensitivity Analysis and Interpretation of Solution. The material is now presented in a more up-to-date fashion and emphasizes the ease of using software to analyze optimization models.

New Management Science in Action, Cases, and Problems

Management Science in Action is the name of the short summaries that describe how the material covered in a chapter have been used in practice. In this edition you will find numerous Management Science in Action vignettes, cases, and homework problems.

Other Content Changes

A variety of other changes, too numerous to mention individually, have been made throughout the text in responses to suggestions of users and our students.

COMPUTER SOFTWARE INTEGRATION

We have been careful to write the text so that it is not dependent on any particular software package. But, we have included materials that facilitate using our text with several of the more popular software packages. The following software and files are available on the website for the text:

- LINGO trial version,
- LINGO and Excel Solver models for every optimization model presented in the text,
- Microsoft® Excel worksheets for most of the examples used throughout the text,
- TreePlan™ Excel add-in for decision analysis and manual.

Microsoft Project is provided on the CD that is packaged with every new copy of the text.

FEATURES AND PEDAGOGY

We have continued many of the features that appeared in previous editions. Some of the important ones are noted here.

Annotations

Annotations that highlight key points and provide additional insights for the student are a continuing feature of this edition. These annotations, which appear in the margins, are designed to provide emphasis and enhance understanding of the terms and concepts being presented in the text.

Notes and Comments

At the end of many sections, we provide Notes and Comments designed to give the student additional insights about the statistical methodology and its application. Notes and Comments include warnings about or limitations of the methodology, recommendations for application, brief descriptions of additional technical considerations, and other matters.

Self-Test Exercises

Certain exercises are identified as self-test exercises. Completely worked-out solutions for those exercises are provided in an appendix at the end of the text. Students can attempt the self-test exercises and immediately check the solution to evaluate their understanding of the concepts presented in the chapter.

ACKNOWLEDGMENTS

We owe a debt to many of our academic colleagues and friends for their helpful comments and suggestions during the development of this and previous editions. Our associates from organizations who supplied several of the Management Science in Action vignettes make a major contribution to the text. These individuals are cited in a credit line associated with each vignette.

We are also indebted to our senior acquisitions editor, Charles McCormick, Jr.; our marketing communications manager, Libby Shipp; our developmental editor, Maggie Kubale; our content project manager, Jacquelyn K Featherly; our media editor, Chris Valentine; and others at Cengage Business and Economics for their counsel and support during the preparation of this text. We also wish to thank Lynn Lustberg, Project Manager at MPS Content Services for her help in manuscript preparation.

David R. Anderson
Dennis J. Sweeney
Thomas A. Williams
Jeffrey D. Camm
Kipp Martin

About the Authors

David R. Anderson.   David R. Anderson is Professor Emeritus of Quantitative Analysis in the College of Business Administration at the University of Cincinnati. Born in Grand Forks, North Dakota, he earned his B.S., M.S., and Ph.D. degrees from Purdue University. Professor Anderson has served as Head of the Department of Quantitative Analysis and Operations Management and as Associate Dean of the College of Business Administration. In addition, he was the coordinator of the College's first Executive Program.

At the University of Cincinnati, Professor Anderson has taught introductory statistics for business students as well as graduate-level courses in regression analysis, multivariate analysis, and management science. He has also taught statistical courses at the Department of Labor in Washington, D.C. He has been honored with nominations and awards for excellence in teaching and excellence in service to student organizations.

Professor Anderson has coauthored ten textbooks in the areas of statistics, management science, linear programming, and production and operations management. He is an active consultant in the field of sampling and statistical methods.

Dennis J. Sweeney.   Dennis J. Sweeney is Professor Emeritus of Quantitative Analysis and Founder of the Center for Productivity Improvement at the University of Cincinnati. Born in Des Moines, Iowa, he earned a B.S.B.A. degree from Drake University and his M.B.A. and D.B.A. degrees from Indiana University, where he was an NDEA Fellow. During 1978–79, Professor Sweeney worked in the management science group at Procter & Gamble; during 1981–82, he was a visiting professor at Duke University. Professor Sweeney served as Head of the Department of Quantitative Analysis and as Associate Dean of the College of Business Administration at the University of Cincinnati.

Professor Sweeney has published more than thirty articles and monographs in the area of management science and statistics. The National Science Foundation, IBM, Procter & Gamble, Federated Department Stores, Kroger, and Cincinnati Gas & Electric have funded his research, which has been published in *Management Science, Operations Research, Mathematical Programming, Decision Sciences,* and other journals.

Professor Sweeney has coauthored ten textbooks in the areas of statistics, management science, linear programming, and production and operations management.

Thomas A. Williams.   Thomas A. Williams is Professor Emeritus of Management Science in the College of Business at Rochester Institute of Technology. Born in Elmira, New York, he earned his B.S. degree at Clarkson University. He did his graduate work at Rensselaer Polytechnic Institute, where he received his M.S. and Ph.D. degrees.

Before joining the College of Business at RIT, Professor Williams served for seven years as a faculty member in the College of Business Administration at the University of Cincinnati, where he developed the undergraduate program in information systems and then served as its coordinator. At RIT he was the first chairman of the Decision Sciences Department. He teaches courses in management science and statistics, as well as graduate courses in regression and decision analysis.

Professor Williams is the coauthor of eleven textbooks in the areas of management science, statistics, production and operations management, and mathematics. He has been a consultant for numerous *Fortune* 500 companies and has worked on projects ranging from the use of data analysis to the development of large-scale regression models.

Jeffrey D. Camm.   Jeffrey D. Camm is Professor of Quantitative Analysis and Head of the Department of Quantitative Analysis and Operations Management at the University of Cincinnati. Dr. Camm earned a Ph.D. in management science from Clemson University and a B.S. in mathematics from Xavier University. He has been at the University of Cincinnati since 1984, has been a visiting scholar at Stanford University, and a visiting professor of business administration at the Tuck School of Business at Dartmouth College. Dr. Camm has published over 30 papers in the general area of optimization applied to problems in operations management and his research has been funded by the Air Force Office of Scientific Research, the Office of Naval Research, and the U.S. Department of Energy. He was named the Dornoff Fellow of Teaching Excellence by the University of Cincinnati College of Business and he was the 2006 recipient of the INFORMS Prize for the Teaching of Operations Research Practice. He currently serves as editor-in-chief of *Interfaces,* and is on the editorial board of *INFORMS Transactions on Education.*

Kipp Martin.   Kipp Martin is Professor of Operations Research and Computing Technology at the Booth School of Business, University of Chicago. Born in St. Bernard, Ohio, he earned a B.A. in mathematics, an MBA, and a Ph.D. in management science from the University of Cincinnati. While at the University of Chicago, Professor Martin has taught courses in management science, operations management, business mathematics, and information systems.

Research interests include incorporating Web technologies such as XML, XSLT, XQuery, and Web Services into the mathematical modeling process; the theory of how to construct good mixed integer linear programming models; symbolic optimization; polyhedral combinatorics; methods for large scale optimization; bundle pricing models; computing technology; and database theory. Professor Martin has published in *INFORMS Journal of Computing, Management Science, Mathematical Programming, Operations Research, The Journal of Accounting Research,* and other professional journals. He is also the author of *The Essential Guide to Internet Business Technology* (with Gail Honda) and *Large Scale Linear and Integer Optimization.*

CHAPTER 1

Introduction

CONTENTS

1.1 PROBLEM SOLVING AND
DECISION MAKING

1.2 QUANTITATIVE ANALYSIS
AND DECISION MAKING

1.3 QUANTITATIVE ANALYSIS
Model Development
Data Preparation
Model Solution
Report Generation
A Note Regarding Implementation

1.4 MODELS OF COST, REVENUE,
AND PROFIT
Cost and Volume Models
Revenue and Volume Models
Profit and Volume Models
Breakeven Analysis

1.5 MANAGEMENT SCIENCE
TECHNIQUES
Methods Used Most Frequently

Management science, an approach to decision making based on the scientific method, makes extensive use of quantitative analysis. A variety of names exists for the body of knowledge involving quantitative approaches to decision making; in addition to management science, two other widely known and accepted names are operations research and decision science. Today, many use the terms *management science, operations research,* and *decision science* interchangeably.

The scientific management revolution of the early 1900s, initiated by Frederic W. Taylor, provided the foundation for the use of quantitative methods in management. But modern management science research is generally considered to have originated during the World War II period, when teams were formed to deal with strategic and tactical problems faced by the military. These teams, which often consisted of people with diverse specialties (e.g., mathematicians, engineers, and behavioral scientists), were joined together to solve a common problem by utilizing the scientific method. After the war, many of these team members continued their research in the field of management science.

According to Irv Lustig of IBM ILOG, Inc., solution methods developed today are 10,000 times faster than the ones used 15 years ago.

Two developments that occurred during the post–World War II period led to the growth and use of management science in nonmilitary applications. First, continued research resulted in numerous methodological developments. Probably the most significant development was the discovery by George Dantzig, in 1947, of the simplex method for solving linear programming problems. At the same time these methodological developments were taking place, digital computers prompted a virtual explosion in computing power. Computers enabled practitioners to use the methodological advances to solve a large variety of problems. The computer technology explosion continues, and personal computers can now be used to solve problems larger than those solved on mainframe computers in the 1990s.

As stated in the Preface, the purpose of the text is to provide students with a sound conceptual understanding of the role that management science plays in the decision-making process. We also said that the text is applications oriented. To reinforce the applications nature of the text and provide a better understanding of the variety of applications in which management science has been used successfully, Management Science in Action articles are presented throughout the text. Each Management Science in Action article summarizes an application of management science in practice. The first Management Science in Action in this chapter, Revenue Management at American Airlines, describes one of the most significant applications of management science in the airline industry.

MANAGEMENT SCIENCE IN ACTION

REVENUE MANAGEMENT AT AMERICAN AIRLINES*

One of the great success stories in management science involves the work done by the operations research (OR) group at American Airlines. In 1982, Thomas M. Cook joined a group of 12 operations research analysts at American Airlines. Under Cook's guidance, the OR group quickly grew to a staff of 75 professionals who developed models and conducted studies to support senior management decision making. Today the OR group is called Sabre and employs 10,000 professionals worldwide.

One of the most significant applications developed by the OR group came about because of the deregulation of the airline industry in the late

1970s. As a result of deregulation, a number of low-cost airlines were able to move into the market by selling seats at a fraction of the price charged by established carriers such as American Airlines. Facing the question of how to compete, the OR group suggested offering different fare classes (discount and full fare) and in the process created a new area of management science referred to as yield or revenue management.

The OR group used forecasting and optimization techniques to determine how many seats to sell at a discount and how many seats to hold for full fare. Although the initial implementation was relatively crude, the group continued to improve the forecasting and optimization models that drive the system and to obtain better data. Tom Cook counts at least four basic generations of revenue management during his tenure. Each produced in excess of $100 million in incremental profitability over its predecessor. This revenue management system at American Airlines generates nearly $1 billion annually in incremental revenue.

Today, virtually every airline uses some sort of revenue management system. The cruise, hotel, and car rental industries also now apply revenue management methods, a further tribute to the pioneering efforts of the OR group at American Airlines and its leader, Thomas M. Cook.

*Based on Peter Horner, "The Sabre Story," *OR/MS Today* (June 2000).

1.1   PROBLEM SOLVING AND DECISION MAKING

Problem solving can be defined as the process of identifying a difference between the actual and the desired state of affairs and then taking action to resolve the difference. For problems important enough to justify the time and effort of careful analysis, the problem-solving process involves the following seven steps:

1. Identify and define the problem.
2. Determine the set of alternative solutions.
3. Determine the criterion or criteria that will be used to evaluate the alternatives.
4. Evaluate the alternatives.
5. Choose an alternative.
6. Implement the selected alternative.
7. Evaluate the results to determine whether a satisfactory solution has been obtained.

Decision making is the term generally associated with the first five steps of the problem-solving process. Thus, the first step of decision making is to identify and define the problem. Decision making ends with the choosing of an alternative, which is the act of making the decision.

Let us consider the following example of the decision-making process. For the moment assume that you are currently unemployed and that you would like a position that will lead to a satisfying career. Suppose that your job search has resulted in offers from companies in Rochester, New York; Dallas, Texas; Greensboro, North Carolina; and Pittsburgh, Pennsylvania. Thus, the alternatives for your decision problem can be stated as follows:

1. Accept the position in Rochester.
2. Accept the position in Dallas.
3. Accept the position in Greensboro.
4. Accept the position in Pittsburgh.

The next step of the problem-solving process involves determining the criteria that will be used to evaluate the four alternatives. Obviously, the starting salary is a factor of some importance. If salary were the only criterion of importance to you, the alternative selected as "best" would be the one with the highest starting salary. Problems in which the objective is to find the best solution with respect to one criterion are referred to as **single-criterion decision problems.**

Suppose that you also conclude that the potential for advancement and the location of the job are two other criteria of major importance. Thus, the three criteria in your decision problem are starting salary, potential for advancement, and location. Problems that involve more than one criterion are referred to as **multicriteria decision problems.**

The next step of the decision-making process is to evaluate each of the alternatives with respect to each criterion. For example, evaluating each alternative relative to the

TABLE 1.1   DATA FOR THE JOB EVALUATION DECISION-MAKING PROBLEM

Alternative	Starting Salary	Potential for Advancement	Job Location
1. Rochester	$48,500	Average	Average
2. Dallas	$46,000	Excellent	Good
3. Greensboro	$46,000	Good	Excellent
4. Pittsburgh	$47,000	Average	Good

starting salary criterion is done simply by recording the starting salary for each job alternative. Evaluating each alternative with respect to the potential for advancement and the location of the job is more difficult to do, however, because these evaluations are based primarily on subjective factors that are often difficult to quantify. Suppose for now that you decide to measure potential for advancement and job location by rating each of these criteria as poor, fair, average, good, or excellent. The data that you compile are shown in Table 1.1.

You are now ready to make a choice from the available alternatives. What makes this choice phase so difficult is that the criteria are probably not all equally important, and no one alternative is "best" with regard to all criteria. Although we will present a method for dealing with situations like this one later in the text, for now let us suppose that after a careful evaluation of the data in Table 1.1, you decide to select alternative 3; alternative 3 is thus referred to as the **decision.**

At this point in time, the decision-making process is complete. In summary, we see that this process involves five steps:

1. Define the problem.
2. Identify the alternatives.
3. Determine the criteria.
4. Evaluate the alternatives.
5. Choose an alternative.

Note that missing from this list are the last two steps in the problem-solving process: implementing the selected alternative and evaluating the results to determine whether a satisfactory solution has been obtained. This omission is not meant to diminish the importance of each of these activities, but to emphasize the more limited scope of the term *decision making* as compared to the term *problem solving.* Figure 1.1 summarizes the relationship between these two concepts.

1.2   QUANTITATIVE ANALYSIS AND DECISION MAKING

Consider the flowchart presented in Figure 1.2. Note that it combines the first three steps of the decision-making process under the heading of "Structuring the Problem" and the latter two steps under the heading "Analyzing the Problem." Let us now consider in greater detail how to carry out the set of activities that make up the decision-making process.

Figure 1.3 shows that the analysis phase of the decision-making process may take two basic forms: qualitative and quantitative. Qualitative analysis is based primarily on the manager's judgment and experience; it includes the manager's intuitive "feel" for the problem and is more an art than a science. If the manager has had experience with similar

FIGURE 1.1   THE RELATIONSHIP BETWEEN PROBLEM SOLVING
AND DECISION MAKING

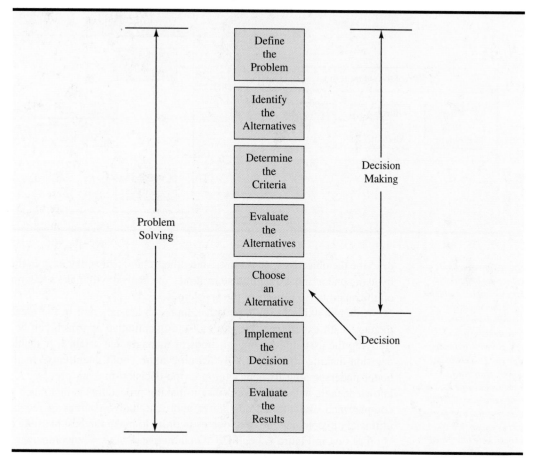

problems or if the problem is relatively simple, heavy emphasis may be placed upon a qualitative analysis. However, if the manager has had little experience with similar problems, or if the problem is sufficiently complex, then a quantitative analysis of the problem can be an especially important consideration in the manager's final decision.

When using the quantitative approach, an analyst will concentrate on the quantitative facts or data associated with the problem and develop mathematical expressions that

FIGURE 1.2   AN ALTERNATE CLASSIFICATION OF THE DECISION-MAKING PROCESS

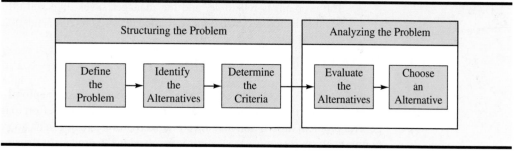

FIGURE 1.3   THE ROLE OF QUALITATIVE AND QUANTITATIVE ANALYSIS

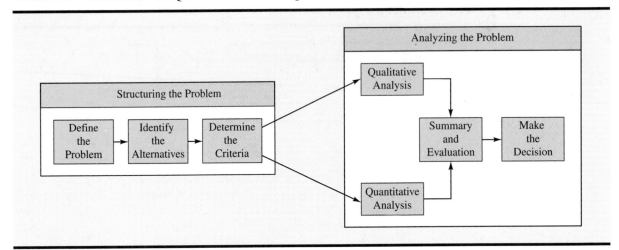

Quantitative methods are especially helpful with large, complex problems. For example, in the coordination of the thousands of tasks associated with landing Apollo 11 safely on the moon, quantitative techniques helped to ensure that more than 300,000 pieces of work performed by more than 400,000 people were integrated smoothly.

describe the objectives, constraints, and other relationships that exist in the problem. Then, by using one or more quantitative methods, the analyst will make a recommendation based on the quantitative aspects of the problem.

Although skills in the qualitative approach are inherent in the manager and usually increase with experience, the skills of the quantitative approach can be learned only by studying the assumptions and methods of management science. A manager can increase decision-making effectiveness by learning more about quantitative methodology and by better understanding its contribution to the decision-making process. A manager who is knowledgeable in quantitative decision-making procedures is in a much better position to compare and evaluate the qualitative and quantitative sources of recommendations and ultimately to combine the two sources in order to make the best possible decision.

The box in Figure 1.3 entitled "Quantitative Analysis" encompasses most of the subject matter of this text. We will consider a managerial problem, introduce the appropriate quantitative methodology, and then develop the recommended decision.

In closing this section, let us briefly state some of the reasons why a quantitative approach might be used in the decision-making process:

Try Problem 4 to test your understanding of why quantitative approaches might be needed in a particular problem.

1. The problem is complex, and the manager cannot develop a good solution without the aid of quantitative analysis.
2. The problem is especially important (e.g., a great deal of money is involved), and the manager desires a thorough analysis before attempting to make a decision.
3. The problem is new, and the manager has no previous experience from which to draw.
4. The problem is repetitive, and the manager saves time and effort by relying on quantitative procedures to make routine decision recommendations.

1.3   QUANTITATIVE ANALYSIS

From Figure 1.3, we see that quantitative analysis begins once the problem has been structured. It usually takes imagination, teamwork, and considerable effort to transform a rather general problem description into a well-defined problem that can be approached via quantitative analysis. The more the analyst is involved in the process of structuring the problem, the more likely the ensuing quantitative analysis will make an important contribution to the decision-making process.

To successfully apply quantitative analysis to decision making, the management scientist must work closely with the manager or user of the results. When both the management scientist and the manager agree that the problem has been adequately structured, work can begin on developing a model to represent the problem mathematically. Solution procedures can then be employed to find the best solution for the model. This best solution for the model then becomes a recommendation to the decision maker. The process of developing and solving models is the essence of the quantitative analysis process.

Model Development

Models are representations of real objects or situations and can be presented in various forms. For example, a scale model of an airplane is a representation of a real airplane. Similarly, a child's toy truck is a model of a real truck. The model airplane and toy truck are examples of models that are physical replicas of real objects. In modeling terminology, physical replicas are referred to as **iconic models.**

A second classification includes models that are physical in form but do not have the same physical appearance as the object being modeled. Such models are referred to as **analog models.** The speedometer of an automobile is an analog model; the position of the needle on the dial represents the speed of the automobile. A thermometer is another analog model representing temperature.

A third classification of models—the type we will primarily be studying—includes representations of a problem by a system of symbols and mathematical relationships or expressions. Such models are referred to as **mathematical models** and are a critical part of any quantitative approach to decision making. For example, the total profit from the sale of a product can be determined by multiplying the profit per unit by the quantity sold. If we let x represent the number of units sold and P the total profit, then, with a profit of $10 per unit, the following mathematical model defines the total profit earned by selling x units:

$$P = 10x \tag{1.1}$$

The purpose, or value, of any model is that it enables us to make inferences about the real situation by studying and analyzing the model. For example, an airplane designer might test an iconic model of a new airplane in a wind tunnel to learn about the potential flying characteristics of the full-size airplane. Similarly, a mathematical model may be used to make inferences about how much profit will be earned if a specified quantity of a particular product is sold. According to the mathematical model of equation (1.1), we would expect selling three units of the product ($x = 3$) would provide a profit of $P = 10(3) = \$30$.

In general, experimenting with models requires less time and is less expensive than experimenting with the real object or situation. A model airplane is certainly quicker and less expensive to build and study than the full-size airplane. Similarly, the mathematical model in equation (1.1) allows a quick identification of profit expectations without actually requiring the manager to produce and sell x units. Models also have the advantage of reducing the risk associated with experimenting with the real situation. In particular, bad designs or bad decisions that cause the model airplane to crash or a mathematical model to project a $10,000 loss can be avoided in the real situation.

The value of model-based conclusions and decisions is dependent on how well the model represents the real situation. The more closely the model airplane represents the real

Herbert A. Simon, a Nobel Prize winner in economics and an expert in decision making, said that a mathematical model does not have to be exact; it just has to be close enough to provide better results than can be obtained by common sense.

airplane, the more accurate the conclusions and predictions will be. Similarly, the more closely the mathematical model represents the company's true profit-volume relationship, the more accurate the profit projections will be.

Because this text deals with quantitative analysis based on mathematical models, let us look more closely at the mathematical modeling process. When initially considering a managerial problem, we usually find that the problem definition phase leads to a specific objective, such as maximization of profit or minimization of cost, and possibly a set of restrictions or **constraints,** such as production capacities. The success of the mathematical model and quantitative approach will depend heavily on how accurately the objective and constraints can be expressed in terms of mathematical equations or relationships.

A mathematical expression that describes the problem's objective is referred to as the **objective function.** For example, the profit equation $P = 10x$ would be an objective function for a firm attempting to maximize profit. A production capacity constraint would be necessary if, for instance, 5 hours are required to produce each unit and only 40 hours of production time are available per week. Let x indicate the number of units produced each week. The production time constraint is given by

$$5x \leq 40 \tag{1.2}$$

The value of $5x$ is the total time required to produce x units; the symbol $\leq$ indicates that the production time required must be less than or equal to the 40 hours available.

The decision problem or question is the following: How many units of the product should be scheduled each week to maximize profit? A complete mathematical model for this simple production problem is

$$\text{Maximize} \quad P = 10x \quad \text{objective function}$$
$$\text{subject to (s.t.)}$$
$$\left.\begin{array}{r} 5x \leq 40 \\ x \geq 0 \end{array}\right\} \text{constraints}$$

The $x \geq 0$ constraint requires the production quantity x to be greater than or equal to zero, which simply recognizes the fact that it is not possible to manufacture a negative number of units. The optimal solution to this model can be easily calculated and is given by $x = 8$, with an associated profit of \$80. This model is an example of a linear programming model. In subsequent chapters we will discuss more complicated mathematical models and learn how to solve them in situations where the answers are not nearly so obvious.

In the preceding mathematical model, the profit per unit (\$10), the production time per unit (5 hours), and the production capacity (40 hours) are environmental factors that are not under the control of the manager or decision maker. Such environmental factors, which can affect both the objective function and the constraints, are referred to as **uncontrollable inputs** to the model. Inputs that are controlled or determined by the decision maker are referred to as **controllable inputs** to the model. In the example given, the production quantity x is the controllable input to the model. Controllable inputs are the decision alternatives specified by the manager and thus are also referred to as the **decision variables** of the model.

Once all controllable and uncontrollable inputs are specified, the objective function and constraints can be evaluated and the output of the model determined. In this sense, the output of the model is simply the projection of what would happen if those particular

FIGURE 1.4 FLOWCHART OF THE PROCESS OF TRANSFORMING MODEL INPUTS INTO OUTPUT

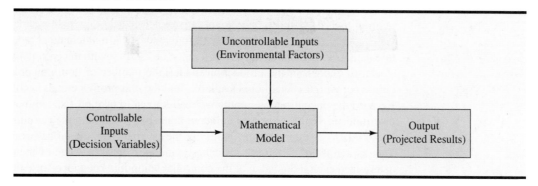

environmental factors and decisions occurred in the real situation. A flowchart of how controllable and uncontrollable inputs are transformed by the mathematical model into output is shown in Figure 1.4. A similar flowchart showing the specific details of the production model is shown in Figure 1.5.

As stated earlier, the uncontrollable inputs are those the decision maker cannot influence. The specific controllable and uncontrollable inputs of a model depend on the particular problem or decision-making situation. In the production problem, the production time available (40) is an uncontrollable input. However, if it were possible to hire more employees or use overtime, the number of hours of production time would become a controllable input and therefore a decision variable in the model.

Uncontrollable inputs can either be known exactly or be uncertain and subject to variation. If all uncontrollable inputs to a model are known and cannot vary, the model is referred to as a **deterministic model.** Corporate income tax rates are not under the influence of the manager and thus constitute an uncontrollable input in many decision models. Because these rates are known and fixed (at least in the short run), a mathematical model with corporate income tax rates as the only uncontrollable input would be a deterministic

FIGURE 1.5 FLOWCHART FOR THE PRODUCTION MODEL

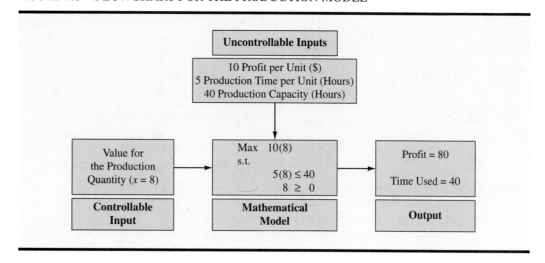

model. The distinguishing feature of a deterministic model is that the uncontrollable input values are known in advance.

If any of the uncontrollable inputs are uncertain and subject to variation, the model is referred to as a **stochastic** or **probabilistic model.** An uncontrollable input to many production planning models is demand for the product. A mathematical model that treats future demand—which may be any of a range of values—with uncertainty would be called a stochastic model. In the production model, the number of hours of production time required per unit, the total hours available, and the unit profit were all uncontrollable inputs. Because the uncontrollable inputs were all known to take on fixed values, the model was deterministic. If, however, the number of hours of production time per unit could vary from 3 to 6 hours depending on the quality of the raw material, the model would be stochastic. The distinguishing feature of a stochastic model is that the value of the output cannot be determined even if the value of the controllable input is known because the specific values of the uncontrollable inputs are unknown. In this respect, stochastic models are often more difficult to analyze.

Data Preparation

Another step in the quantitative analysis of a problem is the preparation of the data required by the model. Data in this sense refer to the values of the uncontrollable inputs to the model. All uncontrollable inputs or data must be specified before we can analyze the model and recommend a decision or solution for the problem.

In the production model, the values of the uncontrollable inputs or data were $10 per unit for profit, 5 hours per unit for production time, and 40 hours for production capacity. In the development of the model, these data values were known and incorporated into the model as it was being developed. If the model is relatively small and the uncontrollable input values or data required are few, the quantitative analyst will probably combine model development and data preparation into one step. In these situations the data values are inserted as the equations of the mathematical model are developed.

However, in many mathematical modeling situations, the data or uncontrollable input values are not readily available. In these situations the management scientist may know that the model will need profit per unit, production time, and production capacity data, but the values will not be known until the accounting, production, and engineering departments can be consulted. Rather than attempting to collect the required data as the model is being developed, the analyst will usually adopt a general notation for the model development step, and then a separate data preparation step will be performed to obtain the uncontrollable input values required by the model.

Using the general notation

$$c = \text{profit per unit}$$
$$a = \text{production time in hours per unit}$$
$$b = \text{production capacity in hours}$$

the model development step of the production problem would result in the following general model:

$$\text{Max} \quad cx$$
$$\text{s.t.}$$
$$ax \leq b$$
$$x \geq 0$$

A separate data preparation step to identify the values for c, a, and b would then be necessary to complete the model.

Many inexperienced quantitative analysts assume that once the problem has been defined and a general model developed, the problem is essentially solved. These individuals tend to believe that data preparation is a trivial step in the process and can be easily handled by clerical staff. Actually, this assumption could not be further from the truth, especially with large-scale models that have numerous data input values. For example, a small linear programming model with 50 decision variables and 25 constraints could have more than 1300 data elements that must be identified in the data preparation step. The time required to prepare these data and the possibility of data collection errors will make the data preparation step a critical part of the quantitative analysis process. Often, a fairly large database is needed to support a mathematical model, and information systems specialists may become involved in the data preparation step.

Model Solution

Once the model development and data preparation steps are completed, we can proceed to the model solution step. In this step, the analyst will attempt to identify the values of the decision variables that provide the "best" output for the model. The specific decision-variable value or values providing the "best" output will be referred to as the **optimal solution** for the model. For the production problem, the model solution step involves finding the value of the production quantity decision variable x that maximizes profit while not causing a violation of the production capacity constraint.

One procedure that might be used in the model solution step involves a trial-and-error approach in which the model is used to test and evaluate various decision alternatives. In the production model, this procedure would mean testing and evaluating the model under various production quantities or values of x. Note, in Figure 1.5, that we could input trial values for x and check the corresponding output for projected profit and satisfaction of the production capacity constraint. If a particular decision alternative does not satisfy one or more of the model constraints, the decision alternative is rejected as being **infeasible,** regardless of the objective function value. If all constraints are satisfied, the decision alternative is **feasible** and a candidate for the "best" solution or recommended decision. Through this trial-and-error process of evaluating selected decision alternatives, a decision maker can identify a good—and possibly the best—feasible solution to the problem. This solution would then be the recommended decision for the problem.

Table 1.2 shows the results of a trial-and-error approach to solving the production model of Figure 1.5. The recommended decision is a production quantity of 8 because the feasible solution with the highest projected profit occurs at $x = 8$.

Although the trial-and-error solution process is often acceptable and can provide valuable information for the manager, it has the drawbacks of not necessarily providing the best solution and of being inefficient in terms of requiring numerous calculations if many decision alternatives are tried. Thus, quantitative analysts have developed special solution procedures for many models that are much more efficient than the trial-and-error approach. Throughout this text, you will be introduced to solution procedures that are applicable to the specific mathematical models that will be formulated. Some relatively small models or problems can be solved by hand computations, but most practical applications require the use of a computer.

Model development and model solution steps are not completely separable. An analyst will want both to develop an accurate model or representation of the actual problem situation and to be able to find a solution to the model. If we approach the model development

TABLE 1.2   TRIAL-AND-ERROR SOLUTION FOR THE PRODUCTION MODEL
OF FIGURE 1.5

Decision Alternative (Production Quantity) x	Projected Profit	Total Hours of Production	Feasible Solution? (Hours Used ≤ 40)
0	0	0	Yes
2	20	10	Yes
4	40	20	Yes
6	60	30	Yes
8	80	40	Yes
10	100	50	No
12	120	60	No

step by attempting to find the most accurate and realistic mathematical model, we may find the model so large and complex that it is impossible to obtain a solution. In this case, a simpler and perhaps more easily understood model with a readily available solution procedure is preferred even if the recommended solution is only a rough approximation of the best decision. As you learn more about quantitative solution procedures, you will have a better idea of the types of mathematical models that can be developed and solved.

Try Problem 8 to test your understanding of the concept of a mathematical model and what is referred to as the optimal solution to the model.

After a model solution is obtained, both the management scientist and the manager will be interested in determining how good the solution really is. Even though the analyst has undoubtedly taken many precautions to develop a realistic model, often the goodness or accuracy of the model cannot be assessed until model solutions are generated. Model testing and validation are frequently conducted with relatively small "test" problems that have known or at least expected solutions. If the model generates the expected solutions, and if other output information appears correct, the go-ahead may be given to use the model on the full-scale problem. However, if the model test and validation identify potential problems or inaccuracies inherent in the model, corrective action, such as model modification and/or collection of more accurate input data, may be taken. Whatever the corrective action, the model solution will not be used in practice until the model has satisfactorily passed testing and validation.

Report Generation

An important part of the quantitative analysis process is the preparation of managerial reports based on the model's solution. In Figure 1.3, we see that the solution based on the quantitative analysis of a problem is one of the inputs the manager considers before making a final decision. Thus, the results of the model must appear in a managerial report that can be easily understood by the decision maker. The report includes the recommended decision and other pertinent information about the results that may be helpful to the decision maker.

A Note Regarding Implementation

As discussed in Section 1.2, the manager is responsible for integrating the quantitative solution with qualitative considerations in order to make the best possible decision. After completing the decision-making process, the manager must oversee the implementation and follow-up evaluation of the decision. The manager should continue to monitor the contribution of the model during the implementation and follow-up. At times this process may lead to requests for model expansion or refinement that will cause the management scientist to return to an earlier step of the quantitative analysis process.

Successful implementation of results is of critical importance to the management scientist as well as the manager. If the results of the quantitative analysis process are not correctly implemented, the entire effort may be of no value. It doesn't take too many unsuccessful implementations before the management scientist is out of work. Because implementation often requires people to do things differently, it often meets with resistance. People want to know, "What's wrong with the way we've been doing it?" and so on. One of the most effective ways to ensure successful implementation is to include users throughout the modeling process. A user who feels a part of identifying the problem and developing the solution is much more likely to enthusiastically implement the results. The success rate for implementing the results of a management science project is much greater for those projects characterized by extensive user involvement. The Management Science in Action, Quantitative Analysis at Merrill Lynch, discusses some of the reasons behind the success Merrill Lynch realized from using quantitative analysis.

MANAGEMENT SCIENCE IN ACTION

QUANTITATIVE ANALYSIS AT MERRILL LYNCH*

Merrill Lynch, a brokerage and financial services firm with more than 56,000 employees in 45 countries, serves its client base through two business units. The Merrill Lynch Corporate and Institutional Client Group serves more than 7000 corporations, institutions, and governments. The Merrill Lynch Private Client Group (MLPC) serves approximately 4 million households, as well as 225,000 small to mid-sized businesses and regional financial institutions, through more than 14,000 financial consultants in 600-plus branch offices. The management science group, established in 1986, has been part of MLPC since 1991. The mission of this group is to provide high-end quantitative analysis to support strategic management decisions and to enhance the financial consultant–client relationship.

The management science group has successfully implemented models and developed systems for asset allocation, financial planning, marketing information technology, database marketing, and portfolio performance measurement. Although technical expertise and objectivity are clearly important factors in any analytical group, the management science group attributes much of its success to communications skills, teamwork, and consulting skills.

Each project begins with face-to-face meetings with the client. A proposal is then prepared to outline the background of the problem, the objectives of the project, the approach, the required resources, the time schedule, and the implementation issues. At this stage, analysts focus on developing solutions that provide significant value and are easily implemented.

As the work progresses, frequent meetings keep the clients up to date. Because people with different skills, perspectives, and motivations must work together for a common goal, teamwork is essential. The group's members take classes in team approaches, facilitation, and conflict resolution. They possess a broad range of multifunctional and multidisciplinary capabilities and are motivated to provide solutions that focus on the goals of the firm. This approach to problem solving and the implementation of quantitative analysis has been a hallmark of the management science group. The impact and success of the group translates into hard dollars and repeat business. The group received the annual Edelman award given by the Institute for Operations Research and the Management Sciences for effective use of management science for organizational success.

*Based on Russ Labe, Raj Nigam, and Steve Spence, "Management Science at Merrill Lynch Private Client Group," *Interfaces* 29, no. 2 (March/April 1999): 1–14.

NOTES AND COMMENTS

1. Developments in computer technology have increased the availability of management science techniques to decision makers. Many software packages are now available for personal computers. Microsoft Excel, and LINGO are widely used in management science courses and in industry.

2. Various chapter appendices provide step-by-step instructions for using Excel and LINGO to solve problems in the text. Microsoft Excel has become the most used analytical modeling software in business and industry. We recommend that you read Appendix A, Building Spreadsheet Models, located in the back of this text.

1.4   MODELS OF COST, REVENUE, AND PROFIT

Some of the most basic quantitative models arising in business and economic applications are those involving the relationship between a volume variable—such as production volume or sales volume—and cost, revenue, and profit. Through the use of these models, a manager can determine the projected cost, revenue, and/or profit associated with an established production quantity or a forecasted sales volume. Financial planning, production planning, sales quotas, and other areas of decision making can benefit from such cost, revenue, and profit models.

Cost and Volume Models

The cost of manufacturing or producing a product is a function of the volume produced. This cost can usually be defined as a sum of two costs: fixed cost and variable cost. **Fixed cost** is the portion of the total cost that does not depend on the production volume; this cost remains the same no matter how much is produced. **Variable cost,** on the other hand, is the portion of the total cost that is dependent on and varies with the production volume. To illustrate how cost and volume models can be developed, we will consider a manufacturing problem faced by Nowlin Plastics.

Nowlin Plastics produces a variety of compact disc (CD) storage cases. Nowlin's best-selling product is the CD-50, a slim, plastic CD holder with a specially designed lining that protects the optical surface of the disc. Several products are produced on the same manufacturing line, and a setup cost is incurred each time a changeover is made for a new product. Suppose that the setup cost for the CD-50 is $3000. This setup cost is a fixed cost that is incurred regardless of the number of units eventually produced. In addition, suppose that variable labor and material costs are $2 for each unit produced. The cost-volume model for producing x units of the CD-50 can be written as

$$C(x) = 3000 + 2x \qquad (1.3)$$

where

$$x = \text{production volume in units}$$
$$C(x) = \text{total cost of producing } x \text{ units}$$

Once a production volume is established, the model in equation (1.3) can be used to compute the total production cost. For example, the decision to produce $x = 1200$ units would result in a total cost of $C(1200) = 3000 + 2(1200) = \$5400$.

Marginal cost is defined as the rate of change of the total cost with respect to production volume. That is, it is the cost increase associated with a one-unit increase in the production volume. In the cost model of equation (1.3), we see that the total cost $C(x)$ will increase by \$2 for each unit increase in the production volume. Thus, the marginal cost is \$2. With more complex total cost models, marginal cost may depend on the production volume. In such cases, we could have marginal cost increasing or decreasing with the production volume x.

Revenue and Volume Models

Management of Nowlin Plastics will also want information on the projected revenue associated with selling a specified number of units. Thus, a model of the relationship between revenue and volume is also needed. Suppose that each CD-50 storage unit sells for \$5. The model for total revenue can be written as

$$R(x) = 5x \tag{1.4}$$

where

$$x = \text{sales volume in units}$$
$$R(x) = \text{total revenue associated with selling } x \text{ units}$$

Marginal revenue is defined as the rate of change of total revenue with respect to sales volume. That is, it is the increase in total revenue resulting from a one-unit increase in sales volume. In the model of equation (1.4), we see that the marginal revenue is \$5. In this case, marginal revenue is constant and does not vary with the sales volume. With more complex models, we may find that marginal revenue increases or decreases as the sales volume x increases.

Profit and Volume Models

One of the most important criteria for management decision making is profit. Managers need to be able to know the profit implications of their decisions. If we assume that we will only produce what can be sold, the production volume and sales volume will be equal. We can combine equations (1.3) and (1.4) to develop a profit-volume model that will determine the total profit associated with a specified production-sales volume. Total profit, denoted $P(x)$, is total revenue minus total cost; therefore, the following model provides the total profit associated with producing and selling x units:

$$
\begin{aligned}
P(x) &= R(x) - C(x) \\
&= 5x - (3000 + 2x) = -3000 + 3x
\end{aligned}
\tag{1.5}
$$

Thus, the profit-volume model can be derived from the revenue-volume and cost-volume models.

Breakeven Analysis

Using equation (1.5), we can now determine the total profit associated with any production volume x. For example, suppose that a demand forecast indicates that 500 units of the product can be sold. The decision to produce and sell the 500 units results in a projected profit of

$$P(500) = -3000 + 3(500) = -1500$$

In other words, a loss of $1500 is predicted. If sales are expected to be 500 units, the manager may decide against producing the product. However, a demand forecast of 1800 units would show a projected profit of

$$P(1800) = -3000 + 3(1800) = 2400$$

This profit may be enough to justify proceeding with the production and sale of the product.

We see that a volume of 500 units will yield a loss, whereas a volume of 1800 provides a profit. The volume that results in total revenue equaling total cost (providing $0 profit) is called the **breakeven point.** If the breakeven point is known, a manager can quickly infer that a volume above the breakeven point will result in a profit, whereas a volume below the breakeven point will result in a loss. Thus, the breakeven point for a product provides valuable information for a manager who must make a yes/no decision concerning production of the product.

Let us now return to the Nowlin Plastics example and show how the total profit model in equation (1.5) can be used to compute the breakeven point. The breakeven point can be found by setting the total profit expression equal to zero and solving for the production volume. Using equation (1.5), we have

$$P(x) = -3000 + 3x = 0$$
$$3x = 3000$$
$$x = 1000$$

Try Problem 12 to test your ability to determine the breakeven point for a quantitative model.

With this information, we know that production and sales of the product must be greater than 1000 units before a profit can be expected. The graphs of the total cost model, the total revenue model, and the location of the breakeven point are shown in Figure 1.6. In Appendix 1.1 we also show how Excel can be used to perform a breakeven analysis for the Nowlin Plastics production example.

1.5   MANAGEMENT SCIENCE TECHNIQUES

In this section we present a brief overview of the management science techniques covered in this text. Over the years, practitioners have found numerous applications for the following techniques:

Linear Programming   Linear programming is a problem-solving approach developed for situations involving maximizing or minimizing a linear function subject to linear constraints that limit the degree to which the objective can be pursued. The production model developed in Section 1.3 (see Figure 1.5) is an example of a simple linear programming model.

Integer Linear Programming   Integer linear programming is an approach used for problems that can be set up as linear programs, with the additional requirement that some or all of the decision variables be integer values.

FIGURE 1.6   GRAPH OF THE BREAKEVEN ANALYSIS FOR NOWLIN PLASTICS

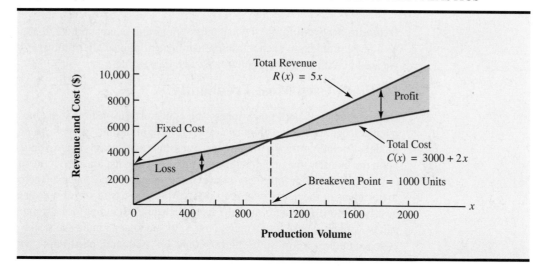

Network Models   A network is a graphical description of a problem consisting of circles called nodes that are interconnected by lines called arcs. Specialized solution procedures exist for these types of problems, enabling us to quickly solve problems in such areas as transportation system design, information system design, and project scheduling.

Project Scheduling: PERT/CPM   In many situations, managers are responsible for planning, scheduling, and controlling projects that consist of numerous separate jobs or tasks performed by a variety of departments, individuals, and so forth. The PERT (Program Evaluation and Review Technique) and CPM (Critical Path Method) techniques help managers carry out their project scheduling responsibilities.

Inventory Models   Inventory models are used by managers faced with the dual problems of maintaining sufficient inventories to meet demand for goods and, at the same time, incurring the lowest possible inventory holding costs.

Waiting-Line or Queueing Models   Waiting-line or queueing models have been developed to help managers understand and make better decisions concerning the operation of systems involving waiting lines.

Simulation   Simulation is a technique used to model the operation of a system. This technique employs a computer program to model the operation and perform simulation computations.

Decision Analysis   Decision analysis can be used to determine optimal strategies in situations involving several decision alternatives and an uncertain or risk-filled pattern of events.

Goal Programming   Goal programming is a technique for solving multicriteria decision problems, usually within the framework of linear programming.

Analytic Hierarchy Process   This multicriteria decision-making technique permits the inclusion of subjective factors in arriving at a recommended decision.

Forecasting   Forecasting methods are techniques that can be used to predict future aspects of a business operation.

Markov Process Models   Markov process models are useful in studying the evolution of certain systems over repeated trials. For example, Markov processes have been used to describe the probability that a machine, functioning in one period, will function or break down in another period.

Dynamic Programming   Dynamic programming is an approach that allows us to break up a large problem in such a fashion that once all the smaller problems have been solved, we are left with an optimal solution to the large problem.

Methods Used Most Frequently

Our experience as both practitioners and educators has been that the most frequently used management science techniques are linear programming, integer programming, network models (including transportation and transshipment models), and simulation. Depending upon the industry, the other methods in the preceding list are used more or less frequently.

Helping to bridge the gap between the manager and the management scientist is a major focus of the text. We believe that the barriers to the use of management science can best be removed by increasing the manager's understanding of how management science can be applied. The text will help you develop an understanding of which management science techniques are most useful, how they are used, and, most importantly, how they can assist managers in making better decisions.

The Management Science in Action, Impact of Operations Research on Everyday Living, describes some of the many ways quantitative analysis affects our everyday lives.

MANAGEMENT SCIENCE IN ACTION

IMPACT OF OPERATIONS RESEARCH ON EVERYDAY LIVING*

Mark Eisner, associate director of the School of Operations Research and Industrial Engineering at Cornell University, once said that operations research "is probably the most important field nobody's ever heard of." The impact of operations research on everyday living over the past 20 years is substantial.

Suppose you schedule a vacation to Florida and use Orbitz to book your flights. An algorithm developed by operations researchers will search among millions of options to find the cheapest fare. Another algorithm will schedule the flight crews and aircraft used by the airline. If you rent a car in Florida, the price you pay for the car is determined by a mathematical model that seeks to maximize revenue for the car rental firm. If you do some shopping on your trip and decide to ship your purchases home using UPS, another algorithm tells UPS which truck to put the packages on, the route the truck should follow, and where the packages

should be placed on the truck to minimize loading and unloading time.

If you enjoy watching college basketball, operations research plays a role in which games you see. Michael Trick, a professor at the Tepper School of Business at Carnegie-Mellon, designed a system for scheduling each year's Atlantic Coast Conference men's and women's basketball games. Even though it might initially appear that scheduling 16 games among the nine men's teams would be easy, it requires sorting through hundreds of millions of possible combinations of possible schedules. Each of those possibilities entails some desirable and some undesirable characteristics. For example, you do not want to schedule too many consecutive home games, and you want to ensure that each team plays the same number of weekend games.

*Based on Virginia Postrel, "Operations Everything," *The Boston Globe,* June 27, 2004.

NOTES AND COMMENTS

The Institute for Operations Research and the Management Sciences (INFORMS) and the Decision Sciences Institute (DSI) are two professional societies that publish journals and newsletters dealing with current research and applications of operations research and management science techniques.

SUMMARY

This text is about how management science may be used to help managers make better decisions. The focus of this text is on the decision-making process and on the role of management science in that process. We discussed the problem orientation of this process and in an overview showed how mathematical models can be used in this type of analysis.

The difference between the model and the situation or managerial problem it represents is an important point. Mathematical models are abstractions of real-world situations and, as such, cannot capture all the aspects of the real situation. However, if a model can capture the major relevant aspects of the problem and can then provide a solution recommendation, it can be a valuable aid to decision making.

One of the characteristics of management science that will become increasingly apparent as we proceed through the text is the search for a best solution to the problem. In carrying out the quantitative analysis, we shall be attempting to develop procedures for finding the "best" or optimal solution.

GLOSSARY

Problem solving   The process of identifying a difference between the actual and the desired state of affairs and then taking action to resolve the difference.

Decision making   The process of defining the problem, identifying the alternatives, determining the criteria, evaluating the alternatives, and choosing an alternative.

Single-criterion decision problem   A problem in which the objective is to find the "best" solution with respect to just one criterion.

Multicriteria decision problem   A problem that involves more than one criterion; the objective is to find the "best" solution, taking into account all the criteria.

Decision   The alternative selected.

Model   A representation of a real object or situation.

Iconic model   A physical replica, or representation, of a real object.

Analog model   Although physical in form, an analog model does not have a physical appearance similar to the real object or situation it represents.

Mathematical model   Mathematical symbols and expressions used to represent a real situation.

Constraints   Restrictions or limitations imposed on a problem.

Objective function   A mathematical expression that describes the problem's objective.

Uncontrollable inputs   The environmental factors or inputs that cannot be controlled by the decision maker.

Controllable inputs   The inputs that are controlled or determined by the decision maker.

Decision variable   Another term for controllable input.

Deterministic model   A model in which all uncontrollable inputs are known and cannot vary.

Stochastic (probabilistic) model   A model in which at least one uncontrollable input is uncertain and subject to variation; stochastic models are also referred to as probabilistic models.

Optimal solution   The specific decision-variable value or values that provide the "best" output for the model.

Infeasible solution   A decision alternative or solution that does not satisfy one or more constraints.

Feasible solution   A decision alternative or solution that satisfies all constraints.

Fixed cost   The portion of the total cost that does not depend on the volume; this cost remains the same no matter how much is produced.

Variable cost   The portion of the total cost that is dependent on and varies with the volume.

Marginal cost   The rate of change of the total cost with respect to volume.

Marginal revenue   The rate of change of total revenue with respect to volume.

Breakeven point   The volume at which total revenue equals total cost.

PROBLEMS

1. Define the terms *management science* and *operations research*.

2. List and discuss the steps of the decision-making process.

3. Discuss the different roles played by the qualitative and quantitative approaches to managerial decision making. Why is it important for a manager or decision maker to have a good understanding of both of these approaches to decision making?

4. A firm just completed a new plant that will produce more than 500 different products, using more than 50 different production lines and machines. The production scheduling decisions are critical in that sales will be lost if customer demands are not met on time. If no individual in the firm has experience with this production operation and if new production schedules must be generated each week, why should the firm consider a quantitative approach to the production scheduling problem?

5. What are the advantages of analyzing and experimenting with a model as opposed to a real object or situation?

6. Suppose that a manager has a choice between the following two mathematical models of a given situation: (a) a relatively simple model that is a reasonable approximation of the real situation, and (b) a thorough and complex model that is the most accurate mathematical representation of the real situation possible. Why might the model described in part (a) be preferred by the manager?

7. Suppose you are going on a weekend trip to a city that is *d* miles away. Develop a model that determines your round-trip gasoline costs. What assumptions or approximations are necessary to treat this model as a deterministic model? Are these assumptions or approximations acceptable to you?

8. Recall the production model from Section 1.3:

$$\text{Max} \quad 10x$$
$$\text{s.t.}$$
$$5x \leq 40$$
$$x \geq 0$$

Suppose the firm in this example considers a second product that has a unit profit of $5 and requires 2 hours of production time for each unit produced. Use *y* as the number of units of product 2 produced.

a. Show the mathematical model when both products are considered simultaneously.
b. Identify the controllable and uncontrollable inputs for this model.
c. Draw the flowchart of the input-output process for this model (see Figure 1.5).
d. What are the optimal solution values of x and y?
e. Is the model developed in part (a) a deterministic or a stochastic model? Explain.

9. Suppose we modify the production model in Section 1.3 to obtain the following mathematical model:

$$\text{Max} \quad 10x$$
$$\text{s.t.}$$
$$ax \leq 40$$
$$x \geq 0$$

where a is the number of hours of production time required for each unit produced. With $a = 5$, the optimal solution is $x = 8$. If we have a stochastic model with $a = 3, a = 4, a = 5$, or $a = 6$ as the possible values for the number of hours required per unit, what is the optimal value for x? What problems does this stochastic model cause?

10. A retail store in Des Moines, Iowa, receives shipments of a particular product from Kansas City and Minneapolis. Let

$$x = \text{number of units of the product received from Kansas City}$$
$$y = \text{number of units of the product received from Minneapolis}$$

a. Write an expression for the total number of units of the product received by the retail store in Des Moines.
b. Shipments from Kansas City cost $0.20 per unit, and shipments from Minneapolis cost $0.25 per unit. Develop an objective function representing the total cost of shipments to Des Moines.
c. Assuming the monthly demand at the retail store is 5000 units, develop a constraint that requires 5000 units to be shipped to Des Moines.
d. No more than 4000 units can be shipped from Kansas City, and no more than 3000 units can be shipped from Minneapolis in a month. Develop constraints to model this situation.
e. Of course, negative amounts cannot be shipped. Combine the objective function and constraints developed to state a mathematical model for satisfying the demand at the Des Moines retail store at minimum cost.

11. For most products, higher prices result in a decreased demand, whereas lower prices result in an increased demand. Let

$$d = \text{annual demand for a product in units}$$
$$p = \text{price per unit}$$

Assume that a firm accepts the following price-demand relationship as being realistic:

$$d = 800 - 10p$$

where p must be between $20 and $70.
a. How many units can the firm sell at the $20 per-unit price? At the $70 per-unit price?
b. Show the mathematical model for the total revenue (TR), which is the annual demand multiplied by the unit price.

    c. Based on other considerations, the firm's management will only consider price alternatives of $30, $40, and $50. Use your model from part (b) to determine the price alternative that will maximize the total revenue.

    d. What are the expected annual demand and the total revenue corresponding to your recommended price?

12. The O'Neill Shoe Manufacturing Company will produce a special-style shoe if the order size is large enough to provide a reasonable profit. For each special-style order, the company incurs a fixed cost of $1000 for the production setup. The variable cost is $30 per pair, and each pair sells for $40.

    a. Let x indicate the number of pairs of shoes produced. Develop a mathematical model for the total cost of producing x pairs of shoes.

    b. Let P indicate the total profit. Develop a mathematical model for the total profit realized from an order for x pairs of shoes.

    c. How large must the shoe order be before O'Neill will break even?

13. Micromedia offers computer training seminars on a variety of topics. In the seminars each student works at a personal computer, practicing the particular activity that the instructor is presenting. Micromedia is currently planning a two-day seminar on the use of Microsoft Excel in statistical analysis. The projected fee for the seminar is $300 per student. The cost for the conference room, instructor compensation, lab assistants, and promotion is $4800. Micromedia rents computers for its seminars at a cost of $30 per computer per day.

    a. Develop a model for the total cost to put on the seminar. Let x represent the number of students who enroll in the seminar.

    b. Develop a model for the total profit if x students enroll in the seminar.

    c. Micromedia has forecasted an enrollment of 30 students for the seminar. How much profit will be earned if their forecast is accurate?

    d. Compute the breakeven point.

14. Eastman Publishing Company is considering publishing a paperback textbook on spreadsheet applications for business. The fixed cost of manuscript preparation, textbook design, and production setup is estimated to be $80,000. Variable production and material costs are estimated to be $3 per book. Demand over the life of the book is estimated to be 4000 copies. The publisher plans to sell the text to college and university bookstores for $20 each.

    a. What is the breakeven point?

    b. What profit or loss can be anticipated with a demand of 4000 copies?

    c. With a demand of 4000 copies, what is the minimum price per copy that the publisher must charge to break even?

    d. If the publisher believes that the price per copy could be increased to $25.95 and not affect the anticipated demand of 4000 copies, what action would you recommend? What profit or loss can be anticipated?

15. Preliminary plans are under way for the construction of a new stadium for a major league baseball team. City officials have questioned the number and profitability of the luxury corporate boxes planned for the upper deck of the stadium. Corporations and selected individuals may buy the boxes for $100,000 each. The fixed construction cost for the upper-deck area is estimated to be $1,500,000, with a variable cost of $50,000 for each box constructed.

    a. What is the breakeven point for the number of luxury boxes in the new stadium?

    b. Preliminary drawings for the stadium show that space is available for the construction of up to 50 luxury boxes. Promoters indicate that buyers are available and that all 50 could be sold if constructed. What is your recommendation concerning the construction of luxury boxes? What profit is anticipated?

16. Financial Analysts, Inc., is an investment firm that manages stock portfolios for a number of clients. A new client is requesting that the firm handle an $80,000 portfolio. As an initial investment strategy, the client would like to restrict the portfolio to a mix of the following two stocks:

Stock	Price/ Share	Maximum Estimated Annual Return/Share	Possible Investment
Oil Alaska	$50	$6	$50,000
Southwest Petroleum	$30	$4	$45,000

Let

$$x = \text{number of shares of Oil Alaska}$$
$$y = \text{number of shares of Southwest Petroleum}$$

a. Develop the objective function, assuming that the client desires to maximize the total annual return.
b. Show the mathematical expression for each of the following three constraints:
   (1) Total investment funds available are $80,000.
   (2) Maximum Oil Alaska investment is $50,000.
   (3) Maximum Southwest Petroleum investment is $45,000.

Note: Adding the $x \geq 0$ and $y \geq 0$ constraints provides a linear programming model for the investment problem. A solution procedure for this model will be discussed in Chapter 2.

17. Models of inventory systems frequently consider the relationships among a beginning inventory, a production quantity, a demand or sales, and an ending inventory. For a given production period j, let

s_{j-1} = ending inventory from the previous period (beginning inventory for period j)
x_j = production quantity in period j
d_j = demand in period j
s_j = ending inventory for period j

a. Write the mathematical relationship or model that describes how these four variables are related.
b. What constraint should be added if production capacity for period j is given by C_j?
c. What constraint should be added if inventory requirements for period j mandate an ending inventory of at least I_j?

Case Problem   SCHEDULING A GOLF LEAGUE

Chris Lane, the head professional at Royal Oak Country Club, must develop a schedule of matches for the couples' golf league that begins its season at 4:00 P.M. tomorrow. Eighteen couples signed up for the league, and each couple must play every other couple over the course of the 17-week season. Chris thought it would be fairly easy to develop a schedule, but after working on it for a couple of hours, he has been unable to come up with a schedule. Because Chris must have a schedule ready by tomorrow afternoon, he asked you to help him. A possible complication is that one of the couples told Chris that they may have to cancel for the season. They told Chris they will let him know by 1:00 P.M. tomorrow whether they will be able to play this season.

Managerial Report

Prepare a report for Chris Lane. Your report should include, at a minimum, the following items:

1. A schedule that will enable each of the 18 couples to play every other couple over the 17-week season.
2. A contingency schedule that can be used if the couple that contacted Chris decides to cancel for the season.

Appendix 1.1   USING EXCEL FOR BREAKEVEN ANALYSIS

In Section 1.4 we introduced the Nowlin Plastics production example to illustrate how quantitative models can be used to help a manager determine the projected cost, revenue, and/or profit associated with an established production quantity or a forecasted sales volume. In this appendix we introduce spreadsheet applications by showing how to use Microsoft Excel to perform a quantitative analysis of the Nowlin Plastics example.

Refer to the worksheet shown in Figure 1.7. We begin by entering the problem data into the top portion of the worksheet. The value of 3000 in cell B3 is the fixed cost, the value

FIGURE 1.7   FORMULA WORKSHEET FOR THE NOWLIN PLASTICS
PRODUCTION EXAMPLE

	A	B
1	**Nowlin Plastics**	
2		
3	**Fixed Cost**	3000
4		
5	**Variable Cost Per Unit**	2
6		
7	**Selling Price Per Unit**	5
8		
9		
10	**Models**	
11		
12	**Production Volume**	800
13		
14	**Total Cost**	=B3+B5*B12
15		
16	**Total Revenue**	=B7*B12
17		
18	**Total Profit (Loss)**	=B16-B14

of 2 in cell B5 is the variable labor and material costs per unit, and the value of 5 in cell B7 is the selling price per unit. As discussed in Appendix A, whenever we perform a quantitative analysis using Excel, we will enter the problem data in the top portion of the worksheet and reserve the bottom portion for model development. The label "Models" in cell A10 helps to provide a visual reminder of this convention.

Cell B12 in the models portion of the worksheet contains the proposed production volume in units. Because the values for total cost, total revenue, and total profit depend upon the value of this decision variable, we have placed a border around cell B12 and screened the cell for emphasis. Based upon the value in cell B12, the cell formulas in cells B14, B16, and B18 are used to compute values for total cost, total revenue, and total profit (loss), respectively. First, recall that the value of total cost is the sum of the fixed cost (cell B3) and the total variable cost. The total variable cost—the product of the variable cost per unit (cell B5) and the production volume (cell B12)—is given by B5*B12. Thus, to compute the value of total cost we entered the formula =B3+B5*B12 in cell B14. Next, total revenue is the product of the selling price per unit (cell B7) and the number of units produced (cell B12), which is entered in cell B16 as the formula =B7*B12. Finally, the total profit (or loss) is the difference between the total revenue (cell B16) and the total cost (cell B14). Thus, in cell B18 we have entered the formula =B16-B14. The worksheet shown in Figure 1.8 shows the formulas used to make these computations; we refer to it as a formula worksheet.

To examine the effect of selecting a particular value for the production volume, we entered a value of 800 in cell B12. The worksheet shown in Figure 1.8 shows the values obtained by the formulas; a production volume of 800 units results in a total cost of $4600, a total revenue of $4000, and a loss of $600. To examine the effect of other production volumes, we only need to enter a different value into cell B12. To examine the

FIGURE 1.8   SOLUTION USING A PRODUCTION VOLUME OF 800 UNITS FOR THE
NOWLIN PLASTICS PRODUCTION EXAMPLE

WEB file

Nowlin

	A	B
1	**Nowlin Plastics**	
2		
3	**Fixed Cost**	$3,000
4		
5	**Variable Cost Per Unit**	$2
6		
7	**Selling Price Per Unit**	$5
8		
9		
10	**Models**	
11		
12	**Production Volume**	800
13		
14	**Total Cost**	$4,600
15		
16	**Total Revenue**	$4,000
17		
18	**Total Profit (Loss)**	−$600

effect of different costs and selling prices, we simply enter the appropriate values in the data portion of the worksheet; the results will be displayed in the model section of the worksheet.

In Section 1.4 we illustrated breakeven analysis. Let us now see how Excel's Goal Seek tool can be used to compute the breakeven point for the Nowlin Plastics production example.

Determining the Breakeven Point Using Excel's Goal Seek Tool

Tutorial 1:
Breakeven Analysis

The breakeven point is the production volume that results in total revenue equal to total cost and hence a profit of $0. One way to determine the breakeven point is to use a trial-and-error approach. For example, in Figure 1.8 we saw that a trial production volume of 800 units resulted in a loss of $600. Because this trial solution resulted in a loss, a production volume of 800 units cannot be the breakeven point. We could continue to experiment with other production volumes by simply entering different values into cell B12 and observing the resulting profit or loss in cell B18. A better approach is to use Excel's Goal Seek tool to determine the breakeven point.

Excel's Goal Seek tool allows the user to determine the value for an input cell that will cause the value of a related output cell to equal some specified value (called the *goal*). In the case of breakeven analysis, the "goal" is to set Total Profit to zero by "seeking" an appropriate value for Production Volume. Goal Seek will allow us to find the value of production volume that will set Nowlin Plastics' total profit to zero. The following steps describe how to use Goal Seek to find the breakeven point for Nowlin Plastics:

Step 1. Select the **Data** tab at the top of the Ribbon
Step 2. Select **What-If Analysis** in the **Data Tools** group
Step 3. Select **Goal Seek** in What-if Analysis
Step 4. When the **Goal Seek** dialog box appears:
      Enter B18 in the **Set cell** box
      Enter 0 in the **To value** box
      Enter B12 in the **By changing cell** box
      Click **OK**

FIGURE 1.9   GOAL SEEK DIALOG BOX FOR THE NOWLIN PLASTICS
                      PRODUCTION EXAMPLE

FIGURE 1.10   BREAKEVEN POINT FOUND USING EXCEL'S GOAL SEEK TOOL
FOR THE NOWLIN PLASTICS PRODUCTION EXAMPLE

	A	B
1	**Nowlin Plastics**	
2		
3	**Fixed Cost**	$3,000
4		
5	**Variable Cost Per Unit**	$2
6		
7	**Selling Price Per Unit**	$5
8		
9		
10	**Models**	
11		
12	**Production Volume**	1000
13		
14	**Total Cost**	$5,000
15		
16	**Total Revenue**	$5,000
17		
18	**Total Profit (Loss)**	$0

The completed Goal Seek dialog box is shown in Figure 1.9, and the worksheet obtained after selecting **OK** is shown in Figure 1.10. The Total Profit in cell B18 is zero, and the Production Volume in cell B12 has been set to the breakeven point of 1000.

CHAPTER 2

An Introduction to Linear Programming

CONTENTS

2.1 A SIMPLE MAXIMIZATION
PROBLEM
Problem Formulation
Mathematical Statement of the Par,
Inc., Problem

2.2 GRAPHICAL SOLUTION
PROCEDURE
A Note on Graphing Lines
Summary of the Graphical Solution
Procedure for Maximization
Problems
Slack Variables

2.3 EXTREME POINTS AND THE
OPTIMAL SOLUTION

2.4 COMPUTER SOLUTION OF THE
PAR, INC., PROBLEM
Interpretation of Computer Output

2.5 A SIMPLE MINIMIZATION
PROBLEM
Summary of the Graphical Solution
Procedure for Minimization
Problems
Surplus Variables
Computer Solution of the M&D
Chemicals Problem

2.6 SPECIAL CASES
Alternative Optimal Solutions
Infeasibility
Unbounded

2.7 GENERAL LINEAR
PROGRAMMING NOTATION

Linear programming is a problem-solving approach developed to help managers make decisions. Numerous applications of linear programming can be found in today's competitive business environment. For instance, Eastman Kodak uses linear programming to determine where to manufacture products throughout their worldwide facilities, and GE Capital uses linear programming to help determine optimal lease structuring. Marathon Oil Company uses linear programming for gasoline blending and to evaluate the economics of a new terminal or pipeline. The Management Science in Action, Timber Harvesting Model at MeadWestvaco Corporation, provides another example of the use of linear programming. Later in the chapter another Management Science in Action illustrates how the Hanshin Expressway Public Corporation uses linear programming for traffic control on an urban toll expressway in Osaka, Japan.

To illustrate some of the properties that all linear programming problems have in common, consider the following typical applications:

1. A manufacturer wants to develop a production schedule and an inventory policy that will satisfy sales demand in future periods. Ideally, the schedule and policy will enable the company to satisfy demand and at the same time *minimize* the total production and inventory costs.

2. A financial analyst must select an investment portfolio from a variety of stock and bond investment alternatives. The analyst would like to establish the portfolio that *maximizes* the return on investment.

3. A marketing manager wants to determine how best to allocate a fixed advertising budget among alternative advertising media such as radio, television, newspaper, and magazine. The manager would like to determine the media mix that *maximizes* advertising effectiveness.

4. A company has warehouses in a number of locations throughout the United States. For a set of customer demands, the company would like to determine how much each warehouse should ship to each customer so that total transportation costs are *minimized.*

MANAGEMENT SCIENCE IN ACTION

TIMBER HARVESTING MODEL AT MEADWESTVACO CORPORATION*

MeadWestvaco Corporation is a major producer of premium papers for periodicals, books, commercial printing, and business forms. The company also produces pulp and lumber, designs and manufactures packaging systems for beverage and other consumables markets, and is a world leader in the production of coated board and shipping containers. Quantitative analyses at MeadWestvaco are developed and implemented by the company's Decision Analysis Department. The department assists decision makers by providing them with analytical tools of quantitative methods as well as personal analysis and recommendations.

MeadWestvaco uses quantitative models to assist with the long-range management of the company's timberland. Through the use of large-scale linear programs, timber harvesting plans are developed to cover a substantial time horizon. These models consider wood market conditions, mill pulpwood requirements, harvesting capacities, and general forest management principles. Within these constraints, the model arrives at an optimal harvesting and purchasing schedule based on discounted cash flow. Alternative schedules reflect changes in the various assumptions concerning forest growth, wood availability, and general economic conditions.

Quantitative methods are also used in the development of the inputs for the linear programming models. Timber prices and supplies as well as mill requirements must be forecast over the time horizon, and advanced sampling techniques are used to evaluate land holdings and to project forest growth. The harvest schedule is then developed using quantitative methods.

*Based on information provided by Dr. Edward P. Winkofsky.

Linear programming was initially referred to as "programming in a linear structure." In 1948 Tjalling Koopmans suggested to George Dantzig that the name was much too long; Koopmans suggested shortening it to linear programming. George Dantzig agreed and the field we now know as linear programming was named.

These examples are only a few of the situations in which linear programming has been used successfully, but they illustrate the diversity of linear programming applications. A close scrutiny reveals one basic property they all have in common. In each example, we were concerned with *maximizing* or *minimizing* some quantity. In example 1, the manufacturer wanted to minimize costs; in example 2, the financial analyst wanted to maximize return on investment; in example 3, the marketing manager wanted to maximize advertising effectiveness; and in example 4, the company wanted to minimize total transportation costs. *In all linear programming problems, the maximization or minimization of some quantity is the objective.*

All linear programming problems also have a second property: restrictions, or **constraints,** that limit the degree to which the objective can be pursued. In example 1, the manufacturer is restricted by constraints requiring product demand to be satisfied and by the constraints limiting production capacity. The financial analyst's portfolio problem is constrained by the total amount of investment funds available and the maximum amounts that can be invested in each stock or bond. The marketing manager's media selection decision is constrained by a fixed advertising budget and the availability of the various media. In the transportation problem, the minimum-cost shipping schedule is constrained by the supply of product available at each warehouse. *Thus, constraints are another general feature of every linear programming problem.*

2.1 A SIMPLE MAXIMIZATION PROBLEM

Par, Inc., is a small manufacturer of golf equipment and supplies whose management has decided to move into the market for medium- and high-priced golf bags. Par's distributor is enthusiastic about the new product line and has agreed to buy all the golf bags Par produces over the next three months.

After a thorough investigation of the steps involved in manufacturing a golf bag, management determined that each golf bag produced will require the following operations:

1. Cutting and dyeing the material
2. Sewing
3. Finishing (inserting umbrella holder, club separators, etc.)
4. Inspection and packaging

The director of manufacturing analyzed each of the operations and concluded that if the company produces a medium-priced standard model, each bag will require $7/10$ hour in the cutting and dyeing department, $\frac{1}{2}$ hour in the sewing department, 1 hour in the finishing department, and $\frac{1}{10}$ hour in the inspection and packaging department. The more expensive deluxe model will require 1 hour for cutting and dyeing, $\frac{5}{6}$ hour for sewing, $\frac{2}{3}$ hour for finishing, and $\frac{1}{4}$ hour for inspection and packaging. This production information is summarized in Table 2.1.

Par's production is constrained by a limited number of hours available in each department. After studying departmental workload projections, the director of manufacturing estimates that 630 hours for cutting and dyeing, 600 hours for sewing, 708 hours for finishing, and 135 hours for inspection and packaging will be available for the production of golf bags during the next three months.

The accounting department analyzed the production data, assigned all relevant variable costs, and arrived at prices for both bags that will result in a profit contribution[1] of $10 for

---

[1]From an accounting perspective, profit contribution is more correctly described as the contribution margin per bag; for example, overhead and other shared costs have not been allocated.

TABLE 2.1 PRODUCTION REQUIREMENTS PER GOLF BAG

	Production Time (hours)	
Department	**Standard Bag**	**Deluxe Bag**
Cutting and Dyeing	$7/10$	1
Sewing	$1/2$	$5/6$
Finishing	1	$2/3$
Inspection and Packaging	$1/10$	$1/4$

It is important to understand that we are maximizing profit contribution, not profit. Overhead and other shared costs must be deducted before arriving at a profit figure.

every standard bag and $9 for every deluxe bag produced. Let us now develop a mathematical model of the Par, Inc., problem that can be used to determine the number of standard bags and the number of deluxe bags to produce in order to maximize total profit contribution.

Problem Formulation

Problem formulation, or **modeling,** is the process of translating the verbal statement of a problem into a mathematical statement. Formulating models is an art that can only be mastered with practice and experience. Even though every problem has some unique features, most problems also have common features. As a result, *some* general guidelines for model formulation can be helpful, especially for beginners. We will illustrate these general guidelines by developing a mathematical model for the Par, Inc., problem.

Understand the Problem Thoroughly We selected the Par, Inc., problem to introduce linear programming because it is easy to understand. However, more complex problems will require much more thinking in order to identify the items that need to be included in the model. In such cases, read the problem description quickly to get a feel for what is involved. Taking notes will help you focus on the key issues and facts.

Describe the Objective The objective is to maximize the total contribution to profit.

Describe Each Constraint Four constraints relate to the number of hours of manufacturing time available; they restrict the number of standard bags and the number of deluxe bags that can be produced.

Constraint 1: Number of hours of cutting and dyeing time used must be less than or equal to the number of hours of cutting and dyeing time available.

Constraint 2: Number of hours of sewing time used must be less than or equal to the number of hours of sewing time available.

Constraint 3: Number of hours of finishing time used must be less than or equal to the number of hours of finishing time available.

Constraint 4: Number of hours of inspection and packaging time used must be less than or equal to the number of hours of inspection and packaging time available.

Define the Decision Variables The controllable inputs for Par, Inc., are (1) the number of standard bags produced, and (2) the number of deluxe bags produced. Let

$$S = \text{number of standard bags}$$
$$D = \text{number of deluxe bags}$$

In linear programming terminology, S and D are referred to as the **decision variables.**

Write the Objective in Terms of the Decision Variables   Par's profit contribution comes from two sources: (1) the profit contribution made by producing S standard bags, and (2) the profit contribution made by producing D deluxe bags. If Par makes $10 for every standard bag, the company will make $10S$ if S standard bags are produced. Also, if Par makes $9 for every deluxe bag, the company will make $9D$ if D deluxe bags are produced. Thus, we have

$$\text{Total Profit Contribution} = 10S + 9D$$

Because the objective—maximize total profit contribution—is a function of the decision variables S and D, we refer to $10S + 9D$ as the *objective function*. Using "Max" as an abbreviation for maximize, we write Par's objective as follows:

$$\text{Max } 10S + 9D$$

Write the Constraints in Terms of the Decision Variables

Constraint 1:

$$\begin{pmatrix} \text{Hours of cutting and} \\ \text{dyeing time used} \end{pmatrix} \leq \begin{pmatrix} \text{Hours of cutting and} \\ \text{dyeing time available} \end{pmatrix}$$

Every standard bag Par produces will use $\frac{7}{10}$ hour cutting and dyeing time; therefore, the total number of hours of cutting and dyeing time used in the manufacture of S standard bags is $\frac{7}{10}S$. In addition, because every deluxe bag produced uses 1 hour of cutting and dyeing time, the production of D deluxe bags will use $1D$ hours of cutting and dyeing time. Thus, the total cutting and dyeing time required for the production of S standard bags and D deluxe bags is given by

$$\text{Total hours of cutting and dyeing time used} = \frac{7}{10}S + 1D$$

The units of measurement on the left-hand side of the constraint must match the units of measurement on the right-hand side.

The director of manufacturing stated that Par has at most 630 hours of cutting and dyeing time available. Therefore, the production combination we select must satisfy the requirement

$$\frac{7}{10}S + 1D \leq 630 \tag{2.1}$$

Constraint 2:

$$\begin{pmatrix} \text{Hours of sewing} \\ \text{time used} \end{pmatrix} \leq \begin{pmatrix} \text{Hours of sewing} \\ \text{time available} \end{pmatrix}$$

From Table 2.1, we see that every standard bag manufactured will require $\frac{1}{2}$ hour for sewing, and every deluxe bag will require $\frac{5}{6}$ hour for sewing. Because 600 hours of sewing time are available, it follows that

$$\frac{1}{2}S + \frac{5}{6}D \leq 600 \tag{2.2}$$

Constraint 3:

$$\binom{\text{Hours of finishing}}{\text{time used}} \leq \binom{\text{Hours of finishing}}{\text{time available}}$$

Every standard bag manufactured will require 1 hour for finishing, and every deluxe bag will require $\frac{2}{3}$ hour for finishing. With 708 hours of finishing time available, it follows that

$$1S + \tfrac{2}{3}D \leq 708 \tag{2.3}$$

Constraint 4:

$$\binom{\text{Hours of inspection and}}{\text{packaging time used}} \leq \binom{\text{Hours of inspection and}}{\text{packaging time available}}$$

Every standard bag manufactured will require $\frac{1}{10}$ hour for inspection and packaging, and every deluxe bag will require $\frac{1}{4}$ hour for inspection and packaging. Because 135 hours of inspection and packaging time are available, it follows that

$$\tfrac{1}{10}S + \tfrac{1}{4}D \leq 135 \tag{2.4}$$

We have now specified the mathematical relationships for the constraints associated with the four departments. Have we forgotten any other constraints? Can Par produce a negative number of standard or deluxe bags? Clearly, the answer is no. Thus, to prevent the decision variables S and D from having negative values, two constraints,

$$S \geq 0 \quad \text{and} \quad D \geq 0 \tag{2.5}$$

must be added. These constraints ensure that the solution to the problem will contain nonnegative values for the decision variables and are thus referred to as the **nonnegativity constraints.** Nonnegativity constraints are a general feature of all linear programming problems and may be written in the abbreviated form:

$$S, D \geq 0$$

Try Problem 24(a) to test your ability to formulate a mathematical model for a maximization linear programming problem with less-than-or-equal-to constraints.

Mathematical Statement of the Par, Inc., Problem

The mathematical statement or mathematical formulation of the Par, Inc., problem is now complete. We succeeded in translating the objective and constraints of the problem into a set of mathematical relationships referred to as a **mathematical model.** The complete mathematical model for the Par problem is as follows:

$$
\begin{aligned}
\text{Max} \quad & 10S + 9D \\
\text{subject to (s.t.)} \quad & \\
& \tfrac{7}{10}S + 1D \leq 630 \quad \text{Cutting and dyeing} \\
& \tfrac{1}{2}S + \tfrac{5}{6}D \leq 600 \quad \text{Sewing} \\
& 1S + \tfrac{2}{3}D \leq 708 \quad \text{Finishing} \\
& \tfrac{1}{10}S + \tfrac{1}{4}D \leq 135 \quad \text{Inspection and packaging} \\
& S, D \geq 0
\end{aligned}
\tag{2.6}
$$

Our job now is to find the product mix (i.e., the combination of S and D) that satisfies all the constraints and, at the same time, yields a value for the objective function that is greater than or equal to the value given by any other feasible solution. Once these values are calculated, we will have found the optimal solution to the problem.

This mathematical model of the Par problem is **a linear programming model,** or **linear program.** The problem has the objective and constraints that, as we said earlier, are common properties of all *linear* programs. But what is the special feature of this mathematical model that makes it a linear program? The special feature that makes it a linear program is that the objective function and all constraint functions are linear functions of the decision variables.

Mathematical functions in which each variable appears in a separate term and is raised to the first power are called **linear functions.** The objective function $(10S + 9D)$ is linear because each decision variable appears in a separate term and has an exponent of 1. The amount of production time required in the cutting and dyeing department $(\tfrac{7}{10}S + 1D)$ is also a linear function of the decision variables for the same reason. Similarly, the functions on the left-hand side of all the constraint inequalities (the constraint functions) are linear functions. Thus, the mathematical formulation of this problem is referred to as a linear program.

Try Problem 1 to test your ability to recognize the types of mathematical relationships that can be found in a linear program.

Linear *programming* has nothing to do with computer programming. The use of the word *programming* here means "choosing a course of action." Linear programming involves choosing a course of action when the mathematical model of the problem contains only linear functions.

NOTES AND COMMENTS

1. The three assumptions necessary for a linear programming model to be appropriate are proportionality, additivity, and divisibility. *Proportionality* means that the contribution to the objective function and the amount of resources used in each constraint are proportional to the value of each decision variable. *Additivity* means that the value of the objective function and the total resources used can be found by summing the objective function contribution and the resources used for all decision variables. *Divisibility* means that the decision variables are continuous. The divisibility assumption plus the nonnegativity constraints mean that decision variables can take on any value greater than or equal to zero.

2. Management scientists formulate and solve a variety of mathematical models that contain an objective function and a set of constraints. Models of this type are referred to as *mathematical programming models*. Linear programming models are a special type of mathematical programming model in that the objective function and all constraint functions are linear.

2.2 GRAPHICAL SOLUTION PROCEDURE

A linear programming problem involving only two decision variables can be solved using a graphical solution procedure. Let us begin the graphical solution procedure by developing a graph that displays the possible solutions (S and D values) for the Par problem. The graph (Figure 2.1) will have values of S on the horizontal axis and values of D on the vertical axis. Any point on the graph can be identified by the S and D values, which indicate the position of the point along the horizontal and vertical axes, respectively. Because every point (S, D) corresponds to a possible solution, every point on the graph is called a *solution point*. The solution point where $S = 0$ and $D = 0$ is referred to as the origin. Because S and D must be nonnegative, the graph in Figure 2.1 only displays solutions where $S \geq 0$ and $D \geq 0$.

Earlier, we saw that the inequality representing the cutting and dyeing constraint is

$$\tfrac{7}{10}S + 1D \leq 630$$

To show all solution points that satisfy this relationship, we start by graphing the solution points satisfying the constraint as an equality. That is, the points where $\tfrac{7}{10}S + 1D = 630$. Because the graph of this equation is a line, it can be obtained by identifying two points that satisfy the equation and then drawing a line through the points. Setting $S = 0$ and solving for D, we see that the point $(S = 0, D = 630)$ satisfies the equation. To find a second point satisfying this equation, we set $D = 0$ and solve for S. By doing so, we obtain

FIGURE 2.1 SOLUTION POINTS FOR THE TWO-VARIABLE PAR, INC., PROBLEM

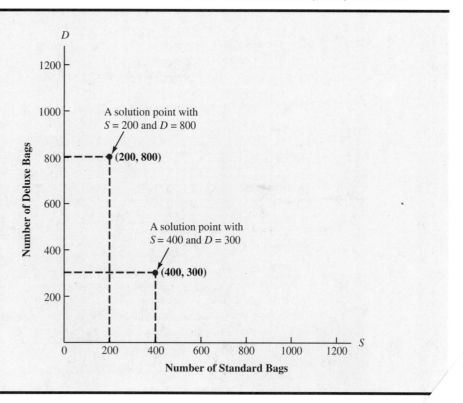

$\frac{7}{10}S + 1(0) = 630$, or $S = 900$. Thus, a second point satisfying the equation is ($S = 900$, $D = 0$). Given these two points, we can now graph the line corresponding to the equation

$$\tfrac{7}{10}S + 1D = 630$$

This line, which will be called the cutting and dyeing *constraint line,* is shown in Figure 2.2. We label this line "C & D" to indicate that it represents the cutting and dyeing constraint line.

Recall that the inequality representing the cutting and dyeing constraint is

$$\tfrac{7}{10}S + 1D \leq 630$$

Can you identify all of the solution points that satisfy this constraint? Because all points on the line satisfy $\frac{7}{10}S + 1D = 630$, we know any point on this line must satisfy the constraint. But where are the solution points satisfying $\frac{7}{10}S + 1D < 630$? Consider two solution points: ($S = 200$, $D = 200$) and ($S = 600$, $D = 500$). You can see from Figure 2.2 that the first solution point is below the constraint line and the second is above the constraint line. Which of these solutions will satisfy the cutting and dyeing constraint? For the point ($S = 200$, $D = 200$), we see that

$$\tfrac{7}{10}S + 1D = \tfrac{7}{10}(200) + 1(200) = 340$$

FIGURE 2.2   THE CUTTING AND DYEING CONSTRAINT LINE

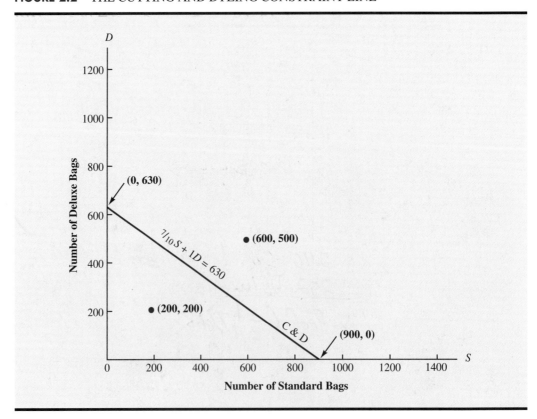

Because the 340 hours is less than the 630 hours available, the ($S = 200, D = 200$) production combination, or solution point, satisfies the constraint. For the point ($S = 600, D = 500$), we have

$$\tfrac{7}{10}S + 1D = \tfrac{7}{10}(600) + 1(500) = 920$$

The 920 hours is greater than the 630 hours available, so the ($S = 600, D = 500$) solution point does not satisfy the constraint and is thus not feasible.

Can you graph a constraint line and find the solution points that are feasible? Try Problem 2.

If a solution point is not feasible for a particular constraint, then all other solution points on the same side of that constraint line are not feasible. If a solution point is feasible for a particular constraint, then all other solution points on the same side of the constraint line are feasible for that constraint. Thus, one has to evaluate the constraint function for only one solution point to determine which side of a constraint line is feasible. In Figure 2.3 we indicate all points satisfying the cutting and dyeing constraint by the shaded region.

We continue by identifying the solution points satisfying each of the other three constraints. The solutions that are feasible for each of these constraints are shown in Figure 2.4.

Four separate graphs now show the feasible solution points for each of the four constraints. In a linear programming problem, we need to identify the solution points that satisfy *all* the constraints *simultaneously*. To find these solution points, we can draw all four constraints on one graph and observe the region containing the points that do in fact satisfy all the constraints simultaneously.

FIGURE 2.3   FEASIBLE SOLUTIONS FOR THE CUTTING AND DYEING CONSTRAINT, REPRESENTED BY THE SHADED REGION

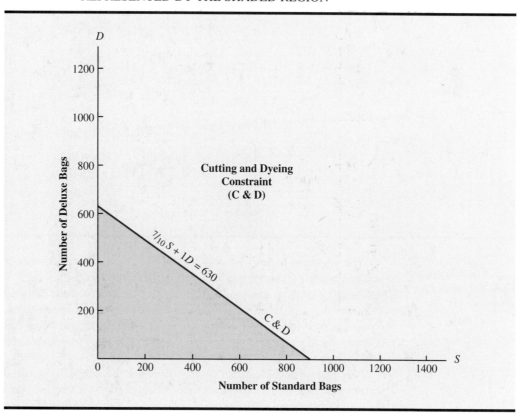

FIGURE 2.4   FEASIBLE SOLUTIONS FOR THE SEWING, FINISHING, AND INSPECTION AND PACKAGING
CONSTRAINTS, REPRESENTED BY THE SHADED REGIONS

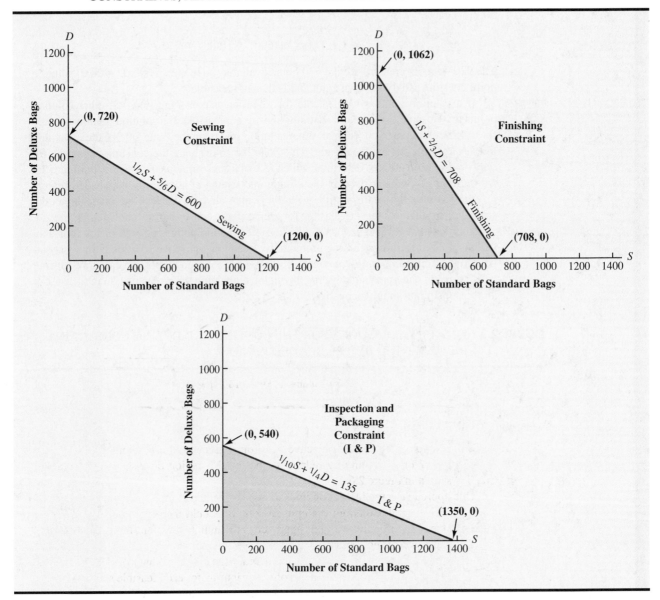

*Try Problem 7 to test your
ability to find the feasible
region given several
constraints.*

The graphs in Figures 2.3 and 2.4 can be superimposed to obtain one graph with all
four constraints. This combined-constraint graph is shown in Figure 2.5. The shaded region
in this figure includes every solution point that satisfies all the constraints simultaneously.
Solutions that satisfy all the constraints are termed **feasible solutions,** and the shaded
region is called the feasible solution region, or simply the **feasible region.** Any solution
point on the boundary of the feasible region or within the feasible region is a *feasible
solution point.*

Now that we have identified the feasible region, we are ready to proceed with the graphical solution procedure and find the optimal solution to the Par, Inc., problem. Recall that
the optimal solution for a linear programming problem is the feasible solution that provides

FIGURE 2.5   COMBINED-CONSTRAINT GRAPH SHOWING THE FEASIBLE REGION
FOR THE PAR, INC., PROBLEM

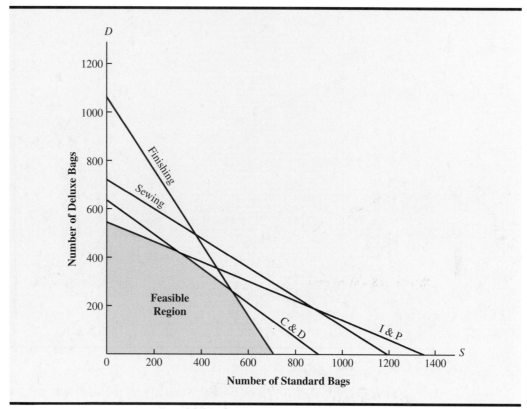

the best possible value of the objective function. Let us start the optimizing step of the graphical solution procedure by redrawing the feasible region on a separate graph. The graph is shown in Figure 2.6.

One approach to finding the optimal solution would be to evaluate the objective function for each feasible solution; the optimal solution would then be the one yielding the largest value. The difficulty with this approach is the infinite number of feasible solutions; thus, because one cannot possibly evaluate an infinite number of feasible solutions, this trial-and-error procedure cannot be used to identify the optimal solution.

Rather than trying to compute the profit contribution for each feasible solution, we select an arbitrary value for profit contribution and identify all the feasible solutions (S, D) that yield the selected value. For example, which feasible solutions provide a profit contribution of $1800? These solutions are given by the values of S and D in the feasible region that will make the objective function

$$10S + 9D = 1800$$

This expression is simply the equation of a line. Thus, all feasible solution points (S, D) yielding a profit contribution of $1800 must be on the line. We learned earlier in this section how to graph a constraint line. The procedure for graphing the profit or objective function line is the same. Letting $S = 0$, we see that D must be 200; thus, the solution

FIGURE 2.6   FEASIBLE REGION FOR THE PAR, INC., PROBLEM

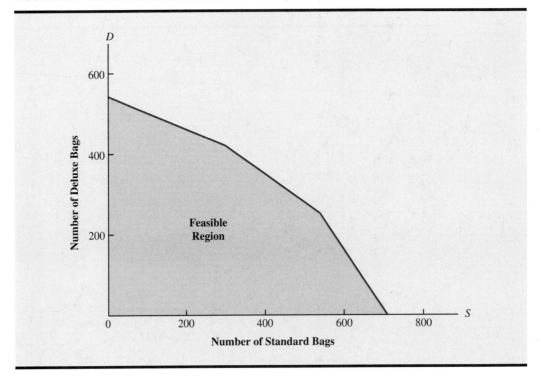

point ($S = 0, D = 200$) is on the line. Similarly, by letting $D = 0$, we see that the solution point ($S = 180, D = 0$) is also on the line. Drawing the line through these two points identifies all the solutions that have a profit contribution of \$1800. A graph of this profit line is presented in Figure 2.7.

Because the objective is to find the feasible solution yielding the largest profit contribution, let us proceed by selecting higher profit contributions and finding the solutions yielding the selected values. For instance, let us find all solutions yielding profit contributions of \$3600 and \$5400. To do so, we must find the S and D values that are on the following lines:

$$10S + 9D = 3600$$

and

$$10S + 9D = 5400$$

Using the previous procedure for graphing profit and constraint lines, we draw the \$3600 and \$5400 profit lines as shown on the graph in Figure 2.8. Although not all solution points on the \$5400 profit line are in the feasible region, at least some points on the line are, and it is therefore possible to obtain a feasible solution that provides a \$5400 profit contribution.

Can we find a feasible solution yielding an even higher profit contribution? Look at Figure 2.8, and see what general observations you can make about the profit lines already drawn. Note the following: (1) the profit lines are *parallel* to each other, and (2) higher

FIGURE 2.7 $1800 PROFIT LINE FOR THE PAR, INC., PROBLEM

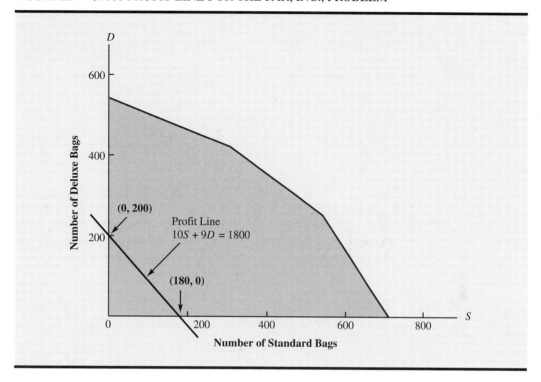

FIGURE 2.8   SELECTED PROFIT LINES FOR THE PAR, INC., PROBLEM

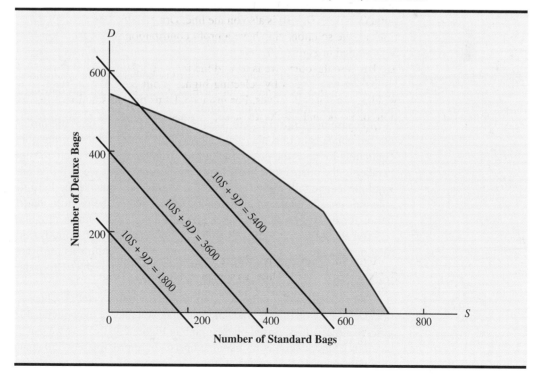

profit lines are obtained as we move farther from the origin. These observations can also be expressed algebraically. Let P represent total profit contribution. The objective function is

$$P = 10S + 9D$$

Solving for D in terms of S and P, we obtain

$$9D = -10S + P$$
$$D = -\tfrac{10}{9}S + \tfrac{1}{9}P \tag{2.7}$$

Equation (2.7) is the *slope-intercept form* of the linear equation relating S and D. The coefficient of S, $-\tfrac{10}{9}$, is the slope of the line, and the term $\tfrac{1}{9}P$ is the D intercept (i.e., the value of D where the graph of equation (2.7) crosses the D axis). Substituting the profit contributions of $P = 1800$, $P = 3600$, and $P = 5400$ into equation (2.7) yields the following slope-intercept equations for the profit lines shown in Figure 2.8:

For $P = 1800$,

$$D = -\tfrac{10}{9}S + 200$$

For $P = 3600$,

$$D = -\tfrac{10}{9}S + 400$$

For $P = 5400$,

$$D = -\tfrac{10}{9}S + 600$$

Can you graph the profit line for a linear program? Try Problem 6.

The slope ($-\tfrac{10}{9}$) is the same for each profit line because the profit lines are parallel. Further, we see that the D intercept increases with larger profit contributions. Thus, higher profit lines are farther from the origin.

Because the profit lines are parallel and higher profit lines are farther from the origin, we can obtain solutions that yield increasingly larger values for the objective function by continuing to move the profit line farther from the origin in such a fashion that it remains parallel to the other profit lines. However, at some point we will find that any further outward movement will place the profit line completely outside the feasible region. Because solutions outside the feasible region are unacceptable, the point in the feasible region that lies on the highest profit line is the optimal solution to the linear program.

You should now be able to identify the optimal solution point for this problem. Use a ruler or the edge of a piece of paper, and move the profit line as far from the origin as you can. What is the last point in the feasible region that you reach? This point, which is the optimal solution, is shown graphically in Figure 2.9.

The optimal values of the decision variables are the S and D values at the optimal solution. Depending on the accuracy of the graph, you may or may not be able to determine the *exact* S and D values. Based on the graph in Figure 2.9, the best we can do is conclude that the optimal production combination consists of approximately 550 standard bags (S) and approximately 250 deluxe bags (D).

FIGURE 2.9 OPTIMAL SOLUTION FOR THE PAR, INC., PROBLEM

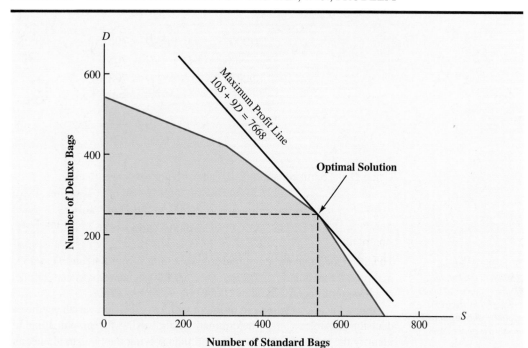

A closer inspection of Figures 2.5 and 2.9 shows that the optimal solution point is at the intersection of the cutting and dyeing and the finishing constraint lines. That is, the optimal solution point is on both the cutting and dyeing constraint line

$$\tfrac{7}{10}S + 1D = 630 \qquad (2.8)$$

and the finishing constraint line

$$1S + \tfrac{2}{3}D = 708 \qquad (2.9)$$

Thus, the optimal values of the decision variables S and D must satisfy both equations (2.8) and (2.9) simultaneously. Using equation (2.8) and solving for S gives

$$\tfrac{7}{10}S = 630 - 1D$$

or

$$S = 900 - \tfrac{10}{7}D \qquad (2.10)$$

Substituting this expression for S into equation (2.9) and solving for D provides the following:

$$1(900 - {}^{10}\!/_{7}D) + {}^{2}\!/_{3}D = 708$$
$$900 - {}^{10}\!/_{7}D + {}^{2}\!/_{3}D = 708$$
$$900 - {}^{30}\!/_{21}D + {}^{14}\!/_{21}D = 708$$
$$-{}^{16}\!/_{21}D = -192$$
$$D = \frac{192}{{}^{16}\!/_{21}} = 252$$

Using $D = 252$ in equation (2.10) and solving for S, we obtain

$$S = 900 - {}^{10}\!/_{7}(252)$$
$$= 900 - 360 = 540$$

Although the optimal solution to the Par, Inc., problem consists of integer values for the decision variables, this result will not always be the case.

The exact location of the optimal solution point is $S = 540$ and $D = 252$. Hence, the optimal production quantities for Par, Inc., are 540 standard bags and 252 deluxe bags, with a resulting profit contribution of $10(540) + 9(252) = \$7668$.

For a linear programming problem with two decision variables, the exact values of the decision variables can be determined by first using the graphical solution procedure to identify the optimal solution point and then solving the two simultaneous constraint equations associated with it.

A Note on Graphing Lines

Try Problem 10 to test your ability to use the graphical solution procedure to identify the optimal solution and find the exact values of the decision variables at the optimal solution.

An important aspect of the graphical method is the ability to graph lines showing the constraints and the objective function of the linear program. The procedure we used for graphing the equation of a line is to find any two points satisfying the equation and then draw the line through the two points. For the Par, Inc., constraints, the two points were easily found by first setting $S = 0$ and solving the constraint equation for D. Then we set $D = 0$ and solved for S. For the cutting and dyeing constraint line

$$\tfrac{7}{10}S + 1D = 630$$

this procedure identified the two points $(S = 0, D = 630)$ and $(S = 900, D = 0)$. The cutting and dyeing constraint line was then graphed by drawing a line through these two points.

All constraints and objective function lines in two-variable linear programs can be graphed if two points on the line can be identified. However, finding the two points on the line is not always as easy as shown in the Par, Inc., problem. For example, suppose a company manufactures two models of a small handheld computer: the Assistant (A) and the Professional (P). Management needs 50 units of the Professional model for its own sales-force, and expects sales of the Professional to be at most one-half of the sales of the Assistant. A constraint enforcing this requirement is

$$P - 50 \leq \tfrac{1}{2}A$$

or

$$2P - 100 \leq A$$

or

$$2P - A \leq 100$$

Using the equality form and setting $P = 0$, we find the point ($P = 0$, $A = -100$) is on the constraint line. Setting $A = 0$, we find a second point ($P = 50$, $A = 0$) on the constraint line. If we have drawn only the nonnegative ($P \geq 0$, $A \geq 0$) portion of the graph, the first point ($P = 0$, $A = -100$) cannot be plotted because $A = -100$ is not on the graph. Whenever we have two points on the line but one or both of the points cannot be plotted in the nonnegative portion of the graph, the simplest approach is to enlarge the graph. In this example, the point ($P = 0$, $A = -100$) can be plotted by extending the graph to include the negative A axis. Once both points satisfying the constraint equation have been located, the line can be drawn. The constraint line and the feasible solutions for the constraint $2P - A \leq 100$ are shown in Figure 2.10.

As another example, consider a problem involving two decision variables, R and T. Suppose that the number of units of R produced had to be at least equal to the number of units of T produced. A constraint enforcing this requirement is

$$R \geq T$$

or

$$R - T \geq 0$$

FIGURE 2.10 FEASIBLE SOLUTIONS FOR THE CONSTRAINT $2P - A \leq 100$

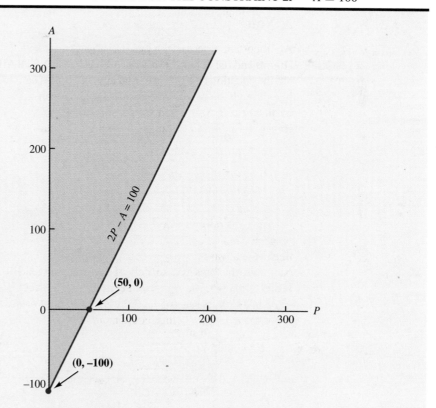

Can you graph a constraint line when the origin is on the constraint line? Try Problem 5.

To find all solutions satisfying the constraint as an equality, we first set $R = 0$ and solve for T. This result shows that the origin ($T = 0$, $R = 0$) is on the constraint line. Setting $T = 0$ and solving for R provides the same point. However, we can obtain a second point on the line by setting T equal to any value other than zero and then solving for R. For instance, setting $T = 100$ and solving for R, we find that the point ($T = 100$, $R = 100$) is on the line. With the two points ($R = 0$, $T = 0$) and ($R = 100$, $T = 100$), the constraint line $R - T = 0$ and the feasible solutions for $R - T \geq 0$ can be plotted as shown in Figure 2.11.

Summary of the Graphical Solution Procedure for Maximization Problems

For additional practice in using the graphical solution procedure, try Problem 24(b), 24(c), and 24(d).

As we have seen, the graphical solution procedure is a method for solving two-variable linear programming problems such as the Par, Inc., problem. The steps of the graphical solution procedure for a maximization problem are summarized here:

1. Prepare a graph of the feasible solutions for each of the constraints.
2. Determine the feasible region by identifying the solutions that satisfy all the constraints simultaneously.
3. Draw an objective function line showing the values of the decision variables that yield a specified value of the objective function.
4. Move parallel objective function lines toward larger objective function values until further movement would take the line completely outside the feasible region.
5. Any feasible solution on the objective function line with the largest value is an optimal solution.

FIGURE 2.11   FEASIBLE SOLUTIONS FOR THE CONSTRAINT $R - T \geq 0$

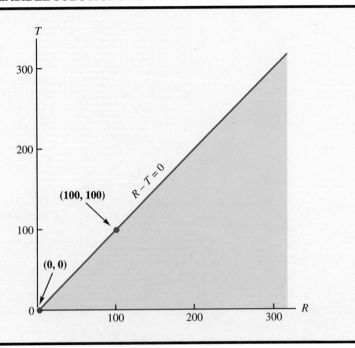

Slack Variables

In addition to the optimal solution and its associated profit contribution, Par's management will probably want information about the production time requirements for each production operation. We can determine this information by substituting the optimal solution values ($S = 540$, $D = 252$) into the constraints of the linear program.

Constraint	Hours Required for $S = 540$ and $D = 252$	Hours Available	Unused Hours
Cutting and dyeing	$\frac{7}{10}(540) + 1(252) = 630$	630	0
Sewing	$\frac{1}{2}(540) + \frac{5}{6}(252) = 480$	600	120
Finishing	$1(540) + \frac{2}{3}(252) = 708$	708	0
Inspection and packaging	$\frac{1}{10}(540) + \frac{1}{4}(252) = 117$	135	18

Thus, the complete solution tells management that the production of 540 standard bags and 252 deluxe bags will require all available cutting and dyeing time (630 hours) and all available finishing time (708 hours), while $600 - 480 = 120$ hours of sewing time and $135 - 117 = 18$ hours of inspection and packaging time will remain unused. The 120 hours of unused sewing time and 18 hours of unused inspection and packaging time are referred to as *slack* for the two departments. In linear programming terminology, any unused capacity for a $\leq$ constraint is referred to as the *slack* associated with the constraint.

Can you identify the slack associated with a constraint? Try Problem 24(e).

Often variables, called **slack variables,** are added to the formulation of a linear programming problem to represent the slack, or idle capacity. Unused capacity makes no contribution to profit; thus, slack variables have coefficients of zero in the objective function. After the addition of four slack variables, denoted S_1, S_2, S_3, and S_4, the mathematical model of the Par, Inc., problem becomes

$$\text{Max} \quad 10S + 9D + 0S_1 + 0S_2 + 0S_3 + 0S_4$$
$$\text{s.t.}$$
$$\frac{7}{10}S + 1D + 1S_1 \qquad\qquad\qquad = 630$$
$$\frac{1}{2}S + \frac{5}{6}D \qquad + 1S_2 \qquad\qquad = 600$$
$$1S + \frac{2}{3}D \qquad\qquad + 1S_3 \qquad = 708$$
$$\frac{1}{10}S + \frac{1}{4}D \qquad\qquad\qquad + 1S_4 = 135$$
$$S, D, S_1, S_2, S_3, S_4 \geq 0$$

Can you write a linear program in standard form? Try Problem 18.

Whenever a linear program is written in a form with all constraints expressed as equalities, it is said to be written in **standard form.**

Referring to the standard form of the Par, Inc., problem, we see that at the optimal solution ($S = 540$ and $D = 252$), the values for the slack variables are

Constraint	Value of Slack Variable
Cutting and dyeing	$S_1 = 0$
Sewing	$S_2 = 120$
Finishing	$S_3 = 0$
Inspection and packaging	$S_4 = 18$

Could we have used the graphical solution to provide some of this information? The answer is yes. By finding the optimal solution point on Figure 2.5, we can see that the cutting and dyeing and the finishing constraints restrict, or *bind,* the feasible region at this point. Thus, this solution requires the use of all available time for these two operations. In other words, the graph shows us that the cutting and dyeing and the finishing departments will have zero slack. On the other hand, the sewing and the inspection and packaging constraints are not binding the feasible region at the optimal solution, which means we can expect some unused time or slack for these two operations.

As a final comment on the graphical analysis of this problem, we call your attention to the sewing capacity constraint as shown in Figure 2.5. Note, in particular, that this constraint did not affect the feasible region. That is, the feasible region would be the same whether the sewing capacity constraint were included or not, which tells us that enough sewing time is available to accommodate any production level that can be achieved by the other three departments. The sewing constraint does not affect the feasible region and thus cannot affect the optimal solution; it is called a **redundant constraint.**

NOTES AND COMMENTS

1. In the standard-form representation of a linear programming model, the objective function coefficients for slack variables are zero. This zero coefficient implies that slack variables, which represent unused resources, do not affect the value of the objective function. However, in some applications, unused resources can be sold and contribute to profit. In such cases, the corresponding slack variables become decision variables representing the amount of unused resources to be sold. For each of these variables, a nonzero coefficient in the objective function would reflect the profit associated with selling a unit of the corresponding resource.

2. Redundant constraints do not affect the feasible region; as a result, they can be removed from a linear programming model without affecting the optimal solution. However, if the linear programming model is to be re-solved later, changes in some of the data might make a previously redundant constraint a binding constraint. Thus, we recommend keeping all constraints in the linear programming model even though at some point in time one or more of the constraints may be redundant.

2.3   EXTREME POINTS AND THE OPTIMAL SOLUTION

Suppose that the profit contribution for Par's standard golf bag is reduced from $10 to $5 per bag, while the profit contribution for the deluxe golf bag and all the constraints remain unchanged. The complete linear programming model of this new problem is identical to the mathematical model in Section 2.1, except for the revised objective function:

$$\text{Max } 5S + 9D$$

How does this change in the objective function affect the optimal solution to the Par, Inc., problem? Figure 2.12 shows the graphical solution of this new problem with the revised objective function. Note that without any change in the constraints, the feasible region does not change. However, the profit lines have been altered to reflect the new objective function.

By moving the profit line in a parallel manner toward higher profit values, we find the optimal solution as shown in Figure 2.12. The values of the decision variables at this point

FIGURE 2.12   OPTIMAL SOLUTION FOR THE PAR, INC., PROBLEM WITH AN
OBJECTIVE FUNCTION OF $5S + 9D$

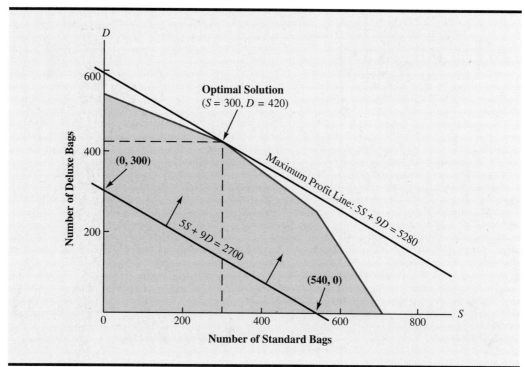

are $S = 300$ and $D = 420$. The reduced profit contribution for the standard bag caused a change in the optimal solution. In fact, as you may have suspected, we are cutting back the production of the lower-profit standard bags and increasing the production of the higher-profit deluxe bags.

What observations can you make about the location of the optimal solutions in the two linear programming problems solved thus far? Look closely at the graphical solutions in Figures 2.9 and 2.12. Notice that the optimal solutions occur at one of the vertices, or "corners," of the feasible region. In linear programming terminology, these vertices are referred to as the **extreme points** of the feasible region. The Par, Inc., feasible region has five vertices, or five extreme points (see Figure 2.13). We can now formally state our observation about the location of optimal solutions as follows:

For additional practice in identifying the extreme points of the feasible region and determining the optimal solution by computing and comparing the objective function value at each extreme point, try Problem 13.

The optimal solution to a linear program can be found at an extreme point of the feasible region.[2]

This property means that if you are looking for the optimal solution to a linear program, you do not have to evaluate all feasible solution points. In fact, you have to consider

[2]We will discuss in Section 2.6 the two special cases (infeasibility and unboundedness) in linear programming that have no optimal solution, and for which this statement does not apply.

FIGURE 2.13   THE FIVE EXTREME POINTS OF THE FEASIBLE REGION
FOR THE PAR, INC., PROBLEM

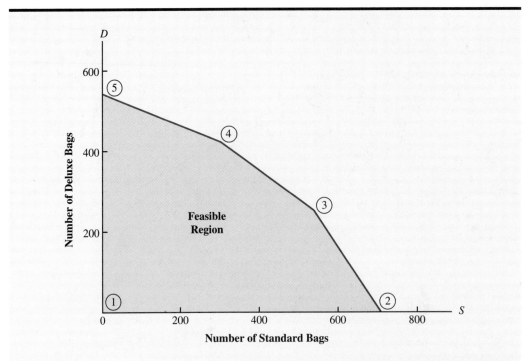

only the feasible solutions that occur at the extreme points of the feasible region. Thus, for the Par, Inc., problem, instead of computing and comparing the profit contributions for all feasible solutions, we can find the optimal solution by evaluating the five extreme-point solutions and selecting the one that provides the largest profit contribution. Actually, the graphical solution procedure is nothing more than a convenient way of identifying an optimal extreme point for two-variable problems.

2.4   COMPUTER SOLUTION OF THE PAR, INC., PROBLEM

In January 1952 the first successful computer solution of a linear programming problem was performed on the SEAC (Standards Eastern Automatic Computer). The SEAC, the first digital computer built by the National Bureau of Standards under U.S. Air Force sponsorship, had a 512-word memory and magnetic tape for external storage.

Computer programs designed to solve linear programming problems are now widely available. After a short period of familiarization with the specific features of the package, users are able to solve linear programming problems with few difficulties. Problems involving thousands of variables and thousands of constraints are now routinely solved with computer packages. Some of the leading commercial packages include CPLEX, Gurobi, LINGO, MOSEK, Risk Solver for Excel, and Xpress-MP. Packages are also available for free download. A good example is Clp (COIN-OR linear programming).

The solution to Par, Inc. is shown in Figure 2.14. The authors have chosen to make this book flexible and not rely on a specific linear programming package. Hence, the output in Figure 2.14 is generic and is not an actual printout from a particular software package. The output provided in Figure 2.14 is typical of most linear programming packages. We use this output format throughout the text. At the website for this course two linear programming packages are provided. A description of the packages is provided in the appendices. In Appendix 2.1 we show how to solve the Par, Inc., problem using LINGO. In Appendix 2.2 we

FIGURE 2.14 THE SOLUTION FOR THE PAR, INC., PROBLEM

Par

```
Optimal Objective Value =              7668.00000

        Variable                Value            Reduced Cost
      ------------          ------------        ------------
           S                 540.00000              0.00000
           D                 252.00000              0.00000

       Constraint          Slack/Surplus          Dual Value
      ------------          ------------        ------------
           1                   0.00000              4.37500
           2                 120.00000              0.00000
           3                   0.00000              6.93750
           4                  18.00000              0.00000

                          Objective          Allowable          Allowable
        Variable         Coefficient          Increase           Decrease
      -----------       ------------        ----------        ----------
           S              10.00000            3.50000            3.70000
           D               9.00000            5.28571            2.33333

                             RHS             Allowable          Allowable
       Constraint           Value            Increase           Decrease
      -----------       ------------        ----------        ----------
           1             630.00000           52.36364          134.40000
           2             600.00000            Infinite         120.00000
           3             708.00000          192.00000          128.00000
           4             135.00000            Infinite          18.00000
```

show how to formulate a spreadsheet model for the Par, Inc., problem and use Excel Solver to solve the problem.

Interpretation of Computer Output

Let us look more closely at the output in Figure 2.14 and interpret the computer solution provided for the Par, Inc., problem. The optimal solution to this problem will provide a profit of $7668. Directly below the objective function value, we find the values of the decision variables at the optimal solution. We have $S = 540$ standard bags and $D = 252$ deluxe bags as the optimal production quantities.

Recall that the Par, Inc., problem had four less-than-or-equal-to constraints corresponding to the hours available in each of four production departments. The information shown in the Slack/Surplus column provides the value of the slack variable for each of the departments. This information is summarized here:

Constraint Number	Constraint Name	Slack
1	Cutting and dyeing	0
2	Sewing	120
3	Finishing	0
4	Inspection and packaging	18

From this information, we see that the binding constraints (the cutting and dyeing and the finishing constraints) have zero slack at the optimal solution. The sewing department has 120 hours of slack or unused capacity, and the inspection and packaging department has 18 hours of slack or unused capacity.

The rest of the output in Figure 2.14 can be used to determine how changes in the input data impact the optimal solution. We shall defer discussion of reduced costs, dual values, allowable increases and decreases of objective function coefficients and right-hand-side values until Chapter 3, when we study the topic of sensitivity analysis.

NOTES AND COMMENTS

Linear programming solvers are now a standard feature of most spreadsheet packages. In Appendix 2.2 we show how spreadsheets can be used to solve linear programs by using Excel to solve the Par, Inc., problem.

2.5   A SIMPLE MINIMIZATION PROBLEM

M&D Chemicals produces two products that are sold as raw materials to companies manufacturing bath soaps and laundry detergents. Based on an analysis of current inventory levels and potential demand for the coming month, M&D's management specified that the combined production for products A and B must total at least 350 gallons. Separately, a major customer's order for 125 gallons of product A must also be satisfied. Product A requires 2 hours of processing time per gallon and product B requires 1 hour of processing time per gallon. For the coming month, 600 hours of processing time are available. M&D's objective is to satisfy these requirements at a minimum total production cost. Production costs are $2 per gallon for product A and $3 per gallon for product B.

To find the minimum-cost production schedule, we will formulate the M&D Chemicals problem as a linear program. Following a procedure similar to the one used for the Par, Inc., problem, we first define the decision variables and the objective function for the problem. Let

$$A = \text{number of gallons of product A}$$
$$B = \text{number of gallons of product B}$$

With production costs at $2 per gallon for product A and $3 per gallon for product B, the objective function that corresponds to the minimization of the total production cost can be written as

$$\text{Min } 2A + 3B$$

Next, consider the constraints placed on the M&D Chemicals problem. To satisfy the major customer's demand for 125 gallons of product A, we know A must be at least 125. Thus, we write the constraint

$$1A \geq 125$$

For the combined production for both products, which must total at least 350 gallons, we can write the constraint

$$1A + 1B \geq 350$$

Finally, for the limitation of 600 hours on available processing time, we add the constraint

$$2A + 1B \leq 600$$

After adding the nonnegativity constraints ($A, B \geq 0$), we arrive at the following linear program for the M&D Chemicals problem:

$$
\begin{aligned}
\text{Min} \quad & 2A + 3B \\
\text{s.t.} \quad & \\
& 1A \qquad\quad \geq 125 \quad \text{Demand for product A} \\
& 1A + 1B \geq 350 \quad \text{Total production} \\
& 2A + 1B \leq 600 \quad \text{Processing time} \\
& A, B \geq 0
\end{aligned}
$$

Because the linear programming model has only two decision variables, the graphical solution procedure can be used to find the optimal production quantities. The graphical solution procedure for this problem, just as in the Par problem, requires us to first graph the constraint lines to find the feasible region. By graphing each constraint line separately and then checking points on either side of the constraint line, the feasible solutions for each constraint can be identified. By combining the feasible solutions for each constraint on the same graph, we obtain the feasible region shown in Figure 2.15.

FIGURE 2.15   THE FEASIBLE REGION FOR THE M&D CHEMICALS PROBLEM

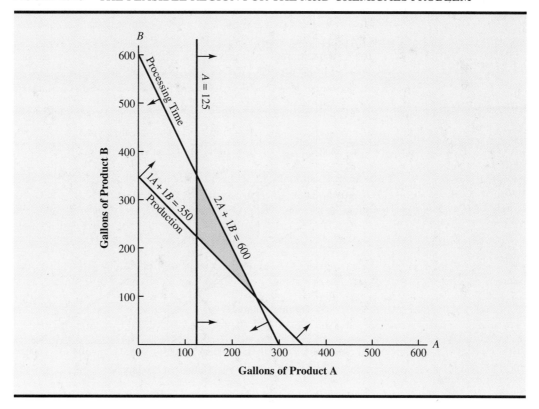

To find the minimum-cost solution, we now draw the objective function line corresponding to a particular total cost value. For example, we might start by drawing the line $2A + 3B = 1200$. This line is shown in Figure 2.16. Clearly, some points in the feasible region would provide a total cost of $1200. To find the values of A and B that provide smaller total cost values, we move the objective function line in a lower left direction until, if we moved it any farther, it would be entirely outside the feasible region. Note that the objective function line $2A + 3B = 800$ intersects the feasible region at the extreme point $A = 250$ and $B = 100$. This extreme point provides the minimum-cost solution with an objective function value of 800. From Figures 2.15 and 2.16, we can see that the total production constraint and the processing time constraint are binding. Just as in every linear programming problem, the optimal solution occurs at an extreme point of the feasible region.

Summary of the Graphical Solution Procedure for Minimization Problems

Can you use the graphical solution procedure to determine the optimal solution for a minimization problem? Try Problem 31.

The steps of the graphical solution procedure for a minimization problem are summarized here:

1. Prepare a graph of the feasible solutions for each of the constraints.
2. Determine the feasible region by identifying the solutions that satisfy all the constraints simultaneously.

FIGURE 2.16   GRAPHICAL SOLUTION FOR THE M&D CHEMICALS PROBLEM

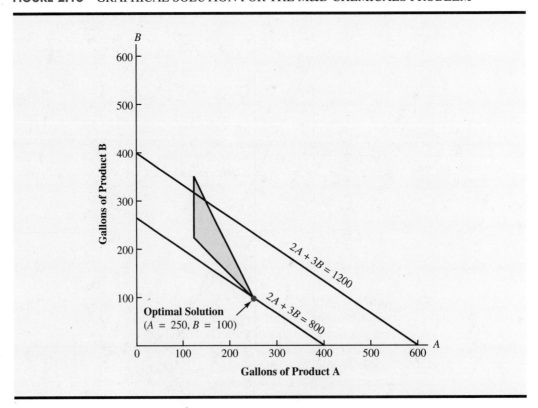

3. Draw an objective function line showing the values of the decision variables that yield a specified value of the objective function.
4. Move parallel objective function lines toward smaller objective function values until further movement would take the line completely outside the feasible region.
5. Any feasible solution on the objective function line with the smallest value is an optimal solution.

Surplus Variables

The optimal solution to the M&D Chemicals problem shows that the desired total production of $A + B = 350$ gallons has been achieved by using all available processing time of $2A + 1B = 2(250) + 1(100) = 600$ hours. In addition, note that the constraint requiring that product A demand be met has been satisfied with $A = 250$ gallons. In fact, the production of product A exceeds its minimum level by $250 - 125 = 125$ gallons. This excess production for product A is referred to as *surplus*. In linear programming terminology, any excess quantity corresponding to a $\geq$ constraint is referred to as surplus.

Recall that with a $\leq$ constraint, a slack variable can be added to the left-hand side of the inequality to convert the constraint to equality form. With a $\geq$ constraint, a **surplus variable** can be subtracted from the left-hand side of the inequality to convert the constraint to equality form. Just as with slack variables, surplus variables are given a coefficient of zero in the objective function because they have no effect on its value. After including two surplus variables, S_1 and S_2, for the $\geq$ constraints and one slack variable, S_3, for the $\leq$ constraint, the linear programming model of the M&D Chemicals problem becomes

$$
\begin{aligned}
\text{Min} \quad & 2A + 3B + 0S_1 + 0S_2 + 0S_3 \\
\text{s.t.} \quad & \\
& 1A \qquad\quad - 1S_1 \qquad\qquad\quad = 125 \\
& 1A + 1B \qquad\quad - 1S_2 \qquad\quad = 350 \\
& 2A + 1B \qquad\qquad\quad + 1S_3 = 600 \\
& A, B, S_1, S_2, S_3 \geq 0
\end{aligned}
$$

Try Problem 35 to test your ability to use slack and surplus variables to write a linear program in standard form.

All the constraints are now equalities. Hence, the preceding formulation is the standard-form representation of the M&D Chemicals problem. At the optimal solution of $A = 250$ and $B = 100$, the values of the surplus and slack variables are as follows:

Constraint	Value of Surplus or Slack Variables
Demand for product A	$S_1 = 125$
Total production	$S_2 = 0$
Processing time	$S_3 = 0$

Refer to Figures 2.15 and 2.16. Note that the zero surplus and slack variables are associated with the constraints that are binding at the optimal solution—that is, the total production and processing time constraints. The surplus of 125 units is associated with the nonbinding constraint on the demand for product A.

In the Par, Inc., problem all the constraints were of the $\leq$ type, and in the M&D Chemicals problem the constraints were a mixture of $\geq$ and $\leq$ types. The number and types of constraints encountered in a particular linear programming problem depend on

Try Problem 34 to practice solving a linear program with all three constraint forms.

the specific conditions existing in the problem. Linear programming problems may have some $\leq$ constraints, some $=$ constraints, and some $\geq$ constraints. For an equality constraint, feasible solutions must lie directly on the constraint line.

An example of a linear program with two decision variables, G and H, and all three constraint forms is given here:

$$\text{Min} \quad 2G + 2H$$
$$\text{s.t.}$$
$$1G + 3H \leq 12$$
$$3G + 1H \geq 13$$
$$1G - 1H = 3$$
$$G, H \geq 0$$

The standard-form representation of this problem is

$$\text{Min} \quad 2G + 2H + 0S_1 + 0S_2$$
$$\text{s.t.}$$
$$1G + 3H + 1S_1 \qquad\quad = 12$$
$$3G + 1H \qquad\quad - 1S_2 = 13$$
$$1G - 1H \qquad\qquad\qquad = 3$$
$$G, H, S_1, S_2 \geq 0$$

The standard form requires a slack variable for the $\leq$ constraint and a surplus variable for the $\geq$ constraint. However, neither a slack nor a surplus variable is required for the third constraint because it is already in equality form.

When solving linear programs graphically, it is not necessary to write the problem in its standard form. Nevertheless, you should be able to compute the values of the slack and surplus variables and understand what they mean, because the values of slack and surplus variables are included in the computer solution of linear programs.

A final point: The standard form of the linear programming problem is equivalent to the original formulation of the problem. That is, the optimal solution to any linear programming problem is the same as the optimal solution to the standard form of the problem. The standard form has not changed the basic problem; it has only changed how we write the constraints for the problem.

Computer Solution of the M&D Chemicals Problem

The optimal solution to M&D is given in Figure 2.17. The computer output shows that the minimum-cost solution yields an objective function value of $800. The values of the decision variables show that 250 gallons of product A and 100 gallons of product B provide the minimum-cost solution.

The Slack/Surplus column shows that the $\geq$ constraint corresponding to the demand for product A (see constraint 1) has a surplus of 125 units. This column tells us that production of product A in the optimal solution exceeds demand by 125 gallons. The Slack/Surplus values are zero for the total production requirement (constraint 2) and the processing time limitation (constraint 3), which indicates that these constraints are binding at the optimal solution. We will discuss the rest of the computer output that appears in Figure 2.17 in Chapter 3 when we study the topic of sensitivity analysis.

FIGURE 2.17   THE SOLUTION FOR THE M&D CHEMICALS PROBLEM

Optimal Objective Value =   800.00000

Variable	Value	Reduced Cost
A	250.00000	0.00000
B	100.00000	0.00000

Constraint	Slack/Surplus	Dual Value
1	125.00000	0.00000
2	0.00000	4.00000
3	0.00000	-1.00000

Variable	Objective Coefficient	Allowable Increase	Allowable Decrease
A	2.00000	1.00000	Infinite
B	3.00000	Infinite	1.00000

Constraint	RHS Value	Allowable Increase	Allowable Decrease
1	125.00000	125.00000	Infinite
2	350.00000	125.00000	50.00000
3	600.00000	100.00000	125.00000

2.6   SPECIAL CASES

In this section we discuss three special situations that can arise when we attempt to solve linear programming problems.

Alternative Optimal Solutions

From the discussion of the graphical solution procedure, we know that optimal solutions can be found at the extreme points of the feasible region. Now let us consider the special case in which the optimal objective function line coincides with one of the binding constraint lines on the boundary of the feasible region. We will see that this situation can lead to the case of **alternative optimal solutions;** in such cases, more than one solution provides the optimal value for the objective function.

To illustrate the case of alternative optimal solutions, we return to the Par, Inc., problem. However, let us assume that the profit for the standard golf bag (S) has been decreased to $6.30. The revised objective function becomes $6.3S + 9D$. The graphical solution of this problem is shown in Figure 2.18. Note that the optimal solution still occurs at an extreme point. In fact, it occurs at two extreme points: extreme point ④ ($S = 300, D = 420$) and extreme point ③ ($S = 540, D = 252$).

The objective function values at these two extreme points are identical; that is,

$$6.3S + 9D = 6.3(300) + 9(420) = 5670$$

FIGURE 2.18   PAR, INC., PROBLEM WITH AN OBJECTIVE FUNCTION OF $6.3S + 9D$
(ALTERNATIVE OPTIMAL SOLUTIONS)

and

$$6.3S + 9D = 6.3(540) + 9(252) = 5670$$

Furthermore, any point on the line connecting the two optimal extreme points also provides an optimal solution. For example, the solution point ($S = 420$, $D = 336$), which is halfway between the two extreme points, also provides the optimal objective function value of

$$6.3S + 9D = 6.3(420) + 9(336) = 5670$$

A linear programming problem with alternative optimal solutions is generally a good situation for the manager or decision maker. It means that several combinations of the decision variables are optimal and that the manager can select the most desirable optimal solution. Unfortunately, determining whether a problem has alternative optimal solutions is not a simple matter.

Infeasibility

Problems with no feasible solution do arise in practice, most often because management's expectations are too high or because too many restrictions have been placed on the problem.

Infeasibility means that no solution to the linear programming problem satisfies all the constraints, including the nonnegativity conditions. Graphically, infeasibility means that a feasible region does not exist; that is, no points satisfy all the constraints and the nonnegativity conditions simultaneously. To illustrate this situation, let us look again at the problem faced by Par, Inc.

Suppose that management specified that at least 500 of the standard bags and at least 360 of the deluxe bags must be manufactured. The graph of the solution region may now be constructed to reflect these new requirements (see Figure 2.19). The shaded area in the lower

FIGURE 2.19   NO FEASIBLE REGION FOR THE PAR, INC., PROBLEM WITH
MINIMUM PRODUCTION REQUIREMENTS OF 500 STANDARD
AND 360 DELUXE BAGS

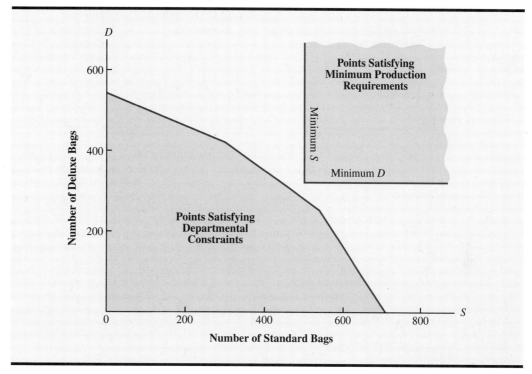

left-hand portion of the graph depicts those points satisfying the departmental constraints on the availability of time. The shaded area in the upper right-hand portion depicts those points satisfying the minimum production requirements of 500 standard and 360 deluxe bags. But no points satisfy both sets of constraints. Thus, we see that if management imposes these minimum production requirements, no feasible region exists for the problem.

How should we interpret infeasibility in terms of this current problem? First, we should tell management that given the resources available (i.e., production time for cutting and dyeing, sewing, finishing, and inspection and packaging), it is not possible to make 500 standard bags and 360 deluxe bags. Moreover, we can tell management exactly how much of each resource must be expended to make it possible to manufacture 500 standard and 360 deluxe bags. Table 2.2 shows the minimum amounts of resources that must be available, the amounts currently available, and additional amounts that would be required to accomplish this level of production. Thus, we need 80 more hours for cutting and dyeing, 32 more hours for finishing, and 5 more hours for inspection and packaging to meet management's minimum production requirements.

If, after reviewing this information, management still wants to manufacture 500 standard and 360 deluxe bags, additional resources must be provided. Perhaps by hiring another person to work in the cutting and dyeing department, transferring a person from elsewhere in the plant to work part-time in the finishing department, or having the sewing people help out periodically with the inspection and packaging, the resource requirements can be met. As you can see, many possibilities are available for corrective management action, once we discover the lack of a feasible solution. The important thing to realize is that linear programming

TABLE 2.2   RESOURCES NEEDED TO MANUFACTURE 500 STANDARD BAGS
AND 360 DELUXE BAGS

Operation	Minimum Required Resources (hours)	Available Resources (hours)	Additional Resources Needed (hours)
Cutting and dyeing	$\frac{7}{10}(500) + 1(360) = 710$	630	80
Sewing	$\frac{1}{2}(500) + \frac{5}{6}(360) = 550$	600	None
Finishing	$1(500) + \frac{2}{3}(360) = 740$	708	32
Inspection and packaging	$\frac{1}{10}(500) + \frac{1}{4}(360) = 140$	135	5

analysis can help determine whether management's plans are feasible. By analyzing the problem using linear programming, we are often able to point out infeasible conditions and initiate corrective action.

Whenever you attempt to solve a problem that is infeasible using either LINGO or Excel Solver, you will get an error message indicating that the problem is infeasible. In this case you know that no solution to the linear programming problem will satisfy all constraints, including the nonnegativity conditions. Careful inspection of your formulation is necessary to try to identify why the problem is infeasible. In some situations, the only reasonable approach is to drop one or more constraints and re-solve the problem. If you are able to find an optimal solution for this revised problem, you will know that the constraint(s) that was omitted, in conjunction with the others, is causing the problem to be infeasible.

Unbounded

The solution to a maximization linear programming problem is **unbounded** if the value of the solution may be made infinitely large without violating any of the constraints; for a minimization problem, the solution is unbounded if the value may be made infinitely small. This condition might be termed *managerial utopia;* for example, if this condition were to occur in a profit maximization problem, the manager could achieve an unlimited profit.

However, in linear programming models of real problems, the occurrence of an unbounded solution means that the problem has been improperly formulated. We know it is not possible to increase profits indefinitely. Therefore, we must conclude that if a profit maximization problem results in an unbounded solution, the mathematical model doesn't represent the real-world problem sufficiently. Usually, what has happened is that a constraint has been inadvertently omitted during problem formulation.

As an illustration, consider the following linear program with two decision variables, X and Y:

$$\text{Max} \quad 20X + 10Y$$

$$\text{s.t.}$$

$$1X \qquad \geq 2$$
$$1Y \leq 5$$
$$X, Y \geq 0$$

In Figure 2.20 we graphed the feasible region associated with this problem. Note that we can only indicate part of the feasible region because the feasible region extends indefinitely in the direction of the X axis. Looking at the objective function lines in Figure 2.20, we see that the solution to this problem may be made as large as we desire. That is, no matter what solution we pick, we will always be able to reach some feasible solution with a larger value. Thus, we say that the solution to this linear program is *unbounded.*

FIGURE 2.20   EXAMPLE OF AN UNBOUNDED PROBLEM

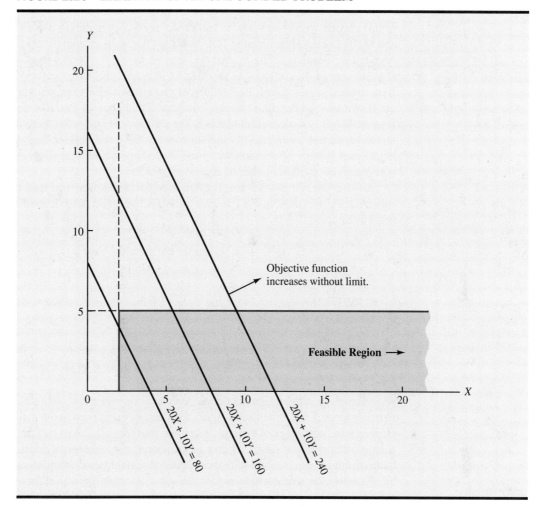

Can you recognize whether
a linear program involves
alternative optimal
solutions or infeasibility,
or is unbounded? Try
Problems 42 and 43.

Whenever you attempt to solve a problem that is unbounded using either LINGO or Excel Solver you will get a message telling you that the problem is unbounded. Because unbounded solutions cannot occur in real problems, the first thing you should do is to review your model to determine whether you incorrectly formulated the problem. In many cases, this error is the result of inadvertently omitting a constraint during problem formulation.

NOTES AND COMMENTS

1. Infeasibility is independent of the objective function. It exists because the constraints are so restrictive that no feasible region for the linear programming model is possible. Thus, when you encounter infeasibility, making changes in the coefficients of the objective function will not help; the problem will remain infeasible.

2. The occurrence of an unbounded solution is often the result of a missing constraint. However,

a change in the objective function may cause a previously unbounded problem to become bounded with an optimal solution. For example, the graph in Figure 2.20 shows an unbounded solution for the objective function Max $20X + 10Y$. However, changing the objective function to Max $-20X - 10Y$ will provide the optimal solution $X = 2$ and $Y = 0$ even though no changes have been made in the constraints.

2.7   GENERAL LINEAR PROGRAMMING NOTATION

In this chapter we showed how to formulate linear programming models for the Par, Inc., and M&D Chemicals problems. To formulate a linear programming model of the Par, Inc., problem we began by defining two decision variables: S = number of standard bags and D = number of deluxe bags. In the M&D Chemicals problem, the two decision variables were defined as A = number of gallons of product A and B = number of gallons of product B. We selected decision-variable names of S and D in the Par, Inc., problem and A and B in the M&D Chemicals problem to make it easier to recall what these decision variables represented in the problem. Although this approach works well for linear programs involving a small number of decision variables, it can become difficult when dealing with problems involving a large number of decision variables.

A more general notation that is often used for linear programs uses the letter x with a subscript. For instance, in the Par, Inc., problem, we could have defined the decision variables as follows:

$$x_1 = \text{number of standard bags}$$
$$x_2 = \text{number of deluxe bags}$$

In the M&D Chemicals problem, the same variable names would be used, but their definitions would change:

$$x_1 = \text{number of gallons of product A}$$
$$x_2 = \text{number of gallons of product B}$$

A disadvantage of using general notation for decision variables is that we are no longer able to easily identify what the decision variables actually represent in the mathematical model. However, the advantage of general notation is that formulating a mathematical model for a problem that involves a large number of decision variables is much easier. For instance, for a linear programming model with three decision variables, we would use variable names of x_1, x_2, and x_3; for a problem with four decision variables, we would use variable names of x_1, x_2, x_3, and x_4, and so on. Clearly, if a problem involved 1000 decision variables, trying to identify 1000 unique names would be difficult. However, using the general linear programming notation, the decision variables would be defined as $x_1, x_2, x_3, \ldots, x_{1000}$.

To illustrate the graphical solution procedure for a linear program written using general linear programming notation, consider the following mathematical model for a maximization problem involving two decision variables:

$$\text{Max} \quad 3x_1 + 2x_2$$
$$\text{s.t.}$$
$$2x_1 + 2x_2 \le 8$$
$$1x_1 + 0.5x_2 \le 3$$
$$x_1, x_2 \ge 0$$

We must first develop a graph that displays the possible solutions (x_1 and x_2 values) for the problem. The usual convention is to plot values of x_1 along the horizontal axis and values of x_2 along the vertical axis. Figure 2.21 shows the graphical solution for this two-variable problem. Note that for this problem the optimal solution is $x_1 = 2$ and $x_2 = 2$, with an objective function value of 10.

FIGURE 2.21   GRAPHICAL SOLUTION OF A TWO-VARIABLE LINEAR PROGRAM
WITH GENERAL NOTATION

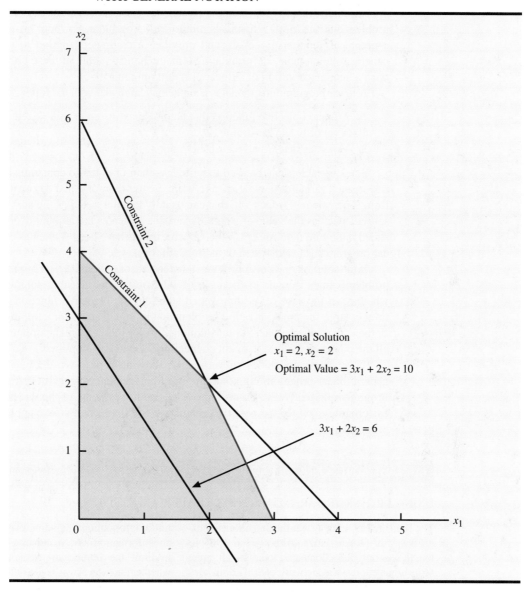

Using general linear programming notation, we can write the standard form of the preceding linear program as follows:

$$\text{Max}\quad 3x_1 + \ 2x_2 + 0s_1 + 0s_2$$

s.t.

$$2x_1 + \ 2x_2 + 1s_1 \qquad\qquad = 8$$
$$1x_1 + 0.5x_2 + \qquad\quad 1s_2 = 3$$
$$x_1, x_2, s_1, s_2 \ge 0$$

Thus, at the optimal solution $x_1 = 2$ and $x_2 = 2$; the values of the slack variables are $s_1 = s_2 = 0$.

SUMMARY

We formulated linear programming models for two problems: the Par, Inc., maximization problem and the M&D Chemicals minimization problem. For both problems we showed a graphical solution procedure and provided a computer solution to the problem in a generic solution table. In formulating a mathematical model of these problems, we developed a general definition of a linear programming model.

A linear programming model is a mathematical model with the following characteristics:

1. A linear objective function that is to be maximized or minimized
2. A set of linear constraints
3. Variables that are all restricted to nonnegative values

Slack variables may be used to write less-than-or-equal-to constraints in equality form and surplus variables may be used to write greater-than-or-equal-to constraints in equality form. The value of a slack variable can usually be interpreted as the amount of unused resource, whereas the value of a surplus variable indicates the amount over and above some stated minimum requirement. When all constraints have been written as equalities, the linear program has been written in its standard form.

If the solution to a linear program is infeasible or unbounded, no optimal solution to the problem can be found. In the case of infeasibility, no feasible solutions are possible, whereas, in the case of an unbounded solution, the objective function can be made infinitely large for a maximization problem and infinitely small for a minimization problem. In the case of alternative optimal solutions, two or more optimal extreme points exist, and all the points on the line segment connecting them are also optimal.

This chapter concludes with a section showing how to write a linear program using general linear programming notation. The Management Science in Action, Using Linear Programming for Traffic Control, provides another example of the widespread use of linear programming. In the next two chapters we will see many more applications of linear programming.

MANAGEMENT SCIENCE IN ACTION

USING LINEAR PROGRAMMING FOR TRAFFIC CONTROL*

The Hanshin Expressway was the first urban toll expressway in Osaka, Japan. Although in 1964 its length was only 2.3 kilometers, today it is a large-scale urban expressway network of 200 kilometers. The Hanshin Expressway provides service for the Hanshin (Osaka-Kobe) area, the second-most populated area in Japan. An average of 828,000 vehicles use the expressway each day, with daily traffic sometimes exceeding 1 million vehicles. In 1990, the Hanshin Expressway Public Corporation started using an automated traffic control system in order to maximize the number of vehicles flowing into the expressway network.

The automated traffic control system relies on two control methods: (1) limiting the number of cars that enter the expressway at each entrance ramp; and (2) providing drivers with up-to-date and accurate traffic information, including expected travel times and information about accidents. The approach used to limit the number of vehicles depends upon whether the expressway is in a normal or steady state of operation, or whether some type of unusual event, such as an accident or a breakdown, has occurred.

In the first phase of the steady-state case, the Hanshin system uses a linear programming model to maximize the total number of vehicles entering the system, while preventing traffic congestion and adverse effects on surrounding road networks. The data that drive the linear programming model are collected from detectors installed every 500 meters along the expressway and at all entrance and exit ramps. Every five minutes the real-time data collected from the detectors are used to update the model coefficients, and a new linear program computes the maximum number of vehicles the expressway can accommodate.

The automated traffic control system has been successful. According to surveys, traffic control decreased the length of congested portions of the expressway by 30% and the duration by 20%. It proved to be extremely cost effective, and drivers consider it an indispensable service.

*Based on T. Yoshino, T. Sasaki, and T. Hasegawa, "The Traffic-Control System on the Hanshin Expressway," *Interfaces* (January/February 1995): 94–108.

GLOSSARY

Constraint   An equation or inequality that rules out certain combinations of decision variables as feasible solutions.

Problem formulation   The process of translating the verbal statement of a problem into a mathematical statement called the *mathematical model.*

Decision variable   A controllable input for a linear programming model.

Nonnegativity constraints   A set of constraints that requires all variables to be nonnegative.

Mathematical model   A representation of a problem where the objective and all constraint conditions are described by mathematical expressions.

Linear programming model   A mathematical model with a linear objective function, a set of linear constraints, and nonnegative variables.

Linear program   Another term for linear programming model.

Linear functions   Mathematical expressions in which the variables appear in separate terms and are raised to the first power.

Feasible solution   A solution that satisfies all the constraints.

Feasible region   The set of all feasible solutions.

Slack variable   A variable added to the left-hand side of a less-than-or-equal-to constraint to convert the constraint into an equality. The value of this variable can usually be interpreted as the amount of unused resource.

Standard form   A linear program in which all the constraints are written as equalities. The optimal solution of the standard form of a linear program is the same as the optimal solution of the original formulation of the linear program.

Redundant constraint   A constraint that does not affect the feasible region. If a constraint is redundant, it can be removed from the problem without affecting the feasible region.

Extreme point   Graphically speaking, extreme points are the feasible solution points occurring at the vertices or "corners" of the feasible region. With two-variable problems, extreme points are determined by the intersection of the constraint lines.

Surplus variable   A variable subtracted from the left-hand side of a greater-than-or-equal-to constraint to convert the constraint into an equality. The value of this variable can usually be interpreted as the amount over and above some required minimum level.

Alternative optimal solutions   The case in which more than one solution provides the optimal value for the objective function.

Infeasibility   The situation in which no solution to the linear programming problem satisfies all the constraints.

Unbounded   If the value of the solution may be made infinitely large in a maximization linear programming problem or infinitely small in a minimization problem without violating any of the constraints, the problem is said to be unbounded.

PROBLEMS

1. Which of the following mathematical relationships could be found in a linear programming model, and which could not? For the relationships that are unacceptable for linear programs, state why.
   a. $-1A + 2B \leq 70$
   b. $2A - 2B = 50$
   c. $1A - 2B^2 \leq 10$
   d. $3\sqrt{A} + 2B \geq 15$
   e. $1A + 1B = 6$
   f. $2A + 5B + 1AB \leq 25$

2. Find the solutions that satisfy the following constraints:
   a. $4A + 2B \leq 16$
   b. $4A + 2B \geq 16$
   c. $4A + 2B = 16$

3. Show a separate graph of the constraint lines and the solutions that satisfy each of the following constraints:
   a. $3A + 2B \leq 18$
   b. $12A + 8B \geq 480$
   c. $5A + 10B = 200$

4. Show a separate graph of the constraint lines and the solutions that satisfy each of the following constraints:
   a. $3A - 4B \geq 60$
   b. $-6A + 5B \leq 60$
   c. $5A - 2B \leq 0$

5. Show a separate graph of the constraint lines and the solutions that satisfy each of the following constraints:
   a. $A \geq 0.25 (A + B)$
   b. $B \leq 0.10 (A + B)$
   c. $A \leq 0.50 (A + B)$

6. Three objective functions for linear programming problems are $7A + 10B$, $6A + 4B$, and $-4A + 7B$. Show the graph of each for objective function values equal to 420.

7. Identify the feasible region for the following set of constraints:

$$0.5A + 0.25B \geq 30$$
$$1A + 5B \geq 250$$
$$0.25A + 0.5B \leq 50$$
$$A, B \geq 0$$

8. Identify the feasible region for the following set of constraints:

$$2A - 1B \leq 0$$
$$-1A + 1.5B \leq 200$$
$$A, B \geq 0$$

9. Identify the feasible region for the following set of constraints:

$$3A - 2B \geq 0$$
$$2A - 1B \leq 200$$
$$1A \leq 150$$
$$A, B \geq 0$$

10. For the linear program

$$\text{Max} \quad 2A + 3B$$
s.t.
$$1A + 2B \le 6$$
$$5A + 3B \le 15$$
$$A, B \ge 0$$

find the optimal solution using the graphical solution procedure. What is the value of the objective function at the optimal solution?

11. Solve the following linear program using the graphical solution procedure:

$$\text{Max} \quad 5A + 5B$$
s.t.
$$1A \qquad \le 100$$
$$1B \le 80$$
$$2A + 4B \le 400$$
$$A, B \ge 0$$

12. Consider the following linear programming problem:

$$\text{Max} \quad 3A + 3B$$
s.t.
$$2A + 4B \le 12$$
$$6A + 4B \le 24$$
$$A, B \ge 0$$

a. Find the optimal solution using the graphical solution procedure.
b. If the objective function is changed to $2A + 6B$, what will the optimal solution be?
c. How many extreme points are there? What are the values of A and B at each extreme point?

13. Consider the following linear program:

$$\text{Max} \quad 1A + 2B$$
s.t.
$$1A \qquad \le 5$$
$$1B \le 4$$
$$2A + 2B = 12$$
$$A, B \ge 0$$

a. Show the feasible region.
b. What are the extreme points of the feasible region?
c. Find the optimal solution using the graphical procedure.

14. RMC, Inc., is a small firm that produces a variety of chemical products. In a particular production process, three raw materials are blended (mixed together) to produce two products: a fuel additive and a solvent base. Each ton of fuel additive is a mixture of $\frac{2}{5}$ ton of material 1 and $\frac{3}{5}$ of material 3. A ton of solvent base is a mixture of $\frac{1}{2}$ ton of material 1, $\frac{1}{5}$ ton of material 2, and $\frac{3}{10}$ ton of material 3. After deducting relevant costs, the profit contribution is $40 for every ton of fuel additive produced and $30 for every ton of solvent base produced.

RMC's production is constrained by a limited availability of the three raw materials. For the current production period, RMC has available the following quantities of each raw material:

Raw Material	Amount Available for Production
Material 1	20 tons
Material 2	5 tons
Material 3	21 tons

Assuming that RMC is interested in maximizing the total profit contribution, answer the following:

a. What is the linear programming model for this problem?
b. Find the optimal solution using the graphical solution procedure. How many tons of each product should be produced, and what is the projected total profit contribution?
c. Is there any unused material? If so, how much?
d. Are any of the constraints redundant? If so, which ones?

15. Refer to the Par, Inc., problem described in Section 2.1. Suppose that Par's management encounters the following situations:

a. The accounting department revises its estimate of the profit contribution for the deluxe bag to $18 per bag.
b. A new low-cost material is available for the standard bag, and the profit contribution per standard bag can be increased to $20 per bag. (Assume that the profit contribution of the deluxe bag is the original $9 value.)
c. New sewing equipment is available that would increase the sewing operation capacity to 750 hours. (Assume that $10A + 9B$ is the appropriate objective function.) If each of these situations is encountered separately, what is the optimal solution and the total profit contribution?

16. Refer to the feasible region for Par, Inc., problem in Figure 2.13.

a. Develop an objective function that will make extreme point ⑤ the optimal extreme point.
b. What is the optimal solution for the objective function you selected in part (a)?
c. What are the values of the slack variables associated with this solution?

17. Write the following linear program in standard form:

$$\text{Max} \quad 5A + 2B$$
$$\text{s.t.}$$
$$1A - 2B \leq 420$$
$$2A + 3B \leq 610$$
$$6A - 1B \leq 125$$
$$A, B \geq 0$$

18. For the linear program

$$\text{Max} \quad 4A + 1B$$
$$\text{s.t.}$$
$$10A + 2B \leq 30$$
$$3A + 2B \leq 12$$
$$2A + 2B \leq 10$$
$$A, B \geq 0$$

a. Write this problem in standard form.
b. Solve the problem using the graphical solution procedure.
c. What are the values of the three slack variables at the optimal solution?

19. Given the linear program

$$\text{Max} \quad 3A + 4B$$
$$\text{s.t.}$$
$$-1A + 2B \leq 8$$
$$1A + 2B \leq 12$$
$$2A + 1B \leq 16$$
$$A, B \geq 0$$

a. Write the problem in standard form.
b. Solve the problem using the graphical solution procedure.
c. What are the values of the three slack variables at the optimal solution?

20. For the linear program

$$\text{Max} \quad 3A + 2B$$
$$\text{s.t.}$$
$$A + B \geq 4$$
$$3A + 4B \leq 24$$
$$A \qquad \geq 2$$
$$A - B \leq 0$$
$$A, B \geq 0$$

a. Write the problem in standard form.
b. Solve the problem.
c. What are the values of the slack and surplus variables at the optimal solution?

21. Consider the following linear program:

$$\text{Max} \quad 2A + 3B$$
$$\text{s.t.}$$
$$5A + 5B \leq 400 \quad \text{Constraint 1}$$
$$-1A + 1B \leq 10 \quad \text{Constraint 2}$$
$$1A + 3B \geq 90 \quad \text{Constraint 3}$$
$$A, B \geq 0$$

Figure 2.22 shows a graph of the constraint lines.
a. Place a number (1, 2, or 3) next to each constraint line to identify which constraint it represents.
b. Shade in the feasible region on the graph.
c. Identify the optimal extreme point. What is the optimal solution?
d. Which constraints are binding? Explain.
e. How much slack or surplus is associated with the nonbinding constraint?

22. Reiser Sports Products wants to determine the number of All-Pro (A) and College (C) footballs to produce in order to maximize profit over the next four-week planning horizon. Constraints affecting the production quantities are the production capacities in three departments: cutting and dyeing; sewing; and inspection and packaging. For

FIGURE 2.22   GRAPH OF THE CONSTRAINT LINES FOR EXERCISE 21

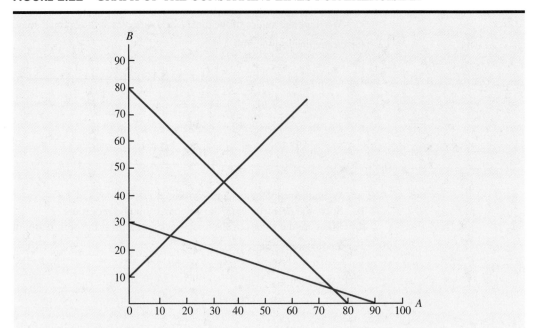

the four-week planning period, 340 hours of cutting and dyeing time, 420 hours of sewing time, and 200 hours of inspection and packaging time are available. All-Pro footballs provide a profit of $5 per unit and College footballs provide a profit of $4 per unit. The linear programming model with production times expressed in minutes is as follows:

$$\text{Max}\quad 5A + 4C$$
$$\text{s.t.}$$

$$
\begin{aligned}
12A + 6C &\le 20{,}400 \quad \text{Cutting and dyeing}\\
9A + 15C &\le 25{,}200 \quad \text{Sewing}\\
6A + 6C &\le 12{,}000 \quad \text{Inspection and packaging}\\
A, C &\ge 0
\end{aligned}
$$

A portion of the graphical solution to the Reiser problem is shown in Figure 2.23.

a.   Shade the feasible region for this problem.

b.   Determine the coordinates of each extreme point and the corresponding profit. Which extreme point generates the highest profit?

c.   Draw the profit line corresponding to a profit of $4000. Move the profit line as far from the origin as you can in order to determine which extreme point will provide the optimal solution. Compare your answer with the approach you used in part (b).

d.   Which constraints are binding? Explain.

e.   Suppose that the values of the objective function coefficients are $4 for each All-Pro model produced and $5 for each College model. Use the graphical solution procedure to determine the new optimal solution and the corresponding value of profit.

FIGURE 2.23   PORTION OF THE GRAPHICAL SOLUTION FOR EXERCISE 22

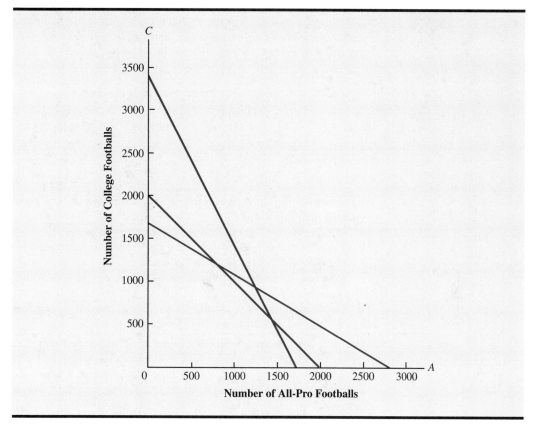

23. Embassy Motorcycles (EM) manufacturers two lightweight motorcycles designed for easy handling and safety. The EZ-Rider model has a new engine and a low profile that make it easy to balance. The Lady-Sport model is slightly larger, uses a more traditional engine, and is specifically designed to appeal to women riders. Embassy produces the engines for both models at its Des Moines, Iowa, plant. Each EZ-Rider engine requires 6 hours of manufacturing time and each Lady-Sport engine requires 3 hours of manufacturing time. The Des Moines plant has 2100 hours of engine manufacturing time available for the next production period. Embassy's motorcycle frame supplier can supply as many EZ-Rider frames as needed. However, the Lady-Sport frame is more complex and the supplier can only provide up to 280 Lady-Sport frames for the next production period. Final assembly and testing requires 2 hours for each EZ-Rider model and 2.5 hours for each Lady-Sport model. A maximum of 1000 hours of assembly and testing time are available for the next production period. The company's accounting department projects a profit contribution of $2400 for each EZ-Rider produced and $1800 for each Lady-Sport produced.

   a. Formulate a linear programming model that can be used to determine the number of units of each model that should be produced in order to maximize the total contribution to profit.

   b. Solve the problem graphically. What is the optimal solution?

   c. Which constraints are binding?

24. Kelson Sporting Equipment, Inc., makes two different types of baseball gloves: a regular model and a catcher's model. The firm has 900 hours of production time available in its cutting and sewing department, 300 hours available in its finishing department, and 100 hours available in its packaging and shipping department. The production time requirements and the profit contribution per glove are given in the following table:

| | Production Time (hours) | | | |
Model	Cutting and Sewing	Finishing	Packaging and Shipping	Profit/Glove
Regular model	1	$\frac{1}{2}$	$\frac{1}{8}$	$5
Catcher's model	$\frac{3}{2}$	$\frac{1}{3}$	$\frac{1}{4}$	$8

Assuming that the company is interested in maximizing the total profit contribution, answer the following:
  a. What is the linear programming model for this problem?
  b. Find the optimal solution using the graphical solution procedure. How many gloves of each model should Kelson manufacture?
  c. What is the total profit contribution Kelson can earn with the given production quantities?
  d. How many hours of production time will be scheduled in each department?
  e. What is the slack time in each department?

25. George Johnson recently inherited a large sum of money; he wants to use a portion of this money to set up a trust fund for his two children. The trust fund has two investment options: (1) a bond fund and (2) a stock fund. The projected returns over the life of the investments are 6% for the bond fund and 10% for the stock fund. Whatever portion of the inheritance he finally decides to commit to the trust fund, he wants to invest at least 30% of that amount in the bond fund. In addition, he wants to select a mix that will enable him to obtain a total return of at least 7.5%.
  a. Formulate a linear programming model that can be used to determine the percentage that should be allocated to each of the possible investment alternatives.
  b. Solve the problem using the graphical solution procedure.

26. The Sea Wharf Restaurant would like to determine the best way to allocate a monthly advertising budget of $1000 between newspaper advertising and radio advertising. Management decided that at least 25% of the budget must be spent on each type of media, and that the amount of money spent on local newspaper advertising must be at least twice the amount spent on radio advertising. A marketing consultant developed an index that measures audience exposure per dollar of advertising on a scale from 0 to 100, with higher values implying greater audience exposure. If the value of the index for local newspaper advertising is 50 and the value of the index for spot radio advertising is 80, how should the restaurant allocate its advertising budget in order to maximize the value of total audience exposure?
  a. Formulate a linear programming model that can be used to determine how the restaurant should allocate its advertising budget in order to maximize the value of total audience exposure.
  b. Solve the problem using the graphical solution procedure.

27. Blair & Rosen, Inc. (B&R), is a brokerage firm that specializes in investment portfolios designed to meet the specific risk tolerances of its clients. A client who contacted B&R this past week has a maximum of $50,000 to invest. B&R's investment advisor decides to recommend a portfolio consisting of two investment funds: an Internet fund and a Blue

Chip fund. The Internet fund has a projected annual return of 12%, whereas the Blue Chip fund has a projected annual return of 9%. The investment advisor requires that at most $35,000 of the client's funds should be invested in the Internet fund. B&R services include a risk rating for each investment alternative. The Internet fund, which is the more risky of the two investment alternatives, has a risk rating of 6 per thousand dollars invested. The Blue Chip fund has a risk rating of 4 per thousand dollars invested. For example, if $10,000 is invested in each of the two investment funds, B&R's risk rating for the portfolio would be $6(10) + 4(10) = 100$. Finally, B&R developed a questionnaire to measure each client's risk tolerance. Based on the responses, each client is classified as a conservative, moderate, or aggressive investor. Suppose that the questionnaire results classified the current client as a moderate investor. B&R recommends that a client who is a moderate investor limit his or her portfolio to a maximum risk rating of 240.

a. What is the recommended investment portfolio for this client? What is the annual return for the portfolio?

b. Suppose that a second client with $50,000 to invest has been classified as an aggressive investor. B&R recommends that the maximum portfolio risk rating for an aggressive investor is 320. What is the recommended investment portfolio for this aggressive investor? Discuss what happens to the portfolio under the aggressive investor strategy.

c. Suppose that a third client with $50,000 to invest has been classified as a conservative investor. B&R recommends that the maximum portfolio risk rating for a conservative investor is 160. Develop the recommended investment portfolio for the conservative investor. Discuss the interpretation of the slack variable for the total investment fund constraint.

28. Tom's, Inc., produces various Mexican food products and sells them to Western Foods, a chain of grocery stores located in Texas and New Mexico. Tom's, Inc., makes two salsa products: Western Foods Salsa and Mexico City Salsa. Essentially, the two products have different blends of whole tomatoes, tomato sauce, and tomato paste. The Western Foods Salsa is a blend of 50% whole tomatoes, 30% tomato sauce, and 20% tomato paste. The Mexico City Salsa, which has a thicker and chunkier consistency, consists of 70% whole tomatoes, 10% tomato sauce, and 20% tomato paste. Each jar of salsa produced weighs 10 ounces. For the current production period, Tom's, Inc., can purchase up to 280 pounds of whole tomatoes, 130 pounds of tomato sauce, and 100 pounds of tomato paste; the price per pound for these ingredients is $0.96, $0.64, and $0.56, respectively. The cost of the spices and the other ingredients is approximately $0.10 per jar. Tom's, Inc., buys empty glass jars for $0.02 each, and labeling and filling costs are estimated to be $0.03 for each jar of salsa produced. Tom's contract with Western Foods results in sales revenue of $1.64 for each jar of Western Foods Salsa and $1.93 for each jar of Mexico City Salsa.

a. Develop a linear programming model that will enable Tom's to determine the mix of salsa products that will maximize the total profit contribution.

b. Find the optimal solution.

29. AutoIgnite produces electronic ignition systems for automobiles at a plant in Cleveland, Ohio. Each ignition system is assembled from two components produced at AutoIgnite's plants in Buffalo, New York, and Dayton, Ohio. The Buffalo plant can produce 2000 units of component 1, 1000 units of component 2, or any combination of the two components each day. For instance, 60% of Buffalo's production time could be used to produce component 1 and 40% of Buffalo's production time could be used to produce component 2; in this case, the Buffalo plant would be able to produce $0.6(2000) = 1200$ units of component 1 each day and $0.4(1000) = 400$ units of component 2 each day. The Dayton plant can produce 600 units of component 1, 1400 units of component 2, or any combination of the two components each day. At the end of each day, the component production at Buffalo and Dayton is sent to Cleveland for assembly of the ignition systems on the following workday.

a. Formulate a linear programming model that can be used to develop a daily production schedule for the Buffalo and Dayton plants that will maximize daily production of ignition systems at Cleveland.

b. Find the optimal solution.

30. A financial advisor at Diehl Investments identified two companies that are likely candidates for a takeover in the near future. Eastern Cable is a leading manufacturer of flexible cable systems used in the construction industry, and ComSwitch is a new firm specializing in digital switching systems. Eastern Cable is currently trading for $40 per share, and ComSwitch is currently trading for $25 per share. If the takeovers occur, the financial advisor estimates that the price of Eastern Cable will go to $55 per share and ComSwitch will go to $43 per share. At this point in time, the financial advisor has identified ComSwitch as the higher risk alternative. Assume that a client indicated a willingness to invest a maximum of $50,000 in the two companies. The client wants to invest at least $15,000 in Eastern Cable and at least $10,000 in ComSwitch. Because of the higher risk associated with ComSwitch, the financial advisor has recommended that at most $25,000 should be invested in ComSwitch.

a. Formulate a linear programming model that can be used to determine the number of shares of Eastern Cable and the number of shares of ComSwitch that will meet the investment constraints and maximize the total return for the investment.

b. Graph the feasible region.

c. Determine the coordinates of each extreme point.

d. Find the optimal solution.

31. Consider the following linear program:

$$\text{Min} \quad 3A + 4B$$
$$\text{s.t.}$$
$$1A + 3B \geq 6$$
$$1A + 1B \geq 4$$
$$A, B \geq 0$$

Identify the feasible region and find the optimal solution using the graphical solution procedure. What is the value of the objective function?

32. Identify the three extreme-point solutions for the M&D Chemicals problem (see Section 2.5). Identify the value of the objective function and the values of the slack and surplus variables at each extreme point.

33. Consider the following linear programming problem:

$$\text{Min} \quad A + 2B$$
$$\text{s.t.}$$
$$A + 4B \leq 21$$
$$2A + B \geq 7$$
$$3A + 1.5B \leq 21$$
$$-2A + 6B \geq 0$$
$$A, B \geq 0$$

a. Find the optimal solution using the graphical solution procedure and the value of the objective function.

b. Determine the amount of slack or surplus for each constraint.

c. Suppose the objective function is changed to max $5A + 2B$. Find the optimal solution and the value of the objective function.

34. Consider the following linear program:

$$\text{Min} \quad 2A + 2B$$

s.t.

$$1A + 3B \leq 12$$
$$3A + 1B \geq 13$$
$$1A - 1B = 3$$
$$A, B \geq 0$$

a. Show the feasible region.
b. What are the extreme points of the feasible region?
c. Find the optimal solution using the graphical solution procedure.

35. For the linear program

$$\text{Min} \quad 6A + 4B$$

s.t.

$$2A + 1B \geq 12$$
$$1A + 1B \geq 10$$
$$1B \leq 4$$
$$A, B \geq 0$$

a. Write the problem in standard form.
b. Solve the problem using the graphical solution procedure.
c. What are the values of the slack and surplus variables?

36. As part of a quality improvement initiative, Consolidated Electronics employees complete a three-day training program on teaming and a two-day training program on problem solving. The manager of quality improvement has requested that at least 8 training programs on teaming and at least 10 training programs on problem solving be offered during the next six months. In addition, senior-level management has specified that at least 25 training programs must be offered during this period. Consolidated Electronics uses a consultant to teach the training programs. During the next quarter, the consultant has 84 days of training time available. Each training program on teaming costs $10,000 and each training program on problem solving costs $8000.
a. Formulate a linear programming model that can be used to determine the number of training programs on teaming and the number of training programs on problem solving that should be offered in order to minimize total cost.
b. Graph the feasible region.
c. Determine the coordinates of each extreme point.
d. Solve for the minimum cost solution.

37. The New England Cheese Company produces two cheese spreads by blending mild cheddar cheese with extra sharp cheddar cheese. The cheese spreads are packaged in 12-ounce containers, which are then sold to distributors throughout the Northeast. The Regular blend contains 80% mild cheddar and 20% extra sharp, and the Zesty blend contains 60% mild cheddar and 40% extra sharp. This year, a local dairy cooperative offered to provide up to 8100 pounds of mild cheddar cheese for $1.20 per pound and up to 3000 pounds of extra sharp cheddar cheese for $1.40 per pound. The cost to blend and package the cheese spreads, excluding the cost of the cheese, is $0.20 per container. If each container of Regular is sold for $1.95 and each container of Zesty is sold for $2.20, how many containers of Regular and Zesty should New England Cheese produce?

38. Applied Technology, Inc. (ATI), produces bicycle frames using two fiberglass materials that improve the strength-to-weight ratio of the frames. The cost of the standard grade material is $7.50 per yard and the cost of the professional grade material is $9.00 per yard. The standard and professional grade materials contain different amounts of fiberglass, carbon fiber, and Kevlar as shown in the following table:

	Standard Grade	**Professional Grade**
Fiberglass	84%	58%
Carbon fiber	10%	30%
Kevlar	6%	12%

ATI signed a contract with a bicycle manufacturer to produce a new frame with a carbon fiber content of at least 20% and a Kevlar content of not greater than 10%. To meet the required weight specification, a total of 30 yards of material must be used for each frame.

a. Formulate a linear program to determine the number of yards of each grade of fiberglass material that ATI should use in each frame in order to minimize total cost. Define the decision variables and indicate the purpose of each constraint.

b. Use the graphical solution procedure to determine the feasible region. What are the coordinates of the extreme points?

c. Compute the total cost at each extreme point. What is the optimal solution?

d. The distributor of the fiberglass material is currently overstocked with the professional grade material. To reduce inventory, the distributor offered ATI the opportunity to purchase the professional grade for $8 per yard. Will the optimal solution change?

e. Suppose that the distributor further lowers the price of the professional grade material to $7.40 per yard. Will the optimal solution change? What effect would an even lower price for the professional grade material have on the optimal solution? Explain.

39. Innis Investments manages funds for a number of companies and wealthy clients. The investment strategy is tailored to each client's needs. For a new client, Innis has been authorized to invest up to $1.2 million in two investment funds: a stock fund and a money market fund. Each unit of the stock fund costs $50 and provides an annual rate of return of 10%; each unit of the money market fund costs $100 and provides an annual rate of return of 4%.

The client wants to minimize risk subject to the requirement that the annual income from the investment be at least $60,000. According to Innis's risk measurement system, each unit invested in the stock fund has a risk index of 8, and each unit invested in the money market fund has a risk index of 3; the higher risk index associated with the stock fund simply indicates that it is the riskier investment. Innis's client also specified that at least $300,000 be invested in the money market fund.

a. Determine how many units of each fund Innis should purchase for the client to minimize the total risk index for the portfolio.

b. How much annual income will this investment strategy generate?

c. Suppose the client desires to maximize annual return. How should the funds be invested?

40. Photo Chemicals produces two types of photographic developing fluids. Both products cost Photo Chemicals $1 per gallon to produce. Based on an analysis of current inventory levels and outstanding orders for the next month, Photo Chemicals' management specified that at least 30 gallons of product 1 and at least 20 gallons of product 2 must be produced during the next two weeks. Management also stated that an existing inventory of highly perishable raw material required in the production of both fluids must be used within the next two weeks. The current inventory of the perishable raw material is 80 pounds. Although more of this raw material can be ordered if necessary, any of the current inventory that is not used within the next two weeks will spoil—hence, the management requirement that at least 80 pounds be used in the next two weeks. Furthermore, it is known that product 1 requires 1 pound of this perishable raw material per gallon and product 2 requires 2 pounds of the raw material per gallon. Because Photo Chemicals' objective is to keep its production costs at the minimum possible level, the firm's management is looking for a minimum cost production plan that uses all the 80 pounds of perishable raw material and provides at least 30 gallons of product 1 and at least 20 gallons of product 2. What is the minimum cost solution?

41. Southern Oil Company produces two grades of gasoline: regular and premium. The profit contributions are \$0.30 per gallon for regular gasoline and \$0.50 per gallon for premium gasoline. Each gallon of regular gasoline contains 0.3 gallons of grade A crude oil and each gallon of premium gasoline contains 0.6 gallons of grade A crude oil. For the next production period, Southern has 18,000 gallons of grade A crude oil available. The refinery used to produce the gasolines has a production capacity of 50,000 gallons for the next production period. Southern Oil's distributors have indicated that demand for the premium gasoline for the next production period will be at most 20,000 gallons.

   a. Formulate a linear programming model that can be used to determine the number of gallons of regular gasoline and the number of gallons of premium gasoline that should be produced in order to maximize total profit contribution.
   b. What is the optimal solution?
   c. What are the values and interpretations of the slack variables?
   d. What are the binding constraints?

42. Does the following linear program involve infeasibility, unbounded, and/or alternative optimal solutions? Explain.

$$\text{Max} \quad 4A + 8B$$
$$\text{s.t.}$$
$$2A + 2B \leq 10$$
$$-1A + 1B \geq 8$$
$$A, B \geq 0$$

43. Does the following linear program involve infeasibility, unbounded, and/or alternative optimal solutions? Explain.

$$\text{Max} \quad 1A + 1B$$
$$\text{s.t.}$$
$$8A + 6B \geq 24$$
$$2B \geq 4$$
$$A, B \geq 0$$

44. Consider the following linear program:

$$\text{Max} \quad 1A + 1B$$
$$\text{s.t.}$$
$$5A + 3B \leq 15$$
$$3A + 5B \leq 15$$
$$A, B \geq 0$$

    a. What is the optimal solution for this problem?

    b. Suppose that the objective function is changed to $1A + 2B$. Find the new optimal solution.

45. Consider the following linear program:

$$\text{Max} \quad 1A - 2B$$
$$\text{s.t.}$$
$$-4A + 3B \leq 3$$
$$1A - 1B \leq 3$$
$$A, B \geq 0$$

    a. Graph the feasible region for the problem.

    b. Is the feasible region unbounded? Explain.

    c. Find the optimal solution.

    d. Does an unbounded feasible region imply that the optimal solution to the linear program will be unbounded?

46. The manager of a small independent grocery store is trying to determine the best use of her shelf space for soft drinks. The store carries national and generic brands and currently has 200 square feet of shelf space available. The manager wants to allocate at least 60% of the space to the national brands and, regardless of the profitability, allocate at least 10% of the space to the generic brands. How many square feet of space should the manager allocate to the national brands and the generic brands under the following circumstances?

    a. The national brands are more profitable than the generic brands.

    b. Both brands are equally profitable.

    c. The generic brand is more profitable than the national brand.

47. Discuss what happens to the M&D Chemicals problem (see Section 2.5) if the cost per gallon for product A is increased to $3.00 per gallon. What would you recommend? Explain.

48. For the M&D Chemicals problem in Section 2.5, discuss the effect of management's requiring total production of 500 gallons for the two products. List two or three actions M&D should consider to correct the situation you encounter.

49. PharmaPlus operates a chain of 30 pharmacies. The pharmacies are staffed by licensed pharmacists and pharmacy technicians. The company currently employs 85 full-time equivalent pharmacists (combination of full time and part time) and 175 full-time equivalent technicians. Each spring management reviews current staffing levels and makes hiring plans for the year. A recent forecast of the prescription load for the next year shows that at least 250 full-time equivalent employees (pharmacists and technicians) will be required to staff the pharmacies. The personnel department expects 10 pharmacists and 30 technicians to leave over the next year. To accommodate the expected attrition and prepare for future growth, management stated that at least 15 new pharmacists must be hired. In addition, PharmaPlus's new service quality guidelines specify no more than two technicians per licensed pharmacist. The average salary for licensed pharmacists is $40 per hour and the average salary for technicians is $10 per hour.

    a. Determine a minimum-cost staffing plan for PharmaPlus. How many pharmacists and technicians are needed?

    b. Given current staffing levels and expected attrition, how many new hires (if any) must be made to reach the level recommended in part (a)? What will be the impact on the payroll?

50. Expedition Outfitters manufactures a variety of specialty clothing for hiking, skiing, and mountain climbing. Its management decided to begin production on two new parkas designed for use in extremely cold weather: the Mount Everest Parka and the Rocky Mountain Parka. The manufacturing plant has 120 hours of cutting time and 120 hours of sewing time available for producing these two parkas. Each Mount Everest Parka requires 30 minutes of cutting time and 45 minutes of sewing time, and each Rocky Mountain Parka requires 20 minutes of cutting time and 15 minutes of sewing time. The labor and material cost is $150 for each Mount Everest Parka and $50 for each Rocky Mountain Parka, and the retail prices through the firm's mail order catalog are $250 for the Mount Everest Parka and $200 for the Rocky Mountain Parka. Because management believes that the Mount Everest Parka is a unique coat that will enhance the image of the firm, they specified that at least 20% of the total production must consist of this model. Assuming that Expedition Outfitters can sell as many coats of each type as it can produce, how many units of each model should it manufacture to maximize the total profit contribution?

51. English Motors, Ltd. (EML), developed a new all-wheel-drive sports utility vehicle. As part of the marketing campaign, EML produced a video tape sales presentation to send to both owners of current EML four-wheel-drive vehicles as well as to owners of four-wheel-drive sports utility vehicles offered by competitors; EML refers to these two target markets as the current customer market and the new customer market. Individuals who receive the new promotion video will also receive a coupon for a test drive of the new EML model for one weekend. A key factor in the success of the new promotion is the response rate, the percentage of individuals who receive the new promotion and test drive the new model. EML estimates that the response rate for the current customer market is 25% and the response rate for the new customer market is 20%. For the customers who test drive the new model, the sales rate is the percentage of individuals that make a purchase. Marketing research studies indicate that the sales rate is 12% for the current customer market and 20% for the new customer market. The cost for each promotion, excluding the test drive costs, is $4 for each promotion sent to the current customer market and $6 for each promotion sent to the new customer market. Management also specified that a minimum of 30,000 current customers should test drive the new model and a minimum of 10,000 new customers should test drive the new model. In addition, the number of current customers who test drive the new vehicle must be at least twice the number of new customers who test drive the new vehicle. If the marketing budget, excluding test drive costs, is $1.2 million, how many promotions should be sent to each group of customers in order to maximize total sales?

52. Creative Sports Design (CSD) manufactures a standard-size racket and an oversize racket. The firm's rackets are extremely light due to the use of a magnesium-graphite alloy that was invented by the firm's founder. Each standard-size racket uses 0.125 kilograms of the alloy and each oversize racket uses 0.4 kilograms; over the next two-week production period only 80 kilograms of the alloy are available. Each standard-size racket uses 10 minutes of manufacturing time and each oversize racket uses 12 minutes. The profit contributions are $10 for each standard-size racket and $15 for each oversize racket, and 40 hours of manufacturing time are available each week. Management specified that at least 20% of the total production must be the standard-size racket. How many rackets of each type should CSD manufacture over the next two weeks to maximize the total profit contribution? Assume that because of the unique nature of their products, CSD can sell as many rackets as they can produce.

53. Management of High Tech Services (HTS) would like to develop a model that will help allocate their technicians' time between service calls to regular contract customers and new customers. A maximum of 80 hours of technician time is available over the two-week planning period. To satisfy cash flow requirements, at least $800 in revenue (per technician) must be generated during the two-week period. Technician time for regular customers generates $25 per hour. However, technician time for new customers only

generates an average of $8 per hour because in many cases a new customer contact does not provide billable services. To ensure that new customer contacts are being maintained, the technician time spent on new customer contacts must be at least 60% of the time spent on regular customer contacts. Given these revenue and policy requirements, HTS would like to determine how to allocate technician time between regular customers and new customers so that the total number of customers contacted during the two-week period will be maximized. Technicians require an average of 50 minutes for each regular customer contact and 1 hour for each new customer contact.

a. Develop a linear programming model that will enable HTS to allocate technician time between regular customers and new customers.

b. Find the optimal solution.

54. Jackson Hole Manufacturing is a small manufacturer of plastic products used in the automotive and computer industries. One of its major contracts is with a large computer company and involves the production of plastic printer cases for the computer company's portable printers. The printer cases are produced on two injection molding machines. The M-100 machine has a production capacity of 25 printer cases per hour, and the M-200 machine has a production capacity of 40 cases per hour. Both machines use the same chemical material to produce the printer cases; the M-100 uses 40 pounds of the raw material per hour and the M-200 uses 50 pounds per hour. The computer company asked Jackson Hole to produce as many of the cases during the upcoming week as possible; it will pay $18 for each case Jackson Hole can deliver. However, next week is a regularly scheduled vacation period for most of Jackson Hole's production employees; during this time, annual maintenance is performed for all equipment in the plant. Because of the downtime for maintenance, the M-100 will be available for no more than 15 hours, and the M-200 will be available for no more than 10 hours. However, because of the high setup cost involved with both machines, management requires that, each machine must be operated for at least 5 hours. The supplier of the chemical material used in the production process informed Jackson Hole that a maximum of 1000 pounds of the chemical material will be available for next week's production; the cost for this raw material is $6 per pound. In addition to the raw material cost, Jackson Hole estimates that the hourly cost of operating the M-100 and the M-200 are $50 and $75, respectively.

a. Formulate a linear programming model that can be used to maximize the contribution to profit.

b. Find the optimal solution.

55. The Kartick Company is trying to determine how much of each of two products to produce over the coming planning period. There are three departments, A, B and C, with limited labor hours available in each department. Each product must be processed by each department and the per-unit requirements for each product, labor hours available, and per-unit profit are as shown below.

	Labor required in each department		
	Product (hrs./unit)		Labor Hours
Department	Product 1	Product 2	Available
A	1.00	0.30	100
B	0.30	0.12	36
C	0.15	0.56	50
Profit Contribution	$33.00	$24.00	

A linear program for this situation is as follows:

Let
$$x_1 = \text{the amount of product 1 to produce}$$
$$x_2 = \text{the amount of product 2 to produce}$$

Maximize $\quad 33\,x_1 + 24\,x_2$

s.t.

$$1.0\,x_1 + .30\,x_2 \le 100 \qquad \text{Department A}$$
$$.30\,x_1 + .12\,x_2 \le 36 \qquad \text{Department B}$$
$$.15\,x_1 + .56\,x_2 \le 50 \qquad \text{Department C}$$
$$x_1, x_2 \ge 0$$

Mr. Kartick (the owner) used trial and error with a spreadsheet model to arrive at a solution. His proposed solution is $x_1 = 75$ and $x_2 = 60$, as shown below in Figure 2.24. He said he felt his proposed solution is optimal.

Is his solution optimal? Without solving the problem, explain why you believe this solution is optimal or not optimal.

FIGURE 2.24 MR. KARTICK'S TRIAL-AND-ERROR MODEL

	A	B	C	D	E
1	**Kartick**				
2	**Data**				
3				Hours	
4	Department	Prod 1	Prod 2	Available	
5	A	1.00	0.30	100	
6	B	0.30	0.12	36	
7	C	0.15	0.56	50	
8	Per unit				
9	Contribution	$33.00	$24.00		
10					
11	**Decisions**				
12					
13		Prod 1	Prod 2		
14	Quantity	75	60		
15					
16					
17	**Model**				
18		Hours	Unused		
19	Department	Used	Hours		
20	A	93	7		
21	B	29.7	6.3		
22	C	44.85	5.15		
23					
24	Contribution	$3,915.00			

56. Assume you are given a minimization linear program that has an optimal solution. The problem is then modified by changing an equality constraint in the problem to a less-than-or-equal-to constraint. Is it possible that the modified problem is infeasible? Answer yes or no and justify.

57. Assume you are given a minimization linear program that has an optimal solution. The problem is then modified by changing a greater-than-or-equal-to constraint in the problem to a less-than-or-equal-to constraint. Is it possible that the modified problem is infeasible? Answer yes or no and justify.

58. A consultant was hired to build an optimization model for a large marketing research company. The model is based on a consumer survey that was taken in which each person was asked to rank 30 new products in descending order based on their likelihood of purchasing the product. The consultant was assigned the task of building a model that selects the minimum number of products (which would then be introduced into the marketplace) such that the first, second, and third choice of every subject in the survey is included in the list of selected products. While building a model to figure out which products to introduce, the consultant's boss walked up to her and said: "Look, if the model tells us we need to introduce more than 15 products, then add a constraint which limits the number of new products to 15 or less. It's too expensive to introduce more than 15 new products." Evaluate this statement in terms of what you have learned so far about constrained optimization models.

Case Problem 1   WORKLOAD BALANCING

Digital Imaging (DI) produces photo printers for both the professional and consumer markets. The DI consumer division recently introduced two photo printers that provide color prints rivaling those produced by a professional processing lab. The DI-910 model can produce a 4" × 6" borderless print in approximately 37 seconds. The more sophisticated and faster DI-950 can even produce a 13" × 19" borderless print. Financial projections show profit contributions of $42 for each DI-910 and $87 for each DI-950.

The printers are assembled, tested, and packaged at DI's plant located in New Bern, North Carolina. This plant is highly automated and uses two manufacturing lines to produce the printers. Line 1 performs the assembly operation with times of 3 minutes per DI-910 printer and 6 minutes per DI-950 printer. Line 2 performs both the testing and packaging operations. Times are 4 minutes per DI-910 printer and 2 minutes per DI-950 printer. The shorter time for the DI-950 printer is a result of its faster print speed. Both manufacturing lines are in operation one 8-hour shift per day.

Managerial Report

Perform an analysis for Digital Imaging in order to determine how many units of each printer to produce. Prepare a report to DI's president presenting your findings and recommendations. Include (but do not limit your discussion to) a consideration of the following:

1. The recommended number of units of each printer to produce to maximize the total contribution to profit for an 8-hour shift. What reasons might management have for not implementing your recommendation?

2. Suppose that management also states that the number of DI-910 printers produced must be at least as great as the number of DI-950 units produced. Assuming that the objective is to maximize the total contribution to profit for an 8-hour shift, how many units of each printer should be produced?

3. Does the solution you developed in part (2) balance the total time spent on line 1 and the total time spent on line 2? Why might this balance or lack of it be a concern to management?

4. Management requested an expansion of the model in part (2) that would provide a better balance between the total time on line 1 and the total time on line 2. Management wants to limit the difference between the total time on line 1 and the total time on line 2 to 30 minutes or less. If the objective is still to maximize the total contribution to profit, how many units of each printer should be produced? What effect does this workload balancing have on total profit in part (2)?

5. Suppose that in part (1) management specified the objective of maximizing the total number of printers produced each shift rather than total profit contribution. With this objective, how many units of each printer should be produced per shift? What effect does this objective have on total profit and workload balancing?

For each solution that you develop, include a copy of your linear programming model and graphical solution in the appendix to your report.

Case Problem 2   PRODUCTION STRATEGY

Better Fitness, Inc. (BFI), manufactures exercise equipment at its plant in Freeport, Long Island. It recently designed two universal weight machines for the home exercise market. Both machines use BFI-patented technology that provides the user with an extremely wide range of motion capability for each type of exercise performed. Until now, such capabilities have been available only on expensive weight machines used primarily by physical therapists.

At a recent trade show, demonstrations of the machines resulted in significant dealer interest. In fact, the number of orders that BFI received at the trade show far exceeded its manufacturing capabilities for the current production period. As a result, management decided to begin production of the two machines. The two machines, which BFI named the BodyPlus 100 and the BodyPlus 200, require different amounts of resources to produce.

The BodyPlus 100 consists of a frame unit, a press station, and a pec-dec station. Each frame produced uses 4 hours of machining and welding time and 2 hours of painting and finishing time. Each press station requires 2 hours of machining and welding time and 1 hour of painting and finishing time, and each pec-dec station uses 2 hours of machining and welding time and 2 hours of painting and finishing time. In addition, 2 hours are spent assembling, testing, and packaging each BodyPlus 100. The raw material costs are $450 for each frame, $300 for each press station, and $250 for each pec-dec station; packaging costs are estimated to be $50 per unit.

The BodyPlus 200 consists of a frame unit, a press station, a pec-dec station, and a leg-press station. Each frame produced uses 5 hours of machining and welding time and 4 hours of painting and finishing time. Each press station requires 3 hours machining and welding time and 2 hours of painting and finishing time, each pec-dec station uses 2 hours of machining and welding time and 2 hours of painting and finishing time, and each leg-press station requires 2 hours of machining and welding time and 2 hours of painting and finishing time. In addition, 2 hours are spent assembling, testing, and packaging each Body-Plus 200. The raw material costs are $650 for each frame, $400 for each press station, $250 for each pec-dec station, and $200 for each leg-press station; packaging costs are estimated to be $75 per unit.

For the next production period, management estimates that 600 hours of machining and welding time, 450 hours of painting and finishing time, and 140 hours of assembly, testing, and packaging time will be available. Current labor costs are $20 per hour for machining and welding time, $15 per hour for painting and finishing time, and $12 per hour for assembly, testing, and packaging time. The market in which the two machines must compete suggests a retail price of $2400 for the BodyPlus 100 and $3500 for the BodyPlus 200, although some flexibility may be available to BFI because of the unique capabilities of the new machines. Authorized BFI dealers can purchase machines for 70% of the suggested retail price.

BFI's president believes that the unique capabilities of the BodyPlus 200 can help position BFI as one of the leaders in high-end exercise equipment. Consequently, he has stated that the number of units of the BodyPlus 200 produced must be at least 25% of the total production.

Managerial Report

Analyze the production problem at Better Fitness, Inc., and prepare a report for BFI's president presenting your findings and recommendations. Include (but do not limit your discussion to) a consideration of the following items:

1. What is the recommended number of BodyPlus 100 and BodyPlus 200 machines to produce?
2. How does the requirement that the number of units of the BodyPlus 200 produced be at least 25% of the total production affect profits?
3. Where should efforts be expended in order to increase profits?

Include a copy of your linear programming model and graphical solution in an appendix to your report.

Case Problem 3   HART VENTURE CAPITAL

Hart Venture Capital (HVC) specializes in providing venture capital for software development and Internet applications. Currently HVC has two investment opportunities: (1) Security Systems, a firm that needs additional capital to develop an Internet security software package, and (2) Market Analysis, a market research company that needs additional capital to develop a software package for conducting customer satisfaction surveys. In exchange for Security Systems stock, the firm has asked HVC to provide $600,000 in year 1, $600,000 in year 2, and $250,000 in year 3 over the coming three-year period. In exchange for their stock, Market Analysis has asked HVC to provide $500,000 in year 1, $350,000 in year 2, and $400,000 in year 3 over the same three-year period. HVC believes that both investment opportunities are worth pursuing. However, because of other investments, they are willing to commit at most $800,000 for both projects in the first year, at most $700,000 in the second year, and $500,000 in the third year.

HVC's financial analysis team reviewed both projects and recommended that the company's objective should be to maximize the net present value of the total investment in Security Systems and Market Analysis. The net present value takes into account the estimated value of the stock at the end of the three-year period as well as the capital outflows that are necessary during each of the three years. Using an 8% rate of return, HVC's financial analysis team estimates that 100% funding of the Security Systems project has a net present value of $1,800,000, and 100% funding of the Market Analysis project has a net present value of $1,600,000.

HVC has the option to fund any percentage of the Security Systems and Market Analysis projects. For example, if HVC decides to fund 40% of the Security Systems project, investments of 0.40($600,000) = $240,000 would be required in year 1, 0.40($600,000) = $240,000 would be required in year 2, and 0.40($250,000) = $100,000 would be required in year 3. In this case, the net present value of the Security Systems project would be 0.40($1,800,000) = $720,000. The investment amounts and the net present value for partial funding of the Market Analysis project would be computed in the same manner.

Managerial Report

Perform an analysis of HVC's investment problem and prepare a report that presents your findings and recommendations. Include (but do not limit your discussion to) a consideration of the following items:

1. What is the recommended percentage of each project that HVC should fund and the net present value of the total investment?
2. What capital allocation plan for Security Systems and Market Analysis for the coming three-year period and the total HVC investment each year would you recommend?
3. What effect, if any, would HVC's willingness to commit an additional $100,000 during the first year have on the recommended percentage of each project that HVC should fund?
4. What would the capital allocation plan look like if an additional $100,000 is made available?
5. What is your recommendation as to whether HVC should commit the additional $100,000 in the first year?

Provide model details and relevant computer output in a report appendix.

Appendix 2.1   SOLVING LINEAR PROGRAMS WITH LINGO

LINGO is a product of LINDO Systems. It was developed by Linus E. Schrage and Kevin Cunningham at the University of Chicago.

In this appendix we describe how to use LINGO to solve the Par, Inc., problem. When you start LINGO, two windows are immediately displayed. The outer or main frame window contains all the command menus and the command toolbar. The smaller window is the model window; this window is used to enter and edit the linear programming model you want to solve. The first item we enter into the model window is the objective function. Recall that the objective function for the Par, Inc., problem is Max $10S + 9D$. Thus, in the first line of the LINGO model window, we enter the following expression:

$$MAX = 10*S + 9*D;$$

Note that in LINGO the symbol * is used to denote multiplication and that the objective function line ends with a semicolon. In general, each mathematical expression (objective function and constraints) in LINGO is terminated with a semicolon.

Next, we press the enter key to move to a new line. The first constraint in the Par, Inc., problem is $0.7S + 1D \leq 630$. Thus, in the second line of the LINGO model window we enter the following expression:

$$0.7*S + 1*D <= 630$$

Note that LINGO interprets the <= symbol as $\leq$. Alternatively, we could enter < instead of <=. As was the case when entering the objective function, a semicolon is required at the end of the first constraint. Pressing the enter key moves us to a new line as we continue the process by entering the remaining constraints as shown here:

$$0.5*S + \tfrac{5}{6}*D <= 600$$
$$1*S + \tfrac{2}{3}*D <= 708$$
$$0.1*S + 0.25*D <= 135$$

The model window will now appear as follows:

$$\text{MAX} = 10*S + 9*D$$
$$0.7*S + 1*D <= 630$$
$$0.5*S + \tfrac{5}{6}*D <= 600$$
$$1*S + \tfrac{2}{3}*D <= 708$$
$$0.1*S + 0.25*D <= 135$$

When entering a fraction into LINGO it is not necessary to convert the fraction into an equivalent or rounded decimal number. For example, simply enter the fraction $\tfrac{2}{3}$ into LINGO as $\tfrac{2}{3}$ and do not worry about converting to a decimal or how many decimal places to use. Enter $\tfrac{7}{10}$ either as $\tfrac{7}{10}$ or .7. Let LINGO act as a calculator for you.

LINGO is very flexible about the format of an equation and it is not necessary to have the variables on the left hand side of an equation and the constant term on the right. For example,

$$0.7*S + 1*D <= 630$$

could also be entered as

$$0.7*S <= 630 - 1*D$$

This feature will be very useful later when writing models in a clear and understandable form. Finally, note that although we have expressly included a coefficient of 1 on the variable D above, this is not necessary. In LINGO, 1*D and D are equivalent.

If you make an error in entering the model, you can correct it at any time by simply positioning the cursor where you made the error and entering the necessary correction.

To solve the model, select the Solve command from the LINGO menu or press the Solve button on the toolbar at the top of the main frame window. LINGO will begin the solution process by determining whether the model conforms to all syntax requirements. If the LINGO model doesn't pass these tests, you will be informed by an error message. If LINGO does not find any errors in the model input, it will begin to solve the model. As part of the solution process, LINGO displays a Solver Status window that allows you to monitor the progress of the solver. LINGO displays the solution in a new window titled "Solution Report." The output that appears in the Solution Report window for the Par, Inc., problem is shown in Figure 2.25.

The first part of the output shown in Figure 2.25 indicates that an optimal solution has been found and that the value of the objective function is 7668. We see that the optimal solution is $S = 540$ and $D = 252$, and that the slack variables for the four constraints (rows 2–5) are 0, 120, 0, and 18. We will discuss the use of the information in the Reduced Cost column and the Dual Price column in Chapter 3 when we study the topic of sensitivity analysis.

FIGURE 2.25 PAR, INC., SOLUTION REPORT USING LINGO

```
Global optimal solution found.
Objective value:                            7668.000
Total solver iterations:                          2

          Variable              Value          Reduced Cost
        --------------      --------------      ----------------
                 S            540.0000             0.000000
                 D            252.0000             0.000000

              Row      Slack or Surplus          Dual Price
        --------------      --------------      ----------------
                 1            7668.000             1.000000
                 2            0.000000             4.375000
                 3            120.0000             0.000000
                 4            0.000000             6.937500
                 5            18.00000             0.000000
```

Appendix 2.2   SOLVING LINEAR PROGRAMS WITH EXCEL

In this appendix we will use an Excel worksheet to solve the Par, Inc., linear programming problem. We will enter the problem data for the Par problem in the top part of the worksheet and develop the linear programming model in the bottom part of the worksheet.

Formulation

Whenever we formulate a worksheet model of a linear program, we perform the following steps:

Step 1.   Enter the problem data in the top part of the worksheet.
Step 2.   Specify cell locations for the decision variables.
Step 3.   Select a cell and enter a formula for computing the value of the objective function.
Step 4.   Select a cell and enter a formula for computing the left-hand side of each constraint.
Step 5.   Select a cell and enter a formula for computing the right-hand side of each constraint.

The formula worksheet that we developed for the Par, Inc., problem using these five steps is shown in Figure 2.26. Note that the worksheet consists of two sections: a data section and a model section. The four components of the model are screened, and the cells reserved for the decision variables are enclosed in a boldface box. Figure 2.26 is called a formula worksheet because it displays the formulas that we have entered and not the values computed from those formulas. In a moment we will see how Excel's Solver is used to find the optimal solution to the Par, Inc., problem. But first, let's review each of the preceding steps as they apply to the Par, Inc., problem.

Step 1.   Enter the problem data in the top part of the worksheet.
          Cells B5:C8 show the production requirements per unit for each product. Note that in cells C6 and C7, we have entered the exact fractions. That is, in cell C6 we have entered $=\frac{5}{6}$ and in cell C7 we have entered $=\frac{2}{3}$.

FIGURE 2.26   FORMULA WORKSHEET FOR THE PAR, INC., PROBLEM

	A	B	C	D
1	Par, Inc.			
2				
3		**Production Time**		
4	**Operation**	**Standard**	**Deluxe**	**Time Available**
5	Cutting and Dyeing	0.7	1	630
6	Sewing	0.5	0.83333	600
7	Finishing	1	0.66667	708
8	Inspection and Packaging	0.1	0.25	135
9	**Profit Per Bag**	10	9	
10				
11				
12	**Model**			
13				
14		**Decision Variables**		
15		**Standard**	**Deluxe**	
16	**Bags Produced**			
17				
18	**Maximize Total Profit**	=B9*B16+C9*C16		
19				
20	**Constraints**	**Hours Used (LHS)**		**Hours Available (RHS)**
21	Cutting and Dyeing	=B5*B16+C5*C16	<=	=D5
22	Sewing	=B6*B16+C6*C16	<=	=D6
23	Finishing	=B7*B16+C7*C16	<=	=D7
24	Inspection and Packaging	=B8*B16+C8*C16	<=	=D8

Cells B9:C9 show the profit contribution per unit for the two products.

Cells D5:D8 show the number of hours available in each department.

Step 2. Specify cell locations for the decision variables.

Cell B16 will contain the number of standard bags produced, and cell C16 will contain the number of deluxe bags produced.

Step 3. Select a cell and enter a formula for computing the value of the objective function.

Cell B18: =B9*B16+C9*C16

Step 4. Select a cell and enter a formula for computing the left-hand side of each constraint.

With four constraints, we have

Cell B21: =B5*B16+C5*C16
Cell B22: =B6*B16+C6*C16
Cell B23: =B7*B16+C7*C16
Cell B24: =B8*B16+C8*C16

Step 5. Select a cell and enter a formula for computing the right-hand side of each constraint.

With four constraints, we have

Cell D21: =D5
Cell D22: =D6
Cell D23: =D7
Cell D24: =D8

Note that descriptive labels make the model section of the worksheet easier to read and understand. For example, we added "Standard," "Deluxe," and "Bags Produced" in rows 15 and 16 so that the values of the decision variables appearing in cells B16 and C16 can be easily interpreted. In addition, we entered "Maximize Total Profit" in cell A18 to indicate that the value of the objective function appearing in cell B18 is the maximum profit contribution. In the constraint section of the worksheet we added the constraint names as well as the "$<=$" symbols to show the relationship that exists between the left-hand side and the right-hand side of each constraint. Although these descriptive labels are not necessary to use Excel Solver to find a solution to the Par, Inc., problem, the labels make it easier for the user to understand and interpret the optimal solution.

Appendix A provides a discussion of how to properly build and structure a good spreadsheet model.

Excel Solution

The standard Excel Solver developed by Frontline Systems can be used to solve all of the linear programming problems presented in this text.

The following steps describe how Excel Solver can be used to obtain the optimal solution to the Par, Inc., problem:

Step 1. Select the **Data tab** on the **Ribbon**
Step 2. Select **Solver** from the **Analysis Group**
Step 3. When the **Solver Parameters** dialog box appears (see Figure 2.27):
    Enter B18 into the **Set Target Cell** box
    Select the **Equal To: Max** option
    Enter B16:C16 into the **By Changing Cells** box
Step 4. Select **Add**
    When the **Add Constraint** dialog box appears:
    Enter B21:B24 in the left-hand box of the **Cell Reference** area
    Select <= from the middle drop-down button.
    Enter D21:D24 in the **Constraint** area
    Click **OK**
Step 5. When the **Solver Parameters** dialog box reappears:
    Choose **Options**
Step 6. When the **Solver Options** dialog box appears:
    Select **Assume Linear Model**
    Select **Assume Non-Negative**
    Click **OK**
Step 7. When the **Solver Parameters** dialog box appears:
    Choose **Solve**
Step 8. When the **Solver Results** dialog box appears:
    Select **Keep Solver Solution**
    Click **OK**

Figure 2.27 shows the completed **Solver Parameters** dialog box, and Figure 2.28 shows the optimal solution in the worksheet. The optimal solution of 540 standard bags and 252 deluxe bags is the same as we obtained using the graphical solution procedure. In addition to the output information shown in Figure 2.28, Solver has an option to provide sensitivity analysis information. We discuss sensitivity analysis in Chapter 3.

In Step 6 we selected the **Assume Non-Negative** option in the **Solver Options** dialog box to avoid having to enter nonnegativity constraints for the decision variables. In general, whenever we want to solve a linear programming model in which the decision variables are

FIGURE 2.27   SOLVER PARAMETERS DIALOG BOX FOR THE PAR, INC., PROBLEM

FIGURE 2.28   EXCEL SOLUTION FOR THE PAR, INC., PROBLEM

	A	B	C	D
4	**Operation**	**Standard**	**Deluxe**	**Time Available**
5	Cutting and Dyeing	0.7	1	630
6	Sewing	0.5	0.833333333	600
7	Finishing	1	0.666666667	708
8	Inspection and Packaging	0.1	0.25	135
9	**Profit Per Bag**	10	9	
10				
11				
12	**Model**			
13				
14		**Decision Variables**		
15		**Standard**	**Deluxe**	
16	**Bags Produced**	540.00000	252.00000	
17				
18	**Maximize Total Profit**	7668		
19				
20	**Constraints**	**Hours Used (LHS)**		**Hours Available (RHS)**
21	Cutting and Dyeing	630	<=	630
22	Sewing	480.00000	<=	600
23	Finishing	708	<=	708
24	Inspection and Packaging	117.00000	<=	135

all restricted to be nonnegative, we will select this option. In addition, in Step 4 we entered all four less-than-or-equal-to constraints simultaneously by entering B21:B24 in the left-hand box of the **Cell Reference** area, selecting $<=$, and entering D21:D24 in the right-hand box. Alternatively, we could have entered the four constraints one at a time.

As a reminder, when entering a fraction into Excel, it is not necessary to convert the fraction into an equivalent or rounded decimal number. For example, simply enter the fraction $2/3$ into Excel as $=2/3$ and do not worry about converting to a decimal or how many decimal places to use. Enter $7/10$ either as $=7/10$ or $=.7$. When entering a fraction, the "$=$" sign is necessary; otherwise, Excel will treat the fraction as text rather than a number.

CHAPTER 3

Linear Programming: Sensitivity Analysis and Interpretation of Solution

CONTENTS

3.1 INTRODUCTION TO SENSITIVITY ANALYSIS

3.2 GRAPHICAL SENSITIVITY ANALYSIS
Objective Function Coefficients
Right-Hand Sides

3.3 SENSITIVITY ANALYSIS: COMPUTER SOLUTION
Interpretation of Computer Output
Cautionary Note on the Interpretation of Dual Values
The Modified Par, Inc., Problem

3.4 LIMITATIONS OF CLASSICAL SENSITIVITY ANALYSIS
Simultaneous Changes
Changes in Constraint Coefficients
Nonintuitive Dual Values

3.5 THE ELECTRONIC COMMUNICATIONS PROBLEM
Problem Formulation
Computer Solution and Interpretation

Sensitivity analysis is the study of how the changes in the coefficients of an optimization model affect the optimal solution. Using sensitivity analysis, we can answer questions such as the following:

1. How will a change *in a coefficient of the objective function* affect the optimal solution?
2. How will a change in the *right-hand-side value for a constraint* affect the optimal solution?

Because sensitivity analysis is concerned with how these changes affect the optimal solution, the analysis does not begin until the optimal solution to the original linear programming problem has been obtained. For that reason, sensitivity analysis is often referred to as *postoptimality analysis.*

Our approach to sensitivity analysis parallels the approach used to introduce linear programming in Chapter 2. We begin by showing how a graphical method can be used to perform sensitivity analysis for linear programming problems with two decision variables. Then, we show how optimization software provides sensitivity analysis information.

Finally, we extend the discussion of problem formulation started in Chapter 2 by formulating and solving three larger linear programming problems. In discussing the solution for each of these problems, we focus on managerial interpretation of the optimal solution and sensitivity analysis information.

MANAGEMENT SCIENCE IN ACTION

ASSIGNING PRODUCTS TO WORLDWIDE FACILITIES AT EASTMAN KODAK*

One of the major planning issues at Eastman Kodak involves the determination of which products should be manufactured at Kodak's facilities located throughout the world. The assignment of products to facilities is called the "world load." In determining the world load, Kodak faces a number of interesting trade-offs. For instance, not all manufacturing facilities are equally efficient for all products, and the margins by which some facilities are better varies from product to product. In addition to manufacturing costs, the transportation costs and the effects of duty and duty drawbacks can significantly affect the allocation decision.

To assist in determining the world load, Kodak developed a linear programming model that accounts for the physical nature of the distribution problem and the various costs (manufacturing, transportation, and duties) involved. The model's objective is to minimize the total cost subject to constraints such as satisfying demand and capacity constraints for each facility.

The linear programming model is a static representation of the problem situation, and the real world is always changing. Thus, the linear programming model must be used in a dynamic way. For instance, when demand expectations change, the model can be used to determine the effect the change will have on the world load. Suppose that the currency of country A rises compared to the currency of country B. How should the world load be modified? In addition to using the linear programming model in a "how-to-react" mode, the model is useful in a more active mode by considering questions such as the following: Is it worthwhile for facility F to spend *d* dollars to lower the unit manufacturing cost of product P from *x* to *y*? The linear programming model helps Kodak evaluate the overall effect of possible changes at any facility.

In the final analysis, managers recognize that they cannot use the model by simply turning it on, reading the results, and executing the solution. The model's recommendation combined with managerial judgment provide the final decision.

*Based on information provided by Greg Sampson of Eastman Kodak.

Sensitivity analysis and the interpretation of the optimal solution are important aspects of applying linear programming. The Management Science in Action, Assigning Products to Worldwide Facilities at Eastman Kodak, shows some of the sensitivity analysis and interpretation issues encountered at Kodak in determining the optimal product assignments. Later in the chapter, other Management Science in Action articles illustrate how Performance Analysis Corporation uses sensitivity analysis as part of an evaluation model for a chain of fast-food outlets, how GE Plastics uses a linear programming model involving thousands of variables and constraints to determine optimal production quantities, how the Nutrition Coordinating Center of the University of Minnesota uses a linear programming model to estimate the nutrient amounts in new food products, and how Duncan Industries Limited's linear programming model for tea distribution convinced management of the benefits of using quantitative analysis techniques to support the decision-making process.

3.1   INTRODUCTION TO SENSITIVITY ANALYSIS

Sensitivity analysis is important to decision makers because real-world problems exist in a changing environment. Prices of raw materials change, product demand changes, companies purchase new machinery, stock prices fluctuate, employee turnover occurs, and so on. If a linear programming model has been used in such an environment, we can expect some of the coefficients to change over time. We will then want to determine how these changes affect the optimal solution to the original linear programming problem. Sensitivity analysis provides us with the information needed to respond to such changes without requiring the complete solution of a revised linear program.

Recall the Par, Inc., problem:

$$\text{Max} \quad 10S + 9D$$

s.t.

$$\frac{7}{10}S + 1D \leq 630 \quad \text{Cutting and dyeing}$$
$$\frac{1}{2}S + \frac{5}{6}D \leq 600 \quad \text{Sewing}$$
$$1S + \frac{2}{3}D \leq 708 \quad \text{Finishing}$$
$$\frac{1}{10}S + \frac{1}{4}D \leq 135 \quad \text{Inspection and packaging}$$
$$S, D \geq 0$$

The optimal solution, $S = 540$ standard bags and $D = 252$ deluxe bags, was based on profit contribution figures of $10 per standard bag and $9 per deluxe bag. Suppose we later learn that a price reduction causes the profit contribution for the standard bag to fall from $10 to $8.50. Sensitivity analysis can be used to determine whether the production schedule calling for 540 standard bags and 252 deluxe bags is still best. If it is, solving a modified linear programming problem with $8.50S + 9D$ as the new objective function will not be necessary.

Sensitivity analysis can also be used to determine which coefficients in a linear programming model are crucial. For example, suppose that management believes the $9 profit contribution for the deluxe bag is only a rough estimate of the profit contribution that will actually be obtained. If sensitivity analysis shows that 540 standard bags and 252 deluxe bags will be the optimal solution as long as the profit contribution for the deluxe bag is between $6.67 and $14.29, management should feel comfortable with the $9-per-bag estimate and the recommended production quantities. However, if sensitivity analysis shows that 540 standard bags and 252 deluxe bags will be the optimal solution only if the profit contribution for the deluxe bags is between $8.90 and $9.25, management may want to review the accuracy of the $9-per-bag estimate. Management would especially want to consider how the optimal production quantities should be revised if the profit contribution per deluxe bag were to drop.

Another aspect of sensitivity analysis concerns changes in the right-hand-side values of the constraints. Recall that in the Par, Inc., problem the optimal solution used all available time in the cutting and dyeing department and the finishing department. What would happen to the optimal solution and total profit contribution if Par could obtain additional quantities of either of these resources? Sensitivity analysis can help determine how much each additional hour of production time is worth and how many hours can be added before diminishing returns set in.

3.2   GRAPHICAL SENSITIVITY ANALYSIS

For linear programming problems with two decision variables, graphical solution methods can be used to perform sensitivity analysis on the objective function coefficients and the right-hand-side values for the constraints.

Objective Function Coefficients

Let us consider how changes in the objective function coefficients might affect the optimal solution to the Par, Inc., problem. The current contribution to profit is $10 per unit for the standard bag and $9 per unit for the deluxe bag. It seems obvious that an increase in the profit contribution for one of the bags might lead management to increase production of that bag, and a decrease in the profit contribution for one of the bags might lead management to decrease production of that bag. It is not as obvious, however, how much the profit contribution would have to change before management would want to change the production quantities.

The current optimal solution to this problem calls for producing 540 standard golf bags and 252 deluxe golf bags. The **range of optimality** for each objective function coefficient provides the range of values over which the current solution will remain optimal. Managerial attention should be focused on those objective function coefficients that have a narrow range of optimality and coefficients near the end points of the range. With these coefficients, a small change can necessitate modifying the optimal solution. Let us now compute the ranges of optimality for this problem.

Figure 3.1 shows the graphical solution. A careful inspection of this graph shows that as long as the slope of the objective function line is between the slope of line A (which coincides with the cutting and dyeing constraint line) and the slope of line B (which coincides with the finishing constraint line), extreme point ③ with $S = 540$ and $D = 252$ will be optimal. Changing an objective function coefficient for S or D will cause the slope of the objective function line to change. In Figure 3.1 we see that such changes cause the objective function line to rotate around extreme point ③. However, as long as the objective function line stays within the shaded region, extreme point ③ will remain optimal.

Rotating the objective function line *counterclockwise* causes the slope to become less negative, and the slope increases. When the objective function line rotates counterclockwise (slope increased) enough to coincide with line A, we obtain alternative optimal solutions between extreme points ③ and ④. Any further counterclockwise rotation of the objective function line will cause extreme point ③ to be nonoptimal. Hence, the slope of line A provides an upper limit for the slope of the objective function line.

Rotating the objective function line *clockwise* causes the slope to become more negative, and the slope decreases. When the objective function line rotates clockwise (slope decreases) enough to coincide with line B, we obtain alternative optimal solutions between extreme points ③ and ②. Any further clockwise rotation of the objective function line

The slope of the objective function line usually is negative; hence, rotating the objective function line clockwise makes the line steeper even though the slope is getting smaller (more negative).

FIGURE 3.1   GRAPHICAL SOLUTION OF PAR, INC., PROBLEM WITH SLOPE OF
OBJECTIVE FUNCTION LINE BETWEEN SLOPES OF LINES A AND B;
EXTREME POINT ③ IS OPTIMAL

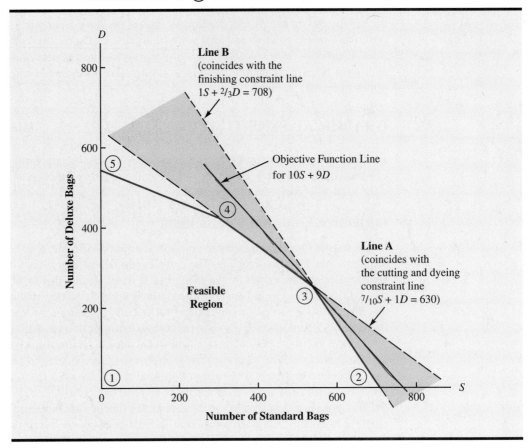

will cause extreme point ③ to be nonoptimal. Hence, the slope of line B provides a lower limit for the slope of the objective function line.

Thus, extreme point ③ will be the optimal solution as long as

Slope of line B ≤ slope of the objective function line ≤ slope of line A

In Figure 3.1 we see that the equation for line A, the cutting and dyeing constraint line, is as follows:

$$\tfrac{7}{10}S + 1D = 630$$

By solving this equation for D, we can write the equation for line A in its slope-intercept form, which yields

$$D = -\tfrac{7}{10}S + 630$$

↑ Slope of line A   ↑ Intercept of line A on D axis

Thus, the slope for line A is $-\tfrac{7}{10}$, and its intercept on the D axis is 630.

The equation for line B in Figure 3.1 is

$$1S + \tfrac{2}{3}D = 708$$

Solving for D provides the slope-intercept form for line B. Doing so yields

$$\tfrac{2}{3}D = -1S + 708$$
$$D = -\tfrac{3}{2}S + 1062$$

Thus, the slope of line B is $-\tfrac{3}{2}$, and its intercept on the D axis is 1062.

Now that the slopes of lines A and B have been computed, we see that for extreme point ③ to remain optimal we must have

$$-\tfrac{3}{2} \leq \text{slope of objective function} \leq -\tfrac{7}{10} \qquad (3.1)$$

Let us now consider the general form of the slope of the objective function line. Let C_S denote the profit of a standard bag, C_D denote the profit of a deluxe bag, and P denote the value of the objective function. Using this notation, the objective function line can be written as

$$P = C_S S + C_D D$$

Writing this equation in slope-intercept form, we obtain

$$C_D D = -C_S S + P$$

and

$$D = -\frac{C_S}{C_D} S + \frac{P}{C_D}$$

Thus, we see that the slope of the objective function line is given by $-C_S/C_D$. Substituting $-C_S/C_D$ into expression (3.1), we see that extreme point ③ will be optimal as long as the following expression is satisfied:

$$-\tfrac{3}{2} \leq -\frac{C_S}{C_D} \leq -\tfrac{7}{10} \qquad (3.2)$$

To compute the range of optimality for the standard-bag profit contribution, we hold the profit contribution for the deluxe bag fixed at its initial value $C_D = 9$. Doing so in expression (3.2), we obtain

$$-\tfrac{3}{2} \leq -\frac{C_S}{9} \leq -\tfrac{7}{10}$$

From the left-hand inequality, we have

$$-\tfrac{3}{2} \leq -\frac{C_S}{9} \qquad \text{or} \qquad \tfrac{3}{2} \geq \frac{C_S}{9}$$

Thus,

$$\tfrac{27}{2} \geq C_S \qquad \text{or} \qquad C_S \leq \tfrac{27}{2} = 13.5$$

From the right-hand inequality, we have

$$-\frac{C_S}{9} \leq -\tfrac{7}{10} \qquad \text{or} \qquad \frac{C_S}{9} \geq \tfrac{7}{10}$$

Thus,

$$C_S \geq \tfrac{63}{10} \qquad \text{or} \qquad C_S \geq 6.3$$

Combining the calculated limits for C_S provides the following range of optimality for the standard-bag profit contribution:

$$6.3 \leq C_S \leq 13.5$$

In the original problem for Par, Inc., the standard bag had a profit contribution of $10. The resulting optimal solution was 540 standard bags and 252 deluxe bags. The range of optimality for C_S tells Par's management that, with other coefficients unchanged, the profit contribution for the standard bag can be anywhere between $6.30 and $13.50 and the production quantities of 540 standard bags and 252 deluxe bags will remain optimal. Note, however, that even though the production quantities will not change, the total profit contribution (value of objective function) will change due to the change in profit contribution per standard bag.

These computations can be repeated, holding the profit contribution for standard bags constant at $C_S = 10$. In this case, the range of optimality for the deluxe-bag profit contribution can be determined. Check to see that this range is $6.67 \leq C_D \leq 14.29$.

In cases where the rotation of the objective function line about an optimal extreme point causes the objective function line to become *vertical*, there will be either no upper limit or no lower limit for the slope as it appears in the form of expression (3.2). To show how this special situation can occur, suppose that the objective function for the Par, Inc., problem is $18C_S + 9C_D$; in this case, extreme point ② in Figure 3.2 provides the optimal solution. Rotating the objective function line counterclockwise around extreme point ② provides an upper limit for the slope when the objective function line coincides with line B. We showed previously that the slope of line B is $-\tfrac{3}{2}$, so the upper limit for the slope of the objective function line must be $-\tfrac{3}{2}$. However, rotating the objective function line clockwise results in the slope becoming more and more negative, approaching a value of minus infinity as the objective function line becomes vertical; in this case, the slope of the objective function has no lower limit. Using the upper limit of $-\tfrac{3}{2}$, we can write

$$-\frac{C_S}{C_D} \leq -\tfrac{3}{2}$$

Slope of the
objective function line

FIGURE 3.2   GRAPHICAL SOLUTION OF PAR, INC., PROBLEM WITH AN OBJECTIVE
FUNCTION OF $18S + 9D$; OPTIMAL SOLUTION AT EXTREME POINT ②

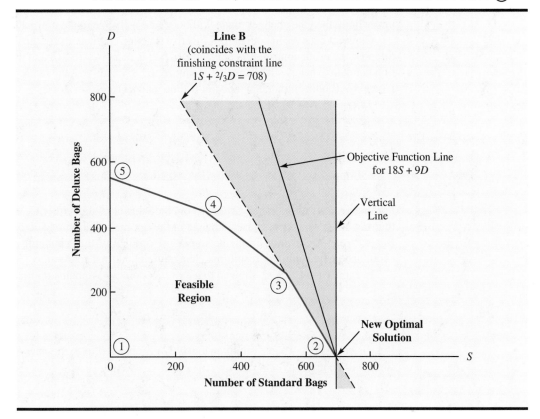

Following the previous procedure of holding C_D constant at its original value, $C_D = 9$,
we have

$$-\frac{C_S}{9} \leq -\frac{3}{2} \quad \text{or} \quad \frac{C_S}{9} \geq \frac{3}{2}$$

Solving for C_S provides the following result:

$$C_S \geq \frac{27}{2} = 13.5$$

In reviewing Figure 3.2 we note that extreme point ② remains optimal for all values of C_S
above 13.5. Thus, we obtain the following range of optimality for C_S at extreme point ②:

$$13.5 \leq C_S < \infty$$

Simultaneous Changes   The range of optimality for objective function coefficients is only
applicable for changes made to one coefficient at a time. All other coefficients are assumed
to be fixed at their initial values. If two or more objective function coefficients are changed
simultaneously, further analysis is necessary to determine whether the optimal solution will
change. However, when solving two-variable problems graphically, expression (3.2) suggests an easy way to determine whether simultaneous changes in both objective function

coefficients will cause a change in the optimal solution. Simply compute the slope of the objective function $(-C_S/C_D)$ for the new coefficient values. If this ratio is greater than or equal to the lower limit on the slope of the objective function and less than or equal to the upper limit, then the changes made will not cause a change in the optimal solution.

Consider changes in both of the objective function coefficients for the Par, Inc., problem. Suppose the profit contribution per standard bag is increased to $13 and the profit contribution per deluxe bag is simultaneously reduced to $8. Recall that the ranges of optimality for C_S and C_D (both computed in a one-at-a-time manner) are

$$6.3 \leq C_S \leq 13.5 \tag{3.3}$$
$$6.67 \leq C_D \leq 14.29 \tag{3.4}$$

For these ranges of optimality, we can conclude that changing either C_S to $13 or C_D to $8 (but not both) would not cause a change in the optimal solution of $S = 540$ and $D = 252$. But we cannot conclude from the ranges of optimality that changing both coefficients simultaneously would not result in a change in the optimal solution.

In expression (3.2) we showed that extreme point ③ remains optimal as long as

$$-\tfrac{3}{2} \leq -\frac{C_S}{C_D} \leq -\tfrac{7}{10}$$

If C_S is changed to 13 and simultaneously C_D is changed to 8, the new objective function slope will be given by

$$-\frac{C_S}{C_D} = -\frac{13}{8} = -1.625$$

Because this value is less than the lower limit of $-\tfrac{3}{2}$, the current solution of $S = 540$ and $D = 252$ will no longer be optimal. By re-solving the problem with $C_S = 13$ and $C_D = 8$, we will find that extreme point ② is the new optimal solution.

Looking at the ranges of optimality, we concluded that changing either C_S to $13 or C_D to $8 (but not both) would not cause a change in the optimal solution. But in recomputing the slope of the objective function with simultaneous changes for both C_S and C_D, we saw that the optimal solution did change. This result emphasizes the fact that a range of optimality, by itself, can only be used to draw a conclusion about changes made to *one objective function coefficient at a time.*

Right-Hand Sides

Let us now consider how a change in the right-hand side for a constraint may affect the feasible region and perhaps cause a change in the optimal solution to the problem. To illustrate this aspect of sensitivity analysis, let us consider what happens if an additional 10 hours of production time become available in the cutting and dyeing department of Par, Inc. The right-hand side of the cutting and dyeing constraint is changed from 630 to 640, and the constraint is rewritten as

$$\tfrac{7}{10}S + 1D \leq 640$$

FIGURE 3.3 EFFECT OF A 10-UNIT CHANGE IN THE RIGHT-HAND SIDE
OF THE CUTTING AND DYEING CONSTRAINT

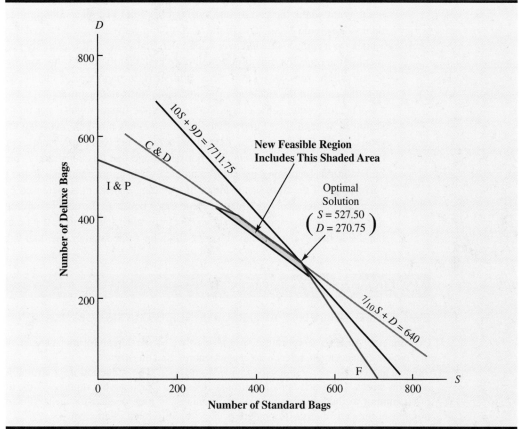

By obtaining an additional 10 hours of cutting and dyeing time, we expand the feasible region for the problem, as shown in Figure 3.3. With an enlarged feasible region, we now want to determine whether one of the new feasible solutions provides an improvement in the value of the objective function. Application of the graphical solution procedure to the problem with the enlarged feasible region shows that the extreme point with $S = 527.5$ and $D = 270.75$ now provides the optimal solution. The new value for the objective function is $10(527.5) + 9(270.75) = \$7711.75$, with an increase in profit of $\$7711.75 - \$7668.00 = \$43.75$. Thus, the increased profit occurs at a rate of $\$43.75/10$ hours $= \$4.375$ per hour added.

The *change* in the value of the optimal solution per unit increase in the right-hand side of the constraint is called the **dual value.** Here, the dual value for the cutting and dyeing constraint is $\$4.375$; in other words, if we increase the right-hand side of the cutting and dyeing constraint by 1 hour, the value of the objective function will increase by $\$4.375$. Conversely, if the right-hand side of the cutting and dyeing constraint were to decrease by 1 hour, the objective function would go down by $\$4.375$. The dual value can generally be used to determine what will happen to the value of the objective function when we make a one-unit change in the right-hand side of a constraint.

We caution here that the value of the dual value may be applicable only for small changes in the right-hand side. As more and more resources are obtained and the right-hand-side value continues to increase, other constraints will become binding and limit the change in the value of the objective function. For example, in the problem for Par, Inc., we would eventually reach a point where more cutting and dyeing time would be of no value; it would occur at the point where the cutting and dyeing constraint becomes nonbinding. At this point, the dual value would equal zero. In the next section we will show how to determine the range of values for a right-hand side over which the dual value will accurately predict the improvement in the objective function. Finally, we note that the dual value for any nonbinding constraint will be zero because an increase in the right-hand side of such a constraint will affect only the value of the slack or surplus variable for that constraint.

The dual value is the change in the objective function value per unit increase in a constraint right-hand side. Suppose that we now solve a problem involving the minimization of total cost and that the value of the optimal solution is $100. Furthermore, suppose that the first constraint is a less-than-or-equal-to constraint and that this constraint is binding for the optimal solution. Increasing the right-hand side of this constraint makes the problem easier to solve. Thus, if the right-hand side of this binding constraint is increased by one unit, we expect the optimal objective function value to get better. In the case of a minimization problem, this means that the optimal objective function value gets smaller. If an increase in the right-hand side makes the optimal objective function value smaller, the dual value is negative.

MANAGEMENT SCIENCE IN ACTION

EVALUATING EFFICIENCY AT PERFORMANCE ANALYSIS CORPORATION*

Performance Analysis Corporation specializes in the use of management science to design more efficient and effective operations for a wide variety of chain stores. One such application uses linear programming methodology to provide an evaluation model for a chain of fast-food outlets.

According to the concept of Pareto optimality, a restaurant in a given chain is relatively inefficient if other restaurants in the same chain exhibit the following characteristics:

1. Operates in the same or worse environment
2. Produces at least the same level of *all* outputs
3. Utilizes no more of *any* resource and *less* of at least one of the resources

To determine which of the restaurants are Pareto inefficient, Performance Analysis Corporation developed and solved a linear programming model. Model constraints involve requirements concerning the minimum acceptable levels of output and conditions imposed by uncontrollable elements in the environment, and the objective function calls for the minimization of the resources necessary to produce the output. Solving the model produces the following output for each restaurant:

1. A score that assesses the level of so-called relative technical efficiency achieved by the

particular restaurant over the time period in question
2. The reduction in controllable resources or the increase of outputs over the time period in question needed for an inefficient restaurant to be rated as efficient
3. A peer group of other restaurants with which each restaurant can be compared in the future

Sensitivity analysis provides important managerial information. For example, for each constraint concerning a minimum acceptable output level, the dual value tells the manager how much one more unit of output would change the efficiency measure.

The analysis typically identifies 40% to 50% of the restaurants as underperforming, given the previously stated conditions concerning the inputs available and outputs produced. Performance Analysis Corporation finds that if all the relative inefficiencies identified are eliminated simultaneously, corporate profits typically increase approximately 5% to 10%. This increase is truly substantial given the large scale of operations involved.

*Based on information provided by Richard C. Morey of Performance Analysis Corporation.

The Management Science in Action, Evaluating Efficiency at Performance Analysis Corporation, illustrates the use of dual values as part of an evaluation model for a chain of fast-food outlets. This type of model will be studied in more detail in Chapter 5 when we discuss an application referred to as data envelopment analysis.

NOTES AND COMMENTS

1. If two objective function coefficients change simultaneously, both may move outside their respective ranges of optimality and not affect the optimal solution. For instance, in a two-variable linear program, the slope of the objective function will not change at all if both coefficients are changed by the same percentage.

2. Some textbooks and optimization solvers, for example Excel Solver, use the term *shadow price* rather than dual value.

3.3   SENSITIVITY ANALYSIS: COMPUTER SOLUTION

In Section 2.4 we showed how to interpret the output of a linear programming solver. In this section we continue that discussion and show how to interpret the sensitivity analysis output. We use the Par, Inc., problem restated below.

$$\text{Max}\quad 10S + 9D$$

s.t.

$$\begin{aligned}
\tfrac{7}{10}S + 1D &\leq 630 \quad \text{Cutting and dyeing} \\
\tfrac{1}{2}S + \tfrac{5}{6}D &\leq 600 \quad \text{Sewing} \\
1S + \tfrac{2}{3}D &\leq 708 \quad \text{Finishing} \\
\tfrac{1}{10}S + \tfrac{1}{4}D &\leq 135 \quad \text{Inspection and packaging} \\
S, D &\geq 0
\end{aligned}$$

Let us demonstrate interpreting the sensitivity analysis by considering the solution to the Par, Inc., linear program shown in Figure 3.4.

Interpretation of Computer Output

In Section 2.4 we discussed the output in the top portion of Figure 3.4. We see that the optimal solution is $S = 540$ standard bags and $D = 252$ deluxe bags; the value of the optimal solution is $7668. Associated with each decision variable is reduced cost. We will interpret the reduced cost after our discussion on dual values.

Immediately following the optimal S and D values and the reduced cost information, the computer output provides information about the constraints. Recall that the Par, Inc., problem had four less-than-or-equal-to constraints corresponding to the hours available in each of four production departments. The information shown in the Slack/Surplus column provides the value of the slack variable for each of the departments. This information is summarized here:

Constraint Number	Constraint Name	Slack
1	Cutting and dyeing	0
2	Sewing	120
3	Finishing	0
4	Inspection and packaging	18

FIGURE 3.4   THE SOLUTION FOR THE PAR, INC., PROBLEM

```
Optimal Objective Value =        7668.00000

        Variable              Value           Reduced Cost
       ------------        ------------       ------------
           S               540.00000            0.00000
           D               252.00000            0.00000

       Constraint          Slack/Surplus        Dual Value
       ------------        ------------       ------------
           1                 0.00000             4.37500
           2               120.00000             0.00000
           3                 0.00000             6.93750
           4                18.00000             0.00000
```

WEB file

Par

Variable	Objective Coefficient	Allowable Increase	Allowable Decrease
S	10.00000	3.50000	3.70000
D	9.00000	5.28571	2.33333

Constraint	RHS Value	Allowable Increase	Allowable Decrease
1	630.00000	52.36364	134.40000
2	600.00000	Infinite	120.00000
3	708.00000	192.00000	128.00000
4	135.00000	Infinite	18.00000

From this information, we see that the binding constraints (the cutting and dyeing and the finishing constraints) have zero slack at the optimal solution. The sewing department has 120 hours of slack, or unused capacity, and the inspection and packaging department has 18 hours of slack, or unused capacity.

     The Dual Value column contains information about the marginal value of each of the four resources at the optimal solution. In Section 3.2 we defined the *dual value* as follows:

> The dual value associated with a constraint is the *change* in the optimal value of the solution per unit increase in the right-hand side of the constraint.

Try Problem 5 to test your ability to use computer output to determine the optimal solution and to interpret the dual values.

Thus, the nonzero dual values of 4.37500 for constraint 1 (cutting and dyeing constraint) and 6.93750 for constraint 3 (finishing constraint) tell us that an additional hour of cutting and dyeing time increases the value of the optimal solution by $4.37, and an additional hour of finishing time increases the value of the optimal solution by $6.94. Thus, if the cutting and dyeing time were increased from 630 to 631 hours, with all other coefficients in the problem remaining the same, Par's profit would be increased by $4.37, from $7668 to $7668 + $4.37 = $7672.37. A similar interpretation for the finishing constraint implies that an increase from 708 to 709 hours of available finishing time, with all other coefficients in the problem remaining the same, would increase Par's profit to $7668 + $6.94 = $7674.94. Because the sewing and the inspection and packaging constraints both have slack, or unused capacity, available, the dual values of zero show that additional hours of these two resources will not improve the value of the objective function.

Now that the concept of a dual value has been explained, we define the reduced cost associated with each variable. The **reduced cost** associated with a variable is equal to the dual value for the nonnegativity constraint associated with the variable. From Figure 3.4, we see that the reduced cost on variable S is zero and on variable D is zero. This makes sense. Consider variable S. The nonnegativity constraint is $S \geq 0$. The current value of S is 540, so changing the nonnegativity constraint to $S \geq 1$ has no effect on the optimal solution value. Because increasing the right-hand side by one unit has no effect on the optimal objective function value, the dual value (i.e., reduced cost) of this nonnegativity constraint is zero. A similar argument applies to variable D. In general, if a variable has a nonzero value in the optimal solution, then it will have a reduced cost equal to zero. Later in this section we give an example where the reduced cost of a variable is nonzero, and this example provides more insight on why the term *reduced cost* is used for the nonnegativity constraint dual value.

Referring again to the computer output in Figure 3.4, we see that after providing the constraint information on slack/surplus variables and dual values, the solution output provides ranges for the objective function coefficients and the right-hand sides of the constraints.

Considering the objective function coefficient range analysis, we see that variable S, which has a current profit coefficient of 10, has an *allowable increase* of 3.5 and an *allowable decrease* of 3.7. Therefore, as long as the profit contribution associated with the standard bag is between $10 - $3.7 = $6.30 and $10 + $3.5 = $13.50, the production of $S = 540$ standard bags and $D = 252$ deluxe bags will remain the optimal solution. Therefore, the range of optimality for the objective function coefficient on variable S is from 6.3 to 13.5. Note that the range of optimality is the same as obtained by performing graphical sensitivity analysis for C_S in Section 3.2.

Using the objective function coefficient range information for deluxe bags, we see the following range of optimality (after rounding to two decimal places):

$$9 - 2.33 = 6.67 \leq C_p \leq 9 + 5.29 = 14.29$$

This result tells us that as long as the profit contribution associated with the deluxe bag is between $6.67 and $14.29, the production of $S = 540$ standard bags and $D = 252$ deluxe bags will remain the optimal solution.

The final section of the computer output provides the allowable increase and allowable decrease in the right-hand sides of the constraints relative to the dual values holding. As long as the constraint right-hand side is not increased (decreased) by more than the allowable increase (decrease), the associated dual value gives the exact change in the value of the optimal solution per unit increase in the right-hand side. For example, let us consider the cutting and dyeing constraint with a current right-hand-side value of 630. Because the dual value for this constraint is $4.37, we can conclude that additional hours will increase the objective function by $4.37 per hour. It is also true that a reduction in the hours available will reduce the value of the objective function by $4.37 per hour. From the range information given, we see that the dual value of $4.37 has an allowable increase of 52.36364 and is therefore valid for right-hand side values up to 630 + 52.36364 = 682.363364. The allowable decrease is 134.4, so the dual value of $4.37 is valid for right-hand side values down to 630 - 134.4 = 495.6. A similar interpretation for the finishing constraint's right-hand

Try Problem 6 to test your ability to use computer output to determine the ranges of optimality and the ranges of feasibility.

side (constraint 3) shows that the dual value of $6.94 is applicable for increases up to 900 hours and decreases down to 580 hours.

As mentioned, the right-hand-side ranges provide limits within which the dual values give the exact change in the optimal objective function value. For changes outside the range, the problem must be re-solved to find the new optimal solution and the new dual value. We shall call the range over which the dual value is applicable the **range of feasibility.** The ranges of feasibility for the Par, Inc., problem are summarized here:

Constraint	Min RHS	Max RHS
Cutting and dyeing	495.6	682.4
Sewing	480.0	No upper limit
Finishing	580.0	900.0
Inspection and packaging	117.0	No upper limit

As long as the values of the right-hand sides are within these ranges, the dual values shown on the computer output will not change. Right-hand-side values outside these limits will result in changes in the dual value information.

Cautionary Note on the Interpretation of Dual Values

As stated previously, the dual value is the change in the value of the optimal solution per unit increase in the right-hand side of a constraint. When the right-hand side of the constraint represents the amount of a resource available, the associated dual value is often interpreted as the maximum amount one should be willing to pay for one additional unit of the resource. However, such an interpretation is not always correct. To see why, we need to understand the difference between sunk and relevant costs. A **sunk cost** is one that is not affected by the decision made. It will be incurred no matter what values the decision variables assume. A **relevant cost** is one that depends on the decision made. The amount of a relevant cost will vary depending on the values of the decision variables.

Let us reconsider the Par, Inc., problem. The amount of cutting and dyeing time available is 630 hours. The cost of the time available is a sunk cost if it must be paid regardless of the number of standard and deluxe golf bags produced. It would be a relevant cost if Par only had to pay for the number of hours of cutting and dyeing time actually used to produce golf bags. All relevant costs should be reflected in the objective function of a linear program. Sunk costs should not be reflected in the objective function. For Par, Inc., we have been assuming that the company must pay its employees' wages regardless of whether their time on the job is completely utilized. Therefore, the cost of the labor-hours resource for Par, Inc., is a sunk cost and has not been reflected in the objective function.

Only relevant costs should be included in the objective function.

When the cost of a resource is *sunk,* the dual value can be interpreted as the maximum amount the company should be willing to pay for one additional unit of the resource. When the cost of a resource used is relevant, the dual value can be interpreted as the amount by which the value of the resource exceeds its cost. Thus, when the resource cost is relevant, the dual value can be interpreted as the maximum premium over the normal cost that the company should be willing to pay for one unit of the resource.

The Modified Par, Inc., Problem

The graphical solution procedure is useful only for linear programs involving two decision variables. In practice, the problems solved using linear programming usually involve a large number of variables and constraints. For instance, the Management Science in Action, Determining Optimal Production Quantities at GE Plastics, describes how a linear programming model with 3100 variables and 1100 constraints was solved in less than 10 seconds to determine the optimal production quantities at GE Plastics. In this section we discuss the formulation and computer solution for two linear programs with three decision variables. In doing so, we will show how to interpret the reduced-cost portion of the computer output.

The original Par, Inc., problem is restated as follows:

$$\text{Max} \quad 10S + 9D$$

s.t.

$$\frac{7}{10}S + 1D \leq 630 \quad \text{Cutting and dyeing}$$
$$\frac{1}{2}S + \frac{5}{6}D \leq 600 \quad \text{Sewing}$$
$$1S + \frac{2}{3}D \leq 708 \quad \text{Finishing}$$
$$\frac{1}{10}S + \frac{1}{4}D \leq 135 \quad \text{Inspection and packaging}$$
$$S, D \geq 0$$

Recall that S is the number of standard golf bags produced and D is the number of deluxe golf bags produced. Suppose that management is also considering producing a lightweight model designed specifically for golfers who prefer to carry their bags. The design department estimates that each new lightweight model will require 0.8 hours for cutting and dyeing, 1 hour for sewing, 1 hour for finishing, and 0.25 hours for inspection and packaging. Because of the unique capabilities designed into the new model, Par's management feels they will realize a profit contribution of $12.85 for each lightweight model produced during the current production period.

Let us consider the modifications in the original linear programming model that are needed to incorporate the effect of this additional decision variable. We will let L denote the number of lightweight bags produced. After adding L to the objective function and to each of the four constraints, we obtain the following linear program for the modified problem:

$$\text{Max} \quad 10S + 9D + 12.85L$$

s.t.

$$\frac{7}{10}S + 1D + 0.8L \leq 630 \quad \text{Cutting and dyeing}$$
$$\frac{1}{2}S + \frac{5}{6}D + 1L \leq 600 \quad \text{Sewing}$$
$$1S + \frac{2}{3}D + 1L \leq 708 \quad \text{Finishing}$$
$$\frac{1}{10}S + \frac{1}{4}D + \frac{1}{4}L \leq 135 \quad \text{Inspection and packaging}$$
$$S, D, L \geq 0$$

Figure 3.5 shows the solution to the modified problem. We see that the optimal solution calls for the production of 280 standard bags, 0 deluxe bags, and 428 of the new lightweight bags; the value of the optimal solution is $8299.80.

Let us now look at the information contained in the Reduced Cost column. Recall that the reduced costs are the dual values of the corresponding nonnegativity constraints. As the computer output shows, the reduced costs for S and L are zero because these decision variables already have positive values in the optimal solution. However, the reduced cost for decision variable D is –1.15. The interpretation of this number is that if the production of deluxe bags is increased from the current level of 0 to 1, then the optimal objective function value will decrease by 1.15. Another interpretation is that if we "reduce the cost" of deluxe bags by 1.15 (i.e., increase the contribution margin by 1.15), then there is an optimal solution where we produce a nonzero number of deluxe bags.

FIGURE 3.5   SOLUTION FOR THE MODIFIED PAR, INC., PROBLEM

Optimal Objective Value =   8299.80000

Variable	Value	Reduced Cost
S	280.00000	0.00000
D	0.00000	-1.15000
L	428.00000	0.00000

Constraint	Slack/Surplus	Dual Value
1	91.60000	0.00000
2	32.00000	0.00000
3	0.00000	8.10000
4	0.00000	19.00000

Variable	Objective Coefficient	Allowable Increase	Allowable Decrease
S	10.00000	2.07000	4.86000
D	9.00000	1.15000	Infinite
L	12.85000	12.15000	0.94091

Constraint	RHS Value	Allowable Increase	Allowable Decrease
1	630.00000	Infinite	91.60000
2	600.00000	Infinite	32.00000
3	708.00000	144.63158	168.00000
4	135.00000	9.60000	64.20000

Suppose we increase the coefficient of D by exactly $1.15 so that the new value is $9 + $1.15 = $10.15 and then re-solve. Figure 3.6 shows the new solution. Note that although D assumes a positive value in the new solution, the value of the optimal solution has not changed. In other words, increasing the profit contribution of D by *exactly* the amount of the reduced cost has resulted in alternative optimal solutions. Depending on the computer software package used to optimize this model, you may or may not see D assume a positive value if you re-solve the problem with an objective function coefficient of exactly 10.15 for D—that is, the software package may show a different alternative optimal solution. However, if the profit contribution of D is increased by *more than* $1.15, then D will not remain at zero in the optimal solution.

We also note from Figure 3.6 that the dual values for constraints 3 and 4 are 8.1 and 19, respectively, indicating that these two constraints are binding in the optimal solution. Thus, each additional hour in the finishing department would increase the value of the optimal solution by $8.10, and each additional hour in the inspection and packaging department would increase the value of the optimal solution by $19.00. Because of a slack of 91.6 hours in the cutting and dyeing department and 32 hours in the sewing department (see Figure 3.6), management might want to consider the possibility of utilizing these unused labor-hours in the finishing or inspection and packaging departments. For example, some of the employees

FIGURE 3.6 SOLUTION FOR THE MODIFIED PAR, INC., PROBLEM WITH THE COEFFICIENT OF *D* INCREASED BY $1.1500

Optimal Objective Value =   8299.80000

Variable	Value	Reduced Cost
S	403.78378	0.00000
D	222.81081	0.00000
L	155.67568	0.00000

Constraint	Slack/Surplus	Dual Value
1	0.00000	0.00000
2	56.75676	0.00000
3	0.00000	8.10000
4	0.00000	19.00000

Variable	Objective Coefficient	Allowable Increase	Allowable Decrease
S	10.00000	2.51071	0.00000
D	10.15000	5.25790	0.00000
L	12.85000	0.00000	2.19688

Constraint	RHS Value	Allowable Increase	Allowable Decrease
1	630.00000	52.36364	91.60000
2	600.00000	Infinite	56.75676
3	708.00000	144.63158	128.00000
4	135.00000	16.15385	18.00000

in the cutting and dyeing department could be used to perform certain operations in either the finishing department or the inspection and packaging department. In the future, Par's management may want to explore the possibility of cross-training employees so that unused capacity in one department could be shifted to other departments. In the next chapter we will consider similar modeling situations.

NOTES AND COMMENTS

1. Computer software packages for solving linear programs are readily available. Most of these provide the optimal solution, dual or shadow price information, the range of optimality for the objective function coefficients, and the range of feasibility for the right-hand sides. The labels used for the ranges of optimality and feasibility may vary, but the meaning is the same as what we have described here.

2. Whenever one of the right-hand sides is at an end point of its range of feasibility, the dual and shadow prices only provide one-sided information. In this case, they only predict the change in the optimal value of the objective function for changes toward the interior of the range.

(continued)

3. A condition called *degeneracy* can cause a subtle difference in how we interpret changes in the objective function coefficients beyond the end points of the range of optimality. Degeneracy occurs when the dual value equals zero for one of the binding constraints. Degeneracy does not affect the interpretation of changes toward the interior of the range of optimality. However, when degeneracy is present, changes beyond the end points of the range do not necessarily mean a different solution will be optimal. From a practical point of view, changes beyond the end points of the range of optimality necessitate re-solving the problem.

4. Managers are frequently called on to provide an economic justification for new technology. Often the new technology is developed, or purchased, in order to conserve resources. The dual value can be helpful in such cases because it can be used to determine the savings attributable to the new technology by showing the savings per unit of resource conserved.

MANAGEMENT SCIENCE IN ACTION

DETERMINING OPTIMAL PRODUCTION QUANTITIES AT GE PLASTICS*

General Electric Plastics (GEP) is a $5 billion global materials supplier of plastics and raw materials to many industries (e.g., automotive, computer, and medical equipment). GEP has plants all over the globe. In the past, GEP followed a pole-centric manufacturing approach wherein each product was manufactured in the geographic area (Americas, Europe, or Pacific) where it was to be delivered. When many of GEP's customers started shifting their manufacturing operations to the Pacific, a geographic imbalance was created between GEP's capacity and demand in the form of overcapacity in the Americas and undercapacity in the Pacific.

Recognizing that a pole-centric approach was no longer effective, GEP adopted a global approach to its manufacturing operations. Initial work focused on the high-performance polymers (HPP) division. Using a linear programming model, GEP was able to determine the optimal production quantities at each HPP plant to maximize the total contribution margin for the division. The model included demand constraints, manufacturing capacity constraints, and constraints that modeled the flow of materials produced at resin plants to the finishing plants and on to warehouses in three geographical regions (Americas, Europe, and Pacific). The mathematical model for a one-year problem has 3100 variables and 1100 constraints, and can be solved in less than 10 seconds. The new system proved successful at the HPP division, and other GE Plastics divisions are adapting it for their supply chain planning.

*Based on R. Tyagi, P. Kalish, and K. Akbay, "GE Plastics Optimizes the Two-Echelon Global Fulfillment Network at Its High-Performance Polymers Division," *Interfaces* (September/October 2004): 359–366.

3.4   LIMITATIONS OF CLASSICAL SENSITIVITY ANALYSIS

As we have seen, classical sensitivity analysis obtained from computer output can provide useful information on the sensitivity of the solution to changes in the model input data. However, classical sensitivity analysis provided by most computer packages does have its limitations. In this section we discuss three such limitations: simultaneous changes in input data, changes in constraint coefficients, and nonintuitive dual values. We give examples of these three cases and discuss how to effectively deal with these through re-solving the model with changes. In fact, in our experience, it is rarely the case that one solves a model once and makes a recommendaiton. More often than not, a series of models are solved using a variety of input data sets before a final plan is adopted. With improved algorithms and more powerful computers, solving multiple runs of a model is extremely cost and time effective.

Simultaneous Changes

The sensitivity analysis information in computer output is based on the assumption that only one coefficient changes; it is assumed that all other coefficients will remain as stated in the original problem. Thus, the range analysis for the objective function coefficients and the constraint right-hand sides is only applicable for changes in a single coefficient. In many cases, however, we are interested in what would happen if two or more coefficients are changed simultaneously.

Let us consider again the modified Par, Inc., problem, whose solution appears in Figure 3.5. Suppose that after we have solved the problem, we find a new supplier and can purchase the leather required for these bags at a lower cost. Leather is an important component of each of the three types of bags, but is used in different amounts in each type. After factoring in the new cost of leather, the profit margin per bag is found to be $10.30 for a standard bag, $11.40 for a deluxe bag and $12.97 for a lightweight bag. Does the current plan from Figure 3.5 remain optimal? We can easily answer this question by simply re-solving the model using the new profit margins as the objective function coefficients. That is, we use as our objective function: Maximize $10.3S + 11.4D + 12.97L$ with the same set of constraints as in the original model. The solution to this problem appears in Figure 3.7. The new optimal profit is $8718.13. All three types of bags should be produced.

FIGURE 3.7 THE SOLUTION FOR THE MODIFIED PAR, INC., PROBLEM WITH REVISED OBJECTIVE FUNCTION COEFFICIENTS

```
Optimal Objective Value =        8718.12973
```

Variable	Value	Reduced Cost
S	403.78378	0.00000
D	222.81081	0.00000
L	155.67568	0.00000

Constraint	Slack/Surplus	Dual Value
1	0.00000	3.08919
2	56.75676	0.00000
3	0.00000	6.56351
4	0.00000	15.74054

Variable	Objective Coefficient	Allowable Increase	Allowable Decrease
S	10.30000	2.08000	2.28600
D	11.40000	4.26053	1.27000
L	12.97000	1.03909	1:82000

Constraint	RHS Value	Allowable Increase	Allowable Decrease
1	630.00000	52.36364	91.60000
2	600.00000	Infinite	56.75676
3	708.00000	144.63158	128.00000
4	135.00000	16.15385	18.00000

Suppose we had not re-solved the model with the new objective function coefficients. We would have used the solution from the original model, the solution found in Figure 3.5. Our profit would have therefore been $10.3(280) + $11.40(0) + $12.97(428) = $8435.16. By re-solving the model with the new information and using the revised plan in Figure 3.7, we have increased total profit by $8718.13 – $8435.16 = $282.97.

Changes in Constraint Coefficients

Classical sensitivity analysis provides no information about changes resulting from a change in the coefficient of a variable in a constraint. To illustrate such a case and how we may deal with it, let us again consider the Modified Par, Inc., problem discussed in Section 3.3.

Suppose we are considering the adoption of a new technology that will allow us to more efficiently finish standard bags. This technology is dedicated to standard bags and would decrease the finishing time on a standard bag from its current value of 1 to ½ of an hour. The technology would not impact the finishing time of deluxe or lightweight bags. The finishing constraint under the new sceanario is:

$$\tfrac{1}{2}S + \tfrac{2}{3}D + 1L \leq 708 \quad \text{Finishing with new technology}$$

Even though this is a single change in a coefficient in the model, there is no way to tell from classical sensitivity analysis what impact the change in the coefficient of S will have on the solution. Instead, we must simply change the coefficient and rerun the model. The solution appears in Figure 3.8. Note that the optimal number of standard bags has increased from 280 to 521.1 and the optimal number of lightweight bags decreased from 428 to 331.6. It remains optimal to produce no deluxe bags. Most importantly, with the new technology, the optimal profit increased from $8299.80 to $9471.32, an increase of $1171.52. Using this information with the cost of the new technology will provide an estimate for mangement as to how long it will take to pay off the new technology based on the increase in profits.

Nonintuitive Dual Values

Constraints with variables naturally on both the left-hand and right-hand sides often lead to dual values that have a nonintuitve explantion. To illustrate such a case and how we may deal with it, let us reconsider the Modified Par, Inc., problem discussed in Section 3.3.

Suppose that after reviewing the solution shown in Figure 3.5, management states that they will not consider any solution that does not include the production of some deluxe bags. Management then decides to add the requirement that the number of deluxe bags produced must be at least 30% of the number of standard bags produced. Writing this requirement using the decision variables S and D, we obtain

$$D \geq 0.3S$$

This new constraint is constraint 5 in the modified Par, Inc., linear program. Re-solving the problem with the new constraint 5 yields the optimal solution shown in Figure 3.9.

Let us consider the interpretation of the dual value for constraint 5, the requirement that the number of deluxe bags produced must be at least 30% of the number of standard bags produced. The dual value of −1.38 indicates that a one-unit increase in the right-hand side of the constraint will lower profits by $1.38. Thus, what the dual value of −1.38 is really

FIGURE 3.8 THE SOLUTION FOR THE MODIFIED PAR, INC., PROBLEM WITH NEW STANDARD BAG FINISHING TECHNOLOGY

Optimal Objective Value =   9471.31579

Variable	Value	Reduced Cost
S	521.05263	0.00000
D	0.00000	-6.40789
L	331.57895	0.00000

Constraint	Slack/Surplus	Dual Value
1	0.00000	12.78947
2	7.89474	0.00000
3	115.89474	0.00000
4	0.00000	10.47368

Variable	Objective Coefficient	Allowable Increase	Allowable Decrease
S	10.00000	1.24375	4.86000
D	9.00000	6.40789	Infinite
L	12.85000	12.15000	1.42143

Constraint	RHS Value	Allowable Increase	Allowable Decrease
1	630.00000	30.00000	198.00000
2	600.00000	Infinite	7.89474
3	708.00000	Infinite	115.89474
4	135.00000	2.50000	45.00000

telling us is what will happen to the value of the optimal solution if the constraint is changed to

$$D \geq 0.3S + 1$$

The interpretation of the dual value of -1.38 is correctly stated as follows: If we are forced to produce one deluxe bag over and above the minimum 30% requirement, total profits will decrease by $1.38. Conversely, if we relax the minimum 30% requirement by one bag ($D \geq 0.3S - 1$), total profits will increase by $1.38.

We might instead be more interested in what happens when the percentage of 30% is increased to 31%. Note that dual value does *not* tell us what will happen in this case. Also, because 0.30 is the coefficient of a variable in a constraint rather than an objective function coefficient or right-hand side, no range analysis is given. Note that this is the case just discussed in the previous section. Because there is no way to get this information directly from classical sensitivity analysis, to answer such a question, we need to re-solve the problem

FIGURE 3.9   THE SOLUTION FOR THE MODIFIED PAR, INC., PROBLEM WITH THE
DELUXE BAG REQUIREMENT

Optimal Objective Value =   8183.88000

Variable	Value	Reduced Cost
S	336.00000	0.00000
D	100.80000	0.00000
L	304.80000	0.00000

Constraint	Slack/Surplus	Dual Value
1	50.16000	0.00000
2	43.20000	0.00000
3	0.00000	7.41000
4	0.00000	21.76000
5	0.00000	-1.38000

Variable	Objective Coefficient	Allowable Increase	Allowable Decrease
S	10.00000	2.07000	3.70500
D	9.00000	1.15000	12.35000
L	12.85000	5.29286	0.94091

Constraint	RHS Value	Allowable Increase	Allowable Decrease
1	630.00000	Infinite	50.16000
2	600.00000	Infinite	43.20000
3	708.00000	57.00000	168.00000
4	135.00000	12.00000	31.75000
5	0.00000	101.67568	84.00000

using the constraint $D \geq 0.31S$. To test the sensitivity of the solution to changes in the percentage required we can re-solve the model replacing 0.30 with any percentage of interest.

To get a feel for how the required percentage impacts total profit, we solved versions of the Par, Inc., model with the required percentage varying from 5% to 100% in increments of 5%. This resulted in 20 different versions of the model to be solved. The impact of changing this percentage on the total profit is shown in Figure 3.10, and results are shown in Table 3.1.

What have we learned from this analysis? Notice from Figure 3.10 that the slope of the graph becomes steeper for values larger than 55%. This indicates that there is a shift in the rate of deterioration in profit starting at 55%. Hence, we see that percentages less than or equal to 55% result in modest loss of profit. More pronounced loss of profit results from percentages larger than 55%. So, management now knows that 30% is a reasonable requirement from a profit point of view and that extending the requirement beyond 55% will lead to a more significant loss of profit. From Table 3.1, as we increase the percentage required, fewer lightweight bags are produced.

FIGURE 3.10 PROFIT FOR VARIOUS VALUES OF REQUIRED PERCENTAGE FOR DELUXE BAGS AS A PERECENTAGE OF STANDARD BAGS

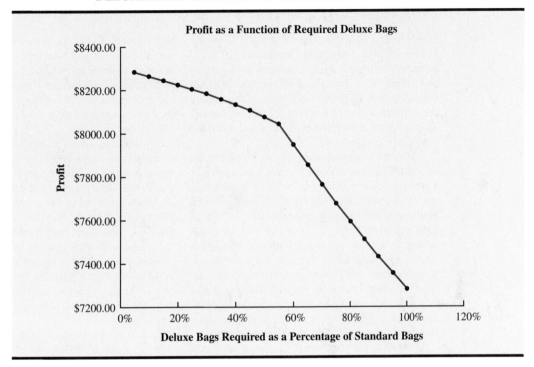

TABLE 3.1 SOLUTIONS VARIOUS VALUES OF REQUIRED PERCENTAGE FOR DELUXE BAGS AS A PERCENTAGE OF STANDARD BAGS

Percent	Profit	Standard	Deluxe	Lightweight
5%	$8283.24	287.9999	14.4000	410.4000
10%	$8265.71	296.4704	29.6470	391.7648
15%	$8247.11	305.4543	45.8181	372.0002
20%	$8227.35	314.9996	62.9999	351.0002
25%	$8206.31	325.1608	81.2902	328.6455
30%	$8183.88	335.9993	100.7998	304.8005
35%	$8159.89	347.5854	121.6549	279.3110
40%	$8134.20	359.9990	143.9996	252.0008
45%	$8106.60	373.3321	167.9994	222.6677
50%	$8076.87	387.6908	193.8454	191.0783
55%	$8044.77	403.1982	221.7590	156.9617
60%	$7948.80	396.0000	237.6000	144.0000
65%	$7854.27	388.2353	252.3529	132.3529
70%	$7763.37	380.7692	266.5385	121.1538
75%	$7675.90	373.5849	280.1887	110.3774
80%	$7591.67	366.6667	293.3333	100.0000
85%	$7510.50	360.0000	306.0000	90.0000
90%	$7432.23	353.5714	318.2143	80.3571
95%	$7356.71	347.3684	330.0000	71.0526
100%	$7283.79	341.3793	341.3793	62.0690

MANAGEMENT SCIENCE IN ACTION

ESTIMATION OF FOOD NUTRIENT VALUES*

The Nutrition Coordinating Center (NCC) of the University of Minnesota maintains a food-composition database that is used by nutritionists and researchers throughout the world. Nutrient information provided by NCC is used to estimate the nutrient intake of individuals, to plan menus, research links between diet and disease, and meet regulatory requirements.

Nutrient intake calculations require data on an enormous number of food nutrient values. NCC's food composition database contains information on 93 different nutrients for each food product. With many new brand-name products introduced each year, NCC has the significant task of maintaining an accurate and timely database. The task is made more difficult by the fact that new brand-name products only provide data on a relatively small number of nutrients. Because of the high cost of chemically analyzing the new products, NCC uses a linear programming model to help estimate thousands of nutrient values per year.

The decision variables in the linear programming model are the amounts of each ingredient in a food product. The objective is to minimize the differences between the estimated nutrient values and the known nutrient values for the food product. Constraints are that ingredients must be in descending order by weight, ingredients must be within nutritionist-specified bounds, and the differences between the calculated nutrient values and the known nutrient values must be within specified tolerances.

In practice, an NCC nutritionist employs the linear programming model to derive estimates of the amounts of each ingredient in a new food product. Given these estimates, the nutritionist refines the estimates based on his or her knowledge of the product formulation and the food composition. Once the amounts of each ingredient are obtained, the amounts of each nutrient in the food product can be calculated. With approximately 1000 products evaluated each year, the time and cost savings provided by using linear programming to help estimate the nutrient values are significant.

*Based on Brian J. Westrich, Michael A. Altmann, and Sandra J. Potthoff, "Minnesota's Nutrition Coordinating Center Uses Mathematical Optimization to Estimate Food Nutrient Values," *Interfaces* (September/October 1998): 86–99.

3.5   THE ELECTRONIC COMMUNICATIONS PROBLEM

The Electronic Communications problem introduced in this section is a maximization problem involving four decision variables, two less-than-or-equal-to constraints, one equality constraint, and one greater-than-or-equal-to constraint. Our objective is to provide a summary of the process of formulating a mathematical model, using software to obtain an optimal solution, and interpreting the solution and sensitivity report information. In the next chapter we will continue to illustrate how linear programming can be applied by showing additional examples from the areas of marketing, finance, and production management. Your ability to formulate, solve, and interpret the solution to problems like the Electronic Communications problem is critical to understanding how more complex problems can be modeled using linear programming.

Electronic Communications manufactures portable radio systems that can be used for two-way communications. The company's new product, which has a range of up to 25 miles, is particularly suitable for use in a variety of business and personal applications. The distribution channels for the new radio are as follows:

1. Marine equipment distributors
2. Business equipment distributors
3. National chain of retail stores
4. Direct mail

TABLE 3.2 PROFIT, ADVERTISING COST, AND PERSONAL SALES TIME DATA
FOR THE ELECTRONIC COMMUNICATIONS PROBLEM

Distribution Channel	Profit per Unit Sold ($)	Advertising Cost per Unit Sold ($)	Personal Sales Effort per Unit Sold (hours)
Marine distributors	90	10	2
Business distributors	84	8	3
National retail stores	70	9	3
Direct mail	60	15	None

Because of differing distribution and promotional costs, the profitability of the product will vary with the distribution channel. In addition, the advertising cost and the personal sales effort required will vary with the distribution channels. Table 3.2 summarizes the contribution to profit, advertising cost, and personal sales effort data pertaining to the Electronic Communications problem. The firm set the advertising budget at $5000, and a maximum of 1800 hours of salesforce time is available for allocation to the sales effort. Management also decided to produce exactly 600 units for the current production period. Finally, an ongoing contract with the national chain of retail stores requires that at least 150 units be distributed through this distribution channel.

Electronic Communications is now faced with the problem of establishing a strategy that will provide for the distribution of the radios in such a way that overall profitability of the new radio production will be maximized. Decisions must be made as to how many units should be allocated to each of the four distribution channels, as well as how to allocate the advertising budget and salesforce effort to each of the four distribution channels.

Problem Formulation

We will now write the objective function and the constraints for the Electronic Communications problem. For the objective function, we can write

Objective function: Maximize profit

Four constraints are necessary for this problem. They are necessary because of (1) a limited advertising budget, (2) limited salesforce availability, (3) a production requirement, and (4) a retail stores distribution requirement.

Constraint 1: Advertising expenditures ≤ Budget
Constraint 2: Sales time used ≤ Time available
Constraint 3: Radios produced = Management requirement
Constraint 4: Retail distribution ≥ Contract requirement

These expressions provide descriptions of the objective function and the constraints. We are now ready to define the decision variables that will represent the decisions the manager must make.

For the Electronic Communications problem, we introduce the following four decision variables:

M = the number of units produced for the marine equipment distribution channel
B = the number of units produced for the business equipment distribution channel
R = the number of units produced for the national retail chain distribution channel
D = the number of units produced for the direct mail distribution channel

Using the data in Table 3.2, the objective function for maximizing the total contribution to profit associated with the radios can be written as follows:

$$\text{Max } 90M + 84B + 70R + 60D$$

Let us now develop a mathematical statement of the constraints for the problem. Because the advertising budget is set at \$5000, the constraint that limits the amount of advertising expenditure can be written as follows:

$$10M + 8B + 9R + 15D \leq 5000$$

Similarly, because the sales time is limited to 1800 hours, we obtain the constraint

$$2M + 3B + 3R \leq 1800$$

Management's decision to produce exactly 600 units during the current production period is expressed as

$$M + B + R + D = 600$$

Finally, to account for the fact that the number of units distributed by the national chain of retail stores must be at least 150, we add the constraint

$$R \geq 150$$

Combining all of the constraints with the nonnegativity requirements enables us to write the complete linear programming model for the Electronic Communications problem as follows:

$$
\begin{array}{lll}
\text{Max} & 90M + 84B + 70R + 60D & \\
\text{s.t.} & & \\
& 10M + 8B + 9R + 15D \leq 5000 & \text{Advertising budget} \\
& 2M + 3B + 3R \leq 1800 & \text{Salesforce availability} \\
& M + B + R + D = 600 & \text{Production level} \\
& R \geq 150 & \text{Retail stores requirement} \\
& M, B, R, D \geq 0 &
\end{array}
$$

Computer Solution and Interpretation

This problem can be solved using either Excel Solver or LINGO. A portion of the standard solution output for the Electronic Communications problem is shown in Figure 3.11. The Objective Function Value section shows that the optimal solution to the problem will provide a maximum profit of \$48,450. The optimal values of the decision variables are given by $M = 25$, $B = 425$, $R = 150$, and $D = 0$.

FIGURE 3.11   A PORTION OF THE COMPUTER OUTPUT FOR THE ELECTRONIC
COMMUNICATIONS PROBLEM

```
Optimal Objective Value =          48450.00000

        Variable              Value              Reduced Cost
     ---------------     ---------------     ------------------
           M                 25.00000               0.00000
           B                425.00000               0.00000
           R                150.00000               0.00000
           D                  0.00000             -45.00000

       Constraint        Slack/Surplus            Dual Value
     ---------------     ---------------     ------------------
           1                  0.00000               3.00000
           2                 25.00000               0.00000
           3                  0.00000              60.00000
           4                  0.00000             -17.00000
```

WEB file

Electronic

Thus, the optimal strategy for Electronic Communications is to concentrate on the business equipment distribution channel with $B = 425$ units. In addition, the firm should allocate 25 units to the marine distribution channel ($M = 25$) and meet its 150-unit commitment to the national retail chain store distribution channel ($R = 150$). With $D = 0$, the optimal solution indicates that the firm should not use the direct mail distribution channel.

Now consider the information contained in the Reduced Cost column. Recall that the reduced cost of a variable is the dual value of the corresponding nonnegativity constraint. As the computer output shows, the first three reduced costs are zero because the corresponding decision variables already have positive values in the optimal solution. However, the reduced cost of –45 for decision variable D tells us that profit will decrease by $45 for every unit produced for the direct mail channel. Stated another way, the profit for the new radios distributed via the direct mail channel would have to increase from its current value of $60 per unit, by $45 per unit, to at least $60 + $45 = $105 per unit before it would be profitable to use the direct mail distribution channel.

The computer output information for the slack/surplus variables and the dual values is restated in Figure 3.12.

The advertising budget constraint has a slack of zero, indicating that the entire budget of $5000 has been used. The corresponding dual value of 3 tells us that an additional dollar added to the advertising budget will increase the objective function (increase the profit) by $3. Thus, the possibility of increasing the advertising budget should be seriously considered by the firm. The slack of 25 hours for the salesforce availability constraint shows that the allocated 1800 hours of sales time are adequate to distribute the radios produced and that 25 hours of sales time will remain unused. Because the production level constraint is an equality constraint, the zero slack/surplus shown on the output is expected. However, the dual value of 60 associated with this constraint shows that if the firm were to consider increasing the production level for the radios, the value of the objective function, or profit, would improve at the rate of $60 per radio produced. Finally, the surplus of zero associated with the retail store distribution channel commitment is a result of this constraint being binding. The negative dual value indicates that increasing the commitment from 150 to 151 units will actually decrease the profit by $17.

FIGURE 3.12   OBJECTIVE COEFFICIENT AND RIGHT-HAND-SIDE RANGES FOR THE ELECTRONIC COMMUNICATIONS PROBLEM

WEB file

Electronic

```
Optimal Objective Value =        48450.00000

        Variable              Value              Reduced Cost
       ------------        ------------         ------------
           M                25.00000                0.00000
           B               425.00000                0.00000
           R               150.00000                0.00000
           D                 0.00000              -45.00000

       Constraint         Slack/Surplus            Dual Value
       ------------        ------------         ------------
           1                 0.00000                3.00000
           2                25.00000                0.00000
           3                 0.00000               60.00000
           4                 0.00000              -17.00000

                        Objective          Allowable          Allowable
        Variable       Coefficient         Increase           Decrease
       ------------    ------------       ------------       ------------
           M            90.00000            Infinite           6.00000
           B            84.00000            6.00000           34.00000
           R            70.00000           17.00000            Infinite
           D            60.00000           45.00000            Infinite

                           RHS             Allowable          Allowable
       Constraint         Value            Increase           Decrease
       ------------    ------------       ------------       ------------
           1           5000.00000          850.00000          50.00000
           2           1800.00000           Infinite          25.00000
           3            600.00000            3.57143          85.00000
           4            150.00000           50.00000         150.00000
```

Thus, Electronic Communications may want to consider reducing its commitment to the retail store distribution channel. A *decrease* in the commitment will actually improve profit at the rate of $17 per unit.

We now consider the additional sensitivity analysis information provided by the computer output shown in Figure 3.12. The allowable increases and decreases for the objective function coefficients are as follows:

Objective Coefficient	Allowable Increase	Allowable Decrease
90.00000	Infinite	6.00000
84.00000	6.00000	34.00000
70.00000	17.00000	Infinite
60.00000	45.00000	Infinite

The current solution or strategy remains optimal, provided that the objective function coefficients do not increase or decrease by more than the allowed amount. Consider the allowable increase and decrease of the direct mail distribution channel coefficient. This information is consistent with the earlier observation for the Reduced Costs portion of the output. In both instances, we see that the per-unit profit would have to increase by $45 to $105 before the direct mail distribution channel could be in the optimal solution with a positive value.

Finally, the sensitivity analysis information on right-hand-side ranges, as shown in Figure 3.12, provides the allowable increase and decrease for the right-hand-side values.

RHS Value	Allowable Increase	Allowable Decrease
5000.00000	850.00000	50.00000
1800.00000	Infinite	25.00000
600.00000	3.57143	85.00000
150.00000	50.00000	150.00000

Try Problems 12 and 13 to test your ability at interpreting the computer output for problems involving more than two decision variables.

Several interpretations of these ranges are possible. In particular, recall that the dual value for the advertising budget enabled us to conclude that each $1 increase in the budget would increase the profit by $3. The current advertising budget is $5000. The allowable increase in the advertising budget is $850 and this implies that there is value in increasing the budget up to an advertising budget of $5850. Increases above this level would not necessarily be beneficial. Also note that the dual value of −17 for the retail stores requirement suggested the desirability of reducing this commitment. The allowable decrease for this constraint is 150, and this implies that the commitment could be reduced to zero and the value of the reduction would be at the rate of $17 per unit.

Again, the *sensitivity analysis* or *postoptimality analysis* provided by computer software packages for linear programming problems considers only *one change at a time,* with all other coefficients of the problem remaining as originally specified. As mentioned earlier, simultaneous changes are best handled by re-solving the problem.

Finally, recall that the complete solution to the Electronic Communications problem requested information not only on the number of units to be distributed over each channel, but also on the allocation of the advertising budget and the salesforce effort to each distribution channel. For the optimal solution of $M = 25$, $B = 425$, $R = 150$, and $D = 0$, we can simply evaluate each term in a given constraint to determine how much of the constraint resource is allocated to each distribution channel. For example, the advertising budget constraint of

$$10M + 8B + 9R + 15D \leq 5000$$

shows that $10M = 10(25) = \$250$, $8B = 8(425) = \$3400$, $9R = 9(150) = \$1350$, and $15D = 15(0) = \$0$. Thus, the advertising budget allocations are, respectively, $250, $3400, $1350, and $0 for each of the four distribution channels. Making similar calculations for the salesforce constraint results in the managerial summary of the Electronic Communications optimal solution as shown in Table 3.3.

TABLE 3.3   PROFIT-MAXIMIZING STRATEGY FOR THE ELECTRONIC
COMMUNICATIONS PROBLEM

Distribution Channel	Volume	Advertising Allocation	Salesforce Allocation (hours)
Marine distributors	25	$ 250	50
Business distributors	425	3400	1275
National retail stores	150	1350	450
Direct mail	0	0	0
Totals	600	$5000	1775
Projected total profit = $48,450			

SUMMARY

We began the chapter with a discussion of sensitivity analysis: the study of how changes in the coefficients of a linear program affect the optimal solution. First, we showed how a graphical method can be used to determine how a change in one of the objective function coefficients or a change in the right-hand-side value for a constraint will affect the optimal solution to the problem. Because graphical sensitivity analysis is limited to linear programs with two decision variables, we showed how to use software to produce a sensitivity report containing the same information.

We continued our discussion of problem formulation, sensitivity analysis and its limitations, and the interpretation of the solution by introducing several modifications of the Par, Inc., problem. They involved an additional decision variable and several types of percentage, or ratio, constraints. Then, in order to provide additional practice in formulating and interpreting the solution for linear programs involving more than two decision variables, we introduced the Electronic Communications problem, a maximization problem with four decision variables, two less-than-or-equal-to constraints, one equality constraint, and one greater-than-or-equal-to constraint.

The Management Science in Action, Tea Production and Distribution in India, illustrates the diversity of problems in which linear programming can be applied and the importance of sensitivity analysis. In the next chapter we will see many more applications of linear programming.

MANAGEMENT SCIENCE IN ACTION

TEA PRODUCTION AND DISTRIBUTION IN INDIA*

In India, one of the largest tea producers in the world, approximately $1 billion of tea packets and loose tea are sold. Duncan Industries Limited (DIL), the third largest producer of tea in the Indian tea market, sells about $37.5 million of tea, almost all of which is sold in packets.

DIL has 16 tea gardens, three blending units, six packing units, and 22 depots. Tea from the gardens is sent to blending units, which then mix various grades of tea to produce blends such as Sargam, Double Diamond, and Runglee Rungliot. The blended tea is transported to packing units,

where it is placed in packets of different sizes and shapes to produce about 120 different product lines. For example, one line is Sargam tea packed in 500-gram cartons, another line is Double Diamond packed in 100-gram pouches, and so on. The tea is then shipped to the depots that supply 11,500 distributors through whom the needs of approximately 325,000 retailers are satisfied.

For the coming month, sales managers provide estimates of the demand for each line of tea at each depot. Using these estimates, a team of senior managers would determine the amounts of loose tea of each blend to ship to each packing unit, the quantity of each line of tea to be packed at each packing unit, and the amounts of packed tea of each line to be transported from each packing unit to the various depots. This process requires two to three days each month and often results in stockouts of lines in demand at specific depots.

Consequently, a linear programming model involving approximately 7000 decision variables and 1500 constraints was developed to minimize the company's freight cost while satisfying demand, supply, and all operational constraints. The model was tested on past data and showed that stockouts could be prevented at little or no additional cost. Moreover, the model was able to provide management with the ability to perform various what-if types of exercises, convincing them of the potential benefits of using management science techniques to support the decision-making process.

*Based on Nilotpal Chakravarti, "Tea Company Steeped in OR," *OR/MS Today* (April 2000).

GLOSSARY

Sensitivity analysis   The study of how changes in the coefficients of a linear programming problem affect the optimal solution.

Range of optimality   The range of values over which an objective function coefficient may vary without causing any change in the values of the decision variables in the optimal solution.

Objective Function Allowable Increase (Decrease)   The allowable increase/decrease of an objective function coefficient is the amount the coefficient may increase (decrease) without causing any change in the values of the decision variables in the optimal solution. The allowable increase/decrease for the objective function coefficients can be used to calculate the range of optimality.

Dual value   The change in the value of the objective function per unit increase in the right-hand side of a constraint.

Reduced cost   The reduced cost of a variable is equal to the dual value on the nonnegativity constraint for that variable.

Range of feasibility   The range of values over which the dual value is applicable.

Right-Hand-Side Allowable Increase (Decrease)   The allowable increase (decrease) of the right-hand side of a constraint is the amount the right-hand side may increase (decrease) without causing any change in the dual value for that constraint. The allowable increase (decrease) for the right-hand side can be used to calculate the range of feasibility for that constraint.

Sunk cost   A cost that is not affected by the decision made. It will be incurred no matter what values the decision variables assume.

Relevant cost   A cost that depends upon the decision made. The amount of a relevant cost will vary depending on the values of the decision variables.

PROBLEMS

1. Consider the following linear program:

$$\text{Max} \quad 3A + 2B$$
s.t.
$$1A + 1B \leq 10$$
$$3A + 1B \leq 24$$
$$1A + 2B \leq 16$$
$$A, B \geq 0$$

a. Use the graphical solution procedure to find the optimal solution.
b. Assume that the objective function coefficient for A changes from 3 to 5. Does the optimal solution change? Use the graphical solution procedure to find the new optimal solution.
c. Assume that the objective function coefficient for A remains 3, but the objective function coefficient for B changes from 2 to 4. Does the optimal solution change? Use the graphical solution procedure to find the new optimal solution.
d. The computer solution for the linear program in part (a) provides the following objective coefficient range information:

Variable	Objective Coefficient	Allowable Increase	Allowable Decrease
A	3.00000	3.00000	1.00000
B	2.00000	1.00000	1.00000

Use this objective coefficient range information to answer parts (b) and (c).

2. Consider the linear program in Problem 1. The value of the optimal solution is 27. Suppose that the right-hand side for constraint 1 is increased from 10 to 11.
a. Use the graphical solution procedure to find the new optimal solution.
b. Use the solution to part (a) to determine the dual value for constraint 1.
c. The computer solution for the linear program in Problem 1 provides the following right-hand-side range information:

Constraint	RHS Value	Allowable Increase	Allowable Decrease
1	10.00000	1.20000	2.00000
2	24.00000	6.00000	6.00000
3	16.00000	Infinite	3.00000

What does the right-hand-side range information for constraint 1 tell you about the dual value for constraint 1?
d. The dual value for constraint 2 is 0.5. Using this dual value and the right-hand-side range information in part (c), what conclusion can be drawn about the effect of changes to the right-hand side of constraint 2?

3. Consider the following linear program:

$$\text{Min} \quad 8X + 12Y$$
$$\text{s.t.}$$
$$1X + 3Y \geq 9$$
$$2X + 2Y \geq 10$$
$$6X + 2Y \geq 18$$
$$A, B \geq 0$$

a. Use the graphical solution procedure to find the optimal solution.
b. Assume that the objective function coefficient for X changes from 8 to 6. Does the optimal solution change? Use the graphical solution procedure to find the new optimal solution.

c. Assume that the objective function coefficient for X remains 8, but the objective function coefficient for Y changes from 12 to 6. Does the optimal solution change? Use the graphical solution procedure to find the new optimal solution.

d. The computer solution for the linear program in part (a) provides the following objective coefficient range information:

Variable	Objective Coefficient	Allowable Increase	Allowable Decrease
X	8.00000	4.00000	4.00000
Y	12.00000	12.00000	4.00000

How would this objective coefficient range information help you answer parts (b) and (c) prior to re-solving the problem?

4. Consider the linear program in Problem 3. The value of the optimal solution is 48. Suppose that the right-hand side for constraint 1 is increased from 9 to 10.
   a. Use the graphical solution procedure to find the new optimal solution.
   b. Use the solution to part (a) to determine the dual value for constraint 1.
   c. The computer solution for the linear program in Problem 3 provides the following right-hand-side range information:

Constraint	RHS Value	Allowable Increase	Allowable Decrease
1	9.00000	2.00000	4.00000
2	10.00000	8.00000	1.00000
3	18.00000	4.00000	Infinite

What does the right-hand-side range information for constraint 1 tell you about the dual value for constraint 1?

   d. The dual value for constraint 2 is 3. Using this dual value and the right-hand-side range information in part (c), what conclusion can be drawn about the effect of changes to the right-hand side of constraint 2?

5. Refer to the Kelson Sporting Equipment problem (Chapter 2, Problem 24). Letting

$$R = \text{number of regular gloves}$$
$$C = \text{number of catcher's mitts}$$

leads to the following formulation:

$$\text{Max} \quad 5R + 8C$$
$$\text{s.t.}$$

$$R + \tfrac{3}{2}C \leq 900 \quad \text{Cutting and sewing}$$
$$\tfrac{1}{2}R + \tfrac{1}{3}C \leq 300 \quad \text{Finishing}$$
$$\tfrac{1}{8}R + \tfrac{1}{4}C \leq 100 \quad \text{Packaging and shipping}$$
$$R, C \geq 0$$

FIGURE 3.13   THE SOLUTION FOR THE KELSON SPORTING EQUIPMENT PROBLEM

Optimal Objective Value =   3700.00000

Variable	Value	Reduced Cost
R	500.00000	0.00000
C	150.00000	0.00000

Constraint	Slack/Surplus	Dual Value
1	175.00000	0.00000
2	0.00000	3.00000
3	0.00000	28.00000

Variable	Objective Coefficient	Allowable Increase	Allowable Decrease
R	5.00000	7.00000	1.00000
C	8.00000	2.00000	4.66667

Constraint	RHS Value	Allowable Increase	Allowable Decrease
1	900.00000	Infinite	175.00000
2	300.00000	100.00000	166.66667
3	100.00000	35.00000	25.00000

The computer solution is shown in Figure 3.13.

a. What is the optimal solution, and what is the value of the total profit contribution?
b. Which constraints are binding?
c. What are the dual values for the resources? Interpret each.
d. If overtime can be scheduled in one of the departments, where would you recommend doing so?

6. Refer to the computer solution of the Kelson Sporting Equipment problem in Figure 3.13 (see Problem 5).
a. Determine the objective coefficient ranges.
b. Interpret the ranges in part (a).
c. Interpret the right-hand-side ranges.
d. How much will the value of the optimal solution improve if 20 extra hours of packaging and shipping time are made available?

7. Investment Advisors, Inc., is a brokerage firm that manages stock portfolios for a number of clients. A particular portfolio consists of U shares of U.S. Oil and H shares of Huber Steel. The annual return for U.S. Oil is $3 per share and the annual return for Huber Steel is $5 per share. U.S. Oil sells for $25 per share and Huber Steel sells for $50 per share. The portfolio has $80,000 to be invested. The portfolio risk index (0.50 per share of U.S. Oil and 0.25 per share for Huber Steel) has a maximum of 700. In addition, the portfolio is limited to a maximum of 1000 shares of U.S. Oil. The linear

FIGURE 3.14 THE SOLUTION FOR THE INVESTMENT ADVISORS PROBLEM

```
Optimal Objective Value =           8400.00000
```

Variable	Value	Reduced Cost
U	800.00000	0.00000
H	1200.00000	0.00000

Constraint	Slack/Surplus	Dual Value
1	0.00000	0.09333
2	0.00000	1.33333
3	200.00000	0.00000

Variable	Objective Coefficient	Allowable Increase	Allowable Decrease
U	3.00000	7.00000	0.50000
H	5.00000	1.00000	3.50000

Constraint	RHS Value	Allowable Increase	Allowable Decrease
1	80000.00000	60000.00000	15000.00000
2	700.00000	75.00000	300.00000
3	1000.00000	Infinite	200.00000

programming formulation that will maximize the total annual return of the portfolio is as follows:

$$\text{Max} \quad 3U + 5H \qquad \text{Maximize total annual return}$$

s.t.

$$25U + 50H \leq 80{,}000 \quad \text{Funds available}$$
$$0.50U + 0.25D \leq \quad 700 \quad \text{Risk maximum}$$
$$1U \qquad\qquad \leq \quad 1000 \quad \text{U.S. Oil maximum}$$
$$U, H \geq 0$$

The computer solution of this problem is shown in Figure 3.14.

a. What is the optimal solution, and what is the value of the total annual return?

b. Which constraints are binding? What is your interpretation of these constraints in terms of the problem?

c. What are the dual values for the constraints? Interpret each.

d. Would it be beneficial to increase the maximum amount invested in U.S. Oil? Why or why not?

8. Refer to Figure 3.14, which shows the computer solution of Problem 7.

a. How much would the return for U.S. Oil have to increase before it would be beneficial to increase the investment in this stock?

b. How much would the return for Huber Steel have to decrease before it would be beneficial to reduce the investment in this stock?

c. How much would the total annual return be reduced if the U.S. Oil maximum were reduced to 900 shares?

9. Recall the Tom's, Inc., problem (Chapter 2, Problem 28). Letting

$$W = \text{jars of Western Foods Salsa}$$
$$M = \text{jars of Mexico City Salsa}$$

leads to the formulation:

$$\text{Max} \quad 1W + 1.25M$$
$$\text{s.t.}$$

$5W +$	$7M \le 4480$	Whole tomatoes
$3W +$	$1M \le 2080$	Tomato sauce
$2W +$	$2M \le 1600$	Tomato paste
$W, M \ge 0$		

The computer solution is shown in Figure 3.15.

a. What is the optimal solution, and what are the optimal production quantities?

b. Specify the objective function ranges.

FIGURE 3.15   THE SOLUTION FOR THE TOM'S, INC., PROBLEM

```
Optimal Objective Value =           860.00000

        Variable                Value              Reduced Cost
     --------------        ---------------        ------------------

           W                 560.00000                0.00000
           M                 240.00000                0.00000


        Constraint          Slack/Surplus             Dual Value
     --------------        ---------------        ------------------

           1                   0.00000                0.12500
           2                 160.00000                0.00000
           3                   0.00000                0.18750


                          Objective            Allowable            Allowable
        Variable         Coefficient            Increase             Decrease
     -----------        -----------           ----------           ----------

           W              1.00000               0.25000              0.10714
           M              1.25000               0.15000              0.25000


                            RHS                Allowable            Allowable
        Constraint         Value                Increase             Decrease
     -----------        -----------           ----------           ----------

           1             4480.00000            1120.00000           160.00000
           2             2080.00000             Infinite            160.00000
           3             1600.00000              40.00000           320.00000
```

c. What are the dual values for each constraint? Interpret each.
d. Identify each of the right-hand-side ranges.

10. Recall the Innis Investments problem (Chapter 2, Problem 39). Letting

$$S = \text{units purchased in the stock fund}$$
$$M = \text{units purchased in the money market fund}$$

leads to the following formulation:

Min $8S + 3M$
s.t.

$$50S + 100M \leq 1{,}200{,}000 \quad \text{Funds available}$$
$$5S + 4M \geq 60{,}000 \quad \text{Annual income}$$
$$M \geq 3{,}000 \quad \text{Units in money market}$$
$$S, M \geq 0$$

The computer solution is shown in Figure 3.16.
a. What is the optimal solution, and what is the minimum total risk?
b. Specify the objective coefficient ranges.
c. How much annual income will be earned by the portfolio?

FIGURE 3.16   THE SOLUTION FOR THE INNIS INVESTMENTS PROBLEM

```
Optimal Objective Value =          62000.00000

        Variable                 Value              Reduced Cost
    ----------------        ----------------        ----------------
          S                   4000.00000               0.00000
          M                  10000.00000               0.00000

       Constraint           Slack/Surplus             Dual Value
    ----------------        ----------------        ----------------
           1                    0.00000                -0.05667
           2                    0.00000                 2.16667
           3                 7000.00000                 0.00000

                        Objective           Allowable           Allowable
        Variable        Coefficient         Increase            Decrease
    -----------        ------------        ----------          ----------
          S              8.00000            Infinite            4.25000
          M              3.00000            3.40000             Infinite

                          RHS               Allowable           Allowable
       Constraint        Value              Increase            Decrease
    -----------        ------------        ----------          ----------
           1          1200000.00000        300000.00000        420000.00000
           2            60000.00000         42000.00000         12000.00000
           3             3000.00000          7000.00000         Infinite
```

    d. What is the rate of return for the portfolio?

    e. What is the dual value for the funds available constraint?

    f. What is the marginal rate of return on extra funds added to the portfolio?

11. Refer to Problem 10 and the computer solution shown in Figure 3.16.

    a. Suppose the risk index for the stock fund (the value of C_S) increases from its current value of 8 to 12. How does the optimal solution change, if at all?

    b. Suppose the risk index for the money market fund (the value of C_M) increases from its current value of 3 to 3.5. How does the optimal solution change, if at all?

    c. Suppose C_S increases to 12 and C_M increases to 3.5. How does the optimal solution change, if at all?

12. Quality Air Conditioning manufactures three home air conditioners: an economy model, a standard model, and a deluxe model. The profits per unit are $63, $95, and $135, respectively. The production requirements per unit are as follows:

	Number of Fans	Number of Cooling Coils	Manufacturing Time (hours)
Economy	1	1	8
Standard	1	2	12
Deluxe	1	4	14

For the coming production period, the company has 200 fan motors, 320 cooling coils, and 2400 hours of manufacturing time available. How many economy models (E), standard models (S), and deluxe models (D) should the company produce in order to maximize profit? The linear programming model for the problem is as follows:

$$\text{Max} \quad 63E + 95S + 135D$$

s.t.

$$
\begin{aligned}
1E + 1S + 1D &\le 200 \quad \text{Fan motors} \\
1E + 2S + 4D &\le 320 \quad \text{Cooling coils} \\
8E + 12S + 14D &\le 2400 \quad \text{Manufacturing time} \\
E, S, D &\ge 0
\end{aligned}
$$

The computer solution is shown in Figure 3.17.

    a. What is the optimal solution, and what is the value of the objective function?

    b. Which constraints are binding?

    c. Which constraint shows extra capacity? How much?

    d. If the profit for the deluxe model were increased to $150 per unit, would the optimal solution change? Use the information in Figure 3.17 to answer this question.

13. Refer to the computer solution of Problem 12 in Figure 3.17.

    a. Identify the range of optimality for each objective function coefficient.

    b. Suppose the profit for the economy model is increased by $6 per unit, the profit for the standard model is decreased by $2 per unit, and the profit for the deluxe model is increased by $4 per unit. What will the new optimal solution be?

    c. Identify the range of feasibility for the right-hand-side values.

    d. If the number of fan motors available for production is increased by 100, will the dual value for that constraint change? Explain.

FIGURE 3.17   THE SOLUTION FOR THE QUALITY AIR CONDITIONING PROBLEM

```
Optimal Objective Value =            16440.00000
```

Variable	Value	Reduced Cost
E	80.00000	0.00000
S	120.00000	0.00000
D	0.00000	-24.00000

Constraint	Slack/Surplus	Dual Value
1	0.00000	31.00000
2	0.00000	32.00000
3	320.00000	0.00000

Variable	Objective Coefficient	Allowable Increase	Allowable Decrease
E	63.00000	12.00000	15.50000
S	95.00000	31.00000	8.00000
D	135.00000	24.00000	Infinite

Constraint	RHS Value	Allowable Increase	Allowable Decrease
1	200.00000	80.00000	40.00000
2	320.00000	80.00000	120.00000
3	2400.00000	Infinite	320.00000

14. Digital Controls, Inc. (DCI), manufactures two models of a radar gun used by police to monitor the speed of automobiles. Model A has an accuracy of plus or minus 1 mile per hour, whereas the smaller model B has an accuracy of plus or minus 3 miles per hour. For the next week, the company has orders for 100 units of model A and 150 units of model B. Although DCI purchases all the electronic components used in both models, the plastic cases for both models are manufactured at a DCI plant in Newark, New Jersey. Each model A case requires 4 minutes of injection-molding time and 6 minutes of assembly time. Each model B case requires 3 minutes of injection-molding time and 8 minutes of assembly time. For next week, the Newark plant has 600 minutes of injection-molding time available and 1080 minutes of assembly time available. The manufacturing cost is $10 per case for model A and $6 per case for model B. Depending upon demand and the time available at the Newark plant, DCI occasionally purchases cases for one or both models from an outside supplier in order to fill customer orders that could not be filled otherwise. The purchase cost is $14 for each model A case and $9 for each model B case. Management wants to develop a minimum cost plan that will determine how many cases of each model should be produced at the Newark plant and how many cases of each model

should be purchased. The following decision variables were used to formulate a linear programming model for this problem:

$$AM = \text{number of cases of model A manufactured}$$
$$BM = \text{number of cases of model B manufactured}$$
$$AP = \text{number of cases of model A purchased}$$
$$BP = \text{number of cases of model B purchased}$$

The linear programming model that can be used to solve this problem is as follows:

Min $10AM + 6BM + 14AP + 9BP$

s.t.

$1AM +$	$+ \ 1AP +$	$=$	100	Demand for model A
	$1BM +$	$1BP =$	150	Demand for model B
$4AM + 3BM$		$\leq$	600	Injection molding time
$6AM + 8BM$		$\leq$	1080	Assembly time

$$AM, BM, AP, BP \geq 0$$

The computer solution is shown in Figure 3.18.

a. What is the optimal solution and what is the optimal value of the objective function?
b. Which constraints are binding?
c. What are the dual values? Interpret each.
d. If you could change the right-hand side of one constraint by one unit, which one would you choose? Why?

15. Refer to the computer solution to Problem 14 in Figure 3.18.
   a. Interpret the ranges of optimality for the objective function coefficients.
   b. Suppose that the manufacturing cost increases to $11.20 per case for model A. What is the new optimal solution?
   c. Suppose that the manufacturing cost increases to $11.20 per case for model A and the manufacturing cost for model B decreases to $5 per unit. Would the optimal solution change?

16. Tucker Inc. produces high-quality suits and sport coats for men. Each suit requires 1.2 hours of cutting time and 0.7 hours of sewing time, uses 6 yards of material, and provides a profit contribution of $190. Each sport coat requires 0.8 hours of cutting time and 0.6 hours of sewing time, uses 4 yards of material, and provides a profit contribution of $150. For the coming week, 200 hours of cutting time, 180 hours of sewing time, and 1200 yards of fabric are available. Additional cutting and sewing time can be obtained by scheduling overtime for these operations. Each hour of overtime for the cutting operation increases the hourly cost by $15, and each hour of overtime for the sewing operation increases the hourly cost by $10. A maximum of 100 hours of overtime can be scheduled. Marketing requirements specify a minimum production of 100 suits and 75 sport coats. Let

$$S = \text{number of suits produced}$$
$$SC = \text{number of sport coats produced}$$
$$D1 = \text{hours of overtime for the cutting operation}$$
$$D2 = \text{hours of overtime for the sewing operation}$$

FIGURE 3.18 THE SOLUTION FOR THE DIGITAL CONTROLS, INC., PROBLEM

```
Optimal Objective Value =          2170.00000
```

Variable	Value	Reduced Cost
AB	100.00000	0.00000
BM	60.00000	0.00000
AP	0.00000	1.75000
BP	90.00000	0.00000

Constraint	Slack/Surplus	Dual Value
1	0.00000	12.25000
2	0.00000	9.00000
3	20.00000	0.00000
4	0.00000	-0.37500

Variable	Objective Coefficient	Allowable Increase	Allowable Decrease
AB	10.00000	1.75000	Infinite
BM	6.00000	3.00000	2.33333
AP	14.00000	Infinite	1.75000
BP	9.00000	2.33333	3.00000

Constraint	RHS Value	Allowable Increase	Allowable Decrease
1	100.00000	11.42857	100.00000
2	150.00000	Infinite	90.00000
3	600.00000	Infinite	20.00000
4	1080.00000	53.33333	480.00000

The computer solution is shown in Figure 3.19.

a. What is the optimal solution, and what is the total profit? What is the plan for the use of overtime?

b. A price increase for suits is being considered that would result in a profit contribution of $210 per suit. If this price increase is undertaken, how will the optimal solution change?

c. Discuss the need for additional material during the coming week. If a rush order for material can be placed at the usual price plus an extra $8 per yard for handling, would you recommend the company consider placing a rush order for material? What is the maximum price Tucker would be willing to pay for an additional yard of material? How many additional yards of material should Tucker consider ordering?

d. Suppose the minimum production requirement for suits is lowered to 75. Would this change help or hurt profit? Explain.

FIGURE 3.19   THE SOLUTION FOR THE TUCKER INC. PROBLEM

```
Optimal Objective Value =            40900.00000
```

Variable	Value	Reduced Cost
S	100.00000	0.00000
SC	150.00000	0.00000
D1	40.00000	0.00000
D2	0.00000	-10.00000

Constraint	Slack/Surplus	Dual Value
1	0.00000	15.00000
2	20.00000	0.00000
3	0.00000	34.50000
4	60.00000	0.00000
5	0.00000	-35.00000
6	75.00000	0.00000

Variable	Objective Coefficient	Allowable Increase	Allowable Decrease
S	190.00000	35.00000	Infinite
SC	150.00000	Infinite	23.33333
D1	-15.00000	15.00000	172.50000
D2	-10.00000	10.00000	Infinite

Constraint	RHS Value	Allowable Increase	Allowable Decrease
1	200.00000	40.00000	60.00000
2	180.00000	Infinite	20.00000
3	1200.00000	133.33333	200.00000
4	100.00000	Infinite	60.00000
5	100.00000	50.00000	100.00000
6	75.00000	75.00000	Infinite

17. The Porsche Club of America sponsors driver education events that provide high-performance driving instruction on actual race tracks. Because safety is a primary consideration at such events, many owners elect to install roll bars in their cars. Deegan Industries manufactures two types of roll bars for Porsches. Model DRB is bolted to the car using existing holes in the car's frame. Model DRW is a heavier roll bar that must be welded to the car's frame. Model DRB requires 20 pounds of a special high alloy steel, 40 minutes of manufacturing time, and 60 minutes of assembly time. Model DRW requires 25 pounds of the special high alloy steel, 100 minutes of manufacturing time, and 40 minutes of assembly time. Deegan's steel supplier indicated that at most 40,000 pounds of the high-alloy steel will be available next quarter. In addition, Deegan estimates that 2000 hours of manufacturing time and 1600 hours of assembly time will be available next quarter. The profit

contributions are \$200 per unit for model DRB and \$280 per unit for model DRW. The linear programming model for this problem is as follows:

$$\text{Max} \quad 200DRB + 280DRW$$

s.t.

$$20DRB + \ \ 25DRW \le \ \ 40{,}000 \quad \text{Steel available}$$
$$40DRB + 100DRW \le 120{,}000 \quad \text{Manufacturing minutes}$$
$$60DRB + \ \ 40DRW \le \ \ 96{,}000 \quad \text{Assembly minutes}$$
$$DRB, DRW \ge 0$$

The computer solution is shown in Figure 3.20.

a. What are the optimal solution and the total profit contribution?

b. Another supplier offered to provide Deegan Industries with an additional 500 pounds of the steel alloy at \$2 per pound. Should Deegan purchase the additional pounds of the steel alloy? Explain.

c. Deegan is considering using overtime to increase the available assembly time. What would you advise Deegan to do regarding this option? Explain.

d. Because of increased competition, Deegan is considering reducing the price of model DRB such that the new contribution to profit is \$175 per unit. How would this change in price affect the optimal solution? Explain.

e. If the available manufacturing time is increased by 500 hours, will the dual value for the manufacturing time constraint change? Explain.

FIGURE 3.20 THE SOLUTION FOR THE DEEGAN INDUSTRIES PROBLEM

Optimal Objective Value =   424000.00000

Variable	Value	Reduced Cost
DRB	1000.00000	0.00000
DRW	800.00000	0.00000

Constraint	Slack/Surplus	Dual Value
1	0.00000	8.80000
2	0.00000	0.60000
3	4000.00000	0.00000

Variable	Objective Coefficient	Allowable Increase	Allowable Decrease
DRB	200.00000	24.00000	88.00000
DRW	280.00000	220.00000	30.00000

Constraint	RHS Value	Allowable Increase	Allowable Decrease
1	40000.00000	909.09091	10000.00000
2	120000.00000	40000.00000	5714.28571
3	96000.00000	Infinite	4000.00000

18. Davison Electronics manufactures two LCD television monitors, identified as model A and model B. Each model has its lowest possible production cost when produced on Davison's new production line. However, the new production line does not have the capacity to handle the total production of both models. As a result, at least some of the production must be routed to a higher-cost, old production line. The following table shows the minimum production requirements for next month, the production line capacities in units per month, and the production cost per unit for each production line:

Model	Production Cost per Unit		Minimum Production Requirements
	New Line	Old Line	
A	$30	$50	50,000
B	$25	$40	70,000
Production Line Capacity	80,000	60,000	

Let

AN = Units of model A produced on the new production line
AO = Units of model A produced on the old production line
BN = Units of model B produced on the new production line
BO = Units of model B produced on the old production line

Davison's objective is to determine the minimum cost production plan. The computer solution is shown in Figure 3.21.

a. Formulate the linear programming model for this problem using the following four constraints:

Constraint 1: Minimum production for model A
Constraint 2: Minimum production for model B
Constraint 3: Capacity of the new production line
Constraint 4: Capacity of the old production line

b. Using computer solution in Figure 3.21, what is the optimal solution, and what is the total production cost associated with this solution?
c. Which constraints are binding? Explain.
d. The production manager noted that the only constraint with a positive dual value is the constraint on the capacity of the new production line. The manager's interpretation of the dual value was that a one-unit increase in the right-hand side of this constraint would actually increase the total production cost by $15 per unit. Do you agree with this interpretation? Would an increase in capacity for the new production line be desirable? Explain.
e. Would you recommend increasing the capacity of the old production line? Explain.
f. The production cost for model A on the old production line is $50 per unit. How much would this cost have to change to make it worthwhile to produce model A on the old production line? Explain.
g. Suppose that the minimum production requirement for model B is reduced from 70,000 units to 60,000 units. What effect would this change have on the total production cost? Explain.

FIGURE 3.21   THE SOLUTION FOR THE DAVISON INDUSTRIES PROBLEM

```
Optimal Objective Value =            3850000.00000
```

Variable	Value	Reduced Cost
AN	50000.00000	0.00000
AO	0.00000	5.00000
BN	30000.00000	0.00000
BO	40000.00000	0.00000

Constraint	Slack/Surplus	Dual Value
1	0.00000	45.00000
2	0.00000	40.00000
3	0.00000	-15.00000
4	20000.00000	0.00000

Variable	Objective Coefficient	Allowable Increase	Allowable Decrease
AN	30.00000	5.00000	Infinite
AO	50.00000	Infinite	5.00000
BN	25.00000	15.00000	5.00000
BO	40.00000	5.00000	15.00000

Constraint	RHS Value	Allowable Increase	Allowable Decrease
1	50000.00000	20000.00000	40000.00000
2	70000.00000	20000.00000	40000.00000
3	80000.00000	40000.00000	20000.00000
4	60000.00000	Infinite	20000.00000

Problems 19–32 require formulation and computer solution.

19. Better Products, Inc., manufactures three products on two machines. In a typical week, 40 hours are available on each machine. The profit contribution and production time in hours per unit are as follows:

Category	Product 1	Product 2	Product 3
Profit/unit	$30	$50	$20
Machine 1 time/unit	0.5	2.0	0.75
Machine 2 time/unit	1.0	1.0	0.5

Two operators are required for machine 1; thus, 2 hours of labor must be scheduled for each hour of machine 1 time. Only one operator is required for machine 2. A maximum of 100 labor-hours is available for assignment to the machines during the coming week.

Other production requirements are that product 1 cannot account for more than 50% of the units produced and that product 3 must account for at least 20% of the units produced.

a. How many units of each product should be produced to maximize the total profit contribution? What is the projected weekly profit associated with your solution?
b. How many hours of production time will be scheduled on each machine?
c. What is the value of an additional hour of labor?
d. Assume that labor capacity can be increased to 120 hours. Would you be interested in using the additional 20 hours available for this resource? Develop the optimal product mix assuming the extra hours are made available.

20. Adirondack Savings Bank (ASB) has $1 million in new funds that must be allocated to home loans, personal loans, and automobile loans. The annual rates of return for the three types of loans are 7% for home loans, 12% for personal loans, and 9% for automobile loans. The bank's planning committee has decided that at least 40% of the new funds must be allocated to home loans. In addition, the planning committee has specified that the amount allocated to personal loans cannot exceed 60% of the amount allocated to automobile loans.

a. Formulate a linear programming model that can be used to determine the amount of funds ASB should allocate to each type of loan in order to maximize the total annual return for the new funds.
b. How much should be allocated to each type of loan? What is the total annual return? What is the annual percentage return?
c. If the interest rate on home loans increased to 9%, would the amount allocated to each type of loan change? Explain.
d. Suppose the total amount of new funds available was increased by $10,000. What effect would this have on the total annual return? Explain.
e. Assume that ASB has the original $1 million in new funds available and that the planning committee has agreed to relax the requirement that at least 40% of the new funds must be allocated to home loans by 1%. How much would the annual return change? How much would the annual percentage return change?

21. Round Tree Manor is a hotel that provides two types of rooms with three rental classes: Super Saver, Deluxe, and Business. The profit per night for each type of room and rental class is as follows:

		Rental Class		
		Super Saver	**Deluxe**	**Business**
Room	**Type I**	$30	$35	—
	Type II	$20	$30	$40

Type I rooms do not have Internet access and are not available for the Business rental class.

Round Tree's management makes a forecast of the demand by rental class for each night in the future. A linear programming model developed to maximize profit is used to determine how many reservations to accept for each rental class. The demand forecast for a particular night is 130 rentals in the Super Saver class, 60 rentals in the Deluxe class, and 50 rentals in the Business class. Round Tree has 100 Type I rooms and 120 Type II rooms.

a. Use linear programming to determine how many reservations to accept in each rental class and how the reservations should be allocated to room types. Is the demand by any rental class not satisfied? Explain.
b. How many reservations can be accommodated in each rental class?

    c. Management is considering offering a free breakfast to anyone upgrading from a Super Saver reservation to Deluxe class. If the cost of the breakfast to Round Tree is $5, should this incentive be offered?

    d. With a little work, an unused office area could be converted to a rental room. If the conversion cost is the same for both types of rooms, would you recommend converting the office to a Type I or a Type II room? Why?

    e. Could the linear programming model be modified to plan for the allocation of rental demand for the next night? What information would be needed and how would the model change?

22. Industrial Designs has been awarded a contract to design a label for a new wine produced by Lake View Winery. The company estimates that 150 hours will be required to complete the project. The firm's three graphics designers available for assignment to this project are Lisa, a senior designer and team leader; David, a senior designer; and Sarah, a junior designer. Because Lisa has worked on several projects for Lake View Winery, management specified that Lisa must be assigned at least 40% of the total number of hours assigned to the two senior designers. To provide label-designing experience for Sarah, Sarah must be assigned at least 15% of the total project time. However, the number of hours assigned to Sarah must not exceed 25% of the total number of hours assigned to the two senior designers. Due to other project commitments, Lisa has a maximum of 50 hours available to work on this project. Hourly wage rates are $30 for Lisa, $25 for David, and $18 for Sarah.

    a. Formulate a linear program that can be used to determine the number of hours each graphic designer should be assigned to the project in order to minimize total cost.

    b. How many hours should each graphic designer be assigned to the project? What is the total cost?

    c. Suppose Lisa could be assigned more than 50 hours. What effect would this have on the optimal solution? Explain.

    d. If Sarah were not required to work a minimum number of hours on this project, would the optimal solution change? Explain.

23. Vollmer Manufacturing makes three components for sale to refrigeration companies. The components are processed on two machines: a shaper and a grinder. The times (in minutes) required on each machine are as follows:

	Machine	
Component	**Shaper**	**Grinder**
1	6	4
2	4	5
3	4	2

The shaper is available for 120 hours, and the grinder is available for 110 hours. No more than 200 units of component 3 can be sold, but up to 1000 units of each of the other components can be sold. In fact, the company already has orders for 600 units of component 1 that must be satisfied. The profit contributions for components 1, 2, and 3 are $8, $6, and $9, respectively.

    a. Formulate and solve for the recommended production quantities.

    b. What are the objective coefficient ranges for the three components? Interpret these ranges for company management.

    c. What are the right-hand-side ranges? Interpret these ranges for company management.

    d. If more time could be made available on the grinder, how much would it be worth?

    e. If more units of component 3 can be sold by reducing the sales price by $4, should the company reduce the price?

24. National Insurance Associates carries an investment portfolio of stocks, bonds, and other investment alternatives. Currently $200,000 of funds are available and must be considered for new investment opportunities. The four stock options National is considering and the relevant financial data are as follows:

	Stock			
	A	**B**	**C**	**D**
Price per share	$100	$50	$80	$40
Annual rate of return	0.12	0.08	0.06	0.10
Risk measure per dollar invested	0.10	0.07	0.05	0.08

The risk measure indicates the relative uncertainty associated with the stock in terms of its realizing the projected annual return; higher values indicate greater risk. The risk measures are provided by the firm's top financial advisor.

National's top management has stipulated the following investment guidelines: The annual rate of return for the portfolio must be at least 9% and no one stock can account for more than 50% of the total dollar investment.

a. Use linear programming to develop an investment portfolio that minimizes risk.
b. If the firm ignores risk and uses a maximum return-on-investment strategy, what is the investment portfolio?
c. What is the dollar difference between the portfolios in parts (a) and (b)? Why might the company prefer the solution developed in part (a)?

25. Georgia Cabinets manufactures kitchen cabinets that are sold to local dealers throughout the Southeast. Because of a large backlog of orders for oak and cherry cabinets, the company decided to contract with three smaller cabinetmakers to do the final finishing operation. For the three cabinetmakers, the number of hours required to complete all the oak cabinets, the number of hours required to complete all the cherry cabinets, the number of hours available for the final finishing operation, and the cost per hour to perform the work are shown here.

	Cabinetmaker 1	**Cabinetmaker 2**	**Cabinetmaker 3**
Hours required to complete all the oak cabinets	50	42	30
Hours required to complete all the cherry cabinets	60	48	35
Hours available	40	30	35
Cost per hour	$36	$42	$55

For example, Cabinetmaker 1 estimates it will take 50 hours to complete all the oak cabinets and 60 hours to complete all the cherry cabinets. However, Cabinetmaker 1 only has 40 hours available for the final finishing operation. Thus, Cabinetmaker 1 can only complete 40/50 = 0.80, or 80%, of the oak cabinets if it worked only on oak cabinets. Similarly, Cabinetmaker 1 can only complete 40/60 = 0.67, or 67%, of the cherry cabinets if it worked only on cherry cabinets.

a. Formulate a linear programming model that can be used to determine the percentage of the oak cabinets and the percentage of the cherry cabinets that should be given to each of the three cabinetmakers in order to minimize the total cost of completing both projects.

b. Solve the model formulated in part (a). What percentage of the oak cabinets and what percentage of the cherry cabinets should be assigned to each cabinetmaker? What is the total cost of completing both projects?

c. If Cabinetmaker 1 has additional hours available, would the optimal solution change? Explain.

d. If Cabinetmaker 2 has additional hours available, would the optimal solution change? Explain.

e. Suppose Cabinetmaker 2 reduced its cost to $38 per hour. What effect would this change have on the optimal solution? Explain.

26. Benson Electronics manufactures three components used to produce cell telephones and other communication devices. In a given production period, demand for the three components may exceed Benson's manufacturing capacity. In this case, the company meets demand by purchasing the components from another manufacturer at an increased cost per unit. Benson's manufacturing cost per unit and purchasing cost per unit for the three components are as follows:

Source	Component 1	Component 2	Component 3
Manufacture	$4.50	$5.00	$2.75
Purchase	$6.50	$8.80	$7.00

Manufacturing times in minutes per unit for Benson's three departments are as follows:

Department	Component 1	Component 2	Component 3
Production	2	3	4
Assembly	1	1.5	3
Testing & Packaging	1.5	2	5

For instance, each unit of component 1 that Benson manufactures requires 2 minutes of production time, 1 minute of assembly time, and 1.5 minutes of testing and packaging time. For the next production period, Benson has capacities of 360 hours in the production department, 250 hours in the assembly department, and 300 hours in the testing and packaging department.

a. Formulate a linear programming model that can be used to determine how many units of each component to manufacture and how many units of each component to purchase. Assume that component demands that must be satisfied are 6000 units for component 1, 4000 units for component 2, and 3500 units for component 3. The objective is to minimize the total manufacturing and purchasing costs.

b. What is the optimal solution? How many units of each component should be manufactured and how many units of each component should be purchased?

c. Which departments are limiting Benson's manufacturing quantities? Use the dual value to determine the value of an *extra hour* in each of these departments.

d. Suppose that Benson had to obtain one additional unit of component 2. Discuss what the dual value for the component 2 constraint tells us about the cost to obtain the additional unit.

27. Golf Shafts, Inc. (GSI), produces graphite shafts for several manufacturers of golf clubs. Two GSI manufacturing facilities, one located in San Diego and the other in Tampa, have the capability to produce shafts in varying degrees of stiffness, ranging from regular models used primarily by average golfers to extra stiff models used primarily by low-handicap and professional golfers. GSI just received a contract for the production of 200,000 regular shafts and 75,000 stiff shafts. Because both plants are currently producing shafts for previous orders, neither plant has sufficient capacity by itself to fill the new order. The San Diego plant can produce up to a total of 120,000 shafts, and the Tampa plant can produce up to a total of 180,000 shafts. Because of equipment differences at each of the plants and differing labor costs, the per-unit production costs vary as shown here:

	San Diego Cost	Tampa Cost
Regular shaft	$5.25	$4.95
Stiff shaft	$5.45	$5.70

   a. Formulate a linear programming model to determine how GSI should schedule production for the new order in order to minimize the total production cost.
   b. Solve the model that you developed in part (a).
   c. Suppose that some of the previous orders at the Tampa plant could be rescheduled in order to free up additional capacity for the new order. Would this option be worthwhile? Explain.
   d. Suppose that the cost to produce a stiff shaft in Tampa had been incorrectly computed, and that the correct cost is $5.30 per shaft. What effect, if any, would the correct cost have on the optimal solution developed in part (b)? What effect would it have on total production cost?

28. The Pfeiffer Company manages approximately $15 million for clients. For each client, Pfeiffer chooses a mix of three investment vehicles: a growth stock fund, an income fund, and a money market fund. Each client has different investment objectives and different tolerances for risk. To accommodate these differences, Pfeiffer places limits on the percentage of each portfolio that may be invested in the three funds and assigns a portfolio risk index to each client.

   Here's how the system works for Dennis Hartmann, one of Pfeiffer's clients. Based on an evaluation of Hartmann's risk tolerance, Pfeiffer has assigned Hartmann's portfolio a risk index of 0.05. Furthermore, to maintain diversity, the fraction of Hartmann's portfolio invested in the growth and income funds must be at least 10% for each, and at least 20% must be in the money market fund.

   The risk ratings for the growth, income, and money market funds are 0.10, 0.05, and 0.01, respectively. A portfolio risk index is computed as a weighted average of the risk ratings for the three funds where the weights are the fraction of the portfolio invested in each of the funds. Hartmann has given Pfeiffer $300,000 to manage. Pfeiffer is currently forecasting a yield of 20% on the growth fund, 10% on the income fund, and 6% on the money market fund.

   a. Develop a linear programming model to select the best mix of investments for Hartmann's portfolio.
   b. Solve the model you developed in part (a).
   c. How much may the yields on the three funds vary before it will be necessary for Pfeiffer to modify Hartmann's portfolio?
   d. If Hartmann were more risk tolerant, how much of a yield increase could he expect? For instance, what if his portfolio risk index is increased to 0.06?
   e. If Pfeiffer revised the yield estimate for the growth fund downward to 0.10, how would you recommend modifying Hartmann's portfolio?

f. What information must Pfeiffer maintain on each client in order to use this system to manage client portfolios?

g. On a weekly basis Pfeiffer revises the yield estimates for the three funds. Suppose Pfeiffer has 50 clients. Describe how you would envision Pfeiffer making weekly modifications in each client's portfolio and allocating the total funds managed among the three investment funds.

29. La Jolla Beverage Products is considering producing a wine cooler that would be a blend of a white wine, a rosé wine, and fruit juice. To meet taste specifications, the wine cooler must consist of at least 50% white wine, at least 20% and no more than 30% rosé, and exactly 20% fruit juice. La Jolla purchases the wine from local wineries and the fruit juice from a processing plant in San Francisco. For the current production period, 10,000 gallons of white wine and 8000 gallons of rosé wine can be purchased; an unlimited amount of fruit juice can be ordered. The costs for the wine are $1.00 per gallon for the white and $1.50 per gallon for the rosé; the fruit juice can be purchased for $0.50 per gallon. La Jolla Beverage Products can sell all of the wine cooler they can produce for $2.50 per gallon.

a. Is the cost of the wine and fruit juice a sunk cost or a relevant cost in this situation? Explain.

b. Formulate a linear program to determine the blend of the three ingredients that will maximize the total profit contribution. Solve the linear program to determine the number of gallons of each ingredient La Jolla should purchase and the total profit contribution they will realize from this blend.

c. If La Jolla could obtain additional amounts of the white wine, should they do so? If so, how much should they be willing to pay for each additional gallon, and how many additional gallons would they want to purchase?

d. If La Jolla Beverage Products could obtain additional amounts of the rosé wine, should they do so? If so, how much should they be willing to pay for each additional gallon, and how many additional gallons would they want to purchase?

e. Interpret the dual value for the constraint corresponding to the requirement that the wine cooler must contain at least 50% white wine. What is your advice to management given this dual value?

f. Interpret the dual value for the constraint corresponding to the requirement that the wine cooler must contain exactly 20% fruit juice. What is your advice to management given this dual value?

30. The program manager for Channel 10 would like to determine the best way to allocate the time for the 11:00–11:30 evening news broadcast. Specifically, she would like to determine the number of minutes of broadcast time to devote to local news, national news, weather, and sports. Over the 30-minute broadcast, 10 minutes are set aside for advertising. The station's broadcast policy states that at least 15% of the time available should be devoted to local news coverage; the time devoted to local news or national news must be at least 50% of the total broadcast time; the time devoted to the weather segment must be less than or equal to the time devoted to the sports segment; the time devoted to the sports segment should be no longer than the total time spent on the local and national news; and at least 20% of the time should be devoted to the weather segment. The production costs per minute are $300 for local news, $200 for national news, $100 for weather, and $100 for sports.

a. Formulate and solve a linear program that can determine how the 20 available minutes should be used to minimize the total cost of producing the program.

b. Interpret the dual value for the constraint corresponding to the available time. What advice would you give the station manager given this dual value?

c. Interpret the dual value for the constraint corresponding to the requirement that at least 15% of the available time should be devoted to local coverage. What advice would you give the station manager given this dual value?

d. Interpret the dual value for the constraint corresponding to the requirement that the time devoted to the local and the national news must be at least 50% of the total broadcast time. What advice would you give the station manager given this dual value?

e. Interpret the dual value for the constraint corresponding to the requirement that the time devoted to the weather segment must be less than or equal to the time devoted to the sports segment. What advice would you give the station manager given this dual value?

31. Gulf Coast Electronics is ready to award contracts for printing their annual report. For the past several years, the four-color annual report has been printed by Johnson Printing and Lakeside Litho. A new firm, Benson Printing, inquired into the possibility of doing a portion of the printing. The quality and service level provided by Lakeside Litho has been extremely high; in fact, only 0.5% of their reports have had to be discarded because of quality problems. Johnson Printing has also had a high quality level historically, producing an average of only 1% unacceptable reports. Because Gulf Coast Electronics has had no experience with Benson Printing, they estimated their defective rate to be 10%. Gulf Coast would like to determine how many reports should be printed by each firm to obtain 75,000 acceptable-quality reports. To ensure that Benson Printing will receive some of the contract, management specified that the number of reports awarded to Benson Printing must be at least 10% of the volume given to Johnson Printing. In addition, the total volume assigned to Benson Printing, Johnson Printing, and Lakeside Litho should not exceed 30,000, 50,000, and 50,000 copies, respectively. Because of the long-term relationship with Lakeside Litho, management also specified that at least 30,000 reports should be awarded to Lakeside Litho. The cost per copy is $2.45 for Benson Printing, $2.50 for Johnson Printing, and $2.75 for Lakeside Litho.

a. Formulate and solve a linear program for determining how many copies should be assigned to each printing firm to minimize the total cost of obtaining 75,000 acceptable-quality reports.

b. Suppose that the quality level for Benson Printing is much better than estimated. What effect, if any, would this quality level have?

c. Suppose that management is willing to reconsider their requirement that Lakeside Litho be awarded at least 30,000 reports. What effect, if any, would this consideration have?

32. PhotoTech, Inc., a manufacturer of rechargeable batteries for digital cameras, signed a contract with a digital photography company to produce three different lithium-ion battery packs for a new line of digital cameras. The contract calls for the following:

Battery Pack	Production Quantity
PT-100	200,000
PT-200	100,000
PT-300	150,000

PhotoTech can manufacture the battery packs at manufacturing plants located in the Philippines and Mexico. The unit cost of the battery packs differs at the two plants because of differences in production equipment and wage rates. The unit costs for each battery pack at each manufacturing plant are as follows:

	Plant	
Product	Philippines	Mexico
PT-100	$0.95	$0.98
PT-200	$0.98	$1.06
PT-300	$1.34	$1.15

The PT-100 and PT-200 battery packs are produced using similar production equipment available at both plants. However, each plant has a limited capacity for the total number of PT-100 and PT-200 battery packs produced. The combined PT-100 and PT-200 production capacities are 175,000 units at the Philippines plant and 160,000 units at the Mexico plant. The PT-300 production capacities are 75,000 units at the Philippines plant and 100,000 units at the Mexico plant. The cost of shipping from the Philippines plant is $0.18 per unit, and the cost of shipping from the Mexico plant is $0.10 per unit.

a. Develop a linear program that PhotoTech can use to determine how many units of each battery pack to produce at each plant in order to minimize the total production and shipping cost associated with the new contract.

b. Solve the linear program developed in part (a) to determine the optimal production plan.

c. Use sensitivity analysis to determine how much the production and/or shipping cost per unit would have to change in order to produce additional units of the PT-100 in the Philippines plant.

d. Use sensitivity analysis to determine how much the production and/or shipping cost per unit would have to change in order to produce additional units of the PT-200 in the Mexico plant.

Case Problem 1   PRODUCT MIX

TJ's, Inc., makes three nut mixes for sale to grocery chains located in the Southeast. The three mixes, referred to as the Regular Mix, the Deluxe Mix, and the Holiday Mix, are made by mixing different percentages of five types of nuts.

In preparation for the fall season, TJ's has just purchased the following shipments of nuts at the prices shown:

Type of Nut	Shipment Amount (pounds)	Cost per Shipment ($)
Almond	6000	7500
Brazil	7500	7125
Filbert	7500	6750
Pecan	6000	7200
Walnut	7500	7875

The Regular Mix consists of 15% almonds, 25% Brazil nuts, 25% filberts, 10% pecans, and 25% walnuts. The Deluxe Mix consists of 20% of each type of nut, and the Holiday Mix consists of 25% almonds, 15% Brazil nuts, 15% filberts, 25% pecans, and 20% walnuts.

TJ's accountant analyzed the cost of packaging materials, sales price per pound, and so forth, and determined that the profit contribution per pound is $1.65 for the Regular Mix, $2.00 for the Deluxe Mix, and $2.25 for the Holiday Mix. These figures do not include the cost of specific types of nuts in the different mixes because that cost can vary greatly in the commodity markets.

Customer orders already received are summarized here:

Type of Mix	Orders (pounds)
Regular	10,000
Deluxe	3,000
Holiday	5,000

Because demand is running high, it is expected that TJ's will receive many more orders than can be satisfied.

TJ's is committed to using the available nuts to maximize profit over the fall season; nuts not used will be given to a local charity. Even if it is not profitable to do so, TJ's president indicated that the orders already received must be satisfied.

Managerial Report

Perform an analysis of TJ's product-mix problem, and prepare a report for TJ's president that summarizes your findings. Be sure to include information and analysis on the following:

1. The cost per pound of the nuts included in the Regular, Deluxe, and Holiday mixes
2. The optimal product mix and the total profit contribution
3. Recommendations regarding how the total profit contribution can be increased if additional quantities of nuts can be purchased
4. A recommendation as to whether TJ's should purchase an additional 1000 pounds of almonds for $1000 from a supplier who overbought
5. Recommendations on how profit contribution could be increased (if at all) if TJ's does not satisfy all existing orders

Case Problem 2   INVESTMENT STRATEGY

J. D. Williams, Inc., is an investment advisory firm that manages more than $120 million in funds for its numerous clients. The company uses an asset allocation model that recommends the portion of each client's portfolio to be invested in a growth stock fund, an income fund, and a money market fund. To maintain diversity in each client's portfolio, the firm places limits on the percentage of each portfolio that may be invested in each of the three funds. General guidelines indicate that the amount invested in the growth fund must be between 20% and 40% of the total portfolio value. Similar percentages for the other two funds stipulate that between 20% and 50% of the total portfolio value must be in the income fund, and at least 30% of the total portfolio value must be in the money market fund.

In addition, the company attempts to assess the risk tolerance of each client and adjust the portfolio to meet the needs of the individual investor. For example, Williams just contracted with a new client who has $800,000 to invest. Based on an evaluation of the client's risk tolerance, Williams assigned a maximum risk index of 0.05 for the client. The firm's risk indicators show the risk of the growth fund at 0.10, the income fund at 0.07, and the money market fund at 0.01. An overall portfolio risk index is computed as a weighted average of the risk rating for the three funds where the weights are the fraction of the client's portfolio invested in each of the funds.

Additionally, Williams is currently forecasting annual yields of 18% for the growth fund, 12.5% for the income fund, and 7.5% for the money market fund. Based on the information provided, how should the new client be advised to allocate the $800,000 among the growth, income, and money market funds? Develop a linear programming model that will provide the maximum yield for the portfolio. Use your model to develop a managerial report.

Managerial Report

1. Recommend how much of the $800,000 should be invested in each of the three funds. What is the annual yield you anticipate for the investment recommendation?
2. Assume that the client's risk index could be increased to 0.055. How much would the yield increase and how would the investment recommendation change?

3. Refer again to the original situation where the client's risk index was assessed to be 0.05. How would your investment recommendation change if the annual yield for the growth fund were revised downward to 16% or even to 14%?
4. Assume that the client expressed some concern about having too much money in the growth fund. How would the original recommendation change if the amount invested in the growth fund is not allowed to exceed the amount invested in the income fund?
5. The asset allocation model you developed may be useful in modifying the portfolios for all of the firm's clients whenever the anticipated yields for the three funds are periodically revised. What is your recommendation as to whether use of this model is possible?

Case Problem 3   TRUCK LEASING STRATEGY

Reep Construction recently won a contract for the excavation and site preparation of a new rest area on the Pennsylvania Turnpike. In preparing his bid for the job, Bob Reep, founder and president of Reep Construction, estimated that it would take four months to perform the work and that 10, 12, 14, and 8 trucks would be needed in months 1 through 4, respectively.

The firm currently has 20 trucks of the type needed to perform the work on the new project. These trucks were obtained last year when Bob signed a long-term lease with PennState Leasing. Although most of these trucks are currently being used on existing jobs, Bob estimates that one truck will be available for use on the new project in month 1, two trucks will be available in month 2, three trucks will be available in month 3, and one truck will be available in month 4. Thus, to complete the project, Bob will have to lease additional trucks.

The long-term leasing contract with PennState has a monthly cost of $600 per truck. Reep Construction pays its truck drivers $20 an hour, and daily fuel costs are approximately $100 per truck. All maintenance costs are paid by PennState Leasing. For planning purposes, Bob estimates that each truck used on the new project will be operating eight hours a day, five days a week for approximately four weeks each month.

Bob does not believe that current business conditions justify committing the firm to additional long-term leases. In discussing the short-term leasing possibilities with PennState Leasing, Bob learned that he can obtain short-term leases of 1–4 months. Short-term leases differ from long-term leases in that the short-term leasing plans include the cost of both a truck and a driver. Maintenance costs for short-term leases also are paid by PennState Leasing. The following costs for each of the four months cover the lease of a truck and driver:

Length of Lease	Cost per Month ($)
1	4000
2	3700
3	3225
4	3040

Bob Reep would like to acquire a lease that would minimize the cost of meeting the monthly trucking requirements for his new project, but he also takes great pride in the fact that his company has never laid off employees. Bob is committed to maintaining his no-layoff policy; that is, he will use his own drivers even if costs are higher.

Managerial Report

Perform an analysis of Reep Construction's leasing problem and prepare a report for Bob Reep that summarizes your findings. Be sure to include information on and analysis of the following items:

1. The optimal leasing plan
2. The costs associated with the optimal leasing plan
3. The cost for Reep Construction to maintain its current policy of no layoffs

Appendix 3.1   SENSITIVITY ANALYSIS WITH EXCEL

In Appendix 2.2 we showed how Excel Solver can be used to solve a linear program by using it to solve the Par, Inc., problem. Let us now see how it can be used to provide sensitivity analysis.

When Solver finds the optimal solution to a linear program, the **Solver Results** dialog box (see Figure 3.22) will appear on the screen. If only the solution is desired, you simply click **OK**. To obtain the optimal solution and the sensitivity analysis output, you must select **Sensitivity** in the **Reports** box before clicking **OK;** the sensitivity report is created on another worksheet in the same Excel workbook. Using this procedure for the Par problem, we obtained the optimal solution shown in Figure 3.23 and the sensitivity report shown in Figure 3.24.

Interpretation of Excel Sensitivity Report

In the Adjustable Cells section of the Sensitivity Report, the column labeled Final Value contains the optimal values of the decision variables. For the Par, Inc., problem the optimal solution is 540 standard bags and 252 deluxe bags. Next, let us consider the values in the Reduced Cost column.[1] For the Par, Inc., problem the reduced costs for both decision variables are zero; they are at their optimal values.

FIGURE 3.22   EXCEL SOLVER RESULTS DIALOG BOX

---

[1]In Excel, if the value of a variable in an optimal solution is equal to the upper bound of the variable, then reduced cost will be the dual value of this upper bound constraint.

FIGURE 3.23   EXCEL SOLUTION FOR THE PAR, INC., PROBLEM

WEB file

Par

	A	B	C	D
1	Par, Inc.			
2				
3		Production Time		
4	Operation	Standard	Deluxe	Time Available
5	Cutting and Dyeing	0.7	1	630
6	Sewing	0.5	0.83333	600
7	Finishing	1	0.66667	708
8	Inspection and packaging	0.1	0.25	135
9	**Profit Per Bag**	10	9	
10				
11				
12	**Model**			
13				
14		Decision Variables		
15		Standard	Deluxe	
16	**Bags Produced**	539.99842	252.00110	
17				
18	**Maximize Total Profit**	7668		
19				
20	**Constraints**	Hours Used (LHS)		Hours Available (RHS)
21	Cutting and Dyeing	630	<=	630
22	Sewing	479.99929	<=	600
23	Finishing	708	<=	708
24	Inspection and Packaging	117.00012	<=	135

FIGURE 3.24   EXCEL SENSITIVITY REPORT FOR THE PAR, INC., PROBLEM

Adjustable Cells

Cell	Name	Final Value	Reduced Cost	Objective Coefficient	Allowable Increase	Allowable Decrease
$B$16	Bags Produced Standard	539.99842	0.00000	10	3.4999325	3.7
$C$16	Bags Produced Deluxe	252.00110	0.00000	9	5.285714286	2.3333

Constraints

Cell	Name	Final Value	Shadow Price	Constraint R.H. Side	Allowable Increase	Allowable Decrease
$B$21	Cutting and Dyeing Hours Used (LHS)	630	4.37495664	630	52.36315884	134.4
$B$22	Sewing Hours Used (LHS)	479.99929	0.00000	600	1E+30	120.0007088
$B$23	Finishing Hours Used (LHS)	708	6.937530352	708	192	127.9986
$B$24	Inspection and Packaging Hours Used (LHS)	117.00012	0.00000	135	1E+30	17.99988187

To the right of the Reduced Cost column in Figure 3.24, we find three columns labeled Objective Coefficient, Allowable Increase, and Allowable Decrease. Note that for the standard bag decision variable, the objective function coefficient value is 10, the allowable increase is 3.5, and the allowable decrease is 3.7. Adding 3.5 to and subtracting 3.7 from the current coefficient of 10 provides the range of optimality for C_S.

$$6.3 \leq C_S \leq 13.5$$

Similarly, the range of optimality for C_D is

$$6.67 \leq C_D \leq 14.29$$

Next, consider the information in the Constraints section of the report. The entries in the Final Value column are the number of hours needed in each department to produce the optimal production quantities of 540 standard bags and 252 deluxe bags. Thus, at the optimal solution, 630 hours of cutting and dyeing time, 480 hours of sewing time, 708 hours of finishing time, and 117 hours of inspection and packaging time are required. The values in the Constraint R.H. Side column are just the original right-hand-side values: 630 hours of cutting and dyeing time, 600 hours of sewing time, 708 hours of finishing time, and 135 hours of inspection and packaging time. Note that for the Par, Inc., problem, the values of the slack variables for each constraint are simply the differences between the entries in the Constraint R.H. Side column and the corresponding entries in the Final Value column.

The sensitivity analysis interpretations provided in this appendix are based on the assumption that only one objective function coefficient or only one right-hand-side change occurs at a time.

The entries in the Shadow Price column provide the *shadow price* for each constraint. The shadow price is another, often-used term for the dual value. The last two columns of the Sensitivity Report contain the range of feasibility information for the constraint right-hand sides. For example, consider the cutting and dyeing constraint with an allowable increase value of 52.4 and an allowable decrease value of 134.4. The values in the Allowable Increase and Allowable Decrease columns indicate that the shadow price of $4.375 is valid for increases up to 52.4 hours and decreases to 134.4 hours. Thus, the shadow price of $4.375 is applicable for increases up to $630 + 52.4 = 682.4$ and decreases down to $630 - 134.4 = 495.6$ hours.

In summary, the range of feasibility information provides the limits where the shadow prices are applicable. For changes outside the range, the problem must be re-solved to find the new optimal solution and the new shadow price.

Appendix 3.2   SENSITIVITY ANALYSIS WITH LINGO

In Appendix 2.1 we showed how LINGO can be used to solve a linear program by using it to solve the Par, Inc., problem. A copy of the Solution Report is shown in Figure 3.25. As we discussed previously, the value of the objective function is 7668, the optimal solution is $S = 540$ and $D = 252$, and the values of the slack variables corresponding to the four constraints (rows 2–5) are 0, 120, 0, and 18. Now let us consider the information in the Reduced Cost column and the Dual Price column.

LINGO always takes the absolute value of the reduced cost.

For the Par, Inc., problem, the reduced costs for both decision variables are zero because both variables are at a positive value. LINGO reports a **dual price** rather than a dual value. For a maximization problem, the dual value and dual price are identical. For a minimization problem, the dual price is equal to the negative of the dual value. There are historical reasons for this oddity that are beyond the scope of the book. When interpreting the LINGO output for a minimization problem, multiply the dual prices by −1, treat the resulting number as the dual value, and interpret the number as described in Section 3.2. The nonzero dual prices of 4.374957 for constraint 1 (cutting and dyeing constraint in row 2)

FIGURE 3.25   PAR, INC., SOLUTION REPORT USING LINGO

```
Global optimal solution found.
   Objective value:                7668.000
   Total solver iterations:               2

         Variable              Value          Reduced Cost
         --------          ------------      ------------
            S                540.0000          0.000000
            D                252.0000          0.000000

           Row          Slack or Surplus      Dual Price
         --------          ------------      ------------
            1                7668.000          1.000000
            2                0.000000          4.375000
            3                120.0000          0.000000
            4                0.000000          6.937500
            5                18.00000          0.000000
```

and 6.937530 for constraint 3 (finishing constraint in row 4) tell us that an additional hour of cutting and dyeing time improves (increases) the value of the optimal solution by \$4.37 and an additional hour of finishing time improves (increases) the value of the optimal solution by \$6.94.

Next, let us consider how LINGO can be used to compute the range of optimality for each objective function coefficient and the range of feasibility for each of the dual prices. By default, range computations are not enabled in LINGO. To enable range computations, perform the following steps:

Step 1. Choose the **LINGO** menu
Step 2. Select **Options**
Step 3. When the LINGO Options dialog box appears:
    Select the **General Solver** tab
    Choose **Prices and Ranges** in the **Dual Computations** box
    Click **Apply**
    Click **OK**

You will now have to re-solve the Par, Inc., problem in order for LINGO to perform the range computations. After re-solving the problem, close or minimize the Solution Report window. To display the range information, select the Range command from the LINGO menu. LINGO displays the range information in a new window titled Range Report. The output that appears in the Range Report window for the Par, Inc., problem is shown in Figure 3.26.

We will use the information in the Objective Coefficient Ranges section of the range report to compute the range of optimality for the objective function coefficients. For example, the current objective function coefficient for S is 10. Note that the corresponding allowable increase is 3.5 and the corresponding allowable decrease is 3.700000. Thus, the range of optimality for C_S, the objective function coefficient for S, is $10 - 3.700000 = 6.300000$ to $10 + 3.5 = 13.5$. After rounding, the range of optimality for C_S is $6.30 \leq C_S \leq 13.50$.

FIGURE 3.26   PAR, INC., SENSITIVITY REPORT USING LINGO

Ranges in which the basis is unchanged:

OBJECTIVE COEFFICIENT RANGES

Variable	Current Coefficient	Allowable Increase	Allowable Decrease
S	10.00000	3.500000	3.700000
D	9.000000	5.285714	2.333333

RIGHTHAND SIDE RANGES

Row	Current RHS	Allowable Increase	Allowable Decrease
2	630.0000	52.36364	134.4000
3	600.0000	INFINITY	120.0000
4	708.0000	192.0000	128.0000
5	135.0000	INFINITY	18.00000

Similarly, with an allowable increase of 5.285714 and an allowable decrease of 2.333300, the range of optimality for C_D is $6.67 \leq C_S \leq 14.29$.

To compute the range of feasibility for each dual price, we will use the information in the Right-Hand-Side Ranges section of the range report. For example, the current right-hand-side value for the cutting and dyeing constraint (row 2) is 630, the allowable increase is 52.36316, and the allowable decrease is 134.40000. Because the dual price for this constraint is 4.375 (shown in the LINGO solution report), we can conclude that additional hours will increase the objective function by $4.37 per hour. From the range information given, we see that after rounding the dual price of $4.37 is valid for increases up to 630 + 52.36 = 682.4 and decreases to 630 − 134.4 = 495.6. Thus, the range of feasibility for the cutting and dyeing constraint is 495.6 to 682.4. The ranges of feasibility for the other constraints can be determined in a similar manner.

CHAPTER 4

Linear Programming Applications in Marketing, Finance, and Operations Management

CONTENTS

4.1 MARKETING APPLICATIONS
Media Selection
Marketing Research

4.2 FINANCIAL APPLICATIONS
Portfolio Selection
Financial Planning

4.3 OPERATIONS MANAGEMENT
APPLICATIONS
A Make-or-Buy Decision
Production Scheduling
Workforce Assignment
Blending Problems

Linear programming has proven to be one of the most successful quantitative approaches to decision making. Applications have been reported in almost every industry. These applications include production scheduling, media selection, financial planning, capital budgeting, transportation, distribution system design, product mix, staffing, and blending.

The wide variety of Management Science in Actions presented in Chapters 2 and 3 illustrated the use of linear programming as a flexible problem-solving tool. The Management Science in Action, A Marketing Planning Model at Marathon Oil Company, provides another example of the use of linear programming by showing how Marathon uses a large-scale linear programming model to solve a wide variety of planning problems. Later in the chapter other Management Science in Action features illustrate how GE Capital uses linear programming for optimal lease structuring; how Jeppesen Sanderson uses linear programming to optimize production of flight manuals; and how the Kellogg Company uses a large-scale linear programming model to integrate production, distribution, and inventory planning.

In this chapter we present a variety of applications from the traditional business areas of marketing, finance, and operations management. Modeling, computer solution, and interpretation of output are emphasized. A mathematical model is developed for each problem studied, and solutions are presented for most of the applications. In the chapter appendix we illustrate the use of Excel Solver by solving a financial planning problem.

MANAGEMENT SCIENCE IN ACTION

A MARKETING PLANNING MODEL AT MARATHON OIL COMPANY*

Marathon Oil Company has four refineries within the United States, operates 50 light products terminals, and has product demand at more than 95 locations. The Supply and Transportation Division faces the problem of determining which refinery should supply which terminal and, at the same time, determining which products should be transported via pipeline, barge, or tanker to minimize cost. Product demand must be satisfied, and the supply capability of each refinery must not be exceeded. To help solve this difficult problem, Marathon Oil developed a marketing planning model.

The marketing planning model is a large-scale linear programming model that takes into account sales not only at Marathon product terminals but also at all exchange locations. An exchange contract is an agreement with other oil product marketers that involves exchanging or trading Marathon's products for theirs at different locations. All pipelines, barges, and tankers within Marathon's marketing area are also represented in the linear programming model.

The objective of the model is to minimize the cost of meeting a given demand structure, taking into account sales price, pipeline tariffs, exchange contract costs, product demand, terminal operating costs, refining costs, and product purchases.

The marketing planning model is used to solve a wide variety of planning problems that vary from evaluating gasoline blending economics to analyzing the economics of a new terminal or pipeline. With daily sales of about 10 million gallons of refined light product, a savings of even one-thousandth of a cent per gallon can result in significant long-term savings. At the same time, what may appear to be a savings in one area, such as refining or transportation, may actually add to overall costs when the effects are fully realized throughout the system. The marketing planning model allows a simultaneous examination of this total effect.

*Based on information provided by Robert W. Wernert at Marathon Oil Company, Findlay, Ohio.

4.1   MARKETING APPLICATIONS

Applications of linear programming in marketing are numerous. In this section we discuss applications in media selection and marketing research.

Media Selection

In Section 2.1 we provided some general guidelines for modeling linear programming problems. You may want to review Section 2.1 before proceeding with the linear programming applications in this chapter.

Media selection applications of linear programming are designed to help marketing managers allocate a fixed advertising budget to various advertising media. Potential media include newspapers, magazines, radio, television, and direct mail. In these applications, the objective is to maximize reach, frequency, and quality of exposure. Restrictions on the allowable allocation usually arise during consideration of company policy, contract requirements, and media availability. In the application that follows, we illustrate how a media selection problem might be formulated and solved using a linear programming model.

Relax-and-Enjoy Lake Development Corporation is developing a lakeside community at a privately owned lake. The primary market for the lakeside lots and homes includes all middle- and upper-income families within approximately 100 miles of the development. Relax-and-Enjoy employed the advertising firm of Boone, Phillips, and Jackson (BP&J) to design the promotional campaign.

After considering possible advertising media and the market to be covered, BP&J recommended that the first month's advertising be restricted to five media. At the end of the month, BP&J will then reevaluate its strategy based on the month's results. BP&J collected data on the number of potential customers reached, the cost per advertisement, the maximum number of times each medium is available, and the exposure quality rating for each of the five media. The quality rating is measured in terms of an exposure quality unit, a measure of the relative value of one advertisement in each of the media. This measure, based on BP&J's experience in the advertising business, takes into account factors such as audience demographics (age, income, and education of the audience reached), image presented, and quality of the advertisement. The information collected is presented in Table 4.1.

Relax-and-Enjoy provided BP&J with an advertising budget of $30,000 for the first month's campaign. In addition, Relax-and-Enjoy imposed the following restrictions on how BP&J may allocate these funds: At least 10 television commercials must be used, at least 50,000 potential customers must be reached, and no more than $18,000 may be spent on television advertisements. What advertising media selection plan should be recommended?

TABLE 4.1 ADVERTISING MEDIA ALTERNATIVES FOR THE RELAX-AND-ENJOY LAKE DEVELOPMENT CORPORATION

Advertising Media	Number of Potential Customers Reached	Cost ($) per Advertisement	Maximum Times Available per Month*	Exposure Quality Units
1. Daytime TV (1 min), station WKLA	1000	1500	15	65
2. Evening TV (30 sec), station WKLA	2000	3000	10	90
3. Daily newspaper (full page), *The Morning Journal*	1500	400	25	40
4. Sunday newspaper magazine (½ page color), *The Sunday Press*	2500	1000	4	60
5. Radio, 8:00 A.M. or 5:00 P.M. news (30 sec), station KNOP	300	100	30	20

*The maximum number of times the medium is available is either the maximum number of times the advertising medium occurs (e.g., four Sundays per month) or the maximum number of times BP&J recommends that the medium be used.

The decision to be made is how many times to use each medium. We begin by defining the decision variables:

$$DTV = \text{number of times daytime TV is used}$$
$$ETV = \text{number of times evening TV is used}$$
$$DN = \text{number of times daily newspaper is used}$$
$$SN = \text{number of times Sunday newspaper is used}$$
$$R = \text{number of times radio is used}$$

The data on quality of exposure in Table 4.1 show that each daytime TV (DTV) advertisement is rated at 65 exposure quality units. Thus, an advertising plan with DTV advertisements will provide a total of $65DTV$ exposure quality units. Continuing with the data in Table 4.1, we find evening TV (ETV) rated at 90 exposure quality units, daily newspaper (DN) rated at 40 exposure quality units, Sunday newspaper (SN) rated at 60 exposure quality units, and radio (R) rated at 20 exposure quality units. With the objective of maximizing the total exposure quality units for the overall media selection plan, the objective function becomes

Care must be taken to ensure the linear programming model accurately reflects the real problem. Always review your formulation thoroughly before attempting to solve the model.

$$\text{Max} \quad 65DTV + 90ETV + 40DN + 60SN + 20R \qquad \text{Exposure quality}$$

We now formulate the constraints for the model from the information given:

$$
\begin{aligned}
DTV & & & & & \leq 15 \\
& ETV & & & & \leq 10 \\
& & DN & & & \leq 25 \\
& & & SN & & \leq 4 \\
& & & & R & \leq 30
\end{aligned}
\left.\vphantom{\begin{aligned}1\\1\\1\\1\\1\end{aligned}}\right\} \text{Availability of media}
$$

$$1500DTV + 3000ETV + 400DN + 1000SN + 100R \leq 30{,}000 \quad \text{Budget}$$

$$
\left.
\begin{aligned}
DTV + ETV & \geq 10 \\
1500DTV + 3000ETV & \leq 18{,}000
\end{aligned}
\right\}
\begin{aligned}
& \text{Television} \\
& \text{restrictions}
\end{aligned}
$$

$$1000DTV + 2000ETV + 1500DN + 2500SN + 300R \geq 50{,}000 \quad \text{Customers reached}$$

$$DTV, ETV, DN, SN, R \geq 0$$

Problem 1 provides practice at formulating a similar media selection model.

The optimal solution to this five-variable, nine-constraint linear programming model is shown in Figure 4.1; a summary is presented in Table 4.2.

The optimal solution calls for advertisements to be distributed among daytime TV, daily newspaper, Sunday newspaper, and radio. The maximum number of exposure quality units is 2370, and the total number of customers reached is 61,500. The Reduced Costs column in Figure 4.1 indicates that the number of exposure quality units for evening TV would have to increase by at least 65 before this media alternative could appear in the optimal solution. Note that the budget constraint (constraint 6) has a dual value of 0.060. Therefore, a $1.00 increase in the advertising budget will lead to an increase of 0.06 exposure quality units. The dual value of –25.000 for constraint 7 indicates that increasing the number of television commercials by 1 will decrease the exposure quality of the advertising plan by 25 units. Alternatively, decreasing the number of television commercials by 1 will increase the exposure quality of the advertising plan by 25 units. Thus,

FIGURE 4.1 THE SOLUTION FOR THE RELAX-AND-ENJOY LAKE DEVELOPMENT
                CORPORATION PROBLEM

```
Optimal Objective Value =        2370.00000

      Variable              Value            Reduced Cost
   --------------      ---------------     ------------------

        DTV               10.00000             0.00000
        ETV                0.00000           -65.00000
        DN                25.00000             0.00000
        SN                 2.00000             0.00000
        R                 30.00000             0.00000


     Constraint         Slack/Surplus          Dual Value
   --------------      ---------------     ------------------

         1                 5.00000             0.00000
         2                10.00000             0.00000
         3                 0.00000            16.00000
         4                 2.00000             0.00000
         5                 0.00000            14.00000
         6                 0.00000             0.06000
         7                 0.00000           -25.00000
         8              3000.00000             0.00000
         9             11500.00000             0.00000
```

Media Availability — Budget — Television Restrictions — Audience Coverage

TABLE 4.2 ADVERTISING PLAN FOR THE RELAX-AND-ENJOY LAKE
               DEVELOPMENT CORPORATION

Media	Frequency	Budget
Daytime TV	10	$15,000
Daily newspaper	25	10,000
Sunday newspaper	2	2,000
Radio	30	3,000
		$30,000

Exposure quality units = 2370
Total customers reached = 61,500

Relax-and-Enjoy should consider reducing the requirement of having at least 10 television commercials.

A possible shortcoming of this model is that, even if the exposure quality measure were not subject to error, it offers no guarantee that maximization of total exposure quality will lead to maximization of profit or of sales (a common surrogate for profit). However, this issue is not a shortcoming of linear programming; rather, it is a shortcoming of the use of exposure quality as a criterion. If we could directly measure the effect of an advertisement on profit, we could use total profit as the objective to be maximized.

NOTES AND COMMENTS

1. The media selection model required subjective evaluations of the exposure quality for the media alternatives. Marketing managers may have substantial data concerning exposure quality, but the final coefficients used in the objective function may also include considerations based primarily on managerial judgment. Judgment is an acceptable way of obtaining input for a linear programming model.

2. The media selection model presented in this section uses exposure quality as the objective function and places a constraint on the number of customers reached. An alternative formulation of this problem would be to use the number of customers reached as the objective function and add a constraint indicating the minimum total exposure quality required for the media plan.

Marketing Research

An organization conducts marketing research to learn about consumer characteristics, attitudes, and preferences. Marketing research firms that specialize in providing such information often do the actual research for client organizations. Typical services offered by a marketing research firm include designing the study, conducting market surveys, analyzing the data collected, and providing summary reports and recommendations for the client. In the research design phase, targets or quotas may be established for the number and types of respondents to be surveyed. The marketing research firm's objective is to conduct the survey so as to meet the client's needs at a minimum cost.

Market Survey, Inc. (MSI), specializes in evaluating consumer reaction to new products, services, and advertising campaigns. A client firm requested MSI's assistance in ascertaining consumer reaction to a recently marketed household product. During meetings with the client, MSI agreed to conduct door-to-door personal interviews to obtain responses from households with children and households without children. In addition, MSI agreed to conduct both day and evening interviews. Specifically, the client's contract called for MSI to conduct 1000 interviews under the following quota guidelines.

1. Interview at least 400 households with children.
2. Interview at least 400 households without children.
3. The total number of households interviewed during the evening must be at least as great as the number of households interviewed during the day.
4. At least 40% of the interviews for households with children must be conducted during the evening.
5. At least 60% of the interviews for households without children must be conducted during the evening.

Because the interviews for households with children take additional interviewer time and because evening interviewers are paid more than daytime interviewers, the cost varies with the type of interview. Based on previous research studies, estimates of the interview costs are as follows:

	Interview Cost	
Household	Day	Evening
Children	$20	$25
No children	$18	$20

What is the household, time-of-day interview plan that will satisfy the contract requirements at a minimum total interviewing cost?

In formulating the linear programming model for the MSI problem, we utilize the following decision-variable notation:

DC = the number of daytime interviews of households with children
EC = the number of evening interviews of households with children
DNC = the number of daytime interviews of households without children
ENC = the number of evening interviews of households without children

We begin the linear programming model formulation by using the cost-per-interview data to develop the objective function:

$$\text{Min} \quad 20DC + 25EC + 18DNC + 20ENC$$

The constraint requiring a total of 1000 interviews is

$$DC + EC + DNC + ENC = 1000$$

The five specifications concerning the types of interviews are as follows.

- Households with children:

$$DC + EC \geq 400$$

- Households without children:

$$DNC + ENC \geq 400$$

- At least as many evening interviews as day interviews:

$$EC + ENC \geq DC + DNC$$

- At least 40% of interviews of households with children during the evening:

$$EC \geq 0.4(DC + EC)$$

- At least 60% of interviews of households without children during the evening:

$$ENC \geq 0.6(DNC + ENC)$$

When we add the nonnegativity requirements, the four-variable and six-constraint linear programming model becomes

Min $20DC + 25EC + 18DNC + 20ENC$

s.t.

$DC +$	$EC +$	$DNC +$	$ENC = 1000$	Total interviews
$DC +$	EC		≥ 400	Households with children
		$DNC +$	$ENC \geq 400$	Households without children
	$EC + ENC \geq DC + DNC$			Evening interviews
	$EC \geq 0.4(DC + EC)$			Evening interviews in households with children
	$ENC \geq 0.6(DNC + ENC)$			Evening interviews in households without children

$DC, EC, DNC, ENC \geq 0$

The optimal solution to this linear program is shown in Figure 4.2. The solution reveals that the minimum cost of $20,320 occurs with the following interview schedule.

| | Number of Interviews | | |
Household	Day	Evening	Totals
Children	240	160	400
No children	240	360	600
Totals	480	520	1000

Hence, 480 interviews will be scheduled during the day and 520 during the evening. Households with children will be covered by 400 interviews, and households without children will be covered by 600 interviews.

Selected sensitivity analysis information from Figure 4.2 shows a dual value of 19.200 for constraint 1. In other words, the value of the optimal solution will increase by $19.20 if the number of interviews is increased from 1000 to 1001. Thus, $19.20 is the incremental cost of obtaining additional interviews. It also is the savings that could be realized by reducing the number of interviews from 1000 to 999.

The surplus variable, with a value of 200.000, for constraint 3 shows that 200 more households without children will be interviewed than required. Similarly, the surplus variable, with a value of 40.000, for constraint 4 shows that the number of evening interviews exceeds the number of daytime interviews by 40. The zero values for the surplus variables in constraints 5 and 6 indicate that the more expensive evening interviews are being held at a minimum. Indeed, the dual value of 5.000 for constraint 5 indicates that if one more household (with children) than the minimum requirement must be interviewed during the evening, the total interviewing cost will go up by $5.00. Similarly, constraint 6 shows that requiring one more household (without children) to be interviewed during the evening will increase costs by $2.00.

FIGURE 4.2   THE SOLUTION FOR THE MARKET SURVEY PROBLEM

WEB file

Market

```
Optimal Objective Value =          20320.00000

          Variable              Value            Reduced Cost
       --------------      --------------      ------------------
            DC               240.00000              0.00000
            EC               160.00000              0.00000
            DNC              240.00000              0.00000
            ENC              360.00000              0.00000

       Constraint         Slack/Surplus            Dual Value
       --------------      --------------      ------------------
            1                 0.00000              19.20000
            2                 0.00000               2.80000
            3               200.00000               0.00000
            4                40.00000               0.00000
            5                 0.00000               5.00000
            6                 0.00000               2.00000
```

4.2   FINANCIAL APPLICATIONS

In finance, linear programming can be applied in problem situations involving capital bud-geting, make-or-buy decisions, asset allocation, portfolio selection, financial planning, and many more. In this section, we describe a portfolio selection problem and a problem involving funding of an early retirement program.

Portfolio Selection

Portfolio selection problems involve situations in which a financial manager must select specific investments—for example, stocks and bonds—from a variety of investment alternatives. Managers of mutual funds, credit unions, insurance companies, and banks frequently encounter this type of problem. The objective function for portfolio selection problems usually is maximization of expected return or minimization of risk. The constraints usually take the form of restrictions on the type of permissible investments, state laws, company policy, maximum permissible risk, and so on. Problems of this type have been formulated and solved using a variety of mathematical programming techniques. In this section we formulate and solve a portfolio selection problem as a linear program.

Consider the case of Welte Mutual Funds, Inc., located in New York City. Welte just obtained $100,000 by converting industrial bonds to cash and is now looking for other investment opportunities for these funds. Based on Welte's current investments, the firm's top financial analyst recommends that all new investments be made in the oil industry, steel industry, or in government bonds. Specifically, the analyst identified five investment opportunities and projected their annual rates of return. The investments and rates of return are shown in Table 4.3.

Management of Welte imposed the following investment guidelines.

1. Neither industry (oil or steel) should receive more than $50,000.
2. Government bonds should be at least 25% of the steel industry investments.
3. The investment in Pacific Oil, the high-return but high-risk investment, cannot be more than 60% of the total oil industry investment.

What portfolio recommendations—investments and amounts—should be made for the available $100,000? Given the objective of maximizing projected return subject to the bud-getary and managerially imposed constraints, we can answer this question by formulating and solving a linear programming model of the problem. The solution will provide investment recommendations for the management of Welte Mutual Funds.

TABLE 4.3   INVESTMENT OPPORTUNITIES FOR WELTE MUTUAL FUNDS

Investment	Projected Rate of Return (%)
Atlantic Oil	7.3
Pacific Oil	10.3
Midwest Steel	6.4
Huber Steel	7.5
Government bonds	4.5

Let

$$A = \text{dollars invested in Atlantic Oil}$$
$$P = \text{dollars invested in Pacific Oil}$$
$$M = \text{dollars invested in Midwest Steel}$$
$$H = \text{dollars invested in Huber Steel}$$
$$G = \text{dollars invested in government bonds}$$

Using the projected rates of return shown in Table 4.3, we write the objective function for maximizing the total return for the portfolio as

$$\text{Max} \quad 0.073A + 0.103P + 0.064M + 0.075H + 0.045G$$

The constraint specifying investment of the available $100,000 is

$$A + P + M + H + G = 100{,}000$$

The requirements that neither the oil nor the steel industry should receive more than $50,000 are

$$A + P \leq 50{,}000$$
$$M + H \leq 50{,}000$$

The requirement that government bonds be at least 25% of the steel industry investment is expressed as

$$G \geq 0.25(M + H)$$

Finally, the constraint that Pacific Oil cannot be more than 60% of the total oil industry investment is

$$P \leq 0.60(A + P)$$

By adding the nonnegativity restrictions, we obtain the complete linear programming model for the Welte Mutual Funds investment problem:

Max $0.073A + 0.103P + 0.064M + 0.075H + 0.045G$
s.t.

$A +$	$P +$	$M +$	$H +$	G	$= 100{,}000$	Available funds
$A +$	P				$\leq \ \ 50{,}000$	Oil industry maximum
		$M +$	H		$\leq \ \ 50{,}000$	Steel industry maximum
		$G \geq 0.25\,(M + H)$				Government bonds minimum
		$P \leq 0.60\,(A + P)$				Pacific Oil restriction
		$A, P, M, H, G \geq 0$				

The optimal solution to this linear program is shown in Figure 4.3. Table 4.4 shows how the funds are divided among the securities. Note that the optimal solution indicates that the portfolio should be diversified among all the investment opportunities except

FIGURE 4.3   THE SOLUTION FOR THE WELTE MUTUAL FUNDS PROBLEM

```
Optimal Objective Value =                    8000.00000

          Variable              Value             Reduced Costs
       ---------------       ---------------      ---------------
             A               20000.00000              0.00000
             P               30000.00000              0.00000
             M                   0.00000             -0.01100
             H               40000.00000              0.00000
             G               10000.00000              0.00000


         Constraint         Slack/Surplus          Dual Value
       ---------------       ---------------      ---------------
             1                   0.00000              0.06900
             2                   0.00000              0.02200
             3               10000.00000              0.00000
             4                   0.00000             -0.02400
             5                   0.00000              0.03000
```

WEB file

Welte

Midwest Steel. The projected annual return for this portfolio is $8000, which is an overall return of 8%.

The optimal solution shows the dual value for constraint 3 is zero. The reason is that the steel industry maximum isn't a binding constraint; increases in the steel industry limit of $50,000 will not improve the value of the optimal solution. Indeed, the slack variable for this constraint shows that the current steel industry investment is $10,000 below its limit of $50,000. The dual values for the other constraints are nonzero, indicating that these constraints are binding.

The dual value for the available funds constraint provides information on the rate of return from additional investment funds.

The dual value of 0.069 for constraint 1 shows that the value of the optimal solution can be increased by 0.069 if one more dollar can be made available for the portfolio investment. If more funds can be obtained at a cost of less than 6.9%, management should consider obtaining them. However, if a return in excess of 6.9% can be obtained by investing funds elsewhere (other than in these five securities), management should question the wisdom of investing the entire $100,000 in this portfolio.

Similar interpretations can be given to the other dual values. Note that the dual value for constraint 4 is negative at –0.024. This result indicates that increasing the value on the

TABLE 4.4   OPTIMAL PORTFOLIO SELECTION FOR WELTE MUTUAL FUNDS

Investment	Amount	Expected Annual Return
Atlantic Oil	$ 20,000	$1460
Pacific Oil	30,000	3090
Huber Steel	40,000	3000
Government bonds	10,000	450
Totals	$100,000	$8000

Expected annual return of $8000
Overall rate of return = 8%

right-hand side of the constraint by one unit can be expected to decrease the objective function value of the optimal solution by 0.024. In terms of the optimal portfolio, then, if Welte invests one more dollar in government bonds (beyond the minimum requirement), the total return will decrease by $0.024. To see why this decrease occurs, note again from the dual value for constraint 1 that the marginal return on the funds invested in the portfolio is 6.9% (the average return is 8%). The rate of return on government bonds is 4.5%. Thus, the cost of investing one more dollar in government bonds is the difference between the marginal return on the portfolio and the marginal return on government bonds: $6.9\% - 4.5\% = 2.4\%$.

Practice formulating a variation of the Welte problem by working Problem 9.

Note that the optimal solution shows that Midwest Steel should not be included in the portfolio ($M = 0$). The associated reduced cost for M of -0.011 tells us that the objective function coefficient for Midwest Steel would have to increase by 0.011 before considering the Midwest Steel investment alternative would be advisable. With such an increase the Midwest Steel return would be $0.064 + 0.011 = 0.075$, making this investment just as desirable as the currently used Huber Steel investment alternative.

Finally, a simple modification of the Welte linear programming model permits determining the fraction of available funds invested in each security. That is, we divide each of the right-hand-side values by 100,000. Then the optimal values for the variables will give the fraction of funds that should be invested in each security for a portfolio of any size.

NOTES AND COMMENTS

1. The optimal solution to the Welte Mutual Funds problem indicates that $20,000 is to be spent on the Atlantic Oil stock. If Atlantic Oil sells for $75 per share, we would have to purchase exactly 266⅔ shares in order to spend exactly $20,000. The difficulty of purchasing fractional shares can be handled by purchasing the largest possible integer number of shares with the allotted funds (e.g., 266 shares of Atlantic Oil). This approach guarantees that the budget constraint will not be violated. This approach, of course, introduces the possibility that the solution will no longer be optimal, but the danger is slight if a large number of securities are involved. In cases where the analyst believes that the decision variables *must* have integer values, the problem must be formulated as an integer linear programming model. Integer linear programming is the topic of Chapter 7.

2. Financial portfolio theory stresses obtaining a proper balance between risk and return. In the Welte problem, we explicitly considered return in the objective function. Risk is controlled by choosing constraints that ensure diversity among oil and steel stocks and a balance between government bonds and the steel industry investment.

Financial Planning

Linear programming has been used for a variety of financial planning applications. The Management Science in Action, Optimal Lease Structuring at GE Capital, describes how linear programming is used to optimize the structure of a leveraged lease.

MANAGEMENT SCIENCE IN ACTION

OPTIMAL LEASE STRUCTURING AT GE CAPITAL*

GE Capital is a $70 billion subsidiary of General Electric. As one of the nation's largest and most diverse financial services companies, GE Capital arranges leases in both domestic and international markets, including leases for telecommunications; data processing; construction; and fleets of cars, trucks, and commercial aircraft. To help allocate and schedule the rental and debt payments of a leveraged lease, GE Capital analysts developed an optimization model, which is available as an optional component of the company's lease analysis proprietary software.

Leveraged leases are designed to provide financing for assets with economic lives of at least five years, which require large capital outlays. A leveraged lease represents an agreement among the lessor (the owner of the asset), the lessee (the user of the asset), and the lender who provides a nonrecourse loan of 50% to 80% of the lessor's purchase price. In a nonrecourse loan, the lenders cannot turn to the lessor for repayment in the event of default. As the lessor in such arrangements, GE Capital is able to claim ownership and realize income tax benefits such as depreciation and interest deductions. These deductions usually produce tax losses during the early years of the lease, which reduces the total tax liability. Approximately 85% of all financial leases in the United States are leveraged leases.

In its simplest form, the leveraged lease structuring problem can be formulated as a linear program. The linear program models the after-tax cash flow for the lessor, taking into consideration rental receipts, borrowing and repaying of the loan, and income taxes. Constraints are formulated to ensure compliance with IRS guidelines and to enable customizing of leases to meet lessee and lessor requirements. The objective function can be entered in a custom fashion or selected from a predefined list. Typically, the objective is to minimize the lessee's cost, expressed as the net present value of rental payments, or to maximize the lessor's after-tax yield.

GE Capital developed an optimization approach that could be applied to single-investor lease structuring. In a study with the department most involved with these transactions, the optimization approach yielded substantial benefits. The approach helped GE Capital win some single-investor transactions ranging in size from $1 million to $20 million.

*Based on C. J. Litty, "Optimal Lease Structuring at GE Capital," *Interfaces* (May/June 1994): 34–45.

Hewlitt Corporation established an early retirement program as part of its corporate restructuring. At the close of the voluntary sign-up period, 68 employees had elected early retirement. As a result of these early retirements, the company incurs the following obligations over the next eight years:

Year	1	2	3	4	5	6	7	8
Cash Requirement	430	210	222	231	240	195	225	255

The cash requirements (in thousands of dollars) are due at the beginning of each year.

The corporate treasurer must determine how much money must be set aside today to meet the eight yearly financial obligations as they come due. The financing plan for the retirement program includes investments in government bonds as well as savings. The investments in government bonds are limited to three choices:

Bond	Price	Rate (%)	Years to Maturity
1	$1150	8.875	5
2	1000	5.500	6
3	1350	11.750	7

The government bonds have a par value of $1000, which means that even with different prices each bond pays $1000 at maturity. The rates shown are based on the par value. For purposes of planning, the treasurer assumed that any funds not invested in bonds will be placed in savings and earn interest at an annual rate of 4%.

We define the decision variables as follows:

F = total dollars required to meet the retirement plan's eight-year obligation
B_1 = units of bond 1 purchased at the beginning of year 1
B_2 = units of bond 2 purchased at the beginning of year 1
B_3 = units of bond 3 purchased at the beginning of year 1
S_i = amount placed in savings at the beginning of year i for $i = 1, \ldots, 8$

The objective function is to minimize the total dollars needed to meet the retirement plan's eight-year obligation, or

$$\text{Min} \quad F$$

A key feature of this type of financial planning problem is that a constraint must be formulated for each year of the planning horizon. In general, each constraint takes the form:

$$\left(\begin{array}{c} \text{Funds available at} \\ \text{the beginning of the year} \end{array} \right) - \left(\begin{array}{c} \text{Funds invested in bonds} \\ \text{and placed in savings} \end{array} \right) = \left(\begin{array}{c} \text{Cash obligation for} \\ \text{the current year} \end{array} \right)$$

The funds available at the beginning of year 1 are given by F. With a current price of $1150 for bond 1 and investments expressed in thousands of dollars, the total investment for B_1 units of bond 1 would be $1.15B_1$. Similarly, the total investment in bonds 2 and 3 would be $1B_2$ and $1.35B_3$, respectively. The investment in savings for year 1 is S_1. Using these results and the first-year obligation of 430, we obtain the constraint for year 1:

$$F - 1.15B_1 - 1B_2 - 1.35B_3 - S_1 = 430 \quad \text{Year 1}$$

We do not consider future investments in bonds because the future price of bonds depends on interest rates and cannot be known in advance.

Investments in bonds can take place only in this first year, and the bonds will be held until maturity.

The funds available at the beginning of year 2 include the investment returns of 8.875% on the par value of bond 1, 5.5% on the par value of bond 2, 11.75% on the par value of bond 3, and 4% on savings. The new amount to be invested in savings for year 2 is S_2. With an obligation of 210, the constraint for year 2 is

$$0.08875B_1 + 0.055B_2 + 0.1175B_3 + 1.04S_1 - S_2 = 210 \quad \text{Year 2}$$

Similarly, the constraints for years 3 to 8 are

$$0.08875B_1 + 0.055B_2 + 0.1175B_3 + 1.04S_2 - S_3 = 222 \quad \text{Year 3}$$
$$0.08875B_1 + 0.055B_2 + 0.1175B_3 + 1.04S_3 - S_4 = 231 \quad \text{Year 4}$$
$$0.08875B_1 + 0.055B_2 + 0.1175B_3 + 1.04S_4 - S_5 = 240 \quad \text{Year 5}$$
$$1.08875B_1 + 0.055B_2 + 0.1175B_3 + 1.04S_5 - S_6 = 195 \quad \text{Year 6}$$
$$1.055B_2 + 0.1175B_3 + 1.04S_6 - S_7 = 225 \quad \text{Year 7}$$
$$1.1175B_3 + 1.04S_7 - S_8 = 255 \quad \text{Year 8}$$

Note that the constraint for year 6 shows that funds available from bond 1 are $1.08875B_1$. The coefficient of 1.08875 reflects the fact that bond 1 matures at the end of year 5. As a result, the par value plus the interest from bond 1 during year 5 is available at the beginning of year 6. Also, because bond 1 matures in year 5 and becomes available for use at the beginning of year 6, the variable B_1 does not appear in the constraints for years 7 and 8. Note the similar interpretation for bond 2, which matures at the end of year 6 and has the par value plus interest available at the beginning of year 7. In addition, bond 3 matures at the end of year 7 and has the par value plus interest available at the beginning of year 8.

Finally, note that a variable S_8 appears in the constraint for year 8. The retirement fund obligation will be completed at the beginning of year 8, so we anticipate that S_8 will be zero and no funds will be put into savings. However, the formulation includes S_8 in the event that the bond income plus interest from the savings in year 7 exceed the 255 cash requirement for year 8. Thus, S_8 is a surplus variable that shows any funds remaining after the eight-year cash requirements have been satisfied.

The optimal solution to this 12-variable, 8-constraint linear program is shown in Figure 4.4. With an objective function value of 1728.79385, the total investment required to meet the retirement plan's eight-year obligation is $1,728,794. Using the current prices of $1150, $1000, and $1350 for each of the bonds, respectively, we can summarize the initial investments in the three bonds as follows:

Bond	Units Purchased	Investment Amount
1	$B_1 = 144.988$	$1150(144.988) = $166,736
2	$B_2 = 187.856$	$1000(187.856) = $187,856
3	$B_3 = 228.188$	$1350(228.188) = $308,054

FIGURE 4.4   THE SOLUTION FOR THE HEWLITT CORPORATION CASH
REQUIREMENTS PROBLEM

WEB file

Hewlitt

```
Optimal Objective Value =             1728.79385

        Variable                 Value              Reduced Cost
     --------------          ---------------       -----------------
          F                   1728.79385               0.00000
          B1                   144.98815               0.00000
          B2                   187.85585               0.00000
          B3                   228.18792               0.00000
          S1                   636.14794               0.00000
          S2                   501.60571               0.00000
          S3                   349.68179               0.00000
          S4                   182.68091               0.00000
          S5                     0.00000               0.06403
          S6                     0.00000               0.01261
          S7                     0.00000               0.02132
          S8                     0.00000               0.67084


       Constraint            Slack/Surplus            Dual Value
     --------------          ---------------       -----------------
           1                     0.00000               1.00000
           2                     0.00000               0.96154
           3                     0.00000               0.92456
           4                     0.00000               0.88900
           5                     0.00000               0.85480
           6                     0.00000               0.76036
           7                     0.00000               0.71899
           8                     0.00000               0.67084
```

The solution also shows that $636,148 (see S_1) will be placed in savings at the beginning of the first year. By starting with $1,728,794, the company can make the specified bond and savings investments and have enough left over to meet the retirement program's first-year cash requirement of $430,000.

The optimal solution in Figure 4.4 shows that the decision variables S_1, S_2, S_3, and S_4 all are greater than zero, indicating investments in savings are required in each of the first four years. However, interest from the bonds plus the bond maturity incomes will be sufficient to cover the retirement program's cash requirements in years 5 through 8.

In this application, the dual value can be thought of as the present value of each dollar in the cash requirement. For example, each dollar that must be paid in year 8 has a present value of $0.67084.

The dual values have an interesting interpretation in this application. Each right-hand-side value corresponds to the payment that must be made in that year. Note that the dual values are positive, indicating that increasing the required payment in any year by $1,000 would *increase* the total funds required for the retirement program's obligation by $1,000 times the dual value. Also note that the dual values show that increases in required payments in the early years have the largest impact. This makes sense in that there is little time to build up investment income in the early years versus the subsequent years. This suggests that if Hewlitt faces increases in required payments it would benefit by deferring those increases to later years if possible.

NOTES AND COMMENTS

1. The optimal solution for the Hewlitt Corporation problem shows fractional numbers of government bonds at 144.988, 187.856, and 228.188 units, respectively. However, fractional bond units usually are not available. If we were conservative and rounded up to 145, 188, and 229 units, respectively, the total funds required for the eight-year retirement program obligation would be approximately $1254 more than the total funds indicated by the objective function. Because of the magnitude of the funds involved, rounding up probably would provide a workable solution. If an optimal integer solution were required, the methods of integer linear programming covered in Chapter 7 would have to be used.

2. We implicitly assumed that interest from the government bonds is paid annually. Investments such as treasury notes actually provide interest payments every six months. In such cases, the model can be reformulated with six-month periods, with interest and/or cash payments occurring every six months.

4.3   OPERATIONS MANAGEMENT APPLICATIONS

Linear programming applications developed for production and operations management include scheduling, staffing, inventory control, and capacity planning. In this section we describe examples with make-or-buy decisions, production scheduling, and workforce assignments.

A Make-or-Buy Decision

We illustrate the use of a linear programming model to determine how much of each of several component parts a company should manufacture and how much it should purchase from an outside supplier. Such a decision is referred to as a make-or-buy decision.

The Janders Company markets various business and engineering products. Currently, Janders is preparing to introduce two new calculators: one for the business market called the Financial Manager and one for the engineering market called the Technician. Each calculator has three components: a base, an electronic cartridge, and a faceplate or top. The same base is used for both calculators, but the cartridges and tops are different. All components can be manufactured by the company or purchased from outside suppliers. The manufacturing costs and purchase prices for the components are summarized in Table 4.5.

TABLE 4.5 MANUFACTURING COSTS AND PURCHASE PRICES FOR JANDERS CALCULATOR COMPONENTS

| | Cost per Unit | |
Component	Manufacture (regular time)	Purchase
Base	$0.50	$0.60
Financial cartridge	$3.75	$4.00
Technician cartridge	$3.30	$3.90
Financial top	$0.60	$0.65
Technician top	$0.75	$0.78

Company forecasters indicate that 3000 Financial Manager calculators and 2000 Technician calculators will be needed. However, manufacturing capacity is limited. The company has 200 hours of regular manufacturing time and 50 hours of overtime that can be scheduled for the calculators. Overtime involves a premium at the additional cost of $9 per hour. Table 4.6 shows manufacturing times (in minutes) for the components.

The problem for Janders is to determine how many units of each component to manufacture and how many units of each component to purchase. We define the decision variables as follows:

$$BM = \text{number of bases manufactured}$$
$$BP = \text{number of bases purchased}$$
$$FCM = \text{number of Financial cartridges manufactured}$$
$$FCP = \text{number of Financial cartridges purchased}$$
$$TCM = \text{number of Technician cartridges manufactured}$$
$$TCP = \text{number of Technician cartridges purchased}$$
$$FTM = \text{number of Financial tops manufactured}$$
$$FTP = \text{number of Financial tops purchased}$$
$$TTM = \text{number of Technician tops manufactured}$$
$$TTP = \text{number of Technician tops purchased}$$

One additional decision variable is needed to determine the hours of overtime that must be scheduled:

$$OT = \text{number of hours of overtime to be scheduled}$$

TABLE 4.6 MANUFACTURING TIMES IN MINUTES PER UNIT FOR JANDERS CALCULATOR COMPONENTS

Component	Manufacturing Time
Base	1.0
Financial cartridge	3.0
Technician cartridge	2.5
Financial top	1.0
Technician top	1.5

The objective function is to minimize the total cost, including manufacturing costs, purchase costs, and overtime costs. Using the cost-per-unit data in Table 4.5 and the overtime premium cost rate of $9 per hour, we write the objective function as

$$\text{Min} \quad 0.5BM + 0.6BP + 3.75FCM + 4FCP + 3.3TCM + 3.9TCP + 0.6FTM$$
$$+ 0.65FTP + 0.75TTM + 0.78TTP + 9OT$$

The first five constraints specify the number of each component needed to satisfy the demand for 3000 Financial Manager calculators and 2000 Technician calculators. A total of 5000 base components are needed, with the number of other components depending on the demand for the particular calculator. The five demand constraints are

$$
\begin{aligned}
BM + BP &= 5000 \quad &\text{Bases} \\
FCM + FCP &= 3000 \quad &\text{Financial cartridges} \\
TCM + TCP &= 2000 \quad &\text{Technician cartridges} \\
FTM + FTP &= 3000 \quad &\text{Financial tops} \\
TTM + TTP &= 2000 \quad &\text{Technician tops}
\end{aligned}
$$

Two constraints are needed to guarantee that manufacturing capacities for regular time and overtime cannot be exceeded. The first constraint limits overtime capacity to 50 hours, or

$$OT \leq 50$$

The same units of measure must be used for both the left-hand side and right-hand side of the constraint. In this case, minutes are used.

The second constraint states that the total manufacturing time required for all components must be less than or equal to the total manufacturing capacity, including regular time plus overtime. The manufacturing times for the components are expressed in minutes, so we state the total manufacturing capacity constraint in minutes, with the 200 hours of regular time capacity becoming $60(200) = 12{,}000$ minutes. The actual overtime required is unknown at this point, so we write the overtime as $60OT$ minutes. Using the manufacturing times from Table 4.6, we have

$$BM + 3FCM + 2.5TCM + FTM + 1.5TTM \leq 12{,}000 + 60OT$$

The complete formulation of the Janders make-or-buy problem with all decision variables greater than or equal to zero is

$$\text{Min} \quad 0.5BM + 0.6BP + 3.75FCM + 4FCP + 3.3TCM + 3.9TCP$$
$$+ 0.6FTM + 0.65FTP + 0.75TTM + 0.78TTP + 9OT$$

s.t.

BM				$+$	$BP =$	5000	Bases
	FCM			$+$	$FCP =$	3000	Financial cartridges
		TCM		$+$	$TCP =$	2000	Technician cartridges
			FTM	$+$	$FTP =$	3000	Financial tops
			$TTM +$		$TTP =$	2000	Technician tops
					$OT \leq$	50	Overtime hours
$BM + 3FCM + 2.5TCM + FTM + 1.5TTM$				$\leq$	$12{,}000 + 60OT$		Manufacturing capacity

The optimal solution to this 11-variable, 7-constraint linear program is shown in Figure 4.5. The optimal solution indicates that all 5000 bases (*BM*), 667 Financial Manager cartridges (*FCM*), and 2000 Technician cartridges (*TCM*) should be manufactured. The remaining 2333 Financial Manager cartridges (*FCP*), all the Financial Manager tops (*FTP*),

FIGURE 4.5   THE SOLUTION FOR THE JANDERS MAKE-OR-BUY PROBLEM

Janders

```
Optimal Objective Value =            24443.33333

        Variable                Value            Reduced Cost
      --------------        ---------------      -----------------
           BM                5000.00000              0.00000
           BP                   0.00000              0.01667
          FCM                 666.66667              0.00000
          FCP                2333.33333              0.00000
          TCM                2000.00000              0.00000
          TCP                   0.00000              0.39167
          FTM                   0.00000              0.03333
          FTP                3000.00000              0.00000
          TTM                   0.00000              0.09500
          TTP                2000.00000              0.00000
           OT                   0.00000              4.00000


       Constraint          Slack/Surplus           Dual Value
      --------------        ---------------      -----------------
            1                   0.00000              0.58333
            2                   0.00000              4.00000
            3                   0.00000              3.50833
            4                   0.00000              0.65000
            5                   0.00000              0.78000
            6                  50.00000              0.00000
            7                   0.00000             -0.08333
```

Variable	Objective Coefficient	Allowable Increase	Allowable Decrease
BM	0.50000	0.01667	Infinite
BP	0.60000	Infinite	0.01667
FCM	3.75000	0.10000	0.05000
FCP	4.00000	0.05000	0.10000
TCM	3.30000	0.39167	Infinite
TCP	3.90000	Infinite	0.39167
FTM	0.60000	Infinite	0.03333
FTP	0.65000	0.03333	Infinite
TTM	0.75000	Infinite	0.09500
TTP	0.78000	0.09500	Infinite
OT	9.00000	Infinite	4.00000

Constraint	RHS Value	Allowable Increase	Allowable Decrease
1	5000.00000	2000.00000	5000.00000
2	3000.00000	Infinite	2333.33333
3	2000.00000	800.00000	2000.00000
4	3000.00000	Infinite	3000.00000
5	2000.00000	Infinite	2000.00000
6	50.00000	Infinite	50.00000
7	12000.00000	7000.00000	2000.00000

and all Technician tops (*TTP*) should be purchased. No overtime manufacturing is necessary, and the total cost associated with the optimal make-or-buy plan is $24,443.33.

Sensitivity analysis provides some additional information about the unused overtime capacity. The Reduced Costs column shows that the overtime (*OT*) premium would have to decrease by $4 per hour before overtime production should be considered. That is, if the overtime premium is $9 − $4 = $5 or less, Janders may want to replace some of the purchased components with components manufactured on overtime.

The dual value for the manufacturing capacity constraint 7 is −0.083. This value indicates that an additional hour of manufacturing capacity is worth $0.083 per minute or ($0.083)(60) = $5 per hour. The right-hand-side range for constraint 7 shows that this conclusion is valid until the amount of regular time increases to 19,000 minutes, or 316.7 hours.

Sensitivity analysis also indicates that a change in prices charged by the outside suppliers can affect the optimal solution. For instance, the objective coefficient range for *BP* is 0.583 (0.600 − 0.017) to no upper limit. If the purchase price for bases remains at $0.583 or more, the number of bases purchased (*BP*) will remain at zero. However, if the purchase price drops below $0.583, Janders should begin to purchase rather than manufacture the base component. Similar sensitivity analysis conclusions about the purchase price ranges can be drawn for the other components.

NOTES AND COMMENTS

The proper interpretation of the dual value for manufacturing capacity (constraint 7) in the Janders problem is that an additional hour of manufacturing capacity is worth ($0.083)(60) = $5 per hour. Thus, the company should be willing to pay a premium of $5 per hour over and above the current regular time cost per hour, which is already included in the manufacturing cost of the product. Thus, if the regular time cost is $18 per hour, Janders should be willing to pay up to $18 + $5 = $23 per hour to obtain additional labor capacity.

Production Scheduling

One of the most important applications of linear programming deals with multiperiod planning such as production scheduling. The solution to a production scheduling problem enables the manager to establish an efficient low-cost production schedule for one or more products over several time periods (weeks or months). Essentially, a production scheduling problem can be viewed as a product-mix problem for each of several periods in the future. The manager must determine the production levels that will allow the company to meet product demand requirements, given limitations on production capacity, labor capacity, and storage space, while minimizing total production costs.

One advantage of using linear programming for production scheduling problems is that they recur. A production schedule must be established for the current month, then again for the next month, for the month after that, and so on. When looking at the problem each month, the production manager will find that, although demand for the products has changed, production times, production capacities, storage space limitations, and so on are roughly the same. Thus, the production manager is basically re-solving the same problem handled in previous months, and a general linear programming model of the production scheduling procedure may be applied frequently. Once the model has been formulated, the manager can simply supply the data—demand, capacities, and so on—for the given production period and use the linear programming model repeatedly to develop the production schedule. The Management Science in Action, Optimizing Production of Flight Manuals at

TABLE 4.7   THREE-MONTH DEMAND SCHEDULE FOR BOLLINGER
ELECTRONICS COMPANY

Component	April	May	June
322A	1000	3000	5000
802B	1000	500	3000

Jeppesen Sanderson, Inc., describes how linear programming is used to minimize the cost of producing weekly revisions to flight manuals.

Let us consider the case of the Bollinger Electronics Company, which produces two different electronic components for a major airplane engine manufacturer. The airplane engine manufacturer notifies the Bollinger sales office each quarter of its monthly requirements for components for each of the next three months. The monthly requirements for the components may vary considerably, depending on the type of engine the airplane engine manufacturer is producing. The order shown in Table 4.7 has just been received for the next three-month period.

After the order is processed, a demand statement is sent to the production control department. The production control department must then develop a three-month production plan for the components. In arriving at the desired schedule, the production manager will want to identify the following:

1. Total production cost
2. Inventory holding cost
3. Change-in-production-level costs

In the remainder of this section, we show how to formulate a linear programming model of the production and inventory process for Bollinger Electronics to minimize the total cost.

MANAGEMENT SCIENCE IN ACTION

OPTIMIZING PRODUCTION OF FLIGHT MANUALS AT JEPPESEN SANDERSON, INC.*

Jeppesen Sanderson, Inc., manufactures and distributes flight manuals that contain safety information to more than 300,000 pilots and 4000 airlines. Every week Jeppesen mails between 5 and 30 million pages of chart revisions to 200,000 customers worldwide, and the company receives about 1500 new orders each week. In the late 1990s, its customer service deteriorated as its existing production and supporting systems failed to keep up with this level of activity. To meet customer service goals, Jeppesen turned to optimization-based decision support tools for production planning.

Jeppesen developed a large-scale linear program called Scheduler to minimize the cost of producing the weekly revisions. Model constraints included capacity constraints and numerous internal business rules. The model includes 250,000 variables, and 40,000 to 50,000 constraints. Immediately after introducing the model, Jeppesen established a new record for the number of consecutive weeks with 100% on-time revisions. Scheduler decreased tardiness of revisions from approximately 9% to 3% and dramatically improved customer satisfaction. Even more importantly, Scheduler provided a model of the production system for Jeppesen to use in strategic economic analysis. Overall, the use of optimization techniques at Jeppesen resulted in cost reductions of nearly 10% and a 24% increase in profit.

*Based on E. Katok, W. Tarantino, and R. Tiedman, "Improving Performance and Flexibility at Jeppesen: The World's Leading Aviation-Information Company," *Interfaces* (January/February 2001): 7–29.

To develop the model, we let x_{im} denote the production volume in units for product i in month m. Here $i = 1, 2$, and $m = 1, 2, 3$; $i = 1$ refers to component 322A, $i = 2$ refers to component 802B, $m = 1$ refers to April, $m = 2$ refers to May, and $m = 3$ refers to June. The purpose of the double subscript is to provide a more descriptive notation. We could simply use x_6 to represent the number of units of product 2 produced in month 3, but x_{23} is more descriptive, identifying directly the product and month represented by the variable.

If component 322A costs \$20 per unit produced and component 802B costs \$10 per unit produced, the total production cost part of the objective function is

$$\text{Total production cost} = 20x_{11} + 20x_{12} + 20x_{13} + 10x_{21} + 10x_{22} + 10x_{23}$$

Because the production cost per unit is the same each month, we don't need to include the production costs in the objective function; that is, regardless of the production schedule selected, the total production cost will remain the same. In other words, production costs are not relevant costs for the production scheduling decision under consideration. In cases in which the production cost per unit is expected to change each month, the variable production costs per unit per month must be included in the objective function. The solution for the Bollinger Electronics problem will be the same regardless of whether these costs are included; therefore, we included them so that the value of the linear programming objective function will include all the costs associated with the problem.

To incorporate the relevant inventory holding costs into the model, we let s_{im} denote the inventory level for product i at the end of month m. Bollinger determined that on a monthly basis inventory holding costs are 1.5% of the cost of the product; that is, $(0.015)(\$20) = \$0.30$ per unit for component 322A and $(0.015)(\$10) = \$0.15$ per unit for component 802B. A common assumption made in using the linear programming approach to production scheduling is that monthly ending inventories are an acceptable approximation to the average inventory levels throughout the month. Making this assumption, we write the inventory holding cost portion of the objective function as

$$\text{Inventory holding cost} = 0.30s_{11} + 0.30s_{12} + 0.30s_{13} + 0.15s_{21} + 0.15s_{22} + 0.15s_{23}$$

To incorporate the costs of fluctuations in production levels from month to month, we need to define two additional variables:

$$I_m = \text{increase in the total production level necessary during month } m$$
$$D_m = \text{decrease in the total production level necessary during month } m$$

After estimating the effects of employee layoffs, turnovers, reassignment training costs, and other costs associated with fluctuating production levels, Bollinger estimates that the cost associated with increasing the production level for any month is \$0.50 per unit increase. A similar cost associated with decreasing the production level for any month is \$0.20 per unit. Thus, we write the third portion of the objective function as

$$\text{Change-in-production-level costs} = 0.50I_1 + 0.50I_2 + 0.50I_3$$
$$+ 0.20D_1 + 0.20D_2 + 0.20D_3$$

Note that the cost associated with changes in production level is a function of the change in the total number of units produced in month m compared to the total number of units produced in month $m - 1$. In other production scheduling applications, fluctuations in production level might be measured in terms of machine hours or labor-hours required rather than in terms of the total number of units produced.

Combining all three costs, the complete objective function becomes

$$\text{Min} \quad 20x_{11} + 20x_{12} + 20x_{13} + 10x_{21} + 10x_{22} + 10x_{23} + 0.30s_{11}$$
$$+ 0.30s_{12} + 0.30s_{13} + 0.15s_{21} + 0.15s_{22} + 0.15s_{23} + 0.50I_1$$
$$+ 0.50I_2 + 0.50I_3 + 0.20D_1 + 0.20D_2 + 0.20D_3$$

We now consider the constraints. First, we must guarantee that the schedule meets customer demand. Because the units shipped can come from the current month's production or from inventory carried over from previous months, the demand requirement takes the form

$$\begin{pmatrix} \text{Ending} \\ \text{inventory} \\ \text{from previous} \\ \text{month} \end{pmatrix} + \begin{pmatrix} \text{Current} \\ \text{production} \end{pmatrix} - \begin{pmatrix} \text{Ending} \\ \text{inventory} \\ \text{for this} \\ \text{month} \end{pmatrix} = \begin{pmatrix} \text{This month's} \\ \text{demand} \end{pmatrix}$$

Suppose that the inventories at the beginning of the three-month scheduling period were 500 units for component 322A and 200 units for component 802B. The demand for both products in the first month (April) was 1000 units, so the constraints for meeting demand in the first month become

$$500 + x_{11} - s_{11} = 1000$$
$$200 + x_{21} - s_{21} = 1000$$

Moving the constants to the right-hand side, we have

$$x_{11} - s_{11} = 500$$
$$x_{21} - s_{21} = 800$$

Similarly, we need demand constraints for both products in the second and third months. We write them as follows:

Month 2

$$s_{11} + x_{12} - s_{12} = 3000$$
$$s_{21} + x_{22} - s_{22} = 500$$

Month 3

$$s_{12} + x_{13} - s_{13} = 5000$$
$$s_{22} + x_{23} - s_{23} = 3000$$

If the company specifies a minimum inventory level at the end of the three-month period of at least 400 units of component 322A and at least 200 units of component 802B, we can add the constraints

$$s_{13} \geq 400$$
$$s_{23} \geq 200$$

TABLE 4.8   MACHINE, LABOR, AND STORAGE CAPACITIES
FOR BOLLINGER ELECTRONICS

Month	Machine Capacity (hours)	Labor Capacity (hours)	Storage Capacity (square feet)
April	400	300	10,000
May	500	300	10,000
June	600	300	10,000

TABLE 4.9   MACHINE, LABOR, AND STORAGE REQUIREMENTS FOR COMPONENTS
322A AND 802B

Component	Machine (hours/unit)	Labor (hours/unit)	Storage (square feet/unit)
322A	0.10	0.05	2
802B	0.08	0.07	3

Suppose that we have the additional information on machine, labor, and storage capacity shown in Table 4.8. Machine, labor, and storage space requirements are given in Table 4.9. To reflect these limitations, the following constraints are necessary:

Machine Capacity

$$0.10x_{11} + 0.08x_{21} \leq 400 \quad \text{Month 1}$$
$$0.10x_{12} + 0.08x_{22} \leq 500 \quad \text{Month 2}$$
$$0.10x_{13} + 0.08x_{23} \leq 600 \quad \text{Month 3}$$

Labor Capacity

$$0.05x_{11} + 0.07x_{21} \leq 300 \quad \text{Month 1}$$
$$0.05x_{12} + 0.07x_{22} \leq 300 \quad \text{Month 2}$$
$$0.05x_{13} + 0.07x_{23} \leq 300 \quad \text{Month 3}$$

Storage Capacity

$$2s_{11} + 3s_{21} \leq 10,000 \quad \text{Month 1}$$
$$2s_{12} + 3s_{22} \leq 10,000 \quad \text{Month 2}$$
$$2s_{13} + 3s_{23} \leq 10,000 \quad \text{Month 3}$$

One final set of constraints must be added to guarantee that I_m and D_m will reflect the increase or decrease in the total production level for month m. Suppose that the production levels for March, the month before the start of the current production scheduling period, had been 1500 units of component 322A and 1000 units of component 802B for a total production level of $1500 + 1000 = 2500$ units. We can find the amount of the change in production for April from the relationship

$$\text{April production} - \text{March production} = \text{Change}$$

Using the April production variables, x_{11} and x_{21}, and the March production of 2500 units, we have

$$(x_{11} + x_{21}) - 2500 = \text{Change}$$

Note that the change can be positive or negative. A positive change reflects an increase in the total production level, and a negative change reflects a decrease in the total production level. We can use the increase in production for April, I_1, and the decrease in production for April, D_1, to specify the constraint for the change in total production for the month of April:

$$(x_{11} + x_{21}) - 2500 = I_1 - D_1$$

Of course, we cannot have an increase in production and a decrease in production during the same one-month period; thus, either, I_1 or D_1 will be zero. If April requires 3000 units of production, $I_1 = 500$ and $D_1 = 0$. If April requires 2200 units of production, $I_1 = 0$ and $D_1 = 300$. This approach of denoting the change in production level as the difference between two nonnegative variables, I_1 and D_1, permits both positive and negative changes in the total production level. If a single variable (say, c_m) had been used to represent the change in production level, only positive changes would be possible because of the non-negativity requirement.

Using the same approach in May and June (always subtracting the previous month's total production from the current month's total production), we obtain the constraints for the second and third months of the production scheduling period:

$$(x_{12} + x_{22}) - (x_{11} + x_{21}) = I_2 - D_2$$
$$(x_{13} + x_{23}) - (x_{12} + x_{22}) = I_3 - D_3$$

Linear programming models for production scheduling are often very large. Thousands of decision variables and constraints are necessary when the problem involves numerous products, machines, and time periods. Data collection for large-scale models can be more time-consuming than either the formulation of the model or the development of the computer solution.

The initially rather small, two-product, three-month scheduling problem has now developed into an 18-variable, 20-constraint linear programming problem. Note that in this problem we were concerned only with one type of machine process, one type of labor, and one type of storage area. Actual production scheduling problems usually involve several machine types, several labor grades, and/or several storage areas, requiring large-scale linear programs. For instance, a problem involving 100 products over a 12-month period could have more than 1000 variables and constraints.

Figure 4.6 shows the optimal solution to the Bollinger Electronics production scheduling problem. Table 4.10 contains a portion of the managerial report based on the optimal solution.

Consider the monthly variation in the production and inventory schedule shown in Table 4.10. Recall that the inventory cost for component 802B is one-half the inventory cost for component 322A. Therefore, as might be expected, component 802B is produced heavily in the first month (April) and then held in inventory for the demand that will occur in future months. Component 322A tends to be produced when needed, and only small amounts are carried in inventory.

FIGURE 4.6   THE SOLUTION FOR THE BOLLINGER ELECTRONICS PROBLEM

Bollinger

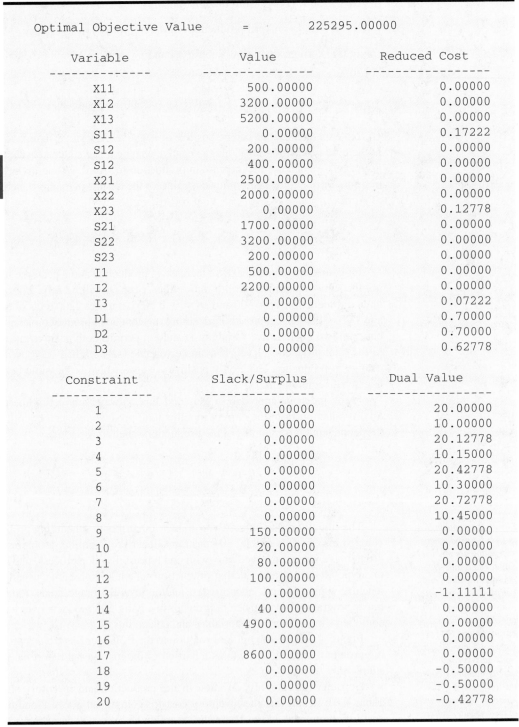

Optimal Objective Value   =   225295.00000

Variable	Value	Reduced Cost
X11	500.00000	0.00000
X12	3200.00000	0.00000
X13	5200.00000	0.00000
S11	0.00000	0.17222
S12	200.00000	0.00000
S12	400.00000	0.00000
X21	2500.00000	0.00000
X22	2000.00000	0.00000
X23	0.00000	0.12778
S21	1700.00000	0.00000
S22	3200.00000	0.00000
S23	200.00000	0.00000
I1	500.00000	0.00000
I2	2200.00000	0.00000
I3	0.00000	0.07222
D1	0.00000	0.70000
D2	0.00000	0.70000
D3	0.00000	0.62778

Constraint	Slack/Surplus	Dual Value
1	0.00000	20.00000
2	0.00000	10.00000
3	0.00000	20.12778
4	0.00000	10.15000
5	0.00000	20.42778
6	0.00000	10.30000
7	0.00000	20.72778
8	0.00000	10.45000
9	150.00000	0.00000
10	20.00000	0.00000
11	80.00000	0.00000
12	100.00000	0.00000
13	0.00000	-1.11111
14	40.00000	0.00000
15	4900.00000	0.00000
16	0.00000	0.00000
17	8600.00000	0.00000
18	0.00000	-0.50000
19	0.00000	-0.50000
20	0.00000	-0.42778

TABLE 4.10 MINIMUM COST PRODUCTION SCHEDULE INFORMATION FOR THE BOLLINGER ELECTRONICS PROBLEM

Activity	April	May	June
Production			
Component 322A	500	3200	5200
Component 802B	2500	2000	0
Totals	3000	5200	5200
Ending inventory			
Component 322A	0	200	400
Component 802B	1700	3200	200
Machine usage			
Scheduled hours	250	480	520
Slack capacity hours	150	20	80
Labor usage			
Scheduled hours	200	300	260
Slack capacity hours	100	0	40
Storage usage			
Scheduled storage	5100	10,000	1400
Slack capacity	4900	0	8600
Total production, inventory, and production-smoothing cost = $225,295			

The costs of increasing and decreasing the total production volume tend to smooth the monthly variations. In fact, the minimum-cost schedule calls for a 500-unit increase in total production in April and a 2200-unit increase in total production in May. The May production level of 5200 units is then maintained during June.

The machine usage section of the report shows ample machine capacity in all three months. However, labor capacity is at full utilization (slack = 0 for constraint 13 in Figure 4.6) in the month of May. The dual value shows that an additional hour of labor capacity in May will decrease total cost by approximately $1.11.

A linear programming model of a two-product, three-month production system can provide valuable information in terms of identifying a minimum-cost production schedule. In larger production systems, where the number of variables and constraints is too large to track manually, linear programming models can provide a significant advantage in developing cost-saving production schedules. The Management Science in Action, Optimizing Production, Inventory, and Distribution at the Kellogg Company, illustrates the use of a large-scale multiperiod linear program for production planning and distribution.

Workforce Assignment

Workforce assignment problems frequently occur when production managers must make decisions involving staffing requirements for a given planning period. Workforce assignments often have some flexibility, and at least some personnel can be assigned to more than one department or work center. Such is the case when employees have been cross-trained on two or more jobs or, for instance, when sales personnel can be transferred between stores. In the following application, we show how linear programming

MANAGEMENT SCIENCE IN ACTION

OPTIMIZING PRODUCTION, INVENTORY, AND DISTRIBUTION AT THE KELLOGG COMPANY*

The Kellogg Company is the largest cereal producer in the world and a leading producer of convenience foods, such as Kellogg's Pop-Tarts and Nutri-Grain cereal bars. Kellogg produces more than 40 different cereals at plants in 19 countries, on six continents. The company markets its products in more than 160 countries and employs more than 15,600 people in its worldwide organization. In the cereal business alone, Kellogg coordinates the production of about 80 products using a total of approximately 90 production lines and 180 packaging lines.

Kellogg has a long history of using linear programming for production planning and distribution. The Kellogg Planning System (KPS) is a large-scale, multiperiod linear program. The operational version of KPS makes production, packaging, inventory, and distribution decisions on a weekly basis. The primary objective of the system is to minimize the total cost of meeting estimated demand; constraints involve processing line capacities, packaging line capacities, and satisfying safety stock requirements.

A tactical version of KPS helps to establish plant budgets and make capacity-expansion and consolidation decisions on a monthly basis. The tactical version was recently used to guide a consolidation of production capacity that resulted in projected savings of $35 to $40 million per year. Because of the success Kellogg has had using KPS in their North American operations, the company is now introducing KPS into Latin America, and is studying the development of a global KPS model.

*Based on G. Brown, J. Keegan, B. Vigus, and K. Wood, "The Kellogg Company Optimizes Production, Inventory, and Distribution," *Interfaces* (November/December 2001): 1–15.

---

can be used to determine not only an optimal product mix, but also an optimal workforce assignment.

McCormick Manufacturing Company produces two products with contributions to profit per unit of $10 and $9, respectively. The labor requirements per unit produced and the total hours of labor available from personnel assigned to each of four departments are shown in Table 4.11. Assuming that the number of hours available in each department is fixed, we can formulate McCormick's problem as a standard product-mix linear program with the following decision variables:

$$P_1 = \text{units of product 1}$$
$$P_2 = \text{units of product 2}$$

TABLE 4.11   DEPARTMENTAL LABOR-HOURS PER UNIT AND TOTAL HOURS AVAILABLE FOR THE McCORMICK MANUFACTURING COMPANY

	Labor-Hours per Unit		
Department	**Product 1**	**Product 2**	**Total Hours Available**
1	0.65	0.95	6500
2	0.45	0.85	6000
3	1.00	0.70	7000
4	0.15	0.30	1400

The linear program is

$$\text{Max} \quad 10P_1 + 9P_2$$

s.t.

$$0.65P_1 + 0.95P_2 \leq 6500$$
$$0.45P_1 + 0.85P_2 \leq 6000$$
$$1.00P_1 + 0.70P_2 \leq 7000$$
$$0.15P_1 + 0.30P_2 \leq 1400$$
$$P_1, P_2 \geq 0$$

The optimal solution to the linear programming model is shown in Figure 4.7. After rounding, it calls for 5744 units of product 1, 1795 units of product 2, and a total profit of $73,590. With this optimal solution, departments 3 and 4 are operating at capacity, and departments 1 and 2 have a slack of approximately 1062 and 1890 hours, respectively. We would anticipate that the product mix would change and that the total profit would increase if the workforce assignment could be revised so that the slack, or unused hours, in departments 1 and 2 could be transferred to the departments currently working at capacity. However, the production manager may be uncertain as to how the workforce should be reallocated among the four departments. Let us expand the linear programming model to include decision variables that will help determine the optimal workforce assignment in addition to the profit-maximizing product mix.

Suppose that McCormick has a cross-training program that enables some employees to be transferred between departments. By taking advantage of the cross-training skills, a limited number of employees and labor-hours may be transferred from one department to another. For example, suppose that the cross-training permits transfers as shown in Table 4.12. Row 1 of this table shows that some employees assigned to department 1 have cross-training skills that permit them to be transferred to department 2 or 3. The right-hand column shows that, for the current production planning period, a maximum of 400 hours can be transferred from department 1. Similar cross-training transfer capabilities and capacities are shown for departments 2, 3, and 4.

FIGURE 4.7 THE SOLUTION FOR THE McCORMICK MANUFACTURING COMPANY PROBLEM WITH NO WORKFORCE TRANSFERS PERMITTED

Optimal Objective Value =   73589.74359

Variable	Value	Reduced Cost
1	5743.58974	0.00000
2	1794.87179	0.00000

Constraint	Slack/Surplus	Dual Value
1	1061.53846	0.00000
2	1889.74359	0.00000
3	0.00000	8.46154
4	0.00000	10.25641

TABLE 4.12   CROSS-TRAINING ABILITY AND CAPACITY INFORMATION

| From Department | Cross-Training Transfers Permitted to Department | | | | Maximum Hours Transferable |
	1	2	3	4	
1	—	yes	yes	—	400
2	—	—	yes	yes	800
3	—	—	—	yes	100
4	yes	yes	—	—	200

When workforce assignments are flexible, we do not automatically know how many hours of labor should be assigned to or be transferred from each department. We need to add decision variables to the linear programming model to account for such changes.

b_i = the labor-hours allocated to department i for i = 1, 2, 3, and 4

t_{ij} = the labor-hours transferred from department i to department j

The right-hand sides are now treated as decision variables.

With the addition of decision variables b_1, b_2, b_3, and b_4, we write the capacity restrictions for the four departments as follows:

$$0.65P_1 + 0.95P_2 \leq b_1$$
$$0.45P_1 + 0.85P_2 \leq b_2$$
$$1.00P_1 + 0.70P_2 \leq b_3$$
$$0.15P_1 + 0.30P_2 \leq b_4$$

The labor-hours ultimately allocated to each department must be determined by a series of labor balance equations, or constraints, that include the number of hours initially assigned to each department plus the number of hours transferred into the department minus the number of hours transferred out of the department. Using department 1 as an example, we determine the workforce allocation as follows:

$$b_1 = \begin{pmatrix} \text{Hours} \\ \text{initially in} \\ \text{department 1} \end{pmatrix} + \begin{pmatrix} \text{Hours} \\ \text{transferred into} \\ \text{department 1} \end{pmatrix} - \begin{pmatrix} \text{Hours} \\ \text{transferred out of} \\ \text{department 1} \end{pmatrix}$$

Table 4.11 shows 6500 hours initially assigned to department 1. We use the transfer decision variables t_{i1} to denote transfers into department 1 and t_{1j} to denote transfers from department 1. Table 4.12 shows that the cross-training capabilities involving department 1 are restricted to transfers from department 4 (variable t_{41}) and transfers to either department 2 or department 3 (variables t_{12} and t_{13}). Thus, we can express the total workforce allocation for department 1 as

$$b_1 = 6500 + t_{41} - t_{12} - t_{13}$$

Moving the decision variables for the workforce transfers to the left-hand side, we have the labor balance equation or constraint

$$b_1 - t_{41} + t_{12} + t_{13} = 6500$$

This form of constraint will be needed for each of the four departments. Thus, the following labor balance constraints for departments 2, 3, and 4 would be added to the model.

$$b_2 - t_{12} - t_{42} + t_{23} + t_{24} = 6000$$
$$b_3 - t_{13} - t_{23} + t_{34} = 7000$$
$$b_4 - t_{24} - t_{34} + t_{41} + t_{42} = 1400$$

Finally, Table 4.12 shows the number of hours that may be transferred from each department is limited, indicating that a transfer capacity constraint must be added for each of the four departments. The additional constraints are

$$t_{12} + t_{13} \leq 400$$
$$t_{23} + t_{24} \leq 800$$
$$t_{34} \leq 100$$
$$t_{41} + t_{42} \leq 200$$

The complete linear programming model has two product decision variables (P_1 and P_2), four department workforce assignment variables (b_1, b_2, b_3, and b_4), seven transfer variables (t_{12}, t_{13}, t_{23}, t_{24}, t_{34}, t_{41}, and t_{42}), and 12 constraints. Figure 4.8 shows the optimal solution to this linear program.

Variations in the workforce assignment model could be used in situations such as allocating raw material resources to products, allocating machine time to products, and allocating salesforce time to stores or sales territories.

McCormick's profit can be increased by $84,011 − $73,590 = $10,421 by taking advantage of cross-training and workforce transfers. The optimal product mix of 6825 units of product 1 and 1751 units of product 2 can be achieved if $t_{13} = 400$ hours are transferred from department 1 to department 3; $t_{23} = 651$ hours are transferred from department 2 to department 3; and $t_{24} = 149$ hours are transferred from department 2 to department 4. The resulting workforce assignments for departments 1 through 4 would provide 6100, 5200, 8051, and 1549 hours, respectively.

If a manager has the flexibility to assign personnel to different departments, reduced workforce idle time, improved workforce utilization, and improved profit should result. The linear programming model in this section automatically assigns employees and labor-hours to the departments in the most profitable manner.

Blending Problems

Blending problems arise whenever a manager must decide how to blend two or more resources to produce one or more products. In these situations, the resources contain one or more essential ingredients that must be blended into final products that will contain specific percentages of each. In most of these applications, then, management must decide how much of each resource to purchase to satisfy product specifications and product demands at minimum cost.

Blending problems occur frequently in the petroleum industry (e.g., blending crude oil to produce different octane gasolines), chemical industry (e.g., blending chemicals to produce fertilizers and weed killers), and food industry (e.g., blending ingredients to produce soft drinks and soups). In this section we illustrate how to apply linear programming to a blending problem in the petroleum industry.

The Grand Strand Oil Company produces regular and premium gasoline for independent service stations in the southeastern United States. The Grand Strand refinery manufactures the gasoline products by blending three petroleum components. The gasolines are sold at different prices, and the petroleum components have different costs. The firm wants

FIGURE 4.8   THE SOLUTION FOR THE McCORMICK MANUFACTURING
COMPANY PROBLEM

```
Optimal Objective Value =              84011.29945

        Variable              Value            Reduced Cost
      ---------------      ---------------     ---------------
            P1             6824.85900              0.00000
            P2             1751.41200              0.00000
            B1             6100.00000              0.00000
            B2             5200.00000              0.00000
            B3             8050.84700              0.00000
            B4             1549.15300              0.00000
            T41               0.00000              7.45763
            T12               0.00000              8.24859
            T13             400.00000              0.00000
            T42               0.00000              8.24859
            T23             650.84750              0.00000
            T24             149.15250              0.00000
            T34               0.00000              0.00000


        Constraint        Slack/Surplus          Dual Value
      ---------------      ---------------     ---------------
             1                0.00000              0.79096
             2              640.11300              0.00000
             3                0.00000              8.24859
             4                0.00000              8.24859
             5                0.00000              0.79096
             6                0.00000              0.00000
             7                0.00000              8.24859
             8                0.00000              8.24859
             9                0.00000              7.45763
            10                0.00000              8.24859
            11              100.00000              0.00000
            12              200.00000              0.00000
```

to determine how to mix or blend the three components into the two gasoline products and maximize profits.

Data available show that regular gasoline can be sold for $2.90 per gallon and premium gasoline for $3.00 per gallon. For the current production planning period, Grand Strand can obtain the three petroleum components at the cost per gallon and in the quantities shown in Table 4.13.

Product specifications for the regular and premium gasolines restrict the amounts of each component that can be used in each gasoline product. Table 4.14 lists the product specifications. Current commitments to distributors require Grand Strand to produce at least 10,000 gallons of regular gasoline.

The Grand Strand blending problem is to determine how many gallons of each component should be used in the regular gasoline blend and how many should be used in the

TABLE 4.13 PETROLEUM COST AND SUPPLY FOR THE GRAND STRAND
BLENDING PROBLEM

Petroleum Component	Cost/Gallon	Maximum Available
1	$2.50	5,000 gallons
2	$2.60	10,000 gallons
3	$2.84	10,000 gallons

TABLE 4.14 PRODUCT SPECIFICATIONS FOR THE GRAND STRAND
BLENDING PROBLEM

Product	Specifications
Regular gasoline	At most 30% component 1
	At least 40% component 2
	At most 20% component 3
Premium gasoline	At least 25% component 1
	At most 45% component 2
	At least 30% component 3

premium gasoline blend. The optimal blending solution should maximize the firm's profit,
subject to the constraints on the available petroleum supplies shown in Table 4.13, the
product specifications shown in Table 4.14, and the required 10,000 gallons of regular
gasoline.

We define the decision variables as

$$x_{ij} = \text{gallons of component } i \text{ used in gasoline } j,$$
$$\text{where } i = 1, 2, \text{ or } 3 \text{ for components } 1, 2, \text{ or } 3,$$
$$\text{and } j = r \text{ if regular or } j = p \text{ if premium}$$

The six decision variables are

$$x_{1r} = \text{gallons of component 1 in regular gasoline}$$
$$x_{2r} = \text{gallons of component 2 in regular gasoline}$$
$$x_{3r} = \text{gallons of component 3 in regular gasoline}$$
$$x_{1p} = \text{gallons of component 1 in premium gasoline}$$
$$x_{2p} = \text{gallons of component 2 in premium gasoline}$$
$$x_{3p} = \text{gallons of component 3 in premium gasoline}$$

The total number of gallons of each type of gasoline produced is the sum of the number of
gallons produced using each of the three petroleum components.

Total Gallons Produced

$$\text{Regular gasoline} = x_{1r} + x_{2r} + x_{3r}$$
$$\text{Premium gasoline} = x_{1p} + x_{2p} + x_{3p}$$

The total gallons of each petroleum component are computed in a similar fashion.

Total Petroleum Component Use

$$\text{Component 1} = x_{1r} + x_{1p}$$
$$\text{Component 2} = x_{2r} + x_{2p}$$
$$\text{Component 3} = x_{3r} + x_{3p}$$

We develop the objective function of maximizing the profit contribution by identifying the difference between the total revenue from both gasolines and the total cost of the three petroleum components. By multiplying the \$2.90 per gallon price by the total gallons of regular gasoline, the \$3.00 per gallon price by the total gallons of premium gasoline, and the component cost per gallon figures in Table 4.13 by the total gallons of each component used, we obtain the objective function:

$$\text{Max}\quad 2.90(x_{1r} + x_{2r} + x_{3r}) + 3.00(x_{1p} + x_{2p} + x_{3p})$$
$$- 2.50(x_{1r} + x_{1p}) - 2.60(x_{2r} + x_{2p}) - 2.84(x_{3r} + x_{3p})$$

When we combine terms, the objective function becomes

$$\text{Max}\quad 0.40x_{1r} + 0.30x_{2r} + 0.06x_{3r} + 0.50x_{1p} + 0.40x_{2p} + 0.16x_{3p}$$

The limitations on the availability of the three petroleum components are

$$
\begin{aligned}
x_{1r} + x_{1p} &\leq 5{,}000 &\quad \text{Component 1}\\
x_{2r} + x_{2p} &\leq 10{,}000 &\quad \text{Component 2}\\
x_{3r} + x_{3p} &\leq 10{,}000 &\quad \text{Component 3}
\end{aligned}
$$

Six constraints are now required to meet the product specifications stated in Table 4.14. The first specification states that component 1 can account for no more than 30% of the total gallons of regular gasoline produced. That is,

$$x_{1r} \leq 0.30(x_{1r} + x_{2r} + x_{3r})$$

The second product specification listed in Table 4.14 becomes

$$x_{2r} \geq 0.40(x_{1r} + x_{2r} + x_{3r})$$

Similarly, we write the four remaining blending specifications listed in Table 4.14 as

$$
\begin{aligned}
x_{3r} &\leq 0.20(x_{1r} + x_{2r} + x_{3r})\\
x_{1p} &\geq 0.25(x_{1p} + x_{2p} + x_{3p})\\
x_{2p} &\leq 0.45(x_{1p} + x_{2p} + x_{3p})\\
x_{3p} &\geq 0.30(x_{1p} + x_{2p} + x_{3p})
\end{aligned}
$$

The constraint for at least 10,000 gallons of regular gasoline is

$$x_{1r} + x_{2r} + x_{3r} \geq 10{,}000$$

The complete linear programming model with six decision variables and 10 constraints is

$$\text{Max}\quad 0.40x_{1r} + 0.30x_{2r} + 0.06x_{3r} + 0.50x_{1p} + 0.40x_{2p} + 0.16x_{3p}$$

s.t.

$$
\begin{array}{llll}
x_{1r} & + \; x_{1p} & \leq 5{,}000 \\
x_{2r} & + \; x_{2p} & \leq 10{,}000 \\
x_{3r} & + \; x_{3p} & \leq 10{,}000 \\
x_{1r} & \leq 0.30(x_{1r} + x_{2r} + x_{3r}) \\
x_{2r} & \geq 0.40(x_{1r} + x_{2r} + x_{3r}) \\
x_{3r} & \leq 0.20(x_{1r} + x_{2r} + x_{3r}) \\
x_{1p} & \geq 0.25(x_{1p} + x_{2p} + x_{3p}) \\
x_{2p} & \leq 0.45(x_{1p} + x_{2p} + x_{3p}) \\
x_{3p} & \geq 0.30(x_{1p} + x_{2p} + x_{3p}) \\
x_{1r} + x_{2r} + x_{2r} & \geq 10{,}000 \\
x_{1r}, x_{2r}, x_{3r}, x_{1p}, x_{2p}, x_{3p} \geq 0
\end{array}
$$

Try Problem 15 as another example of a blending model.

The optimal solution to the Grand Strand blending problem is shown in Figure 4.9. The optimal solution, which provides a profit of $7100, is summarized in Table 4.15. The optimal blending strategy shows that 10,000 gallons of regular gasoline should be produced. The regular gasoline will be manufactured as a blend of 1250 gallons of component 1, 6750 gallons of component 2, and 2000 gallons of component 3. The 15,000 gallons of premium gasoline will be manufactured as a blend of 3750 gallons of component 1, 3250 gallons of component 2, and 8000 gallons of component 3.

FIGURE 4.9 THE SOLUTION FOR THE GRAND STRAND BLENDING PROBLEM

Grand

```
Optimal Objective Value =            7100.00000

        Variable              Value           Reduced Cost
     --------------       ---------------    ------------------
          X1R               1250.00000            0.00000
          X2R               6750.00000            0.00000
          X3R               2000.00000            0.00000
          X1P               3750.00000            0.00000
          X2P               3250.00000            0.00000
          X3P               8000.00000            0.00000

      Constraint         Slack/Surplus           Dual Value
     --------------       ---------------    ------------------
           1                  0.00000             0.50000
           2                  0.00000             0.40000
           3                  0.00000             0.16000
           4               1750.00000             0.00000
           5               2750.00000             0.00000
           6                  0.00000             0.00000
           7                  0.00000             0.00000
           8               3500.00000             0.00000
           9               3500.00000             0.00000
          10                  0.00000            -0.10000
```

TABLE 4.15   GRAND STRAND GASOLINE BLENDING SOLUTION

Gasoline	Gallons of Component (percentage)			Total
	Component 1	Component 2	Component 3	
Regular	1250 (12.5%)	6750 (67.5%)	2000 (20%)	10,000
Premium	3750 (25%)	3250 (21⅔%)	8000 (53⅓%)	15,000

The interpretation of the slack and surplus variables associated with the product specification constraints (constraints 4–9) in Figure 4.9 needs some clarification. If the constraint is a ≤ constraint, the value of the slack variable can be interpreted as the gallons of component use below the maximum amount of the component use specified by the constraint. For example, the slack of 1750.000 for constraint 4 shows that component 1 use is 1750 gallons below the maximum amount of component 1 that could have been used in the production of 10,000 gallons of regular gasoline. If the product specification constraint is a ≥ constraint, a surplus variable shows the gallons of component use above the minimum amount of component use specified by the blending constraint. For example, the surplus of 2750.000 for constraint 5 shows that component 2 use is 2750 gallons above the minimum amount of component 2 that must be used in the production of 10,000 gallons of regular gasoline.

NOTES AND COMMENTS

A convenient way to define the decision variables in a blending problem is to use a matrix in which the rows correspond to the raw materials and the columns correspond to the final products. For example, in the Grand Strand blending problem, we define the decision variables as follows:

This approach has two advantages: (1) it provides a systematic way to define the decision variables for any blending problem; and (2) it provides a visual image of the decision variables in terms of how they are related to the raw materials, products, and each other.

		Final Products	
		Regular Gasoline	Premium Gasoline
Raw Materials	Component 1	x_{1r}	x_{1p}
	Component 2	x_{2r}	x_{2p}
	Component 3	x_{3r}	x_{3p}

SUMMARY

In this chapter we presented a broad range of applications that demonstrate how to use linear programming to assist in the decision-making process. We formulated and solved problems from marketing, finance, and operations management, and interpreted the computer output.

Many of the illustrations presented in this chapter are scaled-down versions of actual situations in which linear programming has been applied. In real-world applications, the problem may not be so concisely stated, the data for the problem may not be as readily available, and the problem most likely will involve numerous decision variables and/or constraints. However, a thorough study of the applications in this chapter is a good place to begin in applying linear programming to real problems.

PROBLEMS

Note: The following problems have been designed to give you an understanding and appreciation of the broad range of problems that can be formulated as linear programs. You should be able to formulate a linear programming model for each of the problems. However, you will need access to a linear programming computer package to develop the solutions and make the requested interpretations.

1. The Westchester Chamber of Commerce periodically sponsors public service seminars and programs. Currently, promotional plans are under way for this year's program. Advertising alternatives include television, radio, and newspaper. Audience estimates, costs, and maximum media usage limitations are as shown.

Constraint	Television	Radio	Newspaper
Audience per advertisement	100,000	18,000	40,000
Cost per advertisement	$2000	$300	$600
Maximum media usage	10	20	10

To ensure a balanced use of advertising media, radio advertisements must not exceed 50% of the total number of advertisements authorized. In addition, television should account for at least 10% of the total number of advertisements authorized.

  a. If the promotional budget is limited to $18,200, how many commercial messages should be run on each medium to maximize total audience contact? What is the allocation of the budget among the three media, and what is the total audience reached?

  b. By how much would audience contact increase if an extra $100 were allocated to the promotional budget?

2. The management of Hartman Company is trying to determine the amount of each of two products to produce over the coming planning period. The following information concerns labor availability, labor utilization, and product profitability.

Department	Product (hours/unit) 1	2	Labor-Hours Available
A	1.00	0.35	100
B	0.30	0.20	36
C	0.20	0.50	50
Profit contribution/unit	$30.00	$15.00	

  a. Develop a linear programming model of the Hartman Company problem. Solve the model to determine the optimal production quantities of products 1 and 2.

  b. In computing the profit contribution per unit, management doesn't deduct labor costs because they are considered fixed for the upcoming planning period. However, suppose that overtime can be scheduled in some of the departments. Which departments would you recommend scheduling for overtime? How much would you be willing to pay per hour of overtime in each department?

  c. Suppose that 10, 6, and 8 hours of overtime may be scheduled in departments A, B, and C, respectively. The cost per hour of overtime is $18 in department A, $22.50 in department B, and $12 in department C. Formulate a linear programming model that can be used to determine the optimal production quantities if overtime is made available. What are the optimal production quantities, and what is the revised total contribution to profit? How much overtime do you recommend using in each department? What is the increase in the total contribution to profit if overtime is used?

3. The employee credit union at State University is planning the allocation of funds for the coming year. The credit union makes four types of loans to its members. In addition, the credit union invests in risk-free securities to stabilize income. The various revenue-producing investments together with annual rates of return are as follows:

Type of Loan/Investment	Annual Rate of Return (%)
Automobile loans	8
Furniture loans	10
Other secured loans	11
Signature loans	12
Risk-free securities	9

The credit union will have $2 million available for investment during the coming year. State laws and credit union policies impose the following restrictions on the composition of the loans and investments.

- Risk-free securities may not exceed 30% of the total funds available for investment.
- Signature loans may not exceed 10% of the funds invested in all loans (automobile, furniture, other secured, and signature loans).
- Furniture loans plus other secured loans may not exceed the automobile loans.
- Other secured loans plus signature loans may not exceed the funds invested in risk-free securities.

How should the $2 million be allocated to each of the loan/investment alternatives to maximize total annual return? What is the projected total annual return?

4. Hilltop Coffee manufactures a coffee product by blending three types of coffee beans. The cost per pound and the available pounds of each bean are as follows:

Bean	Cost per Pound	Available Pounds
1	$0.50	500
2	$0.70	600
3	$0.45	400

Consumer tests with coffee products were used to provide ratings on a scale of 0–100, with higher ratings indicating higher quality. Product quality standards for the blended coffee require a consumer rating for aroma to be at least 75 and a consumer rating for taste to be at least 80. The individual ratings of the aroma and taste for coffee made from 100% of each bean are as follows.

Bean	Aroma Rating	Taste Rating
1	75	86
2	85	88
3	60	75

Assume that the aroma and taste attributes of the coffee blend will be a weighted average of the attributes of the beans used in the blend.

   a. What is the minimum-cost blend that will meet the quality standards and provide 1000 pounds of the blended coffee product?

   b. What is the cost per pound for the coffee blend?

   c. Determine the aroma and taste ratings for the coffee blend.

   d. If additional coffee were to be produced, what would be the expected cost per pound?

5. Ajax Fuels, Inc., is developing a new additive for airplane fuels. The additive is a mixture of three ingredients: A, B, and C. For proper performance, the total amount of additive (amount of A + amount of B + amount of C) must be at least 10 ounces per gallon of fuel. However, because of safety reasons, the amount of additive must not exceed 15 ounces per gallon of fuel. The mix or blend of the three ingredients is critical. At least 1 ounce of ingredient A must be used for every ounce of ingredient B. The amount of ingredient C must be at least one-half the amount of ingredient A. If the costs per ounce for ingredients A, B, and C are $0.10, $0.03, and $0.09, respectively, find the minimum-cost mixture of A, B, and C for each gallon of airplane fuel.

6. G. Kunz and Sons, Inc., manufactures two products used in the heavy equipment industry. Both products require manufacturing operations in two departments. The following are the production time (in hours) and profit contribution figures for the two products.

Product	Profit per Unit	Labor-Hours Dept. A	Dept. B
1	$25	6	12
2	$20	8	10

For the coming production period, Kunz has available a total of 900 hours of labor that can be allocated to either of the two departments. Find the production plan and labor allocation (hours assigned in each department) that will maximize the total contribution to profit.

7. As part of the settlement for a class action lawsuit, Hoxworth Corporation must provide sufficient cash to make the following annual payments (in thousands of dollars).

Year	1	2	3	4	5	6
Payment	190	215	240	285	315	460

The annual payments must be made at the beginning of each year. The judge will approve an amount that, along with earnings on its investment, will cover the annual payments. Investment of the funds will be limited to savings (at 4% annually) and government securities, at prices and rates currently quoted in *The Wall Street Journal.*

    Hoxworth wants to develop a plan for making the annual payments by investing in the following securities (par value = $1000). Funds not invested in these securities will be placed in savings.

Security	Current Price	Rate (%)	Years to Maturity
1	$1055	6.750	3
2	$1000	5.125	4

Assume that interest is paid annually. The plan will be submitted to the judge and, if approved, Hoxworth will be required to pay a trustee the amount that will be required to fund the plan.

a. Use linear programming to find the minimum cash settlement necessary to fund the annual payments.

b. Use the dual value to determine how much more Hoxworth should be willing to pay now to reduce the payment at the beginning of year 6 to $400,000.

c. Use the dual value to determine how much more Hoxworth should be willing to pay to reduce the year 1 payment to $150,000.

d. Suppose that the annual payments are to be made at the end of each year. Reformulate the model to accommodate this change. How much would Hoxworth save if this change could be negotiated?

8. The Clark County Sheriff's Department schedules police officers for 8-hour shifts. The beginning times for the shifts are 8:00 A.M., noon, 4:00 P.M., 8:00 P.M., midnight, and 4:00 A.M. An officer beginning a shift at one of these times works for the next 8 hours. During normal weekday operations, the number of officers needed varies depending on the time of day. The department staffing guidelines require the following minimum number of officers on duty:

Time of Day	Minimum Officers on Duty
8:00 A.M.–Noon	5
Noon–4:00 P.M.	6
4:00 P.M.–8:00 P.M.	10
8:00 P.M.–Midnight	7
Midnight–4:00 A.M.	4
4:00 A.M.–8:00 A.M.	6

Determine the number of police officers that should be scheduled to begin the 8-hour shifts at each of the six times (8:00 A.M., noon, 4:00 P.M., 8:00 P.M., midnight, and 4:00 A.M.) to minimize the total number of officers required. (*Hint:* Let x_1 = the number of officers beginning work at 8:00 A.M., x_2 = the number of officers beginning work at noon, and so on.)

9. Reconsider the Welte Mutual Funds problem from Section 4.2. Define your decision variables as the fraction of funds invested in each security. Also, modify the constraints limiting investments in the oil and steel industries as follows: No more than 50% of the total funds invested in stock (oil and steel) may be invested in the oil industry, and no more than 50% of the funds invested in stock (oil and steel) may be invested in the steel industry.

a. Solve the revised linear programming model. What fraction of the portfolio should be invested in each type of security?

b. How much should be invested in each type of security?

c. What are the total earnings for the portfolio?

d. What is the marginal rate of return on the portfolio? That is, how much more could be earned by investing one more dollar in the portfolio?

10. An investment advisor at Shore Financial Services wants to develop a model that can be used to allocate investment funds among four alternatives: stocks, bonds, mutual funds, and cash. For the coming investment period, the company developed estimates of the annual rate of return and the associated risk for each alternative. Risk is measured using an index between 0 and 1, with higher risk values denoting more volatility and thus more uncertainty.

Investment	Annual Rate of Return (%)	Risk
Stocks	10	0.8
Bonds	3	0.2
Mutual funds	4	0.3
Cash	1	0.0

Because cash is held in a money market fund, the annual return is lower, but it carries essentially no risk. The objective is to determine the portion of funds allocated to each investment alternative in order to maximize the total annual return for the portfolio subject to the risk level the client is willing to tolerate.

Total risk is the sum of the risk for all investment alternatives. For instance, if 40% of a client's funds are invested in stocks, 30% in bonds, 20% in mutual funds, and 10% in cash, the total risk for the portfolio would be $0.40(0.8) + 0.30(0.2) + 0.20(0.3) + 0.10(0.0) = 0.44$. An investment advisor will meet with each client to discuss the client's investment objectives and to determine a maximum total risk value for the client. A maximum total risk value of less than 0.3 would be assigned to a conservative investor; a maximum total risk value of between 0.3 and 0.5 would be assigned to a moderate tolerance to risk; and a maximum total risk value greater than 0.5 would be assigned to a more aggressive investor.

Shore Financial Services specified additional guidelines that must be applied to all clients. The guidelines are as follows:

- No more than 75% of the total investment may be in stocks.
- The amount invested in mutual funds must be at least as much as invested in bonds.
- The amount of cash must be at least 10%, but no more than 30% of the total investment funds.

a. Suppose the maximum risk value for a particular client is 0.4. What is the optimal allocation of investment funds among stocks, bonds, mutual funds, and cash? What is the annual rate of return and the total risk for the optimal portfolio?

b. Suppose the maximum risk value for a more conservative client is 0.18. What is the optimal allocation of investment funds for this client? What is the annual rate of return and the total risk for the optimal portfolio?

c. Another more aggressive client has a maximum risk value of 0.7. What is the optimal allocation of investment funds for this client? What is the annual rate of return and the total risk for the optimal portfolio?

d. Refer to the solution for the more aggressive client in part (c). Would this client be interested in having the investment advisor increase the maximum percentage allowed in stocks or decrease the requirement that the amount of cash must be at least 10% of the funds invested? Explain.

e. What is the advantage of defining the decision variables as is done in this model rather than stating the amount to be invested and expressing the decision variables directly in dollar amounts?

11. Edwards Manufacturing Company purchases two component parts from three different suppliers. The suppliers have limited capacity, and no one supplier can meet all the company's needs. In addition, the suppliers charge different prices for the components. Component price data (in price per unit) are as follows:

Component	Supplier		
	1	2	3
1	$12	$13	$14
2	$10	$11	$10

Each supplier has a limited capacity in terms of the total number of components it can supply. However, as long as Edwards provides sufficient advance orders, each supplier can devote its capacity to component 1, component 2, or any combination of the two components, if the total number of units ordered is within its capacity. Supplier capacities are as follows:

Supplier	1	2	3
Capacity	600	1000	800

If the Edwards production plan for the next period includes 1000 units of component 1 and 800 units of component 2, what purchases do you recommend? That is, how many units of each component should be ordered from each supplier? What is the total purchase cost for the components?

12. The Atlantic Seafood Company (ASC) is a buyer and distributor of seafood products that are sold to restaurants and specialty seafood outlets throughout the Northeast. ASC has a frozen storage facility in New York City that serves as the primary distribution point for all products. One of the ASC products is frozen large black tiger shrimp, which are sized at 16–20 pieces per pound. Each Saturday ASC can purchase more tiger shrimp or sell the tiger shrimp at the existing New York City warehouse market price. The ASC goal is to buy tiger shrimp at a low weekly price and sell it later at a higher price. ASC currently has 20,000 pounds of tiger shrimp in storage. Space is available to store a maximum of 100,000 pounds of tiger shrimp each week. In addition, ASC developed the following estimates of tiger shrimp prices for the next four weeks:

Week	Price/lb.
1	$6.00
2	$6.20
3	$6.65
4	$5.55

ASC would like to determine the optimal buying-storing-selling strategy for the next four weeks. The cost to store a pound of shrimp for one week is $0.15, and to account for unforeseen changes in supply or demand, management also indicated that 25,000 pounds of tiger shrimp must be in storage at the end of week 4. Determine the optimal buying-storing-selling strategy for ASC. What is the projected four-week profit?

13. Romans Food Market, located in Saratoga, New York, carries a variety of specialty foods from around the world. Two of the store's leading products use the Romans Food Market name: Romans Regular Coffee and Romans DeCaf Coffee. These coffees are blends of Brazilian Natural and Colombian Mild coffee beans, which are purchased from a distributor located in New York City. Because Romans purchases large quantities, the coffee beans may be purchased on an as-needed basis for a price 10% higher than the market price the distributor pays for the beans. The current market price is $0.47 per pound for Brazilian Natural and $0.62 per pound for Colombian Mild. The compositions of each coffee blend are as follows:

	Blend	
Bean	Regular	DeCaf
Brazilian Natural	75%	40%
Colombian Mild	25%	60%

Romans sells the Regular blend for $3.60 per pound and the DeCaf blend for $4.40 per pound. Romans would like to place an order for the Brazilian and Colombian coffee beans that will enable the production of 1000 pounds of Romans Regular coffee and 500 pounds of Romans DeCaf coffee. The production cost is $0.80 per pound for the Regular blend. Because of the extra steps required to produce DeCaf, the production cost for the DeCaf blend is $1.05 per pound. Packaging costs for both products are $0.25 per pound. Formulate a linear programming model that can be used to determine the pounds of Brazilian Natural and Colombian Mild that will maximize the total contribution to profit. What is the optimal solution and what is the contribution to profit?

14. The production manager for the Classic Boat Corporation must determine how many units of the Classic 21 model to produce over the next four quarters. The company has a beginning inventory of 100 Classic 21 boats, and demand for the four quarters is 2000 units in quarter 1, 4000 units in quarter 2, 3000 units in quarter 3, and 1500 units in quarter 4. The firm has limited production capacity in each quarter. That is, up to 4000 units can be produced in quarter 1, 3000 units in quarter 2, 2000 units in quarter 3, and 4000 units in quarter 4. Each boat held in inventory in quarters 1 and 2 incurs an inventory holding cost of $250 per unit; the holding cost for quarters 3 and 4 is $300 per unit. The production costs for the first quarter are $10,000 per unit; these costs are expected to increase by 10% each quarter because of increases in labor and material costs. Management specified that the ending inventory for quarter 4 must be at least 500 boats.

   a. Formulate a linear programming model that can be used to determine the production schedule that will minimize the total cost of meeting demand in each quarter subject to the production capacities in each quarter and also to the required ending inventory in quarter 4.

   b. Solve the linear program formulated in part (a). Then develop a table that will show for each quarter the number of units to manufacture, the ending inventory, and the costs incurred.

   c. Interpret each of the dual values corresponding to the constraints developed to meet demand in each quarter. Based on these dual values, what advice would you give the production manager?

   d. Interpret each of the dual values corresponding to the production capacity in each quarter. Based on each of these dual values, what advice would you give the production manager?

15. Seastrand Oil Company produces two grades of gasoline: regular and high octane. Both gasolines are produced by blending two types of crude oil. Although both types of crude oil contain the two important ingredients required to produce both gasolines, the percentage of important ingredients in each type of crude oil differs, as does the cost per gallon. The percentage of ingredients A and B in each type of crude oil and the cost per gallon are shown.

Crude Oil	Cost	Ingredient A	Ingredient B	
1	$0.10	20%	60%	← Crude oil 1 is 60% ingredient B
2	$0.15	50%	30%	

Each gallon of regular gasoline must contain at least 40% of ingredient A, whereas each gallon of high octane can contain at most 50% of ingredient B. Daily demand for regular and high-octane gasoline is 800,000 and 500,000 gallons, respectively. How many gallons of each type of crude oil should be used in the two gasolines to satisfy daily demand at a minimum cost?

16. The Ferguson Paper Company produces rolls of paper for use in adding machines, desk calculators, and cash registers. The rolls, which are 200 feet long, are produced in widths of $1\frac{1}{2}$, $2\frac{1}{2}$, and $3\frac{1}{2}$ inches. The production process provides 200-foot rolls in 10-inch widths only. The firm must therefore cut the rolls to the desired final product sizes. The seven cutting alternatives and the amount of waste generated by each are as follows:

Cutting Alternative	Number of Rolls			Waste (inches)
	$1\frac{1}{2}$ in.	$2\frac{1}{2}$ in.	$3\frac{1}{2}$ in.	
1	6	0	0	1
2	0	4	0	0
3	2	0	2	0
4	0	1	2	$\frac{1}{2}$
5	1	3	0	1
6	1	2	1	0
7	4	0	1	$\frac{1}{2}$

The minimum requirements for the three products are

Roll Width (inches)	$1\frac{1}{2}$	$2\frac{1}{2}$	$3\frac{1}{2}$
Units	1000	2000	4000

a. If the company wants to minimize the number of 10-inch rolls that must be manufactured, how many 10-inch rolls will be processed on each cutting alternative? How many rolls are required, and what is the total waste (inches)?

b. If the company wants to minimize the waste generated, how many 10-inch rolls will be processed on each cutting alternative? How many rolls are required, and what is the total waste (inches)?

c. What are the differences in parts (a) and (b) to this problem? In this case, which objective do you prefer? Explain. What types of situations would make the other objective more desirable?

17. Frandec Company manufactures, assembles, and rebuilds material handling equipment used in warehouses and distribution centers. One product, called a Liftmaster, is assembled from four components: a frame, a motor, two supports, and a metal strap. Frandec's production schedule calls for 5000 Liftmasters to be made next month. Frandec purchases the motors from an outside supplier, but the frames, supports, and straps may be either manufactured by the company or purchased from an outside supplier. Manufacturing and purchase costs per unit are shown.

Component	Manufacturing Cost	Purchase Cost
Frame	$38.00	$51.00
Support	$11.50	$15.00
Strap	$ 6.50	$ 7.50

Three departments are involved in the production of these components. The time (in minutes per unit) required to process each component in each department and the available capacity (in hours) for the three departments are as follows:

	Department		
Component	Cutting	Milling	Shaping
Frame	3.5	2.2	3.1
Support	1.3	1.7	2.6
Strap	0.8	—	1.7
Capacity (hours)	350	420	680

a. Formulate and solve a linear programming model for this make-or-buy application. How many of each component should be manufactured and how many should be purchased?

b. What is the total cost of the manufacturing and purchasing plan?

c. How many hours of production time are used in each department?

d. How much should Frandec be willing to pay for an additional hour of time in the shaping department?

e. Another manufacturer has offered to sell frames to Frandec for $45 each. Could Frandec improve its position by pursuing this opportunity? Why or why not?

18. The Two-Rivers Oil Company near Pittsburgh transports gasoline to its distributors by truck. The company recently contracted to supply gasoline distributors in southern Ohio, and it has $600,000 available to spend on the necessary expansion of its fleet of gasoline tank trucks. Three models of gasoline tank trucks are available.

Truck Model	Capacity (gallons)	Purchase Cost	Monthly Operating Cost, Including Depreciation
Super Tanker	5000	$67,000	$550
Regular Line	2500	$55,000	$425
Econo-Tanker	1000	$46,000	$350

The company estimates that the monthly demand for the region will be 550,000 gallons of gasoline. Because of the size and speed differences of the trucks, the number of deliveries or round trips possible per month for each truck model will vary. Trip capacities are estimated at 15 trips per month for the Super Tanker, 20 trips per month for the Regular Line, and 25 trips per month for the Econo-Tanker. Based on maintenance and driver availability, the firm does not want to add more than 15 new vehicles to its fleet. In addition, the company has decided to purchase at least three of the new Econo-Tankers for use on short-run, low-demand routes. As a final constraint, the company does not want more than half the new models to be Super Tankers.

a. If the company wishes to satisfy the gasoline demand with a minimum monthly operating expense, how many models of each truck should be purchased?

b. If the company did not require at least three Econo-Tankers and did not limit the number of Super Tankers to at most half the new models, how many models of each truck should be purchased?

19. The Silver Star Bicycle Company will be manufacturing both men's and women's models for its Easy-Pedal 10-speed bicycles during the next two months. Management wants to develop a production schedule indicating how many bicycles of each model should be produced in each month. Current demand forecasts call for 150 men's and 125 women's

models to be shipped during the first month and 200 men's and 150 women's models to be shipped during the second month. Additional data are shown:

Model	Production Costs	Labor Requirements (hours)		Current Inventory
		Manufacturing	Assembly	
Men's	$120	2.0	1.5	20
Women's	$ 90	1.6	1.0	30

Last month the company used a total of 1000 hours of labor. The company's labor relations policy will not allow the combined total hours of labor (manufacturing plus assembly) to increase or decrease by more than 100 hours from month to month. In addition, the company charges monthly inventory at the rate of 2% of the production cost based on the inventory levels at the end of the month. The company would like to have at least 25 units of each model in inventory at the end of the two months.

a. Establish a production schedule that minimizes production and inventory costs and satisfies the labor-smoothing, demand, and inventory requirements. What inventories will be maintained and what are the monthly labor requirements?

b. If the company changed the constraints so that monthly labor increases and decreases could not exceed 50 hours, what would happen to the production schedule? How much will the cost increase? What would you recommend?

20. Filtron Corporation produces filtration containers used in water treatment systems. Although business has been growing, the demand each month varies considerably. As a result, the company utilizes a mix of part-time and full-time employees to meet production demands. Although this approach provides Filtron with great flexibility, it has resulted in increased costs and morale problems among employees. For instance, if Filtron needs to increase production from one month to the next, additional part-time employees have to be hired and trained, and costs go up. If Filtron has to decrease production, the workforce has to be reduced and Filtron incurs additional costs in terms of unemployment benefits and decreased morale. Best estimates are that increasing the number of units produced from one month to the next will increase production costs by $1.25 per unit, and that decreasing the number of units produced will increase production costs by $1.00 per unit. In February Filtron produced 10,000 filtration containers but only sold 7500 units; 2500 units are currently in inventory. The sales forecasts for March, April, and May are for 12,000 units, 8000 units, and 15,000 units, respectively. In addition, Filtron has the capacity to store up to 3000 filtration containers at the end of any month. Management would like to determine the number of units to be produced in March, April, and May that will minimize the total cost of the monthly production increases and decreases.

21. Greenville Cabinets received a contract to produce speaker cabinets for a major speaker manufacturer. The contract calls for the production of 3300 bookshelf speakers and 4100 floor speakers over the next two months, with the following delivery schedule:

Model	Month 1	Month 2
Bookshelf	2100	1200
Floor	1500	2600

Greenville estimates that the production time for each bookshelf model is 0.7 hour and the production time for each floor model is 1 hour. The raw material costs are $10 for each bookshelf model and $12 for each floor model. Labor costs are $22 per hour using regular production time and $33 using overtime. Greenville has up to 2400 hours of regular production time available each month and up to 1000 additional hours of overtime available each month. If production for either cabinet exceeds demand in month 1, the cabinets can be stored at a cost of $5 per cabinet. For each product, determine the number of units that should be manufactured each month on regular time and on overtime to minimize total production and storage costs.

22. TriCity Manufacturing (TCM) makes Styrofoam cups, plates, and sandwich and meal containers. Next week's schedule calls for the production of 80,000 small sandwich containers, 80,000 large sandwich containers, and 65,000 meal containers. To make these containers, Styrofoam sheets are melted and formed into final products using three machines: M1, M2, and M3. Machine M1 can process Styrofoam sheets with a maximum width of 12 inches. The width capacity of machine M2 is 16 inches, and the width capacity of machine M3 is 20 inches. The small sandwich containers require 10-inch-wide Styrofoam sheets; thus, these containers can be produced on each of the three machines. The large sandwich containers require 12-inch-wide sheets; thus, these containers can also be produced on each of the three machines. However, the meal containers require 16-inch-wide Styrofoam sheets, so the meal containers cannot be produced on machine M1. Waste is incurred in the production of all three containers because Styrofoam is lost in the heating and forming process as well as in the final trimming of the product. The amount of waste generated varies depending upon the container produced and the machine used. The following table shows the waste in square inches for each machine and product combination. The waste material is recycled for future use.

Machine	Small Sandwich	Large Sandwich	Meal
M1	20	15	—
M2	24	28	18
M3	32	35	36

Production rates also depend upon the container produced and the machine used. The following table shows the production rates in units per minute for each machine and product combination. Machine capacities are limited for the next week. Time available is 35 hours for machine M1, 35 hours for machine M2, and 40 hours for machine M3.

Machine	Small Sandwich	Large Sandwich	Meal
M1	30	25	—
M2	45	40	30
M3	60	52	44

a. Costs associated with reprocessing the waste material have been increasing. Thus, TCM would like to minimize the amount of waste generated in meeting next week's production schedule. Formulate a linear programming model that can be used to determine the best production schedule.

b. Solve the linear program formulated in part (a) to determine the production schedule. How much waste is generated? Which machines, if any, have idle capacity?

23. EZ-Windows, Inc., manufactures replacement windows for the home remodeling business. In January, the company produced 15,000 windows and ended the month with 9000 windows in inventory. EZ-Windows' management team would like to develop a production schedule for the next three months. A smooth production schedule is obviously desirable because it maintains the current workforce and provides a similar month-to-month operation. However, given the sales forecasts, the production capacities, and the storage capabilities as shown, the management team does not think a smooth production schedule with the same production quantity each month possible.

	February	March	April
Sales forecast	15,000	16,500	20,000
Production capacity	14,000	14,000	18,000
Storage capacity	6,000	6,000	6,000

The company's cost accounting department estimates that increasing production by one window from one month to the next will increase total costs by $1.00 for each unit increase in the production level. In addition, decreasing production by one unit from one month to the next will increase total costs by $0.65 for each unit decrease in the production level. Ignoring production and inventory carrying costs, formulate and solve a linear programming model that will minimize the cost of changing production levels while still satisfying the monthly sales forecasts.

24. Morton Financial must decide on the percentage of available funds to commit to each of two investments, referred to as A and B, over the next four periods. The following table shows the amount of new funds available for each of the four periods, as well as the cash expenditure required for each investment (negative values) or the cash income from the investment (positive values). The data shown (in thousands of dollars) reflect the amount of expenditure or income if 100% of the funds available in any period are invested in either A or B. For example, if Morton decides to invest 100% of the funds available in any period in investment A, it will incur cash expenditures of $1000 in period 1, $800 in period 2, $200 in period 3, and income of $200 in period 4. Note, however, if Morton made the decision to invest 80% in investment A, the cash expenditures or income would be 80% of the values shown.

Period	New Investment Funds Available	Investment A	Investment B
1	1500	−1000	−800
2	400	−800	−500
3	500	−200	−300
4	100	200	300

The amount of funds available in any period is the sum of the new investment funds for the period, the new loan funds, the savings from the previous period, the cash income from investment A, and the cash income from investment B. The funds available in any period can be used to pay the loan and interest from the previous period, placed in savings, used to pay the cash expenditures for investment A, or used to pay the cash expenditures for investment B.

Assume an interest rate of 10% per period for savings and an interest rate of 18% per period on borrowed funds. Let

$$S(t) = \text{the savings for period } t$$
$$L(t) = \text{the new loan funds for period } t$$

Then, in any period t, the savings income from the previous period is $1.1S(t-1)$, and the loan and interest expenditure from the previous period is $1.18L(t-1)$.

At the end of period 4, investment A is expected to have a cash value of $3200 (assuming a 100% investment in A), and investment B is expected to have a cash value of $2500 (assuming a 100% investment in B). Additional income and expenses at the end of period 4 will be income from savings in period 4 less the repayment of the period 4 loan plus interest.

Suppose that the decision variables are defined as

$$x_1 = \text{the proportion of investment A undertaken}$$
$$x_2 = \text{the proportion of investment B undertaken}$$

For example, if $x_1 = 0.5$, $500 would be invested in investment A during the first period, and all remaining cash flows and ending investment A values would be multiplied by 0.5. The same holds for investment B. The model must include constraints $x_1 \leq 1$ and $x_2 \leq 1$ to make sure that no more than 100% of the investments can be undertaken.

If no more than $200 can be borrowed in any period, determine the proportions of investments A and B and the amount of savings and borrowing in each period that will maximize the cash value for the firm at the end of the four periods.

25. Western Family Steakhouse offers a variety of low-cost meals and quick service. Other than management, the steakhouse operates with two full-time employees who work 8 hours per day. The rest of the employees are part-time employees who are scheduled for 4-hour shifts during peak meal times. On Saturdays the steakhouse is open from 11:00 A.M. to 10:00 P.M. Management wants to develop a schedule for part-time employees that will minimize labor costs and still provide excellent customer service. The average wage rate for the part-time employees is $7.60 per hour. The total number of full-time and part-time employees needed varies with the time of day as shown.

Time	Total Number of Employees Needed
11:00 A.M.–Noon	9
Noon–1:00 P.M.	9
1:00 P.M.–2:00 P.M.	9
2:00 P.M.–3:00 P.M.	3
3:00 P.M.–4:00 P.M.	3
4:00 P.M.–5:00 P.M.	3
5:00 P.M.–6:00 P.M.	6
6:00 P.M.–7:00 P.M.	12
7:00 P.M.–8:00 P.M.	12
8:00 P.M.–9:00 P.M.	7
9:00 P.M.–10:00 P.M.	7

One full-time employee comes on duty at 11:00 A.M., works 4 hours, takes an hour off, and returns for another 4 hours. The other full-time employee comes to work at 1:00 P.M. and works the same 4-hours-on, 1-hour-off, 4-hours-on pattern.

    a. Develop a minimum-cost schedule for part-time employees.

    b. What is the total payroll for the part-time employees? How many part-time shifts are needed? Use the surplus variables to comment on the desirability of scheduling at least some of the part-time employees for 3-hour shifts.

    c. Assume that part-time employees can be assigned either a 3-hour or a 4-hour shift. Develop a minimum-cost schedule for the part-time employees. How many part-time shifts are needed, and what is the cost savings compared to the previous schedule?

Case Problem 1   PLANNING AN ADVERTISING CAMPAIGN

The Flamingo Grill is an upscale restaurant located in St. Petersburg, Florida. To help plan an advertising campaign for the coming season, Flamingo's management team hired the advertising firm of Haskell & Johnson (HJ). The management team requested HJ's recommendation concerning how the advertising budget should be distributed across television, radio, and newspaper advertisements. The budget has been set at $279,000.

In a meeting with Flamingo's management team, HJ consultants provided the following information about the industry exposure effectiveness rating per ad, their estimate of the number of potential new customers reached per ad, and the cost for each ad.

Advertising Media	Exposure Rating per Ad	New Customers per Ad	Cost per Ad
Television	90	4000	$10,000
Radio	25	2000	$ 3,000
Newspaper	10	1000	$ 1,000

The exposure rating is viewed as a measure of the value of the ad to both existing customers and potential new customers. It is a function of such things as image, message recall, visual and audio appeal, and so on. As expected, the more expensive television advertisement has the highest exposure effectiveness rating along with the greatest potential for reaching new customers.

At this point, the HJ consultants pointed out that the data concerning exposure and reach were only applicable to the first few ads in each medium. For television, HJ stated that the exposure rating of 90 and the 4000 new customers reached per ad were reliable for the first 10 television ads. After 10 ads, the benefit is expected to decline. For planning purposes, HJ recommended reducing the exposure rating to 55 and the estimate of the potential new customers reached to 1500 for any television ads beyond 10. For radio ads, the preceding data are reliable up to a maximum of 15 ads. Beyond 15 ads, the exposure rating declines to 20 and the number of new customers reached declines to 1200 per ad. Similarly, for newspaper ads, the preceding data are reliable up to a maximum of 20; the exposure rating declines to 5 and the potential number of new customers reached declines to 800 for additional ads.

Flamingo's management team accepted maximizing the total exposure rating, across all media, as the objective of the advertising campaign. Because of management's concern with attracting new customers, management stated that the advertising campaign must reach at least 100,000 new customers. To balance the advertising campaign and make use of all advertising media, Flamingo's management team also adopted the following guidelines.

- Use at least twice as many radio advertisements as television advertisements.
- Use no more than 20 television advertisements.

- The television budget should be at least $140,000.
- The radio advertising budget is restricted to a maximum of $99,000.
- The newspaper budget is to be at least $30,000.

HJ agreed to work with these guidelines and provide a recommendation as to how the $279,000 advertising budget should be allocated among television, radio, and newspaper advertising.

Managerial Report

Develop a model that can be used to determine the advertising budget allocation for the Flamingo Grill. Include a discussion of the following in your report.

1. A schedule showing the recommended number of television, radio, and newspaper advertisements and the budget allocation for each medium. Show the total exposure and indicate the total number of potential new customers reached.
2. How would the total exposure change if an additional $10,000 were added to the advertising budget?
3. A discussion of the ranges for the objective function coefficients. What do the ranges indicate about how sensitive the recommended solution is to HJ's exposure rating coefficients?
4. After reviewing HJ's recommendation, the Flamingo's management team asked how the recommendation would change if the objective of the advertising campaign was to maximize the number of potential new customers reached. Develop the media schedule under this objective.
5. Compare the recommendations from parts 1 and 4. What is your recommendation for the Flamingo Grill's advertising campaign?

Case Problem 2   PHOENIX COMPUTER

Phoenix Computer manufactures and sells personal computers directly to customers. Orders are accepted by phone and through the company's website. Phoenix will be introducing several new laptop models over the next few months and management recognizes a need to develop technical support personnel to specialize in the new laptop systems. One option being considered is to hire new employees and put them through a three-month training program. Another option is to put current customer service specialists through a two-month training program on the new laptop models. Phoenix estimates that the need for laptop specialists will grow from 0 to 100 during the months of May through September as follows: May—20; June—30; July—85; August—85; and September—100. After September, Phoenix expects that maintaining a staff of 100 laptop specialists will be sufficient.

The annual salary for a new employee is estimated to be $27,000 whether the person is hired to enter the training program or to replace a current employee who is entering the training program. The annual salary for the current Phoenix employees who are being considered for the training program is approximately $36,000. The cost of the three-month training program is $1500 per person, and the cost of the two-month training program is $1000 per person. Note that the length of the training program means that a lag will occur between the time when a new person is hired and the time a new laptop specialist is available. The number of current employees who will be available for training is limited. Phoenix estimates that the following numbers can be made available in the coming months: March—15; April—20; May—0; June—5; and July—10. The training center has the capacity to start new three-month and two-month training classes each month; however, the total number of students (new and current employees) that begin training each month cannot exceed 25.

Phoenix needs to determine the number of new hires that should begin the three-month training program each month and the number of current employees that should begin the two-month training program each month. The objective is to satisfy staffing needs during May through September at the lowest possible total cost; that is, minimize the incremental salary cost and the total training cost.

It is currently January, and Phoenix Computer would like to develop a plan for hiring new employees and determining the mix of new hires and current employees to place in the training program.

Managerial Report

Perform an analysis of the Phoenix Computer problem and prepare a report that summarizes your findings. Be sure to include information on and analysis of the following items:

1. The incremental salary and training cost associated with hiring a new employee and training him/her to be a laptop specialist.
2. The incremental salary and training cost associated with putting a current employee through the training program. (Don't forget that a replacement must be hired when the current employee enters the program.)
3. Recommendations regarding the hiring and training plan that will minimize the salary and training costs over the February through August period as well as answers to these questions: What is the total cost of providing technical support for the new laptop models? How much higher will monthly payroll costs be in September than in January?

Case Problem 3   TEXTILE MILL SCHEDULING

The Scottsville Textile Mill* produces five different fabrics. Each fabric can be woven on one or more of the mill's 38 looms. The sales department's forecast of demand for the next month is shown in Table 4.16, along with data on the selling price per yard, variable cost per yard, and purchase price per yard. The mill operates 24 hours a day and is scheduled for 30 days during the coming month.

TABLE 4.16   MONTHLY DEMAND, SELLING PRICE, VARIABLE COST, AND PURCHASE PRICE DATA FOR SCOTTSVILLE TEXTILE MILL FABRICS

Fabric	Demand (yards)	Selling Price ($/yard)	Variable Cost ($/yard)	Purchase Price ($/yard)
1	16,500	0.99	0.66	0.80
2	22,000	0.86	0.55	0.70
3	62,000	1.10	0.49	0.60
4	7,500	1.24	0.51	0.70
5	62,000	0.70	0.50	0.70

*This case is based on the Calhoun Textile Mill Case by Jeffrey D. Camm, P. M. Dearing, and Suresh K. Tadisnia, 1987.

TABLE 4.17   LOOM PRODUCTION RATES FOR THE SCOTTSVILLE TEXTILE MILL

	Loom Rate (yards/hour)	
Fabric	Dobbie	Regular
1	4.63	—
2	4.63	—
3	5.23	5.23
4	5.23	5.23
5	4.17	4.17

Note: Fabrics 1 and 2 can be manufactured only on the dobbie loom.

The mill has two types of looms: dobbie and regular. The dobbie looms are more versatile and can be used for all five fabrics. The regular looms can produce only three of the fabrics. The mill has a total of 38 looms: 8 are dobbie and 30 are regular. The rate of production for each fabric on each type of loom is given in Table 4.17. The time required to change over from producing one fabric to another is negligible and does not have to be considered.

The Scottsville Textile Mill satisfies all demand with either its own fabric or fabric purchased from another mill. Fabrics that cannot be woven at the Scottsville Mill because of limited loom capacity will be purchased from another mill. The purchase price of each fabric is also shown in Table 4.16.

Managerial Report

Develop a model that can be used to schedule production for the Scottsville Textile Mill, and at the same time, determine how many yards of each fabric must be purchased from another mill. Include a discussion and analysis of the following items in your report:

1. The final production schedule and loom assignments for each fabric.
2. The projected total contribution to profit.
3. A discussion of the value of additional loom time. (The mill is considering purchasing a ninth dobbie loom. What is your estimate of the monthly profit contribution of this additional loom?)
4. A discussion of the objective coefficients' ranges.
5. A discussion of how the objective of minimizing total costs would provide a different model than the objective of maximizing total profit contribution. (How would the interpretation of the objective coefficients' ranges differ for these two models?)

Case Problem 4   WORKFORCE SCHEDULING

Davis Instruments has two manufacturing plants located in Atlanta, Georgia. Product demand varies considerably from month to month, causing Davis extreme difficulty in workforce scheduling. Recently Davis started hiring temporary workers supplied by WorkForce Unlimited, a company that specializes in providing temporary employees for firms in the greater Atlanta area. WorkForce Unlimited offered to provide temporary employees under three contract options that differ in terms of the length of employment and the cost. The three options are summarized:

Option	Length of Employment	Cost
1	One month	$2000
2	Two months	$4800
3	Three months	$7500

The longer contract periods are more expensive because WorkForce Unlimited experiences greater difficulty finding temporary workers who are willing to commit to longer work assignments.

Over the next six months, Davis projects the following needs for additional employees:

Month	January	February	March	April	May	June
Employees Needed	10	23	19	26	20	14

Each month, Davis can hire as many temporary employees as needed under each of the three options. For instance, if Davis hires five employees in January under Option 2, WorkForce Unlimited will supply Davis with five temporary workers who will work two months: January and February. For these workers, Davis will have to pay 5($4800) = $24,000. Because of some merger negotiations under way, Davis does not want to commit to any contractual obligations for temporary employees that extend beyond June.

Davis's quality control program requires each temporary employee to receive training at the time of hire. The training program is required even if the person worked for Davis Instruments in the past. Davis estimates that the cost of training is $875 each time a temporary employee is hired. Thus, if a temporary employee is hired for one month, Davis will incur a training cost of $875, but will incur no additional training cost if the employee is on a two- or three-month contract.

Managerial Report

Develop a model that can be used to determine the number of temporary employees Davis should hire each month under each contract plan in order to meet the projected needs at a minimum total cost. Include the following items in your report:

1. A schedule that shows the number of temporary employees that Davis should hire each month for each contract option.
2. A summary table that shows the number of temporary employees that Davis should hire under each contract option, the associated contract cost for each option, and the associated training cost for each option. Provide summary totals showing the total number of temporary employees hired, total contract costs, and total training costs.
3. If the cost to train each temporary employee could be reduced to $700 per month, what effect would this change have on the hiring plan? Explain. Discuss the implications that this effect on the hiring plan has for identifying methods for reducing training costs. How much of a reduction in training costs would be required to change the hiring plan based on a training cost of $875 per temporary employee?

4. Suppose that Davis hired 10 full-time employees at the beginning of January in order to satisfy part of the labor requirements over the next six months. If Davis can hire full-time employees for $16.50 per hour, including fringe benefits, what effect would it have on total labor and training costs over the six-month period as compared to hiring only temporary employees? Assume that full-time and temporary employees both work approximately 160 hours per month. Provide a recommendation regarding the decision to hire additional full-time employees.

Case Problem 5   DUKE ENERGY COAL ALLOCATION*

Duke Energy manufactures and distributes electricity to customers in the United States and Latin America. Duke recently purchased Cinergy Corporation, which has generating facilities and energy customers in Indiana, Kentucky, and Ohio. For these customers Cinergy has been spending $725 to $750 million each year for the fuel needed to operate its coal-fired and gas-fired power plants; 92% to 95% of the fuel used is coal. In this region, Duke Energy uses 10 coal-burning generating plants: five located inland and five located on the Ohio River. Some plants have more than one generating unit. Duke Energy uses 28–29 million tons of coal per year at a cost of approximately $2 million every day in this region.

The company purchases coal using fixed-tonnage or variable-tonnage contracts from mines in Indiana (49%), West Virginia (20%), Ohio (12%), Kentucky (11%), Illinois (5%), and Pennsylvania (3%). The company must purchase all of the coal contracted for on fixed-tonnage contracts, but on variable-tonnage contracts it can purchase varying amounts up to the limit specified in the contract. The coal is shipped from the mines to Duke Energy's generating facilities in Ohio, Kentucky, and Indiana. The cost of coal varies from $19 to $35 per ton and transportation/delivery charges range from $1.50 to $5.00 per ton.

A model is used to determine the megawatt-hours (mWh) of electricity that each generating unit is expected to produce and to provide a measure of each generating unit's efficiency, referred to as the heat rate. The heat rate is the total BTUs required to produce 1 kilowatt-hour (kWh) of electrical power.

Coal Allocation Model

Duke Energy uses a linear programming model, called the coal allocation model, to allocate coal to its generating facilities. The objective of the coal allocation model is to determine the lowest-cost method for purchasing and distributing coal to the generating units. The supply/availability of the coal is determined by the contracts with the various mines, and the demand for coal at the generating units is determined indirectly by the megawatt-hours of electricity each unit must produce.

The cost to process coal, called the add-on cost, depends upon the characteristics of the coal (moisture content, ash content, BTU content, sulfur content, and grindability) and the efficiency of the generating unit. The add-on cost plus the transportation cost are added to the purchase cost of the coal to determine the total cost to purchase and use the coal.

---

*The authors are indebted to Thomas Mason and David Bossee of Duke Energy Corporation, formerly Cinergy Corp., for their contribution to this case problem.

Current Problem

Duke Energy signed three fixed-tonnage contracts and four variable-tonnage contracts. The company would like to determine the least-cost way to allocate the coal available through these contracts to five generating units. The relevant data for the three fixed-tonnage contracts are as follows:

Supplier	Number of Tons Contracted For	Cost ($/ton)	BTUs/lb
RAG	350,000	22	13,000
Peabody Coal Sales	300,000	26	13,300
American Coal Sales	275,000	22	12,600

For example, the contract signed with RAG requires Duke Energy to purchase 350,000 tons of coal at a price of $22 per ton; each pound of this particular coal provides 13,000 BTUs.

The data for the four variable-tonnage contracts follow:

Supplier	Number of Tons Available	Cost ($/ton)	BTUs/lb
Consol, Inc.	200,000	32	12,250
Cyprus Amax	175,000	35	12,000
Addington Mining	200,000	31	12,000
Waterloo	180,000	33	11,300

For example, the contract with Consol, Inc., enables Duke Energy to purchase up to 200,000 tons of coal at a cost of $32 per ton; each pound of this coal provides 12,250 BTUs.

The number of megawatt-hours of electricity that each generating unit must produce and the heat rate provided are as follows:

Generating Unit	Electricity Produced (mWh)	Heat Rate (BTUs per kWh)
Miami Fort Unit 5	550,000	10,500
Miami Fort Unit 7	500,000	10,200
Beckjord Unit 1	650,000	10,100
East Bend Unit 2	750,000	10,000
Zimmer Unit 1	1,100,000	10,000

For example, Miami Fort Unit 5 must produce 550,000 megawatt-hours of electricity, and 10,500 BTUs are needed to produce each kilowatt-hour.

The transportation cost and the add-on cost in dollars per ton are shown here:

	Transportation Cost ($/ton)				
Supplier	Miami Fort Unit 5	Miami Fort Unit 7	Beckjord Unit 1	East Bend Unit 2	Zimmer Unit 1
RAG	5.00	5.00	4.75	5.00	4.75
Peabody	3.75	3.75	3.50	3.75	3.50
American	3.00	3.00	2.75	3.00	2.75
Consol	3.25	3.25	2.85	3.25	2.85
Cyprus	5.00	5.00	4.75	5.00	4.75
Addington	2.25	2.25	2.00	2.25	2.00
Waterloo	2.00	2.00	1.60	2.00	1.60

	Add-On Cost ($/ton)				
Supplier	Miami Fort Unit 5	Miami Fort Unit 7	Beckjord Unit 1	East Bend Unit 2	Zimmer Unit 1
RAG	10.00	10.00	10.00	5.00	6.00
Peabody	10.00	10.00	11.00	6.00	7.00
American	13.00	13.00	15.00	9.00	9.00
Consol	10.00	10.00	11.00	7.00	7.00
Cyprus	10.00	10.00	10.00	5.00	6.00
Addington	5.00	5.00	6.00	4.00	4.00
Waterloo	11.00	11.00	11.00	7.00	9.00

Managerial Report

Prepare a report that summarizes your recommendations regarding Duke Energy's coal allocation problem. Be sure to include information and analysis for the following issues:

1. Determine how much coal to purchase from each of the mining companies and how it should be allocated to the generating units. What is the cost to purchase, deliver, and process the coal?
2. Compute the average cost of coal in cents per million BTUs for each generating unit (a measure of the cost of fuel for the generating units).
3. Compute the average number of BTUs per pound of coal received at each generating unit (a measure of the energy efficiency of the coal received at each unit).
4. Suppose that Duke Energy can purchase an additional 80,000 tons of coal from American Coal Sales as an "all or nothing deal" for $30 per ton. Should Duke Energy purchase the additional 80,000 tons of coal?
5. Suppose that Duke Energy learns that the energy content of the coal from Cyprus Amax is actually 13,000 BTUs per pound. Should Duke Energy revise its procurement plan?
6. Duke Energy has learned from its trading group that Duke Energy can sell 50,000 megawatt-hours of electricity over the grid (to other electricity suppliers) at a price of $30 per megawatt-hour. Should Duke Energy sell the electricity? If so, which generating units should produce the additional electricity?

Appendix 4.1   EXCEL SOLUTION OF HEWLITT CORPORATION FINANCIAL PLANNING PROBLEM

In Appendix 2.2 we showed how Excel could be used to solve the Par, Inc., linear programming problem. To illustrate the use of Excel in solving a more complex linear programming problem, we show the solution to the Hewlitt Corporation financial planning problem presented in Section 4.2.

The spreadsheet formulation and solution of the Hewlitt Corporation problem are shown in Figure 4.10. As described in Appendix 2.2, our practice is to put the data required for the problem in the top part of the worksheet and build the model in the bottom part of the worksheet. The model consists of a set of cells for the decision variables, a cell for the objective function, a set of cells for the left-hand-side functions, and a set of cells for the right-hand sides of the constraints. The cells for each of these model components are screened; the cells for the decision variables are also enclosed by a boldface line. Descriptive labels are used to make the spreadsheet easy to read.

Formulation

The data and descriptive labels are contained in cells A1:G12. The screened cells in the bottom portion of the spreadsheet contain the key elements of the model required by the Excel Solver.

Hewlitt

FIGURE 4.10   EXCEL SOLUTION FOR THE HEWLITT CORPORATION PROBLEM

	A	B	C	D	E	F	G	H	I	J	K	L
1	**Hewlitt Corporation Cash Requirements**											
2												
3		**Cash**										
4	**Year**	**Rqmt.**				**Bond**						
5	1	430			1	2	3					
6	2	210		**Price ($1000)**	1.15	1	1.35					
7	3	222		**Rate**	0.08875	0.055	0.1175					
8	4	231		**Years to Maturity**	5	6	7					
9	5	240										
10	6	195		**Annual Savings Multiple**	1.04							
11	7	225										
12	8	255										
13												
14	**Model**											
15												
16	F	B1	B2	B3	S1	S2	S3	S4	S5	S6	S7	S8
17	1728.794	144.988	187.856	228.188	636.148	501.606	349.682	182.681	0	0	0	0
18												
19					**Cash Flow**		**Net Cash**		**Cash**			
20	**Min Funds**	1728.7939		**Constraints**	**In**	**Out**	**Flow**		**Rqmt.**			
21				Year 1	1728.794	1298.794	430	=	430			
22				Year 2	711.6057	501.6057	210	=	210			
23				Year 3	571.6818	349.6818	222	=	222			
24				Year 4	413.6809	182.6809	231	=	231			
25				Year 5	240	0	240	=	240			
26				Year 6	195	0	195	=	195			
27				Year 7	225	0	225	=	225			
28				Year 8	255	0	255	=	255			

Decision Variables	Cells A17:L17 are reserved for the decision variables. The optimal values (rounded to three places), are shown to be $F = 1728.794$, $B_1 = 144.988$, $B_2 = 187.856$, $B_3 = 228.188$, $S_1 = 636.148$, $S_2 = 501.606$, $S_3 = 349.682$, $S_4 = 182.681$, and $S_5 = S_6 = S_7 = S_8 = 0$.
Objective Function	The formula =A17 has been placed into cell B20 to reflect the total funds required. It is simply the value of the decision variable, F. The total funds required by the optimal solution is shown to be $1,728,794.
Left-Hand Sides	The left-hand sides for the eight constraints represent the annual net cash flow. They are placed into cells G21:G28. Cell G21 = E21 – F21 (Copy to G22:G28)

For this problem, some of the left-hand-side cells reference other cells that contain formulas. These referenced cells provide Hewlitt's cash flow in and cash flow out for each of the eight years.* The cells and their formulas are as follows:

Cell E21 = A17

Cell E22 = SUMPRODUCT($E$7:$G$7,$B$17:$D$17)+$F$10*E17

Cell E23 = SUMPRODUCT($E$7:$G$7,$B$17:$D$17)+$F$10*F17

Cell E24 = SUMPRODUCT($E$7:$G$7,$B$17:$D$17)+$F$10*G17

Cell E25 = SUMPRODUCT($E$7:$G$7,$B$17:$D$17)+$F$10*H17

Cell E26 = (1+E7)*B17+F7*C17+G7*D17+F10*I17

Cell E27 = (1+F7)*C17+G7*D17+F10*J17

Cell E28 = (1+G7)*D17+F10*K17

Cell F21 = SUMPRODUCT(E6:G6,B17:D17)+E17

Cell F22 = F17

Cell F23 = G17

Cell F24 = H17

Cell F25 = I17

Cell F26 = J17

Cell F27 = K17

Cell F28 = L17

Right-Hand Sides	The right-hand sides for the eight constraints represent the annual cash requirements. They are placed into cells I21:I28. Cell I21 = B5 (Copy to I22:I28)

Excel Solution

We are now ready to use the information in the worksheet to determine the optimal solution to the Hewlitt Corporation problem. The following steps describe how to use Excel to obtain the optimal solution.

---

*The cash flow in is the sum of the positive terms in each constraint equation in the mathematical model, and the cash flow out is the sum of the negative terms in each constraint equation.

Step 1. Select the **Data** tab
Step 2. Select **Solver** from the **Analysis** group
Step 3. When the **Solver Parameters** dialog box appears (see Figure 4.11):
Enter B20 in the **Set Target Cell** box
Select the **Equal to: Min** option
Enter A17:L17 in the **By Changing Cells** box
Step 4. Choose **Add**
When the **Add Constraint** dialog box appears:
Enter G21:G28 in the left-hand box of the **Cell Reference** area
Select = from the middle drop-down button
Enter I21:I28 in the **Constraint** area
Click **OK**
Step 5. When the **Solver Parameters** dialog box reappears (see Figure 4.11):
Choose **Options**
Step 6. When the **Solver Options** dialog box appears:
Select **Assume Linear Model**
Select **Assume Non-Negative**
Click **OK**
Step 7. When the **Solver Parameters** dialog box reappears:
Choose **Solve**
Step 8. When the **Solver Results** dialog box appears:
Select **Keep Solver Solution**
Select **Sensitivity** in the **Reports** box
Click **OK**

The Solver Parameters dialog box is shown in Figure 4.11. The optimal solution is shown in Figure 4.10; the accompanying sensitivity report is shown in Figure 4.12.

FIGURE 4.11 SOLVER PARAMETERS DIALOG BOX FOR THE HEWLITT
CORPORATION PROBLEM

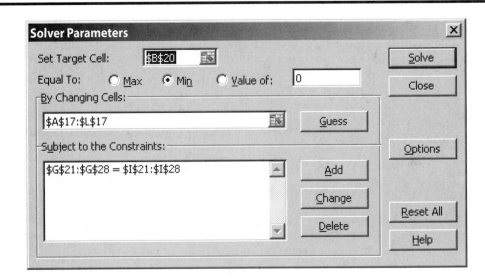

FIGURE 4.12   EXCEL'S SENSITIVITY REPORT FOR THE HEWLITT
CORPORATION PROBLEM

Adjustable Cells

Cell	Name	Final Value	Reduced Cost	Objective Coefficient	Allowable Increase	Allowable Decrease
$A$17	F	1728.793855	0	1	1E + 30	1
$B$17	B1	144.9881496	0	0	0.067026339	0.013026775
$C$17	B2	187.8558478	0	0	0.012795531	0.020273774
$D$17	B3	228.1879195	0	0	0.022906851	0.749663022
$E$17	S1	636.1479438	0	0	0.109559907	0.05507386
$F$17	S2	501.605712	0	0	0.143307365	0.056948823
$G$17	S3	349.681791	0	0	0.210854199	0.059039182
$H$17	S4	182.680913	0	0	0.413598622	0.061382404
$I$17	S5	0	0.064025159	0	1E + 30	0.064025159
$J$17	S6	0	0.012613604	0	1E + 30	0.012613604
$K$17	S7	0	0.021318233	0	1E + 30	0.021318233
$L$17	S8	0	0.670839393	0	1E + 30	0.670839393

Constraints

Cell	Name	Final Value	Shadow Price	Constraint R.H. Side	Allowable Increase	Allowable Decrease
$G$21	Year 1 Flow	430	1	430	1E + 30	1728.793855
$G$22	Year 2 Flow	210	0.961538462	210	1E + 30	661.5938616
$G$23	Year 3 Flow	222	0.924556213	222	1E + 30	521.6699405
$G$24	Year 4 Flow	231	0.888996359	231	1E + 30	363.6690626
$G$25	Year 5 Flow	240	0.854804191	240	1E + 30	189.9881496
$G$26	Year 6 Flow	195	0.760364454	195	2149.927647	157.8558478
$G$27	Year 7 Flow	225	0.718991202	225	3027.962172	198.1879195
$G$28	Year 8 Flow	255	0.670839393	255	1583.881915	255

Discussion

Figures 4.10 and 4.12 contain essentially the same information as that provided in Figure 4.4. Recall that the Excel sensitivity report uses the term *shadow price* to describe the *change* in value of the solution per unit increase in the right-hand side of a constraint. This is the same as the Dual Value in Figure 4.4.

CHAPTER 5

Advanced Linear Programming Applications

CONTENTS

5.1 DATA ENVELOPMENT
   ANALYSIS
   Evaluating the Performance
      of Hospitals
   Overview of the DEA Approach
   DEA Linear Programming
      Model
   Summary of the DEA Approach

5.2 REVENUE MANAGEMENT

5.3 PORTFOLIO MODELS AND
   ASSET ALLOCATION
   A Portfolio of Mutual Funds
   Conservative Portfolio
   Moderate Risk Portfolio

5.4 GAME THEORY
   Competing for Market Share
   Identifying a Pure Strategy Solution
   Identifying a Mixed Strategy
      Solution

This chapter continues the study of linear programming applications. Four new applications of linear programming are introduced. We begin with data envelopment analysis (DEA), which is an application of linear programming used to measure the relative efficiency of operating units with the same goals and objectives. We illustrate how this technique is used to evaluate the performance of hospitals. In Section 5.2, we introduce the topic of revenue management. Revenue management involves managing the short-term demand for a fixed perishable inventory in order to maximize the revenue potential for an organization. Revenue management is critically important in the airline industry, and we illustrate the concept by determining the optimal full-fare and discount-fare seat allocations for flights among five cities.

Management science has a major impact in finance. Section 5.3 shows how linear programming is used to design portfolios that are consistent with a client's risk preferences. In Section 5.4, we introduce game theory, which is the study of how two or more decision makers (players) can compete against each other in an optimal fashion. We illustrate with a linear programming model for two firms competing against each other by trying to gain market share.

5.1 DATA ENVELOPMENT ANALYSIS

Data envelopment analysis (DEA) is an application of linear programming used to measure the relative efficiency of operating units with the same goals and objectives. For example, DEA has been used within individual fast-food outlets in the same chain. In this case, the goal of DEA was to identify the inefficient outlets that should be targeted for further study and, if necessary, corrective action. Other applications of DEA have measured the relative efficiencies of hospitals, banks, courts, schools, and so on. In these applications, the performance of each institution or organization was measured relative to the performance of all operating units in the same system. The Management Science in Action, Efficiency of Bank Branches, describes how a large nationally known bank used DEA to determine which branches were operating inefficiently.

MANAGEMENT SCIENCE IN ACTION

EFFICIENCY OF BANK BRANCHES*

Management of a large, nationally known bank wanted to improve operations at the branch level. A total of 182 branch banks located in four major cities were selected for the study. Data envelopment analysis (DEA) was used to determine which branches were operating inefficiently.

The DEA model compared the actual operating results of each branch with those of all other branches. A less-productive branch was one that required more resources to produce the same output as the best-performing branches. The best-performing branches are identified by a DEA efficiency rating of 100% ($E = 100$). The inefficient or less-productive branches are identified by an efficiency rating less than 100% ($E < 1.00$)

The inputs used for each branch were the number of teller full-time equivalents, the number of nonteller personnel full-time equivalents, the number of parking spaces, the number of ATMs, and the advertising expense per customer. The outputs were the amount of loans (direct, indirect, commercial, and equity), the amount of deposits (checking, savings, and CDs), the average number of accounts per customer, and the customer satisfaction score based on a quarterly customer survey. Data were collected over six consecutive quarters to determine how the branches were operating over time.

(continued)

The solution to the DEA linear programming model showed that 92 of the 182 branches were fully efficient. Only five branches fell below the 70% efficiency level, and approximately 25% of the branches had efficiency ratings between 80% and 89%. DEA identified the specific branches that were relatively inefficient and provided insights as to how these branches could improve productivity. Focusing on the less-productive branches, the bank was able to identify ways to reduce the input resources required without significantly reducing the volume and quality of service. In addition, the DEA analysis provided management with a better understanding of the factors that contribute most to the efficiency of the branch banks.

*Based on B. Golany and J. E. Storbeck, "A Data Envelopment Analysis of the Operational Efficiency of Bank Branches," *Interfaces* (May/June 1999): 14–26.

The operating units of most organizations have multiple inputs such as staff size, salaries, hours of operation, and advertising budget, as well as multiple outputs such as profit, market share, and growth rate. In these situations, it is often difficult for a manager to determine which operating units are inefficient in converting their multiple inputs into multiple outputs. This particular area is where data envelopment analysis has proven to be a helpful managerial tool. We illustrate the application of data envelopment analysis by evaluating the performance of a group of four hospitals.

Evaluating the Performance of Hospitals

The hospital administrators at General Hospital, University Hospital, County Hospital, and State Hospital have been meeting to discuss ways in which they can help one another improve the performance at each of their hospitals. A consultant suggested that they consider using DEA to measure the performance of each hospital relative to the performance of all four hospitals. In discussing how this evaluation could be done, the following three input measures and four output measures were identified:

Input Measures
1. The number of full-time equivalent (FTE) nonphysician personnel
2. The amount spent on supplies
3. The number of bed-days available

Output Measures
1. Patient-days of service under Medicare
2. Patient-days of service not under Medicare
3. Number of nurses trained
4. Number of interns trained

Problem 1 asks you to formulate and solve a linear program to assess the relative efficiency of General Hospital.

Summaries of the input and output measures for a one-year period at each of the four hospitals are shown in Tables 5.1 and 5.2. Let us show how DEA can use these data to identify relatively inefficient hospitals.

Overview of the DEA Approach

In this application of DEA, a linear programming model is developed for each hospital whose efficiency is to be evaluated. To illustrate the modeling process, we formulate a linear program that can be used to determine the relative efficiency of County Hospital.

First, using a linear programming model, we construct a **hypothetical composite,** in this case a composite hospital, based on the outputs and inputs for all operating units with

TABLE 5.1 ANNUAL RESOURCES CONSUMED (INPUTS) BY THE FOUR HOSPITALS

| | Hospital | | | |
Input Measure	General	University	County	State
Full-time equivalent nonphysicians	285.20	162.30	275.70	210.40
Supply expense ($1000s)	123.80	128.70	348.50	154.10
Bed-days available (1000s)	106.72	64.21	104.10	104.04

the same goals. For each of the four hospitals' output measures, the output for the composite hospital is determined by computing a weighted average of the corresponding outputs for all four hospitals. For each of the three input measures, the input for the composite hospital is determined by using the same weights to compute a weighted average of the corresponding inputs for all four hospitals. Constraints in the linear programming model require all outputs for the composite hospital to be *greater than or equal to* the outputs of County Hospital, the hospital being evaluated. If the inputs for the composite unit can be shown to be *less than* the inputs for County Hospital, the composite hospital is shown to have the same, or more, output for *less input*. In this case, the model shows that the composite hospital is more efficient than County Hospital. In other words, the hospital being evaluated is *less efficient* than the composite hospital. Because the composite hospital is based on all four hospitals, the hospital being evaluated can be judged *relatively inefficient* when compared to the other hospitals in the group.

DEA Linear Programming Model

To determine the weight that each hospital will have in computing the outputs and inputs for the composite hospital, we use the following decision variables:

wg = weight applied to inputs and outputs for General Hospital
wu = weight applied to inputs and outputs for University Hospital
wc = weight applied to inputs and outputs for County Hospital
ws = weight applied to inputs and outputs for State Hospital

The DEA approach requires that the sum of these weights equal 1. Thus, the first constraint is

$$wg + wu + wc + ws = 1$$

TABLE 5.2 ANNUAL SERVICES PROVIDED (OUTPUTS) BY THE FOUR HOSPITALS

| | Hospital | | | |
Output Measure	General	University	County	State
Medicare patient-days (1000s)	48.14	34.62	36.72	33.16
Non-Medicare patient-days (1000s)	43.10	27.11	45.98	56.46
Nurses trained	253	148	175	160
Interns trained	41	27	23	84

In general, every DEA linear programming model will include a constraint that requires the weights for the operating units to sum to 1.

As we stated previously, for each output measure, the output for the composite hospital is determined by computing a weighted average of the corresponding outputs for all four hospitals. For instance, for output measure 1, the number of patient days of service under Medicare, the output for the composite hospital is

$$\begin{aligned} \text{Medicare patient-days for Composite Hospital} &= \left(\begin{array}{c} \text{Medicare patient-days} \\ \text{for General Hospital} \end{array} \right) wg + \left(\begin{array}{c} \text{Medicare patient-days} \\ \text{for University Hospital} \end{array} \right) wu \\ &\quad + \left(\begin{array}{c} \text{Medicare patient-days} \\ \text{for County Hospital} \end{array} \right) wc + \left(\begin{array}{c} \text{Medicare patient-days} \\ \text{for State Hospital} \end{array} \right) ws \end{aligned}$$

Substituting the number of Medicare patient-days for each hospital as shown in Table 5.2, we obtain the following expression:

$$\begin{array}{c} \text{Medicare patient-days} \\ \text{for Composite Hospital} \end{array} = 48.14wg + 34.62wu + 36.72wc + 33.16ws$$

The other output measures for the composite hospital are computed in a similar fashion. Figure 5.1 provides a summary of the results.

For each of the four output measures, we need to write a constraint that requires the output for the composite hospital to be greater than or equal to the output for County Hospital. Thus, the general form of the output constraints is

$$\begin{array}{c} \text{Output for the} \\ \text{Composite Hospital} \end{array} \geq \begin{array}{c} \text{Output for} \\ \text{County Hospital} \end{array}$$

FIGURE 5.1   RELATIONSHIP BETWEEN THE OUTPUT MEASURES FOR THE FOUR HOSPITALS AND THE OUTPUT MEASURES FOR THE COMPOSITE HOSPITAL

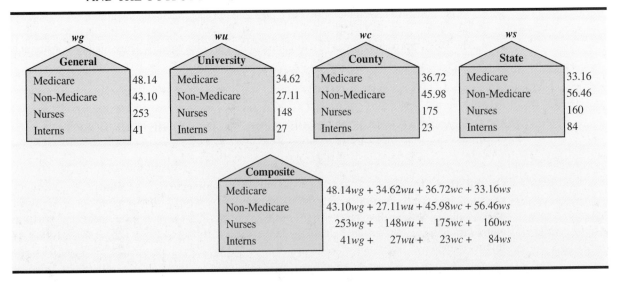

Because the number of Medicare patient-days for County Hospital is 36.72, the output constraint corresponding to the number of Medicare patient-days is

$$48.14wg + 34.62wu + 36.72wc + 33.16ws \geq 36.72$$

In a similar fashion, we formulated a constraint for each of the other three output measures, with the results as shown:

$$
\begin{array}{llll}
43.10wg + 27.11wu + 45.98wc + 56.46ws \geq 45.98 & \text{Non-Medicare} \\
253wg + 148wu + 175wc + 160ws \geq 175 & \text{Nurses} \\
41wg + 27wu + 23wc + 84ws \geq 23 & \text{Interns}
\end{array}
$$

The four output constraints require the linear programming solution to provide weights that will make each output measure for the composite hospital greater than or equal to the corresponding output measure for County Hospital. Thus, if a solution satisfying the output constraints can be found, the composite hospital will have produced at least as much of each output as County Hospital.

Next, we need to consider the constraints needed to model the relationship between the inputs for the composite hospital and the resources available to the composite hospital. A constraint is required for each of the three input measures. The general form for the input constraints is as follows:

$$
\begin{array}{c}
\text{Input for the} \\
\text{Composite Hospital}
\end{array}
\leq
\begin{array}{c}
\text{Resources available to} \\
\text{the Composite Hospital}
\end{array}
$$

For each input measure, the input for the composite hospital is a weighted average of the corresponding input for each of the four hospitals. Thus, for input measure 1, the number of full-time equivalent nonphysicians, the input for the composite hospital is

$$
\begin{array}{c}
\text{FTE nonphysicians} \\
\text{for Composite Hospital}
\end{array}
=
\left(
\begin{array}{c}
\text{FTE nonphysicians} \\
\text{for General Hospital}
\end{array}
\right) wg
+
\left(
\begin{array}{c}
\text{FTE nonphysicians} \\
\text{for University Hospital}
\end{array}
\right) wu
$$
$$
+
\left(
\begin{array}{c}
\text{FTE nonphysicians} \\
\text{for County Hospital}
\end{array}
\right) wc
+
\left(
\begin{array}{c}
\text{FTE nonphysicians} \\
\text{for State Hospital}
\end{array}
\right) ws
$$

Substituting the values for the number of full-time equivalent nonphysicians for each hospital as shown in Table 5.1, we obtain the following expression for the number of full-time equivalent nonphysicians for the composite hospital:

$$285.20wg + 162.30wu + 275.70wc + 210.40ws$$

The logic of a DEA model is to determine whether a hypothetical composite facility can achieve the same or more output while requiring less input. If more output with less input can be achieved, the facility being evaluated is judged to be relatively inefficient.

In a similar manner, we can write expressions for each of the other two input measures as shown in Figure 5.2.

To complete the formulation of the input constraints, we must write expressions for the right-hand-side values for each constraint. First, note that the right-hand-side values are the resources available to the composite hospital. In the DEA approach, these right-hand-side values are a percentage of the input values for County Hospital. Thus, we must introduce the following decision variable:

E = the fraction of County Hospital's input available to the Composite Hospital

FIGURE 5.2 RELATIONSHIP BETWEEN THE INPUT MEASURES FOR THE FOUR HOSPITALS
AND THE INPUT MEASURES FOR THE COMPOSITE HOSPITAL

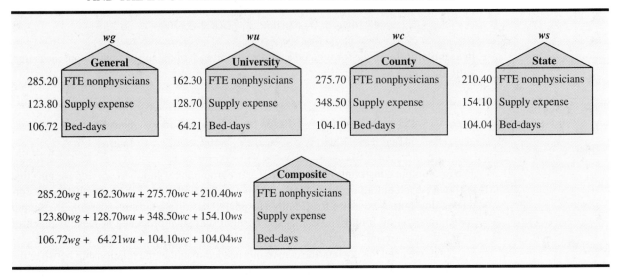

To illustrate the important role that E plays in the DEA approach, we show how to write the expression for the number of FTE nonphysicians available to the composite hospital. Table 5.1 shows that the number of FTE nonphysicians used by County Hospital was 275.70; thus, 275.70E is the number of FTE nonphysicians available to the composite hospital. If $E = 1$, the number of FTE nonphysicians available to the composite hospital is 275.70, the same as the number of FTE nonphysicians used by County Hospital. However, if E is greater than 1, the composite hospital would have available proportionally more nonphysicians, whereas if E is less than 1, the composite hospital would have available proportionally fewer FTE nonphysicians. Because of the effect that E has in determining the resources available to the composite hospital, E is referred to as the **efficiency index.**

We can now write the input constraint corresponding to the number of FTE nonphysicians available to the composite hospital:

$$285.50wg + 162.30wu + 275.70wc + 210.40ws \leq 275.70E$$

In a similar manner, we can write the input constraints for the supplies and bed-days available to the composite hospital. First, using the data in Table 5.1, we note that for each of these resources, the amount that is available to the composite hospital is 348.50E and 104.10E, respectively. Thus, the input constraints for the supplies and bed-days are written as follows:

$$123.80wg + 128.70wu + 348.50wc + 154.10ws \leq 348.50E \quad \text{Supplies}$$
$$106.72wg + 64.21wu + 104.10wc + 104.04ws \leq 104.10E \quad \text{Bed-days}$$

If a solution with $E < 1$ can be found, the composite hospital does not need as many resources as County Hospital needs to produce the same level of output.

The objective function for the DEA model is to minimize the value of E, which is equivalent to minimizing the input resources available to the composite hospital. Thus, the objective function is written as

$$\text{Min } E$$

The DEA efficiency conclusion is based on the optimal objective function value for E. The decision rule is as follows:

If $E = 1$, the composite hospital requires *as much input* as County Hospital does. There is no evidence that County Hospital is inefficient.

If $E < 1$, the composite hospital requires *less input* to obtain the output achieved by County Hospital. The composite hospital is more efficient; thus, County Hospital can be judged relatively inefficient.

The DEA linear programming model for the efficiency evaluation of County Hospital has five decision variables and eight constraints. The complete model is rewritten as follows:

$$\text{Min} \quad E$$

s.t.

$$
\begin{aligned}
wg + wu + wc + ws &= 1 \\
48.14wg + 34.62wu + 36.72wc + 33.16ws &\geq 36.72 \\
43.10wg + 27.11wu + 45.98wc + 56.46ws &\geq 45.98 \\
253wg + 148wu + 175wc + 160ws &\geq 175 \\
41wg + 27wu + 23wc + 84ws &\geq 23 \\
285.20wg + 162.30wu + 275.70wc + 210.40ws &\leq 275.70E \\
123.80wg + 128.70wu + 348.50wc + 154.10ws &\leq 348.50E \\
106.72wg + 64.21wu + 104.10wc + 104.04ws &\leq 104.10E \\
E, wg, wu, wc, ws &\geq 0
\end{aligned}
$$

The optimal solution is shown in Figure 5.3. We first note that the value of the objective function shows that the efficiency score for County Hospital is 0.905. This score tells us that the composite hospital can obtain at least the level of each output that County Hospital obtains by having available no more than 90.5% of the input resources required by County Hospital. Thus, the composite hospital is more efficient, and the DEA analysis identified County Hospital as being relatively inefficient.

From the solution in Figure 5.3, we see that the composite hospital is formed from the weighted average of General Hospital ($wg = 0.212$), University Hospital ($wu = 0.260$), and State Hospital ($ws = 0.527$). Each input and output of the composite hospital is determined by the same weighted average of the inputs and outputs of these three hospitals.

The Slack/Surplus column provides some additional information about the efficiency of County Hospital compared to the composite hospital. Specifically, the composite hospital has at least as much of each output as County Hospital has (constraints 2–5) and provides 1.6 more nurses trained (surplus for constraint 4) and 37 more interns trained (surplus for constraint 5). The slack of zero from constraint 8 shows that the composite hospital uses approximately 90.5% of the bed-days used by County Hospital. The slack values for constraints 6 and 7 show that less than 90.5% of the FTE nonphysician and the supplies expense resources used at County Hospital are used by the composite hospital.

Clearly, the composite hospital is more efficient than County Hospital, and we are justified in concluding that County Hospital is relatively inefficient compared to the other hospitals in the group. Given the results of the DEA analysis, hospital administrators should examine operations to determine how County Hospital resources can be more effectively utilized.

FIGURE 5.3   THE SOLUTION FOR THE COUNTY HOSPITAL DATA ENVELOPMENT
ANALYSIS PROBLEM

```
Optimal Objective Value =         0.90524

        Variable              Value          Reduced Cost
    --------------        --------------     ----------------
         wg                  0.21227            0.00000
         wu                  0.26045            0.00000
         wc                  0.00000            0.09476
         ws                  0.52729            0.00000
         E                   0.90524            0.00000

       Constraint         Slack/Surplus         Dual Value
    --------------        --------------     ------------------
          1                  0.00000            -0.23889
          2                  0.00000             0.01396
          3                  0.00000             0.01373
          4                  1.61539             0.00000
          5                 37.02707             0.00000
          6                 35.82408             0.00000
          7                174.42242             0.00000
          8                  0.00000            -0.00961

                        Objective         Allowable         Allowable
       Variable        Coefficient         Increase         Decrease
    ------------       -----------       -----------       -----------
          wg             0.00000           0.44643           0.19991
          wu             0.00000           0.36384           Infinite
          wc             0.00000           Infinite          0.09476
          ws             0.00000           0.17972           0.42671
          E              1.00000           Infinite          1.00000

                           RHS            Allowable         Allowable
       Constraint         Value            Increase         Decrease
    ------------       -----------       -----------       -----------
          1               1.00000          0.01462           0.08491
          2              36.72000          8.19078           0.23486
          3              45.98000          7.30499           2.15097
          4             175.00000          1.61539           Infinite
          5              23.00000         37.02707           Infinite
          6               0.00000          Infinite         35.82408
          7               0.00000          Infinite        174.42242
          8               0.00000         13.52661           Infinite
```

Summary of the DEA Approach

To use data envelopment analysis to measure the relative efficiency of County Hospital, we used a linear programming model to construct a hypothetical composite hospital based on the outputs and inputs for the four hospitals in the problem. The approach to solving other types of problems using DEA is similar. For each operating unit that we want to measure the efficiency of, we must formulate and solve a linear programming model similar to the linear program we solved to measure the relative efficiency of County Hospital. The following step-by-step procedure should help you in formulating a linear programming model for other types of DEA applications. Note that the operating unit that we want to measure the relative efficiency of is referred to as the jth operating unit.

Step 1. Define decision variables or weights (one for each operating unit) that can be used to determine the inputs and outputs for the composite operating unit.

Step 2. Write a constraint that requires the weights to sum to 1.

Step 3. For each output measure, write a constraint that requires the output for the composite operating unit to be greater than or equal to the corresponding output for the jth operating unit.

Step 4. Define a decision variable, E, which determines the fraction of the jth operating unit's input available to the composite operating unit.

Step 5. For each input measure, write a constraint that requires the input for the composite operating unit to be less than or equal to the resources available to the composite operating unit.

Step 6. Write the objective function as Min E.

NOTES AND COMMENTS

1. Remember that the goal of data envelopment analysis is to identify operating units that are relatively inefficient. The method *does not* necessarily identify the operating units that are *relatively efficient*. Just because the efficiency index is $E = 1$, we cannot conclude that the unit being analyzed is relatively efficient. Indeed, any unit that has the largest output on any one of the output measures cannot be judged relatively inefficient.

2. It is possible for DEA to show all but one unit to be relatively inefficient. Such would be the case if a unit producing the most of every output also consumes the least of every input. Such cases are extremely rare in practice.

3. In applying data envelopment analysis to problems involving a large group of operating units, practitioners have found that roughly 50% of the operating units can be identified as inefficient. Comparing each relatively inefficient unit to the units contributing to the composite unit may be helpful in understanding how the operation of each relatively inefficient unit can be improved.

5.2   REVENUE MANAGEMENT

Revenue management involves managing the short-term demand for a fixed perishable inventory in order to maximize the revenue potential for an organization. The methodology, originally developed for American Airlines, was first used to determine how many airline flight seats to sell at an early reservation discount fare and how many airline flight seats to sell at a full fare. By making the optimal decision for the number of discount-fare seats and the number of full-fare seats on each flight, the airline is able to increase its average number of passengers per flight and maximize the total revenue generated by the combined sale of discount-fare and full-fare seats. Today, all major airlines use some form of revenue management.

Given the success of revenue management in the airline industry, it was not long before other industries began using this approach. Revenue management systems often include pricing strategies, overbooking policies, short-term supply decisions, and the management of nonperishable assets. Application areas now include hotels, apartment rentals, car rentals, cruise lines, and golf courses. The Management Science in Action, Revenue Management at National Car Rental, discusses how National implemented revenue management.

MANAGEMENT SCIENCE IN ACTION

REVENUE MANAGEMENT AT NATIONAL CAR RENTAL*

During its recovery from a near liquidation in the mid-1990s, National Car Rental developed a revenue management system that uses linear programming and other analytical models to help manage rental car capacity, pricing, and reservations. The goal of the revenue management system is to develop procedures that identify unrealized revenue opportunities, improve utilization, and ultimately increase revenue for the company.

Management science models play a key role in revenue management at National. For instance, a linear programming model is used for length-of-rent control. An overbooking model identifies optimal overbooking levels subject to service level constraints, and a planned upgrade algorithm allows cars in a higher-priced class to be used to satisfy excess demand for cars in a lower-priced class.

Another model generates length-of-rent categories for each arrival day, which maximizes revenue. Pricing models are used to manage revenue by segmenting the market between business and leisure travel. For example, fares are adjusted to account for the fact that leisure travelers are willing to commit further in advance than business travelers and are willing to stay over a weekend.

The implementation of the revenue management system is credited with returning National Car Rental to profitability. In the first year of use, revenue management resulted in increased revenues of $56 million.

*Based on M. K. Geraghty and Ernest Johnson, "Revenue Management Saves National Car Rental," *Interfaces* 27, no. 1 (January/February 1997): 107–127.

The development of a revenue management system can be expensive and time-consuming, but the potential payoffs may be substantial. For instance, the revenue management system used at American Airlines generates nearly $1 billion in annual incremental revenue. To illustrate the fundamentals of revenue management, we will use a linear programming model to develop a revenue management plan for Leisure Air, a regional airline that provides service for Pittsburgh, Newark, Charlotte, Myrtle Beach, and Orlando.

Leisure Air has two Boeing 737-400 airplanes, one based in Pittsburgh and the other in Newark. Both airplanes have a coach section with a 132-seat capacity. Each morning the Pittsburgh-based plane flies to Orlando with a stopover in Charlotte, and the Newark-based plane flies to Myrtle Beach, also with a stopover in Charlotte. At the end of the day, both planes return to their home bases. To keep the size of the problem reasonable, we restrict our attention to the Pittsburgh–Charlotte, Charlotte–Orlando, Newark–Charlotte, and Charlotte–Myrtle Beach flight legs for the morning flights. Figure 5.4 illustrates the logistics of the Leisure Air problem situation.

Leisure Air uses two fare classes: a discount-fare Q class and a full-fare Y class. Reservations using the discount-fare Q class must be made 14 days in advance and must include a Saturday night stay in the destination city. Reservations using the full-fare Y class may be made anytime, with no penalty for changing the reservation at a later date. To determine the itinerary and fare alternatives that Leisure Air can offer its customers, we must consider not only the origin and the destination of each flight, but also the fare class. For instance, possible products include Pittsburgh to Charlotte using Q class, Newark to Orlando using Q class, Charlotte to Myrtle Beach using Y class, and so on. Each product is referred to as an origin-destination-itinerary fare (ODIF). For May 5, Leisure Air established fares and developed forecasts of customer demand for each of 16 ODIFs. These data are shown in Table 5.3.

Suppose that on April 4 a customer calls the Leisure Air reservation office and requests a Q class seat on the May 5 flight from Pittsburgh to Myrtle Beach. Should Leisure Air

FIGURE 5.4 LOGISTICS OF THE LEISURE AIR PROBLEM

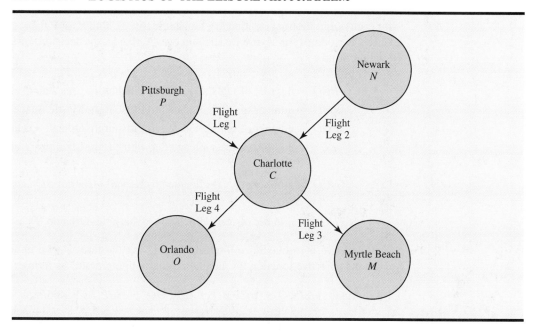

TABLE 5.3 FARE AND DEMAND DATA FOR 16 LEISURE AIR
ORIGIN-DESTINATION-ITINERARY FARES (ODIFs)

ODIF	Origin	Destination	Fare Class	ODIF Code	Fare	Forecasted Demand
1	Pittsburgh	Charlotte	Q	PCQ	$178	33
2	Pittsburgh	Myrtle Beach	Q	PMQ	268	44
3	Pittsburgh	Orlando	Q	POQ	228	45
4	Pittsburgh	Charlotte	Y	PCY	380	16
5	Pittsburgh	Myrtle Beach	Y	PMY	456	6
6	Pittsburgh	Orlando	Y	POY	560	11
7	Newark	Charlotte	Q	NCQ	199	26
8	Newark	Myrtle Beach	Q	NMQ	249	56
9	Newark	Orlando	Q	NOQ	349	39
10	Newark	Charlotte	Y	NCY	385	15
11	Newark	Myrtle Beach	Y	NMY	444	7
12	Newark	Orlando	Y	NOY	580	9
13	Charlotte	Myrtle Beach	Q	CMQ	179	64
14	Charlotte	Myrtle Beach	Y	CMY	380	8
15	Charlotte	Orlando	Q	COQ	224	46
16	Charlotte	Orlando	Y	COY	582	10

accept the reservation? The difficulty in making this decision is that even though Leisure Air may have seats available, the company may not want to accept this reservation at the Q class fare of $268, especially if it is possible to sell the same reservation later at the Y class fare of $456. Thus, determining how many Q and Y class seats to make available are important decisions that Leisure Air must make in order to operate its reservation system.

To develop a linear programming model that can be used to determine how many seats Leisure Air should allocate to each fare class, we need to define 16 decision variables, one for each origin-destination-itinerary fare alternative. Using P for Pittsburgh, N for Newark, C for Charlotte, M for Myrtle Beach, and O for Orlando, the decision variables take the following form:

PCQ = number of seats allocated to Pittsburgh–Charlotte Q class
PMQ = number of seats allocated to Pittsburgh–Myrtle Beach Q class
POQ = number of seats allocated to Pittsburgh–Orlando Q class
PCY = number of seats allocated to Pittsburgh–Charlotte Y class
$\vdots$
NCQ = number of seats allocated to Newark–Charlotte Q class
$\vdots$
COY = number of seats allocated to Charlotte–Orlando Y class

The objective is to maximize total revenue. Using the fares shown in Table 5.3, we can write the objective function for the linear programming model as follows:

$$
\begin{aligned}
\text{Max} \quad & 178PCQ + 268PMQ + 228POQ + 380PCY + 456PMY + 560POY \\
& + 199NCQ + 249NMQ + 349NOQ + 385NCY + 444NMY \\
& + 580NOY + 179CMQ + 380CMY + 224COQ + 582COY
\end{aligned}
$$

Next, we must write the constraints. We need two types of constraints: capacity and demand. We begin with the capacity constraints.

Consider the Pittsburgh–Charlotte flight leg in Figure 5.4. The Boeing 737-400 airplane has a 132-seat capacity. Three possible final destinations for passengers on this flight (Charlotte, Myrtle Beach, or Orlando) and two fare classes (Q and Y) provide six ODIF alternatives: (1) Pittsburgh–Charlotte Q class, (2) Pittsburgh–Myrtle Beach Q class, (3) Pittsburgh–Orlando Q class, (4) Pittsburgh–Charlotte Y class, (5) Pittsburgh–Myrtle Beach Y class, and (6) Pittsburgh–Orlando Y class. Thus, the number of seats allocated to the Pittsburgh–Charlotte flight leg is $PCQ + PMQ + POQ + PCY + PMY + POY$. With the capacity of 132 seats, the capacity constraint is as follows:

$$PCQ + PMQ + POQ + PCY + PMY + POY \leq 132 \quad \text{Pittsburgh–Charlotte}$$

The capacity constraints for the Newark–Charlotte, Charlotte–Myrtle Beach, and Charlotte–Orlando flight legs are developed in a similar manner. These three constraints are as follows:

$$
\begin{aligned}
NCQ + NMQ + NOQ + NCY + NMY + NOY &\leq 132 \quad \text{Newark–Charlotte} \\
PMQ + PMY + NMQ + NMY + CMQ + CMY &\leq 132 \quad \text{Charlotte–Myrtle Beach} \\
POQ + POY + NOQ + NOY + COQ + COY &\leq 132 \quad \text{Charlotte–Orlando}
\end{aligned}
$$

The demand constraints limit the number of seats for each ODIF based on the forecasted demand. Using the demand forecasts in Table 5.3, 16 demand constraints must be added to the model. The first four demand constraints are as follows:

$$
\begin{aligned}
PCQ &\leq 33 \quad \text{Pittsburgh–Charlotte Q class} \\
PMQ &\leq 44 \quad \text{Pittsburgh–Myrtle Beach Q class} \\
POQ &\leq 45 \quad \text{Pittsburgh–Orlando Q class} \\
PCY &\leq 16 \quad \text{Pittsburgh–Charlotte Y class}
\end{aligned}
$$

The complete linear programming model with 16 decision variables, 4 capacity constraints, and 16 demand constraints is as follows:

Max $178PCQ + 268PMQ + 228POQ + 380PCY + 456PMY + 560POY$
$+ 199NCQ + 249NMQ + 349NOQ + 385NCY + 444NMY$
$+ 580NOY + 179CMQ + 380CMY + 224COQ + 582COY$

s.t.

$$PCQ + PMQ + POQ + PCY + PMY + POY \leq 132 \quad \text{Pittsburgh–Charlotte}$$
$$NCQ + NMQ + NOQ + NCY + NMY + NOY \leq 132 \quad \text{Newark–Charlotte}$$
$$PMQ + PMY + NMQ + NMY + CMQ + CMY \leq 132 \quad \text{Charlotte–Myrtle Beach}$$
$$POQ + POY + NOQ + NOY + COQ + COY \leq 132 \quad \text{Charlotte–Orlando}$$

$$
\left.
\begin{aligned}
PCQ &\leq 33 \\
PMQ &\leq 44 \\
POQ &\leq 45 \\
PCY &\leq 16 \\
PMY &\leq 6 \\
POY &\leq 11 \\
NCQ &\leq 26 \\
NMQ &\leq 56 \\
NOQ &\leq 39 \\
NCY &\leq 15 \\
NMY &\leq 7 \\
NOY &\leq 9 \\
CMQ &\leq 64 \\
CMY &\leq 8 \\
COQ &\leq 46 \\
COY &\leq 10
\end{aligned}
\right\} \quad \text{Demand Constraints}
$$

$$PCQ, PMQ, POQ, PCY, \ldots, COY \geq 0$$

The optimal solution to the Leisure Air revenue management problem is shown in Figure 5.5. The value of the optimal solution is $103,103. The optimal solution shows that $PCQ = 33$, $PMQ = 44$, $POQ = 22$, $PCY = 16$, and so on. Thus, to maximize revenue, Leisure Air should allocate 33 Q class seats to Pittsburgh–Charlotte, 44 Q class seats to Pittsburgh–Myrtle Beach, 22 Q class seats to Pittsburgh–Orlando, 16 Y class seats to Pittsburgh–Charlotte, and so on.

Over time, reservations will come into the system and the number of remaining seats available for each ODIF will decrease. For example, the optimal solution allocated 44 Q class seats to Pittsburgh–Myrtle Beach. Suppose that two weeks prior to the departure date of May 5, all 44 seats have been sold. Now, suppose that a new customer calls the Leisure Air reservation office and requests a Q class seat for the Pittsburgh–Myrtle Beach flight. Should Leisure Air accept the new reservation even though it exceeds the original 44-seat allocation? The dual value for the Pittsburgh–Myrtle Beach Q class demand constraint will provide information that will help a Leisure Air reservation agent make this decision.

Dual values tell reservation agents the additional revenue associated with overbooking each ODIF.

Constraint 6, $PMQ \leq 44$, restricts the number of Q class seats that can be allocated to Pittsburgh–Myrtle Beach to 44 seats. In Figure 5.5 we see that the dual value for constraint 6 is $85. The dual value tells us that if one more Q class seat were available from Pittsburgh

FIGURE 5.5   THE SOLUTION FOR THE LEISURE AIR REVENUE
MANAGEMENT PROBLEM

Leisure

```
Optimal Objective Value =              103103.00000

        Variable              Value            Reduced Cost
     --------------      ---------------     ------------------
          PCQ               33.00000             0.00000
          PMQ               44.00000             0.00000
          POQ               22.00000             0.00000
          PCY               16.00000             0.00000
          PMY                6.00000             0.00000
          POY               11.00000             0.00000
          NCQ               26.00000             0.00000
          NMQ               36.00000             0.00000
          NOQ               39.00000             0.00000
          NCY               15.00000             0.00000
          NMY                7.00000             0.00000
          NOY                9.00000             0.00000
          CMQ               31.00000             0.00000
          CMY                8.00000             0.00000
          COQ               41.00000             0.00000
          COY               10.00000             0.00000

       Constraint        Slack/Surplus          Dual Value
     --------------      ---------------     ------------------
            1                0.00000              4.00000
            2                0.00000             70.00000
            3                0.00000            179.00000
            4                0.00000            224.00000
            5                0.00000            174.00000
            6                0.00000             85.00000
            7               23.00000              0.00000
            8                0.00000            376.00000
            9                0.00000            273.00000
           10                0.00000            332.00000
           11                0.00000            129.00000
           12               20.00000              0.00000
           13                0.00000             55.00000
           14                0.00000            315.00000
           15                0.00000            195.00000
           16                0.00000            286.00000
           17               33.00000              0.00000
           18                0.00000            201.00000
           19                5.00000              0.00000
           20                0.00000            358.00000
```

to Myrtle Beach, revenue would increase by $85. This increase in revenue is referred to as the bid price for this origin-destination-itinerary fare. In general, the bid price for an ODIF tells a Leisure Air reservation agent the value of one additional reservation once a particular ODIF has been sold out.

By looking at the dual values for the demand constraints in Figure 5.5, we see that the highest dual value (bid price) is $376 for constraint 8, $PCY \leq 16$. This constraint corresponds to the Pittsburgh–Charlotte Y class itinerary. Thus, if all 16 seats allocated to this itinerary have been sold, accepting another reservation will provide additional revenue of $376. Given this revenue contribution, a reservation agent would most likely accept the additional reservation even if it resulted in an overbooking of the flight. Other dual values for the demand constraints show a value of $358 for constraint 20 ($COY$) and a value of $332 for constraint 10 ($POY$). Thus, accepting additional reservations for the Charlotte–Orlando Y class and the Pittsburgh–Orlando Y class itineraries is a good choice for increasing revenue.

A revenue management system like the one at Leisure Air must be flexible and adjust to the ever-changing reservation status. Conceptually, each time a reservation is accepted for an origin-destination-itinerary fare that is at its capacity, the linear programming model should be updated and re-solved to obtain new seat allocations along with the revised bid price information. In practice, updating the allocations on a real-time basis is not practical because of the large number of itineraries involved. However, the bid prices from a current solution and some simple decision rules enable reservation agents to make decisions that improve the revenue for the firm. Then, on a periodic basis such as once a day or once a week, the entire linear programming model can be updated and re-solved to generate new seat allocations and revised bid price information.

5.3   PORTFOLIO MODELS AND ASSET ALLOCATION

In 1952 Harry Markowitz showed how to develop a portfolio that optimized the trade-off between risk and return. His work earned him a share of the 1990 Nobel Prize in Economics.

Asset allocation refers to the process of determining how to allocate investment funds across a variety of asset classes such as stocks, bonds, mutual funds, real estate, and cash. Portfolio models are used to determine the percentage of the investment funds that should be made in each asset class. The goal is to create a portfolio that provides the best balance between risk and return. In this section we show how linear programming models can be developed to determine an optimal portfolio involving a mix of mutual funds. The first model is designed for conservative investors who are strongly averse to risk. The second model is designed for investors with a variety of risk tolerances.

A Portfolio of Mutual Funds

Hauck Investment Services designs annuities, IRAs, 401(k) plans, and other investment vehicles for investors with a variety of risk tolerances. Hauck would like to develop a portfolio model that can be used to determine an optimal portfolio involving a mix of six mutual funds. A variety of measures can be used to indicate risk, but for portfolios of financial assets all are related to variability in return. Table 5.4 shows the annual return (%) for five 1-year periods for the six mutual funds. Year 1 represents a year in which the annual returns are good for all the mutual funds. Year 2 is also a good year for most of the mutual funds. But year 3 is a bad year for the small-cap value fund; year 4 is a bad year for the intermediate-term bond fund; and year 5 is a bad year for four of the six mutual funds.

It is not possible to predict exactly the returns for any of the funds over the next 12 months, but the portfolio managers at Hauck Financial Services think that the returns for the five years shown in Table 5.4 are scenarios that can be used to represent the possibilities for the next year. For the purpose of building portfolios for their clients, Hauck's portfolio

TABLE 5.4   MUTUAL FUND PERFORMANCE IN FIVE SELECTED YEARS (USED AS
PLANNING SCENARIOS FOR THE NEXT 12 MONTHS)

	Annual Return (%)				
Mutual Fund	**Year 1**	**Year 2**	**Year 3**	**Year 4**	**Year 5**
Foreign Stock	10.06	13.12	13.47	45.42	−21.93
Intermediate-Term Bond	17.64	3.25	7.51	−1.33	7.36
Large-Cap Growth	32.41	18.71	33.28	41.46	−23.26
Large-Cap Value	32.36	20.61	12.93	7.06	−5.37
Small-Cap Growth	33.44	19.40	3.85	58.68	−9.02
Small-Cap Value	24.56	25.32	−6.70	5.43	17.31

managers will choose a mix of these six mutual funds and assume that one of the five possible scenarios will describe the return over the next 12 months.

Conservative Portfolio

One of Hauck's portfolio managers has been asked to develop a portfolio for the firm's conservative clients who express a strong aversion to risk. The manager's task is to determine the proportion of the portfolio to invest in each of the six mutual funds so that the portfolio provides the best return possible with a minimum risk. Let us see how linear programming can be used to develop a portfolio for these clients.

In portfolio models, risk is minimized by diversification. To see the value of diversification, suppose we first consider investing the entire portfolio in just one of the six mutual funds. Assuming the data in Table 5.4 represent the possible outcomes over the next 12 months, the clients run the risk of losing 21.93% over the next 12 months if the entire portfolio is invested in the foreign stock mutual fund. Similarly, if the entire portfolio is invested in any one of the other five mutual funds, the clients will also run the risk of losing money; that is, the possible losses are 1.33% for the intermediate-term bond fund, 23.26% for the large-cap growth fund, 5.37% for the large-cap value fund, 9.02% for the small-cap growth fund, and 6.70% for the small-cap value fund. Let us now see how we can construct a diversified portfolio of these mutual funds that minimizes the risk of a loss.

To determine the proportion of the portfolio that will be invested in each of the mutual funds we use the following decision variables:

FS = proportion of portfolio invested in the foreign stock mutual fund

IB = proportion of portfolio invested in the intermediate-term bond fund

LG = proportion of portfolio invested in the large-cap growth fund

LV = proportion of portfolio invested in the large-cap value fund

SG = proportion of portfolio invested in the small-cap growth fund

SV = proportion of portfolio invested in the small-cap value fund

Because the sum of these proportions must equal 1, we need the following constraint:

$$FS + IB + LG + LV + SG + SV = 1$$

The other constraints are concerned with the return that the portfolio will earn under each of the planning scenarios in Table 5.4.

The portfolio return over the next 12 months depends on which of the possible scenarios (years 1 through 5) in Table 5.4 occurs. Let $R1$ denote the portfolio return if the scenario represented by year 1 occurs, $R2$ denote the portfolio return if the scenario represented by year 2 occurs, and so on. The portfolio returns for the five planning scenarios are as follows:

Scenario 1 return:

$$R1 = 10.06FS + 17.64IB + 32.41LG + 32.36LV + 33.44SG + 24.56SV$$

Scenario 2 return:

$$R2 = 13.12FS + 3.25IB + 18.71LG + 20.61LV + 19.40SG + 25.32SV$$

Scenario 3 return:

$$R3 = 13.47FS + 7.51IB + 33.28LG + 12.93LV + 3.85SG - 6.70SV$$

Scenario 4 return:

$$R4 = 45.42FS - 1.33IB + 41.46LG + 7.06LV + 58.68SG + 5.43SV$$

Scenario 5 return:

$$R5 = -21.93FS + 7.36IB - 23.26LG - 5.37LV - 9.02SG + 17.31SV$$

Let us now introduce a variable M to represent the minimum return for the portfolio. As we have already shown, one of the five possible scenarios in Table 5.4 will determine the portfolio return. Thus, the minimum possible return for the portfolio will be determined by the scenario which provides the worst case return. But we don't know which of the scenarios will turn out to represent what happens over the next 12 months. To ensure that the return under each scenario is at least as large as the minimum return M, we must add the following minimum-return constraints:

$$R1 \geq M \qquad \text{Scenario 1 minimum return}$$
$$R2 \geq M \qquad \text{Scenario 2 minimum return}$$
$$R3 \geq M \qquad \text{Scenario 3 minimum return}$$
$$R4 \geq M \qquad \text{Scenario 4 minimum return}$$
$$R5 \geq M \qquad \text{Scenario 5 minimum return}$$

Substituting the values shown previously for $R1$, $R2$, and so on, provides the following five minimum-return constraints:

$$10.06FS + 17.64IB + 32.41LG + 32.36LV + 33.44SG + 24.56SV \geq M \quad \text{Scenario 1}$$
$$13.12FS + 3.25IB + 18.71LG + 20.61LV + 19.40SG + 25.32SV \geq M \quad \text{Scenario 2}$$
$$13.47FS + 7.51IB + 33.28LG + 12.93LV + 3.85SG - 6.70SV \geq M \quad \text{Scenario 3}$$
$$45.42FS + 1.33IB + 41.46LG + 7.06LV + 58.68SG + 5.43SV \geq M \quad \text{Scenario 4}$$
$$-21.93FS + 7.36IB - 23.26LG - 5.37LV - 9.02SG + 17.31SV \geq M \quad \text{Scenario 5}$$

To develop a portfolio that provides the best return possible with a minimum risk, we need to maximize the minimum return for the portfolio. Thus, the objective function is simple:

$$\text{Max } M$$

With the five minimum-return constraints present, the optimal value of M will equal the value of the minimum return scenario. The objective is to maximize the value of the minimum return scenario.

Because the linear programming model was designed to maximize the minimum return over all the scenarios considered, we refer to it as the *maximin* model. The complete maximin model for the problem of choosing a portfolio of mutual funds for a conservative, risk-averse investor involves seven variables and six constraints. The complete maximin model is written as follows:

Max M

s.t.

$$
\begin{aligned}
10.06FS + 17.64IB + 32.41LG + 32.36LV + 33.44SG + 24.56SV &\ge M \\
13.12FS + 3.25IB + 18.71LG + 20.61LV + 19.40SG + 25.32SV &\ge M \\
13.47FS + 7.51IB + 33.28LG + 12.93LV + 3.85SG - 6.70SV &\ge M \\
45.42FS + 1.33IB + 41.46LG + 7.06LV + 58.68SG + 5.43SV &\ge M \\
-21.93FS + 7.36IB - 23.26LG - 5.37LV - 9.02SG + 17.31SV &\ge M \\
FS + IB + LG + LV + SG + SV &= 1 \\
M, FS, IB, LG, LV, SG, SV &\ge 0
\end{aligned}
$$

Note that we have written the constraint that requires the sum of the proportion of the portfolio invested in each mutual fund as the last constraint in the model. In this way, when we interpret the computer solution of the model, constraint 1 will correspond to planning scenario 1, constraint 2 will correspond to planning scenario 2, and so on.

The optimal solution to the Hauck maximin model is shown in Figure 5.6. The optimal value of the objective function is 6.445; thus, the optimal portfolio will earn 6.445% in the worst-case scenario. The optimal solution calls for 55.4% of the portfolio to be invested in the intermediate-term bond fund, 13.2% of the portfolio to be invested in the large-cap growth fund, and 31.4% of the portfolio to be invested in the small-cap value fund.

Because we do not know at the time of solving the model which of the five possible scenarios will occur, we cannot say for sure that the portfolio return will be 6.445%. However, using the surplus variables, we can learn what the portfolio return will be under each of the scenarios. Constraints 3, 4, and 5 correspond to scenarios 3, 4, and 5 (years 3, 4, and 5 in Table 5.4). The surplus variables for these constraints are zero to indicate that the portfolio return will be $M = 6.445\%$ if any of these three scenarios occur. The surplus variable for constraint 1 is 15.321, indicating that the portfolio return will exceed $M = 6.445$ by 15.321 if scenario 1 occurs. So, if scenario 1 occurs, the portfolio return will be 6.445% + 15.321% = 21.766%. Referring to the surplus variable for constraint 2, we see that the portfolio return will be 6.445% + 5.785% = 12.230% if scenario 2 occurs.

We must also keep in mind that in order to develop the portfolio model, Hauck made the assumption that over the next 12 months one of the five possible scenarios in Table 5.4 will occur. But we also recognize that the actual scenario that occurs over the next 12 months may be different from the scenarios Hauck considered. Thus, Hauck's experience and judgment in selecting representative scenarios plays a key part in determining how valuable the model recommendations will be for the client.

Moderate Risk Portfolio

Hauck's portfolio manager would like to also construct a portfolio for clients who are willing to accept a moderate amount of risk in order to attempt to achieve better returns. Suppose

FIGURE 5.6   THE SOLUTION FOR THE HAUCK MAXIMIN PORTFOLIO MODEL

Maximin

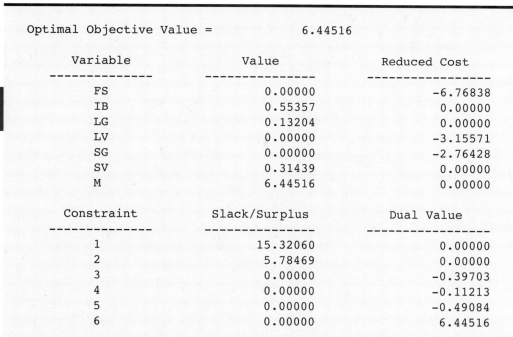

Optimal Objective Value =	6.44516	

Variable	Value	Reduced Cost
FS	0.00000	−6.76838
IB	0.55357	0.00000
LG	0.13204	0.00000
LV	0.00000	−3.15571
SG	0.00000	−2.76428
SV	0.31439	0.00000
M	6.44516	0.00000

Constraint	Slack/Surplus	Dual Value
1	15.32060	0.00000
2	5.78469	0.00000
3	0.00000	−0.39703
4	0.00000	−0.11213
5	0.00000	−0.49084
6	0.00000	6.44516

that clients in this risk category are willing to accept some risk but do not want the annual return for the portfolio to drop below 2%. By setting $M = 2$ in the minimum-return constraints in the maximin model, we can constrain the model to provide a solution with an annual return of at least 2%. The minimum-return constraints needed to provide an annual return of at least 2% are as follows:

$R1 \geq 2$	Scenario 1 minimum return
$R2 \geq 2$	Scenario 2 minimum return
$R3 \geq 2$	Scenario 3 minimum return
$R4 \geq 2$	Scenario 4 minimum return
$R5 \geq 2$	Scenario 5 minimum return

In addition to these five minimum-return constraints, we still need the constraint that requires that the sum of the proportions invested in the separate mutual funds is 1.

$$FS + IB + LG + LV + SG + SV = 1$$

A different objective is needed for this portfolio optimization problem. A common approach is to maximize the expected value of the return for the portfolio. For instance, if we assume that the planning scenarios are equally likely, we would assign a probability of 0.20 to each scenario. In this case, the objective function is to maximize

Expected value of the return $= 0.2R1 + 0.2R2 + 0.2R3 + 0.2R4 + 0.2R5$

Because the objective is to maximize the expected value of the return, we write Hauck's objective as follows:

$$\text{Max} \quad 0.2R1 + 0.2R2 + 0.2R3 + 0.2R4 + 0.2R5$$

The complete linear programming formulation for this version of the portfolio optimization problem involves 11 variables and 11 constraints.

Max $0.2R1 + 0.2R2 + 0.2R3 + 0.2R4 + 0.2R5$	(5.1)
s.t.	
$10.06FS + 17.64IB + 32.41LG + 32.36LV + 33.44SG + 24.56SV = R1$	(5.2)
$13.12FS + 3.25IB + 18.71LG + 20.61LV + 19.40SG + 25.32SV = R2$	(5.3)
$13.47FS + 7.51IB + 33.28LG + 12.93LV + 3.85SG + 6.70SV = R3$	(5.4)
$45.42FS - 1.33IB + 41.46LG + 7.06LV + 58.68SG - 5.43SV = R4$	(5.5)
$-21.93FS + 7.36IB + 23.26LG - 5.37LV + 9.02SG + 17.31SV = R5$	(5.6)
$R1 \geq 2$	(5.7)
$R2 \geq 2$	(5.8)
$R3 \geq 2$	(5.9)
$R4 \geq 2$	(5.10)
$R5 \geq 2$	(5.11)
$FS + \quad IB + \quad LG + \quad LV + \quad SG + \quad SV = 1$	(5.12)
$FS, IB, LG, LV, SG, SV \geq 0$	(5.13)

NOTES AND COMMENTS

1. In this formulation, unlike in the previous maximin model, we keep the variables $R1, R2, R3, R4, R5$ in the model. The variables $R1, R2, R3, R4,$ and $R5$ defined in constraints (5.2)–(5.6) are often called *definitional variables* (a variable that is defined in terms of other variables). These variables could be substituted out of the formulation, resulting in a smaller model. However, we believe that when formulating a model, clarity is of utmost importance and definitional variables often make the model easier to read and understand. Furthermore, stating the model as we have eliminates the need for the user to do the arithmetic calculations necessary to simplify the model. These calculations can lead to error and are best left to the software.

2. Most optimization codes have *preprocessing routines* that will eliminate and substitute out the definitional variables in constraints (5.2)–(5.6). Indeed, the optimization model actually solved by the solver may differ considerably from the actual model formulation. This is why we recommend the user focus on clarity when model building.

3. When building a model such as (5.1)–(5.13) in Excel, we recommend defining adjustable cells for only investment variables, that is, FS, IB, LG, LV, SG, and SV. There will be cells with formulas that calculate the returns given in (5.2)–(5.6), but they need not be adjustable. The Excel Solver model should have only six adjustable cells. See the Excel Web file Moderate Risk that illustrates this point.

The optimal solution is shown in Figure 5.7. The optimal allocation is to invest 10.8% of the portfolio in a large-cap growth mutual fund, 41.5% in a small-cap growth mutual fund, and 47.7% in a small-cap value mutual fund. The objective function value shows that this allocation provides a maximum expected return of 17.33%. From the surplus variables, we see that

FIGURE 5.7   THE SOLUTION FOR THE MODERATE RISK PORTFOLIO MODEL

Optimal Objective Value =   17.33172

Variable	Value	Reduced Cost
R1	29.09269	0.00000
R2	22.14934	0.00000
R3	2.00000	0.00000
R4	31.41658	0.00000
R5	2.00000	0.00000
FS	0.00000	12.24634
IB	0.00000	7.14602
LG	0.10814	0.00000
LV	0.00000	4.35448
SG	0.41484	0.00000
SV	0.47702	0.00000

Constraint	Slack/Surplus	Dual Value
1	0.00000	-0.20000
2	0.00000	-0.20000
3	0.00000	-0.41594
4	0.00000	-0.20000
5	0.00000	-0.59363
6	27.09269	0.00000
7	20.14934	0.00000
8	0.00000	-0.21594
9	29.41658	0.00000
10	0.00000	-0.39363
11	0.00000	18.55087

WEB file

Moderate Risk

the portfolio return will only be 2% if scenarios 3 or 5 occur (constraints 8 and 10 are binding). The returns will be excellent if scenarios 1, 2, or 4 occur: The portfolio return will be 29.093% if scenario 1 occurs, 22.149% if scenario 2 occurs, and 31.417% if scenario 4 occurs.

The moderate risk portfolio exposes Hauck's clients to more risk than the maximin portfolio developed for a conservative investor. With the maximin portfolio, the worst-case scenario provided a return of 6.44%. With this moderate risk portfolio, the worst-case scenarios (scenarios 3 and 5) only provide a return of 2%, but the portfolio also provides the possibility of higher returns.

The formulation we have developed for a moderate risk portfolio can be modified to account for other risk tolerances. If an investor can tolerate the risk of no return, the right-hand sides of the minimum-return constraints would be set to 0. If an investor can tolerate a *loss* of 3%, the right-hand side of the minimum-return constraints would be set equal to –3. In practice, we would expect Hauck to provide the client with a sensitivity analysis that gives the expected return as a function of minimum risk. Linear programming models can be solved quickly, so it is certainly practical to solve a series of linear programs where the minimum return is varied from, for example, –5% to 15% in increments of 1%, and the optimal expected return is calculated for each value of minimum return. Clients can then select an expected value and minimum return combination that they feel is most consistent with their risk preference.

MANAGEMENT SCIENCE IN ACTION

ASSET ALLOCATION AND VARIABLE ANNUITIES*

Insurance companies use portfolio models for asset allocation to structure a portfolio for their clients who purchase variable annuities. A variable annuity is an insurance contract that involves an accumulation phase and a distribution phase. In the accumulation phase the individual either makes a lump sum contribution or contributes to the annuity over a period of time. In the distribution phase the investor receives payments either in a lump sum or over a period of time. The distribution phase usually occurs at retirement, but because a variable annuity is an insurance product, a benefit is paid to a beneficiary should the annuitant die before or during the distribution period.

Most insurance companies selling variable annuities offer their clients the benefit of an asset allocation model to help them decide how to allocate their investment among a family of mutual funds. Usually the client fills out a questionnaire to assess his or her level of risk tolerance. Then, given that risk tolerance, the insurance company's asset allocation model recommends how the client's investment should be allocated over a family of mutual funds. American Skandia, a Prudential Financial Company, markets variable annuities that provide the types of services mentioned. A questionnaire is used to assess the client's risk tolerance, and the Morningstar Asset Allocator is used to develop portfolios for five levels of risk tolerance. Clients with low levels of risk tolerance are guided to portfolios consisting of bond funds and T-bills, and the most risk-tolerant investors are guided to portfolios consisting of a large proportion of growth stock mutual funds. Investors with intermediate, or moderate, risk tolerances are guided to portfolios that may consist of suitable mixtures of value and growth stock funds as well as some bond funds.

*Based on information provided by James R. Martin of the Martin Company, a financial services company.

5.4   GAME THEORY

In **game theory,** two or more decision makers, called players, compete against each other. Each player selects one of several strategies without knowing in advance the strategy selected by the other player or players. The combination of the competing strategies provides the value of the game to the players. Game theory applications have been developed for situations in which the competing players are teams, companies, political candidates, and contract bidders.

In this section, we describe **two-person, zero-sum games.** *Two-person* means that two players participate in the game. *Zero-sum* means that the gain (or loss) for one player is equal to the loss (or gain) for the other player. As a result, the gain and loss balance out (resulting in a zero-sum) for the game. What one player wins, the other player loses. Let us demonstrate a two-person, zero-sum game and its solution by considering two companies competing for market share.

Competing for Market Share

Suppose that two companies are the only manufacturers of a particular product; they compete against each other for market share. In planning a marketing strategy for the coming year, each company will select one of three strategies designed to take market share from the other company. The three strategies, which are assumed to be the same for both companies, are as follows:

Strategy 1: Increase advertising.

Strategy 2: Provide quantity discounts.

Strategy 3: Extend warranty.

TABLE 5.5 PAYOFF TABLE SHOWING THE PERCENTAGE GAIN IN MARKET SHARE FOR COMPANY A

		Company B		
		Increase Advertising b_1	Quantity Discounts b_2	Extend Warranty b_3
Company A	Increase Advertising a_1	4	3	2
	Quantity Discounts a_2	−1	4	1
	Extend Warranty a_3	5	−2	0

A payoff table showing the percentage gain in the market share for Company A for each combination of strategies is shown in Table 5.5. Because it is a zero-sum game, any gain in market share for Company A is a loss in market share for Company B.

In interpreting the entries in the table, we see that if Company A increases advertising (a_1) and Company B increases advertising (b_1), Company A will come out ahead with an increase in market share of 4%, while Company B will have a decrease in market share of 4%. On the other hand, if Company A provides quantity discounts (a_2) and Company B increases advertising (b_1), Company A will lose 1% of market share, while Company B will gain 1% of market share. Therefore, Company A wants to maximize the payoff that is its increase in market share. Company B wants to minimize the payoff because the increase in market share for Company A is the decrease in market share for Company B.

This market-share game meets the requirements of a two-person, zero-sum game. The two companies are the two players, and the zero-sum occurs because the gain (or loss) in market share for Company A is the same as the loss (or gain) in market share for Company B. Each company will select one of its three alternative strategies. Because of the planning horizon, each company will have to select its strategy before knowing the other company's strategy. What is the optimal strategy for each company?

The logic of game theory assumes that each player has the same information and will select a strategy that provides the best possible payoff from its point of view. Suppose Company A selects strategy a_1. Market share increases of 4%, 3%, or 2% are possible depending upon Company B's strategy. At this point, Company A assumes that Company B will select the strategy that is best for it. Thus, if Company A selects strategy a_1, Company A assumes Company B will select its best strategy b_3, which will limit Company A's increase in market share to 2%. Continuing with this logic, Company A analyzes the game by protecting itself against the strategy that may be taken by Company B. Doing so, Company A identifies the minimum payoff for each of its strategies, which is the minimum value in each row of the payoff table. These row minimums are shown in Table 5.6.

The player seeking to maximize the value of the game selects a maximin strategy.

Considering the entries in the Row Minimum column, we see that Company A can be guaranteed an increase in market share of at least 2% by selecting strategy a_1. Strategy a_2 could result in a decrease in market share of 1% and strategy a_3 could result in a decrease in market share of 2%. After comparing the row minimum values, Company A selects the strategy that provides the *maximum* of the row *minimum* values. This is called a **maximin** strategy. Thus, Company A selects strategy a_1 as its optimal strategy; an increase in market share of at least 2% is guaranteed.

Let us now look at the payoff table from the point of view of the other player, Company B. The entries in the payoff table represent gains in market share for Company A, which

TABLE 5.6   PAYOFF TABLE WITH ROW MINIMUMS

		Company B			
		Increase Advertising b_1	Quantity Discounts b_2	Extend Warranty b_3	Row Minimum
	Increase Advertising a_1	4	3	2	② ←Maximum
Company A	Quantity Discounts a_2	−1	4	1	−1
	Extend Warranty a_3	5	−2	0	−2

correspond to losses in market share for Company B. Consider what happens if Company B selects strategy b_1. Company B market share decreases of 4%, −1%, and 5% are possible. Under the assumption that Company A will select the strategy that is best for it, Company B assumes Company A will select strategy a_3, resulting in a gain in market share of 5% for Company A and a loss in market share of 5% for Company B. At this point, Company B analyzes the game by protecting itself against the strategy taken by Company A. Doing so, Company B identifies the maximum payoff to Company A for each of its strategies b_1, b_2, and b_3. This payoff value is the maximum value in each column of the payoff table. These column maximums are shown in Table 5.7.

The player seeking to minimize the value of the game selects a minimax strategy.

Considering the entries in the Column Maximum row, Company B can be guaranteed a decrease in market share of no more than 2% by selecting the strategy b_3. Strategy b_1 could result in a decrease in market share of 5% and strategy b_2 could result in a decrease in market share of 4%. After comparing the column maximum values, Company B selects the strategy that provides the *minimum* of the column *maximum* values. This is called a **minimax** strategy. Thus, Company B selects b_3 as its optimal strategy. Company B has guaranteed that Company A cannot gain more than 2% in market share.

Identifying a Pure Strategy Solution

If it is optimal for both players to select one strategy and stay with that strategy regardless of what the other player does, the game has a **pure strategy** solution. Whenever the maximum of the row minimums *equals* the minimum of the column maximums, the players cannot improve their payoff by changing to a different strategy. The game is said to have a

TABLE 5.7   PAYOFF TABLE WITH COLUMN MAXIMUMS

		Company B			
		Increase Advertising b_1	Quantity Discounts b_2	Extend Warranty b_3	Row Minimum
	Increase Advertising a_1	4	3	2	② ←Maximum
Company A	Quantity Discounts a_2	−1	4	1	−1
	Extend Warranty a_3	5	−2	0	−2
	Column Maximum	5	4	② ←Minimum	

saddle point, or an equilibrium point. Thus, a pure strategy is the optimal strategy for the players. The requirement for a pure strategy solution is as follows:

> **A Game Has a Pure Strategy Solution If:**
>
> Maximum (Row minimums) = Minimum (Column maximums)

Because this equality is the case in our example, the solution to the game is for Company A to increase advertising (strategy a_1) and for Company B to extend the warranty (strategy b_3). Company A's market share will increase by 2% and Company B's market share will decrease by 2%.

With Company A selecting its pure strategy a_1, let us see what happens if Company B tries to change from its pure strategy b_3. Company A's market share will increase 4% if b_1 is selected or will increase 3% if b_2 is selected. Company B must stay with its pure strategy b_3 to limit Company A to a 2% increase in market share. Similarly, with Company B selecting its pure strategy b_3, let us see what happens if Company A tries to change from its pure strategy a_1. Company A's market share will increase only 1% if a_2 is selected or will not increase at all if a_3 is selected. Company A must stay with its pure strategy a_1 in order to keep its 2% increase in market share. Thus, even if one of the companies discovers its opponent's pure strategy in advance, neither company can gain any advantage by switching from its pure strategy.

If a pure strategy solution exists, it is the optimal solution to the game. The following steps can be used to determine when a game has a pure strategy solution and to identify the optimal pure strategy for each player:

Analyze a two-person, zero-sum game by first checking to see whether a pure strategy solution exists.

Step 1. Compute the minimum payoff for each row (Player A).
Step 2. For Player A, select the strategy that provides the maximum of the row minimums.
Step 3. Compute the maximum payoff for each column (Player B).
Step 4. For Player B, select the strategy that provides the minimum of the column maximums.
Step 5. If the maximum of the row minimums is equal to the minimum of the column maximums, this value is the value of the game and a pure strategy solution exists. The optimal pure strategy for Player A is identified in Step 2, and the optimal pure strategy for Player B is identified in Step 4.

If the maximum of the row minimums *does not equal* the minimum of the column maximums, a pure strategy solution does not exist. In this case, a mixed strategy solution becomes optimal. In the following discussion, we define a mixed strategy solution and show how linear programming can be used to identify the optimal mixed strategy for each player.

Identifying a Mixed Strategy Solution

Let us continue with the two-company market-share game and consider a slight modification in the payoff table as shown in Table 5.8. Only one payoff has changed. If both Company A and Company B choose the extended warranty strategy, the payoff to Company A is now a 5% increase in market share rather than the previous 0%. The row minimums do not change, but the column maximums do. Note that the column maximum for strategy b_3 is 5% instead of the previous 2%.

TABLE 5.8   MODIFIED PAYOFF TABLE SHOWING THE PERCENTAGE GAIN IN MARKET SHARE FOR COMPANY A

| | | Company B | | | |
		Increase Advertising b_1	Quantity Discounts b_2	Extend Warranty b_3	Row Minimum
Company A	Increase Advertising a_1	4	3	2	② ←Maximum
	Quantity Discounts a_2	−1	4	1	−1
	Extend Warranty a_3	5	−2	5	−2
	Column Maximum	5	④	5	
			↑ Minimum		

In analyzing the game to determine whether a pure strategy solution exists, we find that the maximum of the row minimums is 2% while the minimum of the row maximums is 4%. Because these values are not equal, a pure strategy solution does not exist. In this case, it is not optimal for each company to be predictable and select a pure strategy regardless of what the other company does. The optimal solution is for both players to adopt a mixed strategy.

With a **mixed strategy,** each player selects its strategy according to a probability distribution. In the market share example, each company will first determine an optimal probability distribution for selecting whether to increase advertising, provide quantity discounts, or extend warranty. Then, when the game is played, each company will use its probability distribution to randomly select one of its three strategies.

First, consider the game from the point of view of Company A. Company A will select one of its three strategies based on the following probabilities:

$$PA1 = \text{the probability that Company A selects strategy } a_1$$

$$PA2 = \text{the probability that Company A selects strategy } a_2$$

$$PA3 = \text{the probability that Company A selects strategy } a_3$$

The expected value, computed by multiplying each payoff by its probability and summing, can be interpreted as a long-run average payoff for a mixed strategy.

Using these probabilities for Company A's mixed strategy, what happens if Company B selects strategy b_1? Using the payoffs in the b_1 column of Table 5.8, we see Company A will experience an increase in market share of 4% with probability $PA1$, a decrease in market share of 1% with probability $PA2$, and an increase in market share of 5% with probability $PA3$. Weighting each payoff by its probability and summing provides the **expected value** of the increase in market share for Company A. If Company B selects strategy b_1, this expected value, referred to as the *expected gain* if strategy b_1 is selected, can be written as follows:

$$EG(b_1) = 4PA1 - 1PA2 = 5PA3$$

The expression for the expected gain in market share for Company A for each Company B strategy is provided in Table 5.9.

TABLE 5.9 EXPECTED GAIN IN MARKET SHARE FOR COMPANY A FOR EACH
COMPANY B STRATEGY

Company B Strategy	Expected Gain for Company A
b_1	$EG(b_1) = 4PA1 - 1PA2 + 5PA3$
b_2	$EG(b_2) = 3PA1 + 4PA2 - 2PA3$
b_3	$EG(b_3) = 2PA1 + 1PA2 + 5PA3$

For example, if Company A uses a mixed strategy with equal probabilities ($PA1 = \frac{1}{3}$, $PA2 = \frac{1}{3}$, and $PA3 = \frac{1}{3}$), Company A's expected gain in market share for each Company B strategy is as follows:

$$EG(b_1) = 4PA1 - 1PA2 + 5PA3 = 4(\tfrac{1}{3}) - 1(\tfrac{1}{3}) + 5(\tfrac{1}{3}) = \tfrac{8}{3} = 2.67$$

$$EG(b_2) = 3PA1 + 4PA2 - 2PA3 = 3(\tfrac{1}{3}) + 4(\tfrac{1}{3}) - 2(\tfrac{1}{3}) = \tfrac{5}{3} = 1.67$$

$$EG(b_3) = 2PA1 + 1PA2 + 5PA3 = 2(\tfrac{1}{3}) + 1(\tfrac{1}{3}) + 5(\tfrac{1}{3}) = \tfrac{8}{3} = 2.67$$

The logic of game theory assumes that if Company A uses a mixed strategy, Company B will select the strategy that will minimize Company A's expected gain. Using these results, Company A assumes Company B will select strategy b_2 and limit Company A's expected gain in market share to 1.67%. Because Company A's pure strategy a_1 provides a 2% increase in market share, the mixed strategy with equal probabilities, $PA1 = \frac{1}{3}$, $PA2 = \frac{1}{3}$, and $PA3 = \frac{1}{3}$, is not the optimal strategy for Company A.

Let us show how Company A can use linear programming to find its optimal mixed strategy. Our goal is to find probabilities, $PA1$, $PA2$, and $PA3$, that maximize the expected gain in market share for Company A regardless of the strategy selected by Company B. In effect, Company A will protect itself against any strategy selected by Company B by being sure its expected gain in market share is as large as possible even if Company B selects its own optimal strategy.

Given the probabilities $PA1$, $PA2$, and $PA3$ and the expected gain expressions in Table 5.9, game theory assumes that Company B will select a strategy that provides the minimum expected gain for Company A. Thus, Company B will select b_1, b_2, or b_3 based on

$$\text{Min } \{EG(b_1), EG(b_2), EG(b_3)\}$$

When Company B selects its strategy, the value of the game will be the minimum expected gain. This strategy will minimize Company A's expected gain in market share.

Company A will select its optimal mixed strategy using a *maximin* strategy, which will maximize the minimum expected gain. This objective is written as follows:

The player seeking to maximize the value of the game selects a maximin strategy by maximizing the minimum expected gain.

$$\text{Max } [\text{Min } \{EG(b_1), EG(b_2), EG(b_3)\}]$$

Company A seeks to maximize the
minimum *EG* Company B can obtain

Company B will select a strategy
to minimize the *EG* for Company A

Define *GAINA* to be the optimal expected gain in market share for Company A. Because Company B will select a strategy that minimizes this expected gain, we know *GAINA* is equal to Min $\{EG(b_1), EG(b_2), EG(b_3)\}$. Thus, the individual expected gains, $EG(b_1)$, $EG(b_2)$, and $EG(b_3)$, must all be *greater than or equal to GAINA*. If Company B selects strategy b_1, we know

$$EG(b_1) \geq GAINA$$

Using the probabilities $PA1$, $PA2$, and $PA3$ and the expected gain expression in Table 5.9, this condition can be written as follows:

$$4PA1 - 1PA2 + 5PA3 \geq GAINA$$

Similarly, for Company B strategies b_2 and b_3, the fact that both $EG(b_2) \geq GAINA$ and $EG(b_3) \geq GAINA$ provides the following two expressions:

$$3PA1 + 4PA2 - 2PA3 \geq GAINA$$
$$2PA1 + 1PA2 + 5PA3 \geq GAINA$$

In addition, we know that the sum of the Company A's mixed strategy probabilities must equal 1.

$$PA1 + PA2 + PA3 = 1$$

Finally, realizing that the objective of Company A is to maximize its expected gain, $GAINA$, we have the following linear programming model. Solving this linear program will provide Company A's optimal mixed strategy.

Max	$GAINA$		
s.t.			Company B strategy
	$4PA1 - 1PA2 + 5PA3 \geq GAINA$		(Strategy b_1)
	$3PA1 + 4PA2 - 2PA3 \geq GAINA$		(Strategy b_2)
	$2PA1 + 1PA2 + 5PA3 \geq GAINA$		(Strategy b_3)
	$PA1 + PA2 + PA3 \qquad = 1$		
	$PA1, PA2, PA3, GAINA \geq 0$		

The solution of Company A's linear program is shown in Figure 5.8.

From Figure 5.8, we see Company A's optimal mixed strategy is to increase advertising (a_1) with a probability of 0.875 and extend warranty (a_3) with a probability of 0.125. Company A should never provide quantity discounts (a_2) because $PA2 = 0$. The expected value of this mixed strategy is a 2.375% increase in market share for Company A.

Let us show what happens to the expected gain if Company A uses this optimal mixed strategy. Company A's expected gain for each Company B strategy follows:

$$EG(b_1) = 4PA1 - 1PA2 + 5PA3 = 4(0.875) - 1(0) + 5(0.125) = 4.125$$
$$EG(b_2) = 3PA1 + 4PA2 - 2PA3 = 3(0.875) + 4(0) - 2(0.125) = 2.375$$
$$EG(b_3) = 2PA1 + 1PA2 + 5PA3 = 2(0.875) + 1(0) + 5(0.125) = 2.375$$

Company B will minimize Company A's expected gain by selecting either strategy b_2 or b_3. However, Company A has selected its optimal mixed strategy by maximizing this

FIGURE 5.8 THE SOLUTION FOR COMPANY A'S OPTIMAL MIXED STRATEGY

WEB file

Strategy A

Optimal Objective Value =   2.37500

Variable	Value	Reduced Costs
PA1	0.87500	0.00000
PA2	0.00000	-0.25000
PA3	0.12500	0.00000
GAINA	2.37500	0.00000

Constraint	Slack/Surplus	Dual Value
1	1.75000	0.00000
2	0.00000	-0.37500
3	0.00000	-0.62500
4	0.00000	2.37500

minimum expected gain. Thus, Company A obtains an expected gain in market share of 2.375% regardless of the strategy selected by Company B. The mixed strategy with $PA1 = 0.875$, $PA2 = 0.0$, and $PA3 = 0.125$ is the optimal strategy for Company A. The expected gain of 2.375% is better than Company A's best pure strategy (a_1), which provides a 2% increase in market share.

Now consider the game from the point of view of Company B. Company B will select one of its strategies based on the following probabilities:

$PB1$ = the probability that Company B selects strategy b_1

$PB2$ = the probability that Company B selects strategy b_2

$PB3$ = the probability that Company B selects strategy b_3

Based on these probabilities for Company B's mixed strategy, what happens if Company A selects strategy a_1? Using the payoffs in the a_1 row of Table 5.8, Company B will experience a decrease in market share of 4% with probability $PB1$, a decrease in market share of 3% with probability $PB2$, and a decrease in market share of 2% with probability $PB3$. If Company A selects strategy a_1, the expected value, referred to as Company B's *expected loss* if strategy a_1 is selected, can be written as follows:

$$EL(a_1) = 4PB1 + 3PB2 + 2PB3$$

The expression for the expected loss in market share for Company B for each Company A strategy is provided in Table 5.10.

Let us show how Company B can use linear programming to find its optimal mixed strategy. Our goal is to find the probabilities, $PB1$, $PB2$, and $PB3$, that minimize the expected loss in market share to Company B regardless of the strategy selected by Company A. In effect, Company B will protect itself from any strategy selected by Company A by being sure its expected loss in market share is as small as possible even if Company A selects its own optimal strategy.

TABLE 5.10   EXPECTED LOSS IN MARKET SHARE FOR COMPANY B FOR EACH COMPANY A STRATEGY

Company A Strategy	Expected Loss for Company B
a_1	$4PB1 + 3PB2 + 2PB3$
a_2	$-1PB1 + 4PB2 + 1PB3$
a_3	$5PB1 - 2PB2 + 5PB3$

Given the probabilities $PB1$, $PB2$, and $PB3$ and the expected loss expressions in Table 5.10, game theory assumes that Company A will select a strategy that provides the maximum expected loss for Company B. Thus, Company A will select a_1, a_2, or a_3 based on

$$\text{Max } \{EL(a_1), EL(a_2), EL(a_3)\}$$

When Company A selects its strategy, the value of the game will be the expected loss, which will maximize Company B's expected loss in market share.

Company B will select its optimal mixed strategy using a *minimax* strategy to minimize the maximum expected loss. This objective is written as follows:

The player seeking to minimize the value of the game selects a minimax strategy by minimizing the maximum expected loss.

$$\text{Min } [\text{Max } \{EL(a_1), EL(a_2), EL(a_3)\}]$$

Company B seeks to maximize the minimum EL Company A can obtain

Company A will select a strategy to minimize the EL for Company B

Define $LOSSB$ to be the optimal expected loss in market share for Company B. Because Company A will select a strategy that maximizes this expected loss, we know $LOSSB$ is equal to Max $\{EL(a_1), EL(a_2), EL(a_3)\}$. Thus, the individual expected losses, $EL(a_1)$, $EL(a_2)$, and $EL(a_3)$, must all be *less than or equal to LOSSB*. If Company A selects strategy, a_1, we know

$$EL(a_1) \leq LOSSB$$

Using the probabilities $PB1$, $PB2$, and $PB3$ and the expected loss expression for $EL(a_1)$ in Table 5.10, this condition can be written as follows:

$$4PB1 + 3PB2 + 2PB3 \leq LOSSB$$

Similarly, for Company A strategies a_2 and a_3, the fact that both $EL(a_2) \leq LOSSB$ and $EL(a_3) \leq LOSSB$ provides the following two expressions:

$$-1PB1 + 4PB2 + 1PB3 \leq LOSSB$$
$$5PB1 - 2PB2 + 5PB3 \leq LOSSB$$

In addition, we know that the sum of the Company B's mixed strategy probabilities must equal 1.

$$PB1 + PB2 + PB3 = 1$$

FIGURE 5.9   THE SOLUTION FOR COMPANY B'S OPTIMAL MIXED STRATEGY

```
Optimal Objective Value =                    2.37500

          Variable              Value              Reduced Cost
      --------------        --------------        ----------------
          PB1                 0.00000                 1.75000
          PB2                 0.37500                 0.00000
          PB3                 0.62500                 0.00000
          LOSSB               2.37500                 0.00000


         Constraint          Slack/Surplus           Dual Value
      --------------        --------------        ----------------
            1                 0.00000                 2.37500
            2                 0.00000                -0.87500
            3                 0.25000                 0.00000
            4                 0.00000                -0.12500
```

Finally, realizing that the objective of Company B is to minimize its expected loss, *LOSSB*, we have the following linear programming model. Solving this linear program will provide Company B's optimal mixed strategy.

$$\text{Min} \quad LOSSB$$

s.t.   Company A strategy

$$4PB1 + 3PB2 + 2PB3 \leq LOSSB \quad (\text{Strategy } a_1)$$
$$-1PB1 + 4PB2 + 1PB3 \leq LOSSB \quad (\text{Strategy } a_2)$$
$$5PB1 - 2PB2 + 5PB3 \leq LOSSB \quad (\text{Strategy } a_3)$$
$$PB1 + PB2 + PB3 \qquad\qquad = 1$$
$$PB1, PB2, PB3, LOSSB \geq 0$$

The solution of Company B's linear program is shown in Figure 5.9.

From Figure 5.9, we see Company B's optimal mixed strategy is to provide quantity discounts (b_2) with a probability of 0.375 and extend warranty (b_3) with a probability of 0.625. Company B should not increase advertising (b_1), because $PB1 = 0$. The expected value or expected loss of this mixed strategy is 2.375%. Note that the expected loss of 2.375% of the market share for Company B is the same as the expected gain in market share for Company A. The mixed strategy solution shows the zero-sum for the expected payoffs.

Let us show what happens to the expected loss if Company B uses this optimal mixed strategy. Company B's expected loss for each Company A strategy follows:

$$EL(a_1) = \quad 4PB1 + 3PB2 + 2PB3 = \quad 4(0) + 3(0.375) + 2(0.625) = 2.375$$
$$EL(a_2) = -1PB1 + 4PB2 + 1PB3 = -1(0) + 4(0.375) + 1(0.625) = 2.125$$
$$EL(a_3) = \quad 5PB1 - 2PB2 + 5PB3 = \quad 5(0) - 2(0.375) + 5(0.625) = 2.375$$

Company A will maximize Company B's expected loss by selecting either strategy a_1 or a_3. However, Company B has selected its optimal mixed strategy by minimizing this maximum expected loss. Thus, Company B obtains an expected loss in market share of 2.375% regardless of the strategy selected by Company A. The mixed strategy with $PB1 = 0.0$, $PB2 = 0.375$, and $PB3 = 0.625$ is the optimal strategy for Company B. The expected loss of 2.375% is better than Company B's best pure strategy (b_2), which provides a 4% loss in market share.

The optimal mixed strategy solution with a value of 2.375% is an equilibrium solution. Given Company A's mixed strategy probabilities, Company B cannot improve the value of the game by changing $PB1$, $PB2$, or $PB3$. Likewise, given Company B's mixed strategy probabilities, Company A cannot improve the value of the game by changing $PA1$, $PA2$, or $PA3$. In general, the solution to the linear program will provide an equilibrium optimal mixed strategy solution for the game.

With a mixed strategy game, only solve the linear program for one of the players. Provided the value of the game is greater than zero, the absolute value of the dual values provides the optimal mixed strategy solution for the other player.

Let us conclude this linear programming application by making some observations and suggestions about using linear programming to solve mixed strategy two-person, zero-sum games. First of all, consider the dual value for constraint 2 in the solution of the Company A linear program in Figure 5.8. This dual value is –0.375. Recall that constraint 2 provides Company A's expected gain if Company B selects strategy b_2. The *absolute value* of the dual value is Company B's optimal probability for this strategy. Thus, we know $PB2 = 0.375$ without having to solve the Company B linear program. Using the absolute value of the dual values for the Company A linear program in Figure 5.8, we know that the optimal mixed strategy solution for Company B is $PB1 = 0.0$, $PB2 = 0.375$, and $PB3 = 0.625$. Therefore, when a two-person, zero-sum game has a mixed strategy, we only need to solve the linear program for one of the players. The optimal mixed strategy for the other player can be found by using the absolute value of the dual values.

Finally, note that a nonnegativity constraint in the linear program for Company A requires the value of the game, *GAINA*, to be greater than or equal to 0. A similar nonnegativity constraint in the linear program for Company B requires the value of the game, *LOSSB*, to be greater than or equal to 0. Because the value of the game in our example was 2.375%, we met these nonnegativity requirements. However, consider a two-person, zero-sum game where the payoff table contains several negative payoffs for player A. It may turn out that when player A selects an optimal mixed strategy, a negative value of the game is the best the player can do. In this case *GAINA* and *LOSSB* would be negative, which causes the linear program to have an infeasible solution.

If this condition exists or may exist, the following strategy can be used to modify the game and ensure that the linear program has a feasible solution. Define a constant c as follows:

If the value of a mixed strategy game may be negative, this procedure will guarantee that the linear program used to determine the optimal mixed strategy will have a feasible solution.

$$c = \text{the absolute value of the largest negative payoff for player A}$$

A revised payoff table can be created by adding c to each payoff, turning it into an equivalent two-person, zero-sum game. Because the revised payoff table contains no negative payoffs, the nonnegativity constraint for the value of the game will be satisfied and a feasible solution will exist for the linear program. More importantly, the optimal mixed strategy using the revised payoffs *will be the same* as the optimal mixed strategy for the original game. By subtracting c from the optimal objective function value for the game with the revised payoffs, you will obtain the objective function value for the original game.

NOTES AND COMMENTS

1. The analysis of a two-person, zero-sum game begins with checking to see whether a pure strategy solution exists. If the maximum of the row minimums for player A, V_A, is not equal to the minimum the column maximums for player B, V_B, a pure strategy solution does not exist. At this point, we can also conclude that a mixed strategy solution is optimal and that the value of the game will be *between* V_A and V_B. For example, in our mixed strategy market-share game, the maximum of the row minimums was 2% and the minimum of the column maximums was 4%. Thus, we can conclude that a mixed strategy solution exists and that the value of the game is between 2% and 4%. We would know this result before solving the mixed strategy linear program.

   If the maximum of the row minimums, V_A, is positive and the minimum of the column maximums, V_B, is positive, we know that the value of the mixed strategy game will be positive. In this case, it is not necessary to revise the payoff table by the constant c to obtain a feasible linear programming solution. However, if one or both V_A and V_B are negative, the value of the mixed strategy game can be negative. In this case, it is desirable to revise the payoff table by adding the constant c to all payoffs prior to solving the linear program.

2. The linear programming formulation presented in this section used nonnegativity constraints $GAINA \geq 0$ and $LOSSB \geq 0$ so that the two-person, mixed strategy game could be solved with traditional linear programming software. If you are using software such as LINGO or Excel, these variables do not have to be nonnegative. In this case, eliminate the nonnegative requirements and make $GAINA$ and $LOSSB$ unrestricted in sign. This treatment guarantees that the linear program will have a feasible solution and eliminates the need to add a constant to the payoffs in situations where $GAINA$ and $LOSSB$ may be negative.

SUMMARY

In this chapter we presented selected advanced linear programming applications. In particular, we applied linear programming to evaluating the performance of hospitals, maximizing revenue for airlines, constructing mutual fund portfolios, and competing for market share. In practice, most of the modeling effort in these types of linear programming applications involves clearly understanding the problem, stating the problem mathematically, and then finding reliable data in the format required by the model.

GLOSSARY

Data envelopment analysis (DEA)   A linear programming application used to measure the relative efficiency of operating units with the same goals and objectives.

Hypothetical composite   A weighted average of outputs and inputs of all operating units with similar goals.

Efficiency index   Percentage of an individual operating unit's resources that are available to the composite operating unit.

Game theory   A decision-making situation in which two or more decision makers compete by each selecting one of several strategies. The combination of the competing strategies provides the value of the game to the players.

Two-person, zero-sum game   A game with two players in which the gain to one player is equal to the loss to the other player.

Maximin strategy   A strategy where the player seeking to maximize the value of the game selects the strategy that maximizes the minimum payoff obtainable by the other player.

Minimax strategy   A strategy where the player seeking to minimize the value of the game selects the strategy that minimizes the maximum payoff obtainable by the other player.

Pure strategy   When one of the available strategies is optimal and the player always selects this strategy regardless of the strategy selected by the other player.

Saddle point   A condition that exists when pure strategies are optimal for both players. Neither player can improve the value of the game by changing from the optimal pure strategy.

Mixed strategy   When a player randomly selects its strategy based on a probability distribution. The strategy selected can vary each time the game is played.

Expected value   In a mixed strategy game, a value computed by multiplying each payoff by its probability and summing. It can be interpreted as the long-run average payoff for the mixed strategy.

PROBLEMS

Note: The following problems have been designed to give you an understanding and appreciation of the broad range of problems that can be formulated as linear programs. You should be able to formulate a linear programming model for each of the problems. However, you will need access to a linear programming computer package to develop the solutions and make the requested interpretations.

1. In Section 5.1 data envelopment analysis was used to evaluate the relative efficiencies of four hospitals. Data for three input measures and four output measures were provided in Tables 5.1 and 5.2.
    a. Use these data to develop a linear programming model that could be used to evaluate the performance of General Hospital.
    b. The following solution is optimal. Does the solution indicate that General Hospital is relatively inefficient?

Objective Function Value = 1.000

Variable	Value	Reduced Costs
E	1.000	0.000
WG	1.000	0.000
WU	0.000	0.000
WC	0.000	0.331
WS	0.000	0.215

    c. Explain which hospital or hospitals make up the composite unit used to evaluate General Hospital and why.

2. Data envelopment analysis can measure the relative efficiency of a group of hospitals. The following data from a particular study involving seven teaching hospitals include three input measures and four output measures:
    a. Formulate a linear programming model so that data envelopment analysis can be used to evaluate the performance of hospital D.

b. Solve the model.
c. Is hospital D relatively inefficient? What is the interpretation of the value of the objective function?

| | **Input Measures** | | |
Hospital	**Full-Time Equivalent Nonphysicians**	**Supply Expense (1000s)**	**Bed-Days Available (1000s)**
A	310.0	134.60	116.00
B	278.5	114.30	106.80
C	165.6	131.30	65.52
D	250.0	316.00	94.40
E	206.4	151.20	102.10
F	384.0	217.00	153.70
G	530.1	770.80	215.00

| | **Output Measures** | | | |
Hospital	**Patient-Days (65 or older) (1000s)**	**Patient-Days (under 65) (1000s)**	**Nurses Trained**	**Interns Trained**
A	55.31	49.52	291	47
B	37.64	55.63	156	3
C	32.91	25.77	141	26
D	33.53	41.99	160	21
E	32.48	55.30	157	82
F	48.78	81.92	285	92
G	58.41	119.70	111	89

d. How many patient-days of each type are produced by the composite hospital?
e. Which hospitals would you recommend hospital D consider emulating to improve the efficiency of its operation?

3. Refer again to the data presented in Problem 2.
   a. Formulate a linear programming model that can be used to perform data envelopment analysis for hospital E.
   b. Solve the model.
   c. Is hospital E relatively inefficient? What is the interpretation of the value of the objective function?
   d. Which hospitals are involved in making up the composite hospital? Can you make a general statement about which hospitals will make up the composite unit associated with a unit that is not inefficient?

4. The Ranch House, Inc., operates five fast-food restaurants. Input measures for the restaurants include weekly hours of operation, full-time equivalent staff, and weekly supply expenses. Output measures of performance include average weekly contribution to profit,

market share, and annual growth rate. Data for the input and output measures are shown in the following tables:

Restaurant	Input Measures		
	Hours of Operation	**FTE Staff**	**Supplies ($)**
Bardstown	96	16	850
Clarksville	110	22	1400
Jeffersonville	100	18	1200
New Albany	125	25	1500
St. Matthews	120	24	1600

Restaurant	Output Measures		
	Weekly Profit	**Market Share (%)**	**Growth Rate (%)**
Bardstown	$3800	25	8.0
Clarksville	$4600	32	8.5
Jeffersonville	$4400	35	8.0
New Albany	$6500	30	10.0
St. Matthews	$6000	28	9.0

    a. Develop a linear programming model that can be used to evaluate the performance of the Clarksville Ranch House restaurant.

    b. Solve the model.

    c. Is the Clarksville Ranch House restaurant relatively inefficient? Discuss.

    d. Where does the composite restaurant have more output than the Clarksville restaurant? How much less of each input resource does the composite restaurant require when compared to the Clarksville restaurant?

    e. What other restaurants should be studied to find suggested ways for the Clarksville restaurant to improve its efficiency?

5. Reconsider the Leisure Airlines problem from Section 5.2. The demand forecasts shown in Table 5.3 represent Leisure Air's best estimates of demand. But because demand cannot be forecasted perfectly, the number of seats actually sold for each origin-destination-itinerary fare (ODIF) may turn out to be smaller or larger than forecasted. Suppose that Leisure Air believes that economic conditions have improved and that their original forecast may be too low. To account for this possibility, Leisure Air is considering switching the Boeing 737-400 airplanes that are based in Pittsburgh and Newark with Boeing 757-200 airplanes that Leisure Air has available in other markets. The Boeing 757-200 airplane has a seating capacity of 158 in the coach section.

    a. Because of scheduling conflicts in other markets, suppose that Leisure Air is only able to obtain one Boeing 757-200. Should the larger plane be based in Pittsburgh or in Newark? Explain.

    b. Based upon your answer in part (a), determine a new allocation for the ODIFs. Briefly summarize the major differences between the new allocation using one Boeing 757-200 and the original allocation summarized in Figure 5.5.

    c. Suppose that two Boeing 757-200 airplanes are available. Determine a new allocation for the ODIFs using the two larger airplanes. Briefly summarize the major differences between the new allocation using two Boeing 757-200 airplanes and the original allocation shown in Figure 5.5.

    d. Consider the new solution obtained in part (b). Which ODIF has the highest bid price? What is the interpretation for this bid price?

6. Reconsider the Leisure Airlines problem from Section 5.2. Suppose that as of May 1 the following number of seats have been sold:

ODIF	1	2	3	4	5	6	7	8	9	10	11	12	13	14	15	16
Seats Sold	25	44	18	12	5	9	20	33	37	11	5	8	27	6	35	7

   a. Determine how many seats are still available for sale on each flight leg.
   b. Using the original demand forecasted for each ODIF, determine the remaining demand for each ODIF.
   c. Revise the linear programming model presented in Section 5.2 to account for the number of seats currently sold and a demand of one additional seat for the Pittsburgh–Myrtle Beach Q class ODIF. Resolve the linear programming model to determine a new allocation schedule for the ODIFs.

7. Hanson Inn is a 96-room hotel located near the airport and convention center in Louisville, Kentucky. When a convention or a special event is in town, Hanson increases its normal room rates and takes reservations based on a revenue management system. The Classic Corvette Owners Association scheduled its annual convention in Louisville for the first weekend in June. Hanson Inn agreed to make at least 50% of its rooms available for convention attendees at a special convention rate in order to be listed as a recommended hotel for the convention. Although the majority of attendees at the annual meeting typically request a Friday and Saturday two-night package, some attendees may select a Friday night only or a Saturday night only reservation. Customers not attending the convention may also request a Friday and Saturday two-night package, or make a Friday night only or Saturday night only reservation. Thus, six types of reservations are possible: Convention customers/two-night package; convention customers/Friday night only; convention customers/Saturday night only; regular customers/two-night package; regular customers/Friday night only; and regular customers/Saturday night only. The cost for each type of reservation is shown here:

	Two-Night Package	Friday Night Only	Saturday Night Only
Convention	$225	$123	$130
Regular	$295	$146	$152

The anticipated demand for each type of reservation is as follows:

	Two-Night Package	Friday Night Only	Saturday Night Only
Convention	40	20	15
Regular	20	30	25

Hanson Inn would like to determine how many rooms to make available for each type of reservation in order to maximize total revenue.
   a. Define the decision variables and state the objective function.
   b. Formulate a linear programming model for this revenue management application.
   c. What are the optimal allocation and the anticipated total revenue?
   d. Suppose that one week before the convention, the number of regular customers/Saturday night only rooms that were made available sell out. If another nonconvention customer calls and requests a Saturday night only room, what is the value of accepting this additional reservation?

TABLE 5.11   RETURNS OVER FIVE 1-YEAR PERIODS FOR SIX MUTUAL FUNDS

Mutual Funds	Planning Scenarios for Next 12 Months				
	Year 1	Year 2	Year 3	Year 4	Year 5
Large-Cap Stock	35.3	20.0	28.3	10.4	−9.3
Mid-Cap Stock	32.3	23.2	−0.9	49.3	−22.8
Small-Cap Stock	20.8	22.5	6.0	33.3	6.1
Energy/Resources Sector	25.3	33.9	−20.5	20.9	−2.5
Health Sector	49.1	5.5	29.7	77.7	−24.9
Technology Sector	46.2	21.7	45.7	93.1	−20.1
Real Estate Sector	20.5	44.0	−21.1	2.6	5.1

8. In the latter part of Section 5.3 we developed a moderate risk portfolio model for Hauck Investment Services. Modify the model given so that it can be used to construct a portfolio for more aggressive investors. In particular, do the following:
   a. Develop a portfolio model for investors who are willing to risk a portfolio with a return as low as 0%.
   b. What is the recommended allocation for this type of investor?
   c. How would you modify your recommendation in part (b) for an investor who also wants to have at least 10% of his or her portfolio invested in the foreign stock mutual fund? How does requiring at least 10% of the portfolio be invested in the foreign stock fund affect the expected return?

9. Table 5.11 shows data on the returns over five 1-year periods for six mutual funds. A firm's portfolio managers will assume that one of these scenarios will accurately reflect the investing climate over the next 12 months. The probabilities of each of the scenarios occurring are 0.1, 0.3, 0.1, 0.1, and 0.4 for years 1 to 5, respectively.
   a. Develop a portfolio model for investors who are willing to risk a portfolio with a return no lower than 2%.
   b. Solve the model in part (a) and recommend a portfolio allocation for the investor with this risk tolerance.
   c. Modify the portfolio model in part (a) and solve it to develop a portfolio for an investor with a risk tolerance of 0%.
   d. Is the expected return higher for investors following the portfolio recommendations in part (c) as compared to the returns for the portfolio in part (b)? If so, do you believe the returns are enough higher to justify investing in that portfolio?

10. Consider the following two-person, zero-sum game. Payoffs are the winnings for Player A. Identify the pure strategy solution. What is the value of the game?

		Player B		
		b_1	b_2	b_3
Player A	a_1	8	5	7
	a_2	2	4	10

11. Assume that a two-person, zero-sum game has a pure strategy solution. If this game were solved using a linear programming formulation, how would you know from the linear programming solution that the game had a pure strategy solution?

12. Consider the payoff table below that shows the percentage increase in market share for Company A for each combination of Company A and Company B strategies. Assume that Company B implements a mixed strategy by using strategy b_2 with probability 0.5 and strategy b_3 with probability 0.5. Company B decides never to use strategy b_1. What is the expected payoff to Company A under each of its three strategies? If Company B were to always use the stated mixed strategy probabilities, what would the optimal strategy for Company A be?

| | | | Company B | |
		Increase Advertising b_1	Quantity Discounts b_2	Extend Warranty b_3
	Increase Advertising a_1	4	3	2
Company A	Quantity Discounts a_2	−1	4	1
	Extend Warranty a_3	5	−2	5

13. Two television stations compete with each other for viewing audience. Local programming options for the 5:00 P.M. weekday time slot include a sitcom rerun, an early news program, or a home improvement show. Each station has the same programming options and must make its preseason program selection before knowing what the other television station will do. The viewing audience gains in thousands of viewers for Station A are shown in the payoff table.

| | | | Station B | |
		Sitcom Rerun b_1	News Program b_2	Home Improvement b_3
	Sitcom Rerun a_1	10	−5	3
Station A	News Program a_2	8	7	6
	Home Improvement a_3	4	8	7

Determine the optimal strategy for each station. What is the value of the game?

14. Two Indiana state senate candidates must decide which city to visit the day before the November election. The same four cities—Indianapolis, Evansville, Fort Wayne, and South Bend—are available for both candidates. Travel plans must be made in advance, so the candidates must decide which city to visit prior to knowing the city the other candidate will visit. Values in the payoff table show thousands of voters gained by the Republican candidate based on the strategies selected by the two candidates. Which city should each candidate visit and what is the value of the game?

| | | | Democratic Candidate | | |
		Indianapolis b_1	Evansville b_2	Fort Wayne b_3	South Bend b_4
	Indianapolis a_1	0	−15	−8	20
Republican	Evansville a_2	30	−5	5	−10
Candidate	Fort Wayne a_3	10	−25	0	20
	South Bend a_4	20	20	10	15

15. Consider a game in which each player selects one of three colored poker chips: red, white, or blue. The players must select a chip without knowing the color of the chip selected by the other player. The players then reveal their chips. Payoffs to Player A in dollars are as follows:

		Player B		
		Red b_1	White b_2	Blue b_3
	Red a_1	0	-1	2
Player A	White a_2	5	4	-3
	Blue a_3	2	3	-4

   a. What is the optimal strategy for each player?
   b. What is the value of the game?
   c. Would you prefer to be Player A or Player B? Why?

16. Two companies compete for a share of the soft drink market. Each has worked with an advertising agency to develop alternative advertising strategies for the coming year. A variety of television advertisements, newspaper advertisements, product promotions, and in-store displays have provided four different strategies for each company. The payoff table summarizes the gain in market share for Company A projected for the various combinations of Company A and Company B strategies. What is the optimal strategy for each company? What is the value of the game?

		Company B		
	b_1	b_2	b_3	b_4
a_1	3	0	2	4
a_2	2	-2	1	0
a_3	4	2	5	6
a_4	-2	6	-1	0

Company A is labeled to the left of rows a_1–a_4.

17. The offensive coordinator for the Chicago Bears professional football team is preparing a game plan for the upcoming game against the Green Bay Packers. A review of game tapes from previous Bears–Packers games provides data on the yardage gained for run plays and pass plays. Data show that when the Bears run against the Packers' run defense, the Bears gain an average of 2 yards. However, when the Bears run against the Packers' pass defense, the Bears gain an average of 6 yards. A similar analysis of pass plays reveals that if the Bears pass against the Packers' run defense, the Bears gain an average of 11 yards. However, if the Bears pass against the Packers' pass defense, the Bears average a loss of 1 yard. This loss, or negative gain of -1, includes the lost yardage due to quarterback sacks and interceptions. Develop a payoff table that shows the Bears' average yardage gain for each combination of the Bears' offensive strategy to run or pass and the Packers' strategy of using a run defense or a pass defense. What is the optimal strategy for the Chicago Bears during the upcoming game against the Green Bay Packers? What is the expected value of this strategy?

CHAPTER 6

Distribution and Network Models

CONTENTS

6.1 TRANSPORTATION PROBLEM
Problem Variations
A General Linear Programming
Model

6.2 ASSIGNMENT PROBLEM
Problem Variations
A General Linear Programming
Model

6.3 TRANSSHIPMENT PROBLEM
Problem Variations
A General Linear Programming
Model

6.4 SHORTEST-ROUTE PROBLEM
A General Linear Programming
Model

6.5 MAXIMAL FLOW PROBLEM

6.6 A PRODUCTION AND
INVENTORY APPLICATION

The models discussed in this chapter belong to a special class of linear programming problems called *network flow* problems. Five different problems are considered:

- Transportation problem
- Assignment problem
- Transshipment problem
- Shortest-route problem
- Maximal flow problem

A separate chapter is devoted to these problems because of the similarity in the problem structure and solution procedure. In each case, we will present a graphical representation of the problem in the form of a *network*. We will then show how the problem can be formulated and solved as a linear program. In the last section of the chapter we present a production and inventory problem that is an interesting application of the transshipment problem.

6.1   TRANSPORTATION PROBLEM

The **transportation problem** arises frequently in planning for the distribution of goods and services from several supply locations to several demand locations. Typically, the quantity of goods available at each supply location (origin) is limited, and the quantity of goods needed at each of several demand locations (destinations) is known. The usual objective in a transportation problem is to minimize the cost of shipping goods from the origins to the destinations.

Let us illustrate by considering a transportation problem faced by Foster Generators. This problem involves the transportation of a product from three plants to four distribution centers. Foster Generators operates plants in Cleveland, Ohio; Bedford, Indiana; and York, Pennsylvania. Production capacities over the next three-month planning period for one particular type of generator are as follows:

Origin	Plant	Three-Month Production Capacity (units)
1	Cleveland	5,000
2	Bedford	6,000
3	York	2,500
	Total	13,500

The firm distributes its generators through four regional distribution centers located in Boston, Chicago, St. Louis, and Lexington; the three-month forecast of demand for the distribution centers is as follows:

Destination	Distribution Center	Three-Month Demand Forecast (units)
1	Boston	6,000
2	Chicago	4,000
3	St. Louis	2,000
4	Lexington	1,500
	Total	13,500

FIGURE 6.1 THE NETWORK REPRESENTATION OF THE FOSTER GENERATORS
TRANSPORTATION PROBLEM

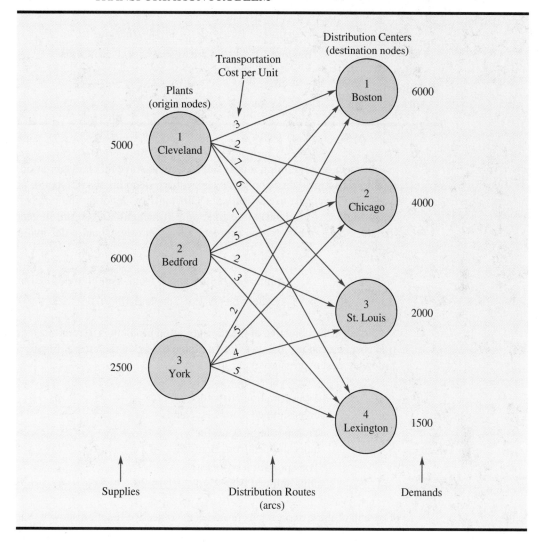

Management would like to determine how much of its production should be shipped
from each plant to each distribution center. Figure 6.1 shows graphically the 12 distribution
routes Foster can use. Such a graph is called a **network;** the circles are referred to as **nodes**
and the lines connecting the nodes as **arcs.** Each origin and destination is represented by a

*Try Problem 1 for practice
in developing a network
model of a transportation
problem.*

*The first subscript identifies
the "from" node of the
corresponding arc and the
second subscript identifies
the "to" node of the arc.*

node, and each possible shipping route is represented by an arc. The amount of the supply
is written next to each origin node, and the amount of the demand is written next to each
destination node. The goods shipped from the origins to the destinations represent the flow
in the network. Note that the direction of flow (from origin to destination) is indicated by
the arrows.

For Foster's transportation problem, the objective is to determine the routes to be used
and the quantity to be shipped via each route that will provide the minimum total transportation cost. The cost for each unit shipped on each route is given in Table 6.1 and is
shown on each arc in Figure 6.1.

TABLE 6.1　TRANSPORTATION COST PER UNIT FOR THE FOSTER GENERATORS TRANSPORTATION PROBLEM

	Destination			
Origin	Boston	Chicago	St. Louis	Lexington
Cleveland	3	2	7	6
Bedford	7	5	2	3
York	2	5	4	5

A linear programming model can be used to solve this transportation problem. We use double-subscripted decision variables, with x_{11} denoting the number of units shipped from origin 1 (Cleveland) to destination 1 (Boston), x_{12} denoting the number of units shipped from origin 1 (Cleveland) to destination 2 (Chicago), and so on. In general, the decision variables for a transportation problem having m origins and n destinations are written as follows:

$$x_{ij} = \text{number of units shipped from origin } i \text{ to destination } j,$$
$$\text{where } i = 1, 2, \ldots, m \text{ and } j = 1, 2, \ldots, n$$

Because the objective of the transportation problem is to minimize the total transportation cost, we can use the cost data in Table 6.1 or on the arcs in Figure 6.1 to develop the following cost expressions:

Transportation costs for
units shipped from Cleveland $= 3x_{11} + 2x_{12} + 7x_{13} + 6x_{14}$

Transportation costs for
units shipped from Bedford $\quad = 7x_{21} + 5x_{22} + 2x_{23} + 3x_{24}$

Transportation costs for
units shipped from York $\quad\quad = 2x_{31} + 5x_{32} + 4x_{33} + 5x_{34}$

The sum of these expressions provides the objective function showing the total transportation cost for Foster Generators.

Transportation problems need constraints because each origin has a limited supply and each destination has a demand requirement. We consider the supply constraints first. The capacity at the Cleveland plant is 5000 units. With the total number of units shipped from the Cleveland plant expressed as $x_{11} + x_{12} + x_{13} + x_{14}$, the supply constraint for the Cleveland plant is

$$x_{11} + x_{12} + x_{13} + x_{14} \leq 5000 \quad \text{Cleveland supply}$$

With three origins (plants), the Foster transportation problem has three supply constraints. Given the capacity of 6000 units at the Bedford plant and 2500 units at the York plant, the two additional supply constraints are

$$x_{21} + x_{22} + x_{23} + x_{24} \leq 6000 \quad \text{Bedford supply}$$
$$x_{31} + x_{32} + x_{33} + x_{34} \leq 2500 \quad \text{York supply}$$

With the four distribution centers as the destinations, four demand constraints are needed to ensure that destination demands will be satisfied:

$$x_{11} + x_{21} + x_{31} = 6000 \quad \text{Boston demand}$$
$$x_{12} + x_{22} + x_{32} = 4000 \quad \text{Chicago demand}$$
$$x_{13} + x_{23} + x_{33} = 2000 \quad \text{St. Louis demand}$$
$$x_{14} + x_{24} + x_{34} = 1500 \quad \text{Lexington demand}$$

To obtain a feasible solution, the total supply must be greater than or equal to the total demand.

Combining the objective function and constraints into one model provides a 12-variable, 7-constraint linear programming formulation of the Foster Generators transportation problem:

Min $\quad 3x_{11} + 2x_{12} + 7x_{13} + 6x_{14} + 7x_{21} + 5x_{22} + 2x_{23} + 3x_{24} + 2x_{31} + 5x_{32} + 4x_{33} + 5x_{34}$

s.t.

$$
\begin{array}{llll}
x_{11} + x_{12} + x_{13} + x_{14} & & & \leq 5000 \\
& x_{21} + x_{22} + x_{23} + x_{24} & & \leq 6000 \\
& & x_{31} + x_{32} + x_{33} + x_{34} & \leq 2500 \\
x_{11} & + x_{21} & + x_{31} & = 6000 \\
x_{12} & + x_{22} & + x_{32} & = 4000 \\
x_{13} & + x_{23} & + x_{33} & = 2000 \\
x_{14} & + x_{24} & + x_{34} & = 1500
\end{array}
$$

$$x_{ij} \geq 0 \quad \text{for } i = 1, 2, 3 \text{ and } j = 1, 2, 3, 4$$

Comparing the linear programming formulation to the network in Figure 6.1 leads to several observations. All the information needed for the linear programming formulation is on the network. Each node has one constraint, and each arc has one variable. The sum of the variables corresponding to arcs from an origin node must be less than or equal to the origin's supply, and the sum of the variables corresponding to the arcs into a destination node must be equal to the destination's demand.

Can you now use the computer to solve a linear programming model of a transportation problem? Try Problem 2.

The solution to the Foster Generators problem (see Figure 6.2) shows that the minimum total transportation cost is $39,500. The values for the decision variables show the

FIGURE 6.2 THE SOLUTION FOR THE FOSTER GENERATORS TRANSPORTATION PROBLEM

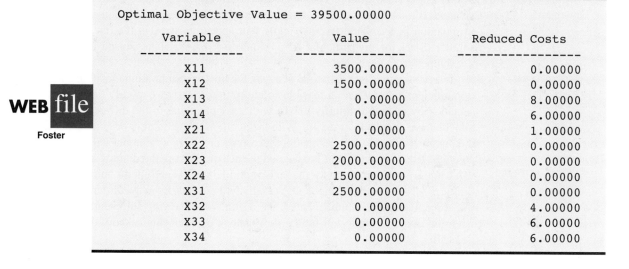

WEB file

Foster

```
Optimal Objective Value = 39500.00000

        Variable            Value           Reduced Costs
      -------------     ---------------     ----------------
          X11            3500.00000            0.00000
          X12            1500.00000            0.00000
          X13               0.00000            8.00000
          X14               0.00000            6.00000
          X21               0.00000            1.00000
          X22            2500.00000            0.00000
          X23            2000.00000            0.00000
          X24            1500.00000            0.00000
          X31            2500.00000            0.00000
          X32               0.00000            4.00000
          X33               0.00000            6.00000
          X34               0.00000            6.00000
```

TABLE 6.2   OPTIMAL SOLUTION TO THE FOSTER GENERATORS
TRANSPORTATION PROBLEM

| Route | | Units | Cost | Total |
From	To	Shipped	per Unit	Cost
Cleveland	Boston	3500	$3	$10,500
Cleveland	Chicago	1500	$2	3,000
Bedford	Chicago	2500	$5	12,500
Bedford	St. Louis	2000	$2	4,000
Bedford	Lexington	1500	$3	4,500
York	Boston	2500	$2	5,000
				$39,500

optimal amounts to ship over each route. For example, with $x_{11} = 3500$, 3500 units should be shipped from Cleveland to Boston, and with $x_{12} = 1500$, 1500 units should be shipped from Cleveland to Chicago. Other values of the decision variables indicate the remaining shipping quantities and routes. Table 6.2 shows the minimum cost transportation schedule and Figure 6.3 summarizes the optimal solution on the network.

Problem Variations

The Foster Generators problem illustrates use of the basic transportation model. Variations of the basic transportation model may involve one or more of the following situations:

1. Total supply not equal to total demand
2. Maximization objective function
3. Route capacities or route minimums
4. Unacceptable routes

With slight modifications in the linear programming model, we can easily accommodate these situations.

Total Supply Not Equal to Total Demand   Often *the total supply is not equal to the total demand.* If total supply exceeds total demand, no modification in the linear programming formulation is necessary. Excess supply will appear as slack in the linear programming solution. Slack for any particular origin can be interpreted as the unused supply or amount not shipped from the origin.

Whenever total supply is less than total demand, the model does not determine how the unsatisfied demand is handled (e.g., backorders). The manager must handle this aspect of the problem.

If total supply is less than total demand, the linear programming model of a transportation problem will not have a feasible solution. In this case, we modify the network representation by adding a **dummy origin** with a supply equal to the difference between the total demand and the total supply. With the addition of the dummy origin, and an arc from the dummy origin to each destination, the linear programming model will have a feasible solution. A zero cost per unit is assigned to each arc leaving the dummy origin so that the value of the optimal solution for the revised problem will represent the shipping cost for the units actually shipped (no shipments actually will be made from the dummy origin). When the optimal solution is implemented, the destinations showing shipments being received from the dummy origin will be the destinations experiencing a shortfall, or unsatisfied demand.

FIGURE 6.3   OPTIMAL SOLUTION TO THE FOSTER GENERATORS
TRANSPORTATION PROBLEM

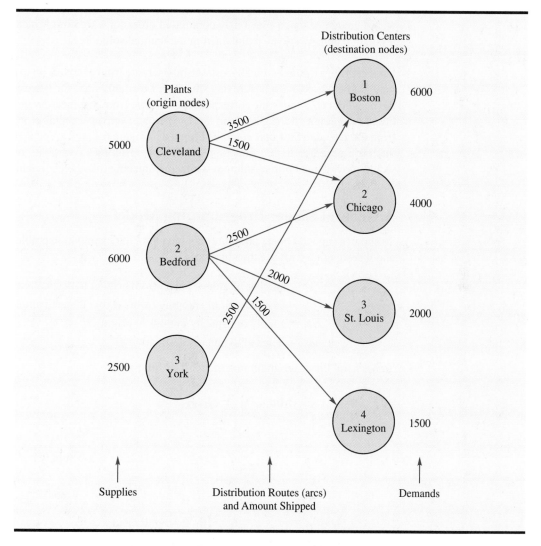

*Try Problem 6 for practice
with a case in which
demand is greater than
supply with a maximization
objective.*

Maximization Objective Function   In some transportation problems, the objective is to find a solution that maximizes profit or revenue. Using the values for profit or revenue per unit as coefficients in the objective function, we simply solve a maximization rather than a minimization linear program. This change does not affect the constraints.

Route Capacities or Route Minimums   The linear programming formulation of the transportation problem also can accommodate capacities or minimum quantities for one or more of the routes. For example, suppose that in the Foster Generators problem the York–Boston route (origin 3 to destination 1) had a capacity of 1000 units because of limited space availability on its normal mode of transportation. With x_{31} denoting the amount shipped from York to Boston, the route capacity constraint for the York–Boston route would be

$$x_{31} \leq 1000$$

Similarly, route minimums can be specified. For example,

$$x_{22} \geq 2000$$

would guarantee that a previously committed order for a Bedford–Chicago delivery of at least 2000 units would be maintained in the optimal solution.

Unacceptable Routes Finally, establishing a route from every origin to every destination may not be possible. To handle this situation, we simply drop the corresponding arc from the network and remove the corresponding variable from the linear programming formulation. For example, if the Cleveland–St. Louis route were unacceptable or unusable, the arc from Cleveland to St. Louis could be dropped in Figure 6.1, and x_{13} could be removed from the linear programming formulation. Solving the resulting 11-variable, 7-constraint model would provide the optimal solution while guaranteeing that the Cleveland–St. Louis route is not used.

A General Linear Programming Model

To show the general linear programming model for a transportation problem with m origins and n destinations, we use the notation:

$$x_{ij} = \text{number of units shipped from origin } i \text{ to destination } j$$
$$c_{ij} = \text{cost per unit of shipping from origin } i \text{ to destination } j$$
$$s_i = \text{supply or capacity in units at origin } i$$
$$d_j = \text{demand in units at destination } j$$

The general linear programming model is as follows:

$$\text{Min} \quad \sum_{i=1}^{m} \sum_{j=1}^{n} c_{ij} x_{ij}$$

s.t.

$$\sum_{j=1}^{n} x_{ij} \leq s_i \quad i = 1, 2, \ldots, m \quad \text{Supply}$$

$$\sum_{i=1}^{m} x_{ij} = d_j \quad j = 1, 2, \ldots, n \quad \text{Demand}$$

$$x_{ij} \geq 0 \quad \text{for all } i \text{ and } j$$

NOTES AND COMMENTS

1. Transportation problems encountered in practice usually lead to large linear programs. Transportation problems with 100 origins and 100 destinations are not unusual. Such a problem would involve $(100)(100) = 10,000$ variables.

2. To handle a situation in which some routes may be unacceptable, we stated that you could drop the corresponding arc from the network and remove the corresponding variable from the linear programming formulation. Another approach often used is to assign an extremely large objective function cost coefficient to any unacceptable arc. If the problem has already been formulated, another option is to add a constraint to the formulation that sets the variable you want to remove equal to zero.

3. The optimal solution to a transportation model will consist of integer values for the decision variables as long as all supply and demand values are integers. The reason is the special mathematical structure of the linear programming model. Each variable appears in exactly one supply and one demand constraint, and all coefficients in the constraint equations are 1 or 0.

MANAGEMENT SCIENCE IN ACTION

EMPTY FREIGHT CAR ASSIGNMENT AT UNION PACIFIC RAILROAD*

Union Pacific Railroad is the largest railroad in North America. The company owns over 32,000 miles of railroad track and has 50,000 employees. It deploys over 8,000 locomotives and over 100,000 freight cars to move goods for its customers.

When goods are delivered to a location, the freight car is left at the customer site to be un-loaded. Therefore, at any particular point in time, empty freight cars are located throughout the North American network of tracks. At the same time, Union Pacific's customers require empty freight cars so they may be loaded for shipments. A critical decision for Union Pacific is how to assign empty freight cars to its customers who are in need of cars. That is, given the location of the empty cars and the demand for empty cars at other loca-tions, which cars should be sent to which demand points? The decision is further complicated by the fact that supply of freight cars is usually smaller than the demand, there are a variety of types of freight cars (for example, box cars, auto transport cars, etc.) and service time expectations must be met while also controlling costs.

Prior to the development of an optimization model for freight car assignment, car managers assigned cars to customers from pools of a particular type of car. These managers had no tool to assess how the assignments they were making impacted the overall rail network.

Union Pacific, working with faculty from Pur-due University, developed a transportation model similar to the one discussed in this section. The model minimizes a linear weighted cost objective subject to supply and demand constraints. The objective function is a weighted combination of trans-portation costs, car-substitution costs (a penalty for assigning a feasible but different type of car than was demanded), penalties for deviating from the delivery schedule, customer priority, and corridor efficiency. The model was successfully imple-mented and resulted in 35% return on investment.

*Based on A.K. Narisetty, J. P. Richard, D. Ramcharan, D. Murphy, G. Minks, and J. Fuller, "An Optimization Model for Empty Freight Car Assignment at Union Pacific Railroad," *Interfaces* (March/April: 2008): 89–102.

As mentioned previously, we can add constraints of the form $x_{ij} \leq L_{ij}$ if the route from origin i to destination j has capacity L_{ij}. A transportation problem that includes constraints of this type is called a **capacitated transportation problem.** Similarly, we can add route minimum constraints of the form $x_{ij} \geq M_{ij}$ if the route from origin i to destination j must handle at least M_{ij} units.

6.2   ASSIGNMENT PROBLEM

The **assignment problem** arises in a variety of decision-making situations; typical assign-ment problems involve assigning jobs to machines, agents to tasks, sales personnel to sales territories, contracts to bidders, and so on. A distinguishing feature of the assignment prob-lem is that *one* agent is assigned to *one and only one* task. Specifically, we look for the set of assignments that will optimize a stated objective, such as minimize cost, minimize time, or maximize profits.

To illustrate the assignment problem, let us consider the case of Fowle Marketing Research, which has just received requests for market research studies from three new clients. The company faces the task of assigning a project leader (agent) to each client (task). Cur-rently, three individuals have no other commitments and are available for the project leader assignments. Fowle's management realizes, however, that the time required to complete each study will depend on the experience and ability of the project leader assigned. The three projects have approximately the same priority, and management wants to assign project leaders to minimize the total number of days required to complete all three projects. If a project leader is to be assigned to one client only, what assignments should be made?

To answer the assignment question, Fowle's management must first consider all possible project leader–client assignments and then estimate the corresponding project completion times. With three project leaders and three clients, nine assignment alternatives are possible. The alternatives and the estimated project completion times in days are summarized in Table 6.3.

Try Problem 9 (part a) for practice in developing a network model for an assignment problem.

Figure 6.4 shows the network representation of Fowle's assignment problem. The nodes correspond to the project leaders and clients, and the arcs represent the possible assignments of project leaders to clients. The supply at each origin node and the demand at

TABLE 6.3 ESTIMATED PROJECT COMPLETION TIMES (DAYS) FOR THE FOWLE MARKETING RESEARCH ASSIGNMENT PROBLEM

	Client		
Project Leader	**1**	**2**	**3**
1. Terry	10	15	9
2. Carle	9	18	5
3. McClymonds	6	14	3

FIGURE 6.4 A NETWORK MODEL OF THE FOWLE MARKETING RESEARCH ASSIGNMENT PROBLEM

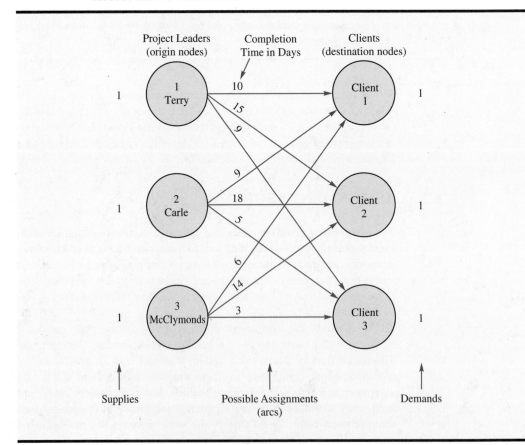

*The assignment problem
is a special case of the
transportation problem.*

each destination node are 1; the cost of assigning a project leader to a client is the time it takes that project leader to complete the client's task. Note the similarity between the network models of the assignment problem (Figure 6.4) and the transportation problem (Figure 6.1). The assignment problem is a special case of the transportation problem in which all supply and demand values equal 1, and the amount shipped over each arc is either 0 or 1.

Because the assignment problem is a special case of the transportation problem, a linear programming formulation can be developed. Again, we need a constraint for each node and a variable for each arc. As in the transportation problem, we use double-subscripted decision variables, with x_{11} denoting the assignment of project leader 1 (Terry) to client 1, x_{12} denoting the assignment of project leader 1 (Terry) to client 2, and so on. Thus, we define the decision variables for Fowle's assignment problem as

$$x_{ij} = \begin{cases} 1 & \text{if project leader } i \text{ is assigned to client } j \\ 0 & \text{otherwise} \end{cases}$$

where $i = 1, 2, 3$, and $j = 1, 2, 3$

Using this notation and the completion time data in Table 6.3, we develop completion time expressions:

Days required for Terry's assignment $\qquad = 10x_{11} + 15x_{12} + 9x_{13}$

Days required for Carle's assignment $\qquad = 9x_{21} + 18x_{22} + 5x_{23}$

Days required for McClymonds's assignment $= 6x_{31} + 14x_{32} + 3x_{33}$

*Because the number of
project leaders equals the
number of clients, all the
constraints could be written
as equalities. But when the
number of project leaders
exceeds the number of
clients, less-than-or-equal-
to constraints must be used
for the project leader
constraints.*

The sum of the completion times for the three project leaders will provide the total days required to complete the three assignments. Thus, the objective function is

$$\text{Min} \quad 10x_{11} + 15x_{12} + 9x_{13} + 9x_{21} + 18x_{22} + 5x_{23} + 6x_{31} + 14x_{32} + 3x_{33}$$

The constraints for the assignment problem reflect the conditions that each project leader can be assigned to at most one client and that each client must have one assigned project leader. These constraints are written as follows:

$$\begin{array}{ll} x_{11} + x_{12} + x_{13} \leq 1 & \text{Terry's assignment} \\ x_{21} + x_{22} + x_{23} \leq 1 & \text{Carle's assignment} \\ x_{31} + x_{32} + x_{33} \leq 1 & \text{McClymonds's assignment} \\ x_{11} + x_{21} + x_{31} = 1 & \text{Client 1} \\ x_{12} + x_{22} + x_{32} = 1 & \text{Client 2} \\ x_{13} + x_{23} + x_{33} = 1 & \text{Client 3} \end{array}$$

Note that each node in Figure 6.4 has one constraint.

*Try Problem 9 (part b) for
practice in formulating
and solving a linear
programming model for an
assignment problem on the
computer.*

Combining the objective function and constraints into one model provides the following 9-variable, 6-constraint linear programming model of the Fowle Marketing Research assignment problem:

$$\text{Min} \quad 10x_{11} + 15x_{12} + 9x_{13} + 9x_{21} + 18x_{22} + 5x_{23} + 6x_{31} + 14x_{32} + 3x_{33}$$

s.t.

$$\begin{array}{lllll} x_{11} + x_{12} + x_{13} & & & \leq 1 \\ & x_{21} + x_{22} + x_{23} & & \leq 1 \\ & & x_{31} + x_{32} + x_{33} & \leq 1 \\ x_{11} & + x_{21} & + x_{31} & = 1 \\ x_{12} & + x_{22} & + x_{32} & = 1 \\ x_{13} & + x_{23} & + x_{33} & = 1 \end{array}$$

$$x_{ij} \geq 0 \quad \text{for } i = 1, 2, 3; \, j = 1, 2, 3$$

FIGURE 6.5   THE SOLUTION FOR THE FOWLE MARKETING RESEARCH ASSIGNMENT
PROBLEM

```
Optimal Objective Value =   26.00000

        Variable                Value              Reduced Costs
     --------------        ---------------        ------------------
          X11                 0.00000                0.00000
          X12                 1.00000                0.00000
          X13                 0.00000                2.00000
          X21                 0.00000                1.00000
          X22                 0.00000                5.00000
          X23                 1.00000                0.00000
          X31                 1.00000                0.00000
          X32                 0.00000                3.00000
          X33                 0.00000                0.00000
```

WEB **file**

Fowle

TABLE 6.4   OPTIMAL PROJECT LEADER ASSIGNMENTS FOR THE FOWLE
MARKETING RESEARCH ASSIGNMENT PROBLEM

Project Leader	Assigned Client	Days
Terry	2	15
Carle	3	5
McClymonds	1	6
	Total	26

Figure 6.5 shows the computer solution for this model. Terry is assigned to client 2
($x_{12} = 1$), Carle is assigned to client 3 ($x_{23} = 1$), and McClymonds is assigned to client 1
($x_{31} = 1$). The total completion time required is 26 days. This solution is summarized in
Table 6.4.

Problem Variations

Because the assignment problem can be viewed as a special case of the transportation problem, the problem variations that may arise in an assignment problem parallel those for the
transportation problem. Specifically, we can handle the following issues:

1. Total number of agents (supply) not equal to the total number of tasks (demand)
2. A maximization objective function
3. Unacceptable assignments

*In the linear programming
formulation of a problem
with five clients and only
three project leaders, we
could get by with one
dummy project leader by
placing a 2 on the right-
hand side of the constraint
for the dummy project
leader.*

The situation in which the number of agents does not equal the number of tasks is analogous to total supply not equaling total demand in a transportation problem. If the number
of agents exceeds the number of tasks, the extra agents simply remain unassigned in the linear programming solution. If the number of tasks exceeds the number of agents, the linear
programming model will not have a feasible solution. In this situation, a simple modification is to add enough dummy agents to equalize the number of agents and the number of

tasks. For instance, in the Fowle problem we might have had five clients (tasks) and only three project leaders (agents). By adding two dummy project leaders, we can create a new assignment problem with the number of project leaders equal to the number of clients. The objective function coefficients for the assignment of dummy project leaders would be zero so that the value of the optimal solution would represent the total number of days required by the assignments actually made (no assignments will actually be made to the clients receiving dummy project leaders).

If the assignment alternatives are evaluated in terms of revenue or profit rather than time or cost, the linear programming formulation can be solved as a maximization rather than a minimization problem. In addition, if one or more assignments are unacceptable, the corresponding decision variable can be removed from the linear programming formulation. This situation could happen, for example, if an agent did not have the experience necessary for one or more of the tasks.

A General Linear Programming Model

To show the general linear programming model for an assignment problem with m agents and n tasks, we use the notation:

$$x_{ij} = \begin{cases} 1 & \text{if agent } i \text{ is assigned to task } j \\ 0 & \text{otherwise} \end{cases}$$

$$c_{ij} = \text{the cost of assigning agent } i \text{ to task } j$$

The general linear programming model is as follows:

$$\text{Min} \quad \sum_{i=1}^{m} \sum_{j=1}^{n} c_{ij} x_{ij}$$

s.t.

$$\sum_{j=1}^{n} x_{ij} \leq 1 \quad i = 1, 2, \ldots, m \quad \text{Agents}$$

$$\sum_{i=1}^{m} x_{ij} = 1 \quad j = 1, 2, \ldots, n \quad \text{Tasks}$$

$$x_{ij} \geq 0 \quad \text{for all } i \text{ and } j$$

NOTES AND COMMENTS

1. As noted, the assignment model is a special case of the transportation model. We stated in the notes and comments at the end of the preceding section that the optimal solution to the transportation problem will consist of integer values for the decision variables as long as the supplies and demands are integers. For the assignment problem, all supplies and demands equal 1; thus, the optimal solution must be integer valued and the integer values must be 0 or 1.

2. Combining the method for handling multiple assignments with the notion of a dummy agent provides another means of dealing with situations when the number of tasks exceeds the number of agents. That is, we add one dummy agent, but provide the dummy agent with the capability to handle multiple tasks. The number of tasks the dummy agent can handle is equal to the difference between the number of tasks and the number of agents.

3. The Management Science in Action, Assigning Project Managers at Heery International, describes how managers are assigned to construction projects. The application involves multiple assignments.

MANAGEMENT SCIENCE IN ACTION

ASSIGNING PROJECT MANAGERS AT HEERY INTERNATIONAL*

Heery International contracts with the State of Tennessee and others for a variety of construction projects including higher education facilities, hotels, and park facilities. At any particular time, Heery typically has more than 100 ongoing projects. Each of these projects must be assigned a single manager. With seven managers available, it means that there are 7(100) = 700 assignment variables. Assisted by an outside consultant, Heery International developed a mathematical model for assigning construction managers to projects.

The assignment problem developed by Heery uses 0-1 decision variables for each manager/project pair, just as in the assignment problem discussed previously. The goal in assigning managers is to balance the workload among managers and, at the same time, to minimize travel cost from the manager's home to the construction site. Thus, an objective function coefficient for each possible assignment was developed that combined project intensity (a function of the size of the project budget) with the travel distance from the manager's home to the construction site. The objective function calls for minimizing the sum over all possible assignments of the product of these coefficients with the assignment variables.

With more construction projects than managers, it was necessary to consider a variation of the standard assignment problem involving multiple assignments. Of the two sets of constraints, one set enforces the requirement that each project receive one and only one manager. The other set of constraints limits the number of assignments each manager can accept by placing an upper bound on the total intensity that is acceptable over all projects assigned.

Heery International implemented this assignment model with considerable success. According to Emory F. Redden, a Heery vice president, "The optimization model . . . has been very helpful for assigning managers to projects. . . . We have been satisfied with the assignments chosen at the Nashville office. . . . We look forward to using the model in our Atlanta office and elsewhere in the Heery organization."

*Based on Larry J. LeBlanc, Dale Randels, Jr., and T. K. Swann, "Heery International's Spreadsheet Optimization Model for Assigning Managers to Construction Projects," *Interfaces* (November/December 2000): 95–106.

At the beginning of this section, we indicated that a distinguishing feature of the assignment problem is that *one* agent is assigned to *one and only one* task. In generalizations of the assignment problem where one agent can be assigned to two or more tasks, the linear programming formulation of the problem can be easily modified. For example, let us assume that in the Fowle Marketing Research problem Terry could be assigned up to two clients; in this case, the constraint representing Terry's assignment would be $x_{11} + x_{12} + x_{13} \leq 2$. In general, if a_i denotes the upper limit for the number of tasks to which agent i can be assigned, we write the agent constraints as

$$\sum_{j=1}^{n} x_{ij} \leq a_i \qquad i = 1, 2, \ldots, m$$

If some tasks require more than one agent, the linear programming formulation can also accommodate the situation. Use the number of agents required as the right-hand side of the appropriate task constraint.

6.3   TRANSSHIPMENT PROBLEM

The **transshipment problem** is an extension of the transportation problem in which intermediate nodes, referred to as *transshipment nodes,* are added to account for locations such as warehouses. In this more general type of distribution problem, shipments may be made between any pair of the three general types of nodes: origin nodes, transshipment nodes, and destination nodes. For example, the transshipment problem permits shipments of goods from origins to intermediate nodes and on to destinations, from one origin to another origin, from one intermediate location to another, from one destination location to another, and directly from origins to destinations.

As was true for the transportation problem, the supply available at each origin is limited, and the demand at each destination is specified. The objective in the transshipment problem is to determine how many units should be shipped over each arc in the network so that all destination demands are satisfied with the minimum possible transportation cost.

Try Problem 17 (part a) for practice in developing a network representation of a transshipment problem.

Let us consider the transshipment problem faced by Ryan Electronics. Ryan is an electronics company with production facilities in Denver and Atlanta. Components produced at either facility may be shipped to either of the firm's regional warehouses, which are located in Kansas City and Louisville. From the regional warehouses, the firm supplies retail outlets in Detroit, Miami, Dallas, and New Orleans. The key features of the problem are shown in the network model depicted in Figure 6.6. Note that the supply at

FIGURE 6.6   NETWORK REPRESENTATION OF THE RYAN ELECTRONICS TRANSSHIPMENT PROBLEM

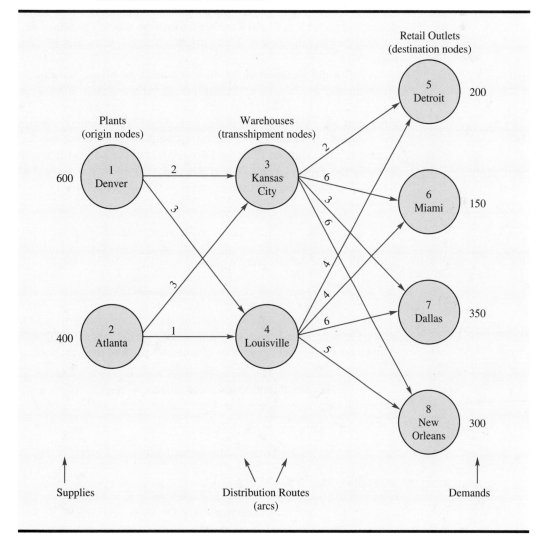

TABLE 6.5   TRANSPORTATION COST PER UNIT FOR THE RYAN ELECTRONICS TRANSSHIPMENT PROBLEM

	Warehouse	
Plant	**Kansas City**	**Louisville**
Denver	2	3
Atlanta	3	1

		Retail Outlet		
Warehouse	**Detroit**	**Miami**	**Dallas**	**New Orleans**
Kansas City	2	6	3	6
Louisville	4	4	6	5

each origin and demand at each destination are shown in the left and right margins, respectively. Nodes 1 and 2 are the origin nodes; nodes 3 and 4 are the transshipment nodes; and nodes 5, 6, 7, and 8 are the destination nodes. The transportation cost per unit for each distribution route is shown in Table 6.5 and on the arcs of the network model in Figure 6.6.

As with the transportation and assignment problems, we can formulate a linear programming model of the transshipment problem from a network representation. Again, we need a constraint for each node and a variable for each arc. Let x_{ij} denote the number of units shipped from node i to node j. For example, x_{13} denotes the number of units shipped from the Denver plant to the Kansas City warehouse, x_{14} denotes the number of units shipped from the Denver plant to the Louisville warehouse, and so on. Because the supply at the Denver plant is 600 units, the amount shipped from the Denver plant must be less than or equal to 600. Mathematically, we write this supply constraint as

$$x_{13} + x_{14} \leq 600$$

Similarly, for the Atlanta plant we have

$$x_{23} + x_{24} \leq 400$$

We now consider how to write the constraints corresponding to the two transshipment nodes. For node 3 (the Kansas City warehouse), we must guarantee that the number of units shipped out must equal the number of units shipped into the warehouse. If

$$\text{Number of units shipped out of node 3} = x_{35} + x_{36} + x_{37} + x_{38}$$

and

$$\text{Number of units shipped into node 3} = x_{13} + x_{23}$$

we obtain

$$x_{35} + x_{36} + x_{37} + x_{38} = x_{13} + x_{23}$$

FIGURE 6.7 LINEAR PROGRAMMING FORMULATION OF THE RYAN ELECTRONICS TRANSSHIPMENT PROBLEM

$$\text{Min } 2x_{13} + 3x_{14} + 3x_{23} + 1x_{24} + 2x_{35} + 6x_{36} + 3x_{37} + 6x_{38} + 4x_{45} + 4x_{46} + 6x_{47} + 5x_{48}$$

s.t.

$$
\begin{array}{llll}
x_{13} + x_{14} & & \leq 600 & \text{Origin node} \\
\quad x_{23} + x_{24} & & \leq 400 & \text{constraints} \\
-x_{13} \quad - x_{23} \quad + x_{35} + x_{36} + x_{37} + x_{38} & & = 0 & \text{Transshipment node} \\
\quad - x_{14} \quad - x_{24} \quad\quad + x_{45} + x_{46} + x_{47} + x_{48} & = 0 & & \text{constraints} \\
x_{35} \quad\quad\quad\quad + x_{45} & & = 200 & \\
x_{36} \quad\quad\quad\quad + x_{46} & & = 150 & \text{Destination node} \\
x_{37} \quad\quad\quad\quad + x_{47} & & = 350 & \text{constraints} \\
x_{38} \quad\quad\quad\quad + x_{48} & = 300 & & \\
\end{array}
$$

$$x_{ij} \geq 0 \text{ for all } i \text{ and } j$$

Similarly, the constraint corresponding to node 4 is

$$x_{45} + x_{46} + x_{47} + x_{48} = x_{14} + x_{24}$$

To develop the constraints associated with the destination nodes, we recognize that for each node the amount shipped to the destination must equal the demand. For example, to satisfy the demand for 200 units at node 5 (the Detroit retail outlet), we write

$$x_{35} + x_{45} = 200$$

Similarly, for nodes 6, 7, and 8, we have

$$x_{36} + x_{46} = 150$$
$$x_{37} + x_{47} = 350$$
$$x_{38} + x_{48} = 300$$

Try Problem 17 (parts b and c) for practice in developing the linear programming model and in solving a transshipment problem on the computer.

As usual, the objective function reflects the total shipping cost over the 12 shipping routes. Combining the objective function and constraints leads to a 12-variable, 8-constraint linear programming model of the Ryan Electronics transshipment problem (see Figure 6.7). Figure 6.8 shows the solution to the Ryan Electronics problem and Table 6.6 summarizes the optimal solution.

As mentioned at the beginning of this section, in the transshipment problem, arcs may connect any pair of nodes. All such shipping patterns are possible in a transshipment problem. We still require only one constraint per node, but the constraint must include a variable for every arc entering or leaving the node. For origin nodes, the sum of the shipments out minus the sum of the shipments in must be less than or equal to the origin supply. For destination nodes, the sum of the shipments in minus the sum of the shipments out must equal demand. For transshipment nodes, the sum of the shipments out must equal the sum of the shipments in, as before.

For an illustration of this more general type of transshipment problem, let us modify the Ryan Electronics problem. Suppose that it is possible to ship directly from Atlanta to New Orleans at $4 per unit and from Dallas to New Orleans at $1 per unit. The network

FIGURE 6.8   THE SOLUTION FOR THE RYAN ELECTRONICS TRANSSHIPMENT
PROBLEM

WEB file

Ryan

```
Optimal Objective Value = 5200.00000

        Variable              Value          Reduced Costs
     ---------------      ---------------    ------------------
          X13               550.00000            0.00000
          X14                50.00000            0.00000
          X23                 0.00000            3.00000
          X24               400.00000            0.00000
          X35               200.00000            0.00000
          X36                 0.00000            1.00000
          X37               350.00000            0.00000
          X38                 0.00000            0.00000
          X45                 0.00000            3.00000
          X46               150.00000            0.00000
          X47                 0.00000            4.00000
          X48               300.00000            0.00000
```

TABLE 6.6   OPTIMAL SOLUTION TO THE RYAN ELECTRONICS
TRANSSHIPMENT PROBLEM

Route			Cost	
From	**To**	**Units Shipped**	**per Unit**	**Total Cost**
Denver	Kansas City	550	$2	$1100
Denver	Louisville	50	$3	150
Atlanta	Louisville	400	$1	400
Kansas City	Detroit	200	$2	400
Kansas City	Dallas	350	$3	1050
Louisville	Miami	150	$4	600
Louisville	New Orleans	300	$5	1500
				$5200

model corresponding to this modified Ryan Electronics problem is shown in Figure 6.9, the
linear programming formulation is shown in Figure 6.10, and the computer solution is
shown in Figure 6.11.

*Try Problem 18 for practice
working with transshipment
problems with this more
general structure.*

In Figure 6.9 we added two new arcs to the network model. Thus, two new variables
are necessary in the linear programming formulation. Figure 6.10 shows that the new variables x_{28} and x_{78} appear in the objective function and in the constraints corresponding to the
nodes to which the new arcs are connected. Figure 6.11 shows that the value of the optimal
solution has been reduced $600 by adding the two new shipping routes; $x_{28} = 250$ units are
being shipped directly from Atlanta to New Orleans, and $x_{78} = 50$ units are being shipped
from Dallas to New Orleans.

FIGURE 6.9 NETWORK REPRESENTATION OF THE MODIFIED RYAN ELECTRONICS TRANSSHIPMENT PROBLEM

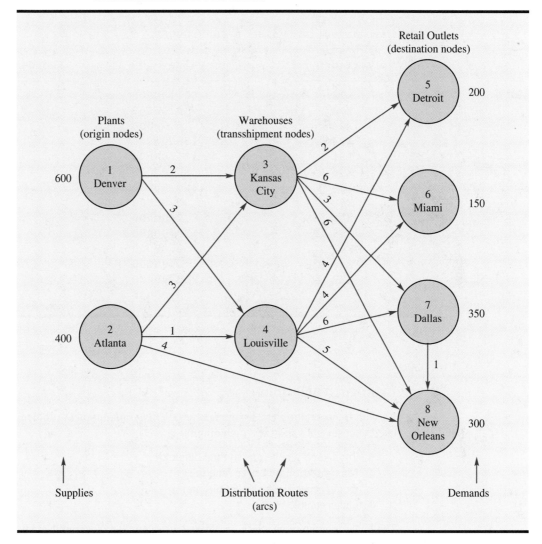

FIGURE 6.10 LINEAR PROGRAMMING FORMULATION OF THE MODIFIED RYAN ELECTRONICS TRANSSHIPMENT PROBLEM

Min $\quad 2x_{13} + 3x_{14} + 3x_{23} + 1x_{24} + 2x_{35} + 6x_{36} + 3x_{37} + 6x_{38} + 4x_{45} + 4x_{46} + 6x_{47} + 5x_{48} + 4x_{28} + 1x_{78}$

s.t.

$$
\begin{array}{ll}
x_{13} + x_{14} & \leq 600 \\
\qquad\qquad x_{23} + x_{24} \qquad\qquad\qquad\qquad + x_{28} & \leq 400 \\
-x_{13} \qquad - x_{23} \quad + x_{35} + x_{36} + x_{37} + x_{38} & = 0 \\
\qquad - x_{14} \qquad - x_{24} \qquad\qquad + x_{45} + x_{46} + x_{47} + x_{48} & = 0 \\
\qquad\qquad\qquad\qquad\quad x_{35} \qquad + x_{45} & = 200 \\
\qquad\qquad\qquad\qquad\qquad\quad x_{36} \qquad\quad + x_{46} & = 150 \\
\qquad\qquad\qquad\qquad\qquad\qquad x_{37} \qquad\quad + x_{47} \qquad\quad - x_{78} & = 350 \\
\qquad\qquad\qquad\qquad\qquad\qquad\quad x_{38} \qquad\qquad + x_{48} + x_{28} + x_{78} & = 300
\end{array}
$$

$\left.\begin{array}{}\\ \\\end{array}\right\}$ Origin node constraints

$\left.\begin{array}{}\\ \\\end{array}\right\}$ Transshipment node constraints

$\left.\begin{array}{}\\ \\ \\ \\\end{array}\right\}$ Destination node constraints

$x_{ij} \geq 0$ for all i and j

FIGURE 6.11   THE SOLUTION FOR THE MODIFIED RYAN ELECTRONICS
TRANSSHIPMENT PROBLEM

```
Optimal Objective Value =  4600.00000

        Variable                  Value              Reduced Costs
    ---------------        ---------------       ------------------
          X13                 600.00000                  0.00000
          X14                   0.00000                  0.00000
          X23                   0.00000                  3.00000
          X24                 150.00000                  0.00000
          X35                 200.00000                  0.00000
          X36                   0.00000                  1.00000
          X37                 400.00000                  0.00000
          X38                   0.00000                  2.00000
          X45                   0.00000                  3.00000
          X46                 150.00000                  0.00000
          X47                   0.00000                  4.00000
          X48                   0.00000                  2.00000
          X28                 250.00000                  0.00000
          X78                  50.00000                  0.00000
```

Problem Variations

As with transportation and assignment problems, transshipment problems may be formulated with several variations, including these:

1. Total supply not equal to total demand
2. Maximization objective function
3. Route capacities or route minimums
4. Unacceptable routes

The linear programming model modifications required to accommodate these variations are identical to the modifications required for the transportation problem described in Section 6.1. When we add one or more constraints of the form $x_{ij} \leq L_{ij}$ to show that the route from node i to node j has capacity L_{ij}, we refer to the transshipment problem as a **capacitated transshipment problem.**

A General Linear Programming Model

To show the general linear programming model for the transshipment problem, we use the notation:

$$x_{ij} = \text{number of units shipped from the node } i \text{ to node } j$$
$$c_{ij} = \text{cost per unit of shipping from node } i \text{ to node } j$$
$$s_i = \text{supply at origin node } i$$
$$d_j = \text{demand at destination node } j$$

The general linear programming model for the transshipment problem is as follows:

$$\text{Min} \quad \sum_{\text{all arcs}} c_{ij} x_{ij}$$

s.t.

$$\sum_{\text{arcs out}} x_{ij} - \sum_{\text{arcs in}} x_{ij} \leq s_i \quad \text{Origin node } i$$

$$\sum_{\text{arcs out}} x_{ij} = \sum_{\text{arcs in}} x_{ij} \quad \text{Transshipment nodes}$$

$$\sum_{\text{arcs in}} x_{ij} - \sum_{\text{arcs out}} x_{ij} = d_j \quad \text{Destination node } j$$

$$x_{ij} \geq 0 \text{ for all } i \text{ and } j$$

NOTES AND COMMENTS

1. The Management Science in Action, Product Sourcing Heuristic at Procter & Gamble, describes how Procter & Gamble used a transshipment model to redesign its North American distribution system.

2. In more advanced treatments of linear programming and network flow problems, the capacitated transshipment problem is called the *pure network flow problem*. Efficient special-purpose solution procedures are available for network flow problems and their special cases.

3. In the general linear programming formulation of the transshipment problem, the constraints for the destination nodes are often written as

$$\sum_{\text{arcs out}} x_{ij} - \sum_{\text{arcs in}} x_{ij} = -d_j$$

The advantage of writing the constraints this way is that the left-hand side of each constraint then represents the flow out of the node minus the flow in. But such constraints would then have to be multiplied by –1 to obtain nonnegative right-hand sides before solving the problem by many linear programming codes.

MANAGEMENT SCIENCE IN ACTION

PRODUCT SOURCING HEURISTIC AT PROCTER & GAMBLE*

A few years ago Procter & Gamble (P&G) embarked on a major strategic planning initiative called the North American Product Sourcing Study. P&G wanted to consolidate its product sources and optimize its distribution system design throughout North America. A decision support system used to aid in this project was called the Product Sourcing Heuristic (PSH) and was based on a transshipment model much like the ones described in this chapter.

In a preprocessing phase, the many P&G products were aggregated into groups that shared the same technology and could be made at the same plant. The PSH employing the transshipment model was then used by product strategy teams responsible for developing product sourcing options for these product groups. The various plants that could produce the product group were the source nodes, the company's regional distribution centers were the transshipment nodes, and P&G's customer zones were the destinations. Direct shipments to customer zones as well as shipments through distribution centers were employed.

The product strategy teams used the heuristic interactively to explore a variety of questions concerning product sourcing and distribution. For instance, the team might be interested in the impact of closing two of five plants and consolidating production in the three remaining plants. The product sourcing heuristic would then delete the source nodes corresponding to the two closed plants,

(continued)

make any capacity modifications necessary to the sources corresponding to the remaining three plants, and re-solve the transshipment problem. The product strategy team could then examine the new solution, make some more modifications, solve again, and so on.

The Product Sourcing Heuristic was viewed as a valuable decision support system by all who used

it. When P&G implemented the results of the study, it realized annual savings in the $200-million range. The PSH proved so successful in North America that P&G used it in other markets around the world.

*Based on information provided by Franz Dill and Tom Chorman of Procter & Gamble.

6.4   SHORTEST-ROUTE PROBLEM

In this section we consider a problem in which the objective is to determine the **shortest route,** or *path,* between two nodes in a network. We will demonstrate the shortest-route problem by considering the situation facing the Gorman Construction Company. Gorman has several construction sites located throughout a three-county area. With multiple daily trips carrying personnel, equipment, and supplies from Gorman's office to the construction sites, the costs associated with transportation activities are substantial. The travel alternatives between Gorman's office and each construction site can be described by the road network shown in Figure 6.12. The road distances in miles between the nodes are shown above the corresponding arcs. In this application, Gorman would like to determine the route that will minimize the total travel distance between Gorman's office (located at node 1) and the construction site located at node 6.

A key to developing a model for the shortest-route problem is to understand that the problem is a special case of the transshipment problem. Specifically, the Gorman shortest-route problem can be viewed as a transshipment problem with one origin node (node 1), one destination node (node 6), and four transshipment nodes (nodes 2, 3, 4, and 5). The

FIGURE 6.12   ROAD NETWORK FOR THE GORMAN COMPANY
SHORTEST-ROUTE PROBLEM

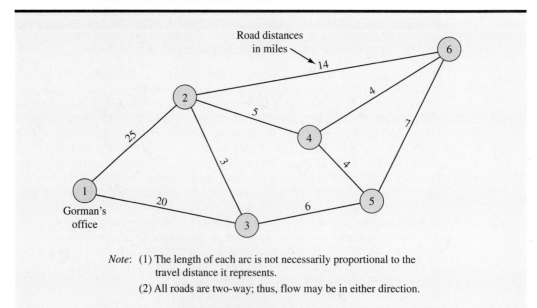

Note: (1) The length of each arc is not necessarily proportional to the travel distance it represents.

(2) All roads are two-way; thus, flow may be in either direction.

FIGURE 6.13   TRANSSHIPMENT NETWORK FOR THE GORMAN
SHORTEST-ROUTE PROBLEM

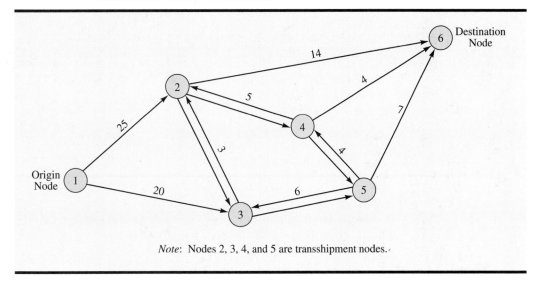

Note: Nodes 2, 3, 4, and 5 are transshipment nodes.

transshipment network for the Gorman shortest-route problem is shown in Figure 6.13. Arrows added to the arcs show the direction of flow, which is always *out* of the origin node and *into* the destination node. Note also that two directed arcs are shown between the pairs of transshipment nodes. For example, one arc going from node 2 to node 3 indicates that the shortest route may go from node 2 to node 3, and one arc going from node 3 to node 2 indicates that the shortest route may go from node 3 to node 2. The distance between two transshipment nodes is the same in either direction.

To find the shortest route between node 1 and node 6, think of node 1 as having a supply of 1 unit and node 6 as having a demand of 1 unit. Let x_{ij} denote the number of units that flow or are shipped from node i to node j. Because only 1 unit will be shipped from node 1 to node 6, the value of x_{ij} will be either 1 or 0. Thus, if $x_{ij} = 1$, the arc from node i to node j is on the shortest route from node 1 to node 6; if $x_{ij} = 0$, the arc from node i to node j is not on the shortest route. Because we are looking for the shortest route between node 1 and node 6, the objective function for the Gorman problem is

$$\text{Min } 25x_{12} + 20x_{13} + 3x_{23} + 3x_{32} + 5x_{24} + 5x_{42} + 14x_{26} + 6x_{35} + 6x_{53} \\ + 4x_{45} + 4x_{54} + 4x_{46} + 7x_{56}$$

To develop the constraints for the model, we begin with node 1. Because the supply at node 1 is 1 unit, the flow out of node 1 must equal 1. Thus, the constraint for node 1 is written

$$x_{12} + x_{13} = 1$$

For transshipment nodes 2, 3, 4, and 5, the flow out of each node must equal the flow into each node; thus, the flow out minus the flow in must be 0. The constraints for the four transshipment nodes are as follows:

	Flow Out		**Flow In**
Node 2	$x_{23} + x_{24} + x_{26}$	=	$x_{12} + x_{32} + x_{42}$
Node 3	$x_{32} + x_{35}$	=	$x_{13} + x_{23} + x_{53}$
Node 4	$x_{42} + x_{45} + x_{46}$	=	$x_{24} + x_{54}$
Node 5	$x_{53} + x_{54} + x_{56}$	=	$x_{35} + x_{45}$

FIGURE 6.14   LINEAR PROGRAMMING FORMULATION OF THE GORMAN SHORTEST-ROUTE PROBLEM

$$\text{Min } 25x_{12} + 20x_{13} + 3x_{23} + 3x_{32} + 5x_{24} + 5x_{42} + 14x_{26} + 6x_{35} + 6x_{53} + 4x_{45} + 4x_{54} + 4x_{46} + 7x_{56}$$

s.t.

$$
\begin{array}{llll}
x_{12} + x_{13} & = 1 & \text{Origin node} \\
-x_{12} + x_{23} - x_{32} + x_{24} - x_{42} + x_{26} & = 0 \\
- x_{13} - x_{23} + x_{32} + x_{35} - x_{53} & = 0 \\
- x_{24} + x_{42} + x_{45} - x_{54} + x_{46} & = 0 \\
- x_{35} + x_{53} - x_{45} + x_{54} + x_{56} & = 0 \\
x_{26} + x_{46} + x_{56} & = 1 & \text{Destination node}
\end{array}
$$

Transshipment nodes

$$x_{ij} \geq 0 \text{ for all } i \text{ and } j$$

Because node 6 is the destination node with a demand of one unit, the flow into node 6 must equal 1. Thus, the constraint for node 6 is written as

$$x_{26} + x_{46} + x_{56} = 1$$

Including the negative constraints $x_{ij} \geq 0$ for all i and j, the linear programming model for the Gorman shortest-route problem is shown in Figure 6.14.

Try Problem 22 to practice solving a shortest-route problem.

The solution to the Gorman shortest-route problem is shown in Figure 6.15. The objective function value of 32 indicates that the shortest route between Gorman's office located at node 1 to the construction site located at node 6 is 32 miles. With $x_{13} = 1$, $x_{32} = 1$, $x_{24} = 1$, and $x_{46} = 1$, the shortest-route from node 1 to node 6 is 1–3–2–4–6; in other words, the shortest route takes us from node 1 to node 3; then from node 3 to node 2; then from node 2 to node 4; and finally from node 4 to node 6.

FIGURE 6.15   THE SOLUTION OF THE GORMAN SHORTEST-ROUTE PROBLEM

```
Optimal Objective Value = 32.00000

        Variable              Value           Reduced Cost
        --------           ------------       ------------
          X12               0.00000             2.00000
          X13               1.00000             0.00000
          X23               0.00000             6.00000
          X32               1.00000             0.00000
          X24               1.00000             0.00000
          X42               0.00000            10.00000
          X26               0.00000             5.00000
          X35               0.00000             0.00000
          X53               0.00000            12.00000
          X45               0.00000             7.00000
          X54               0.00000             1.00000
          X46               1.00000             0.00000
          X56               0.00000             0.00000
```

WEB file

Gorman

A General Linear Programming Model

To show the general linear programming model for the shortest-route problem we use the notation:

$$x_{ij} = \begin{cases} 1 & \text{if the arc from node } i \text{ to node } j \text{ is on the shortest route} \\ 0 & \text{otherwise} \end{cases}$$

$$c_{ij} = \text{the distance, time, or cost associated with the arc from node } i \text{ to node } j$$

The general linear programming model for the shortest-route problem is as follows:

$$\text{Min} \quad \sum_{\text{all arcs}} c_{ij} x_{ij}$$

s.t.

$$\sum_{\text{arcs out}} x_{ij} = 1 \qquad \text{Origin node } i$$

$$\sum_{\text{arcs out}} x_{ij} = \sum_{\text{arcs in}} x_{ij} \quad \text{Transshipment nodes}$$

$$\sum_{\text{arcs in}} x_{ij} = 1 \qquad \text{Destination node } j$$

NOTES AND COMMENTS

In the Gorman problem, we assumed that all roads in the network are two-way. As a result, the road connecting nodes 2 and 3 in the road network resulted in the creation of two corresponding arcs in the transshipment network. Two decision variables, x_{23} and x_{32}, were required to show that the shortest route might go from node 2 to node 3 or from node 3 to node 2. If the road connecting nodes 2 and 3 had been a one-way road allowing flow only from node 2 to node 3, decision variable x_{32} would not have been included in the model.

6.5   MAXIMAL FLOW PROBLEM

The objective in a **maximal flow** problem is to determine the maximum amount of flow (vehicles, messages, fluid, etc.) that can enter and exit a network system in a given period of time. In this problem, we attempt to transmit flow through all arcs of the network as efficiently as possible. The amount of flow is limited due to capacity restrictions on the various arcs of the network. For example, highway types limit vehicle flow in a transportation system, whereas pipe sizes limit oil flow in an oil distribution system. The maximum or upper limit on the flow in an arc is referred to as the **flow capacity** of the arc. Even though we do not specify capacities for the nodes, we do assume that the flow out of a node is equal to the flow into the node.

As an example of the maximal flow problem, consider the north–south interstate highway system passing through Cincinnati, Ohio. The north–south vehicle flow reaches a level of 15,000 vehicles per hour at peak times. Due to a summer highway maintenance program, which calls for the temporary closing of lanes and lower speed limits, a network of alternate routes through Cincinnati has been proposed by a transportation planning committee. The alternate routes include other highways as well as city streets. Because of differences in speed limits and traffic patterns, flow capacities vary, depending on the

FIGURE 6.16 NETWORK OF HIGHWAY SYSTEM AND FLOW CAPACITIES (1000s/HOUR) FOR CINCINNATI

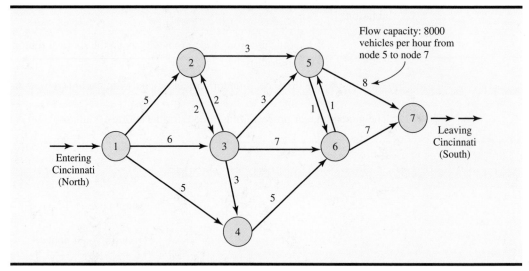

particular streets and roads used. The proposed network with arc flow capacities is shown in Figure 6.16.

The direction of flow for each arc is indicated, and the arc capacity is shown next to each arc. Note that most of the streets are one-way. However, a two-way street can be found between nodes 2 and 3 and between nodes 5 and 6. In both cases, the capacity is the same in each direction.

We will show how to develop a capacitated transshipment model for the maximal flow problem. First, we will add an arc from node 7 back to node 1 to represent the total flow through the highway system. Figure 6.17 shows the modified network. The newly added

FIGURE 6.17 FLOW OVER ARC FROM NODE 7 TO NODE 1 TO REPRESENT TOTAL FLOW THROUGH THE CINCINNATI HIGHWAY SYSTEM

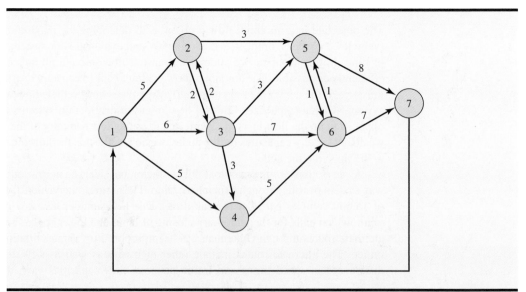

arc shows no capacity; indeed, we will want to maximize the flow over that arc. Maximizing the flow over the arc from node 7 to node 1 is equivalent to maximizing the number of cars that can get through the north–south highway system passing through Cincinnati.

The decision variables are as follows:

$$x_{ij} = \text{amount of traffic flow from node } i \text{ to node } j$$

The objective function that maximizes the flow over the highway system is

$$\text{Max } x_{71}$$

As with all transshipment problems, each arc generates a variable and each node generates a constraint. For each node, a conservation of flow constraint represents the requirement that the flow out must equal the flow in. For node 1, the flow out is $x_{12} + x_{13} + x_{14}$, and the flow in is x_{71}. Therefore, the constraint for node 1 is

$$x_{12} + x_{13} + x_{14} = x_{71}$$

The conservation of flow constraints for the other six nodes are developed in a similar fashion:

	Flow Out		**Flow In**
Node 2	$x_{23} + x_{25}$	$=$	$x_{12} + x_{32}$
Node 3	$x_{32} + x_{34} + x_{35} + x_{36}$	$=$	$x_{13} + x_{23} + x_{53}$
Node 4	x_{46}	$=$	$x_{14} + x_{34}$
Node 5	$x_{56} + x_{57}$	$=$	$x_{25} + x_{35} + x_{65}$
Node 6	$x_{65} + x_{67}$	$=$	$x_{36} + x_{46} + x_{56}$
Node 7	x_{71}	$=$	$x_{57} + x_{67}$

Additional constraints are needed to enforce the capacities on the arcs. These 14 simple upper-bound constraints are given:

$$
\begin{array}{lll}
x_{12} \leq 5 & x_{13} \leq 6 & x_{14} \leq 5 \\
x_{23} \leq 2 & x_{25} \leq 3 & \\
x_{32} \leq 2 & x_{34} \leq 3 & x_{35} \leq 3 \quad x_{36} \leq 7 \\
x_{46} \leq 5 & & \\
x_{56} \leq 1 & x_{57} \leq 8 & \\
x_{65} \leq 1 & x_{67} \leq 7 &
\end{array}
$$

Note that the only arc without a capacity is the one we added from node 7 to node 1.

The solution to this 15-variable, 21-constraint linear programming problem is shown in Figure 6.18. We note that the value of the optimal solution is 14. This result implies that the maximal flow over the highway system is 14,000 vehicles. Figure 6.19 shows how the vehicle flow is routed through the original highway network. We note, for instance, that 5000 vehicles per hour are routed between nodes 1 and 2, 2000 vehicles per hour are routed between nodes 2 and 3, and so on.

The results of the maximal flow analysis indicate that the planned highway network system will not handle the peak flow of 15,000 vehicles per hour. The transportation

Try Problem 29 for practice in solving a maximal flow problem.

FIGURE 6.18   THE SOLUTION TO THE CINCINNATI HIGHWAY SYSTEM MAXIMAL
FLOW PROBLEM

```
Optimal Objective Value = 14.00000

         Variable              Value         Reduced Cost
      ---------------    ---------------    ---------------
           X12               5.00000            0.00000
           X13               6.00000            0.00000
           X14               3.00000            0.00000
           X23               2.00000            0.00000
           X25               3.00000            0.00000
           X34               0.00000            0.00000
           X35               3.00000            0.00000
           X36               5.00000            0.00000
           X32               0.00000            0.00000
           X46               3.00000            0.00000
           X56               0.00000            1.00000
           X57               7.00000            0.00000
           X65               1.00000            0.00000
           X67               7.00000            0.00000
           X71              14.00000            0.00000
```

WEB file

Cincinnati

FIGURE 6.19   MAXIMAL FLOW PATTERN FOR THE CINCINNATI HIGHWAY
SYSTEM NETWORK

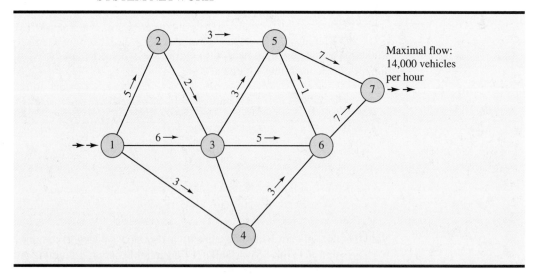

planners will have to expand the highway network, increase current arc flow capacities, or
be prepared for serious traffic problems. If the network is extended or modified, another
maximal flow analysis will determine the extent of any improved flow. The Management
Science in Action, Optimizing Restoration Capacity at AT&T, notes that AT&T solved
shortest-route and maximal flow problems in designing a transmission network.

1. The maximal flow problem of this section can also be solved with a slightly different formulation if the extra arc between nodes 7 and 1 is not used. The alternate approach is to maximize the flow into node 7 ($x_{57} + x_{67}$) and drop the conservation of flow constraints for nodes 1 and 7. However, the formulation used in this section is most common in practice.

2. Network models can be used to describe a variety of management science problems. Unfortunately, no one network solution algorithm can be used to solve every network problem. It is important to recognize the specific type of problem being modeled in order to select the correct specialized solution algorithm.

MANAGEMENT SCIENCE IN ACTION

OPTIMIZING RESTORATION CAPACITY AT AT&T*

AT&T is a global telecommunications company that provides long-distance voice and data, video, wireless, satellite, and Internet services. The company uses state-of-the-art switching and transmission equipment to provide service to more than 80 million customers. In the continental United States, AT&T's transmission network consists of more than 40,000 miles of fiber-optic cable. On peak days AT&T handles as many as 290 million calls of various types.

Power outages, natural disasters, cable cuts, and other events can disable a portion of the transmission network. When such events occur, spare capacity comprising the restoration network must be immediately employed so that service is not disrupted. Critical issues with respect to the restoration network are: How much capacity is necessary? and Where should it be located? In 1997, AT&T assembled a RestNet team to address these issues.

To optimize restoration capacity, the RestNet team developed a large-scale linear programming model. One subproblem in their model involves determining the shortest route connecting an origin and destination whenever a failure occurs in a span of the transmission network. Another subproblem solves a maximal flow problem to find the best restoration paths from each switch to a disaster recovery switch.

The RestNet team was successful, and their work is an example of how valuable management science methodology is to companies. According to C. Michael Armstrong, chair and CEO, "Last year the work of the RestNet team allowed us to reduce capital spending by tens of millions of dollars."

*Based on Ken Ambs, Sebastian Cwilich, Mei Deng, David J. Houck, David F. Lynch, and Dicky Yan, "Optimizing Restoration Capacity in the AT&T Network," *Interfaces* (January/February 2000): 26–44.

6.6   A PRODUCTION AND INVENTORY APPLICATION

The introduction to the transportation and transshipment problems in Sections 6.1 and 6.3 involved applications for the shipment of goods from several supply locations or origins to several demand sites or destinations. Although the shipment of goods is the subject of many transportation and transshipment problems, transportation or transshipment models can be developed for applications that have nothing to do with the physical shipment of goods from origins to destinations. In this section we show how to use a transshipment model to solve a production and inventory problem.

Contois Carpets is a small manufacturer of carpeting for home and office installations. Production capacity, demand, production cost per square yard, and inventory holding cost per square yard for the next four quarters are shown in Table 6.7. Note that production

TABLE 6.7   PRODUCTION, DEMAND, AND COST ESTIMATES FOR CONTOIS CARPETS

Quarter	Production Capacity (square yards)	Demand (square yards)	Production Cost ($/square yard)	Inventory Cost ($/square yard)
1	600	400	2	0.25
2	300	500	5	0.25
3	500	400	3	0.25
4	400	400	3	0.25

The network flows into and out of demand nodes are what make the model a transshipment model.

capacity, demand, and production costs vary by quarter, whereas the cost of carrying inventory from one quarter to the next is constant at $0.25 per yard. Contois wants to determine how many yards of carpeting to manufacture each quarter to minimize the total production and inventory cost for the four-quarter period.

We begin by developing a network representation of the problem. First, we create four nodes corresponding to the production in each quarter and four nodes corresponding to the demand in each quarter. Each production node is connected by an outgoing arc to the demand node for the same period. The flow on the arc represents the number of square yards of carpet manufactured for the period. For each demand node, an outgoing arc represents the amount of inventory (square yards of carpet) carried over to the demand node for the next period. Figure 6.20 shows the network model. Note that nodes 1–4 represent the production for each quarter and that nodes 5–8 represent the demand for each quarter. The quarterly production capacities are shown in the left margin, and the quarterly demands are shown in the right margin.

The objective is to determine a production scheduling and inventory policy that will minimize the total production and inventory cost for the four quarters. Constraints involve production capacity and demand in each quarter. As usual, a linear programming model can be developed from the network by establishing a constraint for each node and a variable for each arc.

Let x_{15} denote the number of square yards of carpet manufactured in quarter 1. The capacity of the facility is 600 square yards in quarter 1, so the production capacity constraint is

$$x_{15} \leq 600$$

Using similar decision variables, we obtain the production capacities for quarters 2–4:

$$x_{26} \leq 300$$
$$x_{37} \leq 500$$
$$x_{48} \leq 400$$

We now consider the development of the constraints for each of the demand nodes. For node 5, one arc enters the node, which represents the number of square yards of carpet produced in quarter 1, and one arc leaves the node, which represents the number of square yards of carpet that will not be sold in quarter 1 and will be carried over for possible sale in quarter 2. In general, for each quarter the beginning inventory plus the production minus the ending inventory must equal demand. However, because quarter 1 has no beginning inventory, the constraint for node 5 is

$$x_{15} - x_{56} = 400$$

FIGURE 6.20 NETWORK REPRESENTATION OF THE CONTOIS CARPETS PROBLEM

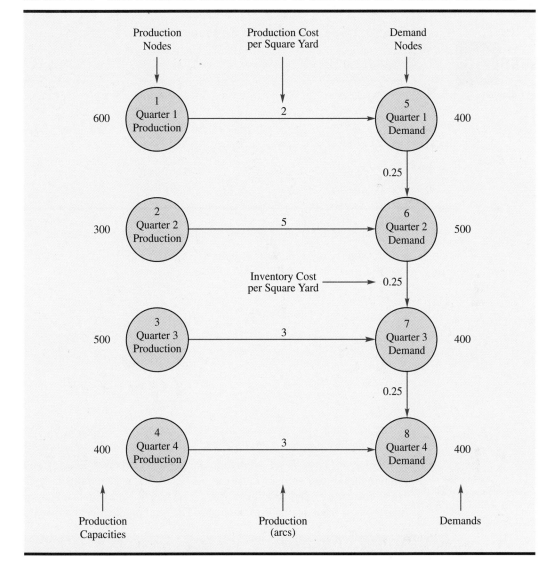

The constraints associated with the demand nodes in quarters 2, 3, and 4 are

$$x_{56} + x_{26} - x_{67} = 500$$
$$x_{67} + x_{37} - x_{78} = 400$$
$$x_{78} + x_{48} = 400$$

Note that the constraint for node 8 (fourth-quarter demand) involves only two variables because no provision is made for holding inventory for a fifth quarter.

The objective is to minimize total production and inventory cost, so we write the objective function as

$$\text{Min} \quad 2x_{15} + 5x_{26} + 3x_{37} + 3x_{48} + 0.25x_{56} + 0.25x_{67} + 0.25x_{78}$$

FIGURE 6.21 THE SOLUTION FOR THE CONTOIS CARPETS PROBLEM

Contois

```
Optimal Objective Value = 5150.00000

    Variable              Value            Reduced Cost
--------------      ---------------      ---------------
        X15             600.00000              0.00000
        X26             300.00000              0.00000
        X37             400.00000              0.00000
        X48             400.00000              0.00000
        X56             200.00000              0.00000
        X67               0.00000              2.25000
        X78               0.00000              0.00000
```

The complete linear programming formulation of the Contois Carpets problem is

Min $2x_{15} + 5x_{26} + 3x_{37} + 3x_{48} + 0.25x_{56} + 0.25x_{67} + 0.25x_{78}$

s.t.

$$
\begin{aligned}
x_{15} &\leq 600 \\
x_{26} &\leq 300 \\
x_{37} &\leq 500 \\
x_{48} &\leq 400 \\
x_{15} \qquad - x_{56} &= 400 \\
x_{26} \qquad + x_{56} - x_{67} &= 500 \\
x_{37} \qquad + x_{67} - x_{78} &= 400 \\
x_{48} \qquad + x_{78} &= 400
\end{aligned}
$$

$x_{ij} \geq 0$ for all i and j

Figure 6.21 shows the solution to the Contois Carpets problem. Contois should manufacture 600 square yards of carpet in quarter 1, 300 square yards in quarter 2, 400 square yards in quarter 3, and 400 square yards in quarter 4. Note also that 200 square yards will be carried over from quarter 1 to quarter 2. The total production and inventory cost is $5150.

NOTES AND COMMENTS

For the network models presented in this chapter, the amount leaving the starting node for an arc is always equal to the amount entering the ending node for that arc. An extension of such a network model is the case where a gain or a loss occurs as an arc is traversed. The amount entering the destination node may be greater or smaller than the amount leaving the origin node. For instance, if cash is the commodity flowing across an arc, the cash earns interest from one period to the next. Thus, the amount of cash entering the next period is greater than the amount leaving the previous period by the amount of interest earned. Networks with gains or losses are treated in more advanced texts on network flow programming.

SUMMARY

In this chapter we introduced transportation, assignment, transshipment, shortest-route, and maximal flow problems. All five types of problems belong to the special category of linear programs called *network flow problems*. In general, the network model for these problems consists of nodes representing origins, destinations, and if necessary, transshipment points in the network system. Arcs are used to represent the routes for shipment, travel, or flow between the various nodes.

The general transportation problem has m origins and n destinations. Given the supply at each origin, the demand at each destination, and unit shipping cost between each origin and each destination, the transportation model determines the optimal amounts to ship from each origin to each destination.

The assignment problem is a special case of the transportation problem in which all supply and all demand values are 1. We represent each agent as an origin node and each task as a destination node. The assignment model determines the minimum cost or maximum profit assignment of agents to tasks.

The transshipment problem is an extension of the transportation problem involving transfer points referred to as transshipment nodes. In this more general model, we allow arcs between any pair of nodes in the network. If desired, capacities can be specified for arcs, which makes it a capacitated transshipment problem.

The shortest-route problem finds the shortest route or path between two nodes of a network. Distance, time, and cost are often the criteria used for this model. The shortest-route problem can be expressed as a transshipment problem with one origin and one destination. By shipping one unit from the origin to the destination, the solution will determine the shortest route through the network.

The maximal flow problem can be used to allocate flow to the arcs of the network so that flow through the network system is maximized. Arc capacities determine the maximum amount of flow for each arc. With these flow capacity constraints, the maximal flow problem is expressed as a capacitated transshipment problem.

In the last section of the chapter, we showed how a variation of the transshipment problem could be used to solve a production and inventory problem. In the chapter appendix we show how to use Excel to solve three of the distribution and network problems presented in the chapter.

GLOSSARY

Transportation problem   A network flow problem that often involves minimizing the cost of shipping goods from a set of origins to a set of destinations; it can be formulated and solved as a linear program by including a variable for each arc and a constraint for each node.

Network   A graphical representation of a problem consisting of numbered circles (nodes) interconnected by a series of lines (arcs); arrowheads on the arcs show the direction of flow. Transportation, assignment, and transshipment problems are network flow problems.

Nodes   The intersection or junction points of a network.

Arcs   The lines connecting the nodes in a network.

Dummy origin   An origin added to a transportation problem to make the total supply equal to the total demand. The supply assigned to the dummy origin is the difference between the total demand and the total supply.

Capacitated transportation problem   A variation of the basic transportation problem in which some or all of the arcs are subject to capacity restrictions.

Assignment problem   A network flow problem that often involves the assignment of agents to tasks; it can be formulated as a linear program and is a special case of the transportation problem.

Transshipment problem   An extension of the transportation problem to distribution problems involving transfer points and possible shipments between any pair of nodes.

Capacitated transshipment problem   A variation of the transshipment problem in which some or all of the arcs are subject to capacity restrictions.

Shortest route   Shortest path between two nodes in a network.

Maximal flow   The maximum amount of flow that can enter and exit a network system during a given period of time.

Flow capacity   The maximum flow for an arc of the network. The flow capacity in one direction may not equal the flow capacity in the reverse direction.

PROBLEMS

1. A company imports goods at two ports: Philadelphia and New Orleans. Shipments of one product are made to customers in Atlanta, Dallas, Columbus, and Boston. For the next planning period, the supplies at each port, customer demands, and shipping costs per case from each port to each customer are as follows:

Port	Atlanta	Dallas	Columbus	Boston	Port Supply
		Customers			
Philadelphia	2	6	6	2	5000
New Orleans	1	2	5	7	3000
Demand	1400	3200	2000	1400	

Develop a network representation of the distribution system (transportation problem).

2. Consider the following network representation of a transportation problem:

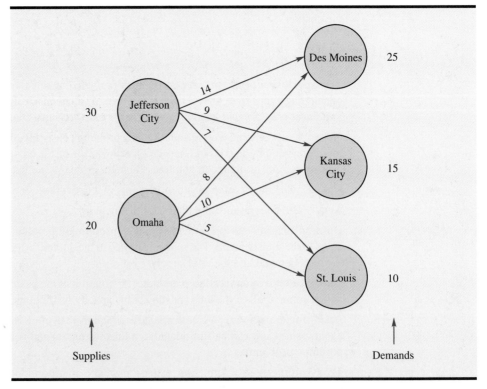

The supplies, demands, and transportation costs per unit are shown on the network.

   a. Develop a linear programming model for this problem; be sure to define the variables in your model.

   b. Solve the linear program to determine the optimal solution.

3. Tri-County Utilities, Inc., supplies natural gas to customers in a three-county area. The company purchases natural gas from two companies: Southern Gas and Northwest Gas. Demand forecasts for the coming winter season are Hamilton County, 400 units; Butler County, 200 units; and Clermont County, 300 units. Contracts to provide the following quantities have been written: Southern Gas, 500 units; and Northwest Gas, 400 units. Distribution costs for the counties vary, depending upon the location of the suppliers. The distribution costs per unit (in thousands of dollars) are as follows:

	To		
From	**Hamilton**	**Butler**	**Clermont**
Southern Gas	10	20	15
Northwest Gas	12	15	18

   a. Develop a network representation of this problem.

   b. Develop a linear programming model that can be used to determine the plan that will minimize total distribution costs.

   c. Describe the distribution plan and show the total distribution cost.

   d. Recent residential and industrial growth in Butler County has the potential for increasing demand by as much as 100 units. Which supplier should Tri-County contract with to supply the additional capacity?

4. Arnoff Enterprises manufactures the central processing unit (CPU) for a line of personal computers. The CPUs are manufactured in Seattle, Columbus, and New York and shipped to warehouses in Pittsburgh, Mobile, Denver, Los Angeles, and Washington, D.C., for further distribution. The following table shows the number of CPUs available at each plant, the number of CPUs required by each warehouse, and the shipping costs (dollars per unit):

	Warehouse					
Plant	**Pittsburgh**	**Mobile**	**Denver**	**Los Angeles**	**Washington**	**CPUs Available**
Seattle	10	20	5	9	10	9000
Columbus	2	10	8	30	6	4000
New York	1	20	7	10	4	8000
CPUs Required	3000	5000	4000	6000	3000	21,000

   a. Develop a network representation of this problem.

   b. Determine the amount that should be shipped from each plant to each warehouse to minimize the total shipping cost.

   c. The Pittsburgh warehouse just increased its order by 1000 units, and Arnoff authorized the Columbus plant to increase its production by 1000 units. Will this production increase lead to an increase or decrease in total shipping costs? Solve for the new optimal solution.

5. Premier Consulting's two consultants, Avery and Baker, can be scheduled to work for clients up to a maximum of 160 hours each over the next four weeks. A third consultant, Campbell, has some administrative assignments already planned and is available for clients up to a maximum of 140 hours over the next four weeks. The company has four clients with projects in process. The estimated hourly requirements for each of the clients over the four-week period are

Client	Hours
A	180
B	75
C	100
D	85

Hourly rates vary for the consultant–client combination and are based on several factors, including project type and the consultant's experience. The rates (dollars per hour) for each consultant–client combination are as follows:

		Client		
Consultant	A	B	C	D
Avery	100	125	115	100
Baker	120	135	115	120
Campbell	155	150	140	130

a. Develop a network representation of the problem.
b. Formulate the problem as a linear program, with the optimal solution providing the hours each consultant should be scheduled for each client to maximize the consulting firm's billings. What is the schedule and what is the total billing?
c. New information shows that Avery doesn't have the experience to be scheduled for client B. If this consulting assignment is not permitted, what impact does it have on total billings? What is the revised schedule?

6. Klein Chemicals, Inc., produces a special oil-based material that is currently in short supply. Four of Klein's customers have already placed orders that together exceed the combined capacity of Klein's two plants. Klein's management faces the problem of deciding how many units it should supply to each customer. Because the four customers are in different industries, different prices can be charged because of the various industry pricing structures. However, slightly different production costs at the two plants and varying transportation costs between the plants and customers make a "sell to the highest bidder" strategy unacceptable. After considering price, production costs, and transportation costs, Klein established the following profit per unit for each plant–customer alternative:

		Customer		
Plant	D_1	D_2	D_3	D_4
Clifton Springs	$32	$34	$32	$40
Danville	$34	$30	$28	$38

The plant capacities and customer orders are as follows:

Plant Capacity (units)		Distributor Orders (units)	
Clifton Springs	5000	D_1	2000
		D_2	5000
Danville	3000	D_3	3000
		D_4	2000

How many units should each plant produce for each customer in order to maximize profits? Which customer demands will not be met? Show your network model and linear programming formulation.

7. Forbelt Corporation has a one-year contract to supply motors for all refrigerators produced by the Ice Age Corporation. Ice Age manufactures the refrigerators at four locations around the country: Boston, Dallas, Los Angeles, and St. Paul. Plans call for the following number (in thousands) of refrigerators to be produced at each location:

Boston	50
Dallas	70
Los Angeles	60
St. Paul	80

Forbelt's three plants are capable of producing the motors. The plants and production capacities (in thousands) are

Denver	100
Atlanta	100
Chicago	150

Because of varying production and transportation costs, the profit that Forbelt earns on each lot of 1000 units depends on which plant produced the lot and which destination it was shipped to. The following table gives the accounting department estimates of the profit per unit (shipments will be made in lots of 1000 units):

	Shipped To			
Produced At	Boston	Dallas	Los Angeles	St. Paul
Denver	7	11	8	13
Atlanta	20	17	12	10
Chicago	8	18	13	16

With profit maximization as a criterion, Forbelt's management wants to determine how many motors should be produced at each plant and how many motors should be shipped from each plant to each destination.

a. Develop a network representation of this problem.
b. Find the optimal solution.

8. The Ace Manufacturing Company has orders for three similar products:

Product	Orders (units)
A	2000
B	500
C	1200

Three machines are available for the manufacturing operations. All three machines can produce all the products at the same production rate. However, due to varying defect percentages of each product on each machine, the unit costs of the products vary depending on the machine used. Machine capacities for the next week, and the unit costs, are as follows:

Machine	Capacity (units)
1	1500
2	1500
3	1000

Machine	Product A	Product B	Product C
1	$1.00	$1.20	$0.90
2	$1.30	$1.40	$1.20
3	$1.10	$1.00	$1.20

Use the transportation model to develop the minimum cost production schedule for the products and machines. Show the linear programming formulation.

9. Scott and Associates, Inc., is an accounting firm that has three new clients. Project leaders will be assigned to the three clients. Based on the different backgrounds and experiences of the leaders, the various leader–client assignments differ in terms of projected completion times. The possible assignments and the estimated completion times in days are as follows:

Project Leader	Client 1	Client 2	Client 3
Jackson	10	16	32
Ellis	14	22	40
Smith	22	24	34

a. Develop a network representation of this problem.
b. Formulate the problem as a linear program, and solve. What is the total time required?

10. CarpetPlus sells and installs floor covering for commercial buildings. Brad Sweeney, a CarpetPlus account executive, was just awarded the contract for five jobs. Brad must now assign a CarpetPlus installation crew to each of the five jobs. Because the commission Brad will earn depends on the profit CarpetPlus makes, Brad would like to determine an assignment that will minimize total installation costs. Currently, five installation crews are available for assignment. Each crew is identified by a color code, which aids in tracking of job progress on a large white board. The following table shows the costs (in hundreds of dollars) for each crew to complete each of the five jobs:

				Job		
		1	**2**	**3**	**4**	**5**
	Red	30	44	38	47	31
	White	25	32	45	44	25
Crew	**Blue**	23	40	37	39	29
	Green	26	38	37	45	28
	Brown	26	34	44	43	28

a. Develop a network representation of the problem.
b. Formulate and solve a linear programming model to determine the minimum cost assignment.

11. A local television station plans to drop four Friday evening programs at the end of the season. Steve Botuchis, the station manager, developed a list of six potential replacement programs. Estimates of the advertising revenue (in dollars) that can be expected for each of the new programs in the four vacated time slots are as follows. Mr. Botuchis asked you to find the assignment of programs to time slots that will maximize total advertising revenue.

	5:00–5:30 P.M.	5:30–6:00 P.M.	7:00–7:30 P.M.	8:00–8:30 P.M.
Home Improvement	5000	3000	6000	4000
World News	7500	8000	7000	5500
NASCAR Live	8500	5000	6500	8000
Wall Street Today	7000	6000	6500	5000
Hollywood Briefings	7000	8000	3000	6000
Ramundo & Son	6000	4000	4500	7000

12. The U.S. Cable Company uses a distribution system with five distribution centers and eight customer zones. Each customer zone is assigned a sole source supplier; each customer zone receives all of its cable products from the same distribution center. In an effort to balance demand and workload at the distribution centers, the company's vice president of logistics specified that distribution centers may not be assigned more than three customer zones. The following table shows the five distribution centers and cost of supplying each customer zone (in thousands of dollars):

				Customer Zones				
Distribution Centers	**Los Angeles**	**Chicago**	**Columbus**	**Atlanta**	**Newark**	**Kansas City**	**Denver**	**Dallas**
Plano	70	47	22	53	98	21	27	13
Nashville	75	38	19	58	90	34	40	26
Flagstaff	15	78	37	82	111	40	29	32
Springfield	60	23	8	39	82	36	32	45
Boulder	45	40	29	75	86	25	11	37

a. Determine the assignment of customer zones to distribution centers that will minimize cost.

b. Which distribution centers, if any, are not used?

c. Suppose that each distribution center is limited to a maximum of two customer zones. How does this constraint change the assignment and the cost of supplying customer zones?

13. United Express Service (UES) uses large quantities of packaging materials at its four distribution hubs. After screening potential suppliers, UES identified six vendors that can provide packaging materials that will satisfy its quality standards. UES asked each of the six vendors to submit bids to satisfy annual demand at each of its four distribution hubs over the next year. The following table lists the bids received (in thousands of dollars). UES wants to ensure that each of the distribution hubs is serviced by a different vendor. Which bids should UES accept, and which vendors should UES select to supply each distribution hub?

	Distribution Hub			
Bidder	1	2	3	4
Martin Products	190	175	125	230
Schmidt Materials	150	235	155	220
Miller Containers	210	225	135	260
D&J Burns	170	185	190	280
Larbes Furnishings	220	190	140	240
Lawler Depot	270	200	130	260

14. The quantitative methods department head at a major midwestern university will be scheduling faculty to teach courses during the coming autumn term. Four core courses need to be covered. The four courses are at the UG, MBA, MS, and Ph.D. levels. Four professors will be assigned to the courses, with each professor receiving one of the courses. Student evaluations of professors are available from previous terms. Based on a rating scale of 4 (excellent), 3 (very good), 2 (average), 1 (fair), and 0 (poor), the average student evaluations for each professor are shown. Professor D does not have a Ph.D. and cannot be assigned to teach the Ph.D.-level course. If the department head makes teaching assignments based on maximizing the student evaluation ratings over all four courses, what staffing assignments should be made?

	Course			
Professor	UG	MBA	MS	Ph.D.
A	2.8	2.2	3.3	3.0
B	3.2	3.0	3.6	3.6
C	3.3	3.2	3.5	3.5
D	3.2	2.8	2.5	—

15. A market research firm's three clients each requested that the firm conduct a sample survey. Four available statisticians can be assigned to these three projects; however, all four statisticians are busy, and therefore each can handle only one client. The following data

show the number of hours required for each statistician to complete each job; the differences in time are based on experience and ability of the statisticians.

		Client	
Statistician	A	B	C
1	150	210	270
2	170	230	220
3	180	230	225
4	160	240	230

a. Formulate and solve a linear programming model for this problem.
b. Suppose that the time statistician 4 needs to complete the job for client A is increased from 160 to 165 hours. What effect will this change have on the solution?
c. Suppose that the time statistician 4 needs to complete the job for client A is decreased to 140 hours. What effect will this change have on the solution?
d. Suppose that the time statistician 3 needs to complete the job for client B increases to 250 hours. What effect will this change have on the solution?

16. Hatcher Enterprises uses a chemical called Rbase in production operations at five divisions. Only six suppliers of Rbase meet Hatcher's quality control standards. All six suppliers can produce Rbase in sufficient quantities to accommodate the needs of each division. The quantity of Rbase needed by each Hatcher division and the price per gallon charged by each supplier are as follows:

Division	Demand (1000s of gallons)	Supplier	Price per Gallon ($)
1	40	1	12.60
2	45	2	14.00
3	50	3	10.20
4	35	4	14.20
5	45	5	12.00
		6	13.00

The cost per gallon (in dollars) for shipping from each supplier to each division is provided in the following table:

	Supplier					
Division	1	2	3	4	5	6
1	2.75	2.50	3.15	2.80	2.75	2.75
2	0.80	0.20	5.40	1.20	3.40	1.00
3	4.70	2.60	5.30	2.80	6.00	5.60
4	2.60	1.80	4.40	2.40	5.00	2.80
5	3.40	0.40	5.00	1.20	2.60	3.60

Hatcher believes in spreading its business among suppliers so that the company will be less affected by supplier problems (e.g., labor strikes or resource availability). Company policy requires that each division have a separate supplier.

a. For each supplier–division combination, compute the total cost of supplying the division's demand.

b. Determine the optimal assignment of suppliers to divisions.

17. The distribution system for the Herman Company consists of three plants, two warehouses, and four customers. Plant capacities and shipping costs per unit (in dollars) from each plant to each warehouse are as follows:

| | Warehouse | | |
Plant	1	2	Capacity
1	4	7	450
2	8	5	600
3	5	6	380

Customer demand and shipping costs per unit (in dollars) from each warehouse to each customer are

| | Customer | | | |
Warehouse	1	2	3	4
1	6	4	8	4
2	3	6	7	7
Demand	300	300	300	400

a. Develop a network representation of this problem.

b. Formulate a linear programming model of the problem.

c. Solve the linear program to determine the optimal shipping plan.

18. Refer to Problem 17. Suppose that shipments between the two warehouses are permitted at $2 per unit and that direct shipments can be made from plant 3 to customer 4 at a cost of $7 per unit.

a. Develop a network representation of this problem.

b. Formulate a linear programming model of this problem.

c. Solve the linear program to determine the optimal shipping plan.

19. Adirondack Paper Mills, Inc., operates paper plants in Augusta, Maine, and Tupper Lake, New York. Warehouse facilities are located in Albany, New York, and Portsmouth, New Hampshire. Distributors are located in Boston, New York, and Philadelphia. The plant capacities and distributor demands for the next month are as follows:

Plant	Capacity (units)
Augusta	300
Tupper Lake	100

Distributor	Demand (units)
Boston	150
New York	100
Philadelphia	150

The unit transportation costs (in dollars) for shipments from the two plants to the two warehouses and from the two warehouses to the three distributors are as follows:

	Warehouse	
Plant	Albany	Portsmouth
Augusta	7	5
Tupper Lake	3	4

	Distributor		
Warehouse	Boston	New York	Philadelphia
Albany	8	5	7
Portsmouth	5	6	10

a. Draw the network representation of the Adirondack Paper Mills problem.
b. Formulate the Adirondack Paper Mills problem as a linear programming problem.
c. Solve the linear program to determine the minimum cost shipping schedule for the problem.

20. The Moore & Harman Company is in the business of buying and selling grain. An important aspect of the company's business is arranging for the purchased grain to be shipped to customers. If the company can keep freight costs low, profitability will improve.

   The company recently purchased three rail cars of grain at Muncie, Indiana; six rail cars at Brazil, Indiana; and five rail cars at Xenia, Ohio. Twelve carloads of grain have been sold. The locations and the amount sold at each location are as follows:

Location	Number of Rail Car Loads
Macon, GA	2
Greenwood, SC	4
Concord, SC	3
Chatham, NC	3

All shipments must be routed through either Louisville or Cincinnati. Shown are the shipping costs per bushel (in cents) from the origins to Louisville and Cincinnati and the costs per bushel to ship from Louisville and Cincinnati to the destinations.

	To	
From	Louisville	Cincinnati
Muncie	8	6 ← Cost per bushel
Brazil	3	8 from Muncie to
Xenia	9	3 Cincinnati is 6¢

		To		
From	**Macon**	**Greenwood**	**Concord**	**Chatham**
Louisville	44	34	34	32
Cincinnati	57	35	28	24

Cost per bushel from
Cincinnati to Greenwood is 35¢

Determine a shipping schedule that will minimize the freight costs necessary to satisfy demand. Which (if any) rail cars of grain must be held at the origin until buyers can be found?

21. The following linear programming formulation is for a transshipment problem:

$$\text{Min} \quad 11x_{13} + 12x_{14} + 10x_{21} + 8x_{34} + 10x_{35} + 11x_{42} + 9x_{45} + 12x_{52}$$

s.t.

$$
\begin{aligned}
x_{13} + x_{14} - x_{21} &\leq 5 \\
x_{21} \quad\quad\quad - x_{42} \quad\quad - x_{52} &\leq 3 \\
x_{13} \quad\quad - x_{34} - x_{35} &= 6 \\
- x_{14} \quad\quad - x_{34} \quad\quad + x_{42} + x_{45} &\leq 2 \\
x_{35} \quad\quad\quad + x_{45} - x_{52} &= 4
\end{aligned}
$$

$$x_{ij} \geq 0 \quad \text{for all } i, j$$

Show the network representation of this problem.

22. A rental car company has an imbalance of cars at seven of its locations. The following network shows the locations of concern (the nodes) and the cost to move a car between locations. A positive number by a node indicates an excess supply at the node, and a negative number indicates an excess demand.

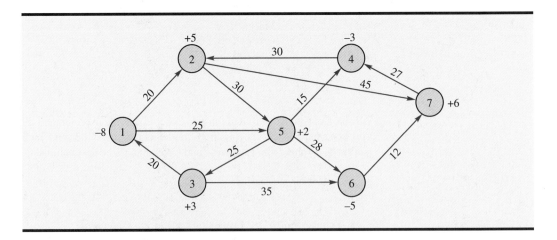

a. Develop a linear programming model of this problem.
b. Solve the model formulated in part (a) to determine how the cars should be redistributed among the locations.

23. Find the shortest route from node 1 to node 7 in the network shown.

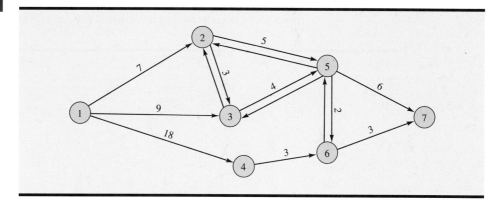

24. In the original Gorman Construction Company problem, we found the shortest distance from the office (node 1) to the construction site located at node 6. Because some of the roads are highways and others are city streets, the shortest-distance routes between the office and the construction site may not necessarily provide the quickest or shortest-time route. Shown here is the Gorman road network with travel time rather than distance. Find the shortest route from Gorman's office to the construction site at node 6 if the objective is to minimize travel time rather than distance.

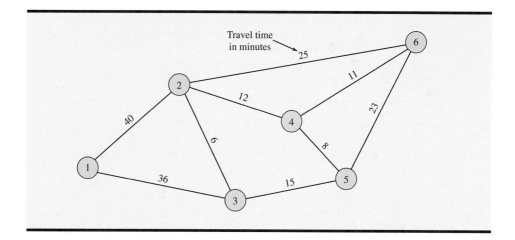

25. CARD, Cleveland Area Rapid Delivery, operates a delivery service in the Cleveland metropolitan area. Most of CARD's business involves rapid delivery of documents and parcels between offices during the business day. CARD promotes its ability to make fast and on-time deliveries anywhere in the metropolitan area. When a customer calls with a delivery request, CARD quotes a guaranteed delivery time. The following network shows the street routes available. The numbers above each arc indicate the travel time in minutes between the two locations.

   a. Develop a linear programming model that can be used to find the minimum time required to make a delivery from location 1 to location 6.

   b. How long does it take to make a delivery from location 1 to location 6?

c. Assume that it is now 1:00 P.M. CARD just received a request for a pickup at location 1, and the closest CARD courier is 8 minutes away from location 1. If CARD provides a 20% safety margin in guaranteeing a delivery time, what is the guaranteed delivery time if the package picked up at location 1 is to be delivered to location 6?

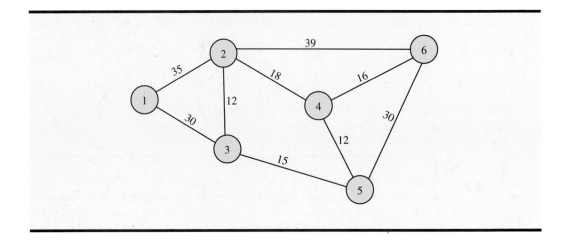

26. Morgan Trucking Company operates a special pickup and delivery service between Chicago and six other cities located in a four-state area. When Morgan receives a request for service, it dispatches a truck from Chicago to the city requesting service as soon as possible. With both fast service and minimum travel costs as objectives for Morgan, it is important that the dispatched truck take the shortest route from Chicago to the specified city. Assume that the following network (not drawn to scale) with distances given in miles represents the highway network for this problem. Find the shortest-route distance from Chicago to node 6.

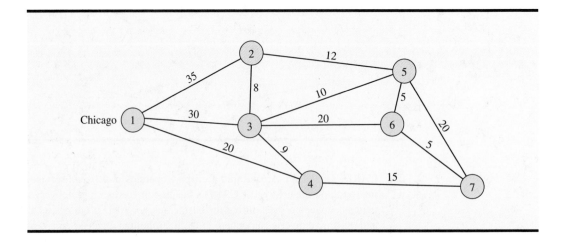

27. City Cab Company identified 10 primary pickup and drop locations for cab riders in New York City. In an effort to minimize travel time and improve customer service and the utilization of the company's fleet of cabs, management would like the cab drivers to take the shortest route between locations whenever possible. Using the following network of roads

and streets, what is the route a driver beginning at location 1 should take to reach location 10? The travel times in minutes are shown on the arcs of the network. Note that there are two one-way streets with the direction shown by the arrows.

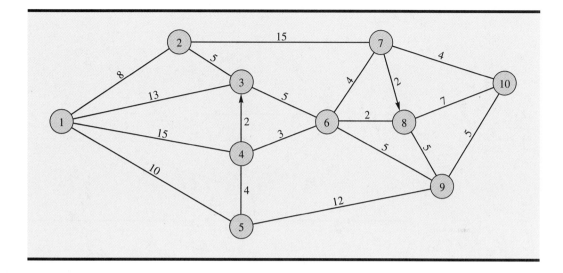

28. The five nodes in the following network represent points one year apart over a four-year period. Each node indicates a time when a decision is made to keep or replace a firm's computer equipment. If a decision is made to replace the equipment, a decision must also be made as to how long the new equipment will be used. The arc from node 0 to node 1 represents the decision to keep the current equipment one year and replace it at the end of the year. The arc from node 0 to node 2 represents the decision to keep the current equipment two years and replace it at the end of year 2. The numbers above the arcs indicate the total cost associated with the equipment replacement decisions. These costs include discounted purchase price, trade-in value, operating costs, and maintenance costs. Use a shortest-route model to determine the minimum cost equipment replacement policy for the four-year period.

29. The north–south highway system passing through Albany, New York, can accommodate the capacities shown:

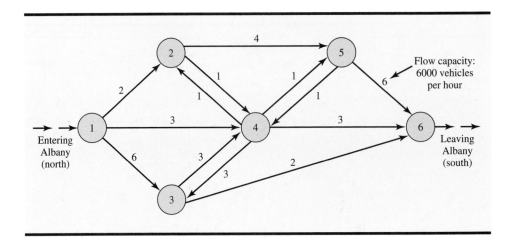

Can the highway system accommodate a north–south flow of 10,000 vehicles per hour?

30. If the Albany highway system described in Problem 29 has revised flow capacities as shown in the following network, what is the maximal flow in vehicles per hour through the system? How many vehicles per hour must travel over each road (arc) to obtain this maximal flow?

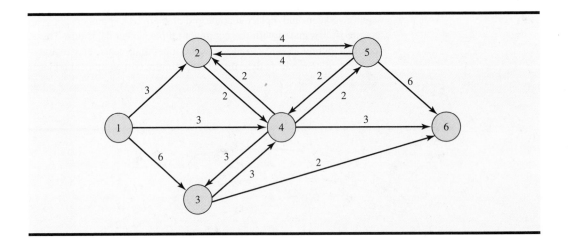

31. A long-distance telephone company uses a fiber-optic network to transmit phone calls and other information between locations. Calls are carried through cable lines and switching nodes. A portion of the company's transmission network is shown here. The numbers above each arc show the capacity in thousands of messages that can be transmitted over that branch of the network.

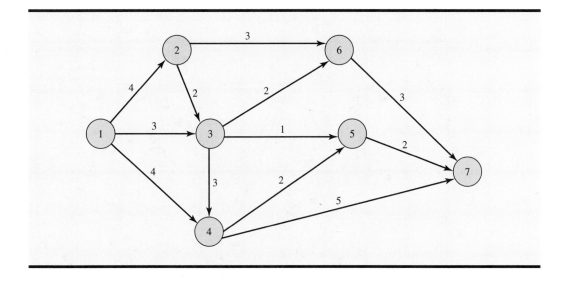

To keep up with the volume of information transmitted between origin and destination points, use the network to determine the maximum number of messages that may be sent from a city located at node 1 to a city located at node 7.

32. The High-Price Oil Company owns a pipeline network that is used to convey oil from its source to several storage locations. A portion of the network is as follows:

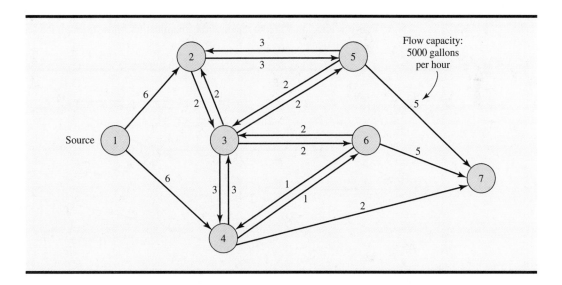

Due to the varying pipe sizes, the flow capacities vary. By selectively opening and closing sections of the pipeline network, the firm can supply any of the storage locations.

a. If the firm wants to fully utilize the system capacity to supply storage location 7, how long will it take to satisfy a location 7 demand of 100,000 gallons? What is the maximal flow for this pipeline system?

b. If a break occurs on line 2–3 and it is closed down, what is the maximal flow for the system? How long will it take to transmit 100,000 gallons to location 7?

33.   For the following highway network system, determine the maximal flow in vehicles per hour.

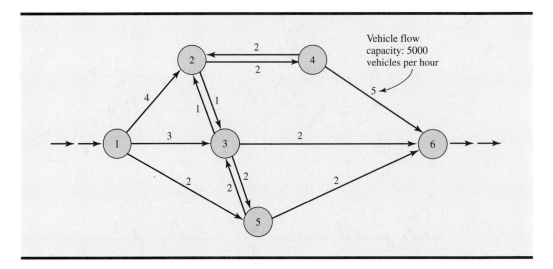

The highway commission is considering adding highway section 3–4 to permit a flow of 2000 vehicles per hour or, at an additional cost, a flow of 3000 vehicles per hour. What is your recommendation for the 3–4 arc of the network?

34.   A chemical processing plant has a network of pipes that are used to transfer liquid chemical products from one part of the plant to another. The following pipe network has pipe flow capacities in gallons per minute as shown. What is the maximum flow capacity for the system if the company wishes to transfer as much liquid chemical as possible from location 1 to location 9? How much of the chemical will flow through the section of pipe from node 3 to node 5?

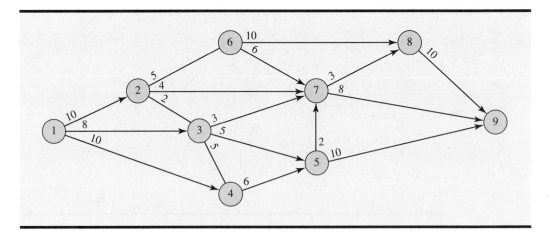

35.   Refer to the Contois Carpets problem for which the network representation is shown in Figure 6.20. Suppose that Contois has a beginning inventory of 50 yards of carpet and requires an inventory of 100 yards at the end of quarter 4.

    a.   Develop a network representation of this modified problem.

    b.   Develop a linear programming model and solve for the optimal solution.

36.   Sanders Fishing Supply of Naples, Florida, manufactures a variety of fishing equipment that it sells throughout the United States. For the next three months, Sanders estimates demand for a particular product at 150, 250, and 300 units, respectively. Sanders can supply this demand by producing on regular time or overtime. Because of other commitments and anticipated cost increases in month 3, the production capacities in units and the production costs per unit are as follows:

Production	Capacity (units)	Cost per Unit
Month 1—Regular	275	$ 50
Month 1—Overtime	100	80
Month 2—Regular	200	50
Month 2—Overtime	50	80
Month 3—Regular	100	60
Month 3—Overtime	50	100

Inventory may be carried from one month to the next, but the cost is $20 per unit per month. For example, regular production from month 1 used to meet demand in month 2 would cost Sanders $50 + $20 = $70 per unit. This same month 1 production used to meet demand in month 3 would cost Sanders $50 + 2($20) = $90 per unit.

a. Develop a network representation of this production scheduling problem as a transportation problem. (*Hint:* Use six origin nodes; the supply for origin node 1 is the maximum that can be produced in month 1 on regular time, and so on.)

b. Develop a linear programming model that can be used to schedule regular and overtime production for each of the three months.

c. What is the production schedule, how many units are carried in inventory each month, and what is the total cost?

d. Is there any unused production capacity? If so, where?

Case Problem 1   SOLUTIONS PLUS

Solutions Plus is an industrial chemicals company that produces specialized cleaning fluids and solvents for a wide variety of applications. Solutions Plus just received an invitation to submit a bid to supply Great North American railroad with a cleaning fluid for locomotives. Great North American needs the cleaning fluid at 11 locations (railway stations); it provided the following information to Solutions Plus regarding the number of gallons of cleaning fluid required at each location (see Table 6.8):

Solutions Plus can produce the cleaning fluid at its Cincinnati plant for $1.20 per gallon. Even though the Cincinnati location is its only plant, Solutions Plus has negotiated with an industrial chemicals company located in Oakland, California, to produce and ship up to 50,000 gallons of the locomotive cleaning fluid to selected Solutions Plus customer locations. The Oakland company will charge Solutions Plus $1.65 per gallon to produce the cleaning fluid, but Solutions Plus thinks that the lower shipping costs from Oakland to some customer locations may offset the added cost to produce the product.

TABLE 6.8   GALLONS OF CLEANING FLUID REQUIRED AT EACH LOCATION

Location	Gallons Required	Location	Gallons Required
Santa Ana	22,418	Glendale	33,689
El Paso	6,800	Jacksonville	68,486
Pendleton	80,290	Little Rock	148,586
Houston	100,447	Bridgeport	111,475
Kansas City	241,570	Sacramento	112,000
Los Angeles	64,761		

TABLE 6.9   FREIGHT COST ($ PER GALLON)

	Cincinnati	Oakland
Santa Ana	—	0.22
El Paso	0.84	0.74
Pendleton	0.83	0.49
Houston	0.45	—
Kansas City	0.36	—
Los Angeles	—	0.22
Glendale	—	0.22
Jacksonville	0.34	—
Little Rock	0.34	—
Bridgeport	0.34	—
Sacramento	—	0.15

The president of Solutions Plus, Charlie Weaver, contacted several trucking companies to negotiate shipping rates between the two production facilities (Cincinnati and Oakland) and the locations where the railroad locomotives are cleaned. Table 6.9 shows the quotes received in terms of dollars per gallon. The — entries in Table 6.9 identify shipping routes that will not be considered because of the large distances involved. These quotes for shipping rates are guaranteed for one year.

To submit a bid to the railroad company, Solutions Plus must determine the price per gallon they will charge. Solutions Plus usually sells its cleaning fluids for 15% more than its cost to produce and deliver the product. For this big contract, however, Fred Roedel, the director of marketing, suggested that maybe the company should consider a smaller profit margin. In addition, to ensure that if Solutions Plus wins the bid, they will have adequate capacity to satisfy existing orders as well as accept orders for other new business, the management team decided to limit the number of gallons of the locomotive cleaning fluid produced in the Cincinnati plant to 500,000 gallons at most.

Managerial Report

You are asked to make recommendations that will help Solutions Plus prepare a bid. Your report should address, but not be limited to, the following issues:

1. If Solutions Plus wins the bid, which production facility (Cincinnati or Oakland) should supply the cleaning fluid to the locations where the railroad locomotives are cleaned? How much should be shipped from each facility to each location?
2. What is the breakeven point for Solutions Plus? That is, how low can the company go on its bid without losing money?
3. If Solutions Plus wants to use its standard 15% markup, how much should it bid?
4. Freight costs are significantly affected by the price of oil. The contract on which Solutions Plus is bidding is for two years. Discuss how fluctuation in freight costs might affect the bid Solutions Plus submits.

Case Problem 2   DISTRIBUTION SYSTEM DESIGN

The Darby Company manufactures and distributes meters used to measure electric power consumption. The company started with a small production plant in El Paso and gradually built a customer base throughout Texas. A distribution center was established in Fort

TABLE 6.10   SHIPPING COST PER UNIT FROM PRODUCTION PLANTS TO
DISTRIBUTION CENTERS (IN $)

	Distribution Center		
Plant	**Fort Worth**	**Santa Fe**	**Las Vegas**
El Paso	3.20	2.20	4.20
San Bernardino	—	3.90	1.20

Worth, Texas, and later, as business expanded, a second distribution center was established in Santa Fe, New Mexico.

The El Paso plant was expanded when the company began marketing its meters in Arizona, California, Nevada, and Utah. With the growth of the West Coast business, the Darby Company opened a third distribution center in Las Vegas and just two years ago opened a second production plant in San Bernardino, California.

Manufacturing costs differ between the company's production plants. The cost of each meter produced at the El Paso plant is $10.50. The San Bernardino plant utilizes newer and more efficient equipment; as a result, manufacturing costs are $0.50 per meter less than at the El Paso plant.

Due to the company's rapid growth, not much attention had been paid to the efficiency of the distribution system, but Darby's management decided that it is time to address this issue. The cost of shipping a meter from each of the two plants to each of the three distribution centers is shown in Table 6.10.

The quarterly production capacity is 30,000 meters at the older El Paso plant and 20,000 meters at the San Bernardino plant. Note that no shipments are allowed from the San Bernardino plant to the Fort Worth distribution center.

The company serves nine customer zones from the three distribution centers. The forecast of the number of meters needed in each customer zone for the next quarter is shown in Table 6.11.

The cost per unit of shipping from each distribution center to each customer zone is given in Table 6.12; note that some distribution centers cannot serve certain customer zones.

In the current distribution system, demand at the Dallas, San Antonio, Wichita, and Kansas City customer zones is satisfied by shipments from the Fort Worth distribution center. In a similar manner, the Denver, Salt Lake City, and Phoenix customer zones are served by the Santa Fe distribution center, and the Los Angeles and San Diego customer zones are

TABLE 6.11   QUARTERLY DEMAND FORECAST

Customer Zone	Demand (meters)
Dallas	6300
San Antonio	4880
Wichita	2130
Kansas City	1210
Denver	6120
Salt Lake City	4830
Phoenix	2750
Los Angeles	8580
San Diego	4460

TABLE 6.12   SHIPPING COST FROM THE DISTRIBUTION CENTERS TO THE CUSTOMER ZONES

Distribution Center	Customer Zone								
	Dallas	San Antonio	Wichita	Kansas City	Denver	Salt Lake City	Phoenix	Los Angeles	San Diego
Fort Worth	0.3	2.1	3.1	4.4	6.0	—	—	—	—
Santa Fe	5.2	5.4	4.5	6.0	2.7	4.7	3.4	3.3	2.7
Las Vegas	—	—	—	—	5.4	3.3	2.4	2.1	2.5

served by the Las Vegas distribution center. To determine how many units to ship from each plant, the quarterly customer demand forecasts are aggregated at the distribution centers, and a transportation model is used to minimize the cost of shipping from the production plants to the distribution centers.

Managerial Report

You are asked to make recommendations for improving the distribution system. Your report should address, but not be limited to, the following issues:

1. If the company does not change its current distribution strategy, what will its distribution costs be for the following quarter?
2. Suppose that the company is willing to consider dropping the distribution center limitations; that is, customers could be served by any of the distribution centers for which costs are available. Can costs be reduced? By how much?
3. The company wants to explore the possibility of satisfying some of the customer demand directly from the production plants. In particular, the shipping cost is $0.30 per unit from San Bernardino to Los Angeles and $0.70 from San Bernardino to San Diego. The cost for direct shipments from El Paso to San Antonio is $3.50 per unit. Can distribution costs be further reduced by considering these direct plant-to-customer shipments?
4. Over the next five years, Darby is anticipating moderate growth (5000 meters) to the North and West. Would you recommend that they consider plant expansion at this time?

Appendix 6.1   EXCEL SOLUTION OF TRANSPORTATION, ASSIGNMENT, AND TRANSSHIPMENT PROBLEMS

In this appendix we will use an Excel Worksheet to solve transportation, assignment, and transshipment problems. We start with the Foster Generators transportation problem (see Section 6.1).

Transportation Problem

The first step is to enter the data for the transportation costs, the origin supplies, and the destination demands in the top portion of the worksheet. Then the linear programming model is developed in the bottom portion of the worksheet. As with all linear programs, the worksheet model has four key elements: the decision variables, the objective function, the constraint left-hand sides, and the constraint right-hand sides. For a transportation problem, the decision variables are the amounts shipped from each origin to each destination; the

FIGURE 6.22   EXCEL SOLUTION OF THE FOSTER GENERATORS PROBLEM

	A	B	C	D	E	F	G	H
1	Foster Generators							
2								
3				Destination				
4	Origin	Boston	Chicago	St. Louis	Lexington	Supply		
5	Cleveland	3	2	7	6	5000		
6	Bedford	7	5	2	3	6000		
7	York	2	5	4	5	2500		
8	Demand	6000	4000	2000	1500			
9								
10								
11	Model							
12								
13		Min Cost	39500					
14								
15				Destination				
16	Origin	Boston	Chicago	St. Louis	Lexington	Total		
17	Cleveland	3500	1500	0	0	5000	<=	5000
18	Bedford	0	2500	2000	1500	6000	<=	6000
19	York	2500	0	0	0	2500	<=	2500
20	Total	6000	4000	2000	1500			
21		=	=	=	=			
22		6000	4000	2000	1500			

WEB **file**

Foster

objective function is the total transportation cost; the left-hand sides are the number of units shipped from each origin and the number of units shipped into each destination; and the right-hand sides are the origin supplies and the destination demands.

The formulation and solution of the Foster Generators problem are shown in Figure 6.22. The data are in the top portion of the worksheet. The model appears in the bottom portion of the worksheet; the key elements are screened.

Formulation

The data and descriptive labels are contained in cells A1:F8. The transportation costs are in cells B5:E7. The origin supplies are in cells F5:F7, and the destination demands are in cells B8:E8. The key elements of the model required by the Excel Solver are the decision variables, the objective function, the constraint left-hand sides, and the constraint right-hand sides. These cells are screened in the bottom portion of the worksheet.

Decision Variables   Cells B17:E19 are reserved for the decision variables. The optimal values are shown to be $x_{11} = 3500$, $x_{12} = 1500$, $x_{22} = 2500$, $x_{23} = 2000$, $x_{24} = 1500$, and $x_{41} = 2500$. All other decision variables equal zero, indicating nothing will be shipped over the corresponding routes.

Objective Function   The formula=SUMPRODUCT(B5:E7,B17:E19) has been placed into cell C13 to compute the cost of the solution. The minimum cost solution is shown to have a value of $39,500.

Left-Hand Sides   Cells F17:F19 contain the left-hand sides for the supply constraints, and cells B20:E20 contain the left-hand sides for the demand constraints.
        Cell F17 = SUM(B17:E17) (Copy to F18:F19)
        Cell B20 = SUM(B17:B19) (Copy to C20:E20)

FIGURE 6.23   SOLVER PARAMETERS DIALOG BOX FOR THE FOSTER
                 GENERATORS PROBLEM

Right-Hand Sides   Cells H17:H19 contain the right-hand sides for the supply constraints and Cells B22:E22 contain the right-hand sides for the demand constraints.

         Cell H17 = F5 (Copy to H18:H19)
         Cell B22 = B8 (Copy to C22:E22)

Excel Solution

The solution shown in Figure 6.22 can be obtained by selecting **Solver** from the **Analysis** group under the **Data** tab, entering the proper values into the **Solver Parameters** dialog box, and specifying the options, **Assume Linear Model** and **Assume Non-Negative.** Then click **Solve.** The information entered into the **Solver Parameters** dialog box is shown in Figure 6.23.

Assignment Problem

The first step is to enter the data for the assignment costs in the top portion of the worksheet. Even though the assignment model is a special case of the transportation model, it is not necessary to enter values for origin supplies and destination demands because they are always equal to one.

     The linear programming model is developed in the bottom portion of the worksheet. As with all linear programs the model has four key elements: the decision variables, the objective function, the constraint left-hand sides, and the constraint right-hand sides. For an assignment problem, the decision variables indicate whether an agent is assigned to a task (with a 1 for yes or 0 for no); the objective function is the total cost of all assignments; the constraint left-hand sides are the number of tasks that are assigned to each agent and the number of agents that are assigned to each task; and the right-hand sides are the number of tasks each agent can handle (1) and the number of agents each task requires (1). The worksheet formulation and solution for the Fowle Marketing Research Problem are shown in Figure 6.24.

FIGURE 6.24   EXCEL SOLUTION OF THE FOWLE MARKETING RESEARCH PROBLEM

WEB file

Fowle

	A	B	C	D	E	F	G
1	**Fowle Marketing Research**						
2							
3			**Client**				
4	**Project Leader**	1	2	3			
5	Terry	10	15	9			
6	Carle	9	18	5			
7	McClymonds	6	14	3			
8							
9							
10	**Model**						
11							
12		**Min Time**	26				
13							
14			**Client**				
15	**Project Leader**	1	2	3	**Total**		
16	Terry	0	1	0	1	<=	1
17	Carle	0	0	1	1	<=	1
18	McClymonds	1	0	0	1	<=	1
19	**Total**	1	1	1			
20		=	=	=			
21		1	1	1			

Formulation

The data and descriptive labels are contained in cells A1:D7. Note that we have not inserted supply and demand values because they are always equal to 1 in an assignment problem. The model appears in the bottom portion of the worksheet with the key elements screened.

Decision Variables
: Cells B16:D18 are reserved for the decision variables. The optimal values are shown to be $x_{12} = 1$, $x_{23} = 1$, and $x_{31} = 1$ with all other variables = 0.

Objective Function
: The formula =SUMPRODUCT(B5:D7,B16:D18) has been placed into cell C12 to compute the number of days required to complete all the jobs. The minimum time solution has a value of 26 days.

Left-Hand Sides
: Cells E16:E18 contain the left-hand sides of the constraints for the number of clients each project leader can handle. Cells B19:D19 contain the left-hand sides of the constraints requiring that each client must be assigned a project leader.
:   Cell E16 = SUM(B16:D16) (Copy to E17:E18)
:   Cell B19 = SUM(B16:B18) (Copy to C19:D19)

Right-Hand Sides
: Cells G16:G18 contain the right-hand sides for the project leader constraints and cells B21:D21 contain the right-hand sides for the client constraints. All right-hand side cell values are 1.

FIGURE 6.25   SOLVER PARAMETERS DIALOG BOX FOR THE FOWLE MARKETING
RESEARCH PROBLEM

Excel Solution

The solution shown in Figure 6.24 can be obtained by selecting **Solver** from the **Analysis** group under the **Data** tab, entering the proper values into the **Solver Parameters** dialog box, and specifying the options **Assume Linear Model** and **Assume Non-Negative.** Then click **Solve.** The information entered into the **Solver Parameters** dialog box is shown in Figure 6.25.

Transshipment Problem

The worksheet model we present for the transshipment problem can be used for all the network flow problems (transportation, assignment, and transshipment) in this chapter. We organize the worksheet into two sections: an arc section and a node section. Let us illustrate by showing the worksheet formulation and solution of the Ryan Electronics transshipment problem. Refer to Figure 6.26 as we describe the steps involved. The key elements are screened.

Formulation

The arc section uses cells A3:D16. For each arc, the start node and end node are identified in cells A5:B16. The arc costs are identified in cells C5:C16, and cells D5:D16 are reserved for the values of the decision variables (the amount shipped over the arcs).

The node section uses cells F5:K14. Each of the nodes is identified in cells F7:F14. The following formulas are entered into cells G7:H14 to represent the flow out and the flow in for each node:

Units shipped in: Cell G9   =D5+D7
                     Cell G10   =D6+D8
                     Cell G11   =D9+D13
                     Cell G12   =D10+D14

FIGURE 6.26   EXCEL SOLUTION FOR THE RYAN ELECTRONICS PROBLEM

Ryan

	A	B	C	D	E	F	G	H	I	J	K
1	**Ryan Electronics Transshipment**										
2											
3		**Arc**		**Units**							
4	Start Node	End Node	Cost	Shipped							
5	Denver	Kansas City	2	550			**Units Shipped**		**Net**		
6	Denver	Louisville	3	50		**Node**	In	Out	**Shipments**		**Supply**
7	Atlanta	Kansas City	3	0		Denver		600	600	<=	600
8	Atlanta	Louisville	1	400		Atlanta		400	400	<=	400
9	Kansas City	Detroit	2	200		Kansas City	550	550	0	=	0
10	Kansas City	Miami	6	0		Louisville	450	450	0	=	0
11	Kansas City	Dallas	3	350		Detroit	200		-200	=	-200
12	Kansas City	New Orleans	6	0		Miami	150		-150	=	-150
13	Louisville	Detroit	4	0		Dallas	350		-350	=	-350
14	Louisville	Miami	4	150		New Orleans	300		-300	=	-300
15	Louisville	Dallas	6	0							
16	Louisville	New Orleans	5	300							
17											
18								**Total Cost**	5200		

$$
\begin{array}{lll}
\text{Cell G13} & =\text{D11+D15} \\
\text{Cell G14} & =\text{D12+D16}
\end{array}
$$

Units shipped out:
$$
\begin{array}{lll}
\text{Cell H7} & =\text{SUM(D5:D6)} \\
\text{Cell H8} & =\text{SUM(D7:D8)} \\
\text{Cell H9} & =\text{SUM(D9:D12)} \\
\text{Cell H10} & =\text{SUM(D13:D16)}
\end{array}
$$

The net shipments in cells I7:I14 are the flows out minus the flows in for each node. For supply nodes, the flow out will exceed the flow in, resulting in positive net shipments. For demand nodes, the flow out will be less than the flow in, resulting in negative net shipments. The "net" supply appears in cells K7:K14. Note that the net supply is negative for demand nodes.

As in previous worksheet formulations, we screened the key elements required by the Excel Solver.

Decision Variables
Cells D5:D16 are reserved for the decision variables. The optimal number of units to ship over each arc is shown.

Objective Function
The formula =SUMPRODUCT(C5:C16,D5:D16) is placed into cell I18 to show the total cost associated with the solution. As shown, the minimum total cost is $5200.

Left-Hand Sides
The left-hand sides of the constraints represent the net shipments for each node. Cells I7:I14 are reserved for these constraints.
Cell I7   = H7-G7   (Copy to I8:I14)

Right-Hand Sides
The right-hand sides of the constraints represent the supply at each node. Cells K7:K14 are reserved for these values. (Note the negative supply at the four demand nodes.)

FIGURE 6.27   SOLVER PARAMETERS DIALOG BOX FOR THE RYAN
                   ELECTRONICS PROBLEM

Excel Solution

The solution can be obtained by selecting **Solver** from the **Analysis** group under the **Data** tab, entering the proper values into the **Solver Parameters** dialog box, and specifying the options **Assume Linear Model** and **Assume Non-Negative.** Then click **Solve.** The information entered into the **Solver Parameters** dialog box is shown in Figure 6.27.

CHAPTER 7

Integer Linear Programming

CONTENTS

7.1 TYPES OF INTEGER LINEAR PROGRAMMING MODELS

7.2 GRAPHICAL AND COMPUTER SOLUTIONS FOR AN ALL-INTEGER LINEAR PROGRAM
Graphical Solution of the LP Relaxation
Rounding to Obtain an Integer Solution
Graphical Solution of the All-Integer Problem
Using the LP Relaxation to Establish Bounds
Computer Solution

7.3 APPLICATIONS INVOLVING 0-1 VARIABLES
Capital Budgeting
Fixed Cost

Distribution System Design
Bank Location
Product Design and Market Share Optimization

7.4 MODELING FLEXIBILITY PROVIDED BY 0-1 INTEGER VARIABLES
Multiple-Choice and Mutually Exclusive Constraints
k out of n Alternatives Constraint
Conditional and Corequisite Constraints
A Cautionary Note About Sensitivity Analysis

In this chapter we discuss a class of problems that are modeled as linear programs with the additional requirement that one or more variables must be integer. Such problems are called **integer linear programs.** If all variables must be integer, we have an all-integer linear program. If some, but not all, variables must be integer, we have a mixed-integer linear program. In many applications of integer linear programming, one or more integer variables are required to equal either 0 or 1. Such variables are called 0-1 or *binary variables.* If all variables are 0-1 variables, we have a 0-1 integer linear program.

Integer variables—especially 0-1 variables—provide substantial modeling flexibility. As a result, the number of applications that can be addressed with linear programming methodology is expanded. For instance, the Management Science in Action, Crew Scheduling at Air New Zealand, describes how that airline company employs 0-1 integer programming models to schedule its pilots and flight attendants. Later Management Science in Actions describe how Valley Metal Containers uses a mixed-integer program for scheduling aluminum can production for Coors beer, and how the modeling flexibility provided by 0-1 variables helped Ketron build a customer order allocation model for a sporting goods company. Many other applications of integer programming are described throughout the chapter.

The objective of this chapter is to provide an applications-oriented introduction to integer linear programming. First, we discuss the different types of integer linear programming models. Then we show the formulation, graphical solution, and computer solution of an all-integer linear program. In Section 7.3 we discuss five applications of integer linear programming that make use of 0-1 variables: capital budgeting, fixed cost, distribution system design, bank location, and market share optimization problems. In Section 7.4 we provide additional illustrations of the modeling flexibility provided by 0-1 variables. Chapter appendices illustrate the use of Excel and LINGO for solving integer programs.

Information about open-source software can be found at the COIN-OR foundation website.

The cost of the added modeling flexibility provided by integer programming is that problems involving integer variables are often much more difficult to solve. A linear programming problem with several thousand continuous variables can be solved with any of several commercial linear programming solvers. However, an all-integer linear programming problem with fewer than 100 variables can be extremely difficult to solve. Experienced management scientists can help identify the types of integer linear programs that are easy, or at least reasonable, to solve. Commercial computer software packages, such as LINGO, CPLEX, Xpress-MP, and the commercial version of Solver have extensive integer programming capability, and very robust open-source software packages for integer programming are also available.

MANAGEMENT SCIENCE IN ACTION

CREW SCHEDULING AT AIR NEW ZEALAND*

As noted in Chapter 1, airlines make extensive use of management science (see Management Science in Action, Revenue Management at American Airlines). Air New Zealand is the largest national and international airline based in New Zealand. Over the past 15 years, Air New Zealand developed integer programming models for crew scheduling.

Air New Zealand finalizes flight schedules at least 12 weeks in advance of when the flights are to take place. At that point the process of assigning crews to implement the flight schedule begins. The crew-scheduling problem involves staffing the flight schedule with pilots and flight attendants. It is solved in two phases. In the first phase, tours of duty (ToD) are generated that will permit constructing sequences of flights for pilots and flight attendants that will allow the airline's flight schedule to be implemented. A tour of duty is a one-day or multiday alternating sequence of duty periods (flight legs, training, etc.) and rest periods (layovers). In the ToD problem, no consideration is given to which individual crew members will perform the tours of duty. In the second phase, individual crew members are assigned to the tours of duty, which is called the rostering problem.

Air New Zealand employs integer programming models to solve both the ToD problem and the rostering problem. In the integer programming model of the ToD problem, each variable is a 0-1 variable that corresponds to a possible tour of duty that could be flown by a crew member (e.g., pilot or flight attendant). Each constraint corresponds to a particular flight and ensures that the flight is included in exactly one tour of duty. The cost of variable *j* reflects the cost of operating the *j*th tour of duty, and the objective is to minimize total cost. Air New Zealand solves a separate ToD problem for each crew type (pilot type or flight attendant type).

In the rostering problem, the tours of duty from the solution to the ToD problem are used to construct lines of work (LoW) for each crew member. In the integer programming model of the rostering problem, a 0-1 variable represents the possible LoWs for each crew member. A separate constraint for each crew member guarantees that

each will be assigned a single LoW. Other constraints correspond to the ToDs that must be covered by any feasible solution to the rostering problem.

The crew-scheduling optimizers developed by Air New Zealand showed a significant impact on profitability. Over the 15 years it took to develop these systems, the estimated development costs were approximately NZ$2 million. The estimated savings are NZ$15.6 million per year. In 1999 the savings from employing these integer programming models represented 11% of Air New Zealand's net operating profit. In addition to the direct dollar savings, the optimization systems provided many intangible benefits such as higher-quality solutions in less time, less dependence on a small number of highly skilled schedulers, flexibility to accommodate small changes in the schedule, and a guarantee that the airline satisfies legislative and contractual rules.

*Based on E. Rod Butchers et al., "Optimized Crew Scheduling at Air New Zealand," *Interfaces* (January/February 2001): 30–56.

NOTES AND COMMENTS

1. Because integer linear programs are harder to solve than linear programs, one should not try to solve a problem as an integer program if simply rounding the linear programming solution is adequate. In many linear programming problems, such as those in previous chapters, rounding has little economic consequence on the objective function, and feasibility is not an issue. But, in problems such as determining how many jet engines to manufacture, the consequences of rounding can be substantial and integer programming methodology should be employed.

2. Some linear programming problems have a special structure, which guarantees that the variables will have integer values. The assignment, transportation, and transshipment problems of Chapter 6 have such structures. If the supply and the demand for transportation and transshipment problems are integer, the optimal linear programming solution will provide integer amounts shipped. For the assignment problem, the optimal linear programming solution will consist of 0s and 1s. So, for these specially structured problems, linear programming methodology can be used to find optimal integer solutions. Integer linear programming algorithms are not necessary.

7.1   TYPES OF INTEGER LINEAR PROGRAMMING MODELS

The only difference between the problems studied in this chapter and the ones studied in earlier chapters on linear programming is that one or more variables are required to be integer. If all variables are required to be integer, we have an **all-integer linear program.** The following is a two-variable, all-integer linear programming model:

$$\text{Max} \quad 2x_1 + 3x_2$$
$$\text{s.t.}$$
$$3x_1 + 3x_2 \leq 12$$
$$\tfrac{2}{3}x_1 + 1x_2 \leq 4$$
$$1x_1 + 2x_2 \leq 6$$
$$x_1, x_2 \geq 0 \text{ and integer}$$

If we drop the phrase "and integer" from the last line of this model, we have the familiar two-variable linear program. The linear program that results from dropping the integer requirements is called the **LP Relaxation** of the integer linear program.

If some, but not necessarily all, variables are required to be integer, we have a **mixed-integer linear program.** The following is a two-variable, mixed-integer linear program:

$$\text{Max} \quad 3x_1 + 4x_2$$
$$\text{s.t.}$$
$$-1x_1 + 2x_2 \leq 8$$
$$1x_1 + 2x_2 \leq 12$$
$$2x_1 + 1x_2 \leq 16$$
$$x_1, x_2 \geq 0 \text{ and } x_2 \text{ integer}$$

We obtain the LP Relaxation of this mixed-integer linear program by dropping the requirement that x_2 be integer.

In some applications, the integer variables may only take on the values 0 or 1. Then we have a **0-1 linear integer program.** As we see later in the chapter, 0-1 variables provide additional modeling capability. The Management Science in Action, Aluminum Can Production at Valley Metal Container, describes how a mixed-integer linear program involving 0-1 integer variables is used to schedule production of aluminum beer cans for Coors breweries. The 0-1 variables are used to model production line changeovers; the continuous variables model production quantities.

MANAGEMENT SCIENCE IN ACTION

ALUMINUM CAN PRODUCTION AT VALLEY METAL CONTAINER*

Valley Metal Container (VMC) produces cans for the seven brands of beer produced by the Coors breweries: Coors Extra Gold, Coors Light, Coors Original, Keystone Ale, Keystone Ice, Keystone Light, and Keystone Premium. VMC produces these cans on six production lines and stores them in three separate inventory storage areas from which they are shipped on to the Coors breweries in Golden, Colorado; Memphis, Tennessee; and Shenandoah, Virginia.

Two important issues face production scheduling at the VMC facility. First, each time a production line must be changed over from producing one type of can to another (label change), it takes time to get the color just right for the new label. As a result, downtime is incurred and scrap is generated.

Second, proper scheduling can reduce the amount of inventory that must be transferred from long-term to short-term storage. Thus, two costs are critical in determining the best production schedule at the VMC facility: the label-change cost and the cost of transferring inventory from one type of storage to another. To determine a production schedule that will minimize these two costs, VMC developed a mixed-integer linear programming model of its production process.

The model's objective function calls for minimizing the sum of the weekly cost of changing labels and the cost of transferring inventory from long-term to short-term storage. Binary (0-1) variables are used to represent a label change in the production process. Continuous variables are used to represent the size of the production run for each type of label on each line during each shift; analogous variables are used to represent inventories for each type of can produced. Additional continuous variables are used to represent the amount of inventory transferred to short-term storage during the week.

The VMC production scheduling problem is solved weekly using a personal computer. Excel worksheets are used for input data preparation and for storing the output report. The GAMS mathe- matical programming system is used to solve the mixed-integer linear program. Susan Schultz, manager of Logistics for Coors Container Operations, reports that using the system resulted in documented annual savings of $169,230.

*Based on Elena Katok and Dennis Ott, "Using Mixed- Integer Programming to Reduce Label Changes in the Coors Aluminum Can Plant," *Interfaces* (March/April 2000): 1–12.

7.2   GRAPHICAL AND COMPUTER SOLUTIONS FOR AN ALL-INTEGER LINEAR PROGRAM

Eastborne Realty has $2 million available for the purchase of new rental property. After an initial screening, Eastborne reduced the investment alternatives to townhouses and apartment buildings. Each townhouse can be purchased for $282,000, and five are available. Each apartment building can be purchased for $400,000, and the developer will construct as many buildings as Eastborne wants to purchase.

Eastborne's property manager can devote up to 140 hours per month to these new properties; each townhouse is expected to require 4 hours per month, and each apartment building is expected to require 40 hours per month. The annual cash flow, after deducting mortgage payments and operating expenses, is estimated to be $10,000 per townhouse and $15,000 per apartment building. Eastborne's owner would like to determine the number of townhouses and the number of apartment buildings to purchase to maximize annual cash flow.

We begin by defining the decision variables as follows:

$$T = \text{number of townhouses}$$
$$A = \text{number of apartment buildings}$$

The objective function for cash flow ($1000s) is

$$\text{Max} \quad 10T + 15A$$

Three constraints must be satisfied:

$$
\begin{array}{llll}
282T & + & 400A \le 2000 & \text{Funds available (\$1000s)} \\
4T & + & 40A \le 140 & \text{Manager's time (hours)} \\
T & & \le 5 & \text{Townhouses available}
\end{array}
$$

The variables T and A must be nonnegative. In addition, the purchase of a fractional number of townhouses and/or a fractional number of apartment buildings is unacceptable. Thus, T and A must be integer. The model for the Eastborne Realty problem is the following all-integer linear program:

$$
\begin{array}{l}
\text{Max} \quad 10T + 15A \\
\text{s.t.} \\
\qquad 282T + 400A \le 2000 \\
\qquad \quad 4T + 40A \le 140 \\
\qquad \quad T \qquad \le 5 \\
\qquad \quad T, A \ge 0 \text{ and integer}
\end{array}
$$

FIGURE 7.1   GRAPHICAL SOLUTION TO THE LP RELAXATION OF THE EASTBORNE REALTY PROBLEM

Graphical Solution of the LP Relaxation

Suppose that we drop the integer requirements for T and A and solve the LP Relaxation of the Eastborne Realty problem. Using the graphical solution procedure, as presented in Chapter 2, the optimal linear programming solution is shown in Figure 7.1. It is $T = 2.479$ townhouses and $A = 3.252$ apartment buildings. The optimal value of the objective function is 73.574, which indicates an annual cash flow of $73,574. Unfortunately, Eastborne cannot purchase fractional numbers of townhouses and apartment buildings; further analysis is necessary.

Rounding to Obtain an Integer Solution

In many cases, a noninteger solution can be rounded to obtain an acceptable integer solution. For instance, a linear programming solution to a production scheduling problem might call for the production of 15,132.4 cases of breakfast cereal. The rounded integer solution of 15,132 cases would probably have minimal impact on the value of the objective function and the feasibility of the solution. Rounding would be a sensible approach. Indeed, whenever rounding has a minimal impact on the objective function and constraints, most managers find it acceptable. A near-optimal solution is fine.

However, rounding may not always be a good strategy. When the decision variables take on small values that have a major impact on the value of the objective function or feasibility, an optimal integer solution is needed. Let us return to the Eastborne Realty problem and examine the impact of rounding. The optimal solution to the LP Relaxation for Eastborne Realty resulted in $T = 2.479$ townhouses and $A = 3.252$ apartment buildings. Because each townhouse costs \$282,000 and each apartment building costs \$400,000, rounding to an integer solution can be expected to have a significant economic impact on the problem.

If a problem has only less-than-or-equal-to constraints with nonnegative coefficients for the variables, rounding down will always provide a feasible integer solution.

Suppose that we round the solution to the LP Relaxation to obtain the integer solution $T = 2$ and $A = 3$, with an objective function value of $10(2) + 15(3) = 65$. The annual cash flow of \$65,000 is substantially less than the annual cash flow of \$73,574 provided by the solution to the LP Relaxation. Do other rounding possibilities exist? Exploring other rounding alternatives shows that the integer solution $T = 3$ and $A = 3$ is infeasible because it requires more funds than the \$2,000,000 Eastborne has available. The rounded solution of $T = 2$ and $A = 4$ is also infeasible for the same reason. At this point, rounding has led to two townhouses and three apartment buildings with an annual cash flow of \$65,000 as the best feasible integer solution to the problem. Unfortunately, we don't know whether this solution is the best integer solution to the problem.

Rounding to an integer solution is a trial-and-error approach. Each rounded solution must be evaluated for feasibility as well as for its impact on the value of the objective function. Even in cases where a rounded solution is feasible, we do not have a guarantee that we have found the optimal integer solution. We will see shortly that the rounded solution ($T = 2$ and $A = 3$) is not optimal for Eastborne Realty.

Graphical Solution of the All-Integer Problem

Try Problem 2 for practice with the graphical solution of an integer program.

Figure 7.2 shows the changes in the linear programming graphical solution procedure required to solve the Eastborne Realty integer linear programming problem. First, the graph of the feasible region is drawn exactly as in the LP Relaxation of the problem. Then, because the optimal solution must have integer values, we identify the feasible integer solutions with the dots shown in Figure 7.2. Finally, instead of moving the objective function line to the best extreme point in the feasible region, we move it in an improving direction as far as possible until reaching the dot (feasible integer point) providing the best value for the objective function. Viewing Figure 7.2, we see that the optimal integer solution occurs at $T = 4$ townhouses and $A = 2$ apartment buildings. The objective function value is $10(4) + 15(2) = 70$, providing an annual cash flow of \$70,000. This solution is significantly better than the best solution found by rounding: $T = 2$, $A = 3$, with an annual cash flow of \$65,000. Thus, we see that rounding would not have been the best strategy for Eastborne Realty.

Using the LP Relaxation to Establish Bounds

An important observation can be made from the analysis of the Eastborne Realty problem. It has to do with the relationship between the value of the optimal integer solution and the value of the optimal solution to the LP Relaxation.

For integer linear programs involving maximization, the value of the optimal solution to the LP Relaxation provides an upper bound on the value of the optimal integer solution. For integer linear programs involving minimization, the value of the optimal solution to the LP Relaxation provides a lower bound on the value of the optimal integer solution.

FIGURE 7.2   GRAPHICAL SOLUTION OF THE EASTBORNE REALTY INTEGER PROBLEM

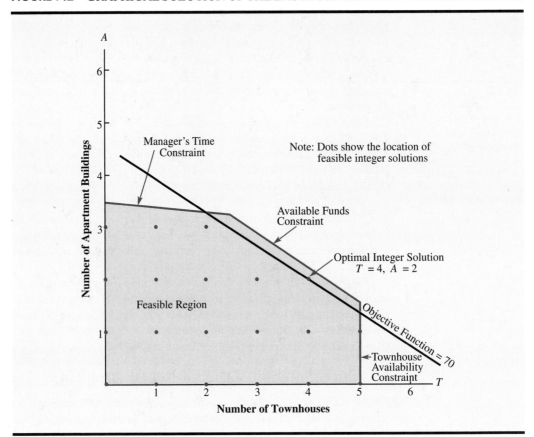

This observation is valid for the Eastborne Realty problem. The value of the optimal integer solution is $70,000, and the value of the optimal solution to the LP Relaxation is $73,574. Thus, we know from the LP Relaxation solution that the upper bound for the value of the objective function is $73,574.

Try Problem 5 for the graphical solution of a mixed-integer program.

The bounding property of the LP Relaxation allows us to conclude that if, by chance, the solution to an LP Relaxation turns out to be an integer solution, it is also optimal for the integer linear program. This bounding property can also be helpful in determining whether a rounded solution is "good enough." If a rounded LP Relaxation solution is feasible and provides a value of the objective function that is "almost as good as" the value of the objective function for the LP Relaxation, we know the rounded solution is a near-optimal integer solution. In this case, we can avoid having to solve the problem as an integer linear program.

Computer Solution

LINGO or Frontline Systems' Solver can be used to solve most of the integer linear programs in this chapter. In the appendices at the end of this chapter, we discuss how to solve integer linear programs using Solver and LINGO.

Specifying both T and A as integers provides the optimal integer solution shown in Figure 7.3. The solution of $T = 4$ townhouses and $A = 2$ apartment buildings has a maximum

FIGURE 7.3 THE SOLUTION FOR THE EASTBORNE REALTY PROBLEM

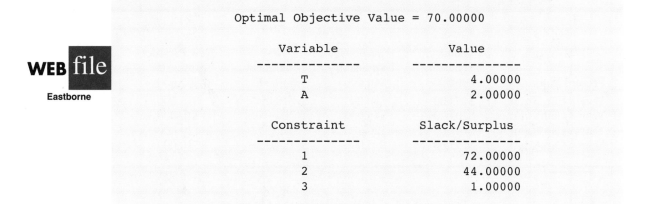

```
          Optimal Objective Value = 70.00000

              Variable              Value
          --------------        --------------
                 T                   4.00000
                 A                   2.00000

              Constraint          Slack/Surplus
          --------------        --------------
                 1                  72.00000
                 2                  44.00000
                 3                   1.00000
```

WEB file

Eastborne

annual cash flow of $70,000. The values of the slack variables tell us that the optimal solution has $72,000 of available funds unused, 44 hours of the manager's time still available, and 1 of the available townhouses not purchased.

NOTES AND COMMENTS

The computer output we show in this chapter for integer programs does not include reduced costs, dual values, or sensitivity ranges because these are not meaningful for integer programs.

7.3 APPLICATIONS INVOLVING 0-1 VARIABLES

Much of the modeling flexibility provided by integer linear programming is due to the use of 0-1 variables. In many applications, 0-1 variables provide selections or choices with the value of the variable equal to 1 if a corresponding activity is undertaken and equal to 0 if the corresponding activity is not undertaken. The capital budgeting, fixed cost, distribution system design, bank location, and product design/market share applications presented in this section make use of 0-1 variables.

Capital Budgeting

The Ice-Cold Refrigerator Company is considering investing in several projects that have varying capital requirements over the next four years. Faced with limited capital each year, management would like to select the most profitable projects. The estimated net present value for each project,[1] the capital requirements, and the available capital over the four-year period are shown in Table 7.1.

---

[1]The estimated net present value is the net cash flow discounted back to the beginning of year 1.

TABLE 7.1   PROJECT NET PRESENT VALUE, CAPITAL REQUIREMENTS, AND AVAILABLE CAPITAL FOR THE ICE-COLD REFRIGERATOR COMPANY

| | Project | | | | |
	Plant Expansion	Warehouse Expansion	New Machinery	New Product Research	Total Capital Available
Present Value	$90,000	$40,000	$10,000	$37,000	
Year 1 Cap Rqmt	$15,000	$10,000	$10,000	$15,000	$40,000
Year 2 Cap Rqmt	$20,000	$15,000		$10,000	$50,000
Year 3 Cap Rqmt	$20,000	$20,000		$10,000	$40,000
Year 4 Cap Rqmt	$15,000	$ 5,000	$ 4,000	$10,000	$35,000

The four 0-1 decision variables are as follows:

$P = 1$ if the plant expansion project is accepted; 0 if rejected
$W = 1$ if the warehouse expansion project is accepted; 0 if rejected
$M = 1$ if the new machinery project is accepted; 0 if rejected
$R = 1$ if the new product research project is accepted; 0 if rejected

In a **capital budgeting problem,** the company's objective function is to maximize the net present value of the capital budgeting projects. This problem has four constraints: one for the funds available in each of the next four years.

A 0-1 integer linear programming model with dollars in thousands is as follows:

$$\text{Max} \quad 90P + 40W + 10M + 37R$$

s.t.

$$15P + 10W + 10M + 15R \leq 40 \quad \text{(Year 1 capital available)}$$
$$20P + 15W + 10R \leq 50 \quad \text{(Year 2 capital available)}$$
$$20P + 20W + 10R \leq 40 \quad \text{(Year 3 capital available)}$$
$$15P + 5W + 4M + 10R \leq 35 \quad \text{(Year 4 capital available)}$$
$$P, W, M, R = 0, 1$$

The integer programming solution is shown in Figure 7.4. The optimal solution is $P = 1$, $W = 1$, $M = 1$, $R = 0$, with a total estimated net present value of $140,000. Thus, the company should fund the plant expansion, the warehouse expansion, and the new machinery projects. The new product research project should be put on hold unless additional capital funds become available. The values of the slack variables (see Figure 7.4) show that the company will have $5,000 remaining in year 1, $15,000 remaining in year 2, and $11,000 remaining in year 4. Checking the capital requirements for the new product research project, we see that enough funds are available for this project in year 2 and year 4. However, the company would have to find additional capital funds of $10,000 in year 1 and $10,000 in year 3 to fund the new product research project.

Fixed Cost

In many applications, the cost of production has two components: a setup cost, which is a fixed cost, and a variable cost, which is directly related to the production quantity. The use of 0-1 variables makes including the setup cost possible in a model for a production application.

FIGURE 7.4   THE SOLUTION FOR THE ICE-COLD REFRIGERATOR COMPANY PROBLEM

```
           Optimal Objective Value = 140.00000

                   Variable                  Value
                 --------------           --------------
                      P                       1.00000
                      W                       1.00000
                      M                       1.00000
                      R                       0.00000


                   Constraint             Slack/Surplus
                 --------------           --------------
                      1                       5.00000
                      2                      15.00000
                      3                       0.00000
                      4                      11.00000
```

WEB file

Ice-Cold

As an example of a **fixed cost problem,** consider the RMC problem. Three raw materials are used to produce three products: a fuel additive, a solvent base, and a carpet cleaning fluid. The following decision variables are used:

$$F = \text{tons of fuel additive produced}$$
$$S = \text{tons of solvent base produced}$$
$$C = \text{tons of carpet cleaning fluid produced}$$

The profit contributions are $40 per ton for the fuel additive, $30 per ton for the solvent base, and $50 per ton for the carpet cleaning fluid. Each ton of fuel additive is a blend of 0.4 tons of material 1 and 0.6 tons of material 3. Each ton of solvent base requires 0.5 tons of material 1, 0.2 tons of material 2, and 0.3 tons of material 3. Each ton of carpet cleaning fluid is a blend of 0.6 tons of material 1, 0.1 tons of material 2, and 0.3 tons of material 3. RMC has 20 tons of material 1, 5 tons of material 2, and 21 tons of material 3 and is interested in determining the optimal production quantities for the upcoming planning period.

A linear programming model of the RMC problem is shown:

$$
\begin{aligned}
\text{Max} \quad & 40F + 30S + 50C \\
\text{s.t.} \quad & \\
& 0.4F + 0.5S + 0.6C \le 20 \quad \text{Material 1} \\
& \phantom{0.4F + {}} 0.2S + 0.1C \le 5 \quad \text{Material 2} \\
& 0.6F + 0.3S + 0.3C \le 21 \quad \text{Material 3} \\
& F, S, C \ge 0
\end{aligned}
$$

The optimal solution consists of 27.5 tons of fuel additive, 0 tons of solvent base, and 15 tons of carpet cleaning fluid, with a value of $1850, as shown in Figure 7.5.

This linear programming formulation of the RMC problem does not include a fixed cost for production setup of the products. Suppose that the following data are available

FIGURE 7.5   THE SOLUTION TO THE RMC PROBLEM

WEB file

RMC

```
Optimal Objective Value = 1850.00000

    Variable               Value              Reduced Costs
 --------------        ----------------      ------------------
       F                  27.50000                0.00000
       S                   0.00000              -12.50000
       C                  15.00000                0.00000
```

concerning the setup cost and the maximum production quantity for each of the three products:

Product	Setup Cost	Maximum Production
Fuel additive	$200	50 tons
Solvent base	$ 50	25 tons
Carpet cleaning fluid	$400	40 tons

The modeling flexibility provided by 0-1 variables can now be used to incorporate the fixed setup costs into the production model. The 0-1 variables are defined as follows:

$$SF = 1 \text{ if the fuel additive is produced; 0 if not}$$
$$SS = 1 \text{ if the solvent base is produced; 0 if not}$$
$$SC = 1 \text{ if the carpet cleaning fluid is produced; 0 if not}$$

Using these setup variables, the total setup cost is

$$200SF + 50SS + 400SC$$

We can now rewrite the objective function to include the setup cost. Thus, the net profit objective function becomes

$$\text{Max} \quad 40F + 30S + 50C - 200SF - 50SS - 400SC$$

Next, we must write production capacity constraints so that if a setup variable equals 0, production of the corresponding product is not permitted and, if a setup variable equals 1, production is permitted up to the maximum quantity. For the fuel additive, we do so by adding the following constraint:

$$F \leq 50SF$$

Note that, with this constraint present, production of the fuel additive is not permitted when $SF = 0$. When $SF = 1$, production of up to 50 tons of fuel additive is permitted. We can think of the setup variable as a switch. When it is off ($SF = 0$), production is not permitted; when it is on ($SF = 1$), production is permitted.

FIGURE 7.6 THE SOLUTION TO THE RMC PROBLEM WITH SETUP COSTS

WEB **file**

RMC Setup

```
           Optimal Objective Value = 1350.00000

                   Variable                    Value
                 --------------              --------------
                        F                       25.00000
                        S                       20.00000
                        C                        0.00000
                       SF                        1.00000
                       SS                        1.00000
                       SC                        0.00000
```

Similar production capacity constraints, using 0-1 variables, are added for the solvent base and carpet cleaning products:

$$S \leq 25SS$$
$$C \leq 40SC$$

We have then the following fixed cost model for the RMC problem:

$$\text{Max} \quad 40F + 30S + 50C - 200SF - 50SS - 400SC$$

s.t.

$0.4F + 0.5S + 0.6C$	$\leq$	20	Material 1
$0.2S + 0.1C$	$\leq$	5	Material 2
$0.6F + 0.3S + 0.3C$	$\leq$	21	Material 3
F	$\leq$	$50SF$	Maximum F
S	$\leq$	$25SS$	Maximum S
C	$\leq$	$40SC$	Maximum C

$$F, S, C \geq 0; \ SF, SS, SC = 0, 1$$

The solution to the RMC problem with setup costs is shown in Figure 7.6. The optimal solution shows 25 tons of fuel additive and 20 tons of solvent base. The value of the objective function after deducting the setup cost is $1350. The setup cost for the fuel additive and the solvent base is $200 + $50 = $250. The optimal solution shows $SC = 0$, which indicates that the more expensive $400 setup cost for the carpet cleaning fluid should be avoided. Thus, the carpet cleaning fluid is not produced.

The Management Science in Action, Aluminum Can Production at Valley Metal Containers (see Section 7.1), employs 0-1 fixed cost variables for production line changeovers.

The key to developing a fixed cost model is the introduction of a 0-1 variable for each fixed cost and the specification of an upper bound for the corresponding production variable. For a production quantity x, a constraint of the form $x \leq My$ can then be used to allow production when the setup variable $y = 1$ and not to allow production when the setup variable $y = 0$. The value of the maximum production quantity M should be large enough to allow for all reasonable levels of production. But research has shown that choosing values of M excessively large will slow the solution procedure.

Distribution System Design

The Martin-Beck Company operates a plant in St. Louis with an annual capacity of 30,000 units. Product is shipped to regional distribution centers located in Boston, Atlanta, and

Houston. Because of an anticipated increase in demand, Martin-Beck plans to increase capacity by constructing a new plant in one or more of the following cities: Detroit, Toledo, Denver, or Kansas City. The estimated annual fixed cost and the annual capacity for the four proposed plants are as follows:

Proposed Plant	Annual Fixed Cost	Annual Capacity
Detroit	$175,000	10,000
Toledo	$300,000	20,000
Denver	$375,000	30,000
Kansas City	$500,000	40,000

The company's long-range planning group developed forecasts of the anticipated annual demand at the distribution centers as follows:

Distribution Center	Annual Demand
Boston	30,000
Atlanta	20,000
Houston	20,000

The shipping cost per unit from each plant to each distribution center is shown in Table 7.2. A network representation of the potential Martin-Beck distribution system is shown in Figure 7.7. Each potential plant location is shown; capacities and demands are shown in thousands of units. This network representation is for a transportation problem with a plant at St. Louis and at all four proposed sites. However, the decision has not yet been made as to which new plant or plants will be constructed.

Let us now show how 0-1 variables can be used in this **distribution system design problem** to develop a model for choosing the best plant locations and for determining how much to ship from each plant to each distribution center. We can use the following 0-1 variables to represent the plant construction decision:

$$y_1 = 1 \text{ if a plant is constructed in Detroit; 0 if not}$$
$$y_2 = 1 \text{ if a plant is constructed in Toledo; 0 if not}$$
$$y_3 = 1 \text{ if a plant is constructed in Denver; 0 if not}$$
$$y_4 = 1 \text{ if a plant is constructed in Kansas City; 0 if not}$$

TABLE 7.2   SHIPPING COST PER UNIT FOR THE MARTIN-BECK DISTRIBUTION SYSTEM

	Distribution Centers		
Plant Site	Boston	Atlanta	Houston
Detroit	5	2	3
Toledo	4	3	4
Denver	9	7	5
Kansas City	10	4	2
St. Louis	8	4	3

FIGURE 7.7 THE NETWORK REPRESENTATION OF THE MARTIN-BECK COMPANY DISTRIBUTION SYSTEM PROBLEM

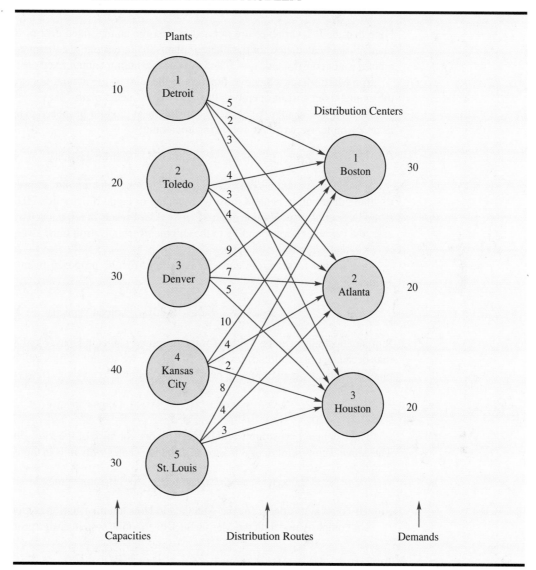

The variables representing the amount shipped from each plant site to each distribution center are defined just as for a transportation problem.

$$x_{ij} = \text{the units shipped in thousands from plant } i \text{ to distribution center } j$$
$$i = 1, 2, 3, 4, 5 \quad \text{and} \quad j = 1, 2, 3$$

Using the shipping cost data in Table 7.2, the annual transportation cost in thousands of dollars is written

$$5x_{11} + 2x_{12} + 3x_{13} + 4x_{21} + 3x_{22} + 4x_{23} + 9x_{31} + 7x_{32} + 5x_{33}$$
$$+ 10x_{41} + 4x_{42} + 2x_{43} + 8x_{51} + 4x_{52} + 3x_{53}$$

The annual fixed cost of operating the new plant or plants in thousands of dollars is written as

$$175y_1 + 300y_2 + 375y_3 + 500y_4$$

Note that the 0-1 variables are defined so that the annual fixed cost of operating the new plants is only calculated for the plant or plants that are actually constructed (i.e., $y_i = 1$). If a plant is not constructed, $y_i = 0$ and the corresponding annual fixed cost is \$0.

The Martin-Beck objective function is the sum of the annual transportation cost plus the annual fixed cost of operating the newly constructed plants.

Now let us consider the capacity constraints at the four proposed plants. Using Detroit as an example, we write the following constraint:

$$x_{11} + x_{12} + x_{13} \leq 10y_1 \quad \text{Detroit capacity}$$

If the Detroit plant is constructed, $y_1 = 1$ and the total amount shipped from Detroit to the three distribution centers must be less than or equal to Detroit's 10,000-unit capacity. If the Detroit plant is not constructed, $y_1 = 0$ will result in a 0 capacity at Detroit. In this case, the variables corresponding to the shipments from Detroit must all equal zero: $x_{11} = 0$, $x_{12} = 0$, and $x_{13} = 0$.

In a similar fashion, the capacity constraint for the proposed plant in Toledo can be written

$$x_{21} + x_{22} + x_{23} \leq 20y_2 \quad \text{Toledo capacity}$$

Similar constraints can be written for the proposed plants in Denver and Kansas City. Note that because a plant already exists in St. Louis, we do not define a 0-1 variable for this plant. Its capacity constraint can be written as follows:

$$x_{51} + x_{52} + x_{53} \leq 30 \quad \text{St. Louis capacity}$$

Three demand constraints will be needed, one for each of the three distribution centers. The demand constraint for the Boston distribution center with units in thousands is written as

$$x_{11} + x_{21} + x_{31} + x_{51} = 30 \quad \text{Boston demand}$$

Similar constraints appear for the Atlanta and Houston distribution centers.

The complete model for the Martin-Beck distribution system design problem is as follows:

$$
\begin{aligned}
\text{Min} \quad & 5x_{11} + 2x_{12} + 3x_{13} + 4x_{21} + 3x_{22} + 4x_{23} + 9x_{31} + 7x_{32} + 5x_{33} + 10x_{41} + 4x_{42} \\
& + 2x_{43} + 8x_{51} + 4x_{52} + 3x_{53} + 175y_1 + 300y_2 + 375y_3 + 500y_4
\end{aligned}
$$

s.t.

$$
\begin{aligned}
x_{11} + x_{12} + x_{13} &\leq 10y_1 \quad && \text{Detroit capacity} \\
x_{21} + x_{22} + x_{23} &\leq 20y_2 \quad && \text{Toledo capacity} \\
x_{31} + x_{32} + x_{33} &\leq 30y_3 \quad && \text{Denver capacity} \\
x_{41} + x_{42} + x_{43} &\leq 40y_4 \quad && \text{Kansas City capacity} \\
x_{51} + x_{52} + x_{53} &\leq 30 \quad && \text{St. Louis capacity} \\
x_{11} + x_{21} + x_{31} + x_{41} + x_{51} &= 30 \quad && \text{Boston demand} \\
x_{12} + x_{22} + x_{32} + x_{42} + x_{52} &= 20 \quad && \text{Atlanta demand} \\
x_{13} + x_{23} + x_{33} + x_{43} + x_{53} &= 20 \quad && \text{Houston demand} \\
\end{aligned}
$$

$$x_{ij} \geq 0 \text{ for all } i \text{ and } j; \ y_1, y_2, y_3, y_4 = 0, 1$$

FIGURE 7.8 THE SOLUTION FOR THE MARTIN-BECK COMPANY DISTRIBUTION SYSTEM PROBLEM

Optimal Objective Value = 860.00000

Variable	Value
X11	0.00000
X12	0.00000
X13	0.00000
X21	0.00000
X22	0.00000
X23	0.00000
X31	0.00000
X32	0.00000
X33	0.00000
X41	0.00000
X42	20.00000
X43	20.00000
X51	30.00000
X52	0.00000
X53	0.00000
Y1	0.00000
Y2	0.00000
Y3	0.00000
Y4	1.00000

Constraint	Slack/Surplus
1	0.00000
2	0.00000
3	0.00000
4	0.00000
5	0.00000
6	0.00000
7	0.00000
8	0.00000

WEB file

Martin-Beck

The solution for the Martin-Beck problem is shown in Figure 7.8. The optimal solution calls for the construction of a plant in Kansas City ($y_4 = 1$); 20,000 units will be shipped from Kansas City to Atlanta ($x_{42} = 20$), 20,000 units will be shipped from Kansas City to Houston ($x_{43} = 20$), and 30,000 units will be shipped from St. Louis to Boston ($x_{51} = 30$). Note that the total cost of this solution including the fixed cost of $500,000 for the plant in Kansas City is $860,000.

This basic model can be expanded to accommodate distribution systems involving direct shipments from plants to warehouses, from plants to retail outlets, and multiple products.[2] Using the special properties of 0-1 variables, the model can also be expanded to accommodate a variety of configuration constraints on the plant locations. For example, suppose in another problem, site 1 were in Dallas and site 2 were in Fort Worth. A company might not want to locate plants in both Dallas and Fort Worth because the cities are so close together. To prevent this result from happening, the following constraint can be added to the model:

Problem 13, which is based on the Martin-Beck distribution system problem, provides additional practice involving 0-1 variables.

$$y_1 + y_2 \leq 1$$

This constraint allows either y_1 or y_2 to equal 1, but not both. If we had written the constraints as an equality, it would require that a plant be located in either Dallas or Fort Worth.

Bank Location

The long-range planning department for the Ohio Trust Company is considering expanding its operation into a 20-county region in northeastern Ohio (see Figure 7.9). Currently, Ohio

FIGURE 7.9   THE 20-COUNTY REGION IN NORTHEASTERN OHIO

Counties

1. Ashtabula	6. Richland	11. Stark	16. Trumbull
2. Lake	7. Ashland	12. Geauga	17. Knox
3. Cuyahoga	8. Wayne	13. Portage	18. Holmes
4. Lorain	9. Medina	14. Columbiana	19. Tuscarawas
5. Huron	10. Summit	15. Mahoning	20. Carroll

---

[2]For computational reasons, it is usually preferable to replace the m plant capacity constraints with mn shipping route capacity constraints of the form $x_{ij} \leq \text{Min } \{s_i, d_j\} y_i$ for $i = 1, \ldots, m$, and $j = 1, \ldots, n$. The coefficient for y_i in each of these constraints is the smaller of the origin capacity (s_i) or the destination demand (d_j). These additional constraints often cause the solution of the LP Relaxation to be integer.

TABLE 7.3 COUNTIES IN THE OHIO TRUST EXPANSION REGION

Counties Under Consideration	Adjacent Counties (by Number)
1. Ashtabula	2, 12, 16
2. Lake	1, 3, 12
3. Cuyahoga	2, 4, 9, 10, 12, 13
4. Lorain	3, 5, 7, 9
5. Huron	4, 6, 7
6. Richland	5, 7, 17
7. Ashland	4, 5, 6, 8, 9, 17, 18
8. Wayne	7, 9, 10, 11, 18
9. Medina	3, 4, 7, 8, 10
10. Summit	3, 8, 9, 11, 12, 13
11. Stark	8, 10, 13, 14, 15, 18, 19, 20
12. Geauga	1, 2, 3, 10, 13, 16
13. Portage	3, 10, 11, 12, 15, 16
14. Columbiana	11, 15, 20
15. Mahoning	11, 13, 14, 16
16. Trumbull	1, 12, 13, 15
17. Knox	6, 7, 18
18. Holmes	7, 8, 11, 17, 19
19. Tuscarawas	11, 18, 20
20. Carroll	11, 14, 19

Trust does not have a principal place of business in any of the 20 counties. According to the banking laws in Ohio, if a bank establishes a principal place of business (PPB) in any county, branch banks can be established in that county and in any adjacent county. However, to establish a new principal place of business, Ohio Trust must either obtain approval for a new bank from the state's superintendent of banks or purchase an existing bank.

Table 7.3 lists the 20 counties in the region and adjacent counties. For example, Ashtabula County is adjacent to Lake, Geauga, and Trumbull counties; Lake County is adjacent to Ashtabula, Cuyahoga, and Geauga counties; and so on.

As an initial step in its planning, Ohio Trust would like to determine the minimum number of PPBs necessary to do business throughout the 20-county region. A 0-1 integer programming model can be used to solve this **location problem** for Ohio Trust. We define the variables as

$$x_i = 1 \text{ if a PPB is established in county } i; 0 \text{ otherwise}$$

To minimize the number of PPBs needed, we write the objective function as

$$\text{Min} \quad x_1 + x_2 + \cdots + x_{20}$$

The bank may locate branches in a county if the county contains a PPB or is adjacent to another county with a PPB. Thus, the linear program will need one constraint for each county. For example, the constraint for Ashtabula County is

$$x_1 + x_2 + x_{12} + x_{16} \geq 1 \quad \text{Ashtabula}$$

Note that satisfaction of this constraint ensures that a PPB will be placed in Ashtabula County *or* in one or more of the adjacent counties. This constraint thus guarantees that Ohio Trust will be able to place branch banks in Ashtabula County.

The complete statement of the bank location problem is

$$\text{Min} \quad x_1 + x_2 + \quad \cdots \quad + x_{20}$$
$$\text{s.t.}$$
$$x_1 + x_2 \qquad + x_{12} + x_{16} \qquad \geq 1 \quad \text{Ashtabula}$$
$$x_1 + x_2 + x_3 \ + x_{12} \qquad\qquad \geq 1 \quad \text{Lake}$$
$$\cdot \qquad\qquad\qquad\qquad\qquad \cdot$$
$$\cdot \qquad\qquad\qquad\qquad\qquad \cdot$$
$$\cdot \qquad\qquad\qquad\qquad\qquad \cdot$$
$$x_{11} + x_{14} + x_{19} + x_{20} \geq 1 \quad \text{Carroll}$$
$$x_i = 0, 1 \quad i = 1, 2, \ldots, 20$$

In Figure 7.10 we show the solution to the Ohio Trust problem. Using the output, we see that the optimal solution calls for principal places of business in Ashland, Stark, and Geauga counties. With PPBs in these three counties, Ohio Trust can place branch banks in all 20 counties (see Figure 7.11). All other decision variables have an optimal value of zero, indicating that a PPB should not be placed in these counties. Clearly the integer

FIGURE 7.10   THE SOLUTION FOR THE OHIO TRUST PPB LOCATION PROBLEM

WEB file

Ohio Trust

Optimal Objective Value = 3.00000

Variable	Value
X1	0.00000
X2	0.00000
X3	0.00000
X4	0.00000
X5	0.00000
X6	0.00000
X7	1.00000
X8	0.00000
X9	0.00000
X10	0.00000
X11	1.00000
X12	1.00000
X13	0.00000
X14	0.00000
X15	0.00000
X16	0.00000
X17	0.00000
X18	0.00000
X19	0.00000
X20	0.00000

FIGURE 7.11 PRINCIPAL PLACE OF BUSINESS COUNTIES FOR OHIO TRUST

Counties

1. Ashtabula	6. Richland	11. Stark	16. Trumbull	★ A principal place
2. Lake	7. Ashland	12. Geauga	17. Knox	of business
3. Cuyahoga	8. Wayne	13. Portage	18. Holmes	should be located
4. Lorain	9. Medina	14. Columbiana	19. Tuscarawas	in these counties.
5. Huron	10. Summit	15. Mahoning	20. Carroll	

programming model could be enlarged to allow for expansion into a larger area or throughout the entire state.

Product Design and Market Share Optimization

Conjoint analysis is a market research technique that can be used to learn how prospective buyers of a product value the product's attributes. In this section we will show how the results of conjoint analysis can be used in an integer programming model of a **product design and market share optimization problem.** We illustrate the approach by considering a problem facing Salem Foods, a major producer of frozen foods.

Salem Foods is planning to enter the frozen pizza market. Currently, two existing brands, Antonio's and King's, have the major share of the market. In trying to develop a sausage pizza that will capture a significant share of the market, Salem determined that the four most important attributes when consumers purchase a frozen sausage pizza are crust, cheese, sauce, and sausage flavor. The crust attribute has two levels (thin and thick); the cheese attribute has two levels (mozzarella and blend); the sauce attribute has two levels (smooth and chunky); and the sausage flavor attribute has three levels (mild, medium, and hot).

In a typical conjoint analysis, a sample of consumers is asked to express their preference for specially prepared pizzas with chosen levels for the attributes. Then regression

TABLE 7.4   PART-WORTHS FOR THE SALEM FOODS PROBLEM

	Crust		Cheese		Sauce		Sausage Flavor		
Consumer	Thin	Thick	Mozzarella	Blend	Smooth	Chunky	Mild	Medium	Hot
1	11	2	6	7	3	17	26	27	8
2	11	7	15	17	16	26	14	1	10
3	7	5	8	14	16	7	29	16	19
4	13	20	20	17	17	14	25	29	10
5	2	8	6	11	30	20	15	5	12
6	12	17	11	9	2	30	22	12	20
7	9	19	12	16	16	25	30	23	19
8	5	9	4	14	23	16	16	30	3

analysis is used to determine the part-worth for each of the attribute levels. In essence, the part-worth is the utility value that a consumer attaches to each level of each attribute. A discussion of how to use regression analysis to compute the part-worths is beyond the scope of this text, but we will show how the part-worths can be used to determine the overall value a consumer attaches to a particular pizza.

Table 7.4 shows the part-worths for each level of each attribute provided by a sample of eight potential Salem customers who are currently buying either King's or Antonio's pizza. For consumer 1, the part-worths for the crust attribute are 11 for thin crust and 2 for thick crust, indicating a preference for thin crust. For the cheese attribute, the part-worths are 6 for the mozzarella cheese and 7 for the cheese blend; thus, consumer 1 has a slight preference for the cheese blend. From the other part-worths, we see that consumer 1 shows a strong preference for the chunky sauce over the smooth sauce (17 to 3) and has a slight preference for the medium-flavored sausage. Note that consumer 2 shows a preference for the thin crust, the cheese blend, the chunky sauce, and mild-flavored sausage. The part-worths for the other consumers are interpreted in a similar manner.

The part-worths can be used to determine the overall value (utility) each consumer attaches to a particular type of pizza. For instance, consumer 1's current favorite pizza is the Antonio's brand, which has a thick crust, mozzarella cheese, chunky sauce, and medium-flavored sausage. We can determine consumer 1's utility for this particular type of pizza using the part-worths in Table 7.4. For consumer 1, the part-worths are 2 for thick crust, 6 for mozzarella cheese, 17 for chunky sauce, and 27 for medium-flavored sausage. Thus, consumer 1's utility for the Antonio's brand pizza is 2 + 6 + 17 + 27 = 52. We can compute consumer 1's utility for a King's brand pizza in a similar manner. The King's brand pizza has a thin crust, a cheese blend, smooth sauce, and mild-flavored sausage. Because the part-worths for consumer 1 are 11 for thin crust, 7 for cheese blend, 3 for smooth sauce, and 26 for mild-flavored sausage, consumer 1's utility for the King's brand pizza is 11 + 7 + 3 + 26 = 47. In general, each consumer's utility for a particular type of pizza is just the sum of the appropriate part-worths.

In order to be successful with its brand, Salem Foods realizes that it must entice consumers in the marketplace to switch from their current favorite brand of pizza to the Salem product. That is, Salem must design a pizza (choose the type of crust, cheese, sauce, and sausage flavor) that will have the highest utility for enough people to ensure sufficient sales to justify making the product. Assuming the sample of eight consumers in the current study is representative of the marketplace for frozen sausage pizza, we can formulate and solve an integer programming model that can help Salem come up with such a design. In marketing literature, the problem being solved is called the *share of choices* problem.

The decision variables are defined as follows:

$$l_{ij} = 1 \text{ if Salem chooses level } i \text{ for attribute } j; 0 \text{ otherwise}$$
$$y_k = 1 \text{ if consumer } k \text{ chooses the Salem brand; } 0 \text{ otherwise}$$

The objective is to choose the levels of each attribute that will maximize the number of consumers preferring the Salem brand pizza. Because the number of customers preferring the Salem brand pizza is just the sum of the y_k variables, the objective function is

$$\text{Max} \quad y_1 + y_2 + \cdots + y_8$$

One constraint is needed for each consumer in the sample. To illustrate how the constraints are formulated, let us consider the constraint corresponding to consumer 1. For consumer 1, the utility of a particular type of pizza can be expressed as the sum of the part-worths:

$$\text{Utility for Consumer 1} = 11l_{11} + 2l_{21} + 6l_{12} + 7l_{22} + 3l_{13} + 17l_{23}$$
$$+ 26l_{14} + 27l_{24} + 8l_{34}$$

In order for consumer 1 to prefer the Salem pizza, the utility for the Salem pizza must be greater than the utility for consumer 1's current favorite. Recall that consumer 1's current favorite brand of pizza is Antonio's, with a utility of 52. Thus, consumer 1 will only purchase the Salem brand if the levels of the attributes for the Salem brand are chosen such that

$$11l_{11} + 2l_{21} + 6l_{12} + 7l_{22} + 3l_{13} + 17l_{23} + 26l_{14} + 27l_{24} + 8l_{34} > 52$$

Given the definitions of the y_k decision variables, we want $y_1 = 1$ when the consumer prefers the Salem brand and $y_1 = 0$ when the consumer does not prefer the Salem brand. Thus, we write the constraint for consumer 1 as follows:

$$11l_{11} + 2l_{21} + 6l_{12} + 7l_{22} + 3l_{13} + 17l_{23} + 26l_{14} + 27l_{24} + 8l_{34} \geq 1 + 52y_1$$

With this constraint, y_1 cannot equal 1 unless the utility for the Salem design (the left-hand side of the constraint) exceeds the utility for consumer 1's current favorite by at least 1. Because the objective function is to maximize the sum of the y_k variables, the optimization will seek a product design that will allow as many y_k as possible to equal 1.

A similar constraint is written for each consumer in the sample. The coefficients for the l_{ij} variables in the utility functions are taken from Table 7.4 and the coefficients for the y_k variables are obtained by computing the overall utility of the consumer's current favorite brand of pizza. The following constraints correspond to the eight consumers in the study:

Antonio's brand is the current favorite pizza for consumers 1, 4, 6, 7, and 8. King's brand is the current favorite pizza for consumers 2, 3, and 5.

$$11l_{11} + 2l_{21} + 6l_{12} + 7l_{22} + 3l_{13} + 17l_{23} + 26l_{14} + 27l_{24} + 8l_{34} \geq 1 + 52y_1$$
$$11l_{11} + 7l_{21} + 15l_{12} + 17l_{22} + 16l_{13} + 26l_{23} + 14l_{14} + 1l_{24} + 10l_{34} \geq 1 + 58y_2$$
$$7l_{11} + 5l_{21} + 8l_{12} + 14l_{22} + 16l_{13} + 7l_{23} + 29l_{14} + 16l_{24} + 19l_{34} \geq 1 + 66y_3$$
$$13l_{11} + 20l_{21} + 20l_{12} + 17l_{22} + 17l_{13} + 14l_{23} + 25l_{14} + 29l_{24} + 10l_{34} \geq 1 + 83y_4$$
$$2l_{11} + 8l_{21} + 6l_{12} + 11l_{22} + 30l_{13} + 20l_{23} + 15l_{14} + 5l_{24} + 12l_{34} \geq 1 + 58y_5$$
$$12l_{11} + 17l_{21} + 11l_{12} + 9l_{22} + 2l_{13} + 30l_{23} + 22l_{14} + 12l_{24} + 20l_{34} \geq 1 + 70y_6$$
$$9l_{11} + 19l_{21} + 12l_{12} + 16l_{22} + 16l_{13} + 25l_{23} + 30l_{14} + 23l_{24} + 19l_{34} \geq 1 + 79y_7$$
$$5l_{11} + 9l_{21} + 4l_{12} + 14l_{22} + 23l_{13} + 16l_{23} + 16l_{14} + 30l_{24} + 3l_{34} \geq 1 + 59y_8$$

Four more constraints must be added, one for each attribute. These constraints are necessary to ensure that one and only one level is selected for each attribute. For attribute 1 (crust), we must add the constraint

$$l_{11} + l_{21} = 1$$

Because l_{11} and l_{21} are both 0-1 variables, this constraint requires that one of the two variables equals 1 and the other equals 0. The following three constraints ensure that one and only one level is selected for each of the other three attributes:

$$l_{12} + l_{22} = 1$$
$$l_{13} + l_{23} = 1$$
$$l_{14} + l_{24} + l_{34} = 1$$

Salem

The optimal solution to this integer linear program is $l_{11} = l_{22} = l_{23} = l_{14} = 1$ and $y_1 = y_2 = y_6 = y_7 = 1$. The value of the optimal solution is 4, indicating that if Salem makes this type of pizza it will be preferable to the current favorite for four of the eight consumers. With $l_{11} = l_{22} = l_{23} = l_{14} = 1$, the pizza design that obtains the largest market share for Salem has a thin crust, a cheese blend, a chunky sauce, and mild-flavored sausage. Note also that with $y_1 = y_2 = y_6 = y_7 = 1$, consumers 1, 2, 6, and 7 will prefer the Salem pizza. With this information Salem may choose to market this type of pizza.

NOTES AND COMMENTS

1. Most practical applications of integer linear programming involve only 0-1 integer variables. Indeed, some mixed-integer computer codes are designed to handle only integer variables with binary values. However, if a clever mathematical trick is employed, these codes can still be used for problems involving general integer variables. The trick is called *binary expansion* and requires that an upper bound be established for each integer variable. More advanced texts on integer programming show how it can be done.

2. The Management Science in Action, Volunteer Scheduling for the Edmonton Folk Festival, describes how a series of three integer programming models was used to schedule volunteers. Two of the models employ 0-1 variables.

3. General-purpose mixed-integer linear programming codes and some spreadsheet packages can be used for linear programming problems, all-integer problems, and problems involving some continuous and some integer variables. General-purpose codes are seldom the fastest for solving problems with special structure (such as the transportation, assignment, and transshipment problems); however, unless the problems are very large, speed is usually not a critical issue. Thus, most practitioners prefer to use one general-purpose computer package that can be used on a variety of problems rather than to maintain a variety of computer programs designed for special problems.

MANAGEMENT SCIENCE IN ACTION

VOLUNTEER SCHEDULING FOR THE EDMONTON FOLK FESTIVAL*

The Edmonton Folk Festival is a four-day outdoor event that is run almost entirely by volunteers. In 2002, 1800 volunteers worked on 35 different crews and contributed more than 50,000 volunteer hours. With this many volunteers, coordination requires a major effort. For instance, in 2002, two volunteer coordinators used a trial-and-error procedure to develop schedules for the volunteers in the two gate crews. However, developing these schedules proved to be time consuming and frustrating; the coordinators spent as much time scheduling as they did supervising volunteers during the festival. To reduce the time spent on gate-crew scheduling, one of the coordinators asked the Centre for Excellence in Operations at the University of Alberta School of Business for help in automating the scheduling process. The Centre agreed to help.

The scheduling system developed consists of three integer programming models. Model 1 is used to determine daily shift schedules. This model determines the length of each shift (number of hours) and how many volunteers are needed for each shift to meet the peaks and valleys in demand. Model 2 is a binary integer program used to assign

volunteers to shifts. The objective is to maximize volunteer preferences subject to several constraints, such as number of hours worked, balance between morning and afternoon shifts, a mix of experienced and inexperienced volunteers on each shift, no conflicting shifts, and so on. Model 3 is used to allocate volunteers between the two gates.

The coordinators of the gate crews were pleased with the results provided by the models and learned to use them effectively. Vicki Fannon, the manager of volunteers for the festival, now has plans to expand the use of the integer programming models to the scheduling of other crews in the future.

*Based on L. Gordon and E. Erkut, "Improving Volunteer Scheduling for the Edmonton Folk Festival," *Interfaces* (September/October 2004): 367–376.

7.4   MODELING FLEXIBILITY PROVIDED BY 0-1 INTEGER VARIABLES

In Section 7.3 we presented four applications involving 0-1 integer variables. In this section we continue the discussion of the use of 0-1 integer variables in modeling. First, we show how 0-1 integer variables can be used to model multiple-choice and mutually exclusive constraints. Then, we show how 0-1 integer variables can be used to model situations in which k projects out of a set of n projects must be selected, as well as situations in which the acceptance of one project is conditional on the acceptance of another. We close the section with a cautionary note on the role of sensitivity analysis in integer linear programming.

Multiple-Choice and Mutually Exclusive Constraints

Recall the Ice-Cold Refrigerator capital budgeting problem introduced in Section 7.3. The decision variables were defined as

$P = 1$ if the plant expansion project is accepted; 0 if rejected

$W = 1$ if the warehouse expansion project is accepted; 0 if rejected

$M = 1$ if the new machinery project is accepted; 0 if rejected

$R = 1$ if the new product research project is accepted; 0 if rejected

Suppose that, instead of one warehouse expansion project, the Ice-Cold Refrigerator Company actually has three warehouse expansion projects under consideration. One of the warehouses *must* be expanded because of increasing product demand, but new demand isn't sufficient to make expansion of more than one warehouse necessary. The following variable definitions and **multiple-choice constraint** could be incorporated into the previous 0-1 integer linear programming model to reflect this situation. Let

$W_1 = 1$ if the original warehouse expansion project is accepted; 0 if rejected

$W_2 = 1$ if the second warehouse expansion project is accepted; 0 if rejected

$W_3 = 1$ if the third warehouse expansion project is accepted; 0 if rejected

The following multiple-choice constraint reflects the requirement that exactly one of these projects must be selected:

$$W_1 + W_2 + W_3 = 1$$

If W_1, W_2, and W_3 are allowed to assume only the values 0 or 1, then one and only one of these projects will be selected from among the three choices.

If the requirement that one warehouse must be expanded did not exist, the multiple-choice constraint could be modified as follows:

$$W_1 + W_2 + W_3 \leq 1$$

This modification allows for the case of no warehouse expansion ($W_1 = W_2 = W_3 = 0$) but does not permit more than one warehouse to be expanded. This type of constraint is often called a **mutually exclusive constraint.**

k out of *n* Alternatives Constraint

An extension of the notion of a multiple-choice constraint can be used to model situations in which *k out of a set of n* projects must be selected—a ***k* out of *n* alternatives constraint.** Suppose that W_1, W_2, W_3, W_4, and W_5 represent five potential warehouse expansion projects and that two of the five projects must be accepted. The constraint that satisfies this new requirement is

$$W_1 + W_2 + W_3 + W_4 + W_5 = 2$$

If no more than two of the projects are to be selected, we would use the following less-than-or-equal-to constraint:

$$W_1 + W_2 + W_3 + W_4 + W_5 \leq 2$$

Again, each of these variables must be restricted to 0-1 values.

Conditional and Corequisite Constraints

Sometimes the acceptance of one project is conditional on the acceptance of another. For example, suppose for the Ice-Cold Refrigerator Company that the warehouse expansion project was conditional on the plant expansion project. That is, management will not consider expanding the warehouse unless the plant is expanded. With P representing plant expansion and W representing warehouse expansion, a **conditional constraint** could be introduced to enforce this requirement:

$$W \leq P$$

Both P and W must be 0 or 1; whenever P is 0, W will be forced to 0. When P is 1, W is also allowed to be 1; thus, both the plant and the warehouse can be expanded. However, we note that the preceding constraint does not force the warehouse expansion project (W) to be accepted if the plant expansion project (P) is accepted.

If the warehouse expansion project had to be accepted whenever the plant expansion project was, and vice versa, we would say that P and W represented **corequisite constraint** projects. To model such a situation, we simply write the preceding constraint as an equality:

$$W = P$$

The constraint forces P and W to take on the same value.

The Management Science in Action, Customer Order Allocation Model at Ketron, describes how the modeling flexibility provided by 0-1 variables helped Ketron build a customer order allocation model for a sporting goods company.

Try Problem 7 for practice with the modeling flexibility provided by 0-1 variables.

CUSTOMER ORDER ALLOCATION MODEL AT KETRON*

Ketron Management Science provides consulting services for the design and implementation of mathematical programming applications. One such application involved the development of a mixed-integer programming model of the customer order allocation problem for a major sporting goods company. The sporting goods company markets approximately 300 products and has about 30 sources of supply (factory and warehouse locations). The problem is to determine how best to allocate customer orders to the various sources of supply such that the total manufacturing cost for the products ordered is minimized. Figure 7.12 provides a graphical representation of this problem. Note in the figure that each customer can receive shipments from only a few of the various sources of supply. For example, we see that customer 1 may be supplied by source A or B, customer 2 may be supplied only by source A, and so on.

The sporting equipment company classifies each customer order as either a "guaranteed" or "secondary" order. Guaranteed orders are single-source orders in that they must be filled by a single supplier to ensure that the complete order will be delivered to the customer at one time. This single-

source requirement necessitates the use of 0-1 integer variables in the model. Approximately 80% of the company's orders are guaranteed orders. Secondary orders can be split among the various sources of supply. These orders are made by customers restocking inventory, and receiving partial shipments from different sources at different times is not a problem. The 0-1 variables are used to represent the assignment of a guaranteed order to a supplier and continuous variables are used to represent the secondary orders.

Constraints for the problem involve raw material capacities, manufacturing capacities, and individual product capacities. A fairly typical problem has about 800 constraints, 2000 0-1 assignment variables, and 500 continuous variables associated with the secondary orders. The customer order allocation problem is solved periodically as orders are received. In a typical period, between 20 and 40 customers are to be supplied. Because most customers require several products, usually between 600 and 800 orders must be assigned to the sources of supply.

*Based on information provided by J. A. Tomlin of Ketron Management Science.

FIGURE 7.12   GRAPHICAL REPRESENTATION OF THE CUSTOMER ORDER ALLOCATION PROBLEM

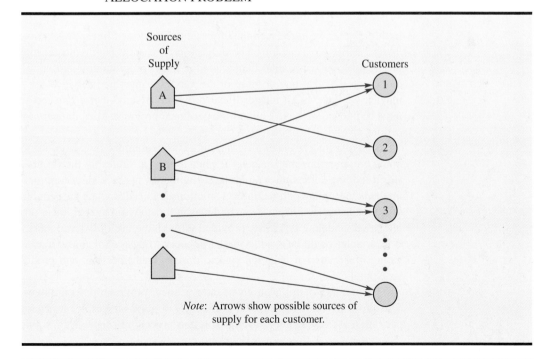

Note: Arrows show possible sources of supply for each customer.

A Cautionary Note About Sensitivity Analysis

Sensitivity analysis often is more crucial for integer linear programming problems than for linear programming problems. A small change in one of the coefficients in the constraints can cause a relatively large change in the value of the optimal solution. To understand why, consider the following integer programming model of a simple capital budgeting problem involving four projects and a budgetary constraint for a single time period:

$$\text{Max} \quad 40x_1 + 60x_2 + 70x_3 + 160x_4$$
$$\text{s.t.}$$
$$16x_1 + 35x_2 + 45x_3 + 85x_4 \leq 100$$
$$x_1, x_2, x_3, x_4 = 0, 1$$

We can obtain the optimal solution to this problem by enumerating the alternatives. It is $x_1 = 1$, $x_2 = 1$, $x_3 = 1$, and $x_4 = 0$, with an objective function value of $170. However, note that if the budget available is increased by $1 (from $100 to $101), the optimal solution changes to $x_1 = 1$, $x_2 = 0$, $x_3 = 0$, and $x_4 = 1$, with an objective function value of $200. That is, one additional dollar in the budget would lead to a $30 increase in the return. Surely management, when faced with such a situation, would increase the budget by $1. Because of the extreme sensitivity of the value of the optimal solution to the constraint coefficients, practitioners usually recommend re-solving the integer linear program several times with slight variations in the coefficients before attempting to choose the best solution for implementation.

SUMMARY

In this chapter we introduced the important extension of linear programming referred to as *integer linear programming*. The only difference between the integer linear programming problems discussed in this chapter and the linear programming problems studied in previous chapters is that one or more of the variables must be integer. If all variables must be integer, we have an all-integer linear program. If some, but not necessarily all, variables must be integer, we have a mixed-integer linear program. Most integer programming applications involve 0-1, or binary, variables.

Studying integer linear programming is important for two major reasons. First, integer linear programming may be helpful when fractional values for the variables are not permitted. Rounding a linear programming solution may not provide an optimal integer solution; methods for finding optimal integer solutions are needed when the economic consequences of rounding are significant. A second reason for studying integer linear programming is the increased modeling flexibility provided through the use of 0-1 variables. We showed how 0-1 variables could be used to model important managerial considerations in capital budgeting, fixed cost, distribution system design, bank location, and product design/market share applications.

The number of applications of integer linear programming continues to grow rapidly. This growth is due in part to the availability of good integer linear programming software packages. As researchers develop solution procedures capable of solving larger integer linear programs and as computer speed increases, a continuation of the growth of integer programming applications is expected.

GLOSSARY

Integer linear program   A linear program with the additional requirement that one or more of the variables must be integer.

All-integer linear program   An integer linear program in which all variables are required to be integer.

LP Relaxation   The linear program that results from dropping the integer requirements for the variables in an integer linear program.

Mixed-integer linear program   An integer linear program in which some, but not necessarily all, variables are required to be integer.

0-1 integer linear program   An all-integer or mixed-integer linear program in which the integer variables are only permitted to assume the values 0 or 1. Also called *binary integer program.*

Capital budgeting problem   A 0-1 integer programming problem that involves choosing which projects or activities provide the best investment return.

Fixed cost problem   A 0-1 mixed-integer programming problem in which the binary variables represent whether an activity, such as a production run, is undertaken (variable = 1) or not (variable = 0).

Distribution system design problem   A mixed-integer linear program in which the binary integer variables usually represent sites selected for warehouses or plants and continuous variables represent the amount shipped over arcs in the distribution network.

Location problem   A 0-1 integer programming problem in which the objective is to select the best locations to meet a stated objective. Variations of this problem (see the bank location problem in Section 7.3) are known as covering problems.

Product design and market share optimization problem   Sometimes called the share of choices problem, it involves choosing a product design that maximizes the number of consumers preferring it.

Multiple-choice constraint   A constraint requiring that the sum of two or more 0-1 variables equal 1. Thus, any feasible solution makes a choice of which variable to set equal to 1.

Mutually exclusive constraint   A constraint requiring that the sum of two or more 0-1 variables be less than or equal to 1. Thus, if one of the variables equals 1, the others must equal 0. However, all variables could equal 0.

k out of n alternatives constraint   An extension of the multiple-choice constraint. This constraint requires that the sum of n 0-1 variables equal k.

Conditional constraint   A constraint involving 0-1 variables that does not allow certain variables to equal 1 unless certain other variables are equal to 1.

Corequisite constraint   A constraint requiring that two 0-1 variables be equal. Thus, they are both in or out of solution together.

PROBLEMS

1. Indicate which of the following is an all-integer linear program and which is a mixed-integer linear program. Write the LP Relaxation for the problem but do not attempt to solve.

   a. Max $30x_1 + 25x_2$

   s.t.

   $$3x_1 + 1.5x_2 \le 400$$
   $$1.5x_1 + 2x_2 \le 250$$
   $$1x_1 + 1x_2 \le 150$$
   $$x_1, x_2 \ge 0 \text{ and } x_2 \text{ integer}$$

   b. Min $3x_1 + 4x_2$

   s.t.

   $$2x_1 + 4x_2 \ge 8$$
   $$2x_1 + 6x_2 \ge 12$$
   $$x_1, x_2 \ge 0 \text{ and integer}$$

 2. Consider the following all-integer linear program:

   $$\text{Max}\quad 5x_1 + 8x_2$$

   s.t.

   $$6x_1 + 5x_2 \le 30$$
   $$9x_1 + 4x_2 \le 36$$
   $$1x_1 + 2x_2 \le 10$$
   $$x_1, x_2 \ge 0 \text{ and integer}$$

   a. Graph the constraints for this problem. Use dots to indicate all feasible integer solutions.
   b. Find the optimal solution to the LP Relaxation. Round down to find a feasible integer solution.
   c. Find the optimal integer solution. Is it the same as the solution obtained in part (b) by rounding down?

3. Consider the following all-integer linear program:

   $$\text{Max}\quad 1x_1 + 1x_2$$

   s.t.

   $$4x_1 + 6x_2 \le 22$$
   $$1x_1 + 5x_2 \le 15$$
   $$2x_1 + 1x_2 \le 9$$
   $$x_1, x_2 \ge 0 \text{ and integer}$$

   a. Graph the constraints for this problem. Use dots to indicate all feasible integer solutions.
   b. Solve the LP Relaxation of this problem.
   c. Find the optimal integer solution.

4. Consider the following all-integer linear program:

   $$\text{Max}\quad 10x_1 + 3x_2$$

   s.t.

   $$6x_1 + 7x_2 \le 40$$
   $$3x_1 + 1x_2 \le 11$$
   $$x_1, x_2 \ge 0 \text{ and integer}$$

a. Formulate and solve the LP Relaxation of the problem. Solve it graphically, and round down to find a feasible solution. Specify an upper bound on the value of the optimal solution.

b. Solve the integer linear program graphically. Compare the value of this solution with the solution obtained in part (a).

c. Suppose the objective function changes to Max $3x_1 + 6x_2$. Repeat parts (a) and (b).

5. Consider the following mixed-integer linear program:

$$\text{Max} \quad 2x_1 + 3x_2$$
$$\text{s.t.}$$
$$4x_1 + 9x_2 \leq 36$$
$$7x_1 + 5x_2 \leq 35$$
$$x_1, x_2 \geq 0 \text{ and } x_1 \text{ integer}$$

a. Graph the constraints for this problem. Indicate on your graph all feasible mixed-integer solutions.

b. Find the optimal solution to the LP Relaxation. Round the value of x_1 down to find a feasible mixed-integer solution. Is this solution optimal? Why or why not?

c. Find the optimal solution for the mixed-integer linear program.

6. Consider the following mixed-integer linear program:

$$\text{Max} \quad 1x_1 + 1x_2$$
$$\text{s.t.}$$
$$7x_1 + 9x_2 \leq 63$$
$$9x_1 + 5x_2 \leq 45$$
$$3x_1 + 1x_2 \leq 12$$
$$x_1, x_2 \geq 0 \text{ and } x_2 \text{ integer}$$

a. Graph the constraints for this problem. Indicate on your graph all feasible mixed-integer solutions.

b. Find the optimal solution to the LP Relaxation. Round the value of x_2 down to find a feasible mixed-integer solution. Specify upper and lower bounds on the value of the optimal solution to the mixed-integer linear program.

c. Find the optimal solution to the mixed-integer linear program.

7. The following questions refer to a capital budgeting problem with six projects represented by 0-1 variables x_1, x_2, x_3, x_4, x_5, and x_6:

a. Write a constraint modeling a situation in which two of the projects 1, 3, 5, and 6 must be undertaken.

b. Write a constraint modeling a situation in which, if projects 3 and 5 must be undertaken, they must be undertaken simultaneously.

c. Write a constraint modeling a situation in which project 1 or 4 must be undertaken, but not both.

d. Write constraints modeling a situation where project 4 cannot be undertaken unless projects 1 and 3 also are undertaken.

e. In addition to the requirement in part (d), assume that when projects 1 and 3 are undertaken, project 4 also must be undertaken.

8. Spencer Enterprises must choose among a series of new investment alternatives. The potential investment alternatives, the net present value of the future stream of returns,

the capital requirements, and the available capital funds over the next three years are summarized as follows:

Alternative	Net Present Value ($)	Capital Requirements ($)		
		Year 1	Year 2	Year 3
Limited warehouse expansion	4,000	3,000	1,000	4,000
Extensive warehouse expansion	6,000	2,500	3,500	3,500
Test market new product	10,500	6,000	4,000	5,000
Advertising campaign	4,000	2,000	1,500	1,800
Basic research	8,000	5,000	1,000	4,000
Purchase new equipment	3,000	1,000	500	900
Capital funds available		10,500	7,000	8,750

    a. Develop and solve an integer programming model for maximizing the net present value.

    b. Assume that only one of the warehouse expansion projects can be implemented. Modify your model of part (a).

    c. Suppose that, if test marketing of the new product is carried out, the advertising campaign also must be conducted. Modify your formulation of part (b) to reflect this new situation.

9. Hawkins Manufacturing Company produces connecting rods for 4- and 6-cylinder automobile engines using the same production line. The cost required to set up the production line to produce the 4-cylinder connecting rods is $2000, and the cost required to set up the production line for the 6-cylinder connecting rods is $3500. Manufacturing costs are $15 for each 4-cylinder connecting rod and $18 for each 6-cylinder connecting rod. Hawkins makes a decision at the end of each week as to which product will be manufactured the following week. If a production changeover is necessary from one week to the next, the weekend is used to reconfigure the production line. Once the line has been set up, the weekly production capacities are 6000 6-cylinder connecting rods and 8000 4-cylinder connecting rods. Let

x_4 = the number of 4-cylinder connecting rods produced next week

x_6 = the number of 6-cylinder connecting rods produced next week

s_4 = 1 if the production line is set up to produce the 4-cylinder connecting rods; 0 if otherwise

s_6 = 1 if the production line is set up to produce the 6-cylinder connecting rods; 0 if otherwise

    a. Using the decision variables x_4 and s_4, write a constraint that limits next week's production of the 4-cylinder connecting rods to either 0 or 8000 units.

    b. Using the decision variables x_6 and s_6, write a constraint that limits next week's production of the 6-cylinder connecting rods to either 0 or 6000 units.

    c. Write three constraints that, taken together, limit the production of connecting rods for next week.

    d. Write an objective function for minimizing the cost of production for next week.

10. Grave City is considering the relocation of several police substations to obtain better enforcement in high-crime areas. The locations under consideration together with the areas that can be covered from these locations are given in the following table:

Potential Locations for Substations	Areas Covered
A	1, 5, 7
B	1, 2, 5, 7
C	1, 3, 5
D	2, 4, 5
E	3, 4, 6
F	4, 5, 6
G	1, 5, 6, 7

    a. Formulate an integer programming model that could be used to find the minimum number of locations necessary to provide coverage to all areas.

    b. Solve the problem in part (a).

11. Hart Manufacturing makes three products. Each product requires manufacturing operations in three departments: A, B, and C. The labor-hour requirements, by department, are as follows:

Department	Product 1	Product 2	Product 3
A	1.50	3.00	2.00
B	2.00	1.00	2.50
C	0.25	0.25	0.25

During the next production period, the labor-hours available are 450 in department A, 350 in department B, and 50 in department C. The profit contributions per unit are $25 for product 1, $28 for product 2, and $30 for product 3.

    a. Formulate a linear programming model for maximizing total profit contribution.

    b. Solve the linear program formulated in part (a). How much of each product should be produced, and what is the projected total profit contribution?

    c. After evaluating the solution obtained in part (b), one of the production supervisors noted that production setup costs had not been taken into account. She noted that setup costs are $400 for product 1, $550 for product 2, and $600 for product 3. If the solution developed in part (b) is to be used, what is the total profit contribution after taking into account the setup costs?

    d. Management realized that the optimal product mix, taking setup costs into account, might be different from the one recommended in part (b). Formulate a mixed-integer linear program that takes setup costs into account. Management also stated that we should not consider making more than 175 units of product 1, 150 units of product 2, or 140 units of product 3.

    e. Solve the mixed-integer linear program formulated in part (d). How much of each product should be produced, and what is the projected total profit contribution? Compare this profit contribution to that obtained in part (c).

12. Yates Company supplies road salt to county highway departments. The company has three trucks, and the dispatcher is trying to schedule tomorrow's deliveries to Polk, Dallas, and Jasper counties. Two trucks have 15-ton capacities, and the third truck has a 30-ton capacity. Based on these truck capacities, two counties will receive 15 tons and the third will receive 30 tons of road salt. The dispatcher wants to determine how much to ship to each county. Let

$$P = \text{amount shipped to Polk County}$$
$$D = \text{amount shipped to Dallas County}$$
$$J = \text{amount shipped to Jasper County}$$

and

$$Y_i = \begin{cases} 1 & \text{if the 30-ton truck is assigned to county } i \\ 0 & \text{otherwise} \end{cases}$$

a. Use these variable definitions and write constraints that appropriately restrict the amount shipped to each county.
b. The cost of assigning the 30-ton truck to the three counties is $100 to Polk, $85 to Dallas, and $50 to Jasper. Formulate and solve a mixed-integer linear program to determine how much to ship to each county.

13. Recall the Martin-Beck Company distribution system problem in Section 7.3.
a. Modify the formulation shown in Section 7.3 to account for the policy restriction that one plant, but not two, must be located either in Detroit or in Toledo.
b. Modify the formulation shown in Section 7.3 to account for the policy restriction that no more than two plants can be located in Denver, Kansas City, and St. Louis.

14. An automobile manufacturer has five outdated plants: one each in Michigan, Ohio, and California and two in New York. Management is considering modernizing these plants to manufacture engine blocks and transmissions for a new model car. The cost to modernize each plant and the manufacturing capacity after modernization are as follows:

Plant	Cost ($ millions)	Engine Blocks (1000s)	Transmissions (1000s)
Michigan	25	500	300
New York	35	800	400
New York	35	400	800
Ohio	40	900	600
California	20	200	300

The projected needs are for total capacities of 900,000 engine blocks and 900,000 transmissions. Management wants to determine which plants to modernize to meet projected manufacturing needs and, at the same time, minimize the total cost of modernization.
a. Develop a table that lists every possible option available to management. As part of your table, indicate the total engine block capacity and transmission capacity for each possible option, whether the option is feasible based on the projected needs, and the total modernization cost for each option.
b. Based on your analysis in part (a), what recommendation would you provide management?
c. Formulate a 0-1 integer programming model that could be used to determine the optimal solution to the modernization question facing management.
d. Solve the model formulated in part (c) to provide a recommendation for management.

15. CHB, Inc., is a bank holding company that is evaluating the potential for expanding into a 13-county region in the southwestern part of the state. State law permits establishing branches in any county that is adjacent to a county in which a PPB (principal place of business) is located. The following map shows the 13-county region with the population of each county indicated.

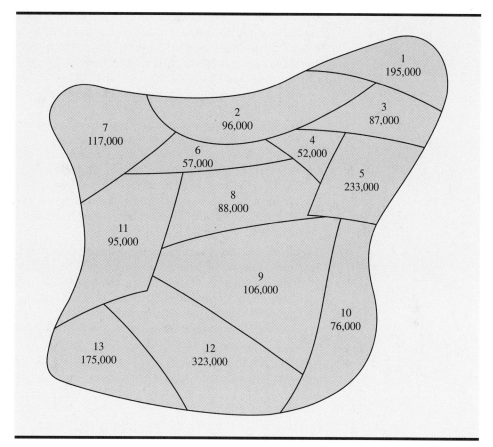

a. Assume that only one PPB can be established in the region. Where should it be located to maximize the population served? (*Hint:* Review the Ohio Trust formulation in Section 7.3. Consider minimizing the population not served, and introduce variable $y_i = 1$ if it is not possible to establish a branch in county i, and $y_i = 0$ otherwise.)

b. Suppose that two PPBs can be established in the region. Where should they be located to maximize the population served?

c. Management learned that a bank located in county 5 is considering selling. If CHB purchases this bank, the requisite PPB will be established in county 5, and a base for beginning expansion in the region will also be established. What advice would you give the management of CHB?

16. The Northshore Bank is working to develop an efficient work schedule for full-time and part-time tellers. The schedule must provide for efficient operation of the bank including adequate customer service, employee breaks, and so on. On Fridays the bank is open from 9:00 A.M. to 7:00 P.M. The number of tellers necessary to provide adequate customer service during each hour of operation is summarized here.

Time	Number of Tellers	Time	Number of Tellers
9:00 A.M.–10:00 A.M.	6	2:00 P.M.–3:00 P.M.	6
10:00 A.M.–11:00 A.M.	4	3:00 P.M.–4:00 P.M.	4
11:00 A.M.–Noon	8	4:00 P.M.–5:00 P.M.	7
Noon–1:00 P.M.	10	5:00 P.M.–6:00 P.M.	6
1:00 P.M.–2:00 P.M.	9	6:00 P.M.–7:00 P.M.	6

Each full-time employee starts on the hour and works a 4-hour shift, followed by 1 hour for lunch and then a 3-hour shift. Part-time employees work one 4-hour shift beginning on the hour. Considering salary and fringe benefits, full-time employees cost the bank $15 per hour ($105 a day), and part-time employees cost the bank $8 per hour ($32 per day).

a. Formulate an integer programming model that can be used to develop a schedule that will satisfy customer service needs at a minimum employee cost. (*Hint:* Let x_i = number of full-time employees coming on duty at the beginning of hour i and y_i = number of part-time employees coming on duty at the beginning of hour i.)

b. Solve the LP Relaxation of your model in part (a).

c. Solve for the optimal schedule of tellers. Comment on the solution.

d. After reviewing the solution to part (c), the bank manager realized that some additional requirements must be specified. Specifically, she wants to ensure that one full-time employee is on duty at all times and that there is a staff of at least five full-time employees. Revise your model to incorporate these additional requirements and solve for the optimal solution.

17. Refer to the Ohio Trust bank location problem introduced in Section 7.3. Table 7.3 shows the counties under consideration and the adjacent counties.

a. Write the complete integer programming model for expansion into the following counties only: Lorain, Huron, Richland, Ashland, Wayne, Medina, and Knox.

b. Use trial and error to solve the problem in part (a).

c. Use a computer program for integer programs to solve the problem.

18. Refer to the Salem Foods share of choices problem in Section 7.3 and address the following issues. It is rumored that King's is getting out of the frozen pizza business. If so, the major competitor for Salem Foods will be the Antonio's brand pizza.

a. Compute the overall utility for the Antonio's brand pizza for each of the consumers in Table 7.4.

b. Assume that Salem's only competitor is the Antonio's brand pizza. Formulate and solve the share of choices problem that will maximize market share. What is the best product design and what share of the market can be expected?

19. Burnside Marketing Research conducted a study for Barker Foods on some designs for a new dry cereal. Three attributes were found to be most influential in determining which cereal had the best taste: ratio of wheat to corn in the cereal flake, type of sweetener (sugar, honey, or artificial), and the presence or absence of flavor bits. Seven children participated in taste tests and provided the following part-worths for the attributes:

	Wheat/Corn		Sweetener			Flavor Bits	
Child	**Low**	**High**	**Sugar**	**Honey**	**Artificial**	**Present**	**Absent**
1	15	35	30	40	25	15	9
2	30	20	40	35	35	8	11
3	40	25	20	40	10	7	14
4	35	30	25	20	30	15	18
5	25	40	40	20	35	18	14
6	20	25	20	35	30	9	16
7	30	15	25	40	40	20	11

a. Suppose the overall utility (sum of part-worths) of the current favorite cereal is 75 for each child. What is the product design that will maximize the share of choices for the seven children in the sample?

b. Assume the overall utility of the current favorite cereal for the first four children in the group is 70, and the overall utility of the current favorite cereal for the last three children in the group is 80. What is the product design that will maximize the share of choices for the seven children in the sample?

20. Refer to Problem 14. Suppose that management determined that its cost estimates to modernize the New York plants were too low. Specifically, suppose that the actual cost is $40 million to modernize each plant.
    a. What changes in your previous 0-1 integer linear programming model are needed to incorporate these changes in costs?
    b. For these cost changes, what recommendations would you now provide management regarding the modernization plan?
    c. Reconsider the solution obtained using the revised cost figures. Suppose that management decides that closing two plants in the same state is not acceptable. How could this policy restriction be added to your 0-1 integer programming model?
    d. Based on the cost revision and the policy restriction presented in part (c), what recommendations would you now provide management regarding the modernization plan?

21. The Bayside Art Gallery is considering installing a video camera security system to reduce its insurance premiums. A diagram of the eight display rooms that Bayside uses for exhibitions is shown in Figure 7.13; the openings between the rooms are numbered 1 through 13. A security firm proposed that two-way cameras be installed at some room openings. Each camera has the ability to monitor the two rooms between which the camera is located. For example, if a camera were located at opening number 4, rooms 1 and 4 would be covered; if a camera were located at opening 11, rooms 7 and 8 would be covered; and so on. Management decided not to locate a camera system at the entrance to the display rooms. The objective is to provide security coverage for all eight rooms using the minimum number of two-way cameras.
    a. Formulate a 0-1 integer linear programming model that will enable Bayside's management to determine the locations for the camera systems.
    b. Solve the model formulated in part (a) to determine how many two-way cameras to purchase and where they should be located.
    c. Suppose that management wants to provide additional security coverage for room 7. Specifically, management wants room 7 to be covered by two cameras. How would your model formulated in part (a) have to change to accommodate this policy restriction?
    d. With the policy restriction specified in part (c), determine how many two-way camera systems will need to be purchased and where they will be located.

22. The Delta Group is a management consulting firm specializing in the health care industry. A team is being formed to study possible new markets, and a linear programming model has been developed for selecting team members. However, one constraint the president imposed is a team size of three, five, or seven members. The staff cannot figure out how to incorporate this requirement in the model. The current model requires that team members be selected from three departments and uses the following variable definitions:

$$x_1 = \text{the number of employees selected from department 1}$$
$$x_2 = \text{the number of employees selected from department 2}$$
$$x_3 = \text{the number of employees selected from department 3}$$

Show the staff how to write constraints that will ensure that the team will consist of three, five, or seven employees. The following integer variables should be helpful:

$$y_1 = \begin{cases} 1 & \text{if team size is 3} \\ 0 & \text{otherwise} \end{cases}$$

$$y_2 = \begin{cases} 1 & \text{if team size is 5} \\ 0 & \text{otherwise} \end{cases}$$

$$y_3 = \begin{cases} 1 & \text{if team size is 7} \\ 0 & \text{otherwise} \end{cases}$$

FIGURE 7.13   DIAGRAM OF DISPLAY ROOMS FOR BAYSIDE ART GALLERY

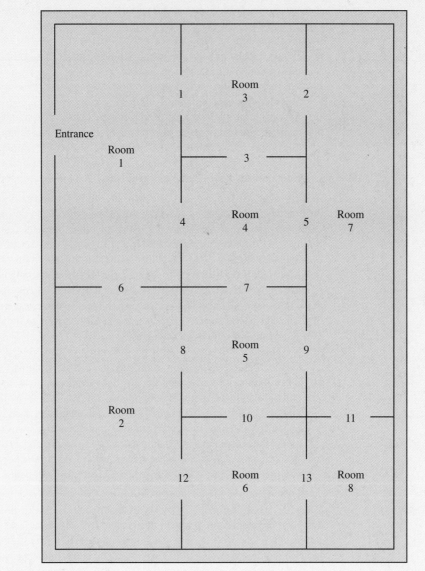

23. Roedel Electronics produces a variety of electrical components, including a remote controller for televisions and a remote controller for VCRs. Each controller consists of three subassemblies that are manufactured by Roedel: a base, a cartridge, and a keypad. Both controllers use the same base subassembly, but different cartridge and keypad subassemblies.

Roedel's sales forecast indicates that 7000 TV controllers and 5000 VCR controllers will be needed to satisfy demand during the upcoming Christmas season. Because only 500 hours of in-house manufacturing time are available, Roedel is considering purchasing some, or all, of the subassemblies from outside suppliers. If Roedel manufactures a subassembly in-house, it incurs a fixed setup cost as well as a variable manufacturing cost. The following table shows the setup cost, the manufacturing time per subassembly, the manufacturing cost per subassembly, and the cost to purchase each of the subassemblies from an outside supplier:

Subassembly	Setup Cost ($)	Manufacturing Time per Unit (min.)	Manufacturing Cost per Unit ($)	Purchase Cost per Unit ($)
Base	1000	0.9	0.40	0.65
TV cartridge	1200	2.2	2.90	3.45
VCR cartridge	1900	3.0	3.15	3.70
TV keypad	1500	0.8	0.30	0.50
VCR keypad	1500	1.0	0.55	0.70

    a. Determine how many units of each subassembly Roedel should manufacture and how many units Roedel should purchase. What is the total manufacturing and purchase cost associated with your recommendation?

    b. Suppose Roedel is considering purchasing new machinery to produce VCR cartridges. For the new machinery, the setup cost is $3000; the manufacturing time is 2.5 minutes per cartridge, and the manufacturing cost is $2.60 per cartridge. Assuming that the new machinery is purchased, determine how many units of each subassembly Roedel should manufacture and how many units of each subassembly Roedel should purchase. What is the total manufacturing and purchase cost associated with your recommendation? Do you think the new machinery should be purchased? Explain.

24. A mathematical programming system named SilverScreener uses a 0-1 integer programming model to help theater managers decide which movies to show on a weekly basis in a multiple-screen theater (*Interfaces,* May/June 2001). Suppose that management of Valley Cinemas would like to investigate the potential of using a similar scheduling system for their chain of multiple-screen theaters. Valley selected a small two-screen movie theater for the pilot testing and would like to develop an integer programming model to help schedule movies for the next four weeks. Six movies are available. The first week each movie is available, the last week each movie can be shown, and the maximum number of weeks that each movie can run are shown here:

Movie	First Week Available	Last Week Available	Max. Run (weeks)
1	1	2	2
2	1	3	2
3	1	1	2
4	2	4	2
5	3	6	3
6	3	5	3

    The overall viewing schedule for the theater is composed of the individual schedules for each of the six movies. For each movie, a schedule must be developed that specifies the week the movie starts and the number of consecutive weeks it will run. For instance, one possible schedule for movie 2 is for it to start in week 1 and run for two weeks. Theater policy requires that once a movie is started it must be shown in consecutive weeks. It cannot be stopped and restarted again. To represent the schedule possibilities for each movie, the following decision variables were developed:

$$x_{ijw} = \begin{cases} 1 & \text{if movie } i \text{ is scheduled to start in week } j \text{ and run for } w \text{ weeks} \\ 0 & \text{otherwise} \end{cases}$$

For example, $x_{532} = 1$ means that the schedule selected for movie 5 is to begin in week 3 and run for two weeks. For each movie, a separate variable is given for each possible schedule.

a. Three schedules are associated with movie 1. List the variables that represent these schedules.

b. Write a constraint requiring that only one schedule be selected for movie 1.

c. Write a constraint requiring that only one schedule be selected for movie 5.

d. What restricts the number of movies that can be shown in week 1? Write a constraint that restricts the number of movies selected for viewing in week 1.

e. Write a constraint that restricts the number of movies selected for viewing in week 3.

25. East Coast Trucking provides service from Boston to Miami using regional offices located in Boston, New York, Philadelphia, Baltimore, Washington, Richmond, Raleigh, Florence, Savannah, Jacksonville, and Tampa. The number of miles between each of the regional offices is provided in the following table:

	New York	Philadelphia	Baltimore	Washington	Richmond	Raleigh	Florence	Savannah	Jacksonville	Tampa	Miami
Boston	211	320	424	459	565	713	884	1056	1196	1399	1669
New York		109	213	248	354	502	673	845	985	1188	1458
Philadelphia			104	139	245	393	564	736	876	1079	1349
Baltimore				35	141	289	460	632	772	975	1245
Washington					106	254	425	597	737	940	1210
Richmond						148	319	491	631	834	1104
Raleigh							171	343	483	686	956
Florence								172	312	515	785
Savannah									140	343	613
Jacksonville										203	473
Tampa											270

The company's expansion plans involve constructing service facilities in some of the cities where a regional office is located. Each regional office must be within 400 miles of a service facility. For instance, if a service facility is constructed in Richmond, it can provide service to regional offices located in New York, Philadelphia, Baltimore, Washington, Richmond, Raleigh, and Florence. Management would like to determine the minimum number of service facilities needed and where they should be located.

a. Formulate an integer linear program that can be used to determine the minimum number of service facilities needed and their location.

b. Solve the linear program formulated in part (a). How many service facilities are required, and where should they be located?

c. Suppose that each service facility can only provide service to regional offices within 300 miles. How many service facilities are required, and where should they be located?

Case Problem 1   TEXTBOOK PUBLISHING

ASW Publishing, Inc., a small publisher of college textbooks, must make a decision regarding which books to publish next year. The books under consideration are listed in the following table, along with the projected three-year sales expected from each book:

Book Subject	Type of Book	Projected Sales ($1000s)
Business calculus	New	20
Finite mathematics	Revision	30
General statistics	New	15
Mathematical statistics	New	10
Business statistics	Revision	25
Finance	New	18
Financial accounting	New	25
Managerial accounting	Revision	50
English literature	New	20
German	New	30

The books listed as revisions are texts that ASW already has under contract; these texts are being considered for publication as new editions. The books that are listed as new have been reviewed by the company, but contracts have not yet been signed.

Three individuals in the company can be assigned to these projects, all of whom have varying amounts of time available; John has 60 days available, and Susan and Monica both have 40 days available. The days required by each person to complete each project are shown in the following table. For instance, if the business calculus book is published, it will require 30 days of John's time and 40 days of Susan's time. An "X" indicates that the person will not be used on the project. Note that at least two staff members will be assigned to each project except the finance book.

Book Subject	John	Susan	Monica
Business calculus	30	40	X
Finite mathematics	16	24	X
General statistics	24	X	30
Mathematical statistics	20	X	24
Business statistics	10	X	16
Finance	X	X	14
Financial accounting	X	24	26
Managerial accounting	X	28	30
English literature	40	34	30
German	X	50	36

ASW will not publish more than two statistics books or more than one accounting text in a single year. In addition, management decided that one of the mathematics books (business calculus or finite math) must be published, but not both.

Managerial Report

Prepare a report for the managing editor of ASW that describes your findings and recommendations regarding the best publication strategy for next year. In carrying out your analysis, assume that the fixed costs and the sales revenues per unit are approximately equal for all books; management is interested primarily in maximizing the total unit sales volume.

The managing editor also asked that you include recommendations regarding the following possible changes:

1. If it would be advantageous to do so, Susan can be moved off another project to allow her to work 12 more days.
2. If it would be advantageous to do so, Monica can also be made available for another 10 days.
3. If one or more of the revisions could be postponed for another year, should they be? Clearly the company will risk losing market share by postponing a revision.

Include details of your analysis in an appendix to your report.

Case Problem 2   YEAGER NATIONAL BANK

Using aggressive mail promotion with low introductory interest rates, Yeager National Bank (YNB) built a large base of credit card customers throughout the continental United States. Currently, all customers send their regular payments to the bank's corporate office located in Charlotte, North Carolina. Daily collections from customers making their regular payments are substantial, with an average of approximately $600,000. YNB estimates that it makes about 15 percent on its funds and would like to ensure that customer payments are credited to the bank's account as soon as possible. For instance, if it takes five days for a customer's payment to be sent through the mail, processed, and credited to the bank's account, YNB has potentially lost five days' worth of interest income. Although the time needed for this collection process cannot be completely eliminated, reducing it can be beneficial given the large amounts of money involved.

Instead of having all its credit card customers send their payments to Charlotte, YNB is considering having customers send their payments to one or more regional collection centers, referred to in the banking industry as lockboxes. Four lockbox locations have been proposed: Phoenix, Salt Lake City, Atlanta, and Boston. To determine which lockboxes to open and where lockbox customers should send their payments, YNB divided its customer base into five geographical regions: Northwest, Southwest, Central, Northeast, and Southeast. Every customer in the same region will be instructed to send his or her payment to the same lockbox. The following table shows the average number of days it takes before a customer's payment is credited to the bank's account when the payment is sent from each of the regions to each of the potential lockboxes:

Customer Zone	Location of Lockbox				Daily Collection ($1000s)
	Phoenix	Salt Lake City	Atlanta	Boston	
Northwest	4	2	4	4	80
Southwest	2	3	4	6	90
Central	5	3	3	4	150
Northeast	5	4	3	2	180
Southeast	4	6	2	3	100

Managerial Report

Dave Wolff, the vice president for cash management, asked you to prepare a report containing your recommendations for the number of lockboxes and the best lockbox locations. Mr. Wolff is primarily concerned with minimizing lost interest income, but he wants you to also consider the effect of an annual fee charged for maintaining a lockbox at any location. Although the amount of the fee is unknown at this time, we can assume that the fees will be in the range of $20,000 to $30,000 per location. Once good potential locations have been selected, Mr. Wolff will inquire as to the annual fees.

Case Problem 3   PRODUCTION SCHEDULING WITH CHANGEOVER COSTS

Buckeye Manufacturing produces heads for engines used in the manufacture of trucks. The production line is highly complex, and it measures 900 feet in length. Two types of engine heads are produced on this line: the P-Head and the H-Head. The P-Head is used in heavy-duty trucks and the H-Head is used in smaller trucks. Because only one type of head can be produced at a time, the line is set up to manufacture either the P-Head or the H-Head, but not both. Changeovers are made over a weekend; costs are $500 in going from a setup for the P-Head to a setup for the H-Head, and vice versa. When set up for the P-Head, the maximum production rate is 100 units per week and when set up for the H-Head, the maximum production rate is 80 units per week.

Buckeye just shut down for the week after using the line to produce the P-Head. The manager wants to plan production and changeovers for the next eight weeks. Currently, Buckeye's inventory consists of 125 P-Heads and 143 H-Heads. Inventory carrying costs are charged at an annual rate of 19.5 percent of the value of inventory. The production cost for the P-Head is $225, and the production cost for the H-Head is $310. The objective in developing a production schedule is to minimize the sum of production cost, plus inventory carrying cost, plus changeover cost.

Buckeye received the following requirements schedule from its customer (an engine assembly plant) for the next nine weeks:

| | **Product Demand** | |
Week	P-Head	H-Head
1	55	38
2	55	38
3	44	30
4	0	0
5	45	48
6	45	48
7	36	58
8	35	57
9	35	58

Safety stock requirements are such that week-ending inventory must provide for at least 80 percent of the next week's demand.

Managerial Report

Prepare a report for Buckeye's management with a production and changeover schedule for the next eight weeks. Be sure to note how much of the total cost is due to production, how much is due to inventory, and how much is due to changeover.

Appendix 7.1   EXCEL SOLUTION OF INTEGER LINEAR PROGRAMS

Worksheet formulation and solution for integer linear programs are similar to that for linear programming problems. Actually the worksheet formulation is exactly the same, but some additional information must be provided when setting up the **Solver Parameters** and **Solver Options** dialog boxes. First, constraints must be added in the **Solver Parameters** dialog box to identify the integer variables. In addition, the value for **Tolerance** in the **Options** dialog box will need to be adjusted to obtain an optimal solution.

Let us demonstrate the Excel solution of an integer linear program by showing how Excel can be used to solve the Eastborne Realty problem. The worksheet with the optimal solution is shown in Figure 7.14. We will describe the key elements of the worksheet and how to obtain the solution, and then interpret the solution.

Formulation

The data and descriptive labels appear in cells A1:G7 of the worksheet in Figure 7.14. The screened cells in the lower portion of the worksheet contain the information required by the

FIGURE 7.14   EXCEL SOLUTION FOR THE EASTBORNE REALTY PROBLEM

WEB file

Eastborne

	A	B	C	D	E	F	G	H
1	Eastborne Realty Problem							
2								
3		Townhouse	Apt. Bldg.					
4	Price($1000s)	282	400		Funds Avl.($1000s)		2000	
5	Mgr. Time	4	40		Mgr. Time Avl.		140	
6					Townhouses Avl.		5	
7	Ann. Cash Flow ($1000s)	10	15					
8								
9								
10	Model							
11								
12								
13	Max Cash Flow	70						
14					Constraints	LHS		RHS
15		Number of			Funds	1928	<=	2000
16		Townhouses	Apt. Bldgs.		Time	96	<=	140
17	Purchase Plan	4	2		Townhouses	4	<=	5
18								

Excel Solver (decision variables, objective function, constraint left-hand sides, and constraint right-hand sides).

Decision Variables	Cells B17:C17 are reserved for the decision variables. The optimal solution is to purchase four townhouses and two apartment buildings.
Objective Function	The formula =SUMPRODUCT(B7:C7,B17:C17) has been placed into cell B13 to reflect the annual cash flow associated with the solution. The optimal solution provides an annual cash flow of $70,000.
Left-Hand Sides	The left-hand sides for the three constraints are placed into cells F15:F17. Cell F15 =SUMPRODUCT(B4:C4,$B$17:$C$17) (Copy to sell F16) Cell F17 =B17
Right-Hand Sides	The right-hand sides for the three constraints are placed into cells H15:H17. Cell H15 =G4 (Copy to cells H16:H17)

Excel Solution

Begin the solution procedure by selecting the Data tab and Solver from the Analysis group, and entering the proper values into the **Solver Parameters** dialog box as shown in Figure 7.15. The first constraint shown is $B$17:$C$17 = integer. This constraint tells Solver that the decision variables in cell B17 and cell C17 must be integer. The integer requirement is created by using the **Add-Constraint** procedure. $B$17:$C17 is entered in the left-hand box of the **Cell Reference** area and **"int"** rather than <= , =, or => is selected as the form of the constraint. When **"int"** is selected, the term integer automatically appears as the right-hand side of the constraint. Figure 7.15 shows the additional information required to complete the **Solver Parameters** dialog box.

FIGURE 7.15   SOLVER PARAMETERS DIALOG BOX FOR THE EASTBORNE
REALTY PROBLEM

FIGURE 7.16　SOLVER OPTIONS DIALOG BOX FOR THE EASTBORNE REALTY PROBLEM

Next the **Options** button must be selected. The options **Assume Non-Negative** and **Assume Linear Model** must be checked. Figure 7.16 shows the **Solver Options** dialog box for the Eastborne Realty problem after completing this step.

0-1 variables are identified with the "bin" designation in the Solver Parameters dialog box.

If binary variables are present in an integer linear programming problem, you must select the designation **"bin"** instead of **"int"** when setting up the constraints in the **Solver Parameters** dialog box.

The time required to obtain an optimal solution can be highly variable for integer linear programs. As shown in Figure 7.16, the **Tolerance** parameter in the **Solver Options** dialog box has a default value of 5%. This means **Solver** will stop its search when it can guarantee that the best solution it has found so far is within 5% of the optimal solution in terms of objective function value. Therefore, to be assured of finding an optimal solution, you must change the default for **Tolerance** from 5% to 0% as shown in Figure 7.17.

To ensure you will find the optimal solution to an integer program using Excel Solver, be sure to set the Tolerance parameter in the Solver Options dialog box to 0%.

Clicking **OK** in the **Solver Options** dialog box and selecting **Solve** in the **Solver Parameters** dialog box will instruct Solver to compute the optimal integer solution. The worksheet in Figure 7.14 shows that the optimal solution is to purchase four townhouses and two apartment buildings. The annual cash flow is $70,000.

Appendix 7.2　LINGO SOLUTION OF INTEGER LINEAR PROGRAMS

LINGO may be used to solve linear integer programs. An integer linear model is entered into LINGO exactly as described in Appendix 7.2, but with additional statements for declaring variables as either general integer or binary. For example, to declare a variable x integer, you need to include the following statement:

@GIN(x) ;

FIGURE 7.17   SOLVER OPTIONS DIALOG BOX WITH TOLERANCE SET TO 0% FOR
THE EASTBORNE REALTY PROBLEM

Note the use of the semicolon to end the statement. GIN stands for "general integer." Likewise to declare a variable *y* a binary variable, the following statement is required:

@BIN(y) ;

BIN stands for "binary."

To illustrate the use of integer variables, the following statements are used to model the Eastborne Reality problem discussed in this chapter:

First, we enter the following:

MODEL:
TITLE   EASTBORNE REALTY;

This statement gives the LINGO model the title Eastborne Realty.

Next, we enter the following two lines to document the definition of our decision variables (recall that ! denotes a comment, and each comment ends with a semicolon).

! T = NUMBER OF TOWNHOUSES PURCHASED;
! A = NUMBER OF APARTMENT BUILDINGS PURCHASED;

Next, we enter the objective function and constraints, each with a descriptive comment.

! MAXIMIZE THE CASH FLOW;
MAX = 10*T + 15*A;

! FUNDS AVAILABLE ($1000);
282*T + 400*A <= 2000;

! TIME AVAILABLILITY;
4*T + 40*A <= 140;

! TOWNHOUSES AVAILABLE;
T <= 5;

Finally, we must declare the variables T and A as general integer variables. Again, to document the model we begin with a descriptive comment and then declare each variable as a general integer variable:

! DECLARE THE VARIABLES TO BE GENERAL INTEGER VARIABLES;
@GIN(T);
@GIN(A);

The complete LINGO model is available on the Web.

CHAPTER 8

Nonlinear Optimization Models

CONTENTS

8.1 A PRODUCTION
APPLICATION—PAR, INC.,
REVISITED
An Unconstrained Problem
A Constrained Problem
Local and Global Optima
Dual Values

8.2 CONSTRUCTING AN INDEX
FUND

8.3 MARKOWITZ PORTFOLIO
MODEL

8.4 BLENDING: THE POOLING
PROBLEM

8.5 FORECASTING ADOPTION OF
A NEW PRODUCT

Many business processes behave in a nonlinear manner. For example, the price of a bond is a nonlinear function of interest rates, and the price of a stock option is a nonlinear function of the price of the underlying stock. The marginal cost of production often decreases with the quantity produced, and the quantity demanded for a product is usually a nonlinear function of the price. These and many other nonlinear relationships are present in many business applications.

A **nonlinear optimization problem** is any optimization problem in which at least one term in the objective function or a constraint is nonlinear. We begin our study of nonlinear applications by considering a production problem in which the objective function is a nonlinear function of the decision variables. In Section 8.2 we develop a nonlinear application that involves designing a portfolio of securities to track a stock market index. We extend our treatment of portfolio models in Section 8.3 by presenting the Nobel Prize–winning Markowitz model for managing the trade-off between risk and return. Section 8.4 provides a nonlinear application of the linear programming blending model introduced in Chapter 4. In Section 8.5, we present a well-known and successful model used in forecasting sales or adoptions of a new product. As further illustrations of the use of nonlinear optimization in practice, the Management Science in Action, Pricing for Environmental Compliance in the Auto Industry, discusses how General Motors uses a mathematical model for coordinating pricing and production while satisfying government regulations on the gas mileage average of the car fleet. The Management Science in Action, Scheduling Flights and Crews for Bombardier Flexjet, discusses how Flexjet uses nonlinear optimization to assign aircraft and crews to flights.

Chapter appendices describe how to solve nonlinear programs using LINGO and Excel Solver.

MANAGEMENT SCIENCE IN ACTION

SCHEDULING FLIGHTS AND CREWS FOR BOMBARDIER FLEXJET*

Bombardier Flexjet is a leading company in the fast-growing fractional aircraft industry. Flexjet sells shares of business jets in share sizes equal to 50 hours of flying per year. A firm with fractional ownership is guaranteed 24-hour access to an aircraft with as little as a 4-hour lead time. Companies with a fractional share pay monthly management and usage fees. In exchange for the management fee, Flexjet provides hangar facilities, maintenance, and flight crews.

Because of the flexibility provided in the fractional aircraft business, the problem of scheduling crews and flights is even more complicated than in the commercial airline industry. Initially, Flexjet attempted to schedule flights by hand. However, this task quickly proved to be infeasible. Indeed, the inadequate manual scheduling resulted in Flexjet maintaining extra business jets and crews. The cost of the extra jets and crews was estimated at several hundred dollars per flight hour. A scheduling system using optimization was clearly required.

The scheduling system developed for Flexjet includes a large nonlinear optimization model that is integrated with a graphical user interface (GUI) used by Flexjet personnel. The model includes "hard" constraints based on Federal Aviation Administration (FAA) regulations, company rules, and aircraft performance characteristics. It also includes "soft constraints" that involve cost trade-offs. The model is used to assign aircraft and crews to flights.

The resulting model is too large to solve directly with commercial optimization software. Models with too many variables to solve directly are often solved using *decomposition* methods. Decomposition methods work with a *master problem* that includes only a small fraction of the total number of variables. Variables that are good candidates to be part of the optimal solution are identified through the solution of a *subproblem*. In the Flexjet model, the subproblem is a nonlinear integer program. The heart of the nonlinearity is the product of a binary variable that is 1 if a particular pair of flight legs is used and a continuous variable that is used to impose a time window on flight times. The subproblem is optimized using a technique called dynamic programming.

The optimization model was a big success. The model initially saved Flexjet $54 million, with a projected annual savings of $27 million. Much of

this cost saving is the result of reducing crew levels by 20% and aircraft inventory by 40%. Aircraft utilization also increased by 10%.

*Based on Richard Hicks et al., "Bombardier Flexjet Significantly Improves Its Fractional Aircraft Ownership Operations," *Interfaces* 35, no. 1 (January/February 2005): 49–60.

8.1   A PRODUCTION APPLICATION—PAR, INC., REVISITED

We introduce constrained and unconstrained nonlinear optimization problems by considering an extension of the Par, Inc., linear program introduced in Chapter 2. We first consider the case in which the relationship between price and quantity sold causes the objective function to become nonlinear. The resulting unconstrained nonlinear program is then solved, and we observe that the unconstrained optimal solution does not satisfy the production constraints. Adding the production constraints back into the problem allows us to show the formulation and solution of a constrained nonlinear program. The section closes with a discussion of local and global optima.

An Unconstrained Problem

Let us consider a revision of the Par, Inc., problem from Chapter 2. Recall that Par, Inc., decided to manufacture standard and deluxe golf bags. In formulating the linear programming model for the Par, Inc., problem, we assumed that it could sell all of the standard and deluxe bags it could produce. However, depending on the price of the golf bags, this assumption may not hold. An inverse relationship usually exists between price and demand. As price goes up, the quantity demanded goes down. Let P_S denote the price Par, Inc., charges for each standard bag and P_D denote the price for each deluxe bag. Assume that the demand for standard bags S and the demand for deluxe bags D are given by

$$S = 2250 - 15P_S \tag{8.1}$$
$$D = 1500 - 5P_D \tag{8.2}$$

The revenue generated from standard bags is the price of each standard bag P_S times the number of standard bags sold S. If the cost to produce a standard bag is $70, the cost to produce S standard bags is 70 S. Thus the profit contribution for producing and selling S standard bags (revenue – cost) is

$$P_S S - 70S \tag{8.3}$$

We can solve equation (8.1) for P_S to show how the price of a standard bag is related to the number of standard bags sold. It is $P_S = 150 - \frac{1}{15}S$. Substituting $150 - \frac{1}{15}S$ for P_S in equation (8.3), the profit contribution for standard bags is

$$P_S S - 70S = (150 - \tfrac{1}{15}S)S - 70S = 80S - \tfrac{1}{15}S^2 \tag{8.4}$$

Suppose that the cost to produce each deluxe golf bag is $150. Using the same logic we used to develop equation (8.4), the profit contribution for deluxe bags is

$$P_D D - 150D = (300 - \tfrac{1}{5}D)D - 150D = 150D - \tfrac{1}{5}D^2$$

Total profit contribution is the sum of the profit contribution for standard bags and the profit contribution for deluxe bags. Thus, total profit contribution is written as

$$\text{Total profit contribution} = 80S - \tfrac{1}{15}S^2 + 150D - \tfrac{1}{5}D^2 \qquad (8.5)$$

Note that the two linear demand functions, equations (8.1) and (8.2), give a nonlinear total profit contribution function, equation (8.5). This function is an example of a *quadratic function* because the nonlinear terms have a power of 2.

Using LINGO (see Appendix 8.1), we find that the values of S and D that maximize the profit contribution function are $S = 600$ and $D = 375$. The corresponding prices are $110 for standard bags and $225 for deluxe bags, and the profit contribution is $52,125. These values provide the optimal solution for Par, Inc., if all production constraints are also satisfied.

A Constrained Problem

Unfortunately, Par, Inc., cannot make the profit contribution associated with the optimal solution to the unconstrained problem because the constraints defining the feasible region are violated. For instance, the cutting and dyeing constraint is

$$\tfrac{7}{10}S + D \le 630$$

A production quantity of 600 standard bags and 375 deluxe bags will require $\tfrac{7}{10}(600) + 1(375) = 795$ hours, which exceeds the limit of 630 hours by 165 hours. The feasible region for the original Par, Inc., problem along with the unconstrained optimal solution point (600, 375) are shown in Figure 8.1. The unconstrained optimum of (600, 375) is obviously outside the feasible region.

Clearly, the problem that Par, Inc., must solve is to maximize the total profit contribution

$$80S - \tfrac{1}{15}S^2 + 150D - \tfrac{1}{5}D^2$$

subject to all of the departmental labor hour constraints that were given in Chapter 2. The complete mathematical model for the Par, Inc., constrained nonlinear maximization problem follows:

WEB file

ParNonlinear

$$\text{Max} \quad 80S - \tfrac{1}{15}S^2 + 150D - \tfrac{1}{5}D^2$$

s.t.

$$
\begin{array}{ll}
\tfrac{7}{10}S + \ D \le 630 & \text{Cutting and dyeing} \\
\tfrac{1}{2}S + \tfrac{5}{6}D \le 600 & \text{Sewing} \\
S + \tfrac{2}{3}D \le 708 & \text{Finishing} \\
\tfrac{1}{10}S + \tfrac{1}{4}D \le 135 & \text{Inspection and packaging} \\
\end{array}
$$

$$S, D \ge 0$$

FIGURE 8.1   THE PAR, INC., FEASIBLE REGION AND THE OPTIMAL SOLUTION FOR THE UNCONSTRAINED OPTIMIZATION PROBLEM

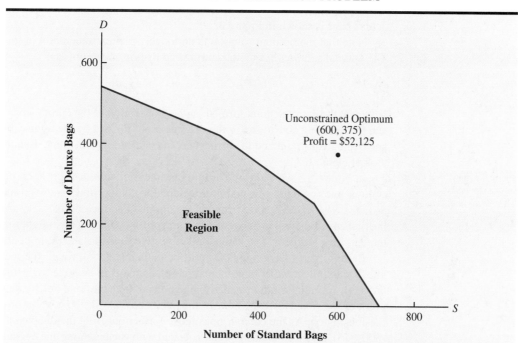

This maximization problem is exactly the same as the Par, Inc., problem in Chapter 2 except for the nonlinear objective function. The solution to this constrained nonlinear maximization problem is shown in Figure 8.2.

The optimal value of the objective function is $49,920.55. The Variable section shows that the optimal solution is to produce 459.7166 standard bags and 308.1984 deluxe bags. In the Constraint section, in the Slack/Surplus column, the value of 0 in Constraint 1 means that

FIGURE 8.2   SOLUTION FOR THE NONLINEAR PAR, INC., PROBLEM

Optimal Objective value = 49920.54655

Variable	Value	Reduced Cost
S	459.71660	0.00000
D	308.19838	0.00000

Constraint	Slack/Surplus	Dual Value
1	0.00000	26.72059
2	113.31074	0.00000
3	42.81679	0.00000
4	11.97875	0.00000

the optimal solution uses all the labor hours in the cutting and dyeing department; but the nonzero values in rows 2–4 indicate that slack hours are available in the other departments.

A graphical view of the optimal solution of 459.7166 standard bags and 308.1984 deluxe bags is shown in Figure 8.3.

Note that the optimal solution is no longer at an extreme point of the feasible region. The optimal solution lies on the cutting and dyeing constraint line

$$\tfrac{7}{10}S + D = 630$$

but *not* at the extreme point formed by the intersection of the cutting and dyeing constraint and the finishing constraint, or the extreme point formed by the intersection of the cutting and dyeing constraint and the inspection and packaging constraint. To understand why, we look at Figure 8.3.

Figure 8.3 shows that the profit contribution contour lines for the nonlinear Par, Inc., problem are ellipses.

In Figure 8.3 we see three profit contribution *contour lines*. Each point on the same contour line is a point of equal profit. Here, the contour lines show profit contributions of $45,000, $49,920.55, and $51,500. In the original Par, Inc., problem described in Chapter 2 the objective function is linear and thus the profit contours are straight lines. However, for the Par, Inc., problem with a quadratic objective function, the profit contours are ellipses.

Because part of the $45,000 profit contour line cuts through the feasible region, we know an infinite number of combinations of standard and deluxe bags will yield a profit of $45,000. An infinite number of combinations of standard and deluxe bags also provide a profit of $51,500. However, none of the points on the $51,500 contour profit line are in the feasible region. As the contour lines move further out from the unconstrained optimum of (600, 375), the profit contribution associated with each contour line decreases. The contour

FIGURE 8.3   THE PAR, INC., FEASIBLE REGION WITH OBJECTIVE FUNCTION
CONTOUR LINES

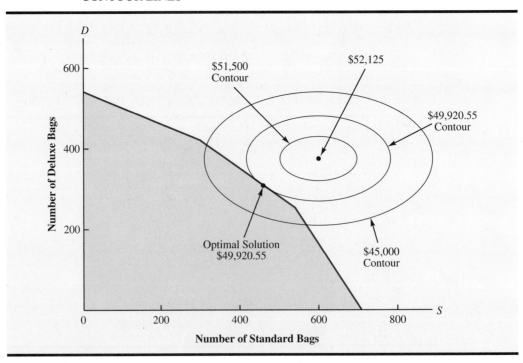

line representing a profit of $49,920.55 intersects the feasible region at a single point. This solution provides the maximum possible profit. No contour line that has a profit contribution greater than $49,920.55 will intersect the feasible region. Because the contour lines are nonlinear, the contour line with the highest profit can touch the boundary of the feasible region at any point, not just an extreme point. In the Par, Inc., case the optimal solution is on the cutting and dyeing constraint line part way between two extreme points.

It is also possible for the optimal solution to a nonlinear optimization problem to lie in the interior of the feasible region. For instance, if the right-hand sides of the constraints in the Par, Inc., problem were all increased by a sufficient amount, the feasible region would expand so that the optimal unconstrained solution point of (600, 375) in Figure 8.3 would be in the interior of the feasible region. Many linear programming algorithms (e.g., the simplex method) optimize by examining only the extreme points and selecting the extreme point that gives the best solution value. As the solution to the constrained Par, Inc., nonlinear problem illustrates, such a method will not work in the nonlinear case because the optimal solution is generally not an extreme point solution. Hence, nonlinear programming algorithms are more complex than linear programming algorithms, and the details are beyond the scope of this text. Fortunately, we don't need to know how nonlinear algorithms work; we just need to know how to use them. Computer software such as LINGO and Excel Solver are available to solve nonlinear programming problems, and we describe how to use these software packages in the chapter appendices.

Local and Global Optima

A feasible solution is a **local optimum** if no other feasible solutions with a better objective function value are found in the immediate neighborhood. For example, for the constrained Par problem, the local optimum corresponds to a **local maximum;** a point is a local maximum if no other feasible solutions with a larger objective function value are in the immediate neighborhood. Similarly, for a minimization problem, a point is a **local minimum** if no other feasible solutions with a smaller objective function value are in the immediate neighborhood.

Nonlinear optimization problems can have multiple local optimal solutions, which means we are concerned with finding the best of the local optimal solutions. A feasible solution is a **global optimum** if no other feasible points with a better objective function value are found in the feasible region. In the case of a maximization problem, the global optimum corresponds to a global maximum. A point is a **global maximum** if no other points in the feasible region give a strictly larger objective function value. For a minimization problem, a point is a **global minimum** if no other feasible points with a strictly smaller objective function value are in the feasible region. Obviously a global maximum is also a local maximum, and a global minimum is also a local minimum.

Nonlinear problems with multiple local optima are difficult to solve. But in many nonlinear applications, a single local optimal solution is also the global optimal solution. For such problems, we only need to find a local optimal solution. We will now present some of the more common classes of nonlinear problems of this type.

Consider the function $f(X, Y) = -X^2 - Y^2$. The shape of this function is illustrated in Figure 8.4. A function that is bowl-shaped down is called a **concave function.** The maximum value for this particular function is 0, and the point $(0, 0)$ gives the optimal value of 0. The point $(0, 0)$ is a local maximum; but it is also a *global maximum* because no point gives a larger function value. In other words, no values of X or Y result in an objective function value greater than 0. Functions that are concave, such as $f(X, Y) = -X^2 - Y^2$, have a single local maximum that is also a global maximum. This type of nonlinear problem is relatively easy to maximize.

FIGURE 8.4   A CONCAVE FUNCTION $f(X, Y) = -X^2 - Y^2$

The objective function for the nonlinear Par, Inc., problem is another example of a concave function.

$$80S - \tfrac{1}{15} S^2 + 150D - \tfrac{1}{5} D^2$$

In general, if all of the squared terms in a quadratic function have a negative coefficient and there are no cross-product terms, such as xy, then the function is a concave quadratic function. Thus, for the Par, Inc., problem, we are assured that the local maximum identified by LINGO in Figure 8.2 is the global maximum.

Let us now consider another type of function with a single local optimum that is also a global optimum. Consider the function $f(X, Y) = X^2 + Y^2$. The shape of this function is illustrated in Figure 8.5. It is bowl-shaped up and called a **convex function.** The minimum value for this particular function is 0, and the point $(0, 0)$ gives the minimum value of 0. The point $(0, 0)$ is a local minimum and a global minimum because no values of X or Y give an objective function value less than 0. Functions that are convex, such as $f(X, Y) = X^2 + Y^2$, have a single local minimum and are relatively easy to minimize.

For a concave function, we can be assured that if our computer software finds a local maximum, it is a global maximum. Similarly, for a convex function, we know that if our computer software finds a local minimum, it is a global minimum. Concave and convex functions are well behaved. However, some nonlinear functions have multiple local optima. For example, Figure 8.6 shows the graph of the following function:[1]

$$f(X, Y) = 3(1 - X)^2 e^{-X^2 - (Y+1)^2} - 10(X/5 - X^3 - Y^5)e^{-X^2 - Y^2} - e^{-(X+1)^2 - Y^2}/3.$$

FIGURE 8.5   A CONVEX FUNCTION $f(X, Y) = X^2 + Y^2$

---

[1] This example is taken from the LINDO API manual available at www.lindo.com.

FIGURE 8.6 A FUNCTION WITH LOCAL MAXIMUMS AND MINIMUMS

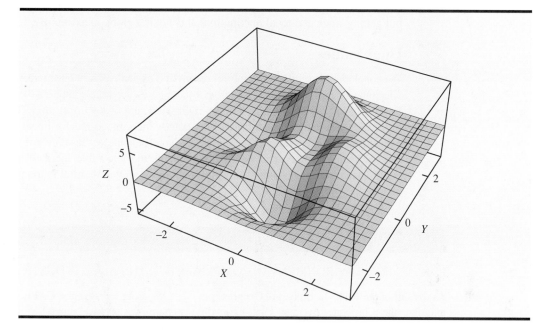

The hills and valleys in this graph show that this function has several local maximums and local minimums. These concepts are further illustrated in Figure 8.7, which is the same function as in Figure 8.6 but from a different viewpoint. It indicates two local minimums and three local maximums. One of the local minimums is also the global minimum, and one of the local maximums is also the global maximum.

Note that the output we use in this chapter for nonlinear optimization uses the label Optimal Objective Value. However, the solution may be either a local or a global optimum, depending on the problem characteristics.

From a technical standpoint, functions with multiple local optima pose a serious challenge for optimization software; most nonlinear optimization software methods can get "stuck" and terminate at a local optimum. Unfortunately, many applications can be nonlinear, and there is a severe penalty for finding a local optimum that is not a global optimum. Developing algorithms capable of finding the global optimum is currently an active research area. But the problem of minimizing a convex quadratic function over a linear constraint set is relatively easy, and for problems of this type there is no danger in getting stuck

FIGURE 8.7 ANOTHER VIEWPOINT OF A FUNCTION WITH LOCAL MAXIMUMS AND MINIMUMS

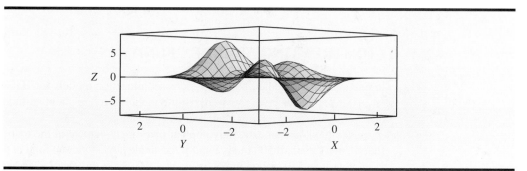

at a local minimum that is not a global minimum. Similarly, the problem of maximizing a concave quadratic function over a linear constraint set is also relatively easy to solve without getting stuck at a local maximum that is not the global maximum.

Dual Values

We conclude this section with a brief discussion of dual values. The concept of a dual value was introduced in Chapter 3. Recall that the dual value is the change in the value of the optimal solution per unit increase in the right-hand side of the constraint. The interpretation of the dual value for nonlinear models is exactly the same as it is for linear programs. However, for nonlinear problems the allowable increase and decrease are not usually reported. This is because for typical nonlinear problems the allowable increase and decrease are zero. That is, if you change the right-hand side by even a small amount, the dual value changes.

MANAGEMENT SCIENCE IN ACTION

PRICING FOR ENVIRONMENTAL COMPLIANCE IN THE AUTO INDUSTRY*

As a result of the 1973 Oil Embargo, Congress put into law the Corporate Average Fuel Economy (CAFE) regulations in 1975. The CAFE standards are designed to promote the sale of fuel-efficient automobiles and light trucks, thus reducing dependence on oil. The CAFE standards were modified when President Bush signed into law the Clean Energy Act of 2007. This law requires that automakers boost fleet gas mileage average to 35 MPG by the year 2020. Although polls reveal strong support for such regulatory action, actual consumer behavior runs counter to supporting the purchase of fuel-efficient cars. Indeed, car manufacturers are faced with the problem of influencing consumers to purchase more fuel-efficient cars in order for the manufacturer to meet the CAFE mandated standard. One way to influence consumer purchase behavior is through price. Lowering the price of fuel-efficient cars is one way to shift demand to this market. Of course, this should be done in a way to keep profits as large as possible subject to the CAFE constraints.

In order to meet the CAFE constraints while maximizing profits, General Motors (GM) used a mathematical model for coordinated pricing and production called Visual CAFE. This was built into an Excel spreadsheet with data input from Microsoft Access. The objective function for this model is much like the objective function for the nonlinear version of Par, Inc., that we develop in this section. In both cases the objective is to maximize profit, and the profit function is the product of quantity sold times the contribution margin of each product. The quantity sold is based on a linear demand function. A key constraint is the CAFE constraint, which is a constraint on the average miles per gallon for the GM fleet of cars. In addition, there are constraints on assembly, engine, and transmission capacity.

*Based on Stephan Biller and Julie Swan, "Pricing for Environmental Compliance in the Auto Industry," *Interfaces* 36, no. 2 (March/April 2007): 118–125.

8.2   CONSTRUCTING AN INDEX FUND

In Section 5.4 we studied portfolio and asset allocation models for Hauck Financial Services. Several linear programs were built to model different client attitudes toward risk. In this section we study an important related application.

Index funds are an extremely popular investment vehicle in the mutual fund industry. Indeed, the Vanguard 500 Index Fund is the single largest mutual fund in the United States, with more than $89 billion in net assets in 2009. An **index fund** is an example of passive

TABLE 8.1   ONE-YEAR RETURNS FOR FOUR VANGUARD INDEX FUNDS

Vanguard Fund	Vanguard Fund Return	Market Index	Market Index Return
500 Index Fund	4.77%	S&P 500	4.91%
Total Stock Index	5.98%	MSCI Broad Market	6.08%
REIT Index	11.90%	MSCI REIT	12.13%
Short-Term Bond	1.31%	Lehman 1-5 Index	1.44%

asset management. The key idea behind an index fund is to construct a portfolio of stocks, mutual funds, or other securities that matches as closely as possible the performance of a broad market index such as the S&P 500.

Table 8.1 shows the one-year returns for four Vanguard Index Funds[2] and the returns for the corresponding market indexes. Several interesting issues are illustrated in this table. First, Vanguard has index funds for numerous types of investments. For example, the first two index funds are stock funds: the S&P 500 Index Fund and the MSCI Broad Market fund. The MSCI REIT fund is an investment in the real estate market, and the Short-Term Bond (Lehman 1-5) fund is an investment in the corporate bond market. Second, notice that even though the returns show considerable variation between the funds, the index funds do a good job of matching the return of the corresponding market index.

Why are index funds so popular? Behind the popularity of index funds is a substantial amount of research in finance that basically says, "You can't beat the market." In fact, the vast majority of mutual fund managers actually underperform leading market indexes such as the S&P 500. Therefore, many investors are satisfied with investments that provide a return that more closely matches the market return.

Now, let's revisit the Hauck Financial Services example from Chapter 5. Assume that Hauck has a substantial number of clients who wish to own a mutual fund portfolio with the characteristic that the portfolio, as a whole, closely matches the performance of the S&P 500 stock index. What percentage of the portfolio should be invested in each mutual fund in order to most closely mimic the performance of the entire S&P 500 index?

In Table 8.2 we reproduce Table 5.4 (see Chapter 5), with an additional row that gives the S&P 500 return for each planning scenario. Recall that the columns show the actual percentage return that was earned by each mutual fund in that year. These five columns represent the most likely scenarios for the coming year.

The variables used in the model presented in Section 5.4 represented the proportion of the portfolio invested in each mutual fund.

FS = proportion of portfolio invested in a foreign stock mutual fund

IB = proportion of portfolio invested in an intermediate-term bond fund

LG = proportion of portfolio invested in a large-cap growth fund

LV = proportion of portfolio invested in a large-cap value fund

SG = proportion of portfolio invested in a small-cap growth fund

SV = proportion of portfolio invested in a small-cap value fund

---

[2] These data were taken from www.vanguard.com and are for the one-year period ending December 31, 2005.

TABLE 8.2 MUTUAL FUND PERFORMANCE IN FIVE SELECTED YEARS USED AS PLANNING SCENARIOS FOR THE NEXT 12 MONTHS

Mutual Fund	Planning Scenarios				
	Year 1	Year 2	Year 3	Year 4	Year 5
Foreign Stock	10.06	13.12	13.47	45.42	−21.93
Intermediate-Term Bond	17.64	3.25	7.51	−1.33	7.36
Large-Cap Growth	32.41	18.71	33.28	41.46	−23.26
Large-Cap Value	32.36	20.61	12.93	7.06	−5.37
Small-Cap Growth	33.44	19.40	3.85	58.68	−9.02
Small-Cap Value	24.56	25.32	−6.70	5.43	17.31
S&P 500 Return	**25.00**	**20.00**	**8.00**	**30.00**	**−10.00**

The portfolio models presented in Section 5.4 chose the proportion of the portfolio to invest in each mutual fund in order to maximize return subject to constraints on the portfolio risk. Here we wish to choose the proportion of the portfolio to invest in each mutual fund in order to track as closely as possible the S&P 500 return.

For clarity of model exposition, we introduce variables $R1$, $R2$, $R3$, $R4$, and $R5$, which measure the portfolio return for each scenario. Consider, for example, variable $R1$. If the scenario represented by year 1 reflects what happens over the next 12 months, the portfolio return under scenario 1 is

$$10.06FS + 17.64IB + 32.41LG + 32.36LV + 33.44SG + 24.56SV = R1$$

Similarly, if scenarios 2–5 reflect the returns obtained over the next 12 months, the portfolio returns under scenarios 2–5 are as follows:

Scenario 2 return:

$$13.12FS + 3.25IB + 18.71LG + 20.61LV + 19.40SG + 25.32SV = R2$$

Scenario 3 return:

$$13.47FS + 7.51IB + 33.28LG + 12.93LV + 3.85SG - 6.70SV = R3$$

Scenario 4 return:

$$45.42FS - 1.33IB + 41.46LG + 7.06LV + 58.68SG + 5.43SV = R4$$

Scenario 5 return:

$$-21.93FS + 7.36IB - 23.26LG - 5.37LV - 9.02SG + 17.31SV = R5$$

Next, for each scenario we compute the deviation between the return for the scenario and the S&P 500 return. Based on the last row of Table 8.2, the deviations are

$$R1 - 25, \quad R2 - 20, \quad R3 - 8, \quad R4 - 30, \quad R5 - (-10) \qquad (8.6)$$

The objective is for the portfolio returns to match as closely as possible the S&P 500 returns. To do so, we might try minimizing the sum of the deviations given in equation (8.6) as follows:

$$\text{Min} \quad (R1 - 25) + (R2 - 20) + (R3 - 8) + (R4 - 30) + (R5 - [-10]) \quad (8.7)$$

Unfortunately, if we use expression (8.7), positive and negative deviations will cancel each other out, so a portfolio that has a small value for expression (8.7) might actually behave quite differently than the target index. Also, because we want to get as close to the target returns as possible, it makes sense to assign a higher marginal penalty cost for large deviations than for small deviations. A function that achieves this goal is

$$\text{Min} \ (R1 - 25)^2 + (R2 - 20)^2 + (R3 - 8)^2 + (R4 - 30)^2 + (R5 - [-10])^2$$

When we square each term, positive and negative deviations do not cancel each other out, and the marginal penalty cost for deviations increases as the deviation gets larger. The complete mathematical model we have developed involves 11 variables and 6 constraints (excluding the nonnegativity constraints).

WEB file

HauckIndex

$$\text{Min} \quad (R1 - 25)^2 + (R2 - 20)^2 + (R3 - 8)^2 + (R4 - 30)^2 + (R5 - [-10])^2$$
$$\text{s.t.}$$
$$10.06FS + 17.64IB + 32.41LG + 32.36LV + 33.44SG + 24.56SV = R1$$
$$13.12FS + 3.25IB + 18.71LG + 20.61LV + 19.40SG + 25.32SV = R2$$
$$13.47FS + 7.51IB + 33.28LG + 12.93LV + 3.85SG - 6.70SV = R3$$
$$45.42FS - 1.33IB + 41.46LG + 7.06LV + 58.68SG + 5.43SV = R4$$
$$-21.93FS + 7.36IB - 23.26LG - 5.37LV - 9.02SG + 17.31SV = R5$$
$$FS + IB + LG + LV + SG + SV = 1$$
$$FS, IB, LG, LV, SG, SV \geq 0$$

This minimization problem is nonlinear because of the quadratic terms that appear in the objective function. For example, in the term $(R1 - 25)^2$ the variable $R1$ is raised to a power of 2 and is therefore nonlinear. However, because the coefficient of each squared term is positive, and there are no cross-product terms, the objective function is a convex function. Therefore, we are guaranteed that any local minimum is also a global minimum.

The solution for the Hauck Financial Services problem is given in Figure 8.8. The optimal value of the objective function is 4.42689, the sum of the squares of the return deviations. The portfolio calls for approximately 30% of the funds to be invested in the foreign stock fund ($FS = 0.30334$), 36% of the funds to be invested in the large-cap value fund ($LV = 0.36498$), 23% of the funds to be invested in the small-cap growth fund ($SG = 0.22655$), and 11% of the funds to be invested in the small-cap value fund ($SV = 0.10513$).

Table 8.3 shows a comparison of the portfolio return (see $R1$, $R2$, $R3$, $R4$, and $R5$ in Figure 8.8) to the S&P 500 return for each scenario. Notice how closely the portfolio returns match the S&P 500 returns. Based on historical data, a portfolio with this mix of Hauck mutual funds will indeed closely match the returns for the S&P 500 stock index.

We just illustrated an important application of nonlinear programming in finance. In the next section we show how the Markowitz model can be used to construct a portfolio that minimizes risk subject to a constraint requiring a minimum level of return.

FIGURE 8.8 SOLUTION FOR THE HAUCK FINANCIAL SERVICES PROBLEM

```
Optimal Objective Value = 4.42689

        Variable              Value            Reduced Cost
     --------------     ----------------     ----------------
           FS                0.30334              0.00000
           IB                0.00000             64.84640
           LG                0.00000             18.51296
           LV                0.36498              0.00000
           SG                0.22655              0.00000
           SV                0.10513              0.00000
           R1               25.02024              0.00000
           R2               18.55903              0.00000
           R3                8.97303              0.00000
           R4               30.21926              0.00000
           R5               -8.83586              0.00000

        Constraint       Slack/Surplus          Dual Value
     --------------     ----------------     ----------------
            1                0.00000              0.04047
            2                0.00000             -2.88192
            3                0.00000              1.94607
            4                0.00000              0.43855
            5                0.00000              2.32829
            6                0.00000            -42.33078
```

TABLE 8.3 PORTFOLIO RETURN VERSUS S&P 500 RETURN

Scenario	Portfolio Return	S&P 500 Return
1	25.02	25
2	18.56	20
3	8.97	8
4	30.22	30
5	−8.84	−10

NOTES AND COMMENTS

1. The returns for the planning scenarios in Table 8.2 are the actual returns for five years in the past. They were chosen as the past data most likely to represent what could happen over the next year. By using actual past data, the correlation among the mutual funds is automatically incorporated into the model.

2. Notice that the return variables ($R1, R2, \ldots, R5$) in the Hauck model are not restricted to be ≥ 0. This is because it might be that the best investment strategy results in a negative return in a given year. From Figure 8.8 you can see that the optimal value of $R5$ is −8.84, a return of −8.84%. A variable may be designated in LINGO as a free variable using the statement @FREE. For example, @FREE(R1); would designate R1 as a free variable. For an Excel model with some variables restricted to be nonnegative and others unrestricted, do not check **Assume Nonnegative** under options and add any nonnegativity constraints in the constraint section of the **Solver Dialog** box.

3. While we used variables $R1, R2, \ldots, R5$ for model clarity in the Hauck model, they are not needed to solve the problem. They do, however, make the model simpler to read and interpret. Also, a model user is likely to be interested in the investment return in each year and these variables provide this information. The use of extra variables for clarity exposes an interesting difference between LINGO models and Excel models. In a LINGO model these quantities must be designated decision variables. In an Excel model the returns can simply be calculated in a cell used in the model and do not have to be designated as adjustable cells (because they are functions of adjustable cells).

4. It would not be practical for an individual investor who desires to receive the same return as the S&P 500 to purchase all the S&P 500 stocks. The index fund we have constructed permits such an investor to approximate the S&P 500 return.

5. In this section we constructed an index fund from among mutual funds. The investment alternatives used to develop the index fund could also be individual stocks that are part of the S&P 500.

8.3   MARKOWITZ PORTFOLIO MODEL

Harry Markowitz received the 1990 Nobel Prize for his path-breaking work in portfolio optimization. The Markowitz mean-variance portfolio model is a classic application of nonlinear programming. In this section we present the **Markowitz mean-variance portfolio model.** Numerous variations of this basic model are used by money management firms throughout the world.

A key trade-off in most portfolio optimization models must be made between risk and return. In order to get greater returns, the investor must also face greater risk. The index fund model of the previous section managed the trade-off passively. An investor in the index fund we constructed must be satisfied with the risk/return characteristics of the S&P 500. Other portfolio models explicitly quantify the trade-off between risk and return. In most portfolio optimization models, the return used is the expected return (or average) of the possible outcomes.

Consider the Hauck Financial Services example developed in the previous section. Five scenarios represented the possible outcomes over a one-year planning horizon. The return under each scenario was defined by the variables $R1, R2, R3, R4,$ and $R5$, respectively. If p_s is the probability of scenario s among n possible scenarios, then the *expected return* for the portfolio $\overline{R}$ is

$$\overline{R} = \sum_{s=1}^{n} p_s R_s \tag{8.8}$$

If we assume that the five planning scenarios in the Hauck Financial Services model are equally likely, then

$$\overline{R} = \sum_{s=1}^{5} \tfrac{1}{5} R_s = \tfrac{1}{5} \sum_{s=1}^{5} R_s$$

Measuring risk is a bit more difficult. Entire books are devoted to the topic. The measure of risk most often associated with the Markowitz portfolio model is the variance of the portfolio. If the expected return is defined by equation (8.8), the portfolio *variance* is

$$Var = \sum_{s=1}^{n} p_s (R_s - \overline{R})^2 \tag{8.9}$$

For the Hauck Financial Services example, the five planning scenarios are equally likely. Thus,

$$Var = \sum_{s=1}^{5} \tfrac{1}{5}(R_s - \overline{R})^2 = \tfrac{1}{5}\sum_{s=1}^{5}(R_s - \overline{R})^2$$

The portfolio variance is the average of the sum of the squares of the deviations from the mean value under each scenario. The larger this number, the more widely dispersed the scenario returns are about their average value. If the portfolio variance were equal to zero, then every scenario return R_i would be equal.

Two basic ways to formulate the Markowitz model are (1) minimize the variance of the portfolio subject to a constraint on the expected return of the portfolio; and (2) maximize the expected return of the portfolio subject to a constraint on variance. Consider the first case. Assume that Hauck clients would like to construct a portfolio from the six mutual funds listed in Table 8.2 that will minimize their risk as measured by the portfolio variance. However, the clients also require the expected portfolio return to be at least 10%. In our notation, the objective function is

$$\text{Min } \tfrac{1}{5}\sum_{s=1}^{5}(R_s - \overline{R})^2$$

The constraint on expected portfolio return is $\overline{R} \geq 10$. The complete Markowitz model involves 12 variables and 8 constraints (excluding the nonnegativity constraints).

WEB file

HauckMarkowitz

$$\text{Min } \tfrac{1}{5}\sum_{s=1}^{5}(R_s - \overline{R})^2 \qquad (8.10)$$

s.t.

$$10.06FS + 17.64IB + 32.41LG + 32.36LV + 33.44SG + 24.56SV = R1 \quad (8.11)$$

$$13.12FS + 3.25IB + 18.71LG + 20.61LV + 19.40SG + 25.32SV = R2 \quad (8.12)$$

$$13.47FS + 7.51IB + 33.28LG + 12.93LV + 3.85SG - 6.70SV = R3 \quad (8.13)$$

$$45.42FS - 1.33IB + 41.46LG + 7.06LV + 58.68SG + 5.43SV = R4 \quad (8.14)$$

$$-21.93FS + 7.36IB - 23.26LG - 5.37LV - 9.02SG + 17.31SV = R5 \quad (8.15)$$

$$FS + IB + LG + LV + SG + SV = 1 \quad (8.16)$$

$$\tfrac{1}{5}\sum_{s=1}^{5}R_s = \overline{R} \quad (8.17)$$

$$\overline{R} \geq 10 \quad (8.18)$$

$$FS, IB, LG, LV, SG, SV \geq 0 \quad (8.19)$$

The objective for the Markowitz model is to minimize portfolio variance. Note that equations (8.11) through (8.15) were present in the index fund model presented in Section 8.2. These equations define the return for each scenario. Equation (8.16), which was also present in the index fund model, requires all of the money to be invested in the mutual funds; this constraint is often called the *unity constraint*. Equation (8.17) defines $\overline{R}$, which is the expected return of the portfolio. Equation (8.18) requires the portfolio return to be at least 10%. Finally, expression (8.19) requires a nonnegative investment in each Hauck mutual fund.

A portion of the solution for this model using a required return of at least 10% appears in Figure 8.9. The minimum value for the portfolio variance is 27.13615. This solution

FIGURE 8.9 SOLUTION FOR THE HAUCK MINIMUM VARIANCE PORTFOLIO WITH A REQUIRED RETURN OF AT LEAST 10%

```
Optimal Objective Value = 27.13615

       Variable            Value          Reduced Cost
   ---------------    ---------------    ------------------
         FS               0.15841            0.00000
         IB               0.52548            0.00000
         LG               0.04207            0.00000
         LV               0.00000           41.64139
         SG               0.00000           15.60953
         SV               0.27405            0.00000
         R1              18.95698            0.00000
         R2              11.51205            0.00000
         R3               5.64390            0.00000
         R4               9.72807            0.00000
         R5               4.15899            0.00000
        RBAR             10.00000            0.00000
```

implies that the clients will get an expected return of 10% (RBAR = 10.00000) and minimize their risk as measured by portfolio variance by investing approximately 16% of the portfolio in the foreign stock fund (FS = 0.15841), 53% in the intermediate bond fund (IB = 0.52548), 4% in the large-cap growth fund (LG = 0.04207), and 27% in the small-cap value fund (SV = 0.27405).

The Markowitz portfolio model provides a convenient way for an investor to trade off risk versus return. In practice, this model is typically solved iteratively for different values of return. Figure 8.10 graphs these minimum portfolio variances versus required expected returns as required expected return is varied from 8% to 12% in increments of 1%. In finance this graph is called the *efficient frontier*. Each point on the efficient frontier is the minimum possible risk (measured by portfolio variance) for the given return. By looking at the graph of the efficient frontier an investor can pick the mean-variance trade-off that he or she is most comfortable with.

FIGURE 8.10 AN EFFICIENT FRONTIER FOR THE MARKOWITZ PORTFOLIO MODEL

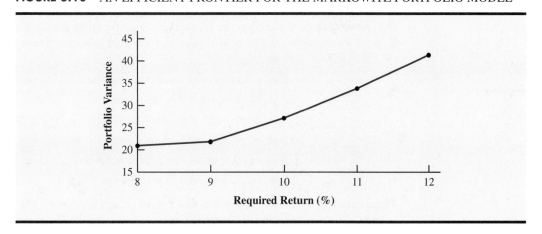

NOTES AND COMMENTS

1. Upper and lower bounds on the amount of an asset type in the portfolio can be easily modeled. Notice that the solution given in Figure 8.9 has more than 50% of the portfolio invested in the intermediate-term bond fund. It may be unwise to let one asset contribute so heavily to the portfolio. Hence upper bounds are often placed on the percentage of the portfolio invested in a single asset. Likewise, it might be undesirable to include an extremely small quantity of an asset in the portfolio. Thus, there may be constraints that require nonzero amounts of an asset to be at least a minimum percentage of the portfolio.

2. In the Hauck example, 100% of the available portfolio was invested in mutual funds. However, risk-averse investors often prefer to have some of their money in a "risk-free" asset such as U.S. Treasury bills. Thus, many portfolio optimization models allow funds to be invested in a risk-free asset.

3. In this section portfolio variance was used to measure risk. However, variance as it is defined counts deviations both above and below the mean. Most investors are happy with returns above the mean but wish to avoid returns below the mean. Hence, numerous portfolio models allow for flexible risk measures.

4. In practice, both brokers and mutual fund companies readjust portfolios as new information becomes available. However, constantly readjusting a portfolio may lead to large transaction costs. Case Problem 1 requires the student to develop a modification of the Markowitz portfolio selection problem in order to account for transaction costs.

8.4   BLENDING: THE POOLING PROBLEM

In Chapter 4 we showed how to use linear programming to solve the Grand Strand Oil Company blending problem. Recall that the Grand Strand refinery wanted to refine three petroleum components into regular and premium gasoline in order to maximize profit. In the Grand Strand model presented in Chapter 4 we assumed that all three petroleum components have separate storage tanks; as a result, components were not mixed together prior to producing gasoline. However, in practice it is often the case that at a blending site the number of storage facilities that hold the blending components is less than the number of components. In this case the components must share a storage tank or storage facility. Similarly, when transporting the components, the components often must share a pipeline or transportation container. Components that share a storage facility or pipeline are called *pooled* components. This pooling is illustrated in Figure 8.11.

Consider Figure 8.11. Components 1 and 2 are pooled in a single storage tank and component 3 has its own storage tank. Regular and premium gasoline are made from blending the pooled components and component 3. Two types of decisions must be made. First, what percentages of component 1 and component 2 should be used in the pooled mixture? Second, how much of the mixture of components 1 and 2 from the pooling tank are to be blended with component 3 to make regular and premium gasoline? These decisions require the following six decision variables:

$$y_1 = \text{gallons of component 1 in the pooling tank}$$
$$y_2 = \text{gallons of component 2 in the pooling tank}$$
$$x_{pr} = \text{gallons of pooled components 1 and 2 in regular gasoline}$$
$$x_{pp} = \text{gallons of pooled components 1 and 2 in premium gasoline}$$
$$x_{3r} = \text{gallons of component 3 in regular gasoline}$$
$$x_{3p} = \text{gallons of component 3 in premium gasoline}$$

These decision variables are shown as flows over the arcs in Figure 8.11.

FIGURE 8.11 THE GRAND STRAND OIL COMPANY POOLING PROBLEM

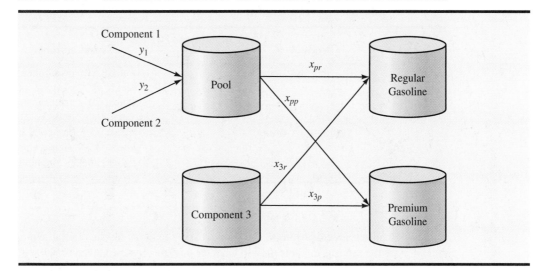

The constraints for the Grand Strand Oil Company pooling problem are similar to the constraints for the original Grand Strand blending problem in Chapter 4. First, we need expressions for the total amount of regular and premium gasoline produced.

Total Gallons Produced   Because the gasoline produced is a blend of the input components, the total number of gallons of each type of gasoline produced is the sum of the pooled components and component 3.

$$\text{Regular gasoline} = x_{pr} + x_{3r}$$
$$\text{Premium gasoline} = x_{pp} + x_{3p}$$

Total Petroleum Component Use   The total gallons of components 1 and 2 consumed are the amount of the pooled mixture used in making regular and premium gasoline. The total gallons of component 3 consumed is the amount of component 3 used in regular gasoline plus the amount used in premium gasoline.

$$\text{Components 1 and 2 consumed:} \quad y_1 + y_2 = x_{pr} + x_{pp}$$
$$\text{Component 3 consumed:} \quad x_{3r} + x_{3p}$$

The equation involving components 1 and 2 is referred to as a *conservation equation;* this equation shows that the total amount of components 1 and 2 consumed must equal the amount of the pooled mixture used to make regular and premium gasoline.

Component Availability   For the current production planning period, the maximum number of gallons available for the three components are 5000, 10,000, and 10,000, respectively. Thus, the three constraints that limit the availability of the three components are

$$\text{Component 1} \quad y_1 \le 5000$$
$$\text{Component 2} \quad y_2 \le 10{,}000$$
$$\text{Component 3} \quad x_{3r} + x_{3p} \le 10{,}000$$

TABLE 8.4   PRODUCT SPECIFICATIONS FOR THE GRAND STRAND
BLENDING PROBLEM

Product	Specifications
Regular gasoline	At most 30% component 1
	At least 40% component 2
	At most 20% component 3
Premium gasoline	At least 25% component 1
	At most 45% component 2
	At least 30% component 3

Product Specifications   The product specifications for the regular and premium gasoline
are the same as in Table 4.14 in Chapter 4. They are reproduced in Table 8.4 for ease of reference. Incorporating the blending specifications from Table 8.4 is a bit more difficult for
the pooling problem because the amount of components 1 and 2 that go into the regular and
premium gasoline depend on the proportion of these components in the pooled tank. For
example, consider the constraint that component 1 can account for no more than 30% of the
total gallons of regular gasoline produced. If x_{pr} gallons of the pooled components are
blended with component 3 to make regular gasoline, it is necessary to know the percentage
of component 1 in x_{pr}. The total gallons of components 1 and 2 in the pooled tank are $y_1 +
y_2$; therefore, the fraction of component 1 in the pooled tank is

$$\left(\frac{y_1}{y_1 + y_2} \right)$$

As a result,

$$\left(\frac{y_1}{y_1 + y_2} \right) x_{pr}$$

is the number of gallons of component 1 used to blend regular gasoline. The total number
of gallons of regular gasoline is $x_{pr} + x_{3r}$. So the constraint that the number of gallons of
component 1 can account for no more than 30% of the total gallons of regular gasoline produced is

$$\left(\frac{y_1}{y_1 + y_2} \right) x_{pr} \leq .3(x_{pr} + x_{3r})$$

This expression is nonlinear because it involves the ratio of variables multiplied by another
variable. The logic is similar for the other constraints required to implement the product
specifications given in Table 8.4.

As in Section 4.4, the objective is to maximize the total profit contribution. Thus, we
want to develop the objective function by maximizing the difference between the total revenue from both gasolines and the total cost of the three petroleum components. Recall that
the price per gallon of the regular gasoline is $2.90 and the price per gallon of premium
gasoline is $3.00. The cost of components 1, 2, and 3 is $2.50, $2.60, and $2.84, respectively. Finally, at least 10,000 gallons of regular gasoline must be produced.

The complete nonlinear model for the Grand Strand pooling problem, containing 6 decision variables and 11 constraints (excluding nonnegativity), follows:

$$\text{Max} \quad 2.9\,(x_{pr} + x_{3r}) + 3.00(x_{pp} + x_{3p}) - 2.5y_1 - 2.6y_2 - 2.84(x_{3r} + x_{3p})$$

s.t.

$$y_1 + y_2 = x_{pr} + x_{pp}$$

$$\left(\frac{y_1}{y_1 + y_2}\right)x_{pr} \le .3(x_{pr} + x_{3r})$$

$$\left(\frac{y_2}{y_1 + y_2}\right)x_{pr} \ge .4(x_{pr} + x_{3r})$$

$$x_{3r} \le .2(x_{pr} + x_{3r})$$

$$\left(\frac{y_1}{y_1 + y_2}\right)x_{pp} \ge .25(x_{pp} + x_{3p})$$

$$\left(\frac{y_2}{y_1 + y_2}\right)x_{pp} \le .45(x_{pp} + x_{3p})$$

$$x_{3p} \ge .3(x_{pp} + x_{3p})$$

$$y_1 \le 5000$$

$$y_2 \le 10{,}000$$

$$x_{3r} + x_{3p} \le 10{,}000$$

$$x_{pr} + x_{3r} \ge 10{,}000$$

$$x_{pr}, x_{pp}, x_{3r}, x_{3p}, y_1, y_2 \ge 0$$

WEB file

GrandPooling

The optimal solution to the Grand Strand pooling problem is shown in Figure 8.12. The number of gallons of each component used and the percentage in regular and premium gasoline are shown in Table 8.5. For example, the 10,000 gallons of regular gasoline contain 2857.143 gallons of component 1. The number 2857.143 does not appear directly in the solution in Figure 8.12. It must be calculated. In the solution, $y_1 = 5000$, $y_2 = 9000$, and $x_{pr} = 8000$, which means that the number of gallons of component 1 in regular gasoline is

$$\left(\frac{y_1}{y_1 + y_2}\right)x_{pr} = \left(\frac{5000}{5000 + 9000}\right)8000 = 2857.143$$

In Figure 8.12 the objective value of 5831.429 corresponds to a total profit contribution of \$5831.43. In Section 4.4 we found that the value of the optimal solution to the original Grand Strand blending problem is \$7100. Why is the total profit contribution smaller for the model where components 1 and 2 are pooled? Note that any feasible solution to the problem with pooled components is feasible to the problem with no pooling. However, the converse is not true. For example, Figure 8.12 shows that the ratio of the number of gallons of component 1 to the number of gallons of component 2 in both regular and premium gasoline is constant. That is,

$$\frac{2857.143}{5142.857} = .5556 = \frac{2142.857}{3857.143}$$

FIGURE 8.12   SOLUTION TO THE GRAND STRAND POOLING PROBLEM

```
Optimal Objective Value = 5831.42857

        Variable              Value           Reduced Cost
      --------------      ---------------    -----------------
           XPR             8000.00000            0.00000
           X3R             2000.00000            0.00000
           XPP             6000.00000            0.00000
           X3P             2571.42857            0.00000
           Y1              5000.00000            0.00000
           Y2              9000.00000            0.00000


       Constraint         Slack/Surplus         Dual Value
      --------------      ---------------    -----------------
            1                 0.00000            1.41200
            2              1000.00000            0.00000
            3              5428.57143            0.00000
            4                 0.00000           -3.06134
            5               142.85714            0.00000
            6              1142.85714            0.00000
            7                 0.00000            0.22857
            8                 0.00000           -2.19657
            9                 0.00000            0.86476
           10                 0.00000            0.00000
           11                 0.00000           -0.12286
```

TABLE 8.5   GRAND STRAND POOLING SOLUTION

| | Gallons of Component (percentage) | | | |
Gasoline	Component 1	Component 2	Component 3	Total
Regular	2857.143 (28.57%)	5142.857 (51.43%)	2000 (20%)	10,000
Premium	2142.857 (25%)	3857.143 (45%)	2571.429 (30%)	8571.429

This must be the case because this ratio is y_1/y_2, the ratio of component 1 to component 2 in the pooled mixture. Table 8.6 shows the solution to the original Grand Strand problem without pooling (this table also appears in Section 4.4). The ratio of component 1 to component 2 in regular gasoline is $1250/6750 = 0.1852$, and the ratio of component 1 to component 2 in premium gasoline is $3750/3250 = 1.1538$, which is a large difference. By forcing us to use the same ratio of component 1 to component 2 in the pooling model, we lose flexibility and must spend more on the petroleum components used to make the gasoline.

The lack of enough storage tanks for all the components reduces the number of blending feasible solutions, which in turn leads to a lower profit. Indeed, one use of this model is to provide management with a good estimate of the profit loss due to a shortage of storage tanks. Management would then be able to assess the profitability of purchasing additional storage tanks.

TABLE 8.6   SOLUTION TO THE GRAND STRAND PROBLEM WITHOUT POOLING

| | Gallons of Component (percentage) | | | |
Gasoline	Component 1	Component 2	Component 3	Total
Regular	1250 (12.50%)	6750 (67.50%)	2000 (20%)	10,000
Premium	3750 (25%)	3250 (21.67%)	8000 (53.33%)	15,000

8.5   FORECASTING ADOPTION OF A NEW PRODUCT

Forecasting new adoptions after a product introduction is an important marketing problem. In this section we introduce a forecasting model developed by Frank Bass that has proven to be particularly effective in forecasting the adoption of innovative and new technologies in the market place.[3] Nonlinear programming is used to estimate the parameters of the Bass forecasting model. The model has three parameters that must be estimated.

m = the number of people estimated to eventually adopt the new product

A company introducing a new product is obviously interested in the value of this parameter.

q = the coefficient of imitation

This parameter measures the likelihood of adoption due to a potential adopter being influenced by someone who has already adopted the product. It measures the "word-of-mouth" effect influencing purchases.

p = the coefficient of innovation

This parameter measures the likelihood of adoption, assuming no influence from someone who has already purchased (adopted) the product. It is the likelihood of someone adopting the product due to her or his own interest in the innovation.

Using these parameters, let us now develop the forecasting model. Let C_{t-1} denote the number of people who have adopted the product through time $t-1$. Because m is the number of people estimated to eventually adopt the product, $m - C_{t-1}$ is the number of potential adopters remaining at time $t-1$. We refer to the time interval between time $t-1$ and time t as time period t. During period t, some percentage of the remaining number of potential adopters, $m - C_{t-1}$, will adopt the product. This value depends upon the likelihood of a new adoption.

Loosely speaking, the likelihood of a new adoption is the likelihood of adoption due to imitation plus the likelihood of adoption due to innovation. The likelihood of adoption due to imitation is a function of the number of people that have already adopted the product. The larger the current pool of adopters, the greater their influence through word of mouth. Because C_{t-1}/m is the fraction of the number of people estimated to adopt the product by time $t-1$, the likelihood of adoption due to imitation is computed by multiplying this fraction by q, the coefficient of imitation. Thus, the likelihood of adoption due to imitation is

$$q(C_{t-1}/m)$$

[3]See Frank M. Bass, "A New Product Growth for Model Consumer Durables," *Management Science* 15 (1969).

The likelihood of adoption due to innovation is simply p, the coefficient of innovation. Thus, the likelihood of adoption is

$$p + q(C_{t-1}/m)$$

Using the likelihood of adoption, we can develop a forecast of the remaining number of potential customers that will adopt the product during time period t. Thus, F_t, the forecast of the number of new adopters during time period t, is

$$F_t = (p + q[C_{t-1}/m])(m - C_{t-1}) \qquad (8.20)$$

The Bass forecasting model given in equation (8.20) can be rigorously derived from statistical principles. Rather than providing such a derivation, we have emphasized the intuitive aspects of the model. In developing a forecast of new adoptions in period t using the Bass model, the value of C_{t-1} will be known from past sales data. But we also need to know the values of the parameters to use in the model. Let us now see how nonlinear programming is used to estimate the parameter values m, p, and q.

Consider Figure 8.13. This figure shows the graph of box office revenues (in \$ millions) for the films *The Doctor* and *Terminator 3* over the first 12 weeks after release.[4] Strictly speaking, box office revenues for time period t are not the same as the number of adopters during time period t. But the number of repeat customers is usually small and box office revenues are a multiple of the number of movie goers. The Bass forecasting model seems appropriate here.

These two films illustrate drastically different adoption patterns. Note that revenues for *The Doctor* grow until they peak in week 4 and then they decline. For this film, much of the revenue is obviously due to word-of-mouth influence. In terms of the Bass model the imitation factor dominates the innovation factor, and we expect $q > p$. However, for

FIGURE 8.13   WEEKLY BOX OFFICE REVENUES FOR *THE DOCTOR* AND *TERMINATOR 3*

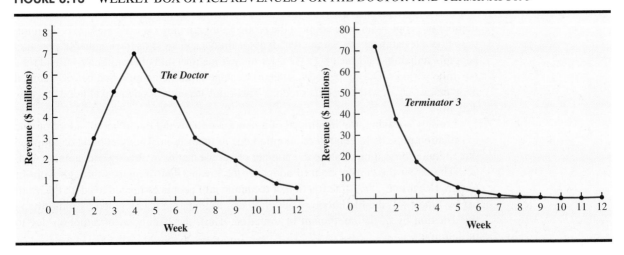

---

[4]The data for *The Doctor* are from Gary Lilien and Arvind Rangaswamy, *Marketing Engineering* (Victoria, BC: Trafford Publishing, 2004). The data for *Terminator 3* came from www.rottentomatoes.com/m/terminator_3_rise_of_the_machines/numbers.php.

the film *Terminator 3,* revenues peak in week 1 and drop sharply afterward. The innovation factor dominates the imitation factor, and we expect $q < p$.

The forecasting model, equation (8.20), can be incorporated into a nonlinear optimization problem to find the values of p, q, and m that give the best forecasts for a set of data. Assume that N periods of data are available. Let S_t denote the actual number of adopters (or a multiple of that number, such as sales) in period t for $t = 1, \ldots, N$. Then the forecast in each period and the corresponding forecast error E_t is defined by

$$F_t = (p + q[C_{t-1}/m])(m - C_{t-1})$$
$$E_t = F_t - S_t$$

Notice that the forecast error is the difference between the forecast value F_t and the actual value, S_t. It is common statistical practice to estimate parameters by minimizing the sum of errors squared.

Doing so for the Bass forecasting model leads to the follow nonlinear optimization problem:

WEB file

BassDoctor

$$\text{Min} \ \sum_{t=1}^{N} E_t^2 \tag{8.21}$$

s.t.

$$F_t = (p + q[C_{t-1}/m])(m - C_{t-1}), \quad t = 1, \ldots, N \tag{8.22}$$

$$E_t = F_t - S_t, \quad t = 1, \ldots, N \tag{8.23}$$

Because equations (8.21) and (8.22) both contain nonlinear terms, this model is a nonlinear minimization problem.

The data in Table 8.7 provide the revenue and cumulative revenues for *The Doctor* in weeks 1–12. Using these data, the nonlinear model to estimate the parameters of the Bass forecasting model for *The Doctor* follows:

$$
\begin{aligned}
\text{Min} \quad & E_1^2 + E_2^2 + \cdots + E_{12}^2 \\
\text{s.t.} \quad & F_1 = (p)m \\
& F_2 = [p + q(0.10/m)](m - 0.10) \\
& F_3 = [p + q(3.10/m)](m - 3.10) \\
& \qquad \cdot \\
& \qquad \cdot \\
& \qquad \cdot \\
& F_{12} = [p + q(34.85/m)](m - 34.85) \\
& E_1 = F_1 - 0.10 \\
& E_2 = F_2 - 3.00 \\
& \qquad \cdot \\
& \qquad \cdot \\
& \qquad \cdot \\
& E_{12} = F_{12} - 0.60
\end{aligned}
$$

TABLE 8.7   BOX OFFICE REVENUES AND CUMULATIVE REVENUES IN $ MILLIONS
FOR *THE DOCTOR*

Week	Revenues S_t	Cumulative Revenues C_t
1	0.10	0.10
2	3.00	3.10
3	5.20	8.30
4	7.00	15.30
5	5.25	20.55
6	4.90	25.45
7	3.00	28.45
8	2.40	30.85
9	1.90	32.75
10	1.30	34.05
11	0.80	34.85
12	0.60	35.45

Problem 21 asks you to formulate and solve a nonlinear model for Terminator 3.

The solution to this nonlinear program and the solution to a similar nonlinear program for *Terminator 3* are given in Table 8.8.

The optimal forecasting parameter values given in Table 8.8 are intuitively appealing and consistent with Figure 8.13. For the film *The Doctor,* which has the largest revenues in week 4, the value of the imitation parameter q is 0.49; this value is substantially larger than the innovation parameter $p = 0.074$. The film picks up momentum over time due to favorable word of mouth. After week 4 revenues decline as more and more of the potential market for the film has already seen it. Contrast these data with those for *Terminator 3*, which has a negative value of –0.018 for the imitation parameter and an innovation parameter of 0.49. The greatest number of adoptions are in week 1, and new adoptions decline afterward. Obviously the word-of-mouth influence was not favorable.

In Figure 8.14 we show the forecast values based on the parameters in Table 8.8 and the observed values in the same graph. The forecast values are denoted by a ■. The Bass forecasting model does a good job of tracking revenue for *The Doctor.* For *Terminator 3*, the Bass model does an outstanding job; it is virtually impossible to distinguish the forecast line from the actual adoption line.

You may wonder what good a forecasting model is if we must wait until after the adoption cycle is complete to estimate the parameters. One way to use the Bass forecasting

TABLE 8.8   OPTIMAL FORECAST PARAMETERS FOR *THE DOCTOR*
AND *TERMINATOR 3*

Parameter	*The Doctor*	*Terminator*
p	0.074	.49
q	0.49	−.018
m	34.85	149.54

FIGURE 8.14 FORECAST AND ACTUAL WEEKLY BOX OFFICE REVENUES FOR *THE DOCTOR* AND *TERMINATOR 3*

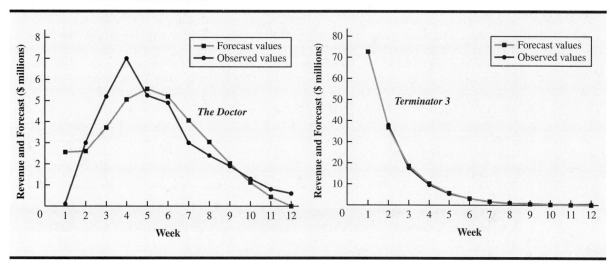

model for a new product is to assume that sales of the new product will behave in a way that is similar to a previous product for which p and q have been calculated and to subjectively estimate m, the potential market for the new product. For example, one might assume that sales of DVD players will be similar to sales of VCRs. Then the p and q used for the DVD forecasts would be the p and q values calculated from the actual sales of VCRs. The Management Science in Action, Forecasting Adoption of Satellite Television, describes how this approach was used to forecast sales of satellite TV, using p and q values from the adoption history of cable television.

A second approach is to wait until several periods of data for the new product are available. For example, if five periods of data are available, the sales data for these five periods could be used to forecast demand for period 6. Then, after six periods of sales are observed, a forecast for period 7 is made. This method is often called a rolling-horizon approach. (See the related discussion in the Management Science in Action just mentioned.)

MANAGEMENT SCIENCE IN ACTION

FORECASTING ADOPTION OF SATELLITE TELEVISION*

DIRECTV was founded in 1991. The goal of this company was to bring to market a direct-broadcast-satellite television service to compete with cable television. Much like cable television, the DIRECTV adoption model was based on new monthly subscription fees. Obviously, a forecast was needed by management to estimate future adoptions. Unfortunately, because it was a completely new product, no historical data were available.

In particular, management wanted to forecast (1) how many television owners in the United States would subscribe to a satellite television

service; and (2) the rate at which they would subscribe to this service. DIRECTV, working in conjunction with the SMART (Strategic Marketing And Research Techniques) consulting firm, developed the required forecast. It was decided to use the Bass forecasting model because of its success in forecasting the adoption and diffusion of new products.

The parameters required to use the Bass model are p, the coefficient of innovation; q, the coefficient of imitation; and m, the estimate of the

(continued)

number of subscribers or adopters. Because no historical data were available it was decided to select values of p and q based on similar products and to estimate m based on survey data.

In order to estimate m a survey was conducted of 1145 potential adopters. Based on the survey results and judgment on the part of the management team, m was set at 16% of the homes having TV. Management also decided that the introduction of cable TV in the 1980s provided a good analogy to the introduction of satellite television in the 1990s because both were subscription-based services. Historical subscription data for cable TV in the 1980s were available for estimating p and q.

The forecasts generated using these parameter values with the Bass model were remarkably good. For example, the forecast made in 1992 for the time period of July 1, 1997, through June 30, 1998, was 6.775 million new subscribers, and the actual number was 7.358 million. The forecast made in 1992 for the time period of July 1, 1998, through June 30, 1999, was 9.391 million new subscribers, and the actual number was 9.989 million.

*Based on Frank M. Bass, Kent Gordon, Teresa L. Ferguson, and Mary Lou Githens, "DIRECTV: Forecasting Diffusion of a New Technology Prior to Product Launch," *Interfaces* (May/June 2001): S82–S93.

NOTES AND COMMENTS

The optimization model used to determine the parameter values for the Bass forecasting model is an example of a hard nonlinear optimization problem. It is neither convex nor concave. For such models, local optima may give values that are much worse than the global optimum. See the discussion in Appendix 8.1 on how to use the LINGO software to find a global optimum.

SUMMARY

In this chapter we introduced nonlinear optimization models. A nonlinear optimization model is a model with a least one nonlinear term in either a constraint or the objective function. Because so many processes in business and nature behave in a nonlinear fashion, allowing nonlinear terms greatly increases the number of important applications that can be modeled as an optimization problem. Numerous problems in portfolio optimization, pricing options, blending, economics, facility location, forecasting, and scheduling lend themselves to nonlinear models.

Unfortunately, nonlinear optimization models are not as easy to solve as linear optimization models, or even linear integer optimization models. As a rule of thumb, if a problem can be modeled realistically as a linear or linear integer problem, then it is probably best to do so. Many nonlinear formulations have local optima that are not globally optimal. Because most nonlinear optimization codes will terminate with a local optimum, the solution returned by the code may not be the best solution available. However, as pointed out in this chapter, numerous important classes of optimization problems, such as the Markowitz portfolio model, are convex optimization problems. For a convex optimization problem, a local optimum is also the global optimum. Additionally, the development of nonlinear optimization codes that do find globally optimal solutions is proceeding at a rapid rate.

GLOSSARY

Nonlinear optimization problem   An optimization problem that contains at least one nonlinear term in the objective function or a constraint.

Local optimum   A feasible solution is a local optimum if there are no other feasible solutions with a better objective function value in the immediate neighborhood. A local optimum may be either a local maximum or a local minimum.

Local maximum A feasible solution is a local maximum if there are no other feasible solutions with a larger objective function value in the immediate neighborhood.

Local minimum A feasible solution is a local minimum if there are no other feasible solutions with a smaller objective function value in the immediate neighborhood.

Global optimum A feasible solution is a global optimum if there are no other feasible points with a better objective function value in the entire feasible region. A global optimum may be either a global maximum or a global minimum.

Global maximum A feasible solution is a global maximum if there are no other feasible points with a larger objective function value in the entire feasible region. A global maximum is also a local maximum.

Global minimum A feasible solution is a global minimum if there are no other feasible points with a smaller objective function value in the entire feasible region. A global minimum is also a local minimum.

Concave function A function that is bowl-shaped down: For example, the functions $f(x) = -5x^2 - 5x$ and $f(x, y) = -x^2 - 11y^2$ are concave functions.

Convex function A function that is bowl-shaped up: For example, the functions $f(x) = x^2 - 5x$ and $f(x, y) = x^2 + 5y^2$ are convex functions.

Index fund A portfolio of stocks, mutual funds, or other securities that matches as closely as possible the performance of a broad market index such as the S&P 500.

Markowitz portfolio model A portfolio optimization model used to construct a portfolio that minimizes risk subject to a constraint requiring a minimum level of return.

PROBLEMS

1. The purpose of this exercise is to provide practice using the LINGO or Excel solvers. Find the values of X and Y that minimize the function

$$\text{Min} \quad X^2 - 4X + Y^2 + 8Y + 20$$

Do not assume nonnegativity of the X and Y variables. Recall that by default LINGO assumes nonnegative variables. In order to allow the variables to take on negative values you can add

$$@FREE(X); \quad @FREE(Y);$$

Alternatively, if you want LINGO to allow for negative values by default, in the LINGO menu select **Options** and then click **General Solver,** and then uncheck the **Variables assumed nonnegative** tab.

2. Consider the problem

$$\text{Min} \quad 2X^2 - 20X + 2XY + Y^2 - 14Y + 58$$
$$\text{s.t.} \quad X + 4Y \le 8$$

   a. Find the minimum solution to this problem.
   b. If the right-hand side of the constraint is increased from 8 to 9, how much do you expect the objective function to change?
   c. Resolve the problem with a new right-hand side of 9. How does the actual change compare with your estimate?

3. The Macon Psychiatric Institute is interested in redesigning its mental health care delivery system in order to maximize the number of people who can benefit from its services.

Unfortunately, having a large number of patients in residence places a burden on the staff and lengthens patient recovery times. Based on patient records and recovery time estimates by the clinic's staff members, the following mathematical relationship has been developed to describe how the number of patients in residence affects the patient recovery time.

$$T = \frac{45}{180 - P}$$

where

T = average patient recovery time in years

P = number of patients in residence

In answering the following questions, think of P as the equilibrium number of patients in residence. We admit a new patient every time we discharge a cured patient in order to keep the number of patients in residence fixed at P.

a. Suppose patients are admitted at a rate that maintains 150 patients in residence at the clinic. What is the average recovery time per patient, and how many patients will recover per year?

b. Using the formula for average patient recovery time, develop an expression for N, which is equal to the number of patients that recover per year as a function of P.

c. Determine the optimal number of patients for the clinic to have in residence if it is interested in maximizing the number of patients that recover per year.

4. Lawn King manufactures two types of riding lawn mowers. One is a low-cost mower sold primarily to residential home owners; the other is an industrial model sold to landscaping and lawn service companies. The company is interested in establishing a pricing policy for the two mowers that will maximize the gross profit for the product line. A study of the relationships between sales prices and quantities sold of the two mowers has validated the following price-quantity relationships.

$$q_1 = 950 - 1.5p_1 + 0.7p_2$$
$$q_2 = 2500 + 0.3p_1 - 0.5p_2$$

where

q_1 = number of residential mowers sold

q_2 = number of industrial mowers sold

p_1 = selling price of the residential mower in dollars

p_2 = selling price of the industrial mower in dollars

The accounting department developed cost information on the fixed and variable cost of producing the two mowers. The fixed cost of production for the residential mower is $10,000 and the variable cost is $1500 per mower. The fixed cost of production for the industrial mower is $30,000 and the variable cost is $4000 per mower.

a. Lawn King traditionally priced the lawn mowers at $2000 and $6000 for the residential and industrial mowers, respectively. Gross profit is computed as the sales revenue minus production cost. How many mowers will be sold, and what is the gross profit with this pricing policy?

b. Following the approach of Section 8.1, develop an expression for gross profit as a function of the selling prices for the two mowers.

c. What are the optimal prices for Lawn King to charge? How many units of each mower will be sold at these prices and what will the gross profit be?

d. Try a different formulation for this problem. Write the objective function as

$$\text{Max} \quad p_1 q_1 + p_2 q_2 - c_1 - c_2$$

where c_1 and c_2 represent the production costs for the two mowers. Then add four constraints to the problem, two based on the price-quantity relationships and two based on the cost functions. Solve this new constrained optimization problem to see whether you get the same answer. What are the advantages of this formulation, if any?

5. GreenLawns provides a lawn fertilizer and weed control service. The company is adding a special aeration treatment as a low-cost extra service option, which it hopes will help attract new customers. Management is planning to promote this new service in two media: radio and direct-mail advertising. A media budget of $3000 is available for this promotional campaign. Based on past experience in promoting its other services, GreenLawns obtained the following estimate of the relationship between sales and the amount spent on promotion in these two media:

$$S = -2R^2 - 10M^2 - 8RM + 18R + 34M$$

where

S = total sales in thousands of dollars
R = thousands of dollars spent on radio advertising
M = thousands of dollars spent on direct-mail advertising

GreenLawns would like to develop a promotional strategy that will lead to maximum sales subject to the restriction provided by the media budget.
   a. What is the value of sales if $2000 is spent on radio advertising and $1000 is spent on direct-mail advertising?
   b. Formulate an optimization problem that can be solved to maximize sales subject to the media budget.
   c. Determine the optimal amount to spend on radio and direct-mail advertising. How much money will be generated in sales?

LINGO must be used to get the global optimal solution for Problem 6.

6. The function

$$f(X, Y) = 3(1 - X)^2 e^{(-X^2 - (Y+1)^2)} - 10\left(X/5 - X^3 - Y^5\right) e^{(-X^2 - Y^2)} - e^{(-(X+1)^2 - Y^2)}/3$$

was used to generate Figures 8.6 and 8.7 in order to illustrate the concept of local optima versus global optima.
   a. Minimize this function using LINGO. (*Warning:* Make sure you use the unary minus sign correctly. In other words, rewrite a term such as $-X^2$ as $-(X)^2$. See Appendix 8.1.)
   b. Now minimize this function using LINGO with the Global Solver option turned on.

7. The Cobb-Douglas production function is a classic model from economics used to model output as a function of capital and labor. It has the form

$$f(L, C) = c_0 L^{c_1} C^{c_2}$$

where c_0, c_1, and c_2 are constants. The variable L represents the units of input of labor and the variable C represents the units of input of capital.
   a. In this example, assume $c_0 = 5$, $c_1 = 0.25$, and $c_2 = 0.75$. Assume each unit of labor costs $25 and each unit of capital costs $75. With $75,000 available in the budget, develop an optimization model for determining how the budgeted amount should be allocated between capital and labor in order to maximize output.
   b. Find the optimal solution to the model you formulated in part (a). *Hint:* When using Excel Solver, start with an initial $L > 0$ and $C > 0$.

8. Let S represent the amount of steel produced (in tons). Steel production is related to the amount of labor used (L) and the amount of capital used (C) by the following function:

$$S = 20L^{0.30}C^{0.70}$$

In this formula L represents the units of labor input and C the units of capital input. Each unit of labor costs \$50, and each unit of capital costs \$100.

   a. Formulate an optimization problem that will determine how much labor and capital are needed in order to produce 50,000 tons of steel at minimum cost.

   b. Solve the optimization problem you formulated in part (a). *Hint:* When using Excel Solver, start with an initial $L > 0$ and $C > 0$.

9.   The profit function for two products is

$$Profit = -3x_1^2 + 42x_1 - 3x_2^2 + 48x_2 + 700$$

where x_1 represents units of production of product 1 and x_2 represents units of production of product 2. Producing one unit of product 1 requires 4 labor-hours and producing one unit of product 2 requires 6 labor-hours. Currently, 24 labor-hours are available. The cost of labor-hours is already factored into the profit function. However, it is possible to schedule overtime at a premium of \$5 per hour.

   a. Formulate an optimization problem that can be used to find the optimal production quantity of products 1 and the optimal number of overtime hours to schedule.

   b. Solve the optimization model you formulated in part (a). How much should be produced and how many overtime hours should be scheduled?

10.   Heller Manufacturing has two production facilities that manufacture baseball gloves. Production costs at the two facilities differ because of varying labor rates, local property taxes, type of equipment, capacity, and so on. The Dayton plant has weekly costs that can be expressed as a function of the number of gloves produced:

$$TCD(X) = X^2 - X + 5$$

where X is the weekly production volume in thousands of units and $TCD(X)$ is the cost in thousands of dollars. The Hamilton plant's weekly production costs are given by

$$TCH(Y) = Y^2 + 2Y + 3$$

where Y is the weekly production volume in thousands of units and $TCH(Y)$ is the cost in thousands of dollars. Heller Manufacturing would like to produce 8000 gloves per week at the lowest possible cost.

   a. Formulate a mathematical model that can be used to determine the optimal number of gloves to produce each week at each facility.

   b. Use LINGO or Excel Solver to find the solution to your mathematical model to determine the optimal number of gloves to produce at each facility.

11.   In the Markowitz portfolio optimization model defined in equations (8.10) through (8.19), the decision variables represent the percentage of the portfolio invested in each of the mutual funds. For example, $FS = 0.25$ in the solution means that 25% of the money in the portfolio is invested in the foreign stock mutual fund. It is possible to define the decision variables to represent the actual dollar amount invested in each mutual fund or stock. Redefine the decision variables so that now each variable represents the dollar amount invested in the mutual fund. Assume an investor has \$50,000 to invest and wants to minimize the variance of his or her portfolio subject to a constraint that the portfolio returns a minimum of 10%. Reformulate the model given by (8.10) through (8.19) based on the new definition of the decision variables. Solve the revised model with LINGO or Excel Solver.

12.   Many forecasting models use parameters that are estimated using nonlinear optimization. A good example is the Bass model introduced in this chapter. Another example is the exponential smoothing forecasting model. The exponential smoothing model is common in

TABLE 8.9   EXPONENTIAL SMOOTHING MODEL FOR $\alpha = 0.3$

Week (t)	Observed Value (Y_t)	Forecast (F_t)	Forecast Error ($Y_t - F_t$)	Squared Forecast Error ($Y_t - F_t)^2$
1	17	17.00	0.00	0.00
2	21	17.00	4.00	16.00
3	19	18.20	0.80	0.64
4	23	18.44	4.56	20.79
5	18	19.81	−1.81	3.27
6	16	19.27	−3.27	10.66
7	20	18.29	1.71	2.94
8	18	18.80	−0.80	0.64
9	22	18.56	3.44	11.83
10	20	19.59	0.41	0.17
11	15	19.71	−4.71	22.23
12	22	18.30	3.70	13.69
				SUM = 102.86

practice and is described in further detail in Chapter 15. For instance, the basic exponential smoothing model for forecasting sales is

$$F_{t+1} = \alpha Y_t + (1 - \alpha)F_t$$

where

$$F_{t+1} = \text{forecast of sales for period } t + 1$$
$$Y_t = \text{actual value of sales for period } t$$
$$F_t = \text{forecast of sales for period } t$$
$$\alpha = \text{smoothing constant } 0 \leq \alpha \leq 1$$

This model is used recursively; the forecast for time period $t + 1$ is based on the forecast for period t, F_t, the observed value of sales in period t, Y_t, and the smoothing parameter α. The use of this model to forecast sales for 12 months is illustrated in Table 8.9 with the smoothing constant $\alpha = 0.3$. The forecast errors, $Y_t - F_t$, are calculated in the fourth column. The value of α is often chosen by minimizing the sum of squared forecast errors, commonly referred to as the mean squared error (MSE). The last column of Table 8.9 shows the square of the forecast error and the sum of squared forecast errors.

In using exponential smoothing models one tries to choose the value of α that provides the best forecasts. Build an Excel Solver or LINGO optimization model that will find the smoothing parameter, α, that minimizes the sum of forecast errors squared. You may find it easiest to put Table 8.9 into an Excel spreadsheet and then use Solver to find the optimal value of α.

13. The purpose of this exercise is to learn how to calculate stock returns for portfolio models using actual stock price data. First, it is necessary to obtain stock price data. One source (of many) is Yahoo! Go to the link http://finance.yahoo.com and type in a ticker symbol such as AAPL (for Apple Computer). Then on the left-hand side of the page, select Historical Data.

These data are easily downloaded to a spreadsheet by clicking on the link Download to Spreadsheet at the bottom of the page. For Apple Computer (AAPL), Advanced Micro Devices (AMD), and Oracle Corporation (ORCL), download the monthly price data for

FIGURE 8.15   YEARLY RETURNS FOR AAPL, AMD, AND ORCL

Date	AAPL Adj. Close	AMD Adj. Close	ORCL Adj. Close	AAPL Return	AMD Return	ORCL Return
2-Jan-97	4.16	17.57	4.32	0.0962	−0.5537	−0.1074
2-Jan-98	4.58	10.1	3.88	0.8104	0.1272	0.8666
4-Jan-99	10.3	11.47	9.23	0.9236	0.4506	0.9956
3-Jan-00	25.94	18	24.98	−0.8753	0.3124	0.1533
2-Jan-01	10.81	24.6	29.12	0.1340	−0.4270	−0.5230
2-Jan-02	12.36	16.05	17.26	−0.5432	−1.1194	−0.3610
2-Jan-03	7.18	5.24	12.03	0.4517	1.0424	0.1416
2-Jan-04	11.28	14.86	13.86	1.2263	0.0613	−0.0065
3-Jan-05	38.45	15.8	13.77	0.6749	0.9729	−0.0912
3-Jan-06	75.51	41.8	12.57			

Data Source: CSI
Web site: http://www.csidata.com

StockReturns

January 1997 through January 2006. These data contain closing prices that are adjusted for stock dividends and splits.

You now have stock prices for 10 years and the objective is to calculate the annual returns for each stock for the years 1997 through 2005. Returns are often calculated using continuous compounding. If the stock prices are adjusted for splits and stock dividends, then the price of stock i in period $t + 1$, $P_{i,t+1}$, is given by

$$p_{i,t+1} = p_t \, e^{r_{it}}$$

where p_{it} is the price of stock i in period t and r_{it} is the return on stock i in period t. This calculation assumes no cash dividends were paid, which is true of Apple Computer, Advanced Micro Devices, and Oracle Corporation. Solving the equation $p_{i,t+1} = p_t \, e^{r_{it}}$ for the return on stock i in period t gives

$$r_{it} = \ln\left(\frac{p_{i,t+1}}{p_t}\right)$$

For example, the Apple Computer adjusted closing price in January 2005 was 38.45. The closing price in January 2006 was 75.51. Thus, the continuously compounded return for Apple Computer from January 2005 to January 2006 is

$$\ln(75.51/38.45) = 0.6749064$$

We use this calculation as our estimate of the annual return for Apple Computer for the year 2005.

Take the closing stock prices that you have downloaded and calculate the annual returns for 1997–2005 for AAPL, AMD, and ORCL using $r_{it} = \ln(p_{i,t+1}/p_t)$. If you calculate the returns properly, your results should appear as in Figure 8.15.

14.   Formulate and solve the Markowitz portfolio optimization model that was defined in equations (8.10) through (8.19) using the data from Problem 13. In this case, nine scenarios correspond to the yearly returns from 1997–2005, inclusive. Treat each scenario as being equally likely and use the scenario returns that were calculated in Problem 13.

15. Using the data obtained in Problem 13, construct a portfolio from Apple, AMD, and Oracle that matches the Information Technology S&P index as closely as possible. Use the return data for the Information Technology S&P index given in the following table. The model for constructing the portfolio should be similar to the one developed for Hauck Financial Services in Section 8.2.

Year	Return
1997	28.54%
1998	78.14
1999	78.74
2000	−40.90
2001	−25.87
2002	−37.41
2003	48.40
2004	2.56
2005	0.99

16. Most investors are happy when their returns are "above average," but not so happy when they are "below average." In the Markowitz portfolio optimization problem given by equations (8.10) through (8.19), the objective function is to minimize variance, which is given by

$$\text{Min } \tfrac{1}{5} \sum_{s=1}^{5} (R_s - \overline{R})^2$$

where R_s is the portfolio return under scenario s and $\overline{R}$ is the expected or average return of the portfolio.

With this objective function, we are choosing a portfolio that minimizes deviations both above and below the average, $\overline{R}$. However, most investors are happy when $R_s > \overline{R}$), but unhappy when $R_s < R$. With this preference in mind, an alternative to the variance measure in the objective function for the Markowitz model is the *semivariance*. The semivariance is calculated by only considering deviations below $\overline{R}$.

Let $D_{sp} - D_{sn} = R_s - \overline{R}$, and restrict D_{sp} and D_{sn} to be nonnegative. Then D_{sp} measures the positive deviation from the mean return in scenario s (i.e., $D_{sp} = R_s - \overline{R}$ when $R_s > \overline{R}$). In the case where the scenario return is below the average return, $R_s < \overline{R}$, we have $-D_{sn} = R_s - \overline{R}$. Using these new variables, we can reformulate the Markowitz model to minimize only the square of negative deviations below the average return. By doing so, we will use the semivariance rather than the variance in the objective function.

Reformulate the Markowitz portfolio optimization model given in equations (8.10) through (8.19) to use semivariance in the objective function. Solve the model using either Excel Solver or LINGO. *Hint:* When using Excel Solver assume $\tfrac{1}{6}$ of the portfolio is allocated to each mutual fund for a starting solution.

17. This problem requires a basic understanding of the normal probability distribution. Investors are often interested in knowing the probabilities of poor returns. For example, for what cutoff return will the probability of the actual return falling below this cutoff value be at most 1%?

Consider the solution to the Markowitz portfolio problem given in Figure 8.9. The mean return of the portfolio is 10% and the standard deviation (calculated by taking the square root of the variance, which is the objective function value) is

$$\sigma = \sqrt{27.13615} = 5.209237$$

Assume that the portfolio scenario returns are normally distributed about the mean return. From the normal probability table, we see that less than 1% of the returns fall more than 2.33 standard deviations below the mean. This result implies a probability of 1% or less that a portfolio return will fall below

$$10 - (2.33)(5.209237) = -2.1375$$

Stated another way, if the initial value of the portfolio is $1, then the investor faces a probability of 1% of incurring a loss of 2.1375 cents or more. The value at risk is 2.1375 cents at 1%. This measure of risk is called the *value at risk,* or VaR. It was popularized by JPMorgan Chase & Co. in the early 1990s (then, just JP Morgan).

A table of normal probabilities appears in Appendix B, but they are also easily calculated in LINGO and Excel. In LINGO the function @PSN(Z) and the equivalent function NORMDIST in Excel provide the probability that a standard normal random variables is less than Z.

a. Consider the Markowitz portfolio problem given in equations (8.10) through (8.19). Delete the required return constraint (8.18), and reformulate this problem to minimize the VaR at 1%.

b. Is minimizing the VaR the same as minimizing the variances of the portfolio? Answer Yes or No, and justify.

c. For a fixed return, is minimizing the VaR the same as minimizing the variances of the portfolio? Answer Yes or No, and justify.

18. Options are popular instruments in the world of finance. A *call option* on a stock gives the owner the right to buy the stock at a predetermined price before the expiration date of the option. For example, on Friday, August 25, 2006, call options were selling for Procter & Gamble stock that gave the owner of the option the right to buy a share of stock for $60 on or before September 15, 2006. The asking price on the option was $1.45 at the market close. How are options priced? A pricing formula for options was developed by Fischer Black and Myron Scholes and published in 1973. Scholes was later awarded the Nobel Prize for this work in 1997 (Black was deceased). The Black-Scholes pricing model is widely used today by hedge funds and traders. The Black-Scholes formula for the price of a call option is

$$C = S[PSN(Z)] - Xe^{-rT}[PSN(Z - \sigma\sqrt{T})]$$

where

$$C = \text{market price of the call option}$$
$$X = \text{strike or exercise price of the stock}$$
$$S = \text{current price of the stock}$$
$$r = \text{annual risk-free interest rate}$$
$$T = \text{time to maturity of the option}$$
$$\sigma = \text{yearly standard deviation}$$

In the Black-Scholes formula, $Z = [(r + \sigma^2/2)T + \ln(S/X)]/(\sigma\sqrt{T})$ and $PSN(Z)$ is the probability of an observation of Z or less for a normal distribution with mean 0 and variance 1.

The purpose of this exercise is to price a Procter & Gamble call option offered on August 25, 2006. The option expires September 15, 2006, which includes 21 days between the market close on August 25, 2006, and the expiration of the option on September 15, 2006. Use the yield on three-month Treasury bills as the risk-free interest rate. As of August 25, 2006, this yield was 0.0494. The strike price on the option is $60 and at the market close on August 25, 2006, the stock was trading at $60.87. In order to use the Black-Scholes formula, the yearly standard deviation, σ is required. One way to obtain this number is to estimate the weekly variance of Procter & Gamble, multiply the weekly variance by 52, and then take the square root to get the annual standard deviation. For this problem, use a weekly variance of 0.000479376. Use these data to calculate the option price using the Black-Scholes formula. For Friday, August 25, 2006, the actual bid on this option was $1.35 and actual ask was $1.45.

LINGO must be used to get the global optimal solution for Problem 19.

19. The port of Lajitas has three loading docks. The distance (in meters) between the loading docks is given in the following table:

	1	2	3
1	0	100	150
2	100	0	50
3	150	50	0

Three tankers currently at sea are coming into Lajitas. It is necessary to assign a dock for each tanker. Also, only one tanker can anchor in a given dock. Currently, ships 2 and 3 are empty and have no cargo. However, ship 1 has cargo that must be loaded onto the other two ships. The number of tons that must be transferred are as follows:

		To		
		1	**2**	**3**
From	**1**	0	60	80

Formulate and solve with Excel Solver or LINGO an optimization problem that will assign ships to docks so that the product of tonnage moved times distance is minimized. (*Hints:* This problem is an extension of the assignment problem introduced in Chapter 6. Also, be careful with the objective function. Only include the nonzero terms. Each of the 12 nonzero terms in the objective function is a quadratic term, or the product of two variables.) There are 12 nonzero terms in the objective function.

This problem formulation is an example of a *quadratic assignment problem.* The quadratic assignment problem is a powerful model. It is used in a number of facility location problems and components on circuit boards. It is also used to assign jets to gates at airports to minimize product of passengers and distance walked.

20. Andalus Furniture Company has two manufacturing plants, one at Aynor and another at Spartanburg. The cost of producing Q_1 kitchen chairs at Aynor is:

$$75Q_1 + 5Q_1^2 + 100$$

and the cost of producing Q_2 kitchen chairs at Spartanburg is

$$25Q_2 + 2.5Q_2^2 + 150$$

Andalus needs to manufacture a total of 40 kitchen chairs to meet an order just received. How many chairs should be made at Aynor and how many should be made at Spartanburg in order to minimize total production cost?

21. The weekly box office revenues (in $ millions) for *Terminator 3* are given here. Use these data in the Bass forecasting model given by equations (8.21) through (8.23) to estimate the parameters p, q, and m. Solve the model in LINGO and see whether you can duplicate the results in Table 8.8.

Week	Terminator 3
1	72.39
2	37.93
3	17.58
4	9.57
5	5.39
6	3.13
7	1.62
8	0.87
9	0.61
10	0.26
11	0.19
12	0.35

The Bass forecasting model is a good example of a "hard" nonlinear program and the answer you get may be a local optimum that is not nearly as good as the result given in Table 8.8. LINGO can find a global optimum for this problem, but the demo version from the website for this text can handle only five variables when finding a global optimum. If you get stuck at a local optimum that is not close to what is reported in Table 8.8, try adding a constraint such as $p \geq .1$ and an initial guess of 100 customers.

Case Problem 1   PORTFOLIO OPTIMIZATION WITH TRANSACTION COSTS[5]

Hauck Financial Services has a number of passive, buy-and-hold clients. For these clients, Hauck offers an investment account whereby clients agree to put their money into a portfolio of mutual funds that is rebalanced once a year. When the rebalancing occurs, Hauck determines the mix of mutual funds in each investor's portfolio by solving an extension of the Markowitz portfolio model that incorporates transaction costs. Investors are charged a small transaction cost for the annual rebalancing of their portfolio. For simplicity, assume the following:

- At the beginning of the time period (in this case one year), the portfolio is rebalanced by buying and selling Hauck mutual funds.
- The transaction costs associated with buying and selling mutual funds are paid at the beginning of the period when the portfolio is rebalanced, which, in effect, reduces the amount of money available to reinvest.
- No further transactions are made until the end of the time period, at which point the new value of the portfolio is observed.
- The transaction cost is a linear function of the dollar amount of mutual funds bought or sold.

[5]The authors appreciate helpful input from Linus Schrage on this case.

Jean Delgado is one of Hauck's buy-and-hold clients. We briefly describe the model as it is used by Hauck for rebalancing her portfolio. The mix of mutual funds that are being considered for her portfolio are a foreign stock fund (*FS*), an intermediate-term bond fund (*IB*), a large-cap growth fund (*LG*), a large-cap value fund (*LV*), a small-cap growth fund (*SG*), and a small-cap value fund (*SV*). In the traditional Markowitz model, the variables are usually interpreted as the *proportion* of the portfolio invested in the asset represented by the variable. For example, *FS* is the proportion of the portfolio invested in the foreign stock fund. However, it is equally correct to interpret *FS* as the dollar amount invested in the foreign stock fund. Then *FS* = 25,000 implies $25,000 is invested in the foreign stock fund. Based on these assumptions, the initial portfolio value must equal the amount of money spent on transaction costs plus the amount invested in all the assets after rebalancing. That is,

$$\text{Initial portfolio value} = \text{Amount invested in all assets after rebalancing} + \text{Transaction costs}$$

The extension of the Markowitz model that Hauck uses for rebalancing portfolios requires a balance constraint for each mutual fund. This balance constraint is

$$\text{Amount invested in fund } i = \text{Initial holding of fund } i + \text{Amount of fund } i \text{ purchased} - \text{Amount of fund } i \text{ sold}$$

Using this balance constraint requires three additional variables for each fund: one for the amount invested prior to rebalancing, one for the amount sold, and one for the amount purchased. For instance, the balance constraint for the foreign stock fund is

$$FS = FS\_START + FS\_BUY - FS\_SELL$$

Jean Delgado has $100,000 in her account prior to the annual rebalancing, and she has specified a minimum acceptable return of 10%. Hauck plans to use the following model to rebalance Ms. Delgado's portfolio. The complete model with transaction costs is

$$\text{Min } \frac{1}{5} \sum_{s=1}^{5} (R_s - \overline{R})^2$$

s.t.

$$0.1006FS + 0.1764IB + 0.3241LG + 0.3236LV + 0.3344SG + 0.2456SV = R1$$
$$0.1312FS + 3.25IB + 0.1871LG + 0.2061LV + 0.1940SG + 0.2532SV = R2$$
$$0.1347FS + 0.0751IB + 0.3328LG + 0.1293LV + 0.385SG - 0.0670SV = R3$$
$$0.4542FS - 0.0133IB + 0.4146LG + 0.0706LV + 0.5868SG + 0.0543SV = R4$$
$$-0.2193FS + 0.0736IB - 0.2326LG - 0.0537LV - 0.0902SG + 0.1731SV = R5$$

$$\frac{1}{5} \sum_{s=1}^{5} R_s = \overline{R}$$

$$\overline{R} \geq 10,000$$

$$FS + IB + LG + LV + SG + SV + TRANS\_COST = 100,000$$
$$FS\_START + FS\_BUY - FS\_SELL = FS$$
$$IB\_START + IB\_BUY - IB\_SELL = IB$$
$$LG\_START + LG\_BUY - LG\_SELL = LG$$
$$LV\_START + LV\_BUY - LV\_SELL = LV$$
$$SG\_START + SG\_BUY - SG\_SELL = SG$$
$$SV\_START + SV\_BUY - SV\_SELL = SV$$

$$TRANS\_FEE * (FS\_BUY + FS\_SELL + IB\_BUY + IB\_SELL +$$
$$LG\_BUY + LG\_SELL + LV\_BUY + LV\_SELL + SG\_BUY + SG\_SELL +$$
$$SV\_BUY + SV\_SELL) = TRANS\_COST$$
$$FS\_START = 10,000$$
$$IB\_START = 10,000$$
$$LG\_START = 10,000$$
$$LV\_START = 40,000$$
$$SG\_START = 10,000$$
$$SV\_START = 20,000$$
$$TRANS\_FEE = 0.01$$
$$FS, IB, LG, LV, SG, SV \geq 0$$

Notice that the transaction fee is set at 1% in the model (the last constraint) and that the transaction cost for buying and selling shares of the mutual funds is a linear function of the amount bought and sold. With this model, the transactions costs are deducted from the client's account at the time of rebalancing and thus reduce the amount of money invested. The LINGO solution for Ms. Delgado's rebalancing problem is shown in Figure 8.16.

Managerial Report

Assume you are a newly employed quantitative analyst hired by Hauck Financial Services. One of your first tasks is to review the portfolio rebalancing model in order to help resolve a dispute with Jean Delgado. Ms. Delgado has had one of the Hauck passively managed portfolios for the last five years and has complained that she is not getting the rate of return of 10% that she specified. After a review of her annual statements for the last five years, she feels that she is actually getting less than 10% on average.

1. According to the model solution in Figure 8.16, $IB\_BUY = \$41,268.51$. How much transaction cost did Ms. Delgado pay for purchasing additional shares of the intermediate-term bond fund?
2. Based on the model solution given in Figure 8.16, what is the total transaction cost associated with rebalancing Ms. Delgado's portfolio?
3. After paying transactions costs, how much did Ms. Delgado have invested in mutual funds after her portfolio was rebalanced?
4. According to the model solution in Figure 8.16, $IB = \$51,268.51$. How much can Ms. Delgado expect to have in the intermediate-term bond fund at the end of the year?
5. According to the model solution in Figure 8.16, the expected return of the portfolio is $10,000. What is the expected dollar amount in Ms. Delgado's portfolio at the end of the year? Can she expect to earn 10% on the $100,000 she had at the beginning of the year?
6. It is now time to prepare a report to management to explain why Ms. Delgado did not earn 10% each year on her investment. Make a recommendation in terms of a revised portfolio model that can be used so that Jean Delgado can have an expected portfolio balance of $110,000 at the end of next year. Prepare a report that includes a modified optimization model that will give an expected return of 10% on the amount of money available at the beginning of the year before paying the transaction costs. Explain why the current model does not do this.
7. Solve the formulation in part (6) for Jean Delgado. How does the portfolio composition differ from that shown in Figure 8.16?

FIGURE 8.16   SOLUTION TO HAUCK MINIMUM VARIANCE PORTFOLIO WITH
TRANSACTION COSTS

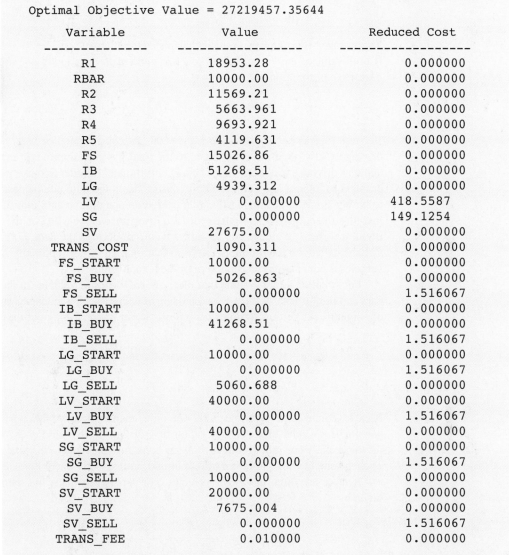

```
Optimal Objective Value = 27219457.35644

       Variable              Value              Reduced Cost
    --------------      ----------------      ------------------
          R1               18953.28               0.000000
         RBAR             10000.00                0.000000
          R2               11569.21               0.000000
          R3               5663.961               0.000000
          R4               9693.921               0.000000
          R5               4119.631               0.000000
          FS               15026.86               0.000000
          IB               51268.51               0.000000
          LG               4939.312               0.000000
          LV                0.000000             418.5587
          SG                0.000000             149.1254
          SV               27675.00               0.000000
      TRANS_COST           1090.311               0.000000
       FS_START           10000.00                0.000000
        FS_BUY            5026.863                0.000000
       FS_SELL             0.000000              1.516067
       IB_START           10000.00                0.000000
        IB_BUY            41268.51                0.000000
       IB_SELL             0.000000              1.516067
       LG_START           10000.00                0.000000
        LG_BUY             0.000000              1.516067
       LG_SELL            5060.688                0.000000
       LV_START           40000.00                0.000000
        LV_BUY             0.000000              1.516067
       LV_SELL            40000.00                0.000000
       SG_START           10000.00                0.000000
        SG_BUY             0.000000              1.516067
       SG_SELL            10000.00                0.000000
       SV_START           20000.00                0.000000
        SV_BUY            7675.004                0.000000
       SV_SELL             0.000000              1.516067
       TRANS_FEE          0.010000                0.000000
```

Case Problem 2   CAFE COMPLIANCE IN THE AUTO INDUSTRY

This case is based on the Management Science in Action, Pricing for Environmental Compliance in the Auto Industry. In this case we build a model similar to the one built for General Motors. The CAFE requirement on fleet miles per gallon is based on an average. The **harmonic average** is used to calculate the CAFE requirement on average miles per gallon.

In order to understand the harmonic average, assume that there is a passenger car and a light truck. The passenger car gets 30 miles per gallon (MPG) and the light truck gets 20 miles per gallon (MPG). Assume each vehicle is driven exactly one mile. Then the passenger car consumes $\frac{1}{30}$ gallon of gasoline in driving one mile and the light truck consumes $\frac{1}{20}$ gallon of gasoline in driving one mile. The amount of gasoline consumed in total is

$$\text{Gas consumption} = (\tfrac{1}{30}) + (\tfrac{1}{20}) = (\tfrac{5}{60}) = (\tfrac{1}{12}) \text{ gallon}$$

The average MPG of the two vehicles calculated the "normal way" is $(30 + 20)/2 = 25$ MPG. If both vehicles are "average," and each vehicle is driven exactly one mile, then the total gasoline consumption is

$$\text{Gas consumption} = (\tfrac{1}{25}) + (\tfrac{1}{25}) = (\tfrac{2}{25}) \text{ gallon}$$

Because $(\frac{2}{25})$ is not equal to $(\frac{5}{60})$, the total gas consumption of two "average vehicles" driving exactly one mile is not equal to the total gas consumption of each of the original vehicles driving exactly one mile. This is unfortunate. In order to make it easy for the government to impose and enforce MPG constraints on the auto companies, it would be nice to have a single target value MPG that every company in the auto industry must meet. As just illustrated, there is a problem with requiring an average MPG on the industry because it will incorrectly estimate the gas mileage consumption of the fleet. Fortunately, there is a statistic called the **harmonic average** so that total gas consumption by harmonic average vehicles is equal to gas consumption of the actual vehicles.

For simplicity, first assume that there are two types of vehicles in the fleet, passenger cars and light trucks. If there is one passenger car getting 30 miles per gallon and there is one light trucks getting 20 miles per gallon, the harmonic average of these two vehicles is

$$\frac{2}{\dfrac{1}{30} + \dfrac{1}{20}} = \frac{2}{\dfrac{5}{60}} = \frac{120}{5} = 24$$

If each vehicle were to drive exactly one mile, each vehicle would consume $\frac{1}{24}$ gallon of gasoline for a total of $\frac{2}{24} = \frac{1}{12}$ gallon of gasoline. In this case each "average" vehicle driving exactly one mile results in total gas consumption equal to the total gas consumption of each vehicle with a different MPG rating driving exactly one mile.

If there are three passenger vehicles and two light trucks, the harmonic average is given by

$$\frac{5}{\dfrac{3}{30} + \dfrac{2}{20}} = \frac{5}{0.1 + 0.1} = \frac{5}{0.2} = 25$$

In general, when calculating the harmonic average, the numerator is the total number of vehicles. The denominator is the sum of two terms. Each term is the ratio of the number of vehicles in that class to the MPG of cars in that class. For example, the first ratio in the denominator is $\frac{3}{30}$ because there are 3 cars (the numerator) each getting 30 MPG (the denominator). These calculations are illustrated in Figure 8.17.

Based on Figure 8.17, if each of the 5 cars is average and drives exactly one mile, $(\frac{5}{25}) = (\frac{1}{5})$ gallon of gas is consumed. If three cars getting 30 MPG drive exactly one mile each and two cars getting 20 MPG drive exactly one mile, then $(\frac{3}{30}) + (\frac{2}{20}) = (\frac{2}{10}) = (\frac{1}{5})$ gallon is consumed. Thus, the average cars exactly duplicate the gas consumption of the fleet with varying MPG.

FIGURE 8.17   AN EXCEL SPREADSHEET WITH A CAFE CALCULATION

	A	B	C	D
1			**Number**	
2		**MPG**	**of Vehicles**	**CAFÉ Weight**
3	**Passenger Cars**	30	3	0.1000
4	**Light Trucks**	20	2	0.1000
5			5	0.2000
6				
7	**CAFÉ Average**	25		

Now assume that the demand function for passenger cars is

$$\text{Demand} = 750 - P_C \qquad (8.24)$$

where P_C is the price of a passenger car. Similarly, the demand function for light trucks is

$$\text{Demand} = 830 - P_T \qquad (8.25)$$

where P_T is the price of a light truck.

Managerial Report

1. Using the formulas given in (8.24) and (8.25), develop an expression for the total profit contribution as a function of the price of cars and the price of light trucks.
2. Using Excel Solver or LINGO, find the price for each car so that the total profit contribution is maximized.
3. Given the prices determined in Question 2, calculate the number of passenger cars sold and the number of light trucks sold.
4. Duplicate the spreadsheet in Figure 8.17. Your spreadsheet should have formulas in cells D3:D5 and B7 and be able to calculate the harmonic (CAFE) average for any MPG rating and any number of vehicles in each category.
5. Again, assume that passenger cars get 30 MPG and light trucks get 20 MPG; calculate the CAFE average for the fleet size from part (3).
6. If you do the calculation in part (5) correctly, the CAFE average of the fleet is 23.57. Add a constraint that the fleet average must be 25 MPG and resolve the model to get the maximum total profit contribution subject to meeting the CAFE constraint.

Appendix 8.1   SOLVING NONLINEAR PROBLEMS WITH LINGO

Appendix 2.1 shows how to use LINGO to solve linear programs.

Solving a nonlinear optimization problem in LINGO is no different from solving a linear optimization problem in LINGO. Simply type in the formulation, select the **LINGO** menu and choose the **Solve** option. Just remember that LINGO uses the ^ sign for exponentiation and the / sign for division. Also note that an asterisk (*) must be used to indicate multiplication.

We show how the unconstrained Par, Inc., problem from Section 8.1 is solved using LINGO. After starting LINGO, we type in the problem formulation in the model window as follows:

$$MAX = 80*S - (1/15)*S\char`\^2 + 150*D - (1/5)*D\char`\^2;$$

The solution obtained is shown in Figure 8.18. To solve the problem, select the **Solve** command from the **LINGO** menu or press the **Solve** button on the toolbar. Note that the value of the objective function is 52125.00, $S = 600$, and $D = 375$.

Now solve the constrained Par, Inc., problem from Section 8.1 using LINGO. The only difference from the constrained problem is that four lines must be added to the formulation to account for the production constraints. After starting LINGO, we type in the problem formulation in the model window as follows.

$$MAX = 80*S - (1/15)*S\char`\^2 + 150*D - (1/5)*D\char`\^2;$$
$$(7/10)*S + D < 630;$$
$$(1/2)*S + (5/6)*D < 600;$$
$$S + (2/3)*D < 708;$$
$$(1/10)*S + (1/4)*D < 135;$$

Note that at the end of the objective function and each constraint a semicolon is used. After selecting the **Solve** command from the **LINGO** menu, the solution shown in Figure 8.2 is obtained.

In the Par, Inc., problem, all the variables are constrained to be nonnegative. If some of the variables may assume negative values, extra lines must be added to the LINGO formulation and the @FREE command must be used. For instance, the Hauck index fund model

FIGURE 8.18   THE LINGO OPTIMAL SOLUTION FOR THE UNCONSTRAINED
PAR, INC., PROBLEM

```
Local optimal solution found.
   Objective value:                      52125.00
   Extended solver steps:                       5
   Total solver iterations:                    40

        Variable              Value          Reduced Cost
      -----------       -------------       ---------------
            S              600.0000             0.000000
            D              375.0000             0.000000

          Row          Slack or Surplus        Dual Price
      -----------       -------------       ---------------
            1               52125.00             1.000000
```

shown in Section 8.2 did not contain nonnegativity constraints for variables $R1$, $R2$, $R3$, $R4$, and $R5$ because these variables are allowed to assume negative values. Thus, after entering the objective function and constraints, the following five lines must be added to the LINGO model to produce the solution shown in Figure 8.8.

@FREE(R1);

@FREE(R2);

@FREE(R3);

@FREE(R4);

@FREE(R5);

LINGO also provides the user with a wide variety of nonlinear functions that are useful in finance, inventory management, statistics, and other applications. To get a list of these functions, use the online LINGO User's Manual that is available under the Help menu. In the User's Manual you will find a chapter entitled "LINGO's Operators and Functions." This chapter contains a list of the available functions. When using a LINGO function you must precede the function name with the @ sign. For example, if you wanted to take the natural logarithm of X you would write @LOG(X).

The demo LINGO provided on the website accompanying this text allows only five variables for problems that use the global solver.

We have discussed the concept of global versus local optimum. By default, LINGO finds a local optimum and the global solver is turned off. In order to turn on the global solver, select **Options** from the **LINGO** menu. When the Options dialog box appears, select the **Global Solver** tab and check the **Use Global Solver** box.

When using LINGO one must exercise care in how the minus sign is used. When used in an expression such as $y - x^2$, the minus sign is a binary operator because it connects two terms y and x^2. By convention, exponentiation has higher "precedence" than the minus; so if $y = 2$ and $x = -1$, the expression $y - x^2$ evaluates to

$$y - x^2 = 2 - (-1)^2 = 2 - 1 = 1$$

However, in the expression $-x^2 + y$, the minus sign is a unary operator because it does not combine terms. LINGO, by default, assigns the unary minus sign higher precedence than exponentiation. Thus, if $y = 2$ and $x = -1$ the expression $-x^2 + y$ evaluates to

$$-x^2 + y = (-x)^2 + y = 1^2 + 2 = 3$$

This is a potential source of confusion. In this text we, like many authors, expect $-x^2$ to be interpreted as $-(x^2)$, not $(-x)^2$. Excel also treats the unary minus sign in this fashion.

Appendix 8.2   SOLVING NONLINEAR PROBLEMS WITH EXCEL SOLVER

Excel Solver can be used for nonlinear optimization. The Excel formulation of the nonlinear version of the Par, Inc., problem developed in Section 8.1 is shown in Figure 8.19. A worksheet model is constructed just as in the linear case. The formula in cell B18 is the objective function. The formulas in cells B21:B24 are the left-hand sides of constraint inequalities. And the formulas in cells D21:D24 provide the right-hand sides for the constraint inequalities.

Note how the nonlinearity comes into the model. The formula in cell B18, the objective function cell, is

$$=B27*B16 + B28*C16 - B9*B16 - C9*C16$$

FIGURE 8.19   THE MODIFIED PAR, INC., PROBLEM IN EXCEL SOLVER

ParNonlinear

	A	B	C	D
1	Par, Inc.			
2				
3		**Production Time**		
4	**Operation**	**Standard**	**Deluxe**	**Time Available**
5	Cutting and Dyeing	0.7	1	630
6	Sewing	0.5	0.83333	600
7	Finishing	1	0.66667	708
8	Inspection and Packaging	0.1	0.25	135
9	**Marginal Cost**	70	150	
10				
11				
12	**Model**			
13				
14		**Decision Variables**		
15		**Standard**	**Deluxe**	
16	**Bags Produced**			
17				
18	**Maximize Total Profit**	=B27*B16+B28*C16-B9*B16-C9*C16		
19				
20	**Constraints**	**Hours Used (LHS)**		**Hours Available (RHS)**
21	Cutting and Dyeing	=B5*B16+C5*C16	<=	=D5
22	Sewing	=B6*B16+C6*C16	<=	=D6
23	Finishing	=B7*B16+C7*C16	<=	=D7
24	Inspection and Packaging	=B8*B16+C8*C16	<=	=D8
25				
26				
27	Standard Bag Price Function	=150-(1/15)*SB$16		
28	Deluxe Bag Price Function	=300-(1/15)*SC$16		

This formula takes the product of the variable cell B16 corresponding to the number of standard bags produced and multiplies it by cell B27 which is the price function for standard bags. But cell B27 also contains the standard bag variable cell B16 in the formula. This creates a nonlinear term and means Excel cannot solve using the standard LP Simplex Solver engine.

Refer to Figure 8.20, which is the **Solver Parameters** dialog box. To solve nonlinear models with Excel Solver, simply do not check **Assume Linear Model** from the Solver **Options**. If the **Assume Linear Model** option is not checked, Solver uses a nonlinear algorithm known as the Generalized Reduced Gradient (GRG) technique. GRG uses a tool from calculus called the gradient. The gradient essentially calculates a direction of improvement for the objective function based on contour lines.

When using Excel, one must exercise care in how the minus sign is used. When used in a cell formula such as $=A1 - B1^2$, the minus sign is a binary operator because it connects

FIGURE 8.20   THE MODIFIED PAR, INC., PROBLEM WITH SOLVER OPTIONS

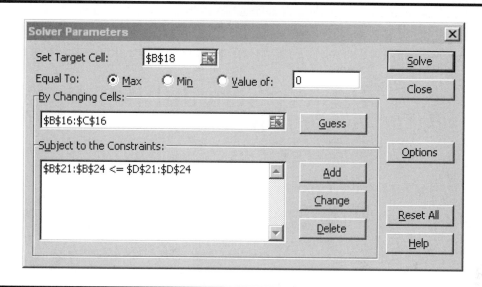

two terms, A1 and B1^2. By convention, exponentiation has higher "precedence" than the minus, so if cell A1 contains 2 and cell B1 contains –1, the expression =A1 – B1^2 evaluates to

$$=A1 - B1\texttt{\^{}}2 = 2 - (-1)^2 = 2 - 1 = 1$$

However, in the expression –B1^2 + A1, the minus sign is a unary operator because it does not combine terms. Excel, by default, assigns the unary minus sign higher precedence than exponentiation. Thus, if cell A1 contains 2 and cell B1 contains –1, the expression –B1^2 + A1 evaluates to

$$-B1\texttt{\^{}}2 + A1 = (-B1)\texttt{\^{}}2 + A1 + 1^2 + 2 = 3$$

LINGO also treats the unary minus sign in this fashion. This is a potential source of confusion. In this text we, like many authors, expect $-x^2$ to be interpreted as $-(x^2)$, not $(-x)^2$.

CHAPTER 9

Project Scheduling: PERT/CPM

CONTENTS

9.1 PROJECT SCHEDULING WITH
KNOWN ACTIVITY TIMES
The Concept of a Critical Path
Determining the Critical Path
Contributions of PERT/CPM
Summary of the PERT/CPM
  Critical Path Procedure

9.2 PROJECT SCHEDULING WITH
UNCERTAIN ACTIVITY TIMES
The Daugherty Porta-Vac Project
Uncertain Activity Times

The Critical Path
Variability in Project Completion
  Time

9.3 CONSIDERING TIME-COST
TRADE-OFFS
Crashing Activity Times
Linear Programming Model
  for Crashing

In many situations, managers are responsible for planning, scheduling, and controlling projects that consist of numerous separate jobs or tasks performed by a variety of departments and individuals. Often these projects are so large or complex that the manager cannot possibly remember all the information pertaining to the plan, schedule, and progress of the project. In these situations the **program evaluation and review technique (PERT)** and the **critical path method (CPM)** have proven to be extremely valuable.

Henry L. Gantt developed the Gantt Chart as a graphical aid to scheduling jobs on machines in 1918. This application was the first of what has become known as project scheduling techniques.

PERT and CPM can be used to plan, schedule, and control a wide variety of projects:

1. Research and development of new products and processes
2. Construction of plants, buildings, and highways
3. Maintenance of large and complex equipment
4. Design and installation of new systems

In these types of projects, project managers must schedule and coordinate the various jobs or **activities** so that the entire project is completed on time. A complicating factor in carrying out this task is the interdependence of the activities; for example, some activities depend on the completion of other activities before they can be started. Because projects may have as many as several thousand activities, project managers look for procedures that will help them answer questions such as the following:

1. What is the total time to complete the project?
2. What are the scheduled start and finish dates for each specific activity?
3. Which activities are "critical" and must be completed *exactly* as scheduled to keep the project on schedule?
4. How long can "noncritical" activities be delayed before they cause an increase in the total project completion time?

PERT and CPM can help answer these questions.

PERT (Navy) and CPM (DuPont and Remington Rand) differ because they were developed by different people working on different projects. Today, the best aspects of each have been combined to provide a valuable project scheduling technique.

Although PERT and CPM have the same general purpose and utilize much of the same terminology, the techniques were developed independently. PERT was developed in the late 1950s specifically for the Polaris missile project. Many activities associated with this project had never been attempted previously, so PERT was developed to handle uncertain activity times. CPM was developed primarily for industrial projects for which activity times were known. CPM offered the option of reducing activity times by adding more workers and/or resources, usually at an increased cost. Thus, a distinguishing feature of CPM was that it identified trade-offs between time and cost for various project activities.

Today's computerized versions of PERT and CPM combine the best features of both approaches. Thus, the distinction between the two techniques is no longer necessary. As a result, we refer to the project scheduling procedures covered in this chapter as PERT/CPM. We begin the discussion of PERT/CPM by considering a project for the expansion of the Western Hills Shopping Center. At the end of the section we describe how the investment securities firm of Seasongood & Mayer used PERT/CPM to schedule a $31 million hospital revenue bond project.

9.1 PROJECT SCHEDULING WITH KNOWN ACTIVITY TIMES

The owner of the Western Hills Shopping Center is planning to modernize and expand the current 32-business shopping center complex. The project is expected to provide room for 8 to 10 new businesses. Financing has been arranged through a private investor. All that remains is for the owner of the shopping center to plan, schedule, and complete the expansion project. Let us show how PERT/CPM can help.

TABLE 9.1   LIST OF ACTIVITIES FOR THE WESTERN HILLS SHOPPING CENTER PROJECT

Activity	Activity Description	Immediate Predecessor	Activity Time
A	Prepare architectural drawings	—	5
B	Identify potential new tenants	—	6
C	Develop prospectus for tenants	A	4
D	Select contractor	A	3
E	Prepare building permits	A	1
F	Obtain approval for building permits	E	4
G	Perform construction	D, F	14
H	Finalize contracts with tenants	B, C	12
I	Tenants move in	G, H	2
		Total	51

The effort that goes into identifying activities, determining interrelationships among activities, and estimating activity times is crucial to the success of PERT/CPM. A significant amount of time may be needed to complete this initial phase of the project scheduling process.

Immediate predecessor information determines whether activities can be completed in parallel (worked on simultaneously) or in series (one completed before another begins). Generally, the more series relationships present in a project, the more time will be required to complete the project.

A project network is extremely helpful in visualizing the interrelationships among the activities. No rules guide the conversion of a list of activities and immediate predecessor information into a project network. The process of constructing a project network generally improves with practice and experience.

The first step in the PERT/CPM scheduling process is to develop a list of the activities that make up the project. Table 9.1 shows the list of activities for the Western Hills Shopping Center expansion project. Nine activities are described and denoted A through I for later reference. Table 9.1 also shows the immediate predecessor(s) and the activity time (in weeks) for each activity. For a given activity, the **immediate predecessor** column identifies the activities that must be completed *immediately prior* to the start of that activity. Activities A and B do not have immediate predecessors and can be started as soon as the project begins; thus, a dash is written in the immediate predecessor column for these activities. The other entries in the immediate predecessor column show that activities C, D, and E cannot be started until activity A has been completed; activity F cannot be started until activity E has been completed; activity G cannot be started until both activities D and F have been completed; activity H cannot be started until both activities B and C have been completed; and, finally, activity I cannot be started until both activities G and H have been completed. The project is finished when activity I is completed.

The last column in Table 9.1 shows the number of weeks required to complete each activity. For example, activity A takes 5 weeks, activity B takes 6 weeks, and so on. The sum of activity times is 51. As a result, you may think that the total time required to complete the project is 51 weeks. However, as we show, two or more activities often may be scheduled concurrently, thus shortening the completion time for the project. Ultimately, PERT/CPM will provide a detailed activity schedule for completing the project in the shortest time possible.

Using the immediate predecessor information in Table 9.1, we can construct a graphical representation of the project, or the **project network.** Figure 9.1 depicts the project network for Western Hills Shopping Center. The activities correspond to the *nodes* of the network (drawn as rectangles), and the *arcs* (the lines with arrows) show the precedence relationships among the activities. In addition, nodes have been added to the network to denote the start and the finish of the project. A project network will help a manager visualize the activity relationships and provide a basis for carrying out the PERT/CPM computations.

The Concept of a Critical Path

To facilitate the PERT/CPM computations, we modified the project network as shown in Figure 9.2. Note that the upper left-hand corner of each node contains the corresponding activity letter. The activity time appears immediately below the letter.

FIGURE 9.1   PROJECT NETWORK FOR THE WESTERN HILLS SHOPPING CENTER

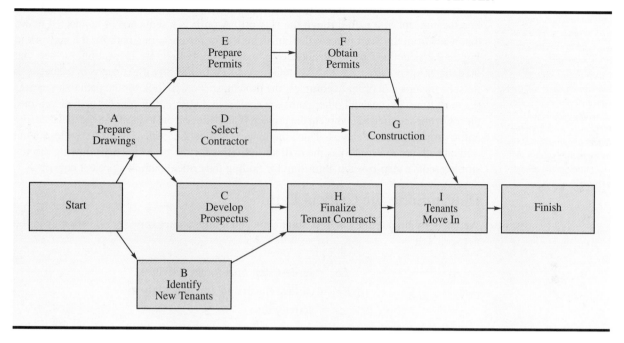

FIGURE 9.2   WESTERN HILLS SHOPPING CENTER PROJECT NETWORK WITH ACTIVITY TIMES

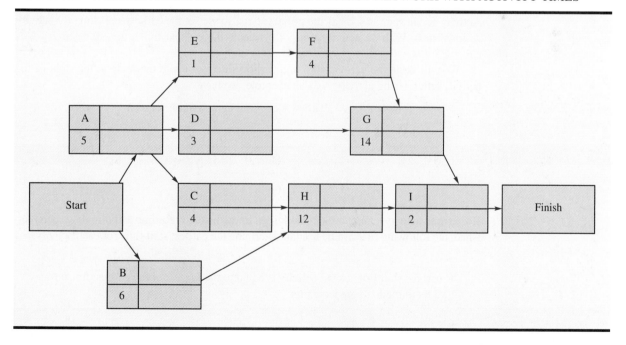

Problem 3 provides the immediate predecessor information for a project with seven activities and asks you to develop the project network.

For convenience, we use the convention of referencing activities with letters. Generally, we assign the letters in approximate order as we move from left to right through the project network.

To determine the project completion time, we have to analyze the network and identify what is called the **critical path** for the network. However, before doing so, we need to define the concept of a path through the network. A **path** is a sequence of connected nodes that leads from the Start node to the Finish node. For instance, one path for the network in Figure 9.2 is defined by the sequence of nodes A–E–F–G–I. By inspection, we see that other paths are possible, such as A–D–G–I, A–C–H–I, and B–H–I. All paths in the network must be traversed in order to complete the project, so we will look for the path that requires the most time. Because all other paths are shorter in duration, this *longest* path determines the total time required to complete the project. If activities on the longest path are delayed, the entire project will be delayed. Thus, the longest path is the *critical path*. Activities on the critical path are referred to as the **critical activities** for the project. The following discussion presents a step-by-step algorithm for finding the critical path in a project network.

Determining the Critical Path

We begin by finding the **earliest start time** and a **latest start time** for all activities in the network. Let

$$ES = \text{earliest start time for an activity}$$
$$EF = \text{earliest finish time for an activity}$$
$$t = \text{activity time}$$

The **earliest finish time** for any activity is

$$EF = ES + t \tag{9.1}$$

Activity A can start as soon as the project starts, so we set the earliest start time for activity A equal to 0. With an activity time of 5 weeks, the earliest finish time for activity A is $EF = ES + t = 0 + 5 = 5$.

We will write the earliest start and earliest finish times in the node to the right of the activity letter. Using activity A as an example, we have

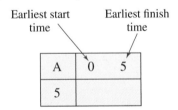

Because an activity cannot be started until *all* immediately preceding activities have been finished, the following rule can be used to determine the earliest start time for each activity:

> The earliest start time for an activity is equal to the *largest* of the earliest finish times for all its immediate predecessors.

Let us apply the earliest start time rule to the portion of the network involving nodes A, B, C, and H, as shown in Figure 9.3. With an earliest start time of 0 and an activity time of 6 for activity B, we show $ES = 0$ and $EF = ES + t = 0 + 6 = 6$ in the node for activity B. Looking at node C, we note that activity A is the only immediate predecessor for activity C.

FIGURE 9.3 A PORTION OF THE WESTERN HILLS SHOPPING CENTER PROJECT NETWORK, SHOWING ACTIVITIES A, B, C, AND H

The earliest finish time for activity A is 5, so the earliest start time for activity C must be $ES = 5$. Thus, with an activity time of 4, the earliest finish time for activity C is $EF = ES + t = 5 + 4 = 9$. Both the earliest start time and the earliest finish time can be shown in the node for activity C (see Figure 9.4).

Continuing with Figure 9.4, we move on to activity H and apply the earliest start time rule for this activity. With both activities B and C as immediate predecessors, the earliest start time for activity H must be equal to the largest of the earliest finish times for activities B and C. Thus, with $EF = 6$ for activity B and $EF = 9$ for activity C, we select the largest value, 9, as the earliest start time for activity H ($ES = 9$). With an activity time of 12, as shown in the node for activity H, the earliest finish time is $EF = ES + t = 9 + 12 = 21$. The $ES = 9$ and $EF = 21$ values can now be entered in the node for activity H in Figure 9.4.

Continuing with this **forward pass** through the network, we can establish the earliest start times and the earliest finish times for all activities in the network. Figure 9.5 shows the Western Hills Shopping Center project network with the *ES* and *EF* values for each activity. Note that the earliest finish time for activity I, the last activity in the project, is 26 weeks. Therefore, we now know that the total completion time for the project is 26 weeks.

We now continue the algorithm for finding the critical path by making a **backward pass** through the network. Because the total completion time for the project is 26 weeks, we begin the backward pass with a **latest finish time** of 26 for activity I. Once the latest finish time for an activity is known, the *latest start time* for an activity can be computed as follows. Let

$$LS = \text{latest start time for an activity}$$
$$LF = \text{latest finish time for an activity}$$

Then

$$LS = LF - t \tag{9.2}$$

FIGURE 9.4   DETERMINING THE EARLIEST START TIME FOR ACTIVITY H

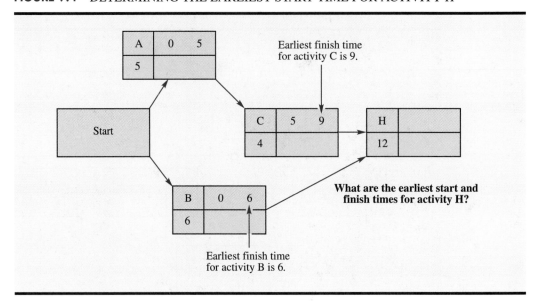

FIGURE 9.5   WESTERN HILLS SHOPPING CENTER PROJECT NETWORK WITH EARLIEST START AND EARLIEST FINISH TIMES SHOWN FOR ALL ACTIVITIES

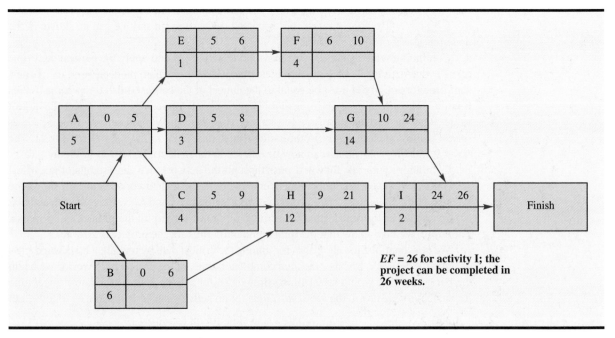

Beginning the backward pass with activity I, we know that the latest finish time is $LF = 26$ and that the activity time is $t = 2$. Thus, the latest start time for activity I is $LS = LF - t = 26 - 2 = 24$. We will write the LS and LF values in the node directly below the earliest start (ES) and earliest finish (EF) times. Thus, for node I, we have

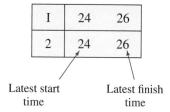

Latest start time   Latest finish time

The following rule can be used to determine the latest finish time for each activity in the network:

> The latest finish time for an activity is the smallest of the latest start times for all activities that immediately follow the activity.

Logically, this rule states that the latest time an activity can be finished equals the earliest (smallest) value for the latest start time of the following activities. Figure 9.6 shows the complete project network with the LS and LF backward pass results. We can use the latest finish time rule to verify the LS and LF values shown for activity H. The latest finish time for activity H must be the latest start time for activity I. Thus, we set $LF = 24$ for activity H. Using equation (9.2), we find that $LS = LF - t = 24 - 12 = 12$ as the latest start time for activity H. These values are shown in the node for activity H in Figure 9.6.

FIGURE 9.6   WESTERN HILLS SHOPPING CENTER PROJECT NETWORK WITH LATEST START AND LATEST FINISH TIMES SHOWN IN EACH NODE

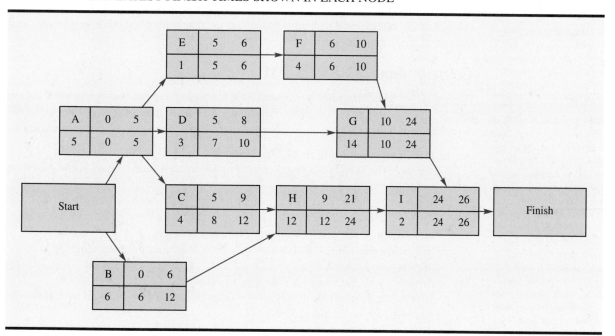

Activity A requires a more involved application of the latest start time rule. First, note that three activities (C, D, and E) immediately follow activity A. Figure 9.6 shows that the latest start times for activities C, D, and E are $LS = 8$, $LS = 7$, and $LS = 5$, respectively. The latest finish time rule for activity A states that the LF for activity A is the smallest of the latest start times for activities C, D, and E. With the smallest value being 5 for activity E, we set the latest finish time for activity A to $LF = 5$. Verify this result and the other latest start times and latest finish times shown in the nodes in Figure 9.6.

The slack for each activity indicates the length of time the activity can be delayed without increasing the project completion time.

After we complete the forward and backward passes, we can determine the amount of slack associated with each activity. **Slack** is the length of time an activity can be delayed without increasing the project completion time. The amount of slack for an activity is computed as follows:

$$\text{Slack} = LS - ES = LF - EF \tag{9.3}$$

For example, the slack associated with activity C is $LS - ES = 8 - 5 = 3$ weeks. Hence, activity C can be delayed up to 3 weeks, and the entire project can still be completed in 26 weeks. In this sense, activity C is not critical to the completion of the entire project in 26 weeks. Next, we consider activity E. Using the information in Figure 9.6, we find that the slack is $LS - ES = 5 - 5 = 0$. Thus, activity E has zero, or no, slack. Thus, this activity cannot be delayed without increasing the completion time for the entire project. In other words, completing activity E exactly as scheduled is critical in terms of keeping the project on schedule. Thus, activity E is a critical activity. In general, the *critical activities* are the activities with zero slack.

One of the primary contributions of PERT/CPM is the identification of the critical activities. The project manager will want to monitor critical activities closely because a delay in any one of these activities will lengthen the project completion time.

The start and finish times shown in Figure 9.6 can be used to develop a detailed start time and finish time schedule for all activities. Putting this information in tabular form provides the activity schedule shown in Table 9.2. Note that the slack column shows that activities A, E, F, G, and I have zero slack. Hence, these activities are the critical activities for the project. The path formed by nodes A–E–F–G–I is the *critical path* in the Western Hills Shopping Center project network. The detailed schedule shown in Table 9.2 indicates the slack or delay that can be tolerated for the noncritical activities before these activities will increase project completion time.

The critical path algorithm is essentially a longest path algorithm. From the start node to the finish node, the critical path identifies the path that requires the most time.

Contributions of PERT/CPM

If the total time required to complete the project is too long, judgment about where and how to shorten the time of critical activities must be exercised. If any activity times are altered, the critical path calculations should be repeated to determine the impact on the activity schedule and the impact on total project completion time. In Section 9.3 we show how to use linear programming to find the least-cost way to shorten the project completion time.

Previously, we stated that project managers look for procedures that will help answer important questions regarding the planning, scheduling, and controlling of projects. Let us reconsider these questions in light of the information that the critical path calculations have given us.

1. How long will the project take to complete?
   Answer: The project can be completed in 26 weeks if each activity is completed on schedule.
2. What are the scheduled start and completion times for each activity?
   Answer: The activity schedule (see Table 9.2) shows the earliest start, latest start, earliest finish, and latest finish times for each activity.
3. Which activities are critical and must be completed *exactly* as scheduled to keep the project on schedule?
   Answer: A, E, F, G, and I are the critical activities.
4. How long can noncritical activities be delayed before they cause an increase in the completion time for the project?
   Answer: The activity schedule (see Table 9.2) shows the slack associated with each activity.

TABLE 9.2   ACTIVITY SCHEDULE FOR THE WESTERN HILLS SHOPPING
CENTER PROJECT

Activity	Earliest Start (ES)	Latest Start (LS)	Earliest Finish (EF)	Latest Finish (LF)	Slack (LS − ES)	Critical Path?
A	0	0	5	5	0	Yes
B	0	6	6	12	6	
C	5	8	9	12	3	
D	5	7	8	10	2	
E	5	5	6	6	0	Yes
F	6	6	10	10	0	Yes
G	10	10	24	24	0	Yes
H	9	12	21	24	3	
I	24	24	26	26	0	Yes

Software packages such as Microsoft Office Project perform the critical path calculations quickly and efficiently. The project manager can modify any aspect of the project and quickly determine how the modification affects the activity schedule and the total time required to complete the project.

Such information is valuable in managing any project. Although larger projects usually increase the effort required to develop the immediate predecessor relationships and the activity time estimates, the procedure and contribution of PERT/CPM to larger projects are identical to those shown for the shopping center expansion project. The Management Science in Action, Hospital Revenue Bond at Seasongood & Mayer, describes a 23-activity project that introduced a $31-million hospital revenue bond. PERT/CPM identified the critical activities, the expected project completion time of 29 weeks, and the activity start times and finish times necessary to keep the entire project on schedule.

Finally, computer packages may be used to carry out the steps of the PERT/CPM procedure. Figure 9.7 shows the activity schedule for the shopping center expansion project produced by Microsoft Office Project. Input to the program included the activities, their immediate predecessors, and the expected activity times. Microsoft Office Project automatically generates the critical path and activity schedule. More details are provided in Appendix 9.1.

Summary of the PERT/CPM Critical Path Procedure

Before leaving this section, let us summarize the PERT/CPM critical path procedure.

Step 1. Develop a list of the activities that make up the project.
Step 2. Determine the immediate predecessor(s) for each activity in the project.
Step 3. Estimate the completion time for each activity.

FIGURE 9.7   MICROSOFT OFFICE PROJECT ACTIVITY SCHEDULE FOR THE WESTERN HILLS
SHOPPING CENTER PROJECT

ID	Task Name	Duration	Early Start	Late Start	Early Finish	Late Finish	Total Slack	Critical
1	A - Prepare architectural drawings	5 wks	Mon 6/8/09	Mon 6/8/09	Fri 7/10/09	Fri 7/10/09	0 wks	Yes
2	B - Identify potential new tenants	6 wks	Mon 6/8/09	Mon 7/20/09	Fri 7/17/09	Fri 8/28/09	6 wks	No
3	C - Develop prospectus for tenants	4 wks	Mon 7/13/09	Mon 8/3/09	Fri 8/7/09	Fri 8/28/09	3 wks	No
4	D - Select contractor	3 wks	Mon 7/13/09	Mon 7/27/09	Fri 7/31/09	Fri 8/14/09	2 wks	No
5	E - Prepare building permits	1 wk	Mon 7/13/09	Mon 7/13/09	Fri 7/17/09	Fri 7/17/09	0 wks	Yes
6	F - Obtain approval for building permits	4 wks	Mon 7/20/09	Mon 7/20/09	Fri 8/14/09	Fri 8/14/09	0 wks	Yes
7	G - Perform construction	14 wks	Mon 8/17/09	Mon 8/17/09	Fri 11/20/09	Fri 11/20/09	0 wks	Yes
8	H - Finalize contracts with tenants	12 wks	Mon 8/10/09	Mon 8/31/09	Fri 10/30/09	Fri 11/20/09	3 wks	No
9	I - Tenants move in	2 wks	Mon 11/23/09	Mon 11/23/09	Fri 12/4/09	Fri 12/4/09	0 wks	Yes

Step 4. Draw a project network depicting the activities and immediate predecessors listed in steps 1 and 2.

Step 5. Use the project network and the activity time estimates to determine the earliest start and the earliest finish time for each activity by making a forward pass through the network. The earliest finish time for the last activity in the project identifies the total time required to complete the project.

Step 6. Use the project completion time identified in step 5 as the latest finish time for the last activity and make a backward pass through the network to identify the latest start and latest finish time for each activity.

Step 7. Use the difference between the latest start time and the earliest start time for each activity to determine the slack for each activity.

Step 8. Find the activities with zero slack; these are the critical activities.

Step 9. Use the information from steps 5 and 6 to develop the activity schedule for the project.

MANAGEMENT SCIENCE IN ACTION

HOSPITAL REVENUE BOND AT SEASONGOOD & MAYER

Seasongood & Mayer is an investment securities firm located in Cincinnati, Ohio. The firm engages in municipal financing, including the underwriting of new issues of municipal bonds, acting as a market maker for previously issued bonds, and performing other investment banking services.

Seasongood & Mayer provided the underwriting for a $31-million issue of hospital facilities revenue bonds for Providence Hospital in Hamilton County, Ohio. The project of underwriting this municipal bond issue began with activities such as drafting the legal documents, drafting a description of the existing hospital facilities, and completing a feasibility study. A total of 23 activities defined the project that would be completed when the hospital

signed the construction contract and then made the bond proceeds available. The immediate predecessor relationships for the activities and the activity times were developed by a project management team.

PERT/CPM analysis of the project network identified the 10 critical path activities. The analysis also provided the expected completion time of 29 weeks, or approximately seven months. The activity schedule showed the start time and finish time for each activity and provided the information necessary to monitor the project and keep it on schedule. PERT/CPM was instrumental in helping Seasongood & Mayer obtain the financing for the project within the time specified in the construction bid.

NOTES AND COMMENTS

Suppose that, after analyzing a PERT/CPM network, the project manager finds that the project completion time is unacceptable (i.e., the project is going to take too long). In this case, the manager must take one or both of the following steps. First, review the original PERT/CPM network to see whether any immediate

predecessor relationships can be modified so that at least some of the critical path activities can be done simultaneously. Second, consider adding resources to critical path activities in an attempt to shorten the critical path; we discuss this alternative, referred to as *crashing,* in Section 9.3.

9.2   PROJECT SCHEDULING WITH UNCERTAIN ACTIVITY TIMES

In this section we consider the details of project scheduling for a problem involving new-product research and development. Because many of the activities in this project have never been attempted, the project manager wants to account for uncertainties in the activity times. Let us show how project scheduling can be conducted with uncertain activity times.

The Daugherty Porta-Vac Project

Accurate activity time estimates are important in the development of an activity schedule. When activity times are uncertain, the three time estimates—optimistic, most probable, and pessimistic—allow the project manager to take uncertainty into consideration in determining the critical path and the activity schedule. This approach was developed by the designers of PERT.

The H. S. Daugherty Company has manufactured industrial vacuum cleaning systems for many years. Recently, a member of the company's new-product research team submitted a report suggesting that the company consider manufacturing a cordless vacuum cleaner. The new product, referred to as Porta-Vac, could contribute to Daugherty's expansion into the household market. Management hopes that it can be manufactured at a reasonable cost and that its portability and no-cord convenience will make it extremely attractive.

Daugherty's management wants to study the feasibility of manufacturing the Porta-Vac product. The feasibility study will recommend the action to be taken. To complete this study, information must be obtained from the firm's research and development (R&D), product testing, manufacturing, cost estimating, and market research groups. How long will this feasibility study take? In the following discussion, we show how to answer this question and provide an activity schedule for the project.

Again, the first step in the project scheduling process is to identify all activities that make up the project and then determine the immediate predecessor(s) for each activity. Table 9.3 shows these data for the Porta-Vac project.

The Porta-Vac project network is shown in Figure 9.8. Verify that the network does in fact maintain the immediate predecessor relationships shown in Table 9.3.

Uncertain Activity Times

Once we develop the project network, we will need information on the time required to complete each activity. This information is used in the calculation of the total time required to complete the project and in the scheduling of specific activities. For repeat projects, such as construction and maintenance projects, managers may have the experience and historical data necessary to provide accurate activity time estimates. However, for new or unique projects, estimating the time for each activity may be quite difficult. In fact, in many cases activity times are uncertain and are best described by a range of possible values rather than by one specific time estimate. In these instances, the uncertain activity times are treated as random variables with associated probability distributions. As a result, probability statements will be provided about the ability to meet a specific project completion date.

TABLE 9.3   ACTIVITY LIST FOR THE PORTA-VAC PROJECT

Activity	Description	Immediate Predecessor
A	Develop product design	—
B	Plan market research	—
C	Prepare routing (manufacturing engineering)	A
D	Build prototype model	A
E	Prepare marketing brochure	A
F	Prepare cost estimates (industrial engineering)	C
G	Do preliminary product testing	D
H	Complete market survey	B, E
I	Prepare pricing and forecast report	H
J	Prepare final report	F, G, I

FIGURE 9.8   PORTA-VAC CORDLESS VACUUM CLEANER PROJECT NETWORK

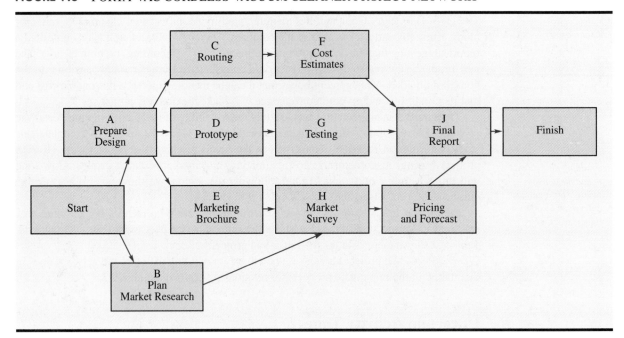

To incorporate uncertain activity times into the analysis, we need to obtain three time estimates for each activity:

Optimistic time a = the minimum activity time if everything progresses ideally
Most probable time m = the most probable activity time under normal conditions
Pessimistic time b = the maximum activity time if significant delays are encountered

To illustrate the PERT/CPM procedure with uncertain activity times, let us consider the optimistic, most probable, and pessimistic time estimates for the Porta-Vac activities as presented in Table 9.4. Using activity A as an example, we see that the most probable time

TABLE 9.4   OPTIMISTIC, MOST PROBABLE, AND PESSIMISTIC ACTIVITY TIME ESTIMATES (IN WEEKS) FOR THE PORTA-VAC PROJECT

Activity	Optimistic (a)	Most Probable (m)	Pessimistic (b)
A	4	5	12
B	1	1.5	5
C	2	3	4
D	3	4	11
E	2	3	4
F	1.5	2	2.5
G	1.5	3	4.5
H	2.5	3.5	7.5
I	1.5	2	2.5
J	1	2	3

is 5 weeks, with a range from 4 weeks (optimistic) to 12 weeks (pessimistic). If the activity could be repeated a large number of times, what is the average time for the activity? This average or **expected time** (*t*) is as follows:

$$t = \frac{a + 4m + b}{6} \tag{9.4}$$

For activity A we have an average or expected time of

$$t_A = \frac{4 + 4(5) + 12}{6} = \frac{36}{6} = 6 \text{ weeks}$$

With uncertain activity times, we can use the *variance* to describe the dispersion or variation in the activity time values. The variance of the activity time is given by the formula[1]

$$\sigma^2 = \left(\frac{b - a}{6}\right)^2 \tag{9.5}$$

The difference between the pessimistic (*b*) and optimistic (*a*) time estimates greatly affects the value of the variance. Large differences in these two values reflect a high degree of uncertainty in the activity time. Using equation (9.5), we obtain the measure of uncertainty—that is, the variance—of activity A, denoted σ_A^2:

$$\sigma_A^2 = \left(\frac{12 - 4}{6}\right)^2 = \left(\frac{8}{6}\right)^2 = 1.78$$

Equations (9.4) and (9.5) are based on the assumption that the activity time distribution can be described by a **beta probability distribution.**[2] With this assumption, the probability distribution for the time to complete activity A is as shown in Figure 9.9. Using equations (9.4) and (9.5) and the data in Table 9.4, we calculated the expected times and variances for all Porta-Vac activities; the results are summarized in Table 9.5. The Porta-Vac project network with expected activity times is shown in Figure 9.10.

The Critical Path

When we have the project network and the expected activity times, we are ready to proceed with the critical path calculations necessary to determine the expected time required to complete the project and determine the activity schedule. In these calculations, we treat the

---

[1] The variance equation is based on the notion that a standard deviation is approximately ⅙ of the difference between the extreme values of the distribution: (*b* − *a*)/6. The variance is the square of the standard deviation.

[2] The equations for *t* and σ^2 require additional assumptions about the parameters of the beta probability distribution. However, even when these additional assumptions are not made, the equations still provide good approximations of *t* and σ^2.

FIGURE 9.9 ACTIVITY TIME DISTRIBUTION FOR PRODUCT DESIGN (ACTIVITY A) FOR THE PORTA-VAC PROJECT

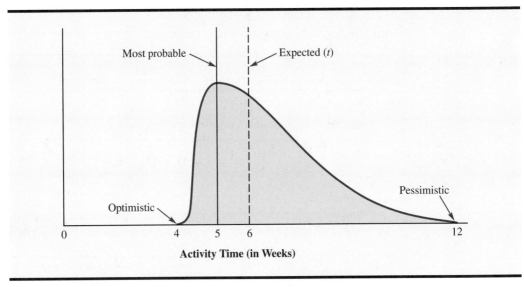

When uncertain activity times are used, the critical path calculations will determine only the expected or average time to complete the project. The actual time required to complete the project may differ. However, for planning purposes, the expected time should be valuable information for the project manager.

expected activity times (Table 9.5) as the fixed length or known duration of each activity. As a result, we can use the critical path procedure introduced in Section 9.1 to find the critical path for the Porta-Vac project. After the critical activities and the expected time to complete the project have been determined, we analyze the effect of the activity time variability.

Proceeding with a forward pass through the network shown in Figure 9.10, we can establish the earliest start (*ES*) and earliest finish (*EF*) times for each activity. Figure 9.11 shows the project network with the *ES* and *EF* values. Note that the earliest finish time for activity J, the last activity, is 17 weeks. Thus, the expected completion time for the project

TABLE 9.5 EXPECTED TIMES AND VARIANCES FOR THE PORTA-VAC PROJECT ACTIVITIES

Activities that have larger variances show a greater degree of uncertainty. The project manager should monitor the progress of any activity with a large variance even if the expected time does not identify the activity as a critical activity.

Activity	Expected Time (weeks)	Variance
A	6	1.78
B	2	0.44
C	3	0.11
D	5	1.78
E	3	0.11
F	2	0.03
G	3	0.25
H	4	0.69
I	2	0.03
J	2	0.11
Total	32	

FIGURE 9.10   PORTA-VAC PROJECT NETWORK WITH EXPECTED ACTIVITY TIMES

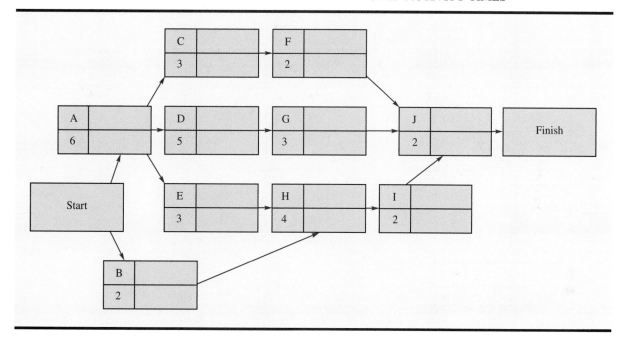

FIGURE 9.11   PORTA-VAC PROJECT NETWORK WITH EARLIEST START AND EARLIEST FINISH TIMES

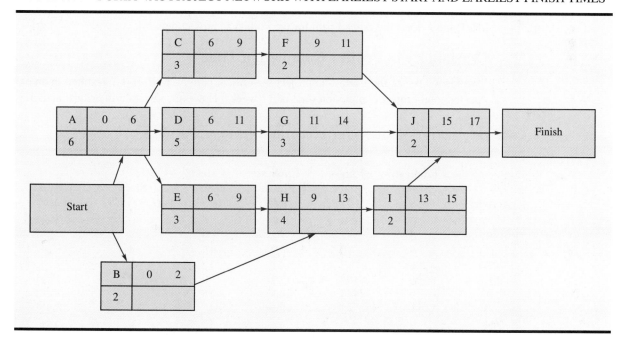

FIGURE 9.12   PORTA-VAC PROJECT NETWORK WITH LATEST START AND LATEST FINISH TIMES

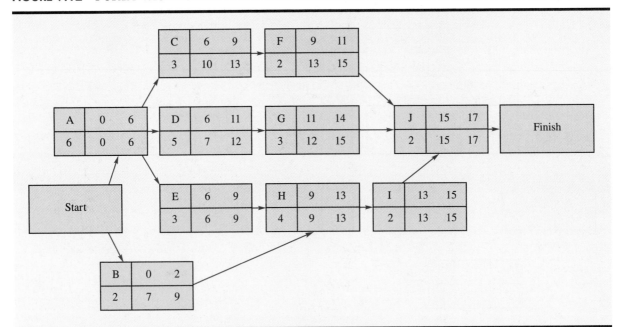

is 17 weeks. Next, we make a backward pass through the network. The backward pass provides the latest start (*LS*) and latest finish (*LF*) times shown in Figure 9.12.

The activity schedule for the Porta-Vac project is shown in Table 9.6. Note that the slack time (*LS* − *ES*) is also shown for each activity. The activities with zero slack (A, E, H, I, and J) form the critical path for the Porta-Vac project network.

Variability in Project Completion Time

We know that for the Porta-Vac project the critical path of A–E–H–I–J resulted in an expected total project completion time of 17 weeks. However, variation in critical activities

TABLE 9.6   ACTIVITY SCHEDULE FOR THE PORTA-VAC PROJECT

Activity	Earliest Start (*ES*)	Latest Start (*LS*)	Earliest Finish (*EF*)	Latest Finish (*LF*)	Slack (*LS* − *ES*)	Critical Path?
A	0	0	6	6	0	Yes
B	0	7	2	9	7	
C	6	10	9	13	4	
D	6	7	11	12	1	
E	6	6	9	9	0	Yes
F	9	13	11	15	4	
G	11	12	14	15	1	
H	9	9	13	13	0	Yes
I	13	13	15	15	0	Yes
J	15	15	17	17	0	Yes

can cause variation in the project completion time. Variation in noncritical activities ordinarily has no effect on the project completion time because of the slack time associated with these activities. However, if a noncritical activity is delayed long enough to expend its slack time, it becomes part of a new critical path and may affect the project completion time. Variability leading to a longer-than-expected total time for the critical activities will always extend the project completion time, and conversely, variability that results in a shorter-than-expected total time for the critical activities will reduce the project completion time, unless other activities become critical. Let us now use the variance in the critical activities to determine the variance in the project completion time.

Let T denote the total time required to complete the project. The expected value of T, which is the sum of the expected times for the critical activities, is

$$E(T) = t_A + t_E + t_H + t_I + t_J$$
$$= 6 + 3 + 4 + 2 + 2 = 17 \text{ weeks}$$

Problem 10 involves a project with uncertain activity times and asks you to compute the expected completion time and the variance for the project.

The variance in the project completion time is the sum of the variances of the critical path activities. Thus, the variance for the Porta-Vac project completion time is

$$\sigma^2 = \sigma_A^2 + \sigma_E^2 + \sigma_H^2 + \sigma_I^2 + \sigma_J^2$$
$$= 1.78 + 0.11 + 0.69 + 0.03 + 0.11 = 2.72$$

where σ_A^2, σ_E^2, σ_H^2, σ_I^2, and σ_J^2 are the variances of the critical activities.

The formula for σ^2 is based on the assumption that the activity times are independent. If two or more activities are dependent, the formula provides only an approximation of the variance of the project completion time. The closer the activities are to being independent, the better the approximation.

Knowing that the standard deviation is the square root of the variance, we compute the standard deviation σ for the Porta-Vac project completion time as

$$\sigma = \sqrt{\sigma^2} = \sqrt{2.72} = 1.65$$

The normal distribution tends to be a better approximation of the distribution of total time for larger projects where the critical path has many activities.

Assuming that the distribution of the project completion time T follows a normal, or bell-shaped, distribution[3] allows us to draw the distribution shown in Figure 9.13. With this distribution, we can compute the probability of meeting a specified project completion date. For example, suppose that management allotted 20 weeks for the Porta-Vac project. What is the probability that we will meet the 20-week deadline? Using the normal probability distribution shown in Figure 9.14, we are asking for the probability that $T \leq 20$; this probability is shown graphically as the shaded area in the figure. The z value for the normal probability distribution at $T = 20$ is

$$z = \frac{20 - 17}{1.65} = 1.82$$

Using $z = 1.82$ and the table for the cumulative standard normal distribution (see Appendix B), we find that the probability of the project meeting the 20-week deadline is 0.9656. Thus,

---

[3]Use of the normal distribution as an approximation is based on the central limit theorem, which indicates that the sum of independent random variables (activity times) follows a normal distribution as the number of random variables becomes large.

FIGURE 9.13   NORMAL DISTRIBUTION OF THE PROJECT COMPLETION TIME
FOR THE PORTA-VAC PROJECT

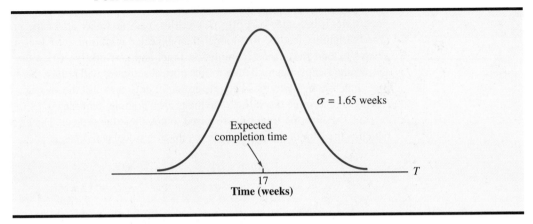

FIGURE 9.14   PROBABILITY THE PORTA-VAC PROJECT WILL MEET
THE 20-WEEK DEADLINE

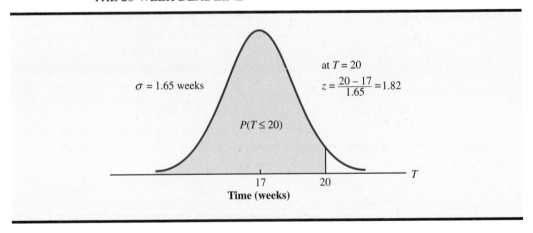

even though activity time variability may cause the completion time to exceed 17 weeks, calculations indicate an excellent chance that the project will be completed before the 20-week deadline. Similar probability calculations can be made for other project deadline alternatives.

NOTES AND COMMENTS

For projects involving uncertain activity times, the probability that the project can be completed within a specified amount of time is helpful managerial information. However, remember that this probability estimate is based *only* on the critical activities. When uncertain activity times exist, longer-than-expected completion times for one or more noncritical activities may cause an original noncritical activity to become critical and hence increase the time required to complete the project. By frequently monitoring the progress of the project to make sure all activities are on schedule, the project manager will be better prepared to take corrective action if a noncritical activity begins to lengthen the duration of the project.

9.3   CONSIDERING TIME-COST TRADE-OFFS

Using more resources to reduce activity times was proposed by the developers of CPM. The shortening of activity times is referred to as crashing.

The original developers of CPM provided the project manager with the option of adding resources to selected activities to reduce project completion time. Added resources (such as more workers, overtime, and so on) generally increase project costs, so the decision to reduce activity times must take into consideration the additional cost involved. In effect, the project manager must make a decision that involves trading reduced activity time for additional project cost.

Table 9.7 defines a two-machine maintenance project consisting of five activities. Because management has had substantial experience with similar projects, the times for maintenance activities are considered to be known; hence, a single time estimate is given for each activity. The project network is shown in Figure 9.15.

The procedure for making critical path calculations for the maintenance project network is the same one used to find the critical path in the networks for both the Western Hills Shopping Center expansion project and the Porta-Vac project. Making the forward pass and backward pass calculations for the network in Figure 9.15, we obtained the activity schedule shown in Table 9.8. The zero slack times, and thus the critical path, are associated with activities A–B–E. The length of the critical path, and thus the total time required to complete the project, is 12 days.

TABLE 9.7   ACTIVITY LIST FOR THE TWO-MACHINE MAINTENANCE PROJECT

Activity	Description	Immediate Predecessor	Expected Time (days)
A	Overhaul machine I	—	7
B	Adjust machine I	A	3
C	Overhaul machine II	—	6
D	Adjust machine II	C	3
E	Test system	B, D	2

FIGURE 9.15   TWO-MACHINE MAINTENANCE PROJECT NETWORK

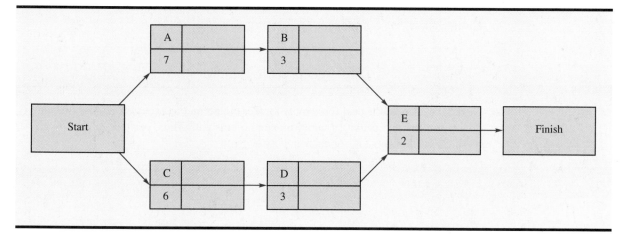

TABLE 9.8   ACTIVITY SCHEDULE FOR THE TWO-MACHINE MAINTENANCE PROJECT

Activity	Earliest Start (ES)	Latest Start (LS)	Earliest Finish (EF)	Latest Finish (LF)	Slack (LS − ES)	Critical Path?
A	0	0	7	7	0	Yes
B	7	7	10	10	0	Yes
C	0	1	6	7	1	
D	6	7	9	10	1	
E	10	10	12	12	0	Yes

Crashing Activity Times

Now suppose that current production levels make completing the maintenance project within 10 days imperative. By looking at the length of the critical path of the network (12 days), we realize that meeting the desired project completion time is impossible unless we can shorten selected activity times. This shortening of activity times, which usually can be achieved by adding resources, is referred to as **crashing.** However, the added resources associated with crashing activity times usually result in added project costs, so we will want to identify the activities that cost the least to crash and then crash those activities only the amount necessary to meet the desired project completion time.

To determine just where and how much to crash activity times, we need information on how much each activity can be crashed and how much the crashing process costs. Hence, we must ask for the following information:

1. Activity cost under the normal or expected activity time
2. Time to complete the activity under maximum crashing (i.e., the shortest possible activity time)
3. Activity cost under maximum crashing

Let

$$\tau_i = \text{expected time for activity } i$$
$$\tau_i' = \text{time for activity } i \text{ under maximum crashing}$$
$$M_i = \text{maximum possible reduction in time for activity } i \text{ due to crashing}$$

Given τ_i and τ_i', we can compute M_i:

$$M_i = \tau_i - \tau_i' \tag{9.6}$$

Next, let C_i denote the cost for activity i under the normal or expected activity time and C_i' denote the cost for activity i under maximum crashing. Thus, per unit of time (e.g., per day), the crashing cost K_i for each activity is given by

$$K_i = \frac{C_i' - C_i}{M_i} \tag{9.7}$$

For example, if the normal or expected time for activity A is 7 days at a cost of $C_A = \$500$ and the time under maximum crashing is 4 days at a cost of $C'_A = \$800$, equations (9.6) and (9.7) show that the maximum possible reduction in time for activity A is

$$M_A = 7 - 4 = 3 \text{ days}$$

with a crashing cost of

$$K_A = \frac{C'_A - C_A}{M_A} = \frac{800 - 500}{3} = \frac{300}{3} = \$100 \text{ per day}$$

We make the assumption that any portion or fraction of the activity crash time can be achieved for a corresponding portion of the activity crashing cost. For example, if we decided to crash activity A by only 1½ days, the added cost would be 1½ ($100) = $150, which results in a total activity cost of $500 + $150 = $650. Figure 9.16 shows the graph of the time-cost relationship for activity A. The complete normal and crash activity data for the two-machine maintenance project are given in Table 9.9.

Which activities should be crashed—and by how much—to meet the 10-day project completion deadline at minimum cost? Your first reaction to this question may be to consider crashing the critical activities—A, B, or E. Activity A has the lowest crashing cost per day of the three, and crashing this activity by 2 days will reduce the A–B–E path to the desired 10 days. Keep in mind, however, that as you crash the current critical activities, other paths may become critical. Thus, you will need to check the critical path in the revised network and perhaps either identify additional activities to crash or modify your initial crashing decision. For a small network, this trial-and-error approach can be used to make crashing decisions; in larger networks, however, a mathematical procedure is required to determine the optimal crashing decisions.

FIGURE 9.16   TIME-COST RELATIONSHIP FOR ACTIVITY A

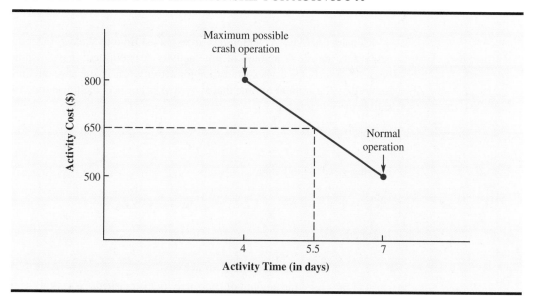

TABLE 9.9   NORMAL AND CRASH ACTIVITY DATA FOR THE TWO-MACHINE MAINTENANCE PROJECT

Activity	Time (days) Normal	Time (days) Crash	Total Cost Normal (C_i)	Total Cost Crash (C_i')	Maximum Reduction in Time (M_i)	Crash Cost per Day $\left(K_i = \dfrac{C_i' - C_i}{M_i} \right)$
A	7	4	$ 500	$ 800	3	$100
B	3	2	200	350	1	150
C	6	4	500	900	2	200
D	3	1	200	500	2	150
E	2	1	300	550	1	250
			$1700	$3100		

Linear Programming Model for Crashing

Let us describe how linear programming can be used to solve the network crashing problem. With PERT/CPM, we know that when an activity starts at its earliest start time, then

$$\text{Finish time} = \text{Earliest start time} + \text{Activity time}$$

However, if slack time is associated with an activity, then the activity need not start at its earliest start time. In this case, we may have

$$\text{Finish time} > \text{Earliest start time} + \text{Activity time}$$

Because we do not know ahead of time whether an activity will start at its earliest start time, we use the following inequality to show the general relationship among finish time, earliest start time, and activity time for each activity:

$$\text{Finish time} \geq \text{Earliest start time} + \text{Activity time}$$

Consider activity A, which has an expected time of 7 days. Let $x_A =$ finish time for activity A, and $y_A =$ amount of time activity A is crashed. If we assume that the project begins at time 0, the earliest start time for activity A is 0. Because the time for activity A is reduced by the amount of time that activity A is crashed, the finish time for activity A must satisfy the relationship

$$x_A \geq 0 + (7 - y_A)$$

Moving y_A to the left side,

$$x_A + y_A \geq 7$$

In general, let

$$x_i = \text{the finish time for activity } i \qquad i = A, B, C, D, E$$
$$y_i = \text{the amount of time activity } i \text{ is crashed} \quad i = A, B, C, D, E$$

If we follow the same approach that we used for activity A, the constraint corresponding to the finish time for activity C (expected time = 6 days) is

$$x_C \geq 0 + (6 - y_C) \quad \text{or} \quad x_C + y_C \geq 6$$

Continuing with the forward pass of the PERT/CPM procedure, we see that the earliest start time for activity B is x_A, the finish time for activity A. Thus, the constraint corresponding to the finish time for activity B is

$$x_B \geq x_A + (3 - y_B) \quad \text{or} \quad x_B + y_B - x_A \geq 3$$

Similarly, we obtain the constraint for the finish time for activity D:

$$x_D \geq x_C + (3 - y_D) \quad \text{or} \quad x_D + y_D - x_C \geq 3$$

Finally, we consider activity E. The earliest start time for activity E equals the *largest* of the finish times for activities B and D. Because the finish times for both activities B and D will be determined by the crashing procedure, we must write two constraints for activity E, one based on the finish time for activity B and one based upon the finish time for activity D:

$$x_E + y_E - x_B \geq 2 \quad \text{and} \quad x_E + y_E - x_D \geq 2$$

Recall that current production levels made completing the maintenance project within 10 days imperative. Thus, the constraint for the finish time for activity E is

$$x_E \leq 10$$

In addition, we must add the following five constraints corresponding to the maximum allowable crashing time for each activity:

$$x_A \leq 3, \quad y_B \leq 1, \quad y_C \leq 2, \quad y_D \leq 2, \quad \text{and} \quad y_E \leq 1$$

As with all linear programs, we add the usual nonnegativity requirements for the decision variables.

All that remains is to develop an objective function for the model. Because the total project cost for a normal completion time is fixed at $1700 (see Table 9.9), we can minimize the total project cost (normal cost plus crashing cost) by minimizing the total crashing costs. Thus, the linear programming objective function becomes

$$\text{Min} \quad 100y_A + 150y_B + 200y_C + 150y_D + 250y_E$$

Thus, to determine the optimal crashing for each of the activities, we must solve a 10-variable, 12-constraint linear programming model. The linear programming solution from either LINGO or Excel Solver provides the optimal solution of crashing activity A by 1 day and activity E by 1 day, with a total crashing cost of $100 + $250 = $350. With the minimum cost crashing solution, the activity times are as follows:

Activity	Time in Days	
A	6	(Crash 1 day)
B	3	
C	6	
D	3	
E	1	(Crash 1 day)

The linear programming solution provided the revised activity times, but not the revised earliest start time, latest start time, and slack information. The revised activity times and the usual PERT/CPM procedure must be used to develop the activity schedule for the project.

NOTES AND COMMENTS

Note that the two-machine maintenance project network for the crashing illustration (see Figure 9.15) has only one activity, activity E, leading directly to the Finish node. As a result, the project completion time is equal to the completion time for activity E. Thus, the linear programming constraint requiring the project completion in 10 days or less could be written $x_E \leq 10$.

If two or more activities lead directly to the Finish node of a project network, a slight modification is required in the linear programming model for crashing. Consider the portion of the project network shown here. In this case, we suggest creating an additional variable, x_{FIN}, which indicates the finish or completion time for the entire project. The fact that the project cannot be finished until both activities E and G are completed can be modeled by the two constraints

$$x_{FIN} \geq x_E \quad \text{or} \quad x_{FIN} - x_E \geq 0$$
$$x_{FIN} \geq x_G \quad \text{or} \quad x_{FIN} - x_G \geq 0$$

The constraint that the project must be finished by time T can be added as $x_{FIN} \leq T$. Problem 22 gives you practice with this type of project network.

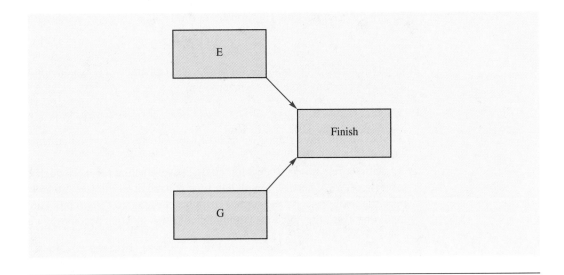

SUMMARY

In this chapter we showed how PERT/CPM can be used to plan, schedule, and control a wide variety of projects. The key to this approach to project scheduling is the development of a PERT/CPM project network that depicts the activities and their precedence relationships. From this project network and activity time estimates, the critical path for the network and the associated critical activities can be identified. In the process, an activity schedule showing the earliest start and earliest finish times, the latest start and latest finish times, and the slack for each activity can be identified.

We showed how we can include capabilities for handling variable or uncertain activity times and how to use this information to provide a probability statement about the chances the project can be completed in a specified period of time. We introduced crashing as a procedure for reducing activity times to meet project completion deadlines, and showed how a linear programming model can be used to determine the crashing decisions that will minimize the cost of reducing the project completion time.

GLOSSARY

Program evaluation and review technique (PERT)   A network-based project scheduling procedure.

Critical path method (CPM)   A network-based project scheduling procedure.

Activities   Specific jobs or tasks that are components of a project. Activities are represented by nodes in a project network.

Immediate predecessors   The activities that must be completed immediately prior to the start of a given activity.

Project network   A graphical representation of a project that depicts the activities and shows the predecessor relationships among the activities.

Critical path   The longest path in a project network.

Path   A sequence of connected nodes that leads from the Start node to the Finish node.

Critical activities   The activities on the critical path.

Earliest start time   The earliest time an activity may begin.

Latest start time   The latest time an activity may begin without increasing the project completion time.

Earliest finish time   The earliest time an activity may be completed.

Forward pass   Part of the PERT/CPM procedure that involves moving forward through the project network to determine the earliest start and earliest finish times for each activity.

Backward pass   Part of the PERT/CPM procedure that involves moving backward through the network to determine the latest start and latest finish times for each activity.

Latest finish time   The latest time an activity may be completed without increasing the project completion time.

Slack   The length of time an activity can be delayed without affecting the project completion time.

Optimistic time   The minimum activity time if everything progresses ideally.

Most probable time   The most probable activity time under normal conditions.

Pessimistic time   The maximum activity time if significant delays are encountered.

Expected time   The average activity time.

Beta probability distribution   A probability distribution used to describe activity times.

Crashing   The shortening of activity times by adding resources and hence usually increasing cost.

PROBLEMS

1. The Mohawk Discount Store is designing a management training program for individuals at its corporate headquarters. The company wants to design the program so that trainees can complete it as quickly as possible. Important precedence relationships must be maintained between assignments or activities in the program. For example, a trainee cannot serve as an assistant to the store manager until the trainee has obtained experience in the credit department and at least one sales department. The following activities are the assignments that must be completed by each trainee in the program. Construct a project network for this problem. Do not perform any further analysis.

Activity	A	B	C	D	E	F	G	H
Immediate Predecessor	—	—	A	A, B	A, B	C	D, F	E, G

2. Bridge City Developers is coordinating the construction of an office complex. As part of the planning process, the company generated the following activity list. Draw a project network that can be used to assist in the scheduling of the project activities.

Activity	A	B	C	D	E	F	G	H	I	J
Immediate Predecessor	—	—	—	A, B	A, B	D	E	C	C	F, G, H, I

3. Construct a project network for the following project. The project is completed when activities F and G are both complete.

Activity	A	B	C	D	E	F	G
Immediate Predecessor	—	—	A	A	C, B	C, B	D, E

4. Assume that the project in Problem 3 has the following activity times (in months):

Activity	A	B	C	D	E	F	G
Time	4	6	2	6	3	3	5

   a. Find the critical path.
   b. The project must be completed in 1½ years. Do you anticipate difficulty in meeting the deadline? Explain.

5. Management Decision Systems (MDS) is a consulting company that specializes in the development of decision support systems. MDS obtained a contract to develop a computer system to assist the management of a large company in formulating its capital expenditure plan. The project leader developed the following list of activities and immediate predecessors. Construct a project network for this problem.

Activity	A	B	C	D	E	F	G	H	I	J
Immediate Predecessor	—	—	—	B	A	B	C, D	B, E	F, G	H

6. Consider the following project network and activity times (in weeks):

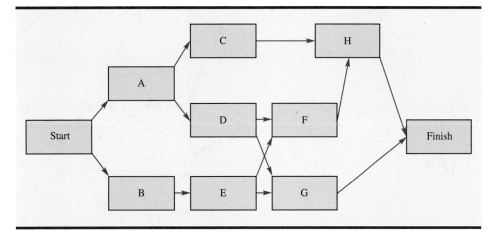

Activity	A	B	C	D	E	F	G	H
Time	5	3	7	6	7	3	10	8

a. Identify the critical path.
b. How much time will be needed to complete this project?
c. Can activity D be delayed without delaying the entire project? If so, by how many weeks?
d. Can activity C be delayed without delaying the entire project? If so, by how many weeks?
e. What is the schedule for activity E?

7. Embassy Club Condominium, located on the west coast of Florida, is undertaking a summer renovation of its main building. The project is scheduled to begin May 1, and a September 1 (17-week) completion date is desired. The condominium manager identified the following renovation activities and their estimated times:

Activity	Immediate Predecessor	Time
A	—	3
B	—	1
C	—	2
D	A, B, C	4
E	C, D	5
F	A	3
G	D, F	6
H	E	4

a. Draw a project network.
b. What are the critical activities?
c. What activity has the most slack time?
d. Will the project be completed by September 1?

8. Colonial State College is considering building a new multipurpose athletic complex on campus. The complex would provide a new gymnasium for intercollegiate basketball games, expanded office space, classrooms, and intramural facilities. The following activities would have to be undertaken before construction can begin:

Activity	Description	Immediate Predecessor	Time (weeks)
A	Survey building site	—	6
B	Develop initial design	—	8
C	Obtain board approval	A, B	12
D	Select architect	C	4
E	Establish budget	C	6
F	Finalize design	D, E	15
G	Obtain financing	E	12
H	Hire contractor	F, G	8

    a. Draw a project network.
    b. Identify the critical path.
    c. Develop the activity schedule for the project.
    d. Does it appear reasonable that construction of the athletic complex could begin one year after the decision to begin the project with the site survey and initial design plans? What is the expected completion time for the project?

9. Hamilton County Parks is planning to develop a new park and recreational area on a recently purchased 100-acre tract. Project development activities include clearing playground and picnic areas, constructing roads, constructing a shelter house, purchasing picnic equipment, and so on. The following network and activity times (in weeks) are being used in the planning, scheduling, and controlling of this project:

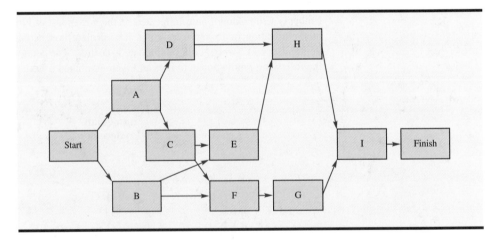

Activity	A	B	C	D	E	F	G	H	I
Time	9	6	6	3	0	3	2	6	3

    a. What is the critical path for this network?
    b. Show the activity schedule for this project.
    c. The park commissioner would like to open the park to the public within six months from the time the work on the project is started. Does this opening date appear to be feasible? Explain.

10. The following estimates of activity times (in days) are available for a small project:

Activity	Optimistic	Most Probable	Pessimistic
A	4	5.0	6
B	8	9.0	10
C	7	7.5	11
D	7	9.0	10
E	6	7.0	9
F	5	6.0	7

    a. Compute the expected activity completion times and the variance for each activity.
    b. An analyst determined that the critical path consists of activities B–D–F. Compute the expected project completion time and the variance.

11. Building a backyard swimming pool consists of nine major activities. The activities and their immediate predecessors are shown. Develop the project network.

Activity	A	B	C	D	E	F	G	H	I
Immediate Predecessor	—	—	A, B	A, B	B	C	D	D, F	E, G, H

12. Assume that the activity time estimates (in days) for the swimming pool construction project in Problem 11 are as follows:

Activity	Optimistic	Most Probable	Pessimistic
A	3	5	6
B	2	4	6
C	5	6	7
D	7	9	10
E	2	4	6
F	1	2	3
G	5	8	10
H	6	8	10
I	3	4	5

    a. What are the critical activities?
    b. What is the expected time to complete the project?
    c. What is the probability that the project can be completed in 25 or fewer days?

13. Suppose that the following estimates of activity times (in weeks) were provided for the network shown in Problem 6:

Activity	Optimistic	Most Probable	Pessimistic
A	4.0	5.0	6.0
B	2.5	3.0	3.5
C	6.0	7.0	8.0
D	5.0	5.5	9.0
E	5.0	7.0	9.0
F	2.0	3.0	4.0
G	8.0	10.0	12.0
H	6.0	7.0	14.0

What is the probability that the project will be completed
a. Within 21 weeks?
b. Within 22 weeks?
c. Within 25 weeks?

14. Davison Construction Company is building a luxury lakefront home in the Finger Lakes region of New York. Coordination of the architect and subcontractors will require a major effort to meet the 44-week (approximately 10-month) completion date requested by the owner. The Davison project manager prepared the following project network:

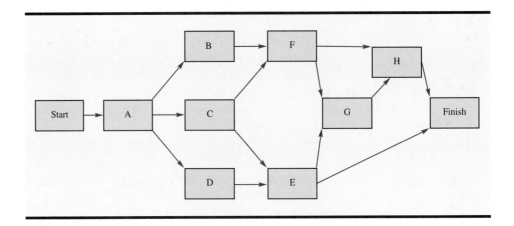

Estimates of the optimistic, most probable, and pessimistic times (in weeks) for the activities are as follows:

Activity	Optimistic	Most Probable	Pessimistic
A	4	8	12
B	6	7	8
C	6	12	18
D	3	5	7
E	6	9	18
F	5	8	17
G	10	15	20
H	5	6	13

a. Find the critical path.
b. What is the expected project completion time?
c. What is the probability the project can be completed in the 44 weeks as requested by the owner?
d. What is the probability the building project could run more than 3 months late? Use 57 weeks for this calculation.
e. What should the construction company tell the owner?

15. Doug Casey is in charge of planning and coordinating next spring's sales management training program for his company. Doug listed the following activity information for this project:

Activity	Description	Immediate Predecessor	Time (weeks)		
			Optimistic	Most Probable	Pessimistic
A	Plan topic	—	1.5	2.0	2.5
B	Obtain speakers	A	2.0	2.5	6.0
C	List meeting locations	—	1.0	2.0	3.0
D	Select location	C	1.5	2.0	2.5
E	Finalize speaker travel plans	B, D	0.5	1.0	1.5
F	Make final check with speakers	E	1.0	2.0	3.0
G	Prepare and mail brochure	B, D	3.0	3.5	7.0
H	Take reservations	G	3.0	4.0	5.0
I	Handle last-minute details	F, H	1.5	2.0	2.5

a. Draw a project network.
b. Prepare an activity schedule.
c. What are the critical activities and what is the expected project completion time?
d. If Doug wants a 0.99 probability of completing the project on time, how far ahead of the scheduled meeting date should he begin working on the project?

16. The Daugherty Porta-Vac project discussed in Section 9.2 has an expected project completion time of 17 weeks. The probability that the project could be completed in 20 weeks or less is 0.9656. The noncritical paths in the Porta-Vac project network are

$$A–D–G–J$$
$$A–C–F–J$$
$$B–H–I–J$$

a. Use the information in Table 9.5 to compute the expected time and variance for each path shown.
b. Compute the probability that each path will be completed in the desired 20-week period.
c. Why is the computation of the probability of completing a project on time based on the analysis of the critical path? In what case, if any, would making the probability computation for a noncritical path be desirable?

17. The Porsche Shop, founded in 1985 by Dale Jensen, specializes in the restoration of vintage Porsche automobiles. One of Jensen's regular customers asked him to prepare an estimate for the restoration of a 1964 model 356SC Porsche. To estimate the time and cost to perform such a restoration, Jensen broke the restoration process into four separate activities: disassembly and initial preparation work (A), body restoration (B), engine restoration (C), and final assembly (D). Once activity A has been completed, activities B and C can be performed independently of each other; however, activity D can be started only if

both activities B and C have been completed. Based on his inspection of the car, Jensen believes that the following time estimates (in days) are applicable:

Activity	Optimistic	Most Probable	Pessimistic
A	3	4	8
B	5	8	11
C	2	4	6
D	4	5	12

Jensen estimates that the parts needed to restore the body will cost $3000 and that the parts needed to restore the engine will cost $5000. His current labor costs are $400 a day.

a. Develop a project network.

b. What is the expected project completion time?

c. Jensen's business philosophy is based on making decisions using a best- and worst-case scenario. Develop cost estimates for completing the restoration based on both a best- and worst-case analysis. Assume that the total restoration cost is the sum of the labor cost plus the material cost.

d. If Jensen obtains the job with a bid that is based on the costs associated with an expected completion time, what is the probability that he will lose money on the job?

e. If Jensen obtains the job based on a bid of $16,800, what is the probability that he will lose money on the job?

18. The manager of the Oak Hills Swimming Club is planning the club's swimming team program. The first team practice is scheduled for May 1. The activities, their immediate predecessors, and the activity time estimates (in weeks) are as follows:

Activity	Description	Immediate Predecessor	Time (weeks) Optimistic	Most Probable	Pessimistic
A	Meet with board	—	1	1	2
B	Hire coaches	A	4	6	8
C	Reserve pool	A	2	4	6
D	Announce program	B, C	1	2	3
E	Meet with coaches	B	2	3	4
F	Order team suits	A	1	2	3
G	Register swimmers	D	1	2	3
H	Collect fees	G	1	2	3
I	Plan first practice	E, H, F	1	1	1

a. Draw a project network.

b. Develop an activity schedule.

c. What are the critical activities, and what is the expected project completion time?

d. If the club manager plans to start the project on February 1, what is the probability the swimming program will be ready by the scheduled May 1 date (13 weeks)? Should the manager begin planning the swimming program before February 1?

19. The product development group at Landon Corporation has been working on a new computer software product that has the potential to capture a large market share. Through outside sources, Landon's management learned that a competitor is working to introduce a similar product. As a result, Landon's top management increased its pressure on the product development group. The group's leader turned to PERT/CPM as an aid to scheduling

the activities remaining before the new product can be brought to the market. The project network is as follows:

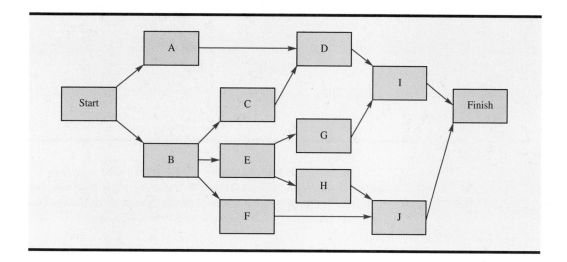

The activity time estimates (in weeks) are

Activity	Optimistic	Most Probable	Pessimistic
A	3.0	4.0	5.0
B	3.0	3.5	7.0
C	4.0	5.0	6.0
D	2.0	3.0	4.0
E	6.0	10.0	14.0
F	7.5	8.5	12.5
G	4.5	6.0	7.5
H	5.0	6.0	13.0
I	2.0	2.5	6.0
J	4.0	5.0	6.0

a. Develop an activity schedule for this project and identify the critical path activities.
b. What is the probability that the project will be completed so that Landon Corporation may introduce the new product within 25 weeks? Within 30 weeks?

20. Norton Industries is installing a new computer system. The activities, the activity times, and the project network are as follows:

Activity	Time	Activity	Time
A	3	E	4
B	6	F	3
C	2	G	9
D	5	H	3

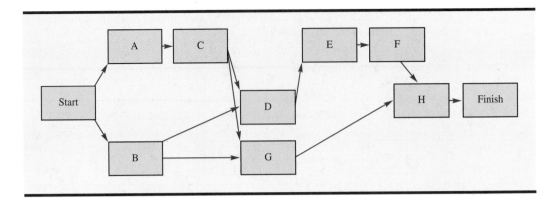

The critical path calculation shows B–D–E–F–H is the critical path, and the expected project completion time is 21 weeks. After viewing this information, management requested overtime be used to complete the project in 16 weeks. Thus, crashing of the project is necessary. The following information is relevant:

	Time (weeks)		Cost ($)	
Activity	**Normal**	**Crash**	**Normal**	**Crash**
A	3	1	900	1700
B	6	3	2000	4000
C	2	1	500	1000
D	5	3	1800	2400
E	4	3	1500	1850
F	3	1	3000	3900
G	9	4	8000	9800
H	3	2	1000	2000

   a. Formulate a linear programming model that can be used to make the crashing decisions for this project.

   b. Solve the linear programming model and make the minimum cost crashing decisions. What is the added cost of meeting the 16-week completion time?

   c. Develop a complete activity schedule based on the crashed activity times.

21. Consider the following project network and activity times (in days):

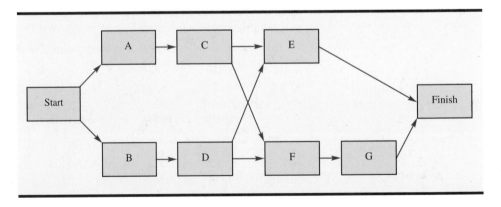

Activity	A	B	C	D	E	F	G
Time	3	2	5	5	6	2	2

The crashing data for this project are as follows:

Activity	Time (days)		Cost ($)	
	Normal	Crash	Normal	Crash
A	3	2	800	1400
B	2	1	1200	1900
C	5	3	2000	2800
D	5	3	1500	2300
E	6	4	1800	2800
F	2	1	600	1000
G	2	1	500	1000

    a. Find the critical path and the expected project completion time.
    b. What is the total project cost using the normal times?

22. Refer to Problem 21. Assume that management desires a 12-day project completion time.

    a. Formulate a linear programming model that can be used to assist with the crashing decisions.
    b. What activities should be crashed?
    c. What is the total project cost for the 12-day completion time?

23. Consider the following project network. Note that the normal or expected activity times are denoted τ_i, $i =$ A, B, . . . , I. Let $x_i =$ the earliest finish time for activity i. Formulate a linear programming model that can be used to determine the length of the critical path.

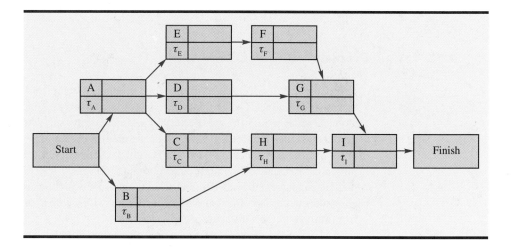

24. Office Automation, Inc., developed a proposal for introducing a new computerized office system that will improve word processing and interoffice communications for a particular company. Contained in the proposal is a list of activities that must be accomplished to complete the new office system project. Use the following relevant information about the activities:

Activity	Description	Immediate Predecessor	Time (weeks)		Cost ($1000s)	
			Normal	Crash	Normal	Crash
A	Plan needs	—	10	8	30	70
B	Order equipment	A	8	6	120	150
C	Install equipment	B	10	7	100	160
D	Set up training lab	A	7	6	40	50
E	Conduct training course	D	10	8	50	75
F	Test system	C, E	3	3	60	—

    a. Develop a project network.
    b. Develop an activity schedule.
    c. What are the critical activities, and what is the expected project completion time?
    d. Assume that the company wants to complete the project in six months or 26 weeks. What crashing decisions do you recommend to meet the desired completion time at the least possible cost? Work through the network and attempt to make the crashing decisions by inspection.
    e. Develop an activity schedule for the crashed project.
    f. What added project cost is required to meet the six-month completion time?

25. Because Landon Corporation (see Problem 19) is being pressured to complete the product development project at the earliest possible date, the project leader requested that the possibility of crashing the project be evaluated.
    a. Formulate a linear programming model that could be used in making the crashing decisions.
    b. What information would have to be provided before the linear programming model could be implemented?

Case Problem   R. C. COLEMAN

R. C. Coleman distributes a variety of food products that are sold through grocery store and supermarket outlets. The company receives orders directly from the individual outlets, with a typical order requesting the delivery of several cases of anywhere from 20 to 50 different products. Under the company's current warehouse operation, warehouse clerks dispatch order-picking personnel to fill each order and have the goods moved to the warehouse shipping area. Because of the high labor costs and relatively low productivity of hand order-picking, management has decided to automate the warehouse operation by installing a computer-controlled order-picking system along with a conveyor system for moving goods from storage to the warehouse shipping area.

    R. C. Coleman's director of material management has been named the project manager in charge of the automated warehouse system. After consulting with members of the engineering staff and warehouse management personnel, the director compiled a list of activities associated with the project. The optimistic, most probable, and pessimistic times (in weeks) have also been provided for each activity.

Activity	Description	Immediate Predecessor
A	Determine equipment needs	—
B	Obtain vendor proposals	—
C	Select vendor	A, B
D	Order system	C
E	Design new warehouse layout	C
F	Design warehouse	E
G	Design computer interface	C
H	Interface computer	D, F, G
I	Install system	D, F
J	Train system operators	H
K	Test system	I, J

Activity	Optimistic	Most Probable	Pessimistic
		Time	
A	4	6	8
B	6	8	16
C	2	4	6
D	8	10	24
E	7	10	13
F	4	6	8
G	4	6	20
H	4	6	8
I	4	6	14
J	3	4	5
K	2	4	6

Managerial Report

Develop a report that presents the activity schedule and expected project completion time for the warehouse expansion project. Include a project network in the report. In addition, take into consideration the following issues:

1. R. C. Coleman's top management established a required 40-week completion time for the project. Can this completion time be achieved? Include probability information in your discussion. What recommendations do you have if the 40-week completion time is required?
2. Suppose that management requests that activity times be shortened to provide an 80% chance of meeting the 40-week completion time. If the variance in the project completion time is the same as you found in part (1), how much should the expected project completion time be shortened to achieve the goal of an 80% chance of completion within 40 weeks?

3. Using the expected activity times as the normal times and the following crashing information, determine the activity crashing decisions and revised activity schedule for the warehouse expansion project:

Activity	Crashed Activity Time (weeks)	Cost ($) Normal	Cost ($) Crashed
A	4	1,000	1,900
B	7	1,000	1,800
C	2	1,500	2,700
D	8	2,000	3,200
E	7	5,000	8,000
F	4	3,000	4,100
G	5	8,000	10,250
H	4	5,000	6,400
I	4	10,000	12,400
J	3	4,000	4,400
K	3	5,000	5,500

Appendix 9.1   USING MICROSOFT OFFICE PROJECT

In this appendix we provide a brief introduction to Microsoft Office Project. A trial version of this software is provided on the CD that is packaged with this book. Microsoft Office Project is software designed to manage and control a project. This software can be used for critical path calculations.

If Microsoft Office Project is properly installed, it will be listed under All Programs in the Start menu along with the other members of the Microsoft Office Family. After starting Microsoft Office Project, you will see what is displayed in Figure 9.17. This is an empty

FIGURE 9.17   MICROSOFT OFFICE PROJECT NETWORK EMPTY PROJECT

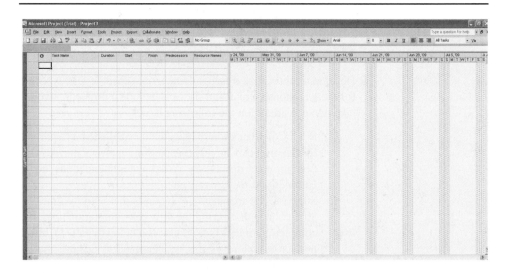

FIGURE 9.18   MICROSOFT OFFICE PROJECT ACTIVITY LIST AND GANTT CHART FOR WESTERN HILLS SHOPPING CENTER

ID		Task Name	Duration	Start	Finish	Predecessors
1		A - Prepare architectural drawings	5 wks	Mon 6/8/09	Fri 7/10/09	
2		B - Identify potential new tenants	6 wks	Mon 6/8/09	Fri 7/17/09	
3		C - Develop propectus for tenants	4 wks	Mon 7/13/09	Fri 8/7/09	1
4		D - Select contractor	3 wks	Mon 7/13/09	Fri 7/31/09	1
5		E - Prepare building permits	1 wk	Mon 7/13/09	Fri 7/17/09	1
6		F - Obtain approval for building permits	4 wks	Mon 7/20/09	Fri 8/14/09	5
7		G - Perform construction	14 wks	Mon 8/17/09	Fri 11/20/09	4,6
8		H - Finalize contracts with tenants	12 wks	Mon 8/10/09	Fri 10/30/09	2,3
9		I - Tenants move in	2 wks	Mon 11/23/09	Fri 12/4/09	7,8

project. Refer back to the list of activities in Table 9.1 for the Western Hills Shopping Center project. Begin entering these activity data. Notice the area of the screen that is much like a spreadsheet. Start in the first row under the column Task Name and type "A - Prepare architectural drawings" and hit return. Next, put the cursor in the column named Duration and type "5 weeks." Note that the default time unit is days, which is why it is important to type "5 weeks" rather than "5 days." Microsoft Office Project will assume that this activity begins on the first available workday. This can be adjusted as well as the number of work days per week, and so on. Enter all of the activities in Table 9.1.

When entering the activities, make sure to enter the appropriate predecessor activities. In Table 9.1 we identified each activity with a letter. However, Microsoft Office Project identifies each activity uniquely with an integer. When entering a predecessor activity use the unique integer identifying it.

In Figure 9.18 we see the result of entering all of the activities in Table 9.1. As mentioned, Microsoft Office Project uses integers to identify activities. In Figure 9.18 we actually started the name of each activity with corresponding letter from Table 9.1 in order to make the correspondence with Table 9.1 more clear. Notice also the second column in Figure 9.18. This is the Indicators column. Double clicking on this column brings up a list of useful possibilities such as % complete.

Notice that the screen in Figure 9.18 is divided into two parts. On the left we see the list of activities, the earliest they can start, and the earliest they can finish. On the right we see the corresponding **Gantt Chart**. This chart has the times superimposed on a calendar. This provides a very useful graphic of when projects can start and end.

The user does not explicitly ask Microsoft Office Project to calculate the critical path. This is automatically done in the background. In order to get the network graphic, select **View** and then **Network Diagram.** The critical path is outlined in red (see Figure 9.19).

FIGURE 9.19   MICROSOFT OFFICE PROJECT NETWORK AND CRITICAL PATH FOR WESTERN HILLS SHOPPING CENTER

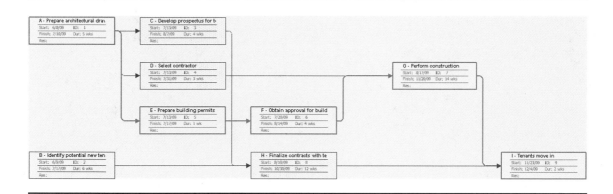

FIGURE 9.20   MICROSOFT OFFICE PROJECT ACTIVITY LIST MODIFIED TO GIVE EARLIEST
AND LATEST START, EARLIEST AND LATEST FINISH,
AND SLACK

In Figure 9.20 we list the earliest start and finish, latest start and finish, and total slack for each activity. Total slack is the Microsoft Office Project terminology for what we are calling slack. We can access these columns by right-clicking on the column bar and selecting the column heading we wish.

CHAPTER 10

Inventory Models

CONTENTS

10.1 ECONOMIC ORDER QUANTITY (EOQ) MODEL
The How-Much-to-Order Decision
The When-to-Order Decision
Sensitivity Analysis for the EOQ Model
Excel Solution of the EOQ Model
Summary of the EOQ Model Assumptions

10.2 ECONOMIC PRODUCTION LOT SIZE MODEL
Total Cost Model
Economic Production Lot Size

10.3 INVENTORY MODEL WITH PLANNED SHORTAGES

10.4 QUANTITY DISCOUNTS FOR THE EOQ MODEL

10.5 SINGLE-PERIOD INVENTORY MODEL WITH PROBABILISTIC DEMAND
Johnson Shoe Company
Nationwide Car Rental

10.6 ORDER-QUANTITY, REORDER POINT MODEL WITH PROBABILISTIC DEMAND
The How-Much-to-Order Decision
The When-to-Order Decision

10.7 PERIODIC REVIEW MODEL WITH PROBABILISTIC DEMAND
More Complex Periodic Review Models

Inventory refers to idle goods or materials held by an organization for use sometime in the future. Items carried in inventory include raw materials, purchased parts, components, subassemblies, work-in-process, finished goods, and supplies. Some reasons organizations maintain inventory include the difficulties in precisely predicting sales levels, production times, demand, and usage needs. Thus, inventory serves as a buffer against uncertain and fluctuating usage and keeps a supply of items available in case the items are needed by the organization or its customers. Even though inventory serves an important and essential role, the expense associated with financing and maintaining inventories is a substantial part of the cost of doing business. In large organizations, the cost associated with inventory can run into millions of dollars.

In applications involving inventory, managers must answer two important questions:

1. *How much* should be ordered when the inventory is replenished?
2. *When* should the inventory be replenished?

Virtually every business uses some sort of inventory management model or system to address the preceding questions. Hewlett-Packard works with its retailers to help determine the retailer's inventory replenishment strategies for printers and other HP products. IBM developed inventory management policies for a range of microelectronic parts that are used in IBM plants as well as sold to a number of outside customers. The Management Science in Action, Inventory Management at CVS Corporation, describes an inventory system used to determine order quantities in the drugstore industry.

The purpose of this chapter is to show how quantitative models can assist in making the how-much-to-order and when-to-order inventory decisions. We will first consider *deterministic* inventory models in which we assume that the rate of demand for the item is constant or nearly constant. Later we will consider *probabilistic* inventory models in which the demand for the item fluctuates and can be described only in probabilistic terms.

MANAGEMENT SCIENCE IN ACTION

INVENTORY MANAGEMENT AT CVS CORPORATION*

The inventory procedure described for the drugstore industry is discussed in detail in Section 10.7.

CVS is the largest drugstore chain in the United States with 4100 stores in 25 states. The primary inventory management area in the drugstore involves the numerous basic products that are carried in inventory on an everyday basis. For these items, the most important issue is the replenishment quantity or order size each time an order is placed. In most drugstore chains, basic products are ordered under a periodic review inventory system, with the review period being one week.

The weekly review system uses electronic ordering equipment that scans an order label affixed to the shelf directly below each item. Among other information on the label is the item's replenishment level, or order-to-quantity. The store employee placing the order determines the weekly order quantity by counting the number of units of the product on the shelf and subtracting this quantity from the replenishment level. A computer program determines the replenishment quantity for each item in each individual store, based on each store's movement, rather than on the company movement. To minimize stockouts the replenishment quantity is set equal to the store's three-week demand, or movement, for the product.

*Based on information provided by Bob Carver. (The inventory system described was originally implemented in the CVS stores formerly known as SupeRx.)

10.1   ECONOMIC ORDER QUANTITY (EOQ) MODEL

The **economic order quantity** (**EOQ**) model is applicable when the demand for an item shows a constant, or nearly constant, rate and when the entire quantity ordered arrives in inventory at one point in time. The **constant demand rate** assumption means that the same number of units is taken from inventory each period of time, such as 5 units every day, 25 units every week, 100 units every four-week period, and so on.

To illustrate the EOQ model, let us consider the situation faced by the R&B Beverage Company. R&B Beverage is a distributor of beer, wine, and soft drink products. From a main warehouse located in Columbus, Ohio, R&B supplies nearly 1000 retail stores with beverage products. The beer inventory, which constitutes about 40% of the company's total inventory, averages approximately 50,000 cases. With an average cost per case of approximately $8, R&B estimates the value of its beer inventory to be $400,000.

The warehouse manager decided to conduct a detailed study of the inventory costs associated with Bub Beer, the number one selling R&B beer. The purpose of the study is to establish the how-much-to-order and the when-to-order decisions for Bub Beer that will result in the lowest possible total cost. As the first step in the study, the warehouse manager obtained the following demand data for the past 10 weeks:

Week	Demand (cases)
1	2000
2	2025
3	1950
4	2000
5	2100
6	2050
7	2000
8	1975
9	1900
10	2000
Total cases	20,000
Average cases per week	2000

Strictly speaking, these weekly demand figures do not show a constant demand rate. However, given the relatively low variability exhibited by the weekly demand, inventory planning with a constant demand rate of 2000 cases per week appears acceptable. In practice, you will find that the actual inventory situation seldom, if ever, satisfies the assumptions of the model exactly. Thus, in any particular application, the manager must determine whether the model assumptions are close enough to reality for the model to be useful. In this situation, because demand varies from a low of 1900 cases to a high of 2100 cases, the assumption of constant demand of 2000 cases per week appears to be a reasonable approximation.

The how-much-to-order decision involves selecting an order quantity that draws a compromise between (1) keeping small inventories and ordering frequently, and (2) keeping large inventories and ordering infrequently. The first alternative can result in undesirably high ordering costs, whereas the second alternative can result in undesirably high inventory holding costs. To find an optimal compromise between these conflicting alternatives, let us consider a mathematical model that shows the total cost as the sum of the holding cost and the ordering cost.[1]

---

[1]Even though analysts typically refer to "total cost" models for inventory systems, often these models describe only the total variable or total relevant costs for the decision being considered. Costs that are not affected by the how-much-to-order decision are considered fixed or constant and are not included in the model.

Holding costs are the costs associated with maintaining or carrying a given level of inventory; these costs depend on the size of the inventory. The first holding cost to consider is the cost of financing the inventory investment. When a firm borrows money, it incurs an interest charge. If the firm uses its own money, it experiences an opportunity cost associated with not being able to use the money for other investments. In either case, an interest cost exists for the capital tied up in inventory. This **cost of capital** is usually expressed as a percentage of the amount invested. R&B estimates its cost of capital at an annual rate of 18%.

A number of other holding costs such as insurance, taxes, breakage, pilferage, and warehouse overhead also depend on the value of the inventory. R&B estimates these other costs at an annual rate of approximately 7% of the value of its inventory. Thus, the total holding cost for the R&B beer inventory is 18% + 7% = 25% of the value of the inventory. The cost of one case of Bub Beer is $8. With an annual holding cost rate of 25%, the cost of holding one case of Bub Beer in inventory for 1 year is 0.25($8) = $2.00.

The next step in the inventory analysis is to determine the **ordering cost.** This cost, which is considered fixed regardless of the order quantity, covers the preparation of the voucher, the processing of the order including payment, postage, telephone, transportation, invoice verification, receiving, and so on. For R&B Beverage, the largest portion of the ordering cost involves the salaries of the purchasers. An analysis of the purchasing process showed that a purchaser spends approximately 45 minutes preparing and processing an order for Bub Beer. With a wage rate and fringe benefit cost for purchasers of $20 per hour, the labor portion of the ordering cost is $15. Making allowances for paper, postage, telephone, transportation, and receiving costs at $17 per order, the manager estimates that the ordering cost is $32 per order. That is, R&B is paying $32 per order regardless of the quantity requested in the order.

The holding cost, ordering cost, and demand information are the three data items that must be known prior to the use of the EOQ model. After developing these data for the R&B problem, we can look at how they are used to develop a total cost model. We begin by defining Q as the order quantity. Thus, the how-much-to-order decision involves finding the value of Q that will minimize the sum of holding and ordering costs.

The inventory for Bub Beer will have a maximum value of Q units when an order of size Q is received from the supplier. R&B will then satisfy customer demand from inventory until the inventory is depleted, at which time another shipment of Q units will be received. Thus, assuming a constant demand, the graph of the inventory for Bub Beer is as shown in Figure 10.1. Note that the graph indicates an average inventory of $\frac{1}{2}Q$ for the period in question. This level should appear reasonable because the maximum inventory is Q, the minimum is zero, and the inventory declines at a constant rate over the period.

Figure 10.1 shows the inventory pattern during one order cycle of length T. As time goes on, this pattern will repeat. The complete inventory pattern is shown in Figure 10.2. If the average inventory during each cycle is $\frac{1}{2}Q$, the average inventory over any number of cycles is also $\frac{1}{2}Q$.

The holding cost can be calculated using the average inventory. That is, we can calculate the holding cost by multiplying the average inventory by the cost of carrying one unit in inventory for the stated period. The period selected for the model is up to you; it could be one week, one month, one year, or more. However, because the holding cost for many industries and businesses is expressed as an *annual* percentage, most inventory models are developed on an *annual* cost basis.

FIGURE 10.1 INVENTORY FOR BUB BEER

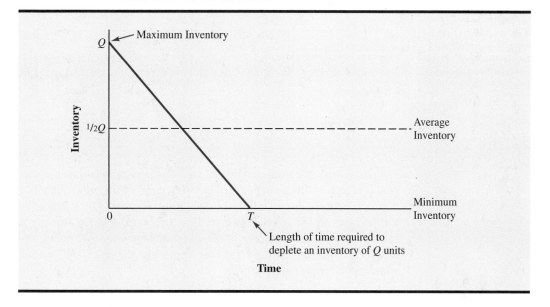

Let

$$I = \text{annual holding cost rate}$$
$$C = \text{unit cost of the inventory item}$$
$$C_h = \text{annual cost of holding one unit in inventory}$$

The annual cost of holding one unit in inventory is

$$C_h = IC \qquad (10.1)$$

FIGURE 10.2 INVENTORY PATTERN FOR THE EOQ INVENTORY MODEL

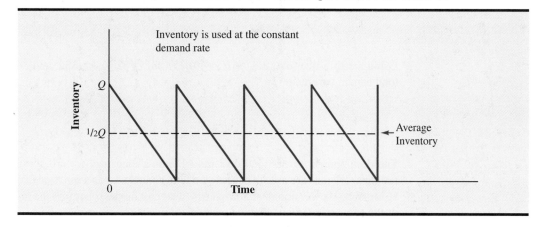

The general equation for the annual holding cost for the average inventory of $\frac{1}{2}Q$ units is as follows:

$$\begin{array}{rcl}
\text{Annual} \\
\text{holding cost}
\end{array} = \left(\begin{array}{c}\text{Average}\\ \text{inventory}\end{array}\right)\left(\begin{array}{c}\text{Annual holding}\\ \text{cost}\\ \text{per unit}\end{array}\right)$$

$$= \frac{1}{2}QC_h \qquad\qquad (10.2)$$

To complete the total cost model, we must now include the annual ordering cost. The goal is to express the annual ordering cost in terms of the order quantity Q. The first question is, How many orders will be placed during the year? Let D denote the annual demand for the product. For R&B Beverage, D = (52 weeks)(2000 cases per week) = 104,000 cases per year. We know that by ordering Q units every time we order, we will have to place D/Q orders per year. If C_o is the cost of placing one order, the general equation for the annual ordering cost is as follows:

$$\begin{array}{rcl}
\text{Annual} \\
\text{ordering cost}
\end{array} = \left(\begin{array}{c}\text{Number of}\\ \text{orders}\\ \text{per year}\end{array}\right)\left(\begin{array}{c}\text{Cost}\\ \text{per}\\ \text{order}\end{array}\right)$$

$$= \left(\frac{D}{Q}\right)C_o \qquad\qquad (10.3)$$

Thus, the total annual cost, denoted TC, can be expressed as follows:

$$\begin{array}{rcl}
\text{Total} \\
\text{annual} \\
\text{cost}
\end{array} = \left(\begin{array}{c}\text{Annual}\\ \text{holding}\\ \text{cost}\end{array}\right)\left(\begin{array}{c}\text{Annual}\\ \text{ordering}\\ \text{cost}\end{array}\right)$$

$$TC = \frac{1}{2}QC_h + \frac{D}{Q}C_o \qquad\qquad (10.4)$$

Using the Bub Beer data [$C_h = IC = (0.25)(\$8) = \$2$, $C_o = \$32$, and $D = 104,000$], the total annual cost model is

$$TC = \frac{1}{2}Q(\$2) + \frac{104,000}{Q}(\$32) = Q + \frac{3,328,000}{Q}$$

The development of the total cost model goes a long way toward solving the inventory problem. We now are able to express the total annual cost as a function of *how much* should be ordered. The development of a realistic total cost model is perhaps the most important part of the application of quantitative methods to inventory decision making. Equation (10.4) is the general total cost equation for inventory situations in which the assumptions of the economic order quantity model are valid.

The How-Much-to-Order Decision

The next step is to find the order quantity Q that will minimize the total annual cost for Bub Beer. Using a trial-and-error approach, we can compute the total annual cost for several possible order quantities. As a starting point, let us consider $Q = 8000$. The total annual cost for Bub Beer is

$$TC = Q + \frac{3,328,000}{Q}$$

$$= 8000 + \frac{3,328,000}{8000} = \$8416$$

A trial order quantity of 5000 gives

$$TC = 5000 + \frac{3,328,000}{5000} = \$5666$$

The results of several other trial order quantities are shown in Table 10.1. It shows the lowest-cost solution to be about 2000 cases. Graphs of the annual holding and ordering costs and total annual costs are shown in Figure 10.3.

    The advantage of the trial-and-error approach is that it is rather easy to do and provides the total annual cost for a number of possible order quantity decisions. In this case, the minimum cost order quantity appears to be approximately 2000 cases. The disadvantage of this approach, however, is that it does not provide the exact minimum cost order quantity.

    Refer to Figure 10.3. The minimum total cost order quantity is denoted by an order size of Q^*. By using differential calculus, it can be shown (see Appendix 10.1) that the value of Q^* that minimizes the total annual cost is given by the formula

The EOQ formula determines the optimal order quantity by balancing the annual holding cost and the annual ordering cost.

In 1915 F. W. Harris derived the mathematical formula for the economic order quantity. It was the first application of quantitative methods to the area of inventory management.

$$Q^* = \sqrt{\frac{2DC_o}{C_h}} \tag{10.5}$$

This formula is referred to as the *economic order quantity (EOQ) formula.*

TABLE 10.1 ANNUAL HOLDING, ORDERING, AND TOTAL COSTS FOR VARIOUS ORDER QUANTITIES OF BUB BEER

	Annual Cost		
Order Quantity	**Holding**	**Ordering**	**Total**
5000	$5000	$ 666	$5666
4000	$4000	$ 832	$4832
3000	$3000	$1109	$4109
2000	$2000	$1664	$3664
1000	$1000	$3328	$4328

FIGURE 10.3   ANNUAL HOLDING, ORDERING, AND TOTAL COSTS FOR BUB BEER

Using equation (10.5), the minimum total annual cost order quantity for Bub Beer is

$$Q^* = \sqrt{\frac{2(104,000)32}{2}} = 1824 \text{ cases}$$

Problem 2 at the end of the chapter asks you to show that equal holding and ordering costs is a property of the EOQ model.

The use of an order quantity of 1824 in equation (10.4) shows that the minimum cost inventory policy for Bub Beer has a total annual cost of $3649. Note that $Q^* = 1824$ balances the holding and ordering costs. Check for yourself to see that these costs are equal.[2]

The When-to-Order Decision

The reorder point is expressed in terms of inventory position, the amount of inventory on hand plus the amount on order. Some people think that the reorder point is expressed in terms of inventory on hand. With short lead times, inventory position is usually the same as the inventory on hand. However, with long lead times, inventory position may be larger than inventory on hand.

Now that we know how much to order, we want to address the question of *when* to order. To answer this question, we need to introduce the concept of inventory position. The **inventory position** is defined as the amount of inventory on hand plus the amount of inventory on order. The when-to-order decision is expressed in terms of a **reorder point**—the inventory position at which a new order should be placed.

The manufacturer of Bub Beer guarantees a two-day delivery on any order placed by R&B Beverage. Hence, assuming R&B Beverage operates 250 days per year, the annual demand of 104,000 cases implies a daily demand of $104,000/250 = 416$ cases. Thus, we expect (2 days)(416 cases per day) = 832 cases of Bub to be sold during the two days it takes a new order to reach the R&B warehouse. In inventory terminology, the two-day

[2]Actually, Q^* from equation (10.5) is 1824.28, but because we cannot order fractional cases of beer, a Q^* of 1824 is shown. This value of Q^* may cause a few cents deviation between the two costs. If Q^* is used at its exact value, the holding and ordering costs will be exactly the same.

delivery period is referred to as the **lead time** for a new order, and the 832-case demand anticipated during this period is referred to as the **lead-time demand.** Thus, R&B should order a new shipment of Bub Beer from the manufacturer when the inventory reaches 832 cases. For inventory systems using the constant demand rate assumption and a fixed lead time, the reorder point is the same as the lead-time demand. For these systems, the general expression for the reorder point is as follows:

$$r = dm \qquad\qquad (10.6)$$

where

$$r = \text{reorder point}$$
$$d = \text{demand per day}$$
$$m = \text{lead time for a new order in days}$$

The question of how frequently the order will be placed can now be answered. The period between orders is referred to as the **cycle time.** Previously in equation (10.2), we defined D/Q as the number of orders that will be placed in a year. Thus, $D/Q^* = 104,000/1824 = 57$ is the number of orders R&B Beverage will place for Bub Beer each year. If R&B places 57 orders over 250 working days, it will order approximately every $250/57 = 4.39$ working days. Thus, the cycle time is 4.39 working days. The general expression for a cycle time[3] of T days is given by

$$T = \frac{250}{D/Q^*} = \frac{250Q^*}{D} \qquad\qquad (10.7)$$

Sensitivity Analysis for the EOQ Model

Even though substantial time may have been spent in arriving at the cost per order ($32) and the holding cost rate (25%), we should realize that these figures are at best good estimates. Thus, we may want to consider how much the recommended order quantity would change with different estimated ordering and holding costs. To determine the effects of various cost scenarios, we can calculate the recommended order quantity under several different cost conditions. Table 10.2 shows the minimum total cost order quantity for several cost possibilities. As you can see from the table, the value of Q^* appears relatively stable, even with some variations in the cost estimates. Based on these results, the best order quantity for Bub Beer is in the range of 1700–2000 cases. If operated properly, the total cost for the Bub Beer inventory system should be close to $3400 to $3800 per year. We also note that little risk is associated with implementing the calculated order quantity of 1824. For example, if holding cost rate = 24%, $C_o = \$34$, and the true optimal order quantity $Q^* = 1919$, R&B experiences only a $5 increase in the total annual cost; that is, $3690 - \$3685 = \$5$, with $Q = 1824$.

From the preceding analysis, we would say that this EOQ model is insensitive to small variations or errors in the cost estimates. This insensitivity is a property of EOQ models in

---

[3]This general expression for cycle time is based on 250 working days per year. If the firm operated 300 working days per year and wanted to express cycle time in terms of working days, the cycle time would be given by $T = 300Q^*/D$.

TABLE 10.2   OPTIMAL ORDER QUANTITIES FOR SEVERAL COST POSSIBILITIES

Possible Inventory Holding Cost (%)	Possible Cost per Order	Optimal Order Quantity (Q^*)	Projected Total Annual Cost	
			Using Q^*	Using $Q = 1824$
24	$30	1803	$3461	$3462
24	34	1919	3685	3690
26	30	1732	3603	3607
26	34	1844	3835	3836

general, which indicates that if we have at least reasonable estimates of ordering cost and holding cost, we can expect to obtain a good approximation of the true minimum cost order quantity.

Excel Solution of the EOQ Model

Inventory models such as the EOQ model are easily implemented with the aid of worksheets. The Excel EOQ worksheet for Bub Beer is shown in Figure 10.4. The formula worksheet is in the background; the value worksheet is in the foreground. Data on annual

FIGURE 10.4   WORKSHEET FOR THE BUB BEER EOQ INVENTORY MODEL

WEB file

EOQ

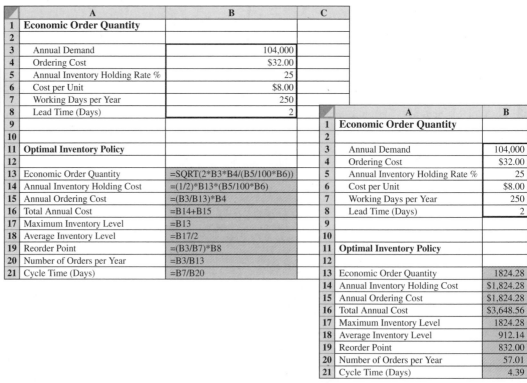

	A	B	C
1	**Economic Order Quantity**		
2			
3	Annual Demand	104,000	
4	Ordering Cost	$32.00	
5	Annual Inventory Holding Rate %	25	
6	Cost per Unit	$8.00	
7	Working Days per Year	250	
8	Lead Time (Days)	2	
9			
10			
11	**Optimal Inventory Policy**		
12			
13	Economic Order Quantity	=SQRT(2*B3*B4/(B5/100*B6))	
14	Annual Inventory Holding Cost	=(1/2)*B13*(B5/100*B6)	
15	Annual Ordering Cost	=(B3/B13)*B4	
16	Total Annual Cost	=B14+B15	
17	Maximum Inventory Level	=B13	
18	Average Inventory Level	=B17/2	
19	Reorder Point	=(B3/B7)*B8	
20	Number of Orders per Year	=B3/B13	
21	Cycle Time (Days)	=B7/B20	

	A	B
1	**Economic Order Quantity**	
2		
3	Annual Demand	104,000
4	Ordering Cost	$32.00
5	Annual Inventory Holding Rate %	25
6	Cost per Unit	$8.00
7	Working Days per Year	250
8	Lead Time (Days)	2
9		
10		
11	**Optimal Inventory Policy**	
12		
13	Economic Order Quantity	1824.28
14	Annual Inventory Holding Cost	$1,824.28
15	Annual Ordering Cost	$1,824.28
16	Total Annual Cost	$3,648.56
17	Maximum Inventory Level	1824.28
18	Average Inventory Level	912.14
19	Reorder Point	832.00
20	Number of Orders per Year	57.01
21	Cycle Time (Days)	4.39

demand, ordering cost, annual inventory holding cost rate, cost per unit, working days per year, and lead time in days are input in cells B3 to B8. The appropriate EOQ model formulas, which determine the optimal inventory policy, are placed in cells B13 to B21. The value worksheet in the foreground shows the optimal economic order quantity 1824.28, the total annual cost $3,648.56, and a variety of additional information. If sensitivity analysis is desired, one or more of the input data values can be modified. The impact of any change or changes on the optimal inventory policy will then appear in the worksheet.

The Excel worksheet in Figure 10.4 is a template that can be used for the EOQ model. This worksheet and similar Excel worksheets for the other inventory models presented in this chapter are available on the website that accompanies this text.

Summary of the EOQ Model Assumptions

You should carefully review the assumptions of the inventory model before applying it in an actual situation. Several inventory models discussed later in this chapter alter one or more of the assumptions of the EOQ model.

To use the optimal order quantity and reorder point model described in this section, an analyst must make assumptions about how the inventory system operates. The EOQ model with its economic order quantity formula is based on some specific assumptions about the R&B inventory system. A summary of the assumptions for this model is provided in Table 10.3. Before using the EOQ formula, carefully review these assumptions to ensure that they are applicable to the inventory system being analyzed. If the assumptions are not reasonable, seek a different inventory model.

Various types of inventory systems are used in practice, and the inventory models presented in the following sections alter one or more of the EOQ model assumptions shown in Table 10.3. When the assumptions change, a different inventory model with different optimal operating policies becomes necessary.

TABLE 10.3 THE EOQ MODEL ASSUMPTIONS

1. Demand D is deterministic and occurs at a constant rate.
2. The order quantity Q is the same for each order. The inventory level increases by Q units each time an order is received.
3. The cost per order, C_o, is constant and does not depend on the quantity ordered.
4. The purchase cost per unit, C, is constant and does not depend on the quantity ordered.
5. The inventory holding cost per unit per time period, C_h, is constant. The total inventory holding cost depends on both C_h and the size of the inventory.
6. Shortages such as stockouts or backorders are not permitted.
7. The lead time for an order is constant.
8. The inventory position is reviewed continuously. As a result, an order is placed as soon as the inventory position reaches the reorder point.

NOTES AND COMMENTS

With relatively long lead times, the lead-time demand and the resulting reorder point r, determined by equation (10.6), may exceed Q^*. If this condition occurs, at least one order will be outstanding when a new order is placed. For example, assume that Bub Beer has a lead time of $m = 6$ days. With a daily demand of $d = 432$ cases, equation (10.6) shows that the reorder point would be $r = dm = 6$ $\times 432 = 2592$ cases. Thus, a new order for Bub Beer should be placed whenever the inventory position (the amount of inventory on hand plus the amount of inventory on order) reaches 2592. With an order quantity of $Q = 2000$ cases, the inventory position of 2592 cases occurs when one order of 2000 cases is outstanding and $2592 - 2000 = 592$ cases are on hand.

10.2   ECONOMIC PRODUCTION LOT SIZE MODEL

The inventory model in this section alters assumption 2 of the EOQ model (see Table 10.3). The assumption concerning the arrival of Q units each time an order is received is changed to a constant production supply rate.

The inventory model presented in this section is similar to the EOQ model in that we are attempting to determine *how much* we should order and *when* the order should be placed. We again assume a constant demand rate. However, instead of assuming that the order arrives in a shipment of size Q^*, as in the EOQ model, we assume that units are supplied to inventory at a constant rate over several days or several weeks. The **constant supply rate** assumption implies that the same number of units is supplied to inventory each period of time (e.g., 10 units every day or 50 units every week). This model is designed for production situations in which, once an order is placed, production begins and a constant number of units is added to inventory each day until the production run has been completed.

If we have a production system that produces 50 units per day and we decide to schedule 10 days of production, we have a 50(10) = 500-unit production lot size. The **lot size** is the number of units in an order. In general, if we let Q indicate the production lot size, the approach to the inventory decisions is similar to the EOQ model; that is, we build a holding and ordering cost model that expresses the total cost as a function of the production lot size. Then we attempt to find the production lot size that minimizes the total cost.

One other condition that should be mentioned at this time is that the model only applies to situations where the production rate is greater than the demand rate; the production system must be able to satisfy demand. For instance, if the constant demand rate is 400 units per day, the production rate must be at least 400 units per day to satisfy demand.

During the production run, demand reduces the inventory while production adds to inventory. Because we assume that the production rate exceeds the demand rate, each day during a production run we produce more units than are demanded. Thus, the excess production causes a gradual inventory buildup during the production period. When the production run is completed, the continuing demand causes the inventory to gradually decline until a new production run is started. The inventory pattern for this system is shown in Figure 10.5.

This model differs from the EOQ model in that a setup cost replaces the ordering cost and the sawtooth inventory pattern shown in Figure 10.5 differs from the inventory pattern shown in Figure 10.2.

As in the EOQ model, we are now dealing with two costs, the holding cost and the ordering cost. Here the holding cost is identical to the definition in the EOQ model, but the interpretation of the ordering cost is slightly different. In fact, in a production situation the ordering cost is more correctly referred to as the production **setup cost.** This cost, which includes labor, material, and lost production costs incurred while preparing the production system for operation, is a fixed cost that occurs for every production run regardless of the production lot size.

FIGURE 10.5   INVENTORY PATTERN FOR THE PRODUCTION LOT SIZE
INVENTORY MODEL

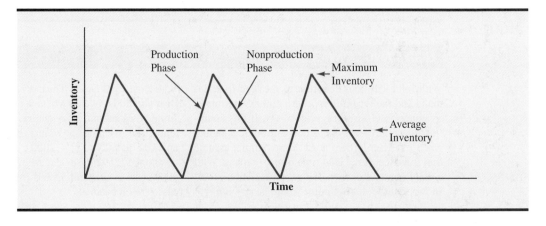

Total Cost Model

Let us begin building the production lot size model by writing the holding cost in terms of the production lot size Q. Again, the approach is to develop an expression for average inventory and then establish the holding costs associated with the average inventory. We use a one-year time period and an annual cost for the model.

In the EOQ model the average inventory is one-half the maximum inventory or $\frac{1}{2}Q$. Figure 10.5 shows that for a production lot size model a constant inventory buildup rate occurs during the production run and a constant inventory depletion rate occurs during the nonproduction period; thus, the average inventory will be one-half the maximum inventory. However, in this inventory system the production lot size Q does not go into inventory at one point in time, and thus the inventory never reaches a level of Q units.

To show how we can compute the maximum inventory, let

$$d = \text{daily demand rate}$$
$$p = \text{daily production rate}$$
$$t = \text{number of days for a production run}$$

At this point, the logic of the production lot size model is easier to follow using a daily demand rate d and a daily production rate p. However, when the total annual cost model is eventually developed, we recommend that inputs to the model be expressed in terms of the annual demand rate D and the annual production rate P.

Because we are assuming that p will be larger than d, the daily inventory buildup rate during the production phase is $p - d$. If we run production for t days and place $p - d$ units in inventory each day, the inventory at the end of the production run will be $(p - d)t$. From Figure 10.5 we can see that the inventory at the end of the production run is also the maximum inventory. Thus,

$$\text{Maximum inventory} = (p - d)t \qquad (10.8)$$

If we know we are producing a production lot size of Q units at a daily production rate of p units, then $Q = pt$, and the length of the production run t must be

$$t = \frac{Q}{p} \text{ days} \qquad (10.9)$$

Thus,

$$\text{Maximum inventory} = (p - d)t = (p - d)\left(\frac{Q}{p}\right)$$
$$= \left(1 - \frac{d}{p}\right)Q \qquad (10.10)$$

The average inventory, which is one-half the maximum inventory, is given by

$$\text{Average inventory} = \frac{1}{2}\left(1 - \frac{d}{p}\right)Q \qquad (10.11)$$

With an annual per unit holding cost of C_h, the general equation for annual holding cost is as follows:

$$\begin{array}{c}
\dfrac{\text{Annual}}{\text{holding cost}} = \left(\begin{array}{c}\text{Average}\\\text{inventory}\end{array}\right)\left(\begin{array}{c}\text{Annual}\\\text{cost}\\\text{per unit}\end{array}\right)\\[2ex]
= \dfrac{1}{2}\left(1 - \dfrac{d}{p}\right)QC_h
\end{array} \qquad (10.12)$$

If D is the annual demand for the product and C_o is the setup cost for a production run, then the annual setup cost, which takes the place of the annual ordering cost in the EOQ model, is as follows:

$$\begin{array}{c}
\text{Annual setup cost} = \left(\begin{array}{c}\text{Number of production}\\\text{runs per year}\end{array}\right)\left(\begin{array}{c}\text{Setup cost}\\\text{per run}\end{array}\right)\\[2ex]
= \dfrac{D}{Q}C_o
\end{array} \qquad (10.13)$$

Thus, the total annual cost (TC) model is

$$TC = \dfrac{1}{2}\left(1 - \dfrac{d}{p}\right)QC_h + \dfrac{D}{Q}C_o \qquad (10.14)$$

Suppose that a production facility operates 250 days per year. Then we can write daily demand d in terms of annual demand D as follows:

$$d = \dfrac{D}{250}$$

Now let P denote the annual production for the product if the product were produced every day. Then

$$P = 250p \qquad \text{and} \qquad p = \dfrac{P}{250}$$

Thus,[4]

$$\dfrac{d}{p} = \dfrac{D/250}{P/250} = \dfrac{D}{P}$$

---

[4]The ratio $d/p = D/P$ holds regardless of the number of days of operation; 250 days is used here merely as an illustration.

Therefore, we can write the total annual cost model as follows:

$$TC = \frac{1}{2}\left(1 - \frac{D}{P}\right)QC_h + \frac{D}{Q}C_o \qquad (10.15)$$

Equations (10.14) and (10.15) are equivalent. However, equation (10.15) may be used more frequently because an *annual* cost model tends to make the analyst think in terms of collecting *annual* demand data (D) and *annual* production data (P) rather than daily data.

Economic Production Lot Size

Given estimates of the holding cost (C_h), setup cost (C_o), annual demand rate (D), and annual production rate (P), we could use a trial-and-error approach to compute the total annual cost for various production lot sizes (Q). However, trial and error is not necessary; we can use the minimum cost formula for Q^* that has been developed using differential calculus (see Appendix 10.2). The equation is as follows:

As the production rate P approaches infinity, D/P approaches zero. In this case, equation (10.16) is equivalent to the EOQ model in equation (10.5).

$$Q^* = \sqrt{\frac{2DC_o}{(1 - D/P)C_h}} \qquad (10.16)$$

WEB file

Lot Size

An Example   Beauty Bar Soap is produced on a production line that has an annual capacity of 60,000 cases. The annual demand is estimated at 26,000 cases, with the demand rate essentially constant throughout the year. The cleaning, preparation, and setup of the production line cost approximately $135. The manufacturing cost per case is $4.50, and the annual holding cost is figured at a 24% rate. Thus, $C_h = IC = 0.24(\$4.50) = \$1.08$. What is the recommended production lot size?

Using equation (10.16), we have

$$Q^* = \sqrt{\frac{2(26,000)(135)}{(1 - 26,000/60,000)(1.08)}} = 3387$$

Work Problem 13 as an example of an economic production lot size model.

The total annual cost using equation (10.15) and $Q^* = 3387$ is $2073.

Other relevant data include a five-day lead time to schedule and set up a production run and 250 working days per year. Thus, the lead-time demand of $(26,000/250)(5) = 520$ cases is the reorder point. The cycle time is the time between production runs. Using equation (10.7), the cycle time is $T = 250Q^*/D = [(250)(3387)]/26,000$, or 33 working days. Thus, we should plan a production run of 3387 units every 33 working days.

10.3   INVENTORY MODEL WITH PLANNED SHORTAGES

A **shortage,** or **stockout,** is a demand that cannot be supplied. In many situations, shortages are undesirable and should be avoided if at all possible. However, in other cases it may be desirable—from an economic point of view—to plan for and allow shortages. In practice, these types of situations are most commonly found where the value of the inventory per unit is high and hence the holding cost is high. An example of this type of situation is a new car dealer's inventory. Often a specific car that a customer wants is not in stock. However, if the customer is willing to wait a few weeks, the dealer is usually able to order the car.

The assumptions of the EOQ model in Table 10.3 apply to this inventory model, with the exception that shortages, referred to as backorders, are now permitted.

The model developed in this section takes into account a type of shortage known as a **backorder.** In a backorder situation, we assume that when a customer places an order and discovers that the supplier is out of stock, the customer waits until the new shipment arrives, and then the order is filled. Frequently, the waiting period in backorder situations is relatively short. Thus, by promising the customer top priority and immediate delivery when the goods become available, companies may be able to convince the customer to wait until the order arrives. In these cases, the backorder assumption is valid.

The backorder model that we develop is an extension of the EOQ model presented in Section 10.1. We use the EOQ model in which all goods arrive in inventory at one time and are subject to a constant demand rate. If we let S indicate the number of backorders that are accumulated when a new shipment of size Q is received, then the inventory system for the backorder case has the following characteristics:

- If S backorders exist when a new shipment of size Q arrives, then S backorders are shipped to the appropriate customers, and the remaining $Q - S$ units are placed in inventory. Therefore, $Q - S$ is the maximum inventory.
- The inventory cycle of T days is divided into two distinct phases: t_1 days when inventory is on hand and orders are filled as they occur, and t_2 days when stockouts occur and all new orders are placed on backorder.

The inventory pattern for the inventory model with backorders, where negative inventory represents the number of backorders, is shown in Figure 10.6.

With the inventory pattern now defined, we can proceed with the basic step of all inventory models—namely, the development of a total cost model. For the inventory model with backorders, we encounter the usual holding costs and ordering costs. We also incur a backorder cost in terms of the labor and special delivery costs directly associated with the handling of the backorders. Another portion of the backorder cost accounts for the loss of goodwill because some customers will have to wait for their orders. Because the **goodwill cost** depends on how long a customer has to wait, it is customary to adopt the convention of expressing backorder cost in terms of the cost of having a unit on backorder for a stated period of time. This method of costing backorders on a time basis is similar to the method

FIGURE 10.6   INVENTORY PATTERN FOR AN INVENTORY MODEL WITH BACKORDERS

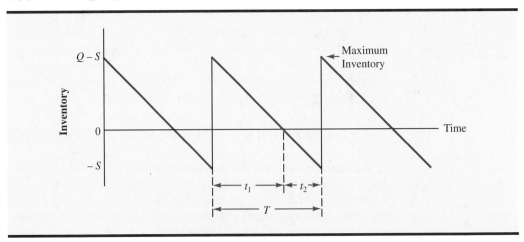

used to compute the inventory holding cost, and we can use it to compute a total annual cost of backorders once the average backorder level and the backorder cost per unit per period are known.

Let us begin the development of a total cost model by calculating the average inventory for a hypothetical problem. If we have an average inventory of two units for three days and no inventory on the fourth day, what is the average inventory over the four-day period? It is

$$\frac{2 \text{ units } (3 \text{ days}) + 0 \text{ units } (1 \text{ day})}{4 \text{ days}} = \frac{6}{4} = 1.5 \text{ units}$$

Refer to Figure 10.6. You can see that this situation is what happens in the backorder model. With a maximum inventory of $Q - S$ units, the t_1 days we have inventory on hand will have an average inventory of $(Q - S)/2$. No inventory is carried for the t_2 days in which we experience backorders. Thus, over the total cycle time of $T = t_1 + t_2$ days, we can compute the average inventory as follows:

$$\text{Average inventory} = \frac{\frac{1}{2}(Q - S)t_1 + 0t_2}{t_1 + t_2} = \frac{\frac{1}{2}(Q - S)t_1}{T} \qquad (10.17)$$

Can we find other ways of expressing t_1 and T? Because we know that the maximum inventory is $Q - S$ and that d represents the constant daily demand, we have

$$t_1 = \frac{Q - S}{d} \text{ days} \qquad (10.18)$$

That is, the maximum inventory of $Q - S$ units will be used up in $(Q - S)/d$ days. Because Q units are ordered each cycle, we know the length of a cycle must be

$$T = \frac{Q}{d} \text{ days} \qquad (10.19)$$

Combining equations (10.18) and (10.19) with equation (10.17), we can compute the average inventory as follows:

$$\text{Average inventory} = \frac{\frac{1}{2}(Q - S)[(Q - S)/d]}{Q/d} = \frac{(Q - S)^2}{2Q} \qquad (10.20)$$

Thus, the average inventory is expressed in terms of two inventory decisions: how much we will order (Q) and the maximum number of backorders (S).

The formula for the annual number of orders placed using this model is identical to that for the EOQ model. With D representing the annual demand, we have

$$\text{Annual number of orders} = \frac{D}{Q} \qquad (10.21)$$

The next step is to develop an expression for the average backorder level. Because we know the maximum for backorders is S, we can use the same logic we used to establish average inventory in finding the average number of backorders. We have an average number of backorders during the period t_2 of $\frac{1}{2}$ the maximum number of backorders, or $\frac{1}{2}S$. We do not have any backorders during the t_1 days we have inventory; therefore, we can calculate the average backorders in a manner similar to equation (10.17). Using this approach, we have

$$\text{Average backorders} = \frac{0t_1 + (S/2)t_2}{T} = \frac{(S/2)t_2}{T} \qquad (10.22)$$

When we let the maximum number of backorders reach an amount S at a daily rate of d, the length of the backorder portion of the inventory cycle is

$$t_2 = \frac{S}{d} \qquad (10.23)$$

Using equations (10.23) and (10.19) in equation (10.22), we have

$$\text{Average backorders} = \frac{(S/2)(S/d)}{Q/d} = \frac{S^2}{2Q} \qquad (10.24)$$

Let

C_h = cost to maintain one unit in inventory for one year

C_o = cost per order

C_b = cost to maintain one unit on backorder for one year

The total annual cost (TC) for the inventory model with backorders becomes

$$TC = \frac{(Q - S)^2}{2Q} C_h + \frac{D}{Q} C_o + \frac{S^2}{2Q} C_b \qquad (10.25)$$

Given C_h, C_o, and C_b and the annual demand D, differential calculus can be used to show that the minimum cost values for the order quantity Q^* and the planned backorders S^* are as follows:

$$Q^* = \sqrt{\frac{2DC_o}{C_h}\left(\frac{C_h + C_b}{C_b}\right)} \qquad (10.26)$$

$$S^* = Q^*\left(\frac{C_h}{C_h + C_b}\right) \qquad (10.27)$$

WEB file

Shortage

An inventory situation that incorporates backorder costs is considered in Problem 15.

The backorder cost C_b is one of the most difficult costs to estimate in inventory models. The reason is that it attempts to measure the cost associated with the loss of goodwill when a customer must wait for an order. Expressing this cost on an annual basis adds to the difficulty.

If backorders can be tolerated, the total cost including the backorder cost will be less than the total cost of the EOQ model. Some people think the model with backorders will have a greater cost because it includes a backorder cost in addition to the usual inventory holding and ordering costs. You can point out the fallacy in this thinking by noting that the backorder model leads to lower inventory and hence lower inventory holding costs.

An Example   Suppose that the Higley Radio Components Company has a product for which the assumptions of the inventory model with backorders are valid. Information obtained by the company is as follows:

$$D = 2000 \text{ units per year}$$
$$I = 20\%$$
$$C = \$50 \text{ per unit}$$
$$C_h = IC = (0.20)(\$50) = \$10 \text{ per unit per year}$$
$$C_o = \$25 \text{ per order}$$

The company is considering the possibility of allowing some backorders to occur for the product. The annual backorder cost is estimated to be \$30 per unit per year. Using equations (10.26) and (10.27), we have

$$Q^* = \sqrt{\frac{2(2000)(25)}{10}\left(\frac{10 + 30}{20}\right)} = 115.47$$

and

$$S^* = 115\left(\frac{10}{10 + 30}\right) = 28.87$$

If this solution is implemented, the system will operate with the following properties:

$$\text{Maximum inventory} = Q - S = 115.47 - 28.87 = 86.6$$
$$\text{Cycle time} = T = \frac{Q}{D}(250) = \frac{115.47}{2000}(250) = 14.43 \text{ working days}$$

The total annual cost is

$$\text{Holding cost} = \frac{(86.6)^2}{2(115.47)}(10) = \$325$$
$$\text{Ordering cost} = \frac{2000}{115.47}(25) \quad = \$433$$
$$\text{Backorder cost} = \frac{(28.87)^2}{2(115.47)}(30) = \$108$$
$$\text{Total cost} = \$866$$

If the company chooses to prohibit backorders and adopts the regular EOQ model, the recommended inventory decision would be

$$Q^* = \sqrt{\frac{2(2000)(25)}{10}} = \sqrt{10{,}000} = 100$$

This order quantity would result in a holding cost and an ordering cost of $500 each, or a total annual cost of $1000. Thus, in this problem, allowing backorders is projecting a $1000 − $866 = $134 or 13.4% savings in cost from the no-stockout EOQ model. The preceding comparison and conclusion are based on the assumption that the backorder model with an annual cost per backordered unit of $30 is a valid model for the actual inventory situation. If the company is concerned that stockouts might lead to lost sales, then the savings might not be enough to warrant switching to an inventory policy that allowed for planned shortages.

NOTES AND COMMENTS

Equation (10.27) shows that the optimal number of planned backorders S^* is proportional to the ratio $C_h/(C_h + C_b)$, where C_h is the annual holding cost per unit and C_b is the annual backorder cost per unit. Whenever C_h increases, this ratio becomes larger, and the number of planned backorders increases. This relationship explains why items that have a high per-unit cost and a correspondingly high annual holding cost are more economically handled on a backorder basis. On the other hand, whenever the backorder cost C_b increases, the ratio becomes smaller, and the number of planned backorders decreases. Thus, the model provides the intuitive result that items with high backorder costs will be handled with few backorders. In fact, with high backorder costs, the backorder model and the EOQ model with no backordering allowed provide similar inventory policies.

10.4   QUANTITY DISCOUNTS FOR THE EOQ MODEL

In the quantity discount model, assumption 4 of the EOQ model in Table 10.3 is altered. The cost per unit varies depending on the quantity ordered.

Quantity discounts occur in numerous situations in which suppliers provide an incentive for large order quantities by offering a lower purchase cost when items are ordered in larger quantities. In this section we show how the EOQ model can be used when quantity discounts are available.

Assume that we have a product in which the basic EOQ model (see Table 10.3) is applicable. Instead of a fixed unit cost, the supplier quotes the following discount schedule:

Discount Category	Order Size	Discount (%)	Unit Cost
1	0 to 999	0	$5.00
2	1000 to 2499	3	4.85
3	2500 and over	5	4.75

The 5% discount for the 2500-unit minimum order quantity looks tempting. However, realizing that higher order quantities result in higher inventory holding costs, we should prepare a thorough cost analysis before making a final ordering and inventory policy recommendation.

Suppose that the data and cost analyses show an annual holding cost rate of 20%, an ordering cost of $49 per order, and an annual demand of 5000 units; what order quantity should we select? The following three-step procedure shows the calculations necessary to make this decision. In the preliminary calculations, we use Q_1 to indicate the order quantity for discount category 1, Q_2 for discount category 2, and Q_3 for discount category 3.

Step 1.   For each discount category, compute a Q^* using the EOQ formula based on the unit cost associated with the discount category.

Recall that the EOQ model provides $Q^* = \sqrt{2DC_o/C_h}$, where $C_h = IC = (0.20)C$. With three discount categories providing three different unit costs C, we obtain

WEB file

Discount

$$Q_1^* = \sqrt{\frac{2(5000)49}{(0.20)(5.00)}} = 700$$

$$Q_2^* = \sqrt{\frac{2(5000)49}{(0.20)(4.85)}} = 711$$

$$Q_3^* = \sqrt{\frac{2(5000)49}{(0.20)(4.75)}} = 718$$

Because the only differences in the EOQ formulas come from slight differences in the holding cost, the economic order quantities resulting from this step will be approximately the same. However, these order quantities will usually not all be of the size necessary to qualify for the discount price assumed. In the preceding case, both Q_2^* and Q_3^* are insufficient order quantities to obtain their assumed discounted costs of $4.85 and $4.75, respectively. For those order quantities for which the assumed price cannot be obtained, the following procedure must be used:

Step 2.   For the Q^* that is too small to qualify for the assumed discount price, adjust the order quantity upward to the nearest order quantity that will allow the product to be purchased at the assumed price.

In our example, this adjustment causes us to set

$$Q_2^* = 1000$$

and

$$Q_3^* = 2500$$

Problem 23 at the end of the chapter asks you to show that this property is true.

In the EOQ model with quantity discounts, the annual purchase cost must be included because purchase cost depends on the order quantity. Thus, it is a relevant cost.

If a calculated Q^* for a given discount price is large enough to qualify for a bigger discount, that value of Q^* cannot lead to an optimal solution. Although the reason may not be obvious, it does turn out to be a property of the EOQ quantity discount model.

In the previous inventory models considered, the annual purchase cost of the item was not included because it was constant and never affected by the inventory order policy decision. However, in the quantity discount model, the annual purchase cost depends on the order quantity and the associated unit cost. Thus, annual purchase cost (annual demand $D \times$ unit cost C) is included in the equation for total cost, as shown here:

$$TC = \frac{Q}{2}C_h + \frac{D}{Q}C_o + DC \qquad (10.28)$$

TABLE 10.4   TOTAL ANNUAL COST CALCULATIONS FOR THE EOQ MODEL
              WITH QUANTITY DISCOUNTS

Discount Category	Unit Cost	Order Quantity	Annual Cost			
			Holding	Ordering	Purchase	Total
1	$5.00	700	$ 350	$350	$25,000	$25,700
2	4.85	1000	$ 485	$245	$24,250	$24,980
3	4.75	2500	$1188	$ 98	$23,750	$25,036

Using this total cost equation, we can determine the optimal order quantity for the EOQ discount model in step 3.

Step 3. For each order quantity resulting from steps 1 and 2, compute the total annual cost using the unit price from the appropriate discount category and equation (10.28). The order quantity yielding the minimum total annual cost is the optimal order quantity.

Problem 21 will give you practice in applying the EOQ model to situations with quantity discounts.

The step 3 calculations for the example problem are summarized in Table 10.4. As you can see, a decision to order 1000 units at the 3% discount rate yields the minimum cost solution. Even though the 2500-unit order quantity would result in a 5% discount, its excessive holding cost makes it the second-best solution. Figure 10.7 shows the total cost curve for each of the three discount categories. Note that $Q^* = 1000$ provides the minimum cost order quantity.

10.5   SINGLE-PERIOD INVENTORY MODEL WITH PROBABILISTIC DEMAND

This inventory model is the first in the chapter that explicitly treats probabilistic demand. Unlike the EOQ model, it is for a single period with unused inventory not carried over to future periods.

The inventory models discussed thus far were based on the assumption that the demand rate is constant and **deterministic** throughout the year. We developed minimum cost order quantity and reorder point policies based on this assumption. In situations in which the demand rate is not deterministic, other models treat demand as **probabilistic** and best described by a probability distribution. In this section we consider a **single-period inventory model** with probabilistic demand.

The single-period inventory model refers to inventory situations in which *one* order is placed for the product; at the end of the period, the product has either sold out or a surplus of unsold items will be sold for a salvage value. The single-period inventory model is applicable in situations involving seasonal or perishable items that cannot be carried in inventory and sold in future periods. Seasonal clothing (such as bathing suits and winter coats) is typically handled in a single-period manner. In these situations, a buyer places one preseason order for each item and then experiences a stockout or holds a clearance sale on the surplus stock at the end of the season. No items are carried in inventory and sold the following year. Newspapers are another example of a product that is ordered one time and is either sold or not sold during the single period. Although newspapers are ordered daily, they cannot be carried in inventory and sold in later periods. Thus, newspaper orders may be treated as a sequence of single-period models; that is, each day or period is separate, and a single-period inventory decision must be made each period (day). Because we order only once for the period, the only inventory decision we must make is *how much* of the product to order at the start of the period.

FIGURE 10.7 TOTAL COST CURVES FOR THE THREE DISCOUNT CATEGORIES

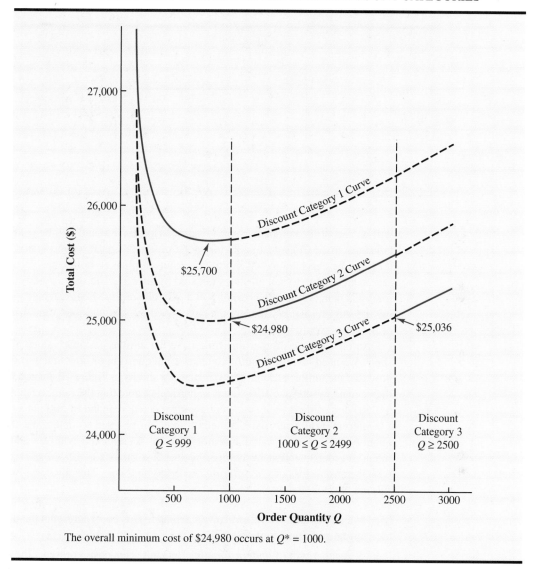

The overall minimum cost of $24,980 occurs at $Q^* = 1000$.

Obviously, if the demand were known for a single-period inventory situation, the solution would be easy; we would simply order the amount we knew would be demanded. However, in most single-period models, the exact demand is not known. In fact, forecasts may show that demand can have a wide variety of values. If we are going to analyze this type of inventory problem in a quantitative manner, we need information about the probabilities associated with the various demand values. Thus, the single-period model presented in this section is based on probabilistic demand.

Johnson Shoe Company

Let us consider a single-period inventory model that could be used to make a how-much-to-order decision for the Johnson Shoe Company. The buyer for the Johnson Shoe Company decided to order a men's shoe shown at a buyers' meeting in New York City. The shoe

FIGURE 10.8   UNIFORM PROBABILITY DISTRIBUTION OF DEMAND FOR THE JOHNSON SHOE COMPANY PROBLEM

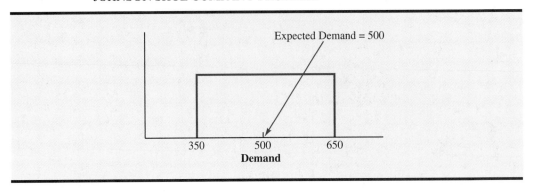

will be part of the company's spring–summer promotion and will be sold through nine retail stores in the Chicago area. Because the shoe is designed for spring and summer months, it cannot be expected to sell in the fall. Johnson plans to hold a special August clearance sale in an attempt to sell all shoes not sold by July 31. The shoes cost $40 a pair and retail for $60 a pair. At the sale price of $30 a pair, all surplus shoes can be expected to sell during the August sale. If you were the buyer for the Johnson Shoe Company, how many pairs of the shoes would you order?

An obvious question at this time is, What are the possible values of demand for the shoe? We need this information to answer the question of how much to order. Let us suppose that the uniform probability distribution shown in Figure 10.8 can be used to describe the demand for the size 10D shoes. In particular, note that the range of demand is from 350 to 650 pairs of shoes, with an average, or expected, demand of 500 pairs of shoes.

Incremental analysis is a method that can be used to determine the optimal order quantity for a single-period inventory model. Incremental analysis addresses the how-much-to-order question by comparing the cost or loss of *ordering one additional unit* with the cost or loss of *not ordering one additional unit*. The costs involved are defined as follows:

c_o = cost per unit of *overestimating* demand. This cost represents the loss of ordering one additional unit and finding that it cannot be sold.

c_u = cost per unit of *underestimating* demand. This cost represents the opportunity loss of not ordering one additional unit and finding that it could have been sold.

The cost of underestimating demand is usually harder to determine than the cost of overestimating demand. The reason is that the cost of underestimating demand includes a lost profit and may include a customer goodwill cost because the customer is unable to purchase the item when desired.

In the Johnson Shoe Company problem, the company will incur the cost of overestimating demand whenever it orders too much and has to sell the extra shoes during the August sale. Thus, the cost per unit of overestimating demand is equal to the purchase cost per unit minus the August sales price per unit; that is, $c_o = \$40 - \$30 = \$10$. Therefore, Johnson will lose $10 for each pair of shoes that it orders over the quantity demanded. The cost of underestimating demand is the lost profit because a pair of shoes that could have been sold was not available in inventory. Thus, the per-unit cost of underestimating demand is the difference between the regular selling price per unit and the purchase cost per unit; that is, $c_u = \$60 - \$40 = \$20$.

Because the exact level of demand for the size 10D shoes is unknown, we have to consider the probability of demand and thus the probability of obtaining the associated costs or losses. For example, let us assume that Johnson Shoe Company management wishes to consider an order quantity equal to the average or expected demand for 500 pairs of shoes. In incremental analysis, we consider the possible losses associated with an order quantity of 501 (ordering one additional unit) and an order quantity of 500 (not ordering one additional unit). The order quantity alternatives and the possible losses are summarized here:

Order Quantity Alternatives	Loss Occurs If	Possible Loss	Probability Loss Occurs
$Q = 501$	Demand overestimated; the additional unit *cannot* be sold	$c_o = \$10$	$P(\text{demand} \leq 500)$
$Q = 500$	Demand underestimated; an additional unit *could have* been sold	$c_u = \$20$	$P(\text{demand} > 500)$

By looking at the demand probability distribution in Figure 10.8, we see that $P(\text{demand} \leq 500) = 0.50$ and that $P(\text{demand} > 500) = 0.50$. By multiplying the possible losses, $c_o = \$10$ and $c_u = \$20$, by the probability of obtaining the loss, we can compute the expected value of the loss, or simply the *expected loss* (EL), associated with the order quantity alternatives. Thus,

$$\text{EL}(Q = 501) = c_o P(\text{demand} \leq 500) = \$10(0.50) = \$5$$
$$\text{EL}(Q = 500) = c_u P(\text{demand} > 500) = \$20(0.50) = \$10$$

Based on these expected losses, do you prefer an order quantity of 501 or 500 pairs of shoes? Because the expected loss is greater for $Q = 500$ and because we want to avoid this higher cost or loss, we should make $Q = 501$ the preferred decision. We could now consider incrementing the order quantity one additional unit to $Q = 502$ and repeating the expected loss calculations.

Although we could continue this unit-by-unit analysis, it would be time-consuming and cumbersome. We would have to evaluate $Q = 502$, $Q = 503$, $Q = 504$, and so on, until we found the value of Q where the expected loss of ordering one incremental unit is equal to the expected loss of not ordering one incremental unit; that is, the optimal order quantity Q^* occurs when the incremental analysis shows that

$$\text{EL}(Q^* + 1) = \text{EL}(Q^*) \qquad (10.29)$$

When this relationship holds, increasing the order quantity by one additional unit has no economic advantage. Using the logic with which we computed the expected losses for the order quantities of 501 and 500, the general expressions for $\text{EL}(Q^* + 1)$ and $\text{EL}(Q^*)$ can be written

$$\text{EL}(Q^* + 1) = c_o P(\text{demand} \leq Q^*) \qquad (10.30)$$
$$\text{EL}(Q^*) = c_u P(\text{demand} > Q^*) \qquad (10.31)$$

Because we know from basic probability that

$$P(\text{demand} \le Q^*) + P(\text{demand} > Q^*) = 1 \qquad (10.32)$$

we can write

$$P(\text{demand} > Q^*) = 1 - P(\text{demand} \le Q^*) \qquad (10.33)$$

Using this expression, equation (10.31) can be rewritten as

$$\text{EL}(Q^*) = c_u[1 - P(\text{demand} \le Q^*)] \qquad (10.34)$$

Equations (10.30) and (10.34) can be used to show that $\text{EL}(Q^* + 1) = \text{EL}(Q^*)$ whenever

$$c_o P(\text{demand} \le Q^*) = c_u[1 - P(\text{demand} \le Q^*)] \qquad (10.35)$$

Solving for $P(\text{demand} \le Q^*)$, we have

$$P(\text{demand} \le Q^*) = \frac{c_u}{c_u + c_o} \qquad (10.36)$$

This expression provides the general condition for the optimal order quantity Q^* in the single-period inventory model.

In the Johnson Shoe Company problem $c_o = \$10$ and $c_u = \$20$. Thus, equation (10.36) shows that the optimal order size for Johnson shoes must satisfy the following condition:

$$P(\text{demand} \le Q^*) = \frac{c_u}{c_u + c_o} = \frac{20}{20 + 10} = \frac{20}{30} = \frac{2}{3}$$

We can find the optimal order quantity Q^* by referring to the probability distribution shown in Figure 10.8 and finding the value of Q that will provide $P(\text{demand} \le Q^*) = \frac{2}{3}$. To find this solution, we note that in the uniform distribution the probability is evenly distributed over the entire range of 350 to 650 pairs of shoes. Thus, we can satisfy the expression for Q^* by moving two-thirds of the way from 350 to 650. Because this range is $650 - 350 = 300$, we move 200 units from 350 toward 650. Doing so provides the optimal order quantity of 550 pairs of shoes.

In summary, the key to establishing an optimal order quantity for single-period inventory models is to identify the probability distribution that describes the demand for the item and the costs of overestimation and underestimation. Then, using the information for the costs of overestimation and underestimation, equation (10.36) can be used to find the location of Q^* in the probability distribution.

Nationwide Car Rental

As another example of a single-period inventory model with probabilistic demand, consider the situation faced by Nationwide Car Rental. Nationwide must decide how many automobiles to have available at each car rental location at specific points in time throughout the year. Using the Myrtle Beach, South Carolina, location as an example, management would like to know the number of full-sized automobiles to have available for the Labor Day weekend. Based on previous experience, customer demand for full-sized automobiles for the Labor Day weekend has a normal distribution with a mean of 150 automobiles and a standard deviation of 14 automobiles.

The Nationwide Car Rental situation can benefit from use of a single-period inventory model. The company must establish the number of full-sized automobiles to have available prior to the weekend. Customer demand over the weekend will then result in either a stock-out or a surplus. Let us denote the number of full-sized automobiles available by Q. If Q is greater than customer demand, Nationwide will have a surplus of cars. The cost of a surplus is the cost of overestimating demand. This cost is set at $80 per car, which reflects, in part, the opportunity cost of not having the car available for rent elsewhere.

If Q is less than customer demand, Nationwide will rent all available cars and experience a stockout, or shortage. A shortage results in an underestimation cost of $200 per car. This figure reflects the cost due to lost profit and the lost goodwill of not having a car available for a customer. Given this information, how many full-sized automobiles should Nationwide make available for the Labor Day weekend?

Using the cost of underestimation, $c_u = \$200$, and the cost of overestimation, $c_o = \$80$, equation (10.36) indicates that the optimal order quantity must satisfy the following condition:

$$P(\text{demand} \leq Q^*) = \frac{c_u}{(c_u + c_o)} = \frac{200}{200 + 80} = 0.7143$$

We can use the normal probability distribution for demand, as shown in Figure 10.9, to find the order quantity that satisfies the condition that $P(\text{demand} \leq Q^*) = 0.7143$. Using the cumulative probabilities for the normal distribution (see Appendix B), the cumulative

FIGURE 10.9   PROBABILITY DISTRIBUTION OF DEMAND FOR THE NATIONWIDE
CAR RENTAL PROBLEM SHOWING THE LOCATION OF Q^*

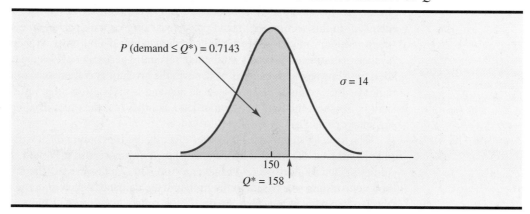

probability closest to 0.7143 occurs at $z = 0.57$. Thus, the optimal order quantity occurs at 0.57 standard deviations above the mean. With a mean demand of $\mu = 150$ automobiles and a standard deviation of $\sigma = 14$ automobiles, we have

$$Q^* = \mu + 0.57\sigma$$
$$= 150 + 0.57(14) = 158$$

WEB file

Single-Period

An example of a single-period inventory model with probabilistic demand described by a normal probability distribution is considered in Problem 25.

Thus, Nationwide Car Rental should plan to have 158 full-sized automobiles available in Myrtle Beach for the Labor Day weekend. Note that in this case the cost of overestimation is less than the cost of underestimation. Thus, Nationwide is willing to risk a higher probability of overestimating demand and hence a higher probability of a surplus. In fact, Nationwide's optimal order quantity has a 0.7143 probability of a surplus and a $1 - 0.7143 = 0.2857$ probability of a stockout. As a result, the probability is 0.2857 that all 158 full-sized automobiles will be rented during the Labor Day weekend.

NOTES AND COMMENTS

1. In any probabilistic inventory model, the assumption about the probability distribution for demand is critical and can affect the recommended inventory decision. In the problems presented in this section, we used the uniform and the normal probability distributions to describe demand. In some situations, other probability distributions may be more appropriate. In using probabilistic inventory models, we must exercise care in selecting the probability distribution that most realistically describes demand.

2. In the single-period inventory model, the value of $c_u/(c_u + c_o)$ plays a critical role in selecting the order quantity the ratio [see equation (10.36)]. Whenever $c_u = c_o$, the ratio $(c_u/(c_u + c_o)) = 0.50$;

in this case, we should select an order quantity corresponding to the median demand. With this choice, a stockout is just as likely as a surplus because the two costs are equal. However, whenever $c_u < c_o$, a smaller order quantity will be recommended. In this case, the smaller order quantity will provide a higher probability of a stockout; however, the more expensive cost of overestimating demand and having a surplus will tend to be avoided. Finally, whenever $c_u > c_o$, a larger order quantity will be recommended. In this case, the larger order quantity provides a lower probability of a stockout in an attempt to avoid the more expensive cost of underestimating demand and experiencing a stockout.

10.6   ORDER-QUANTITY, REORDER POINT MODEL WITH PROBABILISTIC DEMAND

The inventory model in this section is based on the assumptions of the EOQ model shown in Table 10.3, with the exception that demand is probabilistic rather than deterministic. With probabilistic demand, occasional shortages may occur.

In the previous section we considered a single-period inventory model with probabilistic demand. In this section we extend our discussion to a multiperiod order-quantity, reorder point inventory model with probabilistic demand. In the multiperiod model, the inventory system operates continuously with many repeating periods or cycles; inventory can be carried from one period to the next. Whenever the inventory position reaches the reorder point, an order for Q units is placed. Because demand is probabilistic, the time the reorder point will be reached, the time between orders, and the time the order of Q units will arrive in inventory cannot be determined in advance.

The inventory pattern for the order-quantity, reorder point model with probabilistic demand will have the general appearance shown in Figure 10.10. Note that the increases or jumps in the inventory occur whenever an order of Q units arrives. The inventory decreases at a nonconstant rate based on the probabilistic demand. A new order is placed whenever the reorder point is reached. At times, the order quantity of Q units will arrive before

FIGURE 10.10   INVENTORY PATTERN FOR AN ORDER-QUANTITY, REORDER POINT
MODEL WITH PROBABILISTIC DEMAND

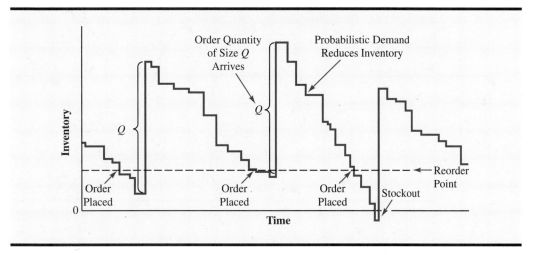

inventory reaches zero. However, at other times, higher demand will cause a stockout before a new order is received. As with other order-quantity, reorder point models, the manager must determine the order quantity Q and the reorder point r for the inventory system.

The exact mathematical formulation of an order-quantity, reorder point inventory model with probabilistic demand is beyond the scope of this text. However, we present a procedure that can be used to obtain good, workable order quantity and reorder point inventory policies. The solution procedure can be expected to provide only an approximation of the optimal solution, but it can yield good solutions in many practical situations.

Let us consider the inventory problem of Dabco Industrial Lighting Distributors. Dabco purchases a special high-intensity lightbulb for industrial lighting systems from a well-known lightbulb manufacturer. Dabco would like a recommendation on how much to order and when to order so that a low-cost inventory policy can be maintained. Pertinent facts are that the ordering cost is $12 per order, one bulb costs $6, and Dabco uses a 20% annual holding cost rate for its inventory ($C_h = IC = 0.20 \times \$6 = \$1.20$). Dabco, which has more than 1000 customers, experiences a probabilistic demand; in fact, the number of units demanded varies considerably from day to day and from week to week. The lead time for a new order of lightbulbs is one week. Historical sales data indicate that demand during a one-week lead time can be described by a normal probability distribution with a mean of 154 lightbulbs and a standard deviation of 25 lightbulbs. The normal distribution of demand during the lead time is shown in Figure 10.11. Because the mean demand during one week is 154 units, Dabco can anticipate a mean or expected annual demand of 154 units per week = 52 weeks per year = 8008 units per year.

The How-Much-to-Order Decision

Although we are in a probabilistic demand situation, we have an estimate of the expected annual demand of 8008 units. We can apply the EOQ model from Section 10.1 as an approximation of the best order quantity, with the expected annual demand used for D. In Dabco's case

WEB file

Q Prob

$$Q^* = \sqrt{\frac{2DC_o}{C_h}} = \sqrt{\frac{2(8008)(12)}{(1.20)}} = 400 \text{ units}$$

FIGURE 10.11   LEAD-TIME DEMAND PROBABILITY DISTRIBUTION
FOR DABCO LIGHTBULBS

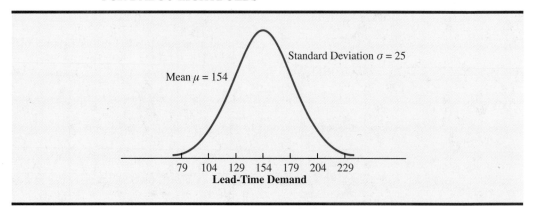

When we studied the sensitivity of the EOQ model, we learned that the total cost of operating an inventory system was relatively insensitive to order quantities that were in the neighborhood of Q^*. Using this knowledge, we expect 400 units per order to be a good approximation of the optimal order quantity. Even if annual demand were as low as 7000 units or as high as 9000 units, an order quantity of 400 units should be a relatively good low-cost order size. Thus, given our best estimate of annual demand at 8008 units, we will use $Q^* = 400$.

We have established the 400-unit order quantity by ignoring the fact that demand is probabilistic. Using $Q^* = 400$, Dabco can anticipate placing approximately $D/Q^* = 8008/400 = 20$ orders per year with an average of approximately $250/20 = 12.5$ working days between orders.

The When-to-Order Decision

We now want to establish a when-to-order decision rule or reorder point that will trigger the ordering process. With a mean lead-time demand of 154 units, you might first suggest a 154-unit reorder point. However, considering the probability of demand now becomes extremely important. If 154 is the mean lead-time demand, and if demand is symmetrically distributed about 154, then the lead-time demand will be more than 154 units roughly 50% of the time. When the demand during the one-week lead time exceeds 154 units, Dabco will experience a shortage, or stockout. Thus, using a reorder point of 154 units, approximately 50% of the time (10 of the 20 orders a year) Dabco will be short of bulbs before the new supply arrives. This shortage rate would most likely be viewed as unacceptable.

The probability of a stockout during any one inventory cycle is easiest to estimate by first determining the number of orders that are expected during the year. The inventory manager can usually state a willingness to allow perhaps one, two, or three stockouts during the year. The allowable stockouts per year divided by the number of orders per year will provide the desired probability of a stockout.

Refer to the **lead-time demand distribution** shown in Figure 10.11. Given this distribution, we can now determine how the reorder point r affects the probability of a stockout. Because stockouts occur whenever the demand during the lead time exceeds the reorder point, we can find the probability of a stockout by using the lead-time demand distribution to compute the probability that demand will exceed r.

We could now approach the when-to-order problem by defining a cost per stockout and then attempting to include this cost in a total cost equation. Alternatively, we can ask management to specify the average number of stockouts that can be tolerated per year. If demand for a product is probabilistic, a manager who will never tolerate a stockout is being somewhat unrealistic because attempting to avoid stockouts completely will require high reorder points, high inventory, and an associated high holding cost.

FIGURE 10.12   REORDER POINT r THAT ALLOWS A 5% CHANCE OF A STOCKOUT
FOR DABCO LIGHTBULBS

Suppose in this case that Dabco management is willing to tolerate an average of one stockout per year. Because Dabco places 20 orders per year, this decision implies that management is willing to allow demand during lead time to exceed the reorder point one time in 20, or 5% of the time. The reorder point r can be found by using the lead-time demand distribution to find the value of r, with a 5% chance of having a lead-time demand that will exceed it. This situation is shown graphically in Figure 10.12.

We can now use the cumulative probabilities for the standard normal distribution (see Appendix B) to determine the reorder point r. In Figure 10.12, the 5% chance of a stockout occurs with the cumulative probability of no stockout being $1.00 - 0.05 = 0.95$. From Appendix B, we see that the cumulative probability of 0.95 occurs at $z = 1.645$ standard deviations above the mean. Therefore, for the assumed normal distribution for lead-time demand with $\mu = 154$ and $\sigma = 25$, the reorder point r is

$$r = 154 + 1.645(25) = 195$$

If a normal distribution is used for lead-time demand, the general equation for r is

$$r = \mu + z\sigma \qquad (10.37)$$

where z is the number of standard deviations necessary to obtain the acceptable stockout probability.

Thus, the recommended inventory decision is to order 400 units whenever the inventory reaches the reorder point of 195. Because the mean or expected demand during the lead time is 154 units, the $195 - 154 = 41$ units serve as a **safety stock,** which absorbs higher than usual demand during the lead time. Roughly 95% of the time, the 195 units will be able to satisfy demand during the lead time. The anticipated annual cost for this system is as follows:

Holding cost, normal inventory $(Q/2)C_h = (400/2)(1.20) = \$240$
Holding cost, safety stock $\qquad\quad (41)C_h = \quad 41(1.20) \quad = \$\ 49$
Ordering cost $\qquad\qquad\qquad (D/Q)C_o = (8008/400)12 = \$240$
$\qquad\qquad\qquad\qquad\qquad\qquad\qquad\qquad\qquad$ Total $\quad \$529$

Try Problem 29 as an example of an order-quantity, reorder point model with probabilistic demand.

If Dabco could assume that a known, constant demand rate of 8008 units per year existed for the lightbulbs, then $Q^* = 400$, $r = 154$, and a total annual cost of $240 + $240 = $480 would be optimal. When demand is uncertain and can only be expressed in probabilistic terms, a larger total cost can be expected. The larger cost occurs in the form of larger holding costs because more inventory must be maintained to limit the number of stockouts. For Dabco, this additional inventory or safety stock was 41 units, with an additional annual holding cost of $49. The Management Science in Action, Lowering Inventory Cost at Dutch Companies, describes how a warehouser in the Netherlands implemented an order-quantity, reorder point system with probabilistic demand.

MANAGEMENT SCIENCE IN ACTION

LOWERING INVENTORY COST AT DUTCH COMPANIES*

In the Netherlands, companies such as Philips, Rank Xerox, and Fokker have followed the trend of developing closer relations between the firm and its suppliers. As teamwork, coordination, and information sharing improve, opportunities are available for better cost control in the operation of inventory systems.

One Dutch public warehouser has a contract with its supplier under which the supplier routinely provides information regarding the status and schedule of upcoming production runs. The warehouser's inventory system operates as an order-quantity, reorder point system with probabilistic demand. When the order quantity Q has been determined, the warehouser selects the desired reorder point for the product. The distribution of the lead-time demand is essential in determining the reorder point. Usually, the lead-time demand distribution is

approximated directly, taking into account both the probabilistic demand and the probabilistic length of the lead-time period.

The supplier's information concerning scheduled production runs provides the warehouser with a better understanding of the lead time involved for a product and the resulting lead-time demand distribution. With this information, the warehouse can modify the reorder point accordingly. Information sharing by the supplier thus enables the order-quantity, reorder point system to operate with a lower inventory holding cost.

*Based on F. A. van der Duyn Schouten, M. J. G. van Eijs, and R. M. J. Heuts, "The Value of Supplier Information to Improve Management of a Retailer's Inventory," *Decision Sciences* 25, no. 1 (January/February 1994): 1–14.

NOTES AND COMMENTS

The Dabco reorder point was based on a 5% probability of a stockout during the lead-time period. Thus, on 95% of all order cycles Dabco will be able to satisfy customer demand without experiencing a stockout. Defining *service level* as the percentage of all order cycles that do not experience a stockout, we would say that Dabco has a 95%

service level. However, other definitions of service level may include the percentage of all customer demand that can be satisfied from inventory. Thus, when an inventory manager expresses a desired service level, it is a good idea to clarify exactly what the manager means by the term *service level*.

10.7   PERIODIC REVIEW MODEL WITH PROBABILISTIC DEMAND

The order-quantity, reorder point inventory models previously discussed require a **continuous review inventory system.** In a continuous review inventory system, the inventory position is monitored continuously so that an order can be placed whenever the reorder point is reached. Computerized inventory systems can easily provide the continuous review required by the order-quantity, reorder point models.

Up to this point, we have assumed that the inventory position is reviewed continuously so that an order can be placed as soon as the inventory position reaches the reorder point. The inventory model in this section assumes probabilistic demand and a periodic review of the inventory position.

An alternative to the continuous review system is the **periodic review inventory system.** With a periodic review system, the inventory is checked and reordering is done only at specified points in time. For example, inventory may be checked and orders placed on a weekly, biweekly, monthly, or some other periodic basis. When a firm or business handles multiple products, the periodic review system offers the advantage of requiring that orders for several items be placed at the same preset periodic review time. With this type of inventory system, the shipping and receiving of orders for multiple products are easily coordinated. Under the previously discussed order-quantity, reorder point systems, the reorder points for various products can be encountered at substantially different points in time, making the coordination of orders for multiple products more difficult.

To illustrate this system, let us consider Dollar Discounts, a firm with several retail stores that carry a wide variety of products for household use. The company operates its inventory system with a two-week periodic review. Under this system, a retail store manager may order any number of units of any product from the Dollar Discounts central warehouse every two weeks. Orders for all products going to a particular store are combined into one shipment. When making the order quantity decision for each product at a given review period, the store manager knows that a reorder for the product cannot be made until the next review period.

Assuming that the lead time is less than the length of the review period, an order placed at a review period will be received prior to the next review period. In this case, the how-much-to-order decision at any review period is determined using the following:

$$Q = M - H \qquad (10.38)$$

where

Q = order quantity

M = replenishment level

H = inventory on hand at the review period

Because the demand is probabilistic, the inventory on hand at the review period, H, will vary. Thus, the order quantity that must be sufficient to bring the inventory position back to its maximum or replenishment level M can be expected to vary each period. For example, if the replenishment level for a particular product is 50 units, and the inventory on hand at the review period is $H = 12$ units, an order of $Q = M - H = 50 - 12 = 38$ units should be made. Thus, under the periodic review model, enough units are ordered each review period to bring the inventory position back up to the replenishment level.

A typical inventory pattern for a periodic review system with probabilistic demand is shown in Figure 10.13. Note that the time between periodic reviews is predetermined and fixed. The order quantity Q at each review period can vary and is shown to be the difference between the replenishment level and the inventory on hand. Finally, as with other probabilistic models, an unusually high demand can result in an occasional stockout.

The decision variable in the periodic review model is the replenishment level M. To determine M, we could begin by developing a total cost model, including holding, ordering, and stockout costs. Instead, we describe an approach that is often used in practice. In this approach, the objective is to determine a replenishment level that will meet a desired performance level, such as a reasonably low probability of stockout or a reasonably low number of stockouts per year.

FIGURE 10.13   INVENTORY PATTERN FOR PERIODIC REVIEW MODEL
WITH PROBABILISTIC DEMAND

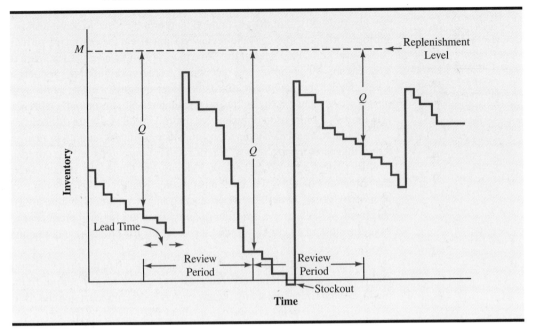

In the Dollar Discounts problem, we assume that management's objective is to deter-mine the replenishment level with only a 0.01 probability of a stockout. In the periodic re-view model, the order quantity at each review period must be sufficient to cover demand for the *review period plus the demand for the following lead time.* That is, the order quantity that brings the inventory position up to the replenishment level M must last until the order made at the next review period is received in inventory. The length of this time is equal to the review period plus the lead time. Figure 10.14 shows the normal probability distribu-tion of demand during the review period plus the lead-time period for one of the Dollar Dis-counts products. The mean demand is 250 units, and the standard deviation of demand is 45 units. Given this situation, the logic used to establish M is similar to the logic used to

FIGURE 10.14   PROBABILITY DISTRIBUTION OF DEMAND DURING THE REVIEW
PERIOD AND LEAD TIME FOR THE DOLLAR DISCOUNTS PROBLEM

FIGURE 10.15   REPLENISHMENT LEVEL *M* THAT ALLOWS A 1% CHANCE
OF A STOCKOUT FOR THE DOLLAR DISCOUNTS PROBLEM

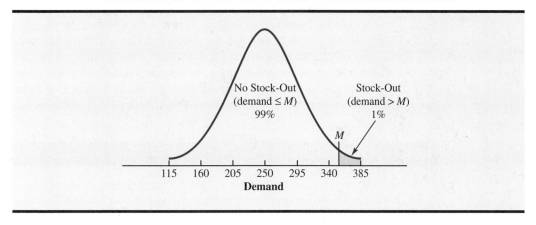

establish the reorder point in Section 10.6. Figure 10.15 shows the replenishment level *M* with a 0.01 probability of a stockout due to demand exceeding the replenishment level. This means that there will be a 0.99 probability of no stockout. Using the cumulative probability 0.99 and the cumulative probability table for the standard normal distribution (Appendix B), we see that the value of *M* must be $z = 2.33$ standard deviations above the mean. Thus, for the given probability distribution, the replenishment level that allows a 0.01 probability of stockout is

Periodic

$$M = 250 = 2.33(45) = 355$$

Problem 33 gives you practice in computing the replenishment level for a periodic review model with probabilistic demand.

Although other probability distributions can be used to express the demand during the review period plus the lead-time period, if the normal probability distribution is used, the general expression for *M* is

$$M = \mu + z\sigma \qquad (10.39)$$

where *z* is the number of standard deviations necessary to obtain the acceptable stockout probability.

Periodic review systems provide advantages of coordinated orders for multiple items. However, periodic review systems require larger safety stock levels than corresponding continuous review systems.

If demand had been deterministic rather than probabilistic, the replenishment level would have been the demand during the review period plus the demand during the lead-time period. In this case, the replenishment level would have been 250 units, and no stockout would have occurred. However, with the probabilistic demand, we have seen that higher inventory is necessary to allow for uncertain demand and to control the probability of a stockout. In the Dollar Discounts problem, $355 - 250 = 105$ is the safety stock that is necessary to absorb any higher than usual demand during the review period plus the demand during the lead-time period. This safety stock limits the probability of a stockout to 1%.

More Complex Periodic Review Models

The periodic review model just discussed is one approach to determining a replenishment level for the periodic review inventory system with probabilistic demand. More complex versions of the periodic review model incorporate a reorder point as another decision variable;

that is, instead of ordering at every periodic review, a reorder point is established. If the inventory on hand at the periodic review is at or below the reorder point, a decision is made to order up to the replenishment level. However, if the inventory on hand at the periodic review is greater than the reorder level, such an order is not placed, and the system continues until the next periodic review. In this case, the cost of ordering is a relevant cost and can be included in a cost model along with holding and stockout costs. Optimal policies can be reached based on minimizing the expected total cost. Situations with lead times longer than the review period add to the complexity of the model. The mathematical level required to treat these more extensive periodic review models is beyond the scope of this text.

NOTES AND COMMENTS

1. The periodic review model presented in this section is based on the assumption that the lead time for an order is less than the periodic review period. Most periodic review systems operate under this condition. However, the case in which the lead time is longer than the review period can be handled by defining H in equation (10.38) as the inventory position, where H includes the inventory on hand plus the inventory on order. In this case, the order quantity at any review period is the amount needed for the inventory on hand plus *all* outstanding orders needed to reach the replenishment level.

2. In the order-quantity, reorder point model discussed in Section 10.6, a continuous review was used to initiate an order whenever the reorder point was reached. The safety stock for this model was based on the probabilistic demand during the lead time. The periodic review model presented in this section also determined a recommended safety stock. However, because the inventory review was only periodic, the safety stock was based on the probabilistic demand during the *review period plus the lead-time period*. This longer period for the safety stock computation means that periodic review systems tend to require a larger safety stock than do continuous review systems.

SUMMARY

In this chapter we presented some of the approaches management scientists use to assist managers in establishing low-cost inventory policies. We first considered cases in which the demand rate for the product is constant. In analyzing these inventory systems, total cost models were developed, which included ordering costs, holding costs, and, in some cases, backorder costs. Then minimum cost formulas for the order quantity Q were presented. A reorder point r can be established by considering the lead-time demand.

In addition, we discussed inventory models in which a deterministic and constant rate could not be assumed, and thus demand was described by a probability distribution. A critical issue with these probabilistic inventory models is obtaining a probability distribution that most realistically approximates the demand distribution. We first described a single-period model where only one order is placed for the product and, at the end of the period, either the product has sold out or a surplus remains of unsold products that will be sold for a salvage value. Solution procedures were then presented for multiperiod models based on either an order-quantity, reorder point, continuous review system or a replenishment-level, periodic review system.

In closing this chapter we reemphasize that inventory and inventory systems can be an expensive phase of a firm's operation. It is important for managers to be aware of the cost of inventory systems and to make the best possible operating policy decisions for the inventory system. Inventory models, as presented in this chapter, can help managers to develop good inventory policies. The Management Science in Action, Multistage Inventory Planning at Deere & Company, provides another example of how computer-based inventory models can be used to provide optimal inventory policies and cost reductions.

MANAGEMENT SCIENCE IN ACTION

MULTISTAGE INVENTORY PLANNING AT DEERE & COMPANY*

Deere & Company's Commercial & Consumer Equipment (C&CE) Division, located in Raleigh, North Carolina, produces seasonal products such as lawn mowers and snow blowers. The seasonal aspect of demand requires the products to be built in advance. Because many of the products involve impulse purchases, the products must be available at dealerships when the customers walk in. Historically, high inventory levels resulted in high inventory costs and an unacceptable return on assets. As a result, management concluded that C&CE needed an inventory planning system that would reduce the average finished goods inventory levels in company warehouses and dealer locations, and at the same time would ensure that stockouts would not cause a negative impact on sales.

In order to optimize inventory levels, Deere moved from an aggregate inventory planning model to a series of individual product inventory models. This approach enabled Deere to determine optimal inventory levels for each product at each dealer, as well as optimal levels for each product at each plant and warehouse. The computerized system developed, known as SmartOps Multistage Inventory Planning and Optimization (MIPO), manages inventory for four C&CE Division plants, 21 dealers, and 150 products. Easily updated, MIPO provides target inventory levels for each product on a weekly basis. In addition, the system provides information about how optimal inventory levels are affected by lead times, forecast errors, and target service levels.

The inventory optimization system enabled the C&CE Division to meet its inventory reduction goals. C&CE management estimates that the company will continue to achieve annual cost savings from lower inventory carrying costs. Meanwhile, the dealers also benefit from lower warehouse expenses, as well as lower interest and insurance costs.

*Based on "Deere's New Software Achieves Inventory Reduction Goals," *Inventory Management Report* (March 2003): 2.

GLOSSARY

Economic order quantity (EOQ)   The order quantity that minimizes the annual holding cost plus the annual ordering cost.

Constant demand rate   An assumption of many inventory models that states that the same number of units are taken from inventory each period of time.

Holding cost   The cost associated with maintaining an inventory investment, including the cost of the capital investment in the inventory, insurance, taxes, warehouse overhead, and so on. This cost may be stated as a percentage of the inventory investment or as a cost per unit.

Cost of capital   The cost a firm incurs to obtain capital for investment. It may be stated as an annual percentage rate, and it is part of the holding cost associated with maintaining inventory.

Ordering cost   The fixed cost (salaries, paper, transportation, etc.) associated with placing an order for an item.

Inventory position   The inventory on hand plus the inventory on order.

Reorder point   The inventory position at which a new order should be placed.

Lead time   The time between the placing of an order and its receipt in the inventory system.

Lead-time demand   The number of units demanded during the lead-time period.

Cycle time   The length of time between the placing of two consecutive orders.

Constant supply rate   A situation in which the inventory is built up at a constant rate over a period of time.

Lot size   The order quantity in the production inventory model.

Setup cost   The fixed cost (labor, materials, lost production) associated with preparing for a new production run.

Shortage, or stockout   Demand that cannot be supplied from inventory.

Backorder   The receipt of an order for a product when no units are in inventory. These backorders become shortages, which are eventually satisfied when a new supply of the product becomes available.

Goodwill cost   A cost associated with a backorder, a lost sale, or any form of stockout or unsatisfied demand. This cost may be used to reflect the loss of future profits because a customer experienced an unsatisfied demand.

Quantity discounts   Discounts or lower unit costs offered by the manufacturer when a customer purchases larger quantities of the product.

Deterministic inventory model   A model where demand is considered known and not subject to uncertainty.

Probabilistic inventory model   A model where demand is not known exactly; probabilities must be associated with the possible values for demand.

Single-period inventory model   An inventory model in which only one order is placed for the product, and at the end of the period either the item has sold out, or a surplus of unsold items will be sold for a salvage value.

Incremental analysis   A method used to determine an optimal order quantity by comparing the cost of ordering an additional unit with the cost of not ordering an additional unit.

Lead-time demand distribution   The distribution of demand that occurs during the lead-time period.

Safety stock   Inventory maintained in order to reduce the number of stockouts resulting from higher than expected demand.

Continuous review inventory system   A system in which the inventory position is monitored or reviewed on a continuous basis so that a new order can be placed as soon as the reorder point is reached.

Periodic review inventory system   A system in which the inventory position is checked or reviewed at predetermined periodic points in time. Reorders are placed only at periodic review points.

PROBLEMS

1. Suppose that the R&B Beverage Company has a soft drink product that shows a constant annual demand rate of 3600 cases. A case of the soft drink costs R&B $3. Ordering costs are $20 per order and holding costs are 25% of the value of the inventory. R&B has 250 working days per year, and the lead time is 5 days. Identify the following aspects of the inventory policy:
   a. Economic order quantity
   b. Reorder point
   c. Cycle time
   d. Total annual cost

2. A general property of the EOQ inventory model is that total inventory holding and total ordering costs are equal at the optimal solution. Use the data in Problem 1 to show that this result is true. Use equations (10.2), (10.3), and (10.5) to show that, in general, total holding costs and total ordering costs are equal whenever Q^* is used.

3. The reorder point [see equation (10.6)] is defined as the lead-time demand for an item. In cases of long lead times, the lead-time demand and thus the reorder point may exceed the economic order quantity Q^*. In such cases, the inventory position will not equal the inventory on hand when an order is placed, and the reorder point may be expressed in terms of either the inventory position or the inventory on hand. Consider the economic order quantity model with $D = 5000$, $C_o = \$32$, $C_h = \$2$, and 250 working days per year. Identify the reorder point in terms of the inventory position and in terms of the inventory on hand for each of the following lead times:
   a. 5 days
   b. 15 days
   c. 25 days
   d. 45 days

4. Westside Auto purchases a component used in the manufacture of automobile generators directly from the supplier. Westside's generator production operation, which is operated at a constant rate, will require 1000 components per month throughout the year (12,000 units annually). Assume that the ordering costs are $25 per order, the unit cost is $2.50 per component, and annual holding costs are 20% of the value of the inventory. Westside has 250 working days per year and a lead time of 5 days. Answer the following inventory policy questions:
   a. What is the EOQ for this component?
   b. What is the reorder point?
   c. What is the cycle time?
   d. What are the total annual holding and ordering costs associated with your recommended EOQ?

5. Suppose that Westside's management in Problem 4 likes the operational efficiency of ordering once each month and in quantities of 1000 units. How much more expensive would this policy be than your EOQ recommendation? Would you recommend in favor of the 1000-unit order quantity? Explain. What would the reorder point be if the 1000-unit quantity were acceptable?

6. Tele-Reco is a new specialty store that sells television sets, videotape recorders, video games, and other television-related products. A new Japanese-manufactured videotape recorder costs Tele-Reco $600 per unit. Tele-Reco's annual holding cost rate is 22%. Ordering costs are estimated to be $70 per order.
   a. If demand for the new videotape recorder is expected to be constant with a rate of 20 units per month, what is the recommended order quantity for the videotape recorder?

b. What are the estimated annual inventory holding and ordering costs associated with this product?

c. How many orders will be placed per year?

d. With 250 working days per year, what is the cycle time for this product?

7. A large distributor of oil-well drilling equipment operated over the past two years with EOQ policies based on an annual holding cost rate of 22%. Under the EOQ policy, a particular product has been ordered with a $Q^* = 80$. A recent evaluation of holding costs shows that because of an increase in the interest rate associated with bank loans, the annual holding cost rate should be 27%.

a. What is the new economic order quantity for the product?

b. Develop a general expression showing how the economic order quantity changes when the annual holding cost rate is changed from I to I'.

8. Nation-Wide Bus Lines is proud of its six-week bus driver training program that it conducts for all new Nation-Wide drivers. As long as the class size remains less than or equal to 35, a six-week training program costs Nation-Wide $22,000 for instructors, equipment, and so on. The Nation-Wide training program must provide the company with approximately five new drivers per month. After completing the training program, new drivers are paid $1600 per month but do not work until a full-time driver position is open. Nation-Wide views the $1600 per month paid to each idle new driver as a holding cost necessary to maintain a supply of newly trained drivers available for immediate service. Viewing new drivers as inventory-type units, how large should the training classes be to minimize Nation-Wide's total annual training and new driver idle-time costs? How many training classes should the company hold each year? What is the total annual cost associated with your recommendation?

9. Cress Electronic Products manufactures components used in the automotive industry. Cress purchases parts for use in its manufacturing operation from a variety of different suppliers. One particular supplier provides a part where the assumptions of the EOQ model are realistic. The annual demand is 5000 units, the ordering cost is $80 per order, and the annual holding cost rate is 25%.

a. If the cost of the part is $20 per unit, what is the economic order quantity?

b. Assume 250 days of operation per year. If the lead time for an order is 12 days, what is the reorder point?

c. If the lead time for the part is seven weeks (35 days), what is the reorder point?

d. What is the reorder point for part (c) if the reorder point is expressed in terms of the inventory on hand rather than the inventory position?

10. All-Star Bat Manufacturing, Inc., supplies baseball bats to major and minor league baseball teams. After an initial order in January, demand over the six-month baseball season is approximately constant at 1000 bats per month. Assuming that the bat production process can handle up to 4000 bats per month, the bat production setup costs are $150 per setup, the production cost is $10 per bat, and the holding costs have a monthly rate of 2%, what production lot size would you recommend to meet the demand during the baseball season? If All-Star operates 20 days per month, how often will the production process operate, and what is the length of a production run?

11. Assume that a production line operates such that the production lot size model of Section 10.2 is applicable. Given $D = 6400$ units per year, $C_o = \$100$, and $C_h = \$2$ per unit per year, compute the minimum cost production lot size for each of the following production rates:

a. 8000 units per year

b. 10,000 units per year

c. 32,000 units per year

d. 100,000 units per year

Compute the EOQ recommended lot size using equation (10.5). What two observations can you make about the relationship between the EOQ model and the production lot size model?

12. Assume that you are reviewing the production lot size decision associated with a production operation where $P = 8000$ units per year, $D = 2000$ units per year, $C_o = \$300$, and $C_h = \$1.60$ per unit per year. Also assume that current practice calls for production runs of 500 units every three months. Would you recommend changing the current production lot size? Why or why not? How much could be saved by converting to your production lot size recommendation?

13. Wilson Publishing Company produces books for the retail market. Demand for a current book is expected to occur at a constant annual rate of 7200 copies. The cost of one copy of the book is $14.50. The holding cost is based on an 18% annual rate, and production setup costs are $150 per setup. The equipment on which the book is produced has an annual production volume of 25,000 copies. Wilson has 250 working days per year, and the lead time for a production run is 15 days. Use the production lot size model to compute the following values:
    a. Minimum cost production lot size
    b. Number of production runs per year
    c. Cycle time
    d. Length of a production run
    e. Maximum inventory
    f. Total annual cost
    g. Reorder point

14. A well-known manufacturer of several brands of toothpaste uses the production lot size model to determine production quantities for its various products. The product known as Extra White is currently being produced in production lot sizes of 5000 units. The length of the production run for this quantity is 10 days. Because of a recent shortage of a particular raw material, the supplier of the material announced that a cost increase will be passed along to the manufacturer of Extra White. Current estimates are that the new raw material cost will increase the manufacturing cost of the toothpaste products by 23% per unit. What will be the effect of this price increase on the production lot sizes for Extra White?

15. Suppose that Westside Auto of Problem 4, with $D = 12{,}000$ units per year, $C_h = (2.50)(0.20) = \$0.50$, and $C_o = \$25$, decided to operate with a backorder inventory policy. Backorder costs are estimated to be $5 per unit per year. Identify the following:
    a. Minimum cost order quantity
    b. Maximum number of backorders
    c. Maximum inventory
    d. Cycle time
    e. Total annual cost

16. Assuming 250 days of operation per year and a lead time of 5 days, what is the reorder point for Westside Auto in Problem 15? Show the general formula for the reorder point for the EOQ model with backorders. In general, is the reorder point when backorders are allowed greater than or less than the reorder point when backorders are not allowed? Explain.

17. A manager of an inventory system believes that inventory models are important decision-making aids. Even though often using an EOQ policy, the manager never considered a backorder model because of the assumption that backorders were "bad" and should be avoided. However, with upper management's continued pressure for cost reduction, you have been asked to analyze the economics of a backorder policy for some products that can possibly be backordered. For a specific product with $D = 800$ units per year,

$C_o = \$150$, $C_h = \$3$, and $C_b = \$20$, what is the difference in total annual cost between the EOQ model and the planned shortage or backorder model? If the manager adds constraints that no more than 25% of the units can be backordered and that no customer will have to wait more than 15 days for an order, should the backorder inventory policy be adopted? Assume 250 working days per year.

18. If the lead time for new orders is 20 days for the inventory system discussed in Problem 17, find the reorder point for both the EOQ and the backorder models.

19. The A&M Hobby Shop carries a line of radio-controlled model racing cars. Demand for the cars is assumed to be constant at a rate of 40 cars per month. The cars cost $60 each, and ordering costs are approximately $15 per order, regardless of the order size. The annual holding cost rate is 20%.
    a. Determine the economic order quantity and total annual cost under the assumption that no backorders are permitted.
    b. Using a $45 per-unit per-year backorder cost, determine the minimum cost inventory policy and total annual cost for the model racing cars.
    c. What is the maximum number of days a customer would have to wait for a backorder under the policy in part (b)? Assume that the Hobby Shop is open for business 300 days per year.
    d. Would you recommend a no-backorder or a backorder inventory policy for this product? Explain.
    e. If the lead time is six days, what is the reorder point for both the no-backorder and backorder inventory policies?

20. Assume that the following quantity discount schedule is appropriate. If annual demand is 120 units, ordering costs are $20 per order, and the annual holding cost rate is 25%, what order quantity would you recommend?

Order Size	Discount (%)	Unit Cost
0 to 49	0	$30.00
50 to 99	5	$28.50
100 or more	10	$27.00

21. Apply the EOQ model to the following quantity discount situation in which $D = 500$ units per year, $C_o = \$40$, and the annual holding cost rate is 20%. What order quantity do you recommend?

Discount Category	Order Size	Discount (%)	Unit Cost
1	0 to 99	0	$10.00
2	100 or more	3	$ 9.70

22. Keith Shoe Stores carries a basic black men's dress shoe that sells at an approximate constant rate of 500 pairs of shoes every three months. Keith's current buying policy is to order 500 pairs each time an order is placed. It costs Keith $30 to place an order. The annual holding cost rate is 20%. With the order quantity of 500, Keith obtains the shoes at the lowest possible unit cost of $28 per pair. Other quantity discounts offered by the manufacturer are as follows. What is the minimum cost order quantity for the shoes? What are the annual savings of your inventory policy over the policy currently being used by Keith?

Order Quantity	Price per Pair
0–99	$36
100–199	$32
200–299	$30
300 or more	$28

23. In the EOQ model with quantity discounts, we stated that if the Q^* for a price category is larger than necessary to qualify for the category price, the category cannot be optimal. Use the two discount categories in Problem 21 to show that this statement is true. That is, plot total cost curves for the two categories and show that if the category 2 minimum cost Q is an acceptable solution, we do not have to consider category 1.

24. The J&B Card Shop sells calendars depicting a different Colonial scene each month. The once-a-year order for each year's calendar arrives in September. From past experience, the September-to-July demand for the calendars can be approximated by a normal probability distribution with $\mu = 500$ and $\sigma = 120$. The calendars cost $1.50 each, and J&B sells them for $3 each.
   a. If J&B throws out all unsold calendars at the end of July (i.e., salvage value is zero), how many calendars should be ordered?
   b. If J&B reduces the calendar price to $1 at the end of July and can sell all surplus calendars at this price, how many calendars should be ordered?

25. The Gilbert Air-Conditioning Company is considering the purchase of a special shipment of portable air conditioners manufactured in Japan. Each unit will cost Gilbert $80, and it will be sold for $125. Gilbert does not want to carry surplus air conditioners over until the following year. Thus, all surplus air conditioners will be sold to a wholesaler for $50 per unit. Assume that the air conditioner demand follows a normal probability distribution with $\mu = 20$ and $\sigma = 8$.
   a. What is the recommended order quantity?
   b. What is the probability that Gilbert will sell all units it orders?

26. The Bridgeport city manager and the chief of police agreed on the size of the police force necessary for normal daily operations. However, they need assistance in determining the number of additional police officers needed to cover daily absences due to injuries, sickness, vacations, and personal leave. Records over the past three years show that the daily demand for additional police officers is normally distributed with a mean of 50 officers and a standard deviation of 10 officers. The cost of an additional police officer is based on the average pay rate of $150 per day. If the daily demand for additional police officers exceeds the number of additional officers available, the excess demand will be covered by overtime at the pay rate of $240 per day for each overtime officer.
   a. If the number of additional police officers available is greater than demand, the city will have to pay for more additional police officers than needed. What is the cost of overestimating demand?
   b. If the number of additional police officers available is less than demand, the city will have to use overtime to meet the demand. What is the cost of underestimating demand?
   c. What is the optimal number of additional police officers that should be included in the police force?
   d. On a typical day, what is the probability that overtime will be necessary?

27. A perishable dairy product is ordered daily at a particular supermarket. The product, which costs $1.19 per unit, sells for $1.65 per unit. If units are unsold at the end of the day, the supplier takes them back at a rebate of $1 per unit. Assume that daily demand is approximately normally distributed with $\mu = 150$ and $\sigma = 30$.

   a.   What is your recommended daily order quantity for the supermarket?
   b.   What is the probability that the supermarket will sell all the units it orders?
   c.   In problems such as these, why would the supplier offer a rebate as high as $1? For example, why not offer a nominal rebate of, say, 25¢ per unit? What happens to the supermarket order quantity as the rebate is reduced?

28.   A retail outlet sells a seasonal product for $10 per unit. The cost of the product is $8 per unit. All units not sold during the regular season are sold for half the retail price in an end-of-season clearance sale. Assume that demand for the product is uniformly distributed between 200 and 800.

   a.   What is the recommended order quantity?
   b.   What is the probability that at least some customers will ask to purchase the product after the outlet is sold out? That is, what is the probability of a stockout using your order quantity in part (a)?
   c.   To keep customers happy and returning to the store later, the owner feels that stock-outs should be avoided if at all possible. What is your recommended order quantity if the owner is willing to tolerate a 0.15 probability of a stockout?
   d.   Using your answer to part (c), what is the goodwill cost you are assigning to a stockout?

29.   Floyd Distributors, Inc., provides a variety of auto parts to small local garages. Floyd purchases parts from manufacturers according to the EOQ model and then ships the parts from a regional warehouse direct to its customers. For a particular type of muffler, Floyd's EOQ analysis recommends orders with $Q^* = 25$ to satisfy an annual demand of 200 mufflers. Floyd's has 250 working days per year, and the lead time averages 15 days.

   a.   What is the reorder point if Floyd assumes a constant demand rate?
   b.   Suppose that an analysis of Floyd's muffler demand shows that the lead-time demand follows a normal probability distribution with $\mu = 12$ and $\sigma = 2.5$. If Floyd's management can tolerate one stockout per year, what is the revised reorder point?
   c.   What is the safety stock for part (b)? If $C_h = \$5/unit/year$, what is the extra cost due to the uncertainty of demand?

30.   For Floyd Distributors in Problem 29, we were given $Q^* = 25$, $D = 200$, $C_h = \$5$, and a normal lead-time demand distribution with $\mu = 12$ and $\sigma = 2.5$.

   a.   What is Floyd's reorder point if the firm is willing to tolerate two stockouts during the year?
   b.   What is Floyd's reorder point if the firm wants to restrict the probability of a stockout on any one cycle to at most 1%?
   c.   What are the safety stock levels and the annual safety stock costs for the reorder points found in parts (a) and (b)?

31.   A product with an annual demand of 1000 units has $C_o = \$25.50$ and $C_h = \$8$. The demand exhibits some variability such that the lead-time demand follows a normal probability distribution with $\mu = 25$ and $\sigma = 5$.

   a.   What is the recommended order quantity?
   b.   What are the reorder point and safety stock if the firm desires at most a 2% probability of stockout on any given order cycle?
   c.   If a manager sets the reorder point at 30, what is the probability of a stockout on any given order cycle? How many times would you expect a stockout during the year if this reorder point were used?

32.   The B&S Novelty and Craft Shop in Bennington, Vermont, sells a variety of quality hand-made items to tourists. B&S will sell 300 hand-carved miniature replicas of a Colonial

soldier each year, but the demand pattern during the year is uncertain. The replicas sell for $20 each, and B&S uses a 15% annual inventory holding cost rate. Ordering costs are $5 per order, and demand during the lead time follows a normal probability distribution with $\mu = 15$ and $\sigma = 6$.

a. What is the recommended order quantity?

b. If B&S is willing to accept a stockout roughly twice a year, what reorder point would you recommend? What is the probability that B&S will have a stockout in any one order cycle?

c. What are the safety stock and annual safety stock costs for this product?

33. A firm uses a one-week periodic review inventory system. A two-day lead time is needed for any order, and the firm is willing to tolerate an average of one stockout per year.

a. Using the firm's service guideline, what is the probability of a stockout associated with each replenishment decision?

b. What is the replenishment level if demand during the review period plus lead-time period is normally distributed with a mean of 60 units and a standard deviation of 12 units?

c. What is the replenishment level if demand during the review period plus lead-time period is uniformly distributed between 35 and 85 units?

34. Foster Drugs, Inc., handles a variety of health and beauty aid products. A particular hair conditioner product costs Foster Drugs $2.95 per unit. The annual holding cost rate is 20%. An order-quantity, reorder point inventory model recommends an order quantity of 300 units per order.

a. Lead time is one week and the lead-time demand is normally distributed with a mean of 150 units and a standard deviation of 40 units. What is the reorder point if the firm is willing to tolerate a 1% chance of stockout on any one cycle?

b. What safety stock and annual safety stock costs are associated with your recommendation in part (a)?

c. The order-quantity, reorder point model requires a continuous review system. Management is considering making a transition to a periodic review system in an attempt to coordinate ordering for many of its products. The demand during the proposed two-week review period and the one-week lead-time period is normally distributed with a mean of 450 units and a standard deviation of 70 units. What is the recommended replenishment level for this periodic review system if the firm is willing to tolerate the same 1% chance of stockout associated with any replenishment decision?

d. What safety stock and annual safety stock costs are associated with your recommendation in part (c)?

e. Compare your answers to parts (b) and (d). The company is seriously considering the periodic review system. Would you support this decision? Explain.

f. Would you tend to favor the continuous review system for more expensive items? For example, assume that the product in the preceding example sold for $295 per unit. Explain.

35. Statewide Auto Parts uses a four-week periodic review system to reorder parts for its inventory stock. A one-week lead time is required to fill the order. Demand for one particular part during the five-week replenishment period is normally distributed with a mean of 18 units and a standard deviation of 6 units.

a. At a particular periodic review, 8 units are in inventory. The parts manager places an order for 16 units. What is the probability that this part will have a stockout before an order that is placed at the next four-week review period arrives?

b. Assume that the company is willing to tolerate a 2.5% chance of a stockout associated with a replenishment decision. How many parts should the manager have ordered in part (a)? What is the replenishment level for the four-week periodic review system?

36. Rose Office Supplies, Inc., which is open six days a week, uses a two-week periodic review for its store inventory. On alternating Monday mornings, the store manager fills out an order sheet requiring a shipment of various items from the company's warehouse. A particular three-ring notebook sells at an average rate of 16 notebooks per week. The standard deviation in sales is 5 notebooks per week. The lead time for a new shipment is three days. The mean lead-time demand is 8 notebooks with a standard deviation of 3.5.

    a. What is the mean or expected demand during the review period plus the lead-time period?

    b. Under the assumption of independent demand from week to week, the variances in demands are additive. Thus, the variance of the demand during the review period plus the lead-time period is equal to the variance of demand during the first week plus the variance of demand during the second week plus the variance of demand during the lead-time period. What is the variance of demand during the review period plus the lead-time period? What is the standard deviation of demand during the review period plus the lead-time period?

    c. Assuming that demand has a normal probability distribution, what is the replenishment level that will provide an expected stockout rate of one per year?

    d. On Monday, March 22, 18 notebooks remain in inventory at the store. How many notebooks should the store manager order?

Case Problem 1   WAGNER FABRICATING COMPANY

Managers at Wagner Fabricating Company are reviewing the economic feasibility of manufacturing a part that it currently purchases from a supplier. Forecasted annual demand for the part is 3200 units. Wagner operates 250 days per year.

Wagner's financial analysts established a cost of capital of 14% for the use of funds for investments within the company. In addition, over the past year $600,000 was the average investment in the company's inventory. Accounting information shows that a total of $24,000 was spent on taxes and insurance related to the company's inventory. In addition, an estimated $9000 was lost due to inventory shrinkage, which included damaged goods as well as pilferage. A remaining $15,000 was spent on warehouse overhead, including utility expenses for heating and lighting.

An analysis of the purchasing operation shows that approximately two hours are required to process and coordinate an order for the part regardless of the quantity ordered. Purchasing salaries average $28 per hour, including employee benefits. In addition, a detailed analysis of 125 orders showed that $2375 was spent on telephone, paper, and postage directly related to the ordering process.

A one-week lead time is required to obtain the part from the supplier. An analysis of demand during the lead time shows it is approximately normally distributed with a mean of 64 units and a standard deviation of 10 units. Service level guidelines indicate that one stockout per year is acceptable.

Currently, the company has a contract to purchase the part from a supplier at a cost of $18 per unit. However, over the past few months, the company's production capacity has been expanded. As a result, excess capacity is now available in certain production departments, and the company is considering the alternative of producing the parts itself.

Forecasted utilization of equipment shows that production capacity will be available for the part being considered. The production capacity is available at the rate of 1000 units per month, with up to five months of production time available. Management believes that with a two-week lead time, schedules can be arranged so that the part can be produced whenever needed. The demand during the two-week lead time is approximately normally distributed, with a mean of 128 units and a standard deviation of 20 units. Production costs are expected to be $17 per part.

A concern of management is that setup costs will be significant. The total cost of labor and lost production time is estimated to be $50 per hour, and a full eight-hour shift will be needed to set up the equipment for producing the part.

Managerial Report

Develop a report for management of Wagner Fabricating that will address the question of whether the company should continue to purchase the part from the supplier or begin to produce the part itself. Include the following factors in your report:

1. An analysis of the holding costs, including the appropriate annual holding cost rate
2. An analysis of ordering costs, including the appropriate cost per order from the supplier
3. An analysis of setup costs for the production operation
4. A development of the inventory policy for the following two alternatives:
   a. Ordering a fixed quantity Q from the supplier
   b. Ordering a fixed quantity Q from in-plant production
5. Include the following in the policies of parts 4(a) and 4(b):
   a. Optimal quantity $Q*$
   b. Number of order or production runs per year
   c. Cycle time
   d. Reorder point
   e. Amount of safety stock
   f. Expected maximum inventory
   g. Average inventory
   h. Annual holding cost
   i. Annual ordering cost
   j. Annual cost of the units purchased or manufactured
   k. Total annual cost of the purchase policy and the total annual cost of the production policy
6. Make a recommendation as to whether the company should purchase or manufacture the part. What savings are associated with your recommendation as compared with the other alternative?

Case Problem 2   RIVER CITY FIRE DEPARTMENT

The River City Fire Department (RCFD) fights fires and provides a variety of rescue operations in the River City metropolitan area. The RCFD staffs 13 ladder companies, 26 pumper companies, and several rescue units and ambulances. Normal staffing requires 186 firefighters to be on duty every day.

RCFD is organized with three firefighting units. Each unit works a full 24-hour day and then has two days (48 hours) off. For example, Unit 1 covers Monday, Unit 2 covers Tuesday, and Unit 3 covers Wednesday. Then Unit 1 returns on Thursday, and so on. Over a three-week (21-day) scheduling period, each unit will be scheduled for seven days. On a rotational basis, firefighters within each unit are given one of the seven regularly scheduled days off. This day off is referred to as a Kelley day. Thus, over a three-week scheduling period, each firefighter in a unit works six of the seven scheduled unit days and gets one Kelley day off.

Determining the number of firefighters to be assigned to each unit includes the 186 firefighters who must be on duty plus the number of firefighters in the unit who are off for a Kelley day. Furthermore, each unit needs additional staffing to cover firefighter absences due to injury, sick leave, vacations, or personal time. This additional staffing involves finding the best mix of adding full-time firefighters to each unit and the selective use of overtime. If the number of absences on a particular day brings the number of available firefighters below the required 186, firefighters who are currently off (e.g., on a Kelley day) must be scheduled to work overtime. Overtime is compensated at 1.55 times the regular pay rate.

Analysis of the records maintained over the last several years concerning the number of daily absences shows a normal probability distribution. A mean of 20 and a standard deviation of 5 provide a good approximation of the probability distribution for the number of daily absences.

Managerial Report

Develop a report that will enable Fire Chief O. E. Smith to determine the necessary numbers for the Fire Department. Include, at a minimum, the following items in your report:

1. Assuming no daily absences and taking into account the need to staff Kelley days, determine the base number of firefighters needed by each unit.
2. Using a minimum cost criterion, how many additional firefighters should be added to each unit in order to cover the daily absences? These extra daily needs will be filled by the additional firefighters and, when necessary, the more expensive use of overtime by off-duty firefighters.
3. On a given day, what is the probability that Kelley-day firefighters will be called in to work overtime?
4. Based on the three-unit organization, how many firefighters should be assigned to each unit? What is the total number of full-time firefighters required for the River City Fire Department?

Appendix 10.1   DEVELOPMENT OF THE OPTIMAL ORDER QUANTITY ($Q*$) FORMULA FOR THE EOQ MODEL

Given equation (10.4) as the total annual cost for the EOQ model,

$$TC = \frac{1}{2} Q C_h + \frac{D}{Q} C_o \tag{10.4}$$

we can find the order quantity Q that minimizes the total cost by setting the derivative, dTC/dQ, equal to zero and solving for $Q*$.

$$\frac{dTC}{dQ} = \frac{1}{2} C_h - \frac{D}{Q^2} C_o = 0$$

$$\frac{1}{2} C_h = \frac{D}{Q^2} C_o$$

$$C_h Q^2 = 2DC_o$$

$$Q^2 = \frac{2DC_o}{C_h}$$

Hence,

$$Q^* = \sqrt{\frac{2DC_o}{C_h}} \tag{10.5}$$

The second derivative is

$$\frac{d^2TC}{dQ^2} = \frac{2D}{Q^3}C_o$$

Because the value of the second derivative is greater than zero, Q^* from equation (10.5) is the minimum cost solution.

Appendix 10.2   DEVELOPMENT OF THE OPTIMAL LOT SIZE (Q^*) FORMULA FOR THE PRODUCTION LOT SIZE MODEL

Given equation (10.15) as the total annual cost for the production lot size model,

$$TC = \frac{1}{2}\left(1 - \frac{D}{P}\right)QC_h + \frac{D}{Q}C_o \tag{10.15}$$

we can find the order quantity Q that minimizes the total cost by setting the derivative, dTC/dQ, equal to zero and solving for Q^*.

$$\frac{dTC}{dQ} = \frac{1}{2}\left(1 - \frac{D}{P}\right)C_h - \frac{D}{Q^2}C_o = 0$$

Solving for Q^*, we have

$$\frac{1}{2}\left(1 - \frac{D}{P}\right)C_h = \frac{D}{Q^2}C_o$$

$$\left(1 - \frac{D}{P}\right)C_hQ^2 = 2DC_o$$

$$Q^2 = \frac{2DC_o}{(1 - D/P)C_h}$$

Hence,

$$Q^* = \sqrt{\frac{2DC_o}{(1 - D/P)C_h}} \tag{10.16}$$

The second derivative is

$$\frac{d^2TC}{dQ^2} = \frac{2DC_o}{Q^3}$$

Because the value of the second derivative is greater than zero, Q^* from equation (10.16) is a minimum cost solution.

CHAPTER 11

Waiting Line Models

CONTENTS

11.1 STRUCTURE OF A WAITING LINE SYSTEM
Single-Channel Waiting Line
Distribution of Arrivals
Distribution of Service Times
Queue Discipline
Steady-State Operation

11.2 SINGLE-CHANNEL WAITING LINE MODEL WITH POISSON ARRIVALS AND EXPONENTIAL SERVICE TIMES
Operating Characteristics
Operating Characteristics for the Burger Dome Problem
Managers' Use of Waiting Line Models
Improving the Waiting Line Operation
Excel Solution of Waiting Line Model

11.3 MULTIPLE-CHANNEL WAITING LINE MODEL WITH POISSON ARRIVALS AND EXPONENTIAL SERVICE TIMES
Operating Characteristics
Operating Characteristics for the Burger Dome Problem

11.4 SOME GENERAL RELATIONSHIPS FOR WAITING LINE MODELS

11.5 ECONOMIC ANALYSIS OF WAITING LINES

11.6 OTHER WAITING LINE MODELS

11.7 SINGLE-CHANNEL WAITING LINE MODEL WITH POISSON ARRIVALS AND ARBITRARY SERVICE TIMES
Operating Characteristics for the $M/G/1$ Model
Constant Service Times

11.8 MULTIPLE-CHANNEL MODEL WITH POISSON ARRIVALS, ARBITRARY SERVICE TIMES, AND NO WAITING LINE
Operating Characteristics for the $M/G/k$ Model with Blocked Customers Cleared

11.9 WAITING LINE MODELS WITH FINITE CALLING POPULATIONS
Operating Characteristics for the $M/M/1$ Model with a Finite Calling Population

Recall the last time that you had to wait at a supermarket checkout counter, for a teller at your local bank, or to be served at a fast-food restaurant. In these and many other waiting line situations, the time spent waiting is undesirable. Adding more checkout clerks, bank tellers, or servers is not always the most economical strategy for improving service, so businesses need to identify other ways to keep waiting times within tolerable limits.

Models have been developed to help managers understand and make better decisions concerning the operation of waiting lines. In management science terminology, a waiting line is also known as a **queue,** and the body of knowledge dealing with waiting lines is known as **queueing theory.** In the early 1900s, A. K. Erlang, a Danish telephone engineer, began a study of the congestion and waiting times occurring in the completion of telephone calls. Since then, queueing theory has grown far more sophisticated, with applications in a wide variety of waiting line situations.

Waiting line models consist of mathematical formulas and relationships that can be used to determine the **operating characteristics** (performance measures) for a waiting line. Operating characteristics of interest include the following:

1. The probability that no units are in the system
2. The average number of units in the waiting line
3. The average number of units in the system (the number of units in the waiting line plus the number of units being served)
4. The average time a unit spends in the waiting line
5. The average time a unit spends in the system (the waiting time plus the service time)
6. The probability that an arriving unit has to wait for service

Managers who have such information are better able to make decisions that balance desirable service levels against the cost of providing the service.

The Management Science in Action, ATM Waiting Times at Citibank, describes how a waiting line model was used to help determine the number of automatic teller machines (ATMs) to place at New York City banking centers. A waiting line model prompted the creation of a new kind of line and a chief line director to implement first-come, first-served queue discipline at Whole Foods Market in the Chelsea neighborhood of New York City. In addition, a waiting line model helped the New Haven, Connecticut, fire department develop policies to improve response time for both fire and medical emergencies.

MANAGEMENT SCIENCE IN ACTION

ATM WAITING TIMES AT CITIBANK*

The waiting line model used at Citibank is discussed in Section 11.3.

The New York City franchise of U.S. Citibanking operates more than 250 banking centers. Each center provides one or more automatic teller machines (ATMs) capable of performing a variety of banking transactions. At each center, a waiting line is formed by randomly arriving customers who seek service at one of the ATMs.

In order to make decisions on the number of ATMs to have at selected banking center locations, management needed information about potential waiting times and general customer service. Waiting line operating characteristics such as average

number of customers in the waiting line, average time a customer spends waiting, and the probability that an arriving customer has to wait would help management determine the number of ATMs to recommend at each banking center.

For example, one busy midtown Manhattan center had a peak arrival rate of 172 customers per hour. A multiple-channel waiting line model with six ATMs showed that 88% of the customers would have to wait, with an average wait time

(*continued*)

between six and seven minutes. This level of service was judged unacceptable. Expansion to seven ATMs was recommended for this location based on the waiting line model's projection of acceptable waiting times. Use of the waiting line model provided guidelines for making incremental ATM decisions at each banking center location.

*Based on information provided by Stacey Karter of Citibank.

11.1   STRUCTURE OF A WAITING LINE SYSTEM

To illustrate the basic features of a waiting line model, we consider the waiting line at the Burger Dome fast-food restaurant. Burger Dome sells hamburgers, cheeseburgers, french fries, soft drinks, and milk shakes, as well as a limited number of specialty items and dessert selections. Although Burger Dome would like to serve each customer immediately, at times more customers arrive than can be handled by the Burger Dome food service staff. Thus, customers wait in line to place and receive their orders.

Burger Dome is concerned that the methods currently used to serve customers are resulting in excessive waiting times. Management wants to conduct a waiting line study to help determine the best approach to reduce waiting times and improve service.

Single-Channel Waiting Line

In the current Burger Dome operation, a server takes a customer's order, determines the total cost of the order, takes the money from the customer, and then fills the order. Once the first customer's order is filled, the server takes the order of the next customer waiting for service. This operation is an example of a **single-channel waiting line.** Each customer entering the Burger Dome restaurant must pass through the *one* channel—one order-taking and order-filling station—to place an order, pay the bill, and receive the food. When more customers arrive than can be served immediately, they form a waiting line and wait for the order-taking and order-filling station to become available. A diagram of the Burger Dome single-channel waiting line is shown in Figure 11.1.

Distribution of Arrivals

Defining the arrival process for a waiting line involves determining the probability distribution for the number of arrivals in a given period of time. For many waiting line situations, the arrivals occur *randomly and independently* of other arrivals, and we cannot predict

FIGURE 11.1   THE BURGER DOME SINGLE-CHANNEL WAITING LINE

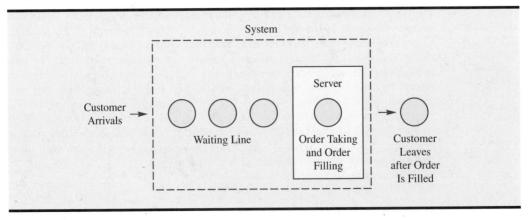

[handwritten note in left margin: One person does all]

when an arrival will occur. In such cases, quantitative analysts have found that the **Poisson probability distribution** provides a good description of the arrival pattern.

The Poisson probability function provides the probability of x arrivals in a specific time period. The probability function is as follows:[1]

$$P(x) = \frac{\lambda^x e^{-\lambda}}{x!} \quad \text{for } x = 0, 1, 2, \ldots \tag{11.1}$$

where

$$x = \text{the number of arrivals in the time period}$$
$$\lambda = \text{the } \textit{mean} \text{ number of arrivals per time period}$$
$$e = 2.71828$$

The mean number of arrivals per time period, λ, is called the **arrival rate.** Values of $e^{-\lambda}$ can be found with a calculator or by using Appendix C.

Suppose that Burger Dome analyzed data on customer arrivals and concluded that the arrival rate is 45 customers per hour. For a one-minute period, the arrival rate would be $\lambda = 45$ customers/60 minutes $= 0.75$ customers per minute. Thus, we can use the following Poisson probability function to compute the probability of x customer arrivals during a one-minute period:

$$P(x) = \frac{\lambda^x e^{-\lambda}}{x!} = \frac{0.75^x e^{-0.75}}{x!} \tag{11.2}$$

Thus, the probabilities of 0, 1, and 2 customer arrivals during a one-minute period are

$$P(0) = \frac{(0.75)^0 e^{-0.75}}{0!} = e^{-0.75} = 0.4724$$

$$P(1) = \frac{(0.75)^1 e^{-0.75}}{1!} = 0.75 e^{-0.75} = 0.75(0.4724) = 0.3543$$

$$P(2) = \frac{(0.75)^2 e^{-0.75}}{2!} = \frac{(0.75)^2 e^{-0.75}}{2!} = \frac{(0.5625)(0.4724)}{2} = 0.1329$$

The probability of no customers in a one-minute period is 0.4724, the probability of one customer in a one-minute period is 0.3543, and the probability of two customers in a one-minute period is 0.1329. Table 11.1 shows the Poisson probabilities for customer arrivals during a one-minute period.

The waiting line models that will be presented in Sections 11.2 and 11.3 use the Poisson probability distribution to describe the customer arrivals at Burger Dome. In practice, you should record the actual number of arrivals per time period for several days or weeks and compare the frequency distribution of the observed number of arrivals to the Poisson probability distribution to determine whether the Poisson probability distribution provides a reasonable approximation of the arrival distribution.

---

[1]The term $x!$, x factorial, is defined as $x! = x(x-1)(x-2)\ldots(2)(1)$. For example, $4! = (4)(3)(2)(1) = 24$. For the special case of $x = 0$, $0! = 1$ by definition.

TABLE 11.1 POISSON PROBABILITIES FOR THE NUMBER OF CUSTOMER ARRIVALS AT A BURGER DOME RESTAURANT DURING A ONE-MINUTE PERIOD ($\lambda = 0.75$)

Number of Arrivals	Probability
0	0.4724
1	0.3543
2	0.1329
3	0.0332
4	0.0062
5 or more	0.0010

Distribution of Service Times

The service time is the time a customer spends at the service facility once the service has started. At Burger Dome, the service time starts when a customer begins to place the order with the food server and continues until the customer receives the order. Service times are rarely constant. At Burger Dome, the number of items ordered and the mix of items ordered vary considerably from one customer to the next. Small orders can be handled in a matter of seconds, but large orders may require more than two minutes.

Quantitative analysts have found that if the probability distribution for the service time can be assumed to follow an **exponential probability distribution,** formulas are available for providing useful information about the operation of the waiting line. Using an exponential probability distribution, the probability that the service time will be less than or equal to a time of length t is

$$P(\text{service time} \leq t) = 1 - e^{-\mu t} \qquad (11.3)$$

where

μ = the *mean* number of units that can be served per time period
e = 2.71828

The mean number of units that can be served per time period, μ, is called the **service rate.**

A property of the exponential probability distribution is that there is a 0.6321 probability that the random variable takes on a value less than its mean. In waiting line applications, the exponential probability distribution indicates that approximately 63 percent of the service times are less than the mean service time and approximately 37 percent of the service times are greater than the mean service time.

Suppose that Burger Dome studied the order-taking and order-filling process and found that the single food server can process an average of 60 customer orders per hour. On a one-minute basis, the service rate would be μ = 60 customers/60 minutes = 1 customer per minute. For example, with $\mu = 1$, we can use equation (11.3) to compute probabilities such as the probability an order can be processed in $\frac{1}{2}$ minute or less, 1 minute or less, and 2 minutes or less. These computations are

$$P(\text{service time} \leq 0.5\,\text{min.}) = 1 - e^{-1(0.5)} = 1 - 0.6065 = 0.3935$$
$$P(\text{service time} \leq 1.0\,\text{min.}) = 1 - e^{-1(1.0)} = 1 - 0.3679 = 0.6321$$
$$P(\text{service time} \leq 2.0\,\text{min.}) = 1 - e^{-1(2.0)} = 1 - 0.1353 = 0.8647$$

Thus, we would conclude that there is a 0.3935 probability that an order can be processed in $\frac{1}{2}$ minute or less, a 0.6321 probability that it can be processed in 1 minute or less, and a 0.8647 probability that it can be processed in 2 minutes or less.

In several waiting line models presented in this chapter, we assume that the probability distribution for the service time follows an exponential probability distribution. In practice, you should collect data on actual service times to determine whether the exponential probability distribution is a reasonable approximation of the service times for your application.

Queue Discipline

In describing a waiting line system, we must define the manner in which the waiting units are arranged for service. For the Burger Dome waiting line, and in general for most customer-oriented waiting lines, the units waiting for service are arranged on a **first-come, first-served** basis; this approach is referred to as an **FCFS** queue discipline. However, some situations call for different queue disciplines. For example, when people wait for an elevator, the last one on the elevator is often the first one to complete service (i.e., the first to leave the elevator). Other types of queue disciplines assign priorities to the waiting units and then serve the unit with the highest priority first. In this chapter we consider only waiting lines based on a first-come, first-served queue discipline. The Management Science in Action, The Serpentine Line and an FCFS Queue Discipline at Whole Foods Market, describes how an FCFS queue discipline is used at a supermarket.

MANAGEMENT SCIENCE IN ACTION

THE SERPENTINE LINE AND AN FCFS QUEUE DISCIPLINE AT WHOLE FOODS MARKET*

The Whole Foods Market in the Chelsea neighborhood of New York City employs a chief line director to implement a first-come, first-served (FCFS) queue discipline. Companies such as Wendy's, American Airlines, and Chemical Bank were among the first to employ serpentine lines to implement an FCFS queue discipline. Such lines are commonplace today. We see them at banks, amusement parks, and fast-food outlets. The line is called *serpentine* because of the way it winds around. When a customer gets to the front of the line, the customer then goes to the first available server. People like serpentine lines because they prevent people who join the line later from being served ahead of an earlier arrival.

As popular as serpentine lines have become, supermarkets have not employed them because of a lack of space. At the typical supermarket, a separate line forms at each checkout counter. When ready to check out, a person picks one of the checkout counters and stays in that line until receiving service. Sometimes a person joining another checkout line later will receive service first,

which tends to upset people. Manhattan's Whole Foods Market solved this problem by creating a new kind of line and employing a chief line director to direct the first person in line to the next available checkout counter.

The waiting line at the Whole Foods Market is actually three parallel lines. Customers join the shortest line and follow a rotation when they reach the front of the line. For instance, if the first customer in line 1 is sent to a checkout counter, the next customer sent to a checkout counter is the first person in line 2, then the first person in line 3, and so on. This way an FCFS queue discipline is implemented without a long, winding serpentine line.

The Whole Foods Market's customers seem to really like the system, and the line director, Bill Jones, has become something of a celebrity. Children point to him on the street and customers invite him over for dinner.

*Based on Ian Parker, "Mr. Next," *The New Yorker* (January 13, 2003).

Steady-State Operation

When the Burger Dome restaurant opens in the morning, no customers are in the restaurant. Gradually, activity builds up to a normal or steady state. The beginning or start-up period is referred to as the **transient period.** The transient period ends when the system reaches the normal or **steady-state operation.** Waiting line models describe the steady-state operating characteristics of a waiting line.

11.2   SINGLE-CHANNEL WAITING LINE MODEL WITH POISSON ARRIVALS AND EXPONENTIAL SERVICE TIMES

Waiting line models are often based on assumptions such as Poisson arrivals and exponential service times. When applying any waiting line model, data should be collected on the actual system to ensure that the assumptions of the model are reasonable.

In this section we present formulas that can be used to determine the steady-state operating characteristics for a single-channel waiting line. The formulas are applicable if the arrivals follow a Poisson probability distribution and the service times follow an exponential probability distribution. As these assumptions apply to the Burger Dome waiting line problem introduced in Section 11.1, we show how formulas can be used to determine Burger Dome's operating characteristics and thus provide management with helpful decision-making information.

The mathematical methodology used to derive the formulas for the operating characteristics of waiting lines is rather complex. However, our purpose in this chapter is not to provide the theoretical development of waiting line models, but rather to show how the formulas that have been developed can provide information about operating characteristics of the waiting line. Readers interested in the mathematical development of the formulas can consult the specialized texts listed in Appendix D at the end of the text.

Operating Characteristics

The following formulas can be used to compute the steady-state operating characteristics for a single-channel waiting line with Poisson arrivals and exponential service times, where

λ = the mean number of arrivals per time period (the arrival rate)

μ = the mean number of services per time period (the service rate)

1. The probability that no units are in the system:

Equations (11.4) through (11.10) do not provide formulas for optimal conditions. Rather, these equations provide information about the steady-state operating characteristics of a waiting line.

$$P_0 = 1 - \frac{\lambda}{\mu} \tag{11.4}$$

2. The average number of units in the waiting line:

$$L_q = \frac{\lambda^2}{\mu(\mu - \lambda)} \tag{11.5}$$

3. The average number of units in the system:

$$L = L_q + \frac{\lambda}{\mu} \tag{11.6}$$

4. The average time a unit spends in the waiting line:

$$W_q = \frac{L_q}{\lambda} \tag{11.7}$$

5. The average time a unit spends in the system:

$$W = W_q + \frac{1}{\mu} \tag{11.8}$$

6. The probability that an arriving unit has to wait for service:

$$P_w = \frac{\lambda}{\mu} \tag{11.9}$$

7. The probability of n units in the system:

$$P_n = \left(\frac{\lambda}{\mu}\right)^n P_0 \tag{11.10}$$

The values of the arrival rate λ and the service rate μ are clearly important components in determining the operating characteristics. Equation (11.9) shows that the ratio of the arrival rate to the service rate, λ/μ, provides the probability that an arriving unit has to wait because the service facility is in use. Hence, λ/μ is referred to as the *utilization factor* for the service facility.

The operating characteristics presented in equations (11.4) through (11.10) are applicable only when the service rate μ is *greater than* the arrival rate λ—in other words, when $\lambda/\mu < 1$. If this condition does not exist, the waiting line will continue to grow without limit because the service facility does not have sufficient capacity to handle the arriving units. Thus, in using equations (11.4) through (11.10), we must have $\mu > \lambda$.

Operating Characteristics for the Burger Dome Problem

Recall that for the Burger Dome problem we had an arrival rate of $\lambda = 0.75$ customers per minute and a service rate of $\mu = 1$ customer per minute. Thus, with $\mu > \lambda$, equations (11.4) through (11.10) can be used to provide operating characteristics for the Burger Dome single-channel waiting line:

$$P_0 = 1 - \frac{\lambda}{\mu} = 1 - \frac{0.75}{1} = 0.25$$

$$L_q = \frac{\lambda^2}{\mu(\mu - \lambda)} = \frac{0.75^2}{1(1 - 0.75)} = 2.25 \text{ customers}$$

$$L = L_q + \frac{\lambda}{\mu} = 2.25 + \frac{0.75}{1} = 3 \text{ customers}$$

$$W_q = \frac{L_q}{\lambda} = \frac{2.25}{0.75} = 3 \text{ minutes}$$

$$W = W_q + \frac{1}{\mu} = 3 + \frac{1}{1} = 4 \text{ minutes} \quad \text{Is this}$$

$$P_w = \frac{\lambda}{\mu} = \frac{0.75}{1} = 0.75$$

TABLE 11.2   THE PROBABILITY OF n CUSTOMERS IN THE SYSTEM FOR THE BURGER
DOME WAITING LINE PROBLEM

Number of Customers	Probability
0	0.2500
1	0.1875
2	0.1406
3	0.1055
4	0.0791
5	0.0593
6	0.0445
7 or more	0.1335

*Problem 5 asks you to
compute the operating
characteristics for a single-
channel waiting line
application.*

Equation (11.10) can be used to determine the probability of any number of customers in
the system. Applying it provides the probability information in Table 11.2.

Managers' Use of Waiting Line Models

The results of the single-channel waiting line for Burger Dome show several important
things about the operation of the waiting line. In particular, customers wait an average of
three minutes before beginning to place an order, which appears somewhat long for a business based on fast service. In addition, the facts that the average number of customers waiting in line is 2.25 and that 75% of the arriving customers have to wait for service are
indicators that something should be done to improve the waiting line operation. Table 11.2
shows a 0.1335 probability that seven or more customers are in the Burger Dome system at
one time. This condition indicates a fairly high probability that Burger Dome will experience some long waiting lines if it continues to use the single-channel operation.

   If the operating characteristics are unsatisfactory in terms of meeting company standards for service, Burger Dome's management should consider alternative designs or plans
for improving the waiting line operation.

Improving the Waiting Line Operation

Waiting line models often indicate when improvements in operating characteristics are desirable. However, the decision of how to modify the waiting line configuration to improve
the operating characteristics must be based on the insights and creativity of the analyst.

   After reviewing the operating characteristics provided by the waiting line model,
Burger Dome's management concluded that improvements designed to reduce waiting
times are desirable. To make improvements in the waiting line operation, analysts often
focus on ways to improve the service rate. Generally, service rate improvements are
obtained by making either or both of the following changes:

1.   Increase the service rate by making a creative design change or by using new
     technology.
2.   Add one or more service channels so that more customers can be served simultaneously.

   Assume that in considering alternative 1, Burger Dome's management decides to employ
an order filler who will assist the order taker at the cash register. The customer begins the
service process by placing the order with the order taker. As the order is placed, the order
taker announces the order over an intercom system, and the order filler begins filling the

TABLE 11.3   OPERATING CHARACTERISTICS FOR THE BURGER DOME SYSTEM
WITH THE SERVICE RATE INCREASED TO $\mu = 1.25$ CUSTOMERS
PER MINUTE

Probability of no customers in the system	0.400
Average number of customers in the waiting line	0.900
Average number of customers in the system	1.500
Average time in the waiting line	1.200 minutes
Average time in the system	2.000 minutes
Probability that an arriving customer has to wait	0.600
Probability that seven or more customers are in the system	0.028

order. When the order is completed, the order taker handles the money, while the order filler continues to fill the order. With this design, Burger Dome's management estimates the service rate can be increased from the current 60 customers per hour to 75 customers per hour. Thus, the service rate for the revised system is $\mu = 75$ customers/60 minutes = 1.25 customers per minute. For $\lambda = 0.75$ customers per minute and $\mu = 1.25$ customers per minute, equations (11.4) through (11.10) can be used to provide the new operating characteristics for the Burger Dome waiting line. These operating characteristics are summarized in Table 11.3.

Problem 11 asks you to determine whether a change in the service rate will meet the company's service guideline for its customers.
The information in Table 11.3 indicates that all operating characteristics have improved because of the increased service rate. In particular, the average time a customer spends in the waiting line has been reduced from 3 to 1.2 minutes and the average time a customer spends in the system has been reduced from 4 to 2 minutes. Are any other alternatives available that Burger Dome can use to increase the service rate? If so, and if the mean service rate μ can be identified for each alternative, equations (11.4) through (11.10) can be used to determine the revised operating characteristics and any improvements in the waiting line system. The added cost of any proposed change can be compared to the corresponding service improvements to help the manager determine whether the proposed service improvements are worthwhile.

As mentioned previously, another option often available is to add one or more service channels so that more customers can be served simultaneously. The extension of the single-channel waiting line model to the multiple-channel waiting line model is the topic of the next section.

Excel Solution of Waiting Line Model

Waiting line models are easily implemented with the aid of worksheets. The Excel worksheet for the Burger Dome single-channel waiting line is shown in Figure 11.2. The formula worksheet is in the background; the value worksheet is in the foreground. The arrival rate and the service rate are entered in cells B7 and B8. The formulas for the waiting line's operating characteristics are placed in cells C13 to C18. The worksheet shows the same values for the operating characteristics that we obtained earlier. Modifications in the waiting line design can be evaluated by entering different arrival rates and/or service rates into cells B7 and B8. The new operating characteristics of the waiting line will be shown immediately.

The Excel worksheet in Figure 11.2 is a template that can be used with any single-channel waiting line model with Poisson arrivals and exponential service times. This worksheet and similar Excel worksheets for the other waiting line models presented in this chapter are available at the website that accompanies this text.

FIGURE 11.2 WORKSHEET FOR THE BURGER DOME SINGLE-CHANNEL WAITING LINE

	A	B	C	D
1	**Single-Channel Waiting Line Model**			
2				
3	**Assumptions**			
4	**Poisson Arrivals**			
5	**Exponential Service Times**			
6				
7	Arrival Rate	0.75		
8	Service Rate	1		
9				
10				
11	**Operating Characteristics**			
12				
13	Probability that no customers are in the system, Po		=1-B7/B8	
14	Average number of customers in the waiting line, Lq		=B7^2/(B8*(B8-B7))	
15	Average number of customers in the system, L		=C14+B7/B8	
16	Average time a customer spends in the waiting line, Wq		=C14/B7	
17	Average time a customer spends in the system, W		=C16+1/B8	
18	Probability an arriving customer has to wait, Pw		=B7/B8	

	A	B	C
1	**Single-Channel Waiting Line Model**		
2			
3	**Assumptions**		
4	**Poisson Arrivals**		
5	**Exponential Service Times**		
6			
7	Arrival Rate	0.75	
8	Service Rate	1	
9			
10			
11	**Operating Characteristics**		
12			
13	Probability that no customers are in the system, Po		0.2500
14	Average number of customers in the waiting line, Lq		2.2500
15	Average number of customers in the system, L		3.0000
16	Average time a customer spends in the waiting line, Wq		3.0000
17	Average time a customer spends in the system, W		4.0000
18	Probability an arriving customer has to wait, Pw		0.7500

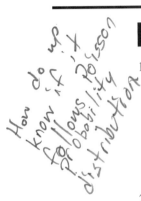

WEB file

Single

NOTES AND COMMENTS

1. The assumption that arrivals follow a Poisson probability distribution is equivalent to the assumption that the time between arrivals has an exponential probability distribution. For example, if the arrivals for a waiting line follow a Poisson probability distribution with a mean of 20 arrivals per hour, the time between arrivals will follow an exponential probability distribution, with a mean time between arrivals of $\frac{1}{20}$, or 0.05, hour.

2. Many individuals believe that whenever the service rate μ is greater than the arrival rate λ, the system should be able to handle or serve all arrivals. However, as the Burger Dome example shows, the variability of arrival times and service times may result in long waiting times even when the service rate exceeds the arrival rate. A contribution of waiting line models is that they can point out undesirable waiting line operating characteristics even when the $\mu > \lambda$ condition appears satisfactory.

11.3 MULTIPLE-CHANNEL WAITING LINE MODEL WITH POISSON ARRIVALS AND EXPONENTIAL SERVICE TIMES

You may be familiar with multiple-channel systems that also have multiple waiting lines. The waiting line model in this section has multiple channels but only a single waiting line. Operating characteristics for a multiple-channel system are better when a single waiting line, rather than multiple waiting lines, is used.

A **multiple-channel waiting line** consists of two or more service channels that are assumed to be identical in terms of service capability. In the multiple-channel system, arriving units wait in a single waiting line and then move to the first available channel to be served. The single-channel Burger Dome operation can be expanded to a two-channel system by opening a second service channel. Figure 11.3 shows a diagram of the Burger Dome two-channel waiting line.

In this section we present formulas that can be used to determine the steady-state operating characteristics for a multiple-channel waiting line. These formulas are applicable if the following conditions exist:

1. The arrivals follow a Poisson probability distribution.
2. The service time for each channel follows an exponential probability distribution.

FIGURE 11.3   THE BURGER DOME TWO-CHANNEL WAITING LINE

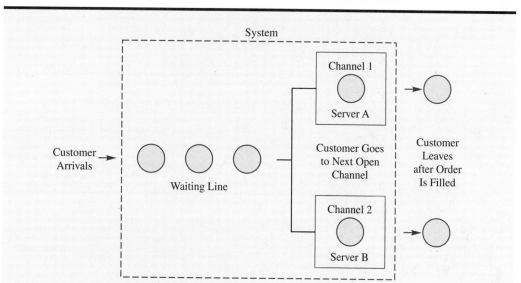

3. The service rate μ is the same for each channel.
4. The arrivals wait in a single waiting line and then move to the first open channel for service.

Operating Characteristics

The following formulas can be used to compute the steady-state operating characteristics for multiple-channel waiting lines, where

$$\lambda = \text{the arrival rate for the system}$$
$$\mu = \text{the service rate for } each \text{ channel}$$
$$k = \text{the number of channels}$$

1. The probability that no units are in the system:

$$P_0 = \frac{1}{\displaystyle\sum_{n=0}^{k-1} \frac{(\lambda/\mu)^n}{n!} + \frac{(\lambda/\mu)^k}{k!}\left(\frac{k\mu}{k\mu - \lambda}\right)} \tag{11.11}$$

2. The average number of units in the waiting line:

$$L_q = \frac{(\lambda/\mu)^k \lambda\mu}{(k-1)!(k\mu - \lambda)^2} P_0 \tag{11.12}$$

3. The average number of units in the system:

$$L = L_q + \frac{\lambda}{\mu} \qquad (11.13)$$

4. The average time a unit spends in the waiting line:

$$W_q = \frac{L_q}{\lambda} \qquad (11.14)$$

5. The average time a unit spends in the system:

$$W = W_q + \frac{1}{\mu} \qquad (11.15)$$

6. The probability that an arriving unit has to wait for service:

$$P_w = \frac{1}{k!} \left(\frac{\lambda}{\mu} \right)^k \left(\frac{k\mu}{k\mu - \lambda} \right) P_0 \qquad (11.16)$$

7. The probability of n units in the system:

$$P_n = \frac{(\lambda/\mu)^n}{n!} P_0 \quad \text{for } n \leq k \qquad (11.17)$$

$$P_n = \frac{(\lambda/\mu)^n}{k! k^{(n-k)}} P_0 \quad \text{for } n > k \qquad (11.18)$$

Because μ is the service rate for each channel, $k\mu$ is the service rate for the multiple-channel system. As was true for the single-channel waiting line model, the formulas for the operating characteristics of multiple-channel waiting lines can be applied only in situations where the service rate for the system is greater than the arrival rate for the system; in other words, the formulas are applicable only if $k\mu$ is greater than λ.

Some expressions for the operating characteristics of multiple-channel waiting lines are more complex than their single-channel counterparts. However, equations (11.11) through (11.18) provide the same information as provided by the single-channel model. To help simplify the use of the multiple-channel equations, Table 11.4 contains values of P_0 for selected values of λ/μ and k. The values provided in the table correspond to cases where $k\mu > \lambda$, and hence the service rate is sufficient to process all arrivals.

TABLE 11.4   VALUES OF P_0 FOR MULTIPLE-CHANNEL WAITING LINES WITH
POISSON ARRIVALS AND EXPONENTIAL SERVICE TIMES

	Number of Channels (k)			
Ratio λ/μ	2	3	4	5
0.15	0.8605	0.8607	0.8607	0.8607
0.20	0.8182	0.8187	0.8187	0.8187
0.25	0.7778	0.7788	0.7788	0.7788
0.30	0.7391	0.7407	0.7408	0.7408
0.35	0.7021	0.7046	0.7047	0.7047
0.40	0.6667	0.6701	0.6703	0.6703
0.45	0.6327	0.6373	0.6376	0.6376
0.50	0.6000	0.6061	0.6065	0.6065
0.55	0.5686	0.5763	0.5769	0.5769
0.60	0.5385	0.5479	0.5487	0.5488
0.65	0.5094	0.5209	0.5219	0.5220
0.70	0.4815	0.4952	0.4965	0.4966
0.75	0.4545	0.4706	0.4722	0.4724
0.80	0.4286	0.4472	0.4491	0.4493
0.85	0.4035	0.4248	0.4271	0.4274
0.90	0.3793	0.4035	0.4062	0.4065
0.95	0.3559	0.3831	0.3863	0.3867
1.00	0.3333	0.3636	0.3673	0.3678
1.20	0.2500	0.2941	0.3002	0.3011
1.40	0.1765	0.2360	0.2449	0.2463
1.60	0.1111	0.1872	0.1993	0.2014
1.80	0.0526	0.1460	0.1616	0.1646
2.00		0.1111	0.1304	0.1343
2.20		0.0815	0.1046	0.1094
2.40		0.0562	0.0831	0.0889
2.60		0.0345	0.0651	0.0721
2.80		0.0160	0.0521	0.0581
3.00			0.0377	0.0466
3.20			0.0273	0.0372
3.40			0.0186	0.0293
3.60			0.0113	0.0228
3.80			0.0051	0.0174
4.00				0.0130
4.20				0.0093
4.40				0.0063
4.60				0.0038
4.80				0.0017

Operating Characteristics for the Burger Dome Problem

To illustrate the multiple-channel waiting line model, we return to the Burger Dome fast-food restaurant waiting line problem. Suppose that management wants to evaluate the desirability of opening a second order-processing station so that two customers can be served simultaneously. Assume a single waiting line with the first customer in line moving to the first available server. Let us evaluate the operating characteristics for this two-channel system.

We use equations (11.12) through (11.18) for the $k = 2$ channel system. For an arrival rate of $\lambda = 0.75$ customers per minute and a service rate of $\mu = 1$ customer per minute for each channel, we obtain the operating characteristics:

WEB file

Multiple

$$P_0 = 0.4545 \quad \text{(from Table 11.4 with } \lambda/\mu = 0.75)$$

$$L_q = \frac{(0.75/1)^2(0.75)(1)}{(2 - 1)![2(1) - 0.75]^2}(0.4545) = 0.1227 \text{ customer}$$

$$L = L_q + \frac{\lambda}{\mu} = 0.1227 + \frac{0.75}{1} = 0.8727 \text{ customer}$$

$$W_q = \frac{L_q}{\lambda} = \frac{0.1227}{0.75} = 0.1636 \text{ minute}$$

$$W = W_q + \frac{1}{\mu} = 0.1636 + \frac{1}{2} = 1.1636 \text{ minutes}$$

$$P_w = \frac{1}{2!}\left(\frac{0.75}{1}\right)^2\left[\frac{2(1)}{2(1) - 0.75}\right](0.4545) = 0.2045$$

Try Problem 18 for practice in determining the operating characteristics for a two-channel waiting line.

Using equations (11.17) and (11.18), we can compute the probabilities of n customers in the system. The results from these computations are summarized in Table 11.5.

We can now compare the steady-state operating characteristics of the two-channel system to the operating characteristics of the original single-channel system discussed in Section 11.2.

1. The average time a customer spends in the system (waiting time plus service time) is reduced from $W = 4$ minutes to $W = 1.1636$ minutes.
2. The average number of customers in the waiting line is reduced from $L_q = 2.25$ customers to $L_q = 0.1227$ customer.
3. The average time a customer spends in the waiting line is reduced from $W_q = 3$ minutes to $W_q = 0.1636$ minute.
4. The probability that a customer has to wait for service is reduced from $P_w = 0.75$ to $P_w = 0.2045$.

Clearly the two-channel system will significantly improve the operating characteristics of the waiting line. However, adding an order filler at each service station would further increase the service rate and improve the operating characteristics. The final decision regarding the staffing policy at Burger Dome rests with the Burger Dome management. The waiting line study simply provides the operating characteristics that can be anticipated

TABLE 11.5   THE PROBABILITY OF n CUSTOMERS IN THE SYSTEM FOR THE BURGER DOME TWO-CHANNEL WAITING LINE

Number of Customers	Probability
0	0.4545
1	0.3409
2	0.1278
3	0.0479
4	0.0180
5 or more	0.0109

under three configurations: a single-channel system with one employee, a single-channel system with two employees, and a two-channel system with an employee for each channel. After considering these results, what action would you recommend? In this case, Burger Dome adopted the following policy statement: For periods when customer arrivals are expected to average 45 customers per hour, Burger Dome will open two order-processing channels with one employee assigned to each.

By changing the arrival rate λ to reflect arrival rates at different times of the day, and then computing the operating characteristics, Burger Dome's management can establish guidelines and policies that tell the store managers when to schedule service operations with a single channel, two channels, or perhaps even three or more channels.

NOTES AND COMMENTS

The multiple-channel waiting line model is based on a single waiting line. You may have also encountered situations where each of the k channels has its own waiting line. Analysts have shown that the operating characteristics of multiple-channel systems are better if a single waiting line is used.

People like them better also; no one who comes in after you can be served ahead of you. Thus, when possible, banks, airline reservation counters, food-service establishments, and other businesses use a single waiting line for a multiple-channel system.

11.4 SOME GENERAL RELATIONSHIPS FOR WAITING LINE MODELS

In Sections 11.2 and 11.3 we presented formulas for computing the operating characteristics for single-channel and multiple-channel waiting lines with Poisson arrivals and exponential service times. The operating characteristics of interest included

$$
\begin{aligned}
L_q &= \text{the average number of units in the waiting line} \\
L &= \text{the average number of units in the system} \\
W_q &= \text{the average time a unit spends in the waiting line} \\
W &= \text{the average time a unit spends in the system}
\end{aligned}
$$

John D. C. Little showed that several relationships exist among these four characteristics and that these relationships apply to a variety of different waiting line systems. Two of the relationships, referred to as *Little's flow equations*, are

$$L = \lambda W \tag{11.19}$$
$$L_q = \lambda W_q \tag{11.20}$$

Equation (11.19) shows that the average number of units in the system, L, can be found by multiplying the arrival rate, λ, by the average time a unit spends in the system, W. Equation (11.20) shows that the same relationship holds between the average number of units in the waiting line, L_q, and the average time a unit spends in the waiting line, W_q.

Using equation (11.20) and solving for W_q, we obtain

$$W_q = \frac{L_q}{\lambda} \tag{11.21}$$

Equation (11.21) follows directly from Little's second flow equation. We used it for the single-channel waiting line model in Section 11.2 and the multiple-channel waiting line model in Section 11.3 [see equations (11.7) and (11.14)]. Once L_q is computed for either of these models, equation (11.21) can then be used to compute W_q.

Another general expression that applies to waiting line models is that the average time in the system, W, is equal to the average time in the waiting line, W_q, plus the average service time. For a system with a service rate μ, the mean service time is $1/\mu$. Thus, we have the general relationship

$$W = W_q + \frac{1}{\mu} \tag{11.22}$$

The advantage of Little's flow equations is that they show how operating characteristics L, L_q, W, and W_q are related in any waiting line system. Arrivals and service times do not have to follow specific probability distributions for the flow equations to be applicable.

Recall that we used equation (11.22) to provide the average time in the system for both the single- and multiple-channel waiting line models [see equations (11.8) and (11.15)].

The importance of Little's flow equations is that they apply to *any waiting line model* regardless of whether arrivals follow the Poisson probability distribution and regardless of whether service times follow the exponential probability distribution. For example, in a study of the grocery checkout counters at Murphy's Foodliner, an analyst concluded that arrivals follow the Poisson probability distribution with an arrival rate of 24 customers per hour or $\lambda = 24/60 = 0.40$ customers per minute. However, the analyst found that service times follow a normal probability distribution rather than an exponential probability distribution. The service rate was found to be 30 customers per hour, or $\mu = 30/60 = 0.50$ customers per minute. A time study of actual customer waiting times showed that, on average, a customer spends 4.5 minutes in the system (waiting time plus checkout time); that is, $W = 4.5$. Using the waiting line relationships discussed in this section, we can now compute other operating characteristics for this waiting line.

First, using equation (11.22) and solving for W_q, we have

$$W_q = W - \frac{1}{\mu} = 4.5 - \frac{1}{0.50} = 2.5 \text{ minutes}$$

With both W and W_q known, we can use Little's flow equations, (11.19) and (11.20), to compute

$$L = \lambda W = 0.40(4.5) = 1.8 \text{ customers}$$
$$L_q = \lambda W_q = 0.40(2.5) = 1 \text{ customer}$$

The application of Little's flow equations is demonstrated in Problem 25.

The manager of Murphy's Foodliner can now review these operating characteristics to see whether action should be taken to improve the service and to reduce the waiting time and the length of the waiting line.

NOTES AND COMMENTS

In waiting line systems where the length of the waiting line is limited (e.g., a small waiting area), some arriving units will be blocked from joining the waiting line and will be lost. In this case, the blocked or lost arrivals will make the mean number of units entering the system something less than the arrival rate. By defining λ as the mean number of units *joining the system*, rather than the arrival rate, the relationships discussed in this section can be used to determine W, L, W_q, and L_q.

11.5   ECONOMIC ANALYSIS OF WAITING LINES

Frequently, decisions involving the design of waiting lines will be based on a subjective evaluation of the operating characteristics of the waiting line. For example, a manager may decide that an average waiting time of one minute or less and an average of two customers or fewer in the system are reasonable goals. The waiting line models presented in the preceding sections can be used to determine the number of channels that will meet the manager's waiting line performance goals.

On the other hand, a manager may want to identify the cost of operating the waiting line system and then base the decision regarding system design on a minimum hourly or daily operating cost. Before an economic analysis of a waiting line can be conducted, a total cost model, which includes the cost of waiting and the cost of service, must be developed.

To develop a total cost model for a waiting line, we begin by defining the notation to be used:

Waiting cost is based on average number of units in the system. It includes the time spent waiting in line plus the time spent being served.

$$c_w = \text{the waiting cost per time period for each unit}$$
$$L = \text{the average number of units in the system}$$
$$c_s = \text{the service cost per time period for each channel}$$
$$k = \text{the number of channels}$$
$$TC = \text{the total cost per time period}$$

The total cost is the sum of the waiting cost and the service cost; that is,

$$TC = c_w L + c_s k \tag{11.23}$$

Adding more channels always improves the operating characteristics of the waiting line and reduces the waiting cost. However, additional channels increase the service cost. An economic analysis of waiting lines attempts to find the number of channels that will minimize total cost by balancing the waiting cost and the service cost.

To conduct an economic analysis of a waiting line, we must obtain reasonable estimates of the waiting cost and the service cost. Of these two costs, the waiting cost is usually the more difficult to evaluate. In the Burger Dome restaurant problem, the waiting cost would be the cost per minute for a customer waiting for service. This cost is not a direct cost to Burger Dome. However, if Burger Dome ignores this cost and allows long waiting lines, customers ultimately will take their business elsewhere. Thus, Burger Dome will experience lost sales and, in effect, incur a cost.

The service cost is generally easier to determine. This cost is the relevant cost associated with operating each service channel. In the Burger Dome problem, this cost would include the server's wages, benefits, and any other direct costs associated with operating the service channel. At Burger Dome, this cost is estimated to be $7 per hour.

To demonstrate the use of equation (11.23), we assume that Burger Dome is willing to assign a cost of $10 per hour for customer waiting time. We use the average number of units in the system, L, as computed in Sections 11.2 and 11.3 to obtain the total hourly cost for the single-channel and two-channel systems.

Single-channel system ($L = 3$ customers)

$$TC = c_w L + c_s k$$
$$= 10(3) + 7(1) = \$37.00 \text{ per hour}$$

Two-channel system ($L = 0.8727$ customer)

$$TC = c_w L + c_s k$$
$$= 10(0.8727) + 7(2) = \$22.73 \text{ per hour}$$

Thus, based on the cost data provided by Burger Dome, the two-channel system provides the most economical operation.

FIGURE 11.4   THE GENERAL SHAPE OF WAITING COST, SERVICE COST, AND TOTAL COST CURVES IN WAITING LINE MODELS

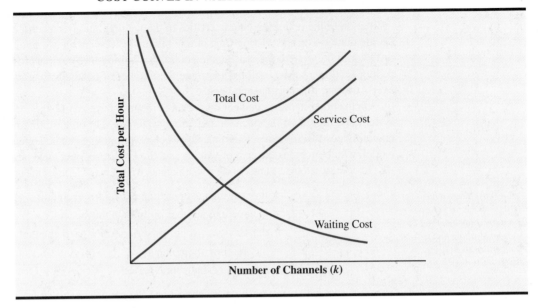

Problem 21 tests your ability to conduct an economic analysis of proposed single-channel and two-channel waiting line systems.

Figure 11.4 shows the general shape of the cost curves in the economic analysis of waiting lines. The service cost increases as the number of channels is increased. However, with more channels, the service is better. As a result, waiting time and cost decrease as the number of channels is increased. The number of channels that will provide a good approximation of the minimum total cost design can be found by evaluating the total cost for several design alternatives.

NOTES AND COMMENTS

1. In dealing with government agencies and utility companies, customers may not be able to take their business elsewhere. In these situations, no lost business occurs when long waiting times are encountered. This condition is one reason that service in such organizations may be poor and that customers in such situations may experience long waiting times.

2. In some instances, the organization providing the service also employs the units waiting for the service. For example, consider the case of a com-pany that owns and operates the trucks used to deliver goods to and from its manufacturing plant. In addition to the costs associated with the trucks waiting to be loaded or unloaded, the firm also pays the wages of the truck loaders and un-loaders who operate the service channel. In this case, the cost of having the trucks wait and the cost of operating the service channel are direct expenses to the firm. An economic analysis of the waiting line system is highly recommended for these types of situations.

11.6   OTHER WAITING LINE MODELS

D. G. Kendall suggested a notation that is helpful in classifying the wide variety of different waiting line models that have been developed. The three-symbol Kendall notation is as follows:

$$A/B/k$$

where

A   denotes the probability distribution for the arrivals

B   denotes the probability distribution for the service time

k   denotes the number of channels

Depending on the letter appearing in the *A* or *B* position, a variety of waiting line systems can be described. The letters that are commonly used are as follows:

M   designates a Poisson probability distribution for the arrivals or an exponential probability distribution for service time

D   designates that the arrivals or the service time is deterministic or constant

G   designates that the arrivals or the service time has a general probability distribution with a known mean and variance

Using the Kendall notation, the single-channel waiting line model with Poisson arrivals and exponential service times is classified as an *M/M/*1 model. The two-channel waiting line model with Poisson arrivals and exponential service times presented in Section 11.3 would be classified as an *M/M/*2 model.

NOTES AND COMMENTS

In some cases, the Kendall notation is extended to five symbols. The fourth symbol indicates the largest number of units that can be in the system, and the fifth symbol indicates the size of the population. The fourth symbol is used in situations where the waiting line can hold a finite or maximum number of units, and the fifth symbol is necessary when the population of arriving units or customers is finite. When the fourth and fifth symbols of the Kendall notation are omitted, the waiting line system is assumed to have infinite capacity, and the population is assumed to be infinite.

11.7   SINGLE-CHANNEL WAITING LINE MODEL WITH POISSON ARRIVALS AND ARBITRARY SERVICE TIMES

When providing input to the M/G/1 model, be consistent in terms of the time period. For example, if λ and μ are expressed in terms of the number of units per hour, the standard deviation of the service time should be expressed in hours. The example that follows uses minutes as the time period for the arrival and service data.

Let us return to the single-channel waiting line model where arrivals are described by a Poisson probability distribution. However, we now assume that the probability distribution for the service times is not an exponential probability distribution. Thus, using the Kendall notation, the waiting line model that is appropriate is an *M/G/*1 model, where *G* denotes a general or unspecified probability distribution.

Operating Characteristics for the *M/G/*1 Model

The notation used to describe the operating characteristics for the *M/G/*1 model is

λ = the arrival rate

μ = the service rate

σ = the standard deviation of the service time

Some of the steady-state operating characteristics of the *M/G/*1 waiting line model are as follows:

1. The probability that no units are in the system:

$$P_0 = 1 - \frac{\lambda}{\mu} \qquad (11.24)$$

2. The average number of units in the waiting line:

$$L_q = \frac{\lambda^2 \sigma^2 + (\lambda/\mu)^2}{2(1 - \lambda/\mu)} \qquad (11.25)$$

3. The average number of units in the system:

$$L = L_q + \frac{\lambda}{\mu} \qquad (11.26)$$

4. The average time a unit spends in the waiting line:

$$W_q = \frac{L_q}{\lambda} \qquad (11.27)$$

5. The average time a unit spends in the system:

$$W = W_q + \frac{1}{\mu} \qquad (11.28)$$

6. The probability that an arriving unit has to wait for service:

$$P_w = \frac{\lambda}{\mu} \qquad (11.29)$$

Note that the relationships for L, W_q, and W are the same as the relationships used for the waiting line models in Sections 11.2 and 11.3. They are given by Little's flow equations.

Problem 27 provides another application of a single-channel waiting line with Poisson arrivals and arbitrary service times.

An Example   Retail sales at Hartlage's Seafood Supply are handled by one clerk. Customer arrivals are random, and the arrival rate is 21 customers per hour, or $\lambda = 21/60 = 0.35$ customers per minute. A study of the service process shows that the service time is 2 minutes per customer, with a standard deviation of $\sigma = 1.2$ minutes. The mean time of

2 minutes per customer shows that the clerk has a service rate of $\mu = \frac{1}{2} = 0.50$ customers per minute. The operating characteristics of this $M/G/1$ waiting line system are

WEB file

Single-Arbitrary

$$P_0 = 1 - \frac{\lambda}{\mu} = 1 - \frac{0.35}{0.50} = 0.30$$

$$L_q = \frac{(0.35)^2 (1.2)^2 + (0.35/0.50)^2}{2(1 - 0.35/0.50)} = 1.1107 \text{ customers}$$

$$L = L_q + \frac{\lambda}{\mu} = 1.1107 + \frac{0.35}{0.50} = 1.8107 \text{ customers}$$

$$W_q = \frac{L_q}{\lambda} = \frac{1.1107}{0.35} = 3.1733 \text{ minutes}$$

$$W = W_q + \frac{1}{\mu} = 3.1733 + \frac{1}{0.50} = 5.1733 \text{ minutes}$$

$$P_w = \frac{\lambda}{\mu} = \frac{0.35}{0.50} = 0.70$$

Hartlage's manager can review these operating characteristics to determine whether scheduling a second clerk appears to be worthwhile.

Constant Service Times

We want to comment briefly on the single-channel waiting line model that assumes random arrivals but constant service times. Such a waiting line can occur in production and manufacturing environments where machine-controlled service times are constant. This waiting line is described by the $M/D/1$ model, with the D referring to the deterministic service times. With the $M/D/1$ model, the average number of units in the waiting line, L_q, can be found by using equation (11.25) with the condition that the standard deviation of the constant service time is $\sigma = 0$. Thus, the expression for the average number of units in the waiting line for the $M/D/1$ waiting line becomes

$$L_q = \frac{(\lambda/\mu)^2}{2(1 - \lambda/\mu)} \tag{11.30}$$

The other expressions presented earlier in this section can be used to determine additional operating characteristics of the $M/D/1$ system.

NOTES AND COMMENTS

Whenever the operating characteristics of a waiting line are unacceptable, managers often try to improve service by increasing the service rate μ. This approach is good, but equation (11.25) shows that the variation in the service times also affects the operating characteristics of the waiting line. Because the standard deviation of service times, σ, appears in the numerator of equation (11.25), a larger variation in service times results in a larger average number of units in the waiting line. Hence, another alternative for improving the service capabilities of a waiting line is to reduce the variation in the service times. Thus, even when the service rate of the service facility cannot be increased, a reduction in σ will reduce the average number of units in the waiting line and improve the operating characteristics of the system.

11.8   MULTIPLE-CHANNEL MODEL WITH POISSON ARRIVALS, ARBITRARY SERVICE TIMES, AND NO WAITING LINE

An interesting variation of the waiting line models discussed so far involves a system in which no waiting is allowed. Arriving units or customers seek service from one of several service channels. If all channels are busy, arriving units are denied access to the system. In waiting line terminology, arrivals occurring when the system is full are **blocked** and are cleared from the system. Such customers may be lost or may attempt a return to the system later.

The specific model considered in this section is based on the following assumptions:

1. The system has k channels.
2. The arrivals follow a Poisson probability distribution, with arrival rate λ.
3. The service times for each channel may have any probability distribution.
4. The service rate μ is the same for each channel.
5. An arrival enters the system only if at least one channel is available. An arrival occurring when all channels are busy is blocked—that is, denied service and not allowed to enter the system.

With G denoting a general or unspecified probability distribution for service times, the appropriate model for this situation is referred to as an *M/G/k* model with "blocked customers cleared." The question addressed in this type of situation is, How many channels or servers should be used?

A primary application of this model involves the design of telephone and other communication systems where the arrivals are the calls and the channels are the number of telephone or communication lines available. In such a system, the calls are made to one telephone number, with each call automatically switched to an open channel if possible. When all channels are busy, additional calls receive a busy signal and are denied access to the system.

Operating Characteristics for the *M/G/k* Model with Blocked Customers Cleared

We approach the problem of selecting the best number of channels by computing the steady-state probabilities that j of the k channels will be busy. These probabilities are

$$P_j = \frac{(\lambda/\mu)^j/j!}{\displaystyle\sum_{i=0}^{k}(\lambda/\mu)^i/i!} \tag{11.31}$$

With no waiting allowed, operating characteristics L_q and W_q considered in previous waiting line models are automatically zero regardless of the number of service channels. In this situation, the more important design consideration involves determining how the percentage of blocked customers is affected by the number of service channels

where

λ = the arrival rate
μ = the service rate for each channel
k = the number of channels
P_j = the probability that j of the k channels are busy
    for $j = 0, 1, 2, \dots, k$

The most important probability value is P_k, which is the probability that all k channels are busy. On a percentage basis, P_k indicates the percentage of arrivals that are blocked and denied access to the system.

Another operating characteristic of interest is the average number of units in the system; note that this number is equivalent to the average number of channels in use. Letting L denote the average number of units in the system, we have

$$L = \frac{\lambda}{\mu}(1 - P_k) \qquad (11.32)$$

An Example   Microdata Software, Inc., uses a telephone ordering system for its computer software products. Callers place orders with Microdata by using the company's 800 telephone number. Assume that calls to this telephone number arrive at a rate of $\lambda = 12$ calls per hour. The time required to process a telephone order varies considerably from order to order. However, each Microdata sales representative can be expected to handle $\mu = 6$ calls per hour. Currently, the Microdata 800 telephone number has three internal lines, or channels, each operated by a separate sales representative. Calls received on the 800 number are automatically transferred to an open line, or channel, if available.

Whenever all three lines are busy, callers receive a busy signal. In the past, Microdata's management assumed that callers receiving a busy signal would call back later. However, recent research on telephone ordering showed that a substantial number of callers who are denied access do not call back later. These lost calls represent lost revenues for the firm, so Microdata's management requested an analysis of the telephone ordering system. Specifically, management wanted to know the percentage of callers who get busy signals and are blocked from the system. If management's goal is to provide sufficient capacity to handle 90% of the callers, how many telephone lines and sales representatives should Microdata use?

We can demonstrate the use of equation (11.31) by computing P_3, the probability that all three of the currently available telephone lines will be in use and additional callers will be blocked:

No Waiting

$$P_3 = \frac{(12/6)^3/3!}{(12/6)^0/0! + (12/6)^1/1! + (12/6)^2/2! + (12/6)^3/3!} = \frac{1.3333}{6.3333} = 0.2105$$

With $P_3 = 0.2105$, approximately 21% of the calls, or slightly more than one in five calls, are being blocked. Only 79% of the calls are being handled immediately by the three-line system.

Let us assume that Microdata expands to a four-line system. Then, the probability that all four channels will be in use and that callers will be blocked is

$$P_4 = \frac{(12/6)^4/4!}{(12/6)^0/0! + (12/6)^1/1! + (12/6)^2/2! + (12/6)^3/3! + (12/6)^4/4!} = \frac{0.667}{7} = 0.0952$$

Problem 30 provides practice in calculating probabilities for multiple-channel systems with no waiting line.

With only 9.52% of the callers blocked, 90.48% of the callers will reach the Microdata sales representatives. Thus, Microdata should expand its order-processing operation to four lines to meet management's goal of providing sufficient capacity to handle at least 90% of the callers. The average number of calls in the four-line system and thus the average number of lines and sales representatives that will be busy is

$$L = \frac{\lambda}{\mu}(1 - P_4) = \frac{12}{6}(1 - 0.0952) = 1.8095$$

TABLE 11.6   PROBABILITIES OF BUSY LINES FOR THE MICRODATA
FOUR-LINE SYSTEM

Number of Busy Lines	Probability
0	0.1429
1	0.2857
2	0.2857
3	0.1905
4	0.0952

Although an average of fewer than two lines will be busy, the four-line system is necessary to provide the capacity to handle at least 90% of the callers. We used equation (11.31) to calculate the probability that 0, 1, 2, 3, or 4 lines will be busy. These probabilities are summarized in Table 11.6.

As we discussed in Section 11.5, an economic analysis of waiting lines can be used to guide system design decisions. In the Microdata system, the cost of the additional line and additional sales representative should be relatively easy to establish. This cost can be balanced against the cost of the blocked calls. With 9.52% of the calls blocked and $\lambda = 12$ calls per hour, an eight-hour day will have an average of $8(12)(0.0952) = 9.1$ blocked calls. If Microdata can estimate the cost of possible lost sales, the cost of these blocked calls can be established. The economic analysis based on the service cost and the blocked-call cost can assist in determining the optimal number of lines for the system.

NOTES AND COMMENTS

Many of the operating characteristics considered in previous sections are not relevant for the $M/G/k$ model with blocked customers cleared. In particular, the average time in the waiting line, W_q, and the average number of units in the waiting line, L_q, are no longer considered because waiting is not permitted in this type of system.

11.9   WAITING LINE MODELS WITH FINITE CALLING POPULATIONS

In previous waiting line models, the arrival rate was constant and independent of the number of units in the system. With a finite calling population, the arrival rate decreases as the number of units in the system increases because, with more units in the system, fewer units are available for arrivals.

For the waiting line models introduced so far, the population of units or customers arriving for service has been considered to be unlimited. In technical terms, when no limit is placed on how many units may seek service, the model is said to have an **infinite calling population.** Under this assumption, the arrival rate λ remains constant regardless of how many units are in the waiting line system. This assumption of an infinite calling population is made in most waiting line models.

In other cases, the maximum number of units or customers that may seek service is assumed to be finite. In this situation, the arrival rate for the system changes, depending on the number of units in the waiting line, and the waiting line model is said to have a **finite calling population.** The formulas for the operating characteristics of the previous waiting line models must be modified to account for the effect of the finite calling population.

The finite calling population model discussed in this section is based on the following assumptions:

1. The arrivals for *each unit* follow a Poisson probability distribution, with arrival rate λ.
2. The service times follow an exponential probability distribution, with service rate μ.
3. The population of units that may seek service is finite.

The arrival rate λ is defined differently for the finite calling population model. Specifically, λ is defined in terms of the arrival rate for each unit.

With a single channel, the waiting line model is referred to as an *M/M/1* model with a finite calling population.

The arrival rate for the *M/M/1* model with a finite calling population is defined in terms of how often *each unit* arrives or seeks service. This situation differs from that for previous waiting line models in which λ denoted the arrival rate for the system. With a finite calling population, the arrival rate for the system varies, depending on the number of units in the system. Instead of adjusting for the changing system arrival rate, in the finite calling population model λ indicates the arrival rate for each unit.

Operating Characteristics for the *M/M/1* Model with a Finite Calling Population

The following formulas are used to determine the steady-state operating characteristics for an *M/M/1* model with a finite calling population, where

$$\lambda = \text{the arrival rate for each unit}$$
$$\mu = \text{the service rate}$$
$$N = \text{the size of the population}$$

1. The probability that no units are in the system:

$$P_0 = \frac{1}{\displaystyle\sum_{n=0}^{N} \frac{N!}{(N-n)!}\left(\frac{\lambda}{\mu}\right)^n} \tag{11.33}$$

2. The average number of units in the waiting line:

$$L_q = N - \frac{\lambda + \mu}{\lambda}(1 - P_0) \tag{11.34}$$

3. The average number of units in the system:

$$L = L_q + (1 - P_0) \tag{11.35}$$

4. The average time a unit spends in the waiting line:

$$W_q = \frac{L_q}{(N-L)\lambda} \tag{11.36}$$

5. The average time a unit spends in the system:

$$W = W_q + \frac{1}{\mu} \tag{11.37}$$

6. The probability an arriving unit has to wait for service:

$$P_w = 1 - P_0 \tag{11.38}$$

7. The probability of n units in the system:

$$P_n = \frac{N!}{(N-n)!} \left(\frac{\lambda}{\mu} \right)^n P_0 \quad \text{for } n = 0, 1, \ldots, N \tag{11.39}$$

One of the primary applications of the $M/M/1$ model with a finite calling population is referred to as the *machine repair problem*. In this problem, a group of machines is considered to be the finite population of "customers" that may request repair service. Whenever a machine breaks down, an arrival occurs in the sense that a new repair request is initiated. If another machine breaks down before the repair work has been completed on the first machine, the second machine begins to form a "waiting line" for repair service. Additional breakdowns by other machines will add to the length of the waiting line. The assumption of first-come, first-served indicates that machines are repaired in the order they break down. The $M/M/1$ model shows that one person or one channel is available to perform the repair service. To return the machine to operation, each machine with a breakdown must be repaired by the single-channel operation.

An Example   The Kolkmeyer Manufacturing Company uses a group of six identical machines; each machine operates an average of 20 hours between breakdowns. Thus, the arrival rate or request for repair service for each machine is $\lambda = \frac{1}{20} = 0.05$ per hour. With randomly occurring breakdowns, the Poisson probability distribution is used to describe the machine breakdown arrival process. One person from the maintenance department provides the single-channel repair service for the six machines. The exponentially distributed service times have a mean of two hours per machine or a service rate of $\mu = \frac{1}{2} = 0.50$ machines per hour.

With $\lambda = 0.05$ and $\mu = 0.50$, we use equations (11.33) through (11.38) to compute the operating characteristics for this system. Note that the use of equation (11.33) makes the computations involved somewhat cumbersome. Confirm for yourself that equation (11.33) provides the value of $P_0 = 0.4845$. The computations for the other operating characteristics are

$$L_q = 6 - \left(\frac{0.05 + 0.50}{0.05} \right)(1 - 0.4845) = 0.3297 \text{ machine}$$

$$L = 0.3295 + (1 - 0.4845) = 0.8451 \text{ machine}$$

$$W_q = \frac{0.3295}{(6 - 0.845)0.50} = 1.279 \text{ hours}$$

$$W = 1.279 + \frac{1}{0.50} = 3.279 \text{ hours}$$

$$P_w = 1 - P_0 = 1 - 0.4845 = 0.5155$$

Operating characteristics of an M/M/1 waiting line with a finite calling population are considered in Problem 34.

Finally, equation (11.39) can be used to compute the probabilities of any number of machines being in the repair system.

As with other waiting line models, the operating characteristics provide the manager with information about the operation of the waiting line. In this case, the fact that a machine breakdown waits an average of $W_q = 1.279$ hours before maintenance begins and the fact that more than 50% of the machine breakdowns must wait for service, $P_w = 0.5155$, indicates a two-channel system may be needed to improve the machine repair service.

An Excel worksheet template at the course website may be used to analyze the multiple-channel finite calling population model.

Computations of the operating characteristics of a multiple-channel finite calling population waiting line are more complex than those for the single-channel model. A computer solution is virtually mandatory in this case. The Excel worksheet for the Kolkmeyer two-channel machine repair system is shown in Figure 11.5. With two repair personnel, the average machine breakdown waiting time is reduced to $W_q = 0.0834$ hours, or 5 minutes, and only 10%, $P_w = 0.1036$, of the machine breakdowns wait for service. Thus, the two-channel system significantly improves the machine repair service operation. Ultimately, by considering the cost of machine downtime and the cost of the repair personnel, management can determine whether the improved service of the two-channel system is cost-effective.

FIGURE 11.5   WORKSHEET FOR THE KOLKMEYER TWO-CHANNEL MACHINE REPAIR PROBLEM

WEB file

Finite

	A	B	C	D
1	**Waiting Line Model with a Finite Calling Population**			
2				
3	**Assumptions**			
4	**Poisson Arrivals**			
5	**Exponential Service Times**			
6	**Finite Calling Population**			
7				
8	Number of Channels	2		
9	Arrival Rate for Each Unit	0.05		
10	Service Rate for Each Channel	0.5		
11	Population Size	6		
12				
13				
14	**Operating Characteristics**			
15				
16	Probability that no machines are in the system, Po		0.5602	
17	Average number of machines in the waiting line, Lq		0.0227	
18	Average number of machines in the system, L		0.5661	
19	Average time a machine spends in the waiting line, Wq		0.0834	
20	Average time a machine spends in the system, W		2.0834	
21	Probability an arriving machine has to wait, Pw		0.1036	

SUMMARY

In this chapter we presented a variety of waiting line models that have been developed to help managers make better decisions concerning the operation of waiting lines. For each model, we presented formulas that could be used to develop operating characteristics or performance measures for the system being studied. The operating characteristics presented include the following:

1. Probability that no units are in the system
2. Average number of units in the waiting line
3. Average number of units in the system
4. Average time a unit spends in the waiting line
5. Average time a unit spends in the system
6. Probability that arriving units will have to wait for service

We also showed how an economic analysis of the waiting line could be conducted by developing a total cost model that includes the cost associated with units waiting for service and the cost required to operate the service facility.

As many of the examples in this chapter show, the most obvious applications of waiting line models are situations in which customers arrive for service such as at a grocery checkout counter, bank, or restaurant. However, with a little creativity, waiting line models can be applied to many different situations such as telephone calls waiting for connections, mail orders waiting for processing, machines waiting for repairs, manufacturing jobs waiting to be processed, and money waiting to be spent or invested. The Management Science in Action, Improving Productivity at the New Haven Fire Department, describes an application in which a waiting line model helped improve emergency medical response time and also provided a significant savings in operating costs.

The complexity and diversity of waiting line systems found in practice often prevent an analyst from finding an existing waiting line model that fits the specific application being studied. Simulation, the topic discussed in Chapter 12, provides an approach to determining the operating characteristics of such waiting line systems.

MANAGEMENT SCIENCE IN ACTION

IMPROVING PRODUCTIVITY AT THE NEW HAVEN FIRE DEPARTMENT*

The New Haven, Connecticut, Fire Department implemented a reorganization plan with cross-trained fire and medical personnel responding to both fire and medical emergencies. A waiting line model provided the basis for the reorganization by demonstrating that substantial improvements in emergency medical response time could be achieved with only a small reduction in fire protection. Annual savings were reported to be $1.4 million.

The model was based on Poisson arrivals and exponential service times for both fire and medical emergencies. It was used to estimate the average time that a person placing a call would have to wait for the appropriate emergency unit to arrive at the location. Waiting times were estimated by the model's prediction of the average travel time to reach each of the city's 28 census tracts.

The model was first applied to the original system of 16 fire units and 4 emergency medical units that operated independently. It was then applied to the proposed reorganization plan that involved cross-trained department personnel qualified to respond to both fire and medical emergencies. Results from the model demonstrated that average travel times could be reduced under the reorganization plan. Various facility location alternatives also were evaluated. When implemented, the reorganization plan reduced operating cost and improved public safety services.

*Based on A. J. Swersey, L. Goldring, and E. D. Geyer, "Improving Fire Department Productivity: Merging Fire and Emergency Medical Units in New Haven," *Interfaces* 23, no. 1 (January/February 1993): 109–129.

GLOSSARY

Queue   A waiting line.

Queueing theory   The body of knowledge dealing with waiting lines.

Operating characteristics   The performance measures for a waiting line including the probability that no units are in the system, the average number of units in the waiting line, the average waiting time, and so on.

Single-channel waiting line   A waiting line with only one service facility.

Poisson probability distribution   A probability distribution used to describe the arrival pattern for some waiting line models.

Arrival rate   The mean number of customers or units arriving in a given period of time.

Exponential probability distribution   A probability distribution used to describe the service time for some waiting line models.

Service rate   The mean number of customers or units that can be served by one service facility in a given period of time.

First-come, first-served (FCFS)   The queue discipline that serves waiting units on a first-come, first-served basis.

Transient period   The start-up period for a waiting line, occurring before the waiting line reaches a normal or steady-state operation.

Steady-state operation   The normal operation of the waiting line after it has gone through a start-up or transient period. The operating characteristics of waiting lines are computed for steady-state conditions.

Multiple-channel waiting line   A waiting line with two or more parallel service facilities.

Blocked   When arriving units cannot enter the waiting line because the system is full. Blocked units can occur when waiting lines are not allowed or when waiting lines have a finite capacity.

Infinite calling population   The population of customers or units that may seek service has no specified upper limit.

Finite calling population   The population of customers or units that may seek service has a fixed and finite value.

PROBLEMS

1. Willow Brook National Bank operates a drive-up teller window that allows customers to complete bank transactions without getting out of their cars. On weekday mornings, arrivals to the drive-up teller window occur at random, with an arrival rate of 24 customers per hour or 0.4 customer per minute.
   a. What is the mean or expected number of customers that will arrive in a five-minute period?
   b. Assume that the Poisson probability distribution can be used to describe the arrival process. Use the arrival rate in part (a) and compute the probabilities that exactly 0, 1, 2, and 3 customers will arrive during a five-minute period.
   c. Delays are expected if more than three customers arrive during any five-minute period. What is the probability that delays will occur?

2. In the Willow Brook National Bank waiting line system (see Problem 1), assume that the service times for the drive-up teller follow an~~exponential~~ probability distribution with a service rate of 36 customers per hour, or 0.6 customer per minute. Use the exponential probability distribution to answer the following questions:
   a. What is the probability the service time is one minute or less?
   b. What is the probability the service time is two minutes or less?
   c. What is the probability the service time is more than two minutes?

3. Use the single-channel drive-up bank teller operation referred to in Problems 1 and 2 to determine the following operating characteristics for the system:
   a. The probability that no customers are in the system
   b. The average number of customers waiting
   c. The average number of customers in the system
   d. The average time a customer spends waiting
   e. The average time a customer spends in the system
   f. The probability that arriving customers will have to wait for service

4. Use the single-channel drive-up bank teller operation referred to in Problems 1–3 to determine the probabilities of 0, 1, 2, and 3 customers in the system. What is the probability that more than three customers will be in the drive-up teller system at the same time?

5. The reference desk of a university library receives requests for assistance. Assume that a Poisson probability distribution with an arrival rate of 10 requests per hour can be used to describe the arrival pattern and that service times follow an exponential probability distribution with a service rate of 12 requests per hour.
   a. What is the probability that no requests for assistance are in the system?
   b. What is the average number of requests that will be waiting for service?
   c. What is the average waiting time in minutes before service begins?
   d. What is the average time at the reference desk in minutes (waiting time plus service time)?
   e. What is the probability that a new arrival has to wait for service?

6. Movies Tonight is a typical video and DVD movie rental outlet for home viewing customers. During the weeknight evenings, customers arrive at Movies Tonight with an arrival rate of 1.25 customers per minute. The checkout clerk has a service rate of 2 customers per minute. Assume Poisson arrivals and exponential service times.
   a. What is the probability that no customers are in the system?
   b. What is the average number of customers waiting for service?
   c. What is the average time a customer waits for service to begin?
   d. What is the probability that an arriving customer will have to wait for service?
   e. Do the operating characteristics indicate that the one-clerk checkout system provides an acceptable level of service?

7. Speedy Oil provides a single-channel automobile oil change and lubrication service. Customers provide an arrival rate of 2.5 cars per hour. The service rate is 5 cars per hour. Assume that arrivals follow a Poisson probability distribution and that service times follow an exponential probability distribution.
   a. What is the average number of cars in the system?
   b. What is the average time that a car waits for the oil and lubrication service to begin?
   c. What is the average time a car spends in the system?
   d. What is the probability that an arrival has to wait for service?

8. For the Burger Dome single-channel waiting line in Section 11.2, assume that the arrival rate is increased to 1 customer per minute and that the service rate is increased to 1.25 customers per minute. Compute the following operating characteristics for the new system: P_0, L_q, L, W_q, W, and P_w. Does this system provide better or poorer service compared to the original system? Discuss any differences and the reason for these differences.

9. Marty's Barber Shop has one barber. Customers have an arrival rate of 2.2 customers per hour, and haircuts are given with a service rate of 5 per hour. Use the Poisson arrivals and exponential service times model to answer the following questions:
   a. What is the probability that no units are in the system?
   b. What is the probability that one customer is receiving a haircut and no one is waiting?
   c. What is the probability that one customer is receiving a haircut and one customer is waiting?
   d. What is the probability that one customer is receiving a haircut and two customers are waiting?
   e. What is the probability that more than two customers are waiting?
   f. What is the average time a customer waits for service?

10. Trosper Tire Company decided to hire a new mechanic to handle all tire changes for customers ordering a new set of tires. Two mechanics applied for the job. One mechanic has limited experience, can be hired for $14 per hour, and can service an average of three customers per hour. The other mechanic has several years of experience, can service an average of four customers per hour, but must be paid $20 per hour. Assume that customers arrive at the Trosper garage at the rate of two customers per hour.
   a. What are the waiting line operating characteristics using each mechanic, assuming Poisson arrivals and exponential service times?
   b. If the company assigns a customer waiting cost of $30 per hour, which mechanic provides the lower operating cost?

11. Agan Interior Design provides home and office decorating assistance to its customers. In normal operation, an average of 2.5 customers arrive each hour. One design consultant is available to answer customer questions and make product recommendations. The consultant averages 10 minutes with each customer.
   a. Compute the operating characteristics of the customer waiting line, assuming Poisson arrivals and exponential service times.
   b. Service goals dictate that an arriving customer should not wait for service more than an average of 5 minutes. Is this goal being met? If not, what action do you recommend?
   c. If the consultant can reduce the average time spent per customer to 8 minutes, what is the mean service rate? Will the service goal be met?

12. Pete's Market is a small local grocery store with only one checkout counter. Assume that shoppers arrive at the checkout lane according to a Poisson probability distribution, with an arrival rate of 15 customers per hour. The checkout service times follow an exponential probability distribution, with a service rate of 20 customers per hour.
   a. Compute the operating characteristics for this waiting line.
   b. If the manager's service goal is to limit the waiting time prior to beginning the checkout process to no more than five minutes, what recommendations would you provide regarding the current checkout system?

13. After reviewing the waiting line analysis of Problem 12, the manager of Pete's Market wants to consider one of the following alternatives for improving service. What alternative would you recommend? Justify your recommendation.
   a. Hire a second person to bag the groceries while the cash register operator is entering the cost data and collecting money from the customer. With this improved single-channel operation, the service rate could be increased to 30 customers per hour.
   b. Hire a second person to operate a second checkout counter. The two-channel operation would have a service rate of 20 customers per hour for each channel.

14. Ocala Software Systems operates a technical support center for its software customers. If customers have installation or use problems with Ocala software products, they may telephone the technical support center and obtain free consultation. Currently, Ocala operates

its support center with one consultant. If the consultant is busy when a new customer call arrives, the customer hears a recorded message stating that all consultants are currently busy with other customers. The customer is then asked to hold and a consultant will provide assistance as soon as possible. The customer calls follow a Poisson probability distribution with an arrival rate of five calls per hour. On average, it takes 7.5 minutes for a consultant to answer a customer's questions. The service time follows an exponential probability distribution.

   a. What is the service rate in terms of customers per hour?

   b. What is the probability that no customers are in the system and the consultant is idle?

   c. What is the average number of customers waiting for a consultant?

   d. What is the average time a customer waits for a consultant?

   e. What is the probability that a customer will have to wait for a consultant?

   f. Ocala's customer service department recently received several letters from customers complaining about the difficulty in obtaining technical support. If Ocala's customer service guidelines state that no more than 35% of all customers should have to wait for technical support and that the average waiting time should be two minutes or less, does your waiting line analysis indicate that Ocala is or is not meeting its customer service guidelines? What action, if any, would you recommend?

15. To improve customer service, Ocala Software Systems (see Problem 14) wants to investigate the effect of using a second consultant at its technical support center. What effect would the additional consultant have on customer service? Would two technical consultants enable Ocala to meet its service guidelines with no more than 35% of all customers having to wait for technical support and an average customer waiting time of two minutes or less? Discuss.

16. The new Fore and Aft Marina is to be located on the Ohio River near Madison, Indiana. Assume that Fore and Aft decides to build a docking facility where one boat at a time can stop for gas and servicing. Assume that arrivals follow a Poisson probability distribution, with an arrival rate of 5 boats per hour, and that service times follow an exponential probability distribution, with a service rate of 10 boats per hour. Answer the following questions:

   a. What is the probability that no boats are in the system?

   b. What is the average number of boats that will be waiting for service?

   c. What is the average time a boat will spend waiting for service?

   d. What is the average time a boat will spend at the dock?

   e. If you were the manager of Fore and Aft Marina, would you be satisfied with the service level your system will be providing? Why or why not?

17. The manager of the Fore and Aft Marina in Problem 16 wants to investigate the possibility of enlarging the docking facility so that two boats can stop for gas and servicing simultaneously. Assume that the arrival rate is 5 boats per hour and that the service rate for each channel is 10 boats per hour.

   a. What is the probability that the boat dock will be idle?

   b. What is the average number of boats that will be waiting for service?

   c. What is the average time a boat will spend waiting for service?

   d. What is the average time a boat will spend at the dock?

   e. If you were the manager of Fore and Aft Marina, would you be satisfied with the service level your system will be providing? Why or why not?

18. All airplane passengers at the Lake City Regional Airport must pass through a security screening area before proceeding to the boarding area. The airport has three screening stations available, and the facility manager must decide how many to have open at any particular time. The service rate for processing passengers at each screening station is 3 passengers per minute. On Monday morning the arrival rate is 5.4 passengers per minute.

Assume that processing times at each screening station follow an exponential distribution and that arrivals follow a Poisson distribution.

a. Suppose two of the three screening stations are open on Monday morning. Compute the operating characteristics for the screening facility.

b. Because of space considerations, the facility manager's goal is to limit the average number of passengers waiting in line to 10 or fewer. Will the two-screening-station system be able to meet the manager's goal?

c. What is the average time required for a passenger to pass through security screening?

19. Refer again to the Lake City Regional Airport described in Problem 18. When the security level is raised to high, the service rate for processing passengers is reduced to 2 passengers per minute at each screening station. Suppose the security level is raised to high on Monday morning. The arrival rate is 5.4 passengers per minute.

a. The facility manager's goal is to limit the average number of passengers waiting in line to 10 or fewer. How many screening stations must be open in order to satisfy the manager's goal?

b. What is the average time required for a passenger to pass through security screening?

20. A Florida coastal community experiences a population increase during the winter months with seasonal residents arriving from northern states and Canada. Staffing at a local post office is often in a state of change due to the relatively low volume of customers in the summer months and the relatively high volume of customers in the winter months. The service rate of a postal clerk is 0.75 customer per minute. The post office counter has a maximum of three work stations. The target maximum time a customer waits in the system is five minutes.

a. For a particular Monday morning in November, the anticipated arrival rate is 1.2 customers per minute. What is the recommended staffing for this Monday morning? Show the operating characteristics of the waiting line.

b. A new population growth study suggests that over the next two years the arrival rate at the post office during the busy winter months can be expected to be 2.1 customers per minute. Use a waiting line analysis to make a recommendation to the post office manager.

21. Refer to the Agan Interior Design situation in Problem 11. Agan's management would like to evaluate two alternatives:
- Use one consultant with an average service time of 8 minutes per customer.
- Expand to two consultants, each of whom has an average service time of 10 minutes per customer.

If the consultants are paid $16 per hour and the customer waiting time is valued at $25 per hour for waiting time prior to service, should Agan expand to the two-consultant system? Explain.

22. A fast-food franchise is considering operating a drive-up window food-service operation. Assume that customer arrivals follow a Poisson probability distribution, with an arrival rate of 24 cars per hour, and that service times follow an exponential probability distribution. Arriving customers place orders at an intercom station at the back of the parking lot and then drive to the service window to pay for and receive their orders. The following three service alternatives are being considered:
- A single-channel operation in which one employee fills the order and takes the money from the customer. The average service time for this alternative is 2 minutes.
- A single-channel operation in which one employee fills the order while a second employee takes the money from the customer. The average service time for this alternative is 1.25 minutes.
- A two-channel operation with two service windows and two employees. The employee stationed at each window fills the order and takes the money from customers arriving at the window. The average service time for this alternative is 2 minutes for each channel.

Answer the following questions and recommend an alternative design for the fast-food franchise:
  a. What is the probability that no cars are in the system?
  b. What is the average number of cars waiting for service?
  c. What is the average number of cars in the system?
  d. What is the average time a car waits for service?
  e. What is the average time in the system?
  f. What is the probability that an arriving car will have to wait for service?

23. The following cost information is available for the fast-food franchise in Problem 22:
  • Customer waiting time is valued at $25 per hour to reflect the fact that waiting time is costly to the fast-food business.
  • The cost of each employee is $6.50 per hour.
  • To account for equipment and space, an additional cost of $20 per hour is attributable to each channel.

What is the lowest-cost design for the fast-food business?

24. Patients arrive at a dentist's office with an arrival rate of 2.8 patients per hour. The dentist can treat patients at a service rate of 3 patients per hour. A study of patient waiting times shows that a patient waits an average of 30 minutes before seeing the dentist.
  a. What are the arrival and service rates in terms of patients per minute?
  b. What is the average number of patients in the waiting room?
  c. If a patient arrives at 10:10 A.M., at what time is the patient expected to leave the office?

25. A study of the multiple-channel food-service operation at the Red Birds baseball park shows that the average time between the arrival of a customer at the food-service counter and his or her departure with a filled order is 10 minutes. During the game, customers arrive at the rate of four per minute. The food-service operation requires an average of 2 minutes per customer order.
  a. What is the service rate per channel in terms of customers per minute?
  b. What is the average waiting time in the line prior to placing an order?
  c. On average, how many customers are in the food-service system?

26. Manning Autos operates an automotive service counter. While completing the repair work, Manning mechanics arrive at the company's parts department counter with an arrival rate of four per hour. The parts coordinator spends an average of 6 minutes with each mechanic, discussing the parts the mechanic needs and retrieving the parts from inventory.
  a. Currently, Manning has one parts coordinator. On average, each mechanic waits 4 minutes before the parts coordinator is available to answer questions or retrieve parts from inventory. Find L_q, W, and L for this single-channel parts operation.
  b. A trial period with a second parts coordinator showed that, on average, each mechanic waited only 1 minute before a parts coordinator was available. Find L_q, W, and L for this two-channel parts operation.
  c. If the cost of each mechanic is $20 per hour and the cost of each parts coordinator is $12 per hour, is the one-channel or the two-channel system more economical?

27. Gubser Welding, Inc., operates a welding service for construction and automotive repair jobs. Assume that the arrival of jobs at the company's office can be described by a Poisson probability distribution with an arrival rate of two jobs per 8-hour day. The time required to complete the jobs follows a normal probability distribution with a mean time of 3.2 hours and a standard deviation of 2 hours. Answer the following questions, assuming that Gubser uses one welder to complete all jobs:
  a. What is the mean arrival rate in jobs per hour?
  b. What is the mean service rate in jobs per hour?
  c. What is the average number of jobs waiting for service?

d. What is the average time a job waits before the welder can begin working on it?

e. What is the average number of hours between when a job is received and when it is completed?

f. What percentage of the time is Gubser's welder busy?

28. Jobs arrive randomly at a particular assembly plant; assume that the arrival rate is five jobs per hour. Service times (in minutes per job) do not follow the exponential probability distribution. Two proposed designs for the plant's assembly operation are shown:

Design	Service Time	
	Mean	Standard Deviation
A	6.0	3.0
B	6.25	0.6

a. What is the service rate in jobs per hour for each design?

b. For the service rates in part (a), what design appears to provide the best or fastest service rate?

c. What are the standard deviations of the service times in hours?

d. Use the $M/G/1$ model to compute the operating characteristics for each design.

e. Which design provides the best operating characteristics? Why?

29. The Robotics Manufacturing Company operates an equipment repair business where emergency jobs arrive randomly at the rate of three jobs per 8-hour day. The company's repair facility is a single-channel system operated by a repair technician. The service time varies, with a mean repair time of 2 hours and a standard deviation of 1.5 hours. The company's cost of the repair operation is $28 per hour. In the economic analysis of the waiting line system, Robotics uses $35 per hour cost for customers waiting during the repair process.

a. What are the arrival rate and service rate in jobs per hour?

b. Show the operating characteristics including the total cost per hour.

c. The company is considering purchasing a computer-based equipment repair system that would enable a constant repair time of 2 hours. For practical purposes, the standard deviation is 0. Because of the computer-based system, the company's cost of the new operation would be $32 per hour. The firm's director of operations said no to the request for the new system because the hourly cost is $4 higher and the mean repair time is the same. Do you agree? What effect will the new system have on the waiting line characteristics of the repair service?

d. Does paying for the computer-based system to reduce the variation in service time make economic sense? How much will the new system save the company during a 40-hour work week?

30. A large insurance company maintains a central computing system that contains a variety of information about customer accounts. Insurance agents in a six-state area use telephone lines to access the customer information database. Currently, the company's central computer system allows three users to access the central computer simultaneously. Agents who attempt to use the system when it is full are denied access; no waiting is allowed. Management realizes that with its expanding business, more requests will be made to the central information system. Being denied access to the system is inefficient as well as annoying for agents. Access requests follow a Poisson probability distribution, with a mean of 42 calls per hour. The service rate per line is 20 calls per hour.

a. What is the probability that 0, 1, 2, and 3 access lines will be in use?

b. What is the probability that an agent will be denied access to the system?

c. What is the average number of access lines in use?

d. In planning for the future, management wants to be able to handle $\lambda = 50$ calls per hour; in addition, the probability that an agent will be denied access to the system should be no greater than the value computed in part (b). How many access lines should this system have?

31. Mid-West Publishing Company publishes college textbooks. The company operates an 800 telephone number whereby potential adopters can ask questions about forthcoming texts, request examination copies of texts, and place orders. Currently, two extension lines are used, with two representatives handling the telephone inquiries. Calls occurring when both extension lines are being used receive a busy signal; no waiting is allowed. Each representative can accommodate an average of 12 calls per hour. The arrival rate is 20 calls per hour.

a. How many extension lines should be used if the company wants to handle 90% of the calls immediately?

b. What is the average number of extension lines that will be busy if your recommendation in part (a) is used?

c. What percentage of calls receive a busy signal for the current telephone system with two extension lines?

32. City Cab, Inc., uses two dispatchers to handle requests for service and to dispatch the cabs. The telephone calls that are made to City Cab use a common telephone number. When both dispatchers are busy, the caller hears a busy signal; no waiting is allowed. Callers who receive a busy signal can call back later or call another cab service. Assume that the arrival of calls follows a Poisson probability distribution, with a mean of 40 calls per hour, and that each dispatcher can handle a mean of 30 calls per hour.

a. What percentage of time are both dispatchers idle?

b. What percentage of time are both dispatchers busy?

c. What is the probability callers will receive a busy signal if two, three, or four dispatchers are used?

d. If management wants no more than 12% of the callers to receive a busy signal, how many dispatchers should be used?

33. Kolkmeyer Manufacturing Company (see Section 11.9) is considering adding two machines to its manufacturing operation. This addition will bring the number of machines to eight. The president of Kolkmeyer asked for a study of the need to add a second employee to the repair operation. The arrival rate is 0.05 machine per hour for each machine, and the service rate for each individual assigned to the repair operation is 0.50 machine per hour.

a. Compute the operating characteristics if the company retains the single-employee repair operation.

b. Compute the operating characteristics if a second employee is added to the machine repair operation.

c. Each employee is paid $20 per hour. Machine downtime is valued at $80 per hour. From an economic point of view, should one or two employees handle the machine repair operation? Explain.

34. Five administrative assistants use an office copier. The average time between arrivals for each assistant is 40 minutes, which is equivalent to an arrival rate of $1/40 = 0.025$ arrival per minute. The mean time each assistant spends at the copier is 5 minutes, which is equivalent to a service rate of $\frac{1}{5} = 0.20$ per minute. Use the $M/M/1$ model with a finite calling population to determine the following:

a. The probability that the copier is idle

b. The average number of administrative assistants in the waiting line

c. The average number of administrative assistants at the copier

d. The average time an assistant spends waiting for the copier

e. The average time an assistant spends at the copier

    f.   During an 8-hour day, how many minutes does an assistant spend at the copier? How much of this time is waiting time?

    g. Should management consider purchasing a second copier? Explain.

35. Schips Department Store operates a fleet of 10 trucks. The trucks arrive at random times throughout the day at the store's truck dock to be loaded with new deliveries or to have incoming shipments from the regional warehouse unloaded. Each truck returns to the truck dock for service two times per 8-hour day. Thus, the arrival rate per truck is 0.25 trucks per hour. The service rate is 4 trucks per hour. Using the Poisson arrivals and exponential service times model with a finite calling population of 10 trucks, determine the following operating characteristics:

    a.   The probability no trucks are at the truck dock

    b. The average number of trucks waiting for loading/unloading

    c. The average number of trucks in the truck dock area

    d. The average waiting time before loading/unloading begins

    e. The average waiting time in the system

    f.   What is the hourly cost of operation if the cost is $50 per hour for each truck and $30 per hour for the truck dock?

    g. Consider a two-channel truck dock operation where the second channel could be operated for an additional $30 per hour. How much would the average number of trucks waiting for loading/unloading have to be reduced to make the two-channel truck dock economically feasible?

    h. Should the company consider expanding to the two-channel truck dock? Explain.

Case Problem 1   REGIONAL AIRLINES

Regional Airlines is establishing a new telephone system for handling flight reservations. During the 10:00 A.M. to 11:00 A.M. time period, calls to the reservation agent occur randomly at an average of one call every 3.75 minutes. Historical service time data show that a reservation agent spends an average of 3 minutes with each customer. The waiting line model assumptions of Poisson arrivals and exponential service times appear reasonable for the telephone reservation system.

Regional Airlines' management believes that offering an efficient telephone reservation system is an important part of establishing an image as a service-oriented airline. If the system is properly implemented, Regional Airlines will establish good customer relations, which in the long run will increase business. However, if the telephone reservation system is frequently overloaded and customers have difficulty contacting an agent, a negative customer reaction may lead to an eventual loss of business. The cost of a ticket reservation agent is $20 per hour. Thus, management wants to provide good service, but it does not want to incur the cost of overstaffing the telephone reservation operation by using more agents than necessary.

At a planning meeting, Regional's management team agreed that an acceptable customer service goal is to answer at least 85% of the incoming calls immediately. During the planning meeting, Regional's vice president of administration pointed out that the data show that the average service rate for an agent is faster than the average arrival rate of the telephone calls. The vice president's conclusion was that personnel costs could be minimized by using one agent and that the single agent should be able to handle the telephone reservations and still have some idle time. The vice president of marketing restated the importance of customer service and expressed support for at least two reservation agents.

The current telephone reservation system design does not allow callers to wait. Callers who attempt to reach a reservation agent when all agents are occupied receive a busy signal and are blocked from the system. A representative from the telephone company suggested that Regional Airlines consider an expanded system that accommodates waiting. In the expanded system, when a customer calls and all agents are busy, a recorded message tells the customer that the call is being held in the order received and that an agent will be available shortly. The customer can stay on the line and listen to background music while waiting for an agent. Regional's management will need more information before switching to the expanded system.

Managerial Report

Prepare a managerial report for Regional Airlines analyzing the telephone reservation system. Evaluate both the system that does not allow waiting and the expanded system that allows waiting. Include the following information in your report:

1. An analysis of the current reservation system that does not allow callers to wait. How many reservation agents are needed to meet the service goal?
2. An analysis of the expanded system proposed by the telephone company. How many agents are needed to meet the service goal?
3. Make a recommendation concerning which system to use and how many agents to hire. Provide supporting rationale for your recommendation.
4. The telephone arrival data presented are for the 10:00 A.M. to 11:00 A.M. time period; however, the arrival rate of incoming calls is expected to change from hour to hour. Describe how your waiting line analysis could be used to develop a ticket agent staffing plan that would enable the company to provide different levels of staffing for the ticket reservation system at different times during the day. Indicate the information that you would need to develop this staffing plan.

Case Problem 2   OFFICE EQUIPMENT, INC.

Office Equipment, Inc. (OEI), leases automatic mailing machines to business customers in Fort Wayne, Indiana. The company built its success on a reputation for providing timely maintenance and repair service. Each OEI service contract states that a service technician will arrive at a customer's business site within an average of three hours from the time that the customer notifies OEI of an equipment problem.

Currently, OEI has 10 customers with service contracts. One service technician is responsible for handling all service calls. A statistical analysis of historical service records indicates that a customer requests a service call at an average rate of one call per 50 hours of operation. If the service technician is available when a customer calls for service, it takes the technician an average of 1 hour of travel time to reach the customer's office and an average of 1.5 hours to complete the repair service. However, if the service technician is busy with another customer when a new customer calls for service, the technician completes the current service call and any other waiting service calls before responding to the new service call. In such cases, once the technician is free from all existing service commitments, the technician takes an average of 1 hour of travel time to reach the new customer's office and an average of 1.5 hours to complete the repair service. The cost of the service technician is $80 per hour. The downtime cost (wait time and service time) for customers is $100 per hour.

OEI is planning to expand its business. Within one year, OEI projects that it will have 20 customers, and within two years, OEI projects that it will have 30 customers. Although OEI is satisfied that one service technician can handle the 10 existing customers, management is concerned about the ability of one technician to meet the average three-hour service call guarantee when the OEI customer base expands. In a recent planning meeting, the marketing manager made a proposal to add a second service technician when OEI reaches 20 customers and to add a third service technician when OEI reaches 30 customers. Before making a final decision, management would like an analysis of OEI service capabilities. OEI is particularly interested in meeting the average three-hour waiting time guarantee at the lowest possible total cost.

Managerial Report

Develop a managerial report summarizing your analysis of the OEI service capabilities. Make recommendations regarding the number of technicians to be used when OEI reaches 20 customers and when OEI reaches 30 customers. Include a discussion of the following in your report:

1. What is the arrival rate for each customer per hour?
2. What is the service rate in terms of the number of customers per hour? Note that the average travel time of 1 hour becomes part of the service time because the time that the service technician is busy handling a service call includes the travel time plus the time required to complete the repair.
3. Waiting line models generally assume that the arriving customers are in the same location as the service facility. Discuss the OEI situation in light of the fact that a service technician travels an average of 1 hour to reach each customer. How should the travel time and the waiting time predicted by the waiting line model be combined to determine the total customer waiting time?
4. OEI is satisfied that one service technician can handle the 10 existing customers. Use a waiting line model to determine the following information:
   - Probability that no customers are in the system
   - Average number of customers in the waiting line
   - Average number of customers in the system
   - Average time a customer waits until the service technician arrives
   - Average time a customer waits until the machine is back in operation
   - Probability that a customer will have to wait more than one hour for the service technician to arrive
   - The number of hours a week the technician is not making service calls
   - The total cost per hour for the service operation

   Do you agree with OEI management that one technician can meet the average three-hour service call guarantee? Explain.
5. What is your recommendation for the number of service technicians to hire when OEI expands to 20 customers? Use the information that you developed in part (4) to justify your answer.
6. What is your recommendation for the number of service technicians to hire when OEI expands to 30 customers? Use the information that you developed in part (4) to justify your answer.
7. What are the annual savings of your recommendation in part (6) compared to the planning committee's proposal that 30 customers will require three service technicians? Assume 250 days of operation per year.

CHAPTER 12

Simulation

CONTENTS

12.1 RISK ANALYSIS
PortaCom Project
What-If Analysis
Simulation
Simulation of the PortaCom Project

12.2 INVENTORY SIMULATION
Butler Inventory Simulation

12.3 WAITING LINE SIMULATION
Hammondsport Savings Bank ATM
Waiting Line
Customer Arrival Times

Customer Service Times
Simulation Model
Hammondsport Savings Bank ATM
Simulation
Simulation with Two ATMs
Simulation Results with Two ATMs

12.4 OTHER SIMULATION ISSUES
Computer Implementation
Verification and Validation
Advantages and Disadvantages of
Using Simulation

Simulation is one of the most widely used quantitative approaches to decision making. It is a method for learning about a real system by experimenting with a model that represents the system. The simulation model contains the mathematical expressions and logical relationships that describe how to compute the value of the outputs given the values of the inputs. Any simulation model has two inputs: controllable inputs and probabilistic inputs. Figure 12.1 shows a conceptual diagram of a simulation model.

In conducting a **simulation experiment,** an analyst selects the value, or values, for the **controllable inputs.** Then values for the **probabilistic inputs** are randomly generated. The simulation model uses the values of the controllable inputs and the values of the probabilistic inputs to compute the value, or values, of the output. By conducting a series of experiments using a variety of values for the controllable inputs, the analyst learns how values of the controllable inputs affect or change the output of the simulation model. After reviewing the simulation results, the analyst is often able to make decision recommendations for the controllable inputs that will provide the desired output for the real system.

Simulation has been successfully applied in a variety of applications. The following examples are typical:

1. *New product development.* The objective of this simulation is to determine the probability that a new product will be profitable. A model is developed relating profit (the output measure) to various probabilistic inputs such as demand, parts cost, and labor cost. The only controllable input is whether to introduce the product. A variety of possible values will be generated for the probabilistic inputs, and the resulting profit will be computed. We develop a simulation model for this type of application in Section 12.1.

2. *Airline overbooking.* The objective of this simulation is to determine the number of reservations an airline should accept for a particular flight. A simulation model is developed relating profit for the flight to a probabilistic input, the number of passengers with a reservation who show up and use their reservation, and a controllable input, the number of reservations accepted for the flight. For each selected value for the controllable input, a variety of possible values will be generated for the number of passengers who show up, and the resulting profit can be computed. Similar simulation models are applicable for hotel and car rental reservation systems.

3. *Inventory policy.* The objective of this simulation is to choose an inventory policy that will provide good customer service at a reasonable cost. A model is developed relating two output measures, total inventory cost and the service level, to probabilistic inputs, such as product demand and delivery lead time from vendors, and controllable inputs, such as the order quantity and the reorder point. For each setting of the controllable inputs, a variety of possible values would be generated for the probabilistic inputs, and the resulting cost and service levels would be computed.

FIGURE 12.1   DIAGRAM OF A SIMULATION MODEL

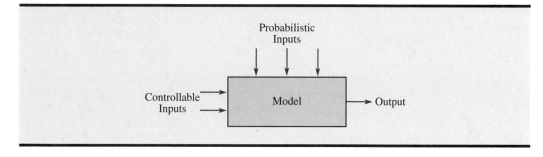

4. *Traffic flow.* The objective of this simulation is to determine the effect of installing a left turn signal on the flow of traffic through a busy intersection. A model is developed relating waiting time for vehicles to get through the intersection to probabilistic inputs such as the number of vehicle arrivals and the fraction that want to make a left turn, and controllable inputs such as the length of time the left turn signal is on. For each setting of the controllable inputs, values would be generated for the probabilistic inputs, and the resulting vehicle waiting times would be computed.

5. *Waiting lines.* The objective of this simulation is to determine the waiting times for customers at a bank's automated teller machine (ATM). A model is developed relating customer waiting times to probabilistic inputs such as customer arrivals and service times, and a controllable input, the number of ATM machines installed. For each value of the controllable input (the number of ATM machines), a variety of values would be generated for the probabilistic inputs, and the customer waiting times would be computed. The Management Science in Action, Call Center Design, describes how simulation of a waiting line system at a call center helped the company balance the service to its customers with the cost of agents providing the service.

Simulation is not an optimization technique. It is a method that can be used to describe or predict how a system will operate given certain choices for the controllable inputs and randomly generated values for the probabilistic inputs. Management scientists often use simulation to determine values for the controllable inputs that are likely to lead to desirable system outputs. In this sense, simulation can be an effective tool in designing a system to provide good performance.

MANAGEMENT SCIENCE IN ACTION

CALL CENTER DESIGN*

A call center is a place where large volumes of calls are made to or received from current or potential customers. More than 60,000 call centers operate in the United States. Saltzman and Mehrotra describe how a simulation model helped make a strategic change in the design of the technical support call center for a major software company. The application used a waiting line simulation model to balance the service to customers calling for assistance with the cost of agents providing the service.

Historically, the software company provided free phone-in technical support, but over time service requests grew to the point where 80% of the callers were waiting between 5 and 10 minutes and abandonment rates were too high. On some days 40% of the callers hung up before receiving service. This service level was unacceptable. As a result, management considered instituting a Rapid Program in which customers would pay a fee for service, but would be guaranteed to receive service within one minute, or the service would be free. Nonpaying customers would continue receiving service but without a guarantee of short service times.

A simulation model was developed to help understand the impact of this new program on the waiting line characteristics of the call center. Data available were used to develop the arrival distribution, the service time distribution, and the probability distribution for abandonment. The key design variables considered were the number of agents (channels) and the percentage of callers subscribing to the Rapid Program. The model was developed using the Arena simulation package.

The simulation results helped the company decide to go ahead with the Rapid Program. Under most of the scenarios considered, the simulation model showed that 95% of the callers in the Rapid Program would receive service within one minute and that free service to the remaining customers could be maintained within acceptable limits. Within nine months, 10% of the software company's customers subscribed to the Rapid Program, generating $2 million in incremental revenue. The company viewed the simulation model as a vehicle for mitigating risk. The model helped evaluate the likely impact of the Rapid Program without experimenting with actual customers.

*Based on Robert M. Saltzman and Vijay Mehrotra, "A Call Center Uses Simulation to Drive Strategic Change," *Interfaces* (May/June 2001): 87–101.

In this chapter we begin by showing how simulation can be used to study the financial risks associated with the development of a new product. We continue with illustrations showing how simulation can be used to establish an effective inventory policy and how simulation can be used to design waiting line systems. Other issues, such as verifying the simulation program, validating the model, and selecting a simulation software package, are discussed in Section 12.4.

12.1   RISK ANALYSIS

Risk analysis is the process of predicting the outcome of a decision in the face of uncertainty. In this section, we describe a problem that involves considerable uncertainty: the development of a new product. We first show how risk analysis can be conducted without using simulation; then we show how a more comprehensive risk analysis can be conducted with the aid of simulation.

PortaCom Project

PortaCom manufactures personal computers and related equipment. PortaCom's product design group developed a prototype for a new high-quality portable printer. The new printer features an innovative design and has the potential to capture a significant share of the portable printer market. Preliminary marketing and financial analyses provided the following selling price, first-year administrative cost, and first-year advertising cost:

$$\text{Selling price} = \$249 \text{ per unit}$$
$$\text{Administrative cost} = \$400{,}000$$
$$\text{Advertising cost} = \$600{,}000$$

In the simulation model for the PortaCom project, the preceding values are constants and are referred to as **parameters** of the model.

The cost of direct labor, the cost of parts, and the first-year demand for the printer are not known with certainty and are considered probabilistic inputs. At this stage of the planning process, PortaCom's best estimates of these inputs are $45 per unit for the direct labor cost, $90 per unit for the parts cost, and 15,000 units for the first-year demand. PortaCom would like an analysis of the first-year profit potential for the printer. Because of PortaCom's tight cash flow situation, management is particularly concerned about the potential for a loss.

What-If Analysis

One approach to risk analysis is called **what-if analysis.** A what-if analysis involves generating values for the probabilistic inputs (direct labor cost, parts cost, and first-year demand) and computing the resulting value for the output (profit). With a selling price of $249 per unit and administrative plus advertising costs equal to $400,000 + $600,000 = $1,000,000, the PortaCom profit model is

$$\text{Profit} = (\$249 - \text{Direct labor cost per unit} - \text{Parts cost per unit}) (\text{Demand}) - \$1{,}000{,}000$$

Letting

$$c_1 = \text{direct labor cost per unit}$$
$$c_2 = \text{parts cost per unit}$$
$$x = \text{first-year demand}$$

the profit model for the first year can be written as follows:

$$\text{Profit} = (249 - c_1 - c_2)x - 1{,}000{,}000 \qquad (12.1)$$

The PortaCom profit model can be depicted as shown in Figure 12.2.

Recall that PortaCom's best estimates of the direct labor cost per unit, the parts cost per unit, and first-year demand are $45, $90, and 15,000 units, respectively. These values constitute the **base-case scenario** for PortaCom. Substituting these values into equation (12.1) yields the following profit projection:

$$\text{Profit} = (249 - 45 - 90)(15{,}000) - 1{,}000{,}000 = 710{,}000$$

Thus, the base-case scenario leads to an anticipated profit of $710,000.

In risk analysis we are concerned with both the probability of a loss and the magnitude of a loss. Although the base-case scenario looks appealing, PortaCom might be interested in what happens if the estimates of the direct labor cost per unit, parts cost per unit, and first-year demand do not turn out to be as expected under the base-case scenario. For instance, suppose that PortaCom believes that direct labor costs could range from $43 to $47 per unit, parts cost could range from $80 to $100 per unit, and first-year demand could range from 1500 to 28,500 units. Using these ranges, what-if analysis can be used to evaluate a **worst-case scenario** and a **best-case scenario.**

The worst-case value for the direct labor cost is $47 (the highest value), the worst-case value for the parts cost is $100 (the highest value), and the worst-case value for demand is 1500 units (the lowest value). Thus, in the worst-case scenario, $c_1 = 47$, $c_2 = 100$, and $x = 1500$. Substituting these values into equation (12.1) leads to the following profit projection:

$$\text{Profit} = (249 - 47 - 100)(1500) - 1{,}000{,}000 = -847{,}000$$

The worst-case scenario leads to a projected loss of $847,000.

The best-case value for the direct labor cost is $43 (the lowest value), the best-case value for the parts cost is $80 (the lowest value), and the best-case value for demand is 28,500 units (the highest value). Substituting these values into equation (12.1) leads to the following profit projection:

Problem 2 will give you practice using what-if analysis.

$$\text{Profit} = (249 - 43 - 80)(28{,}500) - 1{,}000{,}000 = 2{,}591{,}000$$

The best-case scenario leads to a projected profit of $2,591,000.

FIGURE 12.2   PORTACOM PROFIT MODEL

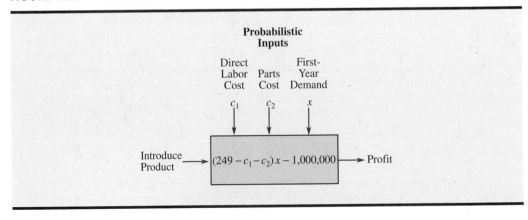

At this point the what-if analysis provides the conclusion that profits can range from a loss of $847,000 to a profit of $2,591,000 with a base-case profit of $710,000. Although the base-case profit of $710,000 is possible, the what-if analysis indicates that either a substantial loss or a substantial profit is possible. Other scenarios that PortaCom might want to consider can also be evaluated. However, the difficulty with what-if analysis is that it does not indicate the likelihood of the various profit or loss values. In particular, we do not know anything about the *probability* of a loss.

Simulation

Using simulation to perform risk analysis for the PortaCom project is like playing out many what-if scenarios by randomly generating values for the probabilistic inputs. The advantage of simulation is that it allows us to assess the probability of a profit and the probability of a loss.

Using the what-if approach to risk analysis, we selected values for the probabilistic inputs [direct labor cost per unit (c_1), parts cost per unit (c_2), and first-year demand (x)], and then computed the resulting profit. Applying simulation to the PortaCom project requires generating values for the probabilistic inputs that are representative of what we might observe in practice. To generate such values, we must know the probability distribution for each probabilistic input. Further analysis by PortaCom led to the following probability distributions for the direct labor cost per unit, the parts cost per unit, and first-year demand:

One advantage of simulation is the ability to use probability distributions that are unique to the system being studied.

Direct Labor Cost   PortaCom believes that the direct labor cost will range from $43 to $47 per unit and is described by the discrete probability distribution shown in Table 12.1. Thus, we see a 0.1 probability that the direct labor cost will be $43 per unit, a 0.2 probability that the direct labor cost will be $44 per unit, and so on. The highest probability of 0.4 is associated with a direct labor cost of $45 per unit.

Parts Cost   This cost depends upon the general economy, the overall demand for parts, and the pricing policy of PortaCom's parts suppliers. PortaCom believes that the parts cost will range from $80 to $100 per unit and is described by the uniform probability distribution shown in Figure 12.3. Costs per unit between $80 and $100 are equally likely.

First-Year Demand   PortaCom believes that first-year demand is described by the normal probability distribution shown in Figure 12.4. The mean or expected value of first-year demand is 15,000 units. The standard deviation of 4500 units describes the variability in the first-year demand.

To simulate the PortaCom project, we must generate values for the three probabilistic inputs and compute the resulting profit. Then we generate another set of values for the

TABLE 12.1   PROBABILITY DISTRIBUTION FOR DIRECT LABOR COST PER UNIT

Direct Labor Cost per Unit	Probability
$43	0.1
$44	0.2
$45	0.4
$46	0.2
$47	0.1

FIGURE 12.3   UNIFORM PROBABILITY DISTRIBUTION FOR THE PARTS COST PER UNIT

probabilistic inputs, compute a second value for profit, and so on. We continue this process until we are satisfied that enough trials have been conducted to describe the probability distribution for profit. This process of generating probabilistic inputs and computing the value of the output is called *simulation*. The sequence of logical and mathematical operations required to conduct a simulation can be depicted with a flowchart. A flowchart for the PortaCom simulation is shown in Figure 12.5.

A flowchart provides a graphical representation that helps describe the logic of the simulation model.

Following the logic described by the flowchart, we see that the model parameters—selling price, administrative cost, and advertising cost—are $249, $400,000, and $600,000, respectively. These values will remain fixed throughout the simulation.

The next three blocks depict the generation of values for the probabilistic inputs. First, a value for the direct labor cost (c_1) is generated. Then a value for the parts cost (c_2) is generated, followed by a value for the first-year demand (x). These probabilistic input values are combined using the profit model given by equation (12.1).

$$\text{Profit} = (249 - c_1 - c_2)x - 1,000,000$$

The computation of profit completes one trial of the simulation. We then return to the block where we generated the direct labor cost and begin another trial. This process is repeated until a satisfactory number of trials has been generated.

FIGURE 12.4   NORMAL PROBABILITY DISTRIBUTION OF FIRST-YEAR DEMAND

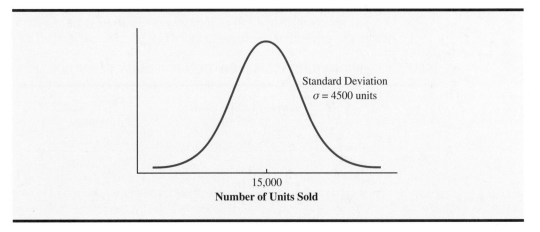

FIGURE 12.5   FLOWCHART FOR THE PORTACOM SIMULATION

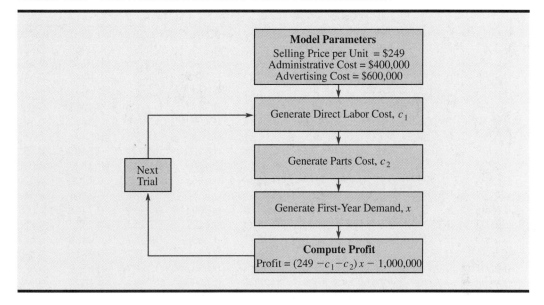

At the end of the simulation, output measures of interest can be developed. For example, we will be interested in computing the average profit and the probability of a loss. For the output measures to be meaningful, the values of the probabilistic inputs must be representative of what is likely to happen when the PortaCom printer is introduced into the market. An essential part of the simulation procedure is the ability to generate representative values for the probabilistic inputs. We now discuss how to generate these values.

Random Numbers and Generating Probabilistic Input Values   In the PortaCom simulation, representative values must be generated for the direct labor cost per unit (c_1), the parts cost per unit (c_2), and the first-year demand (x). Random numbers and the probability distributions associated with each probabilistic input are used to generate representative values. To illustrate how to generate these values, we need to introduce the concept of *computer-generated random numbers*.

Because random numbers are equally likely, management scientists can assign ranges of random numbers to corresponding values of probabilistic inputs so that the probability of any input value to the simulation model is identical to the probability of its occurrence in the real system.

Computer-generated random numbers[1] are randomly selected decimal numbers from 0 up to, but not including, 1. The computer-generated random numbers are equally likely and are uniformly distributed over the interval from 0 to 1. Computer-generated random numbers can be obtained using built-in functions available in computer simulation packages and spreadsheets. For instance, placing =RAND() in a cell of an Excel worksheet will result in a random number between 0 and 1 being placed into that cell.

Table 12.2 contains 500 random numbers generated using Excel. These numbers can be viewed as a random sample of 500 values from a uniform probability distribution over the interval from 0 to 1. Let us show how random numbers can be used to generate values for the PortaCom probability distributions. We begin by showing how to generate a value for the direct labor cost per unit. The approach described is applicable for generating values from any discrete probability distribution.

---

[1]Computer-generated random numbers are called *pseudorandom numbers*. Because they are generated through the use of mathematical formulas, they are not technically random. The difference between random numbers and pseudorandom numbers is primarily philosophical, and we use the term *random numbers* regardless of whether they are generated by a computer.

TABLE 12.2   500 COMPUTER-GENERATED RANDOM NUMBERS

0.6953	0.5247	0.1368	0.9850	0.7467	0.3813	0.5827	0.7893	0.7169	0.8166
0.0082	0.9925	0.6874	0.2122	0.6885	0.2159	0.4299	0.3467	0.2186	0.1033
0.6799	0.1241	0.3056	0.5590	0.0423	0.6515	0.2750	0.8156	0.2871	0.4680
0.8898	0.1514	0.1826	0.0004	0.5259	0.2425	0.8421	0.9248	0.9155	0.9518
0.6515	0.5027	0.9290	0.5177	0.3134	0.9177	0.2605	0.6668	0.1167	0.7870
0.3976	0.7790	0.0035	0.0064	0.0441	0.3437	0.1248	0.5442	0.9800	0.1857
0.0642	0.4086	0.6078	0.2044	0.0484	0.4691	0.7058	0.8552	0.5029	0.3288
0.0377	0.5250	0.7774	0.2390	0.9121	0.5345	0.8178	0.8443	0.4154	0.2526
0.5739	0.5181	0.0234	0.7305	0.0376	0.5169	0.5679	0.5495	0.7872	0.5321
0.5827	0.0341	0.7482	0.6351	0.9146	0.4700	0.7869	0.1337	0.0702	0.4219
0.0508	0.7905	0.2932	0.4971	0.0225	0.4466	0.5118	0.1200	0.0200	0.5445
0.4757	0.1399	0.5668	0.9569	0.7255	0.4650	0.4084	0.3701	0.9446	0.8064
0.6805	0.9931	0.4166	0.1091	0.7730	0.0691	0.9411	0.3468	0.0014	0.7379
0.2603	0.7507	0.6414	0.9907	0.2699	0.4571	0.9254	0.2371	0.8664	0.9553
0.8143	0.7625	0.1708	0.1900	0.2781	0.2830	0.6877	0.0488	0.8635	0.3155
0.5681	0.7854	0.5016	0.9403	0.1078	0.5255	0.8727	0.3815	0.5541	0.9833
0.1501	0.9363	0.3858	0.3545	0.5448	0.0643	0.3167	0.6732	0.6283	0.2631
0.8806	0.7989	0.7484	0.8083	0.2701	0.5039	0.9439	0.1027	0.9677	0.4597
0.4582	0.7590	0.4393	0.4704	0.6903	0.3732	0.6587	0.8675	0.2905	0.3058
0.0785	0.1467	0.3880	0.5274	0.8723	0.7517	0.9905	0.8904	0.8177	0.6660
0.1158	0.6635	0.4992	0.9070	0.2975	0.5686	0.8495	0.1652	0.2039	0.2553
0.2762	0.7018	0.6782	0.4013	0.2224	0.4672	0.5753	0.6219	0.6871	0.9255
0.9382	0.6411	0.7984	0.0608	0.5945	0.3977	0.4570	0.9924	0.8398	0.8361
0.5102	0.7021	0.4353	0.3398	0.8038	0.2260	0.1250	0.1884	0.3432	0.1192
0.2354	0.7410	0.7089	0.2579	0.1358	0.8446	0.1648	0.3889	0.5620	0.6555
0.9082	0.7906	0.7589	0.8870	0.1189	0.7125	0.6324	0.1096	0.5155	0.3449
0.6936	0.0702	0.9716	0.0374	0.0683	0.2397	0.7753	0.2029	0.1464	0.8000
0.4042	0.8158	0.3623	0.6614	0.7954	0.7516	0.6518	0.3638	0.3107	0.2718
0.9410	0.2201	0.6348	0.0367	0.0311	0.0688	0.2346	0.3927	0.7327	0.9994
0.0917	0.2504	0.2878	0.1735	0.3872	0.6816	0.2731	0.3846	0.6621	0.8983
0.8532	0.4869	0.2685	0.6349	0.9364	0.3451	0.4998	0.2842	0.0643	0.6656
0.8980	0.0455	0.8314	0.8189	0.6783	0.8086	0.1386	0.4442	0.9941	0.6812
0.8412	0.8792	0.2025	0.9320	0.7656	0.3815	0.5302	0.8744	0.4584	0.3585
0.5688	0.8633	0.5818	0.0692	0.2543	0.5453	0.9955	0.1237	0.7535	0.5993
0.5006	0.1215	0.8102	0.1026	0.9251	0.6851	0.1559	0.1214	0.2628	0.9374
0.5748	0.4164	0.3427	0.2809	0.8064	0.5855	0.2229	0.2805	0.9139	0.9013
0.1100	0.0873	0.9407	0.8747	0.0496	0.4380	0.5847	0.4183	0.5929	0.4863
0.5802	0.7747	0.1285	0.0074	0.6252	0.7747	0.0112	0.3958	0.3285	0.5389
0.1019	0.6628	0.8998	0.1334	0.2798	0.7351	0.7330	0.6723	0.6924	0.3963
0.9909	0.8991	0.2298	0.2603	0.6921	0.5573	0.8191	0.0384	0.2954	0.0636
0.6292	0.4923	0.0276	0.6734	0.6562	0.4231	0.1980	0.6551	0.3716	0.0507
0.9430	0.2579	0.7933	0.0945	0.3192	0.3195	0.7772	0.4672	0.7070	0.5925
0.9938	0.7098	0.7964	0.7952	0.8947	0.1214	0.8454	0.8294	0.5394	0.9413
0.4690	0.1395	0.0930	0.3189	0.6972	0.7291	0.8513	0.9256	0.7478	0.8124
0.2028	0.3774	0.0485	0.7718	0.9656	0.2444	0.0304	0.1395	0.1577	0.8625
0.6141	0.4131	0.2006	0.2329	0.6182	0.5151	0.6300	0.9311	0.3837	0.7828
0.2757	0.8479	0.7880	0.8492	0.6859	0.8947	0.6246	0.1574	0.4936	0.8077
0.0561	0.0126	0.6531	0.0378	0.4975	0.1133	0.3572	0.0071	0.4555	0.7563
0.1419	0.4308	0.8073	0.4681	0.0481	0.2918	0.2975	0.0685	0.6384	0.0812
0.3125	0.0053	0.9209	0.9768	0.3584	0.0390	0.2161	0.6333	0.4391	0.6991

TABLE 12.3 RANDOM NUMBER INTERVALS FOR GENERATING VALUES OF DIRECT LABOR COST PER UNIT

Direct Labor Cost per Unit	Probability	Interval of Random Numbers
$43	0.1	0.0 but less than 0.1
$44	0.2	0.1 but less than 0.3
$45	0.4	0.3 but less than 0.7
$46	0.2	0.7 but less than 0.9
$47	0.1	0.9 but less than 1.0

An interval of random numbers is assigned to each possible value of the direct labor cost in such a fashion that the probability of generating a random number in the interval is equal to the probability of the corresponding direct labor cost. Table 12.3 shows how this process is done. The interval of random numbers greater than or equal to 0.0 but less than 0.1 is associated with a direct labor cost of $43, the interval of random numbers greater than or equal to 0.1 but less than 0.3 is associated with a direct labor cost of $44, and so on. With this assignment of random number intervals to the possible values of the direct labor cost, the probability of generating a random number in any interval is equal to the probability of obtaining the corresponding value for the direct labor cost. Thus, to select a value for the direct labor cost, we generate a random number between 0 and 1. If the random number is greater than or equal to 0.0 but less than 0.1, we set the direct labor cost equal to $43. If the random number is greater than or equal to 0.1 but less than 0.3, we set the direct labor cost equal to $44, and so on.

Try Problem 5 for an opportunity to establish intervals of random numbers and simulate demand from a discrete probability distribution.

Each trial of the simulation requires a value for the direct labor cost. Suppose that on the first trial the random number is 0.9109. From Table 12.3, the simulated value for the direct labor cost is $47 per unit. Suppose that on the second trial the random number is 0.2841. From Table 12.3, the simulated value for the direct labor cost is $44 per unit. Table 12.4 shows the results obtained for the first 10 simulation trials.

Each trial in the simulation requires a value of the direct labor cost, parts cost, and first-year demand. Let us now turn to the issue of generating values for the parts cost. The probability distribution for the parts cost per unit is the uniform distribution shown in Figure 12.3. Because this random variable has a different probability distribution than direct labor cost, we use random numbers in a slightly different way to generate values for parts cost. With a

TABLE 12.4 RANDOM GENERATION OF 10 VALUES FOR THE DIRECT LABOR COST PER UNIT

Trial	Random Number	Direct Labor Cost ($)
1	0.9109	47
2	0.2841	44
3	0.6531	45
4	0.0367	43
5	0.3451	45
6	0.2757	44
7	0.6859	45
8	0.6246	45
9	0.4936	45
10	0.8077	46

uniform probability distribution, the following relationship between the random number and the associated value of the parts cost is used:

$$\text{Parts cost} = a + r(b - a) \qquad (12.2)$$

where

$$r = \text{random number between 0 and 1}$$
$$a = \text{smallest value for parts cost}$$
$$b = \text{largest value for parts cost}$$

For PortaCom, the smallest value for the parts cost is $80, and the largest value is $100. Applying equation (12.2) with $a = 80$ and $b = 100$ leads to the following formula for generating the parts cost given a random number, r:

$$\text{Parts cost} = 80 + r(100 - 80) = 80 + r20 \qquad (12.3)$$

Equation (12.3) generates a value for the parts cost. Suppose that a random number of 0.2680 is obtained. The value for the parts cost is

$$\text{Parts cost} = 80 + 0.2680(20) = 85.36 \text{ per unit}$$

Spreadsheet packages such as Excel have built-in functions that make simulations based on probability distributions such as the normal probability distribution relatively easy.

Suppose that a random number of 0.5842 is generated on the next trial. The value for the parts cost is

$$\text{Parts cost} = 80 + 0.5842(20) = 91.68 \text{ per unit}$$

With appropriate choices of a and b, equation (12.2) can be used to generate values for any uniform probability distribution. Table 12.5 shows the generation of 10 values for the parts cost per unit.

Finally, we need a random number procedure for generating the first-year demand. Because first-year demand is normally distributed with a mean of 15,000 units and a standard deviation of 4500 units (see Figure 12.4), we need a procedure for generating random

TABLE 12.5   RANDOM GENERATION OF 10 VALUES FOR THE PARTS COST PER UNIT

Trial	Random Number	Parts Cost ($)
1	0.2680	85.36
2	0.5842	91.68
3	0.6675	93.35
4	0.9280	98.56
5	0.4180	88.36
6	0.7342	94.68
7	0.4325	88.65
8	0.1186	82.37
9	0.6944	93.89
10	0.7869	95.74

values from a normal probability distribution. Because of the mathematical complexity, a detailed discussion of the procedure for generating random values from a normal probability distribution is omitted. However, computer simulation packages and spreadsheets include a built-in function that provides randomly generated values from a normal probability distribution. In most cases the user only needs to provide the mean and standard deviation of the normal distribution. For example, using Excel the following formula can be placed into a cell to obtain a value for a probabilistic input that is normally distributed:

$$= \text{NORMINV(RAND(),Mean,Standard Deviation)}$$

Because the mean for the first-year demand in the PortaCom problem is 15,000 and the standard deviation is 4500, the Excel statement

$$= \text{NORMINV(RAND(),15000,4500)} \tag{12.4}$$

will provide a normally distributed value for first-year demand. For example, if Excel's RAND() function generates the random number 0.7005, the Excel function shown in equation (12.4) will provide a first-year demand of 17,366 units. If RAND() generates the random number 0.3204, equation (12.4) will provide a first-year demand of 12,900. Table 12.6 shows the results for the first 10 randomly generated values for demand. Note that random numbers less than 0.5 generate first-year demand values below the mean and that random numbers greater than 0.5 generate first-year demand values greater than the mean.

Running the Simulation Model Running the simulation model means implementing the sequence of logical and mathematical operations described in the flowchart in Figure 12.5. The model parameters are $249 per unit for the selling price, $400,000 for the administrative cost, and $600,000 for the advertising cost. Each trial in the simulation involves randomly generating values for the probabilistic inputs (direct labor cost, parts cost, and first-year demand) and computing profit. The simulation is complete when a satisfactory number of trials have been conducted.

Let us compute the profit for the first trial assuming the following probabilistic inputs:

Direct labor cost: $C_1 = 47$
Parts cost: $C_2 = 85.36$
First-year demand: $x = 17,366$

TABLE 12.6 RANDOM GENERATION OF 10 VALUES FOR FIRST-YEAR DEMAND

Trial	Random Number	Demand
1	0.7005	17,366
2	0.3204	12,900
3	0.8968	20,686
4	0.1804	10,888
5	0.4346	14,259
6	0.9605	22,904
7	0.5646	15,732
8	0.7334	17,804
9	0.0216	5,902
10	0.3218	12,918

TABLE 12.7   PORTACOM SIMULATION RESULTS FOR 10 TRIALS

Trial	Direct Labor Cost per Unit ($)	Parts Cost per Unit ($)	Units Sold	Profit ($)
1	47	85.36	17,366	1,025,570
2	44	91.68	12,900	461,828
3	45	93.35	20,686	1,288,906
4	43	98.56	10,888	169,807
5	45	88.36	14,259	648,911
6	44	94.68	22,904	1,526,769
7	45	88.65	15,732	814,686
8	45	82.37	17,804	1,165,501
9	45	93.89	5,902	−350,131
10	46	95.74	12,918	385,585
Total	449	912.64	151,359	7,137,432
Average	$44.90	$91.26	15,136	$713,743

Referring to the flowchart in Figure 12.5, we see that the profit obtained is

$$\text{Profit} = (249 - c_1 - c_2)x - 1{,}000{,}000$$
$$= (249 - 47 - 85.36)17{,}366 - 1{,}000{,}000 = 1{,}025{,}570$$

The first row of Table 12.7 shows the result of this trial of the PortaCom simulation.

The simulated profit for the PortaCom printer if the direct labor cost is $47 per unit, the parts cost is $85.36 per unit, and first-year demand is 17,366 units is $1,025,570. Of course, one simulation trial does not provide a complete understanding of the possible profit and loss. Because other values are possible for the probabilistic inputs, we can benefit from additional simulation trials.

Suppose that on a second simulation trial, random numbers of 0.2841, 0.5842, and 0.3204 are generated for the direct labor cost, the parts cost, and first-year demand, respectively. These random numbers will provide the probabilistic inputs of $44 for the direct labor cost, $91.68 for the parts cost, and 12,900 for first-year demand. These values provide a simulated profit of $461,828 on the second simulation trial (see the second row of Table 12.7).

Repetition of the simulation process with different values for the probabilistic inputs is an essential part of any simulation. Through the repeated trials, management will begin to understand what might happen when the product is introduced into the real world. We have shown the results of 10 simulation trials in Table 12.7. For these 10 cases, we find a profit as high as $1,526,769 for the 6th trial and a loss of $350,131 for the 9th trial. Thus, we see both the possibility of a profit and of a loss. Averages for the 10 trials are presented at the bottom of the table. We see that the average profit for the 10 trials is $713,743. The probability of a loss is 0.10, because one of the 10 trials (the 9th) resulted in a loss. We note also that the average values for labor cost, parts cost, and first-year demand are fairly close to their means of $45, $90, and 15,000, respectively.

Simulation of the PortaCom Project

Using an Excel worksheet, we simulated the PortaCom project 500 times. The worksheet used to carry out the simulation is shown in Figure 12.6. Note that the simulation results for trials 6 through 495 have been hidden so that the results can be shown in a reasonably sized

FIGURE 12.6   EXCEL WORKSHEET SIMULATION FOR THE PORTACOM PROJECT

WEB **file**

PortaCom

	A	B	C	D	E	F
1	**PortaCom Risk Analysis**					
2						
3	Selling Price per Unit		$249			
4	Administrative Cost		$400,000			
5	Advertising Cost		$600,000			
6						
7	**Direct Labor Cost**			**Parts Cost (Uniform Distribution)**		
8	Lower	Upper		Smallest Value	$80	
9	Random No.	Random No.	Cost per Unit	Largest Value	$100	
10	0.0	0.1	$43			
11	0.1	0.3	$44			
12	0.3	0.7	$45	**Demand (Normal Distribution)**		
13	0.7	0.9	$46	Mean	15000	
14	0.9	1.0	$47	Std Deviation	4500	
15						
16						
17	**Simulation Trials**					
18						
19		Direct Labor	Parts	First-Year		
20	Trial	Cost per Unit	Cost per Unit	Demand	Profit	
21	1	47	$85.36	17,366	$1,025,570	
22	2	44	$91.68	12,900	$461,828	
23	3	45	$93.35	20,686	$1,288,906	
24	4	43	$98.56	10,888	$169,807	
25	5	45	$88.36	14,259	$648,911	
516	496	44	$98.67	8,730	($71,739)	
517	497	45	$94.38	19,257	$1,110,952	
518	498	44	$90.85	14,920	$703,118	
519	499	43	$90.37	13,471	$557,652	
520	500	46	$92.50	18,614	$1,056,847	
521						
522			**Summary Statistics**			
523			Mean Profit		$698,457	
524			Standard Deviation		$520,485	
525			Minimum Profit		($785,234)	
526			Maximum Profit		$2,367,058	
527			Number of Losses		51	
528			Probability of Loss		0.1020	

Excel worksheets for all simulations presented in this chapter are available on the website that accompanies this text.

figure. If desired, the rows for these trials can be shown and the simulation results displayed for all 500 trials. The details of the Excel worksheet that provided the PortaCom simulation are described in Appendix 12.1.

The simulation summary statistics in Figure 12.6 provide information about the risk associated with PortaCom's new printer. The worst result obtained in a simulation of 500 trials is a loss of $785,234, and the best result is a profit of $2,367,058. The mean profit is

$698,457. Fifty-one of the trials resulted in a loss; thus, the estimated probability of a loss is 51/500 = 0.1020.

A histogram of simulated profit values is shown in Figure 12.7. We note that the distribution of profit values is fairly symmetric with a large number of values in the range of $250,000 to $1,250,000. The probability of a large loss or a large gain is small. Only three trials resulted in a loss of more than $500,000, and only three trials resulted in a profit greater than $2,000,000. However, the probability of a loss is significant. Forty-eight of the 500 trials resulted in a loss in the $0 to $500,000 range—almost 10%. The modal category, the one with the largest number of values, is the range of profits between $750,000 and $1,000,000.

In comparing the simulation approach to risk analysis to the what-if approach, we see that much more information is obtained by using simulation. With the what-if analysis, we learned that the base-case scenario projected a profit of $710,000. The worst-case scenario projected a loss of $847,000, and the best-case scenario projected a profit of $2,591,000. From the 500 trials of the simulation run, we see that the worst- and best-case scenarios, although possible, are unlikely. None of the 500 trials provided a loss as low as the worst-case or a profit as high as the best-case. Indeed, the advantage of simulation for risk analysis is the information it provides on the likely values of the output. We now know the probability of a loss, how the profit values are distributed over their range, and what profit values are most likely.

The simulation results help PortaCom's management better understand the profit/loss potential of the PortaCom portable printer. The 0.1020 probability of a loss may be acceptable to management given a probability of almost 0.80 (see Figure 12.7) that profit will exceed $250,000. On the other hand, PortaCom might want to conduct further market research before deciding whether to introduce the product. In any case, the simulation results should be helpful in reaching an appropriate decision. The Management Science in Action, Meeting Demand Levels at Pfizer, describes how a simulation model helped find ways to meet increasing demand for a product.

Simulation studies enable an objective estimate of the probability of a loss, which is an important aspect of risk analysis.

For practice working through a simulation problem, try Problems 9 and 14.

FIGURE 12.7   HISTOGRAM OF SIMULATED PROFIT FOR 500 TRIALS OF THE PORTACOM SIMULATION

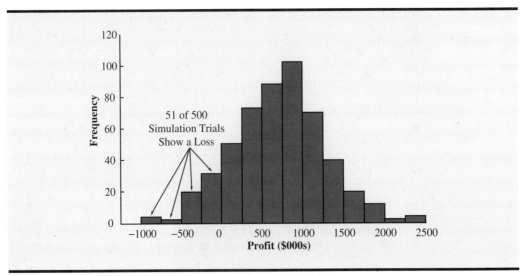

MANAGEMENT SCIENCE IN ACTION

MEETING DEMAND LEVELS AT PFIZER*

Pharmacia & Upjohn's merger with Pfizer created one of the world's largest pharmaceutical firms. Demand for one of Pharmacia & Upjohn's long-standing products remained stable for several years at a level easily satisfied by the company's manufacturing facility. However, changes in market conditions caused an increase in demand to a level beyond the current capacity. A simulation model of the production process was developed to explore ways to increase production to meet the new level of demand in a cost-effective manner.

Simulation results were used to help answer the following questions:

- What is the maximum throughput of the existing facility?
- How can the existing production process be modified to increase throughput?
- How much equipment must be added to the existing facility to meet the increased demand?

- What is the desired size and configuration of the new production process?

The simulation model was able to demonstrate that the existing facilities, with some operating policy improvements, were large enough to satisfy the increased demand for the next several years. Expansion to a new production facility was not necessary. The simulation model also helped determine the number of operators required as the production level increased in the future. This result helped ensure that the proper number of operators would be trained by the time they were needed. The simulation model also provided a way reprocessed material could be used to replace fresh raw materials, resulting in a savings of approximately $3 million per year.

*Based on information provided by David B. Magerlein, James M. Magerlein, and Michael J. Goodrich.

NOTES AND COMMENTS

Appendix 12.2 shows how to perform a simulation of the PortaCom project using Crystal Ball.

1. The PortaCom simulation model is based on independent trials in which the results for one trial do not affect what happens in subsequent trials. Historically, this type of simulation study was referred to as a *Monte Carlo simulation*. The term *Monte Carlo simulation* was used because early practitioners of simulation saw similarities between the models they were developing and the gambling games played in the casinos of Monte Carlo. Today, many individuals interpret the term *Monte Carlo simulation* more broadly to mean any simulation that involves randomly generating values for the probabilistic inputs.

2. The probability distribution used to generate values for probabilistic inputs in a simulation model is often developed using historical data. For instance, suppose that an analysis of daily sales at a new car dealership for the past 50 days showed that on 2 days no cars were sold, on 5 days one car was sold, on 9 days two cars were sold, on 24 days three cars were sold, on 7 days four cars were sold, and on 3 days five cars were

sold. We can estimate the probability distribution of daily demand using the relative frequencies for the observed data. An estimate of the probability that no cars are sold on a given day is $2/50 = 0.04$, an estimate of the probability that one car is sold is $5/50 = 0.10$, and so on. The estimated probability distribution of daily demand is shown in the table below.

3. Spreadsheet add-in packages such as @RISK® and Crystal Ball® have been developed to make spreadsheet simulation easier. For instance, using Crystal Ball we could simulate the PortaCom new product introduction by first entering the formulas showing the relationships between the probabilistic inputs and the output measure, profit. Then, a probability distribution type is selected for each probabilistic input from among a number of available choices. Crystal Ball will generate random values for each probabilistic input, compute the profit, and repeat the simulation for as many trials as specified. Graphical displays and a variety of descriptive statistics can be easily obtained.

Daily Sales	0	1	2	3	4	5
Probability	0.04	0.10	0.18	0.48	0.14	0.06

12.2   INVENTORY SIMULATION

In this section we describe how simulation can be used to establish an inventory policy for a product that has an uncertain demand. The product is a home ventilation fan distributed by the Butler Electrical Supply Company. Each fan costs Butler $75 and sells for $125. Thus Butler realizes a gross profit of $125 − $75 = $50 for each fan sold. Monthly demand for the fan is described by a normal probability distribution with a mean of 100 units and a standard deviation of 20 units.

Butler receives monthly deliveries from its supplier and replenishes its inventory to a level of Q at the beginning of each month. This beginning inventory level is referred to as the replenishment level. If monthly demand is less than the replenishment level, an inventory holding cost of $15 is charged for each unit that is not sold. However, if monthly demand is greater than the replenishment level, a stockout occurs and a shortage cost is incurred. Because Butler assigns a goodwill cost of $30 for each customer turned away, a shortage cost of $30 is charged for each unit of demand that cannot be satisfied. Management would like to use a simulation model to determine the average monthly net profit resulting from using a particular replenishment level. Management would also like information on the percentage of total demand that will be satisfied. This percentage is referred to as the *service level*.

The controllable input to the Butler simulation model is the replenishment level, Q. The probabilistic input is the monthly demand, D. The two output measures are the average monthly net profit and the service level. Computation of the service level requires that we keep track of the number of fans sold each month and the total demand for fans for each month. The service level will be computed at the end of the simulation run as the ratio of total units sold to total demand. A diagram of the relationship between the inputs and the outputs is shown in Figure 12.8.

When demand is less than or equal to the replenishment level ($D \leq Q$), D units are sold, and an inventory holding cost of $15 is incurred for each of the $Q − D$ units that remain in inventory. Net profit for this case is computed as follows:

Case 1: $D \leq Q$

$$
\begin{aligned}
\text{Gross profit} &= \$50D \\
\text{Holding cost} &= \$15(Q - D) \\
\text{Net profit} &= \text{Gross profit} - \text{Holding cost} = \$50D - \$15(Q - D)
\end{aligned}
\tag{12.5}
$$

When demand is greater than the replenishment level ($D > Q$), Q fans are sold, and a shortage cost of $30 is imposed for each of the $D − Q$ units of demand not satisfied. Net profit for this case is computed as follows:

Case 2: $D > Q$

$$
\begin{aligned}
\text{Gross profit} &= \$50Q \\
\text{Shortage cost} &= \$30(D - Q) \\
\text{Net profit} &= \text{Gross profit} - \text{Shortage cost} = \$50Q - \$30(D - Q)
\end{aligned}
\tag{12.6}
$$

Figure 12.9 shows a flowchart that defines the sequence of logical and mathematical operations required to simulate the Butler inventory system. Each trial in the simulation

FIGURE 12.8   BUTLER INVENTORY SIMULATION MODEL

FIGURE 12.9   FLOWCHART FOR THE BUTLER INVENTORY SIMULATION

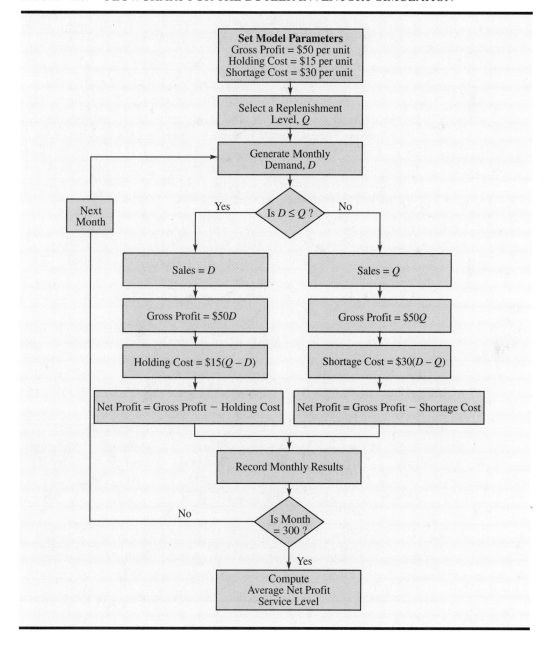

represents one month of operation. The simulation is run for 300 months using a given re-plenishment level, Q. Then the average profit and service level output measures are com-puted. Let us describe the steps involved in the simulation by illustrating the results for the first two months of a simulation run using a replenishment level of $Q = 100$.

The first block of the flowchart in Figure 12.9 sets the values of the model parameters: gross profit = $50 per unit, holding cost = $15 per unit, and shortage cost = $30 per unit. The next block shows that a replenishment level of Q is selected; in our illustration, $Q = 100$. Then a value for monthly demand is generated. Because monthly demand is normally distributed with a mean of 100 units and a standard deviation of 20 units, we can use the Excel function =NORMINV(RAND(),100,20), as described in Section 12.1, to generate a value for monthly demand. Suppose that a value of $D = 79$ is generated on the first trial. This value of demand is then compared with the replenishment level, Q. With the replen-ishment level set at $Q = 100$, demand is less than the replenishment level, and the left branch of the flowchart is followed. Sales are set equal to demand (79), and gross profit, holding cost, and net profit are computed as follows:

$$\text{Gross profit} = 50D = 50(79) = 3950$$
$$\text{Holding cost} = 15(Q - D) = 15(100 - 79) = 315$$
$$\text{Net profit} = \text{Gross profit} - \text{Holding cost} = 3950 - 315 = 3635$$

The values of demand, sales, gross profit, holding cost, and net profit are recorded for the first month. The first row of Table 12.8 summarizes the information for this first trial.

For the second month, suppose that a value of 111 is generated for monthly demand. Because demand is greater than the replenishment level, the right branch of the flowchart is followed. Sales are set equal to the replenishment level (100), and gross profit, shortage cost, and net profit are computed as follows:

$$\text{Gross profit} = 50Q = 50(100) = 5000$$
$$\text{Shortage cost} = 30(D - Q) = 30(111 - 100) = 330$$
$$\text{Net profit} = \text{Gross profit} - \text{Shortage cost} = 5000 - 330 = 4670$$

The values of demand, sales, gross profit, holding cost, shortage cost, and net profit are recorded for the second month. The second row of Table 12.8 summarizes the information generated in the second trial.

Results for the first five months of the simulation are shown in Table 12.8. The totals show an accumulated total net profit of $22,310, which is an average monthly net profit of

TABLE 12.8   BUTLER INVENTORY SIMULATION RESULTS FOR FIVE TRIALS
            WITH $Q = 100$

Month	Demand	Sales	Gross Profit ($)	Holding Cost ($)	Shortage Cost ($)	Net Profit ($)
1	79	79	3,950	315	0	3,635
2	111	100	5,000	0	330	4,670
3	93	93	4,650	105	0	4,545
4	100	100	5,000	0	0	5,000
5	118	100	5,000	0	540	4,460
Totals	501	472	23,600	420	870	22,310
Average	100	94	$4,720	$ 84	$174	$4,462

$22,310/5 = $4462. Total unit sales are 472, and total demand is 501. Thus, the service level is 472/501 = 0.942, indicating Butler has been able to satisfy 94.2% of demand during the five-month period.

Butler Inventory Simulation

Using Excel, we simulated the Butler inventory operation for 300 months. The worksheet used to carry out the simulation is shown in Figure 12.10. Note that the simulation results for months 6 through 295 have been hidden so that the results can be shown in a reasonably sized figure. If desired, the rows for these months can be shown and the simulation results displayed for all 300 months.

FIGURE 12.10   EXCEL WORKSHEET FOR THE BUTLER INVENTORY SIMULATION

WEB file

Butler

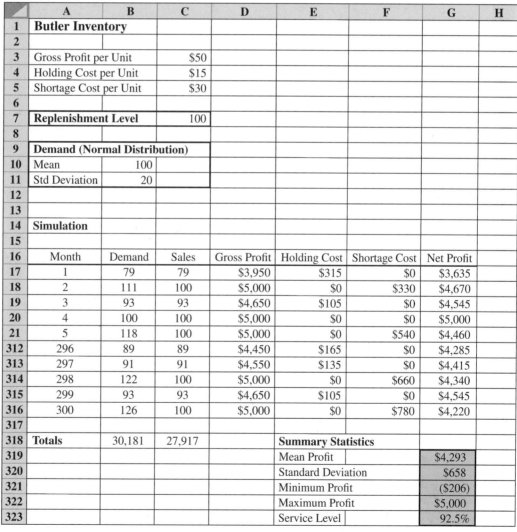

	A	B	C	D	E	F	G	H
1	**Butler Inventory**							
2								
3	Gross Profit per Unit		$50					
4	Holding Cost per Unit		$15					
5	Shortage Cost per Unit		$30					
6								
7	**Replenishment Level**		100					
8								
9	**Demand (Normal Distribution)**							
10	Mean	100						
11	Std Deviation	20						
12								
13								
14	**Simulation**							
15								
16	Month	Demand	Sales	Gross Profit	Holding Cost	Shortage Cost	Net Profit	
17	1	79	79	$3,950	$315	$0	$3,635	
18	2	111	100	$5,000	$0	$330	$4,670	
19	3	93	93	$4,650	$105	$0	$4,545	
20	4	100	100	$5,000	$0	$0	$5,000	
21	5	118	100	$5,000	$0	$540	$4,460	
312	296	89	89	$4,450	$165	$0	$4,285	
313	297	91	91	$4,550	$135	$0	$4,415	
314	298	122	100	$5,000	$0	$660	$4,340	
315	299	93	93	$4,650	$105	$0	$4,545	
316	300	126	100	$5,000	$0	$780	$4,220	
317								
318	**Totals**	30,181	27,917		**Summary Statistics**			
319					Mean Profit		$4,293	
320					Standard Deviation		$658	
321					Minimum Profit		($206)	
322					Maximum Profit		$5,000	
323					Service Level		92.5%	

TABLE 12.9   BUTLER INVENTORY SIMULATION RESULTS FOR 300 TRIALS

Replenishment Level	Average Net Profit ($)	Service Level (%)
100	4293	92.5
110	4524	96.5
120	4575	98.6
130	4519	99.6
140	4399	99.9

Simulation allows the user to consider different operating policies and changes to model parameters and then to observe the impact of the changes on output measures such as profit or service level.

The summary statistics in Figure 12.10 show what can be anticipated over 300 months if Butler operates its inventory system using a replenishment level of 100. The average net profit is $4293 per month. Because 27,917 units of the total demand of 30,181 units were satisfied, the service level is 27,917/30,181 = 92.5%. We are now ready to use the simulation model to consider other replenishment levels that may improve the net profit and the service level.

At this point, we conducted a series of simulation experiments by repeating the Butler inventory simulation with replenishment levels of 110, 120, 130, and 140 units. The average monthly net profits and the service levels are shown in Table 12.9. The highest monthly net profit of $4575 occurs with a replenishment level of $Q = 120$. The associated service level is 98.6%. On the basis of these results, Butler selected a replenishment level of $Q = 120$.

Experimental simulation studies, such as this one for Butler's inventory policy, can help identify good operating policies and decisions. Butler's management used simulation to choose a replenishment level of 120 for its home ventilation fan. With the simulation model in place, management can also explore the sensitivity of this decision to some of the model parameters. For instance, we assigned a shortage cost of $30 for any customer demand not met. With this shortage cost, the replenishment level was $Q = 120$ and the service level was 98.6%. If management felt a more appropriate shortage cost was $10 per unit, running the simulation again using $10 as the shortage cost would be a simple matter.

Problem 18 gives you a chance to develop a different simulation model.

We mentioned earlier that simulation is not an optimization technique. Even though we used simulation to choose a replenishment level, it does not guarantee that this choice is optimal. All possible replenishment levels were not tested. Perhaps a manager would like to consider additional simulation runs with replenishment levels of $Q = 115$ and $Q = 125$ to search for an even better inventory policy. Also, we have no guarantee that with another set of 300 randomly generated demand values the replenishment level with the highest profit would not change. However, with a large number of simulation trials, we should find a good and, at least, near optimal solution. The Management Science in Action, Petroleum Distribution in the Gulf of Mexico, describes a simulation application for 15 petroleum companies in the state of Florida.

MANAGEMENT SCIENCE IN ACTION

PETROLEUM DISTRIBUTION IN THE GULF OF MEXICO*

Domestic suppliers who operate oil refineries along the Gulf Coast are helping to satisfy Florida's increasing demand for refined petroleum products. Barge fleets, operated either by independent shipping companies or by the petroleum companies themselves, are used to transport more than 20 different petroleum products to 15 Florida petroleum companies. The petroleum products are loaded at refineries in Texas, Louisiana, and Mississippi and are discharged at tank terminals concentrated in Tampa, Port Everglades, and Jacksonville.

Barges operate under three types of contracts between the fleet operator and the client petroleum company:

- The client assumes total control of a barge and uses it for trips between its own refinery and one or more discharging ports.
- The client is guaranteed a certain volume will be moved during the contract period. Schedules vary considerably depending upon the customer's needs and the fleet operator's capabilities.
- The client hires a barge for a single trip.

A simulation model was developed to analyze the complex process of operating barge fleets in the Gulf of Mexico. An appropriate probability distribution was used to simulate requests for shipments by the petroleum companies. Additional probability distributions were used to simulate the travel times depending upon the size and type of barge. Using this information, the simulation model was used to track barge loading times, barge discharge times, barge utilization, and total cost.

Analysts used simulation runs with a variety of what-if scenarios to answer questions about the petroleum distribution system and to make recommendations for improving the efficiency of the operation. Simulation helped determine the following:

- The optimal trade-off between fleet utilization and on-time delivery
- The recommended fleet size
- The recommended barge capacities
- The best service contract structure to balance the trade-off between customer service and delivery cost

Implementation of the simulation-based recommendations demonstrated a significant improvement in the operation and a significant lowering of petroleum distribution costs.

*Based on E. D. Chajakis, "Sophisticated Crude Transportation," *OR/MS Today* (December 1997): 30–34.

12.3   WAITING LINE SIMULATION

The simulation models discussed thus far have been based on independent trials in which the results for one trial do not affect what happens in subsequent trials. In this sense, the system being modeled does not change or evolve over time. Simulation models such as these are referred to as **static simulation models.** In this section we develop a simulation model of a waiting line system where the state of the system, including the number of customers in the waiting line and whether the service facility is busy or idle, changes or evolves over time. To incorporate time into the simulation model, we use a simulation clock to record the time that each customer arrives for service as well as the time that each customer completes service. Simulation models that must take into account how the system changes or evolves over time are referred to as **dynamic simulation models.** In situations where the arrivals and departures of customers are **events** that occur at *discrete* points in time, the simulation model is also referred to as a **discrete-event simulation model.**

In Chapter 11 we presented formulas that could be used to compute the steady-state operating characteristics of a waiting line, including the average waiting time, the average number of units in the waiting line, the probability of waiting, and so on. In most cases, the waiting line formulas were based on specific assumptions about the probability distribution for arrivals, the probability distribution for service times, the queue discipline, and so on. Simulation, as an alternative for studying waiting lines, is more flexible. In applications where the assumptions required by the waiting line formulas are not reasonable, simulation may be the only feasible approach to studying the waiting line system. In this section we discuss the simulation of the waiting line for the Hammondsport Savings Bank automated teller machine (ATM).

Hammondsport Savings Bank ATM Waiting Line

Hammondsport Savings Bank will open several new branch banks during the coming year. Each new branch is designed to have one automated teller machine (ATM). A concern is that during busy periods several customers may have to wait to use the ATM. This concern prompted the bank to undertake a study of the ATM waiting line system. The bank's vice president wants to determine whether one ATM will be sufficient. The bank established service guidelines for its ATM system stating that the average customer waiting time for an ATM should be one minute or less. Let us show how a simulation model can be used to study the ATM waiting line at a particular branch.

Customer Arrival Times

One probabilistic input to the ATM simulation model is the arrival times of customers who use the ATM. In waiting line simulations, arrival times are determined by randomly generating the time between two successive arrivals, referred to as the *interarrival time*. For the branch bank being studied, the customer interarrival times are assumed to be uniformly distributed between 0 and 5 minutes, as shown in Figure 12.11. With r denoting a random number between 0 and 1, an interarrival time for two successive customers can be simulated by using the formula for generating values from a uniform probability distribution.

$$\text{Interarrival time} = a + r(b - a) \qquad (12.7)$$

where

$$r = \text{random number between 0 and 1}$$
$$a = \text{minimum interarrival time}$$
$$b = \text{maximum interarrival time}$$

A uniform probability distribution of interarrival times is used here to illustrate the simulation computations. Actually, any interarrival time probability distribution can be assumed, and the logic of the waiting line simulation model will not change.

For the Hammondsport ATM system, the minimum interarrival time is $a = 0$ minutes, and the maximum interarrival time is $b = 5$ minutes; therefore, the formula for generating an interarrival time is

$$\text{Interarrival time} = 0 + r(5 - 0) = 5r \qquad (12.8)$$

Assume that the simulation run begins at time $= 0$. A random number of $r = 0.2804$ generates an interarrival time of $5(0.2804) = 1.4$ minutes for customer 1. Thus, customer 1 arrives 1.4 minutes after the simulation run begins. A second random number of $r = 0.2598$

FIGURE 12.11   UNIFORM PROBABILITY DISTRIBUTION OF INTERARRIVAL TIMES FOR THE ATM WAITING LINE SYSTEM

FIGURE 12.12 NORMAL PROBABILITY DISTRIBUTION OF SERVICE TIMES
FOR THE ATM WAITING LINE SYSTEM

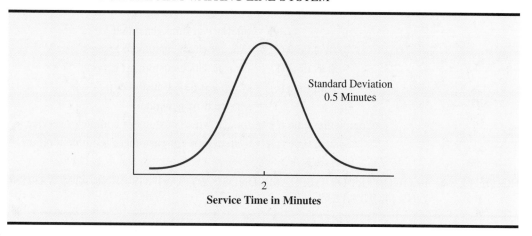

Standard Deviation
0.5 Minutes

2

Service Time in Minutes

generates an interarrival time of 5(0.2598) = 1.3 minutes, indicating that customer 2 arrives 1.3 minutes after customer 1. Thus, customer 2 arrives 1.4 + 1.3 = 2.7 minutes after the simulation begins. Continuing, a third random number of $r = 0.9802$ indicates that customer 3 arrives 4.9 minutes after customer 2, which is 7.6 minutes after the simulation begins.

Customer Service Times

Another probabilistic input in the ATM simulation model is the service time, which is the time a customer spends using the ATM machine. Past data from similar ATMs indicate that a normal probability distribution with a mean of 2 minutes and a standard deviation of 0.5 minutes, as shown in Figure 12.12, can be used to describe service times. As discussed in Sections 12.1 and 12.2, values from a normal probability distribution with mean 2 and standard deviation 0.5 can be generated using the Excel function =NORMINV(RAND(),2,0.5). For example, the random number of 0.7257 generates a customer service time of 2.3 minutes.

Simulation Model

The probabilistic inputs to the Hammondsport Savings Bank ATM simulation model are the interarrival time and the service time. The controllable input is the number of ATMs used. The output will consist of various operating characteristics such as the probability of waiting, the average waiting time, the maximum waiting time, and so on. We show a diagram of the ATM simulation model in Figure 12.13.

FIGURE 12.13 HAMMONDSPORT SAVINGS BANK ATM SIMULATION MODEL

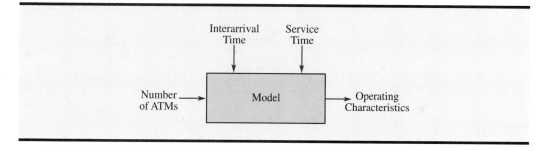

Figure 12.14 shows a flowchart that defines the sequence of logical and mathematical operations required to simulate the Hammondsport ATM system. The flowchart uses the following notation:

$$IAT = \text{interarrival time generated}$$
$$\text{Arrival time } (i) = \text{time at which customer } i \text{ arrives}$$
$$\text{Start time } (i) = \text{time at which customer } I \text{ service}$$
$$\text{Wait time } (i) = \text{waiting time for customer } i$$
$$ST = \text{service time generated}$$
$$\text{Completion time } (i) = \text{time at which customer } i \text{ completes service}$$
$$\text{System time } (i) = \text{system time for customer } i \text{ (completion time } - \text{ arrival time)}$$

FIGURE 12.14   FLOWCHART OF THE HAMMONDSPORT SAVINGS BANK ATM WAITING LINE SIMULATION

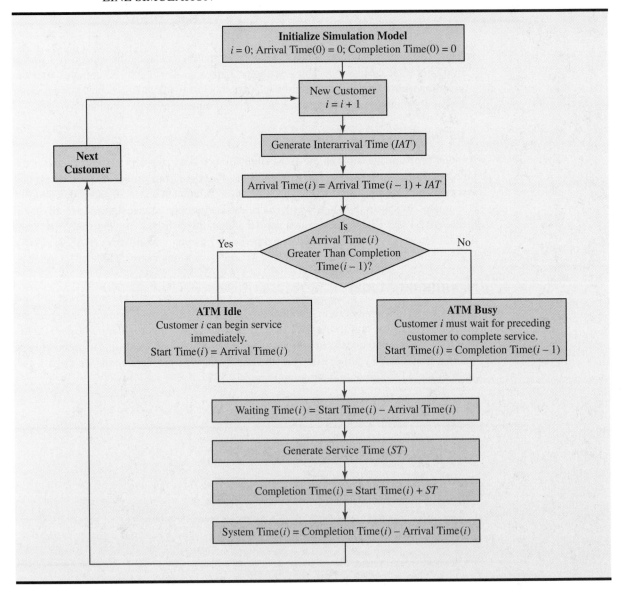

Referring to Figure 12.14, we see that the simulation is initialized in the first block of the flowchart. Then a new customer is created. An interarrival time is generated to determine the time since the preceding customer arrived.[2] The arrival time for the new customer is then computed by adding the interarrival time to the arrival time of the preceding customer.

The decision rule for deciding whether the ATM is idle or busy is the most difficult aspect of the logic in a waiting line simulation model.

The arrival time for the new customer must be compared to the completion time of the preceding customer to determine whether the ATM is idle or busy. If the arrival time of the new customer is greater than the completion time of the preceding customer, the preceding customer will have finished service prior to the arrival of the new customer. In this case, the ATM will be idle, and the new customer can begin service immediately. The service start time for the new customer is equal to the arrival time of the new customer. However, if the arrival time for the new customer is not greater than the completion time of the preceding customer, the new customer arrived before the preceding customer finished service. In this case, the ATM is busy; the new customer must wait to use the ATM until the preceding customer completes service. The service start time for the new customer is equal to the completion time of the preceding customer.

Note that the time the new customer has to wait to use the ATM is the difference between the customer's service start time and the customer's arrival time. At this point, the customer is ready to use the ATM, and the simulation run continues with the generation of the customer's service time. The time at which the customer begins service plus the service time generated determine the customer's completion time. Finally, the total time the customer spends in the system is the difference between the customer's service completion time and the customer's arrival time. At this point, the computations are complete for the current customer, and the simulation continues with the next customer. The simulation is continued until a specified number of customers have been served by the ATM.

Simulation results for the first 10 customers are shown in Table 12.10. We discuss the computations for the first three customers to illustrate the logic of the simulation model and to show how the information in Table 12.10 was developed.

TABLE 12.10   SIMULATION RESULTS FOR 10 ATM CUSTOMERS

Customer	Interarrival Time	Arrival Time	Service Start Time	Waiting Time	Service Time	Completion Time	Time in System
1	1.4	1.4	1.4	0.0	2.3	3.7	2.3
2	1.3	2.7	3.7	1.0	1.5	5.2	2.5
3	4.9	7.6	7.6	0.0	2.2	9.8	2.2
4	3.5	11.1	11.1	0.0	2.5	13.6	2.5
5	0.7	11.8	13.6	1.8	1.8	15.4	3.6
6	2.8	14.6	15.4	0.8	2.4	17.8	3.2
7	2.1	16.7	17.8	1.1	2.1	19.9	3.2
8	0.6	17.3	19.9	2.6	1.8	21.7	4.4
9	2.5	19.8	21.7	1.9	2.0	23.7	3.9
10	1.9	21.7	23.7	2.0	2.3	26.0	4.3
Totals	21.7			11.2	20.9		32.1
Averages	2.17			1.12	2.09		3.21

---

[2]For the first customer, the interarrival time determines the time since the simulation started. Thus, the first interarrival time determines the time the first customer arrives.

Customer 1

- An interarrival time of $IAT = 1.4$ minutes is generated.
- Because the simulation run begins at time 0, the arrival time for customer 1 is $0 + 1.4 = 1.4$ minutes.
- Customer 1 may begin service immediately with a start time of 1.4 minutes.
- The waiting time for customer 1 is the start time minus the arrival time: $1.4 - 1.4 = 0$ minutes.
- A service time of $ST = 2.3$ minutes is generated for customer 1.
- The completion time for customer 1 is the start time plus the service time: $1.4 + 2.3 = 3.7$ minutes.
- The time in the system for customer 1 is the completion time minus the arrival time: $3.7 - 1.4 = 2.3$ minutes.

Customer 2

- An interarrival time of $IAT = 1.3$ minutes is generated.
- Because the arrival time of customer 1 is 1.4, the arrival time for customer 2 is $1.4 + 1.3 = 2.7$ minutes.
- Because the completion time of customer 1 is 3.7 minutes, the arrival time of customer 2 is not greater than the completion time of customer 1; thus, the ATM is busy when customer 2 arrives.
- Customer 2 must wait for customer 1 to complete service before beginning service. Customer 1 completes service at 3.7 minutes, which becomes the start time for customer 2.
- The waiting time for customer 2 is the start time minus the arrival time: $3.7 - 2.7 = 1$ minute.
- A service time of $ST = 1.5$ minutes is generated for customer 2.
- The completion time for customer 2 is the start time plus the service time: $3.7 = 1.5 = 5.2$ minutes.
- The time in the system for customer 2 is the completion time minus the arrival time: $5.2 - 2.7 = 2.5$ minutes.

Customer 3

- An interarrival time of $IAT = 4.9$ minutes is generated.
- Because the arrival time of customer 2 was 2.7 minutes, the arrival time for customer 3 is $2.7 + 4.9 = 7.6$ minutes.
- The completion time of customer 2 is 5.2 minutes, so the arrival time for customer 3 is greater than the completion time of customer 2. Thus, the ATM is idle when customer 3 arrives.
- Customer 3 begins service immediately with a start time of 7.6 minutes.
- The waiting time for customer 3 is the start time minus the arrival time: $7.6 - 7.6 = 0$ minutes.
- A service time of $ST = 2.2$ minutes is generated for customer 3.
- The completion time for customer 3 is the start time plus the service time: $7.6 + 2.2 = 9.8$ minutes.
- The time in the system for customer 3 is the completion time minus the arrival time: $9.8 - 7.6 = 2.2$ minutes.

Using the totals in Table 12.10, we can compute an average waiting time for the 10 customers of $11.2/10 = 1.12$ minutes, and an average time in the system of $32.1/10 = 3.21$ minutes. Table 12.10 shows that seven of the 10 customers had to wait. The total time for the

10-customer simulation is given by the completion time of the 10th customer: 26.0 minutes. However, at this point, we realize that a simulation for 10 customers is much too short a period to draw any firm conclusions about the operation of the waiting line.

Hammondsport Savings Bank ATM Simulation

Using an Excel worksheet, we simulated the operation of the Hammondsport ATM waiting line system for 1000 customers. The worksheet used to carry out the simulation is shown in Figure 12.15. Note that the simulation results for customers 6 through 995 have been hidden so that the results can be shown in a reasonably sized figure. If desired, the rows for these customers can be shown and the simulation results displayed for all 1000 customers.

FIGURE 12.15   EXCEL WORKSHEET FOR THE HAMMONDSPORT SAVINGS BANK
WITH ONE ATM

WEB file

Hammondsport1

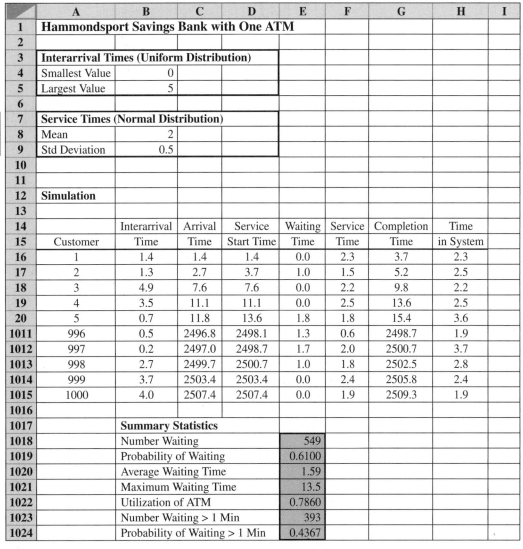

	A	B	C	D	E	F	G	H	I
1	**Hammondsport Savings Bank with One ATM**								
2									
3	**Interarrival Times (Uniform Distribution)**								
4	Smallest Value	0							
5	Largest Value	5							
6									
7	**Service Times (Normal Distribution)**								
8	Mean	2							
9	Std Deviation	0.5							
10									
11									
12	**Simulation**								
13									
14		Interarrival	Arrival	Service	Waiting	Service	Completion	Time	
15	Customer	Time	Time	Start Time	Time	Time	Time	in System	
16	1	1.4	1.4	1.4	0.0	2.3	3.7	2.3	
17	2	1.3	2.7	3.7	1.0	1.5	5.2	2.5	
18	3	4.9	7.6	7.6	0.0	2.2	9.8	2.2	
19	4	3.5	11.1	11.1	0.0	2.5	13.6	2.5	
20	5	0.7	11.8	13.6	1.8	1.8	15.4	3.6	
1011	996	0.5	2496.8	2498.1	1.3	0.6	2498.7	1.9	
1012	997	0.2	2497.0	2498.7	1.7	2.0	2500.7	3.7	
1013	998	2.7	2499.7	2500.7	1.0	1.8	2502.5	2.8	
1014	999	3.7	2503.4	2503.4	0.0	2.4	2505.8	2.4	
1015	1000	4.0	2507.4	2507.4	0.0	1.9	2509.3	1.9	
1016									
1017		**Summary Statistics**							
1018		Number Waiting			549				
1019		Probability of Waiting			0.6100				
1020		Average Waiting Time			1.59				
1021		Maximum Waiting Time			13.5				
1022		Utilization of ATM			0.7860				
1023		Number Waiting > 1 Min			393				
1024		Probability of Waiting > 1 Min			0.4367				

FIGURE 12.16   HISTOGRAM SHOWING THE WAITING TIME FOR 900 ATM CUSTOMERS

Ultimately, summary statistics will be collected in order to describe the results of 1000 customers. Before collecting the summary statistics, let us point out that most simulation studies of dynamic systems focus on the operation of the system during its long-run or steady-state operation. To ensure that the effects of start-up conditions are not included in the steady-state calculations, a dynamic simulation model is usually run for a specified period without collecting any data about the operation of the system. The length of the start-up period can vary depending on the application. For the Hammondsport Savings Bank ATM simulation, we treated the results for the first 100 customers as the start-up period. Thus, the summary statistics shown in Figure 12.15 are for the 900 customers arriving during the steady-state period.

The summary statistics show that 549 of the 900 Hammondsport customers had to wait. This result provides a $549/900 = 0.61$ probability that a customer will have to wait for service. In other words, approximately 61% of the customers will have to wait because the ATM is in use. The average waiting time is 1.59 minutes per customer with at least one customer waiting the maximum time of 13.5 minutes. The utilization rate of 0.7860 indicates that the ATM is in use 78.6% of the time. Finally, 393 of the 900 customers had to wait more than 1 minute (43.67% of all customers). A histogram of waiting times for the 900 customers is shown in Figure 12.16. This figure shows that 45 customers (5%) had a waiting time greater than 6 minutes.

The simulation supports the conclusion that the branch will have a busy ATM system. With an average customer wait time of 1.59 minutes, the branch does not satisfy the bank's customer service guideline. This branch is a good candidate for installation of a second ATM.

Simulation with Two ATMs

We extended the simulation model to the case of two ATMs. For the second ATM we also assume that the service time is normally distributed with a mean of 2 minutes and a standard deviation of 0.5 minutes. Table 12.11 shows the simulation results for the first 10 customers. In comparing the two-ATM system results in Table 12.11 with the single ATM simulation results shown in Table 12.10, we see that two additional columns are needed. These two columns show when each ATM becomes available for customer service. We assume that, when a new customer arrives, the customer will be served by the ATM that frees up first. When the simulation begins, the first customer is assigned to ATM 1.

TABLE 12.11   SIMULATION RESULTS FOR 10 CUSTOMERS FOR A TWO-ATM SYSTEM

Customer	Interarrival Time	Arrival Time	Service Start Time	Waiting Time	Service Time	Completion Time	Time in System	Time Available ATM 1	Time Available ATM 2
1	1.7	1.7	1.7	0.0	2.1	3.8	2.1	3.8	0.0
2	0.7	2.4	2.4	0.0	2.0	4.4	2.0	3.8	4.4
3	2.0	4.4	4.4	0.0	1.4	5.8	1.4	5.8	4.4
4	0.1	4.5	4.5	0.0	0.9	5.4	0.9	5.8	5.4
5	4.6	9.1	9.1	0.0	2.2	11.3	2.2	5.8	11.3
6	1.3	10.4	10.4	0.0	1.6	12.0	1.6	12.0	11.3
7	0.6	11.0	11.3	0.3	1.7	13.0	2.0	12.0	13.0
8	0.3	11.3	12.0	0.7	2.2	14.2	2.9	14.2	13.0
9	3.4	14.7	14.7	0.0	2.9	17.6	2.9	14.2	17.6
10	0.1	14.8	14.8	0.0	2.8	17.6	2.8	17.6	17.6
Totals	14.8			1.0	19.8		20.8		
Averages	1.48			0.1	1.98		2.08		

Table 12.11 shows that customer 7 is the first customer who has to wait to use an ATM. We describe how customers 6, 7, and 8 are processed to show how the logic of the simulation run for two ATMs differs from that with a single ATM.

Customer 6

- An interarrival time of 1.3 minutes is generated, and customer 6 arrives 9.1 + 1.3 = 10.4 minutes into the simulation.
- From the customer 5 row, we see that ATM 1 frees up at 5.8 minutes, and ATM 2 will free up at 11.3 minutes into the simulation. Because ATM 1 is free, customer 6 does not wait and begins service on ATM 1 at the arrival time of 10.4 minutes.
- A service time of 1.6 minutes is generated for customer 6. So customer 6 has a completion time of 10.4 + 1.6 = 12.0 minutes.
- The time ATM 1 will next become available is set at 12.0 minutes; the time available for ATM 2 remains 11.3 minutes.

Customer 7

- An interarrival time of 0.6 minute is generated, and customer 7 arrives 10.4 + 0.6 = 11.0 minutes into the simulation.
- From the previous row, we see that ATM 1 will not be available until 12.0 minutes, and ATM 2 will not be available until 11.3 minutes. So customer 7 must wait to use an ATM. Because ATM 2 will free up first, customer 7 begins service on that machine at a start time of 11.3 minutes. With an arrival time of 11.0 and a service start time of 11.3, customer 7 experiences a waiting time of 11.3 − 11.0 = 0.3 minute.
- A service time of 1.7 minutes is generated, leading to a completion time of 11.3 + 1.7 = 13.0 minutes.
- The time available for ATM 2 is updated to 13.0 minutes, and the time available for ATM 1 remains at 12.0 minutes.

Customer 8

- An interarrival time of 0.3 minute is generated, and customer 8 arrives 11.0 + 0.3 = 11.3 minutes into the simulation.
- From the previous row, we see that ATM 1 will be the first available. Thus, customer 8 starts service on ATM 1 at 12.0 minutes resulting in a waiting time of 12.0 − 11.3 = 0.7 minute.

- A service time of 2.2 minutes is generated, resulting in a completion time of 12.0 + 2.2 = 14.2 minutes and a system time of 0.7 + 2.2 = 2.9 minutes.
- The time available for ATM 1 is updated to 14.2 minutes, and the time available for ATM 2 remains at 13.0 minutes.

From the totals in Table 12.11, we see that the average waiting time for these 10 customers is only 1.0/10 = 0.1 minute. Of course, a much longer simulation will be necessary before any conclusions can be drawn.

Worksheets for the Hammondsport one-ATM and two-ATM systems are available on the website that accompanies this text.

Simulation Results with Two ATMs

The Excel worksheet that we used to conduct a simulation for 1000 customers using two ATMs is shown in Figure 12.17. Results for the first 100 customers were discarded to account for the start-up period. With two ATMs, the number of customers who had to wait was reduced from 549 to 78. This reduction provides a 78/900 = 0.0867 probability that a customer will have to wait for service when two ATMs are used. The two-ATM system also reduced the

FIGURE 12.17   EXCEL WORKSHEET FOR THE HAMMONDSPORT SAVINGS BANK WITH TWO ATMs

WEB file

Hammondsport2

	A	B	C	D	E	F	G	H	I	J	K
1	Hammondsport Savings Bank with Two ATMs										
2											
3	Interarrival Times (Uniform Distribution)										
4	Smallest Value	0									
5	Largest Value	5									
6											
7	Service Times (Normal Distribution)										
8	Mean	2									
9	Std Deviation	0.5									
10											
11											
12	Simulation										
13											
14		Interarrival	Arrival	Service	Waiting	Service	Completion	Time	Time Available		
15	Customer	Time	Time	Start Time	Time	Time	Time	in System	ATM 1	ATM 2	
16	1	1.7	1.7	1.7	0.0	2.1	3.8	2.1	3.8	0.0	
17	2	0.7	2.4	2.4	0.0	2.0	4.4	2.0	3.8	4.4	
18	3	2.0	4.4	4.4	0.0	1.4	5.8	1.4	5.8	4.4	
19	4	0.1	4.5	4.5	0.0	0.9	5.4	0.9	5.8	5.4	
20	5	4.6	9.1	9.1	0.0	2.2	11.3	2.2	5.8	11.3	
1011	996	3.3	2483.2	2483.2	0.0	2.2	2485.4	2.2	2485.4	2482.1	
1012	997	4.5	2487.7	2487.7	0.0	1.9	2489.6	1.9	2485.4	2489.6	
1013	998	3.8	2491.5	2491.5	0.0	3.2	2494.7	3.2	2494.7	2489.6	
1014	999	0.0	2491.5	2491.5	0.0	2.4	2493.9	2.4	2494.7	2493.9	
1015	1000	2.6	2494.1	2494.1	0.0	2.8	2496.9	2.8	2494.7	2496.9	
1016											
1017		Summary Statistics									
1018		Number Waiting			78						
1019		Probability of Waiting			0.0867						
1020		Average Waiting Time			0.07						
1021		Maximum Waiting Time			2.9						
1022		Utilization of ATMs			0.4084						
1023		Number Waiting > 1 Min			23						
1024		Probability of Waiting > 1 Min			0.0256						

average waiting time to 0.07 minute (4.2 seconds) per customer. The maximum waiting time was reduced from 13.5 to 2.9 minutes, and each ATM was in use 40.84% of the time. Finally, only 23 of the 900 customers had to wait more than 1 minute for an ATM to become available. Thus, only 2.56% of customers had to wait more than 1 minute. The simulation results provide evidence that Hammondsport Savings Bank needs to expand to the two-ATM system.

The simulation models that we developed can now be used to study the ATM operation at other branch banks. In each case, assumptions must be made about the appropriate interarrival time and service time probability distributions. However, once appropriate assumptions have been made, the same simulation models can be used to determine the operating characteristics of the ATM waiting line system. The Management Science in Action, Preboard Screening at Vancouver International Airport, describes another use of simulation for a queueing system.

MANAGEMENT SCIENCE IN ACTION

PREBOARD SCREENING AT VANCOUVER INTERNATIONAL AIRPORT*

Following the September 11, 2001, terrorist attacks in the United States, long lines at airport security checkpoints became commonplace. In order to reduce passenger waiting time, the Vancouver International Airport Authority teamed up with students and faculty at the University of British Columbia's Centre for Operations Excellence (COE) to build a simulation model of the airport's preboard screening security checkpoints. The goal was to use the simulation model to help achieve acceptable service standards.

Prior to building the simulation model, students from the COE observed the flow of passengers through the screening process and collected data on the service time at each process step. In addition to service time data, passenger demand data provided input to the simulation model. Two triangular probability distributions were used to simulate passenger arrivals at the preboarding facilities. For flights to Canadian destinations a 90-40-20 triangle was used.

This distribution assumes that, for each flight, the first passenger will arrive at the screening checkpoint 90 minutes before departure, the last passenger will arrive 20 minutes before departure, and the most likely arrival time is 40 minutes before departure. For international flights a 150-80-20 triangle was used.

Output statistics from the simulation model provided information concerning resource utilization, waiting line lengths, and the time passengers spend in the system. The simulation model provided information concerning the number of personnel needed to process 90% of the passengers with a waiting time of 10 minutes or less. Ultimately, the airport authority was able to design and staff the preboarding checkpoints in such a fashion that waiting times for 90% of the passengers were a maximum of 10 minutes.

*Based on Derek Atkins et al., "Right on Queue," *OR/MS Today* (April 2003): 26–29.

NOTES AND COMMENTS

1. The ATM waiting line model was based on uniformly distributed interarrival times and normally distributed service times. One advantage of simulation is its flexibility in accommodating a variety of different probability distributions. For instance, if we believe an exponential distribution is more appropriate for interarrival times, the ATM simulation could be repeated by simply changing the way the interarrival times are generated.

2. At the beginning of this section, we defined *discrete-event simulation* as involving a dynamic system that evolves over time. The simulation computations focus on the sequence of events as they occur at discrete points in time. In the ATM waiting line example, customer arrivals and the customer service completions were the discrete events. Referring to the arrival times and completion times in Table 12.10, we see

(continued)

that the first five discrete events for the ATM waiting line simulation were as follows:

Event	Time
Customer 1 arrives	1.4
Customer 2 arrives	2.7
Customer 1 finished	3.7
Customer 2 finished	5.2
Customer 3 arrives	7.6

3. We did not keep track of the number of customers in the ATM waiting line as we carried out the ATM simulation computations on a customer-by-customer basis. However, we can determine the average number of customers in the waiting line from other information in the simulation output. The following relationship is valid for any waiting line system:

$$\frac{\text{Average number}}{\text{in waiting line}} = \frac{\text{Total waiting time}}{\text{Total time of simulation}}$$

For the system with one ATM, the 100th customer completed service at 247.8 minutes into the simulation. Thus, the total time of the simulation for the next 900 customers was $2509.3 - 247.8 = 2261.5$ minutes. The average waiting time was 1.59 minutes. During the simulation, the 900 customers had a total waiting time of $900(1.59) = 1431$ minutes. Therefore, the average number of customers in the waiting line is

$$\begin{aligned}\text{Average number}\\ \text{in waiting line} &= 1431/2261.5 \\ &= 0.63 \text{ customer}\end{aligned}$$

12.4 OTHER SIMULATION ISSUES

Because simulation is one of the most widely used quantitative analysis techniques, various software tools have been developed to help analysts implement a simulation model on a computer. In this section we comment on the software available and discuss some issues involved in verifying and validating a simulation model. We close the section with a discussion of some of the advantages and disadvantages of using simulation to study a real system.

Computer Implementation

The use of spreadsheets for simulation has grown rapidly in recent years, and third-party software vendors have developed spreadsheet add-ins that make building simulation models on a spreadsheet much easier. These add-in packages provide an easy facility for generating random values from a variety of probability distributions and provide a rich array of statistics describing the simulation output. Two popular spreadsheet add-ins are Crystal Ball from Oracle Corporation and @RISK from Palisade Corporation. Although spreadsheets can be a valuable tool for some simulation studies, they are generally limited to smaller, less complex systems.

With the growth of simulation applications, both users of simulation and software developers began to realize that computer simulations have many common features: model development, generating values from probability distributions, maintaining a record of what happens during the simulation, and recording and summarizing the simulation output. A variety of special-purpose simulation packages are available, including GPSS®, SIMSCRIPT®, SLAM®, and Arena®. These packages have built-in simulation clocks, simplified methods for generating probabilistic inputs, and procedures for collecting and summarizing the simulation output. Special-purpose simulation packages enable quantitative analysts to simplify the process of developing and implementing the simulation model. Indeed, Arena 6.0 was used to develop the simulation model described in the Management Science in Action, Preboard Screening at Vancouver International Airport.

The computational and record-keeping aspects of simulation models are assisted by special simulation software packages. The packages ease the tasks of developing a computer simulation model.

Simulation models can also be developed using general-purpose computer programming languages such as BASIC, FORTRAN, PASCAL, C, and C++. The disadvantage of using these languages is that special simulation procedures are not built in. One command in a special-purpose simulation package often performs the computations and record-keeping tasks that would require several BASIC, FORTRAN, PASCAL, C, or C++ statements to duplicate. The advantage of using a general-purpose programming language is that they offer greater flexibility in terms of being able to model more complex systems.

To decide which software to use, an analyst will have to consider the relative merits of a spreadsheet, a special-purpose simulation package, and a general-purpose computer programming language. The goal is to select the method that is easy to use while still providing an adequate representation of the system being studied.

Verification and Validation

An important aspect of any simulation study involves confirming that the simulation model accurately describes the real system. Inaccurate simulation models cannot be expected to provide worthwhile information. Thus, before using simulation results to draw conclusions about a real system, one must take steps to verify and validate the simulation model.

Verification is the process of determining that the computer procedure that performs the simulation calculations is logically correct. Verification is largely a debugging task to make sure that no errors are in the computer procedure that implements the simulation. In some cases, an analyst may compare computer results for a limited number of events with independent hand calculations. In other cases, tests may be performed to verify that the probabilistic inputs are being generated correctly and that the output from the simulation model seems reasonable. The verification step is not complete until the user develops a high degree of confidence that the computer procedure is error free.

Validation is the process of ensuring that the simulation model provides an accurate representation of a real system. Validation requires an agreement among analysts and managers that the logic and the assumptions used in the design of the simulation model accurately reflect how the real system operates. The first phase of the validation process is done prior to, or in conjunction with, the development of the computer procedure for the simulation process. Validation continues after the computer program has been developed, with the analyst reviewing the simulation output to see whether the simulation results closely approximate the performance of the real system. If possible, the output of the simulation model is compared to the output of an existing real system to make sure that the simulation output closely approximates the performance of the real system. If this form of validation is not possible, an analyst can experiment with the simulation model and have one or more individuals experienced with the operation of the real system review the simulation output to determine whether it is a reasonable approximation of what would be obtained with the real system under similar conditions.

Verification and validation are not tasks to be taken lightly. They are key steps in any simulation study and are necessary to ensure that decisions and conclusions based on the simulation results are appropriate for the real system.

Advantages and Disadvantages of Using Simulation

Using simulation, we can ask what-if questions and project how the real system will behave. Although simulation does not guarantee optimality, it will usually provide near-optimal solutions. In addition, simulation models often warn against poor decision strategies by projecting disastrous outcomes such as system failures, large financial losses, and so on.

The primary advantages of simulation are that it is easy to understand and that the methodology can be used to model and learn about the behavior of complex systems that would be difficult, if not impossible, to deal with analytically. Simulation models are flexible; they can be used to describe systems without requiring the assumptions that are often required by mathematical models. In general, the larger the number of probabilistic inputs a system has, the more likely that a simulation model will provide the best approach for studying the system. Another advantage of simulation is that a simulation model provides a convenient experimental laboratory for the real system. Changing assumptions or operating policies in the simulation model and rerunning it can provide results that help predict how such changes will affect the operation of the real system. Experimenting directly with a real system is often not feasible.

Simulation is not without some disadvantages. For complex systems, the process of developing, verifying, and validating a simulation model can be time-consuming and expensive. In addition, each simulation run provides only a sample of how the real system will operate. As such, the summary of the simulation data provides only estimates or approximations about the real system. Consequently, simulation does not guarantee an optimal solution. Nonetheless, the danger of obtaining poor solutions is slight if the analyst exercises good judgment in developing the simulation model and if the simulation process is run long enough under a wide variety of conditions so that the analyst has sufficient data to predict how the real system will operate.

SUMMARY

Simulation is a method for learning about a real system by experimenting with a model that represents the system. Some of the reasons simulation is frequently used are listed here:

1. It can be used for a wide variety of practical problems.
2. The simulation approach is relatively easy to explain and understand. As a result, management confidence is increased, and acceptance of the results is more easily obtained.
3. Spreadsheet packages now provide another alternative for model implementation, and third-party vendors have developed add-ins that expand the capabilities of the spreadsheet packages.
4. Computer software developers have produced simulation packages that make it easier to develop and implement simulation models for more complex problems.

We first showed how simulation can be used for risk analysis by analyzing a situation involving the development of a new product: the PortaCom printer. We then showed how simulation can be used to select an inventory replenishment level that would provide both a good profit and a good customer service level. Finally, we developed a simulation model for the Hammondsport Savings Bank ATM waiting line system. This model is an example of a dynamic simulation model in which the state of the system changes or evolves over time.

Our approach was to develop a simulation model that contained both controllable inputs and probabilistic inputs. Procedures were developed for randomly generating values for the probabilistic inputs, and a flowchart was developed to show the sequence of logical and mathematical operations that describe the steps of the simulation process. Simulation results obtained by running the simulation for a suitable number of trials or length of time provided the basis for conclusions drawn about the operation of the real system.

The Management Science in Action, Netherlands Company Improves Warehouse Order-Picking Efficiency, describes how a simulation model determined the warehouse storage location for 18,000 products and the sequence in which products were retrieved by order-picking personnel.

MANAGEMENT SCIENCE IN ACTION

NETHERLANDS COMPANY IMPROVES WAREHOUSE ORDER-PICKING EFFICIENCY*

As a wholesaler of tools, hardware, and garden equipment, Ankor, based in The Netherlands, warehouses more than 18,000 different products for customers who are primarily retail store chains, do-it-yourself businesses, and garden centers. Warehouse managers store the fastest-moving products on the ends of the aisles on the ground floor, the medium-moving products in the middle section of the aisles on the ground floor, and the slow-moving products on the mezzanine.

When a new order is received, a warehouse order-picker travels to each product location and selects the requested number of units. An average order includes 25 different products, which requires the order-picker to travel to 25 different locations in the warehouse. In order to minimize damage to the products, heavier products are picked first and breakable products are picked last. Order-picking is typically one of the most time-consuming and expensive aspects of operating the warehouse. The company is under continuous pressure to improve the efficiency of this operation.

To increase efficiency, researchers developed a simulation model of the warehouse order-picking system. Using a sequence of 1098 orders received for 27,790 products over a seven-week period, the researchers used the model to simulate the required order-picking times. The researchers, with the help of the model, varied the assignment of products to storage locations and the sequence in which products were retrieved from the storage locations. The model simulated order-picking times for a variety of product storage location alternatives and four different routing policies that determined the sequence in which products were picked.

Analysis of the simulation results provided a new storage assignment policy for the warehouse as well as new routing rules for the sequence in which to retrieve products from storage. Implementation of the new storage and routing procedures reduced the average route length of the order-picking operation by 31%. Due to the increased efficiency of the operation, the number of order pickers was reduced by more than 25%, saving the company an estimated €140,00 per year.

*Based on R. Dekker, M. B. M. de Koster, K. J. Roodbergen, and H. van Kalleveen, "Improving Order-Picking Response Time at Ankor's Warehouse," *Interfaces* (July/August 2004): 303–313.

GLOSSARY

Simulation A method for learning about a real system by experimenting with a model that represents the system.

Simulation experiment The generation of a sample of values for the probabilistic inputs of a simulation model and computing the resulting values of the model outputs.

Controllable input Input to a simulation model that is selected by the decision maker.

Probabilistic input Input to a simulation model that is subject to uncertainty. A probabilistic input is described by a probability distribution.

Risk analysis The process of predicting the outcome of a decision in the face of uncertainty.

Parameters Numerical values that appear in the mathematical relationships of a model. Parameters are considered known and remain constant over all trials of a simulation.

What-if analysis A trial-and-error approach to learning about the range of possible outputs for a model. Trial values are chosen for the model inputs (these are the what-ifs) and the value of the output(s) is computed.

Base-case scenario Determining the output given the most likely values for the probabilistic inputs of a model.

Worst-case scenario Determining the output given the worst values that can be expected for the probabilistic inputs of a model.

Best-case scenario Determining the output given the best values that can be expected for the probabilistic inputs of a model.

Static simulation model A simulation model used in situations where the state of the system at one point in time does not affect the state of the system at future points in time. Each trial of the simulation is independent.

Dynamic simulation model A simulation model used in situations where the state of the system affects how the system changes or evolves over time.

Event   An instantaneous occurrence that changes the state of the system in a simulation model.

Discrete-event simulation model   A simulation model that describes how a system evolves over time by using events that occur at discrete points in time.

Verification   The process of determining that a computer program implements a simulation model as it is intended.

Validation   The process of determining that a simulation model provides an accurate representation of a real system.

PROBLEMS

Note: Problems 1–12 are designed to give you practice in setting up a simulation model and demonstrating how random numbers can be used to generate values for the probabilistic inputs. These problems, which ask you to provide a small number of simulation trials, can be done with hand calculations. This approach should give you a good understanding of the simulation process, but the simulation results will not be sufficient for you to draw final conclusions or make decisions about the situation. Problems 13–24 are more realistic in that they ask you to generate simulation output(s) for a large number of trials and use the results to draw conclusions about the behavior of the system being studied. These problems require the use of a computer to carry out the simulation computations. The ability to use Excel will be necessary when you attempt Problems 13–24.

1. Consider the PortaCom project discussed in Section 12.1.
   a. An engineer on the product development team believes that first-year sales for the new printer will be 20,000 units. Using estimates of $45 per unit for the direct labor cost and $90 per unit for the parts cost, what is the first-year profit using the engineer's sales estimate?
   b. The financial analyst on the product development team is more conservative, indicating that parts cost may well be $100 per unit. In addition, the analyst suggests that a sales volume of 10,000 units is more realistic. Using the most likely value of $45 per unit for the direct labor cost, what is the first-year profit using the financial analyst's estimates?
   c. Why is the simulation approach to risk analysis preferable to generating a variety of what-if scenarios such as those suggested by the engineer and the financial analyst?

2. The management of Madeira Manufacturing Company is considering the introduction of a new product. The fixed cost to begin the production of the product is $30,000. The variable cost for the product is expected to be between $16 and $24 with a most likely value of $20 per unit. The product will sell for $50 per unit. Demand for the product is expected to range from 300 to 2100 units, with 1200 units the most likely demand.
   a. Develop the profit model for this product.
   b. Provide the base-case, worst-case, and best-case analyses.
   c. Discuss why simulation would be desirable.

3. Use the random numbers 0.3753, 0.9218, 0.0336, 0.5145, and 0.7000 to generate five simulated values for the PortaCom direct labor cost per unit.

4. To generate leads for new business, Gustin Investment Services offers free financial planning seminars at major hotels in Southwest Florida. Attendance is limited to 25 individuals per seminar. Each seminar costs Gustin $3500, and the average first-year commission for each new account opened is $5000. Historical data collected over the past four years show that the number of new accounts opened at a seminar varies from no accounts opened to a maximum of six accounts opened according to the following probability distribution:

Number of New Accounts Opened	Probability
0	0.01
1	0.04
2	0.10
3	0.25
4	0.40
5	0.15
6	0.05

a. Set up intervals of random numbers that can be used to simulate the number of new accounts opened at a seminar.

b. Using the first 10 random numbers in column 9 of Table 12.2, simulate the number of new accounts opened for 10 seminars.

c. Would you recommend that Gustin continue running the seminars?

5. The price of a share of a particular stock listed on the New York Stock Exchange is currently $39. The following probability distribution shows how the price per share is expected to change over a three-month period:

Stock Price Change ($)	Probability
−2	0.05
−1	0.10
0	0.25
+1	0.20
+2	0.20
+3	0.10
+4	0.10

a. Set up intervals of random numbers that can be used to generate the change in stock price over a three-month period.

b. With the current price of $39 per share and the random numbers 0.1091, 0.9407, 0.1941, and 0.8083, simulate the price per share for the next four 3-month periods. What is the ending simulated price per share?

6. The Statewide Auto Insurance Company developed the following probability distribution for automobile collision claims paid during the past year:

Payment($)	Probability
0	0.83
500	0.06
1,000	0.05
2,000	0.02
5,000	0.02
8,000	0.01
10,000	0.01

a. Set up intervals of random numbers that can be used to generate automobile collision claim payments.

b. Using the first 20 random numbers in column 4 of Table 12.2, simulate the payments for 20 policyholders. How many claims are paid and what is the total amount paid to the policyholders?

7. A variety of routine maintenance checks are made on commercial airplanes prior to each takeoff. A particular maintenance check of an airplane's landing gear requires between 10 and 18 minutes of a maintenance engineer's time. In fact, the exact time required is uniformly distributed over this interval. As part of a larger simulation model designed to determine total on-ground maintenance time for an airplane, we will need to simulate the actual time required to perform this maintenance check on the airplane's landing gear. Using random numbers of 0.1567, 0.9823, 0.3419, 0.5572, and 0.7758, compute the time required for each of five simulated maintenance checks of the airplane's landing gear.

8. Baseball's World Series is a maximum of seven games, with the winner being the first team to win four games. Assume that the Atlanta Braves are in the World Series and that the first two games are to be played in Atlanta, the next three games at the opponent's ball park, and the last two games, if necessary, back in Atlanta. Taking into account the projected starting pitchers for each game and the homefield advantage, the probabilities of Atlanta winning each game are as follows:

Game	1	2	3	4	5	6	7
Probability of Win	0.60	0.55	0.48	0.45	0.48	0.55	0.50

a. Set up random number intervals that can be used to determine the winner of each game. Let the smaller random numbers indicate that Atlanta wins the game. For example, the random number interval "0.00 but less than 0.60" corresponds to Atlanta winning game 1.

b. Use the random numbers in column 6 of Table 12.2 beginning with 0.3813 to simulate the playing of the World Series. Do the Atlanta Braves win the series? How many games are played?

c. Discuss how repeated simulation trials could be used to estimate the overall probability of Atlanta winning the series as well as the most likely number of games in the series.

9. A project has four activities (A, B, C, and D) that must be performed sequentially. The probability distributions for the time required to complete each of the activities are as follows:

Activity	Activity Time (weeks)	Probability
A	5	0.25
	6	0.35
	7	0.25
	8	0.15
B	3	0.20
	5	0.55
	7	0.25
C	10	0.10
	12	0.25
	14	0.40
	16	0.20
	18	0.05
D	8	0.60
	10	0.40

a. Provide the base-case, worst-case, and best-case calculations for the time to complete the project.

b. Use the random numbers 0.1778, 0.9617, 0.6849, and 0.4503 to simulate the completion time of the project in weeks.

c. Discuss how simulation could be used to estimate the probability the project can be completed in 35 weeks or less.

10. Blackjack, or 21, is a popular casino game that begins with each player and the dealer being dealt two cards. The value of each hand is determined by the point total of the cards in the hand. Face cards and 10s count 10 points; aces can be counted as either 1 or 11 points; and all other cards count at their face value. For instance, the value of a hand consisting of a jack and an 8 is 18; the value of a hand consisting of an ace and a two is either 3 or 13 depending on whether the ace is counted as 1 or 11 points. The goal is to obtain a hand with a value of 21, or as close to it as possible without exceeding 21. After the initial deal, each player and the dealer may draw additional cards (called taking a "hit") in order to improve their hand. If a player or the dealer takes a hit and the value of their hand exceeds 21, that person "goes broke" and loses. The dealer's advantage is that each player must decide whether to take a hit before the dealer. If a player takes a hit and goes over 21, the player loses even if the dealer later takes a hit and goes over 21. For this reason, players will often decide not to take a hit when the value of their hand is 12 or greater.

The dealer's hand is dealt with one card up and one card down. The player then decides whether to take a hit based on knowledge of the dealer's up card. A gambling professional determined that when the dealer's up card is a 6, the following probabilities describe the ending value of the dealer's hand:

Value of Hand	17	18	19	20	21	Broke
Probability	0.1654	0.1063	0.1063	0.1017	0.0972	0.4231

a. Set up intervals of random numbers that can be used to simulate the ending value of the dealer's hand when the dealer has a 6 as the up card.

b. Use the random numbers in column 4 of Table 12.2 to simulate the ending value of the dealer's hand for 20 plays of the game.

c. Suppose you are playing blackjack and your hand has a value of 16 for the two cards initially dealt. If you decide to take a hit, the following cards will improve your hand: ace, 2, 3, 4, and 5. Any card with a point count greater than 5 will result in you going broke. Suppose you have a hand with a value of 16 and decide to take a hit. The following probabilities describe the ending value of your hand:

Value of Hand	17	18	19	20	21	Broke
Probability	0.0769	0.0769	0.0769	0.0769	0.0769	0.6155

Use the random numbers in column 5 of Table 12.2 to simulate the ending value of your hand after taking a hit for 20 plays of the game.

d. Use the results of parts (b) and (c) to simulate the result of 20 blackjack hands when the dealer has a 6 up and the player chooses to take a hit with a hand that has a value of 16. How many hands result in the dealer winning, a push (a tie), and the player winning?

e. If the player has a hand with a value of 16 and doesn't take a hit, the only way the player can win is if the dealer goes broke. How many of the hands in part (b) result in the player winning without taking a hit? On the basis of this result and the results in part (d), would you recommend the player take a hit if the player has a hand with a value of 16 and the dealer has a 6 up?

580   Chapter 12   Simulation

11. Over a five-year period, the quarterly change in the price per share of common stock for a major oil company ranged from –8% to +12%. A financial analyst wants to learn what can be expected for price appreciation of this stock over the next two years. Using the five-year history as a basis, the analyst is willing to assume the change in price for each quarter is uniformly distributed between –8% and 12%. Use simulation to provide information about the price per share for the stock over the coming two-year period (eight quarters).

    a. Use two-digit random numbers from column 2 of Table 12.2, beginning with 0.52, 0.99, and so on, to simulate the quarterly price change for each of the eight quarters.

    b. If the current price per share is $80, what is the simulated price per share at the end of the two-year period?

    c. Discuss how risk analysis would be helpful in identifying the risk associated with a two-year investment in this stock.

12. The management of Brinkley Corporation is interested in using simulation to estimate the profit per unit for a new product. Probability distributions for the purchase cost, the labor cost, and the transportation cost are as follows:

Purchase Cost ($)	Probability	Labor Cost ($)	Probability	Transportation Cost ($)	Probability
10	0.25	20	0.10	3	0.75
11	0.45	22	0.25	5	0.25
12	0.30	24	0.35		
		25	0.30		

Assume that these are the only costs and that the selling price for the product will be $45 per unit.

    a. Provide the base-case, worst-case, and best-case calculations for the profit per unit.

    b. Set up intervals of random numbers that can be used to randomly generate the three cost components.

    c. Using the random numbers 0.3726, 0.5839, and 0.8275, calculate the profit per unit.

    d. Using the random numbers 0.1862, 0.7466, and 0.6171, calculate the profit per unit.

    e. Management believes the project may not be profitable if the profit per unit is less than $5. Explain how simulation can be used to estimate the probability the profit per unit will be less than $5.

13. Using the PortaCom Risk Analysis worksheet in Figure 12.6 and on the website accompanying the text, develop your own worksheet for the PortaCom simulation model.

    a. Compute the mean profit, the minimum profit, and the maximum profit.

    b. What is your estimate of the probability of a loss?

14. The management of Madeira Manufacturing Company is considering the introduction of a new product. The fixed cost to begin the production of the product is $30,000. The variable cost for the product is uniformly distributed between $16 and $24 per unit. The product will sell for $50 per unit. Demand for the product is best described by a normal probability distribution with a mean of 1200 units and a standard deviation of 300 units. Develop a spreadsheet simulation similar to Figure 12.6. Use 500 simulation trials to answer the following questions:

    a. What is the mean profit for the simulation?

    b. What is the probability the project will result in a loss?

    c. What is your recommendation concerning the introduction of the product?

15. Use a worksheet to simulate the rolling of dice. Use the VLOOKUP function as described in Appendix 12.1 to select the outcome for each die. Place the number for the first die in column B and the number for the second die in column C. Show the sum in column D.

Repeat the simulation for 1000 rolls of the dice. What is your simulation estimate of the probability of rolling a 7?

16. Strassel Investors buys real estate, develops it, and resells it for a profit. A new property is available, and Bud Strassel, the president and owner of Strassel Investors, believes it can be sold for $160,000. The current property owner asked for bids and stated that the property will be sold for the highest bid in excess of $100,000. Two competitors will be submitting bids for the property. Strassel does not know what the competitors will bid, but he assumes for planning purposes that the amount bid by each competitor will be uniformly distributed between $100,000 and $150,000.

   a. Develop a worksheet that can be used to simulate the bids made by the two competitors. Strassel is considering a bid of $130,000 for the property. Using a simulation of 1000 trials, what is the estimate of the probability Strassel will be able to obtain the property using a bid of $130,000?

   b. How much does Strassel need to bid to be assured of obtaining the property? What is the profit associated with this bid?

   c. Use the simulation model to compute the profit for each trial of the simulation run. With maximization of profit as Strassel's objective, use simulation to evaluate Strassel's bid alternatives of $130,000, $140,000, or $150,000. What is the recommended bid, and what is the expected profit?

17. Grear Tire Company has produced a new tire with an estimated mean lifetime mileage of 36,500 miles. Management also believes that the standard deviation is 5000 miles and that tire mileage is normally distributed. Use a worksheet to simulate the miles obtained for a sample of 500 tires.

   a. Use the Excel COUNTIF function to determine the number of tires that last longer than 40,000 miles. What is your estimate of the percentage of tires that will exceed 40,000 miles?

   b. Use COUNTIF to find the number of tires that obtain mileage less than 32,000 miles. Then, find the number with less than 30,000 miles and the number with less than 28,000 miles.

   c. If management would like to advertise a tire mileage guarantee such that approximately no more than 10% of the tires would obtain mileage low enough to qualify for the guarantee, what tire mileage considered in part (b) would you recommend for the guarantee?

18. A building contractor is preparing a bid on a new construction project. Two other contractors will be submitting bids for the same project. Based on past bidding practices, bids from the other contractors can be described by the following probability distributions:

Contractor	Probability Distribution of Bid
A	Uniform probability distribution between $600,000 and $800,000
B	Normal probability distribution with a mean bid of $700,000 and a standard deviation of $50,000

   a. If the building contractor submits a bid of $650,000, what is the probability that the contractor submits the lowest bid and wins the contract for the new construction project? Use a worksheet to simulate 1000 trials of the contract bidding process.

   b. The building contractor is also considering bids of $625,000 and $615,000. If the building contractor would like to bid such that the probability of winning the bid is about 0.80, what bid would you recommend? Repeat the simulation process with bids of $625,000 and $615,000 to justify your recommendation.

19. Develop your own worksheet for the Butler inventory simulation model shown in Figure 12.10. Suppose that management prefers not to charge for loss of goodwill. Run the

Butler inventory simulation model with replenishment levels of 110, 115, 120, and 125. What is your recommendation?

20. In preparing for the upcoming holiday season, Mandrell Toy Company designated a new doll called Freddy. The fixed cost to produce the doll is $100,000. The variable cost, which includes material, labor, and shipping costs, is $34 per doll. During the holiday selling season, Mandrell will sell the dolls for $42 each. If Mandrell overproduces the dolls, the excess dolls will be sold in January through a distributor who has agreed to pay Mandrell $10 per doll. Demand for new toys during the holiday selling season is extremely uncertain. Forecasts are for expected sales of 60,000 dolls with a standard deviation of 15,000. The normal probability distribution is assumed to be a good description of the demand.

a. Create a worksheet similar to the inventory worksheet in Figure 12.10. Include columns showing demand, sales, revenue from sales, amount of surplus, revenue from sales of surplus, total cost, and net profit. Use your worksheet to simulate the sales of the Freddy doll using a production quantity of 60,000 units. Using 500 simulation trials, what is the estimate of the mean profit associated with the production quantity of 60,000 dolls?

b. Before making a final decision on the production quantity, management wants an analysis of a more aggressive 70,000 unit production quantity and a more conservative 50,000 unit production quantity. Run your simulation with these two production quantities. What is the mean profit associated with each? What is your recommendation on the production of the Freddy doll?

c. Assuming that Mandrell's management adopts your recommendation, what is the probability of a stockout and a shortage of the Freddy dolls during the holiday season?

21. South Central Airlines operates a commuter flight between Atlanta and Charlotte. The plane holds 30 passengers, and the airline makes a $100 profit on each passenger on the flight. When South Central takes 30 reservations for the flight, experience has shown that on average, two passengers do not show up. As a result, with 30 reservations, South Central is averaging 28 passengers with a profit of 28(100) = $2800 per flight. The airline operations office has asked for an evaluation of an overbooking strategy where they would accept 32 reservations even though the airplane holds only 30 passengers. The probability distribution for the number of passengers showing up when 32 reservations are accepted is as follows:

Passengers Showing Up	Probability
28	0.05
29	0.25
30	0.50
31	0.15
32	0.05

The airline will receive a profit of $100 for each passenger on the flight up to the capacity of 30 passengers. The airline will incur a cost for any passenger denied seating on the flight. This cost covers added expenses of rescheduling the passenger as well as loss of goodwill, estimated to be $150 per passenger. Develop a worksheet model that will simulate the performance of the overbooking system. Simulate the number of passengers showing up for each of 500 flights by using the VLOOKUP function. Use the results to compute the profit for each flight.

a. Does your simulation recommend the overbooking strategy? What is the mean profit per flight if overbooking is implemented?

b. Explain how your simulation model could be used to evaluate other overbooking levels such as 31, 33, or 34 and for recommending a best overbooking strategy.

22. Develop your own waiting line simulation model for the Hammondsport Savings Bank problem (see Figure 12.14). Assume that a new branch is expected to open with interarrival times uniformly distributed between 0 and 4 minutes. The service times at this branch are anticipated to be normal with a mean of 2 minutes and a standard deviation of 0.5 minute. Simulate the operation of this system for 600 customers using one ATM. What is your assessment of the ability to operate this branch with one ATM? What happens to the average waiting time for customers near the end of the simulation period?

23. The Burger Dome waiting line model in Section 11.2 studies the waiting time of customers at its fast-food restaurant. Burger Dome's single-channel waiting line system has an arrival rate of 0.75 customers per minute and a service rate of 1 customer per minute.

   a. Use a worksheet based on Figure 12.15 to simulate the operation of this waiting line. Assuming that customer arrivals follow a Poisson probability distribution, the interarrival times can be simulated with the cell formula $-(1/\lambda)*LN(RAND())$, where $\lambda = 0.75$. Assuming that the service time follows an exponential probability distribution, the service times can be simulated with the cell formula $-\mu*LN(RAND())$, where $\mu = 1$. Run the Burger Dome simulation for 500 customers. The analytical model in Chapter 11 indicates an average waiting time of 3 minutes per customer. What average waiting time does your simulation model show?

   b. One advantage of using simulation is that a simulation model can be altered easily to reflect other assumptions about the probabilistic inputs. Assume that the service time is more accurately described by a normal probability distribution with a mean of 1 minute and a standard deviation of 0.2 minute. This distribution has less service time variability than the exponential probability distribution used in part (a). What is the impact of this change on the average waiting time?

24. Telephone calls come into an airline reservations office randomly at the mean rate of 15 calls per hour. The time between calls follows an exponential distribution with a mean of 4 minutes. When the two reservation agents are busy, a telephone message tells the caller that the call is important and to please wait on the line until the next reservation agent becomes available. The service time for each reservation agent is normally distributed with a mean of 4 minutes and a standard deviation of 1 minute. Use a two-channel waiting line simulation model to evaluate this waiting line system. Use the worksheet design shown in Figure 12.17. The cell formula $=-4*LN(RAND())$ can be used to generate the interarrival times. Simulate the operation of the telephone reservation system for 600 customers. Discard the first 100 customers, and collect data over the next 500 customers.

   a. Compute the mean interarrival time and the mean service time. If your simulation model is operating correctly, both of these should have means of approximately 4 minutes.

   b. What is the mean customer waiting time for this system?

   c. Use the =COUNTIF function to determine the number of customers who have to wait for a reservation agent. What percentage of the customers have to wait?

Case Problem 1   TRI-STATE CORPORATION

What will your portfolio be worth in 10 years? In 20 years? When you stop working? The Human Resources Department at Tri-State Corporation was asked to develop a financial planning model that would help employees address these questions. Tom Gifford was asked to lead this effort and decided to begin by developing a financial plan for himself. Tom has a degree in business and, at the age of 25, is making $34,000 per year. After two years of contributions to his company's retirement program and the receipt of a small inheritance, Tom has accumulated a portfolio valued at $14,500. Tom plans to work 30 more years and hopes to accumulate a portfolio valued at $1 million. Can he do it?

Tom began with a few assumptions about his future salary, his new investment contributions, and his portfolio growth rate. He assumed 5% annual salary growth rate as reasonable and wanted to make new investment contributions at 4% of his salary. After some research on historical stock market performance, Tom decided that a 10% annual portfolio growth rate was reasonable. Using these assumptions, Tom developed the Excel worksheet shown in Figure 12.18. Tom's specific situation and his assumptions are in the top portion of the worksheet (cells D3:D8). The worksheet provides a financial plan for the next five years. In computing the portfolio earnings for a given year, Tom assumed that his new investment contribution would occur evenly throughout the year and thus half of the new investment could be included in the computation of the portfolio earnings for the year. Using Figure 12.18, we see that at age 29, Tom is projected to have a portfolio valued at $32,898.

Tom's plan was to use this worksheet as a template to develop financial plans for the company's employees. The assumptions in cells D3:D8 would be different for each employee, and rows would be added to the worksheet to reflect the number of years appropriate for each employee. After adding another 25 rows to the worksheet, Tom found that he could expect to have a portfolio of $627,937 after 30 years. Tom then took his results to show his boss, Kate Riegle.

Although Kate was pleased with Tom's progress, she voiced several criticisms. One of the criticisms was the assumption of a constant annual salary growth rate. She noted that most employees experience some variation in the annual salary growth rate from year to year. In addition, she pointed out that the constant annual portfolio growth rate was unrealistic and that the actual growth rate would vary considerably from year to year. She further suggested that a simulation model for the portfolio projection might allow Tom to account for the random variability in the salary growth rate and the portfolio growth rate.

After some research, Tom and Kate decided to assume that the annual salary growth rate would vary from 0% to 10% and that a uniform probability distribution would provide a realistic approximation. Tri-State's accounting firm suggested that the annual portfolio growth rate could be approximated by a normal probability distribution with a mean of 10% and a standard deviation of 5%. With this information, Tom set off to develop a simulation model that could be used by the company's employees for financial planning.

FIGURE 12.18 FINANCIAL PLANNING WORKSHEET FOR TOM GIFFORD

WEB file

Gifford

	A	B	C	D	E	F	G	H
1	Financial Analysis - Portfolio Projection							
2								
3	Age			25				
4	Current Salary			$34,000				
5	Current Portfolio			$14,500				
6	Annual Salary Growth Rate			5%				
7	Annual Investment Rate			4%				
8	Annual Portfolio Growth Rate			10%				
9								
10			Beginning		New	Portfolio	Ending	
11	Year	Age	Portfolio	Salary	Investment	Earnings	Portfolio	
12	1	25	14,500	34,000	1,360	1,518	17,378	
13	2	26	17,378	35,700	1,428	1,809	20,615	
14	3	27	20,615	37,485	1,499	2,136	24,251	
15	4	28	24,251	39,359	1,574	2,504	28,329	
16	5	29	28,329	41,327	1,653	2,916	32,898	

Managerial Report

Play the role of Tom Gifford and develop a simulation model for financial planning. Write a report for Tom's boss and, at a minimum, include the following:

1. Without considering the random variability in growth rates, extend the worksheet in Figure 12.18 to 30 years. Confirm that by using the constant annual salary growth rate and the constant annual portfolio growth rate, Tom can expect to have a 30-year portfolio of $627,937. What would Tom's annual investment rate have to increase to in order for his portfolio to reach a 30-year, $1 million goal?
2. Incorporate the random variability of the annual salary growth rate and the annual portfolio growth rate into a simulation model. Assume that Tom is willing to use the annual investment rate that predicted a 30-year, $1 million portfolio in part 1. Show how to simulate Tom's 30-year financial plan. Use results from the simulation model to comment on the uncertainty associated with Tom reaching the 30-year, $1 million goal. Discuss the advantages of repeating the simulation numerous times.
3. What recommendations do you have for employees with a current profile similar to Tom's after seeing the impact of the uncertainty in the annual salary growth rate and the annual portfolio growth rate?
4. Assume that Tom is willing to consider working 35 years instead of 30 years. What is your assessment of this strategy if Tom's goal is to have a portfolio worth $1 million?
5. Discuss how the financial planning model developed for Tom Gifford can be used as a template to develop a financial plan for any of the company's employees.

Case Problem 2   HARBOR DUNES GOLF COURSE

Harbor Dunes Golf Course was recently honored as one of the top public golf courses in South Carolina. The course, situated on land that was once a rice plantation, offers some of the best views of saltwater marshes available in the Carolinas. Harbor Dunes targets the upper end of the golf market and in the peak spring golfing season, charges green fees of $160 per person and golf cart fees of $20 per person.

Harbor Dunes takes reservations for tee times for groups of four players (foursome) starting at 7:30 each morning. Foursomes start at the same time on both the front nine and the back nine of the course, with a new group teeing off every nine minutes. The process continues with new foursomes starting play on both the front and back nine at noon. To enable all players to complete 18 holes before darkness, the last two afternoon foursomes start their rounds at 1:21 P.M. Under this plan, Harbor Dunes can sell a maximum of 20 afternoon tee times.

Last year Harbor Dunes was able to sell every morning tee time available for every day of the spring golf season. The same result is anticipated for the coming year. Afternoon tee times, however, are generally more difficult to sell. An analysis of the sales data for last year enabled Harbor Dunes to develop the probability distribution of sales for the afternoon tee times as shown in Table 12.12. For the season, Harbor Dunes averaged selling approximately 14 of the 20 available afternoon tee times. The average income from afternoon green fees and cart fees has been $10,240. However, the average of six unused tee times per day resulted in lost revenue.

In an effort to increase the sale of afternoon tee times, Harbor Dunes is considering an idea popular at other golf courses. These courses offer foursomes that play in the morning the option to play another round of golf in the afternoon by paying a reduced fee for the afternoon round. Harbor Dunes is considering two replay options: (1) a green fee of $25

TABLE 12.12   PROBABILITY DISTRIBUTION OF SALES FOR THE AFTERNOON TEE TIMES

Number of Tee Times Sold	Probability
8	0.01
9	0.04
10	0.06
11	0.08
12	0.10
13	0.11
14	0.12
15	0.15
16	0.10
17	0.09
18	0.07
19	0.05
20	0.02

per player plus a cart fee of $20 per player; (2) a green fee of $50 per player plus a cart fee of $20 per player. For option 1, each foursome will generate additional revenues of $180; for option 2, each foursome will generate additional revenues of $280. The key in making a decision as to what option is best depends upon the number of groups that find the option attractive enough to take the replay offer. Working with a consultant who has expertise in statistics and the golf industry, Harbor Dunes developed probability distributions for the number of foursomes requesting a replay for each of the two options. These probability distributions are shown in Table 12.13.

In offering these replay options, Harbor Dunes' first priority will be to sell full-price afternoon advance reservations. If the demand for replay tee times exceeds the number of afternoon tee times available, Harbor Dunes will post a notice that the course is full. In this case, any excess replay requests will not be accepted.

TABLE 12.13   PROBABILITY DISTRIBUTIONS FOR THE NUMBER OF GROUPS
                    REQUESTING A REPLAY

Option 1: $25 per Person + Cart Fee		Option 2: $50 per Person + Cart Fee	
Number of Foursomes Requesting a Replay	Probability	Number of Foursomes Requesting a Replay	Probability
0	0.01	0	0.06
1	0.03	1	0.09
2	0.05	2	0.12
3	0.05	3	0.17
4	0.11	4	0.20
5	0.15	5	0.13
6	0.17	6	0.11
7	0.15	7	0.07
8	0.13	8	0.05
9	0.09		
10	0.06		

Managerial Report

Develop simulation models for both replay options using Crystal Ball. Run each simulation for 5000 trials. Prepare a report that will help management of Harbor Dunes Golf Course decide which replay option to implement for the upcoming spring golf season. In preparing your report be sure to include the following:

1. Statistical summaries of the revenue expected under each replay option.
2. Your recommendation as to the best replay option.
3. Assuming a 90-day spring golf season, what is the estimate of the added revenue using your recommendation?
4. Discuss any other recommendations you have that might improve the income for Harbor Dunes.

Case Problem 3   COUNTY BEVERAGE DRIVE-THRU

County Beverage Drive-Thru, Inc., operates a chain of beverage supply stores in Northern Illinois. Each store has a single service lane; cars enter at one end of the store and exit at the other end. Customers pick up soft drinks, beer, snacks, and party supplies without getting out of their cars. When a new customer arrives at the store, the customer waits until the preceding customer's order is complete and then drives into the store for service.

Typically, three employees operate each store during peak periods; two clerks take and fill orders, and a third clerk serves as cashier and store supervisor. County Beverage is considering a revised store design in which computerized order-taking and payment are integrated with specialized warehousing equipment. Management hopes that the new design will permit operating each store with one clerk. To determine whether the new design is beneficial, management decided to build a new store using the revised design.

County Beverage's new store will be located near a major shopping center. Based on experience at other locations, management believes that during the peak late afternoon and evening hours, the time between arrivals follows an exponential probability distribution with a mean of six minutes. These peak hours are the most critical time period for the company; most of their profit is generated during these peak hours.

An extensive study of times required to fill orders with a single clerk led to the following probability distribution of service times:

Service Time (minutes)	Probability
2	0.24
3	0.20
4	0.15
5	0.14
6	0.12
7	0.08
8	0.05
9	0.02
Total	1.00

In case customer waiting times prove too long with just a single clerk, County Beverage's management is considering two alternatives: add a second clerk to help with bagging, taking orders, and related tasks, or enlarge the drive-thru area so that two cars can be served at once (a two-channel system). With either of these options, two clerks will be needed. With the two-channel option, service times are expected to be the same for each channel.

With the second clerk helping with a single channel, service times will be reduced. The following probability distribution describes service times given that option:

Service Time (minutes)	Probability
1	0.20
2	0.35
3	0.30
4	0.10
5	0.05
Total	1.00

County Beverage's management would like you to develop a spreadsheet simulation model of the new system and use it to compare the operation of the system using the following three designs:

Design	
A	One channel, one clerk
B	One channel, two clerks
C	Two channels, each with one clerk

Management is especially concerned with how long customers have to wait for service. Research has shown that 30% of the customers will wait no longer than 6 minutes and that 90% will wait no longer than 10 minutes. As a guideline, management requires the average waiting time to be less than 1.5 minutes.

Managerial Report

Prepare a report that discusses the general development of the spreadsheet simulation model, and make any recommendations that you have regarding the best store design and staffing plan for County Beverage. One additional consideration is that the design allowing for a two-channel system will cost an additional $10,000 to build.

1. List the information the spreadsheet simulation model should generate so that a decision can be made on the store design and the desired number of clerks.
2. Run the simulation for 1000 customers for each alternative considered. You may want to consider making more than one run with each alternative. [*Note:* Values from an exponential probability distribution with mean μ can be generated in Excel using the following function: $=-\mu*\text{LN}(\text{RAND}())$.]
3. Be sure to note the number of customers County Beverage is likely to lose due to long customer waiting times with each design alternative.

Appendix 12.1   SIMULATION WITH EXCEL

Excel enables small and moderate-sized simulation models to be implemented relatively easily and quickly. In this appendix we show the Excel worksheets for the three simulation models presented in the chapter.

The PortaCom Simulation Model

We simulated the PortaCom problem 500 times. The worksheet used to carry out the simulation is shown again in Figure 12.19. Note that the simulation results for trials 6 through 495

FIGURE 12.19   WORKSHEET FOR THE PORTACOM PROBLEM

PortaCom

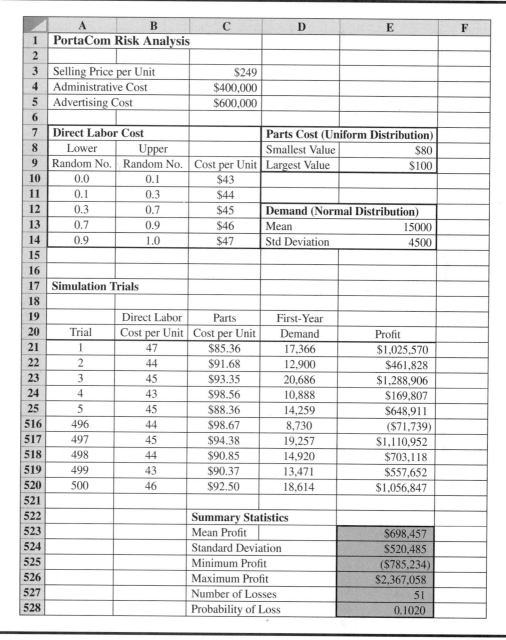

	A	B	C	D	E	F
1	**PortaCom Risk Analysis**					
2						
3	Selling Price per Unit		$249			
4	Administrative Cost		$400,000			
5	Advertising Cost		$600,000			
6						
7	**Direct Labor Cost**			**Parts Cost (Uniform Distribution)**		
8	Lower	Upper		Smallest Value	$80	
9	Random No.	Random No.	Cost per Unit	Largest Value	$100	
10	0.0	0.1	$43			
11	0.1	0.3	$44			
12	0.3	0.7	$45	**Demand (Normal Distribution)**		
13	0.7	0.9	$46	Mean	15000	
14	0.9	1.0	$47	Std Deviation	4500	
15						
16						
17	**Simulation Trials**					
18						
19		Direct Labor	Parts	First-Year		
20	Trial	Cost per Unit	Cost per Unit	Demand	Profit	
21	1	47	$85.36	17,366	$1,025,570	
22	2	44	$91.68	12,900	$461,828	
23	3	45	$93.35	20,686	$1,288,906	
24	4	43	$98.56	10,888	$169,807	
25	5	45	$88.36	14,259	$648,911	
516	496	44	$98.67	8,730	($71,739)	
517	497	45	$94.38	19,257	$1,110,952	
518	498	44	$90.85	14,920	$703,118	
519	499	43	$90.37	13,471	$557,652	
520	500	46	$92.50	18,614	$1,056,847	
521						
522			**Summary Statistics**			
523			Mean Profit		$698,457	
524			Standard Deviation		$520,485	
525			Minimum Profit		($785,234)	
526			Maximum Profit		$2,367,058	
527			Number of Losses		51	
528			Probability of Loss		0.1020	

have been hidden so that the results can be shown in a reasonably sized figure. If desired, the rows for these trials can be shown and the simulation results displayed for all 500 trials. Let us describe the details of the Excel worksheet that provided the PortaCom simulation.

First, the PortaCom data are presented in the first 14 rows of the worksheet. The selling price per unit, administrative cost, and advertising cost parameters are entered directly into cells C3, C4, and C5. The discrete probability distribution for the direct labor cost per unit is shown in a tabular format. Note that the random number intervals are entered first, followed by the corresponding cost per unit. For example, 0.0 in cell A10 and 0.1 in cell B10 show that a cost of $43 per unit will be assigned if the random number is in the interval 0.0 but less than 0.1. Thus, approximately 10% of the simulated direct labor costs will be $43 per unit. The uniform probability distribution with a smallest value of $80 in cell E8 and a largest value of $100 in cell E9 describes the parts cost per unit. Finally, a normal probability distribution with a mean of 15,000 units in cell E13 and a standard deviation of 4500 units in cell E14 describes the first-year demand distribution for the product. At this point we are ready to insert the Excel formulas that will carry out each simulation trial.

Simulation information for the first trial appears in row 21 of the worksheet. The cell formulas for row 21 are as follows:

Cell A21   Enter 1 for the first simulation trial

Cell B21   Simulate the direct labor cost per unit*
$$=VLOOKUP(RAND(),\$A\$10:\$C\$14,3)$$

Cell C21   Simulate the parts cost per unit (uniform distribution)
$$=\$E\$8+(\$E\$9-\$E\$8)*RAND()$$

Cell D21   Simulate the first-year demand (normal distribution)
$$=NORMINV(RAND(),\$E\$13,\$E\$14)$$

Cell E21   The profit obtained for the first trial
$$=(\$C\$3-B21-C21)*D21-\$C\$4-\$C\$5$$

Cells A21:E21 can be copied to A520:E520 in order to provide the 500 simulation trials.

Ultimately, summary statistics will be collected in order to describe the results of the 500 simulated trials. Using the standard Excel functions, the following summary statistics are computed for the 500 simulated profits appearing in cells E21 to E520:

Cell E523   The mean profit per trial = AVERAGE(E21:E520)

Cell E524   The standard deviation of profit = STDEV(E21:E520)

Cell E525   The minimum profit = MIN(E21:E520)

Cell E526   The maximum profit = MAX(E21:E520)

Cell E527   The count of the number of trials where a loss occurred
(i.e., profit < $0) = COUNTIF(E21:E520,"<0")

Cell E528   The percentage or probability of a loss based on the 500 trials
= E527/500

The F9 key can be used to perform another complete simulation of PortaCom. In this case, the entire worksheet will be recalculated and a set of new simulation results will be provided. Any data summaries, measures, or functions that have been built into the worksheet earlier will be updated automatically.

The Butler Inventory Simulation Model

We simulated the Butler inventory operation for 300 months. The worksheet used to carry out the simulation is shown again in Figure 12.20. Note that the simulation results for

---

*The VLOOKUP function generates a random number using the RAND() function. Then, using the table defined by the region from cells $A$10 to $C$14, the function identifies the row containing the RAND() random number and assigns the corresponding direct labor cost per unit shown in column C.

FIGURE 12.20   WORKSHEET FOR THE BUTLER INVENTORY PROBLEM

Butler

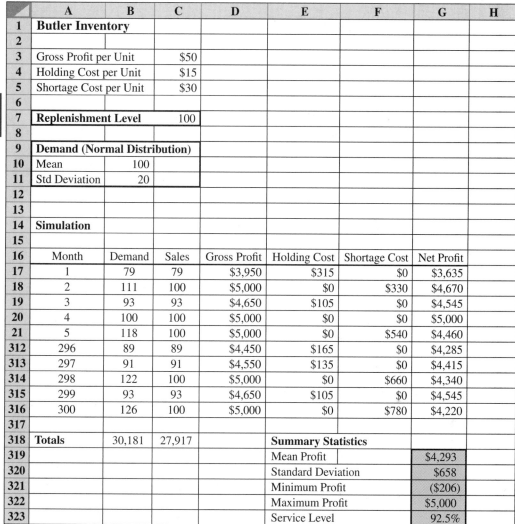

	A	B	C	D	E	F	G	H
1	**Butler Inventory**							
2								
3	Gross Profit per Unit		$50					
4	Holding Cost per Unit		$15					
5	Shortage Cost per Unit		$30					
6								
7	**Replenishment Level**		100					
8								
9	**Demand (Normal Distribution)**							
10	Mean	100						
11	Std Deviation	20						
12								
13								
14	**Simulation**							
15								
16	Month	Demand	Sales	Gross Profit	Holding Cost	Shortage Cost	Net Profit	
17	1	79	79	$3,950	$315	$0	$3,635	
18	2	111	100	$5,000	$0	$330	$4,670	
19	3	93	93	$4,650	$105	$0	$4,545	
20	4	100	100	$5,000	$0	$0	$5,000	
21	5	118	100	$5,000	$0	$540	$4,460	
312	296	89	89	$4,450	$165	$0	$4,285	
313	297	91	91	$4,550	$135	$0	$4,415	
314	298	122	100	$5,000	$0	$660	$4,340	
315	299	93	93	$4,650	$105	$0	$4,545	
316	300	126	100	$5,000	$0	$780	$4,220	
317								
318	**Totals**	30,181	27,917		**Summary Statistics**			
319					Mean Profit		$4,293	
320					Standard Deviation		$658	
321					Minimum Profit		($206)	
322					Maximum Profit		$5,000	
323					Service Level		92.5%	

months 6 through 295 have been hidden so that the results can be shown in a reasonably sized figure. If desired, the rows for these months can be shown and the simulation results displayed for all 300 months. Let us describe the details of the Excel worksheet that provided the Butler inventory simulation.

First, the Butler inventory data are presented in the first 11 rows of the worksheet. The gross profit per unit, holding cost per unit, and shortage cost per unit data are entered directly into cells C3, C4, and C5. The replenishment level is entered into cell C7, and the mean and standard deviation of the normal probability distribution for demand are entered into cells B10 and B11. At this point we are ready to insert Excel formulas that will carry out each simulation month or trial.

Simulation information for the first month or trial appears in row 17 of the worksheet. The cell formulas for row 17 are as follows:

Cell A17   Enter 1 for the first simulation month

Cell B17   Simulate demand (normal distribution)
              =NORMINV(RAND(),$B$10,$B$11)

Next compute the sales, which is equal to demand (cell B17) if demand is less than or equal to the replenishment level, or is equal to the replenishment level (cell C7) if demand is greater than the replenishment level.

Cell C17   Compute sales =IF(B17<=$C$7,B17,$C$7)

Cell D17   Calculate gross profit =$C$3*C17

Cell E17   Calculate the holding cost if demand is less than or equal
              to the replenishment level
              =IF(B17<=$C$7,$C$4*($C$7–B17),0)

Cell F17   Calculate the shortage cost if demand is greater than the replenishment level
              =IF(B17>$C$7,$C$5*(B17–$C$7),0)

Cell G17   Calculate net profit =D17–E17–F17

Cells A17:G17 can be copied to cells A316:G316 in order to provide the 300 simulation months.

Finally, summary statistics will be collected in order to describe the results of the 300 simulated trials. Using the standard Excel functions, the following totals and summary statistics are computed for the 300 months:

Cell B318   Total demand =SUM(B17:B316)

Cell C319   Total sales =SUM(C17:C316)

Cell G319   The mean profit per month =AVERAGE(G17:G316)

Cell G320   The standard deviation of net profit =STDEV(G17:G316)

Cell G321   The minimum net profit =MIN(G17:G316)

Cell G322   The maximum net profit =MAX(G17:G316)

Cell G323   The service level =C318/B318

The Hammondsport ATM Simulation Model

We simulated the operation of the Hammondsport ATM waiting line system for 1000 customers. The worksheet used to carry out the simulation is shown again in Figure 12.21. Note that the simulation results for customers 6 through 995 have been hidden so that the results can be shown in a reasonably sized figure. If desired, the rows for these customers can be shown and the simulation results displayed for all 1000 customers. Let us describe the details of the Excel worksheet that provided the Hammondsport ATM simulation.

The data are presented in the first 9 rows of the worksheet. The interarrival times are described by a uniform distribution with a smallest time of 0 minutes (cell B4) and a largest time of 5 minutes (cell B5). A normal probability distribution with a mean of 2 minutes (cell B8) and a standard deviation of 0.5 minute (cell B9) describes the service time distribution.

FIGURE 12.21   WORKSHEET FOR THE HAMMONDSPORT SAVINGS BANK WITH ONE ATM

WEB file

Hammondsport1

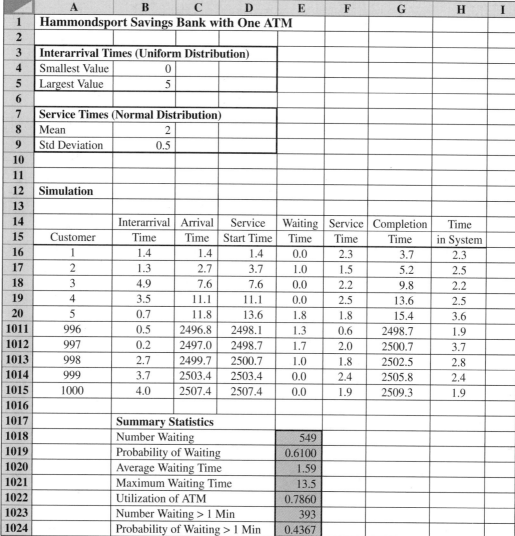

	A	B	C	D	E	F	G	H	I
1	**Hammondsport Savings Bank with One ATM**								
2									
3	**Interarrival Times (Uniform Distribution)**								
4	Smallest Value	0							
5	Largest Value	5							
6									
7	**Service Times (Normal Distribution)**								
8	Mean	2							
9	Std Deviation	0.5							
10									
11									
12	**Simulation**								
13									
14		Interarrival	Arrival	Service	Waiting	Service	Completion	Time	
15	Customer	Time	Time	Start Time	Time	Time	Time	in System	
16	1	1.4	1.4	1.4	0.0	2.3	3.7	2.3	
17	2	1.3	2.7	3.7	1.0	1.5	5.2	2.5	
18	3	4.9	7.6	7.6	0.0	2.2	9.8	2.2	
19	4	3.5	11.1	11.1	0.0	2.5	13.6	2.5	
20	5	0.7	11.8	13.6	1.8	1.8	15.4	3.6	
1011	996	0.5	2496.8	2498.1	1.3	0.6	2498.7	1.9	
1012	997	0.2	2497.0	2498.7	1.7	2.0	2500.7	3.7	
1013	998	2.7	2499.7	2500.7	1.0	1.8	2502.5	2.8	
1014	999	3.7	2503.4	2503.4	0.0	2.4	2505.8	2.4	
1015	1000	4.0	2507.4	2507.4	0.0	1.9	2509.3	1.9	
1016									
1017		**Summary Statistics**							
1018		Number Waiting			549				
1019		Probability of Waiting			0.6100				
1020		Average Waiting Time			1.59				
1021		Maximum Waiting Time			13.5				
1022		Utilization of ATM			0.7860				
1023		Number Waiting > 1 Min			393				
1024		Probability of Waiting > 1 Min			0.4367				

Simulation information for the first customer appears in row 16 of the worksheet. The cell formulas for row 16 are as follows:

Cell A16   Enter 1 for the first customer

Cell B16   Simulate the interarrival time for customer 1 (uniform distribution)
              =$B$4+RAND()*($B$5–$B$4)

Cell C16   Compute the arrival time for customer 1 =B16

Cell D16   Compute the start time for customer 1 =C16

Cell E16   Compute the waiting time for customer 1 =D1–C16

Cell F16	Simulate the service time for customer 1 (normal distribution) =NORMINV(RAND(),$B$8,$B$9)
Cell G16	Compute the completion time for customer 1 =D16+F16
Cell H16	Compute the time in the system for customer 1 =G16–C16

Simulation information for the second customer appears in row 17 of the worksheet. The cell formulas for row 17 are as follows:

Cell A17	Enter 2 for the second customer
Cell B17	Simulate the interarrival time for customer 2 (uniform distribution) =$B$4+RAND()*($B$5–$B$4)
Cell C17	Compute the arrival time for customer 2 =C16+B17
Cell D17	Compute the start time for customer 2 =IF(C17>G16,C17,G16)
Cell E17	Compute the waiting time for customer 2 =D17–C17
Cell F17	Simulate the service time for customer 2 (normal distribution) =NORMINV(RAND(),$B$8,$B$9)
Cell G17	Compute the completion time for customer 2 =D17+F17
Cell H17	Compute the time in the system for customer 2 =G17–C17

Cells A17:H17 can be copied to cells A1015:H1015 in order to provide the 1000-customer simulation.

Ultimately, summary statistics will be collected in order to describe the results of 1000 customers. Before collecting the summary statistics, let us point out that most simulation studies of dynamic systems focus on the operation of the system during its long-run or steady-state operation. To ensure that the effects of start-up conditions are not included in the steady-state calculations, a dynamic simulation model is usually run for a specified period without collecting any data about the operation of the system. The length of the start-up period can vary depending on the application. For the Hammondsport Savings Bank ATM simulation, we treated the results for the first 100 customers as the start-up period. The simulation information for customer 100 appears in row 115 of the spreadsheet. Cell G115 shows that the completion time for the 100th customer is 247.8. Thus the length of the start-up period is 247.8 minutes.

Summary statistics are collected for the next 900 customers corresponding to rows 116 to 1015 of the worksheet. The following Excel formulas provided the summary statistics:

Cell E1018	Number of customers who had to wait (i.e., waiting time > 0) =COUNTIF(E116:E1015,">0")
Cell E1019	Probability of waiting =E1018/900
Cell E1020	The average waiting time =AVERAGE(E116:E1015)
Cell E1021	The maximum waiting time =MAX(E116:E1015)
Cell E1022	The utilization of the ATM* =SUM(F116:F1015)/(G1015–G115)

---

*The proportion of time the ATM is in use is equal to the sum of the 900 customer service times in column F divided by the total elapsed time required for the 900 customers to complete service. This total elapsed time is the difference between the completion time of customer 1000 and the completion time of customer 100.

Cell E1023   The number of customers who had to wait more than 1 minute
=COUNTIF(E116:E1015, ">1")

Cell E1024   Probability of waiting more than 1 minute =E1023/900

Appendix 12.2   SIMULATION USING CRYSTAL BALL

In Section 12.1 we used simulation to perform risk analysis for the PortaCom problem, and in Appendix 12.1 we showed how to construct the Excel worksheet that provided the simulation results. Developing the worksheet simulation for the PortaCom problem using the basic Excel package was relatively easy. The use of add-ins enables larger and more complex simulation problems to be easily analyzed using spreadsheets. In this appendix, we show how Crystal Ball, an add-in package, can be used to perform the PortaCom simulation. We will run the simulation for 1000 trials here. Instructions for installing and starting Crystal Ball are included with the Crystal Ball software.

Formulating a Crystal Ball Model

We begin by entering the problem data into the top portion of the worksheet. For the PortaCom problem, we must enter the following data: selling price, administrative cost, advertising cost, probability distribution for the direct labor cost per unit, smallest and largest values for the parts cost per unit (uniform distribution), and the mean and standard deviation for first-year demand (normal distribution). These data with appropriate descriptive labels are shown in cells A1:E13 of Figure 12.22.

For the PortaCom problem, the Crystal Ball model contains the following two components: (1) cells for the probabilistic inputs (direct labor cost, parts cost, first-year demand), and (2) a cell containing a formula for computing the value of the simulation model output (profit). In Crystal Ball the cells that contain the values of the probabilistic inputs are called *assumption cells*, and the cells that contain the formulas for the model outputs are referred to as *forecast cells*. The PortaCom problem requires only one output (profit), and thus the Crystal Ball model only contains one forecast cell. In more complex simulation problems more than one forecast cell may be necessary.

The assumption cells may only contain simple numeric values. In this model-building stage, we entered PortaCom's best estimates of the direct labor cost ($45), the parts cost ($90), and the first-year demand (15,000) into cells C21:C23, respectively. The forecast cells in a Crystal Ball model contain formulas that refer to one or more of the assumption cells. Because only one forecast cell in the PortaCom problem corresponds to profit, we entered the following formula into cell C27:

$$=(C3-C21-C22)*C23-C4-C5$$

The resulting value of $710,000 is the profit corresponding to the base-case scenario discussed in Section 12.1.

Defining and Entering Assumptions

We are now ready to define the probability distributions corresponding to each of the assumption cells. We begin by defining the probability distribution for the direct labor cost.

Step 1.   Select the Crystal Ball tab
Step 2.   Select cell C21

FIGURE 12.22   CRYSTAL BALL WORKSHEET FOR THE PORTACOM PROBLEM

	A	B	C	D	E	F
1	**PortaCom Risk Analysis**					
2						
3	Selling Price per Unit		$249			
4	Administrative Cost		$400,000			
5	Advertising Cost		$600,000			
6						
7		**Direct Labor**		**Parts Cost (Uniform Distribution)**		
8		Cost per Unit	Probability	Smallest Value	$80	
9		$43	0.1	Largest Value	$100	
10		$44	0.2			
11		$45	0.4	**Demand (Normal Distribution)**		
12		$46	0.2	Mean	15,000	
13		$47	0.1	Standard Dev	4,500	
14						
15						
16						
17	**Crystal Ball Model**					
18						
19			**Assumption**			
20			**Cells**			
21		**Direct Labor Cost**	$45			
22		**Parts Cost**	$90			
23		**Demand**	15,000			
24						
25			**Forecast**			
26			**Cell**			
27		**Profit**	$710,000			

WEB file

PortaCom Crystal

Step 3.   Choose **Define Assumption** from the **Define** group of the **Crystal Ball** ribbon.
Step 4.   When the **Distribution Gallery: Cell 21** dialog box appears:
    Choose **Custom*** (Use the scroll bar to see all possible distributions.)
    Click **OK**
Step 5.   When the **Define Assumption: Cell C21** dialog box appears:

    If the ⌄ button is to the right of the **Name** box, proceed to step 6

    If the ⌃ button is to the right of the **Name** box, click the ⌃ button to

    obtain the ⌄ button
Step 6.   Choose **Load Data**
    Enter B9:C13 in the **Location of data** box
    Click **Keep Linked to Spreadsheet**
    Click **OK** to terminate the data entry process
    Click **OK**

*You may have to click **All** and use the scroll bar to see all possible distributions.

The procedure for defining the probability distribution for the parts cost is similar.

Step 1. Select cell C22
Step 2. Choose **Define Assumption** from the **Define** group of the **Crystal Ball** ribbon.
Step 3. When the **Distribution Gallery: Cell C22** dialog box appears:
    Choose **Uniform** (Use the scroll bar to see all possible distributions.)
    Click **OK**
Step 4. When the **Define Assumption: Cell C22** dialog box appears:
    Enter =E8 in the **Minimum** box
    Enter =E9 in the **Maximum** box
    Click **Enter**
    Click **OK**

Finally, we perform the following steps to define the probability distribution for first-year demand:

Step 1. Select cell C23
Step 2. Choose **Define Assumption** from the **Define** group of the **Crystal Ball** ribbon.
Step 3. When the **Distribution Gallery: Cell 23** dialog box appears:
    Choose **Normal** (Use the scroll bar to see all possible distributions.)
    Click **OK**
Step 4. When the **Define Assumption: Cell C23** dialog box appears:
    Enter =E12 in the **Mean** box
    Enter =E13 in the **Std. Dev.** box
    Click **Enter**
    Click **OK**

Defining Forecasts

After defining the assumption cells, we are ready to define the forecast cells. The following steps show this process for cell C27, which is the profit forecast cell for the PortaCom project:

Step 1. Select cell C27
Step 2. Choose **Define Forecast** from the **Define** group of the **Crystal Ball** ribbon.
Step 3. When the **Define Forecast: Cell C27** dialog box appears:
    Profit will appear in the **Name** box
    Click **OK**

Setting Run Preferences

We must now make the choices that determine how Crystal Ball runs the simulation. For the PortaCom simulation, we only need to specify the number of trials.

Step 1. Choose **Run Preferences** from the **Run** group of the **Crystal Ball** ribbon.
Step 2. When the **Run Preferences** dialog box appears:
    Make sure the **Trials** tab has been selected
    Enter 1000 in the **Number of trials to run:** box
    Click **OK**

Running the Simulation

Crystal Ball repeats three steps on each of the 1000 trials of the PortaCom simulation.

1. Values are generated for the three assumption cells according to the defined probability distributions.
2. A new simulated profit (forecast cell) is computed based on the new values in the three assumption cells.
3. The new simulated profit is recorded.

The simulation is started by selecting the **Start** button .

When the run is complete, Crystal Ball displays a Forecast: Profit window, which shows a frequency distribution of the simulated profit values obtained during the simulation run. See Figure 12.23. Other types of charts and output can be displayed. For instance, the following steps describe how to display the descriptive statistics for the simulation run:

Step 1. Select the **View** menu in the **Forecast: Profit** window
Step 2. Choose **Statistics**

FIGURE 12.23   CRYSTAL BALL FREQUENCY CHART FOR THE PORTACOM SIMULATION

FIGURE 12.24   CRYSTAL BALL STATISTICS FOR THE PORTACOM SIMULATION

Figure 12.24 shows the Forecast: Profit window with descriptive statistics. Note that the worst result obtained in this simulation of 1000 trials is a loss of $1,216,126, and the best result is a profit of $2,415,674. The mean profit is $701,306. These values are similar to the results obtained in Section 12.1. The differences result from the different random numbers used in the two simulations and from the fact that we used 1000 trials with Crystal Ball. If you perform another simulation, your results will differ slightly.

CHAPTER 13

Decision Analysis

CONTENTS

13.1 PROBLEM FORMULATION
Influence Diagrams
Payoff Tables
Decision Trees

13.2 DECISION MAKING
WITHOUT PROBABILITIES
Optimistic Approach
Conservative Approach
Minimax Regret Approach

13.3 DECISION MAKING WITH
PROBABILITIES
Expected Value of Perfect
Information

13.4 RISK ANALYSIS AND
SENSITIVITY ANALYSIS
Risk Analysis
Sensitivity Analysis

13.5 DECISION ANALYSIS WITH
SAMPLE INFORMATION
Influence Diagram
Decision Tree
Decision Strategy
Risk Profile
Expected Value of Sample
Information
Efficiency of Sample Information

13.6 COMPUTING BRANCH
PROBABILITIES

Decision analysis can be used to develop an optimal strategy when a decision maker is faced with several decision alternatives and an uncertain or risk-filled pattern of future events. For example, Ohio Edison used decision analysis to choose the best type of particulate control equipment for coal-fired generating units when it faced future uncertainties concerning sulfur content requirements, construction costs, and so on. The State of North Carolina used decision analysis in evaluating whether to implement a medical screening test to detect metabolic disorders in newborns. Thus, decision analysis repeatedly proves its value in decision making. The Management Science in Action, Decision Analysis at Eastman Kodak, describes how the use of decision analysis added approximately $1 billion in value.

Even when a careful decision analysis has been conducted, uncertain future events make the final consequence uncertain. In some cases, the selected decision alternative may provide good or excellent results. In other cases, a relatively unlikely future event may occur, causing the selected decision alternative to provide only fair or even poor results. The risk associated with any decision alternative is a direct result of the uncertainty associated with the final consequence. A good decision analysis includes risk analysis. Through risk analysis, the decision maker is provided with probability information about favorable as well as unfavorable consequences that may occur.

MANAGEMENT SCIENCE IN ACTION

DECISION ANALYSIS AT EASTMAN KODAK*

Clemen and Kwit conducted a study to determine the value of decision analysis at the Eastman Kodak Company. The study involved an analysis of 178 decision analysis projects over a 10-year period. The projects involved a variety of applications including strategy development, vendor selection, process analysis, new-product brainstorming, product-portfolio selection, and emission-reduction analysis. These projects required 14,372 hours of analyst time and the involvement of many other individuals at Kodak over the 10-year period. The shortest projects took less than 20 hours, and the longest projects took almost a year to complete.

Most decision analysis projects are one-time activities, which makes it difficult to measure the value added to the corporation. Clemen and Kwit used detailed records that were available and some innovative approaches to develop estimates of the incremental dollar value generated by the decision analysis projects. Their conservative estimate of the average value per project was $6.65 million, and their optimistic estimate of the average value per project was $16.35 million. Their analysis led to the conclusion that all projects taken together added more than $1 billion in value to Eastman Kodak. Using these estimates, Clemen and Kwit concluded that decision analysis returned substan-

tial value to the company. Indeed, they concluded that the value added by the projects was at least 185 times the cost of the analysts' time.

In addition to the monetary benefits, the authors point out that decision analysis adds value by facilitating discussion among stakeholders, promoting careful thinking about strategies, providing a common language for discussing the elements of a decision problem, and speeding implementation by helping to build consensus among decision makers. In commenting on the value of decision analysis at Eastman Kodak, Nancy L. S. Sousa said, "As General Manager, New Businesses, VP Health Imaging, Eastman Kodak, I encourage all of the business planners to use the decision and risk principles and processes as part of evaluating new business opportunities. The processes have clearly led to better decisions about entry and exit of businesses."

Although measuring the value of a particular decision analysis project can be difficult, it would be hard to dispute the success that decision analysis had at Kodak.

*Based on Robert T. Clemen and Robert C. Kwit, "The Value of Decision Analysis at Eastman Kodak Company," *Interfaces* (September/October 2001): 74–92.

We begin the study of decision analysis by considering problems that involve reasonably few decision alternatives and reasonably few possible future events. Influence diagrams and payoff tables are introduced to provide a structure for the decision problem and to illustrate the fundamentals of decision analysis. We then introduce decision trees to show the sequential nature of decision problems. Decision trees are used to analyze more complex problems and to identify an optimal sequence of decisions, referred to as an optimal decision strategy. Sensitivity analysis shows how changes in various aspects of the problem affect the recommended decision alternative.

13.1   PROBLEM FORMULATION

The first step in the decision analysis process is problem formulation. We begin with a verbal statement of the problem. We then identify the **decision alternatives,** the uncertain future events, referred to as **chance events,** and the **consequences** associated with each decision alternative and each chance event outcome. Let us begin by considering a construction project of the Pittsburgh Development Corporation.

Pittsburgh Development Corporation (PDC) purchased land that will be the site of a new luxury condominium complex. The location provides a spectacular view of downtown Pittsburgh and the Golden Triangle where the Allegheny and Monongahela Rivers meet to form the Ohio River. PDC plans to price the individual condominium units between $300,000 and $1,400,000.

PDC commissioned preliminary architectural drawings for three different projects: one with 30 condominiums, one with 60 condominiums, and one with 90 condominiums. The financial success of the project depends upon the size of the condominium complex and the chance event concerning the demand for the condominiums. The statement of the PDC decision problem is to select the size of the new luxury condominium project that will lead to the largest profit given the uncertainty concerning the demand for the condominiums.

Given the statement of the problem, it is clear that the decision is to select the best size for the condominium complex. PDC has the following three decision alternatives:

$$d_1 = \text{a small complex with 30 condominiums}$$
$$d_2 = \text{a medium complex with 60 condominiums}$$
$$d_3 = \text{a large complex with 90 condominiums}$$

A factor in selecting the best decision alternative is the uncertainty associated with the chance event concerning the demand for the condominiums. When asked about the possible demand for the condominiums, PDC's president acknowledged a wide range of possibilities but decided that it would be adequate to consider two possible chance event outcomes: a strong demand and a weak demand.

In decision analysis, the possible outcomes for a chance event are referred to as the **states of nature.** The states of nature are defined so that one, and only one, of the possible states of nature will occur. For the PDC problem, the chance event concerning the demand for the condominiums has two states of nature:

$$s_1 = \text{strong demand for the condominiums}$$
$$s_2 = \text{weak demand for the condominiums}$$

Management must first select a decision alternative (complex size); then a state of nature follows (demand for the condominiums); and finally a consequence will occur. In this case, the consequence is PDC's profit.

Influence Diagrams

An **influence diagram** is a graphical device that shows the relationships among the decisions, the chance events, and the consequences for a decision problem. The **nodes** in an influence diagram represent the decisions, chance events, and consequences. Rectangles or squares depict **decision nodes,** circles or ovals depict **chance nodes,** and diamonds depict **consequence nodes.** The lines connecting the nodes, referred to as *arcs,* show the direction of influence that the nodes have on one another. Figure 13.1 shows the influence diagram for the PDC problem. The complex size is the decision node, demand is the chance node, and profit is the consequence node. The arcs connecting the nodes show that both the complex size and the demand influence PDC's profit.

Payoff Tables

Given the three decision alternatives and the two states of nature, which complex size should PDC choose? To answer this question, PDC will need to know the consequence associated with each decision alternative and each state of nature. In decision analysis, we refer to the consequence resulting from a specific combination of a decision alternative and a state of nature as a **payoff.** A table showing payoffs for all combinations of decision alternatives and states of nature is a **payoff table.**

Payoffs can be expressed in terms of profit, cost, time, distance, or any other measure appropriate for the decision problem being analyzed.

Because PDC wants to select the complex size that provides the largest profit, profit is used as the consequence. The payoff table with profits expressed in millions of dollars is shown in Table 13.1. Note, for example, that if a medium complex is built and demand turns out to be strong, a profit of $14 million will be realized. We will use the notation V_{ij} to denote the payoff associated with decision alternative i and state of nature j. Using Table 13.1, $V_{31} = 20$ indicates a payoff of $20 million occurs if the decision is to build a large complex (d_3) and the strong demand state of nature (s_1) occurs. Similarly, $V_{32} = -9$ indicates a loss of $9 million if the decision is to build a large complex (d_3) and the weak demand state of nature (s_2) occurs.

FIGURE 13.1   INFLUENCE DIAGRAM FOR THE PDC PROJECT

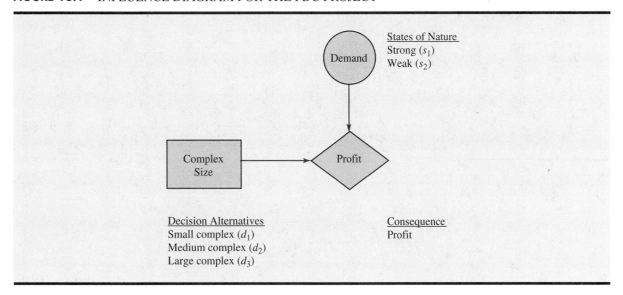

TABLE 13.1　PAYOFF TABLE FOR THE PDC CONDOMINIUM PROJECT
(PAYOFFS IN $ MILLIONS)

	State of Nature	
Decision Alternative	**Strong Demand s_1**	**Weak Demand s_2**
Small complex, d_1	8	7
Medium complex, d_2	14	5
Large complex, d_3	20	−9

Decision Trees

A **decision tree** provides a graphical representation of the decision-making process. Figure 13.2 presents a decision tree for the PDC problem. Note that the decision tree shows the natural or logical progression that will occur over time. First, PDC must make a decision regarding the size of the condominium complex (d_1, d_2, or d_3). Then, after the decision is implemented, either state of nature s_1 or s_2 will occur. The number at each end point of the tree indicates the payoff associated with a particular sequence. For example, the topmost payoff of 8 indicates that an $8 million profit is anticipated if PDC constructs a small condominium complex (d_1) and demand turns out to be strong (s_1). The next payoff of 7 indicates an anticipated profit of $7 million if PDC constructs a small condominium complex (d_1) and demand turns out to be weak (s_2). Thus, the decision tree shows graphically the sequences of decision alternatives and states of nature that provide the six possible payoffs for PDC.

FIGURE 13.2　DECISION TREE FOR THE PDC CONDOMINIUM PROJECT (PAYOFFS IN $ MILLIONS)

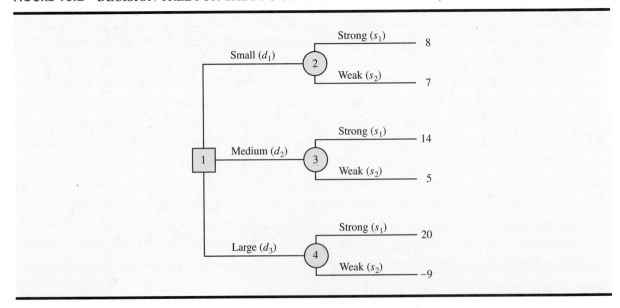

If you have a payoff table, you can develop a decision tree. Try Problem 1(a).

The decision tree in Figure 13.2 shows four nodes, numbered 1–4. Squares are used to depict decision nodes and circles are used to depict chance nodes. Thus, node 1 is a decision node, and nodes 2, 3, and 4 are chance nodes. The **branches** connect the nodes; those leaving the decision node correspond to the decision alternatives. The branches leaving each chance node correspond to the states of nature. The payoffs are shown at the end of the states-of-nature branches. We now turn to the question: How can the decision maker use the information in the payoff table or the decision tree to select the best decision alternative? Several approaches may be used.

NOTES AND COMMENTS

1. Experts in problem solving agree that the first step in solving a complex problem is to decompose it into a series of smaller subproblems. Decision trees provide a useful way to show how a problem can be decomposed and the sequential nature of the decision process.

2. People often view the same problem from different perspectives. Thus, the discussion regarding the development of a decision tree may provide additional insight about the problem.

13.2   DECISION MAKING WITHOUT PROBABILITIES

Many people think of a good decision as one in which the consequence is good. However, in some instances, a good, well-thought-out decision may still lead to a bad or undesirable consequence.

In this section we consider approaches to decision making that do not require knowledge of the probabilities of the states of nature. These approaches are appropriate in situations in which the decision maker has little confidence in his or her ability to assess the probabilities, or in which a simple best-case and worst-case analysis is desirable. Because different approaches sometimes lead to different decision recommendations, the decision maker should understand the approaches available and then select the specific approach that, according to the decision maker's judgment, is the most appropriate.

Optimistic Approach

The **optimistic approach** evaluates each decision alternative in terms of the *best* payoff that can occur. The decision alternative that is recommended is the one that provides the best possible payoff. For a problem in which maximum profit is desired, as in the PDC problem, the optimistic approach would lead the decision maker to choose the alternative corresponding to the largest profit. For problems involving minimization, this approach leads to choosing the alternative with the smallest payoff.

For a maximization problem, the optimistic approach often is referred to as the maximax approach; for a minimization problem, the corresponding terminology is minimin.

To illustrate the optimistic approach, we use it to develop a recommendation for the PDC problem. First, we determine the maximum payoff for each decision alternative; then we select the decision alternative that provides the overall maximum payoff. These steps systematically identify the decision alternative that provides the largest possible profit. Table 13.2 illustrates these steps.

Because 20, corresponding to d_3, is the largest payoff, the decision to construct the large condominium complex is the recommended decision alternative using the optimistic approach.

Conservative Approach

The **conservative approach** evaluates each decision alternative in terms of the *worst* payoff that can occur. The decision alternative recommended is the one that provides the best

TABLE 13.2   MAXIMUM PAYOFF FOR EACH PDC DECISION ALTERNATIVE

Decision Alternative	Maximum Payoff	
Small complex, d_1	8	
Medium complex, d_2	14	
Large complex, d_3	20 ←	Maximum of the maximum payoff values

of the worst possible payoffs. For a problem in which the output measure is profit, as in the PDC problem, the conservative approach would lead the decision maker to choose the alternative that maximizes the minimum possible profit that could be obtained. For problems involving minimization, this approach identifies the alternative that will minimize the maximum payoff.

For a maximization problem, the conservative approach often is referred to as the maximax approach; for a minimization problem, the corresponding terminology is minimax.

To illustrate the conservative approach, we use it to develop a recommendation for the PDC problem. First, we identify the minimum payoff for each of the decision alternatives; then we select the decision alternative that maximizes the minimum payoff. Table 13.3 illustrates these steps for the PDC problem.

Because 7, corresponding to d_1, yields the maximum of the minimum payoffs, the decision alternative of a small condominium complex is recommended. This decision approach is considered conservative because it identifies the worst possible payoffs and then recommends the decision alternative that avoids the possibility of extremely "bad" payoffs. In the conservative approach, PDC is guaranteed a profit of at least $7 million. Although PDC may make more, it *cannot* make less than $7 million.

Minimax Regret Approach

The **minimax regret approach** to decision making is neither purely optimistic nor purely conservative. Let us illustrate the minimax regret approach by showing how it can be used to select a decision alternative for the PDC problem.

Suppose that PDC constructs a small condominium complex (d_1) and demand turns out to be strong (s_1). Table 13.1 showed that the resulting profit for PDC would be $8 million. However, given that the strong demand state of nature (s_1) has occurred, we realize that the decision to construct a large condominium complex (d_3), yielding a profit of $20 million, would have been the best decision. The difference between the payoff for the best decision alternative ($20 million) and the payoff for the decision to construct a small condominium complex ($8 million) is the **opportunity loss,** or **regret,** associated with decision alternative d_1 when state of nature s_1 occurs; thus, for this case, the opportunity loss or regret is $20 million − $8 million = $12 million. Similarly, if PDC makes the decision to construct a medium condominium complex (d_2) and the strong demand state of nature (s_1) occurs, the opportunity loss, or regret, associated with d_2 would be $20 million − $14 million = $6 million.

TABLE 13.3   MINIMUM PAYOFF FOR EACH PDC DECISION ALTERNATIVE

Decision Alternative	Minimum Payoff	
Small complex, d_1	7 ←	Maximum of the minimum payoff values
Medium complex, d_2	5	
Large complex, d_3	−9	

In general, the following expression represents the opportunity loss, or regret:

$$R_{ij} = \left| V_j^* - V_{ij} \right| \qquad (13.1)$$

where

R_{ij} = the regret associated with decision alternative d_i and state of nature s_j
V_j^* = the payoff value[1] corresponding to the best decision for the state of nature s_j
V_{ij} = the payoff corresponding to decision alternative d_i and state of nature s_j

Note the role of the absolute value in equation (13.1). For minimization problems, the best payoff, V_j^*, is the smallest entry in column j. Because this value always is less than or equal to V_{ij}, the absolute value of the difference between V_j^* and V_{ij} ensures that the regret is always the magnitude of the difference.

Using equation (4.1) and the payoffs in Table 13.1, we can compute the regret associated with each combination of decision alternative d_i and state of nature s_j. Because the PDC problem is a maximization problem, V_j^* will be the largest entry in column j of the payoff table. Thus, to compute the regret, we simply subtract each entry in a column from the largest entry in the column. Table 13.4 shows the opportunity loss, or regret, table for the PDC problem.

The next step in applying the minimax regret approach is to list the maximum regret for each decision alternative; Table 13.5 shows the results for the PDC problem. Selecting the decision alternative with the *minimum* of the *maximum* regret values—hence, the name *minimax regret*—yields the minimax regret decision. For the PDC problem, the alternative to construct the medium condominium complex, with a corresponding maximum regret of $6 million, is the recommended minimax regret decision.

For practice in developing a decision recommendation using the optimistic, conservative, and minimax regret approaches, try Problem 1 (part b).

Note that the three approaches discussed in this section provide different recommendations, which in itself isn't bad. It simply reflects the difference in decision-making philosophies that underlie the various approaches. Ultimately, the decision maker will have to choose the most appropriate approach and then make the final decision accordingly. The main criticism of the approaches discussed in this section is that they do not consider any information about the probabilities of the various states of nature. In the next section we discuss an approach that utilizes probability information in selecting a decision alternative.

TABLE 13.4   OPPORTUNITY LOSS, OR REGRET, TABLE FOR THE PDC CONDOMINIUM PROJECT ($ MILLIONS)

	State of Nature	
Decision Alternative	**Strong Demand s_1**	**Weak Demand s_2**
Small complex, d_1	12	0
Medium complex, d_2	6	2
Large complex, d_3	0	16

---

[1] In maximization problems, V_j^* will be the largest entry in column j of the payoff table. In minimization problems, V_j^* will be the smallest entry in column j of the payoff table.

TABLE 13.5   MAXIMUM REGRET FOR EACH PDC DECISION ALTERNATIVE

Decision Alternative	Maximum Regret	
Small complex, d_1	12	
Medium complex, d_2	6	← Minimum of the maximum regret
Large complex, d_3	16	

13.3   DECISION MAKING WITH PROBABILITIES

In many decision-making situations, we can obtain probability assessments for the states of nature. When such probabilities are available, we can use the **expected value approach** to identify the best decision alternative. Let us first define the expected value of a decision alternative and then apply it to the PDC problem.

Let

$$N = \text{the number of states of nature}$$
$$P(s_j) = \text{the probability of state of nature } s_j$$

Because one and only one of the N states of nature can occur, the probabilities must satisfy two conditions:

$$P(s_j) \geq 0 \qquad \text{for all states of nature} \tag{13.2}$$

$$\sum_{j=1}^{N} P(s_j) = P(s_1) + P(s_2) + \cdots + P(s_N) = 1 \tag{13.3}$$

The **expected value (EV)** of decision alternative d_i is defined as follows:

$$EV(d_i) = \sum_{j=1}^{N} P(s_j)V_{ij} \tag{13.4}$$

In words, the expected value of a decision alternative is the sum of weighted payoffs for the decision alternative. The weight for a payoff is the probability of the associated state of nature and therefore the probability that the payoff will occur. Let us return to the PDC problem to see how the expected value approach can be applied.

PDC is optimistic about the potential for the luxury high-rise condominium complex. Suppose that this optimism leads to an initial subjective probability assessment of 0.8 that demand will be strong (s_1) and a corresponding probability of 0.2 that demand will be weak (s_2). Thus, $P(s_1) = 0.8$ and $P(s_2) = 0.2$. Using the payoff values in Table 13.1 and equation

(13.4), we compute the expected value for each of the three decision alternatives as follows:

$$EV(d_1) = 0.8(8) + 0.2(7) = 7.8$$
$$EV(d_2) = 0.8(14) + 0.2(5) = 12.2$$
$$EV(d_3) = 0.8(20) + 0.2(-9) = 14.2$$

Thus, using the expected value approach, we find that the large condominium complex, with an expected value of $14.2 million, is the recommended decision.

Can you now use the expected value approach to develop a decision recommendation? Try Problem 4.

The calculations required to identify the decision alternative with the best expected value can be conveniently carried out on a decision tree. Figure 13.3 shows the decision tree for the PDC problem with state-of-nature branch probabilities. Working backward through the decision tree, we first compute the expected value at each chance node. That is, at each chance node, we weight each possible payoff by its probability of occurrence. By doing so, we obtain the expected values for nodes 2, 3, and 4, as shown in Figure 13.4.

Because the decision maker controls the branch leaving decision node 1 and because we are trying to maximize the expected profit, the best decision alternative at node 1 is d_3. Thus, the decision tree analysis leads to a recommendation of d_3, with an expected value of $14.2 million. Note that this recommendation is also obtained with the expected value approach in conjunction with the payoff table.

Computer software packages are available to help in constructing more complex decision trees. See Appendix 13.1.

Other decision problems may be substantially more complex than the PDC problem, but if a reasonable number of decision alternatives and states of nature are present, you can use the decision tree approach outlined here. First, draw a decision tree consisting of decision nodes, chance nodes, and branches that describe the sequential nature of the problem. If you use the expected value approach, the next step is to determine the probabilities for each of the states of nature and compute the expected value at each chance node. Then select the decision branch leading to the chance node with the best expected value. The decision alternative associated with this branch is the recommended decision.

FIGURE 13.3   PDC DECISION TREE WITH STATE-OF-NATURE BRANCH PROBABILITIES

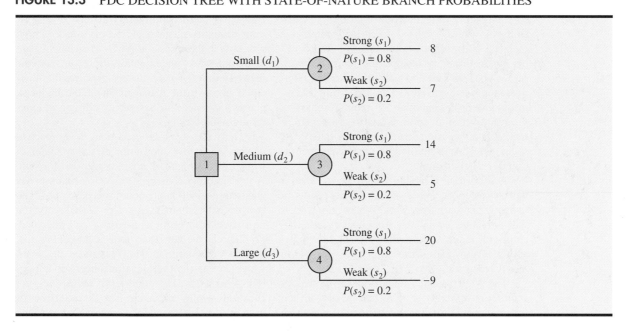

FIGURE 13.4   APPLYING THE EXPECTED VALUE APPROACH USING A DECISION TREE

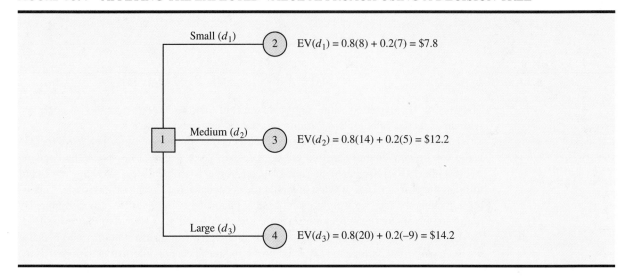

The Management Science in Action, Early Detection of High-Risk Worker Disability Claims, describes how the Workers' Compensation Board of British Columbia used a decision tree and expected cost to help determine whether a short-term disability claim should be considered a high-risk or a low-risk claim.

MANAGEMENT SCIENCE IN ACTION

EARLY DETECTION OF HIGH-RISK WORKER DISABILITY CLAIMS*

The Workers' Compensation Board of British Columbia (WCB) helps workers and employers maintain safe workplaces and helps injured workers obtain disability income and return to work safely. The funds used to make the disability compensation payments are obtained from assessments levied on employers. In return, employers receive protection from lawsuits arising from work-related injuries. In recent years, the WCB spent more than $1 billion on worker compensation and rehabilitation.

A short-term disability claim occurs when a worker suffers an injury or illness that results in temporary absence from work. Whenever a worker fails to recover completely from a short-term disability, the claim is reclassified as a long-term disability claim and more expensive long-term benefits are paid.

The WCB wanted a systematic way to identify short-term disability claims that posed a high financial risk of being converted to the more expensive long-term disability claims. If a short-term disability claim could be classified as high risk early in the process, a WCB management team could intervene and monitor the claim and the recovery process more closely. As a result, WCB could improve the management of the high-risk claims and reduce the cost of any subsequent long-term disability claims.

The WCB used a decision analysis approach to classify each new short-term disability claim as being either a high-risk claim or a low-risk claim. A decision tree consisting of two decision nodes and two states-of-nature nodes was developed. The two decision alternatives were: (1) Classify the new short-term claim as high-risk and intervene. (2) Classify the new short-term claim as low-risk and do not intervene. The two states of nature were: (1) The short-term claim converts to a long-term claim. (2) The short-term claim does not convert to a long-term claim. The characteristics of each new short-term claim were used to determine the probabilities for the states of nature. The pay-offs were the disability claim costs associated with each decision alternative and each state-of-nature outcome. The objective of minimizing the expected cost determined whether a new short-term claim should be classified as high-risk.

Implementation of the decision analysis model improved the practice of claim management for the Workers' Compensation Board. Early intervention

on the high-risk claims saved an estimated $4.7 million per year.

*Based on E. Urbanovich, E. Young, M. Puterman, and S. Fattedad, "Early Detection of High-Risk Claims at the Workers' Compensation Board of British Columbia," *Interfaces* (July/August 2003): 15–26.

Expected Value of Perfect Information

Suppose that PDC has the opportunity to conduct a market research study that would help evaluate buyer interest in the condominium project and provide information that management could use to improve the probability assessments for the states of nature. To determine the potential value of this information, we begin by supposing that the study could provide *perfect information* regarding the states of nature; that is, we assume for the moment that PDC could determine with certainty, prior to making a decision, which state of nature is going to occur. To make use of this perfect information, we will develop a decision strategy that PDC should follow once it knows which state of nature will occur. A decision strategy is simply a decision rule that specifies the decision alternative to be selected after new information becomes available.

To help determine the decision strategy for PDC, we reproduced PDC's payoff table as Table 13.6. Note that, if PDC knew for sure that state of nature s_1 would occur, the best decision alternative would be d_3, with a payoff of $20 million. Similarly, if PDC knew for sure that state of nature s_2 would occur, the best decision alternative would be d_1, with a payoff of $7 million. Thus, we can state PDC's optimal decision strategy when the perfect information becomes available as follows:

If s_1, select d_3 and receive a payoff of $20 million.

If s_2, select d_1 and receive a payoff of $7 million.

What is the expected value for this decision strategy? To compute the expected value with perfect information, we return to the original probabilities for the states of nature: $P(s_1) = 0.8$ and $P(s_2) = 0.2$. Thus, there is a 0.8 probability that the perfect information will indicate state of nature s_1 and the resulting decision alternative d_3 will provide a $20 million profit. Similarly, with a 0.2 probability for state of nature s_2, the optimal decision alternative d_1 will provide a $7 million profit. Thus, from equation (13.4), the expected value of the decision strategy that uses perfect information is

$$0.8(20) + 0.2(7) = 17.4$$

We refer to the expected value of $17.4 million as the *expected value with perfect information* (EVwPI).

Earlier in this section we showed that the recommended decision using the expected value approach is decision alternative d_3, with an expected value of $14.2 million. Because this decision recommendation and expected value computation were made without the benefit of perfect information, $14.2 million is referred to as the *expected value without perfect information* (EVwoPI).

TABLE 13.6   PAYOFF TABLE FOR THE PDC CONDOMINIUM PROJECT ($ MILLIONS)

	State of Nature	
Decision Alternative	**Strong Demand s_1**	**Weak Demand s_2**
Small complex, d_1	8	7
Medium complex, d_2	14	5
Large complex, d_3	20	−9

It would be worth $3.2 million for PDC to learn the level of market acceptance before selecting a decision alternative.

The expected value with perfect information is $17.4 million, and the expected value without perfect information is $14.2; therefore, the expected value of the perfect information (EVPI) is $17.4 − $14.2 = $3.2 million. In other words, $3.2 million represents the additional expected value that can be obtained if perfect information were available about the states of nature.

Generally speaking, a market research study will not provide "perfect" information; however, if the market research study is a good one, the information gathered might be worth a sizable portion of the $3.2 million. Given the EVPI of $3.2 million, PDC might seriously consider a market survey as a way to obtain more information about the states of nature.

In general, the **expected value of perfect information (EVPI)** is computed as follows:

$$EVPI = |EVwPI - EVwoPI| \qquad (13.5)$$

where

EVPI = expected value of perfect information

EVwPI = expected value *with* perfect information about the states of nature

EVwoPI = expected value *without* perfect information about the states of nature

For practice in determining the expected value of perfect information, try Problem 14.

Note the role of the absolute value in equation (13.5). For minimization problems the expected value with perfect information is always less than or equal to the expected value without perfect information. In this case, EVPI is the magnitude of the difference between EVwPI and EVwoPI, or the absolute value of the difference as shown in equation (13.5).

NOTES AND COMMENTS

We restate the *opportunity loss,* or *regret,* table for the PDC problem (see Table 13.4) as follows.

	State of Nature	
	Strong Demand	**Weak Demand**
Decision Alternative	s_1	s_2
Small complex, d_1	12	0
Medium complex, d_2	6	2
Large complex, d_3	0	16

Using $P(s_1)$, $P(s_2)$, and the opportunity loss values, we can compute the *expected opportunity loss* (EOL) for each decision alternative. With $P(s_1) = 0.8$ and $P(s_2) = 0.2$, the expected opportunity loss for each of the three decision alternatives is

$$EOL(d_1) = 0.8(12) + 0.2(0) = 9.6$$
$$EOL(d_2) = 0.8(6) + 0.2(2) = 5.2$$
$$EOL(d_3) = 0.8(0) + 0.2(16) = 3.2$$

Regardless of whether the decision analysis involves maximization or minimization, the *minimum* expected opportunity loss always provides the best decision alternative. Thus, with EOL(d_3) = 3.2, d_3 is the recommended decision. In addition, the minimum expected opportunity loss always is *equal to* *the expected value of perfect information.* That is, EOL(best decision) = EVPI; for the PDC problem, this value is $3.2 million.

13.4 RISK ANALYSIS AND SENSITIVITY ANALYSIS

Risk analysis helps the decision maker recognize the difference between the expected value of a decision alternative and the payoff that may actually occur. **Sensitivity analysis** also helps the decision maker by describing how changes in the state-of-nature probabilities and/or changes in the payoffs affect the recommended decision alternative.

Risk Analysis

A decision alternative and a state of nature combine to generate the payoff associated with a decision. The **risk profile** for a decision alternative shows the possible payoffs along with their associated probabilities.

Let us demonstrate risk analysis and the construction of a risk profile by returning to the PDC condominium construction project. Using the expected value approach, we identified the large condominium complex (d_3) as the best decision alternative. The expected value of $14.2 million for d_3 is based on a 0.8 probability of obtaining a $20 million profit and a 0.2 probability of obtaining a $9 million loss. The 0.8 probability for the $20 million payoff and the 0.2 probability for the −$9 million payoff provide the risk profile for the large complex decision alternative. This risk profile is shown graphically in Figure 13.5.

Sometimes a review of the risk profile associated with an optimal decision alternative may cause the decision maker to choose another decision alternative even though the expected value of the other decision alternative is not as good. For example, the risk profile for the medium complex decision alternative (d_2) shows a 0.8 probability for a $14 million

FIGURE 13.5 RISK PROFILE FOR THE LARGE COMPLEX DECISION ALTERNATIVE FOR THE PDC CONDOMINIUM PROJECT

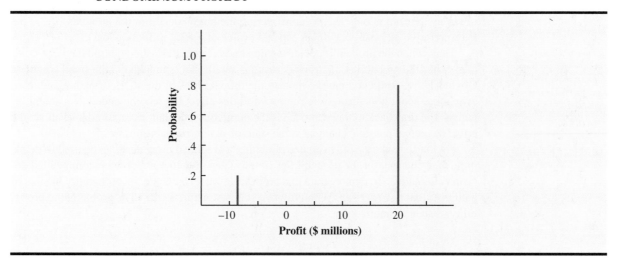

payoff and a 0.2 probability for a $5 million payoff. Because no probability of a loss is associated with decision alternative d_2, the medium complex decision alternative would be judged less risky than the large complex decision alternative. As a result, a decision maker might prefer the less-risky medium complex decision alternative even though it has an expected value of $2 million less than the large complex decision alternative.

Sensitivity Analysis

Sensitivity analysis can be used to determine how changes in the probabilities for the states of nature or changes in the payoffs affect the recommended decision alternative. In many cases, the probabilities for the states of nature and the payoffs are based on subjective assessments. Sensitivity analysis helps the decision maker understand which of these inputs are critical to the choice of the best decision alternative. If a small change in the value of one of the inputs causes a change in the recommended decision alternative, the solution to the decision analysis problem is sensitive to that particular input. Extra effort and care should be taken to make sure the input value is as accurate as possible. On the other hand, if a modest to large change in the value of one of the inputs does not cause a change in the recommended decision alternative, the solution to the decision analysis problem is not sensitive to that particular input. No extra time or effort would be needed to refine the estimated input value.

One approach to sensitivity analysis is to select different values for the probabilities of the states of nature and the payoffs and then re-solve the decision analysis problem. If the recommended decision alternative changes, we know that the solution is sensitive to the changes made. For example, suppose that in the PDC problem the probability for a strong demand is revised to 0.2 and the probability for a weak demand is revised to 0.8. Would the recommended decision alternative change? Using $P(s_1) = 0.2$, $P(s_2) = 0.8$, and equation (13.4), the revised expected values for the three decision alternatives are

$$
\begin{aligned}
EV(d_1) &= 0.2(8)\ \ + 0.8(7)\ \ = \ \ 7.2 \\
EV(d_2) &= 0.2(14) + 0.8(5)\ \ = \ \ 6.8 \\
EV(d_3) &= 0.2(20) + 0.8(-9) = -3.2
\end{aligned}
$$

With these probability assessments the recommended decision alternative is to construct a small condominium complex (d_1), with an expected value of $7.2 million. The probability of strong demand is only 0.2, so constructing the large condominium complex (d_3) is the least preferred alternative, with an expected value of −$3.2 million (a loss).

Computer software packages for decision analysis make it easy to calculate these revised scenarios.

Thus, when the probability of strong demand is large, PDC should build the large complex; when the probability of strong demand is small, PDC should build the small complex. Obviously, we could continue to modify the probabilities of the states of nature and learn even more about how changes in the probabilities affect the recommended decision alternative. The drawback to this approach is the numerous calculations required to evaluate the effect of several possible changes in the state-of-nature probabilities.

For the special case of two states of nature, a graphical procedure can be used to determine how changes for the probabilities of the states of nature affect the recommended decision alternative. To demonstrate this procedure, we let p denote the probability of state of nature s_1; that is, $P(s_1) = p$. With only two states of nature in the PDC problem, the probability of state of nature s_2 is

$$
P(s_2) = 1 - P(s_1) = 1 - p
$$

Using equation (13.4) and the payoff values in Table 13.1, we determine the expected value for decision alternative d_1 as follows:

$$
\begin{aligned}
\text{EV}(d_1) &= P(s_1)(8) + P(s_2)(7) \\
&= p(8) + (1 - p)(7) \\
&= 8p + 7 - 7p = p + 7
\end{aligned}
\tag{13.6}
$$

Repeating the expected value computations for decision alternatives d_2 and d_3, we obtain expressions for the expected value of each decision alternative as a function of p:

$$
\text{EV}(d_2) = 9p + 5 \tag{13.7}
$$
$$
\text{EV}(d_3) = 29p - 9 \tag{13.8}
$$

Thus, we have developed three equations that show the expected value of the three decision alternatives as a function of the probability of state of nature s_1.

We continue by developing a graph with values of p on the horizontal axis and the associated EVs on the vertical axis. Because equations (13.6), (13.7), and (13.8) are linear equations, the graph of each equation is a straight line. For each equation, we can obtain the line by identifying two points that satisfy the equation and drawing a line through the points. For instance, if we let $p = 0$ in equation (13.6), $\text{EV}(d_1) = 7$. Then, letting $p = 1$, $\text{EV}(d_1) = 8$. Connecting these two points, $(0, 7)$ and $(1, 8)$, provides the line labeled $\text{EV}(d_1)$ in Figure 13.6. Similarly, we obtain the lines labeled $\text{EV}(d_2)$ and $\text{EV}(d_3)$; these lines are the graphs of equations (13.7) and (13.8), respectively.

Figure 13.6 shows how the recommended decision changes as p, the probability of the strong demand state of nature (s_1), changes. Note that for small values of p, decision alternative d_1 (small complex) provides the largest expected value and is thus the recommended decision. When the value of p increases to a certain point, decision alternative d_2 (medium complex) provides the largest expected value and is the recommended decision. Finally, for large values of p, decision alternative d_3 (large complex) becomes the recommended decision.

The value of p for which the expected values of d_1 and d_2 are equal is the value of p corresponding to the intersection of the $\text{EV}(d_1)$ and the $\text{EV}(d_2)$ lines. To determine this value, we set $\text{EV}(d_1) = \text{EV}(d_2)$ and solve for the value of p:

$$
\begin{aligned}
p + 7 &= 9p + 5 \\
8p &= 2 \\
p &= \frac{2}{8} = 0.25
\end{aligned}
$$

Graphical sensitivity analysis shows how changes in the probabilities for the states of nature affect the recommended decision alternative. Try Problem 8.

Hence, when $p = 0.25$, decision alternatives d_1 and d_2 provide the same expected value. Repeating this calculation for the value of p corresponding to the intersection of the $\text{EV}(d_2)$ and $\text{EV}(d_3)$ lines, we obtain $p = 0.70$.

Using Figure 13.6, we can conclude that decision alternative d_1 provides the largest expected value for $p \leq 0.25$, decision alternative d_2 provides the largest expected value for

FIGURE 13.6   EXPECTED VALUE FOR THE PDC DECISION ALTERNATIVES AS A FUNCTION OF p

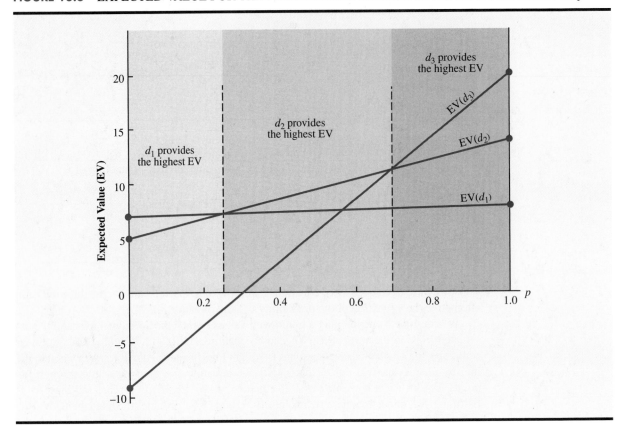

0.25 ≤ p ≤ 0.70, and decision alternative d_3 provides the largest expected value for p ≥ 0.70. Because p is the probability of state of nature s_1 and $(1 - p)$ is the probability of state of nature s_2, we now have the sensitivity analysis information that tells us how changes in the state-of-nature probabilities affect the recommended decision alternative.

Sensitivity analysis calculations can also be made for the values of the payoffs. In the original PDC problem, the expected values for the three decision alternatives were as follows: $EV(d_1) = 7.8$, $EV(d_2) = 12.2$, and $EV(d_3) = 14.2$. Decision alternative d_3 (large complex) was recommended. Note that decision alternative d_2 with $EV(d_2) = 12.2$ was the second best decision alternative. Decision alternative d_3 will remain the optimal decision alternative as long as $EV(d_3)$ is greater than or equal to the expected value of the second best decision alternative. Thus, decision alternative d_3 will remain the optimal decision alternative as long as

$$EV(d_3) \geq 12.2 \qquad (13.9)$$

Let

S = the payoff of decision alternative d_3 when demand is strong

W = the payoff of decision alternative d_3 when demand is weak

Using $P(s_1) = 0.8$ and $P(s_2) = 0.2$, the general expression for $EV(d_3)$ is

$$EV(d_3) = 0.8S + 0.2W \tag{13.10}$$

Assuming that the payoff for d_3 stays at its original value of $-\$9$ million when demand is weak, the large complex decision alternative will remain optimal as long as

$$EV(d_3) = 0.8S + 0.2(-9) \geq 12.2 \tag{13.11}$$

Solving for S, we have

$$0.8S - 1.8 \geq 12.2$$
$$0.8S \geq 14$$
$$S \geq 17.5$$

Recall that when demand is strong, decision alternative d_3 has an estimated payoff of $\$20$ million. The preceding calculation shows that decision alternative d_3 will remain optimal as long as the payoff for d_3 when demand is strong is at least $\$17.5$ million.

Assuming that the payoff for d_3 when demand is strong stays at its original value of $\$20$ million, we can make a similar calculation to learn how sensitive the optimal solution is with regard to the payoff for d_3 when demand is weak. Returning to the expected value calculation of equation (13.10), we know that the large complex decision alternative will remain optimal as long as

$$EV(d_3) = 0.8(20) + 0.2W \geq 12.2 \tag{13.12}$$

Solving for W, we have

$$16 + 0.2W \geq 12.2$$
$$0.2W \geq -3.8$$
$$W \geq -19$$

Recall that when demand is weak, decision alternative d_3 has an estimated payoff of $-\$9$ million. The preceding calculation shows that decision alternative d_3 will remain optimal as long as the payoff for d_3 when demand is weak is at least $-\$19$ million.

Based on this sensitivity analysis, we conclude that the payoffs for the large complex decision alternative (d_3) could vary considerably, and d_3 would remain the recommended decision alternative. Thus, we conclude that the optimal solution for the PDC decision problem is not particularly sensitive to the payoffs for the large complex decision alternative. We note, however, that this sensitivity analysis has been conducted based on only one change at a time. That is, only one payoff was changed and the probabilities for the states

Sensitivity analysis can assist management in deciding whether more time and effort should be spent obtaining better estimates of payoffs and probabilities.

of nature remained $P(s_1) = 0.8$ and $P(s_2) = 0.2$. Note that similar sensitivity analysis calculations can be made for the payoffs associated with the small complex decision alternative d_1 and the medium complex decision alternative d_2. However, in these cases, decision alternative d_3 remains optimal only if the changes in the payoffs for decision alternatives d_1 and d_2 meet the requirements that $EV(d_1) \leq 14.2$ and $EV(d_2) \leq 14.2$.

NOTES AND COMMENTS

1. Some decision analysis software automatically provides the risk profiles for the optimal decision alternative. These packages also allow the user to obtain the risk profiles for other decision alternatives. After comparing the risk profiles, a decision maker may decide to select a decision alternative with a good risk profile even though the expected value of the decision alternative is not as good as the optimal decision alternative.

2. A *tornado diagram,* a graphical display, is particularly helpful when several inputs combine to determine the value of the optimal solution. By varying each input over its range of values, we obtain information about how each input affects the value of the optimal solution. To display this information, a bar is constructed for the input with the width of the bar showing how the input affects the value of the optimal solution. The widest bar corresponds to the input that is most sensitive. The bars are arranged in a graph with the widest bar at the top, resulting in a graph that has the appearance of a tornado.

13.5   DECISION ANALYSIS WITH SAMPLE INFORMATION

In applying the expected value approach, we showed how probability information about the states of nature affects the expected value calculations and thus the decision recommendation. Frequently, decision makers have preliminary or **prior probability** assessments for the states of nature that are the best probability values available at that time. However, to make the best possible decision, the decision maker may want to seek additional information about the states of nature. This new information can be used to revise or update the prior probabilities so that the final decision is based on more accurate probabilities for the states of nature. Most often, additional information is obtained through experiments designed to provide **sample information** about the states of nature. Raw material sampling, product testing, and market research studies are examples of experiments (or studies) that may enable management to revise or update the state-of-nature probabilities. These revised probabilities are called **posterior probabilities.**

Let us return to the PDC problem and assume that management is considering a six-month market research study designed to learn more about potential market acceptance of the PDC condominium project. Management anticipates that the market research study will provide one of the following two results:

1. Favorable report: A significant number of the individuals contacted express interest in purchasing a PDC condominium.
2. Unfavorable report: Very few of the individuals contacted express interest in purchasing a PDC condominium.

Influence Diagram

By introducing the possibility of conducting a market research study, the PDC problem becomes more complex. The influence diagram for the expanded PDC problem is shown in Figure 13.7. Note that the two decision nodes correspond to the research study and the

FIGURE 13.7   INFLUENCE DIAGRAM FOR THE PDC PROBLEM WITH SAMPLE INFORMATION

complex-size decisions. The two chance nodes correspond to the research study results and demand for the condominiums. Finally, the consequence node is the profit. From the arcs of the influence diagram, we see that demand influences both the research study results and profit. Although demand is currently unknown to PDC, some level of demand for the condominiums already exists in the Pittsburgh area. If existing demand is strong, the research study is likely to find a significant number of individuals who express an interest in purchasing a condominium. However, if the existing demand is weak, the research study is more likely to find a significant number of individuals who express little interest in purchasing a condominium. In this sense, existing demand for the condominiums will influence the research study results, and clearly, demand will have an influence upon PDC's profit.

The arc from the research study decision node to the complex-size decision node indicates that the research study decision precedes the complex-size decision. No arc spans from the research study decision node to the research study results node, because the decision to conduct the research study does not actually influence the research study results. The decision to conduct the research study makes the research study results available, but it does not influence the results of the research study. Finally, the complex-size node and the demand node both influence profit. Note that if a stated cost to conduct the research study were given, the decision to conduct the research study would also influence profit. In such a case, we would need to add an arc from the research study decision node to the profit node to show the influence that the research study cost would have on profit.

Decision Tree

The decision tree for the PDC problem with sample information shows the logical sequence for the decisions and the chance events in Figure 13.8.

First, PDC's management must decide whether the market research should be conducted. If it is conducted, PDC's management must be prepared to make a decision about the size of the condominium project if the market research report is favorable and, possibly, a different decision about the size of the condominium project if the market research report is unfavorable. In Figure 13.8, the squares are decision nodes and the circles are chance nodes. At each decision node, the branch of the tree that is taken is based on the decision made. At each chance node, the branch of the tree that is taken is based on probability or chance. For example, decision node 1 shows that PDC must first make the decision

FIGURE 13.8   THE PDC DECISION TREE INCLUDING THE MARKET RESEARCH STUDY

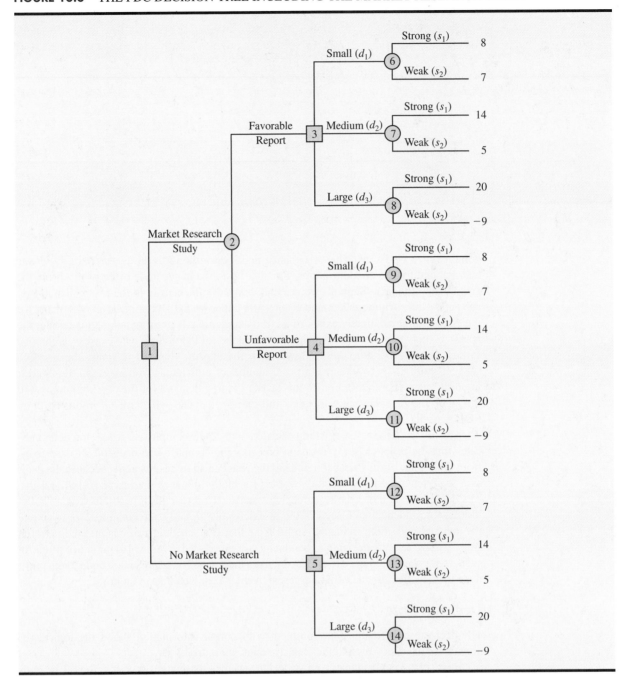

of whether to conduct the market research study. If the market research study is undertaken, chance node 2 indicates that both the favorable report branch and the unfavorable report branch are not under PDC's control and will be determined by chance. Node 3 is a decision node, indicating that PDC must make the decision to construct the small, medium, or large complex if the market research report is favorable. Node 4 is a decision node showing that

PDC must make the decision to construct the small, medium, or large complex if the market research report is unfavorable. Node 5 is a decision node indicating that PDC must make the decision to construct the small, medium, or large complex if the market research is not undertaken. Nodes 6 to 14 are chance nodes indicating that the strong demand or weak demand state-of-nature branches will be determined by chance.

We explain in Section 13.6 how these probabilities can be developed.

Analysis of the decision tree and the choice of an optimal strategy require that we know the branch probabilities corresponding to all chance nodes. PDC has developed the following branch probabilities:

If the market research study is undertaken

$$P(\text{Favorable report}) = 0.77$$
$$P(\text{Unfavorable report}) = 0.23$$

If the market research report is favorable

$$P(\text{Strong demand given a favorable report}) = 0.94$$
$$P(\text{Weak demand given a favorable report}) = 0.06$$

If the market research report is unfavorable

$$P(\text{Strong demand given an unfavorable report}) = 0.35$$
$$P(\text{Weak demand given an unfavorable report}) = 0.65$$

If the market research report is not undertaken, the prior probabilities are applicable.

$$P(\text{Strong demand}) = 0.80$$
$$P(\text{Weak demand}) = 0.20$$

The branch probabilities are shown on the decision tree in Figure 13.9.

Decision Strategy

A **decision strategy** is a sequence of decisions and chance outcomes where the decisions chosen depend on the yet-to-be-determined outcomes of chance events.

The approach used to determine the optimal decision strategy is based on a backward pass through the decision tree using the following steps:

1. At chance nodes, compute the expected value by multiplying the payoff at the end of each branch by the corresponding branch probabilities.
2. At decision nodes, select the decision branch that leads to the best expected value. This expected value becomes the expected value at the decision node.

Starting the backward pass calculations by computing the expected values at chance nodes 6 to 14 provides the following results:

$$
\begin{aligned}
EV(\text{Node 6}) &= 0.94(8) &+ 0.06(7) &= 7.94 \\
EV(\text{Node 7}) &= 0.94(14) &+ 0.06(5) &= 13.46 \\
EV(\text{Node 8}) &= 0.94(20) &+ 0.06(-9) &= 18.26 \\
EV(\text{Node 9}) &= 0.35(8) &+ 0.65(7) &= 7.35 \\
EV(\text{Node 10}) &= 0.35(14) &+ 0.65(5) &= 8.15 \\
EV(\text{Node 11}) &= 0.35(20) &+ 0.65(-9) &= 1.15 \\
EV(\text{Node 12}) &= 0.80(8) &+ 0.20(7) &= 7.80 \\
EV(\text{Node 13}) &= 0.80(14) &+ 0.20(5) &= 12.20 \\
EV(\text{Node 14}) &= 0.80(20) &+ 0.20(-9) &= 14.20
\end{aligned}
$$

622   Chapter 13   Decision Analysis

FIGURE 13.9   THE PDC DECISION TREE WITH BRANCH PROBABILITIES

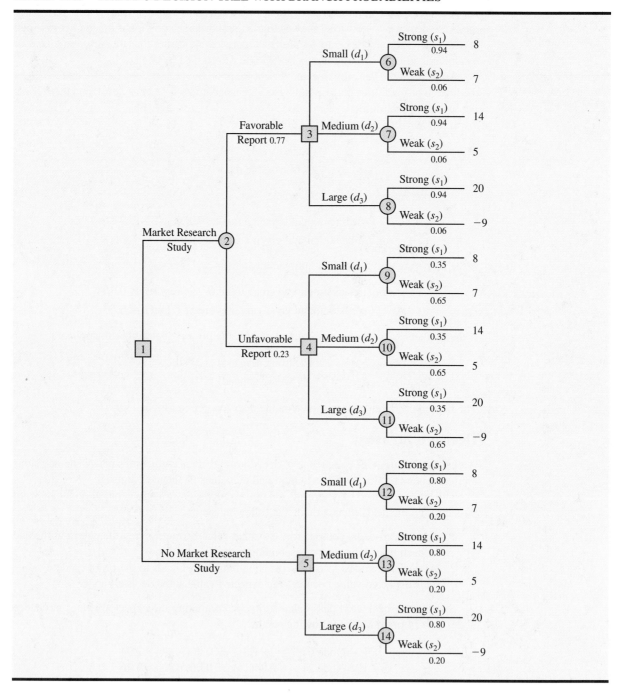

Figure 13.10 shows the reduced decision tree after computing expected values at these chance nodes.

Next, move to decision nodes 3, 4, and 5. For each of these nodes, we select the decision alternative branch that leads to the best expected value. For example, at node 3 we have the choice of the small complex branch with EV(Node 6) = 7.94, the medium complex branch with EV(Node 7) = 13.46, and the large complex branch with EV(Node 8) = 18.26. Thus,

FIGURE 13.10   PDC DECISION TREE AFTER COMPUTING EXPECTED VALUES AT CHANCE
NODES 6 TO 14

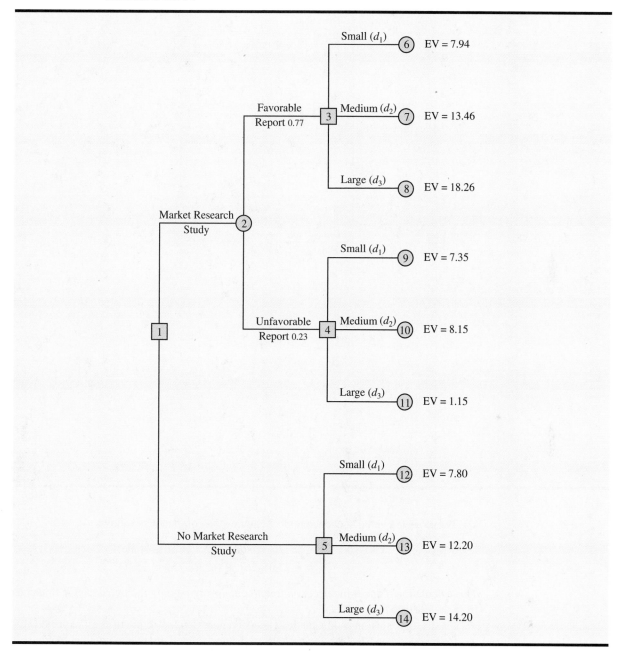

we select the large complex decision alternative branch and the expected value at node 3
becomes EV(Node 3) = 18.26.

    For node 4, we select the best expected value from nodes 9, 10, and 11. The best deci-
sion alternative is the medium complex branch that provides EV(Node 4) = 8.15. For node
5, we select the best expected value from nodes 12, 13, and 14. The best decision alternative is the large complex branch that provides EV(Node 5) = 14.20. Figure 13.11 shows the
reduced decision tree after choosing the best decisions at nodes 3, 4, and 5.

FIGURE 13.11   PDC DECISION TREE AFTER CHOOSING BEST DECISIONS AT NODES 3, 4, AND 5

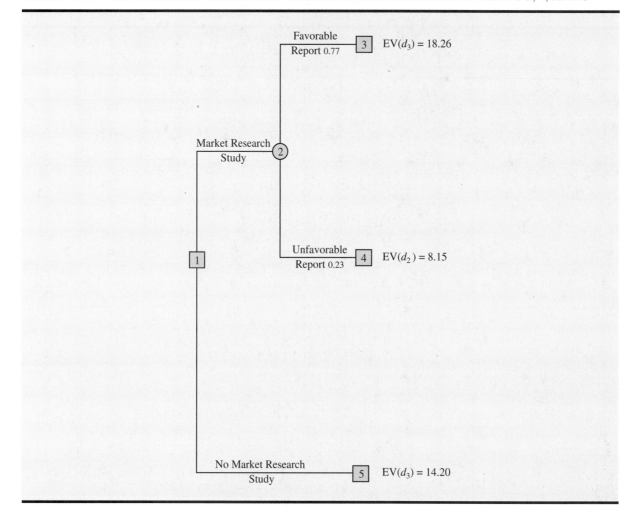

The expected value at chance node 2 can now be computed as follows:

$$EV(\text{Node 2}) = 0.77EV(\text{Node 3}) + 0.23EV(\text{Node 4})$$
$$= 0.77(18.26) + 0.23(8.15) = 15.93$$

This calculation reduces the decision tree to one involving only the two decision branches from node 1 (see Figure 13.12).

Finally, the decision can be made at decision node 1 by selecting the best expected values from nodes 2 and 5. This action leads to the decision alternative to conduct the market research study, which provides an overall expected value of 15.93.

The optimal decision for PDC is to conduct the market research study and then carry out the following decision strategy:

If the market research is favorable, construct the large condominium complex.

If the market research is unfavorable, construct the medium condominium complex.

Problem 16 will test your ability to develop an optimal decision strategy.

The analysis of the PDC decision tree describes the methods that can be used to analyze more complex sequential decision problems. First, draw a decision tree consisting of

FIGURE 13.12   PDC DECISION TREE REDUCED TO TWO DECISION BRANCHES

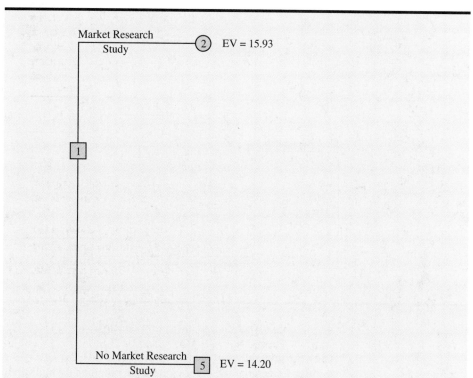

decision and chance nodes and branches that describe the sequential nature of the problem. Determine the probabilities for all chance outcomes. Then, by working backward through the tree, compute expected values at all chance nodes and select the best decision branch at all decision nodes. The sequence of optimal decision branches determines the optimal decision strategy for the problem.

The Management Science in Action, New Drug Decision Analysis at Bayer Pharmaceuticals, describes how an extension of the decision analysis principles presented in this section enabled Bayer to make decisions about the development and marketing of a new drug.

Risk Profile

Figure 13.13 provides a reduced decision tree showing only the sequence of decision alternatives and chance events for the PDC optimal decision strategy. By implementing the optimal decision strategy, PDC will obtain one of the four payoffs shown at the terminal branches of the decision tree. Recall that a risk profile shows the possible payoffs with their associated probabilities. Thus, in order to construct a risk profile for the optimal decision strategy, we will need to compute the probability for each of the four payoffs.

Note that each payoff results from a sequence of branches leading from node 1 to the payoff. For instance, the payoff of $20 million is obtained by following the upper branch from node 1, the upper branch from node 2, the lower branch from node 3, and the upper branch from node 8. The probability of following that sequence of branches can be found by multiplying the probabilities for the branches from the chance nodes in the sequence.

FIGURE 13.13   PDC DECISION TREE SHOWING ONLY BRANCHES ASSOCIATED WITH OPTIMAL DECISION STRATEGY

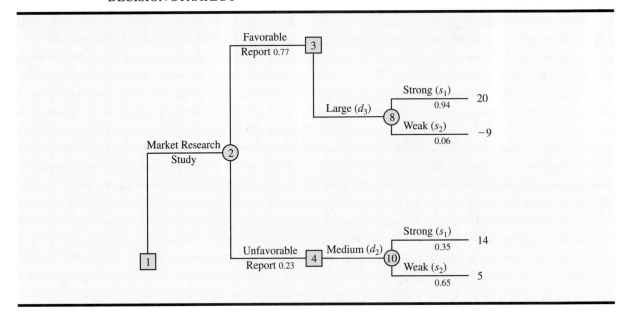

Thus, the probability of the $20 million payoff is $(0.77)(0.94) = 0.72$. Similarly, the probabilities for each of the other payoffs are obtained by multiplying the probabilities for the branches from the chance nodes leading to the payoffs. Doing so, we find the probability of the –$9 million payoff is $(0.77)(0.06) = 0.05$; the probability of the $14 million payoff is $(0.23)(0.35) = 0.08$; and the probability of the $5 million payoff is $(0.23)(0.65) = 0.15$. The following table showing the probability distribution for the payoffs for the PDC optimal decision strategy is the tabular representation of the risk profile for the optimal decision strategy.

Payoff ($ millions)	Probability
−9	0.05
5	0.15
14	0.08
20	0.72
	1.00

Figure 13.14 provides a graphical representation of the risk profile. Comparing Figures 13.5 and 13.14, we see that the PDC risk profile is changed by the strategy to conduct the market research study. In fact, the use of the market research study lowered the probability of the $9 million loss from 0.20 to 0.05. PDC's management would most likely view that change as a significant reduction in the risk associated with the condominium project.

FIGURE 13.14   RISK PROFILE FOR PDC CONDOMINIUM PROJECT WITH SAMPLE
INFORMATION SHOWING PAYOFFS ASSOCIATED WITH OPTIMAL
DECISION STRATEGY

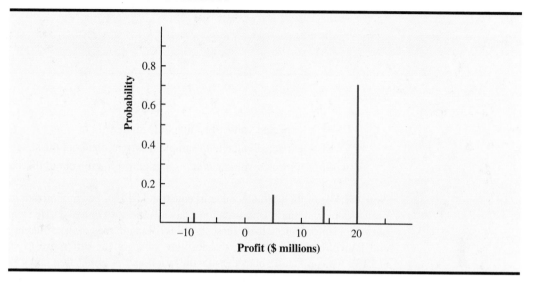

MANAGEMENT SCIENCE IN ACTION

NEW DRUG DECISION ANALYSIS AT BAYER PHARMACEUTICALS*

Drug development in the United States requires substantial investment and is very risky. It takes nearly 15 years to research and develop a new drug. The Bayer Biological Products (BP) group used decision analysis to evaluate the potential for a new blood clot–busting drug. An influence diagram was used to describe the complex structure of the decision analysis process. Six key yes-or-no decision nodes were identified: (1) begin preclinical development; (2) begin testing in humans; (3) continue development into phase 3; (4) continue development into phase 4; (5) file a license application with the FDA; and (6) launch the new drug into the marketplace. More than 50 chance nodes appeared in the influence diagram. The chance nodes showed how uncertainties—related to factors such as direct labor costs, process development costs, market share, tax rate, and pricing—affected the outcome. Net present value provided the consequence and the decision-making criterion.

Probability assessments were made concerning both the technical risk and market risk at each stage of the process. The resulting sequential decision tree had 1955 possible paths that led to different net present value outcomes. Cost inputs, judgments of potential outcomes, and the assignment of probabilities helped evaluate the project's potential contribution. Sensitivity analysis was used to identify key variables that would require special attention by the project team and management during the drug development process. Application of decision analysis principles allowed Bayer to make good decisions about how to develop and market the new drug.

*Based on Jeffrey S. Stonebraker, "How Bayer Makes Decisions to Develop New Drugs," *Interfaces,* no. 6 (November/December 2002): 77–90.

Expected Value of Sample Information

The EVSI = $1.73 million suggests PDC should be willing to pay up to $1.73 million to conduct the market research study.

In the PDC problem, the market research study is the sample information used to determine the optimal decision strategy. The expected value associated with the market research study is $15.93. In Section 13.3 we showed that the best expected value if the market research study is *not* undertaken is \$14.20. Thus, we can conclude that the difference, \$15.93 – \$14.20 = \$1.73, is the **expected value of sample information (EVSI).** In other words, conducting the market research study adds \$1.73 million to the PDC expected value. In general, the expected value of sample information is as follows:

$$EVSI = |EVwSI - EVwoSI| \qquad (13.13)$$

where

$$EVSI = \text{expected value of sample information}$$
$$EVwSI = \text{expected value } with \text{ sample information about the states of nature}$$
$$EVwoSI = \text{expected value } without \text{ sample information about the states of nature}$$

Note the role of the absolute value in equation (13.13). For minimization problems the expected value with sample information is always less than or equal to the expected value without sample information. In this case, EVSI is the magnitude of the difference between EVwSI and EVwoSI; thus, by taking the absolute value of the difference as shown in equation (13.13), we can handle both the maximization and minimization cases with one equation.

Efficiency of Sample Information

In Section 13.3 we showed that the expected value of perfect information (EVPI) for the PDC problem is \$3.2 million. We never anticipated that the market research report would obtain perfect information, but we can use an **efficiency** measure to express the value of the market research information. With perfect information having an efficiency rating of 100%, the efficiency rating E for sample information is computed as follows:

$$E = \frac{EVSI}{EVPI} \times 100 \qquad (13.14)$$

For the PDC problem,

$$E = \frac{1.73}{3.2} \times 100 = 54.1\%$$

In other words, the information from the market research study is 54.1% as efficient as perfect information.

Low efficiency ratings for sample information might lead the decision maker to look for other types of information. However, high efficiency ratings indicate that the sample information is almost as good as perfect information and that additional sources of information would not yield significantly better results.

13.6   COMPUTING BRANCH PROBABILITIES

In Section 13.5 the branch probabilities for the PDC decision tree chance nodes were specified in the problem description. No computations were required to determine these probabilities. In this section we show how **Bayes' theorem** can be used to compute branch probabilities for decision trees.

FIGURE 13.15   THE PDC DECISION TREE

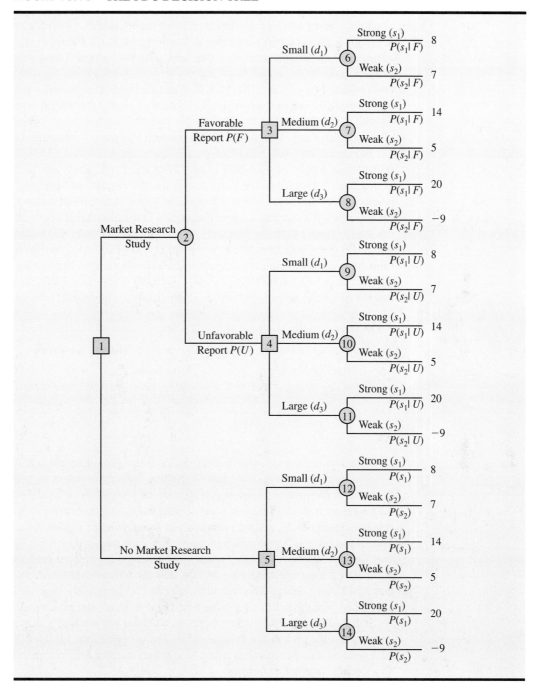

The PDC decision tree is shown again in Figure 13.15. Let

F = Favorable market research report
U = Unfavorable market research report
s_1 = Strong demand (state of nature 1)
s_2 = Weak demand (state of nature 2)

At chance node 2, we need to know the branch probabilities $P(F)$ and $P(U)$. At chance nodes 6, 7, and 8, we need to know the branch probabilities $P(s_1 \mid F)$, the probability of state of nature 1 given a favorable market research report, and $P(s_2 \mid F)$, the probability of state of nature 2 given a favorable market research report. $P(s_1 \mid F)$ and $P(s_2 \mid F)$ are referred to as *posterior probabilities* because they are conditional probabilities based on the outcome of the sample information. At chance nodes 9, 10, and 11, we need to know the branch probabilities $P(s_1 \mid U)$ and $P(s_2 \mid U)$; note that these are also posterior probabilities, denoting the probabilities of the two states of nature *given* that the market research report is unfavorable. Finally, at chance nodes 12, 13, and 14, we need the probabilities for the states of nature, $P(s_1)$ and $P(s_2)$, if the market research study is not undertaken.

In making the probability computations, we need to know PDC's assessment of the probabilities for the two states of nature, $P(s_1)$ and $P(s_2)$, which are the prior probabilities as discussed earlier. In addition, we must know the **conditional probability** of the market research outcomes (the sample information) *given* each state of nature. For example, we need to know the conditional probability of a favorable market research report given that the state of nature is strong demand for the PDC project; note that this conditional probability of F given state of nature s_1 is written $P(F \mid s_1)$. To carry out the probability calculations, we will need conditional probabilities for all sample outcomes given all states of nature, that is, $P(F \mid s_1)$, $P(F \mid s_2)$, $P(U \mid s_1)$, and $P(U \mid s_2)$. In the PDC problem we assume that the following assessments are available for these conditional probabilities:

	Market Research	
State of Nature	**Favorable, *F***	**Unfavorable, *U***
Strong demand, s_1	$P(F \mid s_1) = 0.90$	$P(U \mid s_1) = 0.10$
Weak demand, s_2	$P(F \mid s_2) = 0.25$	$P(U \mid s_2) = 0.75$

Note that the preceding probability assessments provide a reasonable degree of confidence in the market research study. If the true state of nature is s_1, the probability of a favorable market research report is 0.90, and the probability of an unfavorable market research report is 0.10. If the true state of nature is s_2, the probability of a favorable market research report is 0.25, and the probability of an unfavorable market research report is 0.75. The reason for a 0.25 probability of a potentially misleading favorable market research report for state of nature s_2 is that when some potential buyers first hear about the new condominium project, their enthusiasm may lead them to overstate their real interest in it. A potential buyer's initial favorable response can change quickly to a "no thank you" when later faced with the reality of signing a purchase contract and making a down payment.

In the following discussion we present a tabular approach as a convenient method for carrying out the probability computations. The computations for the PDC problem based on a favorable market research report (F) are summarized in Table 13.7. The steps used to develop this table are as follows:

Step 1. In column 1 enter the states of nature. In column 2 enter the *prior probabilities* for the states of nature. In column 3 enter the *conditional probabilities* of a favorable market research report (F) given each state of nature.

Step 2. In column 4 compute the **joint probabilities** by multiplying the prior probability values in column 2 by the corresponding conditional probability values in column 3.

TABLE 13.7 BRANCH PROBABILITIES FOR THE PDC CONDOMINIUM PROJECT BASED ON A FAVORABLE MARKET RESEARCH REPORT

States of Nature s_j	Prior Probabilities $P(s_j)$	Conditional Probabilities $P(F \mid s_j)$	Joint Probabilities $P(F > s_j)$	Posterior Probabilities $P(s_j \mid F)$
s_1	0.8	0.90	0.72	0.94
s_2	0.2	0.25	0.05	0.06
	1.0		$P(F) = 0.77$	1.00

Step 3. Sum the joint probabilities in column 4 to obtain the probability of a favorable market research report, $P(F)$.

Step 4. Divide each joint probability in column 4 by $P(F) = 0.77$ to obtain the revised or *posterior probabilities*, $P(s_1 \mid F)$ and $P(s_2 \mid F)$.

Table 13.7 shows that the probability of obtaining a favorable market research report is $P(F) = 0.77$. In addition, $P(s_1 \mid F) = 0.94$ and $P(s_2 \mid F) = 0.06$. In particular, note that a favorable market research report will prompt a revised or posterior probability of 0.94 that the market demand of the condominium will be strong, s_1.

The tabular probability computation procedure must be repeated for each possible sample information outcome. Thus, Table 13.8 shows the computations of the branch probabilities of the PDC problem based on an unfavorable market research report. Note that the probability of obtaining an unfavorable market research report is $P(U) = 0.23$. If an unfavorable report is obtained, the posterior probability of a strong market demand, s_1, is 0.35 and of a weak market demand, s_2, is 0.65. The branch probabilities from Tables 13.7 and 13.8 were shown on the PDC decision tree in Figure 13.9.

Problem 23 asks you to compute the posterior probabilities.

The discussion in this section shows an underlying relationship between the probabilities on the various branches in a decision tree. To assume different prior probabilities, $P(s_1)$ and $P(s_2)$, without determining how these changes would alter $P(F)$ and $P(U)$, as well as the posterior probabilities $P(s_1 \mid F)$, $P(s_2 \mid F)$, $P(s_1 \mid U)$, and $P(s_2 \mid U)$, would be inappropriate.

The Management Science in Action, Medical Screening Test at Duke University Medical Center, shows how posterior probability information and decision analysis helped management understand the risks and costs associated with a new screening procedure.

TABLE 13.8 BRANCH PROBABILITIES FOR THE PDC CONDOMINIUM PROJECT BASED ON AN UNFAVORABLE MARKET RESEARCH REPORT

States of Nature s_j	Prior Probabilities $P(s_j)$	Conditional Probabilities $P(U \mid s_j)$	Joint Probabilities $P(U > s_j)$	Posterior Probabilities $P(s_j \mid U)$
s_1	0.8	0.10	0.08	0.35
s_2	0.2	0.75	0.15	0.65
	1.0		$P(U) = 0.23$	1.00

MANAGEMENT SCIENCE IN ACTION

MEDICAL SCREENING TEST AT DUKE UNIVERSITY MEDICAL CENTER*

A medical screening test developed at the Duke University Medical Center involved using blood samples from newborns to screen for metabolic disorders. A positive test result indicated that a deficiency was present, while a negative test result indicated that a deficiency was not present. However, it was understood that the screening test was not a perfect predictor; that is, false-positive test results as well as false-negative test results were possible. A false-positive test result meant that the test detected a deficiency when in fact no deficiency was present. This case resulted in unnecessary further testing as well as unnecessary worry for the parents of the newborn. A false-negative test result meant that the test did not detect the presence of an existing deficiency. Using probability and decision analysis, a research team analyzed the role and value of the screening test.

A decision tree with six nodes, 13 branches, and eight outcomes was used to model the screening test procedure. A decision node with the decision branches Test and No Test was placed at the start of the decision tree. Chance nodes and branches were used to describe the possible sequences of a positive test result, a negative test result, a deficiency present, and a deficiency not present.

The particular deficiency in question was rare, occurring at a rate of one case for every 250,000 newborns. Thus, the prior probability of a deficiency was $1/250,000 = 0.000004$. Based on judgments about the probabilities of false-positive and false-negative test results, Bayes' theorem was used to calculate the posterior probability that a newborn with a positive test result actually had a deficiency. This posterior probability was 0.074. Thus, while a positive test result increased the probability the newborn had a deficiency from 0.000004 to 0.074, the probability that the newborn had a deficiency was still relatively low (0.074).

The probability information was helpful to doctors in reassuring worried parents that even though further testing was recommended, the chances were greater than 90% that a deficiency was not present. After the assignment of costs to the eight possible outcomes, decision analysis showed that the decision alternative to conduct the test provided the optimal decision strategy. The expected cost criterion established the expected cost to be approximately $6 per test. Decision analysis helped provide a realistic understanding of the risks and costs associated with the screening test.

*Based on James E. Smith and Robert L. Winkler, "Casey's Problem: Interpreting and Evaluating a New Test," *Interfaces* 29, no. 3 (May/June 1999): 63–76.

SUMMARY

Decision analysis can be used to determine a recommended decision alternative or an optimal decision strategy when a decision maker is faced with an uncertain and risk-filled pattern of future events. The goal of decision analysis is to identify the best decision alternative or the optimal decision strategy given information about the uncertain events and the possible consequences or payoffs. The uncertain future events are called chance events and the outcomes of the chance events are called states of nature.

We showed how influence diagrams, payoff tables, and decision trees could be used to structure a decision problem and describe the relationships among the decisions, the chance events, and the consequences. We presented three approaches to decision making without probabilities: the optimistic approach, the conservative approach, and the minimax regret approach. When probability assessments are provided for the states of nature, the expected value approach can be used to identify the recommended decision alternative or decision strategy.

In cases where sample information about the chance events is available, a sequence of decisions has to be made. First we must decide whether to obtain the sample information.

If the answer to this decision is yes, an optimal decision strategy based on the specific sample information must be developed. In this situation, decision trees and the expected value approach can be used to determine the optimal decision strategy.

Even though the expected value approach can be used to obtain a recommended decision alternative or optimal decision strategy, the payoff that actually occurs will usually have a value different from the expected value. A risk profile provides a probability distribution for the possible payoffs and can assist the decision maker in assessing the risks associated with different decision alternatives. Finally, sensitivity analysis can be conducted to determine the effect changes in the probabilities for the states of nature and changes in the values of the payoffs have on the recommended decision alternative.

Decision analysis has been widely used in practice. The Management Science in Action, Investing in a Transmission System at Oglethorpe Power, describes the use of decision analysis to decide whether to invest in a major transmission system between Georgia and Florida.

MANAGEMENT SCIENCE IN ACTION

INVESTING IN A TRANSMISSION SYSTEM AT OGLETHORPE POWER*

Oglethorpe Power Corporation (OPC) provides wholesale electrical power to consumer-owned cooperatives in the state of Georgia. Florida Power Corporation proposed that OPC join in the building of a major transmission line from Georgia to Florida. Deciding whether to become involved in the building of the transmission line was a major decision for OPC because it would involve the commitment of substantial OPC resources. OPC worked with Applied Decision Analysis, Inc., to conduct a comprehensive decision analysis of the problem.

In the problem formulation step, three decisions were identified: (1) build a transmission line from Georgia to Florida; (2) upgrade existing transmission facilities; and (3) who would control the new facilities. Oglethorpe was faced with five chance events: (1) construction costs, (2) competition, (3) demand in Florida, (4) OPC's share of the operation, and (5) pricing. The consequence or payoff was measured in terms of dollars saved. The influence diagram for the problem had three decision nodes, five chance nodes, a consequence node, and several intermediate nodes that described

intermediate calculations. The decision tree for the problem had more than 8000 paths from the starting node to the terminal branches.

An expected value analysis of the decision tree provided an optimal decision strategy for OPC. However, the risk profile for the optimal decision strategy showed that the recommended strategy was very risky and had a significant probability of increasing OPC's cost rather than providing a savings. The risk analysis led to the conclusion that more information about the competition was needed in order to reduce OPC's risk. Sensitivity analysis involving various probabilities and payoffs showed that the value of the optimal decision strategy was stable over a reasonable range of input values. The final recommendation from the decision analysis was that OPC should begin negotiations with Florida Power Corporation concerning the building of the new transmission line.

*Based on Adam Borison, "Oglethorpe Power Corporation Decides About Investing in a Major Transmission System," *Interfaces* (March/April 1995): 25–36.

GLOSSARY

Decision alternatives   Options available to the decision maker.

Chance event   An uncertain future event affecting the consequence, or payoff, associated with a decision.

Consequence   The result obtained when a decision alternative is chosen and a chance event occurs. A measure of the consequence is often called a payoff.

States of nature   The possible outcomes for chance events that affect the payoff associated with a decision alternative.

Influence diagram   A graphical device that shows the relationship among decisions, chance events, and consequences for a decision problem.

Node   An intersection or junction point of an influence diagram or a decision tree.

Decision nodes   Nodes indicating points where a decision is made.

Chance nodes   Nodes indicating points where an uncertain event will occur.

Consequence nodes   Nodes of an influence diagram indicating points where a payoff will occur.

Payoff   A measure of the consequence of a decision such as profit, cost, or time. Each combination of a decision alternative and a state of nature has an associated payoff (consequence).

Payoff table   A tabular representation of the payoffs for a decision problem.

Decision tree   A graphical representation of the decision problem that shows the sequential nature of the decision-making process.

Branch   Lines showing the alternatives from decision nodes and the outcomes from chance nodes.

Optimistic approach   An approach to choosing a decision alternative without using probabilities. For a maximization problem, it leads to choosing the decision alternative corresponding to the largest payoff; for a minimization problem, it leads to choosing the decision alternative corresponding to the smallest payoff.

Conservative approach   An approach to choosing a decision alternative without using probabilities. For a maximization problem, it leads to choosing the decision alternative that maximizes the minimum payoff; for a minimization problem, it leads to choosing the decision alternative that minimizes the maximum payoff.

Minimax regret approach   An approach to choosing a decision alternative without using probabilities. For each alternative, the maximum regret is computed, which leads to choosing the decision alternative that minimizes the maximum regret.

Opportunity loss, or regret   The amount of loss (lower profit or higher cost) from not making the best decision for each state of nature.

Expected value approach   An approach to choosing a decision alternative based on the expected value of each decision alternative. The recommended decision alternative is the one that provides the best expected value.

Expected value (EV)   For a chance node, it is the weighted average of the payoffs. The weights are the state-of-nature probabilities.

Expected value of perfect information (EVPI)   The expected value of information that would tell the decision maker exactly which state of nature is going to occur (i.e., perfect information).

Risk analysis   The study of the possible payoffs and probabilities associated with a decision alternative or a decision strategy.

Sensitivity analysis   The study of how changes in the probability assessments for the states of nature or changes in the payoffs affect the recommended decision alternative.

Risk profile   The probability distribution of the possible payoffs associated with a decision alternative or decision strategy.

Prior probabilities   The probabilities of the states of nature prior to obtaining sample information.

Sample information   New information obtained through research or experimentation that enables an updating or revision of the state-of-nature probabilities.

Posterior (revised) probabilities   The probabilities of the states of nature after revising the prior probabilities based on sample information.

Decision strategy   A strategy involving a sequence of decisions and chance outcomes to provide the optimal solution to a decision problem.

Expected value of sample information (EVSI)   The difference between the expected value of an optimal strategy based on sample information and the "best" expected value without any sample information.

Efficiency   The ratio of EVSI to EVPI as a percentage; perfect information is 100% efficient.

Bayes' theorem   A theorem that enables the use of sample information to revise prior probabilities.

Conditional probability   The probability of one event given the known outcome of a (possibly) related event.

Joint probabilities   The probabilities of both sample information and a particular state of nature occurring simultaneously.

PROBLEMS

1. The following payoff table shows profit for a decision analysis problem with two decision alternatives and three states of nature:

	State of Nature		
Decision Alternative	s_1	s_2	s_3
d_1	250	100	25
d_2	100	100	75

   a. Construct a decision tree for this problem.
   b. If the decision maker knows nothing about the probabilities of the three states of nature, what is the recommended decision using the optimistic, conservative, and minimax regret approaches?

2. Suppose that a decision maker faced with four decision alternatives and four states of nature develops the following profit payoff table:

	State of Nature			
Decision Alternative	s_1	s_2	s_3	s_4
d_1	14	9	10	5
d_2	11	10	8	7
d_3	9	10	10	11
d_4	8	10	11	13

a. If the decision maker knows nothing about the probabilities of the four states of nature, what is the recommended decision using the optimistic, conservative, and minimax regret approaches?

b. Which approach do you prefer? Explain. Is establishing the most appropriate approach before analyzing the problem important for the decision maker? Explain.

c. Assume that the payoff table provides *cost* rather than profit payoffs. What is the recommended decision using the optimistic, conservative, and minimax regret approaches?

3. Southland Corporation's decision to produce a new line of recreational products resulted in the need to construct either a small plant or a large plant. The best selection of plant size depends on how the marketplace reacts to the new product line. To conduct an analysis, marketing management has decided to view the possible long-run demand as low, medium, or high. The following payoff table shows the projected profit in millions of dollars:

	Long-Run Demand		
Plant Size	Low	Medium	High
Small	150	200	200
Large	50	200	500

a. What is the decision to be made, and what is the chance event for Southland's problem?
b. Construct an influence diagram.
c. Construct a decision tree.
d. Recommend a decision based on the use of the optimistic, conservative, and minimax regret approaches.

4. The following profit payoff table was presented in Problem 1. Suppose that the decision maker obtained the probability assessments $P(s_1) = 0.65$, $P(s_2) = 0.15$, and $P(s_3) = 0.20$. Use the expected value approach to determine the optimal decision.

	State of Nature		
Decision Alternative	s_1	s_2	s_3
d_1	250	100	25
d_2	100	100	75

5. An investor wants to select one of seven mutual funds for the coming year. Data showing the percentage annual return for each fund during five typical one-year periods are shown here. The assumption is that one of these five-year periods will occur again during the coming year. Thus, years A, B, C, D, and E are the states of nature for the mutual fund decision.

	State of Nature				
Mutual Fund	Year A	Year B	Year C	Year D	Year E
Large-Cap Stock	35.3	20.0	28.3	10.4	−9.3
Mid-Cap Stock	32.3	23.2	−0.9	49.3	−22.8
Small-Cap Stock	20.8	22.5	6.0	33.3	6.1
Energy/Resources Sector	25.3	33.9	−20.5	20.9	−2.5
Health Sector	49.1	5.5	29.7	77.7	−24.9
Technology Sector	46.2	21.7	45.7	93.1	−20.1
Real Estate Sector	20.5	44.0	−21.1	2.6	5.1

a. Assume that the investor is conservative. What is the recommended mutual fund? Using this mutual fund, what are the minimum and maximum annual returns?

b. Suppose that an experienced financial analyst reviews the five states of nature and provides the following probabilities: 0.1, 0.3, 0.1, 0.1, and 0.4. Using the expected value, what is the recommended mutual fund? What is the expected annual return? Using this mutual fund, what are the minimum and maximum annual returns?

c. What is the expected annual return for the mutual fund recommended in part (a)? How much of an increase in the expected annual return can be obtained by following the recommendation in part (b)?

d. Which of the two mutual funds appears to have more risk? Why? Is the expected annual return greater for the mutual fund with more risk?

e. What mutual fund would you recommend to the investor? Explain.

6. Amy Lloyd is interested in leasing a new Saab and has contacted three automobile dealers for pricing information. Each dealer offered Amy a closed-end 36-month lease with no down payment due at the time of signing. Each lease includes a monthly charge and a mileage allowance. Additional miles receive a surcharge on a per-mile basis. The monthly lease cost, the mileage allowance, and the cost for additional miles follow:

Dealer	Monthly Cost	Mileage Allowance	Cost per Additional Mile
Forno Saab	$299	36,000	$0.15
Midtown Motors	$310	45,000	$0.20
Hopkins Automotive	$325	54,000	$0.15

Amy decided to choose the lease option that will minimize her total 36-month cost. The difficulty is that Amy is not sure how many miles she will drive over the next three years. For purposes of this decision she believes it is reasonable to assume that she will drive 12,000 miles per year, 15,000 miles per year, or 18,000 miles per year. With this assumption Amy estimated her total costs for the three lease options. For example, she figures that the Forno Saab lease will cost her $10,764 if she drives 12,000 miles per year, $12,114 if she drives 15,000 miles per year, or $13,464 if she drives 18,000 miles per year.

a. What is the decision, and what is the chance event?

b. Construct a payoff table for Amy's problem.

c. If Amy has no idea which of the three mileage assumptions is most appropriate, what is the recommended decision (leasing option) using the optimistic, conservative, and minimax regret approaches?

d. Suppose that the probabilities that Amy drives 12,000, 15,000, and 18,000 miles per year are 0.5, 0.4, and 0.1, respectively. What option should Amy choose using the expected value approach?

e. Develop a risk profile for the decision selected in part (d). What is the most likely cost, and what is its probability?

f. Suppose that after further consideration Amy concludes that the probabilities that she will drive 12,000, 15,000, and 18,000 miles per year are 0.3, 0.4, and 0.3, respectively. What decision should Amy make using the expected value approach?

7. Hudson Corporation is considering three options for managing its data processing operation: continuing with its own staff, hiring an outside vendor to do the managing (referred to as *outsourcing*), or using a combination of its own staff and an outside vendor. The cost of the operation depends on future demand. The annual cost of each option (in thousands of dollars) depends on demand as follows:

	Demand		
Staffing Options	High	Medium	Low
Own staff	650	650	600
Outside vendor	900	600	300
Combination	800	650	500

a. If the demand probabilities are 0.2, 0.5, and 0.3, which decision alternative will minimize the expected cost of the data processing operation? What is the expected annual cost associated with that recommendation?

b. Construct a risk profile for the optimal decision in part (a). What is the probability of the cost exceeding $700,000?

8. The following payoff table shows the profit for a decision problem with two states of nature and two decision alternatives:

	State of Nature	
Decision Alternative	s_1	s_2
d_1	10	1
d_2	4	3

a. Use graphical sensitivity analysis to determine the range of probabilities of state of nature s_1 for which each of the decision alternatives has the largest expected value.

b. Suppose $P(s_1) = 0.2$ and $P(s_2) = 0.8$. What is the best decision using the expected value approach?

c. Perform sensitivity analysis on the payoffs for decision alternative d_1. Assume the probabilities are as given in part (b) and find the range of payoffs under states of nature s_1 and s_2 that will keep the solution found in part (b) optimal. Is the solution more sensitive to the payoff under state of nature s_1 or s_2?

9. Myrtle Air Express decided to offer direct service from Cleveland to Myrtle Beach. Management must decide between a full-price service using the company's new fleet of jet aircraft and a discount service using smaller capacity commuter planes. It is clear that the best choice depends on the market reaction to the service Myrtle Air offers. Management developed estimates of the contribution to profit for each type of service based upon two possible levels of demand for service to Myrtle Beach: strong and weak. The following table shows the estimated quarterly profits (in thousands of dollars):

	Demand for Service	
Service	Strong	Weak
Full price	$960	−$490
Discount	$670	$320

a. What is the decision to be made, what is the chance event, and what is the consequence for this problem? How many decision alternatives are there? How many outcomes are there for the chance event?

b. If nothing is known about the probabilities of the chance outcomes, what is the recommended decision using the optimistic, conservative, and minimax regret approaches?

c. Suppose that management of Myrtle Air Express believes that the probability of strong demand is 0.7 and the probability of weak demand is 0.3. Use the expected value approach to determine an optimal decision.

d. Suppose that the probability of strong demand is 0.8 and the probability of weak demand is 0.2. What is the optimal decision using the expected value approach?

e. Use graphical sensitivity analysis to determine the range of demand probabilities for which each of the decision alternatives has the largest expected value.

10. Video Tech is considering marketing one of two new video games for the coming holiday season: Battle Pacific or Space Pirates. Battle Pacific is a unique game and appears to have no competition. Estimated profits (in thousands of dollars) under high, medium, and low demand are as follows:

Battle Pacific	Demand		
	High	**Medium**	**Low**
Profit	$1000	$700	$300
Probability	0.2	0.5	0.3

Video Tech is optimistic about its Space Pirates game. However, the concern is that profitability will be affected by a competitor's introduction of a video game viewed as similar to Space Pirates. Estimated profits (in thousands of dollars) with and without competition are as follows:

Space Pirates with Competition	Demand		
	High	**Medium**	**Low**
Profit	$800	$400	$200
Probability	0.3	0.4	0.3

Space Pirates without Competition	Demand		
	High	**Medium**	**Low**
Profit	$1600	$800	$400
Probability	0.5	0.3	0.2

a. Develop a decision tree for the Video Tech problem.

b. For planning purposes, Video Tech believes there is a 0.6 probability that its competitor will produce a new game similar to Space Pirates. Given this probability of competition, the director of planning recommends marketing the Battle Pacific video game. Using expected value, what is your recommended decision?

c. Show a risk profile for your recommended decision.

d. Use sensitivity analysis to determine what the probability of competition for Space Pirates would have to be for you to change your recommended decision alternative.

11. For the Pittsburgh Development Corporation problem in Section 13.3, the decision alternative to build the large condominium complex was found to be optimal using the expected value approach. In Section 13.4 we conducted a sensitivity analysis for the payoffs associated with this decision alternative. We found that the large complex remained optimal as long as the payoff for the strong demand was greater than or equal to $17.5 million and as long as the payoff for the weak demand was greater than or equal to –$19 million.

   a. Consider the medium complex decision. How much could the payoff under strong demand increase and still keep decision alternative d_3 the optimal solution?

   b. Consider the small complex decision. How much could the payoff under strong demand increase and still keep decision alternative d_3 the optimal solution?

12. The distance from Potsdam to larger markets and limited air service have hindered the town in attracting new industry. Air Express, a major overnight delivery service, is considering establishing a regional distribution center in Potsdam. However, Air Express will not establish the center unless the length of the runway at the local airport is increased. Another candidate for new development is Diagnostic Research, Inc. (DRI), a leading producer of medical testing equipment. DRI is considering building a new manufacturing plant. Increasing the length of the runway is not a requirement for DRI, but the planning commission feels that doing so will help convince DRI to locate their new plant in Potsdam. Assuming that the town lengthens the runway, the Potsdam planning commission believes that the probabilities shown in the following table are applicable:

	DRI Plant	No DRI Plant
Air Express Center	0.30	0.10
No Air Express Center	0.40	0.20

For instance, the probability that Air Express will establish a distribution center and DRI will build a plant is 0.30.

The estimated annual revenue to the town, after deducting the cost of lengthening the runway, is as follows:

	DRI Plant	No DRI Plant
Air Express Center	$600,000	$150,000
No Air Express Center	$250,000	–$200,000

If the runway expansion project is not conducted, the planning commission assesses the probability DRI will locate their new plant in Potsdam at 0.6; in this case, the estimated annual revenue to the town will be $450,000. If the runway expansion project is not conducted and DRI does not locate in Potsdam, the annual revenue will be $0 because no cost will have been incurred and no revenues will be forthcoming.

   a. What is the decision to be made, what is the chance event, and what is the consequence?

   b. Compute the expected annual revenue associated with the decision alternative to lengthen the runway.

   c. Compute the expected annual revenue associated with the decision alternative not to lengthen the runway.

d. Should the town elect to lengthen the runway? Explain.

e. Suppose that the probabilities associated with lengthening the runway were as follows:

	DRI Plant	No DRI Plant
Air Express Center	0.40	0.10
No Air Express Center	0.30	0.20

What effect, if any, would this change in the probabilities have on the recommended decision?

13. Seneca Hill Winery recently purchased land for the purpose of establishing a new vineyard. Management is considering two varieties of white grapes for the new vineyard: Chardonnay and Riesling. The Chardonnay grapes would be used to produce a dry Chardonnay wine, and the Riesling grapes would be used to produce a semidry Riesling wine. It takes approximately four years from the time of planting before new grapes can be harvested. This length of time creates a great deal of uncertainty about future demand and makes the decision concerning the type of grapes to plant difficult. Three possibilities are being considered: Chardonnay grapes only; Riesling grapes only; and both Chardonnay and Riesling grapes. Seneca management decided that for planning purposes it would be adequate to consider only two demand possibilities for each type of wine: strong or weak. With two possibilities for each type of wine it was necessary to assess four probabilities. With the help of some forecasts in industry publications management made the following probability assessments:

	Riesling Demand	
Chardonnay Demand	**Weak**	**Strong**
Weak	0.05	0.50
Strong	0.25	0.20

Revenue projections show an annual contribution to profit of $20,000 if Seneca Hill only plants Chardonnay grapes and demand is weak for Chardonnay wine, and $70,000 if they only plant Chardonnay grapes and demand is strong for Chardonnay wine. If they only plant Riesling grapes, the annual profit projection is $25,000 if demand is weak for Riesling grapes and $45,000 if demand is strong for Riesling grapes. If Seneca plants both types of grapes, the annual profit projections are shown in the following table:

	Riesling Demand	
Chardonnay Demand	**Weak**	**Strong**
Weak	$22,000	$40,000
Strong	$26,000	$60,000

a. What is the decision to be made, what is the chance event, and what is the consequence? Identify the alternatives for the decisions and the possible outcomes for the chance events.

b. Develop a decision tree.

c. Use the expected value approach to recommend which alternative Seneca Hill Winery should follow in order to maximize expected annual profit.

d. Suppose management is concerned about the probability assessments when demand for Chardonnay wine is strong. Some believe it is likely for Riesling demand to also be strong in this case. Suppose the probability of strong demand for Chardonnay and weak demand for Riesling is 0.05 and that the probability of strong demand for Chardonnay and strong demand for Riesling is 0.40. How does this change the recommended decision? Assume that the probabilities when Chardonnay demand is weak are still 0.05 and 0.50.

e. Other members of the management team expect the Chardonnay market to become saturated at some point in the future, causing a fall in prices. Suppose that the annual profit projections fall to $50,000 when demand for Chardonnay is strong and Chardonnay grapes only are planted. Using the original probability assessments, determine how this change would affect the optimal decision.

14. The following profit payoff table was presented in Problems 1 and 4:

| | State of Nature | | |
Decision Alternative	s_1	s_2	s_3
d_1	250	100	25
d_2	100	100	75

The probabilities for the states of nature are $P(s_1) = 0.65$, $P(s_2) = 0.15$, and $P(s_3) = 0.20$.

a. What is the optimal decision strategy if perfect information were available?

b. What is the expected value for the decision strategy developed in part (a)?

c. Using the expected value approach, what is the recommended decision without perfect information? What is its expected value?

d. What is the expected value of perfect information?

15. The Lake Placid Town Council decided to build a new community center to be used for conventions, concerts, and other public events, but considerable controversy surrounds the appropriate size. Many influential citizens want a large center that would be a showcase for the area. But the mayor feels that if demand does not support such a center, the community will lose a large amount of money. To provide structure for the decision process, the council narrowed the building alternatives to three sizes: small, medium, and large. Everybody agreed that the critical factor in choosing the best size is the number of people who will want to use the new facility. A regional planning consultant provided demand estimates under three scenarios: worst case, base case, and best case. The worst-case scenario corresponds to a situation in which tourism drops significantly; the base-case scenario corresponds to a situation in which Lake Placid continues to attract visitors at current levels; and the best-case scenario corresponds to a significant increase in tourism. The consultant has provided probability assessments of 0.10, 0.60, and 0.30 for the worst-case, base-case, and best-case scenarios, respectively.

The town council suggested using net cash flow over a five-year planning horizon as the criterion for deciding on the best size. The following projections of net cash flow (in thousands of dollars) for a five-year planning horizon have been developed. All costs, including the consultant's fee, have been included.

Center Size	Demand Scenario		
	Worst Case	Base Case	Best Case
Small	400	500	660
Medium	−250	650	800
Large	−400	580	990

a. What decision should Lake Placid make using the expected value approach?
b. Construct risk profiles for the medium and large alternatives. Given the mayor's concern over the possibility of losing money and the result of part (a), which alternative would you recommend?
c. Compute the expected value of perfect information. Do you think it would be worth trying to obtain additional information concerning which scenario is likely to occur?
d. Suppose the probability of the worst-case scenario increases to 0.2, the probability of the base-case scenario decreases to 0.5, and the probability of the best-case scenario remains at 0.3. What effect, if any, would these changes have on the decision recommendation?
e. The consultant has suggested that an expenditure of $150,000 on a promotional campaign over the planning horizon will effectively reduce the probability of the worst-case scenario to zero. If the campaign can be expected to also increase the probability of the best-case scenario to 0.4, is it a good investment?

16. Consider a variation of the PDC decision tree shown in Figure 13.9. The company must first decide whether to undertake the market research study. If the market research study is conducted, the outcome will either be favorable (F) or unfavorable (U). Assume there are only two decision alternatives d_1 and d_2 and two states of nature s_1 and s_2. The payoff table showing profit is as follows:

Decision Alternative	State of Nature	
	s_1	s_2
d_1	100	300
d_2	400	200

a. Show the decision tree.
b. Using the following probabilities, what is the optimal decision strategy?

$$P(F) = 0.56 \quad P(s_1 \mid F) = 0.57 \quad P(s_1 \mid U) = 0.18 \quad P(s_1) = 0.40$$
$$P(U) = 0.44 \quad P(s_2 \mid F) = 0.43 \quad P(s_2 \mid U) = 0.82 \quad P(s_2) = 0.60$$

17. Hemmingway, Inc., is considering a $5 million research and development (R&D) project. Profit projections appear promising, but Hemmingway's president is concerned because the probability that the R&D project will be successful is only 0.50. Secondly, the president knows that even if the project is successful, it will require that the company build a new production facility at a cost of $20 million in order to manufacture the product. If the facility is built, uncertainty remains about the demand and thus uncertainty about the profit

FIGURE 13.16　DECISION TREE FOR HEMMINGWAY, INC.

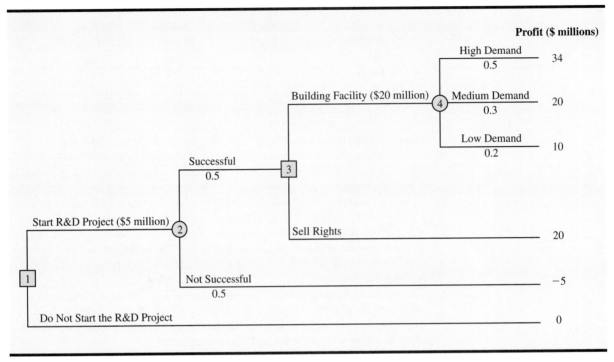

that will be realized. Another option is that if the R&D project is successful, the company could sell the rights to the product for an estimated $25 million. Under this option, the company would not build the $20 million production facility.

The decision tree is shown in Figure 13.16. The profit projection for each outcome is shown at the end of the branches. For example, the revenue projection for the high demand outcome is $59 million. However, the cost of the R&D project ($5 million) and the cost of the production facility ($20 million) show the profit of this outcome to be $59 − $5 − $20 = $34 million. Branch probabilities are also shown for the chance events.

   a. Analyze the decision tree to determine whether the company should undertake the R&D project. If it does, and if the R&D project is successful, what should the company do? What is the expected value of your strategy?
   b. What must the selling price be for the company to consider selling the rights to the product?
   c. Develop a risk profile for the optimal strategy.

18. Dante Development Corporation is considering bidding on a contract for a new office building complex. Figure 13.17 shows the decision tree prepared by one of Dante's analysts. At node 1, the company must decide whether to bid on the contract. The cost of preparing the bid is $200,000. The upper branch from node 2 shows that the company has a 0.8 probability of winning the contract if it submits a bid. If the company wins the bid, it will have to pay $2,000,000 to become a partner in the project. Node 3 shows that the company will then consider doing a market research study to forecast demand for the office units prior to beginning construction. The cost of this study is $150,000. Node 4 is a chance node showing the possible outcomes of the market research study.

Nodes 5, 6, and 7 are similar in that they are the decision nodes for Dante to either build the office complex or sell the rights in the project to another developer. The decision to build the complex will result in an income of $5,000,000 if demand is high and

FIGURE 13.17 DECISION TREE FOR THE DANTE DEVELOPMENT CORPORATION

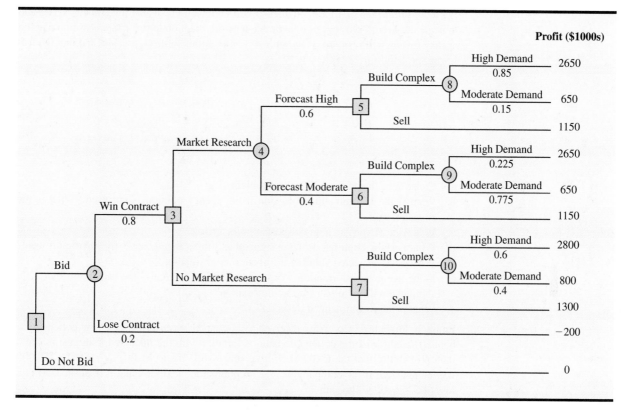

$3,000,000 if demand is moderate. If Dante chooses to sell its rights in the project to another developer, income from the sale is estimated to be $3,500,000. The probabilities shown at nodes 4, 8, and 9 are based on the projected outcomes of the market research study.

a. Verify Dante's profit projections shown at the ending branches of the decision tree by calculating the payoffs of $2,650,000 and $650,000 for first two outcomes.

b. What is the optimal decision strategy for Dante, and what is the expected profit for this project?

c. What would the cost of the market research study have to be before Dante would change its decision about the market research study?

d. Develop a risk profile for Dante.

19. Hale's TV Productions is considering producing a pilot for a comedy series in the hope of selling it to a major television network. The network may decide to reject the series, but it may also decide to purchase the rights to the series for either one or two years. At this point in time, Hale may either produce the pilot and wait for the network's decision or transfer the rights for the pilot and series to a competitor for $100,000. Hale's decision alternatives and profits (in thousands of dollars) are as follows:

	State of Nature		
Decision Alternative	Reject, s_1	1 Year, s_2	2 Years, s_3
Produce pilot, d_1	-100	50	150
Sell to competitor, d_2	100	100	100

The probabilities for the states of nature are $P(s_1) = 0.20$, $P(s_2) = 0.30$, and $P(s_3) = 0.50$. For a consulting fee of $5000, an agency will review the plans for the comedy series and indicate the overall chances of a favorable network reaction to the series. Assume that the agency review will result in a favorable (F) or an unfavorable (U) review and that the following probabilities are relevant:

$$P(F) = 0.69 \qquad P(s_1 \mid F) = 0.09 \qquad P(s_1 \mid U) = 0.45$$
$$P(U) = 0.31 \qquad P(s_2 \mid F) = 0.26 \qquad P(s_2 \mid U) = 0.39$$
$$P(s_3 \mid F) = 0.65 \qquad P(s_3 \mid U) = 0.16$$

a.   Construct a decision tree for this problem.
b.   What is the recommended decision if the agency opinion is not used? What is the expected value?
c.   What is the expected value of perfect information?
d.   What is Hale's optimal decision strategy assuming the agency's information is used?
e.   What is the expected value of the agency's information?
f.   Is the agency's information worth the $5000 fee? What is the maximum that Hale should be willing to pay for the information?
g.   What is the recommended decision?

20.   Embassy Publishing Company received a six-chapter manuscript for a new college textbook. The editor of the college division is familiar with the manuscript and estimated a 0.65 probability that the textbook will be successful. If successful, a profit of $750,000 will be realized. If the company decides to publish the textbook and it is unsuccessful, a loss of $250,000 will occur.

Before making the decision to accept or reject the manuscript, the editor is considering sending the manuscript out for review. A review process provides either a favorable (F) or unfavorable (U) evaluation of the manuscript. Past experience with the review process suggests probabilities $P(F) = 0.7$ and $P(U) = 0.3$ apply. Let $s_1 =$ the textbook is successful, and $s_2 =$ the textbook is unsuccessful. The editor's initial probabilities of s_1 and s_2 will be revised based on whether the review is favorable or unfavorable. The revised probabilities are as follows:

$$P(s_1 \mid F) = 0.75 \qquad P(s_1 \mid U) = 0.417$$
$$P(s_2 \mid F) = 0.25 \qquad P(s_2 \mid U) = 0.583$$

a.   Construct a decision tree assuming that the company will first make the decision of whether to send the manuscript out for review and then make the decision to accept or reject the manuscript.
b.   Analyze the decision tree to determine the optimal decision strategy for the publishing company.
c.   If the manuscript review costs $5000, what is your recommendation?
d.   What is the expected value of perfect information? What does this EVPI suggest for the company?

21.   A real estate investor has the opportunity to purchase land currently zoned residential. If the county board approves a request to rezone the property as commercial within the next year, the investor will be able to lease the land to a large discount firm that wants to open a new store on the property. However, if the zoning change is not approved, the investor

will have to sell the property at a loss. Profits (in thousands of dollars) are shown in the following payoff table:

	State of Nature	
	Rezoning Approved	Rezoning Not Approved
Decision Alternative	s_1	s_2
Purchase, d_1	600	-200
Do not purchase, d_2	0	0

a. If the probability that the rezoning will be approved is 0.5, what decision is recommended? What is the expected profit?

b. The investor can purchase an option to buy the land. Under the option, the investor maintains the rights to purchase the land anytime during the next three months while learning more about possible resistance to the rezoning proposal from area residents. Probabilities are as follows:

$$\text{Let} \quad H = \text{High resistance to rezoning}$$
$$L = \text{Low resistance to rezoning}$$

$$P(H) = 0.55 \quad P(s_1 \mid H) = 0.18 \quad P(s_2 \mid H) = 0.82$$
$$P(L) = 0.45 \quad P(s_1 \mid L) = 0.89 \quad P(s_2 \mid L) = 0.11$$

What is the optimal decision strategy if the investor uses the option period to learn more about the resistance from area residents before making the purchase decision?

c. If the option will cost the investor an additional $10,000, should the investor purchase the option? Why or why not? What is the maximum that the investor should be willing to pay for the option?

22. Lawson's Department Store faces a buying decision for a seasonal product for which demand can be high, medium, or low. The purchaser for Lawson's can order 1, 2, or 3 lots of the product before the season begins but cannot reorder later. Profit projections (in thousands of dollars) are shown.

	State of Nature		
	High Demand	Medium Demand	Low Demand
Decision Alternative	s_1	s_2	s_3
Order 1 lot, d_1	60	60	50
Order 2 lots, d_2	80	80	30
Order 3 lots, d_3	100	70	10

a. If the prior probabilities for the three states of nature are 0.3, 0.3, and 0.4, respectively, what is the recommended order quantity?

b. At each preseason sales meeting, the vice president of sales provides a personal opinion regarding potential demand for this product. Because of the vice president's enthusiasm and optimistic nature, the predictions of market conditions have always been either "excellent" (E) or "very good" (V). Probabilities are as follows:

$$P(E) = 0.70 \quad P(s_1 \mid E) = 0.34 \quad P(s_1 \mid V) = 0.20$$
$$P(V) = 0.30 \quad P(s_2 \mid E) = 0.32 \quad P(s_2 \mid V) = 0.26$$
$$P(s_3 \mid E) = 0.34 \quad P(s_3 \mid V) = 0.54$$

What is the optimal decision strategy?

c.   Use the efficiency of sample information and discuss whether the firm should consider a consulting expert who could provide independent forecasts of market conditions for the product.

23.   Suppose that you are given a decision situation with three possible states of nature: s_1, s_2, and s_3. The prior probabilities are $P(s_1) = 0.2$, $P(s_2) = 0.5$, and $P(s_3) = 0.3$. With sample information I, $P(I \mid s_1) = 0.1$, $P(I \mid s_2) = 0.05$, and $P(I \mid s_3) = 0.2$. Compute the revised or posterior probabilities: $P(s_1 \mid I)$, $P(s_2 \mid I)$, and $P(s_3 \mid I)$.

24.   To save on expenses, Rona and Jerry agreed to form a carpool for traveling to and from work. Rona preferred to use the somewhat longer but more consistent Queen City Avenue. Although Jerry preferred the quicker expressway, he agreed with Rona that they should take Queen City Avenue if the expressway had a traffic jam. The following payoff table provides the one-way time estimate in minutes for traveling to or from work:

	State of Nature	
	Expressway Open	Expressway Jammed
Decision Alternative	s_1	s_2
Queen City Avenue, d_1	30	30
Expressway, d_2	25	45

Based on their experience with traffic problems, Rona and Jerry agreed on a 0.15 probability that the expressway would be jammed.

In addition, they agreed that weather seemed to affect the traffic conditions on the expressway. Let

$$C = \text{clear}$$
$$O = \text{overcast}$$
$$R = \text{rain}$$

The following conditional probabilities apply:

$$P(C \mid s_1) = 0.8 \qquad P(O \mid s_1) = 0.2 \qquad P(R \mid s_1) = 0.0$$
$$P(C \mid s_2) = 0.1 \qquad P(O \mid s_2) = 0.3 \qquad P(R \mid s_2) = 0.6$$

a.   Use Bayes' theorem for probability revision to compute the probability of each weather condition and the conditional probability of the expressway open s_1 or jammed s_2 given each weather condition.
b.   Show the decision tree for this problem.
c.   What is the optimal decision strategy, and what is the expected travel time?

25.   The Gorman Manufacturing Company must decide whether to manufacture a component part at its Milan, Michigan, plant or purchase the component part from a supplier. The resulting profit is dependent upon the demand for the product. The following payoff table shows the projected profit (in thousands of dollars):

	State of Nature		
	Low Demand	Medium Demand	High Demand
Decision Alternative	s_1	s_2	s_3
Manufacture, d_1	−20	40	100
Purchase, d_2	10	45	70

The state-of-nature probabilities are $P(s_1) = 0.35$, $P(s_2) = 0.35$, and $P(s_3) = 0.30$.

a. Use a decision tree to recommend a decision.
b. Use EVPI to determine whether Gorman should attempt to obtain a better estimate of demand.
c. A test market study of the potential demand for the product is expected to report either a favorable (F) or unfavorable (U) condition. The relevant conditional probabilities are as follows:

$$P(F \mid s_1) = 0.10 \qquad P(U \mid s_1) = 0.90$$
$$P(F \mid s_2) = 0.40 \qquad P(U \mid s_2) = 0.60$$
$$P(F \mid s_3) = 0.60 \qquad P(U \mid s_3) = 0.40$$

What is the probability that the market research report will be favorable?
d. What is Gorman's optimal decision strategy?
e. What is the expected value of the market research information?
f. What is the efficiency of the information?

Case Problem 1   PROPERTY PURCHASE STRATEGY

Glenn Foreman, president of Oceanview Development Corporation, is considering submitting a bid to purchase property that will be sold by sealed bid at a county tax foreclosure. Glenn's initial judgment is to submit a bid of $5 million. Based on his experience, Glenn estimates that a bid of $5 million will have a 0.2 probability of being the highest bid and securing the property for Oceanview. The current date is June 1. Sealed bids for the property must be submitted by August 15. The winning bid will be announced on September 1.

If Oceanview submits the highest bid and obtains the property, the firm plans to build and sell a complex of luxury condominiums. However, a complicating factor is that the property is currently zoned for single-family residences only. Glenn believes that a referendum could be placed on the voting ballot in time for the November election. Passage of the referendum would change the zoning of the property and permit construction of the condominiums.

The sealed-bid procedure requires the bid to be submitted with a certified check for 10% of the amount bid. If the bid is rejected, the deposit is refunded. If the bid is accepted, the deposit is the down payment for the property. However, if the bid is accepted and the bidder does not follow through with the purchase and meet the remainder of the financial obligation within six months, the deposit will be forfeited. In this case, the county will offer the property to the next highest bidder.

To determine whether Oceanview should submit the $5 million bid, Glenn conducted some preliminary analysis. This preliminary work provided an assessment of 0.3 for the probability that the referendum for a zoning change will be approved and resulted in the following estimates of the costs and revenues that will be incurred if the condominiums are built:

Cost and Revenue Estimates

Revenue from condominium sales	$15,000,000
Cost	
Property	$5,000,000
Construction expenses	$8,000,000

If Oceanview obtains the property and the zoning change is rejected in November, Glenn believes that the best option would be for the firm not to complete the purchase of the property. In this case, Oceanview would forfeit the 10% deposit that accompanied the bid.

Because the likelihood that the zoning referendum will be approved is such an important factor in the decision process, Glenn suggested that the firm hire a market research service to conduct a survey of voters. The survey would provide a better estimate of the likelihood that the referendum for a zoning change would be approved. The market research firm that Oceanview Development has worked with in the past has agreed to do the study for $15,000. The results of the study will be available August 1, so that Oceanview will have this information before the August 15 bid deadline. The results of the survey will be either a prediction that the zoning change will be approved or a prediction that the zoning change will be rejected. After considering the record of the market research service in previous studies conducted for Oceanview, Glenn developed the following probability estimates concerning the accuracy of the market research information:

$$P(A \mid s_1) = 0.9 \qquad P(N \mid s_1) = 0.1$$
$$P(A \mid s_2) = 0.2 \qquad P(N \mid s_2) = 0.8$$

where

A = prediction of zoning change approval
N = prediction that zoning change will not be approved
s_1 = the zoning change is approved by the voters
s_2 = the zoning change is rejected by the voters

Managerial Report

Perform an analysis of the problem facing the Oceanview Development Corporation, and prepare a report that summarizes your findings and recommendations. Include the following items in your report:

1. A decision tree that shows the logical sequence of the decision problem
2. A recommendation regarding what Oceanview should do if the market research information is not available
3. A decision strategy that Oceanview should follow if the market research is conducted
4. A recommendation as to whether Oceanview should employ the market research firm, along with the value of the information provided by the market research firm

Include the details of your analysis as an appendix to your report.

Case Problem 2   LAWSUIT DEFENSE STRATEGY

John Campbell, an employee of Manhattan Construction Company, claims to have injured his back as a result of a fall while repairing the roof at one of the Eastview apartment buildings. He filed a lawsuit against Doug Reynolds, the owner of Eastview Apartments, asking for damages of $1,500,000. John claims that the roof had rotten sections and that his fall could have been prevented if Mr. Reynolds had told Manhattan Construction about the problem. Mr. Reynolds notified his insurance company, Allied Insurance, of the lawsuit. Allied must defend Mr. Reynolds and decide what action to take regarding the lawsuit.

Some depositions and a series of discussions took place between both sides. As a result, John Campbell offered to accept a settlement of $750,000. Thus, one option is for Allied to pay John $750,000 to settle the claim. Allied is also considering making John a counteroffer of $400,000 in the hope that he will accept a lesser amount to avoid the time and cost of going to trial. Allied's preliminary investigation shows that John's case is strong; Allied is concerned that John may reject their counteroffer and request a jury trial. Allied's lawyers spent some time exploring John's likely reaction if they make a counteroffer of $400,000.

The lawyers concluded that it is adequate to consider three possible outcomes to represent John's possible reaction to a counteroffer of $400,000: (1) John will accept the counteroffer and the case will be closed; (2) John will reject the counteroffer and elect to have a jury decide the settlement amount; or (3) John will make a counteroffer to Allied of $600,000. If John does make a counteroffer, Allied has decided that they will not make additional counteroffers. They will either accept John's counteroffer of $600,000 or go to trial.

If the case goes to a jury trial, Allied considers three outcomes possible: (1) the jury may reject John's claim and Allied will not be required to pay any damages; (2) the jury will find in favor of John and award him $750,000 in damages; or (3) the jury will conclude that John has a strong case and award him the full amount of $1,500,000.

Key considerations as Allied develops its strategy for disposing of the case are the probabilities associated with John's response to an Allied counteroffer of $400,000 and the probabilities associated with the three possible trial outcomes. Allied's lawyers believe the probability that John will accept a counteroffer of $400,000 is 0.10, the probability that John will reject a counteroffer of $400,000 is 0.40, and the probability that John will, himself, make a counteroffer to Allied of $600,000 is 0.50. If the case goes to court, they believe that the probability the jury will award John damages of $1,500,000 is 0.30, the probability that the jury will award John damages of $750,000 is 0.50, and the probability that the jury will award John nothing is 0.20.

Managerial Report

Perform an analysis of the problem facing Allied Insurance and prepare a report that summarizes your findings and recommendations. Be sure to include the following items:

1. A decision tree
2. A recommendation regarding whether Allied should accept John's initial offer to settle the claim for $750,000
3. A decision strategy that Allied should follow if they decide to make John a counteroffer of $400,000
4. A risk profile for your recommended strategy

Appendix 13.1   DECISION ANALYSIS WITH TREEPLAN

TreePlan* is an Excel add-in that can be used to develop decision trees for decision analysis problems. The software package is provided at the website that accompanies this text. Instructions for installing TreePlan are included with the software. A manual containing additional information on starting and using TreePlan is also at the website. In this

---

*TreePlan was developed by Professor Michael R. Middleton at the University of San Francisco and modified for use by Professor James E. Smith at Duke University. The TreePlan website is www.treeplan.com.

FIGURE 13.18   PDC DECISION TREE

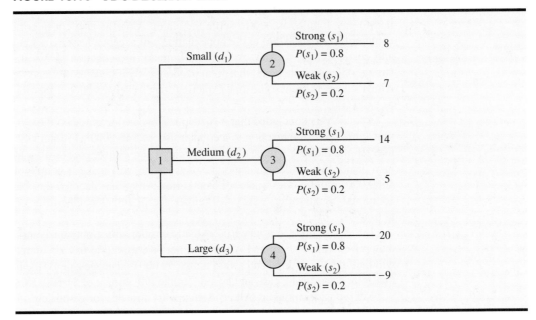

appendix we show how to use TreePlan to build a decision tree and solve the PDC problem presented in Section 13.3. The decision tree for the PDC problem is shown in Figure 13.18.

Getting Started: An Initial Decision Tree

We begin by assuming that TreePlan has been installed and an Excel worksheet is open. To build a TreePlan version of the PDC decision tree, proceed as follows:

Step 1. Select cell A1
Step 2. Select the **Add-Ins** tab and choose **Decision Tree** from the **Menu Commands** group
Step 3. When the **TreePlan New** dialog box appears:
Click **New Tree**

A decision tree with one decision node and two branches appears as follows:

	A	B	C	D	E	F	G
1							
2				Decision 1			
3							0
4				0	0		
5			1				
6		0					
7				Decision 2			
8							0
9				0	0		

Adding a Branch

The PDC problem has three decision alternatives (small, medium, and large condominium complexes), so we must add another decision branch to the tree.

Step 1. Select cell B5
Step 2. Select **Decision Tree** from the **Menu Commands** group
Step 3. When the **TreePlan Decision** dialog box appears:
         Select **Add branch**
         Click **OK**

A revised tree with three decision branches now appears in the Excel worksheet.

Naming the Decision Alternatives

The decision alternatives can be named by selecting the cells containing the labels Decision 1, Decision 2, and Decision 3, and then entering the corresponding PDC names Small, Medium, and Large. After naming the alternatives, the PDC tree with three decision branches appears as follows:

	A	B	C	D	E	F	G
1							
2				Small			
3							0
4				0	0		
5							
6							
7				Medium			
8			1				0
9		0		0	0		
10							
11							
12				Large			
13							0
14				0	0		

Adding Chance Nodes

The chance event for the PDC problem is the demand for the condominiums, which may be either strong or weak. Thus, a chance node with two branches must be added at the end of each decision alternative branch.

Step 1. Select cell F3
Step 2. Select **Decision Tree** from the **Menu Commands** group
Step 3. When the **TreePlan Terminal** dialog box appears:
         Select **Change to event node**
         Select **Two** in the **Branches** section
         Click **OK**

The tree now appears as follows:

	A	B	C	D	E	F	G	H	I	J	K
1								0.5			
2								Event 4			
3											0
4				Small				0	0		
5											
6					0	0			0.5		
7								Event 5			
8											0
9								0	0		
10											
11			1								
12		0		Medium							
13											0
14					0	0					
15											
16											
17				Large							
18											0
19					0	0					

We next select the cells containing Event 4 and Event 5 and rename them Strong and Weak to provide the proper names for the PDC states of nature. After doing so we can copy the subtree for the chance node in cell F5 to the other two decision branches to complete the structure of the PDC decision tree.

Step 1. Select cell F5
Step 2. Select **Decision Tree** from the **Menu Commands** group
Step 3. When the **TreePlan Event** dialog box appears:
Select **Copy subtree**
Click **OK**
Step 4. Select cell F13
Step 5. Select **Decision Tree** from the **Menu Commands** group
Step 6. When the **TreePlan Terminal** dialog box appears:
Select **Paste subtree**
Click **OK**

This copy/paste procedure places a chance node at the end of the Medium decision branch. Repeating the same copy/paste procedure for the Large decision branch completes the structure of the PDC decision tree as shown in Figure 13.19.

Inserting Probabilities and Payoffs

TreePlan provides the capability of inserting probabilities and payoffs into the decision tree. In Figure 13.19 we see that TreePlan automatically assigned an equal probability 0.5 to each of the chance outcomes. For PDC, the probability of strong demand is 0.8 and the probability of weak demand is 0.2. We can select cells H1, H6, H11, H16, H21, and H26 and insert the appropriate probabilities. The payoffs for the chance outcomes are inserted in cells H4, H9, H14, H19, H24, and H29. After inserting the PDC probabilities and payoffs, the PDC decision tree appears as shown in Figure 13.20.

FIGURE 13.19   THE PDC DECISION TREE DEVELOPED BY TREEPLAN

Note that the payoffs also appear in the right-hand margin of the decision tree. The payoffs in the right margin are computed by a formula that adds the payoffs on all of the branches leading to the associated terminal node. For the PDC problem, no payoffs are associated with the decision alternatives branches so we leave the default values of zero in cells D6, D16, and D24. The PDC decision tree is now complete.

Interpreting the Result

When probabilities and payoffs are inserted, TreePlan automatically makes the backward pass computations necessary to determine the optimal solution. Optimal decisions are identified by the number in the corresponding decision node. In the PDC decision tree in Figure 13.20, cell B15 contains the decision node. Note that a 3 appears in this node, which tells us that decision alternative branch 3 provides the optimal decision. Thus, decision analysis recommends PDC construct the Large condominium complex. The expected value of this decision appears at the beginning of the tree in cell A16. Thus, we see the optimal expected value is $14.2 million. The expected values of the other decision alternatives are displayed at the end of the corresponding decision branch. Thus, referring to cells E6 and E16, we see that the expected value of the Small complex is $7.8 million and the expected value of the Medium complex is $12.2 million.

FIGURE 13.20   THE PDC DECISION TREE WITH BRANCH PROBABILITIES AND PAYOFFS

WEB file

PDC Tree

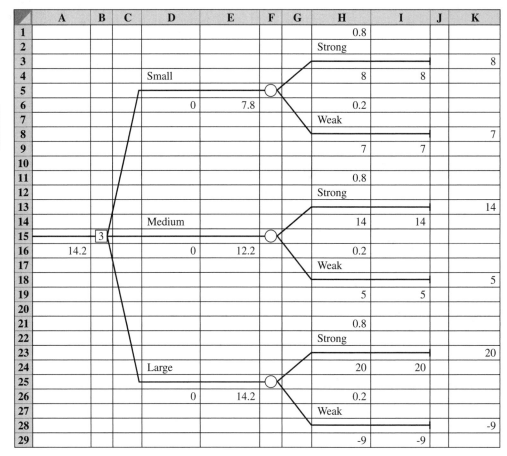

Other Options

TreePlan defaults to a maximization objective. If you would like a minimization objective, follow these steps:

Step 1. Select **Decision Tree** from the **Menu Commands** group
Step 2. Select **Options**
Step 3. Choose **Minimize (costs)**
         Click **OK**

In using a TreePlan decision tree, we can modify probabilities and payoffs and quickly observe the impact of the changes on the optimal solution. Using this "what-if" type of sensitivity analysis, we can identify changes in probabilities and payoffs that would change the optimal decision. Also, because TreePlan is an Excel add-in, most of Excel's capabilities are available. For instance, we could use boldface to highlight the name of the optimal decision alternative on the final decision tree solution. A variety of other options TreePlan provides are contained in the TreePlan manual at the website that accompanies this text. Computer software packages such as TreePlan make it easier to do a thorough analysis of a decision problem.

CHAPTER 14

Multicriteria Decisions

CONTENTS

14.1 GOAL PROGRAMMING:
FORMULATION AND
GRAPHICAL SOLUTION
Developing the Constraints and the
    Goal Equations
Developing an Objective Function
    with Preemptive Priorities
Graphical Solution Procedure
Goal Programming Model

14.2 GOAL PROGRAMMING:
SOLVING MORE COMPLEX
PROBLEMS
Suncoast Office Supplies Problem
Formulating the Goal Equations
Formulating the Objective Function
Computer Solution

14.3 SCORING MODELS

14.4 ANALYTIC HIERARCHY
PROCESS
Developing the Hierarchy

14.5 ESTABLISHING PRIORITIES
USING AHP
Pairwise Comparisons
Pairwise Comparison Matrix
Synthesization
Consistency
Other Pairwise Comparisons for the
    Car Selection Problem

14.6 USING AHP TO DEVELOP AN
OVERALL PRIORITY RANKING

In previous chapters we showed how a variety of quantitative methods can help managers make better decisions. Whenever we desired an optimal solution, we utilized a single criterion (e.g., maximize profit, minimize cost, minimize time). In this chapter we discuss techniques that are appropriate for situations in which the decision maker needs to consider multiple criteria in arriving at the overall best decision. For example, consider a company involved in selecting a location for a new manufacturing plant. The cost of land and construction may vary from location to location, so one criterion in selecting the best site could be the cost involved in building the plant; if cost were the sole criterion of interest, management would simply select the location that minimizes land cost plus construction cost. Before making any decision, however, management might also want to consider additional criteria such as the availability of transportation from the plant to the firm's distribution centers, the attractiveness of the proposed location in terms of hiring and retaining employees, energy costs at the proposed site, and state and local taxes. In such situations the complexity of the problem increases because one location may be more desirable in terms of one criterion and less desirable in terms of one or more of the other criteria.

To introduce the topic of multicriteria decision making, we consider a technique referred to as **goal programming.** This technique has been developed to handle multiple-criteria situations within the general framework of linear programming. We next consider a *scoring model* as a relatively easy way to identify the best decision alternative for a multicriteria problem. Finally, we introduce a method known as the *analytical hierarchy process (AHP)*, which allows the user to make pairwise comparisons among the criteria and a series of pairwise comparisons among the decision alternatives in order to arrive at a prioritized ranking of the decision alternatives.

14.1 GOAL PROGRAMMING: FORMULATION AND GRAPHICAL SOLUTION

To illustrate the goal programming approach to multicriteria decision problems, let us consider a problem facing Nicolo Investment Advisors. A client has $80,000 to invest and, as an initial strategy, would like the investment portfolio restricted to two stocks:

Stock	Price/Share	Estimated Annual Return/Share	Risk Index/Share
U.S. Oil	$25	$3	0.50
Hub Properties	$50	$5	0.25

U.S. Oil, which has a return of $3 on a $25 share price, provides an annual rate of return of 12%, whereas Hub Properties provides an annual rate of return of 10%. The risk index per share, 0.50 for U.S. Oil and 0.25 for Hub Properties, is a rating Nicolo assigned to measure the relative risk of the two investments. Higher risk index values imply greater risk; hence, Nicolo judged U.S. Oil to be the riskier investment. By specifying a maximum portfolio risk index, Nicolo will avoid placing too much of the portfolio in high-risk investments.

To illustrate how to use the risk index per share to measure the total portfolio risk, suppose that Nicolo chooses a portfolio that invests all $80,000 in U.S. Oil, the higher risk, but higher return, investment. Nicolo could purchase $80,000/$25 = 3200 shares of U.S. Oil, and the portfolio would have a risk index of 3200(0.50) = 1600. Conversely, if Nicolo purchases no shares of either stock, the portfolio will have no risk, but also no return. Thus, the portfolio risk index will vary from 0 (least risk) to 1600 (most risk).

Nicolo's client would like to avoid a high-risk portfolio; thus, investing all funds in U.S. Oil would not be desirable. However, the client agreed that an acceptable level of risk would correspond to portfolios with a maximum total risk index of 700. Thus, considering only risk, one *goal* is to find a portfolio with a risk index of 700 or less.

Another goal of the client is to obtain an annual return of at least $9000. This goal can be achieved with a portfolio consisting of 2000 shares of U.S. Oil [at a cost of 2000($25) = $50,000] and 600 shares of Hub Properties [at a cost of 600($50) = $30,000]; the annual return in this case would be 2000($3) + 600($5) = $9000. Note, however, that the portfolio risk index for this investment strategy would be 2000(0.50) + 600(0.25) = 1150; thus, this portfolio achieves the annual return goal but does not satisfy the portfolio risk index goal.

Thus, the portfolio selection problem is a multicriteria decision problem involving two conflicting goals: one dealing with risk and one dealing with annual return. The goal programming approach was developed precisely for this kind of problem. Goal programming can be used to identify a portfolio that comes closest to achieving both goals. Before applying the methodology, the client must determine which, if either, goal is more important.

Suppose that the client's top-priority goal is to restrict the risk; that is, keeping the portfolio risk index at 700 or less is so important that the client is not willing to trade the achievement of this goal for any amount of an increase in annual return. As long as the portfolio risk index does not exceed 700, the client seeks the best possible return. Based on this statement of priorities, the goals for the problem are as follows:

Primary Goal (Priority Level 1)

Goal 1:   Find a portfolio that has a risk index of 700 or less.

Secondary Goal (Priority Level 2)

Goal 2:   Find a portfolio that will provide an annual return of at least $9000.

In goal programming with preemptive priorities, we never permit trade-offs between higher and lower level goals.

The primary goal is called a *priority level 1 goal*, and the secondary goal is called a *priority level 2 goal*. In goal programming terminology, they are called **preemptive priorities** because the decision maker is not willing to sacrifice any amount of achievement of the priority level 1 goal for the lower priority goal. The portfolio risk index of 700 is the **target value** for the priority level 1 (primary) goal, and the annual return of $9000 is the target value for the priority level 2 (secondary) goal. The difficulty in finding a solution that will achieve these goals is that only $80,000 is available for investment.

Developing the Constraints and the Goal Equations

We begin by defining the decision variables:

$$U = \text{number of shares of U.S. Oil purchased}$$
$$H = \text{number of shares of Hub Properties purchased}$$

Constraints for goal programming problems are handled in the same way as in an ordinary linear programming problem. In the Nicolo Investment Advisors problem, one constraint corresponds to the funds available. Because each share of U.S. Oil costs $25 and each share of Hub Properties costs $50, the constraint representing the funds available is

$$25U + 50H \leq 80,000$$

To complete the formulation of the model, we must develop a **goal equation** for each goal. Let us begin by writing the goal equation for the primary goal. Each share of U.S. Oil has a risk index of 0.50 and each share of Hub Properties has a risk index of 0.25; therefore, the portfolio risk index is $0.50U + 0.25H$. Depending on the values of U and H, the portfolio risk index may be less than, equal to, or greater than the target value of 700. To represent these possibilities mathematically, we create the goal equation

$$0.50U + 0.25H = 700 + d_1^+ - d_1^-$$

where

d_1^+ = the amount by which the portfolio risk index exceeds the target
 value of 700

d_1^- = the amount by which the portfolio risk index is less than the target
 value of 700

To achieve a goal exactly, the two deviation variables must both equal zero.

In goal programming, d_1^+ and d_1^- are called **deviation variables.** The purpose of deviation variables is to allow for the possibility of not meeting the target value exactly. Consider, for example, a portfolio that consists of $U = 2000$ shares of U.S. Oil and $H = 0$ shares of Hub Properties. The portfolio risk index is $0.50(2000) = 0.25(0) = 1000$. In this case, $d_1^+ = 300$ reflects the fact that the portfolio risk index exceeds the target value by 300 units; note also that because d_1^+ is greater than zero, the value of d_1^- must be zero. For a portfolio consisting of $U = 0$ shares of U.S. Oil and $H = 1000$ shares of Hub Properties, the portfolio risk index would be $0.50(0) + 0.25(1000) = 250$. In this case, $d_1^- = 450$ and $d_1^+ = 0$, indicating that the solution provides a portfolio risk index of 450 less than the target value of 700.

In general, the letter d is used for deviation variables in a goal programming model. A superscript of plus $(+)$ or minus $(-)$ is used to indicate whether the variable corresponds to a positive or negative deviation from the target value. If we bring the deviation variables to the left-hand side, we can rewrite the goal equation for the primary goal as

$$0.50U + 0.25H - d_1^+ + d_1^- = 700$$

Note that the value on the right-hand side of the goal equation is the target value for the goal. The left-hand side of the goal equation consists of two parts:

1. A function that defines the amount of goal achievement in terms of the decision variables (e.g., $0.50U + 0.25H$)
2. Deviation variables representing the difference between the target value for the goal and the level achieved

To develop a goal equation for the secondary goal, we begin by writing a function representing the annual return for the investment:

$$\text{Annual return} = 3U + 5H$$

Then we define two deviation variables that represent the amount of over- or underachievement of the goal. Doing so, we obtain

d_2^+ = the amount by which the annual return for the portfolio is greater
 than the target value of $9000

d_2^- = the amount by which the annual return for the portfolio is less
 than the target value of $9000

Using these two deviation variables, we write the goal equation for goal 2 as

$$3U + 5H = 9000 + d_2^+ - d_2^-$$

or

$$3U + 5H - d_2^+ + d_2^- = 9000$$

This step completes the development of the goal equations and the constraints for the Nicolo portfolio problem. We are now ready to develop an appropriate objective function for the problem.

Developing an Objective Function with Preemptive Priorities

The objective function in a goal programming model calls for minimizing a function of the deviation variables. In the portfolio selection problem, the most important goal, denoted P_1, is to find a portfolio with a risk index of 700 or less. This problem has only two goals, and the client is unwilling to accept a portfolio risk index greater than 700 to achieve the secondary annual return goal. Therefore, the secondary goal is denoted P_2. As we stated previously, these goal priorities are referred to as preemptive priorities because the satisfaction of a higher level goal cannot be traded for the satisfaction of a lower level goal.

Goal programming problems with preemptive priorities are solved by treating priority level 1 goals (P_1) first in an objective function. The idea is to start by finding a solution that comes closest to satisfying the priority level 1 goals. This solution is then modified by solving a problem with an objective function involving only priority level 2 goals (P_2); however, revisions in the solution are permitted only if they do not hinder achievement of the P_1 goals. In general, solving a goal programming problem with preemptive priorities involves solving a sequence of linear programs with different objective functions; P_1 goals are considered first, P_2 goals second, P_3 goals third, and so on. At each stage of the procedure, a revision in the solution is permitted only if it causes no reduction in the achievement of a higher priority goal.

We must solve one linear program for each priority level.

The number of linear programs that we must solve in sequence to develop the solution to a goal programming problem is determined by the number of priority levels. One linear program must be solved for each priority level. We will call the first linear program solved the priority level 1 problem, the second linear program solved the priority level 2 problem, and so on. Each linear program is obtained from the one at the next higher level by changing the objective function and adding a constraint.

We first formulate the objective function for the priority level 1 problem. The client stated that the portfolio risk index should not exceed 700. Is underachieving the target value of 700 a concern? Clearly, the answer is no because portfolio risk index values of less than 700 correspond to less risk. Is overachieving the target value of 700 a concern? The answer is yes because portfolios with a risk index greater than 700 correspond to unacceptable levels of risk. Thus, the objective function corresponding to the priority level 1 linear program should minimize the value of d_1^+.

The goal equations and the funds available constraint have already been developed. Thus, the priority level 1 linear program can now be stated.

P_1 **Problem**

$$\text{Min} \quad d_1^+$$

s.t.

$$
\begin{array}{rcll}
25U + 50H & \leq & 80{,}000 & \text{Funds available} \\
0.50U + 0.25H - d_1^+ + d_1^- & = & 700 & P_1 \text{ goal} \\
3U + 5H - d_2^+ + d_2^- & = & 9000 & P_2 \text{ goal} \\
U, H, d_1^+, d_1^-, d_2^+, d_2^- \geq 0 & & &
\end{array}
$$

Graphical Solution Procedure

One approach that can often be used to solve a difficult problem is to break the problem into two or more smaller or easier problems. The linear programming procedure we use to solve the goal programming problem is based on this approach.

The graphical solution procedure for goal programming is similar to that for linear programming presented in Chapter 2. The only difference is that the procedure for goal programming involves a separate solution for each priority level. Recall that the linear programming graphical solution procedure uses a graph to display the values for the decision variables. Because the decision variables are nonnegative, we consider only that portion of the graph where $U \geq 0$ and $H \geq 0$. Recall also that every point on the graph is called a *solution point*.

We begin the graphical solution procedure for the Nicolo Investment problem by identifying all solution points that satisfy the available funds constraint:

$$25U + 50H \leq 80,000$$

The shaded region in Figure 14.1, feasible portfolios, consists of all points that satisfy this constraint—that is, values of U and H for which $25U + 50H \leq 80,000$.

The objective for the priority level 1 linear program is to minimize d_1^+, the amount by which the portfolio index exceeds the target value of 700. Recall that the P_1 goal equation is

$$0.50U + 0.25H - d_1^+ + d_1^- = 700$$

When the P_1 goal is met exactly, $d_1^+ = 0$ and $d_1^- = 0$; the goal equation then reduces to $0.50U + 0.25H = 700$. Figure 14.2 shows the graph of this equation; the shaded region identifies all solution points that satisfy the available funds constraint and also result in the value of $d_1^+ = 0$. Thus, the shaded region contains all the feasible solution points that achieve the priority level 1 goal.

At this point, we have solved the priority level 1 problem. Note that alternative optimal solutions are possible; in fact, all solution points in the shaded region in Figure 14.2 maintain a portfolio risk index of 700 or less, and hence $d_1^+ = 0$.

FIGURE 14.1   PORTFOLIOS THAT SATISFY THE AVAILABLE FUNDS CONSTRAINT

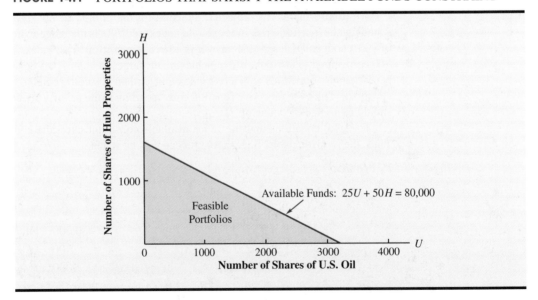

FIGURE 14.2   PORTFOLIOS THAT SATISFY THE P_1 GOAL

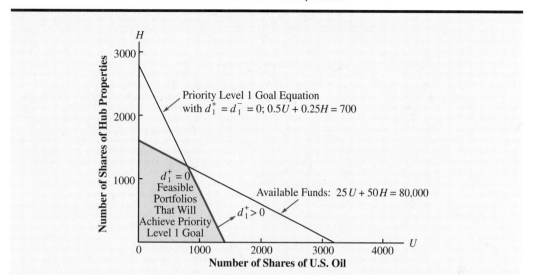

The priority level 2 goal for the Nicolo Investment problem is to find a portfolio that will provide an annual return of at least $9000. Is overachieving the target value of $9000 a concern? Clearly, the answer is no because portfolios with an annual return of more than $9000 correspond to higher returns. Is underachieving the target value of $9000 a concern? The answer is yes because portfolios with an annual return of less than $9000 are not acceptable to the client. Thus, the objective function corresponding to the priority level 2 linear program should minimize the value of d_2^-. However, because goal 2 is a secondary goal, the solution to the priority level 2 linear program must not degrade the optimal solution to the priority level 1 problem. Thus, the priority level 2 linear program can now be stated.

P_2 Problem

$$\text{Min} \quad d_2^-$$

s.t.

$$
\begin{array}{rcll}
25U + 50H & \leq & 80{,}000 & \text{Funds available} \\
0.50U + 0.25H - d_1^+ + d_1^- & = & 700 & P_1 \text{ goal} \\
3U + 5H \quad\quad\quad - d_2^+ + d_2^+ & = & 9000 & P_2 \text{ goal} \\
d_1^+ & = & 0 & \text{Maintain achievement} \\
& & & \text{of } P_1 \text{ goal}
\end{array}
$$

$$U, H, d_1^+, d_1^-, d_2^+, d_2^- \geq 0$$

Note that the priority level 2 linear program differs from the priority level 1 linear program in two ways. The objective function involves minimizing the amount by which the portfolio annual return underachieves the level 2 goal, and another constraint has been added to ensure that no amount of achievement of the priority level 1 goal is sacrificed.

Let us now continue the graphical solution procedure. The goal equation for the priority level 2 goal is

$$3U + 5H - d_2^+ + d_2^- = 9000$$

FIGURE 14.3   BEST SOLUTION WITH RESPECT TO BOTH GOALS
(SOLUTION TO P_2 PROBLEM)

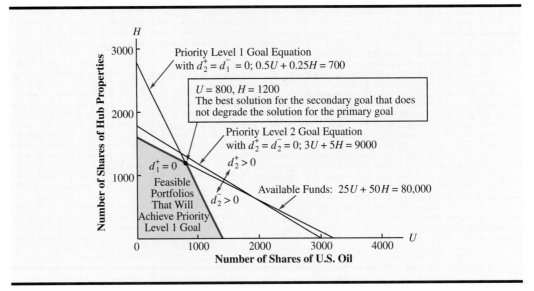

When both d_2^+ and d_2^- equal zero, this equation reduces to $3U + 5H = 9000$; we show the graph with this equation in Figure 14.3.

At this stage, we cannot consider any solution point that will degrade the achievement of the priority level 1 goal. Figure 14.3 shows that no solution points will achieve the priority level 2 goal and maintain the values we were able to achieve for the priority level 1 goal. In fact, the best solution that can be obtained when considering the priority level 2 goal is given by the point ($U = 800$, $H = 1200$); in other words, this point comes the closest to satisfying the priority level 2 goal from among those solutions satisfying the priority level 1 goal. Because the annual return corresponding to this solution point is $3(800) + $5(1200) = 8400, identifying a portfolio that will satisfy both the priority level 1 and the priority level 2 goals is impossible. In fact, the best solution underachieves goal 2 by $d_2^- = $9000 - $8400 = 600.

Thus, the goal programming solution for the Nicolo Investment problem recommends that the $80,000 available for investment be used to purchase 800 shares of U.S. Oil and 1200 shares of Hub Properties. Note that the priority level 1 goal of a portfolio risk index of 700 or less has been achieved. However, the priority level 2 goal of at least a $9000 annual return is not achievable. The annual return for the recommended portfolio is $8400.

In summary, the graphical solution procedure for goal programming involves the following steps:

Step 1. Identify the feasible solution points that satisfy the problem constraints.

Step 2. Identify all feasible solutions that achieve the highest priority goal; if no feasible solutions will achieve the highest priority goal, identify the solution(s) that comes closest to achieving it.

Step 3. Move down one priority level, and determine the "best" solution possible without sacrificing any achievement of higher priority goals.

Step 4. Repeat step 3 until all priority levels have been considered.

Problem 2 will test your ability to formulate a goal programming model and use the graphical solution procedure to obtain a solution.

Although the graphical solution procedure is a convenient method for solving goal programming problems involving two decision variables, the solution of larger problems requires a computer-aided approach. In Section 14.2 we illustrate how to use a computer software package to solve more complex goal programming problems.

Goal Programming Model

As we stated, preemptive goal programming problems are solved as a sequence of linear programs: one linear program for each priority level. However, notation that permits writing a goal programming problem in one concise statement is helpful.

In writing the overall objective for the portfolio selection problem, we must write the objective function in a way that reminds us of the preemptive priorities. We can do so by writing the objective function as

$$\text{Min} \quad P_1(d_1^+) + P_2(d_2^-)$$

The priority levels P_1 and P_2 are not numerical weights on the deviation variables, but simply labels that remind us of the priority levels for the goals.

We now write the complete goal programming model as

$$\text{Min} \quad P_1(d_1^+) + P_2(d_2^-)$$

s.t.

$$
\begin{array}{rlr}
25U + 50H & \leq 80{,}000 & \text{Funds available} \\
0.50U + 0.25H - d_1^+ + d_1^- & = 700 & P_1 \text{ goal} \\
3U + 5H - d_2^+ + d_2^- & = 9000 & P_2 \text{ goal} \\
U, H, d_1^+, d_1^-, d_2^+, d_2^- & \geq 0 &
\end{array}
$$

With the exception of the P_1 and P_2 priority levels in the objective function, this model is a linear programming model. The solution of this linear program involves solving a sequence of linear programs involving goals at decreasing priority levels.

We now summarize the procedure used to develop a goal programming model.

Step 1. Identify the goals and any constraints that reflect resource capacities or other restrictions that may prevent achievement of the goals.

Step 2. Determine the priority level of each goal; goals with priority level P_1 are most important, those with priority level P_2 are next most important, and so on.

Step 3. Define the decision variables.

Step 4. Formulate the constraints in the usual linear programming fashion.

Step 5. For each goal, develop a goal equation, with the right-hand side specifying the target value for the goal. Deviation variables d_i^+ and d_i^- are included in each goal equation to reflect the possible deviations above or below the target value.

Step 6. Write the objective function in terms of minimizing a prioritized function of the deviation variables.

NOTES AND COMMENTS

1. The constraints in the general goal programming model are of two types: goal equations and ordinary linear programming constraints. Some analysts call the goal equations *goal constraints* and the ordinary linear programming constraints *system constraints*.

(continued)

2. You might think of the general goal programming model as having "hard" and "soft" constraints. The hard constraints are the ordinary linear programming constraints that cannot be violated. The soft constraints are the ones resulting from the goal equations. Soft constraints can be violated but with a penalty for doing so. The penalty is reflected by the coefficient of the deviation variable in the objective function. In Section 14.2 we illustrate this point with a problem that has a coefficient of 2 for one of the deviation variables.

3. Note that the constraint added in moving from the linear programming problem at one priority level to the linear programming problem at the next lower priority level is a hard constraint that ensures that no amount of achievement of the higher priority goal is sacrificed to achieve the lower priority goal.

14.2   GOAL PROGRAMMING: SOLVING MORE COMPLEX PROBLEMS

In Section 14.1 we formulated and solved a goal programming model that involved one priority level 1 goal and one priority level 2 goal. In this section we show how to formulate and solve goal programming models that involve multiple goals within the same priority level. Although specially developed computer programs can solve goal programming models, these programs are not as readily available as general purpose linear programming software packages. Thus, the computer solution procedure outlined in this section develops a solution to a goal programming model by solving a sequence of linear programming models with a general purpose linear programming software package.

Suncoast Office Supplies Problem

The management of Suncoast Office Supplies establishes monthly goals, or quotas, for the types of customers contacted. For the next four weeks, Suncoast's customer contact strategy calls for the salesforce, which consists of four salespeople, to make 200 contacts with established customers who have previously purchased supplies from the firm. In addition, the strategy calls for 120 contacts of new customers. The purpose of this latter goal is to ensure that the salesforce is continuing to investigate new sources of sales.

After making allowances for travel and waiting time, as well as for demonstration and direct sales time, Suncoast allocated two hours of salesforce effort to each contact of an established customer. New customer contacts tend to take longer and require three hours per contact. Normally, each salesperson works 40 hours per week, or 160 hours over the four-week planning horizon; under a normal work schedule, the four salespeople will have $4(160) = 640$ hours of salesforce time available for customer contacts.

Management is willing to use some overtime, if needed, but is also willing to accept a solution that uses less than the scheduled 640 hours available. However, management wants both overtime and underutilization of the workforce limited to no more than 40 hours over the four-week period. Thus, in terms of overtime, management's goal is to use no more than $640 + 40 = 680$ hours of salesforce time; and in terms of labor utilization, management's goal is to use at least $640 - 40 = 600$ hours of salesforce time.

In addition to the customer contact goals, Suncoast established a goal regarding sales volume. Based on its experience, Suncoast estimates that each established customer contacted will generate $250 of sales and that each new customer contacted will generate $125 of sales. Management wants to generate sales revenue of at least $70,000 for the next month.

Given Suncoast's small salesforce and the short time frame involved, management decided that the overtime goal and the labor utilization goal are both priority level 1 goals. Management also concluded that the $70,000 sales revenue goal should be a priority level 2 goal and that the two customer contact goals should be priority level 3 goals. Based on these priorities, we can now summarize the goals.

Priority Level 1 Goals

Goal 1: Do not use any more than 680 hours of salesforce time.

Goal 2: Do not use any less than 600 hours of salesforce time.

Priority Level 2 Goal

Goal 3: Generate sales revenue of at least $70,000.

Priority Level 3 Goals

Goal 4: Call on at least 200 established customers.

Goal 5: Call on at least 120 new customers.

Formulating the Goal Equations

Next, we must define the decision variables whose values will be used to determine whether we are able to achieve the goals. Let

$$E = \text{the number of established customers contacted}$$
$$N = \text{the number of new customers contacted}$$

Using these decision variables and appropriate deviation variables, we can develop a goal equation for each goal. The procedure used parallels the approach introduced in the preceding section. A summary of the results obtained is shown for each goal.

Goal 1

$$2E + 3N - d_1^+ + d_1^- = 680$$

where

$d_1^+ =$ the amount by which the number of hours used by the salesforce is greater than the target value of 680 hours

$d_1^- =$ the amount by which the number of hours used by the salesforce is less than the target value of 680 hours

Goal 2

$$2E + 3N - d_2^+ + d_2^- = 600$$

where

$d_2^+ =$ the amount by which the number of hours used by the salesforce is greater than the target value of 600 hours

$d_2^- =$ the amount by which the number of hours used by the salesforce is less than the target value of 600 hours

Goal 3

$$250E + 125N - d_3^+ + d_3^- = 70,000$$

where

$$d_3^+ = \text{the amount by which the sales revenue is greater than the target value of \$70,000}$$

$$d_3^- = \text{the amount by which the sales revenue is less than the target value of \$70,000}$$

Goal 4

$$E - d_4^+ + d_4^- = 200$$

where

$$d_4^+ = \text{the amount by which the number of established customer contacts is greater than the target value of 200 established customer contacts}$$

$$d_4^- = \text{the amount by which the number of established customer contacts is less than the target value of 200 established customer contacts}$$

Goal 5

$$N - d_5^+ + d_5^- = 120$$

where

$$d_5^+ = \text{the amount by which the number of new customer contacts is greater than the target value of 120 new customer contacts}$$

$$d_5^- = \text{the amount by which the number of new customer contacts is less than the target value of 120 new customer contacts}$$

Formulating the Objective Function

To develop the objective function for the Suncoast Office Supplies problem, we begin by considering the priority level 1 goals. When considering goal 1, if $d_1^+ = 0$, we will have found a solution that uses no more than 680 hours of salesforce time. Because solutions for which d_1^+ is greater than zero represent overtime beyond the desired level, the objective function should minimize the value of d_1^+. When considering goal 2, if $d_2^- = 0$, we will have found a solution that uses *at least* 600 hours of sales force time. If d_2^- is greater than zero, however, labor utilization will not have reached the acceptable level. Thus, the objective function for the priority level 1 goals should minimize the value of d_2^-. Because both priority level 1 goals are equally important, the objective function for the priority level 1 problem is

$$\text{Min} \quad d_1^+ + d_2^-$$

In considering the priority level 2 goal, we note that management wants to achieve sales revenues of at least \$70,000. If $d_3^- = 0$, Suncoast will achieve revenues of *at least* \$70,000, and if $d_3^- > 0$, revenues of less than \$70,000 will be obtained. Thus, the objective function for the priority level 2 problem is

$$\text{Min} \quad d_3^-$$

Next, we consider what the objective function must be for the priority level 3 problem. When considering goal 4, if $d_4^- = 0$, we will have found a solution with *at least* 200 established customer contacts; however, if $d_4^- > 0$, we will have underachieved the goal of contacting at least 200 established customers. Thus, for goal 4 the objective is to minimize d_4^-. When considering goal 5, if $d_5^- = 0$, we will have found a solution with *at least* 120 new customer contacts; however, if $d_5^- > 0$, we will have underachieved the goal of contacting at least 120 new customers. Thus, for goal 5 the objective is to minimize d_5^-. If goals 4 and 5 are equal in importance, the objective function for the priority level 3 problem would be

$$\text{Min} \quad d_4^- + d_5^-$$

However, suppose that management believes that generating new customers is vital to the long-run success of the firm and that goal 5 should be weighted more than goal 4. If management believes that goal 5 is twice as important as goal 4, the objective function for the priority level 3 problem would be

$$\text{Min} \quad d_4^- + 2d_5^-$$

Combining the objective functions for all three priority levels, we obtain the overall objective function for the Suncoast Office Supplies problem:

$$\text{Min} \quad P_1(d_1^+) + P_1(d_2^-) + P_2(d_3^-) + P_3(d_4^-) + P_3(2d_5^-)$$

As we indicated previously, P_1, P_2, and P_3 are simply labels that remind us that goals 1 and 2 are the priority level 1 goals, goal 3 is the priority level 2 goal, and goals 4 and 5 are the priority level 3 goals. We can now write the complete goal programming model for the Sun-coast Office Supplies problem as follows:

$$\text{Min} \quad P_1(d_1^+) + P_1(d_2^-) + P_2(d_3^-) + P_3(d_4^-) + P_3(2d_5^-)$$

s.t.

$$
\begin{array}{rcll}
2E + 3N - d_1^+ + d_1^- & = & 680 & \text{Goal 1} \\
2E + 3N \quad - d_2^+ + d_2^- & = & 600 & \text{Goal 2} \\
250E + 125N \quad - d_3^+ + d_3^- & = & 70{,}000 & \text{Goal 3} \\
E \quad\quad - d_4^+ + d_4^- & = & 200 & \text{Goal 4} \\
N \quad\quad - d_5^+ + d_5^- & = & 120 & \text{Goal 5} \\
\end{array}
$$

$$E, N, d_1^+, d_1^-, d_2^+, d_2^-, d_3^+, d_3^-, d_4^+, d_4^-, d_5^+, d_5^- \geq 0$$

Computer Solution

The following computer procedure develops a solution to a goal programming model by solving a sequence of linear programming problems. The first problem comprises all the constraints and all the goal equations for the complete goal programming model; however, the objective function for this problem involves only the P_1 priority level goals. Again, we refer to this problem as the P_1 problem.

Whatever the solution to the P_1 problem, a P_2 problem is formed by adding a constraint to the P_1 model that ensures that subsequent problems will not degrade the solution obtained for the P_1 problem. The objective function for the priority level 2 problem takes into consideration only the P_2 goals. We continue the process until we have considered all priority levels.

FIGURE 14.4   THE SOLUTION OF THE P_1 PROBLEM

Optimal Objective Value = 0.00000

Variable	Value	Reduced Cost
D1PLUS	0.00000	1.00000
D2MINUS	0.00000	1.00000
E	250.00000	0.00000
N	60.00000	0.00000
D1MINUS	0.00000	0.00000
D2PLUS	80.00000	0.00000
D3PLUS	0.00000	0.00000
D3MINUS	0.00000	0.00000
D4PLUS	50.00000	0.00000
D4MINUS	0.00000	0.00000
D5PLUS	0.00000	0.00000
D5MINUS	60.00000	0.00000

To solve the Suncoast Office Supplies problem, we begin by solving the P_1 problem:

$$\text{Min} \quad d_1^+ + d_2^-$$

s.t.

$$
\begin{array}{llll}
2E + 3N - d_1^+ + d_1^- & = & 680 & \text{Goal 1} \\
2E + 3N - d_2^+ + d_2^- & = & 600 & \text{Goal 2} \\
250E + 125N - d_3^+ + d_3^- & = 70{,}000 & & \text{Goal 3} \\
E - d_4^+ + d_4^- & = & 200 & \text{Goal 4} \\
N - d_5^+ + d_5^- & = & 120 & \text{Goal 5}
\end{array}
$$

$$E, N, d_1^+, d_1^-, d_2^+, d_2^-, d_3^+, d_3^-, d_4^+, d_4^-, d_5^+, d_5^- \geq 0$$

In Figure 14.4 we show the solution for this linear program. Note that D1PLUS refers to d_1^+, D2MINUS refers to d_2^-, D1MINUS refers to d_1^-, and so on. The solution shows $E = 250$ established customer contacts and $N = 60$ new customer contacts. Because D1PLUS $= 0$ and D2MINUS $= 0$, we see that the solution achieves both goals 1 and 2. Alternatively, the value of the objective function is 0, confirming that both priority level 1 goals have been achieved. Next, we consider goal 3, the priority level 2 goal, which is to minimize D3MINUS. The solution in Figure 14.4 shows that D3MINUS $= 0$. Thus, the solution of $E = 250$ established customer contacts and $N = 60$ new customer contacts also achieves goal 3, the priority level 2 goal, which is to generate a sales revenue of at least $70,000. The fact that D3PLUS $= 0$ indicates that the current solution satisfies goal 3 exactly at $70,000. Finally, the solution in Figure 14.4 shows D4PLUS $= 50$ and D5MINUS $= 60$. These values tell us that goal 4 of the priority level 3 goals is overachieved by 50 established customers, but goal 5 is underachieved by 60 new customers. As this point, both the priority level 1 and 2 goals have been achieved, but we need to solve another linear program to determine whether a solution can be identified that will satisfy both of the priority level 3 goals. Therefore, we go directly to the P_3 problem.

FIGURE 14.5   THE SOLUTION OF THE P_3 PROBLEM

```
Optimal Objective Value = 120.00000

        Variable                Value              Reduced Cost
      -------------        ---------------       ---------------

        D1PLUS                0.00000               0.00000
        D2MINUS               0.00000               1.00000
        E                   250.00000               0.00000
        N                    60.00000               0.00000
        D1MINUS               0.00000               1.00000
        D2PLUS               80.00000               0.00000
        D3PLUS                0.00000               0.08000
        D3MINUS               0.00000               0.00000
        D4PLUS               50.00000               0.00000
        D4MINUS               0.00000               1.00000
        D5PLUS                0.00000               2.00000
        D5MINUS              60.00000               0.00000
```

The linear programming model for the P_3 problem is a modification of the linear programming model for the P_1 problem. Specifically, the objective function for the P_3 problem is expressed in terms of the priority level 3 goals. Thus, the P_3 problem objective function becomes to minimize D4MINUS + 2D5MINUS. The original five constraints of the P_1 problem appear in the P_3 problem. However, two additional constraints must be added to ensure that the solution to the P_3 problem continues to satisfy the priority level 1 and priority level 2 goals. Thus, we add the priority level 1 constraint D1PLUS + D2MINUS = 0 and the priority level 2 constraint D3MINUS = 0. Making these modifications to the P_1 problem, we obtain the solution to the P_3 problem shown in Figure 14.5.

Referring to Figure 14.5, we see the objective function value of 120 indicates that the priority level 3 goals cannot be achieved. Because D5MINUS = 60, the optimal solution of $E = 250$ and $N = 60$ results in 60 fewer new customer contacts than desired. However, the fact that we solved the P_3 problem tells us the goal programming solution comes as close as possible to satisfying priority level 3 goals given the achievement of both the priority level 1 and 2 goals. Because all priority levels have been considered, the solution procedure is finished. The optimal solution for Suncoast is to contact 250 established customers and 60 new customers. Although this solution will not achieve management's goal of contacting at least 120 new customers, it does achieve each of the other goals specified. If management isn't happy with this solution, a different set of priorities could be considered. Management must keep in mind, however, that in any situation involving multiple goals at different priority levels, rarely will all the goals be achieved with existing resources.

NOTES AND COMMENTS

1. Not all goal programming problems involve multiple priority levels. For problems with one priority level, only one linear program need be solved to obtain the goal programming solution. The analyst simply minimizes the weighted deviations from the goals. Trade-offs are permitted among the goals because they are all at the same priority level.

(continued)

2. The goal programming approach can be used when the analyst is confronted with an infeasible solution to an ordinary linear program. Reformulating some constraints as goal equations with deviation variables allows a solution that minimizes the weighted sum of the deviation variables. Often, this approach will suggest a reasonable solution.

3. The approach that we used to solve goal programming problems with multiple priority levels is to solve a sequence of linear programs. These linear programs are closely related so that complete reformulation and solution are not necessary. By changing the objective function and adding a constraint, we can go from one linear program to the next.

14.3   SCORING MODELS

A scoring model is a relatively quick and easy way to identify the best decision alternative for a multicriteria decision problem. We will demonstrate the use of a scoring model for a job selection application.

Assume that a graduating college student with a double major in finance and accounting received job offers for the following three positions:

- A financial analyst for an investment firm located in Chicago
- An accountant for a manufacturing firm located in Denver
- An auditor for a CPA firm located in Houston

When asked about which job is preferred, the student made the following comments: "The financial analyst position in Chicago provides the best opportunity for my long-run career advancement. However, I would prefer living in Denver rather than in Chicago or Houston. On the other hand, I liked the management style and philosophy at the Houston CPA firm the best." The student's statement points out that this example is clearly a multicriteria decision problem. Considering only the *long-run career advancement* criterion, the financial analyst position in Chicago is the preferred decision alternative. Considering only the *location* criterion, the best decision alternative is the accountant position in Denver. Finally, considering only the *management style* criterion, the best alternative is the auditor position with the CPA firm in Houston. For most individuals, a multicriteria decision problem that requires a trade-off among the several criteria is difficult to solve. In this section, we describe how a **scoring model** can assist in analyzing a multicriteria decision problem and help identify the preferred decision alternative.

The steps required to develop a scoring model are as follows:

A scoring model enables a decision maker to identify the criteria and indicate the weight or importance of each criterion.

Step 1. Develop a list of the criteria to be considered. The criteria are the factors that the decision maker considers relevant for evaluating each decision alternative.

Step 2. Assign a weight to each criterion that describes the criterion's relative importance. Let

$$w_i = \text{the weight for criterion } i$$

Step 3. Assign a rating for each criterion that shows how well each decision alternative satisfies the criterion. Let

$$r_{ij} = \text{the rating for criterion } i \text{ and decision alternative } j$$

Step 4. Compute the score for each decision alternative. Let

$$S_j = \text{score for decision alternative } j$$

The equation used to compute S_j is as follows:

$$S_j = \sum_i w_i r_{ij} \qquad\qquad (14.1)$$

Step 5.   Order the decision alternatives from the highest score to the lowest score to provide the scoring model's ranking of the decision alternatives. The decision alternative with the highest score is the recommended decision alternative.

Let us return to the multicriteria job selection problem the graduating student was facing and illustrate the use of a scoring model to assist in the decision-making process. In carrying out step 1 of the scoring model procedure, the student listed seven criteria as
important factors in the decision-making process. These criteria are as follows:

- Career advancement
- Location
- Management style
- Salary
- Prestige
- Job security
- Enjoyment of the work

In step 2, a weight is assigned to each criterion to indicate the criterion's relative importance in the decision-making process. For example, using a five-point scale, the question used to assign a weight to the career advancement criterion would be as follows:

Relative to the other criteria you are considering, how important is career advancement?

Importance	Weight
Very important	5
Somewhat important	4
Average importance	3
Somewhat unimportant	2
Very unimportant	1

By repeating this question for each of the seven criteria, the student provided the criterion
weights shown in Table 14.1. Using this table, we see that career advancement and enjoyment of the work are the two most important criteria, each receiving a weight of 5. The

TABLE 14.1   WEIGHTS FOR THE SEVEN JOB SELECTION CRITERIA

Criterion	Importance	Weight (w_i)
Career advancement	Very important	5
Location	Average importance	3
Management style	Somewhat important	4
Salary	Average importance	3
Prestige	Somewhat unimportant	2
Job security	Somewhat important	4
Enjoyment of the work	Very important	5

management style and job security criteria are both considered somewhat important, and thus each received a weight of 4. Location and salary are considered average in importance, each receiving a weight of 3. Finally, because prestige is considered to be somewhat unimportant, it received a weight of 2.

The weights shown in Table 14.1 are subjective values provided by the student. A different student would most likely choose to weight the criteria differently. One of the key advantages of a scoring model is that it uses the subjective weights that most closely reflect the preferences of the individual decision maker.

In step 3, each decision alternative is rated in terms of how well it satisfies each criterion. For example, using a nine-point scale, the question used to assign a rating for the "financial analyst in Chicago" alternative and the career advancement criterion would be as follows:

To what extent does the financial analyst position in Chicago satisfy your career advancement criterion?

Level of Satisfaction	Rating
Extremely high	9
Very high	8
High	7
Slightly high	6
Average	5
Slightly low	4
Low	3
Very low	2
Extremely low	1

A score of 8 on this question would indicate that the student believes the financial analyst position would be rated "very high" in terms of satisfying the career advancement criterion.

This scoring process must be completed for each combination of decision alternative and decision criterion. Because seven decision criteria and three decision alternatives need to be considered, $7 \times 3 = 21$ ratings must be provided. Table 14.2 summarizes the student's responses. Scanning this table provides some insights about how the student rates each decision criterion and decision alternative combination. For example, a rating of 9,

TABLE 14.2   RATINGS FOR EACH DECISION CRITERION AND EACH DECISION ALTERNATIVE COMBINATION

	Decision Alternative		
Criterion	Financial Analyst Chicago	Accountant Denver	Auditor Houston
Career advancement	8	6	4
Location	3	8	7
Management style	5	6	9
Salary	6	7	5
Prestige	7	5	4
Job security	4	7	6
Enjoyment of the work	8	6	5

corresponding to an extremely high level of satisfaction, only appears for the management style criterion and the auditor position in Houston. Thus, considering all combinations, the student rates the auditor position in Houston as the very best in terms of satisfying the management criterion. The lowest rating in the table is a 3 that appears for the location criterion of the financial analyst position in Chicago. This rating indicates that Chicago is rated "low" in terms of satisfying the student's location criterion. Other insights and interpretations are possible, but the question at this point is how a scoring model uses the data in Tables 14.1 and 14.2 to identify the best overall decision alternative.

Step 4 of the procedure shows that equation (14.1) is used to compute the score for each decision alternative. The data in Table 14.1 provide the weight for each criterion (w_i) and the data in Table 14.2 provide the ratings of each decision alternative for each criterion (r_{ij}). Thus, for decision alternative 1, the score for the financial analyst position in Chicago is

By comparing the scores for each criterion, a decision maker can learn why a particular decision alternative has the highest score.

$$S_1 = \sum_i w_i r_{i1} = 5(8) + 3(3) + 4(5) + 3(6) + 2(7) + 4(4) + 5(8) = 157$$

The scores for the other decision alternatives are computed in the same manner. The computations are summarized in Table 14.3.

From Table 14.3, we see that the highest score of 167 corresponds to the accountant position in Denver. Thus, the accountant position in Denver is the recommended decision alternative. The financial analyst position in Chicago, with a score of 157, is ranked second, and the auditor position in Houston, with a score of 149, is ranked third.

The job selection example that illustrates the use of a scoring model involved seven criteria, each of which was assigned a weight from 1 to 5. In other applications the weights assigned to the criteria may be percentages that reflect the importance of each of the criteria. In addition, multicriteria problems often involve additional subcriteria that enable the decision maker to incorporate additional detail into the decision process. For instance, consider the location criterion in the job selection example. This criterion might be further subdivided into the following three subcriteria:

- Affordability of housing
- Recreational opportunities
- Climate

TABLE 14.3 COMPUTATION OF SCORES FOR THE THREE DECISION ALTERNATIVES

		Financial Analyst Chicago		Accountant Denver		Auditor Houston	
Criterion	Weight w_i	Rating r_{i1}	Score $w_i r_{i1}$	Rating r_{i2}	Score $w_i r_{i2}$	Rating r_{i3}	Score $w_i r_{i3}$
Career advancement	5	8	40	6	30	4	20
Location	3	3	9	8	24	7	21
Management style	4	5	20	6	24	9	36
Salary	3	6	18	7	21	5	15
Prestige	2	7	14	5	10	4	8
Job security	4	4	16	7	28	6	24
Enjoyment of the work	5	8	40	6	30	5	25
Score			157		167		149

In this case, the three subcriteria would have to be assigned weights, and a score for each decision alternative would have to be computed for each subcriterion. The Management Science in Action, Scoring Model at Ford Motor Company, illustrates how scoring models can be applied for a problem involving four criteria, each of which has several subcriteria. This example also demonstrates the use of percentage weights for the criteria and the wide applicability of scoring models in more complex problem situations.

MANAGEMENT SCIENCE IN ACTION

SCORING MODEL AT FORD MOTOR COMPANY*

Ford Motor Company needed benchmark data in order to set performance targets for future and current model automobiles. A detailed proposal was developed and sent to five suppliers. Three suppliers were considered acceptable for the project.

Because the three suppliers had different capabilities in terms of teardown analysis and testing, Ford developed three project alternatives:

Alternative 1: Supplier C does the entire project alone.

Alternative 2: Supplier A does the testing portion of the project and works with Supplier B to complete the remaining parts of the project.

Alternative 3: Supplier A does the testing portion of the project and works with Supplier C to complete the remaining parts of the project.

For routine projects, selecting the lowest cost alternative might be appropriate. However, because this project involved many nonroutine tasks, Ford incorporated four criteria into the decision process. The four criteria selected by Ford were as follows:

1. Skill level (effective project leader and a skilled team)
2. Cost containment (ability to stay within approved budget)
3. Timing containment (ability to meet program timing requirements)
4. Hardware display (location and functionality of teardown center and user friendliness)

Using team consensus, a weight of 25% was assigned to each of these criteria; note that these weights indicate that members of the Ford project team considered each criterion to be equally important in the decision process.

Each of the four criteria was further subdivided into subcriteria. For example, the skill-level criterion had four subcriteria: project manager leadership; team structure organization; team players' communication; and past Ford experience. In total, 17 subcriteria were considered. A team-consensus weighting process was used to develop percentage weights for the subcriteria. The weights assigned to the skill-level subcriteria were 40% for project manager leadership; 20% for team structure organization; 20% for team players' communication; and 20% for past Ford experience.

Team members visited all the suppliers and individually rated them for each subcriterion using a 1–10 scale (1-worst, 10-best). Then, in a team meeting, consensus ratings were developed. For Alternative 1, the consensus ratings developed for the skill-level subcriteria were 8 for project manager leadership, 8 for team structure organization, 7 for team players' communication, and 8 for past Ford experience. Because the weights assigned to the skill-level subcriteria were 40%, 20%, 20%, and 20%, the rating for Alternative 1 corresponding to the skill-level criterion was

$$\text{Rating} = 0.4(8) + 0.2(8) + 0.2(7) + 0.2(8) = 7.8$$

In a similar fashion, ratings for Alternative 1 corresponding to each of the other criteria were developed. The results obtained were a rating of 6.8 for cost containment, 6.65 for timing containment, and 8 for hardware display. Using the initial weights of 25% assigned to each criterion, the final rating for Alternative 1 = 0.25(7.8) + 0.25(6.8) + 0.25(6.65) + 0.25(8) = 7.3. In a similar fashion, a final rating of 7.4 was developed for Alternative 2, and a final rating of 7.5 was developed for Alternative 3. Thus, Alternative 3 was the recommended decision. Subsequent sensitivity analysis on the weights assigned to the criteria showed that Alternative 3 still received equal or higher ratings than Alternative 1 or Alternative 2. These results increased the team's confidence that Alternative 3 was the best choice.

*Based on Senthil A. Gurusami, "Ford's Wrenching Decision," *OR/MS Today* (December 1998): 36–39.

14.4 ANALYTIC HIERARCHY PROCESS

The **analytic hierarchy process (AHP),** developed by Thomas L. Saaty,[1] is designed to solve complex multicriteria decision problems. AHP requires the decision maker to provide judgments about the relative importance of each criterion and then specify a preference for each decision alternative using each criterion. The output of AHP is a prioritized ranking of the decision alternatives based on the overall preferences expressed by the decision maker.

To introduce AHP, we consider a car purchasing decision problem faced by Diane Payne. After a preliminary analysis of the makes and models of several used cars, Diane narrowed her list of decision alternatives to three cars: a Honda Accord, a Saturn, and a Chevrolet Cavalier. Table 14.4 summarizes the information Diane collected about these cars.

Diane decided that the following criteria were relevant for her car selection decision process:

- Price
- Miles per gallon (MPG)
- Comfort
- Style

Data regarding the Price and MPG are provided in Table 14.4. However, measures of Comfort and Style cannot be specified so directly. Diane will need to consider factors such as the car's interior, type of audio system, ease of entry, seat adjustments, and driver visibility in order to determine the comfort level of each car. The style criterion will have to be based on Diane's subjective evaluation of the color and the general appearance of each car.

AHP allows a decision maker to express personal preferences and subjective judgments about the various aspects of a multicriteria problem.

Even when a criterion such as price can be easily measured, subjectivity becomes an issue whenever a decision maker indicates his or her personal preference for the decision alternatives based on price. For instance, the price of the Accord ($13,100) is $3600 more than the price of the Cavalier ($9500). The $3600 difference might represent a great deal of money to one person, but not much of a difference to another person. Thus, whether the Accord is considered "extremely more expensive" than the Cavalier or perhaps only "moderately more expensive" than the Cavalier depends upon the financial status and the subjective opinion of the person making the comparison. An advantage of AHP is that it can handle situations in which the unique subjective judgments of the individual decision maker constitute an important part of the decision-making process.

TABLE 14.4 INFORMATION FOR THE CAR SELECTION PROBLEM

	Decision Alternative		
Characteristics	**Accord**	**Saturn**	**Cavalier**
Price	$13,100	$11,200	$9500
Color	Black	Red	Blue
Miles per gallon	19	23	28
Interior	Deluxe	Above Average	Standard
Body type	4-door midsize	2-door sport	2-door compact
Sound system	AM/FM, tape, CD	AM/FM	AM/FM

[1] T. Saaty, *Decision Making for Leaders: The Analytic Hierarchy Process for Decisions in a Complex World*, 3d. ed., RWS, 1999.

FIGURE 14.6   HIERARCHY FOR THE CAR SELECTION PROBLEM

Developing the Hierarchy

The first step in AHP is to develop a graphical representation of the problem in terms of the overall goal, the criteria to be used, and the decision alternatives. Such a graph depicts the **hierarchy** for the problem. Figure 14.6 shows the hierarchy for the car selection problem. Note that the first level of the hierarchy shows that the overall goal is to select the best car. At the second level, the four criteria (Price, MPG, Comfort, and Style) each contribute to the achievement of the overall goal. Finally, at the third level, each decision alternative—Accord, Saturn, and Cavalier—contributes to each criterion in a unique way.

Using AHP, the decision maker specifies judgments about the relative importance of each of the four criteria in terms of its contribution to the achievement of the overall goal. At the next level, the decision maker indicates a preference for each decision alternative based on each criterion. A mathematical process is used to synthesize the information on the relative importance of the criteria and the preferences for the decision alternatives to provide an overall priority ranking of the decision alternatives. In the car selection problem, AHP will use Diane's personal preferences to provide a priority ranking of the three cars in terms of how well each car meets the overall goal of being the *best* car.

14.5   ESTABLISHING PRIORITIES USING AHP

In this section we show how AHP uses pairwise comparisons expressed by the decision maker to establish priorities for the criteria and priorities for the decision alternatives based on each criterion. Using the car selection example, we show how AHP determines priorities for each of the following:

1. How the four criteria contribute to the overall goal of selecting the best car
2. How the three cars compare using the Price criterion
3. How the three cars compare using the MPG criterion
4. How the three cars compare using the Comfort criterion
5. How the three cars compare using the Style criterion

In the following discussion we demonstrate how to establish priorities for the four criteria in terms of how each contributes to the overall goal of selecting the best car. The priorities of the three cars using each criterion can be determined similarly.

TABLE 14.5 COMPARISON SCALE FOR THE IMPORTANCE OF CRITERIA USING AHP

Verbal Judgment	Numerical Rating
Extremely more important	9
	8
Very strongly more important	7
	6
Strongly more important	5
	4
Moderately more important	3
	2
Equally important	1

Pairwise Comparisons

Pairwise comparisons form the fundamental building blocks of AHP. In establishing the priorities for the four criteria, AHP will require Diane to state how important each criterion is relative to each other criterion when the criteria are compared two at a time (pairwise). That is, with the four criteria (Price, MPG, Comfort, and Style) Diane must make the following pairwise comparisons:

Price compared to MPG

Price compared to Comfort

Price compared to Style

MPG compared to Comfort

MPG compared to Style

Comfort compared to Style

In each comparison, Diane must select the more important criterion and then express a judgment of how much more important the selected criterion is.

For example, in the Price-MPG pairwise comparison, assume that Diane indicates that Price is more important than MPG. To measure how much more important Price is compared to MPG, AHP uses a scale with values from 1 to 9. Table 14.5 shows how the decision maker's verbal description of the relative importance between the two criteria is converted into a numerical rating. In the car selection example, suppose that Diane states that Price is "moderately more important" than MPG. In this case, a numerical rating of 3 is assigned to the Price-MPG pairwise comparison. From Table 14.5, we see "strongly more important" receives a numerical rating of 5, whereas "very strongly more important" receives a numerical rating of 7. Intermediate judgments such as "strongly to very strongly more important" are possible and would receive a numerical rating of 6.

Table 14.6 provides a summary of the six pairwise comparisons Diane provided for the car selection problem. Using the information in this table, Diane has specified that

Price is moderately more important than MPG.

Price is equally to moderately more important than Comfort.

Price is equally to moderately more important than Style.

Comfort is moderately to strongly more important than MPG.

Style is moderately to strongly more important than MPG.

Style is equally to moderately more important than Comfort.

TABLE 14.6   SUMMARY OF DIANE PAYNE'S PAIRWISE COMPARISONS OF THE FOUR CRITERIA FOR THE CAR SELECTION PROBLEM

Pairwise Comparison	More Important Criterion	How Much More Important	Numerical Rating
Price–MPG	Price	Moderately	3
Price–Comfort	Price	Equally to moderately	2
Price–Style	Price	Equally to moderately	2
MPG–Comfort	Comfort	Moderately to strongly	4
MPG–Style	Style	Moderately to strongly	4
Comfort–Style	Style	Equally to moderately	2

AHP uses the numerical ratings from the pairwise comparisons to establish a priority or importance measure for each criterion.

As shown, the flexibility of AHP can accommodate the unique preferences of each individual decision maker. First, the choice of the criteria that are considered can vary depending upon the decision maker. Not everyone would agree that Price, MPG, Comfort, and Style are the only criteria to be considered in a car selection problem. Perhaps you would want to add safety, resale value, and/or other criteria if you were making the car selection decision. AHP can accommodate any set of criteria specified by the decision maker. Of course, if additional criteria are added, more pairwise comparisons will be necessary. In addition, if you agree with Diane that Price, MPG, Comfort, and Style are the four criteria to use, you would probably disagree with her as to the relative importance of the criteria. Using the format of Table 14.6, you could provide your own assessment of the importance of each pairwise comparison, and AHP would adjust the numerical ratings to reflect your personal preferences.

Pairwise Comparison Matrix

To determine the priorities for the four criteria, we need to construct a matrix of the pairwise comparison ratings provided in Table 14.6. Using the four criteria, the **pairwise comparison matrix** will consist of four rows and four columns as shown here:

	Price	MPG	Comfort	Style
Price				
MPG				
Comfort				
Style				

Each of the numerical ratings in Table 14.6 must be entered into the pairwise comparison matrix. As an illustration of this process consider the numerical rating of 3 for the Price-MPG pairwise comparison. Table 14.6 shows that for this pairwise comparison that Price is the most important criterion. Thus, we must enter a 3 into the row labeled Price and the column labeled MPG in the pairwise comparison matrix. In general, the entries in the column labeled Most Important Criterion in Table 14.6 indicate which row of the pairwise comparison matrix the numerical rating must be placed in. As another illustration, consider the MPG-Comfort pairwise comparison. Table 14.6 shows that Comfort is the most important criterion for this pairwise comparison and that the numerical rating is 4. Thus, we enter a 4 into the row labeled Comfort and into the column labeled MPG. Following this procedure for the other pairwise comparisons shown in Table 14.6, we obtain the following pairwise comparison matrix:

	Price	MPG	Comfort	Style
Price		3	2	2
MPG				
Comfort		4		
Style		4	2	

Because the diagonal elements are comparing each criterion to itself, the diagonal elements of the pairwise comparison matrix are always equal to 1. For example, if Price is compared to Price, the verbal judgment would be "equally important" with a rating of 1; thus, a 1 would be placed into the row labeled Price and into the column labeled Price in the pairwise comparison matrix. At this point, the pairwise comparison matrix appears as follows:

	Price	MPG	Comfort	Style
Price	1	3	2	2
MPG		1		
Comfort		4	1	
Style		4	2	1

All that remains is to complete the entries for the remaining cells of the matrix. To illustrate how these values are obtained, consider the numerical rating of 3 for the Price-MPG pairwise comparison. This rating implies that the MPG-Price pairwise comparison should have a rating of $\frac{1}{3}$. That is, because Diane already indicated Price is moderately more important than MPG (a rating of 3), we can infer that a pairwise comparison of MPG relative to Price should be $\frac{1}{3}$. Similarly, because the Comfort-MPG pairwise comparison has a rating of 4, the MPG-Comfort pairwise comparison would be $\frac{1}{4}$. Thus, the complete pairwise comparison matrix for the car selection criteria is as follows:

	Price	MPG	Comfort	Style
Price	1	3	2	2
MPG	$\frac{1}{3}$	1	$\frac{1}{4}$	$\frac{1}{4}$
Comfort	$\frac{1}{2}$	4	1	$\frac{1}{2}$
Style	$\frac{1}{2}$	4	2	1

Synthesization

Using the pairwise comparison matrix, we can now calculate the priority of each criterion in terms of its contribution to the overall goal of selecting the best car. This aspect of AHP is referred to as **synthesization.** The exact mathematical procedure required to perform synthesization is beyond the scope of this text. However, the following three-step procedure provides a good approximation of the synthesization results:

1. Sum the values in each column of the pairwise comparison matrix.
2. Divide each element in the pairwise comparison matrix by its column total; the resulting matrix is referred to as the **normalized pairwise comparison matrix.**
3. Compute the average of the elements in each row of the normalized pairwise comparison matrix; these averages provide the priorities for the criteria.

To show how the synthesization process works, we carry out this three-step procedure for the criteria pairwise comparison matrix.

Step 1. Sum the values in each column.

	Price	MPG	Comfort	Style
Price	1	3	2	2
MPG	⅓	1	¼	¼
Comfort	½	4	1	½
Style	½	4	2	1
Sum	2.333	12.000	5.250	3.750

Step 2. Divide each element of the matrix by its column total.

	Price	MPG	Comfort	Style
Price	0.429	0.250	0.381	0.533
MPG	0.143	0.083	0.048	0.067
Comfort	0.214	0.333	0.190	0.133
Style	0.214	0.333	0.381	0.267

Step 3. Average the elements in each row to determine the priority of each criterion.

	Price	MPG	Comfort	Style	Priority
Price	0.429	0.250	0.381	0.533	0.398
MPG	0.143	0.083	0.048	0.067	0.085
Comfort	0.214	0.333	0.190	0.133	0.218
Style	0.214	0.333	0.381	0.267	0.299

The AHP synthesization procedure provides the priority of each criterion in terms of its contribution to the overall goal of selecting the best car. Thus, using Diane's pairwise comparisons provided in Table 14.6, AHP determines that Price, with a priority of 0.398, is the most important criterion in the car selection process. Style, with a priority of 0.299, ranks second in importance and is closely followed by Comfort, with a priority of 0.218. MPG is the least important criterion, with a priority of 0.085.

Consistency

A key step in AHP is the making of several pairwise comparisons, as previously described. An important consideration in this process is the **consistency** of the pairwise judgments provided by the decision maker. For example, if criterion A compared to criterion B has a numerical rating of 3 and if criterion B compared to criterion C has a numerical rating of 2, perfect consistency of criterion A compared to criterion C would have a numerical rating of $3 \times 2 = 6$. If the A to C numerical rating assigned by the decision maker was 4 or 5, some inconsistency would exist among the pairwise comparison.

With numerous pairwise comparisons, perfect consistency is difficult to achieve. In fact, some degree of inconsistency can be expected to exist in almost any set of pairwise comparisons. To handle the consistency issue, AHP provides a method for measuring the degree of consistency among the pairwise comparisons provided by the decision maker. If the degree of consistency is unacceptable, the decision maker should review and revise the pairwise comparisons before proceeding with the AHP analysis.

A consistency ratio greater than 0.10 indicates inconsistency in the pairwise comparisons. In such cases, the decision maker should review the pairwise comparisons before proceeding.

AHP provides a measure of the consistency for the pairwise comparisons by computing a **consistency ratio.** This ratio is designed in such a way that a value *greater than* 0.10 indicates an inconsistency in the pairwise judgments. Thus, if the consistency ratio is 0.10 or less, the consistency of the pairwise comparisons is considered reasonable, and the AHP process can continue with the synthesization computations.

Although the exact mathematical computation of the consistency ratio is beyond the scope of this text, an approximation of the ratio can be obtained with little difficulty. The step-by-step procedure for estimating the consistency ratio for the criteria of the car selection problem follows:

Step 1. Multiply each value in the first column of the pairwise comparison matrix by the priority of the first item; multiply each value in the second column of the pairwise comparison matrix by the priority of the second item; continue this process for all columns of the pairwise comparison matrix. Sum the values across the rows to obtain a vector of values labeled "weighted sum." This computation for the car selection problem is as follows:

$$0.398 \begin{bmatrix} 1 \\ \frac{1}{3} \\ \frac{1}{2} \\ \frac{1}{2} \end{bmatrix} + 0.085 \begin{bmatrix} 3 \\ 1 \\ 4 \\ 4 \end{bmatrix} + 0.218 \begin{bmatrix} 2 \\ \frac{1}{2} \\ 1 \\ 2 \end{bmatrix} + 0.299 \begin{bmatrix} 2 \\ \frac{1}{4} \\ \frac{1}{2} \\ 1 \end{bmatrix} =$$

$$\begin{bmatrix} 0.398 \\ 0.133 \\ 0.199 \\ 0.199 \end{bmatrix} + \begin{bmatrix} 0.255 \\ 0.085 \\ 0.340 \\ 0.340 \end{bmatrix} + \begin{bmatrix} 0.436 \\ 0.054 \\ 0.218 \\ 0.436 \end{bmatrix} + \begin{bmatrix} 0.598 \\ 0.075 \\ 0.149 \\ 0.299 \end{bmatrix} = \begin{bmatrix} 1.687 \\ 0.347 \\ 0.907 \\ 1.274 \end{bmatrix}$$

Step 2. Divide the elements of the weighted sum vector obtained in step 1 by the corresponding priority for each criterion.

$$\text{Price} \qquad \frac{1.687}{0.398} = 4.236$$

$$\text{MPG} \qquad \frac{0.347}{0.085} = 4.077$$

$$\text{Comfort} \qquad \frac{0.907}{0.218} = 4.163$$

$$\text{Style} \qquad \frac{1.274}{0.299} = 4.264$$

Step 3. Compute the average of the values found in step 2; this average is denoted λ_{max}.

$$\lambda_{max} = \frac{(4.236 + 4.077 + 4.163 + 4.264)}{4} = 4.185$$

Step 4. Compute the consistency index (CI) as follows:

$$CI = \frac{\lambda_{max} - n}{n - 1}$$

where n is the number of items being compared. Thus, we have

$$CI = \frac{4.185 - 4}{4 - 1} = 0.0616$$

Step 5. Compute the consistency ratio, which is defined as

$$CR = \frac{CI}{RI}$$

where RI is the consistency index of a *randomly* generated pairwise comparison matrix. The value of RI depends on the number of items being compared and is given as follows:

n	3	4	5	6	7	8
RI	0.58	0.90	1.12	1.24	1.32	1.41

Thus, for the car selection problem with $n = 4$ criteria, we have RI = 0.90 and a consistency ratio

$$CR = \frac{0.0616}{0.90} = 0.068$$

Problem 16 will give you practice with the synthesization calculations and determining the consistency ratio.

As mentioned previously, a consistency ratio of 0.10 or less is considered acceptable. Because the pairwise comparisons for the car selection criteria show CR = 0.068, we can conclude that the degree of consistency in the pairwise comparisons is acceptable.

Other Pairwise Comparisons for the Car Selection Problem

Continuing with the AHP analysis of the car selection problem, we need to use the pairwise comparison procedure to determine the priorities for the three cars using each of the criteria: Price, MPG, Comfort, and Style. Determining these priorities requires Diane to express pairwise comparison preferences for the cars using each criterion one at a time. For example, using the Price criterion, Diane must make the following pairwise comparisons:

the Accord compared to the Saturn

the Accord compared to the Cavalier

the Saturn compared to the Cavalier

In each comparison, Diane must select the more preferred car and then express a judgment of how much more preferred the selected car is.

For example, using Price as the basis for comparison, assume that Diane considers the Accord-Saturn pairwise comparison and indicates that the less expensive Saturn is preferred. Table 14.7 shows how AHP uses Diane's verbal description of the preference between the Accord and Saturn to determine a numerical rating of the preference. For example, suppose that Diane states that based on Price, the Saturn is "moderately more preferred" to the Accord. Thus, using the Price criterion, a numerical rating of 3 is assigned to the Saturn row and Accord column of the pairwise comparison matrix.

Table 14.8 shows the summary of the car pairwise comparisons that Diane provided for each criterion of the car selection problem. Using this table and referring to selected pairwise comparison entries, we see that Diane stated the following preferences:

In terms of Price, the Cavalier is moderately to strongly more preferred than the Accord.

In terms of MPG, the Cavalier is moderately more preferred than the Saturn.

In terms of Comfort, the Accord is very strongly to extremely more preferred than the Cavalier.

In terms of Style, the Saturn is moderately more preferred than the Accord.

Practice setting up a pairwise comparison matrix and determine whether judgments are consistent by working Problem 20.

Using the pairwise comparison matrixes in Table 14.8, many other insights may be gained about the preferences Diana expressed for the cars. However, at this point AHP continues by synthesizing each of the four pairwise comparison matrixes in Table 14.8 in order to determine the priority of each car using each criterion. A synthesization is conducted for each pairwise comparison matrix, using the three-step procedure described previously for the criteria pairwise comparison matrix. Four synthesization computations provide the four

TABLE 14.7 PAIRWISE COMPARISON SCALE FOR THE PREFERENCE OF DECISION ALTERNATIVES USING AHP

Verbal Judgment	Numerical Rating
Extremely preferred	9
	8
Very strongly preferred	7
	6
Strongly preferred	5
	4
Moderately preferred	3
	2
Equally preferred	1

TABLE 14.8   PAIRWISE COMPARISON MATRIXES SHOWING PREFERENCES FOR THE CARS USING EACH CRITERION

Price	Accord	Saturn	Cavalier		MPG	Accord	Saturn	Cavalier
Accord	1	$1/3$	$1/4$		Accord	1	$1/4$	$1/6$
Saturn	3	1	$1/2$		Saturn	4	1	$1/3$
Cavalier	4	2	1		Cavalier	6	3	1

Comfort	Accord	Saturn	Cavalier		Style	Accord	Saturn	Cavalier
Accord	1	2	8		Accord	1	$1/3$	4
Saturn	$1/2$	1	6		Saturn	3	1	7
Cavalier	$1/8$	$1/6$	1		Cavalier	$1/4$	$1/7$	1

TABLE 14.9   PRIORITIES FOR EACH CAR USING EACH CRITERION

	Criterion			
	Price	MPG	Comfort	Style
Accord	0.123	0.087	0.593	0.265
Saturn	0.320	0.274	0.341	0.656
Cavalier	0.557	0.639	0.065	0.080

sets of priorities shown in Table 14.9. Using this table, we see that the Cavalier is the preferred alternative based on Price (0.557), the Cavalier is the preferred alternative based on MPG (0.639), the Accord is the preferred alternative based on Comfort (0.593), and the Saturn is the preferred alternative based on Style (0.656). At this point, no car is the clear, overall best. The next section shows how to combine the priorities for the criteria and the priorities in Table 14.9 to develop an overall priority ranking for the three cars.

14.6   USING AHP TO DEVELOP AN OVERALL PRIORITY RANKING

In Section 14.5 we used Diane's pairwise comparisons of the four criteria to develop the priorities of 0.398 for Price, 0.085 for MPG, 0.218 for Comfort, and 0.299 for Style. We now want to use these priorities and the priorities shown in Table 14.9 to develop an overall priority ranking for the three cars.

The procedure used to compute the overall priority is to weight each car's priority shown in Table 14.9 by the corresponding criterion priority. For example, the Price criterion has a priority of 0.398, and the Accord has a priority of 0.123 in terms of the Price criterion. Thus, $0.398 \times 0.123 = 0.049$ is the priority value of the Accord based on the Price criterion. To obtain the overall priority of the Accord, we need to make similar computations for the MPG, Comfort, and Style criteria and then add the values to obtain the overall priority. This calculation is as follows:

Overall Priority of the Accord:

$$0.398(0.123) + 0.085(0.087) + 0.218(0.593) + 0.299(0.265) = 0.265$$

Repeating this calculation for the Saturn and the Cavalier, we obtain the following results:

Overall Priority of the Saturn:

$$0.398(0.320) + 0.085(0.274) + 0.218(0.341) + 0.299(0.656) = 0.421$$

Overall Priority of the Cavalier:

$$0.398(0.557) + 0.085(0.639) + 0.218(0.065) + 0.299(0.080) = 0.314$$

Ranking these priorities, we have the AHP ranking of the decision alternatives:

Car	Priority
1. Saturn	0.421
2. Cavalier	0.314
3. Accord	0.265

Work Problem 24 and determine the AHP priorities for the two decision alternatives.

These results provide a basis for Diane to make a decision regarding the purchase of a car. As long as Diane believes that her judgments regarding the importance of the criteria and her preferences for the cars using each criterion are valid, the AHP priorities show that the Saturn is preferred. In addition to the recommendation of the Saturn as the best car, the AHP analysis helped Diane gain a better understanding of the trade-offs in the decision-making process and a clearer understanding of why the Saturn is the AHP recommended alternative.

NOTES AND COMMENTS

1. The scoring model in Section 14.3 used the following equation to compute the overall score of a decision alternative:

$$S_j = \sum_i w_i r_{ij}$$

where

w_i = the weight for criterion i

r_{ij} = the rating for criterion i and decision alternative j

In Section 14.5 AHP used the same calculation to determine the overall priority of each decision alternative. The difference between the two approaches is that the scoring model required the decision maker to estimate the values of w_i and r_{ij} directly. AHP used synthesization to compute the criterion priorities w_i and the decision alternative priorities r_{ij} based on the pairwise comparison information provided by the decision maker.

2. The software package Expert Choice® marketed by Decision Support Software provides a user-friendly procedure for implementing AHP on a personal computer. Expert Choice takes the decision maker through the pairwise comparison process in a step-by-step manner. Once the decision maker responds to the pairwise comparison prompts, Expert Choice automatically constructs the pairwise comparison matrix, conducts the synthesization calculations, and presents the overall priorities. Expert Choice is a software package that should warrant consideration by a decision maker who anticipates solving a variety of multicriteria decision problems.

SUMMARY

In this chapter we used goal programming to solve problems with multiple goals within the linear programming framework. We showed that the goal programming model contains one or more goal equations and an objective function designed to minimize deviations from the goals. In situations where resource capacities or other restrictions affect the achievement of the goals, the model will contain constraints that are formulated and treated in the same manner as constraints in an ordinary linear programming model.

In goal programming problems with preemptive priorities, priority level 1 goals are treated first in an objective function to identify a solution that will best satisfy these goals. This solution is then revised by considering an objective function involving only the priority level 2 goals; solution modifications are considered only if they do not degrade the solution obtained for the priority level 1 goals. This process continues until all priority levels have been considered.

We showed how a variation of the linear programming graphical solution procedure can be used to solve goal programming problems with two decision variables. Specialized goal programming computer packages are available for solving the general goal programming problem, but such computer codes are not as readily available as are general purpose linear programming computer packages. As a result, we showed how linear programming can be used to solve a goal programming problem.

We then presented a scoring model as a quick and relatively easy way to identify the most desired decision alternative in a multicriteria problem. The decision maker provides a subjective weight indicating the importance of each criterion. Then the decision maker rates each decision alternative in terms of how well it satisfies each criterion. The end result is a score for each decision alternative that indicates the preference for the decision alternative considering all criteria.

We also presented an approach to multicriteria decision making called the analytic hierarchy process (AHP). We showed that a key part of AHP is the development of judgments concerning the relative importance of, or preference for, the elements being compared. A consistency ratio is computed to determine the degree of consistency exhibited by the decision maker in making the pairwise comparisons. Values of the consistency ratio less than or equal to 0.10 are considered acceptable.

Once the set of all pairwise comparisons has been developed, a process referred to as synthesization is used to determine the priorities for the elements being compared. The final step of the analytic hierarchy process involves multiplying the priority levels established for the decision alternatives relative to each criterion by the priority levels reflecting the importance of the criteria themselves; the sum of these products over all the criteria provides the overall priority level for each decision alternative.

GLOSSARY

Goal programming A linear programming approach to multicriteria decision problems whereby the objective function is designed to minimize the deviations from goals.

Preemptive priorities Priorities assigned to goals that ensure that the satisfaction of a higher level goal cannot be traded for the satisfaction of a lower level goal.

Target value A value specified in the statement of the goal. Based on the context of the problem, management will want the solution to the goal programming problem to result in a value for the goal that is less than, equal to, or greater than the target value.

Goal equation An equation whose right-hand side is the target value for the goal; the left-hand side of the goal equation consists of (1) a function representing the level of achievement and (2) deviation variables representing the difference between the target value for the goal and the level achieved.

Deviation variables Variables that are added to the goal equation to allow the solution to deviate from the goal's target value.

Scoring model An approach to multicriteria decision making that requires the user to assign weights to each criterion that describe the criterion's relative importance and to assign a rating that shows how well each decision alternative satisfies each criterion. The output is a score for each decision alternative.

Analytic hierarchy process (AHP) An approach to multicriteria decision making based on pairwise comparisons for elements in a hierarchy.

Hierarchy A diagram that shows the levels of a problem in terms of the overall goal, the criteria, and the decision alternatives.

Pairwise comparison matrix A matrix that consists of the preference, or relative importance, ratings provided during a series of pairwise comparisons.

Synthesization A mathematical process that uses the preference or relative importance values in the pairwise comparison matrix to develop priorities.

Normalized pairwise comparison matrix The matrix obtained by dividing each element of the pairwise comparison matrix by its column total. This matrix is computed as an intermediate step in the synthesization of priorities.

Consistency A concept developed to assess the quality of the judgments made during a series of pairwise comparisons. It is a measure of the internal consistency of these comparisons.

Consistency ratio A numerical measure of the degree of consistency in a series of pairwise comparisons. Values less than or equal to 0.10 are considered reasonable.

PROBLEMS

1. The RMC Corporation blends three raw materials to produce two products: a fuel additive and a solvent base. Each ton of fuel additive is a mixture of $\frac{2}{5}$ ton of material 1 and $\frac{3}{5}$ ton of material 3. A ton of solvent base is a mixture of $\frac{1}{2}$ ton of material 1, $\frac{1}{5}$ ton of material 2, and $\frac{3}{10}$ ton of material 3. RMC's production is constrained by a limited availability of the three raw materials. For the current production period, RMC has the following quantities of each raw material: material 1, 20 tons; material 2, 5 tons; material 3, 21 tons. Management wants to achieve the following P_1 priority level goals:

   Goal 1: Produce at least 30 tons of fuel additive.

   Goal 2: Produce at least 15 tons of solvent base.

   Assume there are no other goals.
   a. Is it possible for management to achieve both P_1 level goals given the constraints on the amounts of each material available? Explain.
   b. Treating the amounts of each material available as constraints, formulate a goal programming model to determine the optimal product mix. Assume that both P_1 priority level goals are equally important to management.
   c. Use the graphical goal programming procedure to solve the model formulated in part (b).
   d. If goal 1 is twice as important as goal 2, what is the optimal product mix?

2. DJS Investment Services must develop an investment portfolio for a new client. As an initial investment strategy, the new client would like to restrict the portfolio to a mix of two stocks:

Stock	Price/Share	Estimated Annual Return (%)
AGA Products	$ 50	6
Key Oil	100	10

The client wants to invest $50,000 and established the following two investment goals:

Priority Level 1 Goal

Goal 1: Obtain an annual return of at least 9%.

Priority Level 2 Goal

Goal 2: Limit the investment in Key Oil, the riskier investment, to no more than 60% of the total investment.

a. Formulate a goal programming model for the DJS Investment problem.
b. Use the graphical goal programming procedure to obtain a solution.

3. The L. Young & Sons Manufacturing Company produces two products, which have the following profit and resource requirement characteristics:

Characteristic	Product 1	Product 2
Profit/unit	$4	$2
Dept. A hours/unit	1	1
Dept. B hours/unit	2	5

Last month's production schedule used 350 hours of labor in department A and 1000 hours of labor in department B.

Young's management has been experiencing workforce morale and labor union problems during the past six months because of monthly departmental workload fluctuations. New hiring, layoffs, and interdepartmental transfers have been common because the firm has not attempted to stabilize workload requirements.

Management would like to develop a production schedule for the coming month that will achieve the following goals:

Goal 1: Use 350 hours of labor in department A.

Goal 2: Use 1000 hours of labor in department B.

Goal 3: Earn a profit of at least $1300.

a. Formulate a goal programming model for this problem, assuming that goals 1 and 2 are P_1 level goals and goal 3 is a P_2 level goal; assume that goals 1 and 2 are equally important.
b. Solve the model formulated in part (a) using the graphical goal programming procedure.
c. Suppose that the firm ignores the workload fluctuations and considers the 350 hours in department A and the 1000 hours in department B as the maximum available. Formulate and solve a linear programming problem to maximize profit subject to these constraints.
d. Compare the solutions obtained in parts (b) and (c). Discuss which approach you favor, and why.

e. Reconsider part (a) assuming that the priority level 1 goal is goal 3 and the priority level 2 goals are goals 1 and 2; as before, assume that goals 1 and 2 are equally important. Solve this revised problem using the graphical goal programming procedure, and compare your solution to the one obtained for the original problem.

4. Industrial Chemicals produces two adhesives used in the manufacturing process for airplanes. The two adhesives, which have different bonding strengths, require different amounts of production time: the IC-100 adhesive requires 20 minutes of production time per gallon of finished product, and the IC-200 adhesive uses 30 minutes of production time per gallon. Both products use 1 pound of a highly perishable resin for each gallon of finished product. Inventory currently holds 300 pounds of the resin, and more can be obtained if necessary. However, because of the limited shelf life of the material, any amount not used in the next two weeks will be discarded.

The firm has existing orders for 100 gallons of IC-100 and 120 gallons of IC-200. Under normal conditions, the production process operates eight hours per day, five days per week. Management wants to schedule production for the next two weeks to achieve the following goals:

Priority Level 1 Goals

Goal 1: Avoid underutilization of the production process.

Goal 2: Avoid overtime in excess of 20 hours for the two weeks.

Priority Level 2 Goals

Goal 3: Satisfy existing orders for the IC-100 adhesive; that is, produce at least 100 gallons of IC-100.

Goal 4: Satisfy existing orders for the IC-200 adhesive; that is, produce at least 120 gallons of IC-200.

Priority Level 3 Goal

Goal 5: Use all the available resin.

a. Formulate a goal programming model for the Industrial Chemicals problem. Assume that both priority level 1 goals and both priority level 2 goals are equally important.

b. Use the graphical goal programming procedure to develop a solution for the model formulated in part (a).

5. Standard Pump recently won a $14 million contract with the U.S. Navy to supply 2000 custom-designed submersible pumps over the next four months. The contract calls for the delivery of 200 pumps at the end of May, 600 pumps at the end of June, 600 pumps at the end of July, and 600 pumps at the end of August. Standard's production capacity is 500 pumps in May, 400 pumps in June, 800 pumps in July, and 500 pumps in August. Management would like to develop a production schedule that will keep monthly ending inventories low while at the same time minimizing the fluctuations in inventory levels from month to month. In attempting to develop a goal programming model of the problem, the company's production scheduler let x_m denote the number of pumps produced in month m and s_m denote the number of pumps in inventory at the end of month m. Here, $m = 1$ refers to May, $m = 2$ refers to June, $m = 3$ refers to July, and $m = 4$ refers to August. Management asks you to assist the production scheduler in model development.

a. Using these variables, develop a constraint for each month that will satisfy the following demand requirement:

$$\begin{pmatrix} \text{Beginning} \\ \text{Inventory} \end{pmatrix} + \begin{pmatrix} \text{Current} \\ \text{Production} \end{pmatrix} - \begin{pmatrix} \text{Ending} \\ \text{Inventory} \end{pmatrix} = \begin{pmatrix} \text{This Month's} \\ \text{Demand} \end{pmatrix}$$

b. Write goal equations that represent the fluctuations in the production level from May to June, June to July, and July to August.

c. Inventory carrying costs are high. Is it possible for Standard to avoid carrying any monthly ending inventories over the scheduling period of May to August? If not, develop goal equations with a target of zero for the ending inventory in May, June, and July.

d. Besides the goal equations developed in parts (b) and (c), what other constraints are needed in the model?

e. Assuming the production fluctuation and inventory goals are of equal importance, develop and solve a goal programming model to determine the best production schedule.

f. Can you find a way to reduce the variables and constraints needed in your model by eliminating the goal equations and deviation variables for ending inventory levels? Explain.

6. Michigan Motors Corporation (MMC) just introduced a new luxury touring sedan. As part of its promotional campaign, the marketing department decided to send personalized invitations to test-drive the new sedan to two target groups: (1) current owners of an MMC luxury automobile and (2) owners of luxury cars manufactured by one of MMC's competitors. The cost of sending a personalized invitation to each customer is estimated to be $1 per letter. Based on previous experience with this type of advertising, MMC estimates that 25% of the customers contacted from group 1 and 10% of the customers contacted from group 2 will test-drive the new sedan. As part of this campaign, MMC set the following goals:

Goal 1: Get at least 10,000 customers from group 1 to test-drive the new sedan.

Goal 2: Get at least 5000 customers from group 2 to test-drive the new sedan.

Goal 3: Limit the expense of sending out the invitations to $70,000.

Assume that goals 1 and 2 are P_1 priority level goals and that goal 3 is a P_2 priority level goal.

a. Suppose that goals 1 and 2 are equally important; formulate a goal programming model of the MMC problem.

b. Use the goal programming computer procedure illustrated in Section 14.2 to solve the model formulated in part (a).

c. If management believes that contacting customers from group 2 is twice as important as contacting customers from group 1, what should MMC do?

7. A committee in charge of promoting a Ladies Professional Golf Association tournament is trying to determine how best to advertise the event during the two weeks prior to the tournament. The committee obtained the following information about the three advertising media they are considering using:

Category	Audience Reached per Advertisement	Cost per Advertisement	Maximum Number of Advertisements
TV	200,000	$2500	10
Radio	50,000	$ 400	15
Newspaper	100,000	$ 500	20

The last column in this table shows the maximum number of advertisements that can be run during the next two weeks; these values should be treated as constraints. The committee established the following goals for the campaign:

Priority Level 1 Goal

Goal 1: Reach at least 4 million people.

Priority Level 2 Goal

Goal 2: The number of television advertisements should be at least 30% of the total number of advertisements.

Priority Level 3 Goal

Goal 3: The number of radio advertisements should not exceed 20% of the total number of advertisements.

Priority Level 4 Goal

Goal 4:   Limit the total amount spent for advertising to $20,000.

a.   Formulate a goal programming model for this problem.
b.   Use the goal programming computer procedure illustrated in Section 14.2 to solve the
model formulated in part (a).

8.   Morley Company is attempting to determine the best location for a new machine in an
existing layout of three machines. The existing machines are located at the following x_1,
x_2 coordinates on the shop floor:

$$\text{Machine 1:}\quad x_1 = 1, x_2 = 7$$
$$\text{Machine 2:}\quad x_1 = 5, x_2 = 9$$
$$\text{Machine 3:}\quad x_1 = 6, x_2 = 2$$

a.   Develop a goal programming model that can be solved to minimize the total distance
of the new machine from the three existing machines. The distance is to be measured
rectangularly. For example, if the location of the new machine is ($x_1 = 3, x_2 = 5$), it is
considered to be a distance of $|3 - 1| + |5 - 7| = 2 + 2 = 4$ from machine 1. *Hint:* In
the goal programming formulation, let

$$x_1 = \text{first coordinate of the new machine location}$$
$$x_2 = \text{second coordinate of the new machine location}$$
$$d_i^+ = \text{amount by which the } x_1 \text{ coordinate of the new machine}$$
$$\text{exceeds the } x_1 \text{ coordinate of machine } i\ (i = 1, 2, 3)$$
$$d_i^- = \text{amount by which the } x_1 \text{ coordinate of machine } i$$
$$\text{exceeds the } x_1 \text{ coordinate of the new machine } (i = 1, 2, 3)$$
$$e_i^+ = \text{amount by which the } x_2 \text{ coordinate of the new machine}$$
$$\text{exceeds the } x_2 \text{ coordinate of machine } i\ (i = 1, 2, 3)$$
$$e_i^- = \text{amount by which the } x_2 \text{ coordinate of machine } i$$
$$\text{exceeds the } x_2 \text{ coordinate of the new machine } (i = 1, 2, 3)$$

b.   What is the optimal location for the new machine?

9.   One advantage of using the multicriteria decision-making methods presented in this chapter is that the criteria weights and the decision alternative ratings may be modified to reflect the unique interests and preferences of each individual decision maker. For example,
assume that another graduating college student had the same three job offers described in
Section 14.3. This student provided the following scoring model information. Rank the
overall preference for the three positions. Which position is recommended?

Criteria	Weight	Analyst Chicago	Accountant Denver	Auditor Houston
Career advancement	5	7	4	4
Location	2	5	6	4
Management style	5	6	5	7
Salary	4	7	8	4
Prestige	4	8	5	6
Job security	2	4	5	8
Enjoyment of the work	4	7	5	5

Ratings

10. The Kenyon Manufacturing Company is interested in selecting the best location for a new plant. After a detailed study of 10 sites, the three location finalists are Georgetown, Kentucky; Marysville, Ohio; and Clarksville, Tennessee. The Kenyon management team provided the following data on location criteria, criteria importance, and location ratings. Use a scoring model to determine the best location for the new plant.

| | | Ratings | | |
| | | Georgetown, | Marysville, | Clarksville, |
Criteria	Weight	Kentucky	Ohio	Tennessee
Land cost	4	7	4	5
Labor cost	3	6	5	8
Labor availability	5	7	8	6
Construction cost	4	6	7	5
Transportation	3	5	7	4
Access to customers	5	6	8	5
Long-range goals	4	7	6	5

11. The Davis family of Atlanta, Georgia, is planning its annual summer vacation. Three vacation locations along with criteria weights and location ratings follow. What is the recommended vacation location?

| | | Ratings | | |
| | | Myrtle Beach, | Smoky | Branson, |
Criteria	Weight	South Carolina	Mountains	Missouri
Travel distance	2	5	7	3
Vacation cost	5	5	6	4
Entertainment available	3	7	4	8
Outdoor activities	2	9	6	5
Unique experience	4	6	7	8
Family fun	5	8	7	7

12. A high school senior is considering attending one of the following four colleges or universities. Eight criteria, criteria weights, and school ratings are also shown. What is the recommended choice?

| | | Ratings | | | |
| | | Midwestern | State College | Handover | Tecumseh |
Criteria	Weight	University	at Newport	College	State
School prestige	3	8	6	7	5
Number of students	4	3	5	8	7
Average class size	5	4	5	8	7
Cost	5	5	8	3	6
Distance from home	2	7	8	7	6
Sports program	4	9	5	4	6
Housing desirability	4	6	5	7	6
Beauty of campus	3	5	3	8	5

13. A real estate investor is interested in purchasing condominium property in Naples, Florida. The three most preferred condominiums are listed along with criteria weights and rating information. Which condominium is preferred?

		Ratings		
Criteria	Weight	Park Shore	The Terrace	Gulf View
Cost	5	5	6	5
Location	4	7	4	9
Appearance	5	7	4	7
Parking	2	5	8	5
Floor plan	4	8	7	5
Swimming pool	1	7	2	3
View	3	5	4	9
Kitchen	4	8	7	6
Closet space	3	6	8	4

14. Clark and Julie Anderson are interested in purchasing a new boat and have limited their choice to one of three boats manufactured by Sea Ray, Inc.: the 220 Bowrider, the 230 Overnighter, and the 240 Sundancer. The Bowrider weighs 3100 pounds, has no overnight capability, and has a price of $28,500. The 230 Overnighter weighs 4300 pounds, has a reasonable overnight capability, and has a price of $37,500. The 240 Sundancer weighs 4500 pounds, has an excellent overnight capability (kitchen, bath, and bed), and has a price of $48,200. The Andersons provided the scoring model information separately, as shown here:

Clark Anderson

		Ratings		
		220	230	240
Criteria	Weight	Bowrider	Overnighter	Sundancer
Cost	5	8	5	3
Overnight capability	3	2	6	9
Kitchen/bath facilities	2	1	4	7
Appearance	5	7	7	6
Engine/speed	5	6	8	4
Towing/handling	4	8	5	2
Maintenance	4	7	5	3
Resale value	3	7	5	6

Julie Anderson

		Ratings		
		220	230	240
Criteria	Weight	Bowrider	Overnighter	Sundancer
Cost	3	7	6	5
Overnight capability	5	1	6	8
Kitchen/bath facilities	5	1	3	7
Appearance	4	5	7	7
Engine/speed	2	4	5	3
Towing/handling	2	8	6	2
Maintenance	1	6	5	4
Resale value	2	5	6	6

a. Which boat does Clark Anderson prefer?
b. Which boat does Julie Anderson prefer?

15. Use the pairwise comparison matrix for the price criterion shown in Table 14.8 to verify that the priorities after synthesization are 0.123, 0.320, and 0.557. Compute the consistency ratio and comment on its acceptability.

16. Use the pairwise comparison matrix for the style criterion, as shown in Table 14.8, to verify that the priorities after synthesization are 0.265, 0.656, and 0.080. Compute the consistency ratio and comment on its acceptability.

17. Dan Joseph was considering entering one of two graduate schools of business to pursue studies for an MBA degree. When asked how he compared the two schools with respect to reputation, he responded that he preferred school A strongly to very strongly to school B.
a. Set up the pairwise comparison matrix for this problem.
b. Determine the priorities for the two schools relative to this criterion.

18. An organization was investigating relocating its corporate headquarters to one of three possible cities. The following pairwise comparison matrix shows the president's judgments regarding the desirability for the three cities:

	City 1	City 2	City 3
City 1	1	5	7
City 2	1/5	1	3
City 3	1/7	1/3	1

a. Determine the priorities for the three cities.
b. Is the president consistent in terms of the judgments provided? Explain.

19. The following pairwise comparison matrix contains the judgments of an individual regarding the fairness of two proposed tax programs, A and B:

	A	B
A	1	3
B	1/3	1

a. Determine the priorities for the two programs.
b. Are the individual's judgments consistent? Explain.

20. Asked to compare three soft drinks with respect to flavor, an individual stated that

A is moderately more preferable than B.

A is equally to moderately more preferable than C.

B is strongly more preferable than C.

a. Set up the pairwise comparison matrix for this problem.
b. Determine the priorities for the soft drinks with respect to the flavor criterion.
c. Compute the consistency ratio. Are the individual's judgments consistent? Explain.

21. Refer to Problem 20. Suppose that the individual had stated the following judgments instead of those given in Problem 20:

> A is strongly more preferable than C.
>
> B is equally to moderately more preferable than A.
>
> B is strongly more preferable than C.

Answer parts (a), (b), and (c) as stated in Problem 20.

22. The national sales director for Jones Office Supplies needs to determine the best location for the next national sales meeting. Three locations have been proposed: Dallas, San Francisco, and New York. One criterion considered important in the decision is the desirability of the location in terms of restaurants, entertainment, and so on. The national sales manager made the following judgments with regard to this criterion:

> New York is very strongly more preferred than Dallas.
>
> New York is moderately more preferred than San Francisco.
>
> San Francisco is moderately to strongly more preferred than Dallas.

   a. Set up the pairwise comparison matrix for this problem.
   b. Determine the priorities for the desirability criterion.
   c. Compute the consistency ratio. Are the sales manager's judgments consistent? Explain.

23. A study comparing four personal computers resulted in the following pairwise comparison matrix for the performance criterion:

	1	2	3	4
1	1	3	7	$\frac{1}{3}$
2	$\frac{1}{3}$	1	4	$\frac{1}{4}$
3	$\frac{1}{7}$	$\frac{1}{4}$	1	$\frac{1}{6}$
4	3	4	6	1

   a. Determine the priorities for the four computers relative to the performance criterion.
   b. Compute the consistency ratio. Are the judgments regarding performance consistent? Explain.

SELF test

24. An individual was interested in determining which of two stocks to invest in, Central Computing Company (CCC) or Software Research, Inc. (SRI). The criteria thought to be most relevant in making the decision are the potential yield of the stock and the risk associated with the investment. The pairwise comparison matrixes for this problem are

Criterion	Yield	Risk
Yield	1	2
Risk	$\frac{1}{2}$	1

Yield	CCC	SRI
CCC	1	3
SRI	$\frac{1}{3}$	1

Risk	CCC	SRI
CCC	1	$\frac{1}{2}$
SRI	2	1

   a. Compute the priorities for each pairwise comparison matrix.
   b. Determine the overall priority for the two investments, CCC and SRI. Which investment is preferred based on yield and risk?

25. The vice president of Harling Equipment needs to select a new director of marketing. The two possible candidates are Bill Jacobs and Sue Martin, and the criteria thought to be most relevant in the selection are leadership ability (L), personal skills (P), and administrative skills (A). The following pairwise comparison matrixes were obtained:

	Criterion		
	L	**P**	**A**
L	1	⅓	¼
P	3	1	2
A	4	½	1

	Leadership	
	Jacobs	**Martin**
Jacobs	1	4
Martin	¼	1

	Personal	
	Jacobs	**Martin**
Jacobs	1	⅓
Martin	3	1

	Administrative	
	Jacobs	**Martin**
Jacobs	1	2
Martin	½	1

a. Compute the priorities for each pairwise comparison matrix.
b. Determine an overall priority for each candidate. Which candidate is preferred?

26. A woman considering the purchase of a custom sound stereo system for her car looked at three different systems (A, B, and C), which varied in terms of price, sound quality, and FM reception. The following pairwise comparison matrixes were developed:

	Criterion		
	Price	**Sound**	**Reception**
Price	1	3	4
Sound	⅓	1	3
Reception	¼	⅓	1

	Price		
	A	**B**	**C**
A	1	4	2
B	¼	1	⅓
C	½	3	1

	Sound		
	A	**B**	**C**
A	1	½	¼
B	2	1	⅓
C	4	3	1

	Reception		
	A	**B**	**C**
A	1	4	2
B	¼	1	1
C	½	1	1

a. Compute the priorities for each pairwise comparison matrix.
b. Determine an overall priority for each system. Which stereo system is preferred?

Case Problem   EZ TRAILERS, INC.

EZ Trailers, Inc., manufactures a variety of general-purpose trailers, including a complete line of boat trailers. Two of their best-selling boat trailers are the EZ-190 and the EZ-250. The EZ-190 is designed for boats up to 19 feet in length, and the EZ-250 can be used for boats up to 25 feet in length.

EZ Trailers would like to schedule production for the next two months for these two models. Each unit of the EZ-190 requires four hours of production time, and each unit of the EZ-250 uses six hours of production time. The following orders have been received for March and April:

Model	March	April
EZ-190	800	600
EZ-250	1100	1200

The ending inventory from February was 200 units of the EZ-190 and 300 units of the EZ-250. The total number of hours of production time used in February was 6300 hours.

The management of EZ Trailers is concerned about being able to satisfy existing orders for the EZ-250 for both March and April. In fact, it believes that this goal is the most important one that a production schedule should meet. Next in importance is satisfying existing orders for the EZ-190. In addition, management doesn't want to implement any production schedule that would involve significant labor fluctuations from month to month. In this regard, its goal is to develop a production schedule that would limit fluctuations in labor hours used to a maximum of 1000 hours from one month to the next.

Managerial Report

Perform an analysis of EZ Trailers' production scheduling problem, and prepare a report for EZ's president that summarizes your findings. Include a discussion and analysis of the following items in your report:

1. The production schedule that best achieves the goals as specified by management.
2. Suppose that EZ Trailers' storage facilities would accommodate only a maximum of 300 trailers in any one month. What effect would this have on the production schedule?
3. Suppose that EZ Trailers can store only a maximum of 300 trailers in any one month. In addition, suppose management would like to have an ending inventory in April of at least 100 units of each model. What effect would both changes have on the production schedule?
4. What changes would occur in the production schedule if the labor fluctuation goal were the highest priority goal?

Appendix 14.1   SCORING MODELS WITH EXCEL

Excel provides an efficient way to analyze a multicriteria decision problem that can be described by a scoring model. We will use the job selection application from Section 14.3 to demonstrate this procedure.

A worksheet for the job selection scoring model is shown in Figure 14.7. The criteria weights are placed into cells B6 to B12. The ratings for each criterion and decision alternative are entered into cells C6 to E12.

The calculations used to compute the score for each decision alternative are shown in the bottom portion of the worksheet. The calculation for cell C18 is provided by the cell formula

$$=\$B6*C6$$

FIGURE 14.7   WORKSHEET FOR THE JOB SELECTION SCORING MODEL

	A	B	C	D	E	F
1	**Job Selection Scoring Model**					
2						
3				**Ratings**		
4			**Analyst**	**Accountant**	**Auditor**	
5	**Criteria**	**Weight**	**Chicago**	**Denver**	**Houston**	
6	Career Advancement	5	8	6	4	
7	Location	3	3	8	7	
8	Management	4	5	6	9	
9	Salary	3	6	7	5	
10	Prestige	2	7	5	4	
11	Job Security	4	4	7	6	
12	Enjoy the Work	5	8	6	5	
13						
14						
15	**Scoring Calculations**					
16			**Analyst**	**Accountant**	**Auditor**	
17	**Criteria**		**Chicago**	**Denver**	**Houston**	
18	Career Advancement		40	30	20	
19	Location		9	24	21	
20	Management		20	24	36	
21	Salary		18	21	15	
22	Prestige		14	10	8	
23	Job Security		16	28	24	
24	Enjoy the Work		40	30	25	
25						
26	**Score**		157	167	149	

Scoring

This cell formula can be copied from cell C18 to cells C18:E24 to provide the results shown in rows 18 to 24. The score for the financial analyst position in Chicago is found by placing the following formula in cell C26:

$$= \text{SUM(C18:C24)}$$

Copying cell C26 to cells D26:E26 provides the scores for the accountant in Denver and the auditor in Houston positions.

CHAPTER 15

Time Series Analysis and Forecasting

CONTENTS

15.1 TIME SERIES PATTERNS
Horizontal Pattern
Trend Pattern
Seasonal Pattern
Trend and Seasonal Pattern
Cyclical Pattern
Selecting a Forecasting Method

15.2 FORECAST ACCURACY

15.3 MOVING AVERAGES AND
EXPONENTIAL SMOOTHING
Moving Averages
Weighted Moving Averages
Exponential Smoothing

15.4 TREND PROJECTION
Linear Trend
Nonlinear Trend

15.5 SEASONALITY
Seasonality Without Trend
Seasonality and Trend
Models Based on Monthly Data

A forecast is simply a prediction of what will happen in the future. Managers must learn to accept the fact that regardless of the technique used, they will not be able to develop perfect forecasts.

The purpose of this chapter is to provide an introduction to time series analysis and forecasting. Suppose we are asked to provide quarterly forecasts of sales for one of our company's products over the coming one-year period. Production schedules, raw material purchasing, inventory policies, and sales quotas will all be affected by the quarterly forecasts we provide. Consequently, poor forecasts may result in poor planning and increased costs for the company. How should we go about providing the quarterly sales forecasts? Good judgment, intuition, and an awareness of the state of the economy may give us a rough idea or "feeling" of what is likely to happen in the future, but converting that feeling into a number that can be used as next year's sales forecast is difficult.

Forecasting methods can be classified as qualitative or quantitative. Qualitative methods generally involve the use of expert judgment to develop forecasts. Such methods are appropriate when historical data on the variable being forecast are either not applicable or unavailable. Quantitative forecasting methods can be used when (1) past information about the variable being forecast is available, (2) the information can be quantified, and (3) it is reasonable to assume that the pattern of the past will continue into the future. We will focus exclusively on quantitative forecasting methods in this chapter.

If the historical data are restricted to past values of the variable to be forecast, the forecasting procedure is called a time series method and the historical data are referred to as a time series. The objective of time series analysis is to discover a pattern in the historical data or time series and then extrapolate the pattern into the future; the forecast is based solely on past values of the variable and/or on past forecast errors.

In Section 15.1 we discuss the various kinds of time series that a forecaster might be faced with in practice. These include a constant or horizontal pattern, trends, seasonal patterns, both a trend and a seasonal pattern, and cyclical patterns. In order to build a quantitative forecasting model, it is necessary to have a measurement of forecast accuracy. Different measurements, and their respective advantages and disadvantages, are discussed in Section 15.2. In Section 15.3 we consider the simplest case, which is a horizontal or constant pattern. For this pattern, we develop the classical moving average and exponential smoothing models. We show how the best parameters can be selected using an optimization model, which provides a good application of the optimization tools developed in Chapters 2 through 8. Many time series have a trend, and taking this trend into account is important. In Section 15.4 we give optimization models for finding the best model parameters when a trend is present. Finally, in Section 15.5 we show how to incorporate both a trend and seasonality into a forecasting model.

MANAGEMENT SCIENCE IN ACTION

FORECASTING ENERGY NEEDS IN THE UTILITY INDUSTRY*

Duke Energy is a diversified energy company with a portfolio of natural gas and electric businesses and an affiliated real estate company. In 2006, Duke Energy merged with Cinergy of Cincinnati, Ohio, to create one of North America's largest energy companies, with assets totaling more than $70 billion. As a result of this merger the Cincinnati Gas & Electric Company became part of Duke Energy. Today, Duke Energy services over 5.5 million retail electric and gas customers in North Carolina, South Carolina, Ohio, Kentucky, Indiana, and Ontario, Canada.

Forecasting in the utility industry offers some unique perspectives. Because electricity cannot take the form of finished goods or in-process inventories, this product must be generated to meet the instantaneous requirements of the customers. Electrical shortages are not just lost sales, but "brownouts" or "blackouts." This situation places an unusual burden on the utility forecaster. On the positive side, the demand for energy and the sale of energy are more predictable than for many other products. Also, unlike the situation in a multiproduct firm, a great amount of forecasting effort and expertise can be concentrated on the two products: gas and electricity.

The largest observed electric demand for any given period, such as an hour, a day, a month, or a year, is defined as the peak load. The forecast of the annual electric peak load guides the timing decision for constructing future generating units, and the financial impact of this decision is great. Obviously, a timing decision that leads to having the unit available no sooner than necessary is crucial.

The energy forecasts are important in other ways also. For example, purchases of coal as fuel for the generating units are based on the forecast levels of energy needed. The revenue from the electric operations of the company is determined from forecasted sales, which in turn enters into the planning of rate changes and external financing. These planning and decision-making processes are among the most important managerial activities in the company. It is imperative that the decision makers have the best forecast information available to assist them in arriving at these decisions.

*Based on information provided by Dr. Richard Evans of Cincinnati Gas & Electric Company, Cincinnati, Ohio.

15.1   TIME SERIES PATTERNS

A time series is a sequence of observations on a variable measured at successive points in time or over successive periods of time. The measurements may be taken every hour, day, week, month, or year, or at any other regular interval.[1] The pattern of the data is an important factor in understanding how the time series has behaved in the past. If such behavior can be expected to continue in the future, we can use it to guide us in selecting an appropriate forecasting method.

To identify the underlying pattern in the data, a useful first step is to construct a time series plot. A time series plot is a graphical presentation of the relationship between time and the time series variable; time is on the horizontal axis and the time series values are shown on the vertical axis. Let us review some of the common types of data patterns that can be identified when examining a time series plot.

Horizontal Pattern

A horizontal pattern exists when the data fluctuate around a constant mean. To illustrate a time series with a horizontal pattern, consider the 12 weeks of data in Table 15.1. These data show the number of gallons of gasoline sold by a gasoline distributor in Bennington, Vermont, over the past 12 weeks. The average value or mean for this time series is 19.25, or 19,250 gallons per week. Figure 15.1 shows a time series plot for these data. Note how the data fluctuate around the sample mean of 19,250 gallons. Although random variability is present, we would say that these data follow a horizontal pattern.

The term stationary time series[2] is used to denote a time series whose statistical properties are independent of time. In particular this means that

1. The process generating the data has a constant mean.
2. The variability of the time series is constant over time.

---

[1] We limit our discussion to time series in which the values of the series are recorded at equal intervals. Cases in which the observations are made at unequal intervals are beyond the scope of this text.

[2] For a formal definition of stationarity see Box, G. E. P., G. M. Jenkins, and G. C. Reinsell (1994), *Time Series Analysis: Forecasting and Control*, 3rd ed., Prentice-Hall, p. 23.

TABLE 15.1   GASOLINE SALES TIME SERIES

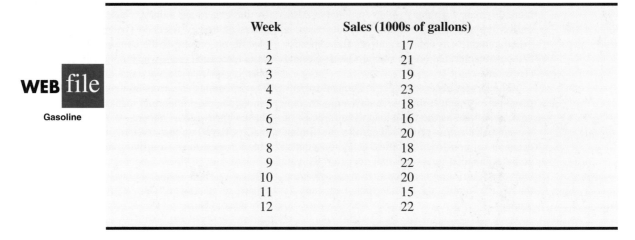

Week	Sales (1000s of gallons)
1	17
2	21
3	19
4	23
5	18
6	16
7	20
8	18
9	22
10	20
11	15
12	22

WEB file

Gasoline

A time series plot for a stationary time series will always exhibit a horizontal pattern. But simply observing a horizontal pattern is not sufficient evidence to conclude that the time series is stationary. More advanced texts on forecasting discuss procedures for determining whether a time series is stationary and provide methods for transforming a time series that is not stationary into a stationary series.

FIGURE 15.1   GASOLINE SALES TIME SERIES PLOT

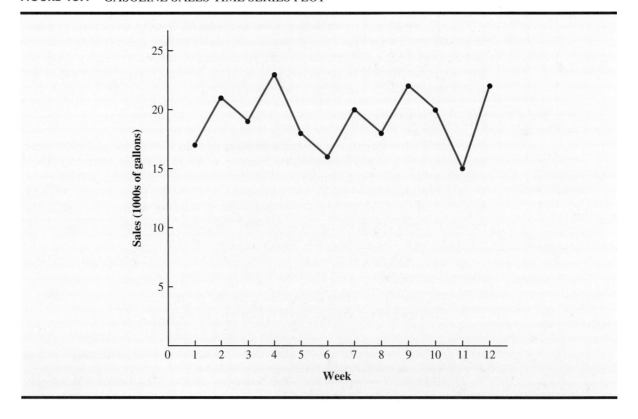

Changes in business conditions can often result in a time series that has a horizontal pattern shifting to a new level. For instance, suppose the gasoline distributor signs a contract with the Vermont Sate Police to provide gasoline for state police cars located in southern Vermont. With this new contract, the distributor expects to see a major increase in weekly sales starting in week 13. Table 15.2 shows the number of gallons of gasoline sold for the original time series and the 10 weeks after signing the new contract. Figure 15.2 shows the corresponding time series plot. Note the increased level of the time series beginning in week 13. This change in the level of the time series makes it more difficult to choose an appropriate forecasting method. Selecting a forecasting method that adapts well to changes in the level of a time series is an important consideration in many practical applications.

Trend Pattern

Although time series data generally exhibit random fluctuations, a time series may also show gradual shifts or movements to relatively higher or lower values over a longer period of time. If a time series plot exhibits this type of behavior, we say that a trend pattern exists. Trend is usually the result of long-term factors such as population increases or decreases, changing demographic characteristics of the population, technology, and/or consumer preferences.

TABLE 15.2   GASOLINE SALES TIME SERIES AFTER OBTAINING THE CONTRACT
WITH THE VERMONT STATE POLICE

GasolineRevised

Week	Sales (1000s of gallons)
1	17
2	21
3	19
4	23
5	18
6	16
7	20
8	18
9	22
10	20
11	15
12	22
13	31
14	34
15	31
16	33
17	28
18	32
19	30
20	29
21	34
22	33

FIGURE 15.2   GASOLINE SALES TIME SERIES PLOT AFTER OBTAINING THE CONTRACT WITH THE VERMONT STATE POLICE

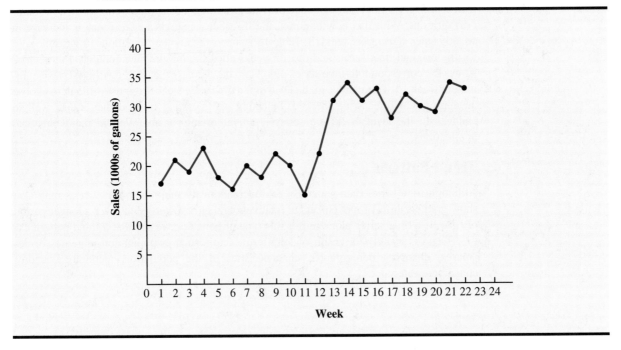

To illustrate a time series with a trend pattern, consider the time series of bicycle sales for a particular manufacturer over the past 10 years, as shown in Table 15.3 and Figure 15.3. Note that 21,600 bicycles were sold in year 1, 22,900 were sold in year 2, and so on. In year 10, the most recent year, 31,400 bicycles were sold. Visual inspection of the time series plot shows some up and down movement over the past 10 years, but the time series seems to also have a systematically increasing or upward trend.

The trend for the bicycle sales time series appears to be linear and increasing over time, but sometimes a trend can be described better by other types of patterns. For instance, the

TABLE 15.3   BICYCLE SALES TIME SERIES

WEB file

Bicycle

Year	Sales (1000s)
1	21.6
2	22.9
3	25.5
4	21.9
5	23.9
6	27.5
7	31.5
8	29.7
9	28.6
10	31.4

FIGURE 15.3   BICYCLE SALES TIME SERIES PLOT

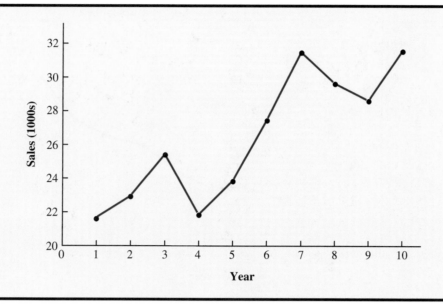

data in Table 15.4 and the corresponding time series plot in Figure 15.4 show the sales revenue for a cholesterol drug since the company won FDA approval for it 10 years ago. The time series increases in a nonlinear fashion; that is, the rate of change of revenue does not increase by a constant amount from one year to the next. In fact the revenue appears to be growing in an exponential fashion. Exponential relationships such as this are appropriate when the percentage change from one period to the next is relatively constant.

Seasonal Pattern

The trend of a time series can be identified by analyzing multiyear movements in historical data. Seasonal patterns are recognized by seeing the same repeating patterns over successive periods of time. For example, a manufacturer of swimming pools expects low sales

TABLE 15.4   CHOLESTEROL REVENUE TIME SERIES ($ MILLIONS)

Year	Revenue
1	23.1
2	21.3
3	27.4
4	34.6
5	33.8
6	43.2
7	59.5
8	64.4
9	74.2
10	99.3

WEB file

Cholesterol

FIGURE 15.4   CHOLESTEROL REVENUE TIMES SERIES PLOT ($ MILLIONS)

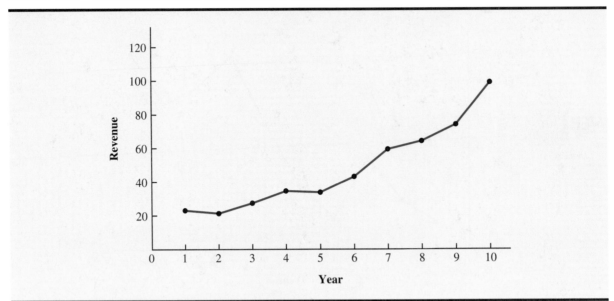

activity in the fall and winter months, with peak sales in the spring and summer months. Manufacturers of snow removal equipment and heavy clothing, however, expect just the opposite yearly pattern. Not surprisingly, the pattern for a time series plot that exhibits a repeating pattern over a one-year period due to seasonal influences is called a *seasonal pattern*. Although we generally think of seasonal movement in a time series as occurring within one year, time series data can also exhibit seasonal patterns of less than one year in duration. For example, daily traffic volume shows within-the-day "seasonal" behavior, with peak levels occurring during rush hours, moderate flow during the rest of the day and early evening, and light flow from midnight to early morning.

As an example of a seasonal pattern, consider the number of umbrellas sold at a clothing store over the past five years. Table 15.5 shows the time series and Figure 15.5 shows the corresponding time series plot. The time series plot does not indicate any long-term trend in sales. In fact, unless you look carefully at the data, you might conclude that the data follow a horizontal pattern. But closer inspection of the time series plot reveals a regular pattern in the data. That is, the first and third quarters have moderate sales, the second quarter has the highest sales, and the fourth quarter tends to have the lowest sales volume. Thus, we would conclude that a quarterly seasonal pattern is present.

Trend and Seasonal Pattern

Some time series include a combination of a trend and seasonal pattern. For instance, the data in Table 15.6 and the corresponding time series plot in Figure 15.6 show television set sales for a particular manufacturer over the past four years. Clearly, an increasing trend is present. But Figure 15.6 also indicates that sales are lowest in the second quarter of each year and increase in quarters 3 and 4. Thus, we conclude that a seasonal pattern also exists for television set sales. In such cases we need to use a forecasting method that has the capability to deal with both trend and seasonality.

TABLE 15.5 UMBRELLA SALES TIME SERIES

WEB file

Umbrella

Year	Quarter	Sales
1	1	125
	2	153
	3	106
	4	88
2	1	118
	2	161
	3	133
	4	102
3	1	138
	2	144
	3	113
	4	80
4	1	109
	2	137
	3	125
	4	109
5	1	130
	2	165
	3	128
	4	96

FIGURE 15.5 UMBRELLA SALES TIME SERIES PLOT

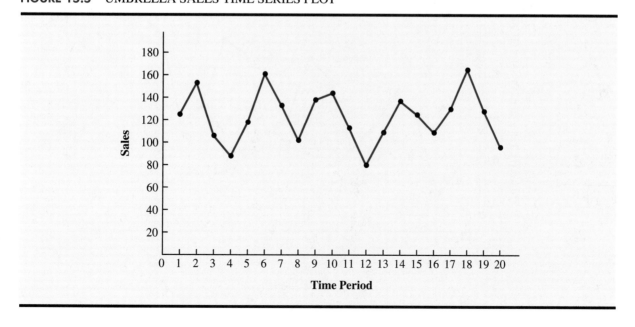

TABLE 15.6   QUARTERLY TELEVISION SET SALES TIME SERIES

Year	Quarter	Sales (1000s)
1	1	4.8
	2	4.1
	3	6.0
	4	6.5
2	1	5.8
	2	5.2
	3	6.8
	4	7.4
3	1	6.0
	2	5.6
	3	7.5
	4	7.8
4	1	6.3
	2	5.9
	3	8.0
	4	8.4

FIGURE 15.6   QUARTERLY TELEVISION SET SALES TIME SERIES PLOT

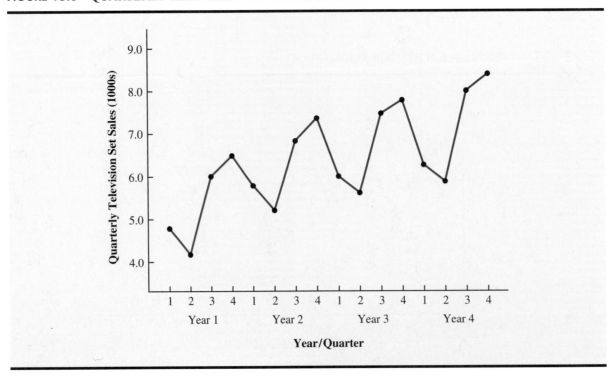

Cyclical Pattern

A cyclical pattern exists if the time series plot shows an alternating sequence of points below and above the trend line lasting more than one year. Many economic time series exhibit cyclical behavior with regular runs of observations below and above the trend line. Often, the cyclical component of a time series is due to multiyear business cycles. For example, periods of moderate inflation followed by periods of rapid inflation can lead to time series that alternate below and above a generally increasing trend line (e.g., a time series for housing costs). Business cycles are extremely difficult, if not impossible, to forecast. As a result, cyclical effects are often combined with long-term trend effects and referred to as trend-cycle effects. In this chapter we do not deal with cyclical effects that may be present in the time series.

Selecting a Forecasting Method

The underlying pattern in the time series is an important factor in selecting a forecasting method. Thus, a time series plot should be one of the first things developed when trying to determine which forecasting method to use. If we see a horizontal pattern, then we need to select a method appropriate for this type of pattern. Similarly, if we observe a trend in the data, then we need to use a forecasting method that has the capability to handle trends effectively. The next two sections illustrate methods that can be used in situations where the underlying pattern is horizontal; in other words, no trend or seasonal effects are present. We then consider methods appropriate when trend and or seasonality are present in the data.

15.2 FORECAST ACCURACY

In this section we begin by developing forecasts for the gasoline time series shown in Table 15.1, using the simplest of all the forecasting methods, an approach that uses the most recent week's sales volume as the forecast for the next week. For instance, the distributor sold 17 thousand gallons of gasoline in week 1; this value is used as the forecast for week 2. Next, we use 21, the actual value of sales in week 2, as the forecast for week 3, and so on. The forecasts obtained for the historical data using this method are shown in Table 15.7 in the column labeled Forecast. Because of its simplicity, this method is often referred to as a naïve forecasting method.

How accurate are the forecasts obtained using this naïve forecasting method? To answer this question, we will introduce several measures of forecast accuracy. These measures are used to determine how well a particular forecasting method is able to reproduce the time series data that are already available. By selecting the method that has the best accuracy for the data already known, we hope to increase the likelihood that we will obtain better forecasts for future time periods.

The key concept associated with measuring forecast accuracy is forecast error, defined as follows:

$$\text{Forecast Error} = \text{Actual Value} - \text{Forecast}$$

For instance, because the distributor actually sold 21 thousand gallons of gasoline in week 2 and the forecast, using the sales volume in week 1, was 17 thousand gallons, the forecast error in week 2 is

$$\text{Forecast Error in week 2} = 21 - 17 = 4$$

TABLE 15.7   COMPUTING FORECASTS AND MEASURES OF FORECAST ACCURACY
USING THE MOST RECENT VALUE AS THE FORECAST FOR THE
NEXT PERIOD

Week	Time Series Value	Forecast	Forecast Error	Absolute Value of Forecast Error	Squared Forecast Error	Percentage Error	Absolute Value of Percentage Error
1	17						
2	21	17	4	4	16	19.05	19.05
3	19	21	−2	2	4	−10.53	10.53
4	23	19	4	4	16	17.39	17.39
5	18	23	−5	5	25	−27.78	27.78
6	16	18	−2	2	4	−12.50	12.50
7	20	16	4	4	16	20.00	20.00
8	18	20	−2	2	4	−11.11	11.11
9	22	18	4	4	16	18.18	18.18
10	20	22	−2	2	4	−10.00	10.00
11	15	20	−5	5	25	−33.33	33.33
12	22	15	7	7	49	31.82	31.82
		Totals	5	41	179	1.19	211.69

The fact that the forecast error is positive indicates that in week 2 the forecasting method underestimated the actual value of sales. Next, we use 21, the actual value of sales in week 2, as the forecast for week 3. Because the actual value of sales in week 3 is 19, the forecast error for week 3 is 19 − 21 = −2. In this case the negative forecast error indicates that in week 3 the forecast overestimated the actual value. Thus, the forecast error may be positive or negative, depending on whether the forecast is too low or too high. A complete summary of the forecast errors for this naïve forecasting method is shown in Table 15.7 in the column labeled Forecast Error.

A simple measure of forecast accuracy is the mean or average of the forecast errors. Table 15.7 shows that the sum of the forecast errors for the gasoline sales time series is 5; thus, the mean or average error is 5/11 = 0.45. Note that although the gasoline time series consists of 12 values, to compute the mean error we divided the sum of the forecast errors by 11 because there are only 11 forecast errors. Because the mean forecast error is positive, the method is under-forecasting; in other words, the observed values tend to be greater than the forecasted values. Because positive and negative forecast errors tend to offset one another, the mean error is likely to be small; thus, the mean error is not a very useful measure of forecast accuracy.

The mean absolute error, denoted MAE, is a measure of forecast accuracy that avoids the problem of positive and negative forecast errors offsetting one another. As you might expect given its name, MAE is the average of the absolute values of the forecast errors. Table 15.7 shows that the sum of the absolute values of the forecast errors is 41; thus

$$\text{MAE} = \text{average of the absolute value of forecast errors} = \frac{41}{11} = 3.73$$

Another measure that avoids the problem of positive and negative errors offsetting each other is obtained by computing the average of the squared forecast errors. This measure of forecast accuracy, referred to as the mean squared error, is denoted MSE. From Table 15.7, the sum of the squared errors is 179; hence,

$$\text{MSE} = \text{average of the sum of squared forecast errors} = \frac{179}{11} = 16.27$$

The size of MAE and MSE depend upon the scale of the data. As a result it is difficult to make comparisons for different time intervals, such as comparing a method of forecasting monthly gasoline sales to a method of forecasting weekly sales, or to make comparisons across different time series. To make comparisons like these, we need to work with relative or percentage error measures. The mean absolute percentage error, denoted MAPE, is such a measure. To compute MAPE, we must first compute the percentage error for each forecast. For example, the percentage error corresponding to the forecast of 17 in week 2 is computed by dividing the forecast error in week 2 by the actual value in week 2 and multiplying the result by 100. For week 2 the percentage error is computed as follows:

$$\text{Percentage error for week 2} = \frac{4}{21}(100) = 19.05\%$$

Thus, the forecast error for week 2 is 19.05% of the observed value in week 2. A complete summary of the percentage errors is shown in Table 15.7 in the column labeled Percentage Error. In the next column, we show the absolute value of the percentage error.

Table 15.7 shows that the sum of the absolute values of the percentage errors is 211.69; thus

$$\text{MAPE} = \text{average of the absolute value of percentage}$$
$$\text{forecast errors} = \frac{211.69}{11} = 19.24\%$$

Summarizing, using the naïve (most recent observation) forecasting method, we obtained the following measures of forecast accuracy:

$$\text{MAE} = 3.73$$
$$\text{MSE} = 16.27$$
$$\text{MAPE} = 19.24\%$$

These measures of forecast accuracy simply measure how well the forecasting method is able to forecast historical values of the time series. Now, suppose we want to forecast sales for a future time period, such as week 13. In this case the forecast for week 13 is 22, the actual value of the time series in week 12. Is this an accurate estimate of sales for week 13? Unfortunately, there is no way to address the issue of accuracy associated with forecasts for future time periods. However, if we select a forecasting method that works well for the historical data and we think that the historical pattern will continue into the future, we should obtain results that will ultimately be shown to be good.

Before closing this section, let us consider another method for forecasting the gasoline sales time series in Table 15.1. Suppose we use the average of all the historical data available as the forecast for the next period. We begin by developing a forecast for week 2. Because there is only one historical value available prior to week 2, the forecast for week 2 is just the time series value in week 1; thus, the forecast for week 2 is 17 thousand gallons of gasoline. To compute the forecast for week 3, we take the average of the sales values in weeks 1 and 2. Thus,

$$\text{Forecast for week 3} = \frac{17 + 21}{2} = 19$$

Similarly, the forecast for week 4 is

$$\text{Forecast for week 4} = \frac{17 + 21 + 19}{3} = 19$$

The forecasts obtained using this method for the gasoline time series are shown in Table 15.8 in the column labeled Forecast. Using the results shown in Table 15.8, we obtained the following values of MAE, MSE, and MAPE:

$$\text{MAE} = \frac{26.81}{11} = 2.44$$

$$\text{MSE} = \frac{89.07}{11} = 8.10$$

$$\text{MAPE} = \frac{141.34}{11} = 12.85\%$$

We can now compare the accuracy of the two forecasting methods we have considered in this section by comparing the values of MAE, MSE, and MAPE for each method.

	Naïve Method	Average of Past Values
MAE	3.73	2.44
MSE	16.27	8.10
MAPE	19.24%	12.85%

For every measure, the average of past values provides more accurate forecasts than using the most recent observation as the forecast for the next period. In general, if the underlying time series is stationary, the average of all the historical data will always provide the best results.

TABLE 15.8   COMPUTING FORECASTS AND MEASURES OF FORECAST ACCURACY USING THE AVERAGE OF ALL THE HISTORICAL DATA AS THE FORECAST FOR THE NEXT PERIOD

Week	Time Series Value	Forecast	Forecast Error	Absolute Value of Forecast Error	Squared Forecast Error	Percentage Error	Absolute Value of Percentage Error
1	17						
2	21	17.00	4.00	4.00	16.00	19.05	19.05
3	19	19.00	0.00	0.00	0.00	0.00	0.00
4	23	19.00	4.00	4.00	16.00	17.39	17.39
5	18	20.00	−2.00	2.00	4.00	−11.11	11.11
6	16	19.60	−3.60	3.60	12.96	−22.50	22.50
7	20	19.00	1.00	1.00	1.00	5.00	5.00
8	18	19.14	−1.14	1.14	1.31	−6.35	6.35
9	22	19.00	3.00	3.00	9.00	13.64	13.64
10	20	19.33	0.67	0.67	0.44	3.33	3.33
11	15	19.40	−4.40	4.40	19.36	−29.33	29.33
12	22	19.00	3.00	3.00	9.00	13.64	13.64
		Totals	4.52	26.81	89.07	2.75	141.34

But suppose that the underlying time series is not stationary. In Section 15.1 we mentioned that changes in business conditions can often result in a time series that has a horizontal pattern shifting to a new level. We discussed a situation in which the gasoline distributor signed a contract with the Vermont Sate Police to provide gasoline for state police cars located in southern Vermont. Table 15.2 shows the number of gallons of gasoline sold for the original time series and the 10 weeks after signing the new contract, and Figure 15.2 shows the corresponding time series plot. Note the change in level in week 13 for the resulting time series. When a shift to a new level like this occurs, it takes a long time for the forecasting method that uses the average of all the historical data to adjust to the new level of the time series. But in this case the simple naïve method adjusts very rapidly to the change in level because it uses the most recent observation available as the forecast.

Measures of forecast accuracy are important factors in comparing different forecasting methods; but we have to be careful to not rely upon them too heavily. Good judgment and knowledge about business conditions that might affect the forecast also have to be carefully considered when selecting a method. In addition, historical forecast accuracy is not the only consideration, especially if the time series is likely to change in the future.

In the next section we will introduce more sophisticated methods for developing forecasts for a time series that exhibits a horizontal pattern. Using the measures of forecast accuracy developed here, we will be able to determine whether such methods provide more accurate forecasts than we obtained using the simple approaches illustrated in this section. The methods that we will introduce also have the advantage that they adapt well in situations where the time series changes to a new level. The ability of a forecasting method to adapt quickly to changes in level is an important consideration, especially in short-term forecasting situations.

15.3   MOVING AVERAGES AND EXPONENTIAL SMOOTHING

In this section we discuss three forecasting methods that are appropriate for a time series with a horizontal pattern: moving averages, weighted moving averages, and exponential smoothing. These methods also adapt well to changes in the level of a horizontal pattern such as what we saw with the extended gasoline sales time series (Table 15.2 and Figure 15.2). However, without modification they are not appropriate when significant trend, cyclical, or seasonal effects are present. Because the objective of each of these methods is to "smooth out" the random fluctuations in the time series, they are referred to as smoothing methods. These methods are easy to use and generally provide a high level of accuracy for short-range forecasts, such as a forecast for the next time period.

Moving Averages

The moving averages method uses the average of the most recent k data values in the time series as the forecast for the next period. Mathematically, a moving average forecast of order k is as follows:

$$F_{t+1} = \frac{\sum(\text{most recent } k \text{ data values})}{k} = \frac{Y_1 + Y_{t-1} + \cdots + Y_{t-k+1}}{k} \qquad (15.1)$$

where

$$F_{t+1} = \text{forecast of the time series for period } t + 1$$

The term *moving* is used because every time a new observation becomes available for the time series, it replaces the oldest observation in the equation and a new average is computed. As a result, the average will change, or move, as new observations become available.

To illustrate the moving averages method, let us return to the gasoline sales data in Table 15.1 and Figure 15.1. The time series plot in Figure 15.1 indicates that the gasoline sales time series has a horizontal pattern. Thus, the smoothing methods of this section are applicable.

To use moving averages to forecast a time series, we must first select the order, or number of time series values, to be included in the moving average. If only the most recent values of the time series are considered relevant, a small value of k is preferred. If more past values are considered relevant, then a larger value of k is better. As mentioned earlier, a time series with a horizontal pattern can shift to a new level over time. A moving average will adapt to the new level of the series and resume providing good forecasts in k periods. Thus, a smaller value of k will track shifts in a time series more quickly. But larger values of k will be more effective in smoothing out the random fluctuations over time. So managerial judgment based on an understanding of the behavior of a time series is helpful in choosing a good value for k.

To illustrate how moving averages can be used to forecast gasoline sales, we will use a three-week moving average ($k = 3$). We begin by computing the forecast of sales in week 4 using the average of the time series values in weeks 1–3.

$$F_4 = \text{average of weeks } 1\text{--}3 = \frac{17 + 21 + 19}{3} = 19$$

Thus, the moving average forecast of sales in week 4 is 19, or 19,000 gallons of gasoline. Because the actual value observed in week 4 is 23, the forecast error in week 4 is $23 - 19 = 4$.

Next, we compute the forecast of sales in week 5 by averaging the time series values in weeks 2–4.

$$F_5 = \text{average of weeks } 2\text{--}4 = \frac{21 + 19 + 23}{3} = 21$$

Hence, the forecast of sales in week 5 is 21 and the error associated with this forecast is $18 - 21 = -3$. A complete summary of the three-week moving average forecasts for the gasoline sales time series is provided in Table 15.9. Figure 15.7 shows the original time series plot and the three-week moving average forecasts. Note how the graph of the moving average forecasts has tended to smooth out the random fluctuations in the time series.

To forecast sales in week 13, the next time period in the future, we simply compute the average of the time series values in weeks 10, 11, and 12.

$$F_{13} = \text{average of weeks } 10\text{--}12 = \frac{20 + 15 + 22}{3} = 19$$

Thus, the forecast for week 13 is 19, or 19,000 gallons of gasoline.

Forecast Accuracy   In Section 15.2 we discussed three measures of forecast accuracy: mean absolute error (MAE), mean squared error (MSE), and mean absolute percentage error (MAPE). Using the three-week moving average calculations in Table 15.9, the values for these three measures of forecast accuracy are

TABLE 15.9   SUMMARY OF THREE-WEEK MOVING AVERAGE CALCULATIONS

Week	Time Series Value	Forecast	Forecast Error	Absolute Value of Forecast Error	Squared Forecast Error	Percentage Error	Absolute Value of Percentage Error
1	17						
2	21						
3	19						
4	23	19	4	4	16	17.39	17.39
5	18	21	−3	3	9	−16.67	16.67
6	16	20	−4	4	16	−25.00	25.00
7	20	19	1	1	1	5.00	5.00
8	18	18	0	0	0	0.00	0.00
9	22	18	4	4	16	18.18	18.18
10	20	20	0	0	0	0.00	0.00
11	15	20	−5	5	25	−33.33	33.33
12	22	19	3	3	9	13.64	13.64
		Totals	0	24	92	−20.79	129.21

FIGURE 15.7   GASOLINE SALES TIME SERIES PLOT AND THREE-WEEK MOVING AERAGE FORECASTS

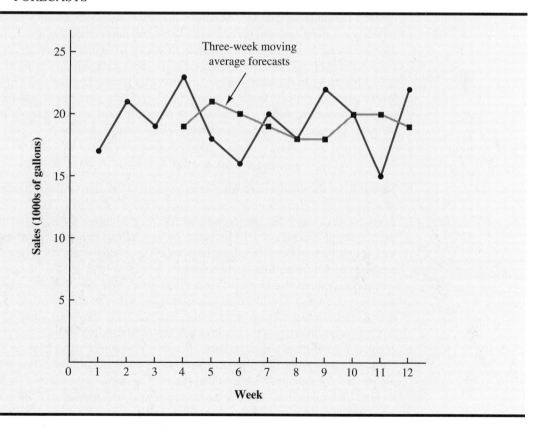

$$\text{MAE} = \frac{24}{9} = 2.67$$

$$\text{MSE} = \frac{92}{9} = 10.22$$

$$\text{MAPE} = \frac{129.21}{9} = 14.36\%$$

In situations where you need to compare forecasting methods for different time periods, such as comparing a forecast of weekly sales to a forecast of monthly sales, relative measures such as MAPE are preferred.

In Section 15.2 we showed that using the most recent observation as the forecast for the next week (a moving average of order $k = 1$) resulted in values of MAE = 3.73; MSE = 16.27; and MAPE = 19.24%. Thus, in each case the three-week moving average approach provided more accurate forecasts than simply using the most recent observation as the forecast.

To determine whether a moving average with a different order k can provide more accurate forecasts, we recommend using trial and error to determine the value of k that minimizes MSE. For the gasoline sales time series, it can be shown that the minimum value of MSE corresponds to a moving average of order $k = 6$ with MSE = 6.79. If we are willing to assume that the order of the moving average that is best for the historical data will also be best for future values of the time series, the most accurate moving average forecasts of gasoline sales can be obtained using a moving average of order $k = 6$.

Weighted Moving Averages

In the moving averages method, each observation in the moving average calculation receives the same weight. One variation, known as weighted moving averages, involves selecting a different weight for each data value and then computing a weighted average of the most recent k values as the forecast. In most cases, the most recent observation receives the most weight, and the weight decreases for older data values. Let us use the gasoline sales time series to illustrate the computation of a weighted three-week moving average. We assign a weight of ³⁄₆ to the most recent observation, a weight of ²⁄₆ to the second most recent observation, and a weight of ¹⁄₆ to the third most recent observation. Using this weighted average, our forecast for week 4 is computed as follows:

$$\text{Forecast for week 4} = \tfrac{1}{6}(17) + \tfrac{2}{6}(21) + \tfrac{3}{6}(19) = 19.33$$

Note that for the weighted moving average method the sum of the weights is equal to 1.

A moving average forecast of order $k = 3$ is just a special case of the weighted moving averages method in which each weight is equal to ⅓.

Forecast Accuracy   To use the weighted moving averages method, we must first select the number of data values to be included in the weighted moving average and then choose weights for each of the data values. In general, if we believe that the recent past is a better predictor of the future than the distant past, larger weights should be given to the more recent observations. However, when the time series is highly variable, selecting approximately equal weights for the data values may be best. The only requirements in selecting the weights are that they be nonnegative and that their sum must equal 1. To determine whether one particular combination of number of data values and weights provides a more accurate forecast than another combination, we recommend using MSE as the measure of forecast accuracy. That is, if we assume that the combination that is best for the past will also be best for the future, we would use the combination of the number of data values and weights that minimized MSE for the historical time series to forecast the next value in the time series.

Exponential Smoothing

Exponential smoothing also uses a weighted average of past time series values as a forecast; it is a special case of the weighted moving averages method in which we select only one weight—the weight for the most recent observation. The weights for the other data values are computed automatically and become smaller as the observations move farther into the past. The exponential smoothing model follows:

$$F_{t+1} = \alpha Y_t + (1 - \alpha)F_t \tag{15.2}$$

where

$$F_{t+1} = \text{forecast of the time series for period } t + 1$$
$$Y_t = \text{actual value of the time series in period } t$$
$$F_t = \text{forecast of the time series for period } t$$
$$\alpha = \text{smoothing constant } (0 \leq \alpha \leq 1)$$

Equation (15.2) shows that the forecast for period $t + 1$ is a weighted average of the actual value in period t and the forecast for period t. The weight given to the actual value in period t is the smoothing constant α and the weight given to the forecast in period t is $1 - \alpha$. It turns out that the exponential smoothing forecast for any period is actually a weighted average of *all the previous actual values* of the time series. Let us illustrate by working with a time series involving only three periods of data: Y_1, Y_2, and Y_3.

To initiate the calculations, we let F_1 equal the actual value of the time series in period 1; that is, $F_1 = Y_1$. Hence, the forecast for period 2 is

$$F_2 = \alpha Y_1 + (1 - \alpha)F_1$$
$$= \alpha Y_1 + (1 - \alpha)Y_1$$
$$= Y_1$$

We see that the exponential smoothing forecast for period 2 is equal to the actual value of the time series in period 1.

The forecast for period 3 is

$$F_3 = \alpha Y_2 + (1-\alpha)F_2 = \alpha Y_2 + (1-\alpha)Y_1$$

Finally, substituting this expression for F_3 into the expression for F_4, we obtain

$$F_4 = \alpha Y_3 + (1-\alpha)F_3$$
$$= \alpha Y_3 + (1-\alpha)[\alpha Y_2 + (1-\alpha)Y_1]$$
$$= \alpha Y_3 + \alpha(1-\alpha)Y_2 + (1-\alpha)^2 Y_1$$

We now see that F_4 is a weighted average of the first three time series values. The sum of the coefficients, or weights, for Y_1, Y_2, and Y_3 equals 1. A similar argument can be made to show that, in general, any forecast F_{t+1} is a weighted average of all the previous time series values.

Despite the fact that exponential smoothing provides a forecast that is a weighted average of all past observations, all past data do not need to be saved to compute the forecast for the next period. In fact, Equation (15.2) shows that once the value for the smoothing constant α is selected, only two pieces of information are needed to compute the forecast: Y_t, the actual value of the time series in period t; and F_t, the forecast for period t.

To illustrate the exponential smoothing approach to forecasting, let us again consider the gasoline sales time series in Table 15.1 and Figure 15.2. As indicated previously, to start the calculations we set the exponential smoothing forecast for period 2 equal to the actual value of the time series in period 1. Thus, with $Y_1 = 17$, we set $F_2 = 17$ to initiate the computations. Referring to the time series data in Table 15.1, we find an actual time series value in period 2 of $Y_2 = 21$. Thus, period 2 has a forecast error of $21 - 17 = 4$.

Continuing with the exponential smoothing computations using a smoothing constant of $\alpha = 0.2$, we obtain the following forecast for period 3:

$$F_3 = 0.2Y_2 + 0.8F_2 = 0.2(21) + 0.8(17) = 17.8$$

Once the actual time series value in period 3, $Y_3 = 19$, is known, we can generate a forecast for period 4 as follows:

$$F_4 = 0.2Y_3 + 0.8F_3 = 0.2(19) + 0.8(17.8) = 18.04$$

Continuing the exponential smoothing calculations, we obtain the weekly forecast values shown in Table 15.10. Note that we have not shown an exponential smoothing forecast or a forecast error for week 1 because no forecast was made. For week 12, we have $Y_{12} = 22$ and $F_{12} = 18.48$. We can use this information to generate a forecast for week 13.

$$F_{13} = 0.2Y_{12} + 0.8F_{12} = 0.2(22) + 0.8(18.48) = 19.18$$

Thus, the exponential smoothing forecast of the amount sold in week 13 is 19.18, or 19,180 gallons of gasoline. With this forecast, the firm can make plans and decisions accordingly.

TABLE 15.10   SUMMARY OF THE EXPONENTIAL SMOOTHING FORECASTS AND FORECAST ERRORS FOR THE GASOLINE SALES TIME SERIES WITH SMOOTHING CONSTANT $\alpha = 0.2$

Week	Time Series Value	Forecast	Forecast Error	Squared Forecast Error
1	17			
2	21	17.00	4.00	16.00
3	19	17.80	1.20	1.44
4	23	18.04	4.96	24.60
5	18	19.03	−1.03	1.06
6	16	18.83	−2.83	8.01
7	20	18.26	1.74	3.03
8	18	18.61	−0.61	0.37
9	22	18.49	3.51	12.32
10	20	19.19	0.81	0.66
11	15	19.35	−4.35	18.92
12	22	18.48	3.52	12.39
		Totals	10.92	98.80

FIGURE 15.9   BICYCLE SALES TIME SERIES PLOT

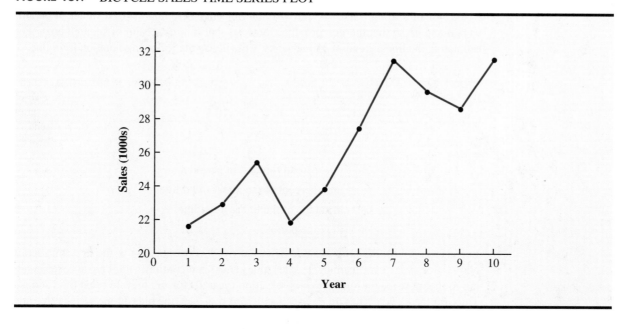

a reasonable approximation of the long-run movement in the series. We can use curve fitting to develop such a linear trend line for the bicycle sales time series.

Curve fitting can be used to find a best-fitting line to a set of data that exhibits a linear trend. The criterion used to determine the best-fitting line is one we used in the previous section. Curve fitting minimizes the sum of squared error between the observed and fitted time series data where the model is a trend line. We build a nonlinear optimization model

FIGURE 15.10   TREND REPRESENTED BY A LINEAR FUNCTION FOR THE BICYCLE SALES
                   TIME SERIES

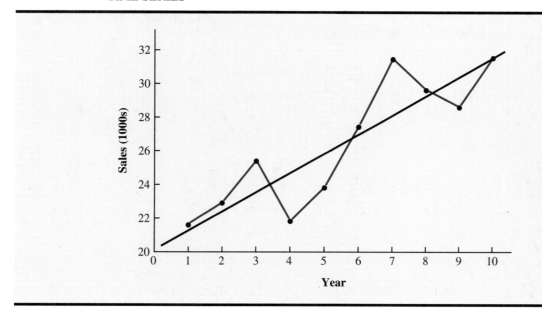

that is similar to the model we used to find the best value of α for exponential smoothing. In the case of a straight line $y = a + mx$, our objective is to find the best values of parameters a and m, so that the line provides forecasts that minimize sum of squared error. For estimating the linear trend in a time series, we will use the following notation for a line:

$$T_t = b_0 + b_1 t \qquad (15.8)$$

where

$$T_t = \text{linear trend forecast in period } t$$
$$b_0 = \text{the intercept of the linear trend line}$$
$$b_1 = \text{the slope of the linear trend line}$$
$$t = \text{the time period}$$

In equation (15.8), the time variable begins at $t = 1$ corresponding to the first time series observation (year 1 for the bicycle sales time series) and continues until $t = n$ corresponding to the most recent time series observation (year 10 for the bicycle sales time series). Thus, for the bicycle sales time series $t = 1$ corresponds to the oldest time series value and $t = 10$ corresponds to the most recent year.

Let us formulate the curve-fitting model that will give us the best values of b_0 and b_1 in equation (15.8) for the bicycle sales data. The objective is to minimize the sum of squared error between the observed values of the time series given in Table 15.11 and the forecasted values for each period:

$$\text{Min } \{(21.6 - T_1)^2 + (22.9 - T_2)^2 + (22.5 - T_3)^2 + (21.9 - T_4)^2 + (23.9 - T_5)^2$$
$$(27.5 - T_6)^2 + (31.5 - T_7)^2 + (29.7 - T_8)^2 + (28.6 - T_9)^2 + (31.4 - T_{10})^2\}$$

The only constraints then are to define the forecasts as a linear function of parameters b_0 and b_1 as described by equation (15.8):

$$T_1 = b_0 + b_1 1$$
$$T_2 = b_0 + b_1 2$$
$$T_3 = b_0 + b_1 3$$
$$T_4 = b_0 + b_1 4$$
$$T_5 = b_0 + b_1 5$$
$$T_6 = b_0 + b_1 6$$
$$T_7 = b_0 + b_1 7$$
$$T_8 = b_0 + b_1 8$$
$$T_9 = b_0 + b_1 9$$
$$T_{10} = b_0 + b_1 10$$

The entire nonlinear curve-fitting optimization model is:

$$\text{Min } \{(21.6 - T_1)^2 + (22.9 - T_2)^2 + (22.5 - T_3)^2 + (21.9 - T_4)^2 + (23.9 - T_5)^2$$
$$(27.5 - T_6)^2 + (31.5 - T_7)^2 + (29.7 - T_8)^2 + (28.6 - T_9)^2 + (31.4 - T_{10})^2\}$$

s.t.

$$T_1 = b_0 + b_1 1$$
$$T_2 = b_0 + b_1 2$$
$$T_3 = b_0 + b_1 3$$
$$T_4 = b_0 + b_1 4$$
$$T_5 = b_0 + b_1 5$$
$$T_6 = b_0 + b_1 6$$
$$T_7 = b_0 + b_1 7$$
$$T_8 = b_0 + b_1 8$$
$$T_9 = b_0 + b_1 9$$
$$T_{10} = b_0 + b_1 10$$

WEB file

Bicycle_Linear

Note that b_0, b_1, and T_t are decision variables and that none are restricted to be nonnegative.

The solution to this problem may be obtained using Excel Solver or LINGO. The solution is $b_0 = 20.4$ and $b_1 = 1.1$ with a sum of squared error of 30.7. Therefore, the trend equation is

$$T_t = 20.4 + 1.1t$$

The slope of 1.1 indicates that over the past 10 years the firm experienced an average growth in sales of about 1100 units per year. If we assume that the past 10-year trend in sales is a good indicator of the future, this trend equation can be used to develop forecasts for future time periods. For example, substituting $t = 11$ into the equation yields next year's trend projection or forecast, T_{11}.

$$T_{11} = 20.4 + 1.1(11) = 32.5$$

Thus, using trend projection, we would forecast sales of 32,500 bicycles for year 11.

Table 15.12 shows the computation of the minimized sum of squared errors for the bicycle sales time series. As previously noted, minimizing sum of squared error also minimizes the commonly used measure of accuracy, mean squared error (MSE). For the bicycle sales time series

$$\text{MSE} = \frac{\sum_{t=1}^{n} (Y_t - F_t)^2}{n} = \frac{30.7}{10} = 3.07$$

We may write a general optimization curve-fitting model for linear trend curve fitting for a time series with n data points. Let Y_t = the observed value of the time series in period t. The general model is

$$\text{Min} \sum_{t=1}^{n} (Y_t - T_t)^2 \tag{15.9}$$

s.t.
$$T_t = b_0 + b_1 t \qquad t = 1,2,3 \ldots . n \tag{15.10}$$

TABLE 15.12   SUMMARY OF THE LINEAR TREND FORECASTS AND FORECAST ERRORS FOR THE BICYCLE SALES TIME SERIES

Week	Sales (1000s) Y_t	Forecast T_t	Forecast Error	Squared Forecast Error
1	21.6	21.5	0.1	0.01
2	22.9	22.6	0.3	0.09
3	25.5	23.7	1.8	3.24
4	21.9	24.8	−2.9	8.41
5	23.9	25.9	−2.0	4.00
6	27.5	27.0	0.5	0.25
7	31.5	28.1	3.4	11.56
8	29.7	29.2	0.5	0.25
9	28.6	30.3	−1.7	2.89
10	31.4	31.4	0.0	0.00
			Total	30.70

The decision variables in this optimization model are b_0 the intercept and b_1 the slope of the line. The variables T_t, the fitted forecast for period t, are definitional variables, as discussed in Chapter 5. Note that none of these are restricted to be nonnegative. This model will have $n + 2$ decision variables and n constraints, one for each data point in the time series.

NOTES AND COMMENTS

1. The optimization model given by equations (15.9) and (15.10) is easily generalized for other types of models. Given the objective is to minimize the sum of squared errors, to test a different forecasting model, you only need to change the form of equation (15.10). We will see an example of this in the forthcoming seciton on nonlinear trend. Examples of both LINGO and Excel Solver models are provided in the appendices to this chapter.

2. Statistical packages such as Minitab and SAS, as well as Excel have routines to perform curve fitting under the label regression analysis. Regression analysis solves the curve-fitting problem of minimizing the sum of squared error, but also under certain assumptions, allows the analyst to make statistical statements about the parameters and the forecasts.

Nonlinear Trend

The use of a linear function to model trend is common. However, as we discussed previously, sometimes time series have a curvilinear or nonlinear trend. As an example, consider the annual revenue in millions of dollars for a cholesterol drug for the first ten years of sales. Table 15.13 shows the time series and Figure 15.11 shows the corresponding time series plot. For instance, revenue in year 1 was \$23.1 million; revenue in year 2 was \$21.3 million; and so on. The time series plot indicates an overall increasing or upward trend. But, unlike the bicycle sales time series, a linear trend does not appear to be appropriate. Instead, a curvilinear function appears to be needed to model the long-term trend.

TABLE 15.13 CHOLESTEROL REVENUE TIME SERIES ($ MILLIONS)

Year	Revenue ($ millions)
1	23.1
2	21.3
3	27.4
4	34.6
5	33.8
6	43.2
7	59.5
8	64.4
9	74.2
10	99.3

WEB file

Cholesterol

Quadratic Trend Equation A variety of nonlinear functions can be used to develop an estimate of the trend for the cholesterol time series. For instance, consider the following quadratic trend equation:

$$T_t = b_0 + b_1 t + b_2 t^2 \tag{15.11}$$

For the cholesterol time series, $t = 1$ corresponds to year 1, $t = 2$ corresponds to year 2, and so on.

Let us construct the optimization model to find the values of b_0, b_1, and b_2 that minimize the sum of squared errors. Note that we need the value of t and the value of t^2 for each period.

FIGURE 15.11 CHOLESTEROL REVENUE TIMES SERIES PLOT ($ MILLIONS)

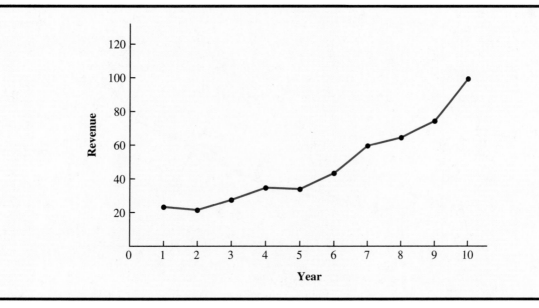

The model to find the best values of b_0, b_1, and b_2 so that the sum of squared error is minimized is as follows:

$$\text{Min } \{(23.1 - T_1)^2 + (21.3 - T_2)^2 + (27.4 - T_3)^2 + (34.6 - T_4)^2 + (33.8 - T_5)^2$$
$$(43.2 - T_6)^2 + (59.5 - T_7)^2 + (64.4 - T_8)^2 + (74.2 - T_9)^2 + (99.3 - T_{10})^2\}$$

s.t.

$$T_1 = b_0 + b_1 1 + b_2 1$$
$$T_2 = b_0 + b_1 2 + b_2 4$$
$$T_3 = b_0 + b_1 3 + b_2 9$$
$$T_4 = b_0 + b_1 4 + b_2 16$$
$$T_5 = b_0 + b_1 5 + b_2 25$$
$$T_6 = b_0 + b_1 6 + b_2 36$$
$$T_7 = b_0 + b_1 7 + b_2 49$$
$$T_8 = b_0 + b_1 8 + b_2 64$$
$$T_9 = b_0 + b_1 9 + b_2 81$$
$$T_{10} = b_0 + b_1 10 + b_2 100$$

Cholesterol_Quad

This model may be solved with Excel Solver or LINGO. The optimal values from this optimization are $b_0 = 24.182$, $b_1 = -2.11$, and $b_2 = 0.922$ with a sum of squared errors of 110.65 and an MSE $= 110.65/10 = 11.065$. The fitted curve is therefore

$$T_t = 24.182 - 2.11\,t + 0.922\,t^2$$

Figure 15.12 shows the observed data along with this curve.

FIGURE 15.12   TIME SERIES QUADRATIC TREND FOR THE CHOLESTEROL SALES TIME SERIES

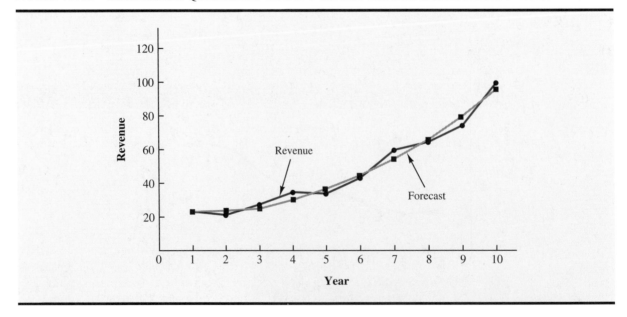

Exponential Trend Equation Another alternative that can be used to model the nonlinear pattern exhibited by the cholesterol time series is to fit an exponential model to the data. For instance, consider the following exponential growth trend equation:

$$T_t = b_0 (b_1)^t \qquad (15.12)$$

Like equation (15.11), this model is a nonlinear function of period t. As with the quadratic case, we can update equation (15.12) to yield the values of b_0 and b_1 that minimize the sum of squared errors. For the cholesterol sales data, minimizing the sum of squared errors yields the following curve-fitting model:

Min $\{(23.1 - T_1)^2 + (21.3 - T_2)^2 + (27.4 - T_3)^2 + (34.6 - T_4)^2 + (33.8 - T_5)^2$

$(43.2 - T_6)^2 + (59.5 - T_7)^2 + (64.4 - T_8)^2 + (74.2 - T_9)^2 + (99.3 - T_{10})^2\}$

s.t.

$$T_1 = b_0 b_1{}^1$$
$$T_2 = b_0 b_1{}^2$$
$$T_3 = b_0 b_1{}^3$$
$$T_4 = b_0 b_1{}^4$$
$$T_5 = b_0 b_1{}^5$$
$$T_6 = b_0 b_1{}^6$$
$$T_7 = b_0 b_1{}^7$$
$$T_8 = b_0 b_1{}^8$$
$$T_9 = b_0 b_1{}^9$$
$$T_{10} = b_0 b_1{}^{10}$$

This may be solved with LINGO or Excel Solver. The optimal values are $b_0 = 15.42$ and $b_1 = 1.2$ with a sum of squared errors of 123.12 and an MSE $= 123.12/10 = 12.312$. Based on MSE, the quadratic model provides a better fit than the exponential model.

NOTES AND COMMENTS

The exponential model (15.12) is nonlinear and the curve-fitting optimization based on it can be difficult to solve. We suggest using a number of different starting values to ensure that the solution found is a global optimum. Also, we found it helpful to bound b_0 and b_1 away from zero (add constraints $b_0 \geq 0.01$ and $b_1 \geq 0.01$).

15.5 SEASONALITY

In this section we show how to develop forecasts for a time series that has a seasonal pattern. To the extent that seasonality exists, we need to incorporate it into our forecasting models to ensure accurate forecasts. We begin the section by considering a seasonal time series with no trend and then discuss how to model seasonality with trend.

Seasonality Without Trend

As an example, consider the number of umbrellas sold at a clothing store over the past five years. Table 15.14 shows the time series and Figure 15.13 shows the corresponding time series plot. The time series plot does not indicate any long-term trend in sales. In fact, unless you look carefully at the data, you might conclude that the data follow a horizontal pattern and that single exponential smoothing could be used to forecast sales. However, closer inspection of the time series plot reveals a pattern in the data. That is, the first and third quarters have moderate sales, the second quarter has the highest sales, and the fourth quarter tends to be the lowest quarter in terms of sales volume. Thus, we would conclude that a quarterly seasonal pattern is present.

   We can model a time series with a seasonal pattern by treating the season as a *categorical variable*. Categorical variables are data used to categorize observations of data. When a categorical variable has k levels, $k - 1$ dummy or 0-1 variables are required. So, if there are four seasons, we need three dummy variables. For instance, in the umbrella sales time series the quarter each observation corresponds to is treated as a season; it is a categorical variable with four levels: Quarter 1, Quarter 2, Quarter 3, and Quarter 4. Thus, to model the seasonal effects in the umbrella time series we need $4 - 1 = 3$ dummy variables. The three dummy variables can be coded as follows:

$$\text{Qtr1}=\begin{cases}1 \text{ if Quarter 1} \\ 0 \text{ otherwise}\end{cases} \qquad \text{Qtr2}=\begin{cases}1 \text{ if Quarter 2} \\ 0 \text{ otherwise}\end{cases} \qquad \text{Qtr3}=\begin{cases}1 \text{ if Quarter 3} \\ 0 \text{ otherwise}\end{cases}$$

Using F_t to denote the forecasted value of sales for period t, the general form of the equation relating the number of umbrellas sold to the quarter the sale takes place follows:

$$F_t = b_0 + b_1 \text{ Qtr1}_t + b_2 \text{ Qtr2}_t + b_3 \text{ Qtr3}_t$$

TABLE 15.14   UMBRELLA SALES TIME SERIES

Umbrella

Year	Quarter	Sales
1	1	125
	2	153
	3	106
	4	88
2	1	118
	2	161
	3	133
	4	102
3	1	138
	2	144
	3	113
	4	80
4	1	109
	2	137
	3	125
	4	109
5	1	130
	2	165
	3	128
	4	96

FIGURE 15.13 UMBRELLA SALES TIME SERIES PLOT

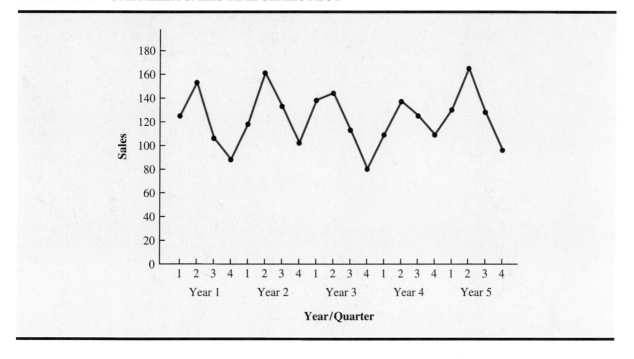

Table 15.15 is the umbrella sales time series with the coded values of the dummy variables shown. We may use an optimization model to find the values of b_0, b_1, b_2, and b_3 that minimize the sum of squared error. The model is as follows:

$$\text{Min } \{(125 - F_1)^2 + (153 - F_2)^2 + (106 - F_3)^2 \cdots + (96 - F_{20})^2\}$$

s.t.

$$F_1 = b_0 + 1b_1 + 0b_2 + 0b_3$$
$$F_2 = b_0 + 0b_1 + 1b_2 + 0b_3$$
$$F_3 = b_0 + 0b_1 + 0b_2 + 1b_3$$
$$F_4 = b_0 + 0b_1 + 0b_2 + 0b_3$$
$$\vdots$$
$$F_{17} = b_0 + 1b_1 + 0b_2 + 0b_3$$
$$F_{18} = b_0 + 0b_1 + 1b_2 + 0b_3$$
$$F_{19} = b_0 + 0b_1 + 0b_2 + 1b_3$$
$$F_{20} = b_0 + 0b_1 + 0b_2 + 0b_3$$

Umbrella_Seas

Note that we have numbered the observations in Table 15.15 as periods 1–20. For example, year 3, quarter 3 is observation 11.

This model may be solved with LINGO or Excel Solver. Using the data in Table 15.15 and the above optimization model, we obtained the following equation:

$$F_t = 95.0 + 29.0 \text{ Qtr1}_t + 57.0 \text{ Qtr2}_t + 26.0 \text{ Qtr3}_t \qquad (15.13)$$

TABLE 15.15   UMBRELLA SALES TIME SERIES WITH DUMMY VARIABLES

Period	Year	Quarter	Qtr1	Qtr2	Qtr3	Sales
1	1	1	1	0	0	125
2		2	0	1	0	153
3		3	0	0	1	106
4		4	0	0	0	88
5	2	1	1	0	0	118
6		2	0	1	0	161
7		3	0	0	1	133
8		4	0	0	0	102
9	3	1	1	0	0	138
10		2	0	1	0	144
11		3	0	0	1	113
12		4	0	0	0	80
13	4	1	1	0	0	109
14		2	0	1	0	137
15		3	0	0	1	125
16		4	0	0	0	109
17	5	1	1	0	0	130
18		2	0	1	0	165
19		3	0	0	1	128
20		4	0	0	0	96

We can use equation (15.13) to forecast quarterly sales for next year.

$$\text{Quarter 1: Sales} = 95.0 + 29.0(1) + 57.0(0) + 26.0(0) = 124$$

$$\text{Quarter 2: Sales} = 95.0 + 29.0(0) + 57.0(1) + 26.0(0) = 152$$

$$\text{Quarter 3: Sales} = 95.0 + 29.0(0) + 57.0(0) + 26.0(1) = 121$$

$$\text{Quarter 4: Sales} = 95.0 + 29.0(0) + 57.0(1) + 26.0(0) = 95$$

It is interesting to note that we could have obtained the quarterly forecasts for next year by simply computing the average number of umbrellas sold in each quarter, as shown in the following table:

Year	Quarter 1	Quarter 2	Quarter 3	Quarter 4
1	125	153	106	88
2	118	161	133	102
3	138	144	113	80
4	109	137	125	109
5	130	165	128	96
Average	124	152	121	95

Nonetheless, for more complex types of problem situations, such as dealing with a time series that has both trend and seasonal effects, this simple averaging approach will not work.

TABLE 15.16   TELEVISION SET SALES TIME SERIES

TVSales

Year	Quarter	Sales (1000s)
1	1	4.8
	2	4.1
	3	6.0
	4	6.5
2	1	5.8
	2	5.2
	3	6.8
	4	7.4
3	1	6.0
	2	5.6
	3	7.5
	4	7.8
4	1	6.3
	2	5.9
	3	8.0
	4	8.4

Seasonality and Trend

We now extend the curve-fitting approach to include situations where the time series contains both a seasonal effect and a linear trend, by showing how to forecast the quarterly television set sales time series introduced in Section 15.1. The data for the television set time series are shown in Table 15.16. The time series plot in Figure 15.14 indicates that sales are lowest in the second quarter of each year and increase in quarters 3 and 4. Thus, we conclude that a seasonal pattern exists for television set sales. But the time series also has an upward linear trend that will need to be accounted for in order to develop accurate forecasts of quarterly sales. This is easily done by combining the dummy variable approach for handling seasonality with the approach we discussed in Section 15.3 for handling linear trend.

The general form of the equation for modeling both the quarterly seasonal effects and the linear trend in the television set time series is

$$F_t = b_0 + b_1 \, \text{Qtr1}_t + b_2 \, \text{Qtr2}_t + b_3 \, \text{Qtr3}_t + b_4 t$$

where

F_t = forecast of sales in period t

Qtr1_t = 1 if time period t corresponds to the first quarter of the year; 0 otherwise

Qtr2_t = 1 if time period t corresponds to the second quarter of the year; 0 otherwise

Qtr3_t = 1 if period t corresponds to the third quarter of the year; 0 otherwise

t = time period

WEB file

TVSales_Seas_Trend

Table 15.17 is the revised television set sales time series that includes the coded values of the dummy variables and the time period t. Using the data in Table 15.17 with the sum

FIGURE 15.14   TELEVISION SET SALES TIME SERIES PLOT

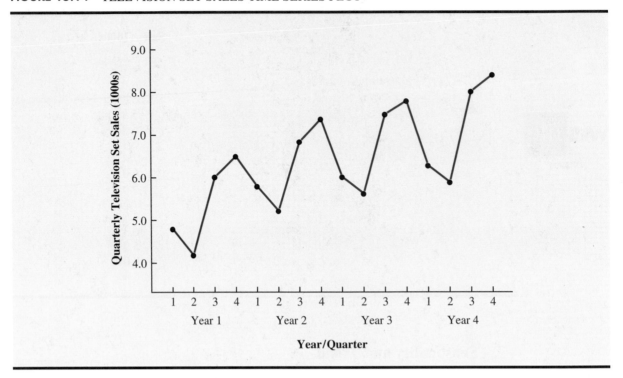

TABLE 15.17   TELEVISION SET SALES TIME SERIES WITH DUMMY VARIABLES
AND TIME PERIOD

Period	Year	Quarter	Qtr1	Qtr2	Qtr3	Period	Sales (1000s)
1	1	1	1	0	0	1	4.8
2		2	0	1	0	2	4.1
3		3	0	0	1	3	6.0
4		4	0	0	0	4	6.5
5	2	1	1	0	0	5	5.8
6		2	0	1	0	6	5.2
7		3	0	0	1	7	6.8
8		4	0	0	0	8	7.4
9	3	1	1	0	0	9	6.0
10		2	0	1	0	10	5.6
11		3	0	0	1	11	7.5
12		4	0	0	0	12	7.8
13	4	1	1	0	0	13	6.3
14		2	0	1	0	14	5.9
15		3	0	0	1	15	8.0
16		4	0	0	0	16	8.4

of squared error minimization model with the seasonal and trend components, we obtain the following equation:

$$F_t = 6.07 - 1.36 \, \text{Qtr1}_t - 2.03 \, \text{Qtr2}_t - 0.304 \, \text{Qtr3}_t + 0.146 \, t \qquad (15.14)$$

We can now use equation (15.14) to forecast quarterly sales for next year. Next year is year 5 for the television set sales time series; that is, time periods 17, 18, 19, and 20.

Forecast for Time Period 17 (quarter 1 in year 5)

$$F_{17} = 6.07 - 1.36(1) - 2.03(0) - 0.304(0) + 0.146(17) = 7.19$$

Forecast for Time Period 18 (quarter 2 in year 5)

$$F_{18} = 6.07 - 1.36(0) - 2.03(1) - 0.304(0) + 0.146(18) = 6.67$$

Forecast for Time Period 19 (quarter 3 in year 5)

$$F_{19} = 6.07 - 1.36(0) - 2.03(0) - 0.304(1) + 0.146(19) = 8.54$$

Forecast for Time Period 20 (quarter 4 in year 5)

$$F_{20} = 6.07 - 1.36(0) - 2.03(0) - 0.304(0) + 0.146(20) = 8.99$$

Thus, accounting for the seasonal effects and the linear trend in television set sales, the estimates of quarterly sales in year 5 are 7190, 6670, 8540, and 8990.

The dummy variables in the equation actually provide four equations, one for each quarter. For instance, if time period t corresponds to quarter 1, the estimate of quarterly sales is

Quarter 1: Sales $= 6.07 - 1.36(1) - 2.03(0) - 0.304(0) + 0.146t = 4.71 + 0.146t$

Similarly, if time period t corresponds to quarters 2, 3, and 4, the estimates of quarterly sales are

Quarter 2: Sales $= 6.07 - 1.36(0) - 2.03(1) - 0.304(0) + 0.146t = 4.04 + 0.146t$

Quarter 3: Sales $= 6.07 - 1.36(0) - 2.03(0) - 0.304(1) + 0.146t = 5.77 + 0.146t$

Quarter 4: Sales $= 6.07 - 1.36(0) - 2.03(0) - 0.304(0) + 0.146t = 6.07 + 0.146t$

The slope of the trend line for each quarterly forecast equation is 0.146, indicating a growth in sales of about 146 sets per quarter. The only difference in the four equations is that they have different intercepts.

Models Based on Monthly Data

In the preceding television set sales example, we showed how dummy variables can be used to account for the quarterly seasonal effects in the time series. Because there were four levels for the categorical variable season, three dummy variables were required. However, many businesses use monthly rather than quarterly forecasts. For monthly data, season is a categorical variable with 12 levels and thus $12 - 1 = 11$ dummy variables are required. For example, the 11 dummy variables could be coded as follows:

$$\text{Month1} = \begin{cases} 1 \text{ if January} \\ 0 \text{ otherwise} \end{cases}$$

$$\text{Month2} = \begin{cases} 1 \text{ if February} \\ 0 \text{ otherwise} \end{cases}$$

$$\vdots$$

$$\text{Month11} = \begin{cases} 1 \text{ if November} \\ 0 \text{ otherwise} \end{cases}$$

Whenever a categorical variable such as season has k levels, k – 1 dummy variables are required.

Other than this change, the approach for handling seasonality remains the same.

SUMMARY

This chapter provided an introduction to the basic methods of time series analysis and forecasting. First, we showed that the underlying pattern in the time series can often be identified by constructing a time series plot. Several types of data patterns can be distinguished, including a horizontal pattern, a trend pattern, and a seasonal pattern. The forecasting methods we have discussed are based on which of these patterns are present in the time series.

For a time series with a horizontal pattern, we showed how moving averages and exponential smoothing can be used to develop a forecast. The moving averages method consists of computing an average of past data values and then using that average as the forecast for the next period. In the exponential smoothing method, a weighted average of past time series values is used to compute a forecast. These methods also adapt well when a horizontal pattern shifts to a different level but maintains a horizontal pattern at the new level.

An important factor in determining what forecasting method to use involves the accuracy of the method. We discussed three measures of forecast accuracy: mean absolute error (MAE), mean squared error (MSE), and mean absolute percentage error (MAPE). Each of these measures is designed to determine how well a particular forecasting method is able to reproduce the time series data that are already available. By selecting a method that has the best accuracy for the data already known, we hope to increase the likelihood that we will obtain better forecasts for future time periods.

For time series that have only a long-term linear trend, we showed how curve fitting can be used to make trend projections. For a time series with a curvilinear or nonlinear trend, we showed how curve-fitting optimization can be used to fit a quadratic trend equation or an exponential trend equation to the data.

For a time series with a seasonal trend, we showed how the use of dummy variables can be used to develop an equation with seasonal effects. We then extended the approach to include situations where the time series contains both a seasonal and a linear trend effect by showing how to combine the dummy variable approach for handling seasonality with the approach for handling linear trend.

GLOSSARY

Time series A sequence of observations on a variable measured at successive points in time or over successive periods of time.

Time series plot A graphical presentation of the relationship between time and the time series variable. Time is shown on the horizontal axis and the time series values are shown on the verical axis.

Stationary time series A time series whose statistical properties are independent of time. For a stationary time series the process generating the data has a constant mean and the variability of the time series is constant over time.

Trend pattern A trend pattern exists if the time series plot shows gradual shifts or movements to relatively higher or lower values over a longer period of time.

Seasonal pattern A seasonal pattern exists if the time series plot exhibits a repeating pattern over successive periods. The successive periods are often one-year intervals, which is where the name seasonal pattern comes from.

Cyclical pattern A cyclical pattern exists if the time series plot shows an alternating sequence of points below and above the trend line lasting more than one year.

Forecast error The difference between the actual time series value and the forecast.

Mean absolute error (MAE) The average of the absolute values of the forecast errors.

Mean squared error (MSE) The average of the sum of squared forecast errors.

Mean absolute percentage error (MAPE) The average of the absolute values of the percentage forecast errors.

Moving averages A forecasting method that uses the average of the most recent k data values in the time series as the forecast for the next period.

Weighted moving averages A forecasting method that involves selecting a different weight for the most recent k data values values in the time series and then computing a weighted average of the values. The sum of the weights must equal 1.

Exponential smoothing A forecasting method that uses a weighted average of past time series values as the forecast; it is a special case of the weighted moving averages method in which we select only one weight—the weight for the most recent observation.

Smoothing constant A parameter of the exponential smoothing model that provides the weight given to the most recent time series value in the calculation of the forecast value.

PROBLEMS

1. Consider the following time series data:

Week	1	2	3	4	5	6
Value	18	13	16	11	17	14

Using the naïve method (most recent value) as the forecast for the next week, compute the following measures of forecast accuracy:
a. Mean absolute error
b. Mean squared error

    c. Mean absolute percentage error
    d. What is the forecast for week 7?

2. Refer to the time series data in Problem 1. Using the average of all the historical data as a forecast for the next period, compute the following measures of forecast accuracy:
    a. Mean absolute error
    b. Mean squared error
    c. Mean absolute percentage error
    d. What is the forecast for week 7?

3. Problems 1 and 2 used different forecasting methods. Which method appears to provide the more accurate forecasts for the historical data? Explain.

4. Consider the following time series data:

Month	1	2	3	4	5	6	7
Value	24	13	20	12	19	23	15

    a. Compute MSE using the most recent value as the forecast for the next period. What is the forecast for month 8?
    b. Compute MSE using the average of all the data available as the forecast for the next period. What is the forecast for month 8?
    c. Which method appears to provide the better forecast?

5. Consider the following time series data:

Week	1	2	3	4	5	6
Value	18	13	16	11	17	14

    a. Construct a time series plot. What type of pattern exists in the data?
    b. Develop a three-week moving average for this time series. Compute MSE and a forecast for week 7.
    c. Use $\alpha = 0.2$ to compute the exponential smoothing values for the time series. Compute MSE and a forecast for week 7.
    d. Compare the three-week moving average forecast with the exponential smoothing forecast using $\alpha = 0.2$. Which appears to provide the better forecast based on MSE? Explain.
    e. Use Excel Solver or LINGO to find the value of α that minimizes MSE. (*Hint:* Minimize the sum of squared error.)

6. Consider the following time series data:

Month	1	2	3	4	5	6	7
Value	24	13	20	12	19	23	15

    a. Construct a time series plot. What type of pattern exists in the data?
    b. Develop a three-week moving average for this time series. Compute MSE and a forecast for week 8.
    c. Use $\alpha = 0.2$ to compute the exponential smoothing values for the time series. Compute MSE and a forecast for week 8.

d. Compare the three-week moving average forecast with the exponential smoothing forecast using $\alpha = 0.2$. Which appears to provide the better forecast based on MSE?

e. Use Excel Solver or LINGO to find the value of α that minimizes MSE. (*Hint:* Minimize the sum of squared error.)

7. Refer to the gasoline sales time series data in Table 15.1.

Gasoline

a. Compute four-week and five-week moving averages for the time series.

b. Compute the MSE for the four-week and five-week moving average forecasts.

c. What appears to be the best number of weeks of past data (three, four, or five) to use in the moving average computation? Recall that MSE for the three-week moving average is 10.22.

8. Refer again to the gasoline sales time series data in Table 15.1.

Gasoline

a. Using a weight of $\frac{1}{2}$ for the most recent observation, $\frac{1}{3}$ for the second most recent, and $\frac{1}{6}$ for third most recent, compute a three-week weighted moving average for the time series.

b. Compute the MSE for the weighted moving average in part (a). Do you prefer this weighted moving average to the unweighted moving average? Remember that the MSE for the unweighted moving average is 10.22.

c. Suppose you are allowed to choose any weights as long as they sum to 1. Could you always find a set of weights that would make the MSE at least as small as for a weighted moving average than for an unweighted moving average? Why or why not?

9. With the gasoline time series data from Table 15.1, show the exponential smoothing forecasts using $\alpha = 0.1$.

Gasoline

a. Applying the MSE measure of forecast accuracy, would you prefer a smoothing constant of $\alpha = 0.1$ or $\alpha = 0.2$ for the gasoline sales time series?

b. Are the results the same if you apply MAE as the measure of accuracy?

c. What are the results if MAPE is used?

10. With a smoothing constant of $\alpha = 0.2$, equation (15.5) shows that the forecast for week 13 of the gasoline sales data from Table 15.1 is given by $F_{13} = 0.2Y_{12} + 0.8F_{12}$. However, the forecast for week 12 is given by $F_{12} = 0.2Y_{11} + 0.8F_{11}$. Thus, we could combine these two results to show that the forecast for week 13 can be written

$$F_{13} = 0.2Y_{12} + 0.8(0.2Y_{11} + 0.8F_{11}) = 0.2Y_{12} + 0.16Y_{11} + 0.64F_{11}$$

a. Making use of the fact that $F_{11} = 0.2Y_{10} + 0.8F_{10}$ (and similarly for F_{10} and F_9), continue to expand the expression for F_{13} until it is written in terms of the past data values Y_{12}, Y_{11}, Y_{10}, Y_9, Y_8, and the forecast for period 8.

b. Refer to the coefficients or weights for the past values Y_{12}, Y_{11}, Y_{10}, Y_9, Y_8; what observation can you make about how exponential smoothing weights past data values in arriving at new forecasts? Compare this weighting pattern with the weighting pattern of the moving averages method.

11. For the Hawkins Company, the monthly percentages of all shipments received on time over the past 12 months are 80, 82, 84, 83, 83, 84, 85, 84, 82, 83, 84, and 83.

a. Construct a time series plot. What type of pattern exists in the data?

b. Compare a three-month moving average forecast with an exponential smoothing forecast for $\alpha = 0.2$. Which provides the better forecasts using MSE as the measure of model accuracy?

c. What is the forecast for next month?

12. Corporate triple A bond interest rates for 12 consecutive months follow:

9.5   9.3   9.4   9.6   9.8   9.7   9.8   10.5   9.9   9.7   9.6   9.6

    a. Construct a time series plot. What type of pattern exists in the data?

    b. Develop three-month and four-month moving averages for this time series. Does the three-month or four-month moving average provide the better forecasts based on MSE? Explain.

    c. What is the moving average forecast for the next month?

13. The values of Alabama building contracts (in millions of dollars) for a 12-month period follow:

    240   350   230   260   280   320   220   310   240   310   240   230

    a. Construct a time series plot. What type of pattern exists in the data?

    b. Compare a three-month moving average forecast with an exponential smoothing forecast. Use $\alpha = 0.2$. Which provides the better forecasts based on MSE?

    c. What is the forecast for the next month?

14. The following time series shows the sales of a particular product over the past 12 months:

Month	Sales	Month	Sales
1	105	7	145
2	135	8	140
3	120	9	100
4	105	10	80
5	90	11	100
6	120	12	110

    a. Construct a time series plot. What type of pattern exists in the data?

    b. Use $\alpha = 0.3$ to compute the exponential smoothing values for the time series.

    c. Use Excel Solver or LINGO to find the value of α that minimizes MSE. (*Hint*: Minimize the sum of squared error.)

15. Ten weeks of data on the Commodity Futures Index are 7.35, 7.40, 7.55, 7.56, 7.60, 7.52, 7.52, 7.70, 7.62, and 7.55.

    a. Construct a time series plot. What type of pattern exists in the data?

    b. Use Excel Solver or LINGO to find the value of α that minimizes MSE. (*Hint:* Minimize the sum of squared error.)

16. The Nielsen ratings (percentage of U.S. households that tuned in) for the Masters golf tournament from 1997 through 2008 follow (*Golf Magazine*, January 2009):

Year	Rating
1997	11.2
1998	8.6
1999	7.9
2000	7.6
2001	10.7
2002	8.1
2003	6.9
2004	6.7
2005	8.0
2006	6.9
2007	7.6
2008	7.3

WEB file

Masters

The rating of 11.2 in 1997 indicates that 11.2% of U.S. households tuned in to watch Tiger Woods win his first major golf tournament and become the first African-American to win the Masters. Tiger Woods also won the Masters in 2001 and 2005.

a. Construct a time series plot. What type of pattern exists in the data? Discuss some of the factors that may have resulted in the pattern exhibited in the time series plot for this time series.

b. Given the pattern of the time series plot developed in part (a), do you think the forecasting methods discussed in this section are appropriate to develop forecasts for this time series? Explain.

c. Would you recommend using only the Nielsen ratings for 2002–2008 to forecast the rating for 2009, or should the entire time series from 1997–2008 be used? Explain.

17. Consider the following time series:

t	1	2	3	4	5
Y_t	6	11	9	14	15

a. Construct a time series plot. What type of pattern exists in the data?
b. Use Excel Solver or LINGO to find the parameters for the line that minimizes MSE this time series.
c. What is the forecast for $t = 6$?

18. The following table reports the percentage of stocks in a portfolio for nine quarters from 2007 to 2009:

Quarter	Stock %
1st—2007	29.8
2nd—2007	31.0
3rd—2007	29.9
4th—2007	30.1
1st—2008	32.2
2nd—2008	31.5
3rd—2008	32.0
4th—2008	31.9
1st—2009	30.0

a. Construct a time series plot. What type of pattern exists in the data?
b. Use exponential smoothing to forecast this time series. Using Excel Solver or LINGO find the value of α that minimizes the sum of squared error.
c. What is the forecast of the percentage of stocks in a typical portfolio for the second quarter of 2009?

19. Consider the following time series:

t	1	2	3	4	5	6	7
Y_t	120	110	100	96	94	92	88

a. Construct a time series plot. What type of pattern exists in the data?
b. Use Excel Solver or LINGO to find the parameters for the line that minimizes MSE this time series.
c. What is the forecast for $t = 8$?

20. Consider the following time series:

t	1	2	3	4	5	6	7
Y_t	82	60	44	35	30	29	35

    a. Construct a time series plot. What type of pattern exists in the data?
    b. Using LINGO or EXCEL Solver, develop the quadratic trend equation for the time series.
    c. What is the forecast for $t = 8$?

21. Because of high tuition costs at state and private universities, enrollments at community colleges have increased dramatically in recent years. The following data show the enrollment (in thousands) for Jefferson Community College from 2001–2009:

Year	Period (t)	Enrollment (1000s)
2001	1	6.5
2002	2	8.1
2003	3	8.4
2004	4	10.2
2005	5	12.5
2006	6	13.3
2007	7	13.7
2008	8	17.2
2009	9	18.1

    a. Construct a time series plot. What type of pattern exists in the data?
    b. Use Excel Solver or LINGO to find the parameters for the line that minimizes MSE this time series.
    c. What is the forecast for 2010?

22. The Seneca Children's Fund (SCC) is a local charity that runs a summer camp for disadvantaged children. The fund's board of directors has been working very hard over recent years to decrease the amount of overhead expenses, a major factor in how charities are rated by independent agencies. The following data show the percentage of the money SCC has raised that were spent on administrative and fund-raising expenses for 2003–2009:

Year	Period (t)	Expense (%)
2003	1	13.9
2004	2	12.2
2005	3	10.5
2006	4	10.4
2007	5	11.5
2008	6	10.0
2009	7	8.5

    a. Construct a time series plot. What type of pattern exists in the data?
    b. Use Excel Solver or LINGO to find the parameters for the line that minimizes MSE this time series.
    c. Forecast the percentage of administrative expenses for 2010.
    d. If SCC can maintain their current trend in reducing administrative expenses, how long will it take them to achieve a level of 5% or less?

23. The president of a small manufacturing firm is concerned about the continual increase in manufacturing costs over the past several years. The following figures provide a time series of the cost per unit for the firm's leading product over the past eight years:

Year	Cost/Unit ($)	Year	Cost/Unit ($)
1	20.00	5	26.60
2	24.50	6	30.00
3	28.20	7	31.00
4	27.50	8	36.00

    a. Construct a time series plot. What type of pattern exists in the data?
    b. Use Excel Solver or LINGO to find the parameters for the line that minimizes MSE this time series.
    c. What is the average cost increase that the firm has been realizing per year?
    d. Compute an estimate of the cost/unit for next year.

Exchange Rate

24. FRED® (Federal Reserve Economic Data), a database of more than 3000 U.S. economic time series, contains historical data on foreign exchange rates. The following data show the foreign exchange rate for the United States and China (http://research.stlouisfed.org/fred2/). The units for Rate are the number of Chinese yuan renmimbis to one U.S. dollar.

Year	Month	Rate
2007	October	7.5019
2007	November	7.4210
2007	December	7.3682
2008	January	7.2405
2008	February	7.1644
2008	March	7.0722
2008	April	6.9997
2008	May	6.9725
2008	June	6.8993
2008	July	6.8355

    a. Construct a time series plot. Does a linear trend appear to be present?
    b. Use Excel Solver or LINGO to find the parameters for the line that minimizes MSE this time series.
    c. Use the trend equation to forecast the exchange rate for August 2008.
    d. Would you feel comfortable using the trend equation to forecast the exchange rate for December 2008?

25. Automobile unit sales at B. J. Scott Motors, Inc., provided the following 10-year time series:

Year	Sales	Year	Sales
1	400	6	260
2	390	7	300
3	320	8	320
4	340	9	340
5	270	10	370

    a. Construct a time series plot. Comment on the appropriateness of a linear trend.
    b. Using Excel Solver or LINGO, develop a quadratic trend equation that can be used to forecast sales.

c. Using the trend equation developed in part (b), forecast sales in year 11.

d. Suggest an alternative to using a quadratic trend equation to forecast sales. Explain.

Pasta

26. Giovanni Food Products produces and sells frozen pizzas to public schools throughout the eastern United States. Using a very aggressive marketing strategy they have been able to increase their annual revenue by approximately $10 million over the past 10 years. But, increased competition has slowed their growth rate in the past few years. The annual revenue, in millions of dollars, for the previous 10 years is shown below.

Year	Revenue
1	8.53
2	10.84
3	12.98
4	14.11
5	16.31
6	17.21
7	18.37
8	18.45
9	18.40
10	18.43

a. Construct a time series plot. Comment on the appropriateness of a linear trend.

b. Using Excel Solver or LINGO, develop a quadratic trend equation that can be used to forecast revenue.

c. Using the trend equation developed in part (b), forecast revenue in year 11.

NFL Value

27. *Forbes* magazine (www.Forbes.com) ranks NFL teams by value each year. The data below are the value of the Indianapolis Colts from 1998 to 2008.

Year	Period	Value ($ million)
1998	1	227
1999	2	305
2000	3	332
2001	4	367
2002	5	419
2003	6	547
2004	7	609
2005	8	715
2006	9	837
2007	10	911
2008	11	1076

a. Construct a time series plot. What type of pattern exists in the data?

b. Using Excel Solver or LINGO, develop the quadratic trend equation that can be used to forecast the team's value.

c. Using Excel Solver or LINGO, develop the exponential trend equation that can be used to forecast the team's value.

d. Using Excel Solver or LINGO, develop the linear trend equation that can be used to forecast the team's value.

e. Which equation would you recommend using to estimate the team's value in 2009?

f. Use the model you recommended in part (e) to forecast the value of the Colts in 2009.

28. Consider the following time series:

Quarter	Year 1	Year 2	Year 3
1	71	68	62
2	49	41	51
3	58	60	53
4	78	81	72

a. Construct a time series plot. What type of pattern exists in the data?
b. Use an Excel or LINGO model with dummy variables as follows to develop an equation to account for seasonal effects in the data. Qtr1 = 1 if Quarter 1, 0 otherwise; Qtr2 = 1 if Quarter 2, 0 otherwise; Qtr3 = 1 if Quarter 3, 0 otherwise.
c. Compute the quarterly forecasts for next year.

29. Consider the following time series data:

Quarter	Year 1	Year 2	Year 3
1	4	6	7
2	2	3	6
3	3	5	6
4	5	7	8

a. Construct a time series plot. What type of pattern exists in the data?
b. Use an Excel or LINGO model with dummy variables as follows to develop an equation to account for seasonal effects in the data. Qtr1 = 1 if Quarter 1, 0 otherwise; Qtr2 = 1 if Quarter 2, 0 otherwise; Qtr3 = 1 if Quarter 3, 0 otherwise.
c. Compute the quarterly forecasts for next year.

30. The quarterly sales data (number of copies sold) for a college textbook over the past three years follow:

Quarter	Year 1	Year 2	Year 3
1	1690	1800	1850
2	940	900	1100
3	2625	2900	2930
4	2500	2360	2615

a. Construct a time series plot. What type of pattern exists in the data?
b. Use an Excel or LINGO model with dummy variables as follows to develop an equation to account for seasonal effects in the data. Qtr1 = 1 if Quarter 1, 0 otherwise; Qtr2 = 1 if Quarter 2, 0 otherwise; Qtr3 = 1 if Quarter 3, 0 otherwise.
c. Compute the quarterly forecasts for next year.
d. Let $t = 1$ to refer to the observation in quarter 1 of year 1; $t = 2$ to refer to the observation in quarter 2 of year 1; . . . and $t = 12$ to refer to the observation in quarter 4 of year 3. Using the dummy variables defined in part (b) and t, develop an equation to account for seasonal effects and any linear trend in the time series. Based upon the seasonal effects in the data and linear trend, compute the quarterly forecasts for next year.

Pollution

31. Air pollution control specialists in southern California monitor the amount of ozone, carbon dioxide, and nitrogen dioxide in the air on an hourly basis. The hourly time series data exhibit seasonality, with the levels of pollutants showing patterns that vary over the hours in the day. On July 15, 16, and 17, the following levels of nitrogen dioxide were observed for the 12 hours from 6:00 A.M. to 6:00 P.M.

July 15:	25	28	35	50	60	60	40	35	30	25	25	20
July 16:	28	30	35	48	60	65	50	40	35	25	20	20
July 17:	35	42	45	70	72	75	60	45	40	25	25	25

a. Construct a time series plot. What type of pattern exists in the data?

b. Use an Excel or LINGO model with dummy variables as follows to develop an equation to account for seasonal effects in the data:

Hour1 = 1 if the reading was made between 6:00 A.M. and 7:00 A.M.; 0 otherwise
Hour2 = 1 if the reading was made between 7:00 A.M. and 8:00 A.M.; 0 otherwise

.
.
.

Hour11 = 1 if the reading was made between 4:00 P.M. and 5:00 P.M., 0 otherwise. Note that when the values of the 11 dummy variables are equal to 0, the observation corresponds to the 5:00 P.M. to 6:00 P.M. hour.

c. Using the equation developed in part (b), compute estimates of the levels of nitrogen dioxide for July 18.

d. Let $t = 1$ refer to the observation in hour 1 on July 15; $t = 2$ to refer to the observation in hour 2 of July 15; ... and $t = 36$ to refer to the observation in hour 12 of July 17. Using the dummy variables defined in part (b) and ts, develop an equation to account for seasonal effects and any linear trend in the time series. Based upon the seasonal effects in the data and the linear trend, compute estimates of the levels of nitrogen dioxide for July 18.

SouthShore

32. South Shore Construction builds permanent docks and seawalls along the southern shore of Long Island, New York. Although the firm has been in business only five years, revenue has increased from $308,000 in the first year of operation to $1,084,000 in the most recent year. The following data show the quarterly sales revenue in thousands of dollars:

Quarter	Year 1	Year 2	Year 3	Year 4	Year 5
1	20	37	75	92	176
2	100	136	155	202	282
3	175	245	326	384	445
4	13	26	48	82	181

a. Construct a time series plot. What type of pattern exists in the data?

b. Use an Excel or LINGO model with dummy variables as follows to develop an equation to account for seasonal effects in the data. Qtr1 = 1 if Quarter 1, 0 otherwise; Qtr2 = 1 if Quarter 2, 0 otherwise; Qtr3 = 1 if Quarter 3, 0 otherwise.

c. Let Period = 1 to refer to the observation in quarter 1 of year 1; Period = 2 to refer to the observation in quarter 2 of year 1; ... and Period = 20 refer to the observation in quarter 4 of year 5. Using the dummy variables defined in part (b) and Period, develop an equation to account for seasonal effects and any linear trend in the time series. Based upon the seasonal effects in the data and linear trend, compute estimates of quarterly sales for year 6.

TABLE 15.18   FOOD AND BEVERAGE SALES FOR THE VINTAGE RESTAURANT ($1000s)

Month	First Year	Second Year	Third Year
January	242	263	282
February	235	238	255
March	232	247	265
April	178	193	205
May	184	193	210
June	140	149	160
July	145	157	166
August	152	161	174
September	110	122	126
October	130	130	148
November	152	167	173
December	206	230	235

WEB file

Vintage

Case Problem 1   FORECASTING FOOD AND BEVERAGE SALES

The Vintage Restaurant, on Captiva Island near Fort Myers, Florida, is owned and operated by Karen Payne. The restaurant just completed its third year of operation. During that time, Karen sought to establish a reputation for the restaurant as a high-quality dining establishment that specializes in fresh seafood. Through the efforts of Karen and her staff, her restaurant has become one of the best and fastest-growing restaurants on the island.

To better plan for future growth of the restaurant, Karen needs to develop a system that will enable her to forecast food and beverage sales by month for up to one year in advance. Table 15.18 shows the value of food and beverage sales ($1000s) for the first three years of operation.

Managerial Report

Perform an analysis of the sales data for the Vintage Restaurant. Prepare a report for Karen that summarizes your findings, forecasts, and recommendations. Include the following:

1. A time series plot. Comment on the underlying pattern in the time series.
2. Using the dummy variable approach, forecast sales for January through December of the fourth year.

Assume that January sales for the fourth year turn out to be $295,000. What was your forecast error? If this error is large, Karen may be puzzled about the difference between your forecast and the actual sales value. What can you do to resolve her uncertainty in the forecasting procedure?

Case Problem 2   FORECASTING LOST SALES

The Carlson Department Store suffered heavy damage when a hurricane struck on August 31. The store was closed for four months (September through December), and Carlson is now involved in a dispute with its insurance company about the amount of lost sales during the time the store was closed. Two key issues must be resolved: (1) the

TABLE 15.19   SALES FOR CARLSON DEPARTMENT STORE ($ MILLIONS)

CarlsonSales

Month	Year 1	Year 2	Year 3	Year 4	Year 5
January		1.45	2.31	2.31	2.56
February		1.80	1.89	1.99	2.28
March		2.03	2.02	2.42	2.69
April		1.99	2.23	2.45	2.48
May		2.32	2.39	2.57	2.73
June		2.20	2.14	2.42	2.37
July		2.13	2.27	2.40	2.31
August		2.43	2.21	2.50	2.23
September	1.71	1.90	1.89	2.09	
October	1.90	2.13	2.29	2.54	
November	2.74	2.56	2.83	2.97	
December	4.20	4.16	4.04	4.35	

amount of sales Carlson would have made if the hurricane had not struck, and (2) whether Carlson is entitled to any compensation for excess sales due to increased business activity after the storm. More than $8 billion in federal disaster relief and insurance money came into the county, resulting in increased sales at department stores and numerous other businesses.

Table 15.19 gives Carlson's sales data for the 48 months preceding the storm. Table 15.20 reports total sales for the 48 months preceding the storm for all department stores in the county, as well as the total sales in the county for the four months the Carlson Department Store was closed. Carlson's managers asked you to analyze these data and develop estimates of the lost sales at the Carlson Department Store for the months of September through December. They also asked you to determine whether a case can be made for excess storm-related sales during the same period. If such a case can be made, Carlson is entitled to compensation for excess sales it would have earned in addition to ordinary sales.

TABLE 15.20   DEPARTMENT STORE SALES FOR THE COUNTY ($ MILLIONS)

CountySales

Month	Year 1	Year 2	Year 3	Year 4	Year 5
January		46.80	46.80	43.80	48.00
February		48.00	48.60	45.60	51.60
March		60.00	59.40	57.60	57.60
April		57.60	58.20	53.40	58.20
May		61.80	60.60	56.40	60.00
June		58.20	55.20	52.80	57.00
July		56.40	51.00	54.00	57.60
August		63.00	58.80	60.60	61.80
September	55.80	57.60	49.80	47.40	69.00
October	56.40	53.40	54.60	54.60	75.00
November	71.40	71.40	65.40	67.80	85.20
December	117.60	114.00	102.00	100.20	121.80

Managerial Report

Prepare a report for the managers of the Carlson Department Store that summarizes your findings, forecasts, and recommendations. Include the following:

1. An estimate of sales for Carlson Department Store had there been no hurricane
2. An estimate of countywide department store sales had there been no hurricane
3. An estimate of lost sales for the Carlson Department Store for September through December

In addition, use the countywide actual department stores sales for September through December and the estimate in part (2) to make a case for or against excess storm-related sales.

Appendix 15.1   FORECASTING WITH EXCEL DATA ANALYSIS TOOLS

In this appendix we show how Excel can be used to develop forecasts using three forecasting methods: moving averages, exponential smoothing, and trend projection. We also show how to use Excel Solver for least-squares fitting of models to data.

Moving Averages

WEB file

Gasoline

To show how Excel can be used to develop forecasts using the moving averages method, we will develop a forecast for the gasoline sales time series in Table 15.1 and Figure 15.1. The sales data for the 12 weeks are entered into worksheet rows 2 through 13 of column B. The following steps can be used to produce a three-week moving average.

Step 1. Click the **Data** tab on the Ribbon
Step 2. In the **Analysis** group, click **Data Analysis**
Step 3. Choose **Moving Average** from the list of Analysis Tools
        Click **OK**
Step 4. When the Moving Average dialog box appears:
        Enter B2:B13 in the **Input Range** box
        Enter 3 in the **Interval** box
        Enter C2 in the **Output Range** box
        Click OK

The three-week moving averages will appear in column C of the worksheet. The forecast for week 4 appears next to the sales value for week 3, and so on. Forecasts for periods of other length can be computed easily by entering a different value in the Interval box.

Exponential Smoothing

To show how Excel can be used for exponential smoothing, we again develop a forecast for the gasoline sales time series in Table 15.1 and Figure 15.1. The sales data for the 12 weeks are entered into worksheet rows 2 through 13 of column B. The following steps can be used to produce a forecast using a smoothing constant of $\alpha = .2$.

Step 1. Click the **Data** tab on the Ribbon
Step 2. In the **Analysis** group, click **Data Analysis**
Step 3. Choose **Exponential Smoothing** from the list of Analysis Tools
        Click **OK**

Step 4.   When the Exponential Smoothing dialog box appears:
             Enter B2:B13 in the **Input Range** box
             Enter .8 in the **Damping factor** box
             Enter C2 in the **Output Range** box
             Click OK

The exponential smoothing forecasts will appear in column C of the worksheet. Note that the value we entered in the Damping factor box is $1 - \alpha$; forecasts for other smoothing constants can be computed easily by entering a different value for $1 - \alpha$ in the Damping factor box.

Trend Projection

To show how Excel can be used for trend projection, we develop a forecast for the bicycle sales time series in Table 15.3 and Figure 15.3. The data, with appropriate labels in row 1, are entered into worksheet rows 1 through 11 of columns A and B. The following steps can be used to produce a forecast for year 11 by trend projection.

WEB file

Bicycle

Step 1.   Select an empty cell in the worksheet
Step 2.   Select the **Formulas** tab on the Ribbon
Step 3.   In the **Function Library** group, click **Insert** Function
Step 4.   When the Insert Function dialog box appears:
             Choose **Statistical** in the **Or select a category** box
             Choose **Forecast** in the Select a function box
             Click **OK**
Step 5.   When the Forecast Arguments dialog box appears:
             Enter 11 in the **x** box
             Enter B2:B11 in the **Known y's** box
             Enter A2:A11 in the **Known x's** box
             Click OK

The forecast for year 11, in this case 32.5, will appear in the cell selected in step 1.

Appendix 15.2   FORECASTING WITH EXCEL SOLVER

Using Excel Solver for Fitting a Model to Data—Exponential Smoothing

To show how Excel Solver can be used to find the best-fitting value for the exponential smoothing parameter α, we develop a forecast for the gasoline sales time series in Table 15.1 and Figure 15.1. We have developed a model that calculates the exponential smoothing forecasts using equation (15.2). This is shown in Figure 15.15 for the gasoline data. Cell B2 contains the current value of $\alpha = 0.2$. As shown in Figure 15.16, we calculate the forecasts using equation (15.2) in column C. Note that we set the forecast in period 2 to the observed value in period, and for subsequent periods we use equation (15.2). The forecast error for each period is calculated in column D and the squared forecast error in column E. Cell E19 contains the sum of the squared errors.

     We seek the value of α that minimizes the sum of squared errors. We will build the optimization model (15.4)–(15.7), but we will not need the definitional variables, as the

FIGURE 15.15   EXPONENTIAL SMOOTHING MODEL IN EXCEL

WEB file

Gasoline_ES

	A	B	C	D	E
1					
2	Alpha	0.2			
3					
4					**Squared**
5		**Time Series**		**Forecast**	**Forecast**
6	**Week**	**Value**	**Forecast**	**Error**	**Error**
7	1	17			
8	2	21	17	4.00	16.00
9	3	19	17.80	1.20	1.44
10	4	23	18.04	4.96	24.60
11	5	18	19.03	−1.03	1.07
12	6	16	18.83	−2.83	7.98
13	7	20	18.26	1.74	3.03
14	8	18	18.61	−0.61	0.37
15	9	22	18.49	3.51	12.34
16	10	20	19.19	0.81	0.66
17	11	15	19.35	−4.35	18.94
18	12	22	18.48	3.52	12.38
19				**Total**	98.80
20					
21					

FIGURE 15.16   EXPONENTIAL SMOOTHING MODEL IN EXCEL WITH FORMULAS

	A	B	C	D	E
1					
2	Alpha	0.2			
3					
4					**Squared**
5		**Time Series**		**Forecast**	**Forecast**
6	**Week**	**Value**	**Forecast**	**Error**	**Error**
7	1	17			
8	2	21	=B7	=B8-C8	=D8^2
9	3	19	=$B$2*B8+(1-$B$2)*C8	=B9-C9	=D9^2
10	4	23	=$B$2*B9+(1-$B$2)*C9	=B10-C10	=D10^2
11	5	18	=$B$2*B10+(1-$B$2)*C10	=B11-C11	=D11^2
12	6	16	=$B$2*B11+(1-$B$2)*C11	=B12-C12	=D12^2
13	7	20	=$B$2*B12+(1-$B$2)*C12	=B13-C13	=D13^2
14	8	18	=$B$2*B13+(1-$B$2)*C13	=B14-C14	=D14^2
15	9	22	=$B$2*B14+(1-$B$2)*C14	=B15-C15	=D15^2
16	10	20	=$B$2*B15+(1-$B$2)*C15	=B16-C16	=D16^2
17	11	15	=$B$2*B16+(1-$B$2)*C16	=B17-C17	=D17^2
18	12	22	=$B$2*B17+(1-$B$2)*C17	=B18-C18	=D18^2
19				**Total**	=SUM(E8:E18)
20					

forecasts will simply be calculations in the spreadsheet (column C). The only decision variable will be α.

The following steps can be used to find the optimal value of α:

Step 1. Select the **Data** tab
Step 2. From the **Analysis** group select the **Solver** option
Step 3. In the solver dialog box, Enter E19 as the **Set Target Cell**
Choose **Min**
Enter B2 in the **Changing Cells** section
Step 4. In the constraints section of the solver dialog box, click the **Add** button. The constraint dialog box appears. In the constraint dialog enter B2 in the left-hand box of the Cell Reference area
Select $<=$
Enter 1 in the **Constraint** box
Click **OK**
Step 5. Click the **Options** button and choose **Assume Non-Negative**
Click **OK.** The solver dialog box should appear as in Figure 15.17
Step 6. Click **Solve**
Step 7. Click **OK** to return to the spreadsheet.

The optimal value of α of 0.174388 appears in cell B2 and the minimal sum of squared errors of 98.56 is given in cell E19.

Using Excel Solver for Curve Fitting

To show how Excel Solver can be used to find the best-fitting values of the parameters of a proposed model, we use the cholesterol drug revenue data shown in Table 15.4 and Figure 15.4. The proposed model is the quadratic trend equation (15.11). We have constructed a spreadsheet model that calculates the forecasts and the sum of squared error given values for the parameters b_0, b_1, and b_2. This spreadsheet is shown in Figure 15.18.

We seek the value of α that minimizes the sum of squared errors. The decision variables are b_0, b_1, and b_2. Figure 15.19 shows the formulas used. As shown in Figure 15.19,

FIGURE 15.17   SOLVER DIALOG BOX FOR EXPONENTIAL SMOOTHING FOR THE GASOLINE DATA

FIGURE 15.18   CHOLESTEROL DRUG REVENUE QUADRATIC MODEL
IN EXCEL

WEB file

Cholesterol_Quad

	A	B	C	D	E
1					
2		**b0**	5.000		
3		**b1**	1.000		
4		**b2**	1.000		
5					**Squared**
6				**Forecast**	**Forecast**
7	**Year**	**Revenue**	**Forecast**	**Error**	**Error**
8	1	23.10	7.00	16.10	259.21
9	2	21.30	11.00	10.30	106.09
10	3	27.40	17.00	10.40	108.16
11	4	34.60	25.00	9.60	92.16
12	5	33.80	35.00	−1.20	1.44
13	6	43.20	47.00	−3.80	14.44
14	7	59.50	61.00	−1.50	2.25
15	8	64.40	77.00	−12.60	158.76
16	9	74.20	95.00	−20.80	432.64
17	10	99.30	115.00	−15.70	246.49
18				**Total**	1421.64
19					
20					

FIGURE 15.19   CHOLESTEROL DRUG REVENUE QUADRATIC MODEL FORMULAS IN EXCEL

	A	B	C	D	E
1					
2		**b0**	5		
3		**b1**	1		
4		**b2**	1		
5					**Squared**
6				**Forecast**	**Forecast**
7	**Year**	**Revenue**	**Forecast**	**Error**	**Error**
8	1	23.1	=$C$2+$C$3*A8+$C$4*A8^2	=B8-C8	=D8^2
9	2	21.3	=$C$2+$C$3*A9+$C$4*A9^2	=B9-C9	=D9^2
10	3	27.4	=$C$2+$C$3*A10+$C$4*A10^2	=B10-C10	=D10^2
11	4	34.6	=$C$2+$C$3*A11+$C$4*A11^2	=B11-C11	=D11^2
12	5	33.8	=$C$2+$C$3*A12+$C$4*A12^2	=B12-C12	=D12^2
13	6	43.2	=$C$2+$C$3*A13+$C$4*A13^2	=B13-C13	=D13^2
14	7	59.5	=$C$2+$C$3*A14+$C$4*A14^2	=B14-C14	=D14^2
15	8	64.4	=$C$2+$C$3*A15+$C$4*A15^2	=B15-C15	=D15^2
16	9	74.2	=$C$2+$C$3*A16+$C$4*A16^2	=B16-C16	=D16^2
17	10	99.3	=$C$2+$C$3*A17+$C$4*A17^2	=B17-C17	=D17^2
18				**Total**	=SUM(E8:E17)
19					

FIGURE 15.20   SOLVER DIALOG BOX FOR QUADRATIC CURVE FITTING FOR THE CHOLESTEROL
SALES DATA

we calculate the forecasts using equation (15.11) in column C. The forecast error for each
period is calculated in column D and the squared forecast error in column E. Cell E18 contains the sum of the squared errors.

*To fit a different model, (for
example, equation 15.12),
change the formula in cell
C8 and copy to cells C9
through C17. Be sure to use
absolute references for
the cell locations C2, C3,
and C4.*

Step 1. Select the **Data** tab.

Step 2. From the **Analysis** group select the **Solver** option

Step 3. In the solver dialog box, Enter E18 as the **Set Target Cell**
Choose **Min**
Enter C2:C4 in the **Changing Cells** section
The solver dialog box should appear as in **Figure 15.20**

Step 4. Click **Solve**

Step 5. Click **OK** to return to the spreadsheet

The optimal values of the decision variables are $b_0 = 24.182$, $b_1 = -2.106$, and $b_2 = 0.922$
with a minimum sum of squared error of 110.65.

Appendix 15.3   FORECASTING WITH LINGO

To show how LINGO can be used to find the best-fitting values of the parameters of a proposed model, we use the cholesterol drug revenue data shown in Table 15.4 and Figure 15.4. In the main window of LINGO, we enter the following model (be sure to end each
statement with a semicolon):

MODEL:
TITLE Cholesterol Revenue Quadratic Least Squares Optimization;

```
! MINIMIZE SUM OF SQUARED ERROR ;
MIN = (23.1 − T1)^2 + (21.3 − T2)^2 + (27.4 − T3)^2 + (34.6 − T4)^2
        + (33.8 − T5)^2 + (43.2 − T6)^2 + (59.5 − T7)^2 + (64.4 − T8)^2
        + (74.2 − T9)^2 + (99.3 − T10)^2 ;

T1 = b0 + b1*1 + b2*1 ;
T2 = b0 + b1*2 + b2*4 ;
T3 = b0 + b1*3 + b2*9 ;
T4 = b0 + b1*4 + b2*16 ;
T5 = b0 + b1*5 + b2*25 ;
T6 = b0 + b1*6 + b2*36 ;
T7 = b0 + b1*7 + b2*49 ;
T8 = b0 + b1*8 + b2*64 ;
T9 = b0 + b1*9 + b2*81 ;
T10 = b0 + b1*10 + b2*100 ;

@free(b0) ;
@free(b1) ;
@free(b2) ;
@free(T1) ;
@free(T2) ;
@free(T3) ;
@free(T4) ;
@free(T5) ;
@free(T6) ;
@free(T7) ;
@free(T8) ;
@free(T9) ;
@free(T10) ;
```

To solve the model, select the Solve command from the LINGO menu or press the Solve button on the toolbar at the top of the main frame window. LINGO will begin the solution process by determining whether the model conforms to all syntax requirements. If the LINGO model doesn't pass these tests, you will be informed by an error message. If LINGO does not find any errors in the model input, it will begin to solve the model. As part of the solution process, LINGO displays a Solver Status window that allows you to monitor the progress of the solver. LINGO displays the solution in a new window titled "Solution Report." The output that appears in the Solution Report window for the fitting of the cholesterol drug revenue data is shown in Figure 15.21.

Note that the minimum sum of squared errors is 110.6479 and the optimal values of the parameters are $b_0 = 24.18167$, $b_1 = -2.105989$, and $b_2 = 0.9215909$. The best fitting curve is therefore

$$T_t = 24.18167 - 2.105989\,t + 0.9215909\,t^2$$

FIGURE 15.21   LINGO SOLUTION TO THE CHOLESTEROL DRUG REVENUE LEAST-SQUARES DATA
WITH QUADRATIC MODEL

```
Local optimal solution found.
   Objective value:                         110.6479
   Infeasibilities:                      0.8009451E-09
   Total solver iterations:                       13


   Model Title: Cholesterol Revenue Quadratic Least Squares Regression
Optimization

                    Variable           Value      Reduced Cost
                          T1        22.99727          0.000000
                          T2        23.65606          0.000000
                          T3        26.15803          0.000000
                          T4        30.50318          0.000000
                          T5        36.69152          0.000000
                          T6        44.72303          0.000000
                          T7        54.59773          0.000000
                          T8        66.31561          0.000000
                          T9        79.87667          0.000000
                         T10        95.28091          0.000000
                          B0        24.18167          0.000000
                          B1       -2.105985          0.000000
                          B2       0.9215909          0.000000

                         Row   Slack or Surplus        Dual Price
                           1          110.6479         -1.000000
                           2          0.000000          0.2054545
                           3          0.000000         -4.712121
                           4          0.000000          2.483939
                           5          0.000000          8.193636
                           6          0.000000         -5.783030
                           7          0.000000         -3.046061
                           8          0.000000          9.804545
                           9          0.000000         -3.831212
                          10          0.000000        -11.35333
                          11          0.000000          8.038182
```

Markov Processes

CONTENTS

16.1 MARKET SHARE ANALYSIS

16.2 ACCOUNTS RECEIVABLE
ANALYSIS
Fundamental Matrix and Associated
Calculations
Establishing the Allowance for
Doubtful Accounts

Markov process models are useful in studying the evolution of systems over repeated trials. The repeated trials are often successive time periods where the state of the system in any particular period cannot be determined with certainty. Rather, transition probabilities are used to describe the manner in which the system makes transitions from one period to the next. Hence, we are interested in the probability of the system being in a particular state at a given time period.

Markov process models can be used to describe the probability that a machine that is functioning in one period will continue to function or will break down in the next period. Models can also be used to describe the probability that a consumer purchasing brand A in one period will purchase brand B in the next period. The Management Science in Action, Benefit of Health Care Services, describes how a Markov process model was used to determine the health status probabilities for persons aged 65 and older. Such information was helpful in understanding the future need for health care services and the benefits of expanding current health care programs.

In this chapter we present a marketing application that involves an analysis of the store-switching behavior of supermarket customers. As a second illustration, we consider an accounting application that is concerned with the transitioning of accounts receivable dollars to different account-aging categories. Because an in-depth treatment of Markov processes is beyond the scope of this text, the analysis in both illustrations is restricted to situations consisting of a finite number of states, the transition probabilities remaining constant over time, and the probability of being in a particular state at any one time period depending only on the state in the immediately preceding time period. Such Markov processes are referred to as *Markov chains with stationary transition probabilities.*

MANAGEMENT SCIENCE IN ACTION

BENEFIT OF HEALTH CARE SERVICES*

The U.S. General Accountability Office (GAO) is an independent, nonpolitical audit organization in the legislative branch of the federal government. GAO evaluators obtained data on the health conditions of individuals aged 65 and older. The individuals were identified as being in three possible states:

Best: Able to perform daily activities without assistance

Next Best: Able to perform some daily activities without assistance

Worst: Unable to perform daily activities without assistance

Using a two-year period, the evaluators developed estimates of the transition probabilities among the three states. For example, a transition probability that a person in the Best state is still in the Best state one year later was 0.80, while the transition probability that a person in the Best state moves to the Next Best state one year later is 0.10. The Markov analysis of the full set of transition probabilities determined the steady-state probabilities that individuals would be in each state. Thus, for a given population aged 65 and older, the steady-state probabilities would indicate the percentage of the population that would be in each state in future years.

The GAO study further subdivided individuals into two groups: those receiving appropriate health care and those not receiving appropriate health care. For individuals not receiving appropriate health care, the kind of additional care and the cost of that care were estimated. The revised transition probabilities showed that with appropriate health care, the steady-state probabilities indicated the larger percentage of the population that would be in the Best and Next Best health states in future years. Using these results, the model provided evidence of the future benefits that would be achieved by expanding current health care programs.

*Based on information provided by Bill Ammann, U.S. General Accounting Office.

16.1   MARKET SHARE ANALYSIS

Suppose we are interested in analyzing the market share and customer loyalty for Murphy's Foodliner and Ashley's Supermarket, the only two grocery stores in a small town. We focus on the sequence of shopping trips of one customer and assume that the customer makes one shopping trip each week to either Murphy's Foodliner or Ashley's Supermarket, but not both.

Using the terminology of Markov processes, we refer to the weekly periods or shopping trips as the **trials of the process.** Thus, at each trial, the customer will shop at either Murphy's Foodliner or Ashley's Supermarket. The particular store selected in a given week is referred to as the **state of the system** in that period. Because the customer has two shopping alternatives at each trial, we say the system has two states. With a finite number of states, we identify the states as follows:

State 1. The customer shops at Murphy's Foodliner.
State 2. The customer shops at Ashley's Supermarket.

If we say the system is in state 1 at trial 3, we are simply saying that the customer shops at Murphy's during the third weekly shopping period.

As we continue the shopping trip process into the future, we cannot say for certain where the customer will shop during a given week or trial. In fact, we realize that during any given week, the customer may be either a Murphy's customer or an Ashley's customer. However, using a Markov process model, we will be able to compute the probability that the customer shops at each store during any period. For example, we may find a 0.6 probability that the customer will shop at Murphy's during a particular week and a 0.4 probability that the customer will shop at Ashley's.

To determine the probabilities of the various states occurring at successive trials of the Markov process, we need information on the probability that a customer remains with the same store or switches to the competing store as the process continues from trial to trial or week to week.

Suppose that, as part of a market research study, we collect data from 100 shoppers over a 10-week period. Suppose further that these data show each customer's weekly shopping trip pattern in terms of the sequence of visits to Murphy's and Ashley's. To develop a Markov process model for the sequence of weekly shopping trips, we need to express the probability of selecting each store (state) in a given period solely in terms of the store (state) that was selected during the previous period. In reviewing the data, suppose that we find that of all customers who shopped at Murphy's in a given week, 90% shopped at Murphy's the following week while 10% switched to Ashley's. Suppose that similar data for the customers who shopped at Ashley's in a given week show that 80% shopped at Ashley's the following week while 20% switched to Murphy's. Probabilities based on these data are shown in Table 16.1. Because these probabilities indicate that a customer moves, or makes a transition, from a state in a given period to each state in the following period, these probabilities are called **transition probabilities.**

An important property of the table of transition probabilities is that the sum of the probabilities in each row is 1; each row of the table provides a probability distribution. For example, a customer who shops at Murphy's one week must shop at either Murphy's or Ashley's the next week. The entries in row 1 give the probabilities associated with each of these events. The 0.9 and 0.8 probabilities in Table 16.1 can be interpreted as measures of store loyalty in that they indicate the probability of a repeat visit to the same store. Similarly, the 0.1 and 0.2 probabilities are measures of the store-switching characteristics of the customers. In developing a Markov process model for this problem, we are assuming that the transition probabilities will be the same for any customer and that the transition probabilities will not change over time.

TABLE 16.1   TRANSITION PROBABILITIES FOR MURPHY'S AND ASHLEY'S
                GROCERY SALES

Current Weekly Shopping Period	Next Weekly Shopping Period	
	Murphy's Foodliner	Ashley's Supermarket
Murphy's Foodliner	0.9	0.1
Ashley's Supermarket	0.2	0.8

Appendix 16.1 contains a review of matrix notation and operations.

Note that Table 16.1 has one row and one column for each state of the system. We will use the symbol p_{ij} to represent the transition probabilities and the symbol P to represent the matrix of transition probabilities; that is,

$$p_{ij} = \text{probability of making a transition from state } i \text{ in a given period to state } j \text{ in the next period}$$

For the supermarket problem, we have

A quick check for a valid matrix of transition probabilities is to make sure the sum of the probabilities in each row equals 1.

$$P = \begin{bmatrix} p_{11} & p_{12} \\ p_{21} & p_{22} \end{bmatrix} = \begin{bmatrix} 0.9 & 0.1 \\ 0.2 & 0.8 \end{bmatrix}$$

Using the matrix of transition probabilities, we can now determine the probability that a customer will be a Murphy's customer or an Ashley's customer at some period in the future. Let us begin by assuming that we have a customer whose last weekly shopping trip was to Murphy's. What is the probability that this customer will shop at Murphy's on the next weekly shopping trip, period 1? In other words, what is the probability that the system will be in state 1 after the first transition? The matrix of transition probabilities indicates that this probability is $p_{11} = 0.9$.

Now let us consider the state of the system in period 2. A useful way of depicting what can happen on the second weekly shopping trip is to draw a tree diagram of the possible outcomes (see Figure 16.1). Using this tree diagram, we see that the probability that the customer shops at Murphy's during both the first and the second weeks is $(0.9)(0.9) = 0.81$. Also, note that the probability of the customer switching to Ashley's on the first trip and then switching back to Murphy's on the second trip is $(0.1)(0.2) = 0.02$. Because these options are the only two ways that the customer can be in state 1 (shopping at Murphy's) during the second period, the probability of the system being in state 1 during the second period is $0.81 + 0.02 = 0.83$. Similarly, the probability of the system being in state 2 during the second period is $0.09 + 0.08 = 0.17$.

As desirable as the tree diagram approach may be from an intuitive point of view, it becomes cumbersome when we want to extend the analysis to three or more periods. Fortunately, we have an easier way to calculate the probabilities of the system being in state 1 or state 2 for any subsequent period. First, we introduce a notation that will allow us to represent these probabilities for any given period. Let

$$\pi_i(n) = \text{probability that the system is in state } i \text{ in period } n$$

Index denotes
the state

Denotes the time
period or number of transitions

FIGURE 16.1   TREE DIAGRAM DEPICTING TWO WEEKLY SHOPPING TRIPS
OF A CUSTOMER WHO SHOPPED LAST AT MURPHY'S

For example, $\pi_1(1)$ denotes the probability of the system being in state 1 in period 1, while $\pi_2(1)$ denotes the probability of the system being in state 2 in period 1. Because $\pi_i(n)$ is the probability that the system is in state i in period n, this probability is referred to as a **state probability.**

The terms $\pi_1(0)$ and $\pi_2(0)$ will denote the probability of the system being in state 1 or state 2 at some initial or starting period. Week 0 represents the most recent period, when we are beginning the analysis of a Markov process. If we set $\pi_1(0) = 1$ and $\pi_2(0) = 0$, we are saying that as an initial condition the customer shopped last week at Murphy's; alternatively, if we set $\pi_1(0) = 0$ and $\pi_2(0) = 1$, we would be starting the system with a customer who shopped last week at Ashley's. In the tree diagram of Figure 16.1, we consider the situation in which the customer shopped last at Murphy's. Thus,

$$\begin{bmatrix} \pi_1(0) & \pi_2(0) \end{bmatrix} = \begin{bmatrix} 1 & 0 \end{bmatrix}$$

is a vector that represents the initial state probabilities of the system. In general, we use the notation

$$\Pi(n) = \begin{bmatrix} \pi_1(n) & \pi_2(n) \end{bmatrix}$$

to denote the vector of state probabilities for the system in period n. In the example, $\Pi(1)$ is a vector representing the state probabilities for the first week, $\Pi(2)$ is a vector representing the state probabilities for the second week, and so on.

Appendix 16.1 provides the step-by-step procedure for vector and matrix multiplication.

Using this notation, we can find the state probabilities for period $n + 1$ by simply multiplying the known state probabilities for period n by the transition probability matrix. Using the vector of state probabilities and the matrix of transition probabilities, the multiplication can be expressed as follows:

$$\Pi(\text{next period}) = \Pi(\text{current period})P$$

or

$$\Pi(n + 1) = \Pi(n)P \qquad (16.1)$$

Beginning with the system in state 1 at period 0, we have $\Pi(0) = [1 \ 0]$. We can compute the state probabilities for period 1 as follows:

$$\Pi(1) = \Pi(0)P$$

or

$$[\pi_1(1) \quad \pi_2(1)] = [\pi_1(0) \quad \pi_2(0)]\begin{bmatrix} p_{11} & p_{12} \\ p_{21} & p_{22} \end{bmatrix}$$

$$= [1 \quad 0]\begin{bmatrix} 0.9 & 0.1 \\ 0.2 & 0.8 \end{bmatrix}$$

$$= [0.9 \quad 0.1]$$

The state probabilities $\pi_1(1) = 0.9$ and $\pi_2(1) = 0.1$ are the probabilities that a customer who shopped at Murphy's during week 0 will shop at Murphy's or at Ashley's during week 1.

Using equation (16.1), we can compute the state probabilities for the second week as follows:

$$\Pi(2) = \Pi(1)P$$

or

$$[\pi_1(2) \quad \pi_2(2)] = [\pi_1(1) \quad \pi_2(1)]\begin{bmatrix} p_{11} & p_{12} \\ p_{21} & p_{22} \end{bmatrix}$$

$$= [0.9 \quad 0.1]\begin{bmatrix} 0.9 & 0.1 \\ 0.2 & 0.8 \end{bmatrix}$$

$$= [0.83 \quad 0.17]$$

We see that the probability of shopping at Murphy's during the second week is 0.83, while the probability of shopping at Ashley's during the second week is 0.17. These same results

TABLE 16.2 STATE PROBABILITIES FOR FUTURE PERIODS BEGINNING INITIALLY
WITH A MURPHY'S CUSTOMER

State Probability	Period (n)										
	0	**1**	**2**	**3**	**4**	**5**	**6**	**7**	**8**	**9**	**10**
$\pi_1(n)$	1	0.9	0.83	0.781	0.747	0.723	0.706	0.694	0.686	0.680	0.676
$\pi_2(n)$	0	0.1	0.17	0.219	0.253	0.277	0.294	0.306	0.314	0.320	0.324

were previously obtained using the tree diagram of Figure 16.1. By continuing to apply
equation (16.1), we can compute the state probabilities for any future period; that is,

$$\Pi(3) = \Pi(2)P$$
$$\Pi(4) = \Pi(3)P$$
$$\vdots \qquad \vdots$$
$$\Pi(n + 1) = \Pi(n)P$$

Table 16.2 shows the result of carrying out these calculations for 10 periods.

The vectors $\Pi(1)$, $\Pi(2)$, $\Pi(3)$, ... contain the probabilities that a customer who started
out as a Murphy customer will be in state 1 or state 2 in the first period, the second period,
the third period, and so on. In Table 16.2 we see that after a few periods these probabilities
do not change much from one period to the next.

If we had started with 1000 Murphy customers—that is, 1000 customers who last
shopped at Murphy's—our analysis indicates that during the fifth weekly shopping period,
723 would be customers of Murphy's, and 277 would be customers of Ashley's. Moreover,
during the 10th weekly shopping period, 676 would be customers of Murphy's, and 324
would be customers of Ashley's.

Now let us repeat the analysis, but this time we will begin the process with a customer
who shopped last at Ashley's. Thus,

$$\Pi(0) = [\pi_1(0) \quad \pi_2(0)] = [0 \quad 1]$$

Using equation (16.1), the probability of the system being in state 1 or state 2 in period 1 is
given by

$$\Pi(1) = \Pi(0)P$$

or

$$[\pi_1(1) \quad \pi_2(1)] = [\pi_1(0) \quad \pi_2(0)]\begin{bmatrix} p_{11} & p_{12} \\ p_{21} & p_{22} \end{bmatrix}$$
$$= [0 \quad 1]\begin{bmatrix} 0.9 & 0.1 \\ 0.2 & 0.8 \end{bmatrix}$$
$$= [0.2 \quad 0.8]$$

Proceeding as before, we can calculate subsequent state probabilities. Doing so, we obtain
the results shown in Table 16.3.

TABLE 16.3   STATE PROBABILITIES FOR FUTURE PERIODS BEGINNING INITIALLY
WITH AN ASHLEY'S CUSTOMER

State Probability	0	1	2	3	4	5	6	7	8	9	10
						Period (*n*)					
$\pi_1(n)$	0	0.2	0.34	0.438	0.507	0.555	0.589	0.612	0.628	0.640	0.648
$\pi_2(n)$	1	0.8	0.66	0.562	0.493	0.445	0.411	0.388	0.372	0.360	0.352

In the fifth shopping period, the probability that the customer will be shopping at Murphy's is 0.555, and the probability that the customer will be shopping at Ashley's is 0.445. In the tenth period, the probability that a customer will be shopping at Murphy's is 0.648, and the probability that a customer will be shopping at Ashley's is 0.352.

As we continue the Markov process, we find that the probability of the system being in a particular state after a large number of periods is independent of the beginning state of the system. The probabilities that we approach after a large number of transitions are referred to as the **steady-state probabilities.** We shall denote the steady-state probability for state 1 with the symbol π_1 and the steady-state probability for state 2 with the symbol π_2. In other words, in the steady-state case, we simply omit the period designation from $\pi_i(n)$ because it is no longer necessary.

Analyses of Tables 16.2 and 16.3 indicate that as n gets larger, the difference between the state probabilities for the nth period and the $(n + 1)$th period becomes increasingly smaller. This analysis leads us to the conclusion that as n gets large, the state probabilities at the $(n + 1)$th period are very close to those at the nth period. This observation provides the basis of a simple method for computing the steady-state probabilities without having to actually carry out a large number of calculations.

In general, we know from equation (16.1) that

$$[\pi_1(n + 1) \quad \pi_2(n + 1)] = [\pi_1(n) \quad \pi_2(n)]\begin{bmatrix} p_{11} & p_{12} \\ p_{21} & p_{22} \end{bmatrix}$$

Because for sufficiently large n the difference between $\Pi(n + 1)$ and $\Pi(n)$ is negligible, we see that in the steady state $\pi_1(n + 1) = \pi_1(n) = \pi_1$, and $\pi_2(n + 1) = \pi_2(n) = \pi_2$. Thus, we have

$$[\pi_1 \quad \pi_2] = [\pi_1 \quad \pi_2]\begin{bmatrix} p_{11} & p_{12} \\ p_{21} & p_{22} \end{bmatrix}$$

$$= [\pi_1 \quad \pi_2]\begin{bmatrix} 0.9 & 0.1 \\ 0.2 & 0.8 \end{bmatrix}$$

After carrying out the multiplications, we obtain

$$\pi_1 = 0.9\pi_1 + 0.2\pi_2 \tag{16.2}$$

and

$$\pi_2 = 0.1\pi_1 + 0.8\pi_2 \qquad (16.3)$$

However, we also know the steady-state probabilities must sum to 1 with

$$\pi_1 + \pi_2 = 1 \qquad (16.4)$$

Using equation (16.4) to solve for π_2 and substituting the result in equation (16.2), we obtain

$$\pi_1 = 0.9\pi_1 + 0.2(1 - \pi_1)$$
$$\pi_1 = 0.9\pi_1 + 0.2 - 0.2\pi_1$$
$$\pi_1 - 0.7\pi_1 = 0.2$$
$$0.3\pi_1 = 0.2$$
$$\pi_1 = \tfrac{2}{3}$$

Can you now compute the steady-state probabilities for Markov processes with two states? Problem 3 provides an application.

Then, using equation (16.4), we can conclude that $\pi_2 = 1 - \pi_1 = \frac{1}{3}$. Thus, using equations (16.2) and (16.4), we can solve for the steady-state probabilities directly. You can check for yourself that we could have obtained the same result using equations (16.3) and (16.4).[1]

Thus, if we have 1000 customers in the system, the Markov process model tells us that in the long run, with steady-state probabilities $\pi_1 = \frac{2}{3}$ and $\pi_2 = \frac{1}{3}$, $\frac{2}{3}(1000) = 667$ customers will be Murphy's and $\frac{1}{3}(1000) = 333$ customers will be Ashley's. The steady-state probabilities can be interpreted as the market shares for the two stores.

Market share information is often quite valuable in decision making. For example, suppose Ashley's Supermarket is contemplating an advertising campaign to attract more of Murphy's customers to its store. Let us suppose further that Ashley's believes this promotional strategy will increase the probability of a Murphy's customer switching to Ashley's from 0.10 to 0.15. The revised transition probabilities are given in Table 16.4.

TABLE 16.4   REVISED TRANSITION PROBABILITIES FOR MURPHY'S AND ASHLEY'S GROCERY STORES

Current Weekly Shopping Period	Next Weekly Shopping Period	
	Murphy's Foodliner	**Ashley's Supermarket**
Murphy's Foodliner	0.85	0.15
Ashley's Supermarket	0.20	0.80

---

[1]Even though equations (16.2) and (16.3) provide two equations and two unknowns, we must include equation (16.4) when solving for π_1 and π_2 to ensure that the sum of steady-state probabilities will equal 1.

Given the new transition probabilities, we can modify equations (16.2) and (16.4) to solve for the new steady-state probabilities or market shares. Thus, we obtain

$$\pi_1 = 0.85\pi_1 + 0.20\pi_2$$

Substituting $\pi_2 = 1 - \pi_1$ from equation (16.4), we have

With three states, the steady-state probabilities are found by solving three equations for the three unknown steady-state probabilities. Try Problem 7 as a slightly more difficult problem involving three states.

$$\pi_1 = 0.85\pi_1 + 0.20(1 - \pi_1)$$
$$\pi_1 = 0.85\pi_1 + 0.20 - 0.20\pi_1$$
$$\pi_1 - 0.65\pi_1 = 0.20$$
$$0.35\pi_1 = 0.20$$
$$\pi_1 = 0.57$$

and

$$\pi_2 = 1 - 0.57 = 0.43$$

Other examples of Markov processes include the promotion of managers to various positions within an organization, the migration of people into and out of various regions of the country, and the progression of students through the years of college, including eventually dropping out or graduating.

We see that the proposed promotional strategy will increase Ashley's market share from $\pi_2 = 0.33$ to $\pi_2 = 0.43$. Suppose that the total market consists of 6000 customers per week. The new promotional strategy will increase the number of customers doing their weekly shopping at Ashley's from 2000 to 2580. If the average weekly profit per customer is $10, the proposed promotional strategy can be expected to increase Ashley's profits by $5800 per week. If the cost of the promotional campaign is less than $5800 per week, Ashley should consider implementing the strategy.

This example demonstrates how a Markov analysis of a firm's market share can be useful in decision making. Suppose that instead of trying to attract customers from Murphy's Foodliner, Ashley's directed a promotional effort at increasing the loyalty of its own customers. In this case, p_{22} would increase and p_{21} would decrease. Once we knew the amount of the change, we could calculate new steady-state probabilities and compute the impact on profits.

NOTES AND COMMENTS

1. The Markov processes presented in this section have what is called the *memoryless property*: the current state of the system together with the transition probabilities contain all the information necessary to predict the future behavior of the system. The prior states of the system do not have to be considered. Such Markov processes are considered first-order Markov processes. Higher-order Markov processes are ones in which future states of the system depend on two or more previous states.

2. Analysis of a Markov process model is not intended to optimize any particular aspect of a system. Rather, the analysis predicts or describes the future and steady-state behavior of the system. For instance, in the grocery store example, the analysis of the steady-state behavior provided a forecast or prediction of the market shares for the two competitors. In other applications, quantitative analysts have extended the study of Markov processes to what are called *Markov decision processes*. In these models, decisions can be made at each period, which affect the transition probabilities and hence influence the future behavior of the system. Markov decision processes have been used in analyzing machine breakdown and maintenance operations, planning the movement of patients in hospitals, developing inspection strategies, determining newspaper subscription duration, and analyzing equipment replacement.

16.2   ACCOUNTS RECEIVABLE ANALYSIS

An accounting application in which Markov processes have produced useful results involves the estimation of the allowance for doubtful accounts receivable. This allowance is an estimate of the amount of accounts receivable that will ultimately prove to be uncollectible (i.e., bad debts).

Let us consider the accounts receivable situation for Heidman's Department Store. Heidman's uses two aging categories for its accounts receivable: (1) accounts that are classified as 0–30 days old, and (2) accounts that are classified as 31–90 days old. If any portion of an account balance exceeds 90 days, that portion is written off as a bad debt. Heidman's follows the procedure of aging the total balance in any customer's account according to the oldest unpaid bill. For example, suppose that one customer's account balance on September 30 is as follows:

Date of Purchase	Amount Charged
August 15	$25
September 18	10
September 28	50
	Total $85

An aging of accounts receivable on September 30 would assign the total balance of $85 to the 31–90-day category because the oldest unpaid bill of August 15 is 46 days old. Let us assume that one week later, October 7, the customer pays the August 15 bill of $25. The remaining total balance of $60 would now be placed in the 0–30-day category because the oldest unpaid amount, corresponding to the September 18 purchase, is less than 31 days old. This method of aging accounts receivable is called the *total balance method* because the total account balance is placed in the age category corresponding to the oldest unpaid amount.

Note that under the total balance method of aging accounts receivable, dollars appearing in a 31–90-day category at one point in time may appear in a 0–30-day category at a later point in time. In the preceding example, this movement between categories was true for $60 of September billings, which shifted from a 31–90-day to a 0–30-day category after the August bill had been paid.

Let us assume that on December 31 Heidman's shows a total of $3000 in its accounts receivable and that the firm's management would like an estimate of how much of the $3000 will eventually be collected and how much will eventually result in bad debts. The estimated amount of bad debts will appear as an allowance for doubtful accounts in the year-end financial statements.

Let us see how we can view the accounts receivable operation as a Markov process. First, concentrate on what happens to *one* dollar currently in accounts receivable. As the firm continues to operate into the future, we can consider each week as a trial of a Markov process with a dollar existing in one of the following states of the system:

State 1. Paid category
State 2. Bad debt category
State 3. 0–30-day category
State 4. 31–90-day category

Thus, we can track the week-by-week status of one dollar by using a Markov analysis to identify the state of the system at a particular week or period.

Using a Markov process model with the preceding states, we define the transition probabilities as follows:

p_{ij} = probability of a dollar in state i in one week moving to state j in the next week

Based on historical transitions of accounts receivable dollars, the following matrix of transition probabilities, P, has been developed for Heidman's Department Store:

$$
P = \begin{bmatrix}
p_{11} & p_{12} & p_{13} & p_{14} \\
p_{21} & p_{22} & p_{23} & p_{24} \\
p_{31} & p_{32} & p_{33} & p_{34} \\
p_{41} & p_{42} & p_{43} & p_{44}
\end{bmatrix} = \begin{bmatrix}
1.0 & 0.0 & 0.0 & 0.0 \\
0.0 & 1.0 & 0.0 & 0.0 \\
0.4 & 0.0 & 0.3 & 0.3 \\
0.4 & 0.2 & 0.3 & 0.1
\end{bmatrix}
$$

Note that the probability of a dollar in the 0–30-day category (state 3) moving to the paid category (state 1) in the next period is 0.4. Also, this dollar has a 0.3 probability it will remain in the 0–30-day category (state 3) one week later, and a 0.3 probability that it will be in the 31–90-day category (state 4) one week later. Note also that a dollar in a 0–30-day account cannot make the transition to a bad debt (state 2) in one week.

When absorbing states are present, each row of the transition matrix corresponding to an absorbing state will have a single 1 and all other probabilities will be 0.

An important property of the Markov process model for Heidman's accounts receivable situation is the presence of *absorbing states*. For example, once a dollar makes a transition to state 1, the paid state, the probability of making a transition to any other state is zero. Similarly, once a dollar is in state 2, the bad debt state, the probability of a transition to any other state is zero. Thus, once a dollar reaches state 1 or state 2, the system will remain in this state forever. We can conclude that all accounts receivable dollars will eventually be absorbed into either the paid or the bad debt state, and hence the name **absorbing state.**

Fundamental Matrix and Associated Calculations

Whenever a Markov process has absorbing states, we do not compute steady-state probabilities because each unit ultimately ends up in one of the absorbing states. With absorbing states present, we are interested in knowing the probability that a unit will end up in each of the absorbing states. For the Heidman's Department Store problem, we want to know the probability that a dollar currently in the 0–30-day age category will end up paid (absorbing state 1) as well as the probability that a dollar in this age category will end up a bad debt (absorbing state 2). We also want to know these absorbing-state probabilities for a dollar currently in the 31–90-day age category.

The computation of the absorbing-state probabilities requires the determination and use of what is called a **fundamental matrix.** The mathematical logic underlying the fundamental matrix is beyond the scope of this text. However, as we show, the fundamental matrix is derived from the matrix of transition probabilities and is relatively easy to compute for Markov processes with a small number of states. In the following example, we show the computation of the fundamental matrix and the determination of the absorbing-state probabilities for Heidman's Department Store.

We begin the computations by partitioning the matrix of transition probabilities into the following four parts:

$$
P = \left[\begin{array}{cc|cc}
1.0 & 0.0 & 0.0 & 0.0 \\
0.0 & 1.0 & 0.0 & 0.0 \\
\hline
0.4 & 0.0 & 0.3 & 0.3 \\
0.4 & 0.2 & 0.3 & 0.1
\end{array}\right] = \left[\begin{array}{cc|cc}
1.0 & 0.0 & 0.0 & 0.0 \\
0.0 & 1.0 & 0.0 & 0.0 \\
\hline
\multicolumn{2}{c|}{R} & \multicolumn{2}{c}{Q} \\
\end{array}\right]
$$

where

$$R = \begin{bmatrix} 0.4 & 0.0 \\ 0.4 & 0.2 \end{bmatrix} \qquad Q = \begin{bmatrix} 0.3 & 0.3 \\ 0.3 & 0.1 \end{bmatrix}$$

A matrix N, called a *fundamental matrix,* can be calculated using the following formula:

$$N = (I - Q)^{-1} \tag{16.5}$$

where I is an identity matrix with 1s on the main diagonal and 0s elsewhere. The superscript -1 is used to indicate the inverse of the matrix $(I - Q)$. In Appendix 16.1 we present formulas for finding the inverse of a matrix with two rows and two columns. In Appendix 16.2 we show how Excel's MINVERSE function can be used to compute an inverse.

Before proceeding, we note that to use equation (16.5), the identity matrix I must be chosen such that it has the *same size or dimensionality* as the matrix Q. In our example problem, Q has two rows and two columns, so we must choose

$$I = \begin{bmatrix} 1.0 & 0.0 \\ 0.0 & 1.0 \end{bmatrix}$$

Let us now continue with the example problem by computing the fundamental matrix

$$I - Q = \begin{bmatrix} 1.0 & 0.0 \\ 0.0 & 1.0 \end{bmatrix} - \begin{bmatrix} 0.3 & 0.3 \\ 0.3 & 0.1 \end{bmatrix}$$
$$= \begin{bmatrix} 0.7 & -0.3 \\ -0.3 & 0.9 \end{bmatrix}$$

and (see Appendix 16.1)

$$N = (I - Q)^{-1} = \begin{bmatrix} 1.67 & 0.56 \\ 0.56 & 1.30 \end{bmatrix}$$

If we multiply the fundamental matrix N times the R portion of the P matrix, we obtain the probabilities that accounts receivable dollars initially in states 3 or 4 will eventually reach each of the absorbing states. The multiplication of N times R for the Heidman's Department Store problem provides the following results (again, see Appendix 16.1 for the steps of this matrix multiplication):

$$NR = \begin{bmatrix} 1.67 & 0.56 \\ 0.56 & 1.30 \end{bmatrix}\begin{bmatrix} 0.4 & 0.0 \\ 0.4 & 0.2 \end{bmatrix} = \begin{bmatrix} 0.89 & 0.11 \\ 0.74 & 0.26 \end{bmatrix}$$

The first row of the product NR is the probability that a dollar in the 0–30-day age category will end up in each absorbing state. Thus, we see a 0.89 probability that a dollar in the 0–30-day category will eventually be paid and a 0.11 probability that it will become a bad debt. Similarly, the second row shows the probabilities associated with a dollar in the 31–90-day category; that is, a dollar in the 31–90-day category has a 0.74 probability of eventually being paid and a 0.26 probability of proving to be uncollectible. Using this information, we can predict the amount of money that will be paid and the amount that will be lost as bad debts.

Establishing the Allowance for Doubtful Accounts

Let B represent a two-element vector that contains the current accounts receivable balances in the 0–30-day and the 31–90-day categories; that is,

$$B = \begin{bmatrix} b_1 & b_2 \end{bmatrix}$$

Total dollars in the   Total dollars in the
0–30-day category   0–30-day category

Suppose that the December 31 balance of accounts receivable for Heidman's shows $1000 in the 0–30-day category (state 3) and $2000 in the 31–90-day category (state 4).

$$B = \begin{bmatrix} 1000 & 2000 \end{bmatrix}$$

We can multiply B times NR to determine how much of the $3000 will be collected and how much will be lost. For example

$$BNR = \begin{bmatrix} 1000 & 2000 \end{bmatrix} \begin{bmatrix} 0.89 & 0.11 \\ 0.74 & 0.26 \end{bmatrix}$$
$$= \begin{bmatrix} 2370 & 630 \end{bmatrix}$$

Thus, we see that $2370 of the accounts receivable balances will be collected and $630 will be written off as a bad debt expense. Based on this analysis, the accounting department would set up an allowance for doubtful accounts of $630.

The matrix multiplication of BNR is simply a convenient way of computing the eventual collections and bad debts of the accounts receivable. Recall that the NR matrix showed a 0.89 probability of collecting dollars in the 0–30-day category and a 0.74 probability of collecting dollars in the 31–90-day category. Thus, as was shown by the BNR calculation, we expect to collect a total of $(1000)0.89 + (2000)0.74 = 890 + 1480 = \$2370$.

Suppose that on the basis of the previous analysis Heidman's would like to investigate the possibility of reducing the amount of bad debts. Recall that the analysis indicated that a 0.11 probability or 11% of the amount in the 0–30-day age category and 26% of the amount in the 31–90-day age category will prove to be uncollectible. Let us assume that Heidman's is considering instituting a new credit policy involving a discount for prompt payment.

Management believes that the policy under consideration will increase the probability of a transition from the 0–30-day age category to the paid category and decrease the probability of a transition from the 0–30-day to the 31–90-day age category. Let us assume that a careful study of the effects of this new policy leads management to conclude that the following transition matrix would be applicable:

$$P = \begin{bmatrix} 1.0 & 0.0 & | & 0.0 & 0.0 \\ 0.0 & 1.0 & | & 0.0 & 0.0 \\ - & - & - & - & - \\ 0.6 & 0.0 & | & 0.3 & 0.1 \\ 0.4 & 0.2 & | & 0.3 & 0.1 \end{bmatrix}$$

We see that the probability of a dollar in the 0–30-day age category making a transition to the paid category in the next period has increased to 0.6 and that the probability of a dollar in the 0–30-day age category making a transition to the 31–90-day category has decreased to 0.1. To determine the effect of these changes on bad debt expense, we must calculate N, NR, and BNR. We begin by using equation (16.5) to calculate the fundamental matrix N:

$$N = (I - Q)^{-1} = \left\{ \begin{bmatrix} 1.0 & 0.0 \\ 0.0 & 1.0 \end{bmatrix} - \begin{bmatrix} 0.3 & 0.1 \\ 0.3 & 0.1 \end{bmatrix} \right\}^{-1}$$

$$= \begin{bmatrix} 0.7 & -0.1 \\ -0.3 & 0.9 \end{bmatrix}^{-1}$$

$$= \begin{bmatrix} 1.5 & 0.17 \\ 0.5 & 1.17 \end{bmatrix}$$

By multiplying N times R, we obtain the new probabilities that the dollars in each age category will end up in the two absorbing states:

$$NR = \begin{bmatrix} 1.5 & 0.17 \\ 0.5 & 1.17 \end{bmatrix} \begin{bmatrix} 0.6 & 0.0 \\ 0.4 & 0.2 \end{bmatrix}$$

$$= \begin{bmatrix} 0.97 & 0.03 \\ 0.77 & 0.23 \end{bmatrix}$$

We see that with the new credit policy we would expect only 3% of the funds in the 0–30-day age category and 23% of the funds in the 31–90-day age category to prove to be uncollectible. If, as before, we assume a current balance of $1000 in the 0–30-day age category and $2000 in the 31–90-day age category, we can calculate the total amount of accounts receivable that will end up in the two absorbing states by multiplying B times NR. We obtain

$$BNR = \begin{bmatrix} 1000 & 2000 \end{bmatrix} \begin{bmatrix} 0.97 & 0.03 \\ 0.77 & 0.23 \end{bmatrix}$$

$$= \begin{bmatrix} 2510 & 490 \end{bmatrix}$$

Problem 11, which provides a variation of Heidman's Department Store problem, will give you practice in analyzing Markov processes with absorbing states.

Thus, the new credit policy shows a bad debt expense of $490. Under the previous credit policy, we found the bad debt expense to be $630. Thus, a savings of $630 − $490 = $140 could be expected as a result of the new credit policy. Given the total accounts receivable balance of $3000, this savings represents a 4.7% reduction in bad debt expense. After considering the costs involved, management can evaluate the economics of adopting the new credit policy. If the cost, including discounts, is less than 4.7% of the accounts receivable balance, we would expect the new policy to lead to increased profits for Heidman's Department Store.

SUMMARY

In this chapter we presented Markov process models as well as examples of their application. We saw that a Markov analysis could provide helpful decision-making information about a situation that involves a sequence of repeated trials with a finite number of possible states on each trial. A primary objective is obtaining information about the probability of each state after a large number of transitions or time periods.

A market share application showed the computational procedure for determining the steady-state probabilities that could be interpreted as market shares for two competing supermarkets. In an accounts receivable application, we introduced the notion of absorbing states; for the two absorbing states, referred to as the paid and bad debt categories, we showed how to determine the percentage of an accounts receivable balance that would be absorbed in each of these states.

Markov process models have also been used to analyze strategies in sporting events. The Management Science in Action, Markov Processes and Canadian Curling, describes the advantage gained in the sport of curling from winning the opening coin toss.

MANAGEMENT SCIENCE IN ACTION

MARKOV PROCESSES AND CANADIAN CURLING*

Curling is a sport played on a strip of ice 14 feet wide and 146 feet long—about half the length of a football field. At the end of each strip is a "house" composed of four concentric circles etched in the ice, much like the target in a dartboard. The object is to slide a curling stone—called a rock—down the strip of ice and have it finish as close to the center of the house (the bulls-eye) as possible. A game consists of 10 ends. In an end, each team slides eight rocks down the strip and then the score is tallied. The team with the rock closest to the center of the house wins one or more points. A point is scored for every rock inside the closest rock for the other team. No rocks in the house means no score for the end.

The team that goes last has an advantage. For instance, that team has the opportunity to execute a "take out" by knocking the other team's rock(s) out of the house with their last shot. The team that goes last in an end is said to have the hammer. At the beginning of the game a coin toss determines which team starts with the hammer. As the game progresses, the hammer switches sides after any end in which the team with the hammer scores. If no score is made in an end, the hammer does not switch sides.

A Markov model was developed to determine the expected value of winning the coin toss to start the game with the hammer. Data were obtained for 8421 games played in the Canadian Men's Curling Championship over the 13 years from 1985 to 1997. The transition probabilities were based on the probability distributions for points scored in each of the 10 ends. An interesting finding was that the transition probabilities for the first end and the last end (and any extra ends) differed from those for the middle ends (ends 2 through 9).

Results of the Markov analysis showed that the expected score differential in favor of the team winning the opening coin toss was 1.115 when using three separate sets of transition probabilities. When one set of aggregate transition probabilities was used for all ends, the expected score differential in favor of the team winning the opening toss was 1.006. These results clearly indicate a significant advantage in winning the opening toss.

*Based on Kent J. Kostuk and Keith A. Willoughby, "OR/MS 'Rocks' the 'House,'" *OR/MS Today* (December 1999): 36–39.

GLOSSARY

Trials of the process   The events that trigger transitions of the system from one state to another. In many applications, successive time periods represent the trials of the process.

State of the system   The condition of the system at any particular trial or time period.

Transition probability Given that the system is in state i during one period, the transition probability p_{ij} is the probability that the system will be in state j during the next period.

State probability The probability that the system will be in any particular state. (That is, $\pi_i(n)$ is the probability of the system being in state i in period n.)

Steady-state probability The probability that the system will be in any particular state after a large number of transitions. Once steady state has been reached, the state probabilities do not change from period to period.

Absorbing state A state is said to be absorbing if the probability of making a transition out of that state is zero. Thus, once the system has made a transition into an absorbing state, it will remain there.

Fundamental matrix A matrix necessary for the computation of probabilities associated with absorbing states of a Markov process.

PROBLEMS

1. In the market share analysis of Section 16.1, suppose that we are considering the Markov process associated with the shopping trips of one customer, but we do not know where the customer shopped during the last week. Thus, we might assume a 0.5 probability that the customer shopped at Murphy's and a 0.5 probability that the customer shopped at Ashley's at period 0; that is, $\pi_1(0) = 0.5$ and $\pi_2(0) = 0.5$. Given these initial state probabilities, develop a table similar to Table 16.2 showing the probability of each state in future periods. What do you observe about the long-run probabilities of each state?

2. Management of the New Fangled Softdrink Company believes that the probability of a customer purchasing Red Pop or the company's major competition, Super Cola, is based on the customer's most recent purchase. Suppose that the following transition probabilities are appropriate:

	To	
From	**Red Pop**	**Super Cola**
Red Pop	0.9	0.1
Super Cola	0.1	0.9

 a. Show the two-period tree diagram for a customer who last purchased Red Pop. What is the probability that this customer purchases Red Pop on the second purchase?
 b. What is the long-run market share for each of these two products?
 c. A Red Pop advertising campaign is being planned to increase the probability of attracting Super Cola customers. Management believes that the new campaign will increase to 0.15 the probability of a customer switching from Super Cola to Red Pop. What is the projected effect of the advertising campaign on the market shares?

3. The computer center at Rockbottom University has been experiencing computer downtime. Let us assume that the trials of an associated Markov process are defined as one-hour periods and that the probability of the system being in a running state or a down state is based on the state of the system in the previous period. Historical data show the following transition probabilities:

	To	
From	**Running**	**Down**
Running	0.90	0.10
Down	0.30	0.70

a. If the system is initially running, what is the probability of the system being down in the next hour of operation?

b. What are the steady-state probabilities of the system being in the running state and in the down state?

4. One cause of the downtime in Problem 3 was traced to a specific piece of computer hardware. Management believes that switching to a different hardware component will result in the following transition probabilities:

	To	
From	**Running**	**Down**
Running	0.95	0.05
Down	0.60	0.40

a. What are the steady-state probabilities of the system being in the running and down states?

b. If the cost of the system being down for any period is estimated to be $500 (including lost profits for time down and maintenance), what is the breakeven cost for the new hardware component on a time-period basis?

5. A major traffic problem in the Greater Cincinnati area involves traffic attempting to cross the Ohio River from Cincinnati to Kentucky using Interstate 75. Let us assume that the probability of no traffic delay in one period, given no traffic delay in the preceding period, is 0.85 and that the probability of finding a traffic delay in one period, given a delay in the preceding period, is 0.75. Traffic is classified as having either a delay or a no-delay state, and the period considered is 30 minutes.

a. Assume that you are a motorist entering the traffic system and receive a radio report of a traffic delay. What is the probability that for the next 60 minutes (two time periods) the system will be in the delay state? Note that this result is the probability of being in the delay state for two consecutive periods.

b. What is the probability that in the long run the traffic will not be in the delay state?

c. An important assumption of the Markov process models presented in this chapter has been the constant or stationary transition probabilities as the system operates in the future. Do you believe this assumption should be questioned for this traffic problem? Explain.

6. Data collected from selected major metropolitan areas in the eastern United States show that 2% of individuals living within the city limits move to the suburbs during a one-year period, while 1% of individuals living in the suburbs move to the city during a one-year period. Answer the following questions assuming that this process is modeled by a Markov process with two states: city and suburbs.

a. Prepare the matrix of transition probabilities.

b. Compute the steady-state probabilities.

c. In a particular metropolitan area, 40% of the population lives in the city, and 60% of the population lives in the suburbs. What population changes do your steady-state probabilities project for this metropolitan area?

7. Assume that a third grocery store, Quick Stop Groceries, enters the market share and customer loyalty situation described in Section 16.1. Quick Stop Groceries is smaller than either Murphy's Foodliner or Ashley's Supermarket. However, Quick Stop's convenience with faster service and gasoline for automobiles can be expected to attract some customers who currently make weekly shopping visits to either Murphy's or Ashley's. Assume that the transition probabilities are as follows:

	To		
From	**Murphy's**	**Ashley's**	**Quick Stop**
Murphy's Foodliner	0.85	0.10	0.05
Ashley's Supermarket	0.20	0.75	0.05
Quick Stop Groceries	0.15	0.10	0.75

   a. Compute the steady-state probabilities for this three-state Markov process.
   b. What market share will Quick Stop obtain?
   c. With 1000 customers, the original two-state Markov process in Section 16.1 projected 667 weekly customer trips to Murphy's Foodliner and 333 weekly customer trips to Ashley's Supermarket. What impact will Quick Stop have on the customer visits at Murphy's and Ashley's? Explain.

8. The purchase patterns for two brands of toothpaste can be expressed as a Markov process with the following transition probabilities:

	To	
From	**Special B**	**MDA**
Special B	0.90	0.10
MDA	0.05	0.95

   a. Which brand appears to have the most loyal customers? Explain.
   b. What are the projected market shares for the two brands?

9. Suppose that in Problem 8 a new toothpaste brand enters the market such that the following transition probabilities exist:

	To		
From	**Special B**	**MDA**	**T-White**
Special B	0.80	0.10	0.10
MDA	0.05	0.75	0.20
T-White	0.40	0.30	0.30

What are the new long-run market shares? Which brand will suffer most from the introduction of the new brand of toothpaste?

10. Given the following transition matrix with states 1 and 2 as absorbing states, what is the probability that units in states 3 and 4 end up in each of the absorbing states?

$$P = \begin{bmatrix} 1.0 & 0.0 & 0.0 & 0.0 \\ 0.0 & 1.0 & 0.0 & 0.0 \\ 0.2 & 0.1 & 0.4 & 0.3 \\ 0.2 & 0.2 & 0.1 & 0.5 \end{bmatrix}$$

11. In the Heidman's Department Store problem of Section 16.2, suppose that the following transition matrix is appropriate:

$$P = \begin{bmatrix} 1.0 & 0.0 & 0.0 & 0.0 \\ 0.0 & 1.0 & 0.0 & 0.0 \\ 0.5 & 0.0 & 0.25 & 0.25 \\ 0.5 & 0.2 & 0.05 & 0.25 \end{bmatrix}$$

If Heidman's has $4000 in the 0–30-day category and $5000 in the 31–90-day category, what is your estimate of the amount of bad debts the company will experience?

12. The KLM Christmas Tree Farm owns a plot of land with 5000 evergreen trees. Each year KLM allows retailers of Christmas trees to select and cut trees for sale to individual customers. KLM protects small trees (usually less than 4 feet tall) so that they will be available for sale in future years. Currently, 1500 trees are classified as protected trees, while the remaining 3500 are available for cutting. However, even though a tree is available for cutting in a given year, it may not be selected for cutting until future years. Most trees not cut in a given year live until the next year, but some diseased trees are lost every year.

In viewing the KLM Christmas tree operation as a Markov process with yearly periods, we define the following four states:

State 1. Cut and sold

State 2. Lost to disease

State 3. Too small for cutting

State 4. Available for cutting but not cut and sold

The following transition matrix is appropriate:

$$P = \begin{bmatrix} 1.0 & 0.0 & 0.0 & 0.0 \\ 0.0 & 1.0 & 0.0 & 0.0 \\ 0.1 & 0.2 & 0.5 & 0.2 \\ 0.4 & 0.1 & 0.0 & 0.5 \end{bmatrix}$$

How many of the farm's 5000 trees will be sold eventually, and how many will be lost?

13. A large corporation collected data on the reasons both middle managers and senior managers leave the company. Some managers eventually retire, but others leave the company prior to retirement for personal reasons including more attractive positions with other firms. Assume that the following matrix of one-year transition probabilities applies with the four states of the Markov process being retirement, leaves prior to retirement for personal reasons, stays as a middle manager, stays as a senior manager.

	Retirement	Leaves—Personal	Middle Manager	Senior Manager
Retirement	1.00	0.00	0.00	0.00
Leaves—Personal	0.00	1.00	0.00	0.00
Middle Manager	0.03	0.07	0.80	0.10
Senior Manager	0.08	0.01	0.03	0.88

a. What states are considered absorbing states? Why?
b. Interpret the transition probabilities for the middle managers.
c. Interpret the transition probabilities for the senior managers.

    d. What percentage of the current middle managers will eventually retire from the company? What percentage will leave the company for personal reasons?

    e. The company currently has 920 managers: 640 middle managers and 280 senior managers. How many of these managers will eventually retire from the company? How many will leave the company for personal reasons?

14. Data for the progression of college students at a particular college are summarized in the following matrix of transition probabilities:

	Graduate	Drop Out	Freshman	Sophomore	Junior	Senior
Graduate	1.00	0.00	0.00	0.00	0.00	0.00
Drop Out	0.00	1.00	0.00	0.00	0.00	0.00
Freshman	0.00	0.20	0.15	0.65	0.00	0.00
Sophomore	0.00	0.15	0.00	0.10	0.75	0.00
Junior	0.00	0.10	0.00	0.00	0.05	0.85
Senior	0.90	0.05	0.00	0.00	0.00	0.05

    a. What states are absorbing states?

    b. Interpret the transition probabilities for a sophomore.

    c. Compute the probabilities that a sophomore will graduate and that a sophomore will drop out.

    d. In an address to the incoming class of 600 freshmen, the dean asks the students to look around the auditorium and realize that about 50% of the freshmen present today will not make it to graduation day. Does your Markov process analysis support the dean's statement? Explain.

    e. Currently, the college has 600 freshmen, 520 sophomores, 460 juniors, and 420 seniors. What percentage of the 2000 students attending the college will eventually graduate?

Case Problem   DEALER'S ABSORBING STATE PROBABILITIES IN BLACKJACK

The game of blackjack (sometimes called "21") is a popular casino game. The goal is to have a hand with a value of 21 or as close to 21 as possible without exceeding 21. The player and the dealer are each dealt two cards initially. Both the player and dealer may draw additional cards (called "taking a hit") in order to improve their hand. If either the player or dealer takes a hit and the value of the hand exceeds 21, the player or dealer is said to have gone broke and loses. Face cards and tens count 10 points, aces can be counted as 1 or 11, and all other cards count at their face value. The dealer's advantage is that the player must decide on whether to take a hit first. The player who takes a hit and goes over 21 goes broke and loses, even if the dealer later goes broke. For instance, if the player has 16 and draws any card with a value higher than a 5, the player goes broke and loses. For this reason, players will often decide not to take a hit when the value of their hand is 12 or greater.

    The dealer's hand is dealt with one card up and one card down. So, the player's decision of whether to take a hit is based on knowledge of the dealer's up card. A gambling professional asks you to help determine the probability of the ending value of the dealer's hand given different up cards. House rules at casinos require that the dealer continue to take a hit until the dealer's hand reaches a value of 17 or higher. Having just studied Markov processes, you suggest that the dealer's process of taking hits can be modeled as a Markov process with absorbing states.

Managerial Report

Prepare a report for the professional gambler that summarizes your findings. Include the following:

1. At some casinos, the dealer is required to stay (stop taking hits) when the dealer hand reaches soft or hard 17. A hand of soft 17 is one including an ace that may be counted as 1 or 11. In all casinos, the dealer is required to stay with soft 18, 19, 20, or 21. For each possible up card, determine the probability that the ending value of the dealer's hand is 17, 18, 19, 20, 21, or broke.
2. At other casinos, the dealer is required to take a hit on soft 17, but must stay on all other hands with a value of 17, 18, 19, 20, or 21. For this situation, determine the probability of the ending value of the dealer's hand.
3. Comment on whether the house rule of staying on soft 17 or hitting on soft 17 appears better for the player.

Appendix 16.1   MATRIX NOTATION AND OPERATIONS

Matrix Notation

A *matrix* is a rectangular arrangement of numbers. For example, consider the following matrix that we have named D:

$$D = \begin{bmatrix} 1 & 3 & 2 \\ 0 & 4 & 5 \end{bmatrix}$$

The matrix D is said to consist of six elements, where each element of D is a number. To identify a particular element of a matrix, we have to specify its location. Therefore, we introduce the concepts of rows and columns.

All elements across some horizontal line in a matrix are said to be in a row of the matrix. For example, elements 1, 3, and 2 in D are in the first row, and elements 0, 4, and 5 are in the second row. By convention, we refer to the top row as row 1, the second row from the top as row 2, and so on.

All elements along some vertical line are said to be in a column of the matrix. Elements 1 and 0 in D are elements in the first column, elements 3 and 4 are elements of the second column, and elements 2 and 5 are elements of the third column. By convention, we refer to the leftmost column as column 1, the next column to the right as column 2, and so on.

We can identify a particular element in a matrix by specifying its row and column position. For example, the element in row 1 and column 2 of D is the number 3. This position is written as

$$d_{12} = 3$$

In general, we use the following notation to refer to the specific elements of D:

$$d_{ij} = \text{element located in the } i\text{th row and } j\text{th column of } D$$

We always use capital letters for the names of matrixes and the corresponding lowercase letters with two subscripts to denote the elements.

The *size* of a matrix is the number of rows and columns in the matrix and is written as the number of rows $\times$ the number of columns. Thus, the size of D is 2×3.

Frequently we will encounter matrixes that have only one row or one column. For example,

$$G = \begin{bmatrix} 6 \\ 4 \\ 2 \\ 3 \end{bmatrix}$$

is a matrix that has only one column. Whenever a matrix has only one column, we call the matrix a *column vector*. In a similar manner, any matrix that has only one row is called a *row vector*. Using our previous notation for the elements of a matrix, we could refer to specific elements in G by writing g_{ij}. However, because G has only one column, the column position is unimportant, and we need only specify the row the element of interest is in. That is, instead of referring to elements in a vector using g_{ij}, we specify only one subscript, which denotes the position of the element in the vector. For example,

$$g_1 = 6 \qquad g_2 = 4 \qquad g_3 = 2 \qquad g_4 = 3$$

Matrix Operations

Matrix Transpose   The transpose of a matrix is formed by making the rows in the original matrix the columns in the transpose matrix, and by making the columns in the original matrix the rows in the transpose matrix. For example, the transpose of the matrix

$$D = \begin{bmatrix} 1 & 3 & 2 \\ 0 & 4 & 5 \end{bmatrix}$$

is

$$D^t = \begin{bmatrix} 1 & 0 \\ 3 & 4 \\ 2 & 5 \end{bmatrix}$$

Note that we use the superscript t to denote the transpose of a matrix.

Matrix Multiplication   We demonstrate how to perform two types of matrix multiplication: (1) multiplying two vectors, and (2) multiplying a matrix times a matrix.

The product of a row vector of size $1 \times n$ times a column vector of size $n \times 1$ is the number obtained by multiplying the first element in the row vector times the first element in the column vector, the second element in the row vector times the second element in the column vector, and continuing on through the last element in the row vector times the last element in the column vector, and then summing the products. Suppose, for example, that we wanted to multiply the row vector H times the column vector G, where

$$H = \begin{bmatrix} 2 & 1 & 5 & 0 \end{bmatrix} \text{ and } G = \begin{bmatrix} 6 \\ 4 \\ 2 \\ 3 \end{bmatrix}$$

The product HG, referred to as a vector product, is given by

$$HG = 2(6) + 1(4) + 5(2) + 0(3) = 26$$

The product of a matrix of size $p \times n$ and a matrix of size $n \times m$ is a new matrix of size $p \times m$. The element in the ith row and jth column of the new matrix is given by the vector product of the ith row of the $p \times n$ matrix times the jth column of the $n \times m$ matrix. Suppose, for example, that we want to multiply D times A, where

$$D = \begin{bmatrix} 1 & 3 & 2 \\ 0 & 4 & 5 \end{bmatrix} \quad A = \begin{bmatrix} 1 & 3 & 5 \\ 2 & 0 & 4 \\ 1 & 5 & 2 \end{bmatrix}$$

Let $C = DA$ denote the product of D times A. The element in row 1 and column 1 of C is given by the vector product of the first row of D times the first column of A. Thus

$$c_{11} = \begin{bmatrix} 1 & 3 & 2 \end{bmatrix} \begin{bmatrix} 1 \\ 2 \\ 1 \end{bmatrix} = 1(1) + 3(2) + 2(1) = 9$$

The element in row 2 and column 1 of C is given by the vector product of the second row of D times the first column of A. Thus,

$$c_{21} = \begin{bmatrix} 0 & 4 & 5 \end{bmatrix} \begin{bmatrix} 1 \\ 2 \\ 1 \end{bmatrix} = 0(1) + 4(2) + 5(1) = 13$$

Calculating the remaining elements of C in a similar fashion, we obtain

$$C = \begin{bmatrix} 9 & 13 & 21 \\ 13 & 25 & 26 \end{bmatrix}$$

Clearly, the product of a matrix and a vector is just a special case of multiplying a matrix times a matrix. For example, the product of a matrix of size $m \times n$ and a vector of size $n \times 1$ is a new vector of size $m \times 1$. The element in the ith position of the new vector is given by the vector product of the ith row of the $m \times n$ matrix times the $n \times 1$ column vector. Suppose, for example, that we want to multiply D times K, where

$$D = \begin{bmatrix} 1 & 3 & 2 \\ 0 & 4 & 5 \end{bmatrix} \quad K = \begin{bmatrix} 1 \\ 4 \\ 2 \end{bmatrix}$$

The first element of DK is given by the vector product of the first row of D times K. Thus,

$$\begin{bmatrix} 1 & 3 & 2 \end{bmatrix} \begin{bmatrix} 1 \\ 4 \\ 2 \end{bmatrix} = 1(1) + 3(4) + 2(2) = 17$$

The second element of DK is given by the vector product of the second row of D and K. Thus,

$$\begin{bmatrix} 0 & 4 & 5 \end{bmatrix} \begin{bmatrix} 1 \\ 4 \\ 2 \end{bmatrix} = 0(1) + 4(4) + 5(2) = 26$$

Hence, we see that the product of the matrix D times the vector K is given by

$$DK = \begin{bmatrix} 1 & 3 & 2 \\ 0 & 4 & 5 \end{bmatrix} \begin{bmatrix} 1 \\ 4 \\ 2 \end{bmatrix} = \begin{bmatrix} 17 \\ 26 \end{bmatrix}$$

Can any two matrixes be multiplied? The answer is no. To multiply two matrixes, the number of the columns in the first matrix must equal the number of rows in the second. If this property is satisfied, the matrixes are said to *conform for multiplication*. Thus, in our example, D and K could be multiplied because D had three columns and K had three rows.

Matrix Inverse   The inverse of a matrix A is another matrix, denoted A^{-1}, such that $A^{-1}A = I$ and $AA^{-1} = I$. The inverse of any square matrix A consisting of two rows and two columns is computed as follows:

$$A = \begin{bmatrix} a_{11} & a_{12} \\ a_{21} & a_{22} \end{bmatrix}$$

$$A^{-1} = \begin{bmatrix} a_{22}/d & -a_{12}/d \\ -a_{21}/d & a_{11}/d \end{bmatrix}$$

where $d = a_{11}a_{22} - a_{21}a_{12}$ is the determinant of the 2×2 matrix A. For example, if

$$A = \begin{bmatrix} 0.7 & -0.3 \\ -0.3 & 0.9 \end{bmatrix}$$

then

$$d = (0.7)(0.9) - (-0.3)(-0.3) = 0.54$$

and

$$A^{-1} = \begin{bmatrix} 0.9/0.54 & 0.3/0.54 \\ 0.3/0.54 & 0.7/0.54 \end{bmatrix} = \begin{bmatrix} 1.67 & 0.56 \\ 0.56 & 1.30 \end{bmatrix}$$

Appendix 16.2   MATRIX INVERSION WITH EXCEL

Excel provides a function called MINVERSE that can be used to compute the inverse of a matrix. This function is extremely useful when the inverse of a matrix of size 3×3 or larger is desired. To see how it is used, suppose we want to invert the following 3×3 matrix:

$$\begin{bmatrix} 3 & 5 & 0 \\ 0 & 1 & 1 \\ 8 & 5 & 0 \end{bmatrix}$$

Enter the matrix into cells B3:D5 of an Excel worksheet. The following steps will compute the inverse and place it in cells B7:D9:

Step 1. Select cells **B7:D9**
Step 2. Type = **MINVERSE(B3:D5)**
Step 3. Press **Ctrl + Shift + Enter**

Step 3 may appear strange. Excel's MINVERSE function returns an array (matrix) and must be used in what Excel calls an array formula. In step 3, we must press the Ctrl and Shift keys while we press Enter. The inverse matrix will then appear as follows in cells B7:D9:

$$\begin{bmatrix} -.20 & 0 & .20 \\ .32 & 0 & -.12 \\ -.32 & 1 & .12 \end{bmatrix}$$

APPENDIXES

APPENDIX A
Building Spreadsheet Models

APPENDIX B
Areas for the Standard Normal Distribution

APPENDIX C
Values of $e^{-\lambda}$

APPENDIX D
References and Bibliography

APPENDIX E
Self-Test Solutions and Answers to Even-Numbered Problems

Appendix A   Building Spreadsheet Models

The purpose of this appendix is twofold. First, we provide an overview of Excel and discuss the basic operations needed to work with Excel workbooks and worksheets. Second, we provide an introduction to building mathematical models using Excel, including a discussion of how to find and use particular Excel functions, how to design and build good spreadsheet models, and how to ensure that these models are free of errors.

OVERVIEW OF MICROSOFT EXCEL

When using Excel for modeling, the data and the model are displayed in workbooks, each of which contains a series of worksheets. Figure A.1 shows the layout of a blank workbook created each time Excel is opened. The workbook is named Book1 and consists of three worksheets named Sheet1, Sheet2, and Sheet3. Excel highlights the worksheet currently displayed (Sheet1) by setting the name on the worksheet tab in bold. To select a different worksheet, simply click on the corresponding tab. Note that cell A1 is initially selected.

A workbook is a file containing one or more worksheets.

    The wide bar located across the top of the workbook is referred to as the Ribbon. Tabs, located at the top of the Ribbon, provide quick access to groups of related commands. There are eight tabs: Home, Insert, Page Layout, Formulas, Data, Review, View, and Add-Ins. Each tab contains several groups of related commands. Note that the Home tab is selected when Excel is opened. Four of the seven groups are displayed in Figure A.2. Under the Home tab there are seven groups of related commands: Clipboard, Font, Alignment, Number, Styles, Cells, and Editing. Commands are arranged within each group. For example, to change selected text to boldface, click the Home tab and click the Bold button in the Font group.

    Figure A.3 illustrates the location of the Office Button, the Quick Access Toolbar, and the Formula Bar. When you click the Office Button, Excel provides a list of workbook options such as opening, saving, and printing (worksheets). The Quick Access Toolbar allows you to quickly access these workbook options. For instance, the Quick Access Toolbar shown in Figure A.3 includes an Open button that can be used to open files without having to first click the Office Button. To add or remove features on the Quick Access Toolbar click the Customize Quick Access Toolbar button on the Quick Access Toolbar.

    The Formula Bar contains a Name box, the Insert Function button f_x, and a Formula box. In Figure A.3, "A1" appears in the Name box because cell A1 is selected. You can select any other cell in the worksheet by using the mouse to move the cursor to another cell and clicking or by typing the new cell location in the name box and pressing the enter key. The Formula box is used to display the formula in the currently selected cell. For instance, if you had entered =A1+A2 into cell A3, whenever you select cell A3, the formula =A1+A2 will be shown in the Formula box. This feature makes it very easy to see and edit a formula in a particular cell. The Insert Function button allows you to quickly access all of the functions available in Excel. Later, we show how to find and use a particular function.

FIGURE A.1   BLANK WORKBOOK CREATED WHEN EXCEL IS STARTED

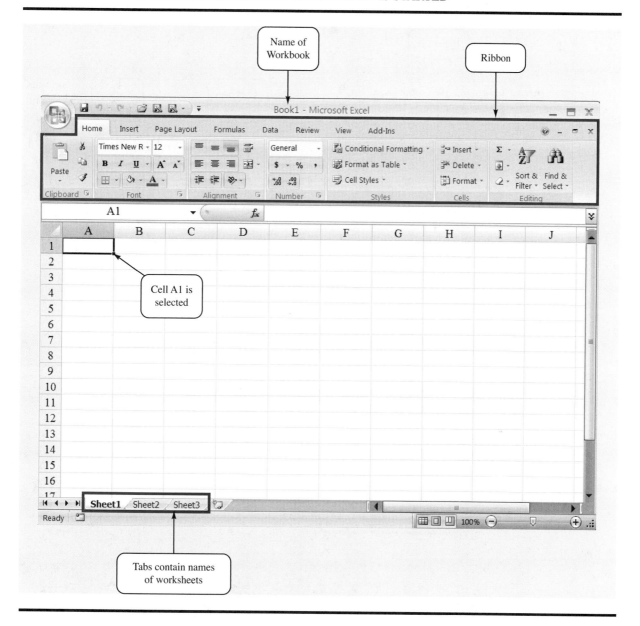

BASIC WORKBOOK OPERATIONS

Figure A.4 illustrates the worksheet options that can be performed after right clicking on a worksheet tab. For instance, to change the name of the current worksheet from "Sheet1" to "NowlinModel," right click the worksheet tab named "Sheet1" and select the Rename option. The current worksheet name (Sheet1) will be highlighted. Then, simply type the new name (NowlinModel) and press the Enter key to rename the worksheet.

FIGURE A.2   PORTION OF THE HOME TAB

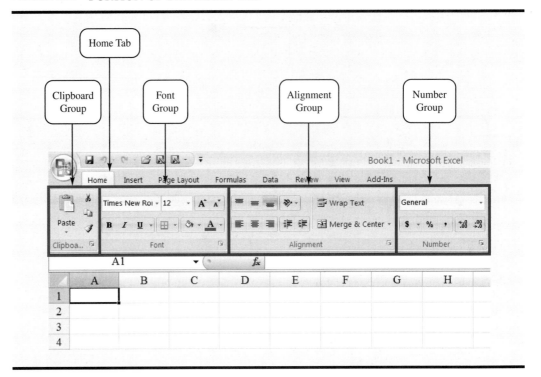

FIGURE A.3   EXCEL OFFICE BUTTON, QUICK ACCESS TOOLBAR, AND
                  FORMULA BAR

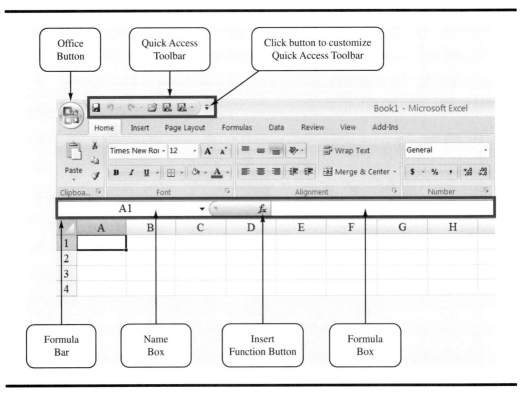

FIGURE A.4   WORKSHEET OPTIONS OBTAINED AFTER RIGHT CLICKING ON A WORKSHEET TAB

Suppose that you wanted to create a copy of "Sheet 1." After right clicking the tab named "Sheet1," select the Move or Copy option. When the Move or Copy dialog box appears, select Create a Copy and click OK. The name of the copied worksheet will appear as "Sheet1 (2)." You can then rename it, if desired.

To add a worksheet to the workbook, right click any worksheet tab and select the Insert option; when the Insert dialog box appears, select Worksheet and click OK. An additional blank worksheet titled "Sheet 4" will appear in the workbook. You can also insert a new worksheet by clicking the Insert Worksheet tab button 📄 that appears to the right of the last worksheet tab displayed. Worksheets can be deleted by right clicking the worksheet tab and choosing Delete. After clicking Delete, a window will appear warning you that any data appearing in the worksheet will be lost. Click Delete to confirm that you do want to delete the worksheet. Worksheets can also be moved to other workbooks or a different position in the current workbook by using the Move or Copy option.

Creating, Saving, and Opening Files

As an illustration of manually entering, saving, and opening a file, we will use the Nowlin Plastics production example from Chapter 1. The objective is to compute the breakeven point for a product that has a fixed cost of $3000, a variable cost per unit of $2, and a selling price per unit of $5. We begin by creating a worksheet containing the problem data.

If you have just opened Excel, a blank workbook containing three worksheets will be displayed. The Nowlin data can now be entered manually by simply typing the fixed cost of $3000, the variable cost of $2, and the selling price of $5 into one of the worksheets. If Excel is currently running and no blank workbook is displayed, you can create a new blank workbook using the following steps:

Step 1.   Click the **Office** button
Step 2.   Click **New** in the list of options

Step 3. When the New Workbook dialog box appears:
Select **Blank and recent** under Templates
Double click **Blank Workbook**

A new workbook containing three worksheets labeled Sheet1, Sheet2, and Sheet3 will appear.

We will place the data for the Nowlin example in the top portion of Sheet1 of the new workbook. First, we enter the label "Nowlin Plastics" into cell A1. To identify each of the three data values we enter the label "Fixed Cost" into cell A3, the label "Variable Cost Per Unit" into cell A5, and the label "Selling Price Per Unit" into cell A7. Next, we enter the actual cost and price data into the corresponding cells in column B: the value of $3000 in cell B3; the value of $2 in cell B5; and the value of $5 into cell B7. Finally, we will change the name of the worksheet from "Sheet1" to "NowlinModel" using the procedure described previously. Figure A.5 shows a portion of the worksheet we have just developed.

Before we begin the development of the model portion of the worksheet, we recommend that you first save the current file; this will prevent you from having to reenter the data in case something happens that causes Excel to close. To save the workbook using the filename "Nowlin," we perform the following steps:

Step 1. Click the **Office** button
Step 2. Click **Save** in the list of options
Step 3. When the **Save As** dialog box appears:
In the **Save in** box select the location where you want to save the file
Type the file name "Nowlin" in the **File name** box
Click **Save**

FIGURE A.5   NOWLIN PLASTICS DATA

	A	B
1	**Nowlin Plastics**	
2		
3	**Fixed Cost**	$3,000
4		
5	**Variable Cost Per Unit**	$2
6		
7	**Selling Price Per Unit**	$5
8		
9		
10		
11		
12		
13		
14		
15		
16		
17		
18		

Excel's Save command is designed to save the file as an Excel workbook. As you work with and build models in Excel, you should follow the practice of periodically saving the file so you will not lose any work. Simply follow the procedure described above, using the Save command.

*Keyboard shortcut: To save the file, press **CTRL S**.*

Sometimes you may want to create a copy of an existing file. For instance, suppose you change one or more of the data values and would like to save the modified file using the filename "NowlinMod." The following steps show how to save the modified workbook using filename "NowlinMod."

Step 1. Click the **Office** button
Step 2. Position the mouse pointer over **Save As**
Step 3. Click **Excel Workbook** from the list of options
Step 4. When the **Save As** dialog box appears:
In the **Save in** box select the location where you want to save the file
Type the filename "NowlinMod" in the **File name** box
Click **Save**

Once the NowlinMod workbook has been saved, you can continue to work with the file to perform whatever type of analysis is appropriate. When you are finished working with the file, simply click the close window button ✕ located at the top right-hand corner of the Ribbon.

You can easily access a saved file at another point in time. For example, the following steps show how to open the previously saved Nowlin workbook.

Step 1. Click the **Office** button
Step 2. Click **Open** in the list of options
Step 3. When the **Open** dialog box appears:
In the **Look in** box select the location where you previously saved the file
Type the filename "Nowlin" in the **File name** box
Click **Open**

The procedures we showed for saving or opening a workbook begin by clicking on the Office Button to access the Save and Open commands. Once you have used Excel for a while, you will probably find it more convenient to add these commands to the Quick Access Toolbar.

CELLS, REFERENCES, AND FORMULAS IN EXCEL

Assume that the Nowlin workbook is open again and that we would like to develop a model that can be used to compute the profit or loss associated with a given production volume. We will use the bottom portion of the worksheet shown in Figure A.5 to develop the model. The model will contain formulas that *refer to the location of the data cells* in the upper section of the worksheet. By putting the location of the data cells in the formula, we will build a model that can be easily updated with new data. This will be discussed in more detail later in this appendix in the section Principles for Building Good Spreadsheet Models.

We enter the label "Models" into cell A10 to provide a visual reminder that the bottom portion of this worksheet will contain the model. Next, we enter the labels "Production Volume" into cell A12, "Total Cost" into cell A14, "Total Revenue" into cell A16, and "Total Profit (Loss)" into cell A18. Cell B12 is used to contain a value for the production volume.

FIGURE A.6   NOWLIN PLASTICS DATA AND MODEL

	A	B
1	**Nowlin Plastics**	
2		
3	**Fixed Cost**	3000
4		
5	**Variable Cost Per Unit**	2
6		
7	**Selling Price Per Unit**	5
8		
9		
10	**Models**	
11		
12	**Production Volume**	
13		
14	**Total Cost**	=B3+B5*B12
15		
16	**Total Revenue**	=B7*B12
17		
18	**Total Profit (Loss)**	=B16-B14

We will now enter formulas into cells B14, B16, and B18 that use the production volume in cell B12 to compute the values for total cost, total revenue, and total profit or loss.

Total cost is the sum of the fixed cost (cell B3) and the total variable cost. The total variable cost is the product of the variable cost per unit (cell B5) and production volume (cell B12). Thus, the formula for total variable cost is B5*B12 and to compute the value of total cost, we enter the formula =B3+B5*B12 into cell B14. Next, total revenue is the product of the selling price per unit (cell B7) and the number of units produced (cell B12), which we enter in cell B16 as the formula =B7*B12. Finally, the total profit or loss is the difference between the total revenue (cell B16) and the total cost (cell B14). Thus, in cell B18 we enter the formula =B16-B14. Figure A.6 shows a portion of the formula worksheet just described.

We can now compute the total profit or loss for a particular production volume by entering a value for the production volume into cell B12. Figure A.7 shows the results after entering a value of 800 into cell B12. We see that a production volume of 800 units results in a total cost of $4600, a total revenue of $4000, and a loss of $600.

USING EXCEL FUNCTIONS

Excel provides a wealth of built-in formulas or functions for developing mathematical models. If we know which function is needed and how to use it, we can simply enter the function into the appropriate worksheet cell. However, if we are not sure which functions are available to accomplish a task or are not sure how to use a particular function, Excel can provide assistance.

FIGURE A.7   NOWLIN PLASTICS RESULTS

	A	B
1	**Nowlin Plastics**	
2		
3	**Fixed Cost**	$3,000
4		
5	**Variable Cost Per Unit**	$2
6		
7	**Selling Price Per Unit**	$5
8		
9		
10	**Models**	
11		
12	**Production Volume**	800
13		
14	**Total Cost**	$4,600
15		
16	**Total Revenue**	$4,000
17		
18	**Total Profit (Loss)**	−$600

Finding the Right Excel Function

To identify the functions available in Excel, click the Formulas tab on the Ribbon and then click the Insert Function button in the Function Library group. Alternatively, click the Insert Function button f_x on the formula bar. Either approach provides the Insert Function dialog box shown in Figure A.8.

The Search for a function box at the top of the Insert Function dialog box enables us to type a brief description for what we want to do. After doing so and clicking Go, Excel will search for and display, in the Select a function box, the functions that may accomplish our task. In many situations, however, we may want to browse through an entire category of functions to see what is available. For this task, the Or select a category box is helpful.

It contains a dropdown list of several categories of functions provided by Excel. Figure A.8 shows that we selected the Math & Trig category. As a result, Excel's Math & Trig functions appear in alphabetical order in the Select a function box. We see the ABS function listed first, followed by the ACOS function, and so on.

Colon Notation

Although many functions, such as the ABS function, have a single argument, some Excel functions depend on arrays. Colon notation provides an efficient way to convey arrays and matrices of cells to functions. The colon notation may be described as follows: B3:B5 means cell B1 "through" cell B5, namely the array of values stored in the locations (B1,B2,B3,B4,B5). Consider for example the following function =SUM(B1:B5). The sum function adds up the elements contained in the function's argument. Hence, =SUM(B1:B5) evaluates the following formula:

$$=B1+B2+B3+B4+B5$$

FIGURE A.8   INSERT FUNCTION DIALOG BOX

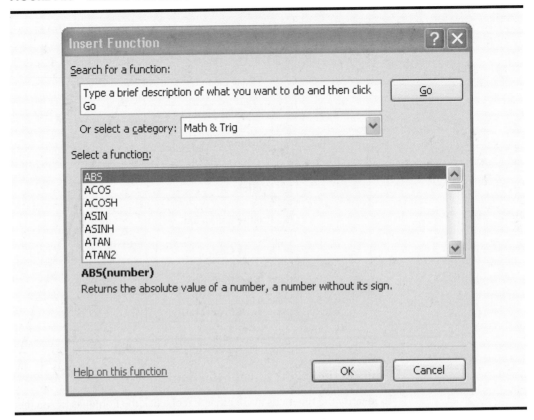

Inserting a Function into a Worksheet Cell

Through the use of an example, we will now show how to use the Insert Function and Function Arguments dialog boxes to select a function, develop its arguments, and insert the function into a worksheet cell. We also illustrate the use of a very useful function, the SUMPRODUCT function, and how to use colon notation in the argument of a function.

The SUMPRODUCT function, as shown in Figure A.9, is used in many of the Solver examples in the textbook. Note that SUMPRODUCT is now highlighted, and that immediately below the Select a function box we see SUMPRODUCT(array1,array2,array3, . . .), which indicates that the SUMPRODUCT function contains the array arguments array1, array2, array3, ... In addition, we see that the description of the SUMPRODUCT function is "Returns the sum of the products of corresponding ranges or arrays." For example, the function =SUMPRODUCT(A1:A3, B1:B3) evaluates the formula A1*B1 + A2*B2 + A3*B3. As shown in the following example, this function can be very useful in calculations of cost, profit, and other such functions involving multiple arrays of numbers.

Figure A.10 displays an Excel worksheet for the Foster Generators Problem that appears in Chapter 6. This problem involves the transportation of a product from three plants (Cleveland, Bedford, and York) to four distribution centers (Boston, Chicago, St. Louis, and Lexington). The costs for each unit shipped from each plant to each distribution center are shown in cells B5:E7, and the values in cells B17:E19 are the number of units shipped

FIGURE A.9   DESCRIPTION OF THE SUMPRODUCT FUNCTION IN THE INSERT
FUNCTION DIALOG BOX

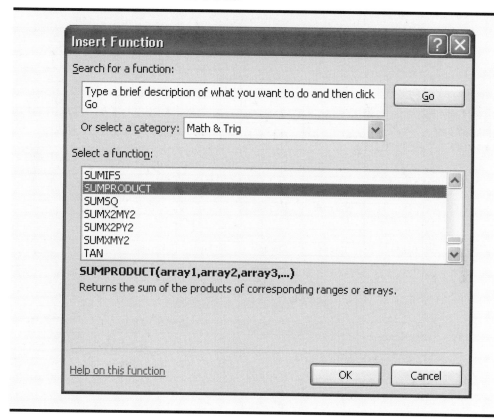

from each plant to each distribution center. Cell B13 will contain the total transportation cost corresponding to the transportation cost values in cells B5:E7 and the values of the number of units shipped in cells B17:E19.

The following steps show how to use the SUMPRODUCT function to compute the total transportation cost for Foster Generators.

Step 1. Select **cell C13**
Step 2. Click f_x on the formula bar
Step 3. When the **Insert Function** dialog box appears:
Select **Math & Trig** in the **Or select a category** box
Select **SUMPRODUCT** in the **Select a function** box (as shown in Figure A.9)
Click **OK**
Step 4. When the **Function Arguments** box appears (see Figure A.11):
Enter B5:E7 in the **Array1** box
Enter B17:E19 in the **Array2** box
Click **OK**

The worksheet then appears as shown in Figure A.12. The value of the total transportation cost in cell C13 is 39500, or $39,500.

FIGURE A.10   EXCEL WORKSHEET USED TO CALCULATE TOTAL SHIPPING COSTS
FOR THE FOSTER GENERATORS TRANSPORTATION PROBLEM

Foster Generators

	A	B	C	D	E	F	G	H
1	**Foster Generators**							
2								
3				**Destination**				
4	**Origin**	Boston	Chicago	St. Louis	Lexington	**Supply**		
5	Cleveland	3	2	7	6	5000		
6	Bedford	7	5	2	3	6000		
7	York	2	5	4	5	2500		
8	**Demand**	6000	4000	2000	1500			
9								
10								
11	**Model**							
12								
13		**Min Cost**						
14								
15				**Destination**				
16	**Origin**	Boston	Chicago	St. Louis	Lexington	**Total**		
17	Cleveland	3500	1500	0	0	5000	<=	5000
18	Bedford	0	2500	2000	1500	6000	<=	6000
19	York	2500	0	0	0	2500	<=	2500
20	**Total**	6000	4000	2000	1500			
21		=	=	=	=			
22		6000	4000	2000	1500			

FIGURE A.11   COMPLETED FUNCTION ARGUMENTS DIALOG BOX FOR THE
SUMPRODUCT FUNCTION

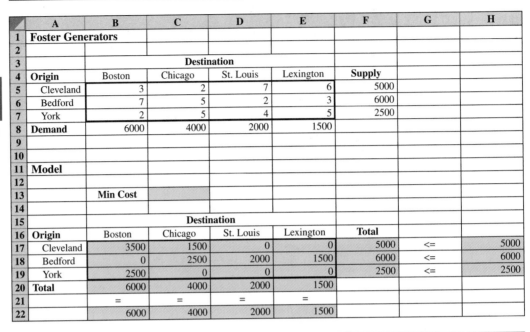

FIGURE A.12 EXCEL WORKSHEET SHOWING THE USE OF EXCEL'S SUMPRODUCT
FUNCTION TO CALCULATE TOTAL SHIPPING COSTS

	A	B	C	D	E	F	G	H
1	Foster Generators							
2								
3				Destination				
4	Origin	Boston	Chicago	St. Louis	Lexington	Supply		
5	Cleveland	3	2	7	6	5000		
6	Bedford	7	5	2	3	6000		
7	York	2	5	4	5	2500		
8	Demand	6000	4000	2000	1500			
9								
10								
11	Model							
12								
13		Min Cost	39500					
14								
15				Destination				
16	Origin	Boston	Chicago	St. Louis	Lexington	Total		
17	Cleveland	3500	1500	0	0	5000	<=	5000
18	Bedford	0	2500	2000	1500	6000	<=	6000
19	York	2500	0	0	0	2500	<=	2500
20	Total	6000	4000	2000	1500			
21		=	=	=	=			
22		6000	4000	2000	1500			

We illustrated the use of Excel's capability to provide assistance in using the SUMPRODUCT function. The procedure is similar for all Excel functions. This capability is especially helpful if you do not know which function to use or forget the proper name and/or syntax for a function.

ADDITIONAL EXCEL FUNCTIONS FOR MODELING

In this section we introduce some additional Excel functions that have proven useful in modeling decision problems.

IF and COUNTIF Functions

Let us consider the case of Gambrell Manufacturing. Gambrell Manufacturing produces car stereos. Stereos are composed of a variety of components that the company must carry in inventory to keep production running smoothly. However, because inventory can be a costly investment, Gambrell generally likes to keep the amount of inventory of the components it uses in manufacturing to a minimum. To help monitor and control its inventory of components, Gambrell uses an inventory policy known as an "order up to" policy. This type of inventory policy and others are discussed in detail in Chapter 14.

The "order up to policy" is as follows. Whenever the inventory on hand drops below a certain level, enough units are ordered to return the inventory to that predetermined level. If the current number of units in inventory, denoted by H, drops below M units, we order

FIGURE A.13   THE GAMBRELL MANUFACTURING COMPONENT ORDERING MODEL

	A	B	C	D	E	F
4	Component ID	570	578	741	755	
5	Inventory On-Hand	5	30	70	17	
6	Up to Order Point	100	55	70	45	
7	Cost per unit	$4.50	$12.50	$3.26	$4.15	
8						
9	Fixed Cost per Order	$120				
10						
11	**Model**					
12						
13	Component ID	570	578	741	755	
14	Order Quantity	95	25	0	28	
15	Cost of Goods	$384.75	$312.50	$0.00	$116.20	
16						
17	Total Number of Orders	3				
18						
19	Total Fixed costs	$360.00				
20	Total Cost of Goods	$813.45				
21	Total Cost	$1,173.45				
22						

WEB file

Gambrell

enough to get the inventory level back up to M units. M is called the Order Up to Point. Stated mathematically, if Q is the amount we order, then

$$Q = M - H$$

An inventory model for Gambrell Manufacturing appears in Figure A.13. In this worksheet, labeled "OrderQuantity" in the upper half of the worksheet, the component ID number, inventory on hand (H), order up to point (M), and cost per unit are given for each of four components. Also given in this sheet is the fixed cost per order. The fixed cost is interpreted as follows: Each time a component is ordered, it costs Gambrell $120 to process the order. The fixed cost of $120 is incurred regardless of how many units are ordered.

The model portion of the worksheet calculates the order quantity for each component. For example, for component 570, $M = 100$ and $H = 5$, so $Q = M - H = 100 - 5 = 95$. For component 741, $M = 70$ and $H = 70$ and no units are ordered because the on-hand inventory of 70 units is equal to the order point of 70. The calculations are similar for the other two components.

Depending on the number of units ordered, Gambrell receives a discount on the cost per unit. If 50 or more units are ordered, there is a quantity discount of 10% on every unit purchased. For example, for component 741, the cost per unit is $4.50 and 95 units are ordered. Because 95 exceeds the 50-unit requirement, there is a 10% discount and the cost per unit is reduced to $4.50 − 0.1($4.50) = $4.50 − $0.45 = $4.05. Not including the fixed cost, the cost of goods purchased is then $4.05(95) = $384.75.

The Excel functions used to perform these calculations are shown in Figure A.14. The IF function is used to calculate the purchase cost of goods for each component in row 15. The general form of the IF function is

=IF(*condition, result if condition is true, result if condition is false*)

FIGURE A.14   FORMULAS AND FUNCTIONS FOR GAMBRELL MANUFACTURING

	A	B	C	D	E
1					
2	**Gambrell Manufacturing**				
3					
4	Component ID	570	578	741	755
5	Inventory On-Hand	5	30	70	17
6	Up to Order Point	100	55	70	45
7	Cost per unit	4.5	12.5	3.26	4.15
8					
9	Fixed Cost per Order	120			
10					
11	**Model**				
12					
13	Component ID	=B4	=C4	=D4	=E4
14	Order Quantity	=B6-B5	=C6-C5	=D6-D5	=E6-E5
15	Cost of Goods	=IF(B14>=50,0.9*B7,B7)*B14	=IF(C14>=50, 0.9*C7,C7)*C14	=IF(D14>=50, 0.9*D7,D7)*D14	=IF(E14>=50, 0.9*E7,E7)*E14
16					
17	Total Number of Orders	=COUNTIF(B14:E14,">0")			
18					
19	Total Fixed Costs	=B17*B9			
20	Total Cost of Goods	=SUM(B15:E15)			
21	Total Cost	=SUM(B19:B20)			
22					

For example, in cell B15 we have =IF(B14>=50,0.9*B7,B7)*B14. This statement says if the order quantity (cell B14) is greater than or equal to 50, then the cost per unit is 0.9*B7 (there is a 10% discount); otherwise, there is no discount and the cost per unit is the amount given in cell B7. The purchase cost of goods for the other components are computed in a like manner.

The total cost in cell B21 is the sum of the purchase cost of goods ordered in row 15 and the fixed ordering costs. Because we place three orders (one each for components 570, 578, and 755), the fixed cost of the orders is 3*120 = $360.

The COUNTIF function in cell B17 is used to count how many times we order. In particular, it counts the number of components having a positive order quantity. The general form of the COUNTIF function is

$$=\text{COUNTIF}(range, condition)$$

The *range* is the range to search for the *condition*. The condition is the test to be counted when satisfied. *Note that quotes are required for the condition with the COUNTIF function.* In the Gambrell model in Figure A.14, cell B17 counts the number of cells that are greater than zero in the range of cells B14:E14. In the model, because only cells B14, C14, and E14 are greater than zero, the COUNTIF function in cell B17 returns 3.

As we have seen, IF and COUNTIF are powerful functions that allow us to make calculations based on a condition holding (or not). There are other such conditional functions available in Excel. In the problems at the end of this appendix, we ask you to investigate one such function, the SUMIF function. Another conditional function that is extremely useful in modeling is the VLOOKUP function. We discuss the VLOOKUP function with an example in the next section.

VLOOKUP Function

Next, consider the workbook named *OM455* shown in Figure A.15. The worksheet named Grades is shown. This worksheet calculates the course grades for the course OM 455. There are 11 students in the course. Each student has a midterm exam score and a final exam score, and these are averaged in column D to get the course average. The scale given in the upper portion of the worksheet is used to determine the course grade for each student. Consider, for example, the performance of student Choi in row 16. This student earned an 82 on the midterm, an 80 on the final, and a course average of 81. From the grading scale, this equates to a course grade of B.

The course average is simply the average of the midterm and final scores, but how do we get Excel to look in the grading scale table and automatically assign the correct course letter grade to each student? The VLOOKUP function allows us to do just that. The formulas and functions used in *OM455* are shown in Figure A.16.

The VLOOKUP function allows the user to pull a subset of data from a larger table of data based on some criterion. The general form of the VLOOKUP function is

$$=VLOOKUP(arg1,arg2,arg3,arg4)$$

where arg1 is the value to search for in the first column of the table, arg2 is the table location, arg3 is the column location in the table to be returned, and arg4 is TRUE if looking for the first partial match of arg1 and FALSE for looking for an exact match of arg1. We will explain the difference between a partial and exact match in a moment. VLOOKUP assumes that the first column of the table is sorted in ascending order.

FIGURE A.15   OM455 GRADE SPREADSHEET

WEB file

OM455

	A	B	C	D	E	F
1	OM455					
2	Section 001					
3	Course Grading Scale Based on Course Average:					
4		Lower	Upper	Course		
5		Limit	Limit	Grade		
6		0	59	F		
7		60	69	D		
8		70	79	C		
9		80	89	B		
10		90	100	A		
11						
12		Midterm	Final	Course	Course	
13	Lastname	Score	Score	Average	Grade	
14	Benson	70	56	63.0	D	
15	Chin	95	91	93.0	A	
16	Choi	82	80	81.0	B	
17	Cruz	45	78	61.5	D	
18	Doe	68	45	56.5	F	
19	Honda	91	98	94.5	A	
20	Hume	87	74	80.5	B	
21	Jones	60	80	70.0	C	
22	Miranda	80	93	86.5	B	
23	Murigami	97	98	97.5	A	
24	Ruebush	90	91	90.5	A	
25						

FIGURE A.16   THE FORMULAS AND FUNCTIONS USED IN OM 455

	A	B	C	D	E
1	OM 455				
2	Section 001				
3	Course Grading Scale Based on Course Average:				
4		Lower	Upper	Course	
5		Limit	Limit	Grade	
6		0	59	F	
7		60	69	D	
8		70	79	C	
9		80	89	B	
10		90	100	A	
11					
12		Midterm	Final	Course	Course
13	Lastname	Score	Score	Average	Grade
14	Benson	70	56	=AVERAGE(B14:C14)	=VLOOKUP(D14,B6:D10,3,TRUE)
15	Chin	95	91	=AVERAGE(B15:C15)	=VLOOKUP(D15,B6:D10,3,TRUE)
16	Choi	82	80	=AVERAGE(B16:C16)	=VLOOKUP(D16,B6:D10,3,TRUE)
17	Cruz	45	78	=AVERAGE(B17:C17)	=VLOOKUP(D17,B6:D10,3,TRUE)
18	Doe	68	45	=AVERAGE(B18:C18)	=VLOOKUP(D18,B6:D10,3,TRUE)
19	Honda	91	98	=AVERAGE(B19:C19)	=VLOOKUP(D19,B6:D10,3,TRUE)
20	Hume	87	74	=AVERAGE(B20:C20)	=VLOOKUP(D20,B6:D10,3,TRUE)
21	Jones	60	80	=AVERAGE(B21:C21)	=VLOOKUP(D21,B6:D10,3,TRUE)
22	Miranda	80	93	=AVERAGE(B22:C22)	=VLOOKUP(D22,B6:D10,3,TRUE)
23	Murigami	97	98	=AVERAGE(B23:C23)	=VLOOKUP(D23,B6:D10,3,TRUE)
24	Ruebush	90	91	=AVERAGE(B24:C24)	=VLOOKUP(D24,B6:D10,3,TRUE)
25					

The VLOOKUP function for student Choi in cell E16 is as follows:

$$=VLOOKUP(D16,B6:D10,3,TRUE)$$

This function uses the course average from cell D16 and searches the first column of the table defined by B6:D10. In the first column of the table (column B), Excel searches from the top until it finds a number strictly greater than the value of D16 (81). It then backs up one row (to row 9). That is, it finds the last value in the first column less than or equal to 81. Because there is a 3 in the third argument of the VLOOKUP function, it takes the element in row 9 in the third column of the table, which is the letter "B." In summary, the VLOOKUP takes the first argument and searches the first column of the table for the last row that is less than or equal to the first argument. It then selects from that row the element in the column number of the third argument.

Note: If the last element of the VLOOKUP function is "False," the only change is that Excel searches for an exact match of the first argument in the first column of the data. VLOOKUP is very useful when you seek subsets of a table based on a condition.

PRINCIPLES FOR BUILDING GOOD SPREADSHEET MODELS

We have covered some of the fundamentals of building spreadsheet models. There are some generally accepted guiding principles for how to build a spreadsheet so that it is more easily used by others and so that the risk of error is mitigated. In this section we discuss some of those principles.

Separate the Data from the Model

One of the first principles of good modeling is to separate the data from the model. This enables the user to update the model parameters without fear of mistakenly typing over a formula or function. For this reason, it is good practice to have a data section at the top of the spreadsheet. A separate model section should contain all calculations and in general should not be updated by a user. For a what-if model or an optimization model, there might also be a separate section for decision cells (values that are not data or calculations, but are the outputs we seek from the model).

The Nowlin model in Figure A.6 is a good example. The data section is in the upper part of the spreadsheet followed by the model section that contains the calculations. The Gambrell model in Figure A.13 does not totally employ the principle of data/model separation. A better model would have the 50-unit hurdle and the 90% cost (10% discount) as data in the upper section. Then the formulas in row 15 would simply refer to the cells in the upper section. This would allow the user to easily change the discount, for example, without having to change all four formulas in row 15.

Document the Model

A good spreadsheet model is well documented. Clear labels and proper formatting and alignment make the spreadsheet easier to navigate and understand. For example, if the values in a worksheet are cost, currency formatting should be used. No cells should be unlabeled. A new user should be able to easily understand the model and its calculations. Figure A.17

FIGURE A.17   A BETTER-DOCUMENTED FOSTER GENERATORS MODEL

Foster Rev

	A	B	C	D	E	F	G	H
1	**Foster Generators**							
2								
3	Origin to Destination—Cost per unit to ship							
4				**Destination**				
5	**Origin**	Boston	Chicago	St. Louis	Lexington	**Units Available**		
6	Cleveland	$3.00	$2.00	$7.00	$6.00	5000		
7	Bedford	$7.00	$5.00	$2.00	$3.00	6000		
8	York	$2.00	$5.00	$4.00	$5.00	2500		
9	**Units Demanded**	6000	4000	2000	1500			
10								
11								
12	**Model**							
13								
14		**Min Cost**	$39,500.00					
15								
16	Origin to Destination—Units Shipped							
17				**Destination**				
18	**Origin**	Boston	Chicago	St. Louis	Lexington	**Units Shipped**		
19	Cleveland	3500	1500	0	0	5000	<=	5000
20	Bedford	0	2500	2000	1500	6000	<=	6000
21	York	2500	0	0	0	2500	<=	2500
22	**Units Received**	6000	4000	2000	1500			
23			=	=	=	=		
24			6000	4000	2000	1500		

shows a better-documented version of the Foster Generators model previously discussed (Figure A.10). The tables are more explicitly labeled, and shading focuses the user on the objective and the decision cells (amount to ship). The per-unit shipping cost data and total (Min) cost have been properly formatted as currency.

Use Simple Formulas and Cell Names

Clear formulas can eliminate unnecessary calculations, reduce errors, and make it easier to maintain your spreadsheet. Long and complex calculations should be divided into several cells. This makes the formula easier to understand and easier to edit. Avoid using numbers in a formula. Instead, put the number in a cell in the data section of your worksheet and refer to the cell location of the data in the formula. Building the formula in this manner avoids having to edit the formula for a simple data change.

Using cell names can make a formula much easier to understand. To assign a name to a cell, use the following steps:

Step 1. Select the cell or range of cells you would like to name
Step 2. Select the **Formulas** tab from the Ribbon
Step 3. Choose **Define Name** from the Define Names section
Step 4. The **New Name** dialog box will appear, as shown in Figure A.18
Enter the name you would like to use in the top portion of the dialog box and Click **OK**

Following this procedure and naming all cells in the *Nowlin Plastics* spreadsheet model leads to the model shown in Figure A.19. Compare this to Figure A.6 to easily understand the formulas in the model.

A name is also easily applied to range as follows. First, highlight the range of interest. Then click on the Name Box in the Formula Bar (refer back to Figure A.3) and type in the desired range name.

FIGURE A.18   THE DEFINE NAME DIALOG BOX

WEB file

Nowlin Plastics

FIGURE A.19   THE NOWLIN PLASTIC MODEL FORMULAS WITH NAMED CELLS

	A	B
1	Nowlin Plastics	
2		
3	Fixed Cost	3000
4		
5	Variable Cost Per Unit	2
6		
7	Selling Price Per Unit	5
8		
9		
10	Models	
11		
12	Production Volume	800
13		
14	Total Cost	=Fixed_Cost+Variable_Cost*Production_Volume
15		
16	Total Revenue	=Selling_Price*Production_Volume
17		
18	Total Profit (Loss)	=Total_Revenue-Total_Cost

Use of Relative and Absolute Cell References

There are a number of ways to copy a formula from one cell to another in an Excel work-sheet. One way to copy the a formula from one cell to another is presented here:

Step 1. Select the cell you would like to copy
Step 2. Right click on the mouse
Step 3. Click **Copy**
Step 4. Select the cell where you would like to put the copy
Step 5. Right click on the mouse
Step 6. Click **Paste**

When copying in Excel, one can use a relative or an absolute address. When copied, a rel-ative address adjusts with the move of the copy, whereas an absolute address stays in its original form. Relative addresses are of the form C7. Absolute addresses have $ in front of the column and row, for example, $C$7. How you use relative and absolute addresses can have an impact on the amount of effort it takes to build a model and the opportunity for error in constructing the model.

Let us reconsider the OM455 grading spreadsheet previously discussed in this ap-pendix and shown in Figure A.16. Recall that we used the VLOOKUP function to retrieve the appropriate letter grade for each student. The following formula is in cell E14:

$$=VLOOKUP(D14,B6:D10,3,TRUE)$$

Note that this formula contains only relative addresses. If we copy this to cell E15, we get the following result:

$$=VLOOKUP(D15,B7:D11,3,TRUE)$$

Although the first argument has correctly changed to D15 (we want to calculate the letter grade for the student in row 15), the table in the function has also shifted to B7:D11. What we desired was for this table location to remain the same. A better approach would have been to use the following formula in cell E14:

$$=VLOOKUP(D14,\$B\$6:\$D\$10,3,TRUE)$$

Copying this formula to cell E15 results in the following formula:

$$=VLOOKUP(D15,\$B\$6:\$D\$10,3,TRUE)$$

This correctly changes the first argument to D15 and keeps the data table intact. Using absolute referencing is extremely useful if you have a function that has a reference that should not change when applied to another cell and you are copying the formula to other locations. In the case of the OM455 workbook, instead of typing the VLOOKUP for each student, we can use absolute referencing on the table and then copy from row 14 to rows 15 through 24.

In this section we have discussed guidelines for good spreadsheet model building. In the next section we discuss EXCEL tools available for checking and debugging spreadsheet models.

AUDITING EXCEL MODELS

EXCEL contains a variety of tools to assist you in the development and debugging of spreadsheet models. These tools are found in the Formula Auditing group of the Formulas Tab as shown in Figure A.20. Let us review each of the tools available in this group.

Trace Precedents and Dependents

The Trace Precedents button ⊞ Trace Precedents creates arrows pointing to the selected cell from cells that are part of the formula in that cell. The Trace Dependents button ⊞ Trace Dependents , on the other hand, shows arrows pointing from the selected cell, to cells that depend on the selected cell. Both of the tools are excellent for quickly ascertaining how parts of a model are linked.

An example of Trace Precedents is shown in Figure A.21. Here we have opened the *Foster Rev* worksheet, selected cell C14, and clicked the Trace Precedents button in the Formula Auditing Group. Recall that the cost in cell C14 is calculated as the SUMPRODUCT of the per-unit shipping cost and units shipped. In Figure A.21, to show this relationship, arrows are drawn to these respective areas of the spreadsheet to cell C14. These arrows may be removed by clicking on the Remove Arrows button in the Auditing Tools Group.

FIGURE A.20   THE FORMULA AUDITING GROUP OF THE FORMULAS TAB

FIGURE A.21 TRACE PRECEDENTS FOR CELL C14 (COST) IN THE FOSTER GENERATORS REV MODEL

	C14		f_x	=SUMPRODUCT(B6:E8,B19:E21)			
	A	**B**	**C**	**D**	**E**	**F**	**G**	**H**
1	**Foster Generators**							
2								
3	Origin to Destination—Cost per unit to ship							
4			**Destination**					
5	**Origin**	Boston	Chicago	St. Louis	Lexington	**Units Available**		
6	Cleveland	$3.00	$2.00	$7.00	$6.00	5000		
7	Bedford	$7.00	$5.00	$2.00	$3.00	6000		
8	York	$2.00	$5.00	$4.00	$5.00	2500		
9	**Units Demanded**	6000	4000	2000	1500			
10								
11								
12	**Model**							
13								
14		**Min Cost**	$39,500.00					
15								
16	Origin to Destination—Units Shipped							
17			**Destination**					
18	**Origin**	Boston	Chicago	St. Louis	Lexington	**Units Shipped**		
19	Cleveland	3500	1500	0	0	5000	<=	5000
20	Bedford	0	2500	2000	1500	6000	<=	6000
21	York	2500	0	0	0	2500	<=	2500
22	**Units Received**	6000	4000	2000	1500			
23		=	=	=	=			
24		6000	4000	2000	1500			

Foster Rev

An example of Trace Dependents is shown in Figure A.22. We have selected cell E20, the units shipped from Bedford to Lexington, and clicked on the Trace Dependents button in the Formula Auditing Group. As shown in Figure A.22, units shipped from Bedford to Lexington impacts the cost function in cell C14, the total units shipped from Bedford given in cell F20, and the total units shipped to Lexington in cell E22. These arrows may be removed by clicking on the Remove Arrows button in the Auditing Tools Group.

Trace Precedents and Trace Dependents can highlight errors in copying and formula construction by showing that incorrect sections of the worksheet are referenced.

Show Formulas

The Show Formulas button, 📊 Show Formulas , does exactly that. To see the formulas in a worksheet, simply click on any cell in the worksheet and then click on Show Formulas. You will see the formulas that exist in that worksheet. To go back to hiding the formulas, click again on the Show Formulas button. Figure A.6 gives an example of the show formulas view. This allows you to inspect each formula in detail in its cell location.

Evaluate Formulas

The Evaluate Formula button, 🔍 Evaluate Formula , allows you to investigate the calculations of particular cell in great detail. To invoke this tool, we simply select a cell containing

FIGURE A.22   TRACE DEPENDENTS FOR CELL C14 (COST) IN THE FOSTER
GENERATORS REV MODEL

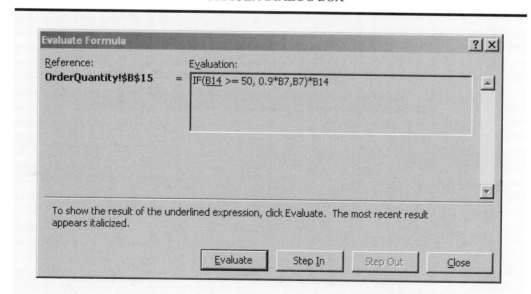

	A	B	C	D	E	F	G	H
	E20		f_x	1500				
12	Model							
13								
14		**Min Cost**	$39,500.00					
15								
16	Origin to Destination—Units Shipped							
17			**Destination**					
18	**Origin**	Boston	Chicago	St. Louis	Lexington	**Units Shipped**		
19	Cleveland	3500	1500	0	0	5000	<=	5000
20	Bedford	0	2500	2000	1500	6000	<=	6000
21	York	2500	0	0	0	2500	<=	2500
22	**Units Received**	6000	4000	2000	1500			
23		=	=	=	=			
24		6000	4000	2000	1500			

a formula and click on the Evaluate Formula button in the Formula Auditing Group. As an
example, we select cell B15 of the Gambrell Manufacturing model (see Figures A.13 and
A.14). Recall we are calculating cost of goods based upon whether or not there is a quantity
discount. Clicking on the Evaluate button allows you to evaluate this formula explicitly. The
Evaluate Formula dialog box appears in Figure A.23. Figure A.24 shows the result of one
click of the Evaluate button. The B14 has changed to its value of 95. Further clicks would
evaluate in order, from left to right, the remaining components of the formula. We ask the
reader to further explore this tool in an exercise at the end of this appendix.

The Evaluate Formula tool provides an excellent means of identifying the exact location of an error in a formula.

FIGURE A.23   THE EVALUATE FORMULA DIALOG BOX

Evaluate Formula	? ✕
Reference:	Evaluation:
OrderQuantity!$B$15 =	IF(B14 >= 50, 0.9*B7,B7)*B14 ▲
	▼
To show the result of the underlined expression, click Evaluate. The most recent result appears italicized.	
	Evaluate Step In Step Out Close

FIGURE A.24   THE EVALUATE FORMULA AFTER ONE CLICK OF THE
EVALUATE BUTTON

Evaluate Formula

Reference: Evaluation:
OrderQuantity!$B$15   =   IF(*95* >= *50*, 0.9*B7,B7)*B14

To show the result of the underlined expression, click Evaluate. The most recent result
appears italicized.

[Evaluate]   [Step In]   [Step Out]   [Close]

Error Checking

The Error Checking Button, Error Checking ▾ , provides an automatic means of checking
for mathematical errors within formulas of a worksheet. Clicking on the Error Checking
button causes Excel to check every formula in the sheet for calculation errors. If an error is
found, the Error Checking dialog box appears. An example for a hypothetical division by
zero error is shown in Figure A.25. From this box, the formula can be edited or the calculation steps can be observed (as in the previous section on Evaluate Formulas).

FIGURE A.25   THE ERROR CHECKING DIALOG BOX FOR A DIVISION
BY ZERO ERROR

Error Checking

Error in cell F22
=F18/F16

Divide by Zero Error
The formula or function used is dividing by
zero or empty cells.

[Help on this error]
[Show Calculation Steps...]
[Ignore Error]
[Edit in Formula Bar]

[Options...]   [Previous]   [Next]

FIGURE A.26 THE WATCH WINDOW FOR THE GAMBRELL MANUFACTURING
MODEL

Book	Sheet	Name	Cell	Value	Formula
Gambr...	Order...		B15	$384.75	=IF(B14 >= 50, 0.9*B7,B7)*B14

Watch Window — Add Watch... / Delete Watch

Watch Window

The Watch Window, located in the Formula Auditing Group, allows the user to observe the values of cells included in the Watch Window box list. This is useful for large models when not all the model is observable on the screen or when multiple worksheets are used. The user can monitor how the listed cells change with a change in the model without searching through the worksheet or changing from one worksheet to another.

A Watch Window for the Gambrell Manufacturing model is shown in Figure A.26. The following steps were used from the OrderQuantity worksheet to add cell B15 of the OrderQuantity worksheet to the watch list:

Step 1. Select the **Formulas** tab
Step 2. Select **Watch Window** from the Formula Auditing Group
The Watch Window will appear
Step 3. Select **Add Watch**
Step 4. Click on the cell you would like to add to the watch list (in this case B15)

As shown in Figure A.26, the list gives the workbook name, worksheet name, cell name (if used), cell location, cell value, and cell formula. To delete a cell from the watch list, select the entry from the list and then click on the Delete Watch button in the upper part of the Watch Window.

The Watch Window, as shown in Figure A.26, allows us to monitor the value of B15 as we make changes elsewhere in the worksheet. Furthermore, if we had other worksheets in this workbook, we could monitor changes to B15 of the OrderQuantity worksheet even from these other worksheets. The Watch Window is observable regardless of where we are in any worksheet of a workbook.

SUMMARY

In this appendix we have discussed how to build effective spreadsheet models using Excel. We provided an overview on workbooks and worksheets and details on useful Excel functions. We also discussed a set of principles for good modeling and tools for auditing spreadsheet models.

PROBLEMS

1. Open the file *Nowlin Plastics*. Recall that we have modeled total profit for the product CD-50 in this spreadsheet. Suppose we have a second product called a CD-100, with the following characteristics:

$$\text{Fixed Cost} = \$2500$$
$$\text{Variable Cost per Unit} = \$1.67$$
$$\text{Selling Price per Unit} = \$4.40$$

Extend the model so that the profit is calculated for each product and then totaled to give an overall profit generated for the two products. Use a CD-100 production volume of 1200. Save this file as *Nowlin Plastics2*. *Hint:* Place the data for CD-100 in column C and copy the formulas in rows 14, 16, and 18 to column C.

2. Assume that in an empty Excel worksheet in cell A1 you enter the formula =B1*$F$3. You now copy this formula into cell E6. What is the modified formula that appears in E6?

3. Open the file *Foster Rev*. Select cells B6:E8 and name these cells Shipping_Cost. Select cells B19:E21 and name these cells Units_Shipped. Use these names in the SUMPRODUCT function in cell C14 to compute cost and verify that you obtain the same cost ($39,500).

4. Open the file *Nowlin Plastics*. Recall that we have modeled total profit for the product CD-50 in this spreadsheet. Modify the spreadsheet to take into account production capacity and forecasted demand. If forecasted demand is less than or equal to capacity, Nowlin will produce only the forecasted demand; otherwise, they will produce the full capacity. For this example, use forecasted demand of 1200 and capacity of 1500. *Hint:* Enter demand and capacity into the data section of the model. Then use an IF statement to calculate production volume.

5. Cox Electric makes electronic components and has estimated the following for a new design of one of its products:

$$\text{Fixed Cost} = \$10,000$$
$$\text{Revenue per unit} = \$0.65$$
$$\text{Material cost per unit} = \$0.15$$
$$\text{Labor cost per unit} = \$0.10$$

These data are given in the spreadsheet *Cox Electric*. Also in the spreadsheet in row 14 is a profit model that gives the profit (or loss) for a specified volume (cell C14).
   a. Use the Show Formula button in the Formula Auditing Group of the Formulas tab to see the formulas and cell references used in row 14.
   b. Use the Trace Precedents tool to see how the formulas are dependent on the elements of the data section.
   c. Use trial and error, by trying various values of volume in cell C14, to arrive at a breakeven volume.

6. Return to the Cox Electric spreadsheet. Build a table of profits based on different volume levels by doing the following: In cell C15, enter a volume of 20,000. Look at each formula in row 14 and decide which references should be absolute or relative for purposes of copying the formulas to row 15. Make the necessary changes to row 14 (change any references that should be absolute by putting in $). Copy cells D14:I14 to row 15. Continue this with new rows until a positive profit is found. Save your file as *Cox_Breakeven*.

OM455

7. Open the workbook *OM455*. Save the file under a new name, *OM455COUNTIF*. Suppose we wish to automatically count the number of each letter grade.
   a. Begin by putting the letters A, B, C, D, and F in cells C29:C33. Use the COUNTIF function in cells D29:D33 to count the number of each letter grade. *Hint:* Create the necessary COUNTIF function in cell D29. Use absolute referencing on the range ($E14:$E$24) and then copy the function to cells D30:D33 to count the number of each of the other letter grades.
   b. We are considering a different grading scale as follows:

Lower	Upper	Grade
0	69	F
70	76	D
77	84	C
85	92	B
93	100	A

For the current list of students, use the COUNTIF function to determine the number of A, B, C, D, and F letter grades earned under this new system.

OM455

8. Open the workbook *OM455*. Save the file under a new name, *OM4555Revised*. Suppose we wish to use a more refined grading system, as shown below:

Lower	Upper	Grade
0	59	F
60	69	D
70	72	C−
73	76	C−
77	79	C+
80	82	B−
83	86	B
87	89	B+
90	92	A−
93	100	A

Update the file to use this more refined grading system. How many of each letter grade are awarded under the new system? *Hint:* Build a new grading table and use VLOOKUP and an absolute reference to the table. Then use COUNTIF to count the number of each letter grade.

Newton_data

9. Newton Manufacturing produces scientific calculators. The models are N350, N450, and the N900. Newton has planned its distribution of these products around eight customer zones: Brazil, China, France, Malaysia, U.S. Northeast, U.S. Southeast, U.S. Midwest, and U.S. West. Data for the current quarter (volume to be shipped in thousands of units) for each product and each customer zone are given in the file *Newton_data*.

   Newton would like to know the total number of units going to each customer zone and also the total units of each product shipped. There are several ways to get this information from the data set. One way is to use the SUMIF function.

   The SUMIF function extends the SUM function by allowing the user to add the values of cells meeting a logical condition. This general form of the function is

$$=\text{SUMIF}(\textit{test range, condition, range to be summed})$$

The *test range* is an area to search to test the *condition,* and the *range to be summed* is the position of the data to be summed. So, for example, using the *Newton_data* file, we would use the following function to get the total units sent to Malaysia:

$$=SUMIF(A3:A26,A3,C3:C26)$$

Here, A3 is Malaysia, A3:A26 is the range of customer zones, and C3:C26 are the volumes for each product for these customer zones. The SUMIF looks for matches of Malaysia in column A and, if a match is found, adds the volume to the total. Use the SUMIF function to get each total volume by zone and each total volume by product.

Williamson

10. Consider the transportation model given in the Excel file *Williamson.* It is a model that is very similar to the Foster Generators model. Williamson produces a single product and has plants in Atlanta, Lexington, Chicago, and Salt Lake City and warehouses in Portland, St. Paul, Las Vegas, Tuscon, and Cleveland. Each plant has a capacity and each warehouse has a demand. Williamson would like to find a low-cost shipping plan. Mr. Williamson has reviewed the results and notices right away that the total cost is way out of line. Use the Formula Auditing Tools under the Formulas tab in Excel to find any errors in this model. Correct the errors. *Hint:* There are two errors in this model. Be sure to check every formula.

Appendix B Areas for the Standard Normal Distribution

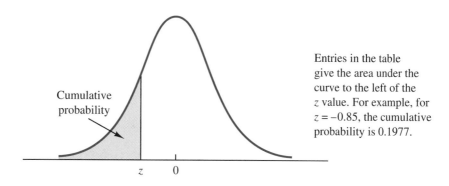

Cumulative probability

Entries in the table give the area under the curve to the left of the z value. For example, for $z = -0.85$, the cumulative probability is 0.1977.

z	0.00	0.01	0.02	0.03	0.04	0.05	0.06	0.07	0.08	0.09
−3.0	0.0013	0.0013	0.0013	0.0012	0.0012	0.0011	0.0011	0.0011	0.0010	0.0010
−2.9	0.0019	0.0018	0.0018	0.0017	0.0016	0.0016	0.0015	0.0015	0.0014	0.0014
−2.8	0.0026	0.0025	0.0024	0.0023	0.0023	0.0022	0.0021	0.0021	0.0020	0.0019
−2.7	0.0035	0.0034	0.0033	0.0032	0.0031	0.0030	0.0029	0.0028	0.0027	0.0026
−2.6	0.0047	0.0045	0.0044	0.0043	0.0041	0.0040	0.0039	0.0038	0.0037	0.0036
−2.5	0.0062	0.0060	0.0059	0.0057	0.0055	0.0054	0.0052	0.0051	0.0049	0.0048
−2.4	0.0082	0.0080	0.0078	0.0075	0.0073	0.0071	0.0069	0.0068	0.0066	0.0064
−2.3	0.0107	0.0104	0.0102	0.0099	0.0096	0.0094	0.0091	0.0089	0.0087	0.0084
−2.2	0.0139	0.0136	0.0132	0.0129	0.0125	0.0122	0.0119	0.0116	0.0113	0.0110
−2.1	0.0179	0.0174	0.0170	0.0166	0.0162	0.0158	0.0154	0.0150	0.0146	0.0143
−2.0	0.0228	0.0222	0.0217	0.0212	0.0207	0.0202	0.0197	0.0192	0.0188	0.0183
−1.9	0.0287	0.0281	0.0274	0.0268	0.0262	0.0256	0.0250	0.0244	0.0239	0.0233
−1.8	0.0359	0.0351	0.0344	0.0336	0.0329	0.0322	0.0314	0.0307	0.0301	0.0294
−1.7	0.0446	0.0436	0.0427	0.0418	0.0409	0.0401	0.0392	0.0384	0.0375	0.0367
−1.6	0.0548	0.0537	0.0526	0.0516	0.0505	0.0495	0.0485	0.0475	0.0465	0.0455
−1.5	0.0668	0.0655	0.0643	0.0630	0.0618	0.0606	0.0594	0.0582	0.0571	0.0559
−1.4	0.0808	0.0793	0.0778	0.0764	0.0749	0.0735	0.0721	0.0708	0.0694	0.0681
−1.3	0.0968	0.0951	0.0934	0.0918	0.0901	0.0885	0.0869	0.0853	0.0838	0.0823
−1.2	0.1151	0.1131	0.1112	0.1093	0.1075	0.1056	0.1038	0.1020	0.1003	0.0985
−1.1	0.1357	0.1335	0.1314	0.1292	0.1271	0.1251	0.1230	0.1210	0.1190	0.1170
−1.0	0.1587	0.1562	0.1539	0.1515	0.1492	0.1469	0.1446	0.1423	0.1401	0.1379
−0.9	0.1841	0.1814	0.1788	0.1762	0.1736	0.1711	0.1685	0.1660	0.1635	0.1611
−0.8	0.2119	0.2090	0.2061	0.2033	0.2005	0.1977	0.1949	0.1922	0.1894	0.1867
−0.7	0.2420	0.2389	0.2358	0.2327	0.2296	0.2266	0.2236	0.2206	0.2177	0.2148
−0.6	0.2743	0.2709	0.2676	0.2643	0.2611	0.2578	0.2546	0.2514	0.2483	0.2451
−0.5	0.3085	0.3050	0.3015	0.2981	0.2946	0.2912	0.2877	0.2843	0.2810	0.2776
−0.4	0.3446	0.3409	0.3372	0.3336	0.3300	0.3264	0.3228	0.3192	0.3156	0.3121
−0.3	0.3821	0.3783	0.3745	0.3707	0.3669	0.3632	0.3594	0.3557	0.3520	0.3483
−0.2	0.4207	0.4168	0.4129	0.4090	0.4052	0.4013	0.3974	0.3936	0.3897	0.3859
−0.1	0.4602	0.4562	0.4522	0.4483	0.4443	0.4404	0.4364	0.4325	0.4286	0.4247
−0.0	0.5000	0.4960	0.4920	0.4880	0.4840	0.4801	0.4761	0.4721	0.4681	0.4641

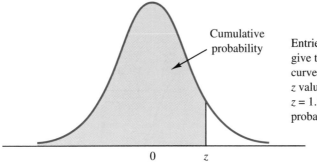

Cumulative probability

Entries in the table give the area under the curve to the left of the z value. For example, for $z = 1.25$, the cumulative probability is 0.8944.

z	0.00	0.01	0.02	0.03	0.04	0.05	0.06	0.07	0.08	0.09
0.0	0.5000	0.5040	0.5080	0.5120	0.5160	0.5199	0.5239	0.5279	0.5319	0.5359
0.1	0.5398	0.5438	0.5478	0.5517	0.5557	0.5596	0.5636	0.5675	0.5714	0.5753
0.2	0.5793	0.5832	0.5871	0.5910	0.5948	0.5987	0.6026	0.6064	0.6103	0.6141
0.3	0.6179	0.6217	0.6255	0.6293	0.6331	0.6368	0.6406	0.6443	0.6480	0.6517
0.4	0.6554	0.6591	0.6628	0.6664	0.6700	0.6736	0.6772	0.6808	0.6844	0.6879
0.5	0.6915	0.6950	0.6985	0.7019	0.7054	0.7088	0.7123	0.7157	0.7190	0.7224
0.6	0.7257	0.7291	0.7324	0.7357	0.7389	0.7422	0.7454	0.7486	0.7517	0.7549
0.7	0.7580	0.7611	0.7642	0.7673	0.7704	0.7734	0.7764	0.7794	0.7823	0.7852
0.8	0.7881	0.7910	0.7939	0.7967	0.7995	0.8023	0.8051	0.8078	0.8106	0.8133
0.9	0.8159	0.8186	0.8212	0.8238	0.8264	0.8289	0.8315	0.8340	0.8365	0.8389
1.0	0.8413	0.8438	0.8461	0.8485	0.8508	0.8531	0.8554	0.8577	0.8599	0.8621
1.1	0.8643	0.8665	0.8686	0.8708	0.8729	0.8749	0.8770	0.8790	0.8810	0.8830
1.2	0.8849	0.8869	0.8888	0.8907	0.8925	0.8944	0.8962	0.8980	0.8997	0.9015
1.3	0.9032	0.9049	0.9066	0.9082	0.9099	0.9115	0.9131	0.9147	0.9162	0.9177
1.4	0.9192	0.9207	0.9222	0.9236	0.9251	0.9265	0.9279	0.9292	0.9306	0.9319
1.5	0.9332	0.9345	0.9357	0.9370	0.9382	0.9394	0.9406	0.9418	0.9429	0.9441
1.6	0.9452	0.9463	0.9474	0.9484	0.9495	0.9505	0.9515	0.9525	0.9535	0.9545
1.7	0.9554	0.9564	0.9573	0.9582	0.9591	0.9599	0.9608	0.9616	0.9625	0.9633
1.8	0.9641	0.9649	0.9656	0.9664	0.9671	0.9678	0.9686	0.9693	0.9699	0.9706
1.9	0.9713	0.9719	0.9726	0.9732	0.9738	0.9744	0.9750	0.9756	0.9761	0.9767
2.0	0.9772	0.9778	0.9783	0.9788	0.9793	0.9798	0.9803	0.9808	0.9812	0.9817
2.1	0.9821	0.9826	0.9830	0.9834	0.9838	0.9842	0.9846	0.9850	0.9854	0.9857
2.2	0.9861	0.9864	0.9868	0.9871	0.9875	0.9878	0.9881	0.9884	0.9887	0.9890
2.3	0.9893	0.9896	0.9898	0.9901	0.9904	0.9906	0.9909	0.9911	0.9913	0.9913
2.4	0.9916	0.9920	0.9922	0.9925	0.9927	0.9929	0.9931	0.9932	0.9934	0.9936
2.5	0.9938	0.9940	0.9941	0.9943	0.9945	0.9946	0.9948	0.9949	0.9951	0.9952
2.6	0.9953	0.9955	0.9956	0.9957	0.9959	0.9960	0.9961	0.9962	0.9963	0.9964
2.7	0.9965	0.9966	0.9967	0.9968	0.9969	0.9970	0.9971	0.9972	0.9973	0.9974
2.8	0.9974	0.9975	0.9976	0.9977	0.9977	0.9978	0.9979	0.9979	0.9980	0.9981
2.9	0.9981	0.9982	0.9982	0.9983	0.9984	0.9984	0.9985	0.9985	0.9986	0.9986
3.0	0.9987	0.9987	0.9987	0.9988	0.9988	0.9989	0.9989	0.9989	0.9990	0.9990

Appendix C   Values of $e^{-\lambda}$

λ	$e^{-\lambda}$	λ	$e^{-\lambda}$	λ	$e^{-\lambda}$
0.05	0.9512	2.05	0.1287	4.05	0.0174
0.10	0.9048	2.10	0.1225	4.10	0.0166
0.15	0.8607	2.15	0.1165	4.15	0.0158
0.20	0.8187	2.20	0.1108	4.20	0.0150
0.25	0.7788	2.25	0.1054	4.25	0.0143
0.30	0.7408	2.30	0.1003	4.30	0.0136
0.35	0.7047	2.35	0.0954	4.35	0.0129
0.40	0.6703	2.40	0.0907	4.40	0.0123
0.45	0.6376	2.45	0.0863	4.45	0.0117
0.50	0.6065	2.50	0.0821	4.50	0.0111
0.55	0.5769	2.55	0.0781	4.55	0.0106
0.60	0.5488	2.60	0.0743	4.60	0.0101
0.65	0.5220	2.65	0.0707	4.65	0.0096
0.70	0.4966	2.70	0.0672	4.70	0.0091
0.75	0.4724	2.75	0.0639	4.75	0.0087
0.80	0.4493	2.80	0.0608	4.80	0.0082
0.85	0.4274	2.85	0.0578	4.85	0.0078
0.90	0.4066	2.90	0.0550	4.90	0.0074
0.95	0.3867	2.95	0.0523	4.95	0.0071
1.00	0.3679	3.00	0.0498	5.00	0.0067
1.05	0.3499	3.05	0.0474	5.05	0.0064
1.10	0.3329	3.10	0.0450	5.10	0.0061
1.15	0.3166	3.15	0.0429	5.15	0.0058
1.20	0.3012	3.20	0.0408	5.20	0.0055
1.25	0.2865	3.25	0.0388	5.25	0.0052
1.30	0.2725	3.30	0.0369	5.30	0.0050
1.35	0.2592	3.35	0.0351	5.35	0.0047
1.40	0.2466	3.40	0.0334	5.40	0.0045
1.45	0.2346	3.45	0.0317	5.45	0.0043
1.50	0.2231	3.50	0.0302	5.50	0.0041
1.55	0.2122	3.55	0.0287	5.55	0.0039
1.60	0.2019	3.60	0.0273	5.60	0.0037
1.65	0.1920	3.65	0.0260	5.65	0.0035
1.70	0.1827	3.70	0.0247	5.70	0.0033
1.75	0.1738	3.75	0.0235	5.75	0.0032
1.80	0.1653	3.80	0.0224	5.80	0.0030
1.85	0.1572	3.85	0.0213	5.85	0.0029
1.90	0.1496	3.90	0.0202	5.90	0.0027
1.95	0.1423	3.95	0.0193	5.95	0.0026
2.00	0.1353	4.00	0.0183	6.00	0.0025
				7.00	0.0009
				8.00	0.000335
				9.00	0.000123
				10.00	0.000045

Appendix D References and Bibliography

Chapter 1 Introduction

Churchman, C. W., R. L. Ackoff, and E. L. Arnoff. *Introduction to Operations Research.* Wiley, 1957.

Horner, Peter. "The Sabre Story," *OR/MS Today* (June 2000).

Leon, Linda, Z. Przasnyski, and K. C. Seal. "Spreadsheets and OR/MS Models: An End-User Perspective," *Interfaces* (March/April 1996).

Powell, S. G. "Innovative Approaches to Management Science," *OR/MS Today* (October 1996).

Savage, S. "Weighing the Pros and Cons of Decision Technology and Spreadsheets," *OR/MS Today* (February 1997).

Winston, W. L. "The Teachers' Forum: Management Science with Spreadsheets for MBAs at Indiana University," *Interfaces* (March/April 1996).

Chapters 2 to 7 Linear, Distribution, Network, and Integer Programming

Ahuja, R. K., T. L. Magnanti, and J. B. Orlin. *Network Flows, Theory, Algorithms, and Applications.* Prentice Hall, 1993.

Bazarra, M. S., J. J. Jarvis, and H. D. Sherali. *Linear Programming and Network Flows,* 2d ed. Wiley, 1990.

Carino, H. F., and C. H. Le Noir, Jr. "Optimizing Wood Procurement in Cabinet Manufacturing," *Interfaces* (March/April 1988): 10–19.

Dantzig, G. B. *Linear Programming and Extensions.* Princeton University Press, 1963.

Davis, Morton D. *Game Theory: A Nontechnical Introduction.* Dover, 1997.

Evans, J. R., and E. Minieka. *Optimization Algorithms for Networks and Graphs,* 2d ed. Marcel Dekker, 1992.

Ford, L. R., and D. R. Fulkerson. *Flows and Networks.* Princeton University Press, 1962.

Geoffrion, A., and G. Graves. "Better Distribution Planning with Computer Models," *Harvard Business Review* (July/August 1976).

Greenberg, H. J. "How to Analyze the Results of Linear Programs—Part 1: Preliminaries," *Interfaces* 23, no. 4 (July/August 1993): 56–67.

Greenberg, H. J. "How to Analyze the Results of Linear Programs—Part 2: Price Interpretation," *Interfaces* 23, no. 5 (September/October 1993): 97–114.

Greenberg, H. J. "How to Analyze the Results of Linear Programs—Part 3: Infeasibility Diagnosis," *Interfaces* 23, no. 6 (November/December 1993): 120–139.

Lillien, G., and A. Rangaswamy. *Marketing Engineering: Computer-Assisted Marketing Analysis and Planning.* Addison-Wesley, 1998.

Martin, R. K. *Large Scale Linear and Integer Optimization: A Unified Approach.* Kluwer Academic Publishers, 1999.

McMillian, John. *Games, Strategies, and Managers.* Oxford University Press, 1992.

Myerson, Roger B. *Game Theory: Analysis of Conflict.* Harvard University Press, 1997.

Nemhauser, G. L., and L. A. Wolsey. *Integer and Combinatorial Optimization.* Wiley, 1999.

Osborne, Martin J. *An Introduction to Game Theory.* Oxford University Press, 2004.

Schrage, Linus. *Optimization Modeling with LINDO,* 4th ed. LINDO Systems Inc., 2000.

Sherman, H. D. "Hospital Efficiency Measurement and Evaluation," *Medical Care* 22, no. 10 (October 1984): 922–938.

Winston, W. L., and S. C. Albright. *Practical Management Science,* 2d ed. Duxbury Press, 2001.

Chapter 8 Nonlinear Optimization Models

Bazarra, M. S., H. D. Sherali, and C. M. Shetty. *Nonlinear Programming Theory and Applications.* Wiley, 1993.

Benninga, Simon. *Financial Modeling.* MIT Press, 2000.

Luenberger, D. *Linear and Nonlinear Programming,* 2d ed. Addison-Wesley, 1984.

Rardin, R. L. *Optimization in Operations Research.* Prentice Hall, 1998.

Chapter 9 Project Scheduling: PERT/CPM

Moder, J. J., C. R. Phillips, and E. W. Davis. *Project Management with CPM, PERT and Precedence Diagramming,* 3d ed. Blitz, 1995.

Wasil, E. A., and A. A. Assad. "Project Management on the PC: Software, Applications, and Trends," *Interfaces* 18, no. 2 (March/April 1988): 75–84.

Wiest, J., and F. Levy. *Management Guide to PERT-CPM,* 2d ed. Prentice Hall, 1977.

Chapter 10 Inventory Models

Fogarty, D. W., J. H. Blackstone, and T. R. Hoffman. *Production and Inventory Management,* 2d ed. South-Western, 1990.

Hillier, F., and G. J. Lieberman. *Introduction to Operations Research,* 7th ed. McGraw-Hill, 2000.

Narasimhan, S. L., D. W. McLeavey, and P. B. Lington. *Production Planning and Inventory Control,* 2d ed. Prentice Hall, 1995.

Orlicky, J., and G. W. Plossi. *Orlicky's Material Requirements Planning.* McGraw-Hill, 1994.

Vollmann, T. E., W. L. Berry, and D. C. Whybark. *Manufacturing Planning and Control Systems,* 4th ed. McGraw-Hill, 1997.

Zipkin, P. H. *Foundations of Inventory Management.* McGraw-Hill/Irwin, 2000.

Chapter 11   Waiting Line Models

Bunday, B. D. *An Introduction to Queueing Theory.* Wiley, 1996.

Gross, D., and C. M. Harris. *Fundamentals of Queueing Theory,* 3d ed. Wiley, 1997.

Hall, R. W. *Queuing Methods: For Services and Manufacturing.* Prentice Hall, 1997.

Hillier, F., and G. J. Lieberman. *Introduction to Operations Research,* 7th ed. McGraw-Hill, 2000.

Kao, E. P. C. *An Introduction to Stochastic Processes.* Duxbury, 1996.

Chapter 12   Simulation

Banks, J., J. S. Carson, and B. L. Nelson. *Discrete-Event System Simulation,* 2d ed. Prentice Hall, 1995.

Fishwick, P. A. *Simulation Model Design and Execution: Building Digital Worlds.* Prentice Hall, 1995.

Harrell, C. R., and K. Tumau. *Simulation Made Easy: A Manager's Guide.* Institute of Industrial Engineers, 1996.

Kelton, W. D., R. P. Sadowski, and D. A. Sadowski. *Simulation with Arena,* 4th ed. McGraw-Hill, 2007.

Law, A. M., and W. D. Kelton. *Simulation Modeling and Analysis,* 3d ed. McGraw-Hill, 1999.

Pidd, M. *Computer Simulation in Management Science,* 4th ed. Wiley, 1998.

Thesen, A., and L. E. Travis. *Simulation for Decision Making.* Wadsworth, 1992.

Chapter 13   Decision Analysis

Berger, J. O. *Statistical Decision Theory and Bayesian Analysis,* 2d ed. Springer-Verlag, 1985.

Chernoff, H., and L. E. Moses. *Elementary Decision Theory.* Dover, 1987.

Clemen, R. T., and T. Reilly. *Making Hard Decisions with Decision Tools.* Duxbury, 2001.

Goodwin, P., and G. Wright. *Decision Analysis for Management Judgment,* 2d ed. Wiley, 1999.

Gregory, G. *Decision Analysis.* Plenum, 1988.

Pratt, J. W., H. Raiffa, and R. Schlaifer. *Introduction to Statistical Decision Theory.* MIT Press, 1995.

Raiffa, H. *Decision Analysis.* McGraw-Hill, 1997.

Schlaifer, R. *Analysis of Decisions Under Uncertainty.* Krieger, 1978.

Chapter 14   Multicriteria Decisions

Dyer, J. S. "A Clarification of Remarks on the Analytic Hierarchy Process," *Management Science* 36, no. 3 (March 1990): 274–275.

Dyer, J. S. "Remarks on the Analytic Hierarchy Process," *Management Science* 36, no. 3 (March 1990): 249–258.

Harker, P. T., and L. G. Vargas. "Reply to Remarks on the Analytic Hierarchy Process by J. S. Dyer," *Management Science* 36, no. 3 (March 1990): 269–273.

Harker, P. T., and L. G. Vargas. "The Theory of Ratio Scale Estimation: Saaty's Analytic Hierarchy Process," *Management Science* 33, no. 11 (November 1987): 1383–1403.

Ignizio, J. *Introduction to Linear Goal Programming.* Sage, 1986.

Keeney, R. L., and H. Raiffa. *Decisions with Multiple Objectives: Preferences and Value Tradeoffs.* Cambridge, 1993.

Saaty, T. *Decision Making for Leaders: The Analytic Hierarchy Process for Decisions in a Complex World,* 3d ed. RWS, 1999.

Saaty, T. *Multicriteria Decision Making,* 2d ed. RWS, 1996.

Saaty, T. L. "An Exposition of the AHP in Reply to the Paper Remarks on the Analytic Hierarchy Process," *Management Science* 36, no. 3 (March 1990): 259–268.

Saaty, T. L. "Rank Generation, Preservation, and Reversal in the Analytic Hierarchy Decision Process," *Decision Sciences* 18 (1987): 157–177.

Winkler, R. L. "Decision Modeling and Rational Choice: AHP and Utility Theory," *Management Science* 36, no. 3 (March 1990): 247–248.

Chapter 15   Forecasting

Bowerman, B. L., and R. T. O'Connell. *Forecasting and Time Series: An Applied Approach,* 3d ed. Duxbury, 2000.

Box, G. E. P., G. M. Jenkins, and G. C. Reinsel. *Time Series Analysis: Forecasting and Control,* 3d ed. Prentice Hall, 1994.

Hanke, J. E., and A. G. Reitsch. *Business Forecasting,* 6th ed. Prentice Hall, 1998.

Makridakis, S. G., S. C. Wheelwright, and R. J. Hyndman. *Forecasting: Methods and Applications,* 3d ed. Wiley, 1997.

Wilson, J. H., and B. Keating. *Business Forecasting,* 3d ed. Irwin, 1998.

Chapter 16   Markov Processes

Bharucha-Reid, A. T. *Elements of the Theory of Markov Processes and Their Applications.* Dover, 1997.

Bhat, U. N. *Elements of Applied Stochastic Processes,* 2d ed. Wiley, 1984.

Filar, J. A., and K. Vrieze. *Competitive Markov Decision Processes.* Springer-Verlag, 1996.

Norris, J. *Markov Chains.* Cambridge, 1997.

Chapter 1

2. Define the problem; identify the alternatives; determine the criteria; evaluate the alternatives; choose an alternative.

4. A quantitative approach should be considered because the problem is large, complex, important, new, and repetitive.

6. Quicker to formulate, easier to solve, and/or more easily understood.

8. a. Max $10x + 5y$
   s.t.
$$5x + 2y \leq 40$$
$$x \geq 0, y \geq 0$$
   b. Controllable inputs: x and y
   Uncontrollable inputs: profit (10, 5), labor-hours (5, 2), and labor-hour availability (40)
   c. See Figure 1.8c.
   d. $x = 0, y = 20$; Profit = \$100 (solution by trial and error)
   e. Deterministic

10. a. Total units received $= x + y$
   b. Total cost $= 0.20x + 0.25y$
   c. $x + y = 5000$
   d. $x \leq 4000$ Kansas City
   $y \leq 3000$ Minneapolis
   e. Min $0.20x + 0.25y$
   s.t.
$$x + \quad y = 5000$$
$$x \quad\quad \leq 4000$$
$$y \leq 3000$$
$$x, y \geq 0$$

FIGURE 1.8c   SOLUTION

Profit:	\$10/unit for x
	\$5/unit for y
Labor-hours:	5/unit for x
	2/unit for y
	40 labor-hour capacity
Uncontrollable Inputs	

Production quantities x and y → **Controllable Input**

Max $10x + 5y$
s.t.
$5x + 2y \leq 40$
$x \quad \geq 0$
$y \geq 0$
Mathematical Model

→ Projected profit and check on production time constraint
Output

12. a. $TC = 1000 + 30x$
   b. $P = 40x - (1000 + 30x) = 10x - 1000$
   c. Break even when $P = 0$
   Thus, $10x - 1000 = 0$
$$10x = 1000$$
$$x = 100$$

14. a. 4706
   b. Loss of \$12,000
   c. \$23
   d. \$11,800 profit

16. a. Max $6x + 4y$
   b. $50x + 30y \leq 80,000$
   $50x \quad\quad \leq 50,000$
   $30y \leq 45,000$

Chapter 2

1. Parts (a), (b), and (e) are acceptable linear programming relationships.
   Part (c) is not acceptable because of $-2x_2^2$.
   Part (d) is not acceptable because of $3\sqrt{x_1}$.
   Part (f) is not acceptable because of $1x_1x_2$.
   Parts (c), (d), and (f) could not be found in a linear programming model because they contain nonlinear terms.

2. a.

b.

c.

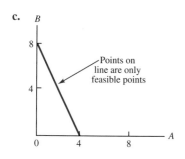

Points on line are only feasible points

6. $7A + 10B = 420$
$6A + 4B = 420$
$-4A + 7B = 420$

7.

10.

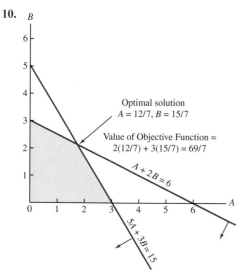

Optimal solution
$A = 12/7, B = 15/7$

Value of Objective Function =
$2(12/7) + 3(15/7) = 69/7$

$A + 2B = 6$

$5A + 3B = 15$

$A + 2B = 6$ (1)
$5A + 3B = 15$ (2)

Equation (1) times 5: $5A + 10B = 30$ (3)
Equation (2) minus equation (3): $-7B = -15$
$B = 15/7$
From equation (1): $A = 6 - 2(15/7)$
$= 6 - 30/7 = 12/7$

12. a. $A = 3, B = 1.5$; value of optimal solution $= 13.5$
b. $A = 0, B = 3$; value of optimal solution $= 18$
c. Four: $(0, 0)$, $(4, 0)$, $(3, 1.5)$, and (0.3)

13. a.

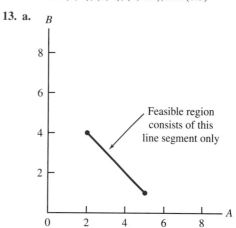

Feasible region consists of this line segment only

b. The extreme points are $(5, 1)$ and $(2, 4)$.

c.

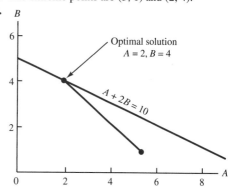

Optimal solution
$A = 2, B = 4$

$A + 2B = 10$

14. a. Let $F =$ number of tons of fuel additive
$S =$ number of tons of solvent base
Max $40F + 30S$
s.t.

$$\frac{2}{5}F + \frac{1}{2}S \le 20 \text{ Material 1}$$
$$\frac{1}{5}S \le 5 \text{ Material 2}$$
$$\frac{3}{5}F + \frac{3}{10}S \le 21 \text{ Material 3}$$
$$F, S \ge 0$$

b. $F = 25, S = 20$
c. Material 2:4 tons are used; 1 ton is unused.
d. No redundant constraints

16. a. $3S + 9D$
b. $(0, 540)$
c. $90, 150, 348, 0$

17. Max $5A + 2B + 0s_1 + 0s_2 + 0s_3$

s.t.

$$
\begin{aligned}
1A - 2B + 1s_1 \quad\quad\quad\quad &= 420 \\
2A + 3B - \quad\; + 1s_2 \quad\quad\; &= 610 \\
6A - 1B + \quad\quad\quad + 1s_3 &= 125 \\
A, B, s_1, s_2, s_3 \geq 0
\end{aligned}
$$

18. b. $A = 18/7, B = 15/7$

    c. $0, 0, 4/7$

20. b. $A = 3.43, B = 3.43$

    c. $2.86, 0, 1.43, 0$

22. b.

Extreme Point	Coordinates	Profit ($)
1	(0, 0)	0
2	(1700, 0)	8500
3	(1400, 600)	9400
4	(800, 1200)	8800
5	(0, 1680)	6720

Extreme point 3 generates the highest profit.

    c. $A = 1400, C = 600$

    d. Cutting and dyeing constraint and the packaging constraint

    e. $A = 800, C = 1200$; profit = $9200

24. a. Let R = number of units of regular model

           C = number of units of catcher's model

    Max $5R + 8C$

$$
\begin{aligned}
1R + \tfrac{3}{2}C &\leq 900 \quad \text{Cutting and sewing} \\
\tfrac{1}{2}R + \tfrac{1}{3}C &\leq 300 \quad \text{Finishing} \\
\tfrac{1}{8}R + \tfrac{1}{4}C &\leq 100 \quad \text{Packaging and shipping} \\
R, C &\geq 0
\end{aligned}
$$

b.

    c. $5(500) + 8(150) = \$3700$

    d. C & S $1(500) + \tfrac{3}{2}(150) = 725$

        F $\tfrac{1}{2}(500) + \tfrac{1}{3}(150) = 300$

        P & S $\tfrac{1}{8}(500) + \tfrac{1}{4}(150) = 100$

e.

Department	Capacity	Usage	Slack
Cutting and sewing	900	725	175 hours
Finishing	300	300	0 hours
Packaging and shipping	100	100	0 hours

26. a. Max $50N + 80R$

s.t.

$$
\begin{aligned}
N + \quad R &= 1000 \\
N \quad\quad &\geq 250 \\
R &\geq 250 \\
N - 2R &\geq 0 \\
N, R &\geq 0
\end{aligned}
$$

    b. $N = 666.67, R = 333.33$; Audience exposure = 60,000

28. a. Max $1W + 1.25M$

s.t.

$$
\begin{aligned}
5W + 7M &\leq 4480 \\
3W + 1M &\leq 2080 \\
2W + 2M &\leq 1600 \\
W, M &\geq 0
\end{aligned}
$$

    b. $W = 560, M = 240$; Profit = 860

30. a. Max $15E + 18C$

s.t.

$$
\begin{aligned}
40E + 25C &\leq 50,000 \\
40E \quad\quad &\geq 15,000 \\
25C &\geq 10,000 \\
25C &\leq 25,000 \\
E, C &\geq 0
\end{aligned}
$$

    c. (375, 400); (1000, 400); (625, 1000); (375, 1000)

    d. $E = 625, C = 1000$

        Total return = $27,375

31.

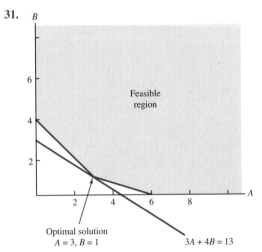

Objective function value = 13

32.

Extreme Points	Objective Function Value	Surplus Demand	Surplus Total Production	Slack Processing Time
(250, 100)	800	125	—	—
(125, 225)	925	—	—	125
(125, 350)	1300	—	125	—

34. a.

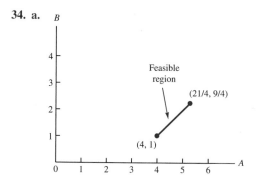

     Feasible region
     (21/4, 9/4)
     (4, 1)

b. The two extreme points are
     $(A = 4, B = 1)$ and $(A = 21/4, B = 9/4)$
c. The optimal solution (see part (a)) is $A = 4, B = 1$.

35. a. Min $6A + 4B + 0s_1 + 0s_2 + 0s_3$
     s.t.

$$2A + 1B - s_1 \qquad\qquad = 12$$
$$1A + 1B \qquad - s_2 \qquad = 10$$
$$1B \qquad\qquad + s_3 = 4$$
$$A, B, s_1, s_2, s_3 \geq 0$$

b. The optimal solution is $A = 6, B = 4$.
c. $s_1 = 4, s_2 = 0, s_3 = 0$

36. a. Min $10{,}000T + 8{,}000P$
     s.t.

$$T \qquad\qquad \geq 8$$
$$P \geq 10$$
$$T + P \geq 25$$
$$3T + 2P \leq 84$$

c. (15, 10); (21.33, 10); (8, 30); (8, 17)
d. $T = 8, P = 17$
     Total cost = \$216,000

38. a. Min $7.50S + 9.00P$
     s.t.

$$0.10S + 0.30P \geq 6$$
$$0.06S + 0.12P \leq 3$$
$$S + P = 30$$
$$S, P \geq 0$$

c. Optional solution is $S = 15, P = 15$.
d. No
e. Yes

40. $P_1 = 30, P_2 = 25$; Cost = \$55

42.

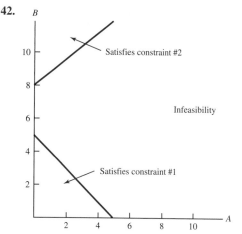

     Satisfies constraint #2
     Infeasibility
     Satisfies constraint #1

43.

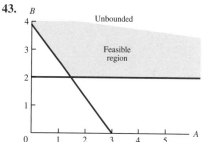

     Unbounded
     Feasible region

44. a. $A = {}^{30}\!/_{16}, B = {}^{30}\!/_{16}$; Value of optimal solution = ${}^{60}\!/_{16}$
b. $A = 0, B = 3$; Value of optimal solution = 6

46. a. 180, 20
b. Alternative optimal solutions
c. 120, 80

48. No feasible solution

50. $M = 65.45, R = 261.82$; Profit = \$45,818

52. $S = 384, O = 80$

54. a. Max $160M_1 + 345M_2$
     s.t.

$$M_1 \qquad\qquad \leq 15$$
$$M_2 \leq 10$$
$$M_1 \qquad\qquad \geq 5$$
$$M_2 \geq 5$$
$$40M_1 + 50M_2 \leq 1000$$
$$M_1, M_2 \geq 0$$

b. $M_1 = 12.5, M_2 = 10$

56. No, this could not make the problem infeasible. Changing an equality constraint to an inequality constraint can only make the feasible region larger, not smaller. No solutions have been eliminated and anything that was feasible before is still feasible.

58. The statement by the boss shows a fundamental misunderstanding of optimization models. If there were an optimal solution with 15 or less products, the model would find it, because it is trying to minimize. If there is no solution with 15 or less, adding this constraint will make the model infeasible.

Chapter 3

1. a.

b. The same extreme point, $A = 7$ and $B = 3$, remains optimal; value of the objective function becomes $5(7) + 2(3) = 41$.

c. A new extreme point, $A = 4$ and $B = 6$, becomes optimal; value of the objective function becomes $3(4) + 4(6) = 36$.

d. The objective coefficient range for variable A is 2 to 6; the optimal solution, $A = 7$ and $B = 3$, does not change. The objective coefficient range for variable B is 1 to 3; re-solve the problem to find the new optimal solution.

2. a. The feasible region becomes larger with the new optimal solution of $A = 6.5$ and $B = 4.5$.

b. Value of the optimal solution to the revised problem is $3(6.5) + 2(4.5) = 28.5$; the one-unit increase in the right-hand side of constraint 1 improves the value of the optimal solution by $28.5 - 27 = 1.5$; therefore, the dual value for constraint 1 is 1.5.

c. The right-hand-side range for constraint 1 is 8 to 11.2; as long as the right-hand side stays within this range, the dual value of 1.5 is applicable.

d. The improvement in the value of the optimal solution will be 0.5 for every unit increase in the right-hand side of constraint 2 as long as the right-hand side is between 18 and 30.

4. a. $X = 2.5$, $Y = 2.5$
   b. -2
   c. 5 to 11
   d. -3 between 9 and 18

5. a. Regular glove = 500; Catcher's mitt = 150; Value = 3700
   b. The finishing, packaging, and shipping constraints are binding; there is no slack.

c. Cutting and sewing = 0
   Finishing = 3
   Packaging and shipping = 28
   Additional finishing time is worth $3 per unit, and additional packaging and shipping time is worth $28 per unit.

d. In the packaging and shipping department, each additional hour is worth $28.

6. a. 4 to 12
   3.33 to 10
   b. As long as the profit contribution for the regular glove is between $4.00 and $12.00, the current solution is optimal; as long as the profit contribution for the catcher's mitt stays between $3.33 and $10.00, the current solution is optimal; the optimal solution is not sensitive to small changes in the profit contributions for the gloves.
   c. The dual values for the resources are applicable over the following ranges:

Constraint	Right-Hand-Side Range
Cutting and sewing	725 to No upper limit
Finishing	133.33 to 400
Packaging and shipping	75 to 135

d. Amount of increase = $(28)(20) = \$560$

8. a. More than $7.00
   b. More than $3.50
   c. None

10. a. $S = 4000$, $M = 10,000$; Total risk = 62,000
   b.

Variable	Objective Coefficient Range
S	3.75 to No upper limit
M	No lower limit to 6.4

   c. $5(4000) + 4(10,000) = \$60,000$
   d. $60,000/1,200,000 = 0.05$ or 5%
   e. 0.057 risk units
   f. $0.057(100) = 5.7\%$

12. a. $E = 80$, $S = 120$, $D = 0$
   Profit = $16,440
   b. Fan motors and cooling coils
   c. Labor hours; 320 hours available
   d. Objective function coefficient range of optimality
      No lower limit to 159
   Because $150 is in this range, the optimal solution would not change.

13. a. Range of optimality
   E 47.5 to 75
   S 87 to 126
   D No lower limit to 159

b.

Model	Profit	Change	Allowable Increase/Decrease	%
E	$ 63	Increase $6(100)	$75 − $63 = $12	$\frac{6}{12}(100) = 50$
S	$ 95	Decrease $2	$95 − $87 = $8	$\frac{2}{8}(100) = 25$
D	$135	Increase $4	$159 − $135 = $24	$\frac{4}{24}(100) = \underline{17}$
				92

Because changes are 92% of allowable changes, the optimal solution of $E = 80$, $S = 120$, $D = 0$ will not change.

The change in total profit will be

$$E \quad 80 \text{ units @ } +\$6 = \$480$$
$$S \quad 120 \text{ units @ } -\$2 = \underline{-240}$$
$$\$240$$

∴ Profit = $16,440 + $240 = $16,680

c. Range of feasibility
Constraint 1   160 to 280
Constraint 2   200 to 400
Constraint 3   2080 to No upper limit

d. Yes, Fan motors = 200 + 100 = 300 is outside the range of feasibility; the dual value will change.

14. a. Manufacture 100 cases of A and 60 cases of B, and purchase 90 cases of B; Total cost = $2170

b. Demand for A, demand for B, assembly time

c. −12.25, −9.0, 0, 0.375

d. Assembly time constraint

16. a. 100 suits, 150 sport coats
Profit = $40,900
40 hours of cutting overtime

b. Optimal solution will not change.

c. Consider ordering additional material $34.50 is the maximum price.

d. Profit will improve by $875.

18. a. The linear programming model is as follows:
Min $30AN + 50AO + 25BN + 40BO$
s.t.

$$AN + \quad AO \qquad\qquad\qquad \geq 50,000$$
$$BN + \quad BO \geq 70,000$$
$$AN \qquad + \quad BN \qquad\qquad \leq 80,000$$
$$AO \qquad\qquad + \quad BO \leq 60,000$$
$$AN, AO, BN, BO \geq 0$$

b. Optimal solution

	New Line	Old Line
Model A	50,000	0
Model B	30,000	40,000

Total cost: $3,850,000

c. The first three constraints are binding.

d. Because the dual value is negative, increasing the right-hand side of constraint 3 will *decrease (improve)* the solution; thus, an increase in capacity for the new production line is desirable.

e. Because constraint 4 is not a binding constraint, any increase in the production line capacity of the old production line will have no effect on the optimal solution; thus, increasing the capacity of the old production line results in no benefit.

f. The reduced cost for model A made on the old production line is 5; thus, the cost would have to decrease by at least $5 before any units of model A would be produced on the old production line.

g. The right-hand-side range for constraint 2 shows a lower limit of 30,000; thus, if the minimum production requirement is reduced 10,000 units to 60,000, the dual value of 40 is applicable; thus, total cost would decrease by 10,000(40) = $400,000.

20. a. Max $0.07H + 0.12P + 0.09A$
s.t.

$$H + \quad P + \quad A = 1,000,000$$
$$0.6H - \quad 0.4P - \quad 0.4A \geq 0$$
$$P - \quad 0.6A \leq 0$$
$$H, P, A \geq 0$$

b. $H = \$400,000$, $P = \$225,000$, $A = \$375,000$
Total annual return = $88,750
Annual percentage return = 8.875%

c. No change

d. Increase of $890

e. Increase of $312.50, or 0.031%

22. a. Min $30L + 25D + 18S$
s.t.

$$L + \quad D + \quad S = 100$$
$$0.6L - \quad 0.4D \qquad \geq 0$$
$$-0.15L - 0.15D + 0.85S \geq 0$$
$$-0.25L - 0.25D + \quad S \leq 0$$
$$L \qquad\qquad\qquad \leq 50$$
$$L, D, S \geq 0$$

b. $L = 48$, $D = 72$, $S = 30$
Total cost = $3780

c. No change

d. No change

24. a. 333.3, 0, 833.3; Risk = 14,666.7; Return = 18,000 or 9%

b. 1000, 0, 0, 2500; Risk = 18,000; Return = 22,000 or 11%

c. $4000

26. a. Let M_1 = units of component 1 manufactured
M_2 = units of component 2 manufactured
M_3 = units of component 3 manufactured
P_1 = units of component 1 purchased
P_2 = units of component 2 purchased
P_3 = units of component 3 purchased

Min $4.50M_1 + 5.00M_2 + 2.75M_3 + 6.50P_1 + 8.80P_2 + 7.00P_3$
s.t.

$2M_1 + 3M_2 + 4M_3$	$\leq 21{,}600$	Production
$1M_1 + 1.5M_2 + 3M_3$	$\leq 15{,}000$	Assembly
$1.5M_1 + 2M_2 + 5M_3$	$\leq 18{,}000$	Testing & Packaging
$1M_1 \qquad\qquad + 1P_1$	$= 6{,}000$	Component 1
$1M_2 \qquad + 1P_2$	$= 4{,}000$	Component 2
$1M_3 \qquad + 1P_3 =$	$3{,}500$	Component 3

$M_1, M_2, M_3, P_1, P_2, P_3 \geq 0$

  b.

Source	Component 1	Component 2	Component 3
Manufacture	2000	4000	1400
Purchase	4000		2100

Total cost = $73,550

  c. Production: $54.36 per hour
   Testing & Packaging: $7.50 per hour
  d. Dual values = $7.969; so it will cost Benson $7.969 to add a unit of component 2.

28. b. $G = 120{,}000$; $S = 30{,}000$; $M = 150{,}000$
  c. 0.15 to 0.60; No lower limit to 0.122; 0.02 to 0.20
  d. 4668
  e. $G = 48{,}000$; $S = 192{,}000$; $M = 60{,}000$
  f. The client's risk index and the amount of funds available

30. a. $L = 3, N = 7, W = 5, S = 5$
  b. Each additional minute of broadcast time increases cost by $100.
  c. If local coverage is increased by 1 minute, total cost will increase by $100.
  d. If the time devoted to local and national news is increased by 1 minute, total cost will increase by $100.
  e. Increasing the sports by 1 minute will have no effect because the dual value is 0.

32. a. Let P_1 = number of PT-100 battery packs produced at the Philippines plant
   P_2 = number of PT-200 battery packs produced at the Philippines plant
   P_3 = number of PT-300 battery packs produced at the Philippines plant
   M_1 = number of PT-100 battery packs produced at the Mexico plant
   M_2 = number of PT-200 battery packs produced at the Mexico plant
   M_3 = number of PT-300 battery packs produced at the Mexico plant

Min $1.13P_1 + 1.16P_2 + 1.52P_3 + 1.08M_1 + 1.16M_2 + 1.25M_3$
s.t.

$P_1 + M_1$	$= 200{,}000$	
$P_2 + M_2$	$= 100{,}000$	
$P_3 + M_3$	$= 150{,}000$	
$P_1 + P_2$	$\leq 175{,}000$	
$M_1 + M_2$	$\leq 160{,}000$	
P_3	$\leq 75{,}000$	
M_3	$\leq 100{,}000$	

$P_1, P_2, P_3, M_1, M_2, M_3 \geq 0$

  b. The optimal solution is as follows:

	Philippines	Mexico
PT-100	40,000	160,000
PT-200	100,000	0
PT-300	50,000	100,000

Total production and transportation cost is $535,000.
  c. The range of optimality for the objective function coefficient for P_1 shows a lower limit of $1.08; thus, the production and/or shipping cost would have to decrease by at least 5 cents per unit.
  d. The range of optimality for the objective function coefficient for M_1 shows a lower limit of $1.11; thus, the production and/or shipping cost would have to decrease by at least 5 cents per unit.

Chapter 4

1. a. Let T = number of television advertisements
   R = number of radio advertisements
   N = number of newspaper advertisements

Max $100{,}000T + 18{,}000R + 40{,}000N$
s.t.

$2000T +$	$300R +$	$600N \leq$	18,200	Budget
T		$\leq$	10	Max TV
	R	$\leq$	20	Max radio
		$N \leq$	10	Max news
$-0.5T +$	$0.5R -$	$0.5N \leq$	0	Max 50% radio
$0.9T -$	$0.1R -$	$0.1N \geq$	0	Min 10% TV
$T, R, N \geq 0$				

		Budget $
Solution:	$T = 4$	$ 8000
	$R = 14$	4200
	$N = 10$	6000
		$18,200

Audience = 1,052,000
  b. The dual value for the budget constraint is 51.30, meaning a $100 increase in the budget should provide an increase in audience coverage of approximately 5130; the right-hand-side range for the budget constraint will show that this interpretation is correct.

2. a. $x_1 = 77.89$, $x_2 = 63.16$, $3284.21
  b. Department A $15.79; Department B $47.37
  c. $x_1 = 87.21$, $x_2 = 65.12$, $3341.34
   Department A 10 hours; Department B 3.2 hours

4. a. $x_1 = 500$, $x_2 = 300$, $x_3 = 200$, $550
  b. $0.55
  c. Aroma, 75; Taste 84.4
  d. −$0.60

6. 50 units of product 1; 0 units of product 2; 300 hours department A; 600 hours department B

8. Schedule 19 officers as follows:
3 begin at 8:00 A.M.; 3 begin at noon; 7 begin at 4:00 P.M.; 4 begin at midnight, 2 begin at 4:00 A.M.

9. a. Decision variables A, P, M, H, and G represent the fraction or proportion of the total investment in each alternative.

Max $0.073A + 0.103P + 0.064M + 0.075H + 0.045G$
s.t.

$$
\begin{array}{rrrrrl}
A + & P + & M + & H + & G = & 1 \\
0.5A + & 0.5P - & 0.5M - & 0.5H & & \le 0 \\
-0.5A - & 0.5P + & 0.5M + & 0.5H & & \le 0 \\
& & -0.25M - & 0.25H + & G \ge & 0 \\
-0.6A + & 0.4P & & & & \le 0 \\
\end{array}
$$
$A, P, M, H, G \ge 0$

Objective function $= 0.079$; $A = 0.178$; $P = 0.267$; $M = 0.000$; $H = 0.444$; $G = 0.111$

b. Multiplying A, P, M, H, and G by the $100,000 invested provides the following:

Atlantic Oil	$ 17,800
Pacific Oil	26,700
Huber Steel	44,400
Government bonds	11,100
	$100,000

c. $0.079(\$100,000) = \$7900$
d. The marginal rate of return is 0.079.

10. a. 40.9%, 14.5%, 14.5%, 30.0%
Annual return = 5.4%
b. 0.0%, 36.0%, 36.0%, 28.0%
Annual return = 2.52%
c. 75.0%, 0.0%, 15.0%, 10.0%
Annual return = 8.2%
d. Yes

12.

Week	Buy	Sell	Store
1	80,000	0	100,000
2	0	0	100,000
3	0	100,000	0
4	25,000	0	25,000

14. b.

Quarter	Production	Ending Inventory
1	4000	2100
2	3000	1100
3	2000	100
4	1900	500

15. Let x_{11} = gallons of crude 1 used to produce regular
x_{12} = gallons of crude 1 used to produce high octane
x_{21} = gallons of crude 2 used to produce regular
x_{22} = gallons of crude 2 used to produce high octane

Min $0.10x_{11} + 0.10x_{12} + 0.15x_{21} + 0.15x_{22}$
s.t.

Each gallon of regular must have at least 40% A.

$x_{11} + x_{21}$ = amount of regular produced
$0.4(x_{11} + x_{21})$ = amount of A required for regular
$0.2x_{11} + 0.50x_{21}$ = amount of A in $(x_{11} + x_{21})$ gallons of regular gas
$\therefore 0.2x_{11} + 0.50x_{21} \ge 0.4x_{11} + 0.40x_{21}$
$\therefore -0.2x_{11} + 0.10x_{21} \ge 0$

Each gallon of high octane can have at most 50% B.

$x_{12} + x_{22}$ = amount high octane
$0.5(x_{12} + x_{22})$ = amount of B required for high octane
$0.60x_{12} + 0.30x_{22}$ = amount of B in $(x_{12} + x_{22})$ gallons of high octane
$\therefore 0.60x_{12} + 0.30x_{22} \le 0.5x_{12} + 0.5x_{22}$
$\therefore 0.1x_{12} - 0.2x_{22} \le 0$
$x_{11} + x_{21} \ge 800,000$
$x_{12} + x_{22} \ge 500,000$
$x_{11}, x_{12}, x_{21}, x_{22} \ge 0$

Optimal solution: $x_{11} = 266,667$, $x_{12} = 333,333$, $x_{21} = 533,333$, $x_{22} = 166,667$
Cost = $165,000

16. x_i = number of 10-inch rolls processed by cutting alternative i
a. $x_1 = 0, x_2 = 125, x_3 = 500, x_4 = 1500, x_5 = 0, x_6 = 0, x_7 = 0$; 2125 rolls with waste of 750 inches
b. 2500 rolls with no waste; however, $1\frac{1}{2}$-inch size is overproduced by 3000 units

18. a. 5 Super, 2 Regular, and 3 Econo-Tankers
Total cost $583,000; monthly operating cost $4650

19. a. Let x_{11} = amount of men's model in month 1
x_{21} = amount of women's model in month 1
x_{12} = amount of men's model in month 2
x_{22} = amount of women's model in month 2
s_{11} = inventory of men's model at end of month 1
s_{21} = inventory of women's model at end of month 1
s_{12} = inventory of men's model at end of month 2
s_{22} = inventory of women's model at end of month 2

Min $120x_{11} + 90x_{21} + 120x_{12} + 90x_{22} + 2.4s_{11} + 1.8s_{21} + 2.4s_{12} + 1.8s_{22}$
s.t.

$$
\left.
\begin{array}{l}
x_{11} - s_{11} = 130 \\
x_{21} - s_{21} = 95 \\
s_{11} + x_{12} - s_{12} = 200 \\
s_{21} + x_{22} - s_{22} = 150
\end{array}
\right\} \text{Satisfy demand}
$$

$$
\left.
\begin{array}{l}
s_{12} \ge 25 \\
s_{22} \ge 25
\end{array}
\right\} \text{Ending inventory requirement}
$$

Labor-hours: Men's $2.0 + 1.5 = 3.5$
Women's $1.6 + 1.0 = 2.6$

$$
\left.
\begin{array}{l}
3.5x_{11} + 2.6x_{21} \ge 900 \\
3.5x_{11} + 2.6x_{21} \le 1100 \\
3.5x_{11} + 2.6x_{21} - 3.5x_{12} - 2.6x_{22} \le 100 \\
-3.5x_{11} - 2.6x_{21} + 3.5x_{12} + 2.6x_{22} \le 100
\end{array}
\right\} \text{Labor smoothing}
$$

$x_{11}, x_{12}, x_{21}, x_{22}, s_{11}, s_{12}, s_{21}, s_{22} \ge 0$

Solution: $x_{11} = 193$; $x_{21} = 95$; $x_{12} = 162$; $x_{22} = 175$
Total cost = $67,156
Inventory levels: $s_{11} = 63$; $s_{12} = 25$; $s_{21} = 0$; $s_{22} = 25$
Labor levels: Previous   1000 hours
                     Month 1   922.25 hours
                     Month 2   1022.25 hours

b. To accommodate the new policy, the right-hand sides of the four labor-smoothing constraints must be changed to 950, 1050, 50, and 50, respectively; the new total cost is $67,175.

20. Produce 10,250 units in March, 10,250 units in April, and 12,000 units in May.

22. b. 5, 515, 887 sq. in. of waste
Machine 3: 492 minutes

24. Investment strategy: 45.8% of A and 100% of B
Objective function = $4340.40
Savings/Loan schedule

	\multicolumn{4}{c}{Period}
	1	**2**	**3**	**4**
Savings	242.11	—	—	341.04
Funds from loan	—	200.00	127.58	—

Chapter 5

2. b. $E = 0.924$
$wa = 0.074$
$wc = 0.436$
$we = 0.489$

c. D is relatively inefficient.
Composite requires 92.4 of D's resources.

d. 34.37 patient days (65 or older)
41.99 patient days (under 65)

e. Hospitals A, C, and E

4. b. $E = 0.960$
$wb = 0.074$
$wc = 0.000$
$wj = 0.436$
$wn = 0.489$
$ws = 0.000$

c. Yes; $E = 0.960$

d. More: $220 profit per week
Less: Hours of Operation 4.4 hours
          FTE Staff 2.6
          Supply Expense $185.61

d. Bardstown, Jeffersonville, and New Albany

6. a. 19, 18, 12, 18

b. PCQ = 8   PMQ = 0   POQ = 27
PCY = 4   PMY = 1   POY = 2
NCQ = 6   NMQ = 23   NOQ = 2
NCY = 4   NMY = 2   NOY = 1
CMQ = 37   CMY = 2
COQ = 11   COY = 3

c. PCQ = 8   PMQ = 1   POQ = 3
PCY = 4   PMY = 1   POY = 2
NCQ = 6   NMQ = 3   NOQ = 2
NCY = 4   NMY = 2   NOY = 1
CMQ = 3   CMY = 2
COQ = 7   COY = 3

8. b. 65.7% small-cap growth fund
34.3% of the portfolio in a small-cap value
Expected return = 18.5%

c. 10% foreign stock
50.8% small-cap growth fund
39.2% of the portfolio in a small-cap value
Expected return = 17.178%

10.

The game has a pure strategy: Player A strategy a_1; Player B strategy b_2; and value of game = 5.

12. 2.5, 2.5, 1.5
Strategy a_1 or a_2
Expected payoff = 2.5

14. Pure strategies a_4 and b_3
Value = 10

15. a. The maximum of the row minimums is not equal to the minimum of the column maximums, so a mixed strategy exists.
Linear program for Player A:
Max $GAINA$
s.t.   Player B strategy
          $5PA2 + 2PA3 - GAINA \geq 0$ (red chip)
$-PA1 + 4PA2 + 3PA3 - GAINA \geq 0$ (white chip)
$2PA1 - 3PA2 - 4PA3 - GAINA \geq 0$ (blue chip)
$PA1 + PA2 + PA3 = 1$
$PA1, PA2, PA3 \geq 0$
Player A: $P(\text{red}) = 0.7$, $P(\text{white}) = 0.3$, $P(\text{blue}) = 0.0$
From dual values:
Player B: $P(\text{red}) = 0.0$, $P(\text{white}) = 0.5$, $P(\text{blue}) = 0.5$

b. The value of the game is a 50-cent expected gain for Player A.

c. Player A

16. Company A: 0.0, 0.0, 0.8, 0.2
Company B: 0.4, 0.6, 0.0, 0.0
Expected gain for A = 2.8

Chapter 6

1.

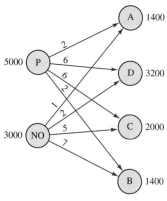

2. a. Let x_{11} = amount shipped from Jefferson City to Des Moines

x_{12} = amount shipped from Jefferson City to Kansas City

.
.
.

x_{23} = amount shipped from Omaha to St. Louis

Min $14x_{11} + 9x_{12} + 7x_{13} + 8x_{21} + 10x_{22} + 5x_{23}$
s.t.

$$
\begin{aligned}
x_{11} + x_{12} + x_{13} &\le 30 \\
x_{21} + x_{22} + x_{23} &\le 20 \\
x_{11} \quad\quad + x_{21} &= 25 \\
x_{12} \quad\quad + x_{22} &= 15 \\
x_{13} \quad\quad + x_{23} &= 10 \\
x_{11}, x_{12}, x_{13}, x_{21}, x_{22}, x_{23} &\ge 0
\end{aligned}
$$

b.

Optimal Solution	Amount	Cost
Jefferson City–Des Moines	5	70
Jefferson City–Kansas City	15	135
Jefferson City–St. Louis	10	70
Omaha–Des Moines	20	160
	Total	435

4. b.

Seattle–Denver	4000	Seattle–Los Angeles	5000
Columbus–Mobile	4000	New York–Pittsburgh	3000
New York–Mobile	1000	New York–Los Angeles	1000
New York–Washington	3000		

Cost = $150,000

c.

Seattle–Denver	4000	Seattle–Los Angeles	5000
Columbus–Mobile	5000	New York–Pittsburgh	4000
New York–Los Angeles	1000	New York–Washington	3000

Cost actually decreases by $9000

6. The network model, the linear programming formulation, and the optimal solution are shown. Note that the third constraint corresponds to the dummy origin; the variables x_{31}, x_{32}, x_{33}, and x_{34} are the amounts shipped out of the dummy origin and do not appear in the objective function because they are given a coefficient of zero.

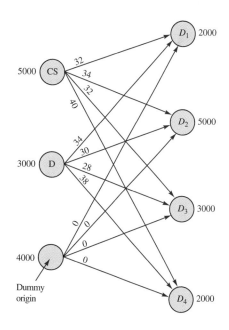

Max $32x_{11} + 34x_{12} + 32x_{13} + 40x_{14} + 34x_{21} + 30x_{22} + 28x_{23} + 38x_{24}$
s.t.

$$
\begin{aligned}
x_{11} + x_{12} + x_{13} + x_{14} &\le 5000 \\
x_{21} + x_{22} + x_{23} + x_{24} &\le 3000 \\
x_{31} + x_{32} + x_{33} + x_{34} &\le 4000 \\
x_{11} \quad + x_{21} \quad\quad + x_{31} &= 2000 \\
x_{12} \quad + x_{22} \quad\quad + x_{32} &= 5000 \\
x_{13} \quad + x_{23} \quad\quad + x_{33} &= 3000 \\
x_{14} \quad + x_{24} \quad\quad + x_{34} &= 2000 \\
x_{ij} \ge 0 \quad \text{for all } i, j
\end{aligned}
$$

Optimal Solution	Units	Cost
Clifton Springs-D_2	4,000	$136,000
Clifton Springs-D_4	1,000	40,000
Danville-D_1	2,000	68,000
Danville-D_4	1,000	38,000
	Total	$282,000

Customer 2 demand has a shortfall of 1000; customer 3 demand of 3000 is not satisfied.

8. 1–A 300; 1–C 1200; 2–A 1200; 3–A 500; 3–B 500

9. a.

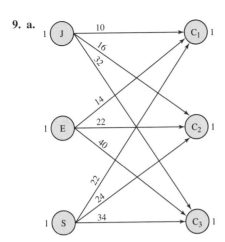

b.

Min $10x_{12} + 16x_{12} + 32x_{13} + 14x_{21} + 22x_{22} + 40x_{23} + 22x_{31} + 24x_{32} + 34x_{33}$

s.t.

$$
\begin{array}{lllll}
x_{11} + & x_{12} + & x_{13} & & \leq 1 \\
& x_{21} + & x_{22} + & x_{23} & \leq 1 \\
& & x_{31} + & x_{32} + & x_{33} \leq 1 \\
x_{11} & + & x_{21} & + & x_{31} & = 1 \\
& x_{12} & + & x_{22} & + & x_{32} & = 1 \\
& & x_{13} & + & x_{23} & + & x_{33} = 1 \\
\end{array}
$$

$x_{ij} \geq 0$ for all i, j

Solution $x_{12} = 1$, $x_{21} = 1$, $x_{33} = 1$; total completion time = 64

10. b.

Green:	Job 1	$ 26
Brown:	Job 2	34
Red:	Job 3	38
Blue:	Job 4	39
White:	Job 5	25
	Total Cost	$162

12. a. Plano: Kansas City and Dallas
Flagstaff: Los Angeles
Springfield: Chicago, Columbus, and Atlanta
Boulder: Newark and Denver
Cost = $216,000
  b. Nashville
  c. Columbus is switched from Springfield to Nashville.
Cost = $227,000

14. A to MS, B to Ph.D., C to MBA, D to undergrad
Maximum total rating = 13.3

16. a.

	Supplier					
Division	1	2	3	4	5	6
1	614	660	534	680	590	630
2	603	639	702	693	693	630
3	865	830	775	850	900	930
4	532	553	511	581	595	553
5	720	648	684	693	657	747

b. Optimal solution:

Supplier 1–Division 2	$ 603
Supplier 2–Division 5	648
Supplier 3–Division 3	775
Supplier 5–Division 1	590
Supplier 6–Division 4	553
Total	$3169

17. a.

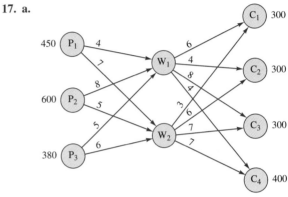

b.

Min $4x_{14} + 7x_{15} + 8x_{24} + 5x_{25} + 5x_{34} + 6x_{35} + 6x_{46} + 4x_{47} + 8x_{48} + 4x_{49} + 3x_{56} + 6x_{57} + 7x_{58} + 7x_{59}$

s.t.

$$
\begin{array}{l}
x_{14} + x_{15} \leq 450 \\
x_{24} + x_{25} \leq 600 \\
x_{34} + x_{35} \leq 380 \\
-x_{14} \quad - x_{24} \quad - x_{34} \quad + x_{46} + x_{47} + x_{48} + x_{49} = 0 \\
\quad - x_{15} \quad - x_{25} \quad - x_{35} \quad + x_{56} + x_{57} + x_{58} + x_{59} = 0 \\
x_{46} \quad + x_{56} = 300 \\
x_{47} \quad + x_{57} = 300 \\
x_{48} \quad + x_{58} = 300 \\
x_{49} \quad + x_{59} = 400 \\
\end{array}
$$

c.

	Warehouse	
Plant	1	2
1	450	—
2	—	600
3	250	—

Total cost = $11,850

	Customer			
Warehouse	1	2	3	4
1	—	300	—	400
2	300	—	300	—

18. c. $x_{14} = 320$, $x_{25} = 600$, $x_{47} = 300$, $x_{49} = 20$, $x_{56} = 300$, $x_{58} = 300$, $x_{39} = 380$
Cost = $11,220

20.

Optimal Solution	Units Shipped	Cost
Muncie–Cincinnati	1	6
Cincinnati–Concord	3	84
Brazil–Louisville	6	18
Louisville–Macon	2	88
Louisville–Greenwood	4	136
Xenia–Cincinnati	5	15
Cincinnati–Chatham	3	72
	Total	419

Two rail cars must be held at Muncie until a buyer is found.

22. b. $x_{25} = 8$, $x_{31} = 8$, $x_{42} = 3$, $x_{53} = 5$, $x_{56} = 5$, $x_{74} = 6$, $x_{56} = 5$
Total cost = $917

23. Min $7x_{12} + 9x_{13} + 18x_{14} + 3x_{23} + 5x_{25} + 3x_{32} + 4x_{35}$
$\quad + 3x_{46} + 5x_{52} + 4x_{53} + 2x_{56} + 6x_{57} + 2x_{65} + 3x_{67}$
s.t.

	Flow Out	Flow In		
Node 1	$x_{12} + x_{13} + x_{14}$		=	1
Node 2	$x_{23} + x_{25}$	$-x_{12} - x_{32} - x_{52}$	=	0
Node 3	$x_{32} + x_{35}$	$-x_{13} - x_{23} - x_{53}$	=	0
Node 4	x_{46}	$-x_{14}$	=	0
Node 5	$x_{52} + x_{53} + x_{56} + x_{57}$	$-x_{25} - x_{35} - x_{65}$	=	0
Node 6	$x_{65} + x_{67}$	$-x_{46} - x_{56}$	=	0
Node 7		$+x_{57} + x_{67}$	=	1

$$x_{ij} \geq 0 \text{ for all } i \text{ and } j$$

Optimal solution: $x_{12} = 1$, $x_{25} = 1$, $x_{56} = 1$, and $x_{67} = 1$
Shortest route 1–2–5–6–7
Length = 17

24. Route: 1–2–4–6
Travel time = 63 minutes

26. Route: 1–4–7–6
Distance = 40 miles

28. Replace years 2, 3, and 4
Total cost = $2500

29. The capacitated transshipment problem to solve is given:

Max x_{61}
s.t.

$$x_{12} + x_{13} + x_{14} - x_{61} = 0$$
$$x_{24} + x_{25} - x_{12} - x_{42} = 0$$
$$x_{34} + x_{36} - x_{13} - x_{43} = 0$$
$$x_{42} + x_{43} + x_{45} + x_{46} - x_{14} - x_{24} - x_{34} - x_{54} = 0$$
$$x_{54} + x_{56} - x_{25} - x_{45} = 0$$
$$x_{61} - x_{36} + x_{46} - x_{56} = 0$$
$$x_{12} \leq 2 \quad x_{13} \leq 6 \quad x_{14} \leq 3$$
$$x_{24} \leq 1 \quad x_{25} \leq 4$$
$$x_{34} \leq 3 \quad x_{36} \leq 2$$
$$x_{42} \leq 1 \quad x_{43} \leq 3 \quad x_{45} \leq 1 \quad x_{46} \leq 3$$
$$x_{54} \leq 1 \quad x_{56} \leq 6$$
$$x_{ij} \geq 0 \text{ for all } i, j$$

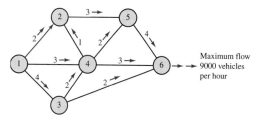

30. Maximal flow = 11,000 vehicles per hour

32. a. 10 hours; 10,000 gallons per hour
    b. 11.1 hours; flow reduced to 9000 gallons per hour

34. Maximal flow = 23 gallons/minute
The total flow from 3 to 5 must be 5 gallons/minute.

36. c. Regular month 1: 275; overtime month 1: 25; inventory at end of month 1: 150
Regular month 2: 200; overtime month 2: 50; inventory at end of month 2: 150
Regular month 3: 100; overtime month 3: 50; inventory at end of month 3: 0

Chapter 7

2. a.

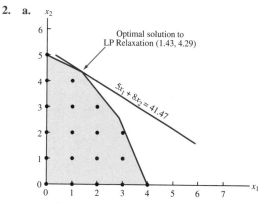

b. The optimal solution to the LP Relaxation is given by $x_1 = 1.43$, $x_2 = 4.29$, with an objective function value of 41.47. Rounding down gives the feasible integer solution $x_1 = 1$, $x_2 = 4$; its value is 37.

c.

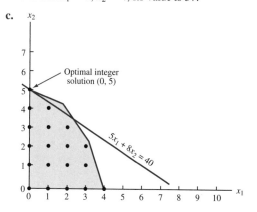

The optimal solution is given by $x_1 = 0$, $x_2 = 5$; its value is 40. It is not the same solution as found by rounding down; it provides a 3-unit increase in the value of the objective function.

4. **a.** $x_1 = 3.67$, $x_2 = 0$; Value $= 36.7$
     Rounded: $x_1 = 3$, $x_2 = 0$; Value $= 30$
     Lower bound $= 30$; Upper bound $= 36.7$
  b. $x_1 = 3$, $x_2 = 2$; Value $= 36$
  c. Alternative optimal solutions: $x_1 = 0$, $x_2 = 5$
                                 $x_1 = 2$, $x_2 = 4$

5. **a.** The feasible mixed-integer solutions are indicated by the boldface vertical lines in the graph.

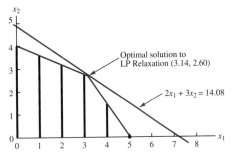

  b. The optimal solution to the LP Relaxation is given by $x_1 = 3.14$, $x_2 = 2.60$; its value is 14.08.
     Rounding down the value of x_1 to find a feasible mixed-integer solution yields $x_1 = 3$, $x_2 = 2.60$ with a value of 13.8; this solution is clearly not optimal; with $x_1 = 3$, x_2 can be made larger without violating the constraints.
  c. The optimal solution to the MILP is given by $x_1 = 3$, $x_2 = 2.67$; its value is 14, as shown in the following figure:

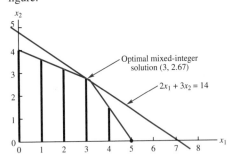

6. **b.** $x_1 = 1.96$, $x_2 = 5.48$; Value $= 7.44$
     Rounded: $x_1 = 1.96$, $x_2 = 5$; Value $= 6.96$
     Lower bound $= 6.96$; Upper bound $= 7.44$
  c. $x_1 = 1.29$, $x_2 = 6$; Value $= 7.29$

7. **a.** $x_1 + x_3 + x_5 + x_6 = 2$
  b. $x_3 - x_5 = 0$
  c. $x_1 + x_4 = 1$
  d. $x_4 \leq x_1$
     $x_4 \leq x_3$
  e. $x_4 \leq x_1$
     $x_4 \leq x_3$
     $x_4 \geq x_1 + x_3 - 1$

8. **a.** $x_3 = 1$, $x_4 = 1$, $x_6 = 1$; Value $= 17,500$
  b. Add $x_1 + x_2 \leq 1$
  c. Add $x_3 - x_4 = 0$

10. **b.** Choose locations B and E.

12. **a.** $P \leq 15 + 15Y_P$
     $D \leq 15 + 15Y_D$
     $J \leq 15 + 15Y_J$
     $Y_P + Y_D + Y_J \leq 1$
  b. $P = 15$, $D = 15$, $J = 30$
     $Y_P = 0$, $Y_D = 0$, $Y_J = 1$; Value $= 50$

13. **a.** Add the following multiple-choice constraint to the problem:
     $y_1 + y_2 = 1$
     New optimal solution: $y_1 = 1$, $y_3 = 1$, $x_{12} = 10$, $x_{31} = 30$,
     $x_{52} = 10$, $x_{53} = 20$
     Value $= 940$
  b. Because one plant is already located in St. Louis, it is only necessary to add the following constraint to the model:
     $y_3 = y_4 \leq 1$
     New optimal solution: $y_4 = 1$, $x_{42} = 20$, $x_{43} = 20$,
     $x_{51} = 30$
     Value $= 860$

14. **b.** Modernize plants 1 and 3 or plants 4 and 5.
  d. Modernize plants 1 and 3.

16. **b.** Use all part-time employees.
     Bring on as follows: 9:00 A.M.–6, 11:00 A.M.–2, 12:00 noon–6, 1:00 P.M.–1, 3:00 P.M.–6
     Cost $= \$672$
  c. Same as in part (b).
  d. New solution is to bring on 1 full-time employee at 9:00 A.M., 4 more at 11:00 A.M., and part-time employees as follows:
     9:00 A.M.–5, 12:00 noon–5, and 3:00 P.M.–2

18. **a.** 52, 49, 36, 83, 39, 70, 79, 59
  b. Thick crust, cheese blend, chunky sauce, medium sausage: Six of eight consumers will prefer this pizza (75%).

20. **a.** New objective function: Min $25x_1 + 40x_2 + 40x_3 + 40x_4 + 25x_5$
  b. $x_4 = x_5 = 1$; modernize the Ohio and California plants.
  c. Add the constraint $x_2 + x_3 = 1$.
  d. $x_1 = x_3 = 1$.

22. $x_1 + x_2 + x_3 = 3y_1 + 5y_2 + 7y_3$
    $y_1 + y_2 + y_3 = 1$

24. **a.** $x_{111}, x_{112}, x_{121}$
  b. $x_{111} + x_{112} + x_{121} \leq 1$
  c. $x_{531} + x_{532} + x_{533} + x_{541} + x_{542} + x_{543} + x_{551} + x_{552} + x_{561} \leq 1$
  d. Only two screens are available.
  e. $x_{222} + x_{231} + x_{422} + x_{431} + x_{531} + x_{531} + x_{532} + x_{533} + x_{631} + x_{632} + x_{633} \leq 2$

Chapter 8

2. a. $X = 4.32$ and $Y = 0.92$, for an optimal solution value of 4.84.

b. The dual value on the constraint $X + 4Y \leq 8$ is 0.88, which is the decrease in the optimal objective function value if we increase the right-hand-side from 8 to 9.

c. The new optimal objective function value is 4.0, so the actual decrease is only 0.84 rather than 0.88.

4. a. $q_1 = 2150$
$q_2 = 100$
Gross profit = \$1,235,000

b. $G = -1.5p_1^2 - 0.5p_2^2 + p_1p_2 + 2000p_1 + 3450p_2 - 11,465,000$

c. $p_1 = \$2725$ and $p_2 = \$6175$; $q_1 = 1185$ and $q_2 = 230$; $G = \$1,911,875$

d. Max $p_1q_1 + p_2q_2 - c_1 - c_2$
s.t.
$c_1 = 10000 + 1500q_1$
$c_2 = 30000 + 4000q_2$
$q_1 = 950 - 1.5p_1 + 0.7p_2$
$q_2 = 2500 + 0.3p_1 - 0.5p_2$

5. a. If \$1000 is spent on radio and \$1000 is spent on direct mail, simply substitute those values into the sales function:

$$S = -2R^2 - 10M^2 - 8RM + 18R + 34M$$
$$= -2(2^2) - 10(1^2) - 8(2)(1) + 18(2) + 34(1)$$
$$= 18$$

Sales = \$18,000

b. Max $-2R^2 - 10M^2 - 8RM + 18R + 34M$
s.t.
$R + M \leq 3$

c. The optimal solution is Radio = \$2500 and Direct mail = \$500
Total sales = \$37,000

6. a. Without the global solver option turned on, LINGO returns $X = 4.978$ and $Y = 1.402$ for a value of 0.3088137E-08, which is a local minimum.

b. With the global solver option turned on, the optimal solution (which is a global minimum) is $X = 0.228$ and $Y = -1.626$ for an objective function value of –6.551.

8. b. $L = 2244.281$ and $C = 2618.328$; Optimal solution = \$374,046.9 (If Excel Solver is used for this problem, we recommend starting with an initial solution that has $L > 0$ and $C > 0$.)

10. a. Min $X^2 - X^2 + 5 + Y^2 + 2Y + 3$
s.t.
$X + Y = 8$
$X, Y \geq 0$

b. $X = 4.75$ and $Y = 3.25$; Optimal objective value = 42.875

11. The LINGO formulation:
Min = (1/5)*((R1 − RBAR)^2 + (R2 − RBAR)^2 + (R3 − RBAR)^2 + (R4 − RBAR)^2 + (R5 − RBAR)^2;

.1006*FS + .1764*IB + .3241*LG + .3236*LV + .3344*SG + .2456*SV = R1;
.1312*FS + .0325*IB + .1871*LG + .2061*LV + .1940*SG + .2532*SV = R2;
.1347*FS + .0751*IB + .3328*LG + .1293*LV + .0385*SG + .0670*SV = R3;
.4542*FS + .0133*IB + .4146*LG + .0706*LV + .5868*SG + .0543*SV = R4;
−.2193*FS + .0736*IB + .2326*LG + .0537*LV + .0902*SG + .1731*SV = R5;
  FS +   IB +   LG +   LV +   SG +   SV = 50000;

(1/5)*(R1 + R2 + R3 + R4 + R5) = RBAR;
RBAR > RMIN;
RMIN = 5000;
@FREE(R1);
@FREE(R2);
@FREE(R3);
@FREE(R4);
@FREE(R5);
Optimal solution:

```
Local optimal solution found.
  Objective value:        6784038
  Total solver iterations:   19

  Model Title: MARKOWITZ
    Variable        Value        Reduced Cost
       R1         9478.492         0.000000
      RBAR        5000.000         0.000000
       R2         5756.023         0.000000
       R3         2821.951         0.000000
       R4         4864.037         0.000000
       R5         2079.496         0.000000
       FS         7920.372         0.000000
       IB         26273.98         0.000000
       LG         2103.251         0.000000
       LV         0.000000         208.2068
       SG         0.000000         78.04764
       SV         13702.40         0.000000
      RMIN        5000.000         0.000000
```

(Excel Solver will produce the same optimal solution.)

12. Optimal value of $\alpha = 0.1743882$
Sum of squared errors = 98.56

14. Optimal solution:

```
Local optimal solution found.
  Objective value:        0.1990478
  Total solver iterations:   12
  Model Title: MARKOWITZ

    Variable        Value        Reduced Cost
       R1        -0.1457056        0.000000
      RBAR        0.1518649        0.000000
       R2         0.7316081        0.000000
       R3         0.8905417        0.000000
       R4        -0.6823468E-02    0.000000
       R5        -0.3873745        0.000000
       R6        -0.5221017        0.000000
       R7         0.3499810        0.000000
       R8         0.2290317        0.000000
       R9         0.2276271        0.000000
      AAPL        0.1817734        0.000000
       AMD        0.1687534        0.000000
      ORCL        0.6494732        0.000000
```

15.

```
MODEL TITLE: MARKOWITZ;
! MINIMIZE VARIANCE OF THE PORTFOLIO;
MIN = (1/9) * ((R1 − RBAR)^2 + (R2 − RBAR)^2 + (R3 − RBAR)^2 +
(R4 − RBAR)^2 + (R5 − RBAR)^2 + (R6 − RBAR)^2 + (R7 − RBAR)^2 +
(R8 − RBAR)^2 + (R9 − RBAR)^2);
! SCENARIO 1 RETURN;
0.0962*AAPL − 0.5537*AMD − 0.1074*ORCL = R1;
! SCENARIO 2 RETURN;
0.8104*AAPL + 0.1272*AMD + 0.8666*ORCL = R2;
! SCENARIO 3 RETURN;
0.9236*AAPL + 0.4506*AMD + 0.9956*ORCL = R3;
! SCENARIO 4 RETURN;
−0.8753*AAPL + 0.3124*AMD + 0.1533*ORCL = R4;
! SCENARIO 5 RETURN;
0.1340*AAPL − 0.4270*AMD − 0.5230*ORCL = R5;
! SCENARIO 6 RETURN;
−0.5432*AAPL − 1.1194*AMD − 0.3610*ORCL = R6;
! SCENARIO 7 RETURN;
0.4517*AAPL + 1.0424*AMD + 0.1416*ORCL = R7;
! SCENARIO 8 RETURN;
1.2263*AAPL + 0.0613*AMD − 0.0065*ORCL = R8;
! SCENARIO 9 RETURN;
0.6749*AAPL + 0.9729*AMD − 0.0912*ORCL = R9;
! MUST BE FULLY INVESTED IN THE MUTUAL FUNDS;
AAPL + AMD + ORCL = 1;
! DEFINE THE MEAN RETURN;
(1/9) * (R1 + R2 + R3 + R4 + R5 + R6 + R7 + R8 + R9) = RBAR;
! THE MEAN RETURN MUST BE AT LEAST 10 PERCENT;
RBAR > 0.12;
! SCENARIO RETURNS MAY BE NEGATIVE;
@FREE(R1);
@FREE(R2);
@FREE(R3);
@FREE(R4);
@FREE(R5);
@FREE(R6);
@FREE(R7);
@FREE(R8);
@FREE(R9);
END
```

Optimal solution:

```
Local optimal solution found.
  Objective value:      0.4120213
  Total solver iterations:      8

  Model Title: MATCHING S&P INFO TECH
  RETURNS

      Variable      Value       Reduced Cost
         R1      −0.5266475E-01   0.000000
         R2       0.8458175       0.000000
         R3       0.9716207       0.000000
         R4      −0.1370104       0.000000
         R5      −0.3362695       0.000000
         R6      −0.4175977       0.000000
         R7       0.2353628       0.000000
         R8       0.3431437       0.000000
         R9       0.1328016       0.000000
       AAPL       0.2832558       0.000000
        AMD       0.6577707E-02   0.000000
       ORCL       0.7101665       0.000000
```

(Excel Solver produces the same return.)

16. Optimal solution:

```
Local optimal solution found.
  Objective value:      7.503540
  Total solver iterations:    18

Model Title: MARKOWITZ WITH SEMIVARIANCE

      Variable      Value       Reduced Cost
        D1N       0.000000       0.000000
        D2N       0.8595142      0.000000
        D3N       3.412762       0.000000
        D4N       2.343876       0.000000
        D5N       4.431505       0.000000
         FS       0.000000       6.491646
         IB       0.6908001      0.000000
         LG       0.6408726E-01  0.000000
         LV       0.000000      14.14185
         SG       0.8613837E-01  0.000000
         SV       0.1589743      0.000000
         R1      21.04766        0.000000
         R2       9.140486       0.000000
         R3       6.587238       0.000000
         R4       7.656124       0.000000
         R5       5.568495       0.000000
       RBAR      10.00000        0.000000
       RMIN      10.00000        0.000000
        D1P      11.04766        0.000000
        D2P       0.000000       0.3438057
        D3P       0.000000       1.365105
        D4P       0.000000       0.9375505
        D5P       0.000000       1.772602
```

The solution calls for investing 69.1% of the portfolio in the intermediate-term bond fund, 6.4% in the large-cap growth fund, 8.6% in the small-cap growth fund, and 15.9% in the small-cap value fund.

(Excel Solver may have trouble with this problem, depending upon the starting solution that is used; a starting solution of each fund at 0.167 will produce the optimal value.)

18. Call option price for Friday, August 25, 2006, is approximately $C = \$1.524709$.

20. Optimal solution: Produce 10 chairs at Aynor, cost = $1350; 30 chairs at Spartanburg, cost = $3150; Total cost = $4500

Chapter 9

2.

3.

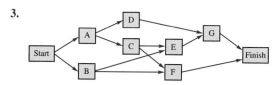

4. a. A–D–G
   b. No; Time = 15 months

6. a. Critical path: A–D–F–H
   b. 22 weeks
   c. No, it is a critical activity.
   d. Yes, 2 weeks
   e. Schedule for activity E:

Earliest start	3
Latest start	4
Earliest finish	10
Latest finish	11

8. b. B–C–E–F–H
   d. Yes, time = 49 weeks

10. a.

Activity	Optimistic	Most Probable	Pessimistic	Expected Times	Variance
A	4	5.0	6	5.00	0.11
B	8	9.0	10	9.00	0.11
C	7	7.5	11	8.00	0.44
D	7	9.0	10	8.83	0.25
E	6	7.0	9	7.17	0.25
F	5	6.0	7	6.00	0.11

   b. Critical activities: B–D–F
   Expected project completion time: $9.00 + 8.83 + 6.00 = 23.83$
   Variance of projection completion time: $0.11 + 0.25 + 0.11 = 0.47$

12. a. A–D–H–I
   b. 25.66 days
   c. 0.2578

13.

Activity	Expected Time	Variance
A	5	0.11
B	3	0.03
C	7	0.11
D	6	0.44
E	7	0.44
F	3	0.11
G	10	0.44
H	8	1.78

From Problem 6, A–D–F–H is the critical path, so
$E(T) = 5 + 6 + 3 + 8 = 22$.
$\sigma^2 = 0.11 + 0.44 + 0.11 + 1.78 = 2.44$
$$z = \frac{\text{Time} - E(T)}{\sigma} = \frac{\text{Time} - 22}{\sqrt{2.44}}$$

   a. Time = 21: $z = -0.64$
   Cumulative Probability = 0.2611
   $P(21 \text{ weeks}) = 0.2611$
   b. Time = 22: $z = 0$
   Cumulative Probability = 0.5000
   $P(22 \text{ weeks}) = 0.5000$
   c. Time = 25: $z = +1.92$
   Cumulative Probability = 0.9726
   $P(25 \text{ weeks}) = 0.9726$

14. a. A–C–E–G–H
   b. 52 weeks (1 year)
   c. 0.0174
   d. 0.0934
   e. 10 month doubtful
   13 month very likely
   Estimate 12 months (1 year)

16. a.

$E(T)$	Variance
16	3.92
13	2.03
10	1.27

   b. 0.9783, approximately 1.00, approximately 1.00

18. c. A–B–D–G–H–I, 14.17 weeks
   d. 0.0951, yes

20. b. Crash B(1 week), D(2 weeks), E(1 week), F(1 week), G(1 week)
   Total cost = $2427
   c. All activities are critical.

21. a.

Activity	Earliest Start	Latest Start	Earliest Finish	Latest Finish	Slack	Critical Activity
A	0	0	3	3	0	Yes
B	0	1	2	3	1	
C	3	3	8	8	0	Yes
D	2	3	7	8	1	
E	8	8	14	14	0	Yes
F	8	10	10	12	2	
G	10	12	12	14	2	

Critical path: A–C–E
Project completion time = $t_A + t_C + t_E = 3 + 5 + 6 = 14$ days
   b. Total cost = $8400

22. a.

Activity	Max Crash Days	Crash Cost/Day
A	1	600
B	1	700
C	2	400
D	2	400
E	2	500
F	1	400
G	1	500

$\text{Min } 600Y_A + 700Y_B + 400Y_C + 400Y_D + 500Y_E + 400Y_F + 400Y_G$

s.t.

$$
\begin{aligned}
X_A + Y_A &\geq 3 \\
X_B + Y_B &\geq 2 \\
-X_A + X_C + Y_C &\geq 5 \\
-X_B + X_D + Y_D &\geq 5 \\
-X_C + X_E + Y_E &\geq 6 \\
-X_D + X_E + Y_E &\geq 6 \\
-X_C + X_F + Y_F &\geq 2 \\
-X_D + X_F + Y_F &\geq 2 \\
-X_F + X_G + Y_G &\geq 2 \\
-X_E + X_{FIN} &\geq 0 \\
-X_G + X_{FIN} &\geq 0 \\
X_{FIN} &\leq 12 \\
Y_A &\leq 1 \\
Y_B &\leq 1 \\
Y_C &\leq 2 \\
Y_D &\leq 2 \\
Y_E &\leq 2 \\
Y_F &\leq 1 \\
Y_G &\leq 1
\end{aligned}
$$

All $X, Y \geq 0$

b. Solution of the linear programming model in part (a) shows

Activity	Crash	Crashing Cost
C	1 day	$400
E	1 day	500
	Total	$900

c. Total cost = Normal cost + Crashing cost
= $8400 + $900 = $9300

24. c. A–B–C–F, 31 weeks
d. Crash A(2 weeks), B(2 weeks), C(1 week), D(1 week), E(1 week)
e. All activities are critical.
f. $112,500

Chapter 10

1. a. $Q^* = \sqrt{\dfrac{2DC_o}{C_h}} = \sqrt{\dfrac{2(3600)(20)}{0.25(3)}} = 438.18$

b. $r = dm = \dfrac{3600}{250}(5) = 72$

c. $T = \dfrac{250Q^*}{D} = \dfrac{250(438.18)}{3600} = 30.43 \text{ days}$

d. $TC = \dfrac{1}{2}QC_h + \dfrac{D}{Q}C_o$

$= \dfrac{1}{2}(438.18)(0.25)(3) + \dfrac{3600}{438.18}(20) = \$328.63$

2. $164.32 for each; Total cost = $328.64

4. a. 1095.45
b. 240
c. 22.82 days
d. $273.86 for each; Total cost = $547.72

6. a. 15.95
b. $2106
c. 15.04
d. 16.62 days

8. $Q^* = 11.73$; use 12
5 classes per year
$225,200

10. $Q^* = 1414.21$
$T = 28.28$ days
Production runs of 7.07 days

12. $Q^* = 1000$; Total cost = $1200
Yes, the change saves $300 per year.

13. a. $Q^* = \sqrt{\dfrac{2DC_o}{(1 - D/P)C_h}}$

$= \sqrt{\dfrac{2(7200)(150)}{(1 - 7200/25,000)(0.18)(14.50)}} = 1078.12$

b. Number of production runs $= \dfrac{D}{Q^*} = \dfrac{7200}{1078.12} = 6.68$

c. $T = \dfrac{250Q}{D} = \dfrac{250(1078.12)}{7200} = 37.43 \text{ days}$

d. Production run length $= \dfrac{Q}{P/250}$

$= \dfrac{1078.12}{25,000/250} = 10.78 \text{ days}$

e. Maximum inventory $= \left(1 - \dfrac{D}{P}\right)Q$

$= \left(1 - \dfrac{7200}{25,000}\right)(1078.12)$

$= 767.62$

f. Holiday cost $= \dfrac{1}{2}\left(a - \dfrac{D}{P}\right)QC_h$

$= \dfrac{1}{2}\left(1 - \dfrac{7200}{25,000}\right)(1078.12)(0.18)(14.50)$

$= \$1001.74$

Ordering cost $= \dfrac{D}{Q}C_o = \dfrac{7200}{1078.12}(150) = \$1001.74$

Total cost $= \$2003.48$

g. $r = dm = \left(\dfrac{D}{250}\right)m = \dfrac{7200}{250}(15) = 432$

14. New $Q^* = 4509$

15. a. $Q^* = \sqrt{\dfrac{2DC_o}{C_h}\left(\dfrac{C_h + C_b}{C_b}\right)}$

$= \sqrt{\dfrac{2(12,000)(25)}{0.50}\left(\dfrac{0.50 + 5}{0.50}\right)} = 1148.91$

b. $S^* = Q^*\left(\dfrac{C_h}{C_h + C_b}\right) = 1148.91\left(\dfrac{0.50}{0.50 + 5}\right) = 104.45$

c. Max inventory $= Q^* - S^* = 1044.46$

d. $T = \dfrac{250Q^*}{D} = \dfrac{250(1148.91)}{12,000} = 23.94$ days

e. Holding $= \dfrac{(Q - S)^2}{2Q}C_h = \$237.38$

Ordering $= \dfrac{D}{Q}C_o = \$261.12$

Backorder $= \dfrac{S^2}{2Q}C_b = \$23.74$

Total cost $= \$522.24$
The total cost for the EOQ model in Problem 4 was $547.72; allowing backorders reduces the total cost.

16. 135.55; $r = dm - S$; less than

18. 64, 24.44

20. $Q^* = 100$; Total cost $= \$3601.50$

21. $Q = \sqrt{\dfrac{2DC_o}{C_h}}$

$Q_1 = \sqrt{\dfrac{2(500)(40)}{0.20(10)}} = 141.42$

$Q_2 = \sqrt{\dfrac{2(500)(40)}{0.20(9.7)}} = 143.59$

Because Q_1 is over its limit of 99 units, Q_1 cannot be optimal (see Problem 23); use $Q_2 = 143.59$ as the optimal order quantity.

Total cost $= \dfrac{1}{2}QC_h + \dfrac{D}{Q}C_o + DC$

$= 139.28 + 139.28 + 4850.00 = \$5128.56$

22. $Q^* = 300$; Savings $= \$480$

24. a. 500
b. 580.4

25. a.
$c_o = 80 - 50 = 30$
$c_u = 125 - 80 = 45$

$P(D \le Q^*) = \dfrac{c_u}{c_u + c_o} = \dfrac{45}{45 + 30} = 0.60$

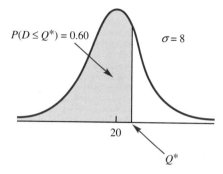

For the cumulative standard normal probability 0.60, $z = 0.25$.
$Q^* = 20 + 0.25(8) = 22$

b. $P(\text{Sell all}) = P(D \ge Q^*) = 1 - 0.60 = 0.40$

26. a. $150
b. $240 - \$150 = \$90$
c. 47
d. 0.625

28. a. 440
b. 0.60
c. 710
d. $c_u = \$17$

29. a. $r = dm = (200/250)15 = 12$

b. $\dfrac{D}{Q} = \dfrac{200}{25} = 8$ orders/year

The limit of 1 stockout per year means that
$P(\text{Stockout/cycle}) = 1/8 = 0.125$.

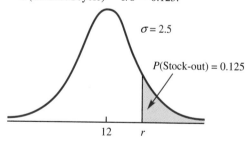

$P(\text{No Stockout/cycle}) = 1 - 0.125 = 0.875$
For cumulative probability 0.875, $z = 1.15$

Thus, $z = \dfrac{r - 12}{2.5} = 1.15$

$r = 12 + 1.15(2.5) = 14.875$ Use 15.

c. Safety stock $= 3$ units
Added cost $= 3(\$5) = \$15/\text{year}$

30. a. 13.68 (14)
b. 17.83 (18)
c. 2, $10; 6, $30

32. a. 31.62
  b. 19.86 (20); 0.2108
  c. 5, $15

33. a. 1/52 = 0.0192
  b. P(No Stockout) = $1 - 0.0192 = 0.9808$
     For cumulative probability 0.9808, $z = 2.07$

     Thus, $z = \dfrac{M - 60}{12} = 2.07$

     $M = \mu + z\sigma = 60 + 2.07(12) = 85$
  c. $M = 35 + (0.9808)(85 - 35) = 84$

34. a. 243
  b. 93, $54.87
  c. 613
  d. 163, $96.17
  e. Yes, added cost would only be $41.30 per year.
  f. Yes, added cost would be $4130 per year.

36. a. 40
  b. 62.25; 7.9
  c. 54
  d. 36

Chapter 11

2. a. 0.4512
  b. 0.6988
  c. 0.3012

4. 0.3333, 0.2222, 0.1481, 0.0988; 0.1976

5. a. $P_0 = 1 - \dfrac{\lambda}{\mu} = 1 - \dfrac{10}{12} = 0.1667$

  b. $L_q = \dfrac{\lambda^2}{\mu(\mu - \lambda)} = \dfrac{10^2}{12(12 - 10)} = 4.1667$

  c. $W_q = \dfrac{L_q}{\lambda} = 0.4167$ hour (25 minutes)

  d. $W = W_q + \dfrac{1}{\lambda} = 0.5$ hour (30 minutes)

  e. $P_w = \dfrac{\lambda}{\mu} = \dfrac{10}{12} = 0.8333$

6. a. 0.3750
  b. 1.0417
  c. 0.8333 minutes (50 seconds)
  d. 0.6250
  e. Yes

8. 0.20, 3.2, 4, 3.2, 4, 0.80
  Slightly poorer service

10. a. New: 0.3333, 1.3333, 2, 0.6667, 1, 0.6667
     Experienced: 0.50, 0.50, 1, 0.25, 0.50, 0.50
  b. New $74; experienced $50; hire experienced

11. a. $\lambda = 2.5$; $\mu = \dfrac{60}{10} = 6$ customers per hour

$L_q = \dfrac{\lambda^2}{\mu(\mu - \lambda)} = \dfrac{(2.5)^2}{6(6 - 2.5)} = 0.2976$

$L = L_q + \dfrac{\lambda}{\mu} = 0.7143$

$W_q = \dfrac{L_q}{\lambda} = 0.1190$ hours (7.14 minutes)

$W = W_q + \dfrac{1}{\mu} = 0.2857$ hours

$P_w = \dfrac{\lambda}{\mu} = \dfrac{2.5}{6} = 0.4167$

  b. No; $W_q = 7.14$ minutes; firm should increase the service rate (μ) for the consultant or hire a second consultant.

  c. $\mu = \dfrac{60}{8} = 7.5$ customers per hour

$L_q = \dfrac{\lambda^2}{\mu(\mu - \lambda)} = \dfrac{(2.5)^2}{7.5(7.5 - 2.5)} = 0.1667$

$W_q = \dfrac{L_q}{\lambda} = 0.0667$ hours (4 minutes)

The service goal is being met.

12. a. 0.25, 2.25, 3, 0.15 hours, 0.20 hours, 0.75
  b. The service needs improvement.

14. a. 8
  b. 0.3750
  c. 1.0417
  d. 12.5 minutes
  e. 0.6250
  f. Add a second consultant.

16. a. 0.50
  b. 0.50
  c. 0.10 hours (6 minutes)
  d. 0.20 hours (12 minutes)
  e. Yes, $W_q = 6$ minutes is most likely acceptable for a marina.

18. a. $k = 2$; $\lambda/\mu = 5.4/3 = 1.8$; $P_0 = 0.0526$

$L_q = \dfrac{(\lambda/\mu)^2 \lambda\mu}{(k - 1)!(2\mu - \lambda)^2}P_0$

$= \dfrac{(1.8)^2(5.4)(3)}{(2 - 1)!(6 - 5.4)^2}(0.0526) = 7.67$

$L = L_q + \lambda/\mu = 7.67 + 1.8 = 9.47$

$W_q = \dfrac{L_q}{\lambda} = \dfrac{7.67}{5.4} = 1.42$ minutes

$W = W_q + 1/\mu = 1.42 + 0.33 = 1.75$ minutes

$$P_w = \frac{1}{k!}\left(\frac{\lambda}{\mu}\right)^k \left(\frac{k\mu}{k\mu - \lambda}\right) P_0$$

$$= \frac{1}{2!}(1.8)^2\left(\frac{6}{6 - 5.4}\right)0.0526 = 0.8526$$

b. $L_q = 7.67$; Yes
c. $W = 1.75$ minutes

20. a. Use $k = 2$
  $W = 3.7037$ minutes
  $L = 4.4444$
  $P_w = 0.7111$
b. For $k = 3$
  $W = 7.1778$ minutes
  $L = 15.0735$ customers
  $P_N = 0.8767$
  Expand post office.

21. From Problem 11, a service time of 8 minutes has
$\mu = 60/8 = 7.5$.

$$L_q = \frac{\lambda^2}{\mu(\mu - \lambda)} = \frac{(2.5)^2}{7.5(7.5 - 2.5)} = 0.1667$$

$$L = L_q + \frac{\lambda}{\mu} = 0.50$$

Total cost $= \$25L + \$16$
$\qquad = 25(0.50) + 16 = \$28.50$

Two channels: $\lambda = 2.5$; $\mu = 60/10 = 6$
With $P_0 = 0.6552$,

$$L_q = \frac{(\lambda/\mu)^2\lambda\mu}{1!(2\mu - \lambda)^2}P_0 = 0.0189$$

$$L = L_q + \frac{\lambda}{\mu} = 0.4356$$

Total cost $= 25(0.4356) + 2(16) = \$42.89$
Use one consultant with an 8-minute service time.

22.

Characteristic	A	B	C
a. P_0	0.2000	0.5000	0.4286
b. L_q	3.2000	0.5000	0.1524
c. L	4.0000	1.0000	0.9524
d. W_q	0.1333	0.0208	0.0063
e. W	0.1667	0.0417	0.0397
f. P_w	0.8000	0.5000	0.2286

The two-channel System C provides the best service.

24. a. 0.0466, 0.05
  b. 1.4
  c. 11:00 A.M.

25. $\lambda = 4$, $W = 10$ minutes
  a. $\mu = \frac{1}{2} = 0.5$
  b. $W_q = W - 1/\mu = 10 - 1/0.5 = 8$ minutes
  c. $L = \lambda W = 4(10) = 40$

26. a. 0.2668, 10 minutes, 0.6667
  b. 0.0667, 7 minutes, 0.4669
  c. \$25.33; \$33.34; one-channel

27. a. ⅘ hours $= 0.25$ per hour
  b. $1/3.2$ hours $= 0.3125$ per hour

  c. $L_q = \dfrac{\lambda^2\sigma^2 + (\lambda/\mu)^2}{2(1 - \lambda/\mu)}$

  $$= \frac{(0.25)^2(2)^2 + (2.5/0.3125)^2}{2(1 - 0.25/0.3125)} = 2.225$$

  d. $W_q = \dfrac{L_q}{\lambda} = \dfrac{2.225}{0.25} = 8.9$ hours

  e. $W = W_q + \dfrac{1}{\mu} = 8.9 + \dfrac{1}{0.3125} = 12.1$ hours

  f. Same as $P_w = \dfrac{\lambda}{\mu} = \dfrac{0.25}{0.3125} = 0.80$
  The welder is busy 80% of the time.

28. a. 10, 9.6
  b. Design A with $\mu = 10$
  c. 0.05, 0.01
  d. A: 0.5, 0.3125, 0.8125, 0.0625, 0.1625, 0.5
  B: 0.4792, 0.2857, 0.8065, 0.0571, 0.1613, 0.5208
  e. Design B has slightly less waiting time.

30. a. $\lambda = 42$; $\mu = 20$

i	$(\lambda/\mu)^i/i!$
0	1.0000
1	2.1000
2	2.2050
3	1.5435
Total	6.8485

j	P_j	
0	1/6.8485	= 0.1460
1	2.1/6.8485	= 0.3066
2	2.2050/6.8485	= 0.3220
3	1.5435/6.8485	= 0.2254
		1.0000

  b. 0.2254
  c. $L = \lambda/\mu(1 - P_k) = 42/20(1 - 0.2254) = 1.6267$

d. Four lines will be necessary; the probability of denied access is 0.1499

32. a. 31.03%
   b. 27.59%
   c. 0.2759, 0.1092, 0.0351
   d. 3, 10.92%

34. $N = 5$; $\lambda = 0.025$; $\mu = 0.20$; $\lambda/\mu = 0.125$
   a.

n	$\dfrac{N!}{(N-n)!}\left(\dfrac{\lambda}{\mu}\right)^n$
0	1.0000
1	0.6250
2	0.3125
3	0.1172
4	0.0293
5	0.0037
Total	2.0877

$P_0 = 1/2.0877 = 0.4790$

   b. $L_q = N - \left(\dfrac{\lambda + \mu}{\lambda}\right)(1 - P_0)$

   $= 5 - \left(\dfrac{0.225}{0.025}\right)(1 - 0.4790) = 0.3110$

   c. $L = L_q + (1 - P_0) = 0.3110 + (1 - 0.4790)$
   $= 0.8321$

   d. $W_q = \dfrac{L_q}{(N - L)\lambda} = \dfrac{0.3110}{(5 - 0.8321)(0.025)}$

   $= 2.9854$ minutes

   e. $W = W_q + \dfrac{1}{\mu} = 2.9854 + \dfrac{1}{0.20} = 7.9854$ minutes

   f. Trips/day $= (8 \text{ hours})(60 \text{ minutes/hour})(\lambda)$
   $= (8)(60)(0.025) = 12$ trips
   Time at copier: $12 \times 7.9854 = 95.8$ minutes/day
   Wait time at copier: $12 \times 2.9854 = 35.8$ minutes/day

   g. Yes, five assistants $\times 35.8 = 179$ minutes (3 hours/day), so 3 hours per day are lost to waiting.
   $(35.8/480)(100) = 7.5\%$ of each assistant's day is spent waiting for the copier.

Chapter 12

2. a. c = variable cost per unit
   x = demand
   Profit $= (50 - c)x - 30,000$
   b. Base: Profit $= (50 - 20)1200 - 30,000 = 6,000$
   Worst: Profit $= (50 - 24)300 - 30,000 = -22,200$
   Best: Profit $= (50 - 16)2100 - 30,000 = 41,400$
   c. Simulation will be helpful in estimating the probability of a loss.

4. a.

Number of New Accounts	Interval
0	0.00 but less than 0.01
1	0.01 but less than 0.05
2	0.05 but less than 0.15
3	0.15 but less than 0.40
4	0.40 but less than 0.80
5	0.80 but less than 0.95
6	0.95 but less than 1.00

   b. 4, 3, 3, 5, 2, 6, 4, 4, 4, 2
   37 new accounts
   c. First-year commission = $185,000
   Cost of 10 seminars = $35,000
   Yes

5. a.

Stock Price Change	Interval
-2	0.00 but less than 0.05
-1	0.05 but less than 0.15
0	0.15 but less than 0.40
$+1$	0.40 but less than 0.60
$+2$	0.60 but less than 0.80
$+3$	0.80 but less than 0.90
$+4$	0.90 but less than 1.00

   b. Beginning price $39
   0.1091 indicates -1 change; $38
   0.9407 indicates $+4$ change; $42
   0.1941 indicates 0 change; $42
   0.8083 indicates $+3$ change; $45 (ending price)

6. a. 0.00–0.83, 0.83–0.89, 0.89–0.94, 0.94–0.96, 0.96–0.98, 0.98–0.99, 0.99–1.00
   b. 4 claims paid; Total = $22,000

8. a. Atlanta wins each game if random number is in interval 0.00–0.60, 0.00–0.55, 0.00–0.48, 0.00–0.45, 0.00–0.48, 0.00–0.55, 0.00–0.50.
   b. Atlanta wins games 1, 2, 4, and 6.
   Atlanta wins series 4 to 2.
   c. Repeat many times; record % of Atlanta wins.

9. a. Base-case based on most likely;
   Time $= 6 + 5 + 14 + 8 = 33$ weeks
   Worst: Time $= 8 + 7 + 18 + 10 = 43$ weeks
   Best: Time $= 5 + 3 + 10 + 8 = 26$ weeks
   b. 0.1778 for A: 5 weeks
   0.9617 for B: 7 weeks
   0.6849 for C: 14 weeks
   0.4503 for D: 8 weeks; Total = 34 weeks
   c. Simulation will provide an estimate of the probability of 35 weeks or less.

10. a.

Hand Value	Interval
17	0.0000 but less than 0.1654
18	0.1654 but less than 0.2717
19	0.2717 but less than 0.3780
20	0.3780 but less than 0.4797
21	0.4797 but less than 0.5769
Broke	0.5769 but less than 1.0000

   b, c, & d. Dealer wins 13 hands, Player wins 5, 2 pushes.
   e. Player wins 7, dealer wins 13.

FIGURE E12.14   WORKSHEET FOR THE MADEIRA MANUFACTURING SIMULATION

	A	B	C	D	E	F	G	H
1	Madeira Manufacturing Company							
2								
3	Selling Price per Unit		$50					
4	Fixed Cost		$30,000					
5								
6	Variable Cost (Uniform Distribution)				Demand (Normal Distribution)			
7	Smallest Value		$16		Mean		1200	
8	Largest Value		$24		Standard Deviation		300	
9								
10	Simulation trials							
11		Variable						
12	Trial	Cost per Unit	Demand	Profit				
13	1	$17.81	788	($4,681)				
14	2	$18.86	1078	$3,580				
15								

12. a. $7, $3, $12

   b. Purchase: 0.00–0.25, 0.25–0.70, 0.70–1.00
   Labor: 0.00–0.10, 0.10–0.35, 0.35–0.70, 0.70–1.00
   Transportation: 0.00–0.75, 0.75–1.00

   c. $5

   d. $7

   e. Provide probability profit less than $5/unit.

14. Selected cell formulas for the worksheet shown in Figure E12.14 are as follows:

Cell	Formula
B13	=$C$7+RAND()*($C$8−$C$7)
C13	=NORMINV(RAND(),$G$7,$G$8)
D13	=($C$3−B13)*C13−$C$4

   a. The mean profit should be approximately $6000; simulation results will vary, with most simulations having a mean profit between $5500 and $6500.

   b. 120 to 150 of the 500 simulation trials should show a loss; thus, the probability of a loss should be between 0.24 and 0.30.

   c. This project appears too risky.

16. a. About 36% of simulation runs will show $130,000 as the winning bid.

   b. $150,000; $10,000

   c. Recommended $140,000

18. Selected cell formulas for the worksheet shown in Figure E12.18 are as follows:

Cell	Formula
B11	=$C$4+RAND()*($C$5−$C$4)
C11	=NORMINV(RAND(),$H$4,$H$5)
D11	=MIN(B11:C11)
G11	=COUNTIF($D$11:$D$1010,">650")
H11	=G11/COUNT($D$11:$D$1010)

   a. $650,000 should win roughly 600 to 650 of the 1000 times; the probability of winning the bid should be between 0.60 and 0.65.

   b. The probability of $625,000 winning should be roughly 0.82, and the probability of $615,000 winning should be roughly 0.88; a contractor's bid of $625,000 is recommended.

20. a. Results vary with each simulation run.
   Approximate results: 50,000 provided $230,000
   60,000 provided $190,000
   70,000 less than $100,000

   b. Recommend 50,000 units.

   c. Roughly 0.75

22. Very poor operation; some customers wait 30 minutes or more.

24. b. Waiting time is approximately 0.8 minutes.

   c. 30% to 35% of customers have to wait.

FIGURE E12.18   WORKSHEET FOR THE CONTRACTOR BIDDING SIMULATION

	A	B	C	D	E	F	G	H	I
1	**Contractor Bidding**								
2									
3	**Contractor A (Uniform Distribution)**					**Contractor B (Normal Distribution)**			
4	Smallest Value		$600			Mean		$700	
5	Largest Value		$800			Standard Deviation		$50	
6									
7									
8	**Simulation**					**Results**			
9		Contractor	Contractor	Lowest		Contractor's	Number	Probability	
10	Trial	A's Bid	B's Bid	Bid		Bid	of Wins	of Winning	
11	1	$673	$720	$673		$650	628	0.628	
12	2	$757	$655	$655		$625	812	0.812	
13	3	$706	$791	$706		$615	875	0.875	
14	4	$638	$677	$638					
15									

Chapter 13

1. a.

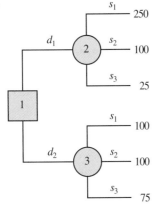

b.

Decision	Maximum Profit	Minimum Profit
d_1	250	25
d_2	100	75

Optimistic approach: Select d_1
Conservative approach: Select d_2

Regret or opportunity loss table:

Decision	s_1	s_2	s_3
d_1	0	0	50
d_2	150	0	0

Maximum regret: 50 for d_1 and 150 for d_2; select d_1

2. a. Optimistic: d_1
   Conservative: d_3
   Minimax regret: d_3
c. Optimistic: d_1
   Conservative: d_2 or d_3
   Minimax regret: d_2

3. a. Decision: Choose the best plant size from the two alternatives—a small plant and a large plant.
   Chance event: market demand for the new product line with three possible outcomes (states of nature)—low, medium, and high
b. Influence diagram:

c.

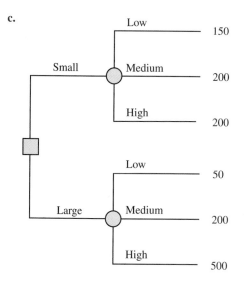

d.

Decision	Maximum Profit	Minimum Profit	Maximum Regret
Small	200	150	300
Large	500	50	100

Optimistic approach: Large plant
Conservative approach: Small plant
Minimax regret: Large plant

4. $EV(d_1) = 0.65(250) + 0.15(100) + 0.20(25) = 182.5$
$EV(d_2) = 0.65(100) + 0.15(100) + 0.20(75) = 95$
The optimal decision is d_1.

6. **a.** Decision: Which lease option to choose
Chance event: Miles driven

b.

	Annual Miles Driven		
	12,000	15,000	18,000
Forno	10,764	12,114	13,464
Midtown	11,160	11,160	12,960
Hopkins	11,700	11,700	11,700

c. Optimistic: Forno Saab
Conservative: Hopkins Automotive
Minimax: Hopkins Automotive
d. Midtown Motors
e. Most likely: $11,160; Probability = 0.9
f. Midtown Motors or Hopkins Automotive

7. **a.** $EV(\text{own staff}) = 0.2(650) + 0.5(650) + 0.3(600) = 635$
$EV(\text{outside vendor}) = 0.2(900) + 0.5(600) + 0.3(300) = 570$
$EV(\text{combination}) = 0.2(800) + 0.5(650) + 0.3(500) = 635$
Optimal decision: Hire an outside vendor with an expected cost of $570,000.

b.

	Cost	Probability
Own staff	300	0.3
Outside vendor	600	0.5
Combination	900	0.2
		1.0

8. **a.** $EV(d_1) = p(10) + (1 - p)(1) = 9p + 1$
$EV(d_2) = p(4) + (1 - p)(3) = 1p + 3$

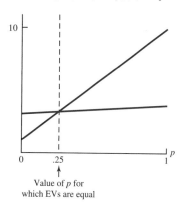

Value of p for
which EVs are equal

$9p + 1 = 1p + 3$ and hence $p = 0.25$
d_2 is optimal for $p \leq 0.25$, d_1 is optimal for $p \geq 0.25$
b. d_2
c. As long as the payoff for $s_1 \geq 2$, then d_2 is optimal.

10. **b.** Space Pirates
EV = $724,000
$84,000 better than Battle Pacific
c. $200   0.18
$400   0.32
$800   0.30
$1600   0.20
d. $P(\text{Competition}) > 0.7273$

12. **a.** Decision: Whether to lengthen the runway
Chance event: The location decisions of Air Express and DRI
Consequence: Annual revenue
b. $255,000
c. $270,000
d. No
e. Lengthen the runway.

14. **a.** If s_1, then d_1; if s_2, then d_1 or d_2; if s_3, then d_2
b. $EVwPI = 0.65(250) + 0.15(100) + 0.20(75) = 192.5$
c. From the solution to Problem 4, we know that $EV(d_1) = 182.5$ and $EV(d_2) = 95$; thus, recommended decision is d_1; hence, $EVwoPI = 182.5$.
d. $EVPI = EVwPI - EVwoPI = 192.5 - 182.5 = 10$

16. a.

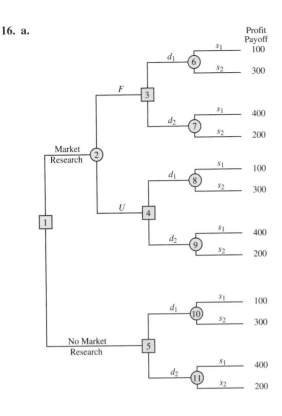

b. EV (node 6) = 0.57(100) + 0.43(300) = 186
EV (node 7) = 0.57(400) + 0.43(200) = 314
EV (node 8) = 0.18(100) + 0.82(300) = 264
EV (node 9) = 0.18(400) + 0.82(200) = 236
EV (node 10) = 0.40(100) + 0.60(300) = 220
EV (node 11) = 0.40(400) + 0.60(200) = 280

EV (node 3) = Max(186,314) = 314 d_2
EV (node 4) = Max(264,236) = 264 d_1
EV (node 5) = Max(220,280) = 280 d_2

EV (node 2) = 0.56(314) + 0.44(264) = 292
EV (node 1) = Max(292,280) = 292

∴ Market research
If favorable, decision d_2
If unfavorable, decision d_1

18. a. 5000 − 200 − 2000 − 150 = 2650
3000 − 200 − 2000 − 150 = 650
b. Expected values at nodes:

8: 2350	5: 2350	9: 1100
6: 1150	10: 2000	7: 2000
4: 1870	3: 2000	2: 1560
1: 1560		

c. Cost would have to decrease by at least $130,000.

d.

Payoff (in millions)	Probability
−$200	0.20
800	0.32
2800	0.48
	1.00

20. b. If Do Not Review, Accept
If Review and *F*, Accept
If Review and *U*, Accept
Always Accept
c. Do not review; EVSI = $0
d. $87,500; better method of predicting success

22. a. Order 2 lots; $60,000
b. If *E*, order 2 lots
If *V*, order 1 lot
EV = $60,500
c. EVPI = $14,000
EVSI = $500
Efficiency = 3.6%
Yes, use consultant.

23.

State of Nature	$P(s_j)$	$P(I/s_j)$	$P(I \cap s_j)$	$P(s_j/I)$
s_1	0.2	0.10	0.020	0.1905
s_2	0.5	0.05	0.025	0.2381
s_3	0.3	0.20	0.060	0.5714
	1.0		$P(I) = 0.105$	1.0000

24. a. 0.695, 0.215, 0.090
0.98, 0.02
0.79, 0.21
0.00, 1.00
c. If *C*, Expressway
If *O*, Expressway
If *R*, Queen City
26.6 minutes

Chapter 14

2. a. Let x_1 = number of shares of AGA Products purchased
x_2 = number of shares of Key Oil purchased

To obtain an annual return of exactly 9%:

$$0.06(50)x_1 + 0.10(100)x_2 = 0.09(50,000)$$
$$3x_1 + 10x_2 = 4500$$

To have exactly 60% of the total investment in Key Oil:

$$100x_2 = 0.60(50,000)$$
$$x_2 = 300$$

Therefore, we can write the goal programming model as follows:

Min $P_1(d_1^-) + P_2(d_2^+)$
s.t.

$$50x_1 + 100x_2 \qquad\qquad \leq 50{,}000 \quad \text{Funds available}$$
$$3x_1 + \ 10x_2 - d_1^+ + d_1^- = \ 4{,}500 \quad P_1 \text{ goal}$$
$$x_2 - d_2^+ + d_2^- = \ \ 300 \quad P_2 \text{ goal}$$
$$x_1, x_2, d_1^+, d_1^-, d_2^+, d_2^- \geq 0$$

b. In the following graphical solution, $x_1 = 250$ and $x_2 = 375$.

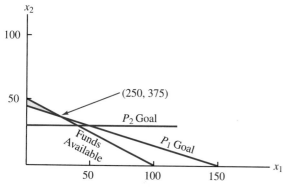

4. a. Min $P_1(d_1^-) + P_2(d_2^l) + P_2(d_3^-) + P_2(d_4^-) + P_3(d_5^-)$
s.t.

$$20x_1 + 30x_2 - d_1^+ + d_1^- = 4800$$
$$20x_1 + 30x_2 - d_2^l + d_2^- = 6000$$
$$x_1 \qquad\quad - d_3^+ + d_3^- = \ 100$$
$$x_2 - d_4^+ + d_4^- = \ 120$$
$$x_1 + \ x_2 - d_3^l + d_5^- = \ 300$$
$$x_1, x_2, \text{ all deviation variables} \geq 0$$

b. $x_1 = 120, x_2 = 120$

6. a. Let $x_1 =$ number of letters mailed to group 1 customers
$x_2 =$ number of letters mailed to group 2 customers

Min $P_1(d_1^-) + P_2(d_2^-) + P_2(d_3^+)$
s.t.

$$x_1 \qquad - d_1^+ + d_1^- = 40{,}000$$
$$x_2 - d_2^+ + d_2^- = 50{,}000$$
$$x_1 + x_2 - d_3^l + d_3^- = 70{,}000$$
$$x_1, x_2, \text{ all deviation variables} \geq 0$$

b. $x_1 = 40{,}000, x_2 = 50{,}000$

c. Optimal solution does not change.

8. a. Min $d_1^- + d_1^+ + e_1^- + e_1^+ + d_2^- + d_2^+ + e_2^- +$
$e_2^+ + d_3^- + d_3^+ + e_3^- + e_3^+$
s.t.

$$x_1 \qquad + d_1^- - d_1^+ = 1$$
$$x_2 + e_1^- - e_1^+ = 7$$

$$x_1 \qquad + d_2^- - d_2^+ = 5$$
$$x_2 + e_2^- - e_2^+ = 9$$
$$x_1 \qquad + d_3^- - d_3^+ = 6$$
$$x_2 + e_3^- - e_3^+ = 2$$
$$\text{all variables} \geq 0$$

b. $x_1 = 5, x_2 = 7$

9. Scoring calculations

Criterion	Analyst Chicago	Accountant Denver	Auditor Houston
Career advancement	35	20	20
Location	10	12	8
Management	30	25	35
Salary	28	32	16
Prestige	32	20	24
Job security	8	10	16
Enjoyment of the work	28	20	20
Totals	171	139	139

The analyst position in Chicago is recommended.

10. 178, 184, 151
Marysville

12. 170, 168, 190, 183
Handover College

14. a. 220 Bowrider (194)
b. 240 Sundancer (144)

16. Step 1: Column totals are $^{17}\!/_{4}$, $^{31}\!/_{21}$, and 12.
Step 2:

Style	Accord	Saturn	Cavalier
Accord	$^4\!/_{17}$	$^7\!/_{31}$	$^4\!/_{12}$
Saturn	$^{12}\!/_{17}$	$^{21}\!/_{31}$	$^7\!/_{12}$
Cavalier	$^1\!/_{17}$	$^3\!/_{31}$	$^1\!/_{12}$

Step 3:

Style	Accord	Saturn	Cavalier	Row Average
Accord	0.235	0.226	0.333	0.265
Saturn	0.706	0.677	0.583	0.656
Cavalier	0.059	0.097	0.083	0.080

Consistency Ratio
Step 1:

$$0.265\begin{bmatrix}1\\3\\1/4\end{bmatrix} + 0.656\begin{bmatrix}1/3\\1\\1/7\end{bmatrix} + 0.080\begin{bmatrix}4\\7\\1\end{bmatrix}$$

$$\begin{bmatrix} 0.265 \\ 0.795 \\ 0.066 \end{bmatrix} + \begin{bmatrix} 0.219 \\ 0.656 \\ 0.094 \end{bmatrix} + \begin{bmatrix} 0.320 \\ 0.560 \\ 0.080 \end{bmatrix} = \begin{bmatrix} 0.802 \\ 2.007 \\ 0.239 \end{bmatrix}$$

Step 2: $0.802/0.265 = 3.028$
$2.007/0.656 = 3.062$
$0.239/0.080 = 3.007$
Step 3: $\lambda_{max} = (3.028 + 3.062 + 3.007)/3 = 3.032$
Step 4: CI $= (3.032 - 3)/2 = 0.016$
Step 5: CR $= 0.016/0.58 = 0.028$
Because CR $= 0.028$ is less than 0.10, the degree of consistency exhibited in the pairwise comparison matrix for style is acceptable.

18. a. 0.724, 0.193, 0.083
   b. CR $= 0.057$, yes

20. a.

Flavor	A	B	C
A	1	3	2
B	1/3	1	5
C	1/2	1/5	1

b. Step 1: Column totals are $^{11}/_6$, $^{21}/_5$, and 8.
Step 2:

Flavor	A	B	C
A	6/11	15/21	2/8
B	2/11	5/21	5/8
C	3/11	1/21	1/8

Step 3:

Flavor	A	B	C	Row Average
A	0.545	0.714	0.250	0.503
B	0.182	0.238	0.625	0.348
C	0.273	0.048	0.125	0.148

c. Step 1:

$$0.503 \begin{bmatrix} 1 \\ 1/3 \\ 1/2 \end{bmatrix} + 0.348 \begin{bmatrix} 3 \\ 1 \\ 1/5 \end{bmatrix} + 0.148 \begin{bmatrix} 2 \\ 5 \\ 1 \end{bmatrix}$$

$$\begin{bmatrix} 0.503 \\ 0.168 \\ 0.252 \end{bmatrix} + \begin{bmatrix} 1.044 \\ 0.348 \\ 0.070 \end{bmatrix} + \begin{bmatrix} 0.296 \\ 0.740 \\ 0.148 \end{bmatrix} = \begin{bmatrix} 1.845 \\ 1.258 \\ 0.470 \end{bmatrix}$$

Step 2: $1.845/0.503 = 3.668$
$1.258/0.348 = 3.615$
$0.470/0.148 = 3.123$
Step 3: $\lambda_{max} = (3.668 + 3.615 + 3.123)/3 = 3.469$
Step 4: CI $= (3.469 - 3)/2 = 0.235$
Step 5: CR $= 0.235/0.58 = 0.415$
Because CR $= 0.415$ is greater than 0.10, the individual's judgments are not consistent.

22. a.

	D	S	N
D	1	1/4	1/7
S	4	1	1/3
N	7	3	1

b. 0.080, 0.265, 0.656
c. CR $= 0.028$, yes

24. Criteria: Yield and Risk
Step 1: Column totals are 1.5 and 3.
Step 2:

	Yield	Risk	Priority
Yield	0.667	0.667	0.667
Risk	0.333	0.333	0.333

With only two criteria, CR $= 0$; no need to compute CR; preceding calculations for Yield and Risk provide

Stocks	Yield Priority	Risk Priority
CCC	0.750	0.333
SRI	0.250	0.667

Overall Priorities:
CCC $0.667(0.750) + 0.333(0.333) = 0.611$
SRI $0.667(0.250) + 0.333(0.667) = 0.389$
CCC is preferred.

26. a. Criterion: 0.608, 0.272, 0.120
Price: 0.557, 0.123, 0.320
Sound: 0.137, 0.239, 0.623
Reception: 0.579, 0.187, 0.046
   b. 0.446, 0.162, 0.392
System A is preferred.

Chapter 15

1. The following table shows the calculations for parts (a), (b), and (c).

Week	Time Series Value	Forecast	Forecast Error	Absolute Value of Forecast Error	Squared Forecast Error	Percentage Error	Absolute Value of Percentage Error
1	18						
2	13	18	−5	5	25	−38.46	38.46
3	16	13	3	3	9	18.75	18.75
4	11	16	−5	5	25	−45.45	45.45
5	17	11	6	6	36	35.29	35.29
6	14	17	−3	3	9	−21.43	21.43
			Totals	22	104	−51.30	159.38

  a. MAE = 22/5 = 4.4
  b. MSE = 104/5 = 20.8
  c. MAPE = 159.38/5 = 31.88
  d. Forecast for week 7 is 14.

2. The following table shows the calculations for parts (a), (b), and (c).

Week	Time Series Value	Forecast	Forecast Error	Absolute Value of Forecast Error	Squared Forecast Error	Percentage Error	Absolute Value of Percentage Error
1	18						
2	13	18.00	−5.00	5.00	25.00	−38.46	38.46
3	16	15.50	0.50	0.50	0.25	3.13	3.13
4	11	15.67	−4.67	4.67	21.81	−42.45	42.45
5	17	14.50	2.50	2.50	6.25	14.71	14.71
6	14	15.00	−1.00	1.00	1.00	−7.14	7.14
			Totals	13.67	54.31	−70.21	105.86

  a. MAE = 13.67/5 = 2.73
  b. MSE = 54.31/5 = 10.86
  c. MAPE = 105.89/5 = 21.18
  d. Forecast for week 7 is (18 + 13 + 16 + 11 + 17 + 14)/6 = 14.83.

3. By every measure, the approach used in problem 2 appears to be the better method.

4. a. MSE = 363/6 = 60.5
    Forecast for month 8 is 15.
  b. MSE = 216.72/6 = 36.12
    Forecast for month 8 is 18.
  c. The average of all the previous values is better because MSE is smaller.

5. a. The data appear to follow a horizontal pattern.

b.

Week	Time Series Value	Forecast	Forecast Error	Squared Forecast Error
1	18			
2	13			
3	16			
4	11	15.67	−4.67	21.78
5	17	13.33	3.67	13.44
6	14	14.67	−0.67	0.44
			Total	35.67

MSE = 35.67/3 = 11.89.
The forecast for week 7 = (11 + 17 + 14)/3 = 14.

c.

Week	Time Series Value	Forecast	Forecast Error	Squared Forecast Error
1	18			
2	13	18.00	−5.00	25.00
3	16	17.00	−1.00	1.00
4	11	16.80	−5.80	33.64
5	17	15.64	1.36	1.85
6	14	15.91	−1.91	3.66
			Total	65.15

MSE = 65.15/5 = 13.03
The forecast for week 7 is 0.2(14) + (1 − 0.2)15.91 = 15.53.

d. The three-week moving average provides a better forecast because it has a smaller MSE.

e.

Alpha   0.367694922

Week	Time Series Value	Forecast	Forecast Error	Squared Forecast Error
1	18			
2	13	18	−5.00	25.00
3	16	16.16	−0.16	0.03
4	11	16.10	−5.10	26.03
5	17	14.23	2.77	7.69
6	14	15.25	−1.25	1.55
			Total	60.30

MSE = 60.30/5 = 12.061

6. a. The data appear to follow a horizontal pattern.
b. MSE = 110/4 = 27.5
The forecast for week 8 is 19.
c. MSE = 252.87/6 = 42.15
The forecast for week 7 is 19.12.

d. The three-week moving average provides a better forecast because it has a smaller MSE.
e. α = 0.351404848   MSE = 39.61428577

8. a.

Week	4	5	6	7	8	9	10	11	12
Forecast	19.3	21.3	19.8	17.8	18.3	18.3	20.3	20.3	17.8

b. MSE = 11.49
Prefer the unweighted moving average here; it has a smaller MSE.
c. You could always find a weighted moving average at least as good as the unweighted one. Actually, the unweighted moving average is a special case of the weighted ones where the weights are equal.

10. b. The more recent data receives the greater weight or importance in determining the forecast. The moving averages method weights the last n data values equally in determining the forecast.

12. a. The data appear to follow a horizontal pattern.
b. MSE(3-month) = 0.12
MSE(4-month) = 0.14
Use 3-month moving averages.
c. 9.63

13. a. The data appear to follow a horizontal pattern.

b.

Month	Time-Series Value	3-Month Moving Average Forecast	(Error)^2	α = 0.2 Forecast	(Error)^2
1	240				
2	350			240.00	12100.00
3	230			262.00	1024.00
4	260	273.33	177.69	255.60	19.36
5	280	280.00	0.00	256.48	553.19
6	320	256.67	4010.69	261.18	3459.79
7	220	286.67	4444.89	272.95	2803.70
8	310	273.33	1344.69	262.36	2269.57
9	240	283.33	1877.49	271.89	1016.97
10	310	256.67	2844.09	265.51	1979.36
11	240	286.67	2178.09	274.41	1184.05
12	230	263.33	1110.89	267.53	1408.50
			17,988.52		27,818.49

MSE(3-Month) = 17,988.52/9 = 1998.72
MSE(α = 0.2) = 27,818.49/11 = 2528.95
Based on the above MSE values, the 3-month moving average appears better. However, exponential smoothing was penalized by including month 2, which was difficult for any method to forecast. Using only the errors for months 4–12, the MSE for exponential smoothing is

$MSE(\alpha = 0.2) = 14{,}694.49/9 = 1632.72$

Thus, exponential smoothing was better considering months 4–12.

c. Using exponential smoothing,

$$F_{13} = \alpha Y_{12} + (1 - \alpha)F_{12} = 0.20(230) + 0.80(267.53)$$
$$= 260$$

14. a. The data appear to follow a horizontal pattern.

b. Values for months 2–12 are as follows:

105.00 114.00 115.80 112.56 105.79 110.05 120.54
126.38 118.46 106.92 104.85
MSE = 510.29

c. $\alpha = 0.032564518$ MSE = 5056.62

16. a. The time series plot indicates a possible linear trend in the data. This could be due to decreasing viewer interest in watching the Masters. But, closer inspection of the data indicates that the two highest ratings correspond to years 1997 and 2001, years in which Tiger Woods won the tournament. The pattern observed may be simply due to the effect Tiger Woods has on ratings and not necessarily on any long-term decrease in viewer interest.

b. The methods discussed in this section are only applicable for a time series that has a horizontal pattern. So, if there is really a long-term linear trend in the data, the methods disucssed in this are not appropriate.

c. The time series plot for the data for years 2002–2008 exhibits a horizontal pattern. It seems reasonable to conclude that the extreme values observed in 1997 and 2001 are more attributable to viewer interest in the performance of Tiger Woods. Basing the forecast on years 2002–2008 does seem reasonable. But, because of the injury that Tiger Woods experienced in the 2008 season, if he is able to play in the 2009 Masters then the rating for 2009 may be significantly higher than suggested by the data for years 2002–2008.

17. a. The time series plot shows a linear trend.

b.

	b0	4.70		
	b1	2.10		
			Forecast	**Squared Forecast**
Year	**Sales**	**Forecast**	**Error**	**Error**
1	6.00	6.80	−0.80	0.64
2	11.00	8.90	2.10	4.41
3	9.00	11.00	−2.00	4.00
4	14.00	13.10	0.90	0.81
5	15.00	15.20	−0.20	0.04
6		17.30	**Total**	9.9

$MSE = 9.9/5 = 1.98$

c. $T_6 = 4.7 + 2.1(6) = 17.3$

18. a.

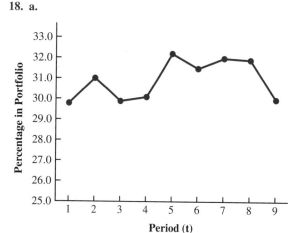

The time series plot indicates a horizontal pattern.

b. $\alpha = 0.467307293$; MSE = 1.222838367

c. Forecast for second quarter 2009 = 30.93

20. a. The time series plot exhibits a curvilinear trend.

b. $T_t = 107.857 - 28.9881\,t + 2.65476\,t^2$

c. 45.86

21. a. The time series plot shows a linear trend.

b.

			b0	4.72		
			b1	1.46		
					Forecast	**Squared Forecast**
Period	**Year**	**Enrollment**	**Forecast**		**Error**	**Error**
1	2001	6.50	6.17		0.33	0.11
2	2002	8.10	7.63		0.47	0.22
3	2003	8.40	9.09		−0.69	0.47
4	2004	10.20	10.54		−0.34	0.12
5	2005	12.50	12.00		0.50	0.25
6	2006	13.30	13.46		−0.16	0.02
7	2007	13.70	14.91		−1.21	1.47
8	2008	17.20	16.37		0.83	0.69
9	2009	18.10	17.83		0.27	0.07
10	2010		19.28		**Total**	3.427333

$T_t = 4.72 + 1.46t$

c. $T_{10} = 4.72 + 1.46(10) = 19.28$

22. a. The time series plot shows a downward linear trend.

b. $T_t = 13.8 - 0.7t$

c. 8.2

d. If SCC can continue to decrease the percentage of funds spent on administrative and fund-raising by 0.7% per year, the forecast of expenses for 2015 is 4.70%.

24. a. The time series plot shows a linear trend.
  b. $T_t = 7.5623 - .07541t$
  c. 6.7328
  d. Given the uncertainty in global market conditions, making a prediction for December using only time is not recommended.

26. a. A linear trend is not appropriate.
  b. $T_t = 5.702 + 2.889t - .1618t^2$
  c. 17.91

28. a. The time series plot shows a horizontal pattern. But, there is a seasonal pattern in the data. For instance, in each year the lowest value occurs in quarter 2 and the highest value occurs in quarter 4.

b.

Year	Quarter	Period	Seasonality QTR1	QTR2	QTR3	Series	Forecast	Forecast Error	Squared Forecast Error
1	1	1	1	0	0	71	67.00	4.00	16.00
	2	2	0	1	0	49	47.00	2.00	4.00
	3	3	0	0	1	58	57.00	1.00	1.00
	4	4	0	0	0	78	77.00	1.00	1.00
2	1	5	1	0	0	68	67.00	1.00	1.00
	2	6	0	1	0	41	47.00	−6.00	36.00
	3	7	0	0	1	60	57.00	3.00	9.00
	4	8	0	0	0	81	77.00	4.00	16.00
3	1	9	1	0	0	62	67.00	−5.00	25.00
	2	10	0	1	0	51	47.00	4.00	16.00
	3	11	0	0	1	53	57.00	−4.00	16.00
	4	12	0	0	0	72	77.00	−5.00	25.00
								Total	166.00
		b0	**b1**	**b2**	**b3**				
		77.00	−10.00	−30.00	−20.00				

c. The quarterly forecasts for next year are as follows:
Quarter 1 forecast = 77.0 − 10.0(1) − 30.0(0) − 20.0(0) = 67
Quarter 2 forecast = 77.0 − 10.0(0) − 30.0(1) − 20.0(0) = 47
Quarter 3 forecast = 77.0 − 10.0(0) − 30.0(0) − 20.0(1) = 57
Quarter 4 forecast = 77.0 − 10.0(0) − 30.0(0) − 20.0(0) = 77

30. a. There appears to be a seasonal pattern in the data and perhaps a moderate upward linear trend.
  b. $Sales_t = 2492 - 712\ Qtr1_t - 1512\ Qtr2_t + 327\ Qtr3_t$
  c. The quarterly forecasts for next year are as follows:
Quarter 1 forecast = 1780
Quarter 2 forecast = 980
Quarter 3 forecast = 2819
Quarter 4 forecast = 2492
  d. $Sales_t = 2307 - 642\ Qtr1_t - 1465\ Qtr2_t + 350\ Qtr3_t + 23.1\ t$

The quarterly forecasts for next year are as follows:
Quarter 1 forecast = 2058
Quarter 2 forecast = 1258
Quarter 3 forecast = 3096
Quarter 4 forecast = 2769

32. a. The time series plot shows both a linear trend and seasonal effects.
  b. $Revenue_t = 70.0 + 10.0\ Qtr1_t + 105\ Qtr2_t + 245\ Qtr3_t$
Quarter 1 forecast = 80
Quarter 1 forecast = 175
Quarter 1 forecast = 315
Quarter 1 forecast = 70
  c. The equation is
$Revenue = -70.1 + 45.0\ Qtr1 + 128\ Qtr2 + 257\ Qtr3 + 11.7\ Period$
Quarter 1 forecast = 221
Quarter 1 forecast = 315
Quarter 1 forecast = 456
Quarter 1 forecast = 211

Chapter 16

2. **a.** 0.82
   b. $\pi_1 = 0.5$, $\pi_2 = 0.5$
   c. $\pi_1 = 0.6$, $\pi_2 = 0.4$

3. **a.** 0.10 as given by the transition probability
   b. $\pi_1 = 0.90\pi_1 + 0.30\pi_2$ (1)
   $\pi_2 = 0.10\pi_1 + 0.70\pi_2$ (2)
   $\pi_1 + \pi_2 = 1$ (1)
   Using (1) and (3),
   $$0.10\pi_1 - 0.30\pi_2 = 0$$
   $$0.10\pi_1 - 0.30(1 - \pi_1) = 0$$
   $$0.10\pi_1 - 0.30 + 0.30\pi_1 = 0$$
   $$0.40\pi_1 = 0.30$$
   $$\pi_1 = 0.75$$
   $$\pi_2 = (1 - \pi_1) = 0.25$$

4. **a.** $\pi_1 = 0.92$, $\pi_2 = 0.08$
   b. $85

6. **a.**

	City	Suburbs
City	0.98	0.02
Suburbs	0.01	0.99

   b. $\pi_1 = 0.333$, $\pi_2 = 0.667$
   c. City will decrease from 40% to 33%; suburbs will increase from 60% to 67%.

7. **a.** $\pi_1 = 0.85\pi_1 + 0.20\pi_2 = 0.15\pi_3$ (1)
   $\pi_2 = 0.10\pi_1 + 0.75\pi_2 = 0.10\pi_3$ (2)
   $\pi_3 = 0.05\pi_1 + 0.05\pi_2 = 0.75\pi_3$ (3)
   $\pi_1 + \pi_2 + \pi_3 = 1$ (4)
   Using (1), (2), and (4) provides three equations with three unknowns; solving provides $\pi_1 = 0.548$, $\pi_2 = 0.286$, and $\pi_3 = 0.166$.
   b. 16.6% as given by π_3
   c. Quick Stop should take
   $667 - 0.548(1000)$ $= 119$ Murphy's customers
   and $333 - 0.286(1000) = \underline{\ 47\ }$ Ashley's customers
   Total   166 Quick Stop customers
   It will take customers from Murphy's and Ashley's.

8. **a.** MDA
   b. $\pi_1 = \frac{1}{3}$, $\pi_2 = \frac{2}{3}$

10. $3 - 1(0.59)$, $4 - 1(0.52)$

11. $I = \begin{bmatrix} 1 & 0 \\ 0 & 1 \end{bmatrix}$ $Q = \begin{bmatrix} 0.25 & 0.25 \\ 0.05 & 0.25 \end{bmatrix}$

   $(I - Q) = \begin{bmatrix} 0.75 & -0.25 \\ -0.05 & 0.75 \end{bmatrix}$

$N = (I - Q)^{-1} = \begin{bmatrix} 1.3636 & 0.4545 \\ 0.0909 & 1.3636 \end{bmatrix}$

$NR = \begin{bmatrix} 1.3636 & 0.4545 \\ 0.0909 & 1.3636 \end{bmatrix}\begin{bmatrix} 0.5 & 0.0 \\ 0.5 & 0.2 \end{bmatrix} = \begin{bmatrix} 0.909 & 0.091 \\ 0.727 & 0.273 \end{bmatrix}$

$BNR = \begin{bmatrix} 4000 & 5000 \end{bmatrix}\begin{bmatrix} 0.909 & 0.091 \\ 0.727 & 0.273 \end{bmatrix} = \begin{bmatrix} 7271 & 1729 \end{bmatrix}$
Estimate $1729 in bad debts.

12. 3580 will be sold eventually; 1420 will be lost.

14. **a.** Graduate and Drop Out
   b. P(Drop Out) $= 0.15$, P(Sophomore) $= 0.10$, P(Junior) $= 0.75$
   c. 0.706, 0.294
   d. Yes; P(Graduate) $= 0.54$
   P(Drop Out) $= 0.46$
   e. 1479 (74%) will graduate.

Appendix A

2. =F6*$F$3

4.

	A	B
1	**Nowlin Plastics**	
2		
3	**Fixed Cost**	$3,000.00
4		
5	**Variable Cost Per Unit**	$2.00
6		
7	**Selling Price Per Unit**	$5.00
8		
9	**Capacity**	1500
10		
11	**Forecasted Demand**	1200
12		
13	**Model**	
14		
15	**Production Volume**	1200
16		
17	**Total Cost**	$5,400.00
18		
19	**Total Revenue**	$6,000.00
20		
21	**Total Profit (Loss)**	$600.00
22		

	A	B
14		
15	**Production Volume**	=IF(B11<B9,B11,B9)
16		
17	**Total Cost**	=B3+B5*B15
18		
19	**Total Revenue**	=B7*B15
20		
21	**Total Profit (Loss)**	=B19-B17
22		

6.

Cell	Formula
D14	=C14*$B$3
E14	=C14*$B$7
F14	=C14*$B$9
G14	=$B$5
H14	=SUM(E14:G14)
I14	=D14-H14

	A	B	C	D	E	F	G	H	I
1	Cox Electric Breakeven Analysis								
2									
3	Revenue per Unit	$0.63							
4									
5	Fixed Costs	$10,000.00							
6									
7	Material Cost per Unit	$0.15							
8									
9	Labor Cost per Unit	$0.10							
10									
11									
12	Model								
13			Volume	Total Revenue	Material Cost	Labor Cost	Fixed Cost	Total Cost	Profit
14			10000	$6,300.00	$1,500.00	$1,000.00	$10,000.00	$12,500.00	-$6,200.00
15			20000	$12,600.00	$3,000.00	$2,000.00	$10,000.00	$15,000.00	-$2,400.00
16			30000	$18,900.00	$4,500.00	$3,000.00	$10,000.00	$17,500.00	$1,400.00
17									

8.

Grade	Count
F	1
D	2
C-	1
C-	1
C+	0
B-	2
B	1
B+	0
A-	1
A	3

10. Error in SUMPRODUCT range in cell B17
Cell A23 should be Lexington.

Index

Note: Entries accompanied by *n* indicate notes. Chapters 17 through 21 are found on the accompanying website and are indicated by the chapter number followed by the page number (i.e., 17-5)

A

Absorbing states, 770
  in blackjack, 779–780
Accounts receivable analysis
  allowance for doubtful accounts, 772–773
  fundamental matrices, 770–772
Activities, 411
Activity time estimates, 421–423
Additivity, 34n1
Advertising campaign problem, 202–203
Air New Zealand, 316–317
All-integer linear programs, 317–318
  graphical and computer solutions for, 319–323
Allowance for doubtful accounts, 772–773
Alternative optimal solutions, 57–58, 64
Aluminum can production problem, 318–319
American Airlines, 2–3, 223
American Skandia, 236
Ammann, Bill, 760
Analog models, 7
Analytic hierarchy process (AHP), 17, 658
  developing overal priority rankings, 686–687
  establishing priorities using, 678–686
  hierarchy development, 678
  pairwise comparisons, 679–686
Annual costs, 454, 456
Arcs, 19-8–19-9, 279
Armstrong, C. Michael, 283
Arrival distribution, 502–504
Arrival rates, 503
  for finite calling population models, 525
Arrivals, blocked or lost, 516n1, 522
Arrival times, 510n1, 562
Artificial variables, 17-21
Asset allocation, 236
Assignment problems, 19-2
  empty freight cart assignment, 263
  finding minimum number of lines, 19-21
  general linear programming model for, 267
  Hungarian method, 19-18–19-21
  maximization objective, 19-22–19-24
  number of agents no equal to number of tasks, 19-22
  problem variations, 19-21–19-25
  project manager assignment, 268
  unacceptable assignments, 19-24
  variations, 266–267

ATM waiting line simulations, 561–571
  average number of customers, 571–572n2
  with two ATMs, 568–571
AT&T, 283
Auto industry pricing problem, 372

B

Backorders, 466–470
Backward pass, 415
Bank branch efficiency, 215–216
Bank location problem, 332–335
Base-case scenarios, 544
Basic feasible solutions, 17-4–17-5
Basic solutions, 17-4
Basic variables, 17-4
Basis, 17-9
Bass, Frank, 385
Bass forecasting model, 385–390, 390n1
Bayer Pharmaceuticals, 627
Bayes' theorem, 628–631
Bellman, Richard, 21-2
Best-case scenarios, 544
Beta probability distribution, 423
Binary expansion, 338n1
Blackjack
  absorbing states in, 779–780
Blending problems, 183–188
Blending the pooling problems, 380–385
Blocked arrivals, 522
Bombardier Flexjet, 364–365
Bossee, David, 207n1
Bounds
  LP Relaxation and, 321–322
Branches, 605
Breakeven analysis, 16
  using Excel, 24–27
Breakeven point, 16
Bush, George W., 372

C

CAFE compliance in auto industry, 403–405
Call center design, 542
Canonical form, 18-14
Canonical form for maximization problem, 18-14
Canonical form for minimization problem, 18-14
Capacitated transportation problem, 263
Capacitated transshipment problem, 274

Capital budgeting, 323–324
Carnegie-Mellon University, 18
Carver, Bob, 452
Central limit theorem, 427n3
Chakravarti, Nilotpal, 123
Chance events, 602
Chance nodes, 603
Chorman, Tom, 276
Citibank, 501–502
Clean Energy Act of 2007, 372
Clemen, Robert T., 601
Coal allocation problem, 207–209
Communications networks, 20-5
Computer-generated random numbers, 547
Computer software packages, 109n1
Computer solutions
    Electronic Communications problem, 118–121
    M&D Chemicals problem, 56–57
    Par, Inc. problem, 50–52
    sensitivity analysis, 103–109
Computer technology, 14n1
Concave functions, 369
Conditional constraints, 340
Conditional probabilities, 630
Consequence nodes, 603
Consequences, 602
Conservative approach to decision making,
    605–606, 633
Consistency, 683
Consistency ratios, 683
Constant demand rate, 452–453
Constant service times, 521
Constant supply rate, 462
Constraint coefficients, 112
Constraint lines, 36
Constraints, 8, 30, 100–102
Continuous review inventory systems, 482
Contribution margin, 30n1
Controllable inputs, 8, 541
Convery, John, 21–21
Convex functions, 370
Cook, Thomas M., 2–3
Corequisite constraints, 340
Cornell University, 18
Corporate Average Fuel Economy (CAFE)
    regulations, 372
Cost and volume models, 14–15
Cost of capital, 454
County Beverage Drive-Thru, Inc., 587–588
CPM (Critical Path Method), 17
Crashing, 420n1
    activity times for, 430–431
    linear programming model for, 432–434
Critical activities, 414
Critical path method (CPM), 411
    concept, 412–414
    determining critical path, 414–418
Critical paths, 414
Crystal Ball® spreadsheet add-in, 555n2, 595–599
Cunningham, Kevin, 85

Curve fitting
    with Excel Solver, 754–756
    linear trend, 724–728
    nonlinear trend, 728–731
Customer order allocation models, 341
CVS Corporation, 452
Cycle time, 459
Cyclical time series patterns, 711

D

Dantzig, George, 2, 30, 17-3
Data envelopment analysis (DEA),
    215–223, 223n1
Data preparation, 10–11
Daugherty Porta-Vac project, 421–428
Decision alternatives, 602
Decision analysis, 17
    computing branch probabilities, 628–631
    decision making without probabilities, 605–608
    decision trees, 604–605
    influence diagrams, 603
    new drugs, 627
    payoff tables, 603–604
    problem formulation, 602–605
    with sample information, 618–628
    software, 618n1
    with TreePlan, 651–656
Decision making
    conservative approach, 605–606
    defined, 3–4
    minimax regret approach to, 606–608
    optimistic approach, 605
    with probabilities, 608–613
    without probabilities, 605–608
Decision nodes, 603
Decisions, 4
Decision Sciences Institute (DSI), 18n1
Decision strategies, 621–625
Decision Support Software, 687n2
Decision trees, 604–605, 619–621
Decision variable d_n, 21-7
Decision variables, 8, 31–32, 188n1
Decomposition methods, 364
Deere & Company, 487
Definitional variables, 234n1
Degeneracy, 110n3, 17-29, 17-33–17-35
Degenerate solutions, 19-12
Delta Airlines, 17-2
Demand, under/overestimating, 474
Demand levels, 555
Dennis, Greg A., 20-5
Destination nodes, 269
Deterministic inventory models, 472
Deterministic models, 9–10
Deviation variables, 660
Dill, Franz, 276
DIRECTV, 389–390
Disability claims, 610–611

Discrete-event simulation models, 561, 571–572n2
Distribution system design, 306–308, 327–332
"Divide and conquer" solution strategy, 21-10n1
Divisibility, 34n1
Duality, 18-14–18-20
Dual prices, 18-6, 18-17
    absolute value of, 18-12n1
Dual problems, 18-14
Dual values, 101–102, 109n2, 110n4, 227, 323n1, 372
    interpretation of, 106
    nonintuitive, 112–115
Dual variables, 18-14, 18-16–18-18
Duke Energy, 207–209, 702–703
Duke University Medical Center, 632
Dummy agents, 267n2
Dummy destinations, 19-18
Dummy origins, 260, 19-2, 19-17, 19-18
Duncan Industries Limited (DIL), 122–123
DuPont, 411
Dutch Companies, 482
Dynamic programming, 18
    knapsack problem, 21-10–21-16
    notation, 21-6–21-10
    production and inventory control problem, 21-16–21-20
    shortest-route problem, 21-2–21-6
    stages of, 21-6
Dynamic simulation models, 561

E

Earliest finish times, 414
Earliest start times, 414
Eastman Kodak, 29, 93, 601
Economic order quantity (EOQ) model, 452–461
    assumptions for, 461
    Excel solution of, 460–461
    formula for, 457
    how-much-to-order decision, 453, 457–458
    optimal order quantity (Q^*), 498–499
    quantity discounts for, 470–472
    sensitivity analysis for, 459–460
    when-to-order decision, 458–459
Economic production lot size, 463
    optimal lot size (Q^*) formula, 499
Economic production lot size model, 462–465
Edmonton Folk Festival, 338–339
EDS, 20-5
Efficiency, 217, 628
Efficiency indexes, 220
Efficient frontiers, 379
Eisner, Mark, 18
Electronic Communications problem, 116–122
Elementary row operations, 17-12
Energy needs forecasting, 702–703
Equilibrium points, 239

Erlang, A. K., 501
Evans, Richard, 703
Events, 561
Excel
    adjustable cells for investment variables, 234n2
    assignment problem with, 310–312
    breakeven analysis using, 24–27
    economic order quantity (EOQ) model, 460–461
    financial planning with, 210–213
    Goal Seek tool, 26–27
    integer linear programming with, 358–360
    linear programs, solving, 87–91
    versus LINGO, 377n3
    matrix inversion with, 783–784
    scoring models with, 699–700
    sensitivity analysis with, 148–150
    simulation with, 588–595
    transportation problem with, 308–310
    transshipment problem with, 312–314
    waiting line models with, 509–510
Excel Solver
    forecasting with, 752–756
    solving nonlinear problems with, 407–409
Expected gains, 240
Expected opportunity loss, 612n1
Expected time (t), 423
Expected values (EV), 240
    approach to decision making, 608
    with perfect information (EPwPI), 611–612
    of perfect information (EVPI), 612
    of sample information (EVSI), 627–628
    without perfect information (EVwoPI), 611–612
Expert Choice® software package, 687n2
Exponential probability distribution, 504
Exponential smoothing, 718–724, 724n1, 724n2
    with Excel data analysis tools, 751–752
    with Excel solver, 752–754
Exponential trend equation, 731
Exposure quality, 155, 158n1, 158n2
Extreme points, 48–50, 64
EZ Trailers, Inc., 698–699

F

Feasible regions, 38
Feasible solution points, 38
Feasible solutions, 11, 38, 369
Financial applications
    financial planning, 164–168
    portfolio selection, 161–164
Financial planning, 164–168
    with Excel, 210–213
Financial portfolio theory, 164n2
Finite calling populations, 524, 525
First-come, first-served (FCFS), 505
Fixed costs, 14, 324–327
Fleet assignment, 17-2
Flexible risk measures, 380n3

Flight and crew scheduling problem, 364–365
Flow capacity, 279
Food nutrient values, 116
Ford Motor Company, 676
Forecast accuracy, 711–715, 716–718, 721–723
Forecast error, 711, 712
Forecasting, 17, 702. *See also* Time series analysis
    adoption of satellite television, 389–390
    energy needs, 702–703
    with Excel data analysis tools, 751–752
    exponential smoothing, 718–724
    food and beverage sales, 749
    with LINGO, 756–758
    lost sales, 749–751
    method selection, 711
    moving averages, 715–718
    seasonality, 731–738
    trend projection, 724–731
    weighted moving averages, 718
Forecasting new adoptions problem, 385–390
Forward pass, 415
Four-stage dynamic programming procedure, 21-6
Fundamental matrices, 770–772
    matrix inversion with Excel, 783–784

G

Game theory
    competing for market share, 236–238
    logic of, 237, 241
    pure strategy solutions, 238–239
    two-person, zero-sum games, 236
Gantt, Henry L., 411
Gantt charts, 411
GE Capital, 29, 164–165
General Electric Plastics (GEP), 110
General linear programming notation, 62–64
General Motors (GM), 372
Global maximums, 369
Global minimums, 369
Global optimums, 369
Goal constraints, 665n1
Goal equations, 659
Goal programming, 17, 658
    complex problems in, 666–671
    constraints and goal equations, 659–661
    formulation and graphical solution, 658–666
    goal programming model, 665
    graphical solution procedure, 662–665
    infeasible solutions and, 672n2
    multiple priority levels, 671n1, 672n2
    objective functions with preemptive priorities, 60
    with preemptive priorities, 661
Goodrich, Michael J., 555
Goodwill costs, 466
Government agencies, 518n1
Graphical sensitivity analysis, 95–102, 615
Graphical solution procedures, 35–44
    for minimization problems, 54–55

Graphing lines, 44–46
Greedy algorithms, 20–5n2

H

Hanshin Expressway Public Corporation, 64–65
Harbor Dunes Golf Course, 585–587
Hard constraints, 666n2
Hard nonlinear optimization problems, 390n1
Harmonic average, 403, 404
Harris, F. W., 457
Health care services, 760
Heery International, 268
Heuristics, 19-2
Hierarchies, 678
Holding costs, 454
Horizontal time series patterns, 703–705
Hospital performance, 216
Hospital revenue bond problem, 420
How-much-to-order decision, 453, 457–458, 479–480
Hungarian method, 19-18–19-21
Hypothetical composites, 216–217

I

Iconic models, 7
IMB ILOG, Inc, 2
Immediate predecessors, 412
Incoming arcs, 19–9
Incremental analysis, 474
Infeasibility, 58–60, 61n1, 64, 17-29–17-31, 17-35
Infeasible solutions, 11
Infinite calling populations, 524
Influence diagrams, 603, 618–619
Inputs, 8, 541
Institute for Operations Research and the Management Sciences (INFORMS), 18n1
Integer linear programming, 16, 164n1, 316–348
    all-integer linear programming, 317–318, 319–323
    computer solutions for, 322–323
    with Excel, 358–360
    versus linear programming, 317n1
    with LINGO, 360–362
    sensitivity analysis and, 342
    types of models in, 317–318
    0-1 variables and, 323–338
Interarrival time, 562, 565
Interior point solution procedures, 17-2n1
Intermediate nodes, 268–269
Inventory cost, lowering, 482
Inventory models, 17, 452–486
    economic order quantity (EOQ) model, 452–461
    economic production lot size model, 462–465
    order-quantity, reorder point with probabilistic demand, 478–482
    periodic review model with probabilistic demand, 482–486

with planned shortages, 465–470
single-period model with probabilistic demand, 472–478
"total cost" models, 453n1
Inventory position, 458
Inventory simultion, 556–560
Investment strategy problem, 146–147
Iteration, 17-11, 17-15

J

Jeppesen Sanderson, Inc., 173
Johnson Shoe Company, 473–476
Joint probabilities, 630

K

Karter, Stacey, 502
Kellogg Company, 180
Kellogg Planning System (KPS), 180
Kendall, D. G., 518
Kendall notation, 518–519
Ketron Management Science, 341
Knapsack problem, 21-10–21-16
Koopmans, Tjolling, 30
k out of n alternatives constraints, 340
Kwit, Robert C., 601

L

Latest finish time, 415, 417
Latest start times, 414
Lawsuit defense strategy, 650–651
Lead time, 459, 486n1
Lead-time demand, 459
Lead-time demand distribution, 480
Less efficient, 217
Leveraged lease structuring problems, 165
Linear functions, 34
0-1 linear integer programs, 318, 323n1
  bank location problem, 332–335
  capital budgeting, 323–324
  distribution system design, 327–332
  fixed costs, 324–327
  modeling flexibility of, 339–342
  product design and market share optimization problems, 335–338
Linear programming, 16, 34
  for crashing, 432–434
  DEA models, 217–222
  defined, 29
  Excel, solving with, 87–91
  general notation for, 62–64
  versus integer linear programming, 317n1
  LINGO, solving with, 85–87
  marketing and, 154–160
  models, 34

multiperiod planning and, 172
network flow problems, 256–287
production scheduling and, 172–179
software packages, 50
special cases in, 57–61
specially structured problems, 317n2
traffic control and, 64–65
LINGO, 14n1, 14n2
  versus Excel, 377n3
  forecasting with, 756–758
  integer linear programming with, 360–362
  nonlinear problems with, 406–407
  sensitivity analysis with, 150–152
  solving linear programs with, 85–87
Little, John D. C., 515
Little's flow equations, 515–516
Local maximums, 369
Local minimums, 369
Local optimums, 369
Location problems, 333
Longest path algorithm, 418
Lot size, 462
Lower bounds, 380n1
LP Relaxation, 318, 320, 321–322
Lustig, Irv, 2

M

Magerlein, David B., 555
Magerlein, James M., 555
Make-or-buy decisions, 168–172
Management science techniques
  analytic hierarchy process, 17
  decision analysis, 17
  dynamic programming, 18
  forecasting, 17
  goal programming, 17
  integer linear programming, 16
  inventory models, 17
  linear programming, 16
  Markov process models, 17–18
  network models, 17
  project scheduling: PERT/CPM, 17
  simulation, 17
  waiting line or queueing models, 17
Managerial judgment, 158n1
Marathon Oil Company, 29, 154
Marginal costs, 15
Marginal revenue, 15
Marketing applications, 154–160
Marketing planning models, 154
Market share, 236–238
Market share analysis, 761–768
Markov process models, 17–18, 760
  accounts receivable analysis, 769–773
  benefit of health care services, 760
  Canadian curling and, 774
  higher order, 768n1
  market share analysis, 761–768

Markov process models (*continued*)
  Markov decision processes, 768n2
  state of the system, 761
  trials of the process, 761
Markowitz, Harry, 229, 377
Markowitz mean-variance portfolio model, 377–380
Martin, James R., 236
Mason, Thomas, 207n1
Master problems, 364
Mathematical models, 7, 34n1
Matrix notation and operations, 780–783
Maximal flow problems, 279–283
Maximax approach to decision making, 605–606
Maximin model, 232
Maximin strategies, 237
Maximization, 30–34
Maximization objective function, 261
MeadWestvaco Corporation
  timber harvesting model, 29
Mean absolute error (MAE), 712
Mean absolute percentage error
    (MAPE), 713
Mean squared error (MSE), 713
Media selection models, 155–158
Medical screening tests, 632
Memoryless properties, 768n1
Merrill Lynch, 13
$M/G/1$ model, 519–521
Microsoft Excel, 14n1, 14n2. *See also* Excel
Microsoft Office Project, 419, 448–450
Middleton, Michael R., 651
Minimal spanning tree algorithm, 20-2–20-5
Minimax regret approach to decision making,
    606–608, 633
Minimax strategies, 238, 244, 605–606
Minimization, 30, 52–54, 18-17
Minimum cost method, 19-5–19-6
Minimum expected opportunity loss, 612–613n1
Minimum ratio test, 17-11
Minitab statistical package, 728n2
Mixed-integer compute codes, 338n1
Mixed-integer computer codes, 338n1
Mixed-integer linear programs, 318, 338n3
Mixed strategy solutions, 239–247
$M/M/1$ model, 519
  with finite calling population, 523–527
  operating characteristics with finite calling
      population, 525–527
$M/M/2$ model, 519
Model development, 7–10
Modelling, 7, 14–16, 31–34
Model solution, 11–12
MODI (modified distribution) method, 19-7
Monte Carlo simulations, 555n1
Morey, Richard C., 102
Morningstar Asset Allocator, 236
Most probable time *m,* 422
Moving averages, 715–718
  with Excel data analysis tools, 751
Multicriteria decision problems, 3

Multiperiod planning, 172
Multiple-channel waiting lines, 510–515
Multiple-choice constraints, 339–340
Multiple priority levels, 671n1
Multistage inventory planning, 487
Mutually exclusive constraints, 340

N

National Bureau of Standards, 50
National Car Rental, 224
Nationwide Car Rental, 477–478
Net evaluation index, 19-8
Net evaluation rows, 17-3
Netherlands Company, 574–575
Network flow problems
  assignment problems, 263–268
  capacitated transportation problem, 263
  capacitated transshipment problem, 274
  maximal flow problems, 279–283
  production and inventory applications, 283–286
  pure, 275n2
  shortest route problems, 276–279
  transportation problems, 256–262
  transshipment problems, 268–275
Network models, 17
Networks, 256, 257
New drug decision analysis, 627
New Haven Fire Department, 528
Nodes, 257, 603
Non-basis variables, 17-4
Nonlinear optimization problems, 364
  blending the pooling problem, 380–385
  constrained problems, 366–369
  forecasting new adoptions problems, 385–390
  hard, 390n1
  index funds, constructing, 372–377
  Markowitz mean-variance portfolio model,
      377–380
  solving with Excel Solver, 407–409
  solving with LINGO, 406–407
  unconstrained problem, 365–366
Nonnegativity constraints, 34n1, 65, 247n2
Nonstationary time series, 724n2
Normal distribution, 427n3
Normalized pairwise comparison matrix, 682
North American Product Sourcing Study, 275–276
Nowlin Plastics, 14, 15
Number of agents not equal to number of tasks,
    19-22

O

Objective function coefficients, 95–100, 103n1,
    18-2–18-6
Objective functions, 8, 32, 105, 123
Office Equipment, Inc. problem, 538–539
Oglethorpe Power, 633
Operating characteristics, 501

Operations management applications
    blending problems, 183–188
    make-or-buy decisions, 168–172
    production scheduling, 172–179
    workforce assignment, 179–183
Opportunity loss (regret), 606, 612n1, 19-23
Optimality, range of. *See* Range of optimality
Optimality criterion, 17-18
Optimal lease structuring, 164–165
Optimal lot size (Q^*) formula, 499
Optimal order quantity (Q^*) formula,
    498–499
Optimal solutions, 11, 48–50, 64
Optimistic approach to decision making, 605
Optimistic time *a,* 422
Orbitz, 18
Ordering costs, 454
Order-quantity, reorder point model with
        probabilistic demand, 478–482
    how-much-to-order decision, 479–480
    when-to-order decision, 480–482
Origin nodes, 268
Outgoing arcs, 19-8–19-9
Overestimating demand, 474

P

Pairwise comparison matrix, 680–681
Pairwise comparisons
    consistency of, 683
    other comparisons, 685–686
    synthesization of, 682–683
Parameters, 543
Paths, 276, 414
Payoffs, 603
Payoff tables, 603–604
100 percent rule, 18-12n2
Perfect information
    expected value of (EVPI), 612
    expected value with (EVwPI), 611–612
    expected value without (EVwoPI), 611–612
Performance Analysis Corporation, 102
Periodic review inventory systems, 483
Periodic review model with probabilistic demand,
    482–486
PERT/CPM. *See* Project scheduling: PERT/CPM
PERT (Program Evaluation and Review
        Technique), 17
Pessimistic time *b,* 422
Petroleum distribution simulation, 560–561
Pfizer, 555
Pharmacia & Upjohn, 555
Phoenix computer problem, 203–204
Pivot columns, 17-12
Pivot elements, 17-12
Pivot rows, 17-12
Poisson probability distribution, 503, 510n1
Portfolio optimization with transaction costs,
    400–403

Portfolio selection, 161–164
    asset allocation and, 236
    conservative portfolios, 230–232
    moderate risk, 232–235
    of mutual funds, 229–230
    upper and lower bounds on assets, 380n1
Portfolio simulation problem, 583–585
Portfolio variance, 377–378, 380n3
Posterior (revised) probabilities, 618, 631
Postoptimality analysis. *See* Sensitivity analysis
Preboard screening problem, 571
Preemptive priorities, 659
Preprocessing routines, 234n2
Pricing for environmental compliance problem, 372
Primal problems, 18-14, 18-17
    finding dual of, 18-18–18-20
    using duals to solve, 18-18
Principle of optimality, 21-2
Priority levels, 671n1
Prior probability assessments, 618
Probabilistic inputs, 541
Probabilistic inventory models, 472
Probabilistic models, 10. *See also* Stochastic models
Problem formulation, 31–34
Problem solving, 3
Process design problem, 21-26–21-27
Proctor & Gamble (P&G), 275–276
Product design and market share optimization
        problems, 335–338
Production and inventory problems, 283–286
Production lot size model. *See* Economic
        production lot size model
Production optimization, 173
Production scheduling, 172–179, 318–319,
    357–358, 698–699
Production strategy, 83–84
Productivity, 528
Product mix problem, 145–146
Product Sourcing Heuristic (PSH), 275–276
Professional societies, 18n1
Profit and volume models, 15
Profit contribution, 30n1
Program evaluation and review technique (PERT), 411
Programming, 34
Project manager assignment problem, 268
Project networks, 412
Project scheduling: PERT/CPM, 17
    activities, 412
    contributions of, 418–419
    crashing, 430–434
    critical path concept, 412–414
    determining critical path, 414–418
    with known activity times, 411–420
    slack, 418
    time-cost trade-offs, 429–434, 430–434
    with uncertain activity times, 420–428
Property purchase strategy, 649–650
Proportionality, 34n1
Prudential Financial Companies, 236
Pseudorandom numbers, 547n1

Purdue University, 263
Pure network flow problem, 275n2
Pure strategy solutions, 238–239, 247n1

Q

Quadratic trend equation, 729
Qualitative forecasting methods, 702
Quantitative analysis, 4–14
Quantitative forecasting methods, 702
Quantity discounts, 470–472
Queue discipline, 505
Queueing theory, 501
Queues, 501

R

R. C. Coleman problem, 446–448
Random number intervals, 549
Random numbers, 547
Range of feasibility, 106, 109n2, 18-9
Range of optimality, 95, 103n1, 18-2
Redden, Emory F., 268
Reduced costs, 323n1
Redundant constraints, 48
Regional Airlines problem, 537–538
Regret (opportunity loss), 606, 612n1
Relative inefficiency, 217, 219, 223n1
Relevant costs, 106
Remington Rand, 411
Reorder point, 458
Replay simulation problem, 585–587
Replenishment levels, 556
Report generation, 12
Restoration capacity, 283
Return function $r_n(x_n, d_n)$, 21–9
Revenue and volume models, 15
Revenue management, 2, 223–229. *See also* Yield
        management
Right-hand sides, 100–102, 109n2, 123,
        18-6–18-13
Risk, Markowitz portfolio model and, 377
Risk analysis, 543–555
    sensitivity analysis and, 613–618
    simulation of PortaCom project, 545–555
    what-if analysis, 543–545
Risk and diversification, 230
Risk-free assets, 380n2
Risk profile, 613
Risk profiles, 625–627
@RISK® spreadsheet add-in, 555n2
Risk tolerance, 236
Risk *versus* return, 164n2, 229
    Markowitz portfolio model and, 379
River City Fire Department problem,
        497–498
Rounding to obtain integer solution, 320–321
Route capacities or route minimums, 261–262

S

Saaty, Thomas L., 677
Saddle points, 239
Safety stock, 481, 486n1
Sample information
    decision analysis with, 618–628
    efficiency of, 628
    expected value of (EVSI), 627–628
Sampson, Greg, 93
SAS statistical package, 728n2
Scheduling flights and crew problem, 364–365
Schrage, Linus E., 85, 400, 400n5
Schultz, Susan, 319
Scoring models, 658, 672–676
    with Excel, 699–700
SEAC (Standards Eastern Automatic Computer), 50
Seasonality
    models based on monthly data, 737–738
    and trend, 735–737
    without trend, 732–735
Seasonal time series patterns, 707–708
Seasongood & Mayer, 420
Sensitivity analysis, 93–95
    changes in constraint coefficients, 112
    computer solution for, 103–109
    economic order quantity (EOQ) model and,
        459–460
    with Excel, 148–150
    graphical, 95–102, 615
    integer linear programming and, 342
    limitation of, 110–116
    with LINGO, 150–152
    nonintuitive dual values and, 112–115
    risk and, 613–618
    simultaneous changes and, 111–112
Sensitivity ranges, 323n1
Serpentine lines, 505
Service calls problem, 538–539
Service costs, 517
Service levels, 482n1, 556
Service rates, 504
Service time distribution, 504–505
Service times, 510n1, 563
Setup cost, 462
Shadow price. *See* Dual prices; Dual values
Shortages, 465–466
Shortest route problem, 276–279
Simon, Herbert A., 8
Simplex-based sensitivity analysis and duality
    duality, 18-14–18-20
    sensitivity analysis with Simples tableu,
        18-2–18-13
Simplex method, 17-2
    algebraic overview of, 17-2–17-5
    alternative optimal solutions, 17-32–17-33
    assignment problems, 19-18–19-24
    basic feasible solutions, 17-4–17-5
    basic solution, 17-4

criterion for removing a variable from the current basis (minimum ratio test), 17-11
degeneracy, 17-33–17-35
equality constraints, 17-24–17-25
general case tableau form, 17-20–17-27
greater-than-or-equal-to constraings, 17-20–17-24
improving the solution, 17-10–17-12
infeasibility, 17-29–17-31, 17-35n1
interpreting optimal solutions, 17-18–17-19
interpreting results of an iteration, 17-15
moving toward a better solution, 17-15–17-18
phase II of, 17-23–17-24
phase I of, 17-23
simplex tableau, 17-7–17-10
solving minimization problems with, 17-27–17-29
special cases, 17-29–17-35
tableau form, 17-5–17-7
unboundedness, 17-31–17-32
Simplex tableau, 17-7–17-10
calculating next, 17-12–17-14
criterion for entering a new variable into Basis, 17-11
Simulation, 17, 541
advantages and disadvantages of, 573–574
ATM waiting lines, 561–571
computer implementation, 572–573
with Crystal Ball® spreadsheet add-in, 595–599
with Excel, 588–595
inventory, 556–560
other issues, 572–574
parameters, 543
risk analysis, 543–555
software packages, 572
verification and validation, 573
waiting line, 561–571
Simulation experiments, 541
Simultaneous changes, 95–96, 103n1, 111–112, 18-13
Single-channel waiting lines, 502
with constant service times, 521
multiple-channel waiting lines and, 515n2
operating characteristics, 506–508
with Poisson arrivals and arbitrary service times, 519–521
with Poisson arrivals and exponential service times, 506–510
Single-criterion decision problems, 3
Single-period inventory model with probabilistic demand, 472–478
Slack, 418
Slack variables, 47–48, 64
Slope-intercept form, 42
SmartOps Multistage Inventory Planning and Optimization (MIPO), 487
SMART (Strategic Marketing and Research Techniques), 389
Smith, James E., 651
Smoothing constant, 719, 721, 722

Soft constraints, 666n2
Solutions Plus problem, 305–306
Sousa, Nancy L. S., 601
Spanning trees, 20-2
Spreadsheet packages, 549, 555, 555n2, 572, 724n1
Stages, 21-6
Stage transformation function, 21-8
Standard form, 47
State of the system, 761
State probabilities, 763
States of nature, 602
State variables x_n and x_{n-1}, 21-8
Static simulation models, 561
Stationary time series, 703, 704, 724n2
Statistical packages, 728n2
Steady-state operations, 505–506
for $M/G/k$ model with blocked customers cleared, 522–524
for multiple-channel waiting lines, 511–515
single-channel waiting lines, 506–508
Steady-state probabilities, 766
Stepping-stone method, 19-8–19-12
Stochastic models, 10. *See also* Probabilistic models
Stockouts, 465–466, 480
Subproblems, 364
Suncoast Office Supplies problem, 666–671
Sunk costs, 106
Surplus variables, 55–56
Synthesization, 682–683
System constraints, 665n1

T

Tableau form, 17-5–17-7
eliminating negative right-hand-side values, 17-25–17-26
equality constrains, 17-24–17-25
general case, 17-20–17-27
steps to create, 17-26–17-27
Target values, 659
Taylor, Frederic W., 2
Tea production and distribution, 122–123
Tee time simulation problem, 585–587
Telephone reservations systems, 537–538
Textbook publishing problem, 355–356
Textile mill scheduling problem, 204–205
Timber harvesting model, 29
Time-cost trade-offs, 429–434
Time series analysis, 702. *See also* Forecasting
method selection, 711
Time series patterns
cyclical patterns, 711
horizontal, 703–705
seasonal patterns, 707–708
trend and seasonal patterns, 708–710
trend patterns, 705–707
Time series plots, 703
Tomlin, J. A., 341

Tornado diagrams, 618n2
Total balance method, 769
Total cost model, 462–463
Transient periods, 505–506
Transition probabilities, 761
Transportation problems, 256–262, 19-2
    assignment model as, 267n1
    general linear programming model, 262
    maximization objective function, 261
    route capacities or route minimums, 261–262
    total supply not equal to total demand, 260
    unacceptable routes, 262
Transportation simplex method
    method summary, 19-17
    phase I: finding initial feasible solution, 19-2–19-6
    phase II: iterating to optimal solution, 19-7–19-16
    problem variations, 19-17–19-18
Transportation tableaux, 19-2
Transshipment nodes, 268
Transshipment problems, 268–275
TreePlan, 651–656
Trend and seasonal time series patterns, 708–710
Trend projection
    with Excel data analysis tools, 752
    linear trend, 724–728
    nonlinear trend, 728–731
Trend time series patterns, 705–707
Trials of the process, 761
Trick, Michael, 18
Tri-State Corporation problem, 583–585
Truck leasing strategy problem, 147–148
Two-person, zero-sum games, 236
Two-variable linear progam, 103n1

U

Unbounded feasible region, 17-35n2
Unboundedness, 17-31–17-32, 17-35n2
Unbounded solutions, 60–61
Uncertain activity times, 421–423
    noncritical activities and, 428n1
    variability in project completion time, 426–428
Uncontrollable inputs, 8
Underestimating demand, 474
Union Pacific Railroad, 263
Unit columns, 17-8
Unit vectors, 17-8
Unity constraint, 378
University of Alberta, 339
University of British Columbia, 571
University of Chicago, 85
University of Minnesota
    Nutrition Coordinating Center (NCC), 116
Upper bounds, 380n1
U.S. Environmental Protection Agency (EPA), 21-21
U.S. General Accountability Office (GAO), 760
U.S. Navy, 411
Utility companies, 518n1
Utilization factors, 507

V

Validation, 573
Valley Metal Container, 318–319
Vancouver International Airport, 571
Variable annuities, 236
Variable costs, 14
Variance, 377
Verification, 573
Visual CAFE, 372
Volunteer scheduling problem, 338–339

W

Wagner Fabricating Company problem, 496–497
Waiting cost, 517
Waiting line or queueing models, 17
    County Beverage Drive-Thru waiting line
        problem, 587–588
    economic analysis of, 517–518
    with finite calling populations, 524–527
    general relationships for, 515–516
    improving operation of, 508–509
    managers' use of, 508
    $M/M/1$ and $M/M/2$ models, 519
    multiple-channel waiting lines, 510–515
    multiple-channel with Poisson arrivals, arbitrary
        service and no waiting line, 522–524
    other models, 518–519
    single-channel with Poisson arrivals and arbitrary
        service times, 519–521
    using Excel, 509–510
    waiting line system structure, 502–506
Waiting line simulations, 561–571
Warehouse order-picking efficiency,
    574–575
Water quality management problem, 21-21
Weighted moving averages, 718
What-if analysis, 543–545
When-to-order decision, 458–459, 480–482
Whole Foods Market, 505
Winkofsky, Edward F., 29
Workers' Compensation Board of British Columbia,
    610–611
Workforce assignments, 179–183
Workforce scheduling problem, 205–207
Workload balancing, 82–83
Worst-case scenarios, 544

Y

Yeager National Bank problem, 356–357
Yield management, 2. *See also* Revenue
    management

Z

Zero-sum, 236